China's National Income, 1952–1995

China's National Income, 1952–1995

EDITED BY

Hsueh Tien-tung
Li Qiang

Westview Press
A Member of the Perseus Books Group

Published in 1999 in the United States of America by Westview Press, 5500 Central Avenue, Boulder, Colorado 80301-2877, and in the United Kingdom by Westview Press, 12 Hid's Copse Road, Cumnor Hill, Oxford OX2 9JJ

A CIP catalog record for this book is available from the Library of Congress.
ISBN 0-8133-3599X

The paper used in this publication meets the requirements of the American National Standard for Permanence of Paper for Printed Library Materials Z39.48-1984.

10 9 8 7 6 5 4 3 2 1

Contents

Preface

Since the implementation of the economic reform and opening policy, China has entered a new era during which she has prepared herself by working hard at joining the international community. The policy itself along with the impact of external influence have enabled China to catch up with the advanced economies of the world in production technology, management science, and economic institution and organization; these are indispensable to China to promote modern economic management and efficiency, which had been a blatant weakness of her past economy. The reform of the statistical system has had to follow suit.

Starting from 1985, the state statistical bureau (SSB) has received a US$0.3 million loan from the World Bank and another 0.3 million in technical aids from the Asian Development Bank for further developing the national income accounts system, particularly the estimation of the gross domestic product and its components in the system of national accounts (SNA) to make up the deficiency of the former system of material product balances (MPS).

By and large, the Chinese statistical reporting system has been under a well organized hierarchical framework, from the top level, SSB down to province, to *xian* (county), and even to *xiang* (township) and *zhen* (town) statistical units. Essentially, these form a regular reporting system for the grass-roots units to submit their statistical data to the statistical authorities.

For the industrial sector, there are generally two formal channels for reporting statistical data from the state enterprises. The first one may be called the government comprehensive statistics channel by which from the *xian* to the district to the province and then to the SSB the bureaucratic administration system submits the data. The second one is referred to as the sectoral statistics which come from the government institutions in charge of some special fields of industry together with the collection of their data. For example, the industrial bureau and the metallurgical bureau receive the statistical data of the enterprises under their jurisdiction. Of course, there is also a possibility that the state organs at channel one may also receive data from channel two because of the bureaucratic administrative system.

Very recently, the SSB established the Organization of Enterprise Surveys to be linked up with the Provincial Enterprise Survey Teams, and Key

Cities Enterprise Survey Teams to proceed with a sampling survey. Moreover, the Rural Enterprise Department under the Ministry of Agriculture has been in charge of the rural enterprises in various fields, such as industrial, construction and transportation enterprises, etc. It should be noted that the Organization of Urban Social and Economic Surveys down to the Provincial and the City/County Urban Social and Economic Survey Teams are responsible for conducting the household budget survey, investigating the residents' income structure and price levels in both the urban and rural areas.

Regarding the agricultural sector, there are also two channels for collecting the statistical data. One is through the bureaucratic administration system from the bottom level, *xiang/zhen* to *xian*, to district/municipality, to province and then to SSB. Another channel is via the organization of Rural Social and Economic Surveys, linked up to Provincial and County Rural Social and Economic Survey Teams, which make samplings in selected *xian* on certain agricultural statistics.

The service sector has been the weakest segment of the statistical reporting system among the tripartite economic sectors. Generally speaking, the urban service industries under the administration of government institutions have to submit their statistical data via the sectoral statistics channels, such as the distribution industries under the administration of the Ministry of Domestic Trade or the transportation enterprises under the Ministry of Railways. The rural service industries employing seven people or more are all under the administration of the Rural Enterprise Department. Those self-employed services which hire less than seven people have to register and obtain the business license from the Industry and Commerce Administration Department or Office concerned at the *xian* and the *xiang/zhen* levels. Apart from the regular reporting system, there are some sampling surveys for collecting data on the services. However, a large-scale sampling survey brings about huge costs that the limited government budget does not allow to be done frequently. It is unavoidable that some portion of the services data is simply out of the statistical accounting sphere.

It is imperative for me to take this opportunity to point out some fundamental issues concerning the estimation of China's national income. The first issue which comes to my mind is that it is very possible that the size of China's national income tends to be underestimated. There are several reasons behind this.

First of all, it has been quite difficult, if not impossible, to change the historical inheritance of the statistical method implemented long before the reform period. I call this the inertia effect. The official position is that the socialist system originating from 1949 should not be reshuffled overnight but should be allowed to adapt to the new situation in a gradualist way. For example, following the economic reform and opening policy, the official value of real estate, fixed assets and produced resources stipulated formerly has been too low to reflect the market value. The revaluation of all these goods takes some time to go through, even though the statistical authorities are fully aware of the deficiency and drawback. Of course, there are some opposite examples. Many of the vehicles on the roads are so old and their outward appearance so worn-out that they should be made obsolete; however, they are still functioning after some repair. The relatively low rate of depreciation naturally causes an overestimate of the national income. Nevertheless, judging by these two conditions, the former is certainly overwhelming the latter.

Secondly, the statistical system lags a behind the needs to account for the actual economic activities after the market-oriented economy has made its appearance. Given the present stage of development, quite a significant portion of market activities is transacted by cash. There is simply no record at all for statistical reporting or investigation; as a result, most of the transactions are out of the scope of statistical accounting. Instead, some indirect measures are carried out. For example, some estimate and/or guesstimate can be made by checking the relevant data and information from various departments for tax, finance and administration. However, the figures so obtained are generally downward biased for the obvious reasons that there are tax evasion and tax avoidance by the production and business units in question.

Thirdly, the actual performance of the service sector has been a large, unknown parameter in the national income accounting. From the mass media reporters interviewing the ordinary people in open cities and municipalities, we know that the supply of community services has become a necessary and indispensable part of people's daily life. As a matter of fact, the services sector has expanded so quickly and widely that its economic outcomes are generally under-reported. Furthermore, tax evasion and avoidance are rampant in the services sector since most of the transactions are dealt in cash with few records for administrative inspection.

The second issue appears to be that the growth rate of the national income tends to be overestimated while, in contrast, the inflationary rate of the national economy may be under-estimated. As will be discussed in some details in Chapter 5, following the historical inheritance of the statistical system, the adoption of the Paasche price index for the calculation of the national economy tends to lower the degree of price inflation under the actual circumstances. And the use of the Laspeyres quantity index tends to raise the growth speed of the national income. The reason behind this is that, on the one hand, the problem of statistical consistency makes the SSB take a long time to work out some fundamental change in statistical methodology. And, on the other hand, the limited budget restrains the SSB from speeding up the compilation of the badly needed price indexes system. Nevertheless, the Chinese authorities have shown the positive attitude that there is no way to get away from the link up with the international statistical system. Thus, the revision of the system has to proceed under such circumstances.

The third issue concerns the uncertain factor regarding the statistical reporting system stemming from the characteristics of Chinese socialism. The hierarchical bureaucratic system of statistical report shows that the grassroots enterprises are all subordinated to the administrative levels of bureaucrats. Very frequently, the upper levels set up higher targets of performance for the grassroots units to fulfill. The latter run their risk to be punished in one way or another if they do not obey the order from the top units.

There have been quite a few cases where the major interest of the bureaucrats in charge has been their promotion to a higher office rather than accurately reporting statistical data. In particular, this applies to the officers who are in the bureaucratic administration category, but not in the Chinese Communist Party system, such as the party secretary. Those in the former category are generally facing the renewal of their term of appointment every three years. The economic performance of the region under their charge constitutes one of the prerequisites for the reappointment; thus, some exaggeration is very possible, for instance, a higher growth rate of output, a larger sown area of grain and cotton or a higher profit rate than the actual case. There is also the temptation of arbitrarily reporting the allocation of investment funds and wilfully assigning the benefit and cost items in order to match the need of certain political and economic purposes. The contrary, some time, also holds when the central authorities advocate a contraction policy on some particular item; the local bureaucrats may endeavor to lower the growth rate of the item in question, for example, a low birth rate and low basic construction investments, etc.

A nationwide investigation of the enforcement of statistical work disclosed that there had been 20,000 cases of falsified reporting (*People's Daily*, 22 April 1995) and some 70,000 occurrences of illegal statistical activities in 1994 (*Economic Daily*, 31 August 1995). Among which, the falsified output value of rural industry, rural birth rate and basic construction investment were most widespread. Thus, it appears that the political regime is overruling the statistical system in such a way that the political cycles give a strong impetus to the national economic accounting through statistical instrumentality.

It is of my belief that the SSB stands its neutral position, and its political interests have little or nothing to do with the actual performance of economic units. The SSB, however, will have to do some crosschecking with the related figures submitted or carry out some sampling survey in order to rectify the doubtful cases, particularly when some discrepancy between the reported figures and the SSB estimates appears to be too large to be credible. In any case, it will take some time for the Chinese statistical system to get on the same track as the international one, as the Chinese are in the course of learning by doing and doing by learning. The international comparability of the Chinese economy with other economies will proceed with little difficulty afterwards.

This book is the outcome of a joint research project between the Department of National Account Statistics, SSB, and this programme. After a research effort of more than two years, we are now able to present the findings to our readers. I would like to take this opportunity to thank Messrs. M.H. Wong, W.C. Hong and Y.M. Lam for a private donation making the project possible. Special appreciation also goes to Dr. Maurice Brosseau for shaping the manuscript for publication purpose, and to Roger Yip Chi-him, Peter Luk Yiu-wang, Sunny Chiang Chi-hang and Ms. Szeto Mei-wah for their kind help with the editorial work. Nevertheless, the editors are solely responsible for any mistakes that still remain.

Hsueh Tien-tung
Programme Director
China's Reform and Development Programme
Hong Kong Institute of Asia-Pacific Studies
The Chinese University of Hong Kong

Provinces

	Abbreviation		Abbreviation
1. Beijing	BJ	16. Henan	HEN
2. Tianjin	TJ	17. Hubei	HUB
3. Hebei	HEB	18. Hunan	HUN
4. Shanxi	SAX	19. Guangdong	GD
5. Inner Mongolia	IM	20. Guangxi	GX
6. Liaoning	LN	21. Hainan	HN
7. Jilin	JL	22. Sichuan	SC
8. Heilongjiang	HLJ	23. Guizhou	GZ
9. Shanghai	SH	24. Yunnan	YN
10. Jiangsu	JS	25. Tibet	TB
11. Zhejiang	ZJ	26. Shaanxi	SHX
12. Anhui	AH	27. Gansu	GS
13. Fujian	FJ	28. Qinghai	QH
14. Jiangxi	JX	29. Ningxia	NX
15. Shandong	SD	30. Xinjiang	XJ

Categories of Variables for National Statistics

1. Gross Domestic Product and Its Composition (by the production approach, at current prices)
2. Growth Rate of Gross Domestic Product and Its Composition (at comparable prices)
3. Gross Domestic Product and Its Composition (by the expenditure approach, at current prices)
4. Final Consumption Expenditure and Its Composition
5. Growth Rate of Final Consumption and Its Composition (at comparable prices)
6. Per Capita Consumption
7. Growth Rate of Per Capita Consumption (at comparable prices)
8. Composition of Gross Capital Formation
9. Growth Rate of Gross Capital Formation and Its Composition (at comparable prices)

Categories of Variables for Provincial Statistics

1. Total Output and Its Composition (at current prices)
2. Growth Rate of Total Output and Its Composition (at comparable prices)
3. Gross Domestic Product and Its Composition (by the production approach)
4. Growth Rate of Gross Domestic Product and Its Composition (at comparable prices)
5. Gross Domestic Product and Its Composition (by the expenditure approach)
6. Composition of Household Consumption Expenditure
7. Growth Rate of Final Consumption Expenditure and Its Composition (at comparable prices)
8. Per Capita Household Consumption
9. Growth Rate of Per Capita Household Consumption (at comparable prices)
10. Gross Capital Formation by Ownership
11. Gross Capital Formation by Type of Industry
12. Growth Rate of Gross Capital Formation (at comparable prices)
13. Gross Domestic Product by Primary Distribution of Income (by the distribution approach)

Variables

Variables for Whole Nation

1. *Gross Domestic Product and Its Composition (by the production approach, at current prices, Renminbi (Rmb) 100 million)*

u1′			Gross National Product
u1			Gross Domestic Product (GDP)
	u1a		Primary industry
	u1b		Secondary industry
		u1b1	industry
		u1b2	construction
	u1c		Tertiary industry
		u1c1	transportation, post and telecommunications
		u1c2	commerce
		u1c3	social services
		u1c4	public utility
		u1c5	banking and insurance
		u1c6	real estate
		u1c7	science, education, culture, health, sports and welfare
		u1c8	government agencies, party agencies and social organizations and others
	u1d		Per capita GDP
	u1e		Tertiary industry (by new industry classification)
		u1e1	farming, forestry, animal husbandary and fishery services
		u1e2	geological prospecting and water conservancy
		u1e3	transportation and storage
		u1e4	post and telecommunications
		u1e5	wholesale, retail trade and food services
		u1e6	banking and insurance
		u1e7	real estate
		u1e8	social services

		u1e9	health, sports and welfare
		u1e10	education, culture, arts and television broadcasting
		u1e11	science research and general technical services
		u1e12	government agencies, party agencies and social organizations and others

2. *Growth Rate of GDP and Its Composition (at comparable prices, preceding year = 100)*

u2′			Gross National Product
u2			Gross Domestic Product
	u2a		Primary industry
	u2b		Secondary industry
		u2b1	industry
		u2b2	construction
	u2c		Tertiary industry
		u2c1	transportation, post and telecommunications
		u2c2	commerce
		u2c3	social services
		u2c4	public utility
		u2c5	banking and insurance
		u2c6	real estate
		u2c7	science, education, culture, health, sports and welfare
		u2c8	government agencies, party agencies and social organizations and others
	u2d		Per capita GDP
	u2e		Tertiary industry (by new industry classification)
		u2e1	farming, forestry, animal husbandary and fishery services
		u2e2	geological prospecting and water conservancy
		u2e3	transportation and storage
		u2e4	post and telecommunications
		u2e5	wholesale, retail trade and food services
		u2e6	banking and insurance
		u2e7	real estate
		u2e8	social services
		u2e9	health, sports and welfare
		u2e10	education, culture, arts and television broadcasting
		u2e11	science research and general technical services

u2e12	government agencies, party agencies and social organizations and others

3. *Gross Domestic Product and Its Composition (by the expenditure approach, at current prices, Rmb 100 million)*

u3	Gross Domestic Product
u3a	Final consumption expenditure
u3b	Gross capital formation
u3c	Net export of goods and services
u3c1	export of goods and services
u3c2	import of goods and services

4. *Final Consumption Expenditure and Its Composition (Rmb 100 million)*

u4a	Household consumption expenditure
u4a1	farmer
u4a1a	self-supplied consumption
u4a1b	commodity consumption
u4a1c	cultural and personal services
u4a1d	housing, water and electricity
u4a2	non-farmer
u4a2b	commodity consumption
u4a2c	cultural and personal services
u4a2d	housing, water and electricity
u4b	Government consumption expenditure

5. *Growth Rate of Final Consumption Expenditure and Its Composition (at comparable prices, preceding year = 100)*

u5	Final Consumption Expenditure
u5a	Household consumption expenditure
u5a1	farmer
u5a2	non-farmer
u5b	Government consumption expenditure

6. *Per Capita Consumption (Rmb)*

u6	Per Capita Household Consumption
u6a	Farmer
u6b	Non-farmer

7. *Growth Rate of Per Capita Consumption (at comparable prices, preceding year = 100)*

u7		Per Capita Household Consumption
	u7a	Farmer
	u7b	Non-farmer

8. *Composition of Gross Capital Formation (Rmb 100 million)*

u8a	Gross fixed capital formation
u8b	Change in inventory

9. Growth Rate of Gross Capital Formation and Its Composition (at comparable prices, preceding year = 100)

u9		Gross Capital Formation
	u9a	Gross fixed capital formation
	u9b	Change in inventory

Variables for Provinces, Municipalities Directly Under the Central Government and Autonomous Regions

1. *Total Output and Its Composition (at current prices, Rmb 100 million)*

v1			Total Output
	v1a		Primary industry
	v1b		Secondary industry
		v1b1	industry
		v1b2	construction
	v1c		Tertiary industry
		v1c1	transportation, post and telecommunications
		v1c2	commerce
		v1c3	others

2. *Growth Rate of Total Output and Its Composition (at comparable prices, preceding year = 100)*

v2			Total Output
	v2a		Primary industry
	v2b		Secondary industry
		v2b1	industry
		v2b2	construction

	v2c		Tertiary industry
		v2c1	transportation, post and telecommunications
		v2c2	commerce

3. *Gross Domestic Product and Its Composition (by the production approach, Rmb 100 million)*

v3′			Gross National Product
v3			Gross Domestic Product (GDP)
	v3a		Primary industry
	v3b		Secondary industry
		v3b1	industry
		v3b2	construction
	v3c		Tertiary industry
		v3c1	transportation, post and telecommunications
		v3c2	commerce
		v3c3	banking and insurance
		v3c4	real estates
		v3c5	social services
		v3c6	health, sports and welfare
		v3c7	education, culture, arts and televsion broadcasting
		v3c8	scientific research and general technical services
		v3c9	government agencies, party agencies and social organizations
		v3c10	others
	v3d		Per capita GDP

4. *Growth Rate of GDP and Its Composition (at comparable prices, preceding year = 100)*

v4′			Gross National Product
v4			Gross Domestic Product
	v4a		Primary industry
	v4b		Secondary industry
		v4b1	industry
		v4b2	construction
	v4c		Tertiary industry
		v4c1	transportation, post and telecommunications
		v4c2	commerce
		v4c3	banking and insurance
		v4c4	real estate
		v4c5	social services

v4c6	health, sports and welfare
v4c7	education, culture, arts and television broadcasting
v4c8	scientific research and general technical services
v4c9	government agencies, party agencies and social organizations
v4c10	others

5. *Gross Domestic Product and Its Composition (by the expenditure approach, Rmb 100 million)*

v5	Gross Domestic Product
v5a	Final consumption expenditure
v5a1	household consumption expenditure
v5a1a	farmer
v5a1b	non-farmer
v5a2	government consumption expenditure
v5b	Gross capital formation
v5b1	gross fixed capital formation
v5b2	changes in inventories
v5c	Net export of goods and services
v5c1	export of goods and services
v5c2	import of goods and services

6. *Composition of Household Consumption Expenditure (Rmb 100 million)*

v6a	Farmer
v6a1	self-supplied consumption
v6a2	commodity consumption
v6a3	cultural and personal services
v6a4	housing, water and electricity
v6b	Non-farmer
v6b2	commodity consumption
v6b3	cultural and personal services
v6b4	housing, water and electricity

7. *Growth Rate of Final Consumption Expenditure and Its Composition (at comparable prices, preceding year = 100)*

v7	Final Consumption Expenditure
v7a	Household consumption expenditure
v7a1	farmer
v7a2	non-farmer

	v7b	Government consumption expenditure

8. Per Capita Household Consumption

v8		Per Capita Household Consumption
	v8a	Farmer
	v8b	Non-farmer

9. Growth Rate of Per Capita Household Consumption (at comparable prices, preceding year = 100)

v9		Per Capita Household Consumption
	v9a	Farmer
	v9b	Non-farmer

10. Gross Capital Formation by Ownership (Rmb 100 million)

v10a			Gross fixed capital formation
	v10a1		state-owned units
	v10a2		collective-owned units
	v10a3		urban and rural households
		v10a3a	urban households
		v10a3b	rural households
	v10a4		others
v10b			Change in inventory
	v10b1		state-owned units
	v10b2		collective-owned units
	v10b4		others

11. Gross Capital Formation by Type of Industry (Rmb 100 million)

a) Primary industry

v11a		Gross capital formation
	v11a1	gross fixed capital formation
	v11a2	change in inventory

b) Secondary industry

v11b		Gross capital formation
	v11b1	gross fixed capital formation
	v11b2	change in inventory

c) Tertiary industry

v11c	Gross capital formation
v11c1	gross fixed capital formation
v11c2	change in inventory

12. *Growth Rate of Gross Capital Formation (at comparable prices, preceding year = 100)*

v12	Gross Capital Formation
v12a	Gross fixed capital formation
v12b	Change in inventory

13. *Gross Domestic Product by Primary Distribution of Income (by the distribution approach, Rmb 100 million)*

v13	Gross Domestic Product
v13i	labor remuneration
v13ii	fixed asset depreciation
v13iii	net production tax
v13iv	operating surplus
v13a	Primary industry
v13ai	labor remuneration
v13aii	fixed asset depreciation
v13aiii	net production tax
v13aiv	operating surplus
v13b	Secondary industry
v13bi	labor remuneration
v13bii	fixed asset depreciation
v13biii	net production tax
v13biv	operating surplus
v13b1	industry
v13b1i	labor remuneration
v13b1ii	fixed asset depreciation
v13b1iii	net production tax
v13b1iv	operating surplus
v13b2	construction
v13b2i	labor remuneration
v13b2ii	fixed asset depreciation
v13b2iii	net production tax
v13b2iv	operating surplus
v13c	Tertiary industry
v13ci	labor remuneration

v13cii	fixed asset depreciation
v13ciii	net production tax
v13civ	operating surplus
v13c1	transportation, post and telecommunications
v13c1i	labor remuneration
v13c1ii	fixed asset depreciation
v13c1iii	net production tax
v13c1iv	operating surplus
v13c2	commerce
v13c2i	labor remuneration
v13c2ii	fixed asset depreciation
v13c2iii	net production tax
v13c2iv	operating surplus
v13c3	banking and insurance
v13c3i	labor remuneration
v13c3ii	fixed asset depreciation
v13c3iii	net production tax
v13c3iv	operating surplus
v13c4	real estate
v13c4i	labor remuneration
v13c4ii	fixed asset depreciation
v13c4iii	net production tax
v13c4iv	operating surplus
v13c5	social services
v13c5i	labor remuneration
v13c5ii	fixed asset depreciation
v13c5iii	net production tax
v13c5iv	operating surplus
v13c6	health, sports and welfare
v13c6i	labor remuneration
v13c6ii	fixed asset depreciation
v13c6iii	net production tax
v13c6iv	operating surplus
v13c7	education, culture, arts and television broadcasting
v13c7i	labor remuneration
v13c7ii	fixed asset depreciation
v13c7iii	net production tax
v13c7iv	operating surplus
v13c8	scientific research and general tenhical services
v13c8i	labor remuneration
v13c8ii	fixed asset depreciation
v13c8iii	net production tax

v13c8iv	operating surplus
v13c9	government agencies, party agencies and social organizations
v13c9i	labor remuneration
v13c9ii	fixed asset depreciation
v13c9iii	net production tax
v13c9iv	operating surplus
v13c10	others
v13c10i	labor remuneration
v13c10ii	fixed asset depreciation
v13c10iii	net production tax
v13c10iv	operating surplus

PART ONE

China's National Income in Theory

1

The Establishment and Evolution of China's National Income

Hsueh Tien-tung
Li Huaju

It is well known that there are two distinct systems of national income accounting in the world. The first is the system of material product balances (MPS) adopted by the former USSR, the Eastern European countries, and the People's Republic of China (PRC); the other is the system of national accounts (SNA) which is being used by most of the western countries. The making of the MPS is tailored to the needs of the socialist economic system, which is characterized by the highly centralized management of its planned economy. The fundamental content of this system is the record of activities in production, distribution, exchange and the usage of material products. Making use of the balance tables, the main aspects of production process of material products can then be reflected. The main aggregative indicators are total output value of society *(shehui zongchanzhi)* and national income *(guomin shouru).* On the other hand, the SNA is an accounting system which, under the conditions of a market economy, employs the concept of value-added to incorporate the macroeconomic variables into a consistent social accounting framework. Economic activities of various sectors of the national economy, including both material production and non-material production departments, are estimated in this system. By means of double-entry accounting, it employs the tools like accounts and matrices to ascertain the various aspects of production, distribution and usage of goods and services.

Because of the distinction in the two systems, the concept of national income differs in each case. In the MPS, the main indicator of national income, *guomin shouru,* is the sum of the net output value of the various material production sectors for a given period. And, in the SNA, national income is the total income of all owners of production factors such as labor, capital and land, etc., who earn their income by producing goods and services within a specified period. This is also what people commonly call the gross national product (GNP), which includes not only the total net output value of the various material production sectors, but also the depreciation allowances and the value-added of various services sectors.

In China, in the process of increasing its understanding of the concept of "social production," different scopes and methods of estimating the national income have been used accordingly. In the following three sections, the development of and changes in the estimation of China's national income are discussed in turn.

National Income Accounting Before 1949

Before 1949, China's statistical organization was very imperfect, and the statistical work was relatively poor.[1] At that time, people in academic and non-academic circles predominantly wrote articles about population and peasant movements, etc. There was little professional statistical study of the national income with the exception of the first national income accounts (1931-1936) made by the past Institute of Social Sciences, Academia Sinica in 1945, under the leadership of Dr. Pao-san Ou.

Witnessing the increasing attention to and the application of national income by economists of the West, Dr. Ou felt an urgent need to estimate China's own national income. As such, the estimated results could be used, on the one hand, for comparisons with the national income of other countries and as the most primary information for further study of the economic and social problems of China, on the other.

However, the paucity of statistics on production, income and population imposed many difficulties on the estimation work. Dr. Ou scrutinized the various statistical data which were contained in the Institute of Social Sciences and adopted the concepts and estimation methods of national income of the West. He managed to find out a better method to estimate the national income under the extremely limited availability of data.

The Concept of National Income

What is meant by national income? Some of its important meanings must be clarified first.

1. National income is not the simple summation of all people's income. Rather, it is the total value-added resulting from a nation's production activities. Without the fruit of net increase in production,

there is simply no national income. However, personal income includes not only labor income, but also received gifts and aid. The latter two items are merely transfer income, hence, from society's point of view, they do not represent any increase in output value.

2. National income is the net income from which intermediate consumption has to be deducted, thus it is not the total value of production.
3. National income includes both the material and non-material products. Material products refer to the production of the various goods, while non-material products refer to the production of the various services. Although the latter does not directly increase material wealth, it does provide services to material production and livelihood, improves the condition for material production and enhances the content and quality of people's living. Generally speaking, the share of services in total production increases as society progresses. The simple truth is that, if there is no change in society's material production and there is some increase in the production of non-material products, we cannot say there is no change in production or income in society because the standard of living has been improved.
4. National income is an indicator of the output value of the national economy. Its real meaning lies in reflecting the amount of goods and services produced in society. Thus, all the different kinds of goods and services newly created have to be included in the calculation, and they are to be measured by a standardized unit of value.
5. National income is the calculable amount of goods and services produced within a year. In principle, all goods and services produced have to be included in the national income. However, since some goods and services have not been exchanged there is no possible way of reckoning their value. Nevertheless, there are some exceptions, like the consumption of self-produced goods which can be approximated by the value of similar goods that are exchanged in the market, or the rent of self-owned housing can be approximated by the market rent of housing of the similar kind.
6. National income includes all goods and services produced, which involves not only those consumed by consumers, but also those used by producers in their economic activities. That is, national income equals the sum of goods and services for consumption and investment purposes.
7. Cognizance is taken of the criterion of inhabitant and nationality. When a country's national income is estimated, it is the income of those inhabiting the country that is calculated, regardless of the

inhabitants' nationality. There are two reasons for the adoption of such criterion. First, in a nation's production and income statistics, the produce and income of the foreigners who live in this nation are usually treated in the same way as those of the nation's own citizens, and it is very difficult to separate them in calculation. Secondly, national income is the total amount of production within a nation's boundary. Many of the important implications of national income would be lost if some of its components were taken away. For instance, when we study the productivity of a nation, we should look not only at its own citizens' income, but also at the total income generated by all inhabitants within its territory, since it is the latter that reflects the whole situation.

Summarizing the above, national income is the total amount of goods and services produced by the inhabitants of a nation within a specified period. Moreover, in order to ascertain the total income under the disposal of a nation, the factor income remitted from abroad is to be added, while the factor income remitted abroad is to be subtracted.

The Method of Estimating National Income

From the broad definition of national income, the state of the national economy is reflected in three ways: production, income and spending. Accordingly, there are three approaches to calculating national income, namely the production approach, the income (or distribution) approach and the expenditure approach. The production approach derives national income from total output value minus the value of intermediate goods consumed; the distribution approach obtains national income by summing up the factor incomes distributed to the various production factors; and the expenditure approach gets the various items of final use, thus national income equals the sum of consumption, investment and net exports.

Given the state of all statistical data available at that time, Dr. Ou employed the production approach to estimate national income. The net value of production was calculated by subtracting the value of intermediate goods (which includes both material goods and services) from the total value of production in the various industries.

The year of estimation chosen was to be 1933, because there was a richer information available for that year. Some of the relevant data unavailable were substituted by those of the nearby years, provided that the economic conditions of the year chosen were not very much different from 1933. After the national income of 1933 had been estimated, various indexes were calculated to extrapolate the national income figures of 1933-1936.

The concrete estimation procedures went as follows:

The first step was to classify all the production sectors into ten categories:

(1) Agriculture, including animal husbandry, forestry and fishing; (2) Mining and metallurgy; (3) Manufacturing, including handicraft; (4) Building and construction; (5) Transportation and communication; (6) Commerce, including hotel, catering trade and entertainment; (7) Finance; (8) Dwelling service; (9) Professional services;(10) Public administration.

The second step was to concretely estimate the income of each sector. Basically, the production approach was being adopted in the process. After the aggregate values of production and the intermediate consumption had been roughly calculated, Dr. Ou then estimated the income of each sector. Yet, some of the relevant data could not be found, such as those for the free-lance occupations and for public administration; so, the product of the average income per employee and the total number of employees was estimated as the substitute. In other words, the estimated income of each sector was equal to the income from the net output value of the national inhabitants.

In the third step, the disposable national income was calculated, which included the income from the net production by the domestic residents by adding or subtracting the international net in-payments, but excluding foreign investment and credit expansion in China.[2]

In his study, Dr. Ou indicated that the result was rather coarse, because the relevant data for all the years, with the exception of 1933, were insufficient and poor. Thus, the results had merely to be seen as a trend,[3] as recorded in Tables 1.1 to 1.5.

Furthermore, the yearly employment figures of 1933 estimated by one of his associates, Djang Gee-hung, and the so calculated rate of labor productivity, are tabulated in Table 1.6. From the provided information, the readers can better understand the national economy before 1949.

According to Dr. Ou, the average income per person in 1933 was 47 Chinese dollars (C$), which was equal to 12 US dollars at the exchange rate of that year. And, the per capita income in the United States was 313 US dollars.[4]

Tackling Some Knotty Problems

Owing to the inadequacies of the data available, some items could not be included in the national income. Some knotty issues and their resolutions are shown as follows.

1. *Labor.* Many services were completely or partially out of the boundary of exchange, as exemplified by the labor force in farming, personal furniture making and self-construction of houses. Only the tangible item, the house, was to be included in the calculation. All the others were omitted simply because of difficulties in the process of estimation.

2. *Transfer income.* Pension and charitable alms were items of a transferable nature. Having taxed the people, the government redistributed the money to others. This transfer income, which was similar to that of making a gift, did not produce immediate services and, thus, was basically excluded from the national income. Yet, it was not the case for the income obtained from pension because it could be explained as a delayed payment of wages and be included in the income of each sector. Meanwhile, though pension often made

TABLE 1.1 Net National Output Value by Sector and Total Income Produced at Current Prices, China, 1931-1936 (in C$ million)

	1931	*1932*	*1933*	*1934*	*1935*	*1936*
Agriculture	15,315	15,094	12,593	11,325	12,906	16,641
Mining & metallurgy	257	234	238	241	258	294
Manufacturing	1,927	1,870	1,889	1,813	2,002	2,475
Building & construction	200	139	221	260	190	195
Transportation & communication	980	885	922	995	1,052	1,042
Commerce	3,989	2,718	2,541	2,286	2,236	2,566
Finance	176	176	200	235	251	294
Dwelling service	934	934	934	934	934	934
Professional & free lance jobs	164	160	171	161	173	215
Domestic servants	141	141	141	141	141	141
Public administration	725	635	642	918	835	1,001
Grand total	24,808	22,986	20,492	19,309	20,978	25,798
Subtraction item[a]	153	153	173	203	217	254
Net national output value	24,655	22,833	20,319	19,106	20,761	25,544
Net international in-payments						
(1)[b]	172	126	68	106	65	171
(2)[c]	216	989	98	337	341	1,214
Disposable national income	24,827	22,959	20,387	19,212	20,826	25,715
Disposable national goods & services	24,871	23,822	20,417	19,443	21,102	26,758

[a]The net output value of the sectors listed has covered the interest income paid to the banking & insurance sector. It would be double counting without deducting the subtraction item.

[b]International net in-payments without foreign investment and its credit expansion, and foreign donation.

[c]International net in-payments including foreign investment and its credit expansion, and foreign donation.

Source: Ou (1947c) p. 97; the revised figures from the first publication in Ou (1947a), Vol. 1, p. 17.

TABLE 1.2 Net National Output Value by Sector and Total Income Produced at Constant Prices, China, 1931-1936 and 1946 (in C$ million)

	1931 prices						1933 prices	1936 prices
	1931	1932	1933	1934	1935	1936	1946	
Agriculture	15,315	16,023	15,027	13,744	14,699	16,860	11,482	14,702
Mining & metallurgy	257	248	284	292	294	298	90	85
Manufacturing	1,927	1,985	2,254	2,200	2,280	2,508	1,202	1,679
Building & construction	200	148	264	316	216	198	21	19
Transportation & communication	980	939	1,100	1,208	1,198	1,056	850	873
Commerce	3,989	2,885	3,032	2,774	2,547	2,600	2,318	2,272
Finance	176	187	239	285	286	298	759	883
Dwelling service	934	880	783	770	820	922	842	842
Professional & free-lance jobs	164	170	204	195	197	218	242	276
Domestic servants	141	150	168	171	161	143	141	141
Public administration	725	674	766	1,114	951	1,014	1,318	1,666
Grand total	24,808	24,289	24,121	23,069	23,649	26,115	19,325	23,438
Subtraction item[a]	153	162	206	246	247	257	301[e]	382[e]
Net national output value	24,655	24,127	23,915	22,823	23,402	25,858	19,024	23,056
Net international in-payments								
(1)[b]	172	134	81	129	74	173	378[f]	337[f]
(2)[c]	216	1,050	117	409	388	1,230	1,887[g]	1,681[g]
Disposable national income	24,827	24,261	23,996	22,952	23,476	26,031	19,402	23,393
Disposable national goods & services	24,871	25,177	24,032	23,232	23,790	27,088	20,911	24,737

[a] [b] and [c] as for Table 1.1 except data for 1946.
[e]Including also the loss of business and public housing services.
[f]Excluding the foreign borrowing funds, donation and aids.
[g]Including the foreign borrowing funds, donation and aids.

Source: Ou (1947c) p. 99; Ou (1947b), p. 19.

its appearance in government expenses, it could not be counted in government income, however.

3. *Appreciation and devaluation of assets.* The ever-changing economic conditions constantly exerted tremendous influence on the fluctuation of the value of assets, such as machinery, real estate and bills. Since there was no corresponding value-added of real goods and services created from the above changes, none of which could be counted as national income. Note that income is generated from assets. The size of income is the basis for the changes in the asset value. Should we include both the income from the assets and that stemming from asset revaluation, we would make a mistake of double-counting.

TABLE 1.3 Revenue and Expenditure of International Payments 1931-1936 (in C$ million)

	1931	*1932*	*1933*	*1934*	*1935*	*1936*
Revenue from international payments						
Overseas Chinese remittances	359.9	327.0	200.0	250.0	260.0	320.0
China's foreign investment revenues	56.7	5.0	5.0			90.0
Foreign investment in China and its credit expansion	43.6	863.0	30.0	230.0	276.0	1,033.0
Total	460.2	1,195.0	235.0	480.0	536.0	1,453.0
Expenditure of international payments						
Principal and interest of government's foreign debts	135.2	90.0	93.0	112.6	107.4	127.8
Profits of foreign investment in China	87.2	89.2	38.3			
Foreigners' remittances from China	21.8	27.0	1.0	31.8	87.6	111.5
Rentals of moving picture films			5.0			
Total	244.2	206.2	137.3	144.4	195.0	239.3
International net in-payments	216.0	988.8	97.7	336.6	341.0	1,213.7

Source: Pao-san Ou et al. (1947a), p. 146.

TABLE 1.4 National Disposable Goods and Services, Consumption and Investment, China, 1931-1936 (in C$ million)

	Disposable goods & services	*Consumption*	*Investment*
1931	24,871	24,173	698
1932	23,822	23,014	718
1933	20,417	20,441	-24
1934	19,443	20,060	-617
1935	21,102	21,675	-573
1936	26,758	25,286	1,472

Source: Pao-san Ou (1947c), pp. 100, 153.

TABLE 1.5 National Consumption and Its Components, China, 1933

Item	*Value (C $million)*	*% share*
Food	9,564	46.8
Clothing	2,193	10.7
Rent	1,431	7.0
Fuel & light	1,851	9.1
Miscellaneous	5,402	26.4
Total	20,441	100.0

Sources: Pao-san Ou et al. (1947a), Vol. 1, p. 16, and Ou (1947c), p. 97.

TABLE 1.6 Net National Product, Labour Force & Labour Productivity, China, 1933

	Net national product		*Labour force*		*Labour productivity (C$/labour)*
	C$ million	*Share (%)*	*'000 persons*	*Share (%)*	
Agriculture	12,593	61.5	143,163	75.7	88
Mining and metallurgy	238	1.2	1,030	0.5	231
Manufacturing	1,889	9.2	15,052	8.0	125
Factories	530	(28.1)	1,106	(7.3)	479
Handicraft	1,359	(71.9)	13,946	(92.7)	97
Building and construction	221	1.1	1,700	0.9	130
Transportation and communication	922	4.5	4,835	2.6	191
Mechanized	363	(39.4)	446	(9.2)	814
Manual labour	493	(53.5)	4,318	(89.3)	114
Posts and telecommunications	66	(7.2)	71	(1.5)	930
Commerce	2,541	12.4	12,400	6.6	205
Shops	2,011	(79.1)	9,000	(72.6)	223
Hawkers	530	(20.9)	3,400	(27.4)	156
Finance	200	1.0	215	0.1	930
Dwelling services	934	4.6	N.A.	N.A.	N.A.
Professional and free lance jobs	171	0.8	1,775	0.9	96
Domestic servants	141	0.7	3,513	1.9	40
Public administration	642	3.1	5,934	2.9	119
Grand total	20,492		189,077		107

Figures in brackets are percentage shares of different subgroups.

Source: Pao-san Ou (1947c), p. 93; Djang (1947), p. 89.

4. *Self-consumed goods of producers.* Many producers consumed self-produced goods like crops and handicraft. In China, the self-consumed part of the farming and handicraft products was so prominent that, if excluded, the national income calculated would have been a misrepresentation. Consumption of this nature included also payment in kind, such as employers providing meals for their workers in the course of farming. The self-consumed products aforementioned should be counted in calculating national income.
5. *Illegal income.* Income obtained from illegal activities, like gambling and smuggling, was neither allowed by government nor increasing the wealth of society. It would not be counted in national income.
6. *Inventory changes.* Inventory changes in factories and stores at the beginning and the end of each year should be counted in calculating national income. Yet in China, the relevant data were lacking, and one could only assume that no adjustment had taken place; such change did not enter the accounting of national income.
7. *Indirect taxes.* Theoretically, indirect tax should be added, and government services subsidized to the production enterprises should be subtracted in the national income estimation. However, it was due to the fact that the number of indirect taxes was impossible to ascertain in various localities and that the government subsidies data were unavailable, thus no account of indirect tax was made, presumably the two items being mutually cancelling out.

The Establishment and Evolution of National Income After 1949

The establishment of the PRC in 1949 was accompanied by a series of fundamental changes during which the nature of her political and social system was altered tremendously. The new system was characterized by a highly centralized and planned management model based on the Marxist economic doctrine. The system of national income accounting adopted by China was similar to the MPS. The fundamental content of this system is the record of activities in production, distribution, exchange and usage of material products, and excludes non-material products. Thus, the net output value of material products, which is within the boundary of national income, makes up China's national income.

The Indispensability of Establishing National Income Statistics

After the establishment of the PRC, the main tasks that China was facing were the restoration and development of the national economy heavily damaged by the prolonged period of warfare, the stability of markets, employment, and the preparation of the planned national economy. In order to understand the situation and evaluate the potential of the nation, Mao Zedong proposed in 1952 to conduct a survey of total output value of the industrial and agricultural sectors, and a survey of national employment (for brevity, refer them as "the two surveys").[5] Thus, the newly established State Statistical Bureau (SSB) looked at the statistical figures of the several major industrial and agricultural product sectors and made comparison with the relevant survey information in order to arrive at an estimate of the total output value of the two sectors.

The "total output value of industry and agriculture" was an indicator that was to be long applied to a wide variety of uses: it depicted the general scale and speed of national economic development. However, it also had its limitations. First, it reflected merely the production status of the two sectors. The scale of the whole nation's economic activities was in reality much greater than these two sectors. Apart from industry and agriculture, other sectors, such as construction, transportation, and post and telecommunications, commerce, etc., needed to be included. Moreover, the output of these two sectors constituted not a constant but a variable component in the total output of the whole national economy, and there did not exist a linear relationship between them. Hence, the use of this indicator in evaluating economic development was apt to engender the phenomenon of imbalance development. Secondly, this indicator was a total output value. It reflected the total value of the products, including both the value newly created by labor and the transferred value of the raw materials used in the process of production. Since the production structure differed among regions and nations, the weight of the transferred value in total output value also differed. Thus, the simple spatial comparison of the total output value of different localities was inappropriate. And, the larger an enterprise's intermediate consumption was the larger was its total output value. Such outcome constituted a distorted picture for the enterprises striving hard to increase their total output value at the expense of economic efficiency. Thirdly, the "factory method" was adopted to evaluate the total output value of industry. Under the method, an enterprise was treated in its entirety, and the departments within the enterprise were not allowed double counting. But, because of the rapid development of specialization and cooperation among enterprises, some of the workshops and production processes were able to gain in importance and become independent factories. Thus, they contributed substantially to the inflated part of the total output.

In regard to the limitations aforesaid, in 1954, the accounting of the total output value of society was expanded. Apart from the agricultural and industrial sectors, other sectors like construction, transportation and post and telecommunications, commerce and catering trade were included. The construction sector directly produced tangible material goods and should have its total output value calculated. Although transportation, post and telecommunications and commerce did not participate directly in the course of tangible material production, they played an important role in the process of circulation by transferring material products from production localities to the areas of consumption and by distributing commodities to consumers. Thus, the use value of the goods could not have been realized and appreciated without them. Actually, they went hand in hand with agriculture, industry and construction, fulfilling the reproduction of social goods, and, thus, had to be treated on an equal footing.

The new indicator of "total output value of society" could be used to illustrate the course of production, the economic proportionality relations, the scale, structure and pace of aggregate production. However, such indicator had the same problem of double counting unsolved, as in the case of the total output value of agriculture and industry. This shortcoming brought about intricate problems which hampered the accurate accounting of enterprise production and, worse still, the realistic reflection of economic efficiency.

With a view to solving the problem of double counting, making use of the newly created statistics encompassing the whole material production domain and illustrating the comprehensive economic efficiency which could be drawn from increasing production and economizing intermediate consumption, the SSB started to estimate China's national income in 1954. National income was defined as the net value of total output of society excluding the intermediate consumption in the course of production.

The Establishment of National Income Statistics and Their Evolution

China took the first step to estimate her national income in 1954. It was a tough task because the actual experience of such work and the statistical data from the specialized sectors were lacking. Perceiving the inadequacies, the staff member engaged in the field tried various methods in the hope of getting the job done. They started by studying the Marxist doctrine of reproduction and the theory and method of national income statistics adopted by the former USSR; they collected relevant data from various specialized departments; especially, they adopted relevant accounting data from various departments, such as finance, taxation, industry and commerce, etc. The so estimated national income data for 1952 and 1953 were a first step towards a better defined statistical system for China's national income.

The above findings were used as the basis for further estimating the national income of 1954 and 1955, through which the general indicators of the structure, pace and level of national income from 1952 to 1955, as well as important economic proportionality data of accumulation and consumption were calculated. The information was important as it enhanced our understanding of the patterns of China's socialist economic reconstruction, strengthened the planned management of the national economy and provided important information for decision-making.

During the 8th National Congress of the Chinese Communist Party in September 1956, Bo Yibo proposed a policy formulation called "Two, Three, Four,"[6] based on the national income data estimated by the SSB and other information. It was suggested that the proportion should be composed of the following shares: 20 percent for accumulation, 30 percent for fiscal revenue in national income, and 40 percent for basic construction investment in public expenditure. By first divulging the national income data, followed by a comprehensive analysis, the congress succeeded in arousing the interest of people from all walks of life, after which the statistical organizations of many provinces and municipalities (directly under the Central Government) started to gather and estimate their local national income and use the data to analyze their economic conditions.

With a view to solving some technical problems in the course of national income accounting and obtaining foreign experience, a working team, headed by the Deputy Director-General of the SSB, Sun Yefang, visited the former USSR from June to September 1956. The visit was intended to seek a better understanding of the Soviet experience and of their method of compiling a national economic balance sheet. A first meeting on the nation's comprehensive balance statistics was called in late 1957 during which the source of data and the method of calculation of the national income statistics were depicted.

The statistical work on the Chinese national income was, however, impeded in the following years. In 1958, when *anti-dogmatism* campaign was prominent, the person-in-charge of the SSB criticized that the workload of the national income statistics was too heavy and the statistics failed to explain the economic problems arising thereof. Such criticism dealt a severe blow to the development of the national income accounting. Nevertheless, in 1959, the SSB verified and amended some sectoral statistics gathered in 1958. However, there were still data overstating the real picture, and thus the estimation of that year was rather biased.

The Cultural Revolution, launched in the second half of 1966, also dealt a severe blow to statistical work. It was not until the 1970s that the nearly stopped statistical work did start again under unfavorable circumstances. At the start of the 1970s, the Statistical Team of the State Planning Commission (into which the SSB was embedded) had allowed only a few to stay and continue the statistical work. Since relevant data were lacking, a simpler approach had then been adopted, and, due to the insufficient data base for calculation, the estimated figures had had to be revised many times. When the SSB was fully restored in 1977, only a limited number of personnel available were authorized to gather and estimate the figures of China's national income over the intervening years. The SSB prepared a *Report on Strengthening and Reforming the Statistical Work*, which was then approved by the State Council. The report emphasized the need to strengthen the collection of comprehensive and balanced statistics and to establish a national economic accounting system, the first objective of which was to be the statistics on China's national income. In 1982, the SSB was able to set up the Department of National Economic Balance Statistics. The national income statistics were then greatly strengthened and became the prevalent statistics throughout the localities of the country.

In 1983, the State Council approved the *Report on Strengthening National Income Statistics* submitted by the State Planning Commission, the State Economic Commission, the Ministry of Finance and SSB. The indicator of national income, from 1984 onwards, was recognized as one of the consolidated indicators to trace the development situation of China's economy. Also, it was requested that the annual planning of the national income for the whole country, each province, municipality and autonomous region, be carefully compiled and reviewed every year. The SSB put forward the *System of National Income Report Forms* (Discussion Draft) in 1986 in order to collaborate with the decision and to establish a sound basis for compiling and assessing the national income. It was also from this year onwards that the system of national income report forms was embedded in national income accounting, through which the national income statistics were able to take another step towards systematization and standardization.

With a view to strengthening the national income accounting system and making further progress, the Department of National Economic Balance Statistics was renamed the Department of National Accounts Statistics in 1994.

Formation of New National Income Accounting System

As a result of the deepening of the economic system reform and open door policy, the development of productivity and the progress in technology, China's economy had undergone significant changes. A new national income accounting system had become necessary because of the increasing importance of the tertiary sector and other rising industries. The material production indicators previously in use to measure the social economic development had been failing to reflect the economic activities and performance of each sector, and had no longer been able to satisfy the need for international comparison. Therefore, based on the demand of

China's actual economic situation and the new requirements of state economic management, a new national income accounting system was urgently needed, which could fulfill the function of a comprehensive economic measure adapted to international practice and which could reflect extensively the total scope of economic development and could facilitate international comparability.

The Inadequacies of National Income Measures

The former approach to national income accounting had been using the MPS method; although it had been functional under the previous type of economic management, being confronted with the conditions of economic system reform and opening, its inadequacies and limitations had become more and more obvious.

1. *Confined definition of production.* China's traditional economic theory had rested on the assumption that only the creation of tangible use value and the services to the creation of tangible use value were productive labor. Only the sectors in which such productive labor was taking place were material production sectors; if not, the other sectors were all non-material production sector. Such assumption confined social production to industry, agriculture, construction, transportation and telecommunications and commerce (including food catering and material supply). As a consequence, from the angle of statistics, the macroeconomic national income indicators represented only material production and the services to material production, but not non-material services production.

   This type of accounting, which concentrated on material production but ignored social services, impeded the development of China's tertiary sector. To such an extent that information was laggard, distribution channels inefficient and facilities outdated. This further inhibited the rational use of labor, the expansion of employment opportunity, the upgrading of productivity as well as the raising of the standards of material culture.
2. *Unreasonable scope of consumption.* Similar to the definition of production, when estimating the national income available by the expenditure approach, the main final consumption parts cover the inhabitants and the government, as well as the non-material production sectors. However, consumer goods were strictly confined to material products. Actually, non-material production sectors, similar to material production ones, were also producers, and not merely consumers. The non-material services consumed by the inhabitants and the government were just the same as the consumption of material goods, which were all legitimate part of the final consumption, indispensable

to the material and cultural life of the people. By defining the non-material production sectors as mere consumers and the consumer goods as merely material goods, the boundary between intermediate consumption and final consumption had become blurred; the needs of cultural life had been neglected. Therefore, a total understanding of the scale of consumption, of its structure and of its direction had been undermined. It became difficult to make correct policies about consumption, to guide its distribution structure and to fulfil to the greatest extent possible the needs of the people's material and cultural life.

3. *Inadequacies of external trade accounting.* When estimating the national income available, only the import and export of material goods were considered; other forms of exchange were not accounted for. Since the reform and opening began, China's various trade activities underwent rapid development. This included not only the import-export of material products and services of a material nature, but also of non-material services, such as overseas transfers and financial transactions which promoted the expansion of the economy. These had to be integrated into the whole accounting practice so as to satisfy the needs of policy-making with regard to foreign trade and its management.
4. *Unscientific nature of national income statistics.* MPS was defining the national economy in territorial terms. Accordingly, the venue of activities, rather than the origin and duration period, were considered the relevant criterion; as long as the economic activities were taking place within the territory, they were a component of the national economy. Correspondingly, activities by Chinese units taking place outside the national boundaries were not to be counted as part of the national economy. This principle was comparatively reasonable in a closed economic system, but under the conditions of reform and opening and increasingly numerous relations with the outside, the inadequacies of the accounting system became obvious. For example, as China's art performing groups came to travel overseas to perform, under territorial principles, these performances were taking place in a foreign land and were not economic activities that could be considered part of China's but of the visited country's economic productive activity. Since these art groups performed both overseas and locally, the corresponding domestic production sectors were faced with inconsistency and variability in the economic estimation of performance.

As a result of the reforms and opening policy, an improved method of national income accounting system had become urgently needed in order to reflect the new economic situation.

Formation of the New National Income Accounting System

The research work on the new national economic accounting system was first launched in 1984. The State Council promulgated the *Decision on Strengthening Statistical Work* in January, proposing a unified and scientific national economic accounting system. In November, the State Council decided to set up the State Council Leading Team on Unified Accounting Standards for the National Economy; the office was located in the SSB, and the team was composed of leading staff from the State Planning Commission, the State Economic Commission, the Ministry of Finance, the People's Bank of China, the Office of Audit, the SSB and the National Standards Bureau.

In April 1985, the State Council further approved the creation of statistics reflecting the gross national product and the tertiary sector. In function of the deepening of the reforms, the tertiary (services) sector had grown rapidly to become one of the important sectors of the national economy. It had become necessary as a condition of the national economy to understand better the nature of its growth and to determine appropriate policies; it was under these circumstances that the State Council thus approved the SSB's *Report on the Establishment of a Statistics System for the Tertiary Industry*.

Specialists and scholars in economics went into a round of academic meetings to tackle the questions concerning the new economic accounting system, such as the theoretical foundation, the guiding principles, the systemic framework and the method of presentation. In addition, foreign experts in national economic accounting were invited to China to deliver lectures, and teams of Chinese experts were sent aboard to investigate the procedures and practical techniques in other countries, such as the United Kingdom, France, the United States, Canada, Japan, the former USSR, the Federal Republic of Germany, etc.

While continuing the scientific research, experts started in 1986 to draft the new national economic accounting system. Then, in November of the same year, the office of the Leadership Team presented the *Tentative Overall Plan for Our National Economic Accounting System* (Discussion Draft). In accordance with subsequent discussions, in February 1987 the staff of the Statistical Bureaux from Heilongjiang, Liaoning, Hebei, Shaanxi, Shanghai, Jiangxi and Sichuan were invited to join in the further amending of the draft. A Consultation Document, *Proposal for Our National Economic Accounting System*, was then put forward and issued to concerned departments and regions for their reactions. A small number of local statistical bureaux of provincial and municipal levels were asked to implement the formula experimentally in order to test its feasibility. A meeting for further discussion was held in April 1988 by representatives of the State Planning

Commission, the Economic System Reform Commission, the Ministry of Finance, various banks, statistics departments, and some of the staff from several provinces and municipalities. The representatives basically agreed with the amended proposal, with the exception of a few areas. After these amendments, the proposal was issued to the government units concerned.

In June 1988, in order to further test in practice the scientific, practical and feasible attributes of the proposed formula, a meeting was called in Chengde, Hebei province, by the SSB to look at the results of the various experiments; then followed a review of the sources of relevant formulations and of the methods of estimation, an investigation of how to reform the related statistical, accounting and business reporting methods and to devise a method of implementation. The discussion clarified the focal points and work procedures of various testing locales. As a result, the State Statistical Bureau conducted a provisional compilation and aggregation of the reports and sectoral accounts from 18 provinces, prefectures and cities using the new accounting system. Then, the SSB tested the value of the gross domestic product statistics from the relevant value-added data of 29 provincial-level regions, excluding Tibet. Through the groundwork and various tests, the proposal found the evidence it needed greatly to improve its reliability and support the further exploration of the way to implement the new method, while finding ways to educate and train a new personnel and, to certain extent, assist in propagating and promoting knowledge in the new system.

A conference on national economic accounting system was held in April 1990. The purpose was to focus the attention of the relevant departments, regions and units and to lead to a comprehensive discussion of the proposal after reviewing the experience that had been gained by the calculation of the GNP of the last few years, the compilation of the 1987 input-output tables and other concrete statistical exercises. Once again in 1991, the proposal was revised as it had become clear that the original mode of presentation and its structure had lacked in clarity. According to the principles of comprehensiveness, systematization and balance, the draft was rationally redesigned, the nature of the tables and the design of the indicators improved. The result was to finally come out as *China's National Economic Accounting System* (trial draft) for preliminary use across the regions and the whole country.

With a view to testing the scientific qualities of the fundamental structure and the various indicators of the draft, the State Council gathered officials from affected departments and concerned experts in a conference in January 1992, during which the draft was further discussed and verified. The gathered experts indicated that they believed that the results were scientific and that the draft could be recommended for implementation.

In April 1992, the State Council held a telephone conference during which the new economic accounting methodology was announced to the whole nation. In August of the same year, the State Council, in promulgating the *Notification on the Enforcement of the New National Economic Accounting System,* indicated that the proposal was going to come into practice all over the country in two stages. The first stage was to establish the fundamental framework of the new system at the national and provincial levels in 1992-1993, as an initial stage of transition; the second stage, which was to extend to 1995, would complete the transformation to the new national economic accounting system.

Notes

1. We would like to thank Dr. Pao-san Ou for the relevant literature offered for the writing of this section.

2. Dr. Ou called it the disposable national goods and services when the foreign investment and credit expansion were included.

3. See Ou et al. (1947a), pp. 16-17 and Ou (1947c), p. 97.

4. See Ou (1947c), p. 94.

5. See Yue Wei (1990), pp. 58-61, 65, and 105-111.

6. See Theory Department, the Central Party School of the Chinese Communist Party (ed.) (1991), p. 48.

References (in Chinese unless otherwise indicated)

Djang, Gee-hung. 1947. "An Estimate of the Working Population of China," *Quarterly Review of Social Sciences*, Vol. IX, No. 2, December, pp. 71-91.

Editorial Board of "Contemporary China" Series. (ed.) 1989. *Statistical Undertakings of Contemporary China.* Beijing: Chinese Social Science Publishing House.

Ou, Pao-san. 1946a. "International Payments in National Income," *Quarterly Journal of Economics* (USA), Vol.VIX, February, pp. 289-98 (in English).

________ . 1946b. "A New Estimate of China's National Income," *Journal of Political Economy* (USA), Vol. LIV, No. 6, December, pp. 547-54 (in English).

________ . 1947b. "National Income of China, 1933, 1936 and 1946," *Quarterly Review of Social Sciences*, Vol. IX, No. 2, December, pp. 12-30.

________ . 1947c. "Revision of National Income of China, 1933," *Quarterly Review of Social Sciences*, Vol. IX, No. 2, December, pp. 92-153.

Ou, Pao-san et al. (eds.) 1947a. *National Income of China (1933)*, Series No. 25, Institute of Social Sciences, Academia Sinica, Vol. I and II (Shanghai: Zhonghua Publishing House).

Research Institute of Statistical Science, State Statistical Bureau (ed.). 1985. *The Establishment and Development of China's Socialist Statistical Work.* Beijing: Chinese Statistical Publishing House.

Theory Department, Central Party School of the Chinese Communist Party (ed.). 1991. *Compendium on Party Construction of the Chinese Communist Party,* Vol. 8. Taiyuan: Shanxi People's Publishing House.

Yang Shuzhuang, Li Qiang, and Liu Chengxiang (eds.). 1993. *Implementation Guidebook of China's New National Economic Accounting System*. Beijing: University of Industry Press.

Yue Wei. 1990. *Theory of Macroeconomic Statistics*. Beijing: Chinese Statistical Publishing House.

2

China's National Income Accounting in MPS

*Zhang Xiyun**
*Hsueh Tien-tung**

The MPS recommended by the United Nations is one of two most influential national income accounting systems in the world. From the beginning of the regime in October, 1949 until August, 1992, the PRC had adopted the MPS. China had basically borrowed the system used by the former USSR and Eastern Europe. However, China had brought some changes to bear on the system according to the real situation, in particular regarding the principles of national income measurements and methods of accounting. MPS takes the view that only material production sectors can create value. Therefore, national income counted by MPS is equal to the net output value of material production sectors, which will be discussed in some details in the following.

Theory of National Income Accounting in MPS

Principle of Differentiation Between Material Production Domain and Non-material Production Domain

Within the social reproduction process, the different types of labor undertaken by various laborers in the various production sectors are all necessary to society. However, some sectors are responsible for material means, (e.g., industry, agriculture, construction). While others provide

*We very much appreciate receiving helpful comments from Xu Xianchun and Liu Liping

services or engaging in management work, (e.g., education, health care, government organizations, national defense, etc.). From the angle of the contribution of the laborers in the various sectors to society whether they provide material products or not, all sectors can be divided into production and non-production domains.

In the production domain, material products provide the basic means for people's survival, which is also the material base for the maintenance of the non-production domain. It is only on the basis of the continuous development of material production that more social wealth can then be built up.

The main characteristic of the various sectors engaged in material production is to transform the invested labor inputs into use value either as means of production or consumption products. Accordingly, industry, agriculture and construction are treated as the basic production sectors in which the labor that is consumed creates a new use value. Although freight transport, post and telecommunications, material supply and marketing, and commerce do not create use value, their labor input is a continuation of the production process. Their labor input is to move material products form the place of production to consumption area so that the use value of the products is realized. As a result, the products gain further in value, and society is assured of the proper continuation of reproduction. Other forms of labor, such as product safekeeping, distributing, packaging, transporting, etc., are also indispensable segments of social reproduction. Through these labor forms, the products can then possibly be used in the production process and in daily consumption. Thus, freight transport, post and telecommunications, material supply and marketing, and commerce should belong to material production domain.

Non-production domain includes all the different kinds of services, culture and education, health care, physical education, tourism, scientific research organizations, finance work, state administration and other non-production sectors.

The labor input into these services is consumed according to the servicing provided, but it is not creating a new social product. Scientific research and state administrative organizations and other services provide non-material services for material production sectors. However, they are not considered as directly linked to the production chain. Nevertheless, they still play an important role in improving people's living conditions, promoting economic, scientific, cultural, health and other development.

Principle Determining the Scope of National Income Statistics

MPS is based on location principle. All material production activities carried out within the boundaries, no matter who manages the enterprises, e.g., Sino-foreign joint ventures, individual investment enterprises, or enterprises with capital of partially or totally foreign origin, are calculated into China's national income. Similarly, for provinces, municipalities directly under the Central Government and autonomous regions, all products actually produced within the boundaries, no matter whether the products are manufactured by locally owned enterprises, or whether the products are made for local use, are all counted as part of the national income of the locality.

However, in recent years, in order to bridge the gap between the national income statistics of the MPS and the new gross domestic product statistics of SNA, and to match the economic indicators and the calculation calibre, some adjustment has been made to the national income statistics originally based on locality principle. This means that only units with permanent residence are included. And during the accounting period, only these resident units' material products are counted into the national income. In this way, since the basic accounting units are the permanent ones in contrast to the within-boundary units, the emphasis is then placed on economic activities within the boundaries and on length of residence. For those units that reside for more than one year, the income belongs to the locality of residence. And the income will be accounted to the original locality the units belonged to in case of residence for less than one year.

Evaluation Principles

National income accounting adopts two different categories of price: the final consumption price and the producer price.

Final consumption price refers to the price accounting for the material products used in production as material consumption, and used in accumulation, and in consumption, or export as final use, which also means the actual price paid for the production means and consumer goods by purchasers; so it is also called the purchaser price.

The producer price means the price which the enterprise uses to sell its product.

Products which have not entered into circulation, such as unfinished products, self-made raw materials, processed materials etc., are generally calculated according to the producer price, i.e., the selling price. The residents' non-commercial sideline product can be evaluated by the selling price of similar product.

Beside the prices aforementioned, the producer price includes production tax which is the set net income the enterprise surrenders to the financial authorities according to the sale of products. The basic price is obtained by deducting the net production tax from the producer price, which can be used to analyze the impact of the production tax on enterprise production.

In the calculation and comparison of national income, both the current prices and the comparable prices need to be used. In practical economic activities, the production, distribution, exchange and consumption of all products proceed according to the current prices. It is under the condition of current prices that the production, distribution and re-distribution of national income take place. And it is only in this way that one can understand the various economic relationships between production scale, distribution and re-distribution of national income under the present situation.

However, it is not enough to adopt the current prices for calculating and comparing the national income. We also want to find out the course and patterns of actual changes; we want to explore also the trends of its real changes and take the corresponding measures, so comparable prices must also be used. National income at comparable prices is employed to eliminate the influence of fluctuation in prices, and to maintain the physical volume of the original national income. By which the dynamic changes in the real volume of the national income can be observed, and the various factors restraining national income can be examined.

Usually, some price index method is used to deflate the nominal price variations, that is to compile the price indexes for the major production means and the major consumption means according to various material production sectors. The indexes are used to deflate the total output value and intermediate consumption in current prices, so as to eliminate the influence of price changes on national income. And for the national income available, the corresponding price indexes are also adopted to deflate the accumulation and consumption in current prices.

Concept and Accounting Meaning of National Income

By national income is meant the value of material production newly created by the laborers of the material production sectors in a country (or a region) during a particular period (usually one year). It is also an important component of the total output value of the whole society made by the sectors during that particular time.

The total output value of society of the period includes, on the one hand, the production means consumed during the production process (material consumption value). During the process, this part of the production means is transferred to the new products gradually. On the other hand, the total value also includes the newly created value. If we use P to represent the total output value of society, then $P = C + V + M$, C represents production means value; $V + M$ is the national income. V designates the remuneration of laborers, that is, wages and welfare funds; M stands for the surplus product value made by laborers, which includes profit, tax and interest. From the view point of physical products, national income comes from two components: firstly, it is the consumption means used by personal and public consumption; secondly, the production means used in accumulation.

Significant Meaning

1. National income designates the value newly created within a year, so it shows the level of the economic strength and development of a country or a region.
2. National income is the result of subtracting material consumption from total output value of society. Therefore, it not only reflects the growth and changes in national income and the state of production development within a certain period, but also shows the economizing of raw materials, processed materials, fuels, etc., during the production process. By means of which, measures to develop more energy sources and to raise economic efficiency can be taken.
3. Since national income deducts the double counting of transferred value, it reflects the development speed, scale and sectoral structure of the production of society more accurately and comprehensively than the total output value of industry and agriculture and the total output value of society.
4. The distribution and usage of national income show the important proportionalities in the national economy: for example, the distribution relationships between state, collective (enterprise) and individual; between consumption and accumulation, between state construction and people livelihood; between fixed assets and circulating assets; between productive accumulation and non-productive accumulation; between personal consumption and social collective consumption; and between rural residents' consumption and non-rural residents' consumption.
5. National income divided according to regions can reflect regional economic features, as well as regional ranking and relations in the whole national economy.

Calculation of the Total Output Value of Society and Its Components

Total Output Value of Society, Material Consumption and Net Output Value

The total output value of society (total product of society) means all the material products produced by the material production sectors within a certain period. The total output value of all production sectors is equal to the total output value of society.

Material consumption designates the production means consumed by the material production sectors during the production process. So, production means as value bearer enter the production process to contribute to the carrying out of society's reproduction.

Consumption during material production mainly includes:

1. The consumption of raw materials, processed materials, fuels and electricity.
2. The consumption of seeds, fodder, fertilizers, pesticides, etc.
3. The expenditures on productive services (e.g., charges for transport, post and telecommunications during the production process; process fees for semi-finished product and repair charges by other enterprises).
4. Losses during the transportation and safekeeping process by commercial, material supply and purchasing trades.
5. Other expenses in the production process, e.g., workers' uniforms, protective measures, nutritious foods and health care.
6. The depreciation and major repair charges on productive fixed assets within the reporting year.

The net output value (i.e., the product of national income) designates the net amount after deducting material consumption from the total output value of society, i.e., the sum of the total net output value of all the material production sectors, such as industry, agriculture, construction, transport, post and telecommunications and commerce (including catering trade and material supply and marketing trade).

There are two points which deserve to be mentioned:

1. When calculating the net output value, a demarcation line must be drawn between the material consumption expenditure, the primary distribution expenditure and the redistribution expenditure. The material consumption during the production process can only be the consumption of production means. Although some goods are bought by the production sectors, they are not for production use, but for individual use or collective welfare, e.g., prizes in kind, nursery schools, hair cuts, bathing and all other cultural life expenses of staff and workers. All these belong to primary distribution, which are components of net output value, and should not be counted into material consumption. For all parts that have already been counted into the primary distribution, e.g., profit, labor insurance and welfare funds, rural public welfare funds, etc., the expenditures drawn from these funds belong to the redistribution domain, thus, they should not be counted twice.
2. The calculation of material consumption by various sectors should

correspond to the calculation of their particular total output value. That is what is usually called "material consumption following output value." Only the material consumption included in total output value should be counted, not the other expenditures.

Total Output Value, Material Consumption and Net Output Value of Industry

Total output value of industry is the monetary value of total products made by industrial enterprises during the reporting period. It includes finished product value and the value of industrial operation,[1] self-made semi-finished goods and the differential value of goods in manufacturing process between end and beginning of term.

The statistical scope of total output value of industry, from economic types, includes state-owned, urban and rural collective-owned, various kinds of jointly owned, co-operative, foreign-owned and urban and rural privately owned industrial enterprises.

Material consumption of industry includes raw materials, processed material, supplementary material, fuel and electricity, productive fixed assets depreciation and other products' consumption.

Industrial net output value is obtained by subtracting the industrial material consumption value from the industrial total output value.

Total Output Value, Material Consumption and Net Output Value of Agriculture

The total output value of agriculture includes the total value of the main products and secondary products of farming, forestry, animal husbandry, sideline production and fishery.

Farming mainly designates all kinds of grain, cotton, oil-bearing crops, hemp, sugar, tobacco, etc., all kinds of cash crops; vegetable, melons, fodder, green manure, etc., and other crops such as tea, mulberry, fruits, and so on.

Forestry mainly designates plant cultivation, forest products collection and bamboo cultivation by cooperative organizations and farmers at village *(cun)* level and below.

Animal husbandry includes raising and shepherding of all animals (except fishery).

Sideline production includes the collection of wild plants, hunting wild animals and fowl, and the handicraft sidelines of peasant households.

Fishery mainly includes fishing aquatic animals as well as cultivating aquatic plants.

The Chinese socialist agriculture is mainly formed of the systems of ownership by the state and by the collective of laborers. There are some peasant households farming by themselves, and other types of farming, mainly including cooperative capital farming, Hong Kong, Macau and overseas Chinese managed farming, and peasant individual farming.

The material consumption of agriculture mainly includes:

1. the actual consumption of seeds, fodder, livestock breeding charges, epidemic prevention charges for domestic animals, fertilizer, fuels, pesticide, electricity, minor farm tools purchase, etc.
2. the wear and tear of fixed assets during the production process, raw and processed materials consumption of sideline production.
3. the expenditure of service charges during the production process, e.g., repairing fees for farm machinery tools and facilities; management fee for administering production; transportation expenses for hired hands; post and telecommunication charges; other labor service expenditures.
4. all other material consumption not listed above.

The net output value of agriculture is the value-added resulting from agricultural laborers' activities (including farming, forestry, animal husbandry, sideline production and fishery) within a given period of time.

Total Output Value, Material Consumption and Net Output Value of Construction

Total output value of construction reflects the overall achievement of construction activities, that means the total value of construction completed by building and installation enterprises or units within a given period of time.

Total output value of construction mainly includes:

1. The value of all kinds of construction projects, e.g., all buildings, houses, bridges, railways, highways, port construction, mine excavation, digging and extension of wells, open-sky strip mining, drilling for oil or natural gas, water reservoir, dykes and dams, irrigation works, river dredging, air defense, underground construction and other special works; the value of subsidiary building materials, heating, sanitary ventilation, lighting, coal gas equipment, etc. All types of construction of pipeline, electric cable and communication installation within the project budget.
2. The value of machinery installation, including the installation of machine tools, boilers, cranes, generators, counting only the value-added of installed works, not the value of the equipment per se.
3. The work related to construction project, such as geological exploration

and prospecting design. Geological exploration can be further divided into engineering and geological resource exploration. Engineering exploration is the activity preceding the constructing of fixed assets, so it should be counted into the total output value of construction. It has been clearly defined in the industry categories of the new national economic accounting. Geological resource exploration generally is not made for a specific project, so it should not be included in the total output value of a construction.

4. The value of major repair of housing and buildings designates the amount of work completed on housing and buildings.
5. Work on rural construction and installation includes all construction of buildings for production or daily life purposes, equipment installation, minor irrigation construction and wasteland reclamation, etc., in the rural area.

Material consumption by construction designates all consumed construction materials and consumption during construction work: water, electricity, gas, fixed asset depreciation, temporary facility write-off charges, transportation, post and telecommunications services, etc.

Net output value of construction designates the value-added created by construction and installation activities. The total output value of construction consists of two components, one is material consumption that has been transferred to the products during construction and installation activities, e.g., raw and processed materials, fuel, structural parts, fixed asset depreciation, etc. The other one is the newly created value by construction and installation activities, e.g., profit, tax, wages and interest expenditures. The net output value of construction is obtained by deducting the material consumption from the total output value of construction.

Total Output Value, Material Consumption and Net Output Value of Transport, Post and Telecommunications

Transport. Transport activity is not only a production process but also a value creation and formation process. The total output value of transport refers to the income from freight traffic, loading and unloading and consigning goods, pipeline transport and transportation agency. This does not include income from passenger transport, services to transportation and other business income.

The statistical scope of transport can be divided into state-owned transport which mainly designates railways, highways, waterways (including loading and unloading, lightering, and storage), port transport, pipeline transport, civil aviation transport; collective-owned transport; private or cooperative transport (mainly referring to road and water transport, of which road transport is more important).

Post and Telecommunications. Total output value of post and telecommunications refers to the business income from post, telecommunications and the distribution of newspapers and magazines. The contents include incomes for letters, parcels, telecommunications, newspapers and magazines distribution, telephone and acting as communication agent (in principle, it should not count the non-production income earned from serving the citizens).

Material consumption by transport and post and telecommunications consists of fuel, material, electricity, vehicle repairing charges and fixed asset depreciation charges consumed in the production process of transportation and post and telecommunications. The concrete material consumption in various sectors can be shown as follows:

- Railways: fuel, material, electricity, fixed asset depreciation, main repair funds, and other material consumption.
- Highways: fuel and energy, material, fixed asset depreciation, major repair funds, upkeep, labor protection charges, travel allowance, damage and compensation, water and electricity fees, administrative fees and consumable products.
- Waterways, ports: port fees, fixed asset depreciation, major repair funds, fuel and energy, lighting, material fees, damage and compensation, and other material consumption.
- Civil aviation: fuel and energy, heating, water and electricity, airport service charges, ground transport fees, consumable products, fixed asset depreciation, major repair funds, and other material consumption.
- Petroleum, natural gas pipeline: energy, fuel, electricity, checking and repairing of line equipment, consumable products, fixed asset depreciation, major repair funds, and other material consumption.
- Post and telecommunications: fixed asset depreciation, major repair funds, line remodelling allowance, fuel, energy and electricity, lighting and heating, water and electricity, parcel transport, equipment repair, labor protection, consumable products, and other material consumption.

Net output value of transport and post and telecommunications is defined as follows:

Net output value of transportation refers to the value obtained by deducting the intermediate goods value (material consumption) from the total output value.

Net output value of post and telecommunications refers to the value obtained by deducting the material consumption from the total business income of the post and telecommunications enterprises.

Total Output Value, Material Consumption and Net Output Value of Commerce (Catering Trade, Material Supply and Marketing)

Commerce includes domestic commerce and foreign trade, which is transferring goods and materials from producer to consumer, hence, increasing the product value through the retailing and purchasing of goods and materials during the circulation process.

The total output value of commerce refers to the margin by deducting the commodity value at entering price from the sale value. That is the so-called commercial extra charges (or the sum total of commodity circulation charges, tax and sale profit). In order to avoid double counting during circulation, the consigning and load and unload charges paid to the transport industry must be deducted from the commodity circulation charges.

The total output value of material supply and marketing designates the product value increased through supply and marketing activities of production means. This increased part is its total output value.

The total output value of the catering trade is usually based on the turnover. That is, one calculates the total production value of catering trade, which includes the value of processed raw and other materials and the processing charges. This is because in this industry, processing, producing and selling take place at the same time.

Material consumption by commerce (including catering trade and supply and marketing) consists of commodity consumption, fixed asset depreciation, consumable products, repair, service charge, upkeeping, selection arranging charges (from which the wages for personnel, which belong to net output value, should be deducted) packaging (consumption of packaging materials, e.g., gunny-bags, oil drum, wood box, expenses or cleaning and repairing, service charges (referring to expenses paid to other trade enterprises to sell the products), advertising and sample charges, post and telecommunications charges, printing, stationery, water and electricity, heating and miscellaneous charges. Consumption of raw material, material, fuel, water and electricity during food processing, depreciation on utensils and furniture, administrative charges, and so on.

However, for the commerce departments it is difficult to directly calculate material consumption in the commerce sector, so the net output value is obtained by taking into account the composing elements of wages, staff and workers welfare funds, profit, taxes, interest and others. Their total is accepted as the net output value.

The statistical scope of total output value of commerce designates commercial and catering trade and material supply of the whole society. It includes trade; supply; foreign trade; grain; medicine; aquatic products; agricultural machines; car parts; Xinhua bookshops; agriculture production means supply companies; the material bureau system, the material handling section of the administration departments responsible for the business, retail departments set up by factories, mines and farms; neighborhood and organized trade units; catering trade owned by state units, supply cooperatives, street collectives, and the private sector; and direct sales by peasants to non-peasants in country fair (not including the service sectors).

The Establishment of Production Accounting for the National Income in MPS

There are two ways for the production accounting of national income: the first is the "production approach," that is to calculate first the total output value and material consumption of each production sector, so as to find for each the net output value. The formula is:

Net Output Value = Total Output Value – Material Consumption

The other is the "distribution approach," i.e., the sum total of the elements making the net output value of each production sector: profits, taxes, interests, wages (or net income of farmers), staff and workers welfare funds, etc. The formula is:

Net Output Value = Profits + Taxes + Interests + Wages + Welfare Funds + Others

Material Consumption = Total Output Value – Net Output Value

Production Value of National Income = Net Output Value of Industry + Net Output Value of Agriculture + Net Output Value of Construction + Net Output Value of Transport and Post and Telecommunications + Net Output Value of Commerce (catering and trade).

The following are explanations of the calculation method and data sources of the total output value, material consumption and net output value of five material production sectors.

A. Total Output Value, Net Output Value and Material Consumption In Current Prices

The principle for calculating the total output value of society and national income (net output value) is to adopt the output value statistics provided by the various specialized statistics departments whenever available. For those incomplete data or partial indicators, supplementary data are taken from other financial, accounting and business sources.

Industry

The "factory method" is used to calculate the total output value at current prices. The relevant data are available directly from the *Annual Reports of Industrial Statistics.*

The net output value at current prices includes the net output value of both independent and non-independent accounting industrial enterprises, that of village (production team) owned and rural cooperative industrial enterprises and that of urban and rural self-employed industrial enterprises.

Data for the net output value of independent accounting industrial enterprises are directly available from the *Annual Report of Industrial Statistics* by the Department of Industrial and Transportation Statistics of SSB.

Data for the non-independent accounting industrial enterprises can be extrapolated from the ratio of net output value to total output value of the independent accounting industrial enterprises. The concrete method is to determine first the net output value ratio and, then, multiply the ratio by the appropriate total output value to obtain the net output value. However, during the process, one must bear in mind that, in order to avoid double counting, once the net output value of the non-independent accounting industrial enterprises has been calculated in the production departments to which the enterprises belong, it should not be counted again with the independent enterprises.

Data regarding the net output value of village (production team) owned industries and rural cooperative industrial enterprises can be gathered from the financial statistics of the administrative department in charge of the rural enterprises. The value can be calculated according to the "distribution approach" or by referring to the net output value ratio estimate of the Rural Enterprise Department for the *xiang*-owned industrial enterprises.[2]

The net output value of urban and rural individual-owned industrial enterprises can be calculated or estimated based on the information from the Industry and Commerce Administrative Department and the Taxation Department.

By adding up the current price total and net output value of the various industrial sectors, we then obtain the total and net output value of industry.

Agriculture

Current-price total and net output value. The total output value of agriculture is usually calculated by the "product method," i.e., the quantity of product times the unit price of the product for the total output value.

Information on total output value can be obtained directly from the

Annual Statistical Report of the Rural Economy by the Organization of Rural Social and Economic Surveys of SSB.

Information on net output value and material consumption can be obtained directly from the *Annual Statistical Report of the Rural Economy* as well.

Construction

One of the characteristics of construction is that the construction enterprise does not own the construction product, while the owner of the product usually is not directly involved in the construction process. The second characteristic is that the production activity of the construction industry is mobile while the construction product is fixed. Therefore, there are two ways of calculating the total output value of construction.

The first method is to carry out the calculation based on the location of the product, i.e., to calculate the output value according to the final output of the construction enterprise or the private construction unit involved in the construction's production activity. Therefore, any construction carried out at other places by the local construction enterprise for more than one year must be excluded from the local calculation, while any local construction carried out by an outside construction enterprise for more than one year must be included in the total output value of local construction.

The second method, called the product method calculation, is to calculate the total output value of construction according to the ownership of the construction. This method can be directly based on the information of fixed assets investment. The second method is commonly adopted due to the difficulty of data collection for the calculation of total output value of the construction industry.

Using the fixed assets investment approach mainly includes the following: (1) construction and installation for state-owned enterprises' basic construction, renovation investment, other fixed assets investment and commercial housing; (2) construction and installation of fixed assets investment carried out by collectives and by other types of ownership at city and town level; (3) construction and installation projects of fixed assets investment by collectives and other ownership types at the village level; (4) investment in private housing in industrial and mining areas and in cities and towns; (5) private housing investment in villages; (6) the workload related to geological prospecting and prospecting design regarding construction projects and the major repairing of housing and structures relevant to construction projects.

The total output value of construction can be obtained by adding up the above items. The data are directly available from the *Annual Report of Investment in Fixed Assets* by the Department of Statistics on Investment

in Fixed Assets of SSB. Information regarding geological prospecting and prospecting design relevant to the projects is available from the year-end financial accounts of the related departments.

The calculation method of the net output value of construction can be based on the net output value ratio (net output value / total output value) of state-owned and collective-owned construction enterprises in the *Annual Report of Construction Statistics* by the Department of Statistics on Investment in Fixed Assets. The following must be taken into consideration when using the net output value ratio for calculation: (1) whether the method adopted by the Specialized Investment Department when calculating the net value of construction is consistent with ours, if not, then adjustment of the net output value is necessary; (2) whether the statistical scope covered by the Specialized Investment Department is corresponding to ours and whether it is comprehensive enough. If not, some supplementary information from standard survey or related data is needed for making adjustment; (3) whether the specifications of the statistics are consistent. In so doing, the link between the production sectors and between regions can be done without repetition and without missing data.

The rate of net output value is also used for the calculation of the private housing investment in cities and towns and rural area. Since it is impossible to collect the relevant financial information, an extrapolation based on a standard survey is calculated. In recent years, with the rise of people's living standards, especially the farmers', the standard of housing constructed by farmers has been rising as well. Investment in housing construction is increasing not only in manpower but in material expenses also, resulting in the decrease of net output value ratio. Therefore, when we calculate the net output value, further confirmation by the actual situation is necessary.

Material consumption of construction can be obtained from the tables of cost of construction enterprises and tables of their management cost. The cost table of a construction enterprise is usually divided into direct cost and indirect cost. Among the direct cost, the material cost means material consumption, while the construction machinery cost and other direct cost are included in material consumption and net output value, so we have to adjust according to the standard survey information in order to get the actual consumption of material. Among the indirect cost, management cost includes some material consumption such as office fees, fixed assets depreciation, renting, low value consumables, water and electricity, heating, etc., and they are to be included in the calculation of material consumption.

Transport, Post and Telecommunications

The output value of transport, post and telecommunications consists of the output of railways, highways, waterways (both individual or joint operations), post and telecommunications, civil aviation and pipelines, etc.

Railway (total output value, net output value at current prices). The total output value of railway transport is the income of its freight traffic. The method of calculation is based on the information in the *Compilation of Nationwide Railway Statistical Data* and the *Annual Accounting Report on Transportation Enterprises* offered by the Ministry of Railways and the Ministry of Communications. Among which, the total output value at current prices is equal to the sum of the income from freight transport, parcels, postal transport, surcharge for short distance transportation, extra charges for over-loading coal, and specific income from coal transportation, etc. Another method is to delete the income that does not belong to the scope of total output value, like passenger traffic income, luggage transport income, etc., from the total income of transportation.

The net output value at current prices of railway transport consists of the sum of wages, staff and workers' welfare funds, profits, taxes, etc., of the railway transport enterprises.

Highway. The total output value of highway transport is the income from highway freight transport. The actual calculation can be divided into transportation system and outside the transportation system. The transportation system can be further divided into central enterprises, local state-owned enterprises and the local collectives.

The calculation of total output value of the transport system is based on the year-end account data within the system. As long as there is a clear indication of freight transport income in the account report, it is directly taken into calculation. Otherwise, the proportion of freight transport has to be extrapolated, which is equal to the cost of freight transport divided by the total cost of transport and then times the total income of transport. The outcome will be the total output value of transport. The net output value of transport consists of the sum of wages, welfare funds, profits, taxes, etc. If the data on the components are lacking, it can be calculated from the net output value ratio and the actual benefits situation.

The total output value from outside the transportation system refers to the income of freight transport by urban privately operated transport enterprises, by rural self-employed, rural collectives and other related independent accounting transport enterprises. The calculation of the total output value can be based on their turnover volume of freight transport with reference to the price of freight transport in the state-owned system.

The composition of net output value of the non-state transportation system is just the same as that of the state transportation system. The relevant data are available in the *Compilation of Nationwide Communications Statistical Data*, or the *Annual Report of Communications, Post and Telecommunications* and *Statistical Data of Rural Enterprises.*

Waterway (river and sea transport). River and sea shipping can be divided into central and local units.

1. The total output value of the centrally operated river and sea shipping is equal to the income from transport and from cargo handling. However, transport income includes also passenger transport and thus can be recalculated by using the ratio of freight transport to total transport cost (i.e., the freight ratio) to get the income of freight transport. Passenger transport can be ignored if small, and the transport income can be used directly. The data can be obtained from the *Compilation of Nationwide Communications Statistical Data.*

   Some river and sea shipping directly under the center has been transferred to the local port management. The total output value of these parts is directly available from the "Operation Income" in the "Major Financial Indicators for Transferred Ports."

   The net output value at current prices includes wages, profits, taxes and welfare funds. The information is available from the "Major Financial Indicators of Transport and Ports Enterprises Directly under the Center."
2. The local shipping transportation is divided into state-owned and collective units.

   The total output value of the state-owned at current prices is available directly from the "Freight Transport Income" in the financial report of the local state-operated transport enterprises in the *Compilation of Nationwide Communications Statistical Data*. The net output value includes wages, profits, taxes and welfare funds.

   The total output value at current prices of the collective units can be obtained by the turnover of goods times the unit price of transport. Information on the turnover of goods and the unit price is available in the *Compilation*.

   Information regarding the composition of the net output value at current prices is available in the *Compilation* and the relevant financial and taxation departments.

Post and Telecommunications. The total output value of post and telecommunications is available from the business income in the annual statistical reports of the post and telecommunications departments. In principle, the non-productive income from services provided to the residents should not be included in the calculation.

Information concerning the net output value of post and telecommunications is available in the final accounting data of the department.

When taking data from the annual statistical reports of the transport and post and telecommunications departments, special attention should be paid regarding the statistical scope and criteria used for the total output value and net output value. Necessary adjustment in accordance with the requirement of national income calculation has to be done in order to avoid double counting among the departments.

Civil Aviation. Data on total output value at current prices of civil aviation transport are available for freight transport in the *Accountant Report of Civil Aviation Transportation Enterprise* by China's Civil Aviation Bureau. The freight transport income includes the incomes of within-country postal freight transport, international postal freight transport, general aviation charges, charges for ground services of foreign and domestic airplanes, ground transport income, etc.

The net output value of civil aviation is taken from the annual final accounts of the Civil Aviation Bureau.

Pipeline Transport. The total output value of pipeline transport at current prices equals its operational income. The data are available from the China Natural Gas and Petroleum Corporation's Pipeline office. The net output value includes profits, taxes, wages and welfare funds. All are available in the financial data.

Commerce and Catering Trade

The total and net output values of commerce and catering trade are calculated according to the types of ownership, i.e., state-owned, collective, individual ownership and others.

The state-owned division includes the units in trade, cereals, foreign trade, pharmaceuticals, materials supply and marketing and catering. Its total output value belongs to the commercial system. The common method of calculation is as follows:

Total output value of commerce = income from commodity sales – original prices at purchase – transportation fee.

Net output value = business profit + sale tax + education fee surcharge + wages + welfare funds + service charge + interests + insurance + rent + staff and workers education fee + travel cost + property tax + vehicle and ship usage tax + stamp duty + land tax + unemployment insurance + labor union fee + partial storage charges + partial selection charge + part of packaging fee + part of other expenditures.

Information is available from the pooled annual accounting report of the Ministry of Commerce, the *Annual Report of Commercial Statistics* by the Department of Trade and External Economic Relation Statistics of SSB and data from *Customs* by the General Administration of Customs.

To be noted: although the method of calculation for the total and net output values for the state-owned units is basically the same, some adjustment according to the nature of individual business, such as scope and calibre is requisite in order to be consistent with the estimation of the national income. For instance, the "additional price for surplus purchase of grain" has to be excluded in calculating the total and net output values of cereal enterprises. The "income from export tax refund" has to be excluded in calculating the total and net output values of foreign trade enterprises (dealing with import and export trade). Since the above two incomes are considered as subsidies that are commonly used to increase income or cut down cost in order to increase the sale profit, they would not actually increase the national income. Therefore, these parts should be excluded from the total and net output values. The total output value of catering trade is equal to the amount of retail sale. Its net output value can be based on the financial information from the responsible administration departments, or based on the total and net output values of the catering trade units under the Ministry of Commerce to get the net output value ratio, and then use the ratio to calculate the net output value of the state-owned catering trade. For the calculation of the net output value of the foreign trade enterprises, the tax information can be obtained directly from the customs duties because the calculation criterion is based on the whole society.

The collective part consists of the supply and marketing cooperatives, the cooperative commerce, and the catering trade.

The calculation method of the total and net output values of the supply and marketing cooperatives is basically the same as for the state-owned commercial units. However, the additional price paid for surplus purchase of cotton must be excluded during the calculation. Information is available from "The General Accounting Report for Supply and Marketing Cooperatives under the Ministry of Commerce" and from the relevant data from the Ministry of Finance.

The total output value of cooperative commerce can be obtained from the retail volume times the gross profit rate of supply and marketing cooperatives. The gross profit rate has to be adjusted according to the actual situation. Information is available from the *Annual Report of Commercial Statistics*. The net output value can be obtained by referring to the net output value ratio of supply and marketing cooperatives times the total output value.

The catering trade part consists of collective owned, jointly owned and catering under the supply and marketing cooperatives. The total output value of the former two is equal to their retail volume. Information is available in the *Annual Report of Commercial Statistics,* while the net output value can be calculated with the help of the net output value ratio. The total output value of catering under supply and marketing cooperative system is its "business income," while the net output value can be obtained with the help of the net output value ratio. Information is available in the "Report of the Catering Service Business Profit" in the general accounting report of supply and marketing cooperatives.

Individually owned catering includes country marketing, individual catering and individual commerce. Its total and net output values can be calculated from *Annual Report of Commercial Statistics* or from survey reports.

The category "others" includes all that are not state-owned, collective or individual-owned, e.g., the commercial turnover of shops dealing in fishery, cigarettes, bookstores, salt, farming machines, fuel, petrol, forest products, publications, etc. under state ownership; the retail business of military service centers, state-farms, government organizations, factories and mines, etc.; the turnover of direct sale to citizens and business units by various industries; the retail sales of other trades, including agriculture, transport and construction of various economic types.

The calculation method for total and net output values is to get the part of commodity turnover under the state ownership first. Then, add the parts from industry and other trades so as to get all sections' turnover, and multiply by the gross profit rate to get the total output value, then times the net output value ratio to get the net output value.

The exact figures for the gross profit rate and the net output value ratio can be obtained through an actual calculation to get a proper ratio or through some type survey.

Illustration of the Calculation Method for the Components of Net Output Value

1. Wage refers to the production worker's wages: it does not include (i) the wages of welfare facilities' employees supported by the staff and workers' welfare funds; (ii) the wages expenditure for employees given for non-production business; (iii) bonuses paid from enterprise funds and retained profits, and wages paid to employees from special-purpose funds.
2. Staff and workers' welfare funds designate those funds drawn according to the proportion stipulated by the state, which are to be counted as cost in financial reports.
3. Profit means the profit to be gained as included in total output value, mainly referring to industrial enterprises. The due profit of industrial enterprises is made up of the profit that should be obtained from up-to-standard products, locally made semi-manufactured goods, and goods in process during the accounting period. Because profits from sold products are sale profits, profits for those qualified unsold products, semi-manufactured products and goods in process

are also to be assigned a profit. Therefore, it is neither sale profit realized from products actually sold, nor total profit (which includes non-production loss or gain and other sale profit). It has to be adjusted when calculating the total output value.

Adjustment formula:

Profit = (output value of saleable goods ± price difference of locally made semi-finished goods, goods in process, tools and dies from the final and initial prices) x sale profit rate ÷ product sale income.

The profits of the commerce, transport, post and telecommunications sectors can be directly obtained from the operation profits recorded in the accountant report forms.

4. Tax designates products tax, value-added tax and business tax (excluding the direct taxes such as income tax, bonus tax, adjustment tax and resources tax) which should be paid by the material production sector. Tax data can be obtained from the accounting report forms of each sector. However, the sales tax of the industrial production sector cannot be obtained from their accounting reports, because industrial enterprises' actual sales of products include the products made in the previous period and sold in this period and exclude those products made in this period and sold in the next term. It's necessary to adjust because the product sale tax is of a different scale from that of total output value. The formula is:

   Product sale tax to be surrendered = gross cost of all products (or total output value in current prices) x product sale tax ÷ product sale cost (product sales income).

5. Interest designates the net expenditure after subtracting interest income from interest expenses. If expenses are bigger than income the net result is to be counted into cost, which should be included in the net output value. Contrarily, if interest income is bigger than expenses, the amount reduces cost and it is entered with a negative sign.
6. The rest refers to expenses which belong to primary distribution of national income besides those above. They mainly include:
   (i) expenses on individuals, e.g., reward for doing enterprise work in household, compensation for missed meals.
   (ii) expenses on non-production departments, e.g., business travel, home visit, insurance, advertising expenses, etc.
   (iii) expenses on non-production units in production departments, e.g., union's fees, recreation and propaganda fees, militia activity expenditure, enterprise education fee. (are excluded expenses for non-business purposes).

(iv) direct and indirect finance payments, e.g., vehicle and ship license tax, stamp tax, property tax, building site use tax, special fuel tax, water and electricity surcharge, pollution emission fees, etc., which are not included in the sales tax.

Moreover, the net output value of agriculture also includes agricultural laborer's remunerations, accumulation fund, public welfare fund, production cost fund and grain reserves fund in addition to the items listed above.

Data for all the items listed above are available from the related topics in accounting reports, or they can be calculated based on ratios from type survey data or related statistics.

B. Total Output Value, Net Output Value and Material Consumption at Comparable Prices

In order to have a dynamic analysis of the national income, and to observe the situation of its growth changes, national income at current prices is also converted into comparable prices. However, due to the still unreliable price indexes, we can only use the current available indexes, or variable methods to make the conversion possible so as to eliminate the impact brought by price fluctuation.

From liberation to 1957, the 1952 prices are the base for the comparable prices, 1957 prices for the years between 1957 to 1970, 1970 prices for 1970 to 1980, and 1980 prices for 1980 to 1990. The years after 1990 are compared at 1990 prices.

The following is the conversion of total output value and net output value into comparable prices for the various sectors.

1. Industry

   Total output value: the industrial total output value in comparable prices is from the Department of Industrial and Transportation Statistics of SSB.

   Net output value: one can use the price change coefficient of total output value of industry in comparable prices to do the conversion.

   Formula:

   Net output value of industry in comparable prices = Net output value of industry at current prices x (total output value of industry in comparable prices ÷ total output value of industry at current prices)

2. Agriculture

   Total output value: it can be directly taken from the total output value of agriculture in comparable prices in the *Annual Report of Rural Economic Statistics.*

Net output value: deduct material consumption in comparable prices from the total output value of agriculture in comparable prices.

Material consumption of agriculture can be calculated according to "Itemized Material Consumption of Agriculture for Whole Nation" in the *Annual Report of Rural Economic Statistics,* in which agricultural seeds consumed in production, fodder, fertilizers, fuel, pesticides, agricultural plastic film, electricity consumed, etc., are recorded. All these items are calculated according to their comparable prices indexes, respectively. In addition, farm implement depreciation and medium and small size farming tools cost can be converted by referring to the retail price indexes of production instruments in the *Annual Report of Price Statistics* by the Organization of Urban Social and Economic Surveys of SSB. All the statistical data are taken from the production division of the Organization of Urban Social and Economic Surveys.

3. Construction

Total output value and net output value can be converted through the price indexes of output value of construction collected by the Department of Statistics on Investment in Fixed Assets of SSB.

4. Transport, Post and Telecommunications

(i) Total output value of transport

There are two ways to convert total output value of transport at current prices into comparable prices:

(a) The turnover value of goods during the report term (turnover of goods at current prices) multiplied by unit price of freight transport in base period (yuan/tn. km);

(b) to multiply price coefficient of unit price by freight transport income during the report term. The formula is:

Total output value of transport in comparable prices = freight transport income (i.e., total output value of freight transport at current prices) x (unit price of freight transport in base period ÷ unit price of freight transport during the report term)

The net output value of transport in comparable prices can be obtained by multiplying the price coefficient of transport unit price by net output value of transport at current prices.

(ii) Total output value of post and telecommunications

The conversion into comparable prices is as follows: Given

the total output value in comparable prices of base year, then, the following year's figures can be calculated by multiplying last year's total output value in comparable prices by this year's growth rate in gross business volume.

5. Commerce and Catering Trade
   (i) Total output value of commerce is affected by input prices and selling prices. When converting the total output value of commerce into comparable prices, we need to calculate first the net sales of commodities at current prices from the various sectors, such as commerce, foreign trade, grain supply and marketing cooperatives, material supply and marketing enterprises, etc. The sectoral retail price indexes are used to convert the figures into the net sales of commodities at base period prices, then, the total output value commerce in comparable prices is obtained by multiplying the ratio of the current year's total output value to net sales of commodities by net sales of commodities in comparable prices.

   There are two methods for the conversion of net output value:
   (a) The ratio of net output value of commerce to total output value of commerce in current prices times the total output value of commerce in comparable prices.
   (b) Net output value of commerce in current prices times the price coefficient of total output value of commerce.

   The formula is:

   Net output value of commerce in comparable prices = net output value of commerce in current prices x (total output value of commerce in comparable prices ÷ total output value of commerce in current prices).

   (ii) Total output value, net output value of catering trade

   The total output value of catering trade includes the value of raw materials, which can be converted into comparable prices by the retail price index of catering trade. Material consumption can be converted by using the raw materials' price indexes of staple and non-staple food. Then, we subtract material consumption in comparable prices from total output value in comparable prices, so as to get the net output value in comparable prices. Besides, we can also directly convert net output value of catering trade by using the retail price index of catering trade.

Establishment of National Income Available in MPS

Once the primary distribution of products of the national income has been done, it forms the enterprises' and worker's income in the material production sectors. A portion goes through a redistribution towards non-material production sectors by various channels. Ultimately, it forms the income of all sectors and all social groups in the society. According to different life and production purpose, part of national income will be used by citizens' living and non-production need of society, this is consumption (total consumption). Another part of the income is used to expand social reproduction and increase the fixed assets of non-production sectors and national accumulation forming reserves (total accumulation). Therefore, the national income available is equal to the sum of total consumption and total accumulation.

The formula is:

National income available = national income from production + net import of material products = total consumption + total accumulation.

In what follows, we discuss the calculation of the national income available in current prices first.

And the conversion of the current prices in comparable prices will be presented later.

The Calculation of Total Consumption

1. The Concept of Total Consumption and Some Problems to be Grasped

   (i) Concept of Total Consumption

   Total consumption means the national income used by all citizens for living expenses and by public organizations for consumption on material products. From the angle of permanent units, total consumption means the total consumption of material products by permanent residents and permanent non-production organizations within a specific period of time.

   Total consumption is divided into two types: total consumption by residents and total social consumption. Total resident consumption designates the total value of material products used within a specific period for personal material consumption and for cultural life, such as culture, education, etc. In material terms, it mainly includes the usual consumption of food, clothing, furniture, sundries, stationery, durable consumer goods, housing repair, water, electricity and various cultural service expenditures with material content.

   Total social consumption includes material consumption by governmental bodies, defense and security units, culture and education, hygiene, science research organizations, financial and insurance organizations, mass organizations and non-production enterprises, in terms of fuel, electricity, office supplies, books, other general purchased facilities, the wear and tear of related housing, etc. Besides, collective welfare facilities consumption furnished by state-owned and city and town collective enterprises, and the collective consumption by rural villager committees should be counted into social consumption, too.

(ii) Some Problems to Be Mastered During Calculation

(a) It must be non-productive consumption. This is different from productive consumption. The latter's material consumption has already been deducted during the production process when calculating the production of national income.

(b) It must be the consumption of material products. Usually, cultural life service expenditures belong to non-material consumption. However, it also has material consumption elements, e.g., movie presentation needs films, electricity, film tickets, etc. Passenger transport needs fuel, vehicle depreciation, etc., kinds of material consumption. Bathing facilities and hair salons also need water, coal, electricity, etc. All these kinds of material consumption should be counted during the calculation of consumption.

(c) Consumption that has not been grouped into the domain of total output value of society should not be regarded as statistics of consumption.

(d) Consumption usually means products which have already passed to the consumer, not necessarily the actual consuming of the product. With the exception of residential housing, building construction and facilities bought by non-production institutions treated as fixed assets and their depreciation to be calculated. In general, the current year's consumption is of the product sold to the consumer.

2. Calculation Method of Total Consumption

Total consumption is divided into personal consumption and public consumption. The former can also be divided into the consumption of the rural and non-rural residents. The latter includes collective consumption. The calculation method and data base are illustrated as follows:

(i) Calculation of Personal Consumption

Usually, there are two approaches for the calculation of personal consumption, i.e., the balanced revenue and expenditure approach and the direct calculation approach. Whichever approach will be chosen depends very much upon the data situation. In general, the direct calculation approach is adopted. The result can be calibrated by the balanced revenue and expenditure approach, provided the data source of the latter is available. Moreover, some adjustment has to be made if there exists a discrepancy between them.

The balanced revenue and expenditure approach is, first, to calculate the residents' total income (both money income and pay in kind), then, to deduct from total income the expenditures of redistribution not belonging to material products' consumption. We thus obtain personal consumption.

(a) Total income includes staff and workers' wages of state-owned, city and town collective-owned and various jointly owned units; net money income of city and town workers; income of workers in other occupations; other incomes from the work unit and from state financial units; other cash incomes; income obtained by peasants from collective unified and cooperative operations and from the sale of farming side-line products; net money income of peasants from industrial or handicraft work and from various kind of labor.

(b) Expenditures not belonging to consumption include all compulsory payments for national treasury bonds, fines, reparations, housing investment bought and built by urban and rural residents in current year, the productive investment by urban and rural entrepreneurs, the accumulation of grain reserves by peasants, the increase of cash and savings by residents, the portion of expenses for cultural life which does not apply to material products, and other cash expenses.

(c) Personal consumption is equal to the difference between total income and expenditure not belonging to personal consumption.

To calculate personal consumption by using the balanced revenue and expenditure approach can reflect residents' source of income and growth situation and the direction of expenses so as to analyze the personal consumption pattern.

The direct calculation approach is to calculate directly residents' material products consumption. However, due to the limitations of data, we can only account for the major categories of residents' consumption. This can be divided into commercial products consumption, self-supplied consumption, cultural life and services consumption, housing, water and electricity consumption.

Commercial products consumption means the direct

money purchase of products for personal consumption purpose. But this does not include buying a house and building materials. Related information can be obtained from the Department of Trade and External Economic Relation Statistics of SSB.

Self-supplied consumption refers to income from resident's self-produced materials, i.e., the portion of the farming and side-line products directly used for individual consumption. In general, we can obtain this by deducting value of marketable agricultural output and non consumable output value from the total output value of agriculture. It can also be estimated by using rural household survey data. Data are obtained from the Organization of Rural Social and Economic Surveys of SSB.

Cultural life services consumption designates expenditure for material products consumption in all kinds of cultural life services. It mainly includes transportation fees, vehicle and boat travel fees, post and telecommunications fees, various school fees, child care, cultural recreation, repairs, medical health care, etc. Data are obtained from *Annual Report of Commercial Statistics*. Public health services enjoyed by staff and workers should also be counted.

Housing consumption implies the wear and tear of housing (including self-owned housing). It is usually estimated from house rent or house depreciation, or by estimating from the building price and service life-span of the house. The related data can be obtained from the "Statistical Year Report" of the Ministry of Construction and its related commission. The above consumption can be calculated according to the data on rural and non-rural residents, so as to find their respective consumption value.

(ii) Calculation of Public Consumption

There are two methods for the calculation of public consumption. One is to survey directly the non-material production sectors, and to compile the revenue and expenditure balance sheet for these sectors based on the survey data. This includes the material expenditures, such as expenses on administration, water and electricity, fuel, materials, transportation and miscellaneous expenses, repairs, renovation, leasing, heating, furniture and tools, and depreciation of fixed assets.

Another one is the calculation according to the source of expenses for all non-material production organizations. For state financial expenditure, calculation can be based on central state's and lower level agencies' financial data. For business units, one adds the constituent items of labor insurance and welfare found in *Annual Report of Labor Wage Statistics.*

It is better to use the second method, which is simpler and more workable, because financial revenue and expenditure statistics for non-material production sectors have not been established yet.

For public finance expenditure, expenses used for non-material production institution include: (1) executive management costs; (2) defense and Armed Police force outlay; (3) culture and education, science, hygiene operating expenses; (4) social welfare expenses; (5) industry, transportation, commerce, farming, forestry, water conservancy and meteorological sectors expenses; (6) urban upkeep expenses; (7) the "three-category" expenses in science and technology;[3] (8) geological survey expenses, and other sectors' operating expenses.

Among these expenses, belong to public consumption the expenses at the lowest level of classification, such as expenses on administration, business, repair, and other expenses by the collectives. Extra-budgetary expenditure used for public consumption includes road maintenance, city upkeep, the three-category expenses in science and technology, operating expenses, administration and other expenses.

Costs for collective welfare facilities by state-owned and city and town collective-owned units can be calculated from the constituent items of labor insurance and welfare in the *Annual Report of Labor Wage Statistics.* Expenses on collective welfare facilities, subsidies for collective welfare institution, and cultural, recreation and sports promotion fees belong to public consumption.

Public consumption in rural area includes expenses by culture, education, propaganda and welfare organizations created by collective funds raised and expenses by villagers' committees, but excluding the expenses under county and town governments which are state finance. Calculation can be done from the related data recorded in surveys of the rural basic economic situation and the statistics on the distribution of rural economic revenues.

Fixed asset depreciation of the non-material production sector designates all depreciation costs for all fixed assets used by state organizations, mass organizations, cultural education, science research and hygiene units, etc. This is the constituent part of public consumption. For profit-making non-material production sectors (e.g., passenger transport, public utilities, banks, etc.) major repair funds should be included. In China, there is no depreciation allowance for fixed assets used by non-material production sectors in the current financial management system. Estimation can be done according to total value of fixed assets occupied by non-material production sectors (excluding residents' houses) and the assured depreciation rate based on the years of service. Usually, the rate is about 2 percent.

(iii) The level of personal consumption is calculated according to the average of consumption by population, divided into rural and non-rural residents' respective averages in order to obtain the respective consumption levels. It is noted that, under the current system, the classification standards are taken from the Public Security department, rural registration for those engaged in agriculture, and non-rural registration for all the others. Therefore, soldiers, laborers in cities and towns, staff and workers in state-managed farms are non-rural residents. Those who work in rural areas in other professions than farming are treated as rural residents. Personal consumption should accordingly be calculated based on rural and non-rural residents. The related figures are available in the table of "Social Commodities Purchasing Power" of *Annual Report of Commercial Statistics*, where they are averaged according to the two categories of population.

Calculation of Total Accumulation

The Concept of Total Accumulation and Calculation Method. From the national income available, a part is consumption; the part remaining after the consumption in the current year is total accumulation. Usually, the latter shows as the value of newly increased fixed assets and circulating assets in the given period.

According to its function in social reproduction, total accumulation can be divided into fixed assets accumulation and circulating assets accumulation; productive accumulation and non-productive accumulation. The process for the calculation, generally, is to figure out fixed assets accumulation and circulating assets accumulation first and, then, to classify them into productive accumulation and non-productive accumulation.

In order to examine the various kinds of ownership and accumulation scales, total accumulation can be divided into 6 constituents as follows: (1) state-owned; (2) cities and towns' collective-owned; (3) village collective-owned; (4) individual economy; (5) other ownership forms (including various kinds of joint ventures owned and foreign-owned enterprises); (6) urban township individual accumulation.

Because of the economic system reform process, the multiplication of foreign economic relations and the variety of domestic cooperative ventures have led to the growth of sino-foreign joint and to various kinds of ownership combinations among enterprises (organizations); it is now very difficult, if not impossible, to categorize their ownership system. In order to do so, we have adopted the following principle: the one who is the main entity in the combined venture is the one to whom is ascribed the investment, then the ownership category is decided accordingly. Based on this ownership system, accumulation is, for the time being, further divided into four constituents: (1) state-owned accumulation; (2) accumulation of city and town collective and other ownership; (3) village collective and other ownership accumulation; (4) private housing accumulation of urban and rural residents.

1. Fixed Asset Accumulation

   Fixed assets are defined as the accumulation of productive material taking place during the process of social reproduction, which can be repeatedly used for long periods of time and which, in the course of production, does not basically change from its original state, such as finished or unfinished houses, structures, machine equipment, transport vehicles, draught animal, etc. But, it does not include small tools of low value and armament purely used for military purpose, because this part is treated as consumed products and is counted as intermediate input. Fixed assets in the material production domain are treated as the major labor means which are the material technical conditions for all production; they are called productive fixed assets. Fixed assets in the non-material production domain are the material goods provided on a long term basis for people's livelihood and non-production organizations; they are called non-productive fixed assets.

   The value of fixed assets that has increased during the calculation period includes not only the various kinds of fixed assets above, but also the value of major repairs to these fixed assets. Must be deducted, however, the value of the fixed assets depreciation fund and the major repair fund drawn; what remains is then the current fixed assets accumulation.

   Usually there are two ways to calculate fixed asset accumulation:

   The first is the difference approach, i.e., the approach calculates the difference of net fixed asset value between the beginning and the end of period from financial data of the current year. However, this method has not been adopted so far because of the limitations on data source.

The second method is the addition-subtraction approach, i.e., from the increased fixed asset value (difference between expenses which do not increase fixed assets from currently completed fixed asset investment), deduct the current basic depreciation and major repair fund of fixed assets to get the fixed asset accumulation. Because of the data availability, it is easier to adopt the second approach.

2. Circulating Asset Accumulation

Circulating assets mean the materials prepared for production, e.g., raw material, material, fuel, repair component parts, packing equipment, low value and easily consumable products, goods in process, self-made semi-finished products and charges to be apportioned, products and unfinished products ready for sale. Inventory of commercial sector also belongs to circulating assets.

There is a difference between circulating assets and working capital. Circulating assets include only the part of physical materials in working capital; other kinds of working capital are reserve cash, cash in transit, bank deposits and reserve bills and bonds. The latter are not counted as circulating assets. During the accounting period, the net increased amount of circulating assets is the circulating asset accumulation. Based on the difference approach, the circulating asset accumulation is calculated by taking the difference of circulating asset value between the beginning and the end of period.

3. Fixed Asset Accumulation for State-owned Units

It is the difference, after deducting basic depreciation and major repair fund outlay of fixed asset from increase in fixed assets. The latter designates the total investment in fixed assets realized by state-owned units during the accounting period, including the basic construction investment, renovation and upgrading investment, housing purchase and other fixed asset investments (deducting the expenses which do not increase fixed assets), actual completed major repair value, geological exploration and prospecting design charges (excluding the part already counted into fixed asset investment). Data on fixed asset investment and expenses not increasing fixed assets can be obtained from the statistic report forms of fixed asset investment. And data on geological exploration and prospecting design charges are available from state finance departments.

Basic depreciation of fixed assets includes the total of fixed asset depreciation and major repair funds of state-owned enterprises, state organizations and institutions. Information on depreciation and major repair funds of state-owned enterprises' fixed assets can be obtained from budget data. However, the current financial management system has not yet stipulated the depreciation allowance for the fixed assets used by state organizations and institutions. The calculation can be done by multiplying the fixed asset value by the depreciation rate or estimated according to relevant data. For units drawing on repair funds, the amount should also be included.

4. Circulating Asset Accumulation for State-owned Units

This is the difference between the circulating assets of the state and state-owned enterprises at the beginning and the end of period. Circulating assets include:

(i) quota circulating assets, e.g., stored assets for industrial enterprises (e.g., raw and processed materials, fuel, auxiliary materials, etc.), production assets (e.g., semi-finished product, goods in process) and finished product assets, etc.; commodities and material assets of commercial enterprises (e.g., inventory, commodities in transit, special reserves, etc.); non-commodity assets (e.g., packaging materials, furniture and tools, low value and easily consumable articles and charges receivable); and planned circulating assets of other sectors.

(ii) material part of non-quota circulating assets, e.g., special reserves of industrial enterprises, materials and issued commodities of idle or closed enterprises, all stored materials in railway and transport enterprises.

The accumulation of circulating assets by state-owned enterprise can be calculated from the materials portion of quota and non quota circulating assets recorded in the financial reports of each responsible department. Data on the state material reserves can be obtained from the state reserve departments. The increased amount in the current year is used to calculate the accumulation.

When using the difference approach to calculate the circulating asset accumulation, one must note that the materials and equipment scrapped and lost during assets-checking process mostly were produced and became inventory in the previous years, they should not be subtracted from circulating asset accumulation in the current year. Hence, we have to deduct the reported discard and loss from quota circulating assets in both the final as well as the initial period when we use the difference of quota circulating assets.

Evaluation of circulating asset accumulation takes the average price of circulating assets during the calculation period. When using the difference approach, the circulating asset value at the beginning of period should be adjusted by the new price level, and then the difference approach is adopted to get the increased amount of circulating assets.

5. City and Town Collectives and Other Ownerships' Fixed Asset Accumulation

   This refers to city & town collectives, individual enterprises and all kinds of other joint enterprises, that is, not belonging to the state-owned category. Data for the city & town collectives are obtained from the *Annual Report of Statistics on Investment in Fixed Assets* in which the completed amount of fixed assets investment and the major repair investments are added up while subtracting the fixed asset depreciation fund and the major repair fund. The amount drawn and expenditure from the basic depreciation and major repair funds for fixed assets can be calculated from the respective departments' financial reports, or from the depreciation rate of the state-owned enterprises if there is no financial report. Asset accumulation for private enterprises and other ownerships can only be estimated from the related data by industrial and commercial administration departments.

6. City and Town Collectives and Other Ownerships' Circulating Asset Accumulation

   The statistical calculation domain of circulating asset accumulation is the same as the fixed asset accumulation of the same types of ownership. The related data on industry and commerce are available in the *Annual Report of Industrial Statistics* and *Annual Report of Commercial Statistics*. The remaining data can be obtained from the industrial and commercial administration departments.

7. Rural Collective and Other Private Ownerships' Fixed Asset Accumulation

   This refers to the actual increased value of fixed assets of all economic organizations in rural area during the calculation period (collective units under unified operation, enterprises at the level of *xiang, cun* and below, and new economic corporate bodies) and peasants' household operation (including specialized households). Data can be obtained by deducting fixed asset depreciation from the fixed asset investment of the rural collective and other ownership units. For the case of no depreciation drawn for large livestock, the investment amount can be directly calculated, or by multiplying by the unit price the difference in number of livestock on hand at the beginning and the end of period. Fixed investment assets of the rural collective and other ownership units include agricultural mechanical implements and tools, irrigation work of farmland, large livestock, *xiang* (commune) and *cun* (production team) factory buildings, warehouse and production equipment, transportation vehicles, bridges, piers, and *xiang* and *cun*-owned culture, education, sanitation, social welfare units' fixed asset investments, and investment in the reclamation of wasteland and in afforestation, etc. Calculation can be done according to the completed amount of fixed asset investments by the rural collective and the private sector investing in production assets in rural area. All information is provided in *Annual Report of Statistics on Investment in Fixed Assets*. The fixed asset depreciation figure can be calculated by multiplying the original value of productive fixed assets and non-production housing and buildings by their depreciation rates. These data are from the "Tables on the Structure of Rural Fixed Assets" recorded in the comprehensive statistical report forms system on the rural economy. The depreciation rate is determined according to the different situations or usages of fixed assets. For instance, for farming mechanical equipment and tools, the service life is about 15 years, and the depreciation rate is at around 6 percent; housing depreciation rate is around 2 percent. Or, it can be estimated according to the figures in the "Tables on the Situation of Villages Fixed Asset Property Survey." About *xiang* (commune) and *cun* (production team) enterprises, one can also get the information from the responsible department (Rural Enterprise Department). Investment in the reclamation of wasteland and in afforestation can be calculated by multiplying the areas of these works by the investment amount on unit area. The data of which are obtained from *Annual Report of Rural Economic Statistics*.

8. Rural Collective and Other Ownerships' Circulating Asset Accumulation

It refers to the increased value between the end and initial period concerning domestic animals (pigs, sheep), domestic fowl and other animal raised by various kinds of rural collective organizations and peasants' households, food reserves and the circulating assets of *xiang* (commune) and *cun* (production team) enterprises, etc. Data are provided in the *Annual Report of Rural Economic Statistics* or can be calculated from the statistics of responsible departments for *xiang, cun* enterprises. In the comprehensive statistical report forms on the rural economy laid down by the SSB, there are "rural economic production accumulation" indicators in the "Table of Income Distribution and Benefits of the Rural Economy". They reflect the increased amount of productive capital from the viewpoint of the distribution of money income, which is not only material production data for calculating rural accumulation. Some adjustments must be made, such as taking out the increased amount to money capital.

9. Private Housing Accumulation of Urban and Rural Residents

This refers to the private housing investment of urban and rural residents, the net increased value of which results from deducting housing depreciation. However, the accumulation of residents' construction for production purposes must be included in the part on fixed asset accumulation of urban and rural collectives and other ownerships.

Private housing accumulation of city and town residents includes private housing accumulation in cities, county seats, towns, factory and mining areas (whether or not the owner permanently lives in the area). The calculation can be based on the *Annual Report of Statistics on Investment in Fixed Assets.* It has to exclude private housing depreciation from the value of private housing completed in the current year in cities and towns, and factory and mining areas.

Rural private housing accumulation can be calculated from the same *Annual Report,* also deducting the housing depreciation from rural private housing investment.

The depreciation of residents' housing in urban and rural areas can be calculated from "Residents' Housing Consumption."

10. Difference between productive and non-productive accumulation

Generally speaking, productive accumulation is composed of the production means (products of first category) of all social products, while non-productive accumulation is composed of the consumption means (products of second category) of the social products. Therefore, the distinction between productive and non-productive accumulation is based on the principle of division between production means and consumption means.

The division between the fixed assets of productive accumulation and non-productive accumulation can be made according to the proportion in fixed assets investment of productive construction and non-productive construction in the *Annual Report.*

The division between the productiveness and non-productiveness of circulating asset accumulation is made basically according to the principle of whether the re-production process has been involved. Commonly speaking, the circulating assets of the construction and communication and transportation departments are productive. The raw and processed materials, fuel, goods in process and semi-finished products of the industrial sector, which are involved in the process of production are considered as productive. The storage of finished products of the industrial sector can be divided into productive and non-productive ones according to their usage. The storage of commodities by the commercial sector can also be divided according to their usage (whether they are to be used for production or consumption). Of which the circulating asset accumulation of the material supply and marketing sector, car parts, farming machinery companies, etc., are basically productive. The small domestic animals, small domestic fowls, other animals of rural collective and other ownerships circulating asset accumulation and food storage are non-productive.

Calculation of Import and Export

Import and export refer to the import and export of goods and material services within a given period.

For the nation as a whole, import and export of goods are divided into two main parts: the first part is the import and export of commodities (goods) that are included in the customs' import and export statistics; the second part consists of the goods directly purchased by Chinese citizens in foreign countries and the goods directly purchased by foreigners in China, both of which are not included in the customs' import and export statistics.

As a whole, import and export of material services consist mainly of the material services activities, such as goods transportation, post and telecommunications, etc., serving the import and export of material products in foreign trade. Since the import and export commodities are calculated according to the c.i.f. (cost, insurance and freight) and f.o.b. (free on board), respectively, the transportation of goods for exportation includes the following four aspects: China's freight transport sectors carry out (1) the transportation provided for exportables and importables; (2) transportation provided for foreign goods passing through China; (3) transportation provided for the trading of goods among other countries; (4) transportation provided for foreigners other than for trading purpose, such as the transportation for the domestic property of foreign officials. Freight transport services for importation include mainly the following two aspects: Foreign freight transport sectors carry out (1) transportation provided for China's goods among other countries; (2) transportation for China's residents other than for trading purposes, such as the transportation provided for the domestic property of China's officials.

The import and export of the material services by the post and telecommunications are calculated mainly through the settlement accounts of international business, such as post, telegram, phone, electronic communication, etc.

Information on the import and export of goods that have passed through the Customs is available directly from the customs statistics. Information for those parts that have not passed through the Customs can be taken from the relevant data of the consumption of commodities. Information regarding the import and export of material services can be obtained from the "Balance of International Payments Table." However, some adjustment according to relevant principles is needed owing to the f.o.b. price used by the Balance of International Payments Table.

The Calculation of the National Income Available in Comparable Prices

1. Total Consumption in Comparable Prices

Total consumption: once personal consumption and public consumption have been converted in comparable prices separately, the two sums are added together to obtain the total consumption in comparable prices.

(i) Personal consumption is obtained by converting separately rural residents' consumption and the non-rural residents' consumption, respectively. Non-rural residents' consumption can be converted directly from the price index of the staff and workers' living cost provided in the *Annual Report of Price Statistics*. Rural residents' consumption can be converted directly from the price index of the farmers' living cost. If more detailed information is available, calculation has to be divided into different items according to the composition of consumption: commodity consumption shall be converted according to the general retail price index in the *Annual Report,* while the self-produced consumption shall be converted according to the procurement price index of farming and sideline products in the *Annual Report*. However, the result may deviate considerably, owing to the differences of constituent items between the farming and sideline product procurement and the self-produced consumption. Adjustment is needed, based on the weighted average price of the main products of the self-sufficient consumption, such as grain, meat, eggs, vegetables, fire-wood, etc., so as to obtain the proper price index for conversion. Conversion can also be made based on the price index of the total output value of agriculture. Cultural life services consumption can be converted according to the price index of the expenditure on cultural life services. The prices for water and electricity have been adjusted in the recent years and thus needed conversion has to be made. The depreciation of the residents' housing can be converted according to the price index of construction output by the construction sector.

The sum of the non-rural residents' consumption and the rural residents' consumption in comparable prices is thus the personal consumption in comparable prices. Divided by the average population, the result is the level of average personal consumption in comparable prices.

(ii) Public consumption mainly refers to the material consumption, such as fuel, water and electricity, office stationery, domestic utensils, fixed assets depreciation, etc., consumed by the non-material production bodies like administrative bodies, scientific research and education bodies, hygiene departments, etc. Conversion can be made by estimating the proportion of various consumption items first and, then, converting by the retail price index of these consumption goods, respectively.

2. Conversion of Total Accumulation in Comparable Prices

Total accumulation is obtained by converting separately fixed asset accumulation and circulating asset accumulation and adding the results to get total accumulation in comparable prices.

(i) Fixed asset accumulation can be deflated by using the price index of fixed asset investment; the result is the fixed asset accumulation in comparable prices. In case the price index is not available, the conversion can be done first by finding out the proportion of the price the respective construction and installation work and the purchase of machine equipment occupies in the price increase of the fixed assets. Then, the accumulation of the fixed assets is divided into the respective portion from construction and installation work and the portion from the purchase of machine equipment; next, the respective values are converted by the price index of the production of the construction industry and the index of the ex-factory price of the machine equipment which can be obtained from the index of ex-factory price for all of industry. The conversion for the fixed assets accumulation from the construction and installation work is calculated according to the price index of the construction industry; and, the conversion for the fixed assets accumulation from the purchase of machine equipment is calculated from the ex-factory price index of the machine equipment.

(ii) Circulating asset accumulation: the deflation can be done according to each sector concerned. The circulating asset accumulation of industry, construction, transport, commerce, etc. can be deflated under the following categories, such as agricultural products, industrial products, production means and livelihood means, which are deflated by the procurement price index of farming and sideline products, the price indexes of production means and livelihood means in the producer price indexes of industrial products, respectively. The accumulation of farming products (like grain reserves, small domestic fowl, etc.) of rural collective and other kinds of ownership can be deflated according to the relevant price index of farming products.

3. Conversion of Imports and Exports in Comparable Prices

The conversion of the imports and the exports in comparable prices is based on the volume and the money value of the imported and exported goods contained in the various commodities lists of the Customs Administration; from which, one seeks the average prices of both imported and exported goods. Taking as criterion the commodity prices of imported and exported commodities during the base period, one obtains the price increase changes for various commodities during the report period; then, for the report period, one compiles a weight value from the values of various imported and exported commodities over the total value of imports and exports, respectively. Then, taking the values of the base period as 100, the weight value is used to create the general value index for the report period with regard to import and to export. Finally, one proceeds to convert the import and the export commodities.

The data are available from the *Statistical Data of Customs* by the General Administration of Customs made for the Department of Trade and External Economic Relation Statistics of SSB.

As a summary of the above, the National Income and Its Use Table in the MPS can be shown as follows:

TABLE 2.1 National Income and Its Use in MPS

Material Production Sectors	*Material Products*
Total output value	Total use value
Intermediate consumption	Intermediate use
Intermediate consumption of material products	Final use
Depreciation of fixed assets	Total consumption
	Personal consumption
	Public consumption
Net output value	Total accumulation
Individual income	Fixed asset accumulation
Net income	Circulating asset accumulation
	Export
	Import

Notes

1. The value of industrial operation is meant to contrast with the production of the finished product. It designates the activities which restore or increase the use value of a product. Thus, it includes the value of repair of industrial products entrusted by other factories and the value of installing equipment by the enterprise per se.

2. The Department which is under the Ministry of Agriculture takes charge of the rural enterprises.

3. These include research and development expenses for new products, intermediate experiment expenses, and subsidies to key science research, which are allocated by the state mainly for the departments under the State Council and for provinces, municipalities and autonomous regions working on projects of national interest and special regional peculiarity.

References

A. General Reference Books

Accounting Department, Accounting Office of the SSB (ed.), *National Income Indicator's Exposition and Calculation Scheme*, 1992 (Internal Document of SSB).

Department of Economic and Social Affairs, Statistical Office of the United Nations, *Basic Principles of The System of Balances of the National Economy* (New York: United Nations, 1971).

Department of Economic and Social Affairs, Statistical Office of the United Nations, *Comparisons of The System of National Accounts and The System of Balances of the National Economy* (New York: United Nations, 1977).

Industry Department, Agricultural Department, Trade and Material Department, Accounting Department et al. (eds.), *Exposition of Major Indicators of National Economy*, Vol. I, II and III, 1987 (Internal Document of SSB).

Liu Ru, Liu Bowu et al. (eds.), *Teaching Material of Economic Statistics* (Tianjin: Tianjin Financial and Economic College, 1965) (Mimeographed Internal Reference Teaching Material).

Statistical Cooperation Standing Committee for the Compilation of the Basic Method and Principle for National Economic Statistics Balance Sheet, The Council of Mutual Economic Assistance (Comecon), *New MPS* (Moscow, 1984, Vol. 1) (Chinese version prepared by SSB).

Yang Jianbai (ed.), *Some Theoretical Issues of Socialist Social National Income* (Beijing: China Social Science Publishing House, 1983).

B. Internal Data in Book Form

Construction Division of the Department of Statistics on Investment in Fixed Assets of SSB (ed.), *Annual Report of Construction Statistics* (Beijing: SSB Printing House, various issues) (Internal Data).

Department of Comprehensive Planning, Ministry of Communications (ed.), *Compilation of Nationwide Communications Statistical Data*, Classified Document for Internal Research Use.

Department of Finance, China Civil Aviation Bureau (ed.), *Accountant Report Forms of Civil Aviation Transportation Enterprise* (to be submitted to the Ministry of Finance, copy of the Accountant Final Accounts Table made for SSB. (Internal Data)

Department of Finance, Ministry of Communications (ed.), *Annual Accountant Report Forms of Transportation Enterprises* (to be submitted to the Ministry of Finance, copy of the Accountant Final Accounts Table made for SSB (Internal Data).

Department of Industrial and Transportation Statistics of SSB (ed.), *Annual Report of Communications, Post and Telecommunications Statistics*, or under another title, *Annual Report of Communications, Transportation and Post and Telecommunications Statistics* (Beijing: SSB Printing House, various issues) (Internal Data).

Department of Industrial and Transportation Statistics of SSB (ed.), *Annual Report of Industrial Statistics* (Beijing: SSB Printing House, various issues) (Internal Data).

Department of Organization of Rural Social and Economic Surveys of SSB (ed.), *Annual Report of Rural Economic Statistics*, or under another title *Annual Report of Agricultural Statistics* (Beijing: SSB Printing House, various issues) (Internal Data).

Department of Planning, Ministry of Railway (ed.), *Compilation of Nationwide Railway Statistical Data.* Various issues (Internal Data).

Department of Population and Labor Statistics of SSB (ed.), *Annual Report of Labor Wage Statistics* (Beijing: SSB Printing House, various issues) (Internal Data).

Department of Statistics, General Administration of Customs (ed.), *Statistical Data of Customs*, the statistical report forms made for the External Economic Relation Division of the Department of Trade and External Economic Relation Statistics, SSB (Internal Data).

Department of Statistics on Investment in Fixed Assets of SSB (ed.), *Annual Report of Statistics on Investment in Fixed Assets* (Beijing: SSB Printing House, various issues) (Internal Data).

Department of Trade and External Economic Relation Statistics of SSB (ed.), *Annual Report of Commercial Statistics* (Beijing: SSB Printing House, various issues) (Internal Data).

Production Division of the Organization of Urban Social and Economic Surveys, SSB (ed.), *Annual Report of Price Statistics* (Beijing: SSB Printing House, various issues) (Internal Data).

Rural Enterprise Department, Ministry of Agriculture (ed.), *Statistical Data of Rural Enterprises* (Beijing) (Internal Data).

C. Internal Data in Report Forms

"Annual Report of Social Commodity Purchasing Power Statistics," which is a part of *Annual Report of Commercial Statistics.*

"Balance of International Payments Table," compiled by the State Foreign Exchange Management Bureau, the statistical table is made for the External Economic Relation Division of the Department of Trade and External Economic Relation Statistics, SSB.

"The Pooled Accountant Report Forms of the Supply and Marketing Cooperatives of the Ministry of Commerce," the Accountant Final Accounts Table collected by the General Agency of Supply and Marketing Cooperative, Ministry of Commerce, mainly reported to the Ministry of Finance, copy of the Table is made for SSB (Internal Data).

"Table of Rural Fixed Assets Structure" and "Table from the Investigation of Rural Fixed Assets Ownership Situation," both are report forms of statistics compiled by the Special Project Division of Organization of Rural Social and Economic Surveys, SSB.

3

China's National Economic Accounting System — SNA

*Li Xiaochao**
*Hsueh Tien-tung**

Reasons for Setting Up the New National Economic Accounting System in SNA

The national economic accounting system is a system which makes use of scientific accounting procedures and principles in order to reflect the development of the economy and organize its key economic indicators in an accounting framework so as to completely, comprehensively and systematically represent the internal relationships and the regularities of the national economy.

As far as national economic accounting system is concerned, there are two systems in the world nowadays, i.e., the Soviet-style MPS and the Western countries' SNA. On the whole, these two accounting systems are distinguished by difference of scope, procedure and principle. One of the most pronounced differences lies in the treatment of non-material product. Non-material product is included in SNA but not in MPS. Due to this difference in production sphere, the scopes of distribution and consumption are greatly affected. While MPS applies balanced table accounting, SNA adopts ledger accounting. This is the second major difference.

In response to an administration model of centralized and planned economy, MPS was used to administer the national accounting since the time of the establishment of the PRC. Under this traditional model, MPS

*Comments from Xu Xianchun and Liu Liping are very helpful

played an important role in the administration of the economy, however, it gradually lagged behind the actual need of national economic management as the economy evolved towards a market-oriented one after China began its economic reform and opening policy. The inadequacy of MPS manifested itself particularly in the following aspects:

Narrow Production Scope

Owing to the fact that China's traditional accounting system is based upon MPS, its range on production is limited to the production of material goods; the non-material products and the related services are neglected. In view of the steady growth of the economy and society and the advance of science, non-material services, as their ratio of the economy has expanded gradually, and their function have become more and more decisive. Their exclusion from the accounting system can no longer be accepted as the non-material sector is part of the coordinated development of the national economy and the growing concern for material and cultural life.

Incomplete Distribution Accounting

Despite using MPS as the foundation, the traditional accounting system of China has not established the entire accounting contents from MPS, especially those related to distribution. Far from it, it has never reached the level requested. The MPS distribution accounting, comprises both the primary distribution of income and its redistribution. Primary distribution refers to the value newly created by enterprise production, i.e., the distribution of net output value between material production enterprises and laborers undertaking material production activities. Then, the distribution of this net output value in relation to other production factors, expenses on non-material services in material production enterprises, the pay for labor in non-material production enterprise, or one-way non-refundable transfer of income among different economic units are all contents of secondary distribution. In addition, within the scope of secondary distribution in MPS are also included the supply of credit funds and their repayment with interests. Indeed, we could obtain the full picture of primary distribution of income in MPS if we categorized appropriately all the components that constitute net output value distribution in the traditional accounting practice. However, although the Chinese traditional accounting used the concept of redistribution, in reality it never followed up by using the redistribution accounting content.

SNA also distinguishes income distribution into primary distribution and redistribution. Primary distribution in SNA comprises the value-added of all production activities (including both material production and non-material service activities) that is distributed among the factors of production and is made as payment to the government. The distribution of the factors of production includes labor remuneration, interest, dividends, land rent, which are paid from the income of properties, while payment to government includes taxes paid for undertaking production and sale, and in reverse subsidy to production from government (negative production tax). Redistribution in SNA is the free transfer of cash and materials. These include, for example, income tax from individuals and enterprises, insurance premiums by individuals to social insurance organizations, pensions and financial assistance given by social insurance organizations to individuals, etc. In the light of this, SNA does not include cash loan funds and their repayments as redistribution.

In spite of different criteria for primary distribution and redistribution contents between MPS and SNA, nevertheless, both have, on their own terms, a complete picture of distribution and redistribution as they take into account both of them in their accounting contents. However, China's traditional accounting system lacks redistribution accounting. Viewed from the extended production domain, it lacks, in its accounting of distribution, the value added of the non-material production sector. Therefore, we can conclude that the Chinese traditional accounting, in view of the above defect, fails to accurately and comprehensively reflect the actual income and its distribution process; it is not so useful for any concrete analysis of distribution activity and the pattern of income distribution. It is not helpful to the government when formulating the proper taxation policy and distribution policy.

Unreasonable Consumption Scope

Reciprocal to production, the final consumption constituents under the traditional accounting system include, in addition to residents and government, the non-material services production sectors. However, consumer goods are strictly confined to material products. Similar to material production sectors, non-material services production sectors (non-material production sectors for short) are also main production units and not consumption units. Services, non-material in nature, consumed by residents or government are an integral part of what is counted as consumption, and they cannot be left out of consumer goods. To look upon non-material production sectors as only consumers and to limit the definition of consumer goods to material products obscure the distinction between intermediary and final consumption and neglect the people's needs regarding cultural life. Moreover, there are detrimental to the comprehensive study of the scale of consumption, of its structure and its trends; harmful to the correct formulation of consumption policies, to the correct guidance of consumption structure and to the maximization of the response to the needs of the people in terms of material and cultural life.

Incomplete Accounting of Investment and Financing Capital

The traditional accounting system reflects only the part of asset accumulation created by the material production activities. These include fixed assets like machinery equipment and housing construction, and stock increase in materials, finished products and semi-finished products. However, they do not cover land and the purchase of non-financial intangible assets like copyright, trademark and patent. Though land and non-financial intangible assets are not the direct products from any production process (except land reclamation and improvements), they are indispensable in any production process of which they are one of the factors of production. They are as contributory as fixed assets during the process of production over long periods and they generate income for their owners. To exclude investment in these assets makes investment accounting defective.

Fixed assets accumulation, inventory increase and land with the purchase of non-financial intangible asset are thus the results of the investment process. A complete investment accounting not only has to show the investment outcome but it also must indicate another aspect of the process, that is, the source of the investment funds. However, the accounting of the sources of investment in the traditional accounting system is extremely weak.

As far as investment activities are concerned, there are two distinct situations where some units have insufficient investment sources whereas others can enjoy a surplus. The former needs to borrow so as to have an adequate cash flow. The other hopes to lend out the extra cash so as to earn income. There happens a mutual financial transaction. Financial institutions, with regard to these transactions, play an important intermediary role. In practice, the financial transactions are completed according to various different ways. They produce an important positive effect on the development of the socialist market economy. It is extremely important to obtain a comprehensive reflection of this type of transaction in order to make effective financial policy and to have a healthy and harmonious guidance of the national economy. However, there is no comprehensive portrayal of these financial transactions in the traditional accounting system.

Insufficient Accounting of Foreign Trade Activities

Foreign trade activity is one of the major elements constituting the whole national economic operation. It ranges from the import and export of material products, the import and export of non-material services, the inflow and outflow of factor income, external transfer payments and financial transactions, etc. From the adoption of the reform and opening policy until now, the exchanges mentioned above have been growing rapidly, and they have worked as a driving force pushing China's economy forward. Their significance is underrated, nevertheless, in traditional accounting practice. What are included are the import and export of material products and services of a material nature; any external activities outside them are ignored. Hence, the traditional practice falls short of the real needs due to its insufficient coverage of foreign trade activities. As a result, it is of little help to the administration of external trade to foreign trade decision making.

Shortfall of the Accounting of the Stock of Assets and Liabilities

Stock of assets and liabilities comprise initial stock of assets and liabilities at the beginning and at the end of the fiscal year. Assets include fixed assets and inventory created through the production process and comprise also some natural resources that are not the result of production like land, mineral reserves, etc. Assets also extend to financial and non-financial intangible assets in different forms. Liabilities designate various forms of financial liabilities.

The stock of assets and liabilities are both the outcome of the operation of the national economy and the basis and conditions for the national economic undertakings. The accounts of their size and growth reflect the strength, the situation and the level of the national economic development, which have a prominent implication for macro-economic administration. However, the calculation of the stock of assets and liabilities is missing in the Chinese traditional national income accounting practice.

Unsound Accounting of Price Index

When we assess the growth performance and structural change of an economy over a period of time, we have to rely on the calculation of constant prices. Such a calculation rests with the price index. Unfortunately, the price index in the Chinese traditional accounting practice is problematic. From the Chinese and international practice for the accounting of the national income, there should be three kinds of price index used in the national economic accounting: they are the producer price index, the purchaser price index and import-export price index. We owe the constant prices' calculation of production, consumption, material products, non-material services, imports and exports, etc., to these three price indexes system. However, there are some prominent problems associated with the traditional Chinese producer price index and purchaser price index. The producer price index does not include the transportation and telecommunications price indexes and the non-material services price index, etc. And, the purchaser price index lacks a raw material purchase price index. Until now, there has been no effort at dealing formally with the deficiencies about the price indexes of the export and import of material products and non-material services by setting up a relevant accounting system. In this connection, there is a relative weakness in the price indexes system; it is not capable of responding to the need of the management of the national economy through the accounting of the price indexes.

Monotonous Accounting Approach

Based upon MPS, the Chinese traditional accounting practice is a balance sheet in nature. The accounting approach is monotonous. Nowadays, most countries use the SNA framework to establish their accounting forms. The ledger account approach applies the principle of double-entry, which assures that each indicator of the accounts does not stand alone, rather that each one is relating to the others. This is of especially great importance because this form of accounting is able to reflect the macro-economic dimensions of the process of the national economic development. As each aspect and each linkage of the national economy have an intrinsic relation to the other elements, the macro-economic accounting cannot limit itself to presenting only the isolated elements but must provide the interdependence. SNA adopts matrix accounting which is of high clarity, has strong synthetic power and allows for the scrutiny of particular sectors and indicators. These advantages, in turn, cannot be found in the traditional practice which lacks interdependence and rigor.

In summary, the traditional accounting system because of its lack of comprehensiveness, completeness, systematicality and efficacy can no longer represent the active process of the national economy; therefore, the adoption of the SNA accounting system is urgently needed for the administration of the Chinese national economy. As a matter of fact, the new national economic accounting system has been formally established since 1992.

Basic Theories of National Economic Accounting in SNA

The gross domestic product (GDP) in SNA is corresponding to national income in MPS. Due to the difference in the understanding of the concept of production, the basic theories upon which these two systems are based are quite distinct.

The Main Object of GDP Accounting

The main object of gross domestic product accounting in SNA, compared to the object for national income accounting in MPS, is very divergent and different. Under MPS, the object is the individuals or the units which are engaged in material production and consumption within the national boundaries. All outputs created by individuals or production units become the object of national income accounting. Correspondingly, the accounting of import and export is made on the basis of the one-on-one relations between individuals and units within the country and individuals and units beyond the boundaries.

According to SNA, the main object of accounting to obtain the GDP statistics is defined as the (permanent) resident unit. Whatever the result of production activity of such resident unit within the country, the GDP must reflect this activity: that is, the GDP is the production of these resident producers, such as resident corporations, resident households (the resident concept is further discussed below), as well as the production made outside the country by Chinese resident producers; however, the production within the country of non-resident producers may not be included in the gross national product. Obviously, the resident concept is very important to the accurate accounting of the GDP statistics.

The Concept of Resident Unit. It applies to any organization unit that possesses a center of economic interest in a country's economic territory. For a better understanding, one needs to grasp first the meaning of "economic territory" and of "center of economic interest."

1. Economic Territory. A country's economic territory refers to the geographical territory under a government's jurisdiction in which there is a free flow of goods, labor and capital. Specifically, a country's economic territory includes: (1) owned or claimed air space, sea territory or continental shelf under a public sea over which a country can exercise its property right, fishing right, seabed resources exploration right and mineral products right; (2) enclaves elsewhere in the world that a country obtains the right to lease or own for diplomatic, military, scientific investigation purposes, like embassy, consulate, military base, etc., through formal political agreements reached with the country where these lands are located; (3) free trade zones, tax-free warehouses and factories, etc., run by coastal enterprises that are under Customs control.
2. Center of Economic Interest. As long as an organization unit in a country's economic territory possesses a place of abode, a place for production or any other buildings and is planning to or is using these places to carry out economic activities and transactions whether on permanent or on long-term basis, it is said to possess a center of economic interest. In the case of a firm's owing at least one place in the territory of a country, that is used or is on the way to be used for massive production on either long-term or permanent basis, that place(s) naturally become(s) its center of economic

interest. In the case of a household, it is said to have a center of economic interest as long as it owns one or more than one residence (normally for one year) and the personnel uses it as the primary residence. Finally, in the case of a government unit, it possesses a center of economic interest as long as governing rights and taxing rights can be exercised.

Resident Household. With regard to the household as integral unit, the qualification to a resident household implies that it is permanent and that the personnel uses residence as their main place of abode. Nevertheless, with regard to an individual member of a household, who may be leaving for a relatively long period for study or work, some further illustrations are needed.

1. Expatriate member of a resident household. This includes traveller, tourist, seasonal worker, cross-boundary worker, international organization staff, short- or long-term staying away from one's economic territory where one's residence is and working in the economic territory of another country, employee in a foreign embassy, consulate, military base, crew member on vessels, aircraft or mobile equipment partially or fully living outside one's own economic territory, expatriate military staff, expatriate clerical official, and diplomat working in overseas enclaves.
2. Expatriate member of a non-resident household. This means a citizen of a country working overseas consistently for over a year, regardless whether the settlement of pay is made by a local or overseas firm. However, the resident status of non-legal entity enterprise mainly rests with the permanence of the residence.

Resident Corporation. A corporation is established in a country according to the law and regulations of the country and is formally recognized and recorded as a legal entity. It is treated as a resident corporation of the country. However, it should be noted that whether the stockholder is resident is irrelevant to the residence issue of the corporation. A resident corporation can be exclusively owned and controlled by a non-resident unit. For example, a coastal enterprise owned by some non residing unit is a resident unit in the country where the enterprise registers and runs its business. This includes enterprises which work on manufacture, assembling spare parts produced outside and financial intermediaries, such as international trade companies, insurance companies, etc. Similarly, following the same way, we can define the resident non profit-making institution.

Accounting Scope of Gross Domestic Product

The present GDP accounting system is much larger in scope than the national income accounting of MPS. It embraces both material goods production and services production; it also covers production for society and production for its own use; and, it includes actual production as well as the production imputed.

Goods and Services. As there are different characteristics about goods and services with regard to the accounting scope, here are some brief definitions for each one of them.

1. Goods. A good is an object which has a clearly defined property attached to it and for which there is a supply and demand. Correspondingly, the production of goods is the creation of products by a concrete process, for example, machinery equipment as a capital asset, consumer goods like television sets and measuring instruments. Production and utilization are the distinctive characteristics of goods. Under normal circumstances, there exits a time lag between the production and use of goods. Television sets for instance, after manufacturing, are not sent directly to consumers; they have to go through the process of storage, delivery, retail sale, etc., before they reach the consumers.
2. Services. Activities carried out by a producer which aim to alter a consumer's circumstances are considered services. For example, activities purporting to improve the conditions of goods for organizational units, like transportation, repair, maintenance, cleaning, etc., are services. Others are activities to improve health, image, skill, knowledge, etc., such as health care, education, consultation, entertainment, etc. Insurance, money lending and credit are included as well. The most important feature of services is that the production is simultaneous with their utilization. For example, a barber provides hair-dressing service to a client, and the client receives his service simultaneously.

Market Production and Non-market Production. Market production refers to the act of provision of goods and services for the market. It is also known as society-oriented production. In contrast, non-market production refers to the act of producing goods or services for one's own consumption. It is also known as self-oriented production.

1. Market Production. The accounting of GDP is manifested by the goods and services that have gone through the market before they are utilized. The major items include marketed agricultural goods, industrial goods, capital goods and consumer goods. This category of production will have a growing share in the prospective economic development in China.

2. Non-market Production. Non-market production in GDP denotes the provision of goods and services that are not transacted in the market but that are available for utilization. Goods and services in this category include self-consumed grain by peasants, the processing of agricultural goods and leather or cloth weaving for self use, etc. It is important to specify here that household cooking is not subject to the accounting scope of GDP.

Actual and Imputed Production. Actual production and imputed production are distinguished according to whether or not some direct calculation of the production outcome is possible. If the product value can be calculated directly, it is actual. If the production result is difficult to obtain or cannot be calculated, its production belongs to imputed production.

1. Actual Production. A major part of the accounting scope of GDP belongs to outputs that can be calculated directly. This includes production of machinery equipment, electrical motors, and motor vehicles; cultivating crops and raising poultry by peasants; transportation, retailing, catering, etc., by any enterprise.
2. Imputed Production. Apart from actual production, the accounting scope of GDP includes also imputed production. Building a house by a household is one example. At first glance, building a house does not imply any exchange or economic activity; it does not belong to production. However, if we interpret one's having one's own premises as a contractual arrangement by which the owner is paying some kind of rent to oneself, the arrangement, in this context, implies an imputed undertaking which is considered as imputed production.

Lastly, there is a need to define the goods and services that we have mentioned. Goods and services, in this sense, must have human labor inputs in the course of production or exploration. Natural resources reserves, e.g., undeveloped land, forest and underground resources, are not goods and services as defined above because they do not involve any human labor inputs in transforming their status. They are not outputs of a production process of any kind. However, natural products should be recorded as economic variables outside production if they already have a market price and are transacted in the market prior to full processing to become goods. Besides, they should be considered products of the current period of production activity. If transaction period is distinct from the production period, only the latter is considered. No matter sold or unsold, the goods are accounted for according to their production period so as to reflect the current production results of the accounting period.

To reiterate, the accounting scope of GDP in China is as follows: (1) the production of goods and services provided by the resident units to other units and individuals; (2) the production of goods for one's own consumption or for fixed assets formation by resident producers; (3) imputed services of self-occupied housing, the pay for housekeepers, and labor on time-scale service paid by the residents units.

Accounting Classification of Gross Domestic Product

GDP accounting in China adopts four groups of classifications: according to institutional sectors; according to industrial sectors; group according to material and non-material production sectors; and according to the primary, secondary, and tertiary type of production.

Classification by Institutional Sectors. The institutional sectors consist of resident organizational units. The range of institutions included in GDP accounting covers the following four types: non-financial enterprises, financial enterprises, government bureaux, and inhabitants (including urban and rural individual production units).

1. Non-financial Enterprise Sector. Non-financial enterprise sector refers to non-financial resident independent accounting enterprises which undertake non-financial activity; they range from state-owned and collective-owned enterprises, various share-based joint ventures, partnerships or foreign-owned resident industrial and commercial enterprises, construction enterprises, transportation and telecommunication enterprises and non-financial service enterprises. However, non-independent accounting enterprises attached to administrative undertaking units and self-employed enterprises fall outside this group. The former belongs to the government group, the latter to the inhabitant sector, because these two types of enterprises do not have an independent authority over their assets and liabilities, and the accounting of their income and expenses are not outside of their respective -- government or private -- sectors. It would be difficult to separate the accounting from the accounts of their particular sectors.
2. Financial Enterprise Sector. The sector refers to those resident independent accounting enterprises that are mainly engaged in financial intermediary activities; it includes the central bank, specialized banks, credit cooperatives, insurance companies, trust and investment organizations, etc. The reason for separating the financial from the non-financial enterprises is that there is a substantive difference in their types of economic activity.
3. Government Sector. Government sector is composed of the various administrative undertaking units, which include the army, non-

independent accounting enterprises attached to the administrative undertaking units, but exclude the independent accounting units which are classified under the enterprise sector.

4. Inhabitant Sector. The sector consists of all resident households. It comprises also self-employed businesses by households and non-legal person enterprises. Because one can not yet distinguish clearly between the assets and liabilities and income and expenses of the businesses in question and the households themselves, it is reasonable to keep them under this general sector.

Classification by Industrial Sectors. Industrial sector denotes the aggregate of grassroots production units engaged in the same type of production activity. Grassroots production unit signifies any production unit running one or mainly one production activity at one location. A firm can be running one or many production activities at one time. In this way, a firm may be a grassroots production unit; however, a large enterprise may combine more than one grassroots production unit simultaneously. And so, we divide our production sectors into groups, according to the present standard classification of industries in China. We classify the whole national economy into the following: (1) agriculture; (2) industry; (3) construction; (4) commerce, catering, material supply and storage; (5) transport, post and telecommunications and information; (6) geological survey and exploration; (7) real estate, public utilities, residents' services and consultation services; (8) hygiene, sports and social welfare services; (9) education, culture, arts, and television and broadcasting; (10) scientific research and comprehensive technical services; (11) finance and insurance; (12) state organs, and party and government organizations, and social organizations; and (13) others.

Classification by Material and Non-material Production Sectors. The reason for this distinction is the historical comparability of statistical data. Strictly speaking, by material production sector is meant the final outcome of production activity which provides production means and consumption goods for social needs. This sector includes both the material products and the services of material nature. Any production sector other than this one will be listed under the non-material sector.

1. Material Production Sector. There are five large subsections under it. They are agriculture; industry; construction; commerce, catering, material supply and marketing as well as storage; and transport, post and telecommunications. However, the last subsection excludes passenger transport.
2. Non-material Production Sector. It includes the sections not classified

under the five subsections mentioned above. They are (1) passenger transport in transport, post and telecommunications sector; (2) geological survey and exploration; (3) real estate administration and public utilities, residents' services and consultation services; (4) hygiene, sports and social welfare services; (5) education, culture, arts, television and radio broadcasting; (6) scientific research and comprehensive technical services; (7) finance and insurance; (8) state organs, party and government organs as well as social organizations; and, (9) others.

Classification by the Primary, Secondary and Tertiary Industries. Classification of this type is a popular and useful one all over the world. It breaks down all undertakings of an economy into three broad industries namely primary industry, secondary industry and tertiary industry.

1. Primary Industry. It refers to agriculture, including farming, forestry, animal husbandry and fishery. Industry at *cun* (village) level and below is not included, which is classified in the industry sector.
2. Secondary Industry. It represents industry and construction. Industry includes extraction industry, manufacturing, water supply, electricity, steam power, hot water, coal gas, etc.; construction includes construction and installation enterprises and private construction units, geological exploration services and construction design.
3. Tertiary Industry. The rest of industries untouched in Primary Industry and Secondary Industry are classified in this category. In view of the great diversity of industries that it includes, it can be further broken down in two sectors according to the situation in China: (1) circulation sector and (2) service sector. Practically, it can also be divided into four levels. At the top, the circulation sector, we have transport, post and telecommunications, commerce, catering trade, material supply and marketing as well as storage. Next is services sector meeting the needs of production and daily life, which include banking, finance and insurance, comprehensive technical services, services to farming, forestry, animal husbandry and fishery, irrigation works, consultancy services, highway, inland waterway maintenance, geological surveying, residents' services, public utilities, real estate, etc. Further below is the service sector for raising scientific level and residents' quality, which includes education, culture, television and broadcasting, scientific research, hygiene, sports and social welfare services. At the bottom is the service sector for the provision of public services, which includes state and party and government organizations, social organizations, army and police force, etc.

Accounting Units of GDP. There are two types of GDP accounting units. They are institutional units and grassroots units, respectively. In principle, no matter which units are our accounting based on, the GDP should be the same. In other words, the aggregate sum of value-added by enterprises will be commensurate with that of value-added by industries.

1. Institutional Unit. There are several requirements for any unit to become an institutional unit. First, a unit has the kind of right to own goods and assets independently. It has the ownership of goods and assets when engaged in exchange with other units and has the authority to settle payments and acknowledge unsettled payments and assume liabilities that come into effect when a transaction is completed. Besides, it has the right to sign contracts and resort to legal action for its own sake. Thirdly, it can make decision and act on its own. Lastly, it has a full set of account records. On fulfilling all these requirements, an unit is recognized as an institutional unit. In practice, there are also two kinds of institutional unit. The first one is the individual who may be a single person or a household grouping several persons. The household in this sense is equivalent to the family. Yet, members of a household are not necessarily of the family. Monks or religious staff in a monastery or church exemplify this fact. In parallel, people living together are not necessarily members of a household; house servants or paid employees are not considered members of this family. The other type of institutional unit is the legal or social entity. It means the corporation, the non profit-making organization and government. Corporation, in this context, is the legal person entity created for making profits through the provision of goods and services, the legal entity owned by the shareholders possessing the right to appoint or remove the managing personnel. The non-for-profit organization is created in law or by society to provide goods and services, but it does not seek income for itself. Government is such a legal entity set up in a particular territory according to specific political procedures. It is endowed with legislative, executive and judicial power over other legal entities.
2. Grassroots Unit. A grassroots unit is a business or an integral part of a business which carries out one production activity at one location. In practice, a grassroots unit can be a farm, a mine, a factory, a workshop, a commercial shop, an office, or a production unit that undertakes another production activity. Most small-size businesses are largely single grassroots units. But, medium- to large-size businesses may be composed of two or more than two grassroots units. According to this definition, we can classify the

national economy into various grassroots units; for example, the classification of the grassroots units according to horizontally integrated enterprises and vertically integrated enterprises. Horizontally integrated enterprises are units within a particular sector, which simultaneously engage in a diversity of businesses and separately market where the goods and services derived from this production. In other words, according to the definition of grassroots organization, these unrelated businesses are individuals, of which each one can be an independent grassroots unit. Vertically integrated enterprises consist of different units which perform different production activities in a multi-stage production, and the output of an earlier stage becomes the input of the following stage. Enterprises at different production stage are also individual grassroots units.

Recording Time of GDP Accounting. GDP accounting touches upon various flows, such as goods and services, revenues and expenditures, etc. Moreover, it is essential to pinpoint and to record these flows in a unified time framework; this implies the question regarding the time when the accounting is recorded. There are two principles of choice by which recording time of GDP accounting can be accomplished. The first is right-liability occurrence principle. A transaction is recorded at the moment a credit right or liability takes place or is transferred or cancelled. The second is delivery-reception realization principle. It records a transaction either at the moment when the products concerned are delivered or are received.

1. Production Accounting. Usually, the production is recorded once the total production of the goods is completed. Finished here does not solely refer to products having gone through the entire production processes. Semi-finished products, goods in process which are partially finished and need further process are included. This applies to most industries which record their products as finished product, semi-finished product, and product in process according to the finished time except for agricultural products which are recorded according to their harvest time. For those products in process which take more than one accounting period to finish, the record is made according to its progress at the completion. About intermediate input recording, it is done when the material is inputed as a record of concrete material use rather than after they have become finished products. As to services, output is recorded according to the time of providing the service, consumption is recorded when a service is received. Since the time of providing a service is identical with the time it is consumed, the recording of provision and consumption of a service is usually the same.

2. Income Accounting. When recording the income accounting, the income item is recorded at the point when payment obligation and income right take place. For example, the accounting of labor remuneration, net production tax and business profits is treated in this way. In principle, the time is recorded on the time the accounting items are entered so that all payable wages, payable taxes and receivable profits are recorded simultaneously and not at the time the real expenditures or income are paid out. The recording time of all income items and the one for production accounting have to be corresponding.
3. Use Accounting. Whenever one proceeds with use accounting, the final use of the item should be recorded according to the time of acquiring the ownership of goods and services. For the accounting of total consumption, total investment and import and export items, if final use is realized through purchase or transfer, its record is done according to the time of changing the ownership of goods. On the other hand, unsold goods and self-produced and self-consumed goods are dated back to the time of their production. The recording time for import and export goods is dated in principle according to the time of the legal change of ownership. In practice, the discharging time of the concerned products by Customs is the time that is usually accepted. In principle, some adjustment has to be done for the recording time according to the right-liability occurrence system.

Price Assessment Principle in GDP Accounting. In measuring the output value, GDP accounting applies the market price as a unified measurement yardstick. No matter sold, unsold or not for sale, any material product should be assessed according to the market price of similar product at the time of its production. For instance, when assessing the value of an unsold tractor, the price of a sold tractor of the same category and same model is used. Similarly, the price of a farmer's self-produced and self-consumed crops is assessed according to the price of the crop of the same category and the same quality on the market. As far as the service sector is concerned, like hairdressing and catering, the price is set with reference to the actual transaction price in the market. For non-marketed services, they are appraised according to the cost of the usual expenses that are implied, such as payment in kind, non-market services provided by the government. Alternatively, some reference from the market price of the similar goods and services is considered, such as the imputed rent for privately owned housing. Intermediate input, fixed asset depreciation, goods going in and out of inventory are assessed in principle according to current market prices instead of the original price. All these are the basic principles for the price assessment of goods and services.

There are two kinds of price assessment for marketable goods and services, i.e., the producer price and the purchaser price. Despite the fact that they are both market prices, they are derived from different standpoints. While the first adopts the production standpoint, the second decides on the price from the angle of consumption. The difference in price is due to the processes accompanying the production of goods and their reaching the consumers and the difference in time and location between production and consumption. The main sources of price difference are the various production expenses on the first hand and circulation expenses on the second. For services, the standpoints mentioned here overlap and the two prices are the same because the service is produced at the same time it is consumed. For the accounting of GDP and its application, total output should be computed according to the producer price whereas intermediate input should be according to the purchaser price.

If necessary for further analysis, there is a third assessment measure, i.e., according to the basic price. The basic price is the final price after deducting from the producer price the net production tax. Because the price has no tax component, it reflects the genuine cost of production and the true producer price. It is the most suitable price for studying the interindustry input-output relation and for analyzing the impact of production tax on production activity.

Basic Method and Indicators of National Income Accounting

The national income accounting of the national economic accounting system in SNA involves a great number of indicators. Some of them deal with the whole picture of the national economy. Some of them reflect a portion of the national economy, some others reveal the whole process of the national economy. And, some just reveal part of the process. This section will give a detailed discussion on these indicators.

Indicators Content of GDP and its Use Table. Viewed from the production standpoint, the indicators of GDP accounting include total output, intermediate input, GDP and net material product value. From the standpoint of usage, the relevant indicators include total expenditure, intermediate use, GDP as well as net material product value. See Table 3.1 and also Table 4.1 in Chapter 4.

1. Indicators Content of Production Side

   (A) Total Output. Total output, also known as total product, refers to the total achievements of all production activities in an accounting period. As an indication of the scale of various

TABLE 3.1 Gross Domestic Product and Its Use

Production and Distribution	*Use*
Total Output	Total Expenditure
Intermediate input	Intermediate use
Material product input	Used by material production sector
Services input	Used by non-material production sector
Gross Domestic Product	Gross Domestic Product
Fixed Asset Depreciation	Gross Final Consumption
Labour Remuneration	Household consumption
Net Production Tax	Government consumption
Operating Surplus	Gross Capital Formation
	Gross fixed capital formation
	Change in inventory
	Export
	Import

production sectors of the national economy, it comprises the sold or unsold material goods and services, self-produced and self-consumed agricultural products and self-manufactured fixed assets in current period. In other words, the total output amounts to the sum of intermediate inputs and value-added, and it is calculated generally according to the producer price.

(B) Intermediate Input. It refers to the total value of material goods and services consumed in the course of production processes undertaken by the resident units in producing their material goods or furnishing their services. It is also called intermediate product. There are two conditions to qualify for inclusion: first of all, those material goods and non-material services that are consumed or transformed into furnished goods during the production process correspond to the total output. Secondly, the non-durable goods not belonging to fixed assets are consumed in current period. Intermediate input can also be divided into two categories: material product inputs and non-material service inputs. Their value is generally calculated in purchaser price. What is counted as material product inputs are materials that are consumed or transformed during production and services of material nature like freight transport, post and telecommunications, commerce and catering trade, etc., except fixed assets depreciation. In the services part, service input refers to the services that are provided in the course of production, with the exception of the services of material nature. They range from finance and insurance, culture and education, scientific research, medical treatment and hygiene, and administration services, etc.

(C) Value-added. It refers to the value increase during the process of producing material products or furnishing services. It reflects the difference in value between the total output and the intermediate input and the final result of the activities of the production units or industrial sectors, their contribution to GDP. Value-added is made up of four elements: fixed asset depreciation, laborers' remuneration, net production tax and operating surplus.

Fixed asset depreciation is a fixed value drawn within the accounting period to compensate for tear and wear of fixed assets during the production process; it represents the value of loss or transfer on the part of the fixed assets during the production. The basic depreciation fund is drawn according to the stipulated ratio. Fixed asset depreciation is not a newly created value; rather, it is a transferred value intended to make up for the loss in value of fixed assets incurred during production. There are a number of reasons for including this transferred value in the calculation of GDP. The first reason is to be objective and accurate in dealing with fixed asset value loss. In response to the lack of a corresponding visible or material measure, the depreciation value foresees some possible factors affecting the depletion value of fixed assets. These factors are, for example, damage by constant wear and tear, foreseeable loss arising from accident, and value change due to technological advance. It is possible for a fixed asset "to be retired" before completing the expected normal service or to be kept in use beyond such period. Hence, depreciation is pre-estimated value which implies some subjectivity. It is due to this feature that the computation of this item among enterprises, industries and countries has no consensual criterion of measurement method or result. For the same fixed asset in the same production process, the depreciation rate adopted can be distinctly different in different industries and countries. The depreciation rate is a difficult measure to determine. Secondly, it is for the sake of disclosing comprehensively the balance of the final product. From a material balance viewpoint, the depletion of fixed assets needs not to be replaced immediately, which implies that this value correspondingly must be utilized by final use, i.e., consumption and investment. The GDP measure will then become defective in reflecting comprehensively the balance relations between production and final use if it does not take depreciation into account. Thirdly, for the sake of thoroughly tracing the flow of funds, the depreciation itself does not require any immediate compensation by real goods; depreciation allowance drawn can be directed to other ends, as ordinary capital flow. Thus, retaining this part in GDP facilitates the illustration of the balance relationship between the source and use of funds. Moreover, fixed assets depreciation is different from other intermediate products. While the former can be used several times, the latter is used just once. Although theoretically fixed asset depreciation should be treated as transferred value, and treated as intermediate product, given a certain price level, this would give rise to fluctuation of the GDP if we treat it as intermediate product. It would be disadvantageous to its comparability. Under this situation, the deduction of depreciation from the GDP is not performed. It enhances the degree of accuracy of calculation and ensures the coherence of GDP accounting. Above all, it raises the level of comparability of the indicators with international practice.

Labor remuneration depicts the value of effective labor or the contributions of human input in the production process. Concretely, laborer remuneration represents what the employer gives, in various forms, as payment for labor. Basically, there are three forms: (1) Money income. It comprises the net money income, such as wages, salaries, bonuses, various subsidies and allowances and the income of private and other laborers. (2) Income in kind. It refers to various material products and services provided to the laborers by the production units to which they belong at lower than cost price or free of charge, and agricultural products grown for self consumption by farmers. (3) Social insurance premiums paid on behalf of the laborers by their production units. Fall in this category premiums to the government and insurance companies for insurance on unemployment, retirement, pension, life, medical care, family property, etc. These kinds of payments should be added to the pay of the laborer at the time they are made.

Net production tax is the remainder amount after subtracting the tax payment made by the resident production units to the government from the subsidy received by the resident production units from the government. Production tax precisely includes the taxation on production, sale, purchase, use of goods and services, levied on resident production units. There are three kinds of production tax in China. The first kind includes tax to the government by producers, such as product tax, business tax, value-added tax, farming and animal husbandry tax, vehicle and ship use tax, real estate tax, slaughter tax, city building tax, domestic animal transaction tax, country market transaction tax, import and export tax, special consumption tax etc. The second kind covers specified revenues and profits surrendered by the monopoly authorities on their profits from cigarette, alcohol sales, etc. The third kind is the tax given to the government according to law and regulations as regulatory fees.

Production subsidy designates subsidy provided to the production sectors as a means to fulfill the dual role of promoting production and controlling market prices. They include price subsidy and loss subsidy.

Operating surplus points to the residual value achieved by taxable factors of production during the production process. It represents the net revenue obtained from undertaking a production activity by the resident production units, i.e., the difference between the total output, on the one hand, and intermediate inputs, fixed assets depreciation, laborers' remuneration and net production tax, on the other. This residual is really what the producers seek to obtain through their production activity, the concrete realization of the enterprise's economic benefits.

2. Indicators Content of the User's Side

(A) Total Expenditure: It refers to the total sum of expenditures on goods and services by resident units in China over a given period of time (normally one year). It comprises two parts: intermediate use expenditure and final use expenditure.

(B) Intermediate Use Expenditure: It refers to the value of goods and services consumed and utilized in all production processes by resident production units, which is also called intermediate consumption, taking place in both material production and non-material production sectors. Utilization in material production sector designates the goods and services used up in production processes and in service industries of material nature like freight transport, post and telecommunications, commerce, and catering trade, etc., except fixed asset depreciation. By the same token, utilization in non-material production sector refers to goods and services consumed and utilized in non-material production sector during production process, such as finance and insurance, culture and education, scientific research, medicine and hygiene, government administration sectors; this also excludes fixed asset depreciation.

(C) Final Use: It refers to the total expenditure on the final use of goods and services by resident units in China over a given period of time (normally one year). So far as its composition is concerned, there are three essential parts: gross final consumption, gross capital formation and net export. Gross final consumption measures the final consumption expenditure on goods and services by the resident units within a specified period (again normally one year), which caters for the need of satisfying the material, cultural as well as spiritual life of individuals. Goods and services purchased in China's economic territory or abroad are included. Yet, consumption within China's economic territory by non-resident inhabitants is not included. What's more, gross consumption is divided into household consumption and government consumption. Household (personal) consumption designates the final expenditure on goods and services by the resident inhabitants during an accounting period. It has four components: (1) direct purchase of durable or non-durable consumer goods for everyday consumption, except housing and expenditure for production purpose; (2) expenditure on direct purchase of services for everyday life, e.g., travel expense, rent, cleaning, repair, medical care, education, culture, household servants, etc.; (3) income in kind at below-market-price or free goods and services received by the residents for various living consumption; (4) resident' self-produced and self-consumed goods which are considered as part of social products during the accounting period, and the imputed rent of self-owned flat, etc.

Government (social, or public) consumption consists of the consumer goods and services provided to society for consumption by the public service sectors. These sectors include those in fields such as culture, education, sports and athletics, medicine and hygiene, scientific research, government agencies, social groups, army, police, etc. The consumption goods and services provided by these agencies are manifested as their total output minus their incomes from sale. The reason for deducting sales income from total output is that, among the goods that are provided by these agencies to society, there are goods which are provided without charging any fee, while other agencies provide goods or services to the individual from which the agencies collect a sales income. This portion that is provided to the individual for a fee has already been accounted among the consumption expenses of residents as direct consumption of goods or services. By deducting sales income from total output, this procedure eliminates the possibility of counting twice the same consumption costs.

Gross capital formation represents the total expenditure

invested in fixed assets and inventory by the resident units during the accounting period, namely, gross fixed capital formation and increase in inventory. Fixed capital formation points to the total investment in building and buying fixed assets by the resident units in the accounting period. Assets into this category are any kind of houses, buildings, machinery equipment, draught animal and breeding stock, long-term growth of economic forests, projects under construction, etc. However, durable consumer goods owned by any residents as well as durable goods for military purpose are excluded. Concretely, gross fixed capital formation consists of four parts. The first part refers to the newly formed fixed asset value by basic construction investment. The second part refers to the increased fixed asset value derived from renovation investment. The third is the increased fixed asset value due to major repairs. The last is the fixed asset value formed by other capital expenditure. Inventory increase expresses the change in market value of the physical stock by the resident units in the accounting period. The difference between the amount at the beginning and the end of the period, if negative, represents an increase in stock, while, if it is positive, a decrease in stock. Concretely, this includes the following: the raw materials, fuels, various materials reserve, etc., purchased by the production units from other units. These commodities in stock have to be accounted for at the purchaser's price in the accounting period in which the purchases take place. Inventory increase includes also the producers' finished products, products in process, semi-finished products. The price of finished products which are put in storage should be valued according to the producer price in the current period.

Net export designates the difference between exports and imports. In an open economy, goods and services so consumed by a country's resident units are often produced by non-resident units. At the same time, resident units may often produce goods and services which are consumed by non-resident units. With a view of use to getting an accurate picture of final products produced by the resident units in the accounting period, we have to get the information about net export. Export refers to the gross value of goods and services sold or gratuitously transferred from the resident units to non-resident units. Import, on the other hand, refers to the gross value of goods and services purchased or gratuitously acquired by the resident units from non-resident units. Net export is thus the difference when subtracting the gross value of import from the gross value of export.

Major Indicators of National Income Accounting.

1. Gross (Net) Domestic Product. The gross domestic product is expressed in three forms, namely value form, income form and material object form. The first form measures the value difference between the total output value of goods and services produced by all resident units minus the total input value of goods and services exclusive of fixed assets in the accounting period. The resultant value is, in other words, the sum of value-added of all resident units. From the income angle, GDP sums up the total value of the primary distribution of income among the resident institution units and non-resident institution units, which is created by the production activities of all resident institution units in the given period. Lastly, the material object form indicates the goods and services of final use minus imported goods and services.

   The net domestic product represents the concept of net value by deducting the total fixed asset depreciation for all resident units of a country from the GDP. One thing to emphasize is that neither the GDP nor the net domestic products indicates a measure of welfare; they represent only the aggregate production activity of the national economy. As a result, the implication is that, to a large extent, its meaning derives from the concept of production and the boundary set by intermediate consumption and final use. For example, activities without visible rewards like housework are outside the concept of production in question, thus ignored in the calculation of GDP. In addition, we use the market price to estimate the GDP and the net domestic product.

2. Gross (Net) National Product. The gross national product is the final result of the primary distribution of income among the resident units over a specific period of time. In effect, the value-added created by the resident units is mainly distributed among the resident units. However, some part is distributed to non-resident institution units in the forms of laborer remuneration and property income: for instance, the earnings from investments in China by foreign resident units. The portion of income distributed to non-resident units should not be counted in the gross national product. However, some resident units will receive laborer remuneration and property income from the value-added created by non-resident units: this creates a discrepancy with the actual production and the actual income of the resident units. It is necessary to work out an indicator for measuring the actual income of the resident units in addition to the GDP measuring the actual production of these units. The new indicator, the gross national income or the gross national product, equals the GDP plus the difference between

laborer remuneration and property income received by local resident units from foreign units and laborer remuneration and property income paid out to foreign ones. Gross domestic product is distinguished from gross national product in that the former is an indicator measuring production, the latter measuring income. And, the net national product (NNP) is a net value concept: it is simply equal to the gross national product minus the fixed asset depreciation of all resident units; the NNP is also equal to the net domestic product to which is added the difference between the income from labor wages and property income paid by foreign sources, on the one hand, and the labor wages and property income paid to foreign interests, on the other hand.

3. Gross (Net) National Disposable Income. It refers to the final result of the redistribution of income among the resident organizational units over a specific period of time. It indicates the redistribution process between the resident and non-resident units once the national economy has gone through the production process and the primary distribution of income. The distributed primary income of the resident units may be transferred to non-resident units, as for example, when foreign resident units in China may transmit their income to their mother companies overseas. It is also true for the resident units in China which receive transferred income from non-resident ones, like relief money received by resident households in China from foreign resident households. This kind of distribution restructuring is also known as the income transfer process. What is meant is that this process involves only one-way and gratuitous transfer of income among different units, implying the lack of goods or services going back in return. It is due to this process that the disposable income of local resident units can change over time. In order to measure the effect of this transfer, it is expedient to bring in the concept of gross national disposable income. It is equal to the sum of the gross national product plus the current transfer of income from foreign resident units minus the current transfer income paid to foreign resident units. In other words, it also reveals the total income of local resident units that is used for final consumption and savings.

   The net national disposable income is equal to the net national product plus the current transfer of income from foreign resident units minus the current transfer of income paid to foreign resident units. It can also be obtained by subtracting the depreciation of fixed assets of all resident units from the gross national disposable income.

4. Final Expenditure. Final expenditure designates the amount paid

for the purchase of goods and services by the resident units in China. The ultimate goal of economic activities is consumption. However, consumption is usually carried out through two channels: direct purchase of goods and services by the household; and, direct purchase of goods and services by government or other social organizations. The former is called personal consumption while the latter is called public consumption. Apart from fulfilling final consumption, another goal of economic activities is to maintain and strengthen the future economic production activity which requires part of the current produced goods to be put into fixed assets investment and is known as the investment part of the final expenditure. We can see that final expenditure includes two parts: final consumption expenditure and final investment expenditure.

We have to point out that the final expenditure does not mean that all of the goods and services need to be purchased by resident units. For instance, the self-produced self-consumed grain by the farmers themselves should be included in the final expenditure. But the farmers do not purchase them. Therefore, such "expenditure" is regarded as imputed expenditure.

5. Gross (Net) National Savings. Gross national savings are the remaining part of the national disposable income that has not been consumed by the current final consumption. It is equal to the difference of the gross national disposable income subtracting the final consumption expenditure. The net national savings are equal to gross national savings minus fixed asset depreciation. It is also equal to the net national disposable income minus final consumption expenditure.

The identities of the above economic variables can be summarized as the following:

Gross National Product = Gross Domestic Product + laborer remuneration and property income from abroad – laborer remuneration and property income paid out abroad;

Net National Product = Gross National Product – fixed asset depreciation of all resident units;

Gross National Disposable Income = Gross National Product + current transfer income from foreign residents – current transfer income paid to foreign residents = final consumption of resident units + total savings;

Net National Disposable Income = Gross National Disposable Income – fixed asset depreciation of all resident units;

Gross National Savings = Gross National Disposable Income – final consumption expenditure;

Net National Saving = Gross National Savings – fixed asset depreciation

Compilation of National Income Accounting in SNA

GDP is the final outcome in terms of value of the production activities within the specified calculation period. It provides a comprehensive description of the production, distribution and use of the economic activities of the society. Owing to its function of reflecting economic activities from different aspects, GDP has three different approaches to calculation: the production approach, the distribution approach and the expenditure approach. The production approach is to observe economic activities from the production aspect and carry out a comprehensive measurement of the newly created value in the calculation period. The distribution approach is to observe the direction of the primary distribution of GDP from the constituent items formed by the newly created value. The expenditure approach is to observe the expenditure composition of GDP through the distribution direction of the final outcome. Among these three approaches of calculation, the production and distribution approaches can be from a micro-angle: by first finding out the value-added of the enterprises or sectors, then, one adds them together to form GDP. The expenditure approach is from a macro point of view, obtained by adding the expenditure items of consumption and investment. Even though these three approaches differ in their angles of calculation and sources of information, the final outcome should be coherent in principle. That is to say, GDP calculated by the three different approaches should be of equivalence in their aggregate amount. This is known as the principle of three-scale equivalent value in the calculation of GDP. The following is the explanation of the three calculation approaches.

The Production Approach

The production approach calculates GDP from the production's point of view. It starts with the value formation of the total output of the various basic accounting units in the national economy. Then, it obtains the value-added -- the newly created value obtained by subtracting the intermediate products (goods and services) during the production process from the total output. The total of value-added from the various sectors is the gross domestic product (GDP).

The formula for the production approach is:

Total output – intermediate input = value-added

The methodology and source of information for calculating the value-added of various sectors in the national economy using the production approach are as follows:

Agriculture. Agriculture includes four sub-sectors: farming, forestry, animal husbandry and fishery. Farming refers to cultivation, i.e., the production of various grains, cash crops and products like tea, mulberry and fruit, etc. It also includes the collection of wild plants, hunting of wild animals and sideline industrial production in which a farming household may engage. Forestry refers to the planting of trees and forests, the collection of forest products, activities by co-operative economic organizations at village level and below, and individuals who are engaged in the cutting and felling of bamboo and timber. Animal husbandry designates the raising and herding of all animals (except fish breeding). Fishery refers to the catching and breeding of animals living in water and the cultivation of aquatic plants. Agricultural production units comprise all the agricultural production activities by farm households, rural collectives and state farms. Several points regarding the compilation of agricultural data need elaborations.

1. The total output of agriculture refers to the total outcome of the agricultural production activities in the accounting period. The "product method" *(chan pin fa)* is adopted for the calculation. That means the output is calculated by multiplying the quantity of the product by its unit price for whatever category of product. One thing needs to be specified: the planting of trees in forestry is calculated according to the unit cost of the various activities in the forestry production process. The concrete calculation method of total output of agriculture is discussed in some details as follows:

   The total output of farming includes the output of main farming products, sideline products and other farming products. The output of main farming products include grain, cash crops, vegetables, melon types, mulberry leaves, fruits and forage crops, etc. The output of sideline products includes the output of products from the leaves, stalks and straw of grains and cash crops. The output of other farming products includes the output value of reeds, lotus roots, sisal hemp and lemongrass, etc., and the output of wild medical plants, mushrooms, starch and faggot, etc. Output value is obtained from multiplying the quantities of various products by the current price.

   The total output of forestry includes bamboo and timber felling, the products of forest cultivation and forest fruit. The formula is as follows:

Total output of forestry = output of felling of bamboo and timber (the quantity in current year x price) + output of forest plantation (the sum of actual costs for various afforestation activities) + output of forest fruit (the quantity of various collected fruit in the forest in current year x price)

The total output of animal husbandry includes (1) the output of animals and fowls which left the farm (for sale or slaughter) that is, the output of pigs, ox, horses, donkeys, mules, sheep and poultry for sale or slaughter; piglets and kids sold or slaughtered for eating and the value of young livestock such as kid killed for their hide. The value is arrived at by multiplying the amount of products by their price. (2) The difference of the amount of livestock on hand at the beginning and by the end of the year. Referring to the total output table of current prices for farming, forestry, animal husbandry and fishery, pigs are counted at half price; large livestocks are divided into different groups for calculation according to age; other livestocks are counted at full price. (3) The output of live livestock: the value for the production of milk, eggs, fur and feathers of various livestock is the quantity of each product multiplied by their prices. (4) Output of breeding and hunting of other wild animal and fowl: the value is the production quantities multiplied by their respective price.

The total output of fishery includes (1) Marine products: the quantities of products both caught and bred multiplied by their respective price. (2) Freshwater products: the quantities of both caught and bred freshwater products multiplied by their respective price. The quantity of products remaining in the water is not included.

2. Intermediate input of agriculture refers to the value of the materials and services both bought from outside and self-produced for self consumption, that are being put into the process for running the farming production. Consumption of material products refers to the value of various material products consumed during the production process of agriculture, including the ones bought from outside and the ones produced by oneself for self consumption, that have been calculated into the total output such as seeds, eggs for incubation, saplings and cocoon kept for further raising, forage, fertilizer, fuel, pesticide, electricity used (according to the current price), the purchase of minor farming tools, use of raw materials for sideline products; various service charges paid to material production departments, such as repair fees, fees of outside hired transport for production, post and telecommunication fees for production,

and other consumed materials. Service consumption refers to the various service charges paid to non-material production departments, such as insemination fees, fees for epidemic prevention of livestock and poultry, research fees, hotel costs, transportation, financial services, insurance and advertising costs, etc.

Total output of agriculture – intermediate input of agriculture = value-added of agriculture

3. Source of data: The calculation of agriculture value-added at present is based mainly on the financial account reports of state farms and army reclamation farms, such as profit and loss tables, cost lists, etc. in the *Annual Report of Rural Economic Statistics* and random surveys of the agriculture sector. We first calculate the total output of each item in the agriculture sector separately. On this basis, we further gather the relevant information of the material consumption of individual items and household budget statistics of the agricultural sector, and after necessary adjustments, we calculate the intermediate input.

Industry. There are four statistical areas for calculating the industrial activities in China: (1) extraction of natural resources (which exclude hunting and fishing which belong to the agricultural sector); (2) the processing and re-processing of farming and sideline products; (3) the processing and re-processing of extracted material; and, (4) the repair and renovation of industrial products. These four parts are further divided into 25 subsectors for individual calculation.

1. Total output of industry refers to the total outcome of the industrial enterprises' production in the accounting period. The method for calculation is the quantity of products multiplied by unit price. However, there is a difference between industry and agriculture; the present method for industry is the "factory method" *(gong chang fa)*. This treats the industrial enterprise as a total unit, and no repetition of counting is allowed therein. Total output of industry includes the production of finished products, the value of operation of an industrial nature, self manufactured equipment, and the value of major repairs to machinery and equipment, and the differential value of products in process and half finished products between the beginning and the end of the accounting period.
2. Intermediate input of industry designates the raw and processed materials, fuel, energy, other physical products, and service charges bought from outside in the process of industrial production activities.

More precise definitions are provided as: (1) Materials bought outside: all raw materials and production materials, half-finished products, supplementary materials, repair parts, low value and easily consumable products, etc., that are bought outside the enterprise for production activities. (2) Fuel bought outside: various fuel bought outside the enterprise for production. (3) Energy bought from outside: various forms of energy bought outside the enterprise for production. (4) Service charges of material nature: service charges of a material nature, distinct from the above mentioned intermediate input products for production, such as the transport fees to other units, post and telecommunication fees, repair charges, storage fees, etc. (5) Non material service charges: the non material service charges paid to other units during the production and running of the industrial enterprise, such as financial service charges, insurance premiums, advertising charges, staff and workers education charges, etc.

Total output of industry – intermediate input of industry = value-added of industry

3. Source of data: information on the total output is directly available from the total output value of industry in the *Annual Report of Industrial Statistics;* the complete information about industrial intermediate inputs can be obtained from "Summary of Industrial Intermediate Consumption" recorded in the "Major Economic Indicators of Independent Accounting Industrial Enterprises."

Construction. The accounting object of construction includes housing, structures, and equipment installation activities. This includes in practice four areas: construction projects and organizations' equipment installation projects; the amount of private housing construction investment; workload related to building projects; such as geological prospecting, exploration design; and workload of major repair of housing and structures.

1. The total output of construction reflects the total outcome of construction production activities and refers to the money value of the total quantity of construction. This includes: (1) output of construction projects such as buildings, housing, bridges and railways, highways, port engineering, opening, extracting and strip-mining, drilling for oil and natural gas, water engineering such as reservoirs, dams, pipe-lines and maintenance of rivers, air-raid shelters, underground construction materials, and the value of supplementary equipment used for heating, ventilating, lighting, hygiene, gas, etc.;

(2) output of machinery equipment installation designates the output value of production equipment installation, such as the installation of machine tools, boilers, cranes, generators, etc., which is calculated on the value-added of installation work alone, leaving out the value of the equipment installed; (3) geological prospecting and exploration design workload that are related to construction projects: geological prospecting is divided into engineering geological prospecting and resource geological prospecting. Engineering geological prospecting designates the production activity carried out for the building of fixed assets and should be included in the total output of construction. Resource geological prospecting refers to exploration which is not serving engineering projects and thus should be excluded from the total output of construction; (4) output value of major repair of housing and structures designates major reparation of houses and structures realized by the construction industry. The original value of the houses and structures and the value of production equipment repaired are not included; (5) rural construction, private construction and equipment installation: this includes the houses built for production and residence purposes and production equipment installation by the rural or city and town dwellers. Minor irrigation works and the reclamation of wasteland are included as well.

There are two methods for the actual calculation. One is to calculate the total output directly from the construction production activities of the construction enterprises and the private construction units; the other is to calculate the cost of construction projects from the owners of the construction products. The results of theses two methods should be the same in principle.

2. The intermediate input of construction industry refers to material products and service charges consumed by the construction and installation enterprises during production activities for the given period. For instance, are included raw materials, structural components, fuel, power, stationery, transport fee, post and telecommunications fee, storage fee, finance and insurance service fees, staff and workers education fee, etc.

   Total output of construction – intermediate input of construction = value-added of construction.

3. Source of data: one source is to obtain the total output and intermediate input of the workload completed by the construction enterprises directly through the collection of financial information from all construction enterprises and self-managed construction

units. Presently, the SSB possesses the survey report forms of independent accounting construction enterprises at the county (*xian*) level and above. From which data "total output value of construction", "intermediate consumption of construction" and "value-added of construction" are available therewith. Another source is to calculate the total output of construction based on the completed investment statistics. Total output of construction includes the construction installation project investment of state-owned basic construction, the renovation of other fixed assets, and commercial housing investment; the construction installation project investment among the cities' and towns' collective-owned fixed asset investments; private housing construction investment in cities and towns and in factory and mining areas; the construction installation project investment among the rural collective-owned investments, and construction investment in water conservancy works and the private housing investment in the rural areas. After calculating the total output of construction, one then proceeds to calculate the intermediate input based on accountants' information of the state-owned and city and town collective construction enterprises, from which one estimates the intermediate input of all the construction enterprises.

Transport. Transport takes on the function of transferring products from the location of production to the location of use, a function by which the value and the use value of the goods can be realized; secondly, it bears the task of transporting passengers to fulfill the need of production and life needs. The production and use of such service is concurrent. The total income of its production activities is its total output.

1. The total output of transport designates the total outcome of the production activities of transport enterprises in the calculating period, which includes: (1) total output of highway transport, i.e., the total income or the operation income of the freight and passenger transport by the highway transport enterprises; (2) total output of water transport refers to the operation income of water transport departments, such as port offices, agencies for foreign shipping companies, ocean-going transport companies, shipping companies, and incomes from loading and unloading, storing, foreign shipping agency work, transportation, etc., by the container shipping companies; (3) total output of air transport designates the business income generated by air transport and services for air transport, which include the incomes of both national and international airlines, general aviation income, ground services income, etc; (4) total output of railway transport refers to the traffic income of railway

transport enterprises, including income from passenger and freight transport and income from loading and unloading operations; (5) total output of pipeline transport which is the income of oil pipeline transportation.

2. Intermediate input of transport industry refers to the material products bought from outside suppliers and service charges that have been consumed in the transport industry during the accounting period, such as materials bought from outside suppliers, fuel, power, repair fees, post and telecommunication fees, printing fees, water and electricity fees, finance and insurance services charges, conference fees, transfer of technology charges, advertising charges, etc.

   Total output of transportation – intermediate input of transportation = value-added of transportation.

3. Source of data: The data of the system are available in the financial accounts data of the transport system. The total output can be found from the profit and loss tables. The intermediate input data can be obtained by decomposing the business cost, management fees and financial fees of the transport enterprises. Information for total output of independent accounting enterprises of non-transport system is available from statistics departments of the non-transport system by multiplying the amount for passenger and freight turnover of various independent accounting transportation modes in the system by the relevant unit prices.

Post and Telecommunications. Post and telecommunications industry provides services by transmitting messages about production and life activities.

1. The total output of post and telecommunications industry designates the outcome of all the business incomes by post and telecommunications activities, like telegraph, telephone, post, etc., which is the total outcome of all the production activities in the industry. The actual elements include service income; saving income which is the income of service charge for handling post saving business (exclusive of the port related to income and expense of the interests on post and telecommunications savings, which belong to the financial sector activity); and the telephone income from local and long-distance services.
2. The intermediate input of post and telecommunications industry refers to power, fuel, lighting, heating bought from outside, and

communication and navigation equipment, goods for business use, low cost and easily consumable products, and the paid service charges, etc.

Total output of post and telecommunications – intermediate input of post and telecommunications = value-added of post and telecommunications

3. Source of data. all the post and telecommunications enterprises are state-owned, the only differences are in the terms of the administrative systems. Therefore, part of the data is available from the central state-owned postal and telecommunication enterprises; another part is from the local state-owned rural telephone, and the independent accounting specialized communication enterprises that do not belong to the post and telecommunications departments. These actually include city *(shi)*, and county *(xian)* post and telecommunications offices, the prefectural post and telecommunication management offices running production operation activities, post and telecommunications head offices, head line stations, and head microwave stations under provincial bureaus. Other information includes the financial account data of communications enterprises, such as independent accounting rural telephone offices, etc. The total output and the intermediate input of the post and telecommunication industry are calculated based on the above information.

Wholesale, Retail and Catering Trades, and Storage.

1. Total Output of Wholesale, Retail and Catering Trades, and Storage
   Wholesale and retail trade, or commerce, involves the transfer of commodities from the producer to the consumer by purchase, wholesale trade, retail trade and storage of commodities (consumption goods and production means). The use value and value of goods are realized through commercial activities; the value increases during the process of circulation. Therefore, the total output of wholesale and retail trades refers to the trade surcharges in principle, which is the difference of the sale value minus the purchase value of the commodities, commonly known as gross profit. The transportation fee and the loading and unloading fees of the goods have to be excluded in order to avoid double counting in the course of the circulation process. The wholesale and retail trades actually include wholesale and retail activities of the domestic trade, foreign trade, material supply and marketing, self retailing by industry, etc.

Total Output of Catering Trade. The activities of catering trade have a dual nature: processing of material products into edible and drinkable finished products; and carrying out of retail activities without passing through the circulation channels. Therefore, catering has the dual nature of both industrial and commercial activities. We believe that the catering activities are closer to the industrial nature of production, thus the total output of catering trade is the business income of the catering trade and not the gross profit.

Total Output of Storage. The activities of storage involve the various kinds of consumer products and production goods and the special storage materials. It is a necessary activity to maintain the original state and function of the goods; it is also a kind of activity which assures the use value and value of the goods. Similar to commercial activities, it increases the value of the goods. There are two types of storage conditions: one implies that the storage fee is charged for storing materials for the state or other units, the total output of which is the income of the storing fee; the second is the state provides storage free of charge, yet there are some expenditures in the process of storage. Such storing activity and inventory expenditure is its total output. The output of the storage industry is exclusive of the value of the stored goods themselves.

2. The intermediate input of wholesale and retail trades, catering trade and storage industry is the material products and the non material services consumed in the production activity. It mainly consists of damaged commodities, storing materials consumed, low value and easily consumable products, storage fees and packing fees (to be noted that the charges exclude those paid to the individuals as labor remuneration, bonus, etc.) printing, stationery, newspapers and books, water and electricity charges, transport and telecommunications charges, financial and insurance service charges, advertising charges, commodity inspection charges, consultation fees, technological research, etc. The intermediate input of catering trade has to include the purchased foods like grain, meat, poultry, eggs, dry or fresh vegetable, etc.

   Total output of wholesale and retail trade, catering trade, storage – their respective intermediate input = value-added.

3. Source of data: Information for the state-owned enterprises can be obtained from financial accounts data of the responsible departments in the commercial system. Information for collective, individual or other ownership's independent accounting enterprises is based

(with the exclusion of data on supply and marketing cooperatives) on data on total amount of retailed commodities plus data from taxation and other relevant industrial or commercial departments. Part of the information on the catering trade and storage industry is available from the accounting data of commerce and supply and marketing cooperatives. The rest of the information on catering trade can be calculated from the data on total amount of retailed commodities plus information from relevant tax departments. Data for storage industry are based on the statistics of the system under the State Reserve Bureau and the system under the Ministry of Domestic Trade.

According to the new classification of national economic categories, storage industry is to be included in the transport and post and telecommunications industry.

Accounting of Profit-making Units in Non-Material Production Sector. Profit-making units of the non-material production sector include social services, real estate management, finance, insurance, etc. For these profit-making businesses, the outlay in the course of economic activities arises from business income. Therefore, the total output of these sectors is their business income.

1. Accounting of profit-making units in non-material production sector

   Social services industry is an activity which provides direct services to people's daily life, such as small repair, bathhouse services, hair styling, hotel and guest house services, etc.

   Total output of social services = business income of social services

   Real estate industry designates the tertiary industry providing housing for residents. There are actually three parts: housing management agencies, housing development agencies, and urban and rural privately owned housing. (1) Total output of housing management agencies: total output = income from housing rent + income from land use charges + fees from appropriation (exclusive of basic construction expenditure) + other business income (charges for moving house and housing sale, etc.). Among them, fees from appropriation refer to income from other departments, mainly from government departments. (2) Housing development companies usually invest in housing construction and then sell the output. Therefore, the activities of this branch are divided into two parts: construction activities and housing management. Construction activity part shall be calculated into construction industry. Here the calculation covers only the price difference of managing house sales. The total output of housing development department is as follows: total output = income from sales -compensation for land commandeered and demolition and removal - primary engineering charge and construction and installation charges - infrastructure construction charges - public accessory facility charges. (3) The private building of urban and rural residents shall be included into the production activities of the real estate industry. The output of which is to be calculated according to the housing rent in the market so that the total output equals the imputed housing rent.

Finance industry refers to business providing financial services by taking in deposits and giving out loans.

> Total output of the finance industry = various interest incomes + administrative fees + fiduciary income + income of financing rent + income from foreign exchange + dividend on investment - various interest expenditures - depositors' interest expenditures.

Insurance industry designates the activity that collects funds from individuals or units which have bought an insurance for a given period, after which will be returned to the individual or unit at the end of the period. The funds can be used for investment from which certain amount of income and return on capital can be generated during the period.

> Total output of insurance industry = income from insurance premiums + income from claims for compensation fees + income from administration fees + interest (dividends from investment) + revolving reserve capital for liability not yet expired + income from underwriters for subcontracted profit and loss insurance - return of capital to insured and compensation expenditure - accumulation into reserve capital for liability not yet expired.[1]

2. The intermediate input of the above units designates the material goods and services used by them during the accounting period, which include mainly fuels, energy and materials bought from outside, water and electricity charges, post and telecommunications charges, printing fees, books and data fees, periodicals charges, packaging charges, low cost and easily consumable products, labor protection fees, security and fire services fees, heating fee, transportation fees, office stationeries, charges for motor vehicles, rental fees, cashier's fees, safety facilities charges, cash transfer fees, common miscellaneous fees, etc. There are also executive fees, insurance service fees,

environmental fees, staff training fees, notarization fees, advertising fees, investigation fees, legal fees, court fees, laboratory test fees, etc.

Total output of the sector = intermediate input of the sector - value-added of the sector

3. Source of data: data for real estate industry can be obtained from the financial income and expenditure report of the relevant financial final accounts. Information on the commercial enterprises and the supply and marketing cooperatives in the services sector is available from the income and expenditure data of the relevant departments, while for other sectors information needs to be estimated. Information on total output of the finance and insurance industries is available directly from their profit and loss tables. Information on intermediate input is available from the cost lists, business income and expense tables, management fee expenditure tables, and charge expenditure tables while estimation is necessary for sectors whose data are missing. Presently, there are "financial status tables" for the above businesses in the new statistic reports. Total output is available therein, while estimation is necessary for the intermediate input.

Accounting of the Non Profit-making Units in the Non-material Production Sector. Calculation for the non profit-making units in the non-material production sector usually refers to those units that do not have business income or the income fails to cover their expenditure. These units mainly include geological prospecting and water conservancy management, services to farming, forestry, animal husbandry and fishery, hygiene, sports, social welfare, education, culture, arts and broadcasting, movie, television, scientific research and comprehensive technological services, national political parties and social groups or other business accounting. The total output of which is the expenses occurring when delivering the services during the calculating period, which is the current expenditures plus the imputed depreciation of fixed assets. However, non current expenditures should be deleted, like purchase of equipment, scholarship for helping people, occasional construction project, etc.

1. Total output

Total output = income of the workers + staff and workers welfare funds + public service fees + renovation fees + business fees + other charges + price subsidies + extra budgetary expenditures + imputed depreciation of fixed assets + spending on specific funding.

It is also noted that revenues and expenditures and taxes of units that operate on a balanced budget or on their own income to pay for expenditures shall be calculated as their total output. The balanced budget units here refer to units whose activity expenditures do not come completely from state finance but obtain income from its own production activities or through other channels.

2. Intermediate input refers to the material products and services consumed in the process of various organization activities. It concretely includes office charges, water and electricity, post and telecommunications, public heating charges, fuel, repair, rent, low cost consumable products, materials, printing, books and newspapers, transportation, storage, insurance services, propaganda and advertising, etc.
3. Source of data: on one hand, information is available from the financial status table in the "administrative organization units statistical reports" by the statistics system. On the other hand, information of the relevant total output and intermediate input is available form the detailed financial final accounts of the financial departments, the relevant accountants and financial statistics in the related departments. However, these two sets of data must be cleared of double counting. Moreover, for estimation if needed one may use the coefficient of "input-output table" for reference.

Conversion into Comparable Prices. There are two ways to convert GDP in current prices into and GDP in comparable prices: deflation and extrapolation.

The deflation method is divided into the double and single deflation approaches. Double deflation refers to the application of the output price index and intermediate input price index to deflate the output and intermediate input (in current prices) of the reported period, and obtain the output and intermediate input in comparable prices; their difference is the value-added in comparable prices. The single deflation has two formats: the first uses the output price index of the reported period to deflate the value-added of that period and obtain the value-added in comparable prices. Another form is to use the intermediate input price index of the reported period to deflate the current price value-added and obtain the value-added in comparable prices of that period. Both single deflation methods carry the assumption that price changes for output and that for intermediate input have maintained the same pace basically.

The extrapolation method uses a suitable material volume index to represent the value-added in comparable prices of the base year then extrapolate for the reported period so as to obtain the value-added in comparable prices for the period. The following depicts the actual application of comparable price conversion in China:

1. The agricultural sector uses the double deflation approach. Total output uses the unified state base year constant prices; the constant price multiplied by the quantities of the products thus provides directly the total output at constant prices at the grassroots. The 1990 constant prices are used now in calculating the total output of agriculture. However, when making the national account and calculating the total output of agriculture in comparable prices, one uses the growth rate of the comparable prices compiled by the Organization of Rural Social and Economic Surveys of SSB, so that on the current prices of the base period extrapolation can be made. For the intermediate input, the currently consumed material products and service expenditures of agriculture are adjusted for price fluctuation according to the corresponding price indexes. For example, the consolidated price index for seeds;[2] the price index for animal feed;[3] the fertilizer price index for fertilizer,[4] the price index for engine oil for agricultural purpose for fuel;[5] the price index for the small and semi mechanized agricultural tools for medium and small agricultural tools. There is no price index available for service expenditures, but it can be obtained from some type survey data or from the adjusted daily life service index. Thus, the intermediate input in comparable prices can be obtained by adjusting for the price factors. Subtracting from the total output in comparable prices the intermediate input in comparable prices, the result will be the value-added in comparable prices.
2. The double or single deflation approaches are used for industry. The calculation of total output of industry in comparable prices is similar to the case for agriculture. Making use of the growth rate of the industrial total production value in comparable prices from the Department of Industrial and Transportation Statistics of SSB, one then carries out the extrapolation on the basis of the current prices in the base period. In effect, the intermediate inputs are adjusted by the suitable price index.[6] However, the double deflation approach is very difficult to carry out for industry, because there are so many types of industries and there are great variations in outputs and intermediate inputs. Therefore, a very detailed information regarding the classification of outputs and intermediate inputs is needed. As a matter of fact, there are very few countries in the world that can apply the double deflation approach to the industry sector. China does not have the conditions to do so. Therefore, the calculation of the value-added for industry in constant prices can be done by using the ratio of the total output of industry in current prices to the total output of industry in constant prices to serve as the price index of the industrial output.

Then using the single deflation approach to adjust for price variation of the value-added of industry and obtain the value-added of industry in comparable prices. At the same time, the extrapolation method is adopted as a supplementary monitor, i.e., using the value-added of industry at constant prices of the previous year multiplied by the growth rate of the current year's total output of industry at constant prices, the result is the value-added of industry at constant prices in the current year, so as to facilitate the checking and eliminating of possible error caused by the single deflation approach. The single deflation is the major approach currently in use in China.

3. Construction. The single deflation approach is mainly adopted. Use is made of the price index for construction output value in the table of the price index of output value of construction industry to adjust the total output value and value-added of construction industry at the same time. It is to be noted that the price index of construction output value is to be first converted into the fixed base index for the year 1990, so as to be coherent with the price indexes of industry and agriculture which take 1990 as the base year.
4. Transport, Post and Telecommunication Industries. Basically, the extrapolation approach is adopted. Multiplying the growth index (the turnover volume in the reported period divided by the turnover volume in the base year) of the turnover volume of passenger and freight transport in the reported period with the operation income of the various kinds of passenger and freight transport in the base year, results in the total output of transport in comparable prices. At the same time, the value-added of the various kinds of transport in the base year multiplied by the corresponding growth index of the turnover volume results in the value-added of the transport industry in comparable prices.

   Post and telecommunication industry is calculated by multiplying the business income of the base year by the growth index of total business amount in the reported period (the total business amount at 1990 constant prices of the report period / that of the base period), the result is the total output of post and telecommunications industry in comparable prices for the reported period. Multiplying the value-added of post and telecommunications industry of the base year by the growth index of the total business amount in the above reported period results in the value-added of post and telecommunications industry in comparable prices in the reported period. In the base year, the total output and value-added of transport, post and telecommunications industries in constant prices are equal to the total output and value-added in current prices, respectively.

5. Commerce and Catering Trade. Use is made of the single deflation approach. Since the total output of commerce is the difference between the purchasing and selling prices, the price of total output is influenced by these two kinds of prices. Therefore, one must first convert the net sales amount of commodities of the reported period in domestic commerce, foreign trade and grain departments into the sales volume at base year prices. Then, multiplying by the price difference rate of the base year (deleting the transportation and miscellaneous expenses of purchase from outside) one gets the total output of commerce at comparable prices. Then, using the price index of total output (total output in current prices of the report period divided by total output in comparable prices of the report period) to adjust the price factor of the value-added in current prices in the report period one obtains the value-added in comparable prices.

   As to the total output of catering trade, using base year 1990 catering trade retail price index to adjust the total output of catering trade in the report period. Similarly, using base year 1990 catering trade retail price index to adjust the value-added of catering trade in the report period one obtains the value-added in comparable prices.

6. Price Conversion of Non-material Production Sector. The total output of the non-material production sector is basically calculated according to the distribution approach. Therefore, the calculation of its total output in constant prices can borrow from the conversion measure adopted in calculating GDP at comparable prices by the distribution approach.

The Distribution Approach

The distribution approach is also known as the income approach. It calculates GDP based on the primary distribution of the value-added from the grassroots statistical units. The value-added created by the grassroots statistical units comes from the operating surplus, that is the residual after value compensation for the fixed assets, remuneration to workers and taxes to the state, the residual shared by the enterprise by participating in the creation of value-added. Therefore, according to the direction of distribution of the value-added, calculation of the value-added by the distribution approach can be divided into four parts: labor remuneration; the depreciation of fixed assets; net production tax (production tax after deducting subsidies); and operating surplus. The formula is as follows:

Value-added = labor remuneration + depreciation of fixed assets + net production tax + operating surplus. And, the sum of the value-added for all the sectors of national economy is equal to GDP.

A. Making Use of the Accounting Materials to Calculate the Value-added Directly. An effective way to calculate an accurate GDP is to use the financial accounting information of the grassroots enterprises. Using the accountant information to calculate the value-added directly is possible, provided that all the final accounts data of all enterprises in all industries in the whole country can be obtained.

The following example is the application of the distribution approach in calculating the value-added.

Labor remuneration

Wages. Regarding wages in the accounting list of the enterprises, they are obtained from the direct wages in the production cost list; wages in the manufacturing, administration and sales expenses; and the wages in the detailed list of companies' outlays in administrative expense tables.

Welfare costs. These include staff and workers welfare outlays among direct expenditures for production, such as manufacturing, sales and administrations; labor insurance and unemployment insurance among the administrative expenses; staff and workers' welfare costs in the detailed list of companies' outlays in administrative expense tables; and the public welfare fund drawn from profit after tax, which is used for staff and workers welfare.

Other Costs. They cover travel fees paid to individuals as contained in the manufacturing, administrative and sales expenses, and labor union outlay paid for individual in the management expenses.

Income in kind. Data can be obtained from the relevant items in the manufacturing expenses, administration expenses, sales expenses and profit after tax.

Depreciation of Fixed Assets. It refers to the depreciation allowances among manufacturing expenses and sales expenses, and the depreciation allowances in the detailed items of company outlay for administrative expenses.

Net Production Tax. Production tax can be obtained from the product sales tax and additional taxes in the profit and loss table, and the taxes, sewage charges, road maintenance charges found in administrative expense list and other local surcharges. Data on subsidies are obtained from subsidy income in the profit and loss table.

Operating Surplus. It designates a balance item in accounting, which is obtained by deducting labor remunerations, fixed asset depreciation and net production tax from the value-added. It corresponds to the accounting items which are equal to business profit plus subsidy income in the profit and loss table.

B. Computation of Value-added for Each Sector of the National Economy Based on Available Statistics

Agriculture.

1. Scope. Agriculture covers farming, forestry, animal husbandry and fishery. Farming comprises grain crops, cash crops, vegetables, melons, feed, green manure as well as other products, such as tea, mulberry, fruits, collection of wild plants, the hunting of wild animals and domestic industries undertaken by farm households.

   Forestry designates tree planting, the gathering of forest products and collection of trees and bamboo by cooperative economic organizations at *cun* (village) level and below and by individuals. Animal husbandry refers to the raising and grazing of all animals, except fishery and fish breeding. Fishery refers to the catching and breeding of fish and other aquatic animals and the cultivation and collection of seaweeds and other aquatic plants.

   As to the management form is concerned, agriculture includes state farms, village and towns agriculture enterprises, collective unified operation, farm household operation and partnership operation.
2. Source of data. The pertinent data are obtained from the *Annual Report of Rural Economic Statistics* on value-added of farming, forestry, animal husbandry and fishery. The four constitutive elements of value-added (labor remuneration, fixed asset depreciation, net production tax and operating surplus) are available under their respective sectors in the *Annual Report, idem.*

Industry.

1. Scope. The scope of industrial statistics covers mainly four aspects: exploitations of natural resources, processing and reprocessing of farming sideline products, processing and reprocessing of mined materials, and the production and distribution of electricity, tap water and cooking gas, and the renovation and repairs of industrial products, etc.
2. Source of data. Data can be found in the *Annual Report of Industrial Statistics* as well as *Statistical Data of Rural Enterprise* from Rural Enterprise Department of the Ministry of Agriculture.
3. Method of calculation: The data can be broadly divided into three kinds according to their origin: (1) state-owned and collective-

owned industries at town *(xiang)* level and above, (2) industries at the village *(cun)* level and below, (3) urban or rural partnership and household *(geti)* industries. State- and collective-owned industry is also distinguished as independent accounting and non-independent accounting enterprises.

Labor Remuneration

(1) State-owned and collective-owned industries at town level and above: For independent accounting units, data are obtained from the reports on industrial comprehensive statistics in which the major economic indicators of the whole independent accounting industry are recorded: payable wages of the current year, payable welfare funds of the current year, and labor and unemployment insurance expenses (Table B302). The labor union fees part of laborer remuneration can be estimated as 2 percent of total wages of the same calibre (a standard set by the Ministry of Finance) since the information is lacking in the *Annual Report of Industrial Statistics*. Then, 10 percent of the labor union fee is to be treated as a part of payments paid to each individual as part of one's labor income. The rest of the union fee is treated as intermediate consumption and is not to be included under the present topic. Likewise, travel expense is not included in the *Report idem*. Through input-output surveys, one can work out the proportion of travel expense to the total enterprise expenses. After getting its actual amount, one has to break it down by means of input-output survey data and calculate what proportion of travel expense is disbursed to each individual in each particular industry, then one further calculates for each industrial sector the portion which is given to individuals. The actual amount of public welfare fund for each individual can be derived by finding the proportion of public welfare fund drawn from profit after tax through a type survey and then make the calculation for the individual portion.

On the other hand, for the non-independent-accounting enterprises, total wages are obtained from the "Production, Sales, Inventory of Subsidiary Industry" set of tables which deal with grassroots enterprises; the relevant information is under the category, "Total Wage Bill of Workers for the Whole Year." Other laborer remuneration can be obtained through a type survey again by looking at the information in accounting topic "Other Expenses" in which enterprise outlays to workers are indicated, such as "welfare expenses," and, thus, by estimation can be found the amount paid to the individual.

(2) Industrial enterprise at village level and below: Actual wages and welfare funds are obtainable from the *Statistical Data of Rural Enterprise*; other parts of labor remuneration can be obtained through a type survey and a proportional estimation.

Urban and rural partnership and household industrial enterprises: in household enterprise, labor remuneration is in two parts: owner's income and employees' wages. The latter can be derived or estimated by referring to the number of employees and their wages provided under "Major Indicators of Urban and Rural Household Industry" in *Annual Report of Industrial Statistics.* Owner's income can be got by using the average net profit ratio of the private household industry from the Industry and Commerce departments and multiplying it by the total output of private industry (revenue from the product sales); other sources are also available. However, as owner's income is a mixed income of employer income as well as operating surplus, hence, we put them all under labor remuneration.

Fixed Asset Depreciation

For state-owned and collective-owned independent accounting enterprises at town *(xiang)* level and above depreciation statistics come from the "Depreciation Drawn in Current Year" from the *Annual Report of Industrial Statistics.* For non-independent accounting enterprises, one should look at "Other Business Expenses" in the data of finance departments for direct calculation, or collect other relevant data for estimation.

For industrial enterprises at village *(cun)* level and below, one may refer to depreciation mentioned in "Major Financial Indicators of Town and Village Enterprises" in the *Statistical Data of Rural Enterprise.*

For urban and rural private household industry, depreciation can be estimated through a type survey or from data from Industry and Commerce taxation departments.

Net Production Tax

Production Tax

For those state-owned and collective-owned independent accounting industrial enterprises at town level and above, the production tax can be obtained under the sections called "Product Sales Tax and Surcharge" and "Tax Payment" under administrative expenses in the *Annual Report of Industrial Statistics*. Surcharges by local finance departments, taxes and road maintenance fees are obtainable from financial expense items. For non-independent accounting enterprises, one obtains the information from the concrete financial data of the enterprises, and, from these, one can calculate or make an estimation.

For enterprises at the village level and below, one has to refer to "Major Financial Indicators of Town and Village Enterprises" in *Statistical Data of Rural Enterprise* to find sale tax, salary and production tax and various surcharges in order to make the calculation according to the sources of information or to make the evaluation. Production tax of enterprises at village level or below is also available under "Tax Payment" in the "Major Indicators of Village-managed Industrial Enterprises" in the *Annual Report of Industrial Statistics*. However, income tax has to be subtracted first.

On the other hand, production tax levied on urban or rural jointly owned and household industries is available under item "Tax Payment" in "Major Indicators of Urban or Rural Cooperative Industries, Urban or Rural Household Industries" from the Department of Industrial and Transportation Statistics of SSB. However, income tax has to be subtracted first.

Subsidy Income

When an enterprise experiences a financial loss and obtains a financial subsidy from the state, the information on this subsidy income can be found in the "Profit and Loss Table" of the enterprise accountant's final accounts.

Operating Surplus

This refers to the portion of value-added distributed to the industrial enterprises as their income share. In computing this item, for state-owned and collective owned at town level and above industrial enterprises one should refer to "Business Profit" of the same calibre enterprises indicated in the major economic indicators of independent accounting industrial enterprises. Some adjustment, however, has to be made. For example, those parts that have been entered as laborer remuneration as well as those profits listed under "Profit from Other Businesses" should be deducted. The latter has its corresponding counterpart in other industries.

In case there is a loss and the state has given a subsidy, this "income" is included in business profit. The "Subsidy Income" has to be deducted from the production tax at the same time that it is added to the operating surplus. "Subsidy Income" can be found in the profit and loss table of an enterprise.

Data for industries at village level and below are available from the item "Total Profit" in the "Major Indicators of Village-owned Industrial Enterprises" section in the *Annual Report of Industrial Statistics*. Yet the item has to be clear of labor remuneration. Since operating surplus has been calculated in labor remuneration for urban or rural partnership and household industry, there is no need to make a separate calculation here.

The operating surplus can also be calculated by deducting labor remuneration, fixed asset depreciation and net production tax from value-added. And, value-added of independent accounting industrial enterprises at town level and above is available in "Value-added of Industry" in "Table B305" of report forms system of industrial comprehensive statistics.

Construction.

1. Scope. This covers civil engineering construction, pipeline and equipment installation, and geological prospecting and prospecting design industries connected with engineering projects.
2. Source of data. The information comes from *Annual Report of Construction Statistics* by the Department of Statistics on Investment in Fixed Assets of SSB and *Annual Report of Investment in Fixed Assets Investment Statistics* by the same department and *Statistical Data of Rural Enterprise.*
3. Method of calculation. The calculation of value-added in respect to operation type and data source of construction industry can be classified as (1) state-owned and collective-owned construction enterprises at county level and above, (2) Town and village and village-owned construction enterprises and (3) urban and rural private construction activities.

Labor Remuneration

Data for state-owned and collective-owned at county level and above independent accounting construction enterprises are obtained from the financial situation for independent accounting construction enterprises, i.e., Table C303. The items are wages and welfare funds payable for current year (in the major business section) and labor and unemployment insurance premiums under administrative expense. Labor unions' fees included in laborer remuneration take a share of 2 percent of total of wages of the same category. And 10 percent of labor unions' fee is treated as individual income. For travel expenses which are not available in the annual report can be estimated through the proportion via input-output survey. The ratio of travel expenses in total operation expenses of an enterprise is first ascertained; then, the estimate of total travel expenses is determined; this amount then is further broken down by means of input-output survey into what proportion is paid to individuals. The proportion allows to estimate the amount of total travel expenses paid to the individuals in the construction industry. Public welfare funds drawn from profit after tax are to be calculated through a type survey, from which is determined the proportion applied to welfare needed to obtain the final estimation.

For the non-independent accounting sector, the employees' remuneration is obtained from the "Production Operation Situation of Subsidiary Construction Industry" (Table 109). The welfare funds and other parts of laborer remuneration can be calculated through a type survey, making use of the accounting item "Other Expenses" of the enterprises for estimation of the ratio needed to arrive at the final estimation.

Data for wages and welfare funds of town-and-village and village-owned construction enterprises are derived from the corresponding items in the "Major Financial Indicators of Nationwide Rural Enterprises" in the *Statistical Data of Rural Enterprise.* For other parts of labor remuneration can be obtained through a type survey, whereby the ratio is determined which allows for an estimation.

For the construction activities of urban and rural household and private enterprises, there are two kinds of activities. One is the formation of a construction team by a household boss; the other takes place when someone builds one's own housing. For the first type, the workers wages can be estimated from Industry and Commerce departments and tax office data; the employer's income and profit can be calculated from the average profit rate found in Industry and Commerce departments' data. Self-employed urban-rural residents' housing construction, on the other hand, only involves labor remuneration for those who participate in the construction work and their pay can be easily obtained by type survey data.

Fixed Asset Depreciation

For state-owned and collective-owned at county level and above construction enterprises, data for current year's extracted depreciation are indicated in the financial situation statistics of independent-accounting construction enterprises by the Department of Statistics on Investment in Fixed Assets of SSB. Town-and-village and village-owned construction enterprises have the report on depreciation allowance posted in the "Major Financial Indicators of Nationwide Village Enterprises" in the *Statistical Data of Rural Enterprise.* Urban-rural household and residents' construction activities can be estimated from type survey data.

Production Tax

Information on state-owned and collective-owned enterprises at county level and above are drawn from "Project Settling Accounts' Tax and Surcharge" in "Financial Situation of Independent Accounting Construction Enterprises" in *Annual Report of Construction Statistics* prepared by the Investment Department (office) of SSB and "Tax Payment" in administrative expenses. Town and village-owned construction enterprises' tax payment can be found in "Major Financial Indicators of Nationwide Town-and-village Enterprises" in *Statistical Data of Rural Enterprise.* Details about taxation for urban and rural household enterprises' and residents' construction activities can be estimated through type surveys; regarding household construction enterprises, one can also consult data from Industry and Commerce tax offices before making the estimation. It is necessary to bear in mind that production tax has to be distinguished from income tax.

Operating Surplus

Operating surplus for state-owned and collective-owned at county level and above is derived from "Business Profit" in the "Financial Situation of Independent Accounting Construction Enterprises" in *Annual Report of Construction Statistics.* However, one must first subtract the part already counted in labor remuneration and the other industries' profit in "Other Business Profit." For town-and-village and village-owned construction enterprises, the source is "Major Financial Indicators of Nationwide Village Enterprises" in the relevant *Statistical Data of Rural Enterprise* but, again, the portion already included under labor remuneration has to be subtracted. Operating surplus of household construction activities can be treated as mixed income and placed under labor remuneration.

Operational surplus can also be obtained by subtracting from value added the parts under labor remuneration, depreciation of fixed assets and net production tax. If the construction production is calculated from the angle of investment, one can obtain the value added by first using the production method, then, using the latter as a gross control value, draw out the value added from its various components.

Transportation, Storage, Post and Telecommunications.

1. Scope. They refer to railway transport, highway transport, waterway transport, air transport, pipeline transport, storage and post and telecommunications.
2. Source of data. The following data are adopted for the purpose: (1) "Final Account Report of Transport Business" from the Ministry of Railways, (2) annual financial final accounts of the Ministry (Bureaus) of Domestic Trade, (3) *Annual Report of Communications, Transportation, and Post and Telecommunications Statistics* from the Department of Industrial and Transportation Statistics of SSB, (4) "Financial Final Accounts of Civil Aviation Enterprises" by Civil Aviation Bureau, (5) "Current Year's Financial Final Accounts" by the Ministry (Bureaus) of Communications, (6) "Financial Final Accounts of Post and Telecommunications" by the Ministry (Bureaus) of Post and Telecommunications, (7) *Annual Report of Labor Wage Statistics* by the Department of Population and Labor Statistics of SSB.
3. Method of Calculation. It is based upon a dichotomy of transport on one side, and storage and post and telecommunications on the other. There is a further subdivision in the transport industry into five subdivisions, namely railway, highway, waterway, air and pipeline transport.

   The value-added of railway transport, air transport, and post and telecommunications can be directly calculated according to the current year's financial final account report forms gathered from the corresponding departments; use is made of the accounting categories. The method is the same as that mentioned previously, regarding the calculation of value added from the direct use of accountants' data.

Highway and waterway transports have four subcategories: (1) highway, waterway, port loading and unloading independent accounting enterprises at county level and above, (2) town-and-village highway and waterway transportation enterprises, (3) non-independent accounting highway, waterway transportation activities and (4) private household highway and waterway transportation undertakings.

(1) For the independent accounting units at county level and above, the labor remuneration can be obtained from payable wages and welfare funds for current year plus labor and unemployment insurance premiums among administrative expenses from the enterprises' financial situation table in the *Annual Report of Communications, Transportation, and Post and Telecommunications Statistics*. Then, 2 percent of the total wages is treated as the outlay for labor unions of which 10 percent will be counted as labor remuneration. Travelling expense can be estimated with reference to the ratio derived from input-output survey and by using the method indicated for industry; public welfare fund can be derived from after-tax profit according to proportion estimation following some type survey.

Fixed asset depreciation can be obtained from "Extracted Fixed Assets Depreciation for Current Year" in enterprise financial situation table of the *Annual Report, idem*.

Production tax is obtained from the "Business Tax and Surcharge" in enterprise financial situation table and "Tax Payment" under administrative expenses of the *Annual Report*.

Operating surplus is derived from "Business Profit" for transport enterprises in the *Annual Report*; as before, first must be subtracted what has been accounted as labor remuneration and profit gained from other independent accounting industries. The latter should be accounted for under each particular industry.

(2) For town-and-village highway and waterway transportation enterprises, data largely come from the *Statistical Data of Rural Enterprise* available at the Rural Enterprise Department. There are several equivalent indicators: for example, wage and welfare funds are converted into labor remuneration, depreciation into fixed asset depreciation, sales tax payment into net production tax and total profit into operating surplus.

(3) For non-independent accounting and individual household highway and waterway transportation: value added for household enterprises is obtained first by multiplying freight turnover volume and passenger turnover volume released by the Department

of Industrial and Transportation Statistics (Division) of SSB by their unit prices (here, passenger and freight transport includes only the portion which is contracted officially). The sum becomes operation revenue, that is total output. Then based on the information collected and the situation of the industry and commerce taxes, one sets the ratio and the composition of the value-added; from which we can then deduce the value-added figure.

Moreover, regarding the non-independent accounting sector, of the set of tables for each speciality at the grassroots,[7] "Business Income" in the table "Operation Situation of Subsidiary Transportation Industry" can be treated as the total output, a gross control figure. And we can, by the same token, take as equivalent "Employees' Remuneration" to "Labor Remuneration." Other parts of value-added have to estimate via the collection of other sources.

Pipeline transportation refers to the transportation mode through the laying of pipeline to carry fuels or natural gas; it is still limited to a few provinces. The calculation method is to collect financial final accounts information about pipeline transportation enterprises from the Petroleum (Natural Gas) Pipeline Transportation Office; from their financial indicators and the elements which imply factors of value-added one can calculate the value-added. Moreover, the wage part in labor remuneration is available as total wages of "Pipeline Transportation Industry" in the *Annual Report of Labor Wage Statistics*.

Storage industry can be divided into profit-making and non-profit-making parts. The profit-making part is included in statistics on transportation enterprise; there is no need to duplicate. The second part is to be found in data from the Ministry of Domestic Trade system; by means of the accounting data one can obtain the value-added already signified. The non-profit-making portion, i.e., enterprises in the state materials reserve system, is computed in the same way as other service industry listed below.

Wholesale, Retail and Catering Trades.

1. Scope. Wholesale and retail trades and catering trade include domestic commerce and foreign trade, materials supply and marketing, and catering trade.
2. Source of data. Yearly accounting reports of commerce, grain trade and supply and marketing cooperatives at the Ministry of Domestic Trade; yearly accounting reports of the foreign trade-enterprises

at the Ministry of Foreign Economic Relations and Trade, yearly accounting reports of material supply enterprise sector; as well as the annual reports of state-owned commercial sectors, and finally *Annual Report of Comprehensive Statistics on Commodity Flow and Catering Trade* at the Department of Trade and External Economic Relation Statistics of SSB.

3. Method of calculation. Depending on the source of information available, our calculation will be divided into three categories: independent accounting commodity exchange enterprises, private commerce and non-independent accounting commerce activities. Some explanation is made as follows:

(1) Independent accounting commodity exchange enterprises. They include domestic commerce (commerce, grain, supply and marketing cooperatives, materials supply and marketing, medicine, sea products, cigarettes, Xinhua Book Shops, agricultural machinery, vehicle sales, and petrochemicals, etc. in the system of the Ministry of Domestic Trade), foreign trade, and catering trade. If the relevant information can be collected from the yearly financial final accounts of these departments under which the above businesses are operating, then the calculation method of value-added discussed above can be directly utilized here. In case there is problem in collecting final accounting information, we can seek the data on the financial situation about commodity exchange and catering trade enterprises at the Department of Trade and External Economic Relation Statistics of SSB. The calculation procedure is as follows:

Labor remuneration is derived from the financial situation tables showing payable wages and welfare funds for the current year as well as labor and unemployment insurance premiums. Labor union payment is set at 2 percent of total wages, and 10 percent of the payment is assumed to be part of labor remuneration. Travelling expense can be determined from input and output survey data, first of all, by obtaining the total travel expense and, then, ascertaining the portion which goes to individuals' receivable income.

Public welfare funds extracted from after-tax profit can be estimated through a type survey to figure out the appropriate ratio for calculation. Fixed assets depreciation is derived from "Extracted Depreciation for Current Year" in the enterprises' financial situation table.

Net production tax: Production tax is taken from the "Commodity Sales Tax And Surcharge" in the enterprises' financial situation table and "Tax Payment" in the administrative expenses. However, one must make sure import-export tariff on foreign trade industry is replaced by the customs tariff since customs tariff can reflect thoroughly the tariff on all import-export activities for the whole economy. First of all, it covers tariff on all foreign trade activities including those conducted by commerce-trade as well as industry trade enterprises. Secondly, it covers the tariff on imported and exported products paid by the owners involved in import and export trading undertaken by some foreign trade department acting as agent. Lastly, it includes tariff on imported raw materials for processing and spare parts imported by Sino-foreign joint-ventures or foreign enterprises. Tariffs on foreign trade enterprises, in contrast, just reflect the part of tariffs on commerce activity only; it ultimately leaves out the tariff levied on the other parts of business activities which the customs tariffs include.

Subsidies are basically an allowance of a policy nature to commerce and trade enterprises by state finance by turning measures into some kind of negative production tax. Instances are "Receivable Subsidy For Current Year" in "Food Price Rise List" when there is a price rise for extra procurement of food and "Tax Refund From Export" in the "Profit And Loss Table" of foreign trade enterprises. Other types of subsidies given out by the government to other state-owned commerce can be collected from financial information of commerce departments and subsidy data of finance departments.

Operating surplus is derived from "Business Profit" of enterprises' financial situation table in the *Annual Report of Comprehensive Statistics on Commodity Flow and Catering Trade*. However, the part of profit that has been realized as labor remuneration and other independent accounting industries' profit derived from "Other Business Profit" has to be excluded.

(2) Private household commerce is made up of country fair trade, catering trade and commerce. In spite of the difficulty in gathering the pertinent information for this part, we can still count on records of private commerce's commodity turnover at Department of Trade and External Economic Relation Statistics of SSB to work out the total output for private commerce. Moreover, it is important to take the total output as a gross control figure and to find out through type survey the proportion of value-added in total output and the proportion of the four constitutive elements of value-added and from these proportions to extrapolate to the whole category. Of the four elements

(because private commerce is special), the main factors of value added are labor remuneration, depreciation and production tax; operating surplus is counted as mixed income already included in laborer remuneration. The size of fixed assets depreciation depends on the scale of business operation; in the course of calculation, one has to refer to industrial and commercial taxation data.

For independent accounting private business at county level and below, there is a lack of records revealing the enterprises' situation statistics, hence we have to collect the financial final account data for calculation, or to make use of commodity turnover statistics and refer to the calculation method of private commerce for estimation.

(3) In the absence of detailed financial information about non-independent accounting commercial enterprises, we can only do some estimation. Fortunately, there are two sources of data of which we can make use. First, it is the gross retail sale in Table 110 in the set of tables for each grassroots speciality i.e., "Commodity Sales and Inventory of Subsidiary Commerce." The second is income from "Major Situation of Other Subsidiary Activities" in Table 111. Thus, we can estimate the total output of non-independent accounting commerce activities. We then refer to the ratio of value-added to total output of the collective-owned commerce as well as the ratios of the constitutive elements to value-added to estimate the value-added of the former. However, if the financial data of non-independent accounting units are obtainable, some estimation can be made.

Finance and Insurance Industry.

1. Scope. Finance industry engages in financial and credit services. Banks, non-banking financial organizations, credit cooperatives and insurance organizations are all included.
2. Source of data. The annual financial final accounts of the People's Bank of China and other specialized banks; the annual financial final accounts of the subsidiary trust and investment corporations of the specialized banks; the annual financial final accounts of the Agricultural Bank of China's Rural Credit Cooperatives; the annual financial final accounts of the Urban Credit Cooperatives provided by the People's Bank of China; the annual financial final accounts of the foreign and joint venture financial organizations provided by the State Foreign Exchange Administration Bureau; the annual financial final accounts of the Ministry (Bureaus) of Post and Telecommunications; the annual financial final accounts of the

Chinese People's Insurance Cooperation; and available data from other financial organizations.

3. Method of calculation. The calculation is divided according to the various categories of banks, credit cooperatives, trust and investment cooperations, the insurance companies and the others.

The finance and insurance portion is basically calculated in accordance with the accounting data. For the method of calculation, one may refer above to "making use of accounting data to calculate value-added directly". However, the operating surplus should be adjusted. To put it in a formula:

operating surplus = business profit + investment income -(non-business income - non-business expenditure)

The interest paid to customers is also calculated in the value added of the financial enterprises; the source is current savings interests, the fixed savings interests, value-assured fixed savings interests, and current and fixed exchangeable savings interests obtained from the banks' profit and loss tables. These items can be found in operating surplus under other items.

Real Estate.

1. Scope. This includes (1) housing administration departments, (2) real estate development and management units, (3) urban and rural self-owned housing.
2. Source of data. The *Annual Report of Labor Wage Statistics* of the Department of Social, Science and Technology Statistics, and data on urban and rural self-owned housing and the *Annual Report of Commodity Flats Management Situation* by the Ministry of Construction.

(1) Housing Administration Departments

The scope of activities includes only flat maintenance and repair, which basically do not yield profit. Therefore, the calculation of their value-added is restricted to labor remuneration and depreciation.

Labor remuneration. In accordance with the total wages of the personnel stated in "Real Estate Management" of the *Annual Report of Labor Wage Statistics.* Welfare funding is calculated as 14 percent of the total wages; labor union fees take up 2 percent of the total wages, of which 10 percent is redistributed into labor remuneration. Other components of labor remuneration can be estimated according to the sources of data.

Fixed assets depreciation. To calculate the depreciation, a

depreciation rate is imputed according to the original value of fixed assets of these departments.

(2) Real Estate Development and Management Units

The value-added of real estate development enterprises is calculated in accordance with the data of the financial situation of service industry by the Department of Social, Science and Technology Statistics of SSB. The calculation of the components of value-added adopts a calculation method similar to that of the industry and construction sectors. In case the data of the financial situation of service industry are lacking, the estimation may be done by referring to the *Annual Report of Commodity Flats Management Situation.*

(3) Urban and Rural Self-owned Housing

Its value-added is to subtract intermediate input from the imputed rent. To ascertain the imputed rent of a flat, all urban and rural self-owned flats as well as current market housing rent is used. The imputed rent of all urban and rural self-owned flats is calculated by multiplying the unit imputed flat rent by the area of flats owned by all urban and rural inhabitants. The imputed rent can also be estimated by taking the imputed depreciation as the basis, putting into consideration also the management and repair expenses of flat maintenance, plus a certain percentage to be added. Intermediate input is the cost of buying and operating materials needed in the course of maintaining one's housing.

Other services industry.

1. Scope. This area comprises the services to farming, forestry, animal husbandry and fishery; geological prospecting and water conservancy administration; social services; hygiene, sports and social welfare services; education; culture and art, television and broadcasting; scientific research and comprehensive technology service; state organs, party and government organizations, social organizations; and others.
2. Source of data. The *Annual Report of the Labor Wage Statistics* of the Department of Social, Science and Technology Statistics, and the detailed administrative operating expenses of the Ministry (Departments) of Finance are the major sources.
3. Method of calculation. The value-added of other services is formed of labor remuneration and imputed depreciation. For organizations that adopt a business management style, such as city public utilities and medical and health organizations, information can be obtained through the financial department or the specific administration

department. Based on the sources of information and with reference to the method of value-added calculation of other industries, the value-added can be calculated directly. For non business type organizations, the calculation method is demonstrated below.

Labor remuneration. The wages can be obtained from the total wages of the same calibre in the *Annual Report of Labor Wage Statistics*. The welfare funds are estimated according to the proportion of labor insurance and welfare to total wages of the same calibre, 14 percent.

Imputed depreciation. Based on the total investment accumulated as fixed assets by these departments or on the original value of the fixed assets of these departments obtained from the census of the tertiary industry, a choice is made of the use period of the fixed assets, then is chosen a depreciation rate, from which one can deduce the imputed depreciation.

All other service industries belong to the tertiary sector. The present situation is that there are some tertiary industries which exist as subsidiaries of state-owned and collective-owned enterprises, and some which exist as urban or rural household-owned and partnership enterprises. For the latter, we are unable to collect information in this area at the present moment. Even information on labor wages is incomplete; we have to do some partial estimation as follows:

(1) Social service organizations under state-owned and collective-owned enterprises.

For the state-owned part, we can refer to the proportion of "Social Service Organization Personnel" under "Services Personnel" in the report on wages for industry and construction staff and workers to get the ratio of service personnel to the total number of workers. After taking the other relevant information, we can estimate the number of people serving in social services and the annual per capita gross wages; then, we can calculate the gross labor wages of this sector. Because the service industries in this sector are not independent accounting units — they are welfare in nature — profit and tax are usually non-existent or minimal; thus, we can use the relevant information to make an estimation or simply note the information without making the calculation. For the collective part, from the proportion of total number of "Social Service Organizations Personnel" to the total number of staff and workers in the state-owned units one then adjusts with the relevant information and proceeds with the estimate. The annual per capita gross wage can be determined from the relevant information of the same collective industry, from which we can deduce the value-added. The gross wages constitute the main content of labor remuneration; if the circumstances indicate that these service organization employees have some additional income, such as welfare or others, one can make some estimation.

(2) Service industries among urban and rural individual households

The estimation of this part is mainly estimated from the size of their labor force. The figure is taken from the year-end labor force in "Number of Self-employed Labor in Cities and Towns" in the *Annual Report of the Labor Wage Statistics,* not counting the number of people serving in agriculture, industry, construction, transport, post and telecommunications and commerce and catering trade. Based on the relevant information from industry and commerce and from taxation, we determine the per capita "Mixed Income" (including labor remuneration and operating surplus); then based on the production tax collected by the tax bureaus for the urban and rural individual household tax data, we obtain the production tax; and with the information about the circumstances of the individual enterprises held by the industry and commerce administration departments, we can estimate depreciation and finally get the value-added.

(3) Peasants concurrently running tertiary industry

This refers to the labor force in rural areas who engages in tertiary industry activities without industrial and commercial registration. To calculate the value-added in this part, we only need to calculate the "Mixed Income." Estimation is made of the proportion of rural labor force engaging in the tripartite industries — apart from the other labor engaged in industry and services already — from "The Number of Social Labor Force of Various Industries Classified by Economic Types" by the Department of Social, Science and Technology Statistics of SSB. Based on the ratios, we categorize the rural labor force according to the tripartite industries; then, we further calculate the number of peasants engaging in tertiary industry as the number of peasants running tertiary industry concurrently. After some type survey, we determine the per capita "Mixed Income" of personnel in this sector. From this, we can get the value-added of peasants concurrently engaging in tertiary industry.

Other service industry refers to the military and the armed police forces. The calculation of the value-added refers to the wages (or subsidy) and the value of food, clothing and sundries of those who engage in this type of industry, together with the imputed depreciation of buildings, facilities and motor vehicles in the forces which can be ascribed as public use. Due to the difficulty in getting the information, the value-added has to be estimated. The number of personnel can be estimated by referring to the total amount of food grain supplied by the grain departments and the per capita consumption. The per capita wages (subsidy) and the value of meals, clothing and sundries can be obtained by investigation. The imputed depreciation of the buildings, facilities and motor vehicles aforementioned has to be estimated from surveys. The value-added is obtained by multiplying the per capita income (including wages and the value of pay in kind) by the number of personnel in question plus the imputed depreciation.

Conversion into Comparable Prices. In what follows, the conversion of GDP according to the net domestic product (NDP) and the depreciation of fixed assets in comparable prices will be discussed.

1. NDP in comparable prices. The NDP is formed by the value-added of various sectors calculated by the production approach and distribution approach minus the depreciation of fixed assets. As far as the conversion of NDP in comparable prices is concerned, for the material production sector, we can use the coefficient of total output value in current prices and their indices in comparable prices to proceed with the calculation. For the non-material production and financial sectors, we adopt the retail price index for the whole society with reference to the index of changes in deposit and loan interest rates of the financial sector. We employ the residents' living expense price index for the real estate industry. For resident service industry and public utilities, we use resident service price index. For the calculation of the comparable prices for comprehensive technology and production service industry, health, sports, social welfare services, education, arts, television and broadcasting industry and scientific research undertakings, we can refer to the conversion procedure of the comparable prices of the public consumption in GDP by the expenditure approach. We can use the residents' living expenses price index for labor remuneration conversion into comparable prices. For consumed fuel, water and electricity, articles for office, furniture and containers, we can refer to the consumer goods' retail price index. For paid services like passenger transport, hotel and training of cadres, etc., we employ the relevant service price indexes. Also, we can refer to the growth rate of average

wages in these industries for crosschecking. For the conversion regarding state government and party organizations, social organizations and other activities, we can refer to the increase in the size of membership.

2. The depreciation of fixed assets in comparable prices.

   Because the depreciation of fixed assets is based on the original value of fixed assets and a certain depreciation rate, and the original value of fixed assets is based on the purchase price of fixed assets at different times, if we directly employ the current year fixed asset price index to deflate the depreciation, it is unavoidable that the depreciation value of the fixed assets in comparable prices will be improperly decreased. To make it closer to the reality, we use the following method: the depreciation of fixed assets in current prices in 1990 is treated as the depreciation in comparable prices based on the 1990 prices. After 1990, we use the fixed assets investment price index (1990=100) to deflate the increased part in current prices in the depreciation of fixed assets drawn each year. Thus, we can obtain the increased part in 1990 comparable prices, plus the last year's part calculated in 1990 comparable prices. This gives the depreciation of fixed assets in 1990 comparable prices in the relevant year.

The Expenditure Approach

The expenditure approach is a means to reflect the ultimate destination of goods and services produced during the accounting period from the standpoint of final use. Theoretically, goods and services produced during the accounting period should be equal to the use of the goods and services in final consumption, investment and net export. According to the expenditure approach, the formula for GDP should be:

GDP = Gross consumption + Gross investment + Net export

The concrete method and sources of data for the calculation of GDP by the expenditure approach are demonstrated in the prescribed order. Gross consumption is formed of personal consumption and public consumption. And net export consists of exportables minus importables.

Household Consumption. There are two ways to calculate personal consumption. One is the balance of revenue and expenditure, the other is the direct calculation method.

Balance of Revenue and Expenditure. It first calculates the total income of residents, then subtracts the parts that do not belong to consumption, so as to get the consumption volume of residents.

Residents' total income includes:

1. The wages and labor remuneration that all staff and workers and other employees get from state-owned economic units.
2. The wages and labor remuneration that all staff and workers and other employees get from cities' and towns' collective-owned economic units.
3. The wages and labor remuneration that all staff and workers and other employees get from various other economic units in cities and towns. Various other economic units include partnerships, economic units under the share system, foreign invested economic units, investment from Hong Kong, Macau and Taiwan, and other economic units besides those mentioned above.
4. Income of people in other occupations. This part mainly refers to the wages, subsidies of people working in military organizations, military forces, enterprises, schools and hospitals, etc. under the system of the Military Commission, and the free meals, clothing and daily necessities provided to the personnel, excluding the wages of non-military staff and workers in the enterprises attached to the General Logistics Department which are counted in the staff and workers statistics of state-owned economic units.
5. Staff and workers' personal income besides wages. This includes insurance and welfare fee, labor protection fee, remuneration for labor not included in the total wages, pay in kind, property income (e.g., interest on savings, treasury bonds, interest and pay back of bonds, etc.), transfer income (e.g., education stipend from public finance, various subsidies, income from overseas, and remittance, etc.) and other income (including service income).
6. The income that peasants get from collective unified operations.
7. The income that peasants get from partnerships.
8. The income peasants get when engaging in business operated by the family in agriculture, industry, handicraft, etc.
9. The income of peasants obtained from public finance.
10. The cash income that peasants get from the sale of farming and sideline products.
11. Other income of peasants (including service income).
12. Residents' income from private-operated economic units (including the income of cities' and towns' self-employed *(geti)* laborers).

The relevant data are taken from the *Annual Report of Comprehensive Statistics on Labor* of SSB and rural housing surveys.

The non-consumption part includes:

1. Obligatory payments of residents (party fee, league fee,[8] taxes, etc.).
2. Purchase of treasury bonds and public bonds, etc.
3. Various fines and compensation fees, etc.
4. The investment in the purchase and construction of houses by urban and rural residents (excluding depreciation).
5. Investments of a business nature by peasants and cities' and towns' self-employed households.
6. The increase in reserve storage of food grain by peasants.
7. The increase in savings of residents (it will be negative if there is a decrease).
8. The increase in cash in hand (it will be negative if there is a decrease).
9. Other monetary expenses.

We should note that the investment in the purchase and construction of houses by urban and rural residents and the productive investment of peasants and cities' and towns' self-employed laborers belong to investment expenses outside household consumption. Therefore, they are categorized as non-consumption and are to be deducted.

The relevant information is taken from survey data on housing, and the *Annual Report of Comprehensive Statistics on Commodity Flow and Catering Trade.*

Direct calculation Method. This is calculated directly according to residents' consumption of material products and services. The consumption of material products and services can be divided into the following categories: (1) commodity consumption; (2) self-provided consumption; (3) cultural life service consumption; (4) housing, water, electricity and gas consumption; (5) public health services; (6) pay in kind and the collective welfare facilities enjoyed by residents, etc.

To put it in a formula:

Household consumption = commodity consumption + self-produced consumption + cultural life service consumption + housing, water, electricity and gas consumption + public health services + pay in kind + collective welfare facilities for staff and workers paid by the enterprises from the public welfare funds.

Commodity consumption. This refers to commodities for personal consumption bought from the domestic and foreign markets by permanent residents in China in the accounting period. These include: (1) food; (2) beverage, tobacco and alcohol; (3) clothing, shoes and hats; (4) textile products; (5) Chinese and Western medicine; (6) cosmetics; (7) books and magazines; (8) cultural and sports products; (9) daily necessities; (10) domestic electrical appliances; (11) ornaments; (12) coal, etc.

When we use the retail value of residents' consumption of commodities to calculate commodity consumption, we need to deduct from it the purchase of housing by residents and the retail value of construction materials and also the retail value of other materials not belonging to consumption goods.

Materials not belonging to consumption goods refer to ferrous metal, nonferrous metals, industrial chemicals, lumber, electrical and mechanical equipment, fuel, etc. They belong to productive means, not consumption goods. Housing and construction materials belong to investment expenditure, thus have to be excluded.

Note the deduction of other materials not belonging to consumption goods may include construction materials, industrial chemicals and lumber, etc., used by residents for maintenance and repair of their houses. These should be treated as the household consumption, not investment or other productive expenditure. Therefore, we should be careful and keep this part when deducting non consumption expenses.

The data are taken from the *Annual Report of Comprehensive Statistics on Commodity Flow and Catering Trade*; the proportion of the construction materials used for maintenance and repair of houses is in the *China's Nationwide (provinces, municipalities) Input-Output Table, 1992*; or it can be obtained from housing survey data.

Self-supplied consumption. This mainly refers to the farming and sideline products produced by residents themselves and consumed by them directly. Usually we only consider the self-supplied consumption of peasants. The vegetables grown by city and town residents and the domestic fowl raised in their backyards are small in amount, and it is difficult to obtain information in this area. Therefore, we can simply ignore them.

To calculate the self-supplied consumption of peasants, we usually use the aggregate balance method. That is, from the total output value of agriculture (i.e., the total output value of farming, forestry, animal husbandry and fishery) as the gross control figure, we then deduct the non-consumable output value from the total output value of agriculture (e.g., the growth of forest and the reproduction and increase in the weight of livestock, etc.). Then we deduct the farming, forestry, animal husbandry and fishery output value of the state farms. Based on the flow of farming and sideline products, we further deduct the commodity part, i.e., the part sold to the state, production sectors and non-agricultural residents. We should also deduct the compensation for the farming and sideline products consumed in the course of production (seeds and forage, etc.); and then deduct the farming and sideline products used to increase storage (grain reserves, etc.). Thus, we obtain the self-supplied consumption of peasants.

We can also use relevant information from rural household surveys about farming and sideline products of self supplied nature relating to cereal crops, other cash crops, livestock-breeding and fishery products for the calculation. At the same time, we may refer to the per capita self-supplied consumption of peasant and the number of agricultural population for the calculation.

Cultural life service consumption. This refers to the various cultural service expenses of residents, which is also the consumption of these services by citizens. For example, urban transportation expenses, travel expenses, post and telecommunications expenses, school fees, entertainment costs, medical and health expenses (directly paid by residents), child care expenses, repair service charges and various cultural service charges. Data are taken from relevant statistical reports and household survey data, etc., by the Department of Trade and External Economic Relation Statistics of SSB.

Consumption of housing, water, electricity and gas designates the expenses on housing rent, water, electricity, and gas and the imputed rent for privately owned housing. Data are taken from relevant statistic reports and housing survey data by the Department aforementioned. For the imputed rent of private urban and town housing, one can refer to "The Amount of Actual Private Housing at the End of the Year" and the construction price of housing and the length of service in the *Annual Report of Urban Construction Statistics* for estimation. The imputed rent for peasant housing can be deduced by reference to the data on surface area, construction price and length of service in rural household surveys.

Public health services refer to the cost of medical treatment and hygiene protection paid by various governments, enterprises and institutions for their employees. The information comes from the "Medical Treatment and Hygiene Fees" in the "Table of the Cost Composition of Insurance and Welfare of the Whole Staff and Workers" in the *Annual Report of Labor Wage Statistics.*

Pay in kind designates the income of residents in material form obtained either freely or at a price lower than the market value. This free material reward is counted as part of household consumption according to its market price. Pay in kind at prices lower than market value is counted into household consumption by calculating the difference between the market price and the paid price of the goods. This part is deduced or estimated on the basis of either type survey information or other relevant data.

Moreover, household consumption should include also the cost of collective welfare facilities and the subsidies of collective welfare undertaking by state-owned, collective and other economic units. Information in this part is taken from "The Table of the Cost Composition of Insurance and Welfare of the Whole Staff and Workers" from the *Annual Report of Labor Wage Statistics.* The above statistics of household consumption can be divided into two main strata: agriculture and non-agriculture personnel. By calculating the two categories separately, we then have farmer personal consumption and non-farmer personal consumption.

Government Consumption. Government consumption is calculated according to the source of outlay for the various administrative and organizational units. They include: (1) financial allocation expenditure from the state and departments at different levels; (2) extra budgetary expenditures; (3) the imputed depreciation of fixed assets of administrative and organizational units; (4) rural public consumption, etc.

To put it in a formula:

Government consumption = Operating expenses of public organizations (including administrative expenditure of the central government in each province) - Parts not belonging to consumption + Relevant items in the extra budgetary expenditures of the local financial departments + Relevant items in the extra budgetary expenditures of national organizations and administrative units + Rural public consumption + Depreciation of fixed assets of administrative and organization units.

1. The operating expenses from public expenditure. This refers mainly to the development cost of new products, national defense and armed police force outlay, operating expenses of industrial, transport and commercial departments, operating expenses for education, science and hygiene, operating expenses of agricultural, forestry, water conservancy and meteorology departments, expenses for urban defense, expenses for geological prospecting, resettlement of city educated youths, social welfare services expenditure, administration expenses and other items of expenditure, etc.
2. Parts not belonging to consumption. Of the expenses for geological prospecting, those related to engineering should not be counted as consumption. Of the expenses for national defense, military construction which can be shifted to public-use, such as housing, pier for military use and airport for military use, etc. According to SNA rules, items among military projects which can be transferred to public use belong to fixed assets. The fees for the design and research of basic construction items from the development expenses of new products, people's education promotion stipend, fees for the purchase of equipment, and public health service outlay at central level which is included in residents' consumption statistics,

etc., should be deducted from relevant items of public expenditure, and not counted as government consumption. The appropriate amount for deduction for the above parts should be estimated from the proportion of relevant items and their shares in the total investment.

3. Extra budgetary expenditure includes the maintenance cost for roads, expenses for urban defense, organization expenses, administrative expenses, and other expenses, etc.
4. Imputed depreciation of fixed assets of administrative and organization units. This can be deduced by multiplying the original value of fixed assets by a certain depreciation rate. The original value of fixed assets is estimated by reference to the accumulated amount of the fixed assets investment completed by the administrative and organization units during the past years until the current year, which is used as the original value of fixed assets at the end of period, and then take the mean (the sum of the original value of fixed assets at the beginning and the original value of fixed assets at the end divided by two). The depreciation rate is to be set by reference to the stipulated depreciation rate of fixed assets of state-owned enterprises and the actual situation. Usually we will take 2 to 4 percent as the reference rate.
5. Rural government consumption refers to the current expenses of villages' people committees below *xiang* level in rural area. The financial expenditures of the county and *xiang* governments and the collective purchase of consumption goods by town-and-village enterprises are not included in this part.

   Data for government consumption are taken from the lowest level's subject indicators of the year-end final accounts of public finance department, including wages, subsidy wages, welfare funds of staff and workers, public affairs expenses, maintenance expenses, operating expenses, other expenses, subsidy expenses for marginal deficits, etc., and the statistics of extra budgetary expenses by public finance departments. Data for the expenses of the village people committees below *xiang* level in rural area are taken from the rural collective purchase consumption in the report forms by the Department of Trade and External Economic Relation Statistics of SSB.

Gross Capital Formation. Gross capital formation is formed by the gross fixed capital formation and the increase in inventories.

1. Gross Fixed Capital Formation

   The calculation of gross fixed capital formation is based on the total social investment in the *Annual Report of Statistics on Investment in Fixed Assets*. This has to be adjusted according to the calibre scope of the gross fixed capital formation.

(1) State-owned Units

i. Fixed assets investment in state-owned units refers to the items listed in the plan for basic construction and renovation and items which are not listed in the plan but the cost of which is over Rmb50,000, and also the investment in the development of real estates. Data can be obtained from the "Tables of Major Indicators for Fixed Asset Investments for the Whole Society" in the *Annual Report* aforementioned.

ii. Investment items between Rmb20,000 - 50,000. This refers to items not included in the statistic scope of the annual report of investment in the range between Rmb20,000 - 50,000; these were included in the investment statistics in the past, but they are excluded at present. So, we have to add this part in our calculation. The data are based on the past years' statistical data by the Department of Statistics on Investment in Fixed Assets of SSB and the current investment information obtained for calculation.

iii. Deduction of investment which does not increase fixed assets. This designates expenses for the training of productive staff and workers, expenses for the moving of construction organizations, expenses for loss in scrapped construction, expenses for agricultural reclamation. There are two methods for calculation. The first one is the balance method, i.e., the difference of the cumulated investment in non-increased fixed assets in two consecutive years. The second one is the deduction method. That is deduced from the investment in non-increased fixed assets according to the input-output survey together with the finished investment in the current year. Between the two methods above, we mainly use the first one. The second one is the basis for adjustment.

For the source of data, the "Table of Total Scale of Fixed Assets Investment and Completion Situation" in the *Annual Report, idem,* and the data pool of input-output survey by the Department of Statistics on National Economic Balances (now renamed as Department of National Accounts Statistics) of SSB.

iv. The purchase of occasional equipments. This designates the purchase of miscellaneous equipment which fits the standard of fixed assets, but is not listed in the investment plan. And each total investment is below Rmb20,000. For the sources of data, we can use the figures of the base year together with the information from the public finance departments for the estimation or the result of a type survey.

v. Fixed assets increased by the expenses of experiments for new products. This designates the expenses of experiments on new products or testing new design data for a particular construction project.

   The data for the experiment expenses on new products are taken from the final accounts of the public finance departments, then from the proportion of experiment expenses related to the project item in the total expenses obtained through type surveys we proceed with our calculation.

vi. Investment by military units refers to the structures, facilities and equipments which are used for not exclusively military purpose but can also be used repeatedly in the process of production, even transferred to public use. For the source of data, we use the part for fixed assets formed by the investment in basic construction projects funded by military expenses and people's air defense outlay; what has already included in the investment statistics is not to be calculated again. For the civil machinery equipment which can have public use and are bought under national defense expenses, the information is taken from the national defense expenditure contained in the financial final accounts of the Ministry of Finance; this is based on a certain ratio to calculate the part pertaining to the fixed assets. The size of which can be drawn from the figures used in previous years or estimated by a type survey.

vii. Value-increased in the sale of commodity housing. Due to the nature of statistics on investment in China, houses and structures are calculated at the construction cost in the current fixed assets investment statistics. For commodity houses purchased through the market, the difference between the sale and the construction values is not recorded in the statistics. Therefore, it should be recalculated and included in the fixed asset formation. For the data, we use the sale value of commodity houses in current year taken from the Department of Statistics on Investment in Fixed Assets of SSB, together with relevant information to deduce the increased value.

viii. The formation of intangible fixed assets includes the exploration for mineral resources, software for computer, literature and art works. The exploration for mineral resources is already included in the fixed asset investment statistics; it is not calculated again. For software of computer, there is no clear rules on this in current accounting practices; some units even treat it as low-cost and easily consumable goods. Information on this cannot be found easily. Therefore, we can reckon the value for regions which provide the conditions and ignore regions where the conditions are inexistent. For entertainment, literature and art works, we will not calculate them since the conditions for calculation are not yet mature.

(2) Collective-owned Units

i. Fixed asset investment by collective-owned units. This includes items of total investment over Rmb50,000 under planning, construction and purchase of fixed assets by cities' and towns' collective units, and the investment in fixed assets by rural collective units. The data can be found in the "Table of the Major Indicators of Fixed Asset Investment for the Whole Society" in the *Annual Report of Statistics on Investment in Fixed Assets.*

ii. Investment by cities' and towns' collective units which ranges between Rmb20,000 - 50,000. The data are available from the same source as for the state-owned units.

iii. Deduction of cities and towns collective units' investment in non-increasing fixed assets. The data can be found in the "Table of the Total Scale of Investment and Completion Situation of the Cities' and Towns' Collective-owned Units" in the *Annual Report, idem.*

iv. Others: Besides the three items mentioned above, we also look at other investment in fixed assets by collective units. For the estimation of this item, we can base the estimation on the actual circumstances of each region and collect the relevant information. If the figure is small or difficult to collect, we can simply ignore it.

(3) Personal Fixed Asset Investment

This refers to the personal housing construction in cities and county towns, towns and mining areas, the personal housing construction in rural area, and the purchase of productive fixed assets. The data can be obtained from the "Table of Major Indicators of Fixed Asset Investment for the Whole Society" in the *Annual Report, idem.*

(4) Other Units

This refers to the total fixed capital formation by economic units in joint-ventures, the share system, foreign investment,

investment by Hong Kong, Macau or Taiwan, and other economic types, besides state-owned units, collective units and personal investment in fixed assets.

i. The investment of total planned investment in items over Rmb50,000. The data are available from the "Table for the Basic Situation of Fixed Assets Investment" in *Statistical Report Forms System of Fixed Assets Investment.*

ii. The investment in fixed assets under Rmb50,000. The estimation and calculation are made from the relevant data collected by the Department of Statistics on Investment in Fixed Assets of SSB and the information obtained from type surveys.

According to the type of industry, gross fixed capital formation can be divided into the investment by the primary, secondary and tertiary industrial sectors. The principle behind this division according to industrial sectors is the nature of the production activities undertaken after the construction units have completed the projects or have handed them to be put into production, or the particular nature of production that other social economic activities take in the process of production.

i. The division into three industrial sectors for the state-owned units

Data can be found in the *Annual Report of Statistics on Investment in Fixed Assets* which contains the "Table on the Overall Scale and Completion Situation by the State-owned Units in Fixed Asset Investment among National Economic Industries."

The primary industrial sector refers to farming, forestry, animal husbandry and fishery; the secondary sector is industry and construction; and production other than the primary and secondary sectors belongs to the tertiary sector.

For the categorization of other items which do not fall in these three categories in the current investment statistics, reference can be made to the proportions among the three sectors from which can be derived the appropriate shares which are then assigned to each of the tripartite sectors concerned.

ii. The division into three industrial sectors for the collective-owned units

The source of data is the "Table on Investments According to Production Sectors by Each Region's Collective-owned Units" in the *Annual Report, idem.*

The primary sector is composed of farming, forestry, animal husbandry and fishery. Since the table includes the above plus water conservancy, the amounts for water conservancy have to be deducted, as well as the data on the services sector to agriculture, forestry, animal husbandry, fishery and water conservancy, so as to get the figure for the primary industry. The ratios for the deduction can be drawn from the ratios for cities' and towns' collective units as a reference.

Here again, the secondary sector is industry and construction; and, the tertiary sector comprises what is not included in the other two. And, the treatment of other items which are not recorded in the investment statistics of the three sectors can be estimated in accordance with the previous proportions.

iii. The division into three industrial sectors for individual fixed asset investment

The categorization into three sectors for individual fixed asset investment is divided into rural areas and city and town areas. The data for the rural areas are taken from the "Table for Rural Individual Fixed Asset Investment by Region Classified According to National Economic Industries" found in the *Annual Report, idem.* The data for city and town individual investment can be drawn from the "Table of the Main Indicators of Fixed Asset Investment for the Whole Society" and the "Table of Investment Amount and Newly Increased Fixed Assets by Urban and Township Collective-Owned Units in the National Economic Industries" to be found in the *Annual Report, idem.*

To categorize the proportion of construction investment into the tripartite sectors, we refer to the proportions of the three industrial sectors classification about the cities' and towns' collectives. Non-productive construction investment comes under the tertiary sector.

iv. The division into three industrial sectors for other units

This item is estimated in accordance with the proportions of the three-sector classification for state-owned units.

2. Increase of Inventory

Inventory increase is estimated in accordance with the balance method; it is based on the difference between the final and initial stock value.

(1) Agriculture

Inventory increase in agriculture refers to the increase in

stock of the agricultural enterprises through their agricultural production activities, and small livestock (such as pigs and sheep), poultry as well as other animals and grain storage which are done by individual farmers.

i. The estimation of stock of agricultural enterprises at county level and above. This comprises the stock of independent accounting farming, forestry, animal husbandry and fishery enterprises. The increase in stock by economic type, i.e., state-owned, collective-owned and others is calculated from the difference between the final and initial period. Data are obtained from the "Table on the Financial Situation of Agricultural Enterprises" in the *Annual Report of Farming, Forestry, Animal Husbandry and Fishery Enterprises Statistics.*

ii. Stock increase of agricultural enterprises at *xiang* and village levels. This refers to the current stock value increase of agricultural enterprises (including self-employed households) at *xiang* and village levels and below. By economic type, these enterprises are counted into the collective economy. Data are obtained for the rural enterprises' from "Statement on Assets and Liabilities" by industries from the Rural Enterprise Department.

iii. The increased value constituted by rearing pigs, sheep and poultry and other animals. To put it in a formula:

    Increased value = (Final amount of stock on hand - Initial amount of stock on hand) x Average unit price.

    Data for the number of pig and sheep stock on hand are directly taken from the "Table of Nationwide Situation on Animal Husbandry Production" in the *Annual Report of Rural Economic Statistics.* The value of pigs is taken as half the price of a fat pig and that of a sheep is half the price of a grown-up sheep. Data concerning the prices of various animals are available from the Organization of Urban Social and Economic Surveys of SSB. The increase by household raising poultry and other animals can be replaced by the output value of household raising poultry and other animals from the Organization of Rural Social and Economic Survey Teams of SSB. The value of the household inventory increase is counted in "others" economic category.

iv. Increase in grain reserve. It designates the value of newly increased grain reserve by the rural collectives and peasant households. It includes both the reserve of seed grain and the reserve of grain for consumption. Grain reserves are listed into "others" economics category. The method to calculate the value is to multiply the stock increase of grain producers by the "Mixed Average Retail Unit Price" of grain in the same period. For the data, the stock increase of grain producers can be taken from the "Balance Sheet of Grain Production and Sales" in the *Annual Report of Commercial Statistics.* And the average unit price of grain is obtained from the table of the "Mixed Average Retail Price of Major Commodities (1)" in the *Annual Report of Price Statistics.*

(2) Industry

The inventory increase in industry refers to the stock increase in all independent accounting industrial enterprises at *xiang* level and above; the subsidiary industrial production units; industrial enterprises at village level and below; urban-rural-cooperative industries; and self-employed industries.

The information regarding inventory increase in independent accounting industrial enterprises at *xiang* level and above comes from the table of "The Major Economic Indicators of All Independent Accounting Industries" in the *Annual Report of Industrial Statistics.* If possible, we can directly estimate the non-independent accounting portion by collecting the relevant financial data. If the data are lacking, we can base our estimation on the ratio of independent accounting output value to non-independent accounting output value, and categorize the stocks according to their economic types. The stock increase in industrial enterprises at village level and below can be estimated from the "Statement of Assets and Liabilities" by industries from the Rural Enterprise Department. The inventory increase in urban-rural-cooperative and self-employed household industries can be estimated from data of the Rural Enterprise Department and Industry and Commerce departments.

The industries at *xiang* level and above are classified into state-owned, collective-owned and other forms of ownership according to the division in annual report data by the Department of Industrial and Transportation Statistics of SSB. The stock increase in industries at village level and below is included in the collective economy. Urban-rural cooperative and self-employed industries, inventory increase is included in the category "other ownership."

(3) Construction

This refers to the increase in inventory value for independent accounting and legal entity construction enterprises between the final and initial period of accounting for state-owned enterprises; cities' and towns' collective-owned units; partnerships; share-holding units; foreign business units and enterprises owned by Hong Kong, Macau and Taiwan investors. And it covers also construction enterprises by rural collectives; private enterprises; and household enterprises, whose stock is in storage, in use, being transported and being processed.

For state owned, city and town collectives, partnerships, share-holdings, foreign businesses and Hong Kong, Macau and Taiwan investments, data are found in the "Financial Situation Table" of the *Annual Report of Construction Statistics.* The increased stock value is estimated and categorized, according to the economic types, into state-owned, collective-owned and other ownerships. The construction enterprises under rural-collective, private-operated and household ownerships are not included in the current statistics of the construction enterprises. Since the direct sources of information are lacking, we can only base the data on information for the construction enterprises supplied by the Rural Enterprise Department using the proportions of inventory figures for the state economy for further estimation. Or alternatively, we can use data gathered by type surveys for estimation. The relevant data will be grouped under collective ownership and other ownership, respectively.

(4) Construction Units' Increase In Inventory

This refers to the newly increased stock equipment, stock materials, equipment in transit, sub-contracted equipment being processed, etc. in the current year for the need of construction unit. The data can be found in "Funds Balance Sheet" of the "Table of Final Accounting Report for Basic Construction" on construction units by the Chinese People's Construction Bank.

The construction units come from all sectors of the national economy. If date allow, the construction units should be divided in accordance with their sector; moreover, an estimate of the inventory increase for the corresponding sector should be made. The stock increase of these major construction units is included in the state-owned sector of the economy.

Inventory increase should be divided into two categories by ownership type and by industrial sector. The categorization according to ownership consists of state-owned, collective-owned and other ownership. State-owned units refer to the state-owned enterprises included in the set of tables for speciality grassroots enterprises; collective-owned units refer to those in the set of tables depicting the collective economy; other ownership form refers to all economic types other than those state- or collective-owned, the components of which are private-operated enterprises, partnerships, share-holding units, as well as other kinds of joint venture enterprises and other forms of ownership. The other categorization consists of the primary, secondary, and tertiary industries.

Inventory increase is usually based on the records of accountants, but the bookkeeper accounting has a different purpose from statistical accounting. Hence, we cannot use directly the stock increase calculated by using the difference between the final and initial period; an adjustment is necessary, which involves two issues. First of all, there is discrepancy between the calculated price at the time of stock delivery and the buying price, resulting in changes in stock. Secondly, some departments (such as material department) adopt market price to calculate stock and, thus, the price as well as the stock value are subject to irregular adjustments, with the result that the inventory value tends to be gaining in value. To handle the first problem, we inquire into the method of pricing stock at the time of delivery adopted by various units, and then adjust the result with corresponding price indexes. To tackle the second one, we put into consideration the current price index of production means and then readjust the initial stock value. These ways of handling the variations have been adopted as no other relatively standardized criteria of adjustment have yet been devised.

(5) Transport and Post and Telecommunications Enterprises

Inventory increase here refers to the increased value between the final and initial period for railway enterprises, transport enterprises, post and telecommunications enterprises, and civil aviation enterprises.

For the method of calculation, the stock increase for railway, post and telecommunication, civil aviation enterprises can be calculated directly by using the stock value taken from the annual "Statement of Assets and Liabilities" by the Ministry of Railway, the Ministry of Post and Telecommunication and the Civil Aviation Bureau. Or alternatively, it can be calculated directly from data of the finance departments. For the stock increase of transport enterprises, the independent accounting transport enterprises of various ownership types at county level and above, inventory variations are taken from "Enterprises' Financial Situation Table" of the *Annual Report of Communications,*

Transportation, and Post and Telecommunications Statistics. The data concerning rural transport enterprises are taken from the corresponding "Statement of Assets and Liabilities" by the Rural Enterprise Department.

To account for stock increase, transport enterprises are divided into state-owned, collective-owned and other ownership in accordance with the economic types found in the *Annual Report, idem.* The data concerning the division of the rural transport enterprises by economic types are taken from the Rural Enterprise Department. The railway, civil aviation, and post and telecommunications enterprises are all categorized state-owned enterprises.

(6) Commerce & Catering Trade

The stock increase in commerce and catering trade refers to the increased value of various commodities and materials between the final and initial period in the commodity trade enterprises (including domestic commerce, foreign trade, material supply and marketing) and catering trade. The commodities and materials that are included involves the goods stored, in transit, on lease or in processing.

The data concerning the stock increase in commodity and catering trade enterprises of all economic types at *xiang* level and above are taken from the "Financial Situation Table" depicting stock changes by the ownership types. The table appears in the *Annual Report of Commercial Statistics.* The source of information concerning the stock of various ownership types of commerce and catering trade at the county level and below is taken from the Rural Enterprise Department's "Statement of Assets and Liabilities" for rural trade. Rural enterprises' data may be incomplete, additional information has to be collected and grouped in the corresponding ownership types. Since data on self-employed commerce and catering trade are lacking, we seek from the Industry and Commerce Administration departments the relevant information for an estimation, which is then grouped into its proper sectors.

(7) Inventory Increase for Administrative Units Being Run as Business

This refers to the various kinds of independent accounting units being run as businesses, which are not included in the enterprises aforementioned. The warehouses attached to the Reserve Bureau system are included in this category. The inventory increase is grouped into the state-owned sector. The data can be obtained from the "Financial Situation Table" in the *Annual Report of Administration and Institution Units' Statistics*. When the financial information of certain regions is lacking, we can estimate in accordance with the data of the speciality departments.

(8) Service Enterprises

The increase in inventory value of service enterprises designate the independent accounting and legal entity service enterprises of all ownership types. This category comprises prospecting companies under the prospecting and engineering industry that engage in the production activities, storage enterprises, real estate development enterprises, consumer service enterprises, city public transport enterprises, cultural enterprises, comprehensive technological development enterprises, financial and insurance enterprises, and the services enterprises of other economic sectors. The data can be obtained from the stock increase shown in the "Financial Situation Table" of the *Annual Report of Service Enterprise Statistics*. And the division of inventory into ownership types as state-owned, collective-owned and other ownership can also be estimated from the data in the *Annual Report, idem*.

Net Export. The value for net export which enters into GDP is constituted of two parts: the net export of material products (material goods and services of material nature) and the net export of services of non-material nature. An explicit account comprises the net export of customs goods, consumer goods and services of material nature purchased by foreigners (net income of freight traffic), net export of services of non-material nature (net income from ports' supply sale and services and net income from tourism).

The source of data:

1. For the net export of material products, the data for the customs net exports are taken from the "Table of Total Export and Import Trade" by the Department of Trade and External Economic Relation Statistics of SSB. Data about consumer goods purchased by foreigners are taken from the statistical data table from the same Department aforesaid. Data about services of material nature (freight traffic income) are from the "Balance of International Payments Table."

   The net export of material products by region mainly comprises four elements: the first is the commodity export and import trade by regions; the second is the direct overseas purchase made by local residents and that made by foreign residents in China, but is excluded from statistics on foreign trade; the third is the import-export of material products exchanged between regions made through organizations such as the commerce and material departments; the fourth is the direct purchase from other regions by local residents and other regions' residents' direct purchase from this locality. The first two elements are the inflow and outflow between internal regions and foreign countries, i.e., the net export of material goods. From the angle of the whole country, the two are seen as import-export trade between China and foreign countries, while the last two are the inflow and outflow of material goods between domestic regions.

The inflow-outflow of material products within regions is calculated according to the experience of each region. The methods adopted are:

(1) Direct Calculation: by directly using the data of material products' inflow and outflow. This mainly includes the relevant data concerning the outflow and inflow via the commerce, foreign trade, material distribution, and business enterprises and institution units, and the direct purchase by residents within and outside the region.

(2) To estimate the inflow and outflow of material products by using the dealings of banks' link-accounts, making sure to deduct the pure currency dealings. In practice, among the data of the incoming and outgoing accounts of inter banks' transactions, only the current account of payment for goods is taken into consideration and are deducted the portions of "pure funds appropriation" and other payments for non-goods transactions: for example, the fund appropriation between regional banks and their headquarters, finance departments' tax submission and appropriation, turning over of profits, appropriation of basic construction investment funds, and financial subsidy, etc.

(3) Measure of the net inflow, net outflow across regions by making use of the difference between Finance Departments upward turn-over and downward appropriation, the difference of profits handed over and funds invested by central enterprises and business organizations; difference of loans and deposit of banks; and difference in increase or decrease of the cash-in-hand among units and residents. When a larger amount of fund is handed upward by the Finance Departments than appropriation downward, it shows that there is a net outflow of products, and vice versa; when deposits are larger than loans in credit business, it shows that there is a net outflow of products, and vice versa. Net cash outflow implies product inflow whereas net cash inflow implies net product outflow. The movement of pure cash *per se* has to be deducted.

(4) Balance Method. This method uses the difference between the production of GDP and the use of GDP (the sum of consumption and investment) to estimate the net inflow and outflow of products.

It is noted that when measuring the flow of goods between regions, better result is achieved by using more than two methods for estimation as this provides a means for comparison and testing.

2. The forms of export and import of non-material services are different from those of material products. Non-material services are characterized by the concurrence of the provision and use of services. The data are taken from "Balance of International Payments Table" from which net income data for ports' labor services and for tourism can be collected. The data gathered from the Table aforementioned is presented in US dollars, and it is necessary to convert them into *Renminbi*. The exchange rate can be obtained from "The Average Exchange Rate of the *Renminbi* to Major Foreign Currencies" prepared by the State Foreign Exchange Administration Bureau.

Apart from the payments between regions and overseas for the non-material product services, there are also interregional payments for non-material product services. However, the relevant data are lacking; and for these regions, one can resort only to the analysis of input-output survey data for further estimation. For the provinces and municipalities which possess such data, one can conduct relevant surveys for estimation. Or else, one may neglect such data and regard the inflow and outflow of services as a mutual cancellation.

The Calculation in Comparable Prices

1. Gross Final Consumption in Comparable Prices

After calculating gross final consumption in current prices, one needs to investigate the circumstances of growth change and proceed with an analysis of the development trends. Thus, on the basis of relevant price indexes applied to the gross final consumption values in current prices, one converts the values in comparable prices for household consumption and government consumption; then, one adds the latter two values to obtain the gross consumption in comparable prices.

(1) Household consumption in comparable prices is divided into the non-farmer household consumption and farmer household consumption, respectively, and converted separately.

1) Non-farmer household consumption in constant prices

This is converted in accordance with the constituent parts of the non-agricultural residents' consumption:

i. Commodity consumption, we may directly use the price index to convert cities' and towns' the value of consumption goods. Such data are taken from the staff and workers living cost price index of the *Annual Report of Price Statistics*. To make the data more reliable, we have to account for the commodity consumption by the non-agricultural residents who buy from urban-rural markets, or outside these markets from rural production teams, and peasants. This portion should be converted according to the country fair trade price index.

ii. The price index of city service items taken from the *Annual Report of Price Statistics* is used to deflate the consumption of services for cultural activities, the rent of flats, water and electricity, and public health services.

iii. For the depreciation of private-owned housing, the current year's increased part can be deflated in accordance with the price index of construction output value, and then add to it the last year's comparable price portion. The sum is, thus, the flats depreciation in comparable prices in the calender year.

2) Farmer household consumption in comparable prices

It is obtained by converting independently the value of the various components of agricultural residents' consumption and, then, adding them up.

i. Commodity consumption is converted by using the rural consumption goods price index of the *Annual Report of Price Statistics*.

ii. Self-supplied consumption can be deflated by taking the prices of major self-produced goods such as grain, meat, eggs, vegetables, etc., to obtain a weighted average price index for conversion purpose. Or alternatively, their value can be deflated by referring to the price index of total output value of agriculture with some suitable adjustment.

iii. Consumption of cultural services can be deflated by using the price index for rural services.

iv. The conversion of housing depreciation is similar to that for non-agricultural residents' housing depreciation.

(2) Government Consumption in Comparable Prices

The government consumption (fixed asset depreciation is calculated individually), is divided into three parts according to the lowest level's subject indicators of final account expenditure of state Finance Ministry: consumption of material products, employees' wages, and services expenses. Different sets of indexes are adopted for conversion purpose.

Consumption of material products can be deflated by various consumption good retail price indexes. Examples of consumption are fuels, water and electricity, articles for office use, furniture, and household utensils consumed by non-material production organizations such as government administrative organizations, science and research or health care organizations etc. The part on employees' wages, such as wages, wage subsidies, and staff and workers welfare funds, etc., is converted by using the price index for the nationwide staff and workers' living expenses of the *Annual Report of Price Statistics*. The part on service expenses is converted in accordance with relevant services' price indexes. The service expenses include staff transportation, hotel, training of administrative cadres, etc.

To calculate the comparable prices of fixed asset depreciation belonging to the administrative and business units, one can refer to the relevant method suggested under income approach to calculate fixed asset depreciation in comparable prices of GDP.

2. Gross Capital Formation in Comparable Prices

(1) Gross Fixed Capital Formation in Comparable Prices

If the price index for fixed asset investment is available from the Organization of Urban Social and Economic Surveys of SSB, we can directly use it to deflate. Or else, the following method may be adopted:

First, we seek the proportions of investment in construction installation projects and the investment in equipment, machines, tools (investments formed by construction and installation projects, equipment, machines and tools), the data of which are taken from the *Annual Report of Statistics on Investment in Fixed Assets*. Then, we use the price index of output value for construction industry and producer price index of mechanical products via the weighted average method to form the price index for gross fixed capital formation, which is used for the conversion. The indexes aforementioned can be found in the *Annual Report of Price Statistics*.

(2) Inventory Increase in Comparable Prices

The first step is to categorize the stock into production means and means of subsistence. On this basis, these are further categorized into industrial inventory and commercial inventory, and out of which is calculated separately the value of the procured farming and sideline products. Next, according to the price index for the means of subsistence, the price index of the procurement farming and sideline products, and the price index for production means, we then calculate the price index of inventory increase through the weighted average method to obtain the value of inventory increase in comparable prices.

For the source of data, the price index for production means, the price index for the means of subsistence, the price index for farming and sideline products procurement are all taken from the *Annual Report of Price Statistics*. The ratio of farming and sideline product inventory to industrial and commercial stock is available in the *Annual Report of Commercial Statistics* and from the Ministry of Commerce.

Pigs, sheep, poultry, other animal raising and grain reserve are deflated respectively according to the changes in their unit prices. The data come from the *Annual Report of Price Statistics*.

3. Net Export in Comparable Prices

This is calculated separately in accordance with the net export of material products and the net export of services:

(1) Net export of goods in comparable prices: Use is made of the Customs' import and export price indexes to convert the value of import and export of goods. Data are obtained from the price survey data by the Organization of Urban Social and Economic Surveys of SSB.

(2) Net export of services in comparable prices: We make use of the service price index for conversion. Information is taken from the *Annual Report of Price Statistics*.

Notes

1. In this formula, the item "accumulation into reserve capital for ongoing liability" stands for the capital reserve for the ongoing period the insurance company draws according to a determined proportion from the income of the insurance premiums; the item "revolving reserve capital for liability not yet expired" refers to the reserve capital for liability not yet expired accumulated in the previous year. In the formula, the accumulation into reserve capital for liability minus the revolving capital for liability not yet expired is equivalent to the difference between the new and previous accumulations; this difference is one part of the income from insurance premiums during the present period; however, the income from insurance premiums is already included in the total output, thus, in order to avoid accounting duplication the portion of new accumulation into the reserve capital must be subtracted. In addition, in the formula, the item called "income from underwriters for subcontracted profit and

loss insurance" refers to the portion of insurance activity that an insurance company transfers to other insurance companies for the purpose of sharing the management burden from which it draws a portion of management profit.

2. The index is compiled from the weighted average of grain and cash crop prices which are under the procurement price indexes of farming and sideline products.

3. The index is obtained from the feed index in the price indexes for the means of agricultural production, recorded in the price categories indexes of country markets.

4. Making use of the fertilizer item in the price indexes for the means of agricultural production.

5. Making use of the index for engine oil in the price indexes for the means of agricultural production.

6. This can be obtained from the weighted average of the price indexes for major industrial raw materials, fuel and energy and for productive services.

7. This is a set of tables organized and designed by the SSB for statistical investigation of the enterprises of various industries for the whole society.

8. The Communist Youth League.

References

A. General Reference Books

Commission of the European Communities, International Monetary Fund, Organization for Economic Cooperation and Development, United Nations and World Bank. *System of National Accounts, 1993*, prepared under the auspices of the Inter-Secretariat Group on National Accounts, Brussels/Luxembourg, New York, Paris, Washington D.C. 1993.

Department of Economic and Social Affairs, Statistical Office of the United Nations. *A System of National Accounts*, New York: United Nations, 1968.

Department of Economic and Social Affairs, Statistical Office of the United Nations. *Basic Methodological Principles Governing the Compilation of the System of Statistical Balances of the National Economy*, New York: United Nations, 1989.

Department of Economic and Social Affairs, Statistical Office of the United Nations. *Basic Principles of The System of Balances of The National Economy*. New York: United Nations, 1971.

Department of Economic and Social Affairs, Statistical Office of the United Nations. *Accounting for Production: Sources and Methods*. New York: United Nations, 1986.

Min Qingquan, *A Concise National Economic Accounting System*. Beijing: Economic Science Publishing House, 1987 (in Chinese).

National Income Department, Economic Planning Agency of Japan. *A Popular Guide to New National Economic Accounting System*. Beijing: China's Statistical Publishing House, 1985 (translated into Chinese).

State Statistical Bureau. *Exposition of Major Statistical Indicators of the National Economy* (Vols. I, II, III), 1987 (internal documents).

Yang Shuzhuang, Li Qiang and Liu Chengxiang (eds.). *An Implementation Guidebook of China's New National Economic Accounting System*. Beijing: Beijing University

of Industry Publishing House, 1993 (in Chinese).
Zhang Sai (ed.). *The Work of New National Economic Accounting*. Beijing: China's Statistical Publishing House, 1993 (in Chinese).

B. Internal Data in Book Form

Construction Division of the Department of Statistics on Investment in Fixed Assets of SSB (ed.). *Annual Report of Construction Statistics*, Beijing: SSB Printing House, various issues (internal data).

Department of Industrial and Transportation Statistics of SSB (ed.). *Annual Report of Communications, Transportation, and Post and Telecommunications Statistics*, Beijing: SSB Printing House, various issues (internal data).

Department of Industrial and Transportation Statistics of SSB (ed.). *Annual Report of Industrial Statistics*, Beijing: SSB Printing House, various issues (internal data).

Department of National Accounts Statistics of SSB (ed.). *China's Nationwide (Provinces, Municipalities) Input-Output Table, 1992* (draft).

Department of Organization of Rural Social and Economic Surveys of SSB (ed.). *Annual Report of Rural Economic Statistics*, Beijing: SSB Printing House, various issues (internal data).

Department of Population and Labor Statistics of SSB (ed.). *Annual Report of Comprehensive Statistics on Labor*, Beijing: SSB Printing House, various issues (internal data).

Department of Population and Labor Statistics of SSB (ed.). *Annual Report of Labor Wage Statistics*, Beijing: SSB Printing House, various issues (internal data).

Department of Social, Science and Technology Statistics of SSB (ed.). *Annual Report of Administration and Institution Units' Statistics*, Beijing: SSB Printing House, various issues (internal data).

Department of Social, Science and Technology Statistics of SSB (ed.). *Annual Report of Service Enterprise Statistics*, Beijing: SSB Printing House, various issues (internal data).

Department of Statistics on Investment in Fixed Assets of SSB (ed.). *Annual Report of Statistics on Investment in Fixed Assets*, Beijing: SSB Printing House, various issues (internal data).

Department of Statistics on Investment in Fixed Assets of SSB (ed.). *Statistical Report Forms System of Fixed Assets Investment*, Beijing: SSB Printing House, (internal data).

Department of Trade and External Economic Relation Statistics of SSB (ed.). *Annual Report of Commercial Statistics*, Beijing: SSB Printing House, various issues (internal data).

Department of Trade and External Economic Relation Statistics of SSB (ed.). *Annual Report of Comprehensive Statistics on Commodity Flow and Catering Trade*, Beijing: SSB Printing House, various issues (internal data).

The Ministry of Construction (ed.). *Annual Report of Commodity Flats Management Situation*, Beijing (internal data).

The Ministry of Construction (ed.). *Annual Report of Urban Construction Statistics*, Beijing (internal data).

Organization of Rural Social and Economic Surveys of SSB (ed.). *Annual Report of Farming, Forestry, Animal Husbandry and Fishery Enterprises Statistics,* Beijing: SSB Printing House, various issues (internal data).

Production Division of the Organization of Urban Social and Economic Surveys, SSB (ed.). *Annual Report of Price Statistics,* Beijing: SSB Printing House, various issues (internal data).

Rural Enterprise Department, Ministry of Agriculture (ed.). *Statistical Data of Rural Enterprise,* Beijing (internal data).

4

The Interchange Between SNA Gross Domestic Product and Its Constituent Elements and MPS National Income and Its Constituent Elements

Xu Xianchun
Hsueh Tien-tung

Basically, the national economic accounting system adopted in the PRC, the estimation of GDP and its constituent elements in SNA corresponds to that used in the Western countries in terms of its accounting scope, object and principle. Yet, it demonstrates its uniqueness by making possible the interchange between GDP of SNA and National Income of MPS. This chapter will focus on these two issues for detailed discussion.

Characteristics of the Calculation of China's Gross Domestic Product

On the whole, the calculation of GDP in China's national economic accounting system has the following characteristics:

First of all, it has a relatively high comparability as the one used in the West. By and large, they share the same accounting scope, object and principle. In fact, its inclusion of activities of both the material production sector and the non-material production sector complies with the GDP of SNA in terms of scope.

In addition, the accounting object of GDP in China is all resident units, whatever the category under which they operate; their activities are subject to inclusion in the GDP as long as they are resident units in China.

The accounting statistical units of GDP in China are grassroots units and organizational units which are similar to those used in the West. The aggregate of the former becomes the industrial sector whereas that of the latter becomes the institutional sector.

Moreover, the way China unifies transaction recording is identical with the West. A transaction is recorded in the GDP exactly at the moment when right and obligation involved become effective with its current market price as the common yardstick of evaluation. Therefore, Chinese measures of GDP are similar to SNA measures in the West. This means that the two measures of GDP can be directly compared, and both have a high level of comparability.

Interchange with National Income of MPS

In view of the corresponding features between China's and the West's GDP of SNA mentioned above, here arise two problems to be tackled: what are the significant differences between the present GDP of SNA and past National Income (NI) of MPS in China? and how can we link the aggregate economic variables involved in a consistent way? In this connection, we are going to elaborate in some details on the related issues.

1. In designing the "Table for Gross Domestic Product and Its Use in SNA" (see Table 4.1), we have deliberately included some relevant MPS items for the sake of such interchange. In the main column for production, intermediate inputs are divided into material production input and service input, with an addition for net output value of material production of the sub-column for production is divided into material production sector and non-material production sector, respectively. Moreover, in the main column for use, intermediate use is divided into use by material production sector and use by non-material production sector, with an addition for net output value of material product. In the use sub-column goods and services are disintegrated into material product and services. As a consequence of this effort to modify the original items and make up the new items, it is easy to convert GDP and its constituent elements of SNA and NI and its constituent elements of MPS into each other.
2. In order to preserve the integrity and consistency of the whole accounting, we revise the main components of the NI in MPS to fit the components of GDP in SNA in Table 4.1. In practice, the main components of the equilibrium table in MPS (see Table 4.2) are the activities of national production and utilization by all production units and individuals that are within the country's

TABLE 4.1 Gross Domestic Product and Its Use in SNA

Production	Ordering	Total	Material Production sector	Non-material production sector	Use	Ordering	Total	Material product	Service
		1	2	3			4	5	6
I. Total output	1		(1, 2)		I. Total expenditure	10		(10, 5)	
II. Intermediate input	2		(2, 2)		II. Intermediate use (Intermediate consumption)	11			
1. Material product input	3		(3, 2)		1. In material production sector	12		(12, 5)	
2. Service input	4		(4, 2)		2. In non-material production sector	13		(13, 5)	
III. Gross domestic product (value-added)	5		(5, 2)		III. Gross domestic product	14		(14, 5)	
					1. Gross final consumption	15			
1. Fixed asset depreciation	6		(6, 2)		(1) Household consumption	16			
					(2) Government consumption	17			
2. Labour remuneration	7		(7, 2)		2. Gross capital formation	18			
					(1) Gross fixed capital formation	19			
3. Net production tax	8		(8, 2)						
4. Operating surplus	9		(9, 2)		(2) Increase in inventory	20			
					3. Export	21		(21, 5)	
					4. Import	22		(22, 5)	

TABLE 4.2 National Income and Its Use in MPS

Income	Ordering	Material production sector	Use	Ordering	Material product
I. Total output value	a		I. Total use value	h	
II. Intermediate consumption	b		II. Intermediate use	i	
			III. Final use	j	
1. Intermediate consumption of material products	c		1. Total consumption	k	
			(1) Personal consumption	l	
2. Depreciation of fixed assets	d		(2) Public consumption	m	
			2. Total accumulation	n	
III. Net output value	e		(1) Fixed asset accumulation	o	
1. Individual income	f				
2. Net income	g		(2) Circulating asset accumulation	p	
			3. Export	q	
			4. Import	r	

territory and their import-export trading activities with units or individuals outside the country's territory. However, the GDP of SNA is concerned about the resident units which are permanent units in China. Once they are resident units in China, regardless of the location of production, whether local or overseas, their production outcome must be counted in China's GDP. Use under GDP is also of the resident units which engage in investment and consumption activities. Import and export trading activities are also defined as exchange between the resident and non-resident units. Thus, in order to facilitate the conversion between the components of GDP in SNA and the components of NI in MPS, the relevant components of NI in MPS recorded in Table 4.2 must first be adjusted to be the resident units before transforming them into the corresponding components of GDP in SNA. Following this necessary design and treatment (supplemented by necessary adjustments) the interchange between them can be done with ease.

Interchange Between Gross Domestic Product of SNA and National Income of MPS

From the particularities of the accounting methods, there are two approaches by which such an interchange can be obtained. They are interchange based either on production or on use.

For the sake of comparison, we first review the accounting table of Gross Domestic Product of SNA and the one of the National Income of MPS.

1. Interchanging production accounting in GDP of SNA and production accounting in NI of MPS can be accomplished by the following series of adjustments:

Step 1: Interchanging total output value with total output as follows:

Total output value (a) in Table 4.2 = Total output of material production sectors (1, 2) in Table 4.1.

Step 2: Interchanging intermediate input with intermediate consumption as follows:

Intermediate consumption (b) in Table 4.2 = Intermediate input of material production sector (2, 2) + Fixed asset depreciation in material production sector (6, 2) – Service input in material production sector (4, 2) in Table 4.1 = Intermediate consumption of material product (c) + Depreciation of fixed assets (d) in Table 4.2.

While, intermediate consumption of material product (c) in Table 4.2 = Material product input in material production sector (3, 2) in Table 4.1 = Intermediate input in material production sector (2, 2) – Service input in material production sector (4, 2) in Table 4.1

And, depreciation of fixed assets (d) in Table 4.2 = Fixed asset depreciation in material production sector (6, 2) in Table 4.1.

Step 3: Interchanging net output value with gross domestic product is illustrated below:

Net output value (e) in Table 4.2 = Gross domestic product in material production sector (5, 2) – Fixed asset depreciation in material production sector (6, 2) – Service input in material production sector (4, 2) in Table 4.1 = Labor remuneration in material production sector (7, 2) + Net production tax in material production sector (8, 2) + Operating surplus in material production sector (9, 2) – Service input in material production sector (4, 2) in Table 4.1 = Individual income (f) + Net income (g) in Table 4.2

However, a problem arises here as there are no interchangeable items in Table 4.1 for individual income (f) and net income (g) in Table 4.2 and hence it is difficult to transform them.

Step 4: Adjusting the basic accounting unit. Since under SNA, the unit of accounting is the permanent resident unit in the country while under MPS, the unit of accounting is each unit within the territory, the previous description of interchange is still only formal. Another adjustment is needed so that information on permanent resident units can be interchanged with units within the territory.

2. Interchanging use of national income in MPS with use of GDP in SNA. The interchange between these two items is achieved through the following steps:

Step 1: Interchanging total use value with total expenditure:

Total use value (h) in Table 4.2 = Total expenditure on material product (10, 5) in Table 4.1

Step 2: Interchanging intermediate use with each other:

Intermediate use (i) in Table 4.2 = Intermediate use of material product in material production sector (12, 5) + Fixed asset depreciation in material production sector (6,2) in Table 4.1

Step 3: Interchanging final use with gross domestic product:

Final use (j) in Table 4.2 = Material goods portion in gross domestic product (14, 5) + Material goods used by non-material production sector (13, 5) – Fixed asset depreciation in material production sector (6, 2) in Table 4.1

Step 4: Interchanging Export and Import:

Export (q) in Table 4.2 = Export (21, 5) in Table 4.1

and,

Import (r) in Table 4.2 = Import (22, 5) in Table 4.1

Step 5: Interchanging within-territory units of MPS with resident units of SNA and vice versa to assure the conversion of accounting between the two systems.

The detailed interchanging procedures are tabulated in Table 4.3.

TABLE 4.3 Conversion between GDP and Its Components in SNA and NI and Its Components in MPS

T1, Gross domestic product (SNA) accounting T2, National income (MPS) accounting	T1, Total expenditure of GDP T2, Total use of NI
1. T2 (a) = T1 (1, 2)	1. T2 (h) = T1 (10, 5)
2. T2 (b) = T1 (3, 2) + (6, 2) - (4, 2)	2. T2 (i) = T1 (12, 5) + (6, 2)
= T2 (c) + (d)	3. T2 (j) = T1 (14, 5) - (13, 5) - (6, 2)
where	4. T2 (q) = T1 (21, 5)
T2 (c) = T1 (3, 2)	T2 (r) = T1 (22, 5)
= T1 (2, 2) - (4, 2)	
T2 (d) = T1 (6, 2)	
3. T2 (e) = T1 (5, 2) - (6, 2) - (4, 2)	
= T1 (7, 2) + (8, 2) + (9, 2) - (4, 2)	
= T2 (f) + (g)	

Note: T1, accounting unit: permanent resident units; T2, accounting unit: within-territory units. Adjustments are needed.

References

Department of Economic and Social Affairs, Statistical Office of the United Nations, *A System of National Accounts*. New York: United Nations, 1968.

Department of Economic and Social Affairs, Statistical Office of the United Nations, *Basic Principles of the System of Balances of the National Economy*. New York: United Nations, 1971.

Department of Economic and Social Affairs, Statistical Office of the United Nations, *Comparisons of the System of National Accounts and the System of Balances of the National Economy*. New York: United Nations, 1977.

Yang Shuzhuang, Li Qiang and Liu Chengxiang (eds.), *An Implementation Guidebook of China's New National Economic Accounting System*. Beijing: Beijing University of Industry Publishing House, 1993 (in Chinese).

5

Some Explanations of the Estimation of Gross Domestic Product and Its Components and Future Improvements

Hsueh Tien-tung
Li Qiang
Liu Liping

The gross domestic product represents a general indicator of the macroeconomic condition of a national economy. Its calculation is closely related to a nation's economic system, economic policy, and price policy. Since 1985, China has begun to estimate her GDP. Apart from some technical problems arising in the process of concrete estimation, it was found that improvement in the methodology and sources of data needed to be addressed. This chapter is going to clarify some important unsolved issues.

Price Index Problem

Gross Domestic Product in Constant Prices

As stated in Chapter III, except for agriculture, the value-added of the other production sectors of the national economy is deflated in accordance with the method of single deflation. The reasons for this are: first, the estimation of GDP has been established for only about 10 years. The value-added of the industrial sectors is partly calculated according to the production approach and partly according to the distribution approach. The value-added of agriculture for which better conditions exist for the calculation by total output and intermediate input, is obtained by subtracting intermediate input from total output on the basis of the production approach. This lays down a good foundation for obtaining value-added in constant prices in the light of the method of double deflation. However, for the majority of production sectors, owing to difficulties in collecting basic data, the distribution approach is adopted instead to find out the value-added, which is not appropriate for the double deflation method. The second important reason is the need of a sound price system. The present price indexes for circulation links and consumption have been set up for a relatively longer period and are, therefore, better and more complete. But, for the production segments, especially those indexes which can be used to deflate the intermediate input, have to be further improved. This creates difficulties for applying double deflation on all other industrial sectors.

With detailed data for the calculation of value-added by the production approach, especially the detailed data of intermediate input, and the corresponding price indexes, the use of double deflation method can better reflect the actual changes in value-added in constant prices. However, if there are no better data available on the total output, intermediate input, and the price indexes aforementioned, the use of single deflation method can eliminate some systematic errors resulting from problems in data source. Moreover, under the condition that the magnitudes of increases in prices of total output and intermediate input are basically consistent, the use of single deflation method can basically reflect the value-added in constant prices.[1]

Price Index of Total Output of Industry and Agriculture

The price index of the total output of industry and agriculture is compiled by adopting a fixed price for products within the base period for the calculation. That is, the quantities of products being considered in the accounting period are first multiplied by the established constant price of these products of a predetermined base period, thus obtaining the total output in constant prices $\sum_i P_{oi} Q_{ni}$ (in this expression, P_{oi} : the price of the product (i=1,2....) in the base period; Q_{ni} : the quantity of the product (i=1,2....) in the current accounting period). At the same time, the total output of the current period is calculated according to the current market prices $\sum_i P_{ni} Q_{ni}$ (where, P_{ni} : the price of the product in the current period). We then divide the total output in current prices $\sum_i P_{ni} Q_{ni}$ by the total output in constant prices $\sum_i P_{oi} Q_{ni}$,so giving the price index of total output. The expression of this index is $\sum_i P_{ni} Q_{ni} / \sum_i P_{oi} Q_{ni}$, which is a Paasche price index.

However, under the Chinese circumstance, compared with the Laspeyres price index, the Paasche price index tends to be lower than the Laspeyres'.[2]

The price index of the total output of industry and agriculture is mainly determined by the setting of the constant price for each of the two sectors, and such a setting was formed under a system of planned economy. Owing to the control of prices of these two sectors by the state in each five-year plan, the prices and the products selected were basically unchanged. Therefore, by using the prices at a given point in the first year of a five-year plan to serve as the constant prices of those products within the whole of the five years, the planning departments easily formulated the development objectives of the national economy (in fact, this was the reason for setting the constant prices) and exercised macroeconomic management. And, it was also easy for the statistics department to calculate within very short periods of time the total output in constant prices by directly using data of output quantities as there was no market behavior. This facilitated the immediate calculation of the growth rate of total output (the growth rate of total output is $\sum_i P_{oi} Q_{ni} / \sum_i P_{oi} Q_{n-1i}$, where P_{oi} (i=1,2....) refers to the price of the base period, Q_{ni} (i=1,2....) refers to the quantity of products in current calculation period, Q_{n-1i} (i=1,2....) refers to the quantity of products in the previous accounting period). The formula designates a kind of Laspeyres quantity index, which tends to inflate the growth rate of total output of industry and agriculture under the Chinese circumstances.[3]

However, in the course of economic system reform and of the change in national economic accounting, the limitations of calculating industrial and agricultural total output growth by Laspeyres' quantity index and by Paasche's price indexes are becoming more conspicuous. The scope of the approach includes only material products of each sector. It is not possible to make a calculation about the price index of the service sector. The price index also has its shortcomings for the industrial and agricultural products, especially for the industrial products as the time between the current calculation period and the base period has been becoming longer. The list of fixed-price products selected for the base period can not include the numerous new products. Although the fixed price of other similar products can be used to substitute for the price of new products, differences between prices still exist. Moreover, there may even be an inappropriate enlargement of the total output in constant prices, an understatement of the price indexes, an overstatement of growth rates as discussed above.

Link-up Between Comparable Prices of Different Time Periods

Since 1952, the PRC has altogether compiled the industrial and agricultural products in constant prices in 1952, 1957, 1970, 1980 and 1990.[4] The compilation in constant prices of the total output of industrial and agricultural products is based on the compilation of the constant prices of these two sectors, divided into several time intervals. Correspondingly, the value-added of these two sectors and GDP in constant prices are also divided into the same different time intervals as those aforementioned. The constant prices of different time intervals are interchangeable, because there are two different constant prices for one single year at each time interval. One is the constant price of the previous time interval, the other is the constant price of the following time interval. The coefficient between the two constant prices of the same year can be used to convert the different constant prices in two consecutive time intervals. Therefore, this allows for converting the constant prices of the previous time interval, and also that of the following time interval. For example, 1957 is the base year for the 1957 constant price index, and, at the same time, the 1952 constant price of 1957 is kept as a reference. The value added of industry in 1957 can be calculated into two constant prices by using the 1952 constant prices and the 1957 constant prices. If the value added of industry for 1956 according to the constant prices of 1952 is to be converted into 1957 constant prices, then the value added of industry for 1956 in 1957 constant prices = value added of industry for 1956 in 1952 constant prices x (value-added of industry for 1957 in 1957 constant prices/value-added of industry for 1957 in 1952 constant prices).[5] Similarly, if one wants to convert the value added in 1957 constant prices of industrial value-added for 1958 into value added in 1952 constant prices, the 1958 value added of industry in 1952 constant prices = the 1958 value added of industry in 1957 constant prices x (1957 value added of industry in 1952 constant prices/1957 value added of industry in 1957 constant prices).[6] The conversion of different constant prices of other years can be made by similar procedures. However, it must be noted that if more than two time intervals are involved, the different conversion coefficients between different constant prices have to be considered at the same time.

Further Improvement of Price Indexes

The establishment and improvement of price indexes need further strengthening in the calculation of GDP and its components in China. The SSB is making a great effort to solve the problems. The trial compilation of the industrial production index in progress will adopt the methods internationally used to evaluate the growth rate of industry. Thus, it will change the method of using growth rate of total output in constant prices to observe the change in the growth of industrial production.[7] At the same time, the producer price index of industrial products is adopted to replace the price index of total output of industry. Further improving the compilation of the producer price index of industrial products and of the purchase price index of raw materials makes possible using the double deflation method to deflate the value-added of industry. This is to replace the single deflation method currently using the deflation index from total industrial output to deflate industrial value-added. Moreover, the price index needed for the value-added of the service sector is being studied and estimated. In short, the further improvement of price indexes will promote the calculation of GDP and its components.

Depreciation of Fixed Assets

Fixed Assets

The formation of fixed assets in GDP calculated by the expenditure approach is estimated by the purchaser price of fixed assets, that is the market price of the fixed assets at the time of purchase. This also applies to the fixed assets which are produced for own use.

The prices of the stock of fixed assets are also appraised by the purchaser price of the fixed assets. Yet there is no re-evaluation. There are historical reasons and problems in practical operation for the absence of re-evaluation of the fixed assets. From a historical point of view, the prices of fixed assets have faced great changes only after the reform and opening policy implemented in 1978. Within the 28 years between the establishment of the PRC and the reform period (1949-1977), the prices of the fixed assets including construction materials for building houses and other buildings, and machinery and equipment were basically controlled by the state, and there was no great change. Therefore, there was not much meaning to re-evaluation of the fixed assets within this period. After the implementation of the reform and opening policy, as the pricing of production means was becoming decentralized, the prices of construction materials and machinery equipment increased much. Prices changed from the original state fixed prices to the double-track price system of state fixed prices and market prices, and then to the complete decentralization to market prices. However, from another aspect, there have also been problems of over-evaluation of the stock of fixed assets, such as the over-evaluation of the fixed assets of certain foreign invested enterprises and the over-extended use of fixed assets of a few small enterprises. Nevertheless, in general, the under-evaluation of the stock of fixed assets engendered by historically fixed prices and the lack of re-appraisal is much greater than the over-evaluation of fixed assets. Following the implementation of the re-evaluation of the fixed assets, the historically fixed price accounting of assets has led to the under-valuing of the capital stock, even during the period after the beginning of the reforms in 1978. In contrast, not a small portion of machinery and equipment, which under international standards would be considered to have become obsolete and in need of replacement, is still continuing to operate and produce or is still being transferred as productive assets from larger to smaller factories or to rural town-and-village enterprises.

In order to handle the reality of the increasing price of the fixed assets, China formally started compiling a price index for fixed asset investment in 1991. Although this price index has existed for just a very short time, and the categorization is also not very detailed, it has created an important condition for the re-evaluation of fixed assets. At present, another reason for the impossibility of re-evaluating such fixed assets relates to the difficulties of practical operation. We can only get data on the accumulation of fixed assets by the state-owned enterprises, and their categorization is too crude. The stock of fixed assets for other than the state-owned units cannot be completely known, and this poses a problem in the practical operation of re-appraisal of the whole nation's fixed assets.

Depreciation

According to the definition, the amount of depreciation depends on two factors: the value of the fixed asset and the rate of depreciation. Because of the absence of re-evaluation of accumulated fixed assets mentioned above, there is a problem of under-evaluation of depreciation based on the value of the fixed assets. On the other hand, a depreciation rate was set in 1993 by the state's finance departments to determine the limit of the service years of fixed assets. The depreciation rate of machinery equipment is generally about 10 percent, even if the durability of different equipment varies. Transportation and electronic equipment which have shorter lives are depreciated at about 20 percent. Tools and communication equipment for non-production use, which have longer lives are depreciated at about 5 percent. Houses and buildings for production uses are depreciated at between 3 to 10 percent, depending on whether they are subject to deterioration. On average, the depreciation rate of production equipment of enterprises is generally about 8 percent, and that for buildings is about 5 percent. As to the imputed depreciation of administrative units and private residential housing, the depreciation is set at about 4 percent at present. That is to say, the usable life of non-production buildings is about 25 years. This mainly refers to the general durability of buildings, which basically reflects the economic condition and income level of nowaday China. For the nation as a whole, the share of depreciation of fixed assets in GDP was about 14 percent in 1993.

By and large, there had been a general tendency for the depreciation rate to be biased towards the relatively low end before the reform and opening period. That is to say, because of the under-evaluation of fixed assets the depreciation allowances had tended to be lower. However, the situation has been ameliorated to a large extent since the beginning of the reforms.

It should be noted that, for the profitable enterprises, the problem of understatement of depreciation engendered by under-evaluation of the original value of fixed assets does not influence their total value-added. In the accounting calculation of enterprises, there is an offsetting relationship between costs and profits. Decreases in costs is reflected in business profits by the same amount. When we are calculating the value-added of an enterprise, the depreciation among the costs and business profits are both included. Depreciation refers to the depreciation of the fixed assets in the value-added; business profits refer to the operating surplus. The understated amount of depreciation actually increases business profits by the same amount and, thus, is taken into calculating the value-added. This does not affect total value-added, although it changes the composition of value-added.

Future Remedies and Improvements

In order to deal with the problem of re-evaluation of fixed assets, the state has prepared the compilation of the 1995 balance sheet for the whole nation. And in the forthcoming years, the price of all fixed assets will be re-evaluated when all conditions become ripe. It is hoped that the re-appraisal problem will be solved in the near future.

The fundamental solution for the understatement of depreciation of fixed assets lies with the re-evaluation of the original value of the fixed assets. This can be done after the completion of re-evaluation of all fixed assets for the whole nation. As for the rate of depreciation, the standard system set by the state is being implemented. This standard is set up according to the present purchase situation and utilization condition of fixed assets as well as the condition of technological updating and the level of economic development in China. In 1993 the Ministry of Finance newly promulgated that the time limits of fixed assets (depreciation rate) were to be generally raised by 20-30 percent on the basis of the original rates set in 1985. We believe that this adjustment is basically in accordance with the present status of China.

Housing Rent

The Rents of Public-owned Housing

In China, the general situations of housing rent tends to be biased downward; rent barely covers the cost of simple maintenance. This implies a tremendous implicit subsidy from government to the residents who are the tenants of housing provided by the state and state enterprises.

The fact is that the housing rent paid by the tenants falls short of the actual cost in terms of maintenance, repair and depreciation to a significant extent. A large portion of the housing space in the cities is owned by the state. Obviously, the SSB authorities are aware of the seriousness of the case. Some remedial measures have been taken to alleviate the enormous discrepancy.

In effect, the rents of public-owned houses are so low that they are just enough for simple maintenance of the houses. But as the housing reform progresses, housing rents have risen much in several steps in recent years. According to estimate figures, housing rents increased from the original 0.1 yuan/square meter to 0.3 yuan/square meter in the period from 1990 to 1994, and reached at 0.55 yuan/square meter in 1995. Thus, housing rents increased more than five-fold within 5 years.

The rent of the public-owned housing is calculated from the actual rental expenditure of residents. Rent reflects the realistic condition of low wages and low consumption of residents in China. Looking at the present state of income level and residence, the share of housing rent in total income is about 1/30 of income for a four-member family with a middle income level and residential housing condition.

Imputed Housing Rent

The imputed private housing rent of residents is calculated at about 4 percent of the original value of private residential housing in GDP accounting. It mainly includes imputed depreciation; in addition, it considers the costs of simple maintenance of the houses made by the residents. According to the actual condition of China, the vast territory, the large agricultural population, and imbalanced regional economic development, the market for rental housing does not yet exist in most of inland, economically undeveloped regions; this holds true even for the eastern region. There is little activity in the property market. Therefore, the imputed housing rent cannot be over-estimated, otherwise the economic status of China will be exaggerated. This is especially true for the villages of the huge agricultural regions. Since the rural economy has not yet diversified enough, if the value of real estate is over-estimated, the structure of the economic sectors in the GDP will be unreasonable and misrepresent the reality of the Chinese economy. In some coastal developed regions, economic growth and the growth of the mobile population promote the development of the housing and land market. Hence, the imputed rents in these regions are basically calculated according to market rents.

Future Improvement

In the near term, urban residential housing has to be improved further.

The direction of reform is roughly as follows: the size of commercial housing owned by individuals is to increase; the rent for public-owned housing is to be raised. In the estimation process, private residential housing will be calculated from imputed housing rent. As the amount of urban private residential housing increases, the proportion of imputed rent in GDP will be enlarged. As the rent of public-owned housing goes up, so will increase the proportion of rent in the value-added of real estate and the rental expenditure in personal consumption.

Subsidy Income

The Content of Subsidy Income

It is due to the characteristics of Chinese socialism that the treatment of subsidies has to be illuminated in some detail from distinct cases. In GDP calculation, subsidy income is treated as a negative tax. Subsidy refers to the financial expenditure given by the state to enterprises for their losses in production due to policy reasons. It includes the expenditure by the state to commercial and trading enterprises which incur losses due to the policy of lower selling price than purchasing price. It also includes the subsidies made to raw material and fuel producers for the loss engendered by the policy that products are to be sold at a restricted low price.

Education and medical and health organizations belong to non-profit institutions. The estimation of their total output and value-added is similar to that of the administration organizations. The current expenditures of these units are treated as the total output, from which the intermediate consumption is deducted to get the value-added. The source of fund for the current expenditures mainly comes from the public finance bureaus. Therefore, the expenditures of the state for education outlay and the subsidies for medical and health organizations are not treated as negative taxes.

The price subsidies to balance consumer price inflation from the state to individual residents are calculated as residents' income, but as value-added.

Future Improvement

As the reform and opening policy becomes more intense and the pricing policy is further reformed, price subsidies from the state will gradually become smaller. The original huge beneficiaries of financial subsidies, i.e., the grain and oil commercial enterprises, have planned to transform themselves from loss to profit makers within three years, thus altering the need to get twenty to thirty billion in yearly subsidies from the state. The foreign trade enterprises are also starting to earn profits rather than suffering losses as the institutional reform further progresses. The price subsidies for vegetables, coal, etc., are to be abandoned step by step. Therefore, as the state macroeconomic price policy proceeds, such subsidy income will be fundamentally changed in the future.

Inventories

According to the definition of inventory under the SNA, are included the raw materials bought by enterprises for production, semi-finished products in the course of production in the calculation period, and finished products that are put in warehouse for future sale.

Due to the feature of the supply-oriented planned economic system, some low quality products treated as inventories are, in fact, unsalable and should be eventually scrapped or sold out at a loss. However, under the Chinese socialism, they are still calculated at full value as current output of the state enterprises. As we know, the portion of unsalable inventories are usually written off in a market-oriented economy.

Thus, the by-product of such treatment of inventories under planning is that the accumulated stock is also reflected in the amount of total output, value-added, and inventory increases of total investment when the economic efficiency of enterprises is not very satisfactory. Nevertheless, when the economic condition is normal and the economic efficiency of enterprises is good, the inflated phenomenon of inventory accumulation should not be very noticeable.

The Valuation of the Agricultural Sector

In the pre-reform period, there was a general situation whereby the total output value of the agricultural sector was underreported and undervalued. In particular, the portion of obligatory crops, vegetables and livestock, etc., were particularly affected by the relatively low price stipulated by the government authorities.

Owing to the prolonged existence of the so-called "scissors difference" *(jian dao cha)* policy, the prices of agricultural products in terms of industrial products had been kept relatively low, thus leading to the problem of understating the value of the total output and value-added of agriculture. However, since 1979, the official procurement prices of sideline farm produce have been repeatedly raised by the government. Payments for above-quota sales of these products were also allowed to go beyond price quotas, while produce markets also spread quickly allowing for free exchange. Thus, the price of the total output and value-added of agriculture is no longer the official price, but the weighted average of three prices, i.e., the official procurement price, the above-quota procurement price, and the produce market price. Therefore, the total output and value-added of agriculture basically reflect the market prices of commercial crop products and are no longer affected by artificially low valuation.

As for the problem of the cost of basic construction and irrigation in rural regions before the reform period, based on "equalitarianism and cost dispersion" *(yi ping er diao)*, the labor force had been apportioned according to administrative decisions. For example, the labor cost incurred in the construction of water conservancy had been relatively low, and the construction price of irrigation and farmland had been very much undervalued. Today's large to medium scale irrigation projects are put out for bidding to engineering and construction teams. The contract price is the realistic market price; the phenomenon of under-valuation has been corrected.

The construction of housing by farmers has now changed from the past practice of free labor from relatives and close neighbors. Now, construction helpers are paid, and such labor costs are measured at the market price. Hence, the problem of under-valuation is no longer noticeable.

The Categorization of Industrial Output Value

Among all national economic sectors in China, the most satisfactory and complete statistics are those of the industrial sector. They include not only the output value of independent accounting, legal-person industrial enterprises, but also that of other small enterprises which are non independent accounting units subordinated to other non-industrial organizations, and possessing no legal-person status.

The self-employed (household) businesses that have less than eight employees are categorized into corresponding national economic sectors according to the nature of their economic activities. And the self-employed units engaged in industrial production are no exceptions.

However, the features of the Chinese socialist economy may easily stimulate a phenomenon called "policy from the top countermeasure from below." Thus, the scope and output value of the industrial sector may be distorted by the grassroots reporting units, since the enterprises in question may purposely misrepresent the submitted figures for reasons relating to specific state policies affecting them. For example, the profit rate stipulated and the amount of profits and tax to be submitted may be related to the output value reported. Similarly, the political motivation of some party members who are in charge of enterprises may distort the factual accounts simply because of the economic and political benefits involved.

The Service Sector

Collecting statistics for the service sector is a recent matter in China. Before the reform period, the service sector had not developed; moreover, because of its theoretical implications for the ideology of that time, the state had given the statistics of the material production sectors the pride of place and ignored those of the service sector. After the start of the economic reforms, especially since the beginning of the estimation of GDP, the value-added of the service sector has been accounted for. However, because of historical reasons, there does exist a lack of basic information about the service sector and lacunae in statistical work.

China has a large territory and a large variety of service industry. There is a significant portion of the service industry which is simply out of reach for the statistical reporting system, particularly services in the rural area. For example, the income of the self-employed such as domestic servants, hawkers, repair traders, restaurant owners, laundry or bathhouse keepers, child care service providers, the "informal" transport service providers, like pedicabs in both urban and rural areas, etc., has all been under-reported. Moreover, enterprises provide services to their employees and employee families, such as education, health care, nursery care, entertainment, etc., either free of charge or at extremely low price. Their output value is probably being under-reported or simply out of the statistical scope of national income accounting.

Since the 1990s, the tertiary sector has accelerated its intensive and extensive development. In order to fully reflect this situation of the national economy and accurately calculate the value-added of the service sector, in 1993 the state initiated a national census of the tertiary industries. The scope of the census included all industries of the service sector, within which both the newly emerging industries and the traditional service sectors were included; the census also covered the tertiary organizations attached to various enterprises. The data obtained from the census indicated that the value-added of the tertiary sector was about 30 percent more than that obtained from standard statistical work. The state and local governments have already adjusted the original value-added statistics of the service sector according to the information obtained from the census. It goes without saying, some further effort has to be put in in order to accurately reflect the present condition of the tertiary sector.

Notes

1. As a matter of fact, the ratio of material consumption to total output value of society appeared to be 42%~43.5% in 1952-1957; 48.7% in 1962; 49.3%~56.2% in 1970-1979; 56.8%~61.8% in 1980-1989; and 62.2%~64.5% in 1990-1992. See also *Statistical Yearbook of China 1993*, p. 64. Moreover, the general price level of

intermediate input was lower than that of finished products under the Chinese socialist planning system.

2. A simple example illustrates the Chinese case.

	Base Year		Current Year	
	P_{oi}	Q_{oi}	P_{ni}	Q_{ni}
Industrial product (i=1)	20	1	25	50
Agricultural product (i=2)	15	10	30	40

The Laspeyres price index $L_p = \frac{\sum_i P_{ni}Q_{oi}}{\sum_i P_{oi}Q_{oi}} = \frac{25 \times 1 + 30 \times 10}{20 \times 1 + 15 \times 10} = \frac{350}{170} = 206\%$

The Paasche price index $P_p = \frac{\sum_i P_{ni}Q_{ni}}{\sum_i P_{oi}Q_{ni}} = \frac{25 \times 50 + 30 \times 40}{20 \times 50 + 15 \times 40} = \frac{2450}{1600} = 153\%$

The developing characteristic of the Chinese economy appears to be a faster-growing output of the industrial sector with a relative slower growth of price level vs a slower-growing output of the agricultural sector with a relative faster growth of price level. As calculated above, $P_p<L_p$.

3. Following the above case,

The Laspeyres quantity index $L_Q = \frac{\sum_i P_{oi}Q_{ni}}{\sum_i P_{oi}Q_{oi}} = \frac{20 \times 50 + 15 \times 40}{20 \times 1 + 15 \times 10} = \frac{1600}{170} = 941\%$

The Paasche quantity index $P_Q = \frac{\sum_i P_{ni}Q_{ni}}{\sum_i P_{ni}Q_{oi}} = \frac{25 \times 50 + 30 \times 40}{20 \times 1 + 30 \times 10} = \frac{2450}{325} = 754\%$

It is very obvious that $L_Q>P_Q$.

4. Because a huge amount of manpower and resources was necessary for the compilation of constant prices, it then became impossible to make one compilation per five-year plan.

5. In a more precise expression, the formula is

$$\sum_i P_{57i}Q_{56i} = \sum_i P_{52i}Q_{56i} \cdot \frac{\sum_i P_{57i}Q_{57i}}{\sum_i P_{52i}Q_{57i}}$$

It is expected that there arises from some offsetting effect of Q_{57i} via $\Sigma P_{57i}Q_{57i}/$

$\Sigma P_{52i}Q_{57i}$ and that of P_{52i} via $\Sigma P_{52i}Q_{56i}$ / $\Sigma P_{52i}Q_{57i}$ so as to get the index $\Sigma P_{57i}Q_{56i}$. In the formula,

$$\left(\frac{\Sigma P_{57i}Q_{57i}}{\Sigma P_{52i}Q_{57i}}\right)$$

can be regarded as a conversion coefficient.

6. By the same token, the formula is

$$\sum_i P_{52i}Q_{58i} = \sum_i P_{57i}Q_{58i} \cdot \frac{\sum_i P_{52i}Q_{57i}}{\sum_i P_{57i}Q_{57i}}$$

7. The SSB is trying out the compilation of the industrial production index by the following formula

$$K = \frac{\sum_i \frac{Q_{ti}}{Q_{t-1i}} P_{oi}Q_{oi}}{\sum_i P_{oi}Q_{oi}}$$

where K : total index or category index

$$\sum_i \frac{Q_{ti}}{Q_{t-1i}} : \text{output index}$$

P_{oi} Q_{oi}: output value of base year as weight.

Taking value-added as the fixed weight, the base period will be chosen by the year of industrial survey (every five years) so that it will also be changed every five years. There are totally 904 industrial products selected as the sample for compiling the yearly industrial production index, and some 400 products for the monthly index purpose. The compilation work will proceed in an all-round way in 1997.

References (in Chinese unless otherwise indicated)

Commission of the European Communities, International Monetary Fund, Organization for Economic Co-operation and Development, United Nations and World Bank, *System of National Accounts, 1993*, prepared under the auspices of the Inter-Secretariat Group on National Accounts, Brussels/Luxembourg, New York, Paris, Washington, D.C. 1993 (in English).

Ministry of Finance, *The Newly Promulgated Financial System of Industry and Tertiary Industries*, Beijing: China's Audit Publishing House, 1993.

Nationwide Tertiary Industry Survey Office, *The First Census of the Tertiary Industry in China, Summary Statistics (1991-1992)*, Beijing: China's Statistical Publishing House, 1995.

Qian Bohai (ed.), *Statistics of the National Economy*, Beijing: China's Statistical Publishing House, 1995.

PART TWO

The National and Provincial Statistics

Whole Nation

Year	u1'	u1	u1a	u1b	u1b1	u1b2	u1c	u1c1	u1c2	u1c3	u1c4	u1c5	u1c6	u1c7	u1c8
1952	679.0	679.0	342.9	141.8	119.8	22.0	194.3	29.0	80.3	14.0	2.0	11.0	14.0	14.0	30.0
1953	824.0	824.0	378.0	192.5	163.5	29.0	253.5	35.0	115.5	15.0	2.0	11.0	13.0	16.0	46.0
1954	859.0	859.0	392.0	211.7	184.7	27.0	255.3	38.0	120.3	15.0	3.0	11.0	13.0	17.0	38.0
1955	910.0	910.0	421.0	222.2	191.2	31.0	266.8	39.0	119.8	16.0	3.0	13.0	17.0	18.0	41.0
1956	1028.0	1028.0	443.9	280.7	224.7	56.0	303.4	46.0	131.4	18.0	4.0	13.0	16.0	24.0	51.0
1957	1068.0	1068.0	430.0	317.0	271.0	46.0	321.0	49.0	133.0	20.0	4.0	15.0	17.0	29.0	54.0
1958	1307.0	1307.0	445.9	483.5	414.5	69.0	377.6	71.0	136.6	35.0	5.0	23.0	16.0	41.0	50.0
1959	1439.0	1439.0	383.8	615.5	538.5	77.0	439.7	94.0	145.7	42.0	7.0	37.0	19.0	44.0	51.0
1960	1457.0	1457.0	340.7	648.2	568.2	80.0	468.1	104.0	133.1	46.0	9.0	61.0	18.0	46.0	51.0
1961	1220.0	1220.0	441.1	388.9	362.1	26.8	390.0	69.2	110.8	27.0	8.0	61.0	20.0	41.0	53.0
1962	1149.3	1149.3	453.1	359.3	325.4	33.9	336.9	57.4	80.5	26.0	8.0	48.0	21.0	39.0	57.0
1963	1233.3	1233.3	497.5	407.6	365.6	42.0	328.2	55.0	76.1	28.0	9.1	36.0	22.0	42.0	60.0
1964	1454.0	1454.0	559.0	513.5	461.1	52.4	381.5	58.4	94.0	29.0	11.1	59.0	20.0	47.0	63.0
1965	1716.1	1716.1	651.1	602.2	546.5	55.7	462.8	77.4	118.3	31.0	10.1	86.0	24.0	52.0	64.0
1966	1868.0	1868.0	702.2	709.5	648.6	60.9	456.3	85.1	148.1	32.0	11.1	35.0	25.0	53.0	67.0
1967	1773.9	1773.9	714.2	602.8	544.9	57.9	456.9	72.3	153.5	33.0	10.1	41.0	29.0	53.0	65.0
1968	1723.1	1723.1	726.3	537.3	490.3	47.0	459.5	70.5	138.9	34.0	10.1	48.0	31.0	56.0	71.0
1969	1937.9	1937.9	736.2	689.1	626.1	63.0	512.6	84.9	163.6	36.0	10.1	54.0	33.0	56.0	75.0
1970	2252.7	2252.7	793.3	912.2	828.1	84.1	547.2	100.2	178.1	36.0	11.1	57.0	34.0	56.0	74.8
1971	2426.4	2426.4	826.3	1022.8	926.6	96.2	577.3	108.4	178.3	38.0	12.1	66.0	35.0	58.0	81.5
1972	2518.1	2518.1	827.4	1084.2	989.9	94.3	606.5	118.0	194.3	40.0	12.1	52.9	38.0	66.0	85.2
1973	2720.9	2720.9	907.5	1173.0	1072.5	100.5	640.4	125.5	211.0	42.0	12.2	52.8	37.0	69.0	90.9
1974	2789.9	2789.9	945.2	1192.0	1083.6	108.4	652.7	126.1	206.6	46.0	13.2	56.8	39.0	71.0	94.0
1975	2997.3	2997.3	971.1	1370.5	1244.9	125.6	655.7	141.6	175.8	48.0	14.3	61.8	42.1	72.0	100.1
1976	2943.7	2943.7	967.0	1337.2	1204.6	132.6	639.5	139.6	147.2	53.0	14.3	62.8	44.1	75.0	103.5
1977	3201.9	3201.9	942.1	1509.1	1372.4	136.7	750.7	156.9	213.8	58.0	15.3	69.8	46.1	83.0	107.8
1978	3624.1	3624.1	1018.4	1745.2	1607.0	138.2	860.5	172.8	265.5	66.0	17.3	77.8	49.1	95.0	117.0
1979	4038.2	4038.2	1258.9	1913.5	1769.7	143.8	865.8	184.2	220.2	76.0	20.4	76.8	52.1	110.0	126.1
1980	4517.8	4517.8	1359.4	2192.0	1996.5	195.5	966.4	205.0	213.6	85.0	26.4	86.5	57.1	138.0	154.8
1981	4860.3	4862.4	1545.6	2255.5	2048.4	207.1	1061.3	211.1	255.7	90.9	28.5	92.5	58.1	151.0	173.5
1982	5301.8	5294.7	1761.6	2383.0	2162.3	220.7	1150.1	236.7	198.6	108.2	32.3	133.7	63.2	178.0	199.4
1983	5957.4	5934.5	1960.8	2646.2	2375.6	270.6	1327.5	264.9	231.4	122.6	34.9	174.4	68.2	203.0	228.1
1984	7206.7	7171.0	2295.5	3105.7	2789.0	316.7	1769.8	327.1	412.4	147.4	38.2	240.0	89.2	254.0	261.5
1985	8989.1	8964.4	2541.6	3866.6	3448.7	417.9	2556.2	406.9	878.4	191.8	40.9	307.4	116.1	307.0	307.7
1986	10201.4	10202.2	2763.9	4492.7	3967.0	525.7	2945.6	475.6	943.2	223.7	44.1	423.7	157.8	336.0	341.5
1987	11954.5	11962.5	3204.3	5251.6	4585.8	665.8	3506.6	544.9	1159.3	269.2	49.1	537.7	198.8	367.8	379.8
1988	14922.3	14928.3	3831.0	6587.2	5777.2	810.0	4510.1	661.0	1618.0	329.1	55.9	703.0	241.6	470.0	431.5
1989	16917.8	16909.2	4228.0	7278.0	6484.0	794.0	5403.2	786.0	1687.0	389.8	62.2	1164.0	283.4	543.0	487.8
1990	18598.4	18547.9	5017.0	7717.4	6858.0	859.4	5813.5	1147.5	1419.7	403.8	69.1	1234.5	325.3	614.3	599.3
1991	21662.5	21617.8	5288.6	9102.2	8087.1	1015.1	7227.0	1409.7	2087.0	543.4	76.2	1288.1	368.2	725.7	728.7
1992	26651.9	26638.1	5800.0	11699.5	10284.5	1415.0	9138.6	1681.8	2735.0	724.2	98.5	1601.0	521.1	878.3	898.7
1993	34560.5	34634.4	6882.1	16428.5	14143.8	2284.7	11323.8	2123.2	3090.7	1033.5	147.7	2057.0	640.7	1124.4	1106.6
1994	46670.0	46759.4	9457.2	22372.2	19359.6	3012.6	14930.0	2685.9	4050.4	1395.6	197.2	2767.2	870.3	1525.1	1438.4
1995	57494.9	58478.1	11993.0	28537.9	24718.3	3819.6	17947.2	3054.7	4932.3	1791.0	254.0	3482.8	1058.6	1755.3	1618.5

Note: The difference between GNP and GDP is net foreign factor income. Net foreign factor income of 1995 is inconsistent with that of previous years due to coverage changed.

Year	u1d	u1e1	u1e2	u1e3	u1e4	u1e5	u1e6	u1e7	u1e8	u1e9	u1e10	u1e11	u1e12	u2'	u2
1952	119														
1953	142													115.6	115.6
1954	144													104.2	104.2
1955	150													106.8	106.8
1956	165													115.0	115.0
1957	168													105.1	105.1
1958	200													121.3	121.3
1959	216													108.8	108.8
1960	218													99.7	99.7
1961	185													72.7	72.7
1962	173													94.4	94.4
1963	181													110.2	110.2
1964	208													118.3	118.3
1965	240													117.0	117.0
1966	254													110.7	110.7
1967	235													94.3	94.3
1968	222													95.9	95.9
1969	243													115.9	116.9
1970	275													119.4	119.4
1971	288													107.0	107.0
1972	292													103.8	103.8
1973	309													107.9	107.9
1974	310													102.3	102.3
1975	327													108.7	108.7
1976	316													98.4	98.4
1977	339													107.6	107.6
1978	379													111.7	111.7
1979	417													107.6	107.6
1980	460													107.8	107.8
1981	489													105.2	105.2
1982	525													109.3	109.1
1983	580													111.1	110.9
1984	692													115.3	115.2
1985	853													113.2	113.5
1986	956													108.5	108.8
1987	1104													111.5	111.6
1988	1355													111.3	111.3
1989	1512													104.2	104.1
1990	1634	45.0	65.0	1038.3	109.2	1419.7	1234.5	325.3	327.9	174.0	393.8	81.5	599.3	104.2	103.8
1991	1879	53.6	76.8	1261.7	148.0	2087.0	1288.1	368.2	447.3	215.2	454.9	97.5	728.7	109.1	109.2
1992	2287	66.6	98.0	1488.0	193.8	2735.0	1601.0	521.1	599.7	264.0	547.7	125.0	898.7	114.1	114.2
1993	2939	76.5	134.5	1823.5	299.7	3090.7	2057.0	640.7	899.2	333.7	709.9	151.8	1106.6	113.1	113.5
1994	3923	101.3	191.2	2204.3	481.6	4050.4	2767.2	870.3	1200.5	433.8	977.6	213.4	1438.4	112.6	112.6
1995	4854	115.8	253.3	2378.0	676.7	4932.3	3482.8	1058.6	1546.4	483.2	1124.5	277.1	1618.5	109.0	110.5

Year	u2a	u2b	u2b1	u2b2	u2c	u2c1	u2c2	u2c3	u2c4	u2c5	u2c6	u2c7	u2c8	u2d	u2e1
1952															
1953	101.9	135.8	135.7	136.4	127.3	124.1	138.0	103.6	100.0	97.3	95.0	110.7	148.7	113.1	
1954	101.7	115.7	119.3	96.7	99.4	110.8	101.8	97.9	145.0	98.1	100.0	104.5	81.2	101.8	
1955	107.9	107.6	106.6	113.8	104.6	102.5	99.9	105.6	96.6	117.1	133.8	104.9	106.9	104.5	
1956	104.7	134.5	128.6	170.0	114.1	121.8	108.5	112.7	139.3	100.0	97.8	134.1	124.0	112.7	
1957	103.1	108.0	111.4	92.9	104.8	107.2	98.9	108.9	100.0	115.4	110.3	119.3	104.6	102.4	
1958	100.4	152.9	153.4	150.0	117.9	146.7	103.6	174.5	125.0	150.0	92.4	140.7	92.0	118.3	
1959	84.1	125.8	129.1	105.7	115.2	131.0	105.9	118.9	136.0	160.1	112.7	106.4	101.2	106.7	
1960	83.6	105.6	106.1	101.4	104.8	110.4	91.2	106.5	126.5	160.3	91.0	101.2	97.2	99.5	
1961	101.4	57.9	61.0	34.6	74.3	65.0	73.0	50.5	77.9	86.3	109.9	77.4	89.8	73.4	
1962	104.5	89.2	86.7	123.8	90.8	81.1	96.0	92.8	97.0	75.8	103.4	92.1	103.6	93.6	
1963	111.3	114.5	113.3	125.9	104.4	98.4	108.2	114.5	118.5	78.6	107.1	114.1	111.6	107.5	
1964	112.9	125.6	125.6	125.6	115.5	105.4	113.2	107.6	126.0	171.1	91.8	115.7	108.9	115.5	
1965	109.7	124.2	125.8	110.6	115.8	134.5	99.5	109.8	93.8	150.5	121.1	113.6	104.3	114.3	
1966	107.2	122.4	123.8	109.4	98.2	110.3	120.4	103.6	111.0	40.8	104.6	102.3	105.0	107.7	
1967	101.9	85.7	84.9	95.0	100.5	86.0	104.1	103.8	91.1	117.4	116.7	100.8	97.7	91.9	
1968	98.4	90.8	91.8	81.1	100.6	97.7	90.7	103.0	100.0	116.7	108.6	105.6	109.3	93.4	
1969	100.8	133.1	133.0	134.5	113.3	122.7	119.2	107.1	102.2	114.5	108.0	101.4	106.8	113.7	
1970	107.7	134.8	135.2	130.4	107.1	116.8	109.4	100.0	110.6	106.0	103.5	100.2	100.1	116.1	
1971	101.9	112.3	112.3	112.1	105.8	108.3	99.9	106.4	109.9	117.0	102.1	104.1	109.6	104.1	
1972	99.1	106.7	107.6	97.9	105.0	109.6	108.8	105.5	107.4	80.8	107.2	113.7	102.9	101.2	
1973	109.0	108.3	108.8	103.4	105.5	106.3	109.0	104.2	99.2	97.4	97.6	104.1	107.8	105.4	
1974	104.1	101.4	101.0	106.2	101.6	100.3	98.0	109.0	100.8	107.4	105.5	102.5	102.6	100.2	
1975	102.0	115.8	116.0	113.8	104.9	111.4	99.9	104.4	108.4	109.1	106.8	101.1	106.3	106.8	
1976	98.2	97.5	96.9	104.3	100.4	98.4	96.3	110.0	99.3	101.8	103.4	103.8	102.6	96.9	
1977	97.8	113.3	114.4	101.7	109.5	112.6	113.4	107.2	105.0	109.6	103.8	108.6	102.1	106.2	
1978	104.1	115.0	116.4	99.4	113.7	108.9	123.1	113.1	112.2	109.8	105.7	113.0	107.7	110.2	
1979	106.1	108.2	108.7	102.0	107.8	107.7	108.8	112.7	115.1	97.2	104.1	114.2	105.4	106.1	
1980	98.5	113.6	112.7	126.7	105.9	105.7	98.7	101.4	112.0	106.6	107.9	119.2	113.7	106.5	
1981	107.0	101.9	101.7	103.2	110.4	101.9	130.0	103.8	103.0	104.3	96.5	106.5	110.7	103.9	
1982	111.5	105.6	105.8	103.4	113.0	111.7	103.9	117.7	108.8	144.6	109.1	115.6	110.4	107.5	
1983	108.3	110.4	109.7	117.1	115.2	110.0	121.9	111.5	104.1	127.0	105.2	112.4	112.6	109.3	
1984	112.9	114.5	114.9	110.9	119.4	115.0	121.5	115.9	105.2	131.1	127.7	122.0	111.1	113.7	
1985	101.8	118.6	118.2	122.2	118.3	113.5	128.9	121.9	104.9	116.9	125.0	112.0	109.2	111.9	
1986	103.3	110.2	109.6	115.9	112.1	112.8	110.6	108.6	102.4	131.6	125.9	101.7	103.9	107.2	
1987	104.7	113.7	113.2	117.9	114.4	110.0	113.5	118.6	108.0	123.3	129.3	107.0	110.0	109.8	
1988	102.5	114.5	115.3	108.0	113.2	113.3	114.3	111.2	105.3	119.5	112.7	110.9	106.7	109.5	
1989	103.1	103.8	105.1	91.6	105.4	104.7	91.7	102.0	103.0	125.9	115.9	106.9	105.1	102.5	
1990	107.3	103.2	103.4	101.2	102.3	108.6	95.2	99.5	102.0	101.9	106.2	103.7	108.0	102.3	
1991	102.4	113.9	114.4	109.6	108.8	111.2	104.5	125.3	102.5	102.3	112.0	110.2	114.5	107.7	110.7
1992	104.7	121.2	121.2	121.0	112.4	110.5	113.1	118.9	115.0	108.0	134.7	108.4	109.6	112.8	110.4
1993	104.7	119.9	120.1	118.0	110.7	112.4	106.6	115.3	118.9	110.9	110.8	113.4	108.7	112.2	102.2
1994	104.0	118.4	118.9	113.7	109.6	109.5	107.7	110.2	108.3	109.4	112.0	113.2	108.5	111.4	110.3
1995	105.0	113.9	114.0	112.4	108.4	112.0	105.9	106.4	105.8	108.5	112.4	107.7	106.3	109.3	108.7

Year	u2e2	u2e3	u2e4	u2e5	u2e6	u2e7	u2e8	u2e9	u2e10	u2e11	u2e12	u3	u3a	u3b	u3c
1952												692.2	546.3	153.7	-7.8
1953												834.3	644.4	198.3	-8.4
1954												878.3	654.1	226.9	-2.7
1955												934.9	722.3	221.5	-8.9
1956												1034.2	772.6	257.6	4.0
1957												1101.9	816.4	230.0	5.5
1958												1291.2	852.6	432.0	6.6
1959												1451.3	821.5	621.7	8.1
1960												1508.0	932.6	575.0	0.4
1961												1275.2	995.1	274.6	5.5
1962												1176.4	985.7	178.1	12.6
1963												1293.1	1014.3	265.3	13.5
1964												1441.8	1078.6	350.3	12.9
1965												1629.2	1158.6	462.1	8.5
1966												1827.3	1251.3	569.8	6.2
1967												1707.7	1275.7	425.7	6.3
1968												1708.7	1269.1	432.2	7.4
1969												1857.7	1359.4	485.9	12.4
1970												2207.0	1459.7	744.9	2.4
1971												2392.5	1557.9	819.0	15.6
1972												2453.8	1644.3	791.1	18.4
1973												2669.6	1751.3	903.5	14.8
1974												2738.7	1809.6	936.1	-7.0
1975												2950.4	1887.4	1062.3	0.7
1976												2968.3	1969.5	990.1	8.7
1977												3166.0	2057.8	1098.1	10.1
1978												3605.6	2239.1	1377.9	-11.4
1979												4073.9	2619.4	1474.2	-19.7
1980												4551.3	2976.1	1590.0	-14.8
1981												4901.4	3309.1	1581.0	11.3
1982												5489.2	3637.9	1760.2	91.1
1983												6076.3	4020.5	2005.0	50.8
1984												7164.4	4694.5	2468.6	1.3
1985												8792.1	5773.0	3386.0	-366.9
1986												10132.8	6542.0	3846.0	-255.2
1987												11784.0	7451.2	4322.0	10.8
1988												14704.0	9360.1	5495.0	-151.1
1989												16466.0	10556.5	6095.0	-185.5
1990												18319.5	11365.2	6444.0	510.3
1991	110.9	108.6	135.5	104.5	102.3	112.0	126.8	114.9	107.8	112.0	114.5	21280.4	13145.9	7517.0	617.5
1992	115.1	107.9	130.3	113.1	108.0	134.7	119.3	109.4	108.0	115.3	109.6	25863.6	15952.1	9636.0	275.5
1993	111.2	105.9	153.3	106.6	110.9	110.8	118.9	111.8	114.9	106.9	108.7	34500.6	20182.1	14998.0	-679.5
1994	116.3	107.1	120.1	107.7	109.4	112.0	108.3	108.2	115.0	117.9	108.5	47110.9	27216.2	19260.6	634.1
1995	105.4	105.0	139.0	105.9	108.5	112.4	105.8	106.4	108.0	110.5	106.3	59404.9	34529.4	23877.0	998.5

Year	u3c1	u3c2	u4a	u4a1	u4a1a	u4a1b	u4a1c	u4a1d	u4a2	u4a2b	u4a2c	u4a2d	u4b	u5	u5a
1952			453.0	312.2	198.1	95.5	18.6		140.8	125.9	14.9		93.3		
1953			529.2	346.7	209.6	117.6	19.5		182.5	164.0	18.5		115.2	112.5	109.8
1954			550.0	363.2	210.4	131.8	21.0		186.8	166.0	20.8		104.1	101.3	103.0
1955			602.6	406.2	237.0	145.2	24.0		196.4	172.7	23.7		119.7	110.6	109.2
1956			646.8	414.2	235.9	153.0	25.3		232.6	201.3	31.3		125.8	106.5	107.2
1957			686.6	430.5	243.8	160.2	26.5		256.1	220.8	35.3		129.8	105.1	105.3
1958			724.0	454.2	231.3	194.9	28.0		269.8	230.3	39.5		128.6	103.4	104.1
1959			691.2	362.6	122.7	207.7	32.2		328.6	280.3	48.3		130.3	94.8	93.4
1960			741.7	370.2	135.1	202.4	32.7		371.5	311.2	60.3		190.9	102.9	94.8
1961			816.7	445.2	233.5	175.7	36.0		371.5	308.0	63.5		178.4	91.3	92.7
1962			838.7	486.4	255.6	194.1	36.7		352.3	294.4	57.9		147.0	99.7	104.5
1963			844.2	513.3	257.0	221.0	35.3		330.9	280.6	50.3		170.1	112.1	112.1
1964			889.6	562.9	280.5	245.9	36.5		326.7	276.5	50.2		189.0	109.2	108.1
1965			951.5	608.3	321.0	247.2	40.1		343.2	292.0	51.2		207.1	112.2	112.4
1966			1021.1	664.5	356.0	267.5	41.0		356.6	310.5	46.1		230.2	107.2	106.1
1967			1081.5	710.5	374.0	291.6	44.9		371.0	325.5	45.5		194.2	101.7	105.9
1968			1076.6	704.0	385.0	272.0	47.0		372.6	329.8	42.8		192.5	99.2	99.3
1969			1127.7	741.1	393.0	298.7	49.4		386.6	341.0	45.6		231.7	108.2	105.5
1970			1206.8	802.2	432.0	322.8	47.4		404.6	350.9	53.7		252.9	107.3	106.9
1971			1262.0	842.7	455.0	333.7	54.0		419.3	365.3	54.0		295.9	106.4	104.1
1972			1334.2	865.2	457.6	350.9	56.7		469.0	409.8	59.2		310.1	105.3	105.4
1973			1432.5	936.6	496.0	381.9	58.7		495.9	434.5	61.4		318.8	106.2	107.1
1974			1467.0	954.3	486.2	407.4	60.7		512.7	448.4	64.3		342.6	103.0	102.0
1975			1528.5	987.0	494.7	429.5	62.8		541.5	470.2	71.3		358.9	104.1	104.0
1976			1588.5	1011.4	499.3	442.8	69.3		577.1	500.7	76.4		381.0	104.2	103.7
1977			1647.8	1021.3	478.1	472.2	71.0		626.5	539.7	86.8		410.0	103.6	102.7
1978			1759.1	1092.4	516.1	499.7	31.0	45.6	666.7	585.4	64.7	16.6	480.0	107.8	105.5
1979			2005.4	1259.7	567.5	612.6	31.6	48.0	745.7	654.0	73.2	18.5	614.0	112.1	108.0
1980			2317.1	1427.3	565.6	772.7	36.0	53.0	889.8	784.2	84.0	21.6	659.0	108.2	110.1
1981	319.7	308.4	2604.1	1630.8	638.7	899.5	38.3	54.3	973.3	857.0	92.0	24.3	705.0	108.7	109.4
1982	448.8	357.7	2867.9	1826.5	691.0	1030.0	44.5	61.0	1041.4	916.6	99.0	25.8	770.0	108.4	108.1
1983	460.0	409.2	3182.5	2063.4	754.3	1190.3	51.1	67.7	1119.1	983.7	109.0	26.4	838.0	109.2	109.4
1984	623.7	622.4	3674.5	2385.7	802.0	1444.6	63.4	75.7	1288.8	1124.9	129.1	34.8	1020.0	114.8	113.1
1985	829.3	1196.2	4589.0	2921.5	858.0	1889.0	80.7	93.8	1667.5	1472.0	155.3	40.2	1184.0	114.2	114.7
1986	1028.3	1283.5	5175.0	3210.0	911.0	2094.0	90.9	114.1	1965.0	1743.0	174.4	47.6	1367.0	107.4	106.0
1987	1458.0	1447.2	5961.2	3630.1	991.0	2383.1	122.5	133.5	2331.1	2058.9	215.2	57.0	1490.0	107.0	107.3
1988	1708.9	1860.0	7633.1	4473.2	1125.0	3010.2	175.5	162.5	3159.9	2742.4	347.7	69.8	1727.0	108.0	109.2
1989	1801.0	1986.5	8523.5	4919.8	1250.0	3261.5	225.5	182.8	3603.7	3057.9	449.3	96.5	2033.0	101.5	101.0
1990	2744.6	2234.3	9113.2	5129.1	1390.0	3263.9	268.2	207.0	3984.1	3248.2	622.4	113.5	2252.0	105.9	104.9
1991	3507.6	2890.1	10315.9	5639.8	1460.0	3589.6	308.0	282.2	4676.1	3767.6	759.0	149.5	2830.0	111.7	109.8
1992	4346.7	4071.1	12459.8	6571.6	1620.0	4223.0	430.7	297.9	5888.2	4622.2	1044.0	222.0	3492.3	114.2	114.3
1993	4987.3	5666.8	15682.4	7867.2	1935.2	4852.2	658.7	421.1	7815.2	6148.5	1346.9	319.8	4499.7	109.3	109.4
1994	10250.0	9615.8	21230.0	10491.3	2680.0	6419.0	919.2	473.1	10738.7	8346.7	1894.0	498.0	5986.2	108.0	107.7
1995	12295.5	11297.0	27838.9	13663.6	4148.2	7439.3	1411.2	664.9	14175.3	10920.3	2630.6	624.4	6690.5	109.2	110.1

Year	u5a1	u5a2	u5b	u6	u6a	u6b	u7	u7a	u7b	u8a	u8b	u9	u9a	u9b
1952				80	65	154				80.7	73.0			
1953	104.2	122.5	125.7	91	72	188	107.5	102.8	115.1	115.3	83.0	129.9	144.6	113.7
1954	104.0	101.3	93.9	92	73	191	100.6	101.2	100.7	140.9	86.0	113.9	123.0	101.2
1955	111.3	105.0	117.5	99	80	198	106.8	108.7	103.7	145.5	76.0	101.5	107.9	90.5
1956	101.7	118.6	103.3	104	81	212	105.0	101.3	107.0	219.6	38.0	120.6	151.4	57.9
1957	104.0	107.7	104.3	108	82	222	102.7	102.0	102.4	187.0	93.0	109.4	88.9	213.2
1958	103.2	105.7	99.3	111	86	212	101.6	102.5	95.8	333.0	99.0	154.2	177.4	107.5
1959	79.8	115.8	102.0	104	70	224	91.7	80.8	100.8	435.7	186.0	135.6	120.7	185.0
1960	93.6	96.1	143.9	111	73	236	94.7	95.5	89.4	473.0	102.0	92.3	108.9	55.2
1961	101.5	83.0	86.6	124	87	248	93.7	101.3	87.2	227.6	47.0	48.1	49.0	44.2
1962	109.6	97.6	82.5	126	93	248	103.7	106.9	102.8	175.1	3.0	59.0	71.7	0.0
1963	111.8	112.7	112.1	124	94	240	109.4	107.5	116.3	215.3	50.0	143.4	117.3	100.0
1964	110.6	104.2	114.3	127	99	253	105.6	105.8	111.3	290.3	60.0	135.4	137.7	125.0
1965	112.7	112.1	111.1	133	104	259	109.8	110.0	109.3	350.1	112.0	140.1	124.7	215.0
1966	107.0	104.5	111.9	139	111	262	103.1	104.1	101.6	406.8	163.0	125.2	118.5	144.4
1967	107.2	103.9	84.5	143	115	268	103.3	104.2	102.4	323.7	102.0	76.1	79.3	63.6
1968	98.7	100.5	98.6	139	111	266	96.8	95.9	99.1	300.2	132.0	106.2	96.0	133.6
1969	106.2	104.4	122.0	142	113	272	102.7	103.0	102.9	406.9	79.0	113.7	138.7	65.0
1970	108.1	104.9	109.2	147	119	281	104.0	104.8	103.5	545.9	199.0	153.4	134.2	233.3
1971	104.3	103.8	117.3	150	121	287	101.3	101.2	102.2	603.0	216.0	109.2	109.3	109.0
1972	102.3	111.4	105.0	155	121	315	102.8	99.7	109.4	622.1	169.0	95.7	101.9	73.8
1973	107.9	105.6	102.4	162	128	325	104.7	105.4	103.3	664.5	239.0	114.4	106.7	141.5
1974	101.5	102.9	107.4	163	128	334	99.9	99.1	102.2	748.1	188.0	103.2	112.4	73.5
1975	103.4	105.2	104.4	167	130	349	102.2	101.5	103.9	880.3	182.0	112.1	116.3	95.3
1976	102.3	106.3	106.5	171	131	365	102.1	100.7	104.6	865.1	125.0	93.1	97.6	72.1
1977	101.1	105.6	107.2	175	130	390	101.3	99.8	103.7	911.1	187.0	109.5	103.8	145.5
1978	105.5	105.7	116.9	184	138	405	104.1	104.3	103.3	1073.9	304.0	125.1	117.2	160.4
1979	106.9	109.8	126.8	207	158	434	106.5	106.1	105.2	1151.2	323.0	103.4	104.9	93.4
1980	109.5	111.0	102.6	236	178	496	108.7	108.8	106.3	1318.0	272.0	105.5	111.1	85.1
1981	111.0	106.8	106.4	262	199	562	108.0	108.4	110.6	1253.0	328.0	96.8	92.1	119.5
1982	110.1	104.8	109.6	284	221	576	106.5	109.1	100.4	1493.2	267.0	108.8	116.5	80.0
1983	111.7	105.3	108.8	311	246	603	107.8	110.4	102.5	1709.0	296.0	111.1	111.7	107.7
1984	113.6	112.2	120.9	354	283	662	111.6	113.0	107.0	2125.6	343.0	118.9	119.5	115.0
1985	114.2	115.6	112.6	437	347	802	113.1	114.1	108.2	2641.0	745.0	128.5	115.9	202.5
1986	103.8	110.1	112.0	485	376	920	104.4	102.5	107.3	3098.0	748.0	107.1	110.2	95.3
1987	106.4	109.0	105.9	550	417	1089	105.6	104.3	108.7	3742.0	580.0	105.9	114.8	71.7
1988	107.3	112.3	104.1	693	508	1431	107.4	106.0	108.9	4624.0	871.0	111.7	108.9	129.6
1989	100.2	102.4	103.3	762	553	1568	99.5	99.2	98.4	4339.0	1756.0	101.2	86.5	177.0
1990	101.4	110.5	109.2	803	571	1686	103.4	100.3	107.5	4732.0	1712.0	99.8	103.4	90.6
1991	107.8	112.4	119.3	896	621	1925	108.3	106.7	109.3	5940.0	1577.0	108.2	115.7	87.4
1992	110.7	118.8	113.6	1070	718	2356	112.9	109.8	115.4	8317.0	1319.0	112.9	123.9	72.4
1993	106.7	112.5	109.1	1331	855	3027	108.1	106.1	108.9	12980.0	2018.0	124.9	124.8	125.5
1994	106.7	108.8	109.1	1781	1138	3979	106.5	106.5	104.1	16856.3	2404.3	115.6	117.7	102.8
1995	109.9	110.3	105.9	2311	1479	5044	108.9	109.6	105.9	20300.5	3576.5	115.5	113.6	123.7

1

Beijing

Year	v1	v1a	v1b	v1b1	v1b2	v1c	v1c1	v1c2	v1c3	v2	v2a	v2b	v2b1	v2b2	v2c
1952	20.13	2.54	10.17	9.07	1.10	7.42	0.60	1.52	5.30	117.1	113.9	114.5	120.2	106.2	130.0
1953	31.97	2.72	16.72	12.96	3.76	12.53	0.95	2.63	8.95	159.1	106.8	164.3	142.0	241.2	176.7
1954	37.41	2.48	20.54	14.95	5.59	14.39	0.96	3.15	10.28	117.0	91.2	122.9	154.0	210.6	114.8
1955	39.89	2.83	21.97	16.63	5.34	15.09	1.14	3.17	10.78	106.6	114.0	107.7	111.2	92.3	106.9
1956	49.17	2.90	25.60	20.03	5.57	20.67	1.87	4.04	14.76	123.3	102.6	115.9	103.9	108.0	128.3
1957	52.50	3.03	27.77	22.00	5.77	21.70	1.32	3.73	16.65	106.7	113.8	108.2	109.8	103.5	96.2
1958	78.86	4.90	50.31	42.78	7.53	23.65	1.59	4.31	17.75	150.2	130.0	181.4	214.8	130.6	124.6
1959	110.34	5.01	75.05	63.33	11.72	30.28	2.12	6.23	21.93	140.0	103.2	149.3	152.7	155.7	130.6
1960	136.10	4.91	97.10	85.87	11.23	34.09	3.46	6.28	24.35	123.4	95.4	129.3	132.9	95.8	112.6
1961	88.98	4.76	58.28	53.17	5.11	25.94	2.41	5.00	18.53	64.4	95.3	60.0	59.0	45.5	70.7
1962	70.65	5.15	45.93	41.87	4.06	19.57	1.94	3.60	14.03	79.4	109.3	79.6	76.3	79.5	72.7
1963	73.74	5.52	49.00	44.47	4.53	19.22	1.94	3.55	13.73	104.4	106.1	106.7	103.8	111.7	98.2
1964	81.30	6.23	55.05	49.40	5.65	20.02	2.20	3.52	14.30	110.3	108.7	113.4	113.2	124.7	105.1
1965	89.91	7.05	62.63	55.90	6.73	20.23	2.23	3.55	14.45	110.6	116.7	113.8	119.8	119.1	104.7
1966	102.31	7.08	74.86	69.01	5.85	20.37	2.17	3.65	14.55	113.8	99.0	117.3	120.0	86.8	102.6
1967	90.48	7.31	62.80	58.22	4.58	20.37	2.04	3.64	14.69	88.2	103.3	85.9	90.4	78.3	98.5
1968	94.10	7.49	65.99	61.39	4.60	20.62	2.11	3.78	14.73	104.0	98.6	104.6	105.4	100.6	102.8
1969	128.50	6.89	93.36	87.51	5.85	28.25	2.52	5.55	20.18	136.3	92.0	138.8	142.5	127.1	128.3
1970	138.82	8.20	103.91	97.14	6.77	26.71	2.98	4.65	19.08	108.0	117.1	114.5	133.1	115.6	96.4
1971	142.85	8.48	105.42	99.32	6.10	28.95	3.09	5.18	20.68	102.9	101.7	102.0	122.0	90.1	108.1
1972	150.91	8.07	111.51	105.28	6.23	31.33	3.45	5.50	22.38	107.7	96.2	104.2	106.0	102.1	108.5
1973	165.59	9.21	121.10	113.09	8.01	35.28	3.73	6.34	25.21	109.7	111.5	109.7	107.4	128.7	109.6
1974	180.97	9.99	133.28	123.29	9.99	37.70	4.05	6.72	26.93	109.3	108.4	110.1	109.0	124.7	107.6
1975	205.04	10.57	146.45	133.79	12.66	48.02	5.73	7.99	34.30	113.3	106.0	110.4	108.5	126.7	126.4
1976	206.90	10.36	150.93	141.21	9.72	45.61	5.77	7.90	31.94	100.9	97.3	103.1	105.3	76.8	103.9
1977	227.22	9.82	162.87	149.27	13.60	54.53	6.63	8.95	38.95	109.8	94.1	107.4	108.0	139.9	119.6
1978	260.87	11.52	187.89	169.97	17.92	61.46	7.70	9.86	43.90	114.8	112.2	116.0	114.0	131.4	115.9
1979	287.21	12.40	208.94	188.61	20.33	65.87	8.31	10.51	47.05	110.1	100.1	110.6	111.5	113.4	105.2
1980	331.11	14.35	239.44	213.37	26.07	77.32	8.53	13.56	55.23	115.3	101.3	115.2	110.2	114.9	110.2
1981	345.02	14.96	246.34	218.96	27.38	83.72	9.37	14.55	59.80	106.3	99.3	102.9	101.2	103.7	108.3
1982	364.28	16.80	261.17	230.84	30.33	86.31	10.24	14.42	61.65	103.5	108.3	104.5	106.1	109.2	106.8
1983	410.89	19.61	297.50	256.81	40.69	93.78	10.86	16.64	66.28	112.8	114.5	114.6	112.4	133.2	104.9
1984	475.60	22.15	342.42	292.36	50.06	111.03	12.77	19.79	78.47	115.7	111.2	113.8	113.8	124.7	113.5
1985	604.85	25.94	405.34	338.70	66.64	173.57	18.43	32.47	122.67	122.3	106.3	109.4	110.3	119.8	134.0
1986	661.57	28.14	441.52	371.24	70.28	191.91	22.46	33.82	135.63	105.4	100.4	105.2	106.1	100.6	118.2
1987	800.48	34.42	519.01	434.63	84.38	247.05	30.40	42.05	174.60	110.9	109.6	113.6	112.8	110.2	129.7
1988	1042.36	52.50	672.63	571.57	101.06	317.23	34.37	58.66	224.20	120.2	111.8	124.4	122.5	112.3	111.3
1989	1195.52	60.35	819.10	700.92	118.18	316.07	37.99	54.70	223.38	106.5	110.6	112.8	107.2	106.0	99.6
1990	1310.85	70.18	876.79	748.94	127.85	363.88	37.69	69.02	257.17	109.6	105.5	122.8	110.5	94.6	138.2
1991	1496.05	76.47	999.04	886.85	112.19	420.54	45.90	80.01	294.63	114.1	108.9	105.9	102.9	86.0	115.9
1992	1776.93	84.52	1243.11	1085.37	157.74	449.30	55.12	98.27	295.91	118.8	106.8	120.3	118.4	119.3	119.3
1993	2543.24	100.47	1770.98	1492.00	278.98	671.79	62.00	162.11	447.68	123.3	115.1	122.3	120.8	135.0	127.6
1994	3048.76	145.56	2101.21	1761.52	339.69	801.99	82.01	202.23	517.75	118.1	112.8	118.2	115.6	137.0	118.9
1995	4073.03	164.47	2174.19	1803.74	370.45	1734.37	280.52	236.22	1217.63	122.6	99.0	108.7	110.0	101.8	164.0

Year	v2c1	v2c2	v3'	v3	v3a	v3b	v3b1	v3b2	v3c	v3c1	v3c2	v3c3	v3c4	v3c5	v3c6
1952	149.4	103.7	7.88	7.88	1.75	3.05	2.69	0.36	3.08	0.40	1.23				
1953	156.2	161.5	19.28	19.28	3.37	7.85	6.12	1.73	8.06	1.23	3.52				
1954	100.7	117.6	21.13	21.13	3.01	9.31	6.85	2.46	8.81	1.24	3.83				
1955	119.1	99.6	23.88	23.88	3.44	10.07	7.60	2.47	10.37	1.48	4.68				
1956	173.1	127.2	26.83	26.83	3.32	11.39	8.67	2.72	12.12	1.71	5.10				
1957	68.9	89.7	32.81	32.81	3.49	15.68	12.40	3.28	13.64	1.86	5.00				
1958	130.1	118.6	34.52	34.52	3.93	20.35	17.32	3.03	10.24	1.52	4.25				
1959	155.4	145.9	46.28	46.28	3.96	28.69	25.13	3.56	13.63	2.00	6.54				
1960	143.9	101.1	57.47	57.47	4.01	37.03	33.57	3.46	16.43	4.21	6.51				
1961	69.4	74.4	36.55	36.55	3.74	20.42	18.80	1.62	12.39	2.75	4.60				
1962	80.2	69.5	29.59	29.59	3.74	16.30	14.83	1.47	9.55	1.94	2.83				
1963	100.0	97.7	31.72	31.72	4.12	18.23	16.60	1.63	9.37	1.61	3.00				
1964	113.1	99.2	35.99	35.99	4.83	20.96	18.95	2.01	10.20	1.96	3.13				
1965	101.7	106.2	39.79	39.79	4.96	23.50	21.00	2.50	11.33	2.60	3.06				
1966	97.2	102.9	44.41	44.41	5.24	28.41	26.31	2.10	10.76	2.00	3.17				
1967	94.1	99.9	37.86	37.86	5.30	22.37	20.73	1.64	10.19	1.82	3.00				
1968	103.2	104.2	37.82	37.82	5.48	22.13	20.49	1.64	10.21	1.83	3.36				
1969	119.9	146.3	50.63	50.63	4.71	33.60	31.53	2.07	12.32	2.15	5.07				
1970	118.6	84.7	63.37	63.37	6.48	45.06	42.61	2.45	11.83	2.88	4.55				
1971	104.1	111.1	61.14	61.14	6.28	41.91	39.75	2.16	12.95	3.07	4.99				
1972	110.8	106.1	67.19	67.19	5.37	47.01	44.80	2.21	14.81	3.37	5.14				
1973	106.5	115.3	73.03	73.03	6.03	50.45	47.59	2.86	16.55	3.76	5.98				
1974	109.3	105.9	80.19	80.19	5.60	56.38	52.95	3.43	18.21	4.54	3.91				
1975	142.9	119.1	90.92	90.92	6.04	60.50	56.09	4.41	24.38	6.10	6.81				
1976	100.8	99.1	93.54	93.54	5.58	63.59	59.85	3.74	24.37	5.86	6.44				
1977	112.6	113.3	99.09	99.09	5.17	67.26	62.55	4.71	26.66	6.55	7.24				
1978	118.9	109.5	108.84	108.84	5.63	77.43	70.22	7.21	25.78	7.00	8.28	1.90	0.85	1.84	1.45
1979	107.8	104.7	120.11	120.11	5.17	85.18	77.37	7.81	29.76	6.55	8.79	3.36	1.55	2.61	1.71
1980	101.4	122.9	139.07	139.07	6.07	95.79	86.94	8.85	37.21	6.96	11.01	6.47	1.79	2.94	2.04
1981	109.1	105.8	139.15	139.15	6.61	92.52	82.71	9.81	40.02	7.60	11.86	5.44	1.92	3.20	2.57
1982	110.2	107.9	154.94	154.94	10.34	99.79	89.30	10.49	44.81	8.25	11.05	9.83	2.01	3.76	2.45
1983	92.0	101.9	183.13	183.13	12.85	112.65	98.76	13.89	57.63	9.06	13.63	16.00	2.42	4.20	3.06
1984	109.2	116.7	216.61	216.61	14.85	130.68	113.99	16.69	71.08	10.43	18.37	18.01	2.35	6.55	3.77
1985	148.8	138.2	257.12	257.12	17.81	153.66	130.65	23.01	85.65	12.74	25.89	18.95	3.03	7.97	4.23
1986	133.3	97.6	284.86	284.86	19.14	165.75	141.17	24.58	99.97	14.98	27.99	21.68	3.10	11.17	4.76
1987	132.6	114.4	326.82	326.82	24.31	182.59	154.54	28.05	119.92	17.70	27.21	30.66	2.90	15.27	6.30
1988	108.1	114.3	410.22	410.22	37.07	221.27	189.48	31.79	151.88	19.03	39.07	42.21	4.21	16.11	7.86
1989	109.1	78.8	455.96	455.96	38.53	252.23	212.83	39.40	165.20	18.72	34.77	55.67	4.13	13.35	9.45
1990	80.0	121.2	500.72	500.82	43.88	262.39	219.27	43.12	194.55	23.96	43.85	56.75	4.27	19.89	11.58
1991	119.1	109.4	598.79	598.89	45.52	291.53	255.59	35.94	261.84	29.61	65.65	54.67	5.48	27.55	8.06
1992	106.0	105.9	709.00	709.10	48.67	345.91	292.97	52.94	314.52	35.49	85.41	64.95	5.58	29.36	10.72
1993	109.6	131.5	863.23	863.53	53.57	414.79	334.00	80.79	395.17	37.58	113.88	82.95	6.69	35.23	12.33
1994	132.3	116.5	1083.73	1084.03	74.77	499.84	405.11	94.73	509.42	61.51	146.62	108.98	10.11	39.94	17.91
1995	176.2	113.9	1395.12	1394.89	81.44	615.17	503.71	111.46	698.28	83.55	174.70	145.27	28.39	94.08	23.09

Year	v3c7	v3c8	v3c9	v3c10	v3d	v4'	v4	v4a	v4b	v4b1	v4b2	v4c	v4c1	v4c2	v4c3
1952				1.45	170	102.1	102.1	99.2	107.8	106.6	116.5	98.7	98.2	96.5	
1953				3.31	394	237.1	237.1	193.1	259.6	227.5	477.3	239.8	292.4	266.8	
1954				3.74	405	109.4	109.4	87.2	119.0	112.1	141.7	109.3	98.2	107.0	
1955				4.21	436	113.0	113.0	116.8	108.0	111.0	100.3	117.3	122.6	121.1	
1956				5.31	465	116.8	116.8	96.5	125.1	130.0	110.3	115.4	120.8	108.7	
1957				6.78	539	125.4	125.4	114.5	137.9	143.4	120.6	114.7	115.9	97.2	
1958				4.47	552	106.6	106.6	81.2	132.9	143.1	92.5	79.0	83.9	94.8	
1959				5.09	703	138.7	138.7	101.9	145.2	149.7	117.1	135.0	133.5	155.3	
1960				5.71	812	123.7	123.7	98.6	127.1	130.9	97.3	121.1	212.6	100.0	
1961				5.04	503	59.4	59.4	91.6	52.8	53.3	47.0	70.1	65.3	66.0	
1962				4.78	412	78.1	78.1	100.9	77.5	76.4	90.6	73.8	70.1	59.3	
1963				4.76	431	105.9	105.9	108.9	109.6	109.4	111.8	97.6	82.6	105.3	
1964				5.11	476	114.8	114.8	113.0	116.9	116.4	121.8	110.7	122.0	104.2	
1965				5.67	513	116.4	116.4	106.0	118.0	117.3	124.7	116.5	132.0	103.3	
1966				5.59	573	111.0	111.0	104.1	118.8	122.7	84.1	94.9	77.7	103.7	
1967				5.37	488	87.9	87.9	101.1	84.0	84.5	77.4	94.4	90.1	94.6	
1968				5.02	482	99.5	99.5	99.7	98.9	98.8	101.1	101.0	101.0	112.2	
1969				5.10	655	137.9	137.9	86.0	152.0	153.9	125.5	121.5	118.8	150.8	
1970				4.40	823	144.3	144.3	137.4	159.8	162.2	118.5	95.9	126.1	90.4	
1971				4.89	786	109.8	109.8	97.5	110.5	111.5	88.2	110.8	112.7	109.5	
1972				6.30	851	86.8	86.8	115.5	80.0	79.3	102.4	113.1	102.2	106.3	
1973				6.81	914	108.2	108.2	109.8	107.2	106.2	129.2	111.4	109.7	116.3	
1974				9.76	990	109.6	109.6	98.9	111.0	110.5	120.0	108.1	121.2	65.4	
1975				11.47	1112	112.9	112.9	101.6	107.8	106.6	128.5	135.3	135.2	174.4	
1976				12.07	1130	103.3	103.3	92.4	105.3	105.2	84.7	100.0	96.3	94.7	
1977				12.87	1188	107.1	107.1	92.4	107.6	98.1	126.1	108.8	108.7	112.4	
1978	1.20	1.49	1.77		1290	110.5	110.5	105.3	114.9	112.4	105.3	97.7	110.5	113.6	139.9
1979	1.41	1.76	2.02		1391	109.7	109.7	86.8	110.0	110.1	108.4	113.2	93.5	104.3	173.8
1980	1.69	2.10	2.21		1582	111.8	111.8	108.0	110.1	110.1	110.3	118.5	103.4	119.4	325.1
1981	2.13	2.64	2.66		1558	98.5	98.5	138.4	93.7	92.3	109.4	106.1	107.7	106.2	83.0
1982	2.03	2.52	2.91		1704	106.8	106.8	148.7	111.3	100.2	111.1	117.7	112.8	114.7	177.1
1983	2.54	3.15	3.57		1977	115.8	115.8	124.1	113.7	111.5	132.3	119.0	97.0	104.9	157.9
1984	3.12	3.88	4.60		2308	117.6	117.6	115.8	116.0	115.7	118.8	121.6	114.2	132.3	113.1
1985	3.51	4.35	4.98		2704	108.6	108.6	100.7	111.2	109.3	124.7	104.3	114.7	118.6	88.7
1986	3.95	4.90	7.44		2955	108.9	108.9	99.9	102.5	102.8	100.4	126.7	101.9	102.3	133.0
1987	5.22	6.48	8.18		3338	109.6	109.6	113.8	104.8	104.5	106.3	118.4	110.6	89.2	136.9
1988	6.51	8.08	8.80		4125	112.8	112.8	126.8	112.1	113.0	106.5	111.7	99.1	118.0	138.0
1989	7.83	9.72	11.56		4496	104.4	104.4	88.5	108.9	108.4	112.2	99.5	136.3	76.1	111.6
1990	9.96	10.67	13.62		4881	105.4	105.4	103.4	101.0	101.9	95.6	114.0	106.2	119.7	111.5
1991	25.48	23.51	21.83		5781	109.5	109.5	103.6	107.7	112.6	81.6	113.0	129.9	97.6	116.9
1992	30.30	27.48	21.91	3.32	6805	111.6	111.6	103.0	112.1	110.3	125.7	112.5	109.9	118.6	110.3
1993	38.56	35.50	28.69	3.75	8240	112.1	112.1	103.1	112.9	110.5	128.5	112.7	110.1	115.7	112.2
1994	43.07	41.68	35.14	4.46	10265	113.5	113.5	102.6	114.6	113.5	120.8	113.7	124.2	109.6	107.9
1995	53.54	51.91	37.95	5.80	13073	112.5	112.4	91.7	107.6	107.7	107.6	120.9	139.9	117.4	118.1

Year	v4c4	v4c5	v4c6	v4c7	v4c8	v4c9	v4c10	v5	v5a	v5a1	v5a1a	v5a1b	v5a2	v5b	v5b1
1952								7.88	8.40	6.90	1.80	5.10	1.50	1.92	0.79
1953								19.28	10.70	9.10	1.60	7.50	1.60	6.53	5.36
1954								21.13	11.70	9.70	1.70	8.00	2.00	9.45	8.19
1955								23.88	12.10	10.50	1.90	8.60	1.60	7.00	5.25
1956								26.83	15.20	13.00	1.90	11.10	2.20	10.60	7.71
1957								32.81	13.30	11.40	2.20	9.20	1.90	11.20	7.10
1958								34.52	14.10	12.20	2.40	9.80	1.90	17.10	11.80
1959								46.28	17.70	13.80	2.30	11.50	3.90	25.30	17.70
1960								57.47	21.40	15.50	2.30	13.20	5.90	25.90	18.40
1961								36.55	20.30	15.90	3.80	12.10	4.40	8.90	8.70
1962								29.59	19.90	16.10	3.30	12.80	3.80	0.80	
1963								31.72	19.00	14.20	2.90	11.30	4.80	2.70	2.30
1964								35.99	19.70	14.60	2.80	11.80	5.10	7.40	6.20
1965								39.79	22.40	18.00	4.20	13.80	4.40	9.70	8.30
1966								44.41	22.80	18.10	4.30	13.80	4.70	12.20	9.00
1967								37.86	21.50	17.70	4.30	13.40	3.80	8.90	6.30
1968								37.82	21.00	17.90	4.40	13.50	3.10	8.70	5.90
1969								50.63	21.10	18.10	4.60	13.50	3.00	13.20	8.70
1970								63.37	20.20	17.20	4.70	12.50	3.00	11.90	7.10
1971								61.14	20.70	17.30	4.70	12.60	3.40	16.90	9.80
1972								67.19	22.00	18.20	4.40	13.80	3.80	15.80	9.90
1973								73.03	25.60	20.70	5.00	15.70	4.90	27.70	14.40
1974								80.19	25.50	20.30	5.30	15.00	5.20	27.50	19.00
1975								90.92	28.70	22.23	5.30	16.93	6.47	22.70	16.80
1976								93.54	29.50	23.39	5.00	18.39	6.11	14.90	3.30
1977								99.09	34.07	26.67	5.90	20.77	7.40	22.10	14.20
1978	101.4	97.6	103.1	101.8	103.0	110.9		108.84	40.98	30.47	7.32	23.15	10.51	31.67	24.84
1979	178.7	139.8	115.7	116.2	116.8	113.5		120.11	49.34	36.24	8.63	27.61	13.10	37.40	29.76
1980	107.5	105.3	112.2	111.5	112.4	104.5		139.07	57.44	44.35	10.53	33.82	13.09	43.69	35.63
1981	106.3	107.6	123.6	124.3	125.0	117.4		139.15	63.72	47.66	11.98	35.68	16.06	38.85	29.53
1982	102.6	114.9	93.6	93.5	96.3	106.9		154.94	71.22	51.24	13.64	37.60	19.98	34.43	26.10
1983	119.7	111.3	124.1	124.7	121.7	121.6		183.13	81.31	56.45	16.57	39.88	24.86	54.76	49.04
1984	94.7	152.1	120.7	119.8	122.2	126.0		216.61	96.14	67.65	21.05	46.60	28.49	78.57	68.60
1985	109.6	103.6	95.5	95.8	112.0	93.8		257.12	112.30	83.14	24.59	58.55	29.16	191.43	98.70
1986	144.6	197.5	158.6	158.8	123.8	154.5		284.86	125.16	92.40	26.10	66.30	32.76	156.33	129.75
1987	92.6	135.4	130.9	119.2	132.1	126.7		326.82	147.87	107.73	29.12	78.61	40.14	208.33	170.12
1988	121.0	87.9	103.7	92.8	121.8	108.4		410.22	178.49	131.98	37.25	94.73	46.51	250.01	197.79
1989	99.4	82.9	120.7	138.0	101.9	123.0		455.96	197.67	138.99	46.78	92.21	58.68	297.00	200.26
1990	102.9	93.9	109.4	210.0	195.0	118.0		500.82	230.96	169.83	49.22	120.61	61.13	307.29	227.95
1991	141.0	138.8	72.6	148.1	133.1	137.4		598.89	225.47	153.62	37.59	116.03	71.85	322.77	184.37
1992	102.4	107.7	125.6	112.2	113.3	109.1		709.10	262.97	177.08	40.11	136.97	85.89	423.71	200.98
1993	110.1	107.0	105.6	112.0	117.0	117.4	101.7	863.53	310.28	207.21	52.95	154.26	103.07	625.15	326.82
1994	117.0	109.2	128.0	111.8	118.8	122.5	123.5	1318.60	396.29	264.55	66.95	197.60	131.74	902.63	519.01
1995	235.3	163.4	110.3	99.5	83.0	101.4	114.0	1694.89	506.58	375.46	78.53	296.93	131.12	1256.28	888.31

Year	v5b2	v5c	v5c1	v5c2	v6a1	v6a2	v6a3	v6a4	v6b2	v6b3	v6b4	v7	v7a	v7a1	v7a2
1952	1.13	-2.44	0.01	2.45											
1953	1.17	2.05	2.07	0.02								127.4	131.9	92.0	147.1
1954	1.26	-0.02	0.01	0.03								109.3	106.6	103.1	110.7
1955	1.75	4.78	4.80	0.02								103.4	108.2	112.1	107.6
1956	2.89	1.03	1.06	0.03								125.6	113.1	100.0	128.9
1957	4.10	8.31	8.35	0.04								87.5	87.7	118.9	82.0
1958	5.30	3.32	3.53	0.21								106.0	107.0	107.3	107.7
1959	7.60	3.28	3.69	0.41								125.5	121.1	93.2	117.6
1960	7.50	10.17	10.59	0.42								120.9	112.3	104.5	114.6
1961	0.20	7.35	8.11	0.76								94.9	102.6	160.9	91.7
1962		8.89	11.21	0.72								98.0	101.3	86.5	105.8
1963	0.40	10.02	10.77	0.75								95.5	88.2	87.5	88.3
1964	1.20	8.89	9.72	0.83								103.7	102.8	100.0	104.4
1965	1.40	7.69	8.50	0.81								113.7	123.3	146.4	116.9
1966	3.20	9.41	10.27	0.86								101.8	100.6	102.4	100.0
1967	2.60	7.46	8.18	0.72								94.3	97.8	100.0	97.1
1968	2.80	8.12	8.91	0.79								97.7	101.1	102.4	100.0
1969	4.50	16.33	17.32	0.99								100.5	101.5	104.7	100.7
1970	4.80	31.27	32.34	1.07								95.7	95.0	102.2	92.6
1971	7.10	23.54	24.76	1.22								102.5	100.5	100.0	100.8
1972	5.90	29.39	30.95	1.56								106.3	104.3	93.5	109.5
1973	13.30	19.73	22.15	2.42								123.7	113.6	114.0	113.0
1974	8.50	27.19	29.75	2.56								112.5	99.0	110.2	96.2
1975	5.90	39.52	42.45	2.93								103.1	109.2	98.1	113.3
1976	11.60	49.14	52.33	3.19								105.5	104.9	94.3	108.8
1977	7.90	42.92	46.70	3.78								120.7	114.5	118.0	112.4
1978	6.83	36.19	40.84	4.65	1.71	5.19	0.06	0.36	21.30	1.15	0.70	112.3	113.7	106.8	95.2
1979	7.64	33.37	39.84	6.47	2.01	6.12	0.08	0.42	25.40	1.38	0.83	120.4	118.8	117.4	119.2
1980	8.06	37.94	46.78	8.84	2.45	7.47	0.09	0.52	31.11	1.70	1.01	116.2	122.5	123.0	122.5
1981	9.32	36.58	47.81	11.23	2.26	9.13	0.07	0.52	31.65	2.64	1.39	111.0	109.4	113.2	105.5
1982	8.33	49.29	61.10	11.81	2.58	10.39	0.08	0.59	33.35	2.78	1.47	111.8	108.1	114.6	105.2
1983	5.72	47.06	58.71	11.65	3.13	12.63	0.10	0.71	35.37	2.95	1.56	114.3	119.9	121.1	106.2
1984	9.97	41.90	55.55	13.65	3.85	16.19	0.21	0.80	41.71	3.21	1.68	118.2	122.8	126.2	116.7
1985	92.73	-46.61	14.12	60.73	3.37	20.09	0.20	0.93	51.99	4.45	2.11	116.8	111.1	117.1	125.9
1986	26.58	3.37	20.65	17.28	3.29	21.24	0.42	1.15	58.08	5.77	2.45	111.4	116.1	111.6	113.2
1987	38.21	-29.38	22.25	51.63	3.90	21.81	0.32	3.09	69.49	6.45	2.67	118.1	116.6	127.9	118.5
1988	52.22	-18.28	24.14	42.42	4.43	26.71	1.98	4.13	86.34	6.21	2.18	120.7	122.5	125.5	120.4
1989	96.74	-38.71	41.81	80.52	6.60	32.79	2.81	4.58	83.82	6.18	2.21	92.4	88.6	100.0	97.4
1990	79.34	-37.43	41.25	78.68	6.84	34.26	3.30	4.82	108.80	9.16	2.65	116.9	121.8	105.2	130.8
1991	138.40	50.65	102.18	51.53	4.51	25.11	3.08	4.89	103.61	9.98	2.44	97.6	90.8	76.4	96.1
1992	222.73	22.42	83.82	61.40	3.97	25.47	4.57	6.10	113.62	14.43	8.92	100.9	106.3	102.0	107.5
1993	298.33	-71.90	87.77	159.67	4.51	32.76	5.24	10.44	125.86	18.54	9.86	106.5	106.9	113.4	105.0
1994	383.62	19.68	180.41	160.73	6.03	42.18	7.03	11.71	159.16	22.59	15.85	108.4	108.6	111.3	107.8
1995	367.97	-67.97	189.58	257.55	6.85	48.75	9.34	13.59	230.54	40.91	25.48	109.0	114.1	107.4	116.3

Year	v7b	v8	v8a	v8b	v9	v9a	v9b	v10a1	v10a2	v10a3	v10a3a	v10a3b	v10a4	v10b1	v10b2
1952		148	66	250	110.5	114.1	105.9								
1953	100.7	185	62	331	113.5	93.8	129.6								
1954	132.6	184	62	312	99.4	100.0	95.1								
1955	75.4	190	68	308	130.6	101.6	95.1								
1956	144.9	224	66	370	117.2	96.8	114.7								
1957	80.0	186	79	282	82.8	116.5	75.0								
1958	106.3	193	84	285	103.6	106.3	98.8								
1959	223.5	207	78	305	106.5	92.9	102.8								
1960	152.6	217	81	307	116.6	104.3	100.8								
1961	74.1	215	130	270	99.0	148.6	87.9								
1962	83.7	222	107	303	103.6	88.8	112.0								
1963	130.6	191	89	265	89.3	83.2	88.9								
1964	104.3	191	87	374	99.4	97.5	119.2								
1965	85.7	230	122	308	120.7	122.1	88.8								
1966	107.1	231	126	311	100.0	103.2	104.6								
1967	76.7	226	124	309	96.2	97.9	96.0								
1968	81.2	235	124	309	104.0	100.0	100.0								
1969	92.9	232	126	324	88.6	100.0	104.9								
1970	103.8	220	124	310	95.2	102.1	95.8								
1971	114.8	271	125	312	124.4	99.0	101.2								
1972	116.1	228	116	337	85.5	102.1	107.2								
1973	127.8	256	131	370	107.7	113.3	118.2								
1974	106.5	251	140	350	103.1	111.6	104.1								
1975	126.5	271	137	394	107.0	97.6	95.2								
1976	95.2	285	130	417	103.7	95.0	106.0								
1977	120.3	322	155	460	124.7	119.1	116.2								
1978	125.3	361	190	505	112.3	122.6	110.1	22.58	1.22	0.42		0.42	0.62	4.64	1.00
1979	124.7	420	229	568	116.2	120.2	112.6	27.05	1.46	0.51		0.51	0.74	5.20	1.07
1980	100.0	504	281	672	119.0	132.2	122.1	32.39	1.75	0.61		0.61	0.88	6.27	1.60
1981	122.5	534	318	691	102.8	114.2	102.3	25.69	1.00	1.92		1.92	0.92	6.41	1.31
1982	138.2	564	358	712	102.7	118.3	103.1	21.97	1.07	2.08		2.08	0.98	5.73	1.17
1983	114.2	594	430	738	102.8	120.6	103.7	42.61	1.67	3.24		3.24	1.52	3.94	0.81
1984	102.5	721	544	845	125.7	118.1	118.1	59.75	2.68	3.43		3.43	2.74	6.78	1.40
1985	112.6	874	635	1039	103.9	138.2	123.5	83.48	8.75	5.03	0.57	4.46	1.44	62.13	12.98
1986	122.3	958	755	1359	107.8	115.6	118.3	109.46	9.26	5.19	0.59	4.60	5.84	18.07	3.73
1987	115.9	1100	754	1325	105.0	102.8	119.5	148.34	8.51	7.32	0.65	6.67	5.95	35.50	1.94
1988	126.1	1327	960	1563	108.1	117.8	104.6	171.29	9.89	9.10	1.27	7.83	7.51	43.66	2.30
1989	104.2	1371	1196	1482	103.4	119.3	91.3	163.21	8.61	8.01	-2.23	10.24	20.43	88.81	4.64
1990	117.6	1435	1080	1628	161.8	103.8	120.9	197.86	10.49	5.24	-1.68	6.92	14.36	38.88	2.06
1991	117.6	1290	825	1904	97.0	72.7	111.3	152.78	8.17	6.64	0.48	6.16	16.78	85.67	4.57
1992	91.6	1699	1026	2104	106.0	112.6	100.9	170.83	9.25	1.97	-0.53	2.50	18.93	186.65	5.79
1993	105.6	1977	1372	2330	106.2	114.9	104.2	263.38	18.97	8.87	3.85	5.02	35.60	265.50	5.29
1994	108.0	2505	1757	2928	107.8	112.7	105.7	425.45	8.08	13.72	5.76	7.96	71.76	341.42	6.91
1995	98.2	3519	2083	4303	112.9	108.6	113.7	531.90	58.15	17.35	7.50	9.85	280.91	123.65	94.49

Year	v10b4	v11a	v11a1	v11a2	v11b	v11b1	v11b2	v11c	v11c1	v11c2	v12	v12a	v12b	v13	v13i
1952											116.6	116.6	116.6		
1953											340.1	679.4	104.1		
1954											144.4	152.8	107.8		
1955											75.9	64.0	136.4		
1956											151.1	146.0	166.7		
1957											105.4	93.3	140.0		
1958											153.6	164.0	131.4		
1959											147.7	151.5	143.5		
1960											102.3	103.5	98.5		
1961											65.8	47.4	125.9		
1962											100.0	100.0	100.0		
1963											100.0	100.0	100.0		
1964											266.3	269.7	250.0		
1965											131.4	133.1	123.0		
1966											126.2	108.6	219.3		
1967											72.6	70.3	80.1		
1968											98.7	93.4	108.4		
1969											150.0	147.9	157.9		
1970											90.4	81.3	159.2		
1971											142.7	139.0	147.9		
1972											93.2	99.1	83.2		
1973											175.9	148.7	184.3		
1974											99.2	131.3	27.6		
1975											82.4	88.4	41.9		
1976											65.8	18.6	196.1		
1977											148.2	456.7	69.0		
1978	1.19	2.63	0.68	1.95	14.76	12.66	2.10	14.28	11.50	2.78	143.2	173.6	85.5	108.84	28.69
1979	1.37	1.61	0.09	1.52	16.27	13.96	2.31	19.52	15.71	3.81	118.2	120.1	111.9	120.11	33.44
1980	0.19	1.18	1.00	0.18	20.45	16.87	3.58	22.06	17.76	4.30	116.0	119.5	106.1	139.07	39.56
1981	1.60	0.89	0.68	0.21	16.20	12.31	3.89	21.76	16.54	5.22	88.9	82.7	84.3	139.15	39.66
1982	1.43	1.34	1.01	0.33	15.05	11.41	3.64	18.04	13.68	4.36	88.5	107.1	29.6	154.94	47.99
1983	0.97	1.81	1.63	0.18	23.05	20.57	2.48	29.90	26.84	3.06	159.2	155.5	204.2	183.13	54.71
1984	1.79	2.12	1.85	0.27	30.25	26.41	3.84	46.20	40.34	5.86	143.5	139.7	177.6	216.61	63.62
1985	17.62	4.59	2.37	2.22	74.08	38.20	35.88	112.76	58.13	54.63	172.9	144.0	379.3	257.12	86.35
1986	4.78	2.50	2.07	0.43	69.25	57.48	11.77	84.58	70.20	14.38	81.7	131.4	70.0	284.86	97.91
1987	1.27	2.51	2.04	0.47	81.65	66.52	15.13	124.67	101.56	23.11	119.7	131.2	145.5	326.82	102.30
1988	6.26	3.50	2.77	0.73	89.75	71.01	18.74	156.76	124.01	32.75	118.8	116.2	135.1	410.22	126.00
1989	3.29	4.46	3.00	1.46	93.26	62.88	30.38	199.28	134.38	64.90	122.9	101.2	185.2	455.96	142.40
1990	38.40	5.22	3.88	1.34	99.56	73.86	25.70	202.51	150.21	52.30	103.4	113.8	82.0	500.82	180.65
1991	48.16	6.13	3.50	2.63	115.87	66.19	49.68	200.77	114.68	86.09	105.1	80.9	174.4	598.89	216.26
1992	30.29	8.05	3.82	4.23	175.84	83.41	92.43	239.82	113.75	126.07	122.9	105.0	145.3	709.10	257.77
1993	27.54	0.63	0.33	0.30	263.81	137.91	125.90	360.71	188.58	172.13	123.9	127.9	120.3	863.53	464.11
1994	35.29	7.47	3.63	3.84	356.12	184.26	171.86	539.04	331.12	207.92	131.1	143.7	119.1	1084.03	500.62
1995	149.83	25.56	3.68	21.88	324.49	161.72	162.77	906.23	722.91	183.32	120.1	150.2	85.3	1394.89	632.08

Year	v13ii	v13iii	v13iv	v13a	v13ai	v13aii	v13aiii	v13aiv	v13b	v13bi	v13bii	v13biii	v13biv	v13b1	v13b1i
1952															
1953															
1954															
1955															
1956															
1957															
1958															
1959															
1960															
1961															
1962															
1963															
1964															
1965															
1966															
1967															
1968															
1969															
1970															
1971															
1972															
1973															
1974															
1975															
1976															
1977															
1978	10.96	16.35	52.84	5.63	4.04	0.14		1.45	77.43	16.07	7.23	14.59	39.54	70.22	12.66
1979	13.51	17.76	55.40	5.17	3.82	0.14		1.21	85.18	19.10	8.69	15.67	41.72	77.37	15.30
1980	15.78	19.04	64.69	6.07	4.52	1.03	0.23	0.29	95.79	22.90	9.22	16.15	47.52	86.94	18.79
1981	16.69	19.31	63.49	6.61	4.56	1.13	0.32	0.60	92.52	21.59	9.29	16.22	45.42	82.71	16.44
1982	16.56	20.67	69.72	10.34	8.63	0.48	0.49	0.74	99.79	22.46	9.31	17.16	50.86	89.30	16.97
1983	19.93	23.12	85.37	12.85	9.93	0.48	0.88	1.56	112.65	25.92	10.52	19.09	57.12	98.76	18.93
1984	21.54	28.27	103.18	14.85	10.42	0.48	0.99	2.96	130.68	30.21	10.95	22.98	66.54	113.99	21.38
1985	25.38	0.64	144.75	17.81	12.08	0.42		5.31	153.66	45.75	12.76		95.15	130.55	32.82
1986	29.41	13.85	143.69	19.14	14.23	0.47		4.44	165.75	47.47	14.28	1.99	102.01	141.17	32.94
1987	36.14	52.43	135.95	24.31	9.30	0.50	1.11	13.40	182.59	49.53	17.89	39.23	75.94	154.54	33.60
1988	40.11	74.22	169.89	37.07	13.33	0.60	10.38	12.76	221.27	60.02	19.40	48.62	93.23	189.48	41.65
1989	44.80	91.71	177.05	38.53	16.88	0.67	10.64	10.34	252.23	68.99	22.64	61.14	99.46	212.33	47.38
1990	57.87	93.56	168.74	43.88	19.31	2.19	11.01	11.37	262.39	84.87	30.01	60.86	86.65	219.27	56.99
1991	78.66	108.74	195.23	45.52	19.98	2.28	11.43	11.83	291.53	89.67	34.26	70.30	97.30	255.59	66.45
1992	91.62	126.67	233.04	48.67	21.37	2.43	12.24	12.63	345.91	110.60	39.92	82.12	113.27	292.97	76.42
1993	84.78	144.31	170.33	53.57	33.88	3.48	2.35	13.86	414.79	202.32	57.45	97.61	57.41	334.00	156.98
1994	178.49	156.29	248.63	74.77	40.06	4.26	2.12	28.33	499.84	191.19	69.65	112.19	126.81	405.11	135.67
1995	225.57	224.52	312.72	81.44	39.91	5.75	3.84	31.94	615.17	289.78	90.60	152.24	82.55	503.71	213.87

Year	v13b1ii	v13b1iii	v13b1iv	v13b2	v13b2i	v13b2ii	v13b2iii	v13b2iv	v13c	v13ci	v13cii	v13ciii	v13civ	v13c1
1952														
1953														
1954														
1955														
1956														
1957														
1958														
1959														
1960														
1961														
1962														
1963														
1964														
1965														
1966														
1967														
1968														
1969														
1970														
1971														
1972														
1973														
1974														
1975														
1976														
1977														
1978	6.67	13.54	37.35	7.21	3.41	0.56	1.05	2.19	25.78	8.58	3.59	1.76	11.85	7.00
1979	7.69	14.57	39.81	7.81	3.80	1.00	1.10	1.91	29.76	10.52	4.68	2.09	12.47	6.55
1980	7.97	16.12	44.06	8.85	4.11	1.25	0.03	3.46	37.21	12.14	5.53	2.66	16.88	6.96
1981	7.97	16.19	42.11	9.81	5.15	1.32	0.03	3.31	40.02	13.51	6.27	2.77	17.47	7.60
1982	7.98	17.13	47.22	10.49	5.49	1.33	0.03	3.64	44.81	16.90	6.77	3.02	18.12	8.25
1983	9.10	17.89	52.84	13.89	6.99	1.42	1.20	4.28	57.63	18.86	8.93	3.15	26.69	9.06
1984	9.52	21.85	61.24	16.69	8.83	1.43	1.13	5.30	71.08	22.99	10.11	4.30	33.68	10.43
1985	11.13		86.70	23.01	12.93	1.63		8.45	85.65	28.52	12.20	0.64	44.29	12.74
1986	12.75		95.48	24.58	14.53	1.53	1.99	6.53	99.97	36.21	14.66	11.86	37.24	14.98
1987	16.09	36.73	68.12	28.05	15.93	1.80	2.50	7.82	119.92	43.47	17.75	12.09	46.61	17.70
1988	17.61	45.43	84.79	31.79	18.37	1.79	3.19	8.44	151.88	52.65	20.11	15.22	63.90	19.03
1989	20.57	56.47	88.41	39.40	21.61	2.07	4.67	11.05	165.20	56.53	21.49	19.93	67.25	18.72
1990	27.85	57.02	77.41	43.12	27.88	2.16	3.84	9.24	194.55	76.47	25.67	21.69	70.72	23.96
1991	32.46	66.45	90.23	35.94	23.22	1.80	3.85	7.07	261.84	106.61	42.12	27.01	86.10	29.61
1992	37.25	76.43	102.87	52.94	34.18	2.67	5.69	10.40	314.52	125.80	49.27	32.31	107.14	35.49
1993	52.77	86.51	37.74	80.79	45.34	4.68	11.10	19.67	395.17	227.91	23.85	44.35	99.06	37.58
1994	64.86	102.33	102.25	94.73	55.52	4.79	9.86	24.56	509.42	269.37	104.58	41.98	93.49	61.51
1995	84.74	138.52	66.58	111.46	75.91	5.86	13.72	15.97	698.28	302.39	129.22	68.44	198.23	83.55

Year	v13c1i	v13c1ii	v13c1iii	v13c1iv	v13c2	v13c2i	v13c2ii	v13c2iii	v13c2iv	v13c3	v13c3i	v13c3ii	v13c3iii	v13c3iv
1952														
1953														
1954														
1955														
1956														
1957														
1958														
1959														
1960														
1961														
1962														
1963														
1964														
1965														
1966														
1967														
1968														
1969														
1970														
1971														
1972														
1973														
1974														
1975														
1976														
1977														
1978	0.87	0.67	0.53	4.93	8.28	1.82	0.25	1.08	5.13	1.90	0.24	0.01		1.65
1979	1.01	0.72	0.55	4.27	8.79	2.10	0.28	1.33	5.08	3.36	0.40	0.03		2.93
1980	1.05	0.80	0.50	4.61	11.01	2.63	0.44	1.92	6.02	6.47	0.73	0.03		5.71
1981	1.08	0.81	0.52	5.19	11.86	2.75	0.50	1.99	6.62	5.44	0.62	0.03		4.79
1982	3.21	0.88	0.62	3.54	11.05	2.66	0.57	2.09	5.73	9.83	1.10	0.04		8.69
1983	3.04	1.22	0.56	4.24	13.63	2.46	1.02	2.25	7.90	16.00	1.70	0.07		14.23
1984	3.33	1.38	0.88	4.84	18.37	2.46	1.33	2.88	11.70	18.01	1.92	0.07		16.02
1985	3.39	1.54		7.81	25.89	5.16	1.44		19.29	18.95	2.03	0.07		16.85
1986	4.39	2.03	4.90	3.66	27.99	6.18	2.06	5.45	14.30	21.68	2.29	0.09	0.59	18.71
1987	4.37	2.42	3.26	7.65	27.21	7.47	1.59	6.28	11.87	30.66	3.10	0.10	1.30	26.16
1988	4.70	2.60	3.51	8.22	39.07	10.39	2.00	9.59	17.09	42.21	3.32	0.10	0.80	37.99
1989	5.22	2.62	5.16	5.72	34.77	10.13	2.46	10.79	11.39	55.67	3.00	0.18	2.89	49.60
1990	6.88	4.14	1.78	11.16	43.85	19.73	1.31	10.99	11.82	56.75	2.27	0.40	7.24	46.84
1991	10.66	4.80	2.58	11.57	65.65	29.41	5.78	15.17	15.29	54.67	2.18	0.38	4.33	47.78
1992	12.74	5.75	3.09	13.91	85.41	38.25	7.60	19.74	19.82	64.95	2.58	1.96	3.65	56.76
1993	13.32	6.22	3.27	14.77	113.88	51.45	6.28	25.08	31.07	82.95	28.06	3.71	8.22	42.96
1994	8.10	45.55	1.73	6.13	146.62	73.57	13.08	8.15	51.82	108.98	23.72	6.20	16.75	62.31
1995	24.62	34.36	5.29	19.28	174.70	80.61	19.89	27.30	46.90	145.27	10.80	12.10	23.31	99.06

Year	v13c4	v13c4i	v13c4ii	v13c4iii	v13c4iv	v13c5	v13c5i	v13c5ii	v13c5iii	v13c5iv	v13c6	v13c6i	v13c6ii	v13c6iii
1952														
1953														
1954														
1955														
1956														
1957														
1958														
1959														
1960														
1961														
1962														
1963														
1964														
1965														
1966														
1967														
1968														
1969														
1970														
1971														
1972														
1973														
1974														
1975														
1976														
1977														
1978	0.85	0.12	0.69		0.04	1.84	1.45	0.20	0.15	0.04	1.45	0.90	0.55	
1979	1.55	0.22	1.27		0.06	2.61	2.05	0.28	0.21	0.07	1.71	1.06	0.65	
1980	1.79	0.25	1.47		0.07	2.94	2.31	0.31	0.24	0.08	2.04	1.26	0.78	
1981	1.92	0.27	1.57		0.08	3.20	2.52	0.34	0.26	0.08	2.57	1.59	0.98	
1982	2.01	0.29	1.65		0.07	3.76	2.96	0.40	0.31	0.09	2.45	1.52	0.93	
1983	2.42	0.34	1.98		0.10	4.20	3.30	0.45	0.34	0.11	3.06	1.90	1.16	
1984	2.35	0.33	1.93		0.09	6.55	5.15	0.70	0.54	0.16	3.77	2.34	1.43	
1985	3.03	0.43	2.48		0.12	7.97	6.26	0.85	0.64	0.22	4.23	2.62	1.61	
1986	3.10	0.44	2.54		0.12	11.17	8.78	1.20	0.92	0.27	4.76	2.95	1.81	
1987	2.90	0.43	2.33		0.14	15.27	12.00	1.63	1.25	0.39	6.30	3.91	2.39	
1988	4.21	0.63	3.39		0.19	16.11	12.66	1.72	1.32	0.41	7.86	4.91	2.95	
1989	4.13	0.61	3.32		0.20	13.35	10.49	1.43	1.09	0.34	9.45	5.91	3.54	
1990	4.27	0.51	3.68	0.02	0.06	19.89	15.29	2.10	1.66	0.84	11.58	6.41	5.17	
1991	5.48	0.66	4.70	0.04	0.08	27.55	21.20	2.95	2.30	1.10	8.06	5.73	2.33	
1992	5.58	0.67	4.78	0.05	0.08	29.36	23.08	3.14	2.41	0.73	10.72	6.68	3.53	0.07
1993	6.69	5.35	0.29	0.25	0.80	35.23	27.69	3.77	2.89	0.88	12.33	10.48	0.50	0.25
1994	10.11	2.73	2.68	2.02	2.68	39.94	59.17	21.31	-3.07	-37.47	17.91	16.50	1.27	0.07
1995	28.39	10.17	9.26	6.40	2.56	94.08	53.46	21.90	-3.98	22.70	23.09	16.52	6.53	0.06

Year	v13c6iv	v13c7	v13c7i	v13c7ii	v13c7iii	v13c7iv	v13c8	v13c8i	v13c8ii	v13c8iii	v13c8iv	v13c9	v13c9i	v13c9ii
1952														
1953														
1954														
1955														
1956														
1957														
1958														
1959														
1960														
1961														
1962														
1963														
1964														
1965														
1966														
1967														
1968														
1969														
1970														
1971														
1972														
1973														
1974														
1975														
1976														
1977														
1978		1.20	0.84	0.36			1.49	0.95	0.54			1.77	1.39	0.32
1979		1.41	0.99	0.42			1.76	1.13	0.63			2.02	1.56	0.40
1980		1.69	1.18	0.51			2.10	1.34	0.76			2.21	1.39	0.43
1981		2.13	1.49	0.64			2.64	1.69	0.95			2.66	1.30	0.45
1982		2.03	1.42	0.61			2.52	1.61	0.91			2.91	2.13	0.78
1983		2.54	1.77	0.77			3.15	2.02	1.13			3.57	2.33	1.13
1984		3.12	2.19	0.93			3.88	2.48	1.40			4.60	2.79	0.94
1985		3.51	2.46	1.05			4.35	2.79	1.56			4.98	3.38	1.60
1986		3.95	2.77	1.18			4.90	3.14	1.76			7.44	5.27	1.99
1987		5.22	3.65	1.57			6.48	4.15	2.33			8.18	4.39	3.39
1988		6.51	4.57	1.94			8.08	5.17	2.91			8.80	6.30	2.50
1989		7.83	5.49	2.34			9.72	6.21	3.51			11.56	9.47	2.09
1990		9.96	6.66	3.30			10.67	7.65	3.02			13.62	11.07	2.55
1991		25.48	13.29	6.48	1.88	3.83	23.51	9.30	7.05	0.71	6.45	21.83	14.18	7.65
1992	0.44	30.30	15.14	8.15	1.32	5.69	27.48	10.73	8.40	0.84	7.51	21.91	13.89	5.29
1993	1.10	38.56	33.39	0.78	0.97	3.42	35.51	29.88	1.55	0.65	3.43	28.69	25.54	0.39
1994	0.07	43.07	30.59	1.33	6.19	4.96	41.68	23.52	11.66	2.52	3.98	35.14	27.70	0.40
1995	-0.02	53.54	38.71	7.47	1.27	6.09	51.91	34.64	8.85	3.65	4.77	37.95	28.22	6.75

Year	v13c9iii	v13c9iv	v13c10	v13c10i	v13c10ii	v13c10iii	v13c10iv
1952							
1953							
1954							
1955							
1956							
1957							
1958							
1959							
1960							
1961							
1962							
1963							
1964							
1965							
1966							
1967							
1968							
1969							
1970							
1971							
1972							
1973							
1974							
1975							
1976							
1977							
1978		0.06					
1979		0.06					
1980		0.39					
1981		0.71					
1982							
1983		0.11					
1984		0.87					
1985							
1986		0.18					
1987		0.40					
1988							
1989							
1990							
1991							
1992	0.53	2.20	3.32	2.04	0.67	0.61	
1993	2.70	0.06	3.75	2.75	0.36	0.07	0.57
1994	7.14	-0.10	4.46	3.77	1.10	0.48	-0.89
1995	4.23	-1.25	5.80	4.64	2.11	0.91	-1.86

2

Tianjin

Year	v1	v1a	v1b	v1b1	v1b2	v1c	v1c1	v1c2	v1c3	v2	v2a	v2b	v2b1	v2b2	v2c
1952	28.54	2.73	20.36	19.71	0.66	5.45	0.76	3.51	1.18	117.1	110.9	113.5	115.6	76.9	133.7
1953	38.89	2.48	27.52	26.21	1.32	8.89	1.01	6.30	1.58	134.6	92.1	136.4	133.7	206.9	154.9
1954	41.78	2.38	31.25	29.43	1.83	8.15	1.16	5.01	1.98	106.1	97.1	114.2	112.5	142.3	88.4
1955	41.57	3.00	31.09	30.09	1.00	7.48	1.16	4.14	2.18	101.2	125.6	101.5	104.9	55.9	90.7
1956	48.88	3.01	36.89	35.69	1.21	8.97	1.39	5.19	2.39	121.6	102.0	124.6	125.2	108.2	121.3
1957	56.11	3.23	42.12	40.43	1.68	10.77	1.66	6.31	2.80	112.1	105.1	111.1	109.2	164.1	119.2
1958	80.21	2.94	65.28	61.94	3.35	11.99	2.04	6.41	3.54	139.1	92.9	152.0	149.6	198.1	111.7
1959	106.19	3.40	88.99	85.15	3.84	13.80	2.62	6.53	4.65	129.0	115.7	133.1	134.8	107.6	113.6
1960	119.54	3.17	100.87	96.03	4.84	15.49	3.22	6.40	5.87	112.2	93.9	113.7	113.1	123.2	109.9
1961	69.70	2.95	53.20	51.54	1.66	13.55	2.18	5.81	5.56	54.8	91.7	48.7	49.6	33.9	80.1
1962	61.47	2.78	46.44	45.39	1.05	12.25	2.06	5.13	4.38	89.5	94.9	89.2	90.2	65.7	88.5
1963	65.81	2.98	50.66	48.94	1.72	12.16	1.91	5.65	4.60	107.5	103.1	109.8	108.1	166.3	100.8
1964	73.19	3.11	57.66	55.21	2.46	12.42	2.09	6.06	4.27	111.9	105.0	116.7	115.5	141.6	95.5
1965	86.43	4.82	67.98	66.35	1.63	13.62	2.50	6.49	4.63	123.5	155.0	120.4	123.2	69.9	125.6
1966	100.88	3.98	82.96	80.62	2.54	13.94	2.32	6.44	5.18	113.2	82.0	118.9	117.7	157.3	102.7
1967	87.46	4.59	69.87	68.27	1.60	13.01	2.00	6.05	4.96	87.7	113.6	84.7	85.6	62.8	93.7
1968	89.55	4.49	70.96	69.13	1.83	14.10	2.04	6.04	6.02	108.4	98.0	109.6	109.4	114.5	108.0
1969	110.22	3.99	91.01	88.47	2.55	15.22	2.57	6.35	6.30	123.8	88.9	130.0	130.3	139.2	107.4
1970	126.77	5.20	105.50	102.77	2.73	16.07	3.07	6.64	6.36	113.7	130.2	113.9	114.1	107.6	107.1
1971	137.30	5.41	115.09	111.58	3.51	16.80	3.74	6.55	6.51	109.7	102.8	111.0	110.5	126.4	104.5
1972	139.03	4.44	116.88	112.24	4.64	17.72	4.02	7.07	6.63	104.0	80.8	105.3	104.4	130.3	105.7
1973	154.64	4.43	129.70	123.50	6.20	20.51	4.83	8.37	7.31	111.8	105.8	111.5	110.6	131.1	115.6
1974	170.51	5.52	142.59	134.55	8.04	22.41	4.99	9.28	8.14	110.2	121.9	109.8	108.9	126.7	109.5
1975	184.06	5.39	156.14	145.57	10.57	22.54	5.15	8.94	8.45	108.0	98.7	109.7	108.4	128.9	100.3
1976	171.25	5.21	142.37	135.60	6.77	23.67	5.99	8.55	9.13	93.4	96.5	91.7	93.9	63.1	104.6
1977	177.42	4.23	147.18	138.12	9.06	26.01	6.69	9.46	9.86	103.5	81.8	103.5	102.1	131.8	109.8
1978	209.64	6.72	171.42	157.91	13.51	31.50	8.02	12.03	11.45	118.0	123.0	117.3	114.3	162.7	121.0
1979	236.38	8.88	192.60	175.52	17.08	34.91	9.39	13.20	12.32	110.6	116.8	110.4	109.6	118.9	110.0
1980	262.33	9.25	213.57	195.94	17.64	39.50	11.31	13.83	14.36	109.7	104.9	110.1	111.4	97.1	108.7
1981	276.51	8.34	224.31	205.86	18.45	43.86	11.93	15.01	16.92	105.9	89.9	105.9	106.6	98.3	109.5
1982	301.66	12.56	244.47	218.40	26.06	44.63	12.76	14.90	16.97	107.9	120.9	108.6	106.4	135.1	101.5
1983	330.96	12.68	264.76	235.33	29.43	53.51	15.26	18.77	19.48	109.9	101.3	108.6	108.5	109.5	119.8
1984	367.81	16.68	291.18	259.10	32.08	59.94	16.86	21.32	21.76	111.1	120.5	110.8	111.7	102.2	110.6
1985	458.30	20.44	356.99	319.47	37.53	80.87	20.74	28.64	31.49	116.1	119.4	114.8	115.7	105.8	122.5
1986	512.00	26.93	387.19	344.73	42.46	97.88	26.03	33.31	38.54	107.2	111.4	106.2	106.2	105.7	111.2
1987	597.65	32.93	452.30	405.49	46.82	112.42	27.76	39.92	44.74	110.3	111.7	110.6	111.4	102.1	108.3
1988	765.90	44.49	574.50	521.10	53.40	146.91	34.02	54.14	58.75	116.0	109.0	117.3	118.7	100.1	111.0
1989	895.76	51.82	692.81	634.24	58.57	151.13	37.42	46.33	67.38	107.1	114.0	108.4	109.1	97.9	98.8
1990	1007.90	54.88	705.93	647.66	58.27	247.09	58.06	74.04	114.99	112.3	107.4	106.9	108.0	88.0	144.9
1991	1179.54	58.05	852.62	786.60	66.02	268.87	61.99	95.96	110.92	110.4	106.9	111.8	112.2	104.3	105.3
1992	1473.80	62.16	1078.69	997.91	80.78	332.95	75.93	117.35	139.67	120.8	104.1	123.4	124.4	101.6	112.2
1993	2012.40	70.62	1512.08	1401.84	110.24	429.70	101.95	146.69	181.06	122.7	104.6	124.2	125.1	110.7	112.0
1994	2591.47	94.97	1902.65	1754.30	148.35	593.85	140.75	183.69	269.41	124.5	107.7	126.8	126.8	127.1	118.0
1995	3328.15	133.25	2417.14	2230.69	186.45	777.76	192.50	221.06	364.20	122.7	112.4	122.9	123.5	112.8	123.5

Year	v2c1	v2c2	v3'	v3	v3a	v3b	v3b1	v3b2	v3c	v3c1	v3c2	v3c3	v3c4	v3c5	v3c6
1952	102.2	109.7	12.80	12.80	1.85	6.31	6.12	0.19	4.64	0.61	3.04				
1953	139.1	165.3	17.58	17.58	1.76	8.49	8.18	0.31	7.33	0.74	5.26				
1954	115.4	78.2	16.98	16.98	1.79	8.93	8.51	0.42	6.26	0.79	3.85				
1955	102.1	82.6	17.12	17.12	2.35	9.16	8.89	0.27	5.61	0.75	3.03				
1956	122.7	125.6	20.70	20.70	2.26	10.83	10.54	0.29	7.61	1.02	4.60				
1957	126.1	119.3	24.11	24.11	2.49	13.28	12.86	0.42	8.34	1.08	4.92				
1958	124.0	102.9	32.49	32.49	2.28	22.21	21.34	0.87	8.00	1.08	3.98				
1959	128.0	101.8	41.25	41.25	2.80	29.10	28.08	1.02	9.35	1.40	4.05				
1960	123.8	96.8	42.66	42.66	2.65	29.65	28.46	1.19	10.36	1.60	3.84				
1961	67.6	82.5	28.41	28.41	2.52	16.56	15.98	0.58	9.33	1.09	3.58				
1962	93.3	85.0	24.25	24.25	2.12	14.08	13.69	0.39	8.05	1.17	2.77				
1963	92.8	109.5	26.65	26.65	2.27	16.20	15.63	0.57	8.18	1.01	3.47				
1964	109.1	109.4	30.59	30.59	2.30	20.08	19.28	0.80	8.21	1.16	3.58				
1965	119.6	112.6	35.96	35.96	3.91	22.96	22.34	0.62	9.09	1.23	4.10				
1966	93.0	100.2	39.31	39.31	2.69	26.87	26.17	0.70	9.75	1.38	4.14				
1967	87.1	94.1	33.62	33.62	3.50	20.93	20.30	0.63	9.19	1.20	3.93				
1968	103.2	100.0	34.77	34.77	3.60	21.26	20.64	0.62	9.91	1.19	3.80				
1969	125.6	104.5	42.87	42.87	3.46	29.03	28.39	0.64	10.38	1.40	3.98				
1970	120.1	106.6	50.99	50.99	3.80	35.80	35.08	0.72	11.39	1.94	4.39				
1971	121.7	98.7	55.12	55.12	3.89	39.52	38.33	1.19	11.71	2.10	4.35				
1972	107.7	107.9	56.37	56.37	3.46	40.53	38.95	1.58	12.38	2.27	4.84				
1973	120.2	117.8	60.33	60.33	3.92	42.51	40.68	1.83	13.90	2.55	5.54				
1974	103.3	111.2	66.69	66.69	4.79	46.81	44.52	2.29	15.09	2.66	5.99				
1975	103.3	96.4	69.73	69.73	4.37	50.29	47.73	2.56	15.07	2.60	5.83				
1976	116.3	95.6	65.25	65.25	4.01	45.57	43.84	1.73	15.67	2.77	5.97				
1977	111.6	110.5	67.73	67.73	3.56	46.97	44.81	2.16	17.20	3.17	6.77				
1978	119.9	125.9	82.65	82.65	5.03	57.53	54.39	3.14	20.09	4.79	6.95	0.13		4 60	0.28
1979	117.1	108.5	93.00	93.00	6.54	64.76	60.95	3.81	21.70	5.51	7.41	0.14		3 69	0.42
1980	120.5	99.3	103.52	103.52	6.53	72.43	67.35	5.08	24.56	6.36	7.12	0.76		5 63	0.14
1981	105.5	106.9	107.96	107.96	5.18	76.77	70.86	5.91	26.01	6.70	8.52	0.57		4 21	1.08
1982	107.0	98.8	114.10	114.10	7.00	79.59	72.03	7.56	27.51	6.59	7.24	0.74		5 46	1.29
1983	119.6	125.2	123.40	123.40	7.60	84.11	76.33	7.78	31.69	7.58	8.89	1.55		5 48	1.78
1984	110.5	111.5	147.47	147.47	11.13	95.97	87.47	8.50	40.37	11.60	14.61	5.64	0.85	3 07	0.63
1985	123.0	118.1	175.71	175.71	12.95	114.23	104.11	10.12	48.53	11.69	15.64	8.94	1.67	3 33	1.39
1986	111.2	108.4	194.67	194.67	16.51	122.49	111.06	11.43	55.67	13.89	17.40	9.80	1.86	3 44	1.85
1987	103.6	112.1	220.00	220.00	19.63	136.96	123.99	12.97	63.41	14.46	20.36	14.54	1.88	3 41	1.48
1988	105.2	115.2	259.64	259.64	26.21	159.58	145.35	14.23	73.85	16.61	21.55	18.32	3.35	3 72	2.02
1989	98.8	97.9	283.34	283.34	26.85	175.88	159.07	16.81	80.61	21.30	14.26	25.31	3.22	3 79	2.41
1990	125.4	139.7	310.95	310.95	27.32	179.51	163.72	15.79	104.12	30.25	15.85	29.04	5.35	5 66	2.77
1991	106.1	122.6	342.75	342.75	29.26	194.41	177.56	16.85	119.08	27.13	27.65	30.37	5.84	6 82	3.36
1992	109.3	111.5	411.24	411.24	30.26	230.61	210.00	20.61	150.37	35.66	41.05	34.71	6.78	7 82	3.84
1993	134.5	109.6	536.10	536.10	35.39	302.48	275.04	27.44	198.23	47.60	51.21	42.61	9.70	17 10	4.58
1994	132.5	108.3	725.14	725.14	46.53	404.08	361.27	42.81	274.53	66.55	65.41	55.50	12.14	34 38	6.02
1995	125.1	120.3	920.11	920.11	63.21	501.22	451.84	49.38	355.68	86.14	78.27	81.40	16.85	45 43	7.21

Year	v3c7	v3c8	v3c9	v3c10	v3d	v4'	v4	v4a	v4b	v4b1	v4b2	v4c	v4c1	v4c2	v4c3
1952				0.99	299	112.2	112.2	112.4	104.4			121.1			
1953				1.33	393	133.4	133.4	96.6	135.6	134.2	172.1	147.8	114.7	162.4	
1954				1.62	364	95.3	95.3	101.9	105.8	104.4	136.3	83.6	101.8	71.3	
1955				1.83	357	102.5	102.5	131.6	104.7	107.1	65.6	89.4	95.5	78.1	
1956				1.99	419	123.6	123.6	97.8	124.2	125.2	95.4	136.4	138.2	153.4	
1957				2.34	468	113.5	113.5	108.3	119.2	117.7	170.3	108.3	104.7	106.1	
1958				2.94	607	129.8	129.8	93.5	163.6	161.9	204.9	97.2	99.4	81.9	
1959				3.90	744	124.4	124.4	122.4	128.1	129.1	110.3	116.5	130.0	100.7	
1960				4.92	746	103.3	103.3	94.5	102.2	101.7	113.3	109.4	112.5	93.0	
1961				4.66	489	64.1	64.1	93.9	51.8	51.9	48.8	83.5	64.5	88.0	
1962				4.11	414	85.5	85.5	85.0	87.0	87.8	70.2	83.5	103.7	75.4	
1963				3.70	442	109.0	109.0	102.8	115.6	114.5	144.6	101.1	86.6	124.7	
1964				3.47	494	115.9	115.9	102.3	126.8	126.0	143.0	102.0	115.8	104.8	
1965				3.76	571	121.5	121.5	169.4	115.9	117.7	80.1	115.4	109.7	118.5	
1966				4.23	618	106.2	106.2	68.7	115.1	115.2	111.8	108.0	112.9	101.1	
1967				4.06	524	87.9	87.9	127.7	78.7	78.2	93.8	94.9	87.5	96.0	
1968				4.92	535	107.9	107.9	103.0	109.1	109.7	94.5	108.1	99.5	96.7	
1969				5.00	661	122.6	122.6	95.7	138.5	139.7	104.9	104.1	117.0	104.0	
1970				5.06	791	117.5	117.5	109.3	121.2	121.5	110.5	111.5	140.3	111.8	
1971				5.26	843	109.0	109.0	100.7	112.5	111.1	166.1	102.7	108.0	98.9	
1972				5.27	849	104.3	104.3	87.3	106.1	105.2	130.9	105.7	108.3	111.4	
1973				5.81	893	107.8	107.8	117.3	105.5	105.1	113.5	111.7	111.7	113.8	
1974				6.44	977	110.5	110.5	119.7	110.0	109.3	124.1	109.0	105.0	108.5	
1975				6.64	1011	104.3	104.3	91.9	107.4	107.4	108.0	99.9	97.7	97.2	
1976				6.93	928	94.1	94.1	91.7	91.2	92.6	66.3	104.0	106.4	102.5	
1977				7.26	961	103.6	103.6	88.2	103.2	102.4	124.0	109.5	114.3	113.2	
1978	1.92	0.33	1.09		1160	120.9	120.9	115.6	123.3	121.1	167.9	116.0	150.3	102.2	
1979	2.97	0.49	1.07		1272	110.0	110.0	117.4	110.4	110.4	110.7	107.0	114.1	105.8	
1980	2.62	0.53	1.40		1392	110.0	110.0	99.8	111.4	110.6	122.0	108.7	112.0	93.2	
1981	3.28	0.53	1.12		1433	104.8	104.8	79.1	107.0	106.6	112.2	104.8	104.5	118.7	
1982	3.93	0.63	1.63		1488	104.3	104.3	112.9	103.5	102.4	117.5	105.3	98.1	84.7	
1983	3.85	0.88	1.68		1583	108.3	108.3	109.2	106.0	106.0	106.3	114.8	114.7	122.4	
1984	2.13	0.66	1.18		1868	119.3	119.3	122.8	116.6	117.5	106.2	125.9	151.4	162.5	
1985	3.54	0.77	1.56		2198	110.6	110.6	121.1	110.5	110.0	116.5	108.8	94.3	100.2	
1986	4.59	0.97	1.87		2406	105.8	105.8	108.0	105.5	105.0	111.8	106.0	108.1	101.3	
1987	4.03	1.05	2.20		2682	107.6	107.6	106.0	108.3	108.2	108.9	106.3	109.9	102.3	
1988	4.58	1.04	2.66		3117	105.8	105.8	107.7	107.7	108.3	101.2	100.4	94.1	94.3	
1989	5.66	1.41	3.25		3353	101.6	101.6	111.4	98.1	97.8	101.2	109.3	119.3	75.2	
1990	5.85	3.52	5.83		3621	105.4	105.4	104.6	101.1	102.0	91.6	116.4	139.6	102.7	
1991	7.66	3.73	6.52		3943	106.0	106.0	103.4	105.5	105.8	102.1	107.5	99.1	130.0	
1992	8.68	4.58	7.25		4696	111.7	111.7	100.7	111.5	112.4	101.2	114.6	120.0	134.9	104.5
1993	10.10	5.54	9.79		6075	112.1	112.1	107.4	112.9	113.6	103.6	111.7	124.0	109.2	107.2
1994	14.05	8.52	11.96		8164	114.3	114.3	105.3	114.7	114.1	122.7	115.6	123.1	111.9	112.7
1995	15.97	10.19	14.22		10308	114.9	114.9	106.3	114.1	114.5	109.9	117.9	120.6	111.1	125.2

Year	v4c4	v4c5	v4c6	v4c7	v4c8	v4c9	v4c10	v5	v5a	v5a1	v5a1a	v5a1b	v5a2	v5b	v5b1
1952								12.80	6.93	6.09	1.20	4.89	0.84	1.59	1.32
1953								17.58	8.47	7.19	1.14	6.05	1.28	4.09	2.03
1954								16.98	8.21	7.15	1.13	6.02	1.06	5.89	2.58
1955								17.12	8.06	7.08	1.46	5.62	0.98	2.72	1.78
1956								20.70	9.22	7.98	1.43	6.55	1.24	0.56	2.59
1957								24.11	9.68	8.64	1.51	7.13	1.04	6.71	3.07
1958								32.49	10.90	9.49	1.65	7.84	1.41	10.53	7.51
1959								41.25	13.11	11.69	2.04	9.65	1.42	17.63	8.22
1960								42.66	14.65	13.26	2.30	10.96	1.39	12.15	9.65
1961								28.41	14.45	13.12	2.35	10.77	1.33	1.21	3.25
1962								24.25	12.45	11.03	1.92	9.11	1.42	0.94	2.38
1963								26.65	13.77	12.25	2.15	10.10	1.52	0.93	3.30
1964								30.59	14.26	12.64	2.21	10.43	1.62	5.13	4.59
1965								35.96	14.97	13.23	2.68	10.55	1.74	8.13	3.73
1966								39.31	16.03	14.48	2.74	11.74	1.55	9.94	4.92
1967								33.62	16.76	15.51	3.37	12.14	1.25	7.32	2.22
1968								34.77	16.83	15.74	3.48	12.26	1.09	7.20	2.72
1969								42.87	17.89	16.52	3.88	12.64	1.37	8.07	4.98
1970								50.99	17.59	16.12	4.44	11.68	1.47	11.21	7.89
1971								55.12	17.73	16.30	4.64	11.66	1.43	15.29	8.40
1972								56.37	18.88	17.35	4.43	12.92	1.53	16.11	10.22
1973								60.33	20.31	18.53	4.83	13.70	1.78	21.78	15.27
1974								66.69	22.13	20.14	5.56	14.58	1.99	27.50	19.98
1975								69.73	23.74	21.55	5.95	15.60	2.19	25.50	20.80
1976								65.25	25.25	22.65	6.11	16.54	2.60	21.58	17.38
1977								67.73	27.36	24.28	6.24	18.04	3.08	24.54	20.18
1978							113.9	82.65	30.18	26.52	6.89	19.63	3.66	26.40	18.55
1979							104.0	93.00	34.01	29.90	8.00	21.90	4.11	33.27	23.91
1980							119.5	103.52	39.62	35.48	9.58	25.90	4.14	35.66	25.56
1981							95.9	107.96	43.72	37.31	10.46	26.85	6.41	25.06	25.00
1982							126.2	114.10	47.22	40.72	12.86	27.86	6.50	34.81	32.36
1983							110.7	123.40	52.92	45.20	13.96	31.24	7.72	41.94	38.27
1984							91.5	147.47	60.37	50.63	16.98	33.65	9.74	48.30	48.67
1985							129.8	175.71	71.86	60.60	19.53	41.07	11.26	88.65	67.60
1986							108.5	194.67	82.11	68.66	20.67	47.99	13.45	101.10	75.89
1987							107.1	220.00	97.23	76.31	22.99	53.32	20.92	92.70	81.63
1988							108.7	259.64	126.42	97.16	28.73	68.43	29.26	142.27	96.85
1989							125.4	283.34	143.10	109.05	32.00	77.05	34.05	137.20	95.43
1990							109.7	310.95	143.68	115.38	31.56	83.82	28.30	134.37	98.03
1991							103.9	342.75	165.26	130.16	34.66	95.50	35.10	163.65	144.19
1992	111.7	101.1	103.5	101.4	101.6	102.6		411.24	190.08	147.90	38.58	109.32	42.18	227.18	185.12
1993	108.3	105.6	105.0	104.0	115.3	109.4		536.10	244.85	186.31	47.11	139.20	58.54	315.61	246.16
1994	108.2	121.5	103.2	104.9	111.2	113.0		725.14	323.76	241.56	55.78	185.78	82.20	430.90	345.46
1995	129.0	127.4	106.0	102.0	119.4	110.1		920.11	386.99	301.66	71.61	230.05	85.33	524.77	428.48

Year	v5b2	v5c	v5c1	v5c2	v6a1	v6a2	v6a3	v6a4	v6b2	v6b3	v6b4	v7	v7a	v7a1	v7a2
1952	0.27	4.28													
1953	2.06	5.02										112.7	108.8	87.6	114.0
1954	3.31	2.88										95.3	97.7	97.4	97.8
1955	0.94	6.34										98.1	98.9	129.1	93.3
1956	-2.03	10.92										114.7	113.0	98.2	116.8
1957	3.64	7.72										103.0	106.3	103.6	106.8
1958	3.02	11.06										114.2	111.4	110.8	111.5
1959	9.41	10.51										120.2	123.1	123.6	123.0
1960	2.50	15.86										110.3	112.0	111.3	112.1
1961	-2.04	12.75										89.6	89.9	92.8	89.3
1962	-1.44	10.86										83.1	81.0	78.8	81.5
1963	-2.37	11.95										109.9	110.4	111.3	110.2
1964	0.54	11.20										105.7	105.3	104.9	105.4
1965	4.40	12.86										110.4	110.1	127.6	106.4
1966	5.02	13.34										108.1	110.4	103.2	112.3
1967	5.10	9.54										104.9	107.4	123.4	103.7
1968	4.48	10.74										100.5	101.6	103.4	101.1
1969	3.09	16.91										105.6	104.3	110.8	102.5
1970	3.32	22.19										100.3	99.6	116.8	94.3
1971	6.89	22.10										100.8	101.1	104.5	99.8
1972	5.89	21.38										106.5	106.5	95.5	110.8
1973	6.51	18.24										107.1	106.4	108.6	105.6
1974	7.52	17.06										109.3	109.1	115.5	106.8
1975	4.80	20.39										107.2	107.0	107.0	106.9
1976	4.20	18.42										106.4	105.1	102.7	106.1
1977	4.36	15.83										108.1	107.0	101.9	108.9
1978	7.85	26.07			2.51	3.69	0.31	0.38	17.79	1.48	0.36	108.1	106.9	106.9	106.9
1979	9.36	25.72			3.07	4.27	0.27	0.39	19.89	1.62	0.39	112.6	111.7	115.5	110.4
1980	10.10	28.24			2.99	5.72	0.40	0.47	23.02	2.52	0.36	110.5	109.6	113.0	108.4
1981	0.06	39.18			2.65	6.82	0.35	0.64	24.06	2.28	0.51	108.7	104.8	108.1	103.6
1982	2.45	32.07			3.16	7.47	1.50	0.73	24.90	2.37	0.59	107.5	107.9	116.9	104.3
1983	3.67	28.54			2.84	9.30	1.10	0.72	27.63	2.92	0.69	111.6	110.2	110.4	110.1
1984	-0.37	38.80			3.67	11.14	1.31	0.86	29.59	3.24	0.82	112.5	111.0	120.8	106.7
1985	21.05	15.20			3.46	13.70	1.48	0.89	36.41	3.83	0.83	108.3	109.0	109.1	108.9
1986	25.21	11.46			3.60	14.83	1.21	1.03	41.81	5.16	1.02	106.5	105.5	103.5	106.6
1987	11.07	30.07			3.94	16.61	1.25	1.19	46.81	5.27	1.24	111.7	105.2	102.5	106.7
1988	45.42	-9.05			4.67	21.59	1.05	1.42	56.17	10.39	1.87	110.9	108.8	109.6	108.5
1989	41.77	3.04			5.36	23.72	1.18	1.74	62.57	12.40	2.08	98.9	98.3	98.6	98.2
1990	36.34	32.90			6.61	21.54	1.42	1.99	67.51	14.20	2.11	100.0	102.4	95.5	105.6
1991	19.46	13.84			7.43	22.83	1.87	2.53	76.96	15.53	3.01	105.5	103.3	102.9	103.4
1992	42.06	-6.02	416.31	422.33	7.99	26.22	1.83	2.54	86.03	18.98	4.31	104.2	102.6	102.2	102.7
1993	69.45	-24.36	592.57	616.93	8.60	28.24	4.20	6.07	101.39	30.59	7.22	108.6	107.0	102.7	108.6
1994	85.44	-29.52		29.52	10.38	34.72	5.31	5.37	137.63	40.05	8.10	109.7	106.9	104.7	107.5
1995	96.29	8.35	8.35		15.35	42.38	6.21	7.67	173.37	45.79	10.89	106.1	107.6	108.4	107.4

Year	v7b	v8	v8a	v8b	v9	v9a	v9b	v10a1	v10a2	v10a3	v10a3a	v10a3b	v10a4	v10b1	v10b2
1952		142	58	222											
1953	140.5	161	53	258	104.5	84.9	107.1								
1954	81.4	153	52	239	93.6	96.8	91.3								
1955	92.4	148	66	217	96.6	125.0	90.5								
1956	126.8	162	63	246	110.1	96.0	113.7								
1957	82.3	168	65	251	101.6	101.4	100.0								
1958	137.5	177	71	259	106.9	111.0	104.6								
1959	100.7	211	87	302	119.3	122.2	116.6								
1960	96.6	232	97	327	108.3	110.1	107.0								
1961	87.0	226	98	217	88.0	91.7	88.0								
1962	102.9	188	76	272	80.1	75.0	82.7								
1963	106.4	203	81	298	107.6	105.3	109.0								
1964	108.7	204	81	301	102.5	102.5	103.1								
1965	113.0	210	96	302	108.3	124.7	105.3								
1966	89.9	228	95	338	109.5	100.0	113.2								
1967	80.9	242	114	351	106.2	119.8	103.9								
1968	87.3	242	115	353	100.4	100.8	100.8								
1969	124.9	255	125	375	104.7	108.2	105.6								
1970	109.5	250	137	365	100.0	112.1	99.2								
1971	97.3	249	138	368	99.6	100.7	100.8								
1972	107.0	261	130	398	104.8	94.0	108.3								
1973	115.9	274	140	413	104.6	107.9	103.3								
1974	112.2	295	159	437	107.8	113.9	106.3								
1975	110.0	312	169	461	106.0	105.8	105.3								
1976	118.8	322	171	478	103.3	101.6	103.8								
1977	118.2	345	174	521	106.9	101.1	108.7								
1978	117.7	373	191	558	105.6	107.0	105.2	16.70	0.89	0.74	0.05	0.69	0.22	7 71	0.13
1979	111.0	409	222	590	108.7	115.0	104.6	20.62	2.07	0.96	0.06	0.90	0.26	8 25	0.24
1980	95.5	477	268	671	107.7	113.9	104.4	22.95	1.65	0.95	0.07	0.88	0.01	9 04	1.04
1981	152.5	516	293	718	103.5	108.4	100.9	23.19	0.23	1.56	0.11	1.45	0.02	-0 70	0.56
1982	100.9	531	356	689	106.1	115.1	102.0	28.62	2.04	1.52	0.11	1.41	0.18	1 55	0.58
1983	118.2	579	383	754	108.1	109.5	107.5	32.16	3.75	2.06	0.20	1.86	0.30	1 89	1.26
1984	124.0	641	464	795	109.7	120.4	104.5	38.92	6.80	2.88	0.50	2.38	0.07	-2 99	1.54
1985	101.5	758	540	952	107.7	110.4	105.2	55.79	7.29	3.84	0.42	3.42	0.68	14 59	5.48
1986	111.4	848	569	1074	104.3	103.2	104.6	62.06	7.69	4.40	0.71	3.69	1.74	18 78	4.48
1987	145.4	930	621	1185	103.7	100.4	105.7	64.10	11.12	5.58	1.27	4.31	0.83	8 03	3.60
1988	118.9	1166	768	1490	107.2	108.5	106.3	79.25	9.48	7.35	1.45	5.90	0.77	30 86	11.42
1989	101.1	1291	856	1635	97.1	98.7	95.8	77.06	9.18	8.80	2.58	6.22	0.39	30 53	9.55
1990	99.8	1344	831	1749	100.7	94.0	103.8	81.47	11.62	4.38	0.58	3.80	0.56	21 84	11.92
1991	114.7	1497	905	1963	101.9	102.0	101.9	119.17	12.18	5.69	1.07	4.62	7.15	-1 53	16.44
1992	109.9	1689	1007	2219	101.9	102.1	101.4	150.45	26.55	6.74	0.66	6.08	1.38	12 85	14.41
1993	113.9	2111	1224	2799	106.2	102.3	107.6	175.81	33.47	8.22	1.86	6.36	28.66	32 15	26.03
1994	119.7	2720	1444	3701	106.2	104.4	106.5	233.90	48.13	10.51	2.00	8.51	52.92	43 64	24.21
1995	101.4	3380	1852	4546	107.1	108.3	106.6	256.84	66.60	10.27	0.97	9.30	94.77	7 26	4.20

Year	v10b4	v11a	v11a1	v11a2	v11b	v11b1	v11b2	v11c	v11c1	v11c2	v12	v12a	v12b	v13	v13i
1952															
1953															
1954															
1955															
1956															
1957															
1958															
1959															
1960															
1961															
1962															
1963															
1964															
1965															
1966															
1967															
1968															
1969															
1970															
1971															
1972															
1973															
1974															
1975															
1976															
1977															
1978	0.01	1.00	0.89	0.11	14.25	10.64	3.61	11.15	7.02	4.13				82.65	26.30
1979	0.87	2.31	2.07	0.24	13.66	11.89	1.77	17.30	9.95	7.35				93.00	31.03
1980	0.02	0.84	0.46	0.38	19.43	15.08	4.35	15.39	10.02	5.37				103.52	30.76
1981	0.20	1.21	0.91	0.30	13.41	10.50	2.91	10.44	13.59	-3.15				107.96	30.95
1982	0.32	3.36	3.51	-0.15	25.39	21.26	4.13	6.06	7.59	-1.53				114.10	33.80
1983	0.52	5.66	5.31	0.35	12.44	11.13	1.31	23.84	21.83	2.01				123.40	35.49
1984	1.08	3.94	2.57	1.37	22.19	17.52	4.67	22.17	28.58	-6.41				147.47	50.33
1985	0.98	2.14	2.01	0.13	34.25	27.04	7.21	52.26	38.55	13.71				175.71	49.40
1986	1.95	4.26	0.76	3.50	49.18	38.70	10.48	47.66	36.43	11.23				194.67	60.61
1987	-0.56	4.02	1.63	2.39	50.82	44.89	5.93	37.86	35.11	2.75				220.00	72.73
1988	3.14	10.83	1.94	8.89	73.16	59.08	14.08	58.28	35.83	22.45				259.64	84.52
1989	1.69	6.04	1.83	4.21	89.60	63.86	25.74	41.56	29.74	11.82	88.3	89.1	86.7	283.34	100.00
1990	2.58	7.86	2.57	5.29	90.32	66.59	23.73	36.19	28.87	7.32	95.8	98.9	89.9	310.95	139.52
1991	4.55	8.95	2.38	6.57	133.30	111.45	21.85	21.40	30.36	-8.96	115.6	137.2	57.1	342.75	150.68
1992	14.80	5.06	1.85	3.21	168.84	132.92	35.92	53.28	50.35	2.93	121.8	113.0	179.4	411.24	169.33
1993	11.27	8.12	2.82	5.30	198.15	138.82	59.33	109.34	104.52	4.82	111.0	108.2	122.5	536.10	225.62
1994	17.59	9.15	0.96	8.19	231.76	184.01	47.75	189.99	160.49	29.50	119.6	120.4	116.2	725.14	328.69
1995	84.83	15.19	0.98	14.21	317.35	238.81	78.54	192.23	188.69	3.54	115.3	117.0	107.7	920.11	422.48

Year	v13ii	v13iii	v13iv	v13a	v13ai	v13aii	v13aiii	v13aiv	v13b	v13bi	v13bii	v13biii	v13biv	v13b1	v13b1i
1952															
1953															
1954															
1955															
1956															
1957															
1958															
1959															
1960															
1961															
1962															
1963															
1964															
1965															
1966															
1967															
1968															
1969															
1970															
1971															
1972															
1973															
1974															
1975															
1976															
1977															
1978	6.10	15.68	34.57	5.03	3.94	0.02	0.42	0.65	57.53	13.50	4.00	13.36	26.67	54.39	10.94
1979	6.81	16.27	38.89	6.54	5.26	0.03	0.41	0.84	64.76	15.70	4.64	14.56	29.86	60.95	12.77
1980	8.75	19.61	44.40	6.53	4.74	0.59	0.34	0.86	72.43	14.95	5.39	18.14	33.95	67 35	11.78
1981	10.41	17.45	49.15	5.18	3.69	0.53	0.00	0.96	76.77	16.87	6.52	16.65	36.73	70 86	13.57
1982	12.00	16.54	51.76	7.00	5.28	0.25	0.54	0.93	79.59	17.08	7.43	15.84	39.24	72 03	13.20
1983	13.85	19.16	54.90	7.60	5.51	0.27	0.58	1.24	84.11	18.94	8.36	18.43	38.38	76 33	14.44
1984	14.50	21.92	60.72	11.13	9.90	0.25	0.12	0.86	95.97	25.97	10.31	21.33	38.36	87 47	21.02
1985	17.56	28.49	80.26	12.95	10.38	0.80	-0.10	1.87	114.23	24.95	11.67	27.17	50.44	104 11	18.80
1986	22.70	30.44	80.92	16.51	12.60	0.95	0.34	2.62	122.49	30.98	14.40	27.68	49.43	111 06	23.39
1987	23.09	30.06	94.12	19.63	15.72	0.43	0.43	3.05	136.96	36.04	15.92	29.81	55.19	123 99	27.31
1988	26.73	26.63	121.76	26.21	18.27	1.46	1.29	5.19	159.58	43.53	17.15	34.26	64.64	145 35	33.77
1989	44.21	26.66	112.47	26.85	20.23	1.62	0.85	4.15	175.88	51.27	30.51	36.85	57.25	159 07	41.22
1990	47.65	25.07	98.71	27.32	24.69	1.12	0.02	1.49	179.51	69.52	29.87	38.23	41.89	163 72	60.13
1991	54.43	37.55	100.09	29.26	24.97	1.20	0.50	2.59	194.41	72.31	35.80	42.17	44.13	177 56	59.99
1992	67.63	41.14	133.14	30.26	26.00	1.13	0.69	2.44	230.61	85.22	43.35	48.93	53.11	210 00	72.47
1993	71.73	67.09	171.66	35.39	26.14	1.76	0.88	6.61	302.48	119.69	47.57	63.55	71.67	275 04	103.04
1994	97.52	95.48	203.45	46.53	36.63	2.30	0.68	6.92	404.08	176.32	61.88	78.42	87.46	361 27	151.17
1995	137.40	122.33	237.90	63.21	49.33	2.45	0.84	10.59	501.22	204.76	94.43	94.75	107.28	451 84	172.65

Year	v13b1ii	v13b1iii	v13b1iv	v13b2	v13b2i	v13b2ii	v13b2iii	v13b2iv	v13c	v13ci	v13cii	v13ciii	v13civ	v13c1
1952														
1953														
1954														
1955														
1956														
1957														
1958														
1959														
1960														
1961														
1962														
1963														
1964														
1965														
1966														
1967														
1968														
1969														
1970														
1971														
1972														
1973														
1974														
1975														
1976														
1977														
1978	3.76	13.35	26.34	3.14	2.56	0.24	0.01	0.33	20.09	8.86	2.08	1.90	7.25	4.79
1979	4.28	14.55	29.35	3.81	2.93	0.36	0.01	0.51	21.70	10.07	2.14	1.30	8.19	5.51
1980	4.51	18.06	33.00	5.08	3.17	0.88	0.08	0.95	24.56	11.07	2.77	1.13	9.59	6.36
1981	5.44	16.57	35.28	5.91	3.30	1.08	0.08	1.45	26.01	10.39	3.36	0.80	11.46	6.70
1982	6.13	15.84	36.86	7.56	3.88	1.30	0.00	2.38	27.51	11.44	4.32	0.16	11.59	6.59
1983	7.59	18.37	35.93	7.78	4.50	0.77	0.06	2.45	31.69	11.04	5.22	0.15	15.28	7.58
1984	9.62	21.14	35.69	8.50	4.95	0.69	0.19	2.67	40.37	14.46	3.94	0.47	21.50	11.60
1985	10.74	26.68	47.89	10.12	6.15	0.93	0.49	2.55	48.53	14.07	5.09	1.42	27.95	10.69
1986	13.03	27.34	47.30	11.43	7.59	1.37	0.34	2.13	55.67	17.03	7.35	2.42	28.87	13.89
1987	14.63	29.20	52.85	12.97	8.73	1.29	0.61	2.34	63.41	20.97	6.74	-0.18	35.88	14.46
1988	15.89	33.32	62.37	14.23	9.76	1.26	0.94	2.27	73.85	22.72	8.12	-8.92	51.93	16.61
1989	26.71	35.77	55.37	16.81	10.05	3.80	1.08	1.88	80.61	28.50	12.08	-11.04	51.07	21.30
1990	27.32	36.93	39.34	15.79	9.39	2.55	1.30	2.55	104.12	45.31	16.66	-13.18	55.33	30.25
1991	33.21	40.55	43.81	16.85	12.32	2.59	1.62	0.32	119.08	53.40	17.43	-5.12	53.37	27.13
1992	40.31	46.54	50.68	20.61	12.75	3.04	2.39	2.43	150.37	58.11	23.15	-8.48	77.59	35.66
1993	45.26	60.63	66.11	27.44	16.65	2.31	2.92	5.56	198.23	79.79	22.40	2.66	93.38	47.60
1994	57.49	73.55	79.06	42.81	25.15	4.39	4.87	8.40	274.53	115.74	33.34	16.38	109.07	66.55
1995	90.90	89.19	99.10	49.38	32.11	3.53	5.56	8.18	355.68	168.39	40.52	26.74	120.03	86.14

Year	v13c1i	v13c1ii	v13c1iii	v13c1iv	v13c2	v13c2i	v13c2ii	v13c2iii	v13c2iv	v13c3	v13c3i	v13c3ii	v13c3iii	v13c3iv
1952														
1953														
1954														
1955														
1956														
1957														
1958														
1959														
1960														
1961														
1962														
1963														
1964														
1965														
1966														
1967														
1968														
1969														
1970														
1971														
1972														
1973														
1974														
1975														
1976														
1977														
1978	1.09	0.83	0.47	2.40	6.95	1.72	0.25	0.87	4.11	0.13	0.11	0.02		
1979	1.23	0.86	0.54	2.88	7.41	2.18	0.31	0.24	4.68	0.14	0.12	0.02		
1980	1.28	0.90	0.64	3.54	7.12	2.03	0.30	-0.17	4.96	0.76	0.23	0.03		0.50
1981	1.85	1.12	0.56	3.17	8.52	2.30	0.37	-0.14	5.99	0.57	0.17	0.02		0.38
1982	1.83	1.01	0.58	3.17	7.24	2.22	0.47	-0.72	5.27	0.74	0.22	0.03		0.49
1983	2.28	1.14	0.74	3.42	8.89	1.73	0.49	-1.47	8.14	1.55	0.19	0.06	0.60	0.70
1984	4.15	2.64	0.51	4.30	14.61	4.03	0.72	-0.74	10.60	5.64	0.18	0.03	0.44	4.99
1985	2.69	1.58	0.92	5.50	16.64	3.35	0.76	-0.58	13.11	8.94	0.22	0.06	0.59	7.97
1986	3.47	2.66	1.63	6.13	17.40	4.15	1.02	-0.76	12.99	9.80	0.27	0.15	0.34	8.54
1987	4.81	2.18	0.97	6.50	20.36	5.98	1.27	-2.79	15.90	14.54	0.36	0.17	1.09	12.92
1988	4.59	2.62	1.23	8.17	21.55	5.66	1.66	-12.31	26.54	18.32	0.42	0.14	1.42	16.34
1989	5.27	5.89	1.21	8.93	14.26	8.13	1.64	-14.74	19.23	25.31	0.48	0.29	2.21	22.33
1990	10.85	7.72	1.91	9.77	15.85	15.52	1.85	-16.86	15.34	29.04	0.57	0.28	2.38	25.81
1991	9.59	6.72	1.90	8.92	27.65	21.79	3.02	-9.50	12.34	30.37	0.84	0.49	2.44	26.60
1992	12.09	10.05	2.58	10.94	41.05	20.42	3.72	-13.97	30.88	34.71	1.15	0.73	2.78	30.05
1993	15.65	10.15	3.63	18.17	51.21	24.74	2.78	-7.90	31.59	42.61	2.51	0.78	3.55	35.77
1994	20.20	17.53	9.29	19.53	65.41	34.48	4.49	-4.05	30.49	55.50	4.21	1.82	5.99	43.48
1995	38.35	21.18	12.41	14.20	78.27	48.94	3.30	-1.28	27.31	81.40	5.75	2.81	7.38	64.96

Year	v13c4	v13c4i	v13c4ii	v13c4iii	v13c4iv	v13c5	v13c5i	v13c5ii	v13c5iii	v13c5iv	v13c6	v13c6i	v13c6ii	v13c6iii
1952														
1953														
1954														
1955														
1956														
1957														
1958														
1959														
1960														
1961														
1962														
1963														
1964														
1965														
1966														
1967														
1968														
1969														
1970														
1971														
1972														
1973														
1974														
1975														
1976														
1977														
1978						4.60	2.65	0.65	0.56	0.74	0.28	0.26	0.02	
1979						3.69	1.91	0.63	0.52	0.63	0.42	0.39	0.03	
1980						5.63	3.06	1.54	0.66	0.37	0.14	0.14		
1981						4.21	1.87	1.25	0.38	0.71	1.08	0.76	0.13	
1982						5.46	2.00	2.05	0.30	1.11	1.29	0.91	0.15	
1983						5.48	1.40	2.64	0.28	1.16	1.78	1.05	0.23	
1984	0.85	0.14	0.05	0.01	0.65	3.07	1.96	0.37	0.15	0.59	0.63	0.62	0.01	
1985	1.67	1.08	0.12	0.02	0.45	3.33	1.98	0.06	0.37	0.92	1.39	0.75	0.64	
1986	1.86	1.36	0.25	0.03	0.22	3.44	1.68	0.23	0.67	0.86	1.85	1.04	0.81	
1987	1.88	0.21	1.67			3.41	2.28	0.22	0.54	0.37	1.48	1.24	0.24	
1988	3.35	0.36	2.33	0.22	0.44	3.72	2.53	0.30	0.51	0.38	2.02	1.69	0.33	
1989	3.22	0.31	2.52	0.03	0.36	3.79	2.86	0.46	0.25	0.22	2.41	2.10	0.31	
1990	5.35	0.43	4.41	0.07	0.44	5.66	3.86	0.83	-1.12	2.09	2.77	2.57	0.33	0.01
1991	5.84	0.60	4.59	0.07	0.58	6.82	5.24	0.35	-0.65	1.88	3.36	2.10	0.83	0.04
1992	6.78	0.63	4.73	0.24	1.18	7.82	4.99	1.14	-0.81	2.50	3.84	3.05	0.34	0.02
1993	9.70	0.90	6.98	0.19	1.63	17.10	9.07	0.96	1.53	5.54	4.58	4.40	0.02	0.15
1994	12.14	1.69	6.20	1.41	2.84	34.48	20.91	1.99	2.90	8.58	6.02	4.83	0.05	0.02
1995	16.85	2.42	10.04	2.25	2.14	45.43	34.41	1.31	4.53	5.18	7.21	6.19	0.07	0.02

Year	v13c6iv	v13c7	v13c7i	v13c7ii	v13c7iii	v13c7iv	v13c8	v13c8i	v13c8ii	v13c8iii	v13c8iv	v13c9	v13c9i	v13c9ii
1952														
1953														
1954														
1955														
1956														
1957														
1958														
1959														
1960														
1961														
1962														
1963														
1964														
1965														
1966														
1967														
1968														
1969														
1970														
1971														
1972														
1973														
1974														
1975														
1976														
1977														
1978		1.92	1.79	0.13			0.33	0.31	0.02			1.09	0.93	0.16
1979		2.97	2.78	0.19			0.49	0.47	0.02			1.07	0.99	0.08
1980		2.62	2.55			0.07	0.53	0.53				1.40	1.25	
1981	0.19	3.28	2.21	0.24		0.83	0.53	0.36	0.04		0.13	1.12	0.87	0.19
1982	0.23	3.93	2.65	0.29		0.99	0.63	0.43	0.05		0.15	1.63	1.18	0.27
1983	0.50	3.85	2.56	0.34		0.95	0.88	0.59	0.07		0.22	1.68	1.24	0.25
1984		2.13	1.87	0.04	0.03	0.19	0.66	0.42	0.03	0.03	0.18	1.18	1.09	0.05
1985		3.54	2.41	1.13			0.77	0.47	0.30			1.56	1.12	0.44
1986		4.59	2.91	1.56	0.01	0.11	0.97	0.61	0.34		0.02	1.87	1.54	0.33
1987		4.03	3.21	0.72	0.01	0.09	1.05	0.88	0.07		0.10	2.20	2.00	0.20
1988		4.58	4.10	0.41	0.01	0.06	1.04	0.96	0.08			2.66	2.41	0.25
1989		5.66	5.11	0.55			1.41	1.27	0.14			3.25	2.97	0.28
1990	-0.14	5.85	5.41	0.35	-0.02	0.11	3.52	2.10	0.44	0.18	0.80	5.83	4.00	0.45
1991	0.39	7.66	6.65	0.64	0.16	0.21	3.73	2.44	0.20	0.39	0.70	6.52	4.15	0.59
1992	0.43	8.68	7.22	0.73	0.18	0.55	4.58	2.25	1.28	0.25	0.80	7.25	6.31	0.43
1993	0.01	10.10	9.00	0.21	0.25	0.64	5.54	4.79	0.30	0.44	0.01	9.79	8.73	0.22
1994	1.12	14.05	12.12	0.11	0.19	1.63	8.52	5.66	0.92	0.58	1.36	11.96	11.64	0.23
1995	0.93	15.97	13.83	0.23	0.25	1.66	10.19	6.46	1.37	0.59	1.77	14.22	12.04	0.21

Year	v13c9iii	v13c9iv	v13c10	v13c10i	v13c10ii	v13c10iii	v13c10iv
1952							
1953							
1954							
1955							
1956							
1957							
1958							
1959							
1960							
1961							
1962							
1963							
1964							
1965							
1966							
1967							
1968							
1969							
1970							
1971							
1972							
1973							
1974							
1975							
1976							
1977							
1978							
1979							
1980		0.15					
1981		0.06					
1982		0.18					
1983		0.19					
1984	0.04						
1985							
1986							
1987							
1988							
1989							
1990	0.27	1.11					
1991	0.03	1.75					
1992	0.25	0.26					
1993	0.82	0.02					
1994	0.05	0.04					
1995	0.09	1.88					

3

Hebei

Year	v1	v1a	v1b	v1b1	v1b2	v1c	v1c1	v1c2	v1c3	v2	v2a	v2b	v2b1	v2b2	v2c
1952	61.93	29.70	18.81	16.56	2.25	13.42	2.25	5.84	5.33						
1953	68.14	29.07	21.53	18.17	3.36	17.54	2.70	7.96	6.88	106.6	91.1	115.9	110.7	154.5	127.6
1954	74.65	30.44	25.28	22.04	3.24	18.93	3.09	8.58	7.26	108.6	103.1	119.4	123.3	98.9	104.0
1955	80.15	34.39	26.36	22.96	3.40	19.40	3.21	8.79	7.40	107.8	113.0	106.1	105.9	106.9	101.7
1956	83.28	30.77	30.25	24.48	5.77	22.26	3.60	9.56	9.10	105.4	88.4	118.4	113.2	152.7	115.1
1957	85.72	30.77	31.09	25.86	5.23	23.86	4.19	9.67	10.00	110.8	118.6	107.2	107.4	106.6	105.8
1958	110.17	33.15	48.58	39.63	8.95	28.44	6.30	10.18	11.96	128.8	104.6	157.0	154.2	170.3	120.4
1959	139.49	31.99	74.25	63.84	10.41	33.25	8.45	10.96	13.84	126.5	94.8	150.7	160.2	109.0	117.3
1960	147.20	28.50	85.72	74.73	10.99	32.98	9.15	10.65	13.18	104.5	84.4	115.9	117.9	103.2	95.0
1961	103.75	31.28	46.08	42.09	3.99	26.39	5.31	9.87	11.21	62.7	86.7	51.6	53.7	35.8	76.4
1962	88.70	31.26	36.75	33.42	3.33	20.69	4.86	8.27	7.56	83.6	101.5	77.4	76.6	86.5	78.1
1963	84.24	26.22	37.85	33.49	4.36	20.17	5.17	8.17	6.83	98.4	84.9	103.7	100.7	133.1	105.3
1964	100.44	34.14	44.51	39.10	5.41	21.79	5.64	8.32	7.83	121.2	132.5	119.5	119.0	123.0	112.4
1965	127.99	45.49	55.72	49.38	6.34	26.78	7.37	9.92	9.49	127.6	124.3	129.8	130.7	123.2	126.5
1966	142.21	49.07	62.62	55.21	7.41	30.52	8.35	11.84	10.33	114.1	107.1	118.0	118.0	118.2	113.9
1967	138.79	48.93	60.79	53.76	7.03	29.07	7.07	11.73	10.27	97.9	99.6	98.1	98.5	94.9	95.4
1968	143.95	49.06	67.18	60.52	6.66	27.71	6.82	11.37	9.52	104.9	97.1	112.6	114.9	94.8	95.4
1969	170.51	53.63	84.85	73.64	11.21	32.03	8.14	12.92	10.97	121.9	108.0	130.0	126.0	168.3	116.1
1970	197.76	59.69	102.60	89.52	13.08	35.47	9.62	14.16	11.69	119.9	111.3	125.7	127.0	116.7	111.1
1971	208.93	57.86	114.34	98.64	15.70	36.73	10.52	14.58	11.63	109.7	105.7	112.5	111.8	118.1	104.3
1972	207.35	51.40	117.22	100.91	16.31	38.73	11.18	15.35	12.20	100.2	87.3	102.9	102.9	102.6	105.1
1973	228.96	59.67	128.70	111.79	16.91	40.59	11.83	17.00	11.76	110.4	115.2	110.2	111.4	101.6	106.2
1974	248.83	65.24	143.90	124.92	18.98	39.69	11.67	17.26	10.76	109.4	109.3	112.2	112.5	109.7	97.9
1975	279.25	72.73	168.67	146.61	22.06	37.85	12.45	16.57	8.83	112.3	103.1	118.4	118.9	114.0	95.4
1976	283.57	65.83	179.18	157.34	21.84	38.56	11.77	17.63	9.16	102.2	94.4	104.0	104.8	97.5	101.7
1977	323.45	67.19	213.21	185.13	28.08	43.05	14.95	19.37	8.73	114.3	92.2	119.4	118.6	126.6	111.5
1978	385.34	75.86	249.61	219.25	30.36	59.87	16.03	20.83	23.01	113.5	122.1	114.7	117.0	106.5	107.9
1979	426.97	91.10	268.21	228.34	39.87	67.66	17.67	24.39	25.60	108.0	106.9	106.0	101.7	128.3	111.9
1980	451.92	97.79	277.40	238.62	38.78	76.73	17.67	24.39	34.67	104.5	93.8	101.5	102.7	95.2	112.9
1981	458.08	100.23	275.18	236.77	38.41	82.67	17.25	26.67	38.75	101.1	103.8	98.7	99.7	96.1	105.2
1982	510.87	118.58	293.09	249.53	43.56	99.20	19.94	29.55	49.71	110.7	117.5	104.6	105.2	101.4	119.0
1983	574.52	139.22	322.10	276.68	45.42	113.20	22.02	35.48	55.70	111.9	117.2	108.7	110.5	99.7	113.6
1984	669.66	153.07	388.52	334.26	54.26	128.07	23.74	42.67	61.66	115.7	109.1	118.4	119.2	112.3	112.3
1985	831.85	167.33	505.64	435.82	69.82	158.88	26.11	52.22	80.55	115.1	103.3	119.2	119.8	115.2	115.1
1986	942.98	174.39	585.97	506.19	79.78	182.62	29.05	58.32	95.25	108.4	98.5	110.9	111.7	104.3	110.1
1987	1150.78	200.66	728.93	640.85	88.08	221.19	35.13	67.48	118.58	114.4	104.5	116.3	117.9	99.7	117.6
1988	1590.94	256.90	962.28	841.12	121.16	371.76	63.82	94.15	213.79	116.9	107.8	119.3	119.5	117.8	121.9
1989	1888.76	306.99	1143.51	1026.09	117.42	438.26	79.81	99.52	258.93	107.2	103.1	107.2	108.8	84.4	110.6
1990	2075.12	357.63	1233.15	1123.23	109.92	484.34	91.04	124.42	268.88	106.8	105.4	105.4	106.8	85.8	110.1
1991	2461.39	377.64	1478.95	1331.96	146.99	604.80	131.25	188.12	285.43	114.5	103.6	114.5	113.3	127.8	122.1
1992	3011.18	419.82	1858.70	1664.26	194.44	732.66	157.07	224.75	350.84	117.8	100.9	122.0	123.3	110.1	121.9
1993	4275.86	511.29	2862.50	2515.73	346.77	902.07	180.22	281.16	440.69	123.6	108.7	129.8	129.9	129.1	117.8
1994	6055.61	796.33	4104.92	3649.19	455.73	1154.36	236.24	367.37	550.75	120.5	116.2	123.2	123.1	124.7	114.6
1995	7489.41	1147.83	4763.82	4182.92	577.90	1577.76	348.18	556.19	673.39	118.6	111.9	120.9	121.1	118.9	115.1

Year	v2c1	v2c2	v3'	v3	v3a	v3b	v3b1	v3b2	v3c	v3c1	v3c2	v3c3	v3c4	v3c5	v3c6
1952			40.49	40.49	25.23	7.61	6.78	0.83	7.65	1.83	5.00				
1953	125.6	130.1	42.48	42.48	24.10	8.38	7.26	1.12	10.00	2.12	6.88				
1954	116.1	105.4	45.31	45.31	25.38	9.14	8.00	1.14	10.79	2.33	7.13				
1955	105.6	102.7	49.20	49.20	28.18	9.96	8.77	1.19	11.06	2.38	7.16				
1956	114.9	108.7	49.83	49.83	25.01	12.13	10.12	2.01	12.69	2.67	7.92				
1957	122.7	98.9	52.30	52.30	26.11	12.59	10.70	1.89	13.60	3.08	7.96				
1958	152.0	105.2	63.61	63.61	27.89	19.51	16.41	3.10	16.21	4.67	8.69				
1959	133.7	107.6	74.21	74.21	27.00	28.26	24.73	3.53	18.95	6.15	9.26				
1960	109.0	96.7	73.44	73.44	23.43	30.88	27.61	3.27	19.13	6.47	8.76				
1961	57.9	81.5	54.87	54.87	23.99	15.84	14.66	1.18	15.04	3.64	7.79				
1962	90.3	97.7	48.73	48.73	24.07	12.66	11.65	1.01	12.00	3.20	5.76				
1963	106.4	106.7	44.83	44.83	19.84	13.29	11.95	1.34	11.70	3.43	5.22				
1964	109.1	101.1	56.68	56.68	27.15	16.89	15.07	1.82	12.64	3.80	5.61				
1965	130.7	100.0	72.72	72.72	37.20	19.99	17.84	2.15	15.53	5.00	7.22				
1966	113.7	120.0	80.24	80.24	40.12	22.42	19.87	2.55	17.70	5.90	9.16				
1967	85.4	100.4	78.11	78.11	40.06	21.19	18.78	2.41	16.86	4.75	9.43				
1968	132.1	96.7	79.43	79.43	40.35	23.01	20.79	2.22	16.07	4.60	8.74				
1969	87.9	114.8	92.16	92.16	44.11	29.47	25.90	3.57	18.58	5.54	10.18				
1970	118.8	111.6	104.25	104.25	46.41	36.91	32.66	4.25	20.93	6.58	11.22				
1971	109.4	102.9	107.60	107.60	44.06	41.87	36.75	5.12	21.67	7.20	11.28				
1972	106.3	105.3	102.50	102.50	38.35	41.91	36.65	5.26	22.24	7.25	11.32				
1973	105.8	111.1	112.57	112.57	43.16	45.46	40.02	5.44	23.95	8.16	11.96				
1974	98.6	101.2	121.39	121.39	45.62	50.24	44.01	6.23	25.52	7.83	11.52				
1975	104.1	105.8	132.79	132.79	50.66	57.19	50.03	7.16	24.94	8.17	9.68				
1976	98.0	113.0	133.95	133.95	45.86	63.00	56.03	6.97	25.06	7.63	10.14				
1977	125.6	96.6	158.18	158.18	48.42	78.74	69.76	8.98	31.02	9.13	10.89				
1978	107.2	107.2	183.06	183.06	52.20	92.38	83.19	9.19	38.48	9.99	9.23	3.08	3.49	2.37	0.84
1979	111.4	122.2	203.22	203.22	61.11	101.76	89.69	12.07	40.35	10.86	8.36	3.31	4.03	2.55	0.97
1980	99.1	110.6	219.24	219.24	68.09	105.88	94.08	11.80	45.27	10.71	9.85	4.19	4.81	2.87	1.16
1981	97.6	108.3	222.54	222.54	71.03	103.15	92.34	10.81	48.36	10.87	10.86	3.84	4.00	3.53	1.34
1982	108.9	109.0	251.45	251.45	85.59	107.83	95.33	12.50	58.03	12.51	12.03	7.61	5.15	3.99	1.56
1983	105.4	122.0	283.21	283.21	102.10	114.89	101.95	12.94	66.22	13.71	15.18	9.01	5.72	4.22	1.78
1984	106.1	119.1	332.22	332.22	111.46	145.84	129.83	16.01	74.92	14.97	17.95	10.90	5.90	5.28	2.05
1985	109.2	113.8	396.75	396.75	120.34	184.26	164.27	19.99	92.15	16.91	22.22	13.89	8.85	5.60	2.40
1986	109.4	106.2	436.65	436.65	123.45	207.28	185.48	21.80	105.92	19.32	25.74	17.02	10.33	6.64	3.06
1987	119.6	106.8	521.98	521.92	137.66	255.97	231.03	24.54	128.29	24.03	29.06	22.22	12.06	9.88	3.81
1988	116.8	127.4	701.40	701.33	162.31	323.40	289.22	34.18	215.62	34.08	54.36	43.38	16.28	21.63	5.02
1989	118.9	102.3	822.89	822.83	196.35	374.92	338.79	36.13	251.56	41.50	56.75	55.51	18.66	25.70	6.44
1990	98.9	115.7	896.41	896.33	227.89	387.52	354.26	33.26	280.92	46.43	56.98	70.58	21.69	19.95	7.61
1991	119.8	125.4	1073.09	1072.07	236.89	459.91	417.17	42.74	375.27	79.35	109.11	63.48	22.84	14.45	10.77
1992	120.3	122.2	1279.55	1278.50	257.08	573.15	517.75	55.40	448.27	93.85	130.37	79.80	25.44	17.70	12.87
1993	114.3	125.7	1694.78	1690.84	301.68	847.92	758.10	89.82	541.24	115.34	161.88	90.96	35.21	21.38	13.57
1994	111.8	113.4	2192.67	2187.49	451.91	1053.12	926.36	126.76	682.46	126.94	205.75	128.22	41.23	26.86	16.09
1995	118.7	113.1	2853.02	2849.52	631.34	1322.77	1150.49	172.28	895.41	179.41	261.69	166.51	46.07	38.45	20.23

Year	v3c7	v3c8	v3c9	v3c10	v3d	v4'	v4	v4a	v4b	v4b1	v4b2	v4c	v4c1	v4c2	v4c3
1952				0.82	125										
1953				1.00	128	99.6	99.6	88.3	109.1	105.5	138.6	127.3	120.2	132.0	
1954				1.33	134	106.8	106.8	103.1	116.0	117.8	107.0	107.3	112.3	101.4	
1955				1.52	141	109.4	109.4	111.6	111.7	113.1	102.4	102.5	102.0	100.4	
1956				2.10	140	103.9	103.9	88.0	130.1	126.3	158.7	115.4	117.5	109.4	
1957				2.56	144	106.6	106.6	111.3	98.7	97.4	106.5	107.2	117.2	98.5	
1958				2.85	172	122.0	122.0	103.4	155.7	154.1	164.3	121.9	154.5	109.9	
1959				3.54	197	116.6	116.6	94.7	142.2	149.9	102.3	117.5	130.8	105.8	
1960				3.90	194	98.3	98.3	81.6	109.9	112.5	90.5	101.1	105.3	93.9	
1961				3.61	145	63.0	63.0	79.8	49.4	50.7	37.3	69.4	56.8	77.2	
1962				3.04	127	89.7	89.7	102.3	77.0	76.5	84.3	90.5	93.1	91.3	
1963				3.05	114	95.5	95.5	83.6	106.2	103.9	133.3	100.2	107.2	103.6	
1964				3.23	143	126.2	126.2	138.1	126.7	125.5	137.5	112.2	111.0	104.8	
1965				3.31	180	122.9	122.9	128.4	125.7	126.0	123.5	111.6	131.0	103.1	
1966				2.64	194	112.0	112.0	107.2	116.5	116.3	118.6	113.3	118.4	122.6	
1967				2.68	185	96.8	96.8	100.0	95.5	95.6	94.5	94.0	81.9	103.4	
1968				2.73	185	101.8	101.8	97.3	110.9	113.2	91.9	95.3	96.8	93.4	
1969				2.86	210	117.8	117.8	108.5	132.1	129.3	160.9	108.3	97.0	117.0	
1970				3.13	232	117.4	117.4	103.0	130.0	131.7	116.2	114.1	118.8	111.0	
1971				3.19	234	105.3	105.3	92.8	113.6	113.1	118.0	103.9	109.6	100.6	
1972				3.67	220	97.9	97.9	86.2	99.9	99.2	106.1	108.1	100.6	100.3	
1973				3.83	236	108.9	108.9	111.8	110.1	111.2	100.2	102.9	112.7	105.8	
1974				6.17	251	108.4	108.4	105.6	110.2	110.0	112.4	107.1	95.8	96.2	
1975				7.09	272	110.5	110.5	110.5	114.9	115.2	112.9	98.7	104.5	84.0	
1976				7.29	272	104.9	104.9	89.5	110.8	112.4	95.9	106.0	94.6	118.5	
1977				11.00	318	116.2	116.2	105.9	119.3	118.5	127.1	125.4	118.2	85.8	
1978	2.12	2.48	1.76	3.12	364	114.5	114.5	110.4	118.0	121.4	113.6	112.0	102.4	118.3	
1979	2.50	2.68	1.97	3.12	400	106.2	106.2	104.2	107.8	105.3	131.4	104.9	108.7	90.6	107.3
1980	3.14	2.93	2.49	3.12	427	103.2	103.2	97.4	102.4	103.1	97.8	112.5	98.7	117.8	126.6
1981	3.49	3.17	2.75	4.51	427	101.0	101.0	105.4	96.6	98.1	84.1	105.1	100.7	108.1	89.5
1982	4.08	3.35	3.24	4.51	474	111.8	111.8	119.7	103.4	103.0	106.9	118.9	114.1	109.2	187.0
1983	4.54	3.62	3.93	4.51	526	111.5	111.5	118.9	105.4	105.9	101.2	112.3	105.0	124.5	117.7
1984	4.91	3.97	4.48	4.51	609	114.4	114.4	107.8	122.6	123.0	119.1	109.8	103.9	115.9	117.4
1985	6.52	5.22	5.93	4.61	719	112.5	112.5	102.1	118.1	117.8	120.1	117.4	111.7	120.7	117.5
1986	7.61	4.49	7.33	4.38	782	105.1	105.1	97.3	107.9	108.5	101.7	109.7	112.8	105.5	118.0
1987	8.97	5.65	8.11	4.50	921	111.6	111.6	101.5	114.8	116.3	100.1	117.1	121.9	104.3	110.6
1988	13.88	8.26	11.53	7.20	1219	113.5	113.5	101.0	116.8	116.6	119.3	120.0	113.1	126.1	125.9
1989	15.16	9.42	14.88	7.54	1409	106.0	106.1	103.6	105.3	106.7	88.1	109.6	114.6	99.9	100.1
1990	19.94	12.02	17.57	8.15	1465	105.8	105.8	105.8	104.1	104.6	95.7	109.1	91.8	114.8	127.1
1991	20.59	7.67	34.59	12.42	1727	111.1	111.0	102.5	110.0	109.3	117.0	121.2	119.4	123.0	86.5
1992	24.04	9.52	40.47	14.21	2040	115.6	115.6	99.4	120.7	122.1	106.9	121.5	119.9	121.6	128.2
1993	27.89	11.51	48.02	15.48	2682	117.8	117.7	104.4	124.6	124.3	128.4	116.6	114.2	124.9	105.0
1994	37.08	19.54	59.05	21.70	3439	114.9	114.9	111.8	116.9	116.2	124.3	113.7	105.8	109.0	124.8
1995	49.03	25.39	81.68	26.95	4444	113.8	113.9	108.6	115.4	115.0	119.5	114.5	118.4	111.4	115.4

Year	v4c4	v4c5	v4c6	v4c7	v4c8	v4c9	v4c10	v5	v5a	v5a1	v5a1a	v5a1b	v5a2	v5b	v5b1
1952								40.49	28.51	27.57	22.20	5.37	0.94	8.51	5.22
1953								42.48	32.64	31.54	25.61	5.93	1.10	8.43	6.16
1954								45.31	34.54	33.01	26.44	6.57	1.50	10.16	6.17
1955								49.20	36.58	34.58	27.38	7.20	2.00	12.45	7.76
1956								49.83	38.94	36.74	28.34	8.40	2.20	12.90	7.98
1957								52.30	41.22	39.14	30.02	9.12	2.08	15.65	10.43
1958								62.61	45.81	43.65	32.39	11.26	2.20	28.65	22.12
1959								74.21	47.46	45.06	32.09	12.97	2.40	30.46	23.72
1960								73.44	48.38	45.88	31.79	14.09	2.50	33.08	25.64
1961								54.87	47.38	45.28	32.15	13.13	2.10	17.92	10.16
1962								48.73	45.54	43.99	32.73	11.26	1.55	-1.08	4.99
1963								44.83	46.33	44.87	34.24	10.63	1.46	10.52	7.49
1964								56.68	48.04	46.46	35.47	10.99	1.58	13.02	9.38
1965								72.72	51.07	49.43	37.63	11.80	1.64	17.10	11.92
1966								80.24	54.34	52.24	39.66	12.58	2.10	14.57	12.39
1967								78.11	56.36	53.51	40.52	13.02	2.82	18.71	12.52
1968								79.43	57.27	54.12	40.95	13.17	3.15	18.86	11.76
1969								92.16	61.59	57.72	44.00	13.72	3.87	23.45	14.66
1970								104.25	66.07	61.94	47.82	14.12	4.13	30.46	18.38
1971								107.60	69.47	65.38	50.26	15.12	4.09	36.16	23.05
1972								103.00	67.87	63.44	47.20	16.24	4.43	33.89	23.63
1973								112.57	74.25	69.61	51.39	18.22	4.64	35.71	24.97
1974								121.39	77.92	73.01	53.41	19.60	4.91	40.36	28.95
1975								132.79	80.76	75.82	54.89	20.93	4.94	47.86	38.15
1976								133.95	82.35	77.08	55.24	21.84	5.27	45.39	37.71
1977								158.18	85.02	79.09	56.15	22.94	5.93	52.01	40.53
1978								183.06	93.28	83.02	61.35	21.67	10.26	64.26	51.39
1979	115.3	107.7	115.9	117.5	107.8	111.9	100.0	203.22	104.43	92.94	68.78	24.16	11.49	68.95	58.37
1980	119.3	112.3	119.3	125.8	109.2	126.3	100.0	219.24	114.68	102.07	74.41	27.66	12.61	63.84	51.86
1981	82.9	120.6	112.9	108.7	106.5	108.2	141.2	222.54	129.06	116.08	85.99	30.09	12.98	50.73	45.44
1982	127.2	112.1	115.7	116.3	104.4	117.1	99.4	251.45	140.19	124.99	91.92	33.07	15.20	73.96	65.12
1983	109.9	105.3	113.6	110.5	107.0	120.4	99.4	283.21	156.34	139.14	104.22	34.92	17.20	90.10	71.35
1984	101.8	114.7	111.6	105.1	110.5	115.9	97.0	332.22	186.56	164.17	123.78	40.39	22.39	114.66	82.12
1985	130.4	98.2	108.8	122.9	114.3	122.2	94.2	396.75	229.73	202.16	152.23	49.93	27.57	156.90	116.38
1986	113.4	114.3	122.6	112.6	83.6	119.1	91.5	436.65	262.33	230.85	171.29	59.56	31.48	162.79	127.62
1987	112.4	128.4	114.5	108.4	116.1	92.7	93.8	521.92	318.27	280.08	205.58	74.50	38.19	176.58	137.63
1988	117.4	137.7	113.6	127.9	127.1	123.6	137.9	701.33	434.25	382.14	274.76	107.38	52.11	242.39	195.17
1989	104.2	103.3	109.7	99.3	99.2	111.3	91.1	822.83	480.95	421.79	291.27	130.52	59.16	295.30	180.90
1990	111.8	77.6	113.6	125.3	122.7	118.1	108.1	896.33	518.86	456.84	318.83	140.01	62.02	334.66	204.02
1991	101.1	72.4	123.1	100.3	60.8	178.9	132.5	1072.07	634.73	525.70	357.43	168.27	109.03	384.84	254.27
1992	113.4	124.7	118.4	113.4	129.8	118.1	125.8	1278.50	712.19	595.43	387.45	207.98	116.76	475.18	390.02
1993	125.9	115.4	105.5	116.9	115.3	122.4	105.8	1690.84	870.45	686.54	442.97	243.57	183.91	679.12	530.37
1994	113.2	118.1	113.7	119.6	126.7	118.1	117.9	2187.49	1059.29	839.97	535.45	304.52	219.32	884.46	704.87
1995	98.2	123.8	109.3	115.0	114.5	120.3	118.7	2849.52	1348.75	1081.09	684.96	396.13	267.66	1226.07	955.21

Year	v5b2	v5c	v5c1	v5c2	v6a1	v6a2	v6a3	v6a4	v6b2	v6b3	v6b4	v7	v7a	v7a1	v7a2
1952	3.29	3.47													
1953	2.27	1.41										114.6	114.4	115.4	110.4
1954	3.99	0.64										102.1	101.0	99.7	106.9
1955	4.69	0.17										104.3	103.0	101.6	108.7
1956	4.92	-2.01										107.1	106.9	104.2	117.0
1957	5.22	-4.57										105.0	105.7	105.2	107.2
1958	6.53	-10.87										112.2	112.5	108.7	125.0
1959	6.74	-3.71										104.0	103.7	99.7	115.1
1960	7.44	-8.02										98.2	98.1	95.8	103.9
1961	7.76	-10.43										96.0	96.9	100.5	88.7
1962	-6.07	4.27										94.9	95.8	99.7	85.8
1963	3.03	-12.02										105.0	105.3	105.7	104.3
1964	3.64	-4.38										105.8	105.6	104.5	109.1
1965	5.18	4.55										108.9	108.9	108.3	110.9
1966	2.18	11.33										106.3	105.6	105.3	107.4
1967	6.19	3.04										103.3	102.1	101.7	102.4
1968	7.10	3.30										101.6	101.1	101.8	101.0
1969	8.79	7.12										108.0	107.1	108.2	104.2
1970	12.08	7.72										107.7	107.8	109.3	103.3
1971	13.11	1.95										105.4	106.4	105.5	109.4
1972	10.26	1.24										98.0	97.4	94.1	107.3
1973	10.74	2.61										109.5	109.8	108.9	112.3
1974	10.41	3.11										105.0	105.0	103.9	107.6
1975	9.71	4.17										103.8	103.9	102.8	106.8
1976	7.68	6.21										101.9	101.7	100.6	104.2
1977	11.48	21.15										103.0	102.5	101.5	104.5
1978	12.87	25.52			29.15	24.64	3.49	4.07	18.38	2.77	0.52	126.0	126.5	131.0	114.6
1979	10.58	29.84			32.68	27.62	3.91	4.57	20.49	3.08	0.59	99.1	97.5	93.7	108.7
1980	11.98	40.72			35.36	29.88	4.23	4.94	23.46	3.53	0.67	104.3	104.6	103.6	107.3
1981	5.29	42.75			28.96	49.46	3.04	4.53	25.64	3.72	0.73	111.8	113.0	114.9	107.8
1982	8.84	37.30			24.97	57.90	3.96	5.09	28.43	3.81	0.83	107.3	106.6	106.0	108.5
1983	18.75	36.77			28.25	66.16	4.18	5.63	29.63	4.43	0.86	111.2	112.0	114.5	104.8
1984	32.54	31.00			31.48	79.89	6.51	5.90	33.89	5.42	1.08	120.9	118.3	119.0	116.0
1985	40.52	10.12			39.77	97.15	7.29	8.02	41.87	6.36	1.70	117.8	118.4	118.6	117.9
1986	35.17	11.53			51.15	101.34	9.26	9.54	50.19	7.38	1.99	106.2	106.3	105.5	108.8
1987	38.95	27.07			57.74	121.30	11.50	15.04	62.72	9.14	2.64	108.9	107.1	106.2	109.9
1988	47.22	24.69			68.84	161.73	14.11	30.08	88.01	15.26	4.11	112.6	114.1	112.0	120.3
1989	114.40	46.58			79.90	165.33	6.99	39.05	106.35	19.16	5.01	95.8	96.1	94.5	100.4
1990	130.64	42.81			89.91	195.00	12.94	18.98	115.94	17.83	6.24	108.7	108.9	107.6	112.2
1991	130.57	52.50	372.47	319.97	96.27	212.19	26.54	22.43	135.42	25.71	7.14	109.4	108.7	106.8	113.0
1992	85.16	91.13	448.79	357.66	105.67	226.10	26.96	28.72	168.81	30.50	8.67	110.4	109.5	107.4	114.2
1993	148.75	141.27	542.27	401.00	124.87	258.76	25.62	33.72	198.19	33.12	12.26	114.3	112.6	110.4	117.1
1994	179.59	243.74	723.74	480.00	178.28	283.76	33.18	40.23	235.17	55.49	13.86	111.6	110.5	108.3	114.8
1995	270.86	274.70	815.96	541.26	264.83	320.67	42.63	56.83	308.55	66.17	21.41	110.5	111.5	111.0	112.5

Year	v7b	v8	v8a	v8b	v9	v9a	v9b	v10a1	v10a2	v10a3	v10a3a	v10a3b	v10a4	v10b1	v10b2
1952		85	74	218											
1953	118.1	95	84	224	111.8	113.5	102.8								
1954	131.5	97	85	231	99.0	97.6	99.6								
1955	132.2	99	86	225	100.0	98.8	100.9								
1956	109.8	103	87	266	105.3	102.5	113.8								
1957	93.4	108	91	266	103.0	104.8	98.4								
1958	107.2	118	98	283	110.8	108.1	107.5								
1959	108.5	120	97	281	101.8	98.9	99.3								
1960	100.0	121	96	290	97.4	95.7	98.9								
1961	79.3	120	96	296	97.3	100.0	97.0								
1962	74.0	115	94	303	94.5	95.5	102.3								
1963	94.4	114	96	311	102.9	102.4	113.6								
1964	110.5	117	98	313	103.8	103.8	106.0								
1965	106.1	122	102	326	107.3	106.7	107.6								
1966	128.0	121	105	342	103.4	102.1	105.9								
1967	134.3	127	105	350	100.0	100.0	100.6								
1968	111.5	126	104	352	99.2	100.0	101.1								
1969	122.9	131	109	368	104.1	105.1	104.6								
1970	107.0	138	116	376	106.4	106.8	102.3								
1971	98.8	142	120	387	103.7	103.6	105.3								
1972	108.1	135	111	383	95.7	93.0	99.0								
1973	104.5	146	119	399	108.3	107.6	103.9								
1974	105.9	151	122	415	103.5	102.6	104.2								
1975	100.8	155	125	431	102.7	101.7	103.8								
1976	106.3	156	125	437	100.7	100.0	101.1								
1977	111.9	159	126	445	102.0	99.2	101.5								
1978	119.8	165	137	402	103.7	104.9	90.9	34.81	11.54	5.04		5.04		11.96	0.91
1979	121.3	183	153	423	99.4	106.3	93.4	39.65	8.75	9.97		9.97		9.83	0.75
1980	100.7	199	164	460	119.9	120.6	119.5	36.62	5.75	9.49		9.45		3.83	8.15
1981	101.8	223	187	481	111.1	113.4	103.7	26.73	6.39	12.32	0.25	12.07		1.69	3.60
1982	113.7	236	198	507	104.5	104.8	104.0	37.57	15.04	12.51	0.20	12.31		2.83	6.01
1983	104.7	258	221	513	110.8	112.8	100.6	41.14	15.46	14.75	0.12	14.63		12.10	6.65
1984	144.5	301	261	569	116.8	118.2	111.0	45.46	23.12	13.54	0.27	13.27		9.68	22.86
1985	113.1	366	319	672	117.1	118.1	112.8	64.47	31.84	20.07	0.51	19.56		18.18	22.34
1986	104.9	413	356	773	104.8	104.6	104.8	71.10	38.29	18.23	0.64	17.59		26.24	8.93
1987	120.9	494	423	917	105.2	105.3	104.3	74.95	32.30	30.38	1.28	29.10		28.45	1.85
1988	102.4	664	557	1300	112.9	110.4	118.3	100.22	55.62	39.33	2.38	36.95		31.78	4.86
1989	93.7	722	583	1557	94.7	93.3	98.9	93.68	44.25	42.97	2.04	40.93		77.42	18.59
1990	107.2	783	605	1592	103.9	102.6	107.0	112.77	37.37	33.77	2.23	31.54	20.11	66.72	36.00
1991	113.1	847	675	1839	107.0	105.6	108.5	125.56	58.52	44.88	2.68	42.20	25.31	76.89	24.56
1992	114.7	950	729	2182	108.6	107.0	109.6	194.07	71.15	59.88	4.90	54.98	64.92	41.11	5.55
1993	122.9	1089	831	2496	111.9	110.2	114.3	288.26	153.64	66.49	20.49	46.00	21.98	20.82	19.65
1994	116.4	1320	1001	3009	109.6	107.9	110.8	333.10	179.54	118.91	24.91	94.00	73.32	-19.97	14.03
1995	106.1	1686	1281	3716	110.6	111.0	106.8	425.77	252.51	168.69	30.19	138.50	108.24	130.80	4.68

Year	v10b4	v11a	v11a1	v11a2	v11b	v11b1	v11b2	v11c	v11c1	v11c2	v12	v12a	v12b	v13	v13i
1952															
1953											97.8	115.9	69.0		
1954											119.8	100.3	171.8		
1955											126.2	130.0	120.3		
1956											95.1	79.3	121.5		
1957											138.6	178.8	94.6		
1958											186.6	215.6	126.4		
1959											100.5	100.2	101.7		
1960											109.4	108.3	113.1		
1961											52.0	37.6	100.1		
1962												45.1			
1963											52.9	154.6	31.8		
1964											125.7	126.0	125.2		
1965											137.4	127.3	164.7		
1966											85.2	105.5	41.9		
1967											134.0	101.0	310.5		
1968											107.2	100.7	118.5		
1969											126.5	121.0	134.6		
1970											127.7	128.0	127.2		
1971											119.2	126.7	109.1		
1972											93.3	102.6	78.8		
1973											105.2	105.4	104.8		
1974											113.0	116.3	106.1		
1975											117.0	131.5	84.6		
1976											95.6	99.2	83.1		
1977											114.3	106.8	145.4		
1978		6.53	7.31	-0.78	39.24	33.30	5.94	18.49	10.78	7.71	112.8	113.7	110.6	183.06	94.04
1979		8.25	7.49	0.76	36.44	33.34	3.10	24.26	17.54	6.72	103.3	114.4	76.1	203.22	106.36
1980		6.48	5.55	0.93	34.27	32.19	2.08	23.09	14.12	8.97	91.2	84.5	115.9	219.24	115.62
1981		2.05	2.05		30.09	29.95	0.14	18.59	13.44	5.15	77.9	85.7	44.0	222.54	120.10
1982		13.01	13.01		24.38	20.98	3.40	36.57	31.13	5.44	143.4	140.9	164.5	251.45	137.36
1983		6.04	6.04		36.82	30.16	6.66	47.24	35.15	12.09	120.5	109.8	197.8	283.21	156.90
1984		7.81	7.81		58.13	36.70	21.43	48.72	37.61	11.11	115.5	98.9	182.3	332.22	179.22
1985		1.97	1.97		72.36	51.71	20.65	82.57	62.70	19.87	126.8	129.6	129.6	396.75	206.73
1986		3.00	3.00		84.30	69.30	15.00	75.49	55.32	20.17	101.5	108.3	85.5	436.65	222.45
1987	8.65	1.58	1.58		96.19	79.58	16.61	78.81	56.47	22.34	109.8	111.0	106.0	521.92	259.88
1988	10.58	8.61	8.61		142.40	111.52	30.88	91.38	75.04	16.34	115.6	116.6	112.5	701.33	344.54
1989	18.39	7.18	7.18		136.02	96.31	39.71	152.10	77.41	74.69	119.6	96.3	194.5	822.83	405.25
1990	27.92	10.71	10.71		155.76	110.41	45.35	168.19	82.90	85.29	104.9	103.6	106.9	896.33	444.71
1991	29.12	10.45	9.15	1.30	190.16	119.28	70.88	184.23	125.84	58.39	113.4	122.9	97.7	1072.07	570.09
1992	38.50	20.96	9.96	11.00	300.61	240.72	59.89	153.61	139.34	14.27	114.1	137.5	65.3	1278.50	593.09
1993	108.28	164.64	15.68	148.96	290.24	284.11	6.13	224.24	230.58	-6.34	124.3	122.1	133.5	1690.84	832.75
1994	185.53	169.63	33.88	135.75	390.44	359.47	30.97	324.39	311.52	12.87	116.1	118.6	106.1	2187.49	1198.47
1995	135.38	195.02	61.13	133.89	528.68	470.14	58.54	502.37	423.94	78.43	121.4	120.0	127.7	2849.52	1643.15

Year	v13ii	v13iii	v13iv	v13a	v13ai	v13aii	v13aiii	v13aiv	v13b	v13bi	v13bii	v13biii	v13biv	v13b1	v13b1i
1952															
1953															
1954															
1955															
1956															
1957															
1958															
1959															
1960															
1961															
1962															
1963															
1964															
1965															
1966															
1967															
1968															
1969															
1970															
1971															
1972															
1973															
1974															
1975															
1976															
1977															
1978	20.81	17.47	50.74	52.20	43.85	1.62	1.10	5.63	92.38	31.62	11.70	13.43	35.63	83.19	25.46
1979	23.00	18.79	55.07	61.11	51.33	1.89	1.28	6.61	101.76	35.54	12.83	14.62	38.77	89.69	27.45
1980	24.81	19.97	58.84	68.09	57.20	2.11	1.43	7.35	105.88	36.70	13.37	15.28	40.53	94.08	28.79
1981	24.14	19.87	58.43	71.03	59.67	2.20	1.49	7.67	103.15	35.50	13.05	14.94	39.66	92.34	28.26
1982	26.95	21.50	65.64	85.59	71.90	2.65	1.80	9.24	107.83	37.55	13.60	15.52	41.16	95.33	29.17
1983	29.63	23.74	72.94	102.10	85.76	3.17	2.14	11.03	114.89	39.87	14.51	16.57	43.94	101.95	31.20
1984	34.84	29.26	88.90	111.46	93.63	3.46	2.34	12.03	145.84	50.46	18.43	21.06	55.89	129.83	39.75
1985	44.17	36.35	109.50	120.34	101.09	3.73	2.53	12.99	184.26	63.66	23.29	26.64	70.67	164.27	50.27
1986	49.59	41.01	123.60	123.45	103.70	3.83	2.59	13.33	207.28	71.36	26.22	30.03	79.67	185.48	56.76
1987	60.28	50.11	151.65	137.66	115.63	4.27	2.89	14.87	255.97	87.26	32.47	37.28	98.96	231.43	70.82
1988	78.86	68.64	209.29	162.31	136.34	5.03	3.41	17.53	323.40	111.40	40.92	46.83	124.25	289.22	88.50
1989	91.45	79.66	246.47	196.35	164.93	6.09	4.12	21.21	374.92	127.87	47.55	54.59	144.91	338.79	103.67
1990	98.31	84.66	268.65	227.89	191.43	7.06	4.79	24.61	387.52	130.68	49.28	56.79	150.77	354.26	108.40
1991	129.76	118.28	253.94	236.89	196.82	6.16	13.33	20.58	459.91	206.68	63.02	85.38	104.83	417.17	173.17
1992	159.88	122.19	403.34	257.08	219.21	7.80	6.69	23.38	573.15	178.13	80.52	89.11	225.39	517.75	141.01
1993	187.51	162.06	508.52	301.68	249.59	9.26	6.25	36.58	847.92	324.03	83.23	120.92	319.74	758.10	264.07
1994	258.96	231.15	498.91	451.91	349.47	13.88	5.39	83.17	1053.12	472.37	125.61	168.17	286.97	926.36	403.03
1995	296.37	304.58	605.42	631.34	534.06	18.78	10.27	68.23	1322.77	586.57	143.25	211.06	381.89	1322.77	586.57

Year	v13b1ii	v13b1iii	v13b1iv	v13b2	v13b2i	v13b2ii	v13b2iii	v13b2iv	v13c	v13ci	v13cii	v13ciii	v13civ	v13c1
1952														
1953														
1954														
1955														
1956														
1957														
1958														
1959														
1960														
1961														
1962														
1963														
1964														
1965														
1966														
1967														
1968														
1969														
1970														
1971														
1972														
1973														
1974														
1975														
1976														
1977														
1978	10.81	12.81	34.11	9.19	6.16	0.89	0.62	1.52	38.48	18.57	7.49	2.94	9.48	9.99
1979	11.66	13.81	36.77	12.07	8.09	1.17	0.81	2.00	40.35	19.49	8.28	2.89	9.69	10.86
1980	12.23	14.49	38.57	11.80	7.91	1.14	0.79	1.96	45.27	21.72	9.33	3.26	10.96	10.71
1981	12.00	14.22	37.86	10.81	7.24	1.05	0.72	1.80	48.36	24.93	8.89	3.44	11.10	10.87
1982	12.39	14.68	39.09	12.50	8.38	1.21	0.84	2.07	58.03	27.91	10.70	4.18	15.24	12.51
1983	13.25	15.70	41.80	12.94	8.67	1.26	0.87	2.14	66.22	31.27	11.95	5.03	17.97	13.71
1984	16.88	19.99	53.23	16.01	10.73	1.55	1.07	2.66	74.92	35.13	12.95	5.86	20.98	14.97
1985	21.35	25.30	67.35	19.99	13.39	1.94	1.34	3.32	92.15	41.98	17.15	7.18	25.84	16.91
1986	24.11	28.56	76.05	21.80	14.60	2.11	1.47	3.62	105.92	47.39	19.54	8.39	30.60	19.32
1987	30.09	35.64	94.88	24.54	16.44	2.38	1.64	4.08	128.29	56.99	23.54	9.94	37.82	24.03
1988	37.60	44.54	48.58	34.18	22.90	3.32	2.29	5.67	215.62	94.64	34.96	17.76	68.26	34.08
1989	44.54	52.17	138.91	36.13	24.20	3.51	2.42	6.00	251.56	109.20	40.60	19.99	81.77	41.50
1990	46.05	54.56	145.25	33.26	22.28	3.23	2.23	5.52	280.92	117.19	45.57	21.97	96.19	46.43
1991	58.76	82.76	101.78	42.74	32.81	4.26	2.62	3.05	375.27	166.59	60.58	19.57	128.53	79.35
1992	75.14	84.85	216.75	55.40	37.12	5.38	4.26	8.64	448.27	195.75	71.56	26.39	154.57	93.85
1993	77.40	113.17	303.46	89.82	59.96	5.83	7.75	16.28	541.24	259.13	95.02	34.89	152.20	115.34
1994	116.04	157.38	249.91	126.76	69.34	9.57	10.79	37.06	682.46	376.63	119.47	57.59	128.77	126.94
1995	143.25	211.06	381.89	172.28	92.60	9.27	18.99	51.42	895.41	522.52	134.34	83.25	155.30	179.41

Year	v13c1i	v13c1ii	v13c1iii	v13c1iv	v13c2	v13c2i	v13c2ii	v13c2iii	v13c2iv	v13c3	v13c3i	v13c3ii	v13c3iii	v13c3iv
1952														
1953														
1954														
1955														
1956														
1957														
1958														
1959														
1960														
1961														
1962														
1963														
1964														
1965														
1966														
1967														
1968														
1969														
1970														
1971														
1972														
1973														
1974														
1975														
1976														
1977														
1978	3.77	2.10	0.79	3.33	9.23	3.54	0.60	1.76	3.33	3.08	0.19	0.08	0.23	2.53
1979	4.09	2.28	0.87	3.62	8.36	3.21	0.54	1.60	3.01	3.31	0.20	0.10	0.30	2.71
1980	4.04	2.25	0.85	3.57	9.85	3.78	0.64	1.88	3.55	4.19	0.26	0.12	0.33	3.43
1981	4.10	2.28	0.87	3.62	10.86	4.17	0.71	2.07	3.91	3.84	0.23	0.11	0.35	3.15
1982	4.72	2.63	0.99	4.17	12.03	4.62	0.78	2.30	4.33	7.61	0.46	0.21	0.70	6.24
1983	5.17	2.88	1.09	4.57	15.18	5.83	0.99	2.90	5.46	9.01	0.55	0.24	0.83	7.39
1984	5.64	3.14	1.20	4.99	17.95	6.89	1.17	3.43	6.46	10.90	0.66	0.30	1.00	8.94
1985	6.38	3.55	1.35	5.63	22.22	8.53	1.44	4.24	8.01	13.89	0.85	0.37	1.23	11.39
1986	7.28	4.06	1.55	6.43	25.74	9.88	1.67	4.92	9.27	17.02	1.04	0.45	1.57	13.96
1987	9.06	5.05	1.92	8.00	29.06	11.16	1.89	5.55	10.46	22.22	1.35	0.61	2.04	18.22
1988	12.84	7.16	2.73	11.35	54.36	20.88	3.54	10.38	19.56	43.38	2.65	1.17	3.99	35.57
1989	15.65	8.72	3.31	13.82	56.75	21.80	3.68	10.83	20.44	55.51	3.39	1.49	5.11	45.52
1990	17.50	9.76	3.71	15.46	56.98	21.88	3.70	10.88	20.52	70.58	4.31	1.90	6.49	57.88
1991	22.58	17.42	5.66	33.69	109.11	61.07	6.44	6.79	34.81	63.48	5.94	1.94	5.09	50.51
1992	35.67	20.66	6.66	30.86	130.37	57.40	8.61	11.16	53.20	79.80	8.30	2.44	6.21	62.85
1993	53.68	23.85	8.17	29.64	161.88	98.93	10.99	16.12	35.84	90.96	6.28	2.30	7.40	74.98
1994	65.89	31.58	21.03	8.44	205.75	157.37	12.75	21.31	15.32	128.22	15.83	4.42	10.66	97.31
1995	104.95	33.15	33.97	7.34	261.69	198.33	15.87	27.86	19.63	166.51	21.47	5.48	13.52	126.04

Year	v13c4	v13c4i	v13c4ii	v13c4iii	v13c4iv	v13c5	v13c5i	v13c5ii	v13c5iii	v13c5iv	v13c6	v13c6i	v13c6ii	v13c6iii
1952														
1953														
1954														
1955														
1956														
1957														
1958														
1959														
1960														
1961														
1962														
1963														
1964														
1965														
1966														
1967														
1968														
1969														
1970														
1971														
1972														
1973														
1974														
1975														
1976														
1977														
1978	3.49	0.07	3.27	0.03	0.12	2.37	2.00	0.33	0.01	0.03	0.84	0.76	0.08	
1979	4.03	0.08	3.78	0.03	0.14	2.55	2.15	0.35	0.01	0.04	0.97	0.88	0.09	
1980	4.81	0.10	4.51	0.04	0.16	2.87	2.42	0.40	0.01	0.04	1.16	1.05	0.11	
1981	4.00	0.08	3.75	0.03	0.14	3.53	2.98	0.49	0.01	0.05	1.34	1.21	0.13	
1982	5.15	0.10	4.83	0.04	0.18	3.99	3.37	0.55	0.01	0.06	1.56	1.41	0.15	
1983	5.72	0.11	5.37	0.05	0.19	4.22	3.57	0.58	0.01	0.06	1.78	1.61	0.17	
1984	5.90	0.12	5.53	0.05	0.20	5.28	4.46	0.73	0.02	0.07	2.05	1.86	0.19	
1985	8.85	0.18	8.30	0.07	0.30	5.60	4.73	0.77	0.02	0.08	2.40	2.17	0.23	
1986	10.33	0.21	9.69	0.08	0.35	6.64	5.61	0.92	0.02	0.09	3.06	2.77	0.29	
1987	12.06	0.24	11.31	0.10	0.41	9.88	8.35	1.36	0.03	0.14	3.81	3.45	0.36	
1988	16.28	0.32	15.27	0.14	0.55	21.63	18.28	2.99	0.05	0.31	5.02	4.54	0.48	
1989	18.66	0.37	17.50	0.15	0.64	25.70	21.72	3.54	0.08	0.36	6.44	5.82	0.62	
1990	21.69	0.44	20.34	0.17	0.74	19.95	16.86	2.75	0.07	0.27	7.61	6.88	0.73	
1991	22.84	0.59	20.96	0.16	1.13	14.45	9.82	1.31	0.94	2.38	10.77	9.02	1.16	0.04
1992	25.44	0.99	23.50	0.34	0.61	17.70	14.50	1.84	1.13	0.23	12.87	10.81	1.37	0.04
1993	35.21	1.08	32.38	0.57	1.18	21.38	10.67	2.29	2.62	5.80	13.57	11.82	1.15	
1994	41.23	1.35	37.79	1.30	0.79	26.86	13.69	3.17	3.76	6.27	16.09	14.73	1.27	0.07
1995	46.07	1.71	41.51	1.69	1.16	38.45	27.73	3.89	5.62	1.21	20.23	18.79	1.71	0.07

Year	v13c6iv	v13c7	v13c7i	v13c7ii	v13c7iii	v13c7iv	v13c8	v13c8i	v13c8ii	v13c8iii	v13c8iv	v13c9	v13c9i	v13c9ii
1952														
1953														
1954														
1955														
1956														
1957														
1958														
1959														
1960														
1961														
1962														
1963														
1964														
1965														
1966														
1967														
1968														
1969														
1970														
1971														
1972														
1973														
1974														
1975														
1976														
1977														
1978		2.12	1.75	0.16	0.07	0.14	2.48	1.73	0.75			1.76	1.64	0.12
1979		2.50	2.06	0.19	0.08	0.17	2.68	1.87	0.81			1.97	1.83	0.14
1980		3.14	2.59	0.24	0.10	0.21	2.93	2.04	0.89			2.49	2.32	0.17
1981		3.49	2.88	0.27	0.11	0.23	3.17	2.21	0.96			2.75	2.56	0.19
1982		4.08	3.37	0.31	0.14	0.26	3.35	2.33	1.02			3.24	3.02	0.22
1983		4.54	3.74	0.35	0.15	0.30	3.62	2.52	1.10			3.93	3.66	0.27
1984		4.91	4.05	0.38	0.16	0.32	3.97	2.77	1.20			4.48	4.17	0.31
1985		6.52	5.37	0.50	0.22	0.43	5.22	3.64	1.58			5.93	5.52	0.41
1986		7.61	6.27	0.59	0.25	0.50	4.49	3.13	1.36			7.33	6.82	0.51
1987		8.97	7.39	0.69	0.30	0.59	5.65	3.94	1.71			8.11	7.55	0.56
1988		13.88	11.43	1.06	0.47	0.92	8.26	5.76	2.50			11.53	10.74	0.79
1989		15.16	12.49	1.17	0.50	1.00	9.42	6.57	2.85			14.88	13.85	1.03
1990		19.94	16.44	1.53	0.65	1.32	12.02	8.38	3.64			17.57	16.35	1.22
1991	0.55	20.59	16.67	3.10	0.14	0.68	7.67	4.89	1.98	0.23	0.57	34.59	27.28	5.64
1992	0.65	24.04	19.74	3.53	0.14	0.63	9.52	6.11	2.22	0.31	0.88	40.47	32.26	6.55
1993	0.60	27.89	23.95	3.23	0.01	0.70	11.51	7.70	3.81			48.02	33.86	14.16
1994	0.02	37.08	33.04	3.66	0.26	0.12	19.54	11.66	7.67	0.12	0.09	59.05	42.24	16.81
1995	-0.34	49.03	43.89	4.61	0.35	0.18	25.39	16.15	8.99	0.17	0.08	81.68	53.63	18.05

Year	v13c9iii	v13c9iv	v13c10	v13c10i	v13c10ii	v13c10iii	v13c10iv
1952							
1953							
1954							
1955							
1956							
1957							
1958							
1959							
1960							
1961							
1962							
1963							
1964							
1965							
1966							
1967							
1968							
1969							
1970							
1971							
1972							
1973							
1974							
1975							
1976							
1977							
1978			3.12	3.12			
1979			3.12	3.12			
1980			3.12	3.12			
1981			4.51	4.51			
1982			4.51	4.51			
1983			4.51	4.51			
1984			4.51	4.51			
1985			4.61	4.61			
1986			4.38	4.38			
1987			4.50	4.50			
1988			7.20	7.20			
1989			7.54	7.54			
1990			8.15	8.15			
1991	0.73	0.94	12.42	8.73	0.63	-0.21	3.27
1992	0.65	1.01	14.21	9.97	0.84	-0.25	3.65
1993			15.48	11.16	0.86	0.00	3.46
1994			21.70	20.83	0.35	0.11	0.41
1995			26.95	25.87	1.08		

4

Shanxi

Year	v1	v1a	v1b	v1b1	v1b2	v1c	v1c1	v1c2	v1c3	v2	v2a	v2b	v2b1	v2b2	v2c
1952	26.12	12.24	6.70	5.57	1.13	7.18	0.84	1.70	4.64						
1953	32.89	14.42	8.57	6.99	1.58	9.90	0.81	2.38	6.71	119.7	105.7	126.6	123.8	140.3	137.2
1954	36.15	14.86	10.92	9.11	1.81	10.37	0.98	2.45	6.94	110.1	101.5	131.6	134.4	119.6	102.9
1955	38.78	15.19	12.46	10.53	1.93	11.13	1.50	2.37	7.26	103.8	91.1	118.8	120.9	108.6	103.7
1956	48.68	17.61	17.12	12.91	4.21	13.95	1.43	3.33	9.19	126.8	120.4	134.2	122.5	197.5	124.9
1957	52.11	15.41	21.44	14.84	6.60	15.26	1.74	3.86	9.66	112.3	92.3	131.3	115.4	184.9	108.4
1958	72.31	17.82	33.72	23.66	10.06	20.77	3.27	4.97	12.53	140.9	115.7	161.5	166.2	151.1	137.3
1959	93.63	17.65	52.08	39.80	12.28	23.90	3.51	5.61	14.78	121.2	99.2	136.4	145.3	114.5	114.9
1960	99.72	11.98	64.11	49.90	14.21	23.63	3.53	4.28	15.82	104.8	73.1	120.9	123.4	113.0	96.4
1961	65.80	14.39	32.41	27.81	4.60	19.00	2.69	4.27	12.04	64.1	102.4	50.6	56.0	32.0	76.1
1962	61.55	15.07	29.47	25.65	3.82	17.01	2.47	4.17	10.37	89.5	103.8	85.9	85.8	86.2	84.7
1963	64.66	15.82	32.15	28.17	3.98	16.69	2.62	4.00	10.07	107.3	110.7	110.1	110.9	105.5	99.5
1964	73.18	17.69	37.42	32.53	4.89	18.07	2.73	4.48	10.86	114.5	115.5	116.1	115.2	121.9	110.6
1965	85.36	17.35	48.16	42.34	5.82	19.85	3.15	4.79	11.91	121.2	104.2	132.5	133.7	125.4	117.4
1966	96.14	19.53	55.93	50.47	5.46	20.68	3.42	4.97	12.29	107.7	100.2	112.0	114.7	94.6	105.4
1967	84.73	19.94	46.48	43.01	3.47	18.31	2.73	4.59	10.99	87.2	107.8	78.4	80.3	63.8	88.8
1968	66.53	19.23	30.70	27.40	3.30	16.60	2.53	4.20	9.87	81.8	87.9	74.3	72.2	94.7	90.5
1969	83.81	21.68	43.47	39.49	3.98	18.66	3.05	4.67	10.94	123.0	112.6	135.9	137.9	120.9	112.7
1970	113.18	20.72	69.73	62.56	7.17	22.73	3.49	6.43	12.81	131.8	97.9	154.6	151.6	180.0	121.7
1971	121.81	24.58	72.84	62.81	10.03	24.39	3.80	6.71	13.88	111.0	106.9	113.4	110.6	137.8	107.5
1972	121.60	22.28	73.83	64.03	9.80	25.49	4.13	6.99	14.37	101.8	90.9	104.0	105.2	95.7	104.6
1973	132.43	26.11	79.96	70.55	9.41	26.36	4.46	6.16	15.74	108.5	116.8	108.2	109.9	95.0	103.1
1974	128.63	27.42	74.65	65.77	8.88	26.56	4.29	6.36	15.91	97.2	105.4	93.9	94.1	92.2	101.1
1975	141.65	29.96	85.06	76.16	8.90	26.63	4.06	6.75	15.82	109.7	109.2	113.6	115.3	98.4	97.9
1976	134.02	28.55	79.09	70.60	8.49	26.38	3.78	7.47	15.13	94.3	95.0	93.4	93.3	93.9	97.2
1977	159.95	28.97	99.96	89.45	10.51	31.02	4.68	8.59	17.75	120.4	102.2	125.4	125.7	122.0	121.5
1978	188.51	29.01	119.40	106.43	12.97	40.10	6.20	9.86	24.04	117.9	93.8	120.4	120.3	121.4	129.5
1979	224.16	36.77	137.15	120.71	16.44	50.24	7.87	12.74	29.63	111.9	113.5	109.1	107.7	123.8	120.5
1980	233.29	38.23	140.56	126.34	14.22	54.50	11.48	10.44	32.58	101.6	93.7	101.1	102.9	84.6	107.6
1981	250.32	46.02	147.60	128.87	18.73	56.70	12.75	12.37	31.58	102.5	103.5	102.6	99.8	127.8	101.6
1982	288.27	53.08	167.94	141.81	26.13	67.25	15.79	14.56	36.90	116.2	121.9	115.1	112.1	135.6	115.1
1983	329.66	53.81	198.46	166.35	32.11	77.39	17.99	17.54	41.86	112.8	101.9	115.7	115.4	117.5	113.4
1984	412.20	65.15	237.81	194.60	43.21	109.24	23.80	20.54	64.90	123.7	117.9	118.4	116.5	129.2	141.8
1985	490.21	62.91	298.68	238.10	60.58	128.62	31.06	25.86	71.70	113.5	92.3	119.7	116.1	138.2	111.6
1986	537.30	58.82	323.43	261.80	61.63	155.05	35.09	30.66	89.30	107.1	91.7	107.0	108.3	101.4	116.6
1987	602.93	61.42	373.92	304.29	69.63	167.59	33.92	37.21	96.46	106.6	97.2	110.7	111.0	109.3	99.7
1988	764.36	87.24	457.16	387.22	69.94	219.96	38.88	58.42	122.66	109.4	112.5	109.2	113.4	89.4	108.7
1989	895.18	104.94	552.68	487.65	65.03	237.56	45.13	62.03	130.40	103.4	107.4	106.3	110.2	83.0	92.5
1990	1002.02	124.78	620.19	538.39	81.80	257.05	55.59	67.40	134.06	107.2	108.5	107.8	106.5	117.6	104.5
1991	1120.34	112.96	687.09	601.45	85.64	320.29	68.14	78.54	173.61	106.1	89.2	104.8	106.1	96.3	117.5
1992	1381.58	131.43	843.15	744.11	99.04	407.00	88.72	104.24	214.04	114.1	113.5	113.0	115.0	98.5	116.8
1993	1870.44	155.34	1242.58	1095.32	147.26	472.52	139.25	134.00	199.27	116.8	110.3	124.1	124.7	119.1	104.1
1994	2411.41	219.20	1625.00	1437.44	187.56	567.21	160.35	172.96	233.90	115.3	106.4	119.9	120.0	119.3	107.1
1995	3071.08	299.68	2032.30	1835.00	197.30	739.10	205.18	217.42	316.50	111.7	104.1	111.9	113.4	98.5	113.9

Year	v2c1	v2c2	v3'	v3	v3a	v3b	v3b1	v3b2	v3c	v3c1	v3c2	v3c3	v3c4	v3c5	v3c6
1952			16.00	16.00	9.38	2.75	2.35	0.40	3.87	0.33	1.12				
1953	94.4	144.5	19.87	19.87	11.05	3.49	2.96	0.53	5.33	0.36	1.57				
1954	118.4	105.7	21.90	21.90	11.55	4.77	4.24	0.53	5.58	0.45	1.57				
1955	149.1	97.1	23.87	23.87	12.08	5.80	5.17	0.63	5.99	0.72	1.52				
1956	94.4	140.3	28.44	28.44	13.59	7.34	5.89	1.45	7.51	0.67	2.05				
1957	115.2	117.9	29.16	29.16	11.54	9.40	7.18	2.22	8.22	0.79	2.38				
1958	186.8	128.6	39.51	39.51	13.67	14.65	11.46	3.19	11.19	1.56	3.01				
1959	107.9	113.1	48.28	48.28	12.45	22.96	19.50	3.46	12.87	1.71	3.41				
1960	99.7	76.6	50.20	50.20	8.87	28.61	24.28	4.33	12.72	1.73	2.73				
1961	76.6	113.8	34.07	34.07	10.38	13.47	12.06	1.41	10.22	1.19	2.46				
1962	93.5	83.7	32.41	32.41	11.07	12.18	10.91	1.27	9.16	1.12	2.30				
1963	106.0	88.9	33.72	33.72	11.52	13.22	11.91	1.31	8.98	1.15	2.07				
1964	103.9	112.7	38.44	38.44	13.09	15.61	13.98	1.63	9.74	1.19	2.35				
1965	114.5	127.5	43.92	43.92	12.70	20.52	18.59	1.93	10.70	1.39	2.57				
1966	109.5	103.0	49.68	49.68	14.22	24.32	22.29	2.03	11.14	1.69	2.32				
1967	78.4	92.0	44.87	44.87	14.34	20.68	19.00	1.68	9.85	1.33	2.26				
1968	91.6	91.7	36.82	36.82	13.72	14.17	12.43	1.74	8.93	1.20	2.03				
1969	121.9	109.7	45.42	45.42	15.68	19.69	17.77	1.92	10.05	1.46	2.25				
1970	113.3	135.3	57.69	57.69	15.19	30.26	27.95	2.31	12.24	1.73	3.04				
1971	108.9	104.3	62.05	62.05	18.19	30.72	27.86	2.86	13.14	1.81	3.08				
1972	108.8	104.1	61.64	61.64	15.67	32.25	27.99	4.26	13.72	1.93	3.07				
1973	108.0	88.1	66.20	66.20	18.70	33.30	30.49	2.81	14.20	2.05	3.02				
1974	96.1	103.4	64.42	64.42	19.23	30.88	28.27	2.61	14.31	2.03	3.04				
1975	94.7	96.2	69.81	69.81	20.80	34.67	32.20	2.47	14.34	1.76	3.18				
1976	93.1	104.3	64.61	64.61	19.05	31.35	29.61	1.74	14.21	1.62	3.09				
1977	123.6	130.4	75.26	75.26	18.99	39.57	37.23	2.34	16.70	2.07	3.74				
1978	132.5	115.4	87.99	87.99	18.20	51.45	48.11	3.34	18.34	2.72	4.81	1.71	1.10	0.65	1.05
1979	127.0	110.4	106.43	106.43	22.65	62.73	56.87	5.86	21.05	3.78	6.58	1.38	1.11	0.71	1.09
1980	145.8	82.9	108.76	108.76	20.63	63.52	58.22	5.30	24.61	6.26	5.11	1.97	1.50	0.85	1.12
1981	111.0	112.6	121.71	121.71	31.13	64.47	58.54	5.93	26.11	4.24	6.24	2.57	1.32	1.29	1.34
1982	123.9	107.0	139.21	139.22	37.33	70.24	62.20	8.04	31.65	6.22	6.49	4.44	1.27	1.76	1.64
1983	113.9	115.7	155.05	155.06	37.79	82.57	71.53	11.04	34.70	7.33	8.30	4.63	1.34	2.04	1.51
1984	132.3	131.3	197.43	197.42	46.25	103.12	89.60	13.52	48.05	13.30	9.87	5.29	1.98	3.51	1.99
1985	130.5	115.4	218.98	218.99	42.26	120.07	102.14	17.93	56.66	14.97	13.08	7.53	2.41	3.20	2.16
1986	111.8	119.2	235.10	235.11	37.90	128.27	108.90	19.37	68.94	17.73	15.55	10.15	2.81	3.73	2.44
1987	87.9	113.3	257.17	257.23	39.06	137.98	118.09	19.89	80.19	18.74	17.29	16.18	3.13	4.21	2.78
1988	103.2	122.1	315.88	316.69	48.54	163.30	142.24	21.06	104.85	22.19	25.69	21.11	3.47	5.43	3.46
1989	104.0	89.1	374.65	376.26	63.75	188.72	169.05	19.67	123.79	22.67	26.79	30.95	3.84	6.38	4.14
1990	110.5	106.4	427.65	429.27	80.81	210.07	186.61	23.46	138.39	24.99	29.06	37.24	4.08	7.20	4.24
1991	120.1	100.6	467.02	468.51	68.77	236.28	210.81	25.47	163.46	33.25	34.71	42.69	4.00	6.97	5.13
1992	124.0	121.0	568.51	570.12	82.94	289.26	259.42	29.84	197.92	43.82	44.31	46.38	5.56	8.70	6.00
1993	136.3	119.7	701.50	704.63	97.27	366.36	326.85	39.51	241.00	56.21	52.46	58.47	6.05	12.01	7.76
1994	119.9	115.9	848.38	853.77	123.85	440.81	390.17	50.64	289.11	70.54	66.35	47.80	7.20	14.62	8.60
1995	113.9	108.7	1088.17	1092.48	168.69	545.13	487.05	58.08	378.66	87.98	84.96	80.39	8.17	19.55	10.29

Year	v3c7	v3c8	v3c9	v3c10	v3d	v4'	v4	v4a	v4b	v4b1	v4b2	v4c	v4c1	v4c2	v4c3
1952				2.42	116										
1953				3.40	141	116.7	116.7	105.6	125.7	124.6	132.0	137.2	104.4	143.7	
1954				3.56	151	110.0	110.0	103.0	140.9	147.4	105.2	102.9	122.6	102.6	
1955				3.75	160	104.0	104.0	93.1	126.9	127.8	120.1	103.7	156.4	96.8	
1956				4.79	186	121.1	121.1	116.9	124.2	113.9	208.1	124.9	92.0	135.4	
1957				5.05	186	107.6	107.6	89.6	133.0	122.2	181.5	108.4	112.0	117.8	
1958				6.62	246	137.4	137.4	118.5	160.8	166.5	142.2	137.3	195.8	126.3	
1959				7.75	294	115.3	115.3	91.2	137.5	147.0	101.6	114.9	110.7	113.5	
1960				8.26	298	102.8	102.8	76.7	122.5	122.5	122.3	96.4	99.8	80.4	
1961				6.57	200	65.4	65.4	99.8	47.2	49.9	32.1	76.1	69.1	102.9	
1962				5.74	188	91.3	91.3	105.7	85.2	84.2	93.9	84.7	96.3	80.0	
1963				5.76	191	106.8	106.8	109.8	109.5	110.2	104.4	99.5	102.6	83.6	
1964				6.20	213	115.8	115.8	117.4	117.8	117.1	123.4	110.6	102.6	114.2	
1965				6.74	238	118.8	118.8	103.1	135.2	136.6	124.5	117.4	116.9	130.4	
1966				7.13	263	107.4	107.4	99.7	114.4	115.4	105.8	105.4	122.2	89.5	
1967				6.26	233	90.3	90.3	106.5	80.6	80.3	83.0	88.8	77.2	97.4	
1968				5.70	187	83.9	83.9	87.2	77.1	74.1	103.5	90.5	89.6	89.6	
1969				6.34	224	120.9	120.9	114.2	133.3	136.9	110.5	112.7	123.0	109.9	
1970				7.47	277	124.4	124.4	99.2	147.0	150.5	120.0	121.7	116.8	132.4	
1971				8.25	290	109.3	109.3	107.9	110.7	109.8	122.3	107.5	104.9	101.4	
1972				8.72	282	101.3	101.3	86.4	107.2	103.7	145.7	104.6	106.4	99.3	
1973				9.13	296	106.9	106.9	119.0	103.7	108.7	65.2	103.1	106.4	98.6	
1974				9.24	283	97.4	97.4	103.2	93.4	93.6	90.8	101.1	99.2	100.8	
1975				9.40	301	107.9	107.9	108.1	112.0	113.4	93.0	97.9	86.6	94.8	
1976				9.50	274	92.4	92.4	91.3	91.2	92.6	69.1	97.2	91.8	91.4	
1977				10.89	315	118.0	118.0	100.4	125.1	124.7	132.6	121.5	127.8	137.5	
1978	2.44	0.58	1.57	1.71	365	117.6	117.6	89.8	131.2	130.7	140.9	109.9	131.2	129.4	
1979	2.44	0.55	1.66	1.75	437	109.8	109.8	107.8	108.7	105.3	172.4	115.2	140.3	137.4	80.3
1980	2.57	0.76	1.75	2.72	442	102.0	102.0	87.6	102.9	104.6	82.6	111.1	158.4	73.7	133.8
1981	3.33	0.91	2.53	2.34	488	100.8	100.8	121.3	93.2	91.8	109.1	103.3	76.5	119.1	125.3
1982	3.90	0.94	2.79	2.20	551	115.6	115.6	123.5	111.8	109.7	131.3	116.5	125.2	102.4	165.6
1983	3.82	0.99	2.92	1.82	604	113.9	113.9	102.6	120.9	119.6	131.3	109.7	114.8	125.0	101.9
1984	4.72	1.06	3.75	2.58	756	121.6	121.6	119.8	118.2	118.3	117.8	131.7	173.2	113.3	109.1
1985	4.93	0.94	4.42	3.02	826	107.0	107.1	82.2	113.1	110.2	133.3	115.8	110.0	130.5	138.3
1986	5.56	1.72	6.34	2.91	873	106.5	106.5	96.3	108.2	108.0	109.3	109.2	108.7	105.5	127.1
1987	5.97	2.31	7.01	2.57	940	105.2	105.2	97.0	107.0	107.3	105.4	105.8	100.7	108.1	121.2
1988	7.63	3.89	8.88	3.10	1138	107.5	107.8	103.8	107.0	110.1	88.8	111.7	102.5	115.2	119.3
1989	8.92	5.14	11.30	3.66	1329	104.9	105.2	107.2	104.7	107.6	83.5	105.3	93.4	93.1	130.0
1990	9.34	5.93	12.11	4.20	1493	105.0	105.0	112.6	101.4	100.4	110.7	108.6	111.3	104.7	108.0
1991	11.27	5.40	15.60	4.44	1604	104.3	104.2	87.4	106.3	106.9	101.3	110.9	131.1	108.9	107.9
1992	13.48	5.29	18.45	5.93	1926	113.9	113.8	112.9	113.9	115.4	101.4	114.1	121.8	121.1	117.6
1993	16.22	5.49	19.82	6.51	2352	111.9	112.2	109.1	114.5	115.1	108.8	110.2	112.8	112.2	116.5
1994	24.25	10.95	30.93	7.87	2819	109.1	109.4	104.5	112.4	112.4	112.5	107.1	117.8	113.0	85.9
1995	29.53	13.45	35.69	8.65	3569	111.4	111.1	103.8	114.3	114.9	107.6	109.3	111.2	109.5	113.7

Year	v4c4	v4c5	v4c6	v4c7	v4c8	v4c9	v4c10	v5	v5a	v5a1	v5a1a	v5a1b	v5a2	v5b	v5b1
1952								16.00	10.68	10.41	8.52	1.89	0.27	2.89	2.24
1953								19.87	12.60	12.18	9.35	2.83	0.42	3.75	2.96
1954								21.90	13.36	12.89	9.36	3.53	0.47	5.52	4.62
1955								23.87	14.05	13.54	9.55	3.99	0.51	5.72	4.86
1956								28.44	16.46	15.74	10.67	5.07	0.72	10.91	10.23
1957								29.16	16.18	15.31	9.58	5.73	0.87	13.37	10.72
1958								39.51	19.01	17.92	11.12	6.80	1.09	21.90	21.09
1959								48.28	20.37	18.71	10.48	8.23	1.66	27.97	22.03
1960								50.20	21.09	19.27	9.50	9.77	1.82	26.00	24.51
1961								34.07	20.59	18.75	10.25	8.50	1.84	8.76	8.37
1962								32.41	20.16	18.88	10.91	7.97	1.28	2.87	4.73
1963								33.72	20.61	19.17	11.70	7.47	1.44	5.61	5.85
1964								38.44	21.41	19.82	12.57	7.25	1.59	6.78	8.15
1965								43.92	21.99	20.31	13.01	7.30	1.68	13.35	10.03
1966								49.68	23.11	21.75	14.04	7.71	1.36	13.82	11.67
1967								44.87	23.75	22.77	14.73	8.04	0.98	8.47	7.48
1968								36.82	22.69	21.97	14.41	7.56	0.72	7.70	5.74
1969								45.42	25.35	24.36	16.46	7.90	0.99	13.71	8.52
1970								57.69	26.13	24.96	16.66	8.30	1.17	17.76	15.77
1971								62.05	28.87	27.19	18.11	9.08	1.68	27.05	20.92
1972								61.64	30.18	28.33	17.44	10.89	1.85	27.95	20.72
1973								66.20	32.68	30.42	19.09	11.33	2.26	22.88	20.46
1974								64.42	34.83	31.95	20.35	11.60	2.88	24.94	19.33
1975								69.81	36.07	32.68	20.81	11.87	3.39	26.06	21.07
1976								64.61	36.86	33.75	20.93	12.82	3.11	21.76	19.58
1977								75.26	39.14	35.72	21.83	13.89	3.42	30.34	24.74
1978								87.99	45.94	42.03	25.81	16.22	3.91	33.93	27.44
1979	99.9	100.6	101.7	99.9	92.0	102.8	99.1	106.43	54.62	46.21	28.51	17.70	8.41	31.92	22.46
1980	132.5	118.3	96.5	99.4	126.8	97.3	138.4	108.76	62.86	54.09	32.49	21.60	8.77	32.74	27.29
1981	87.8	132.7	106.2	106.2	104.7	134.1	82.1	121.71	70.34	61.40	37.59	23.81	8.94	32.96	24.74
1982	98.1	119.4	113.2	110.8	91.4	117.4	91.1	139.22	79.14	67.98	42.52	25.46	11.16	43.27	33.52
1983	102.7	109.0	94.9	114.6	114.4	91.1	91.3	155.06	89.82	75.91	48.13	27.78	13.91	54.65	43.55
1984	139.4	145.4	110.7	120.3	193.8	119.5	111.2	197.42	105.64	87.30	54.73	32.57	18.34	80.89	66.89
1985	126.1	86.4	126.2	102.0	53.7	112.3	115.6	218.99	123.32	102.00	60.48	41.52	21.32	109.28	88.92
1986	104.0	114.4	99.8	98.8	113.3	118.4	78.8	235.11	134.87	109.37	64.37	45.00	25.50	112.00	94.05
1987	105.0	106.2	102.5	101.0	120.2	104.1	74.8	257.23	154.41	124.74	71.44	53.30	29.67	129.95	102.97
1988	97.3	118.6	105.7	106.9	143.6	103.7	113.4	316.69	195.32	157.01	86.83	70.18	38.31	145.29	104.43
1989	99.9	105.3	103.1	100.5	104.4	110.5	99.2	376.26	227.71	176.89	99.30	77.59	50.82	165.89	104.67
1990	107.5	106.6	103.4	105.7	114.9	106.7	114.5	429.27	259.90	191.47	106.25	85.22	68.43	186.99	117.24
1991	98.8	88.7	110.6	103.7	99.5	114.6	99.6	468.51	284.04	218.09	113.19	104.90	65.95	176.67	144.39
1992	104.3	85.3	116.4	106.4	78.6	106.8	108.4	570.12	342.09	262.96	132.15	130.81	79.13	235.33	175.52
1993	105.1	107.1	107.9	106.5	118.7	109.8	93.3	704.63	418.65	333.21	166.03	167.18	85.44	313.50	242.55
1994	116.1	130.0	111.9	115.2	116.4	107.6	121.5	857.62	494.91	378.57	183.15	195.42	116.34	385.71	290.90
1995	106.9	109.9	104.6	107.1	105.2	102.2	95.9	1090.29	627.23	486.52	235.36	251.16	140.71	412.42	314.06

Year	v5b2	v5c	v5c1	v5c2	v6a1	v6a2	v6a3	v6a4	v6b2	v6b3	v6b4	v7	v7a	v7a1	v7a2
1952	0.65	2.43													
1953	0.79	3.52										111.7	110.8	109.0	119.3
1954	0.90	3.02										106.0	105.8	100.3	130.0
1955	0.86	4.10										104.5	104.3	97.6	127.2
1956	0.68	1.07										117.0	116.2	112.1	127.0
1957	2.65	-0.39										97.4	96.5	90.4	110.6
1958	0.81	-1.40										116.2	115.8	114.0	119.0
1959	5.94	-0.06										105.1	102.7	95.9	115.0
1960	1.49	3.11										92.8	91.7	85.4	101.1
1961	0.39	4.72										82.8	81.8	89.5	72.1
1962	-1.86	9.38										99.5	102.6	106.4	96.7
1963	-0.24	7.50										112.1	112.2	112.0	112.7
1964	-1.37	10.25										106.6	106.2	108.4	102.4
1965	3.32	8.58										107.4	107.4	107.4	107.4
1966	2.15	12.75										104.1	105.8	105.5	106.2
1967	0.99	12.65										103.0	104.7	104.9	104.5
1968	1.96	6.43										95.3	96.1	97.4	93.8
1969	5.19	6.36										112.7	112.0	115.5	105.4
1970	1.99	13.80										102.8	102.3	100.9	105.1
1971	6.13	6.13										110.0	108.5	108.1	109.3
1972	7.23	3.51										104.2	103.9	95.8	119.7
1973	2.42	10.64										108.0	107.2	109.2	104.1
1974	5.61	4.65										106.2	104.7	106.5	101.8
1975	4.99	7.68										103.3	102.1	102.3	101.7
1976	2.18	5.99										102.1	103.1	100.4	107.7
1977	5.60	5.78										105.2	104.8	104.4	105.4
1978	6.49	8.12			11.10	11.63	1.75	1.33	15.03	1.08	0.11	116.3	116.5	116.8	116.1
1979	9.46	19.89			11.67	13.02	2.34	1.48	16.30	1.25	0.15	113.2	104.7	103.1	107.2
1980	5.45	13.16			12.26	15.99	2.60	1.64	20.10	1.32	0.18	110.2	111.5	110.2	113.4
1981	8.22	18.41			12.89	19.88	3.00	1.82	22.15	1.43	0.23	109.5	110.9	113.2	107.5
1982	9.75	16.81			15.05	22.03	3.43	2.01	23.36	1.80	0.30	110.9	108.8	111.4	104.7
1983	11.10	10.59			15.69	26.43	3.79	2.22	25.78	1.65	0.35	112.7	110.5	112.6	107.0
1984	14.00	10.89			17.74	30.50	4.33	2.16	30.11	2.04	0.42	113.6	110.2	109.6	111.2
1985	20.36	-13.61			17.10	36.00	4.77	2.61	38.58	2.37	0.57	112.2	112.0	107.9	119.1
1986	17.95	-11.76			13.90	42.67	5.04	2.76	42.51	1.85	0.64	101.9	102.4	102.7	102.1
1987	26.98	-27.13			19.46	43.21	5.41	3.36	50.26	2.16	0.88	108.6	108.7	108.4	109.2
1988	40.86	-23.92			20.53	55.90	6.85	3.55	66.13	2.87	1.18	103.2	102.4	99.2	107.5
1989	61.22	-17.34			24.82	62.45	7.86	4.17	71.66	4.36	1.57	93.9	89.8	86.0	95.4
1990	69.75	-17.62			33.43	60.35	7.87	4.60	74.56	8.81	1.85	117.2	112.5	114.7	109.7
1991	32.28	7.80			37.24	59.34	11.00	5.61	88.99	13.90	2.01	104.6	108.8	103.6	115.9
1992	59.81	-7.30			39.18	78.25	9.11	5.61	111.03	16.62	3.16	112.1	112.8	111.6	114.3
1993	70.95	-27.52			51.50	96.78	11.28	6.47	141.37	20.86	4.95	107.1	111.5	112.5	110.3
1994	94.81	-23.00	362.27	385.27	53.54	109.02	12.54	8.05	157.47	32.61	5.34	107.9	108.0	107.9	108.2
1995	98.36	50.64	455.84	405.20	66.35	139.87	19.68	9.46	199.02	46.12	6.02	109.4	109.7	108.6	111.0

Year	v7b	v8	v8a	v8b	v9	v9a	v9b	v10a1	v10a2	v10a3	v10a3a	v10a3b	v10a4	v10b1	v10b2
1952		76	69	142											
1953	159.5	86	74	186	107.5	107.2	104.8								
1954	114.7	89	73	208	103.5	99.0	116.2								
1955	109.1	91	74	207	100.8	96.1	111.8								
1956	140.8	103	82	228	113.4	111.1	109.8								
1957	121.9	98	72	237	94.1	89.1	102.1								
1958	126.3	112	84	248	113.4	113.3	104.9								
1959	152.3	114	79	259	100.0	96.4	99.3								
1960	107.4	114	70	298	89.6	83.2	98.0								
1961	94.6	110	73	280	80.6	86.5	77.8								
1962	69.0	109	74	310	101.9	102.6	114.0								
1963	109.9	108	76	315	109.4	107.6	122.3								
1964	113.1	110	81	290	103.4	105.9	97.2								
1965	107.7	110	82	275	105.0	105.6	101.3								
1966	81.2	115	87	282	104.0	103.2	102.9								
1967	71.9	118	89	289	102.3	103.1	102.8								
1968	73.5	111	85	266	94.0	95.0	91.8								
1969	139.6	120	95	274	109.5	112.5	103.9								
1970	117.5	120	94	276	99.3	98.1	100.3								
1971	144.5	127	100	285	105.8	105.7	103.8								
1972	109.9	129	94	327	101.4	94.6	114.3								
1973	121.8	136	101	328	104.8	106.6	100.0								
1974	127.5	140	106	328	102.6	104.4	99.7								
1975	117.8	141	106	330	100.6	100.8	100.0								
1976	91.6	143	105	346	101.3	99.2	104.8								
1977	110.0	150	109	368	103.7	103.4	103.1								
1978	113.8	174	128	419	115.0	115.6	113.3	23.60	2.00	1.84	0.02	1.82		4.54	1.30
1979	213.1	190	140	437	103.6	102.8	102.4	19.31	1.64	1.51	0.01	1.50		6.52	1.89
1980	103.2	220	160	505	110.6	110.3	107.4	21.61	3.55	2.13	0.02	2.11		3.82	1.09
1981	100.8	246	184	530	109.5	112.5	102.4	17.21	3.53	4.00	0.15	3.85		5.75	1.64
1982	124.8	269	206	545	107.1	110.6	100.8	24.16	5.31	4.05	0.22	3.83		7.33	0.16
1983	126.0	297	232	576	109.3	111.6	103.6	30.21	7.20	6.14	0.39	5.75		6.33	1.82
1984	131.4	338	262	651	108.9	109.0	107.2	47.26	12.07	7.56	1.21	6.35		6.09	6.43
1985	113.3	390	289	798	110.7	107.4	114.5	64.99	12.90	11.03	2.29	8.74		13.28	6.80
1986	99.8	414	306	833	101.5	102.3	98.2	70.08	9.94	14.03	3.39	10.64		13.62	4.06
1987	108.3	467	338	948	107.5	107.9	104.9	76.82	9.68	16.47	2.77	13.70		19.39	3.95
1988	106.7	579	408	1206	100.8	98.6	103.8	75.40	11.87	17.16	3.04	14.12		25.37	8.17
1989	111.4	643	461	1293	88.5	84.8	92.5	77.15	10.03	17.49	3.82	13.67		46.75	12.24
1990	133.1	681	485	1379	110.3	112.9	106.6	86.96	10.28	20.00	3.55	16.45		41.12	13.95
1991	92.7	741	494	1611	103.8	98.9	110.0	107.53	13.49	23.37	3.15	20.22		16.45	6.46
1992	109.8	882	574	1926	111.3	111.2	109.6	144.42	15.73	15.37	3.43	11.94		31.84	11.96
1993	91.7	1112	717	2459	110.9	111.7	110.1	186.43	24.07	27.08	7.90	19.18	4.97	46.36	2.20
1994	107.4	1250	789	2756	106.9	107.7	103.8	226.82	21.26	30.53	10.41	20.12	12.29	49.62	10.53
1995	108.2	1589	1012	3413	105.5	111.1	100.4	235.87	27.90	37.65	18.77	18.88	12.64	48.86	39.98

Year	v10b4	v11a	v11a1	v11a2	v11b	v11b1	v11b2	v11c	v11c1	v11c2	v12	v12a	v12b	v13	v13i
1952															
1953											130.9	134.8	116.4		
1954											147.2	157.5	102.2		
1955											107.7	109.6	94.6		
1956											197.0	211.5	84.4		
1957											122.1	104.6	465.1		
1958											163.4	194.1	28.3		
1959											121.5	101.7	721.1		
1960											93.0	111.6	13.8		
1961											33.6	33.2	46.6		
1962											30.7	55.1	-565.2		
1963											185.3	118.1	25.2		
1964											124.8	142.8	326.1		
1965											206.7	127.1	-182.7		
1966											105.2	118.5	60.1		
1967											62.5	63.9	53.2		
1968											95.3	79.4	223.0		
1969											179.7	152.0	259.0		
1970											129.3	185.3	34.9		
1971											150.0	127.5	352.0		
1972											103.1	100.7	110.8		
1973											82.0	98.6	33.2		
1974											108.5	94.3	232.8		
1975											103.3	107.8	87.4		
1976											83.4	92.3	44.7		
1977											137.8	124.6	256.7		
1978	0.65	6.51	5.21	1.30	17.04	15.61	1.43	10.38	6.62	3.76	111.4	110.4	115.9	87.99	42.88
1979	0.95	6.16	4.27	1.89	14.86	12.78	2.08	10.90	5.41	5.49	90.8	80.1	135.5	106.43	53.22
1980	0.54	5.48	4.39	1.09	17.03	15.83	1.20	10.23	7.07	3.16	100.5	117.8	57.9	108.76	52.72
1981	0.83	4.24	2.60	1.64	14.45	12.64	1.81	14.27	9.50	4.77	98.1	87.9	149.2	121.71	66.44
1982	2.26	5.92	3.69	2.23	20.44	18.17	2.27	16.91	11.66	5.25	128.2	132.4	116.0	139.22	78.03
1983	2.95	7.67	4.75	2.92	28.12	25.08	3.04	18.86	13.72	5.14	123.5	126.9	112.3	155.06	84.56
1984	1.48	4.36	3.01	1.35	43.85	37.39	6.46	32.68	26.49	6.19	139.1	143.8	121.3	197.42	109.31
1985	0.28	2.57	2.22	0.35	64.22	53.89	10.33	42.49	32.81	9.68	133.0	132.5	135.1	218.99	116.86
1986	0.27	4.16	4.04	0.12	77.21	58.31	18.90	30.63	31.70	-1.07	97.3	100.5	83.4	235.11	113.71
1987	3.64	7.75	4.74	3.01	69.78	57.97	11.81	52.42	40.26	12.16	107.9	100.1	149.0	257.23	116.80
1988	7.32	11.06	5.74	5.32	83.53	64.33	19.20	50.70	34.36	16.34	94.3	86.7	121.5	316.69	144.21
1989	2.23	14.73	5.55	9.18	95.40	64.79	30.61	55.76	34.33	21.43	99.2	89.4	124.3	376.26	174.74
1990	14.68	21.67	9.81	11.86	108.89	71.92	36.97	56.43	35.51	20.92	109.5	104.8	118.3	429.27	211.03
1991	9.37	16.44	10.31	6.13	110.41	92.33	18.08	49.82	41.75	8.07	87.7	113.7	45.3	468.51	243.47
1992	16.01	24.14	11.58	12.56	144.99	109.70	35.29	66.20	54.24	11.96	113.4	104.6	149.3	570.12	277.58
1993	22.39	26.67	9.03	17.64	168.90	123.42	45.48	117.93	110.10	7.83	203.0	206.9	191.8	704.63	356.02
1994	34.66	30.68	6.39	24.29	186.32	127.48	58.84	168.71	157.03	11.68	110.1	110.7	108.0	853.77	431.07
1995	9.52	17.46	7.80	9.66	201.85	128.48	73.37	193.11	177.78	15.33	104.1	102.9	108.1	1092.48	561.85

Year	v13ii	v13iii	v13iv	v13a	v13ai	v13aii	v13aiii	v13aiv	v13b	v13bi	v13bii	v13biii	v13biv	v13b1	v13b1i
1952															
1953															
1954															
1955															
1956															
1957															
1958															
1959															
1960															
1961															
1962															
1963															
1964															
1965															
1966															
1967															
1968															
1969															
1970															
1971															
1972															
1973															
1974															
1975															
1976															
1977															
1978	13.04	11.78	20.29	18.20	14.61	0.25	1.08	2.26	51.45	18.07	10.20	8.59	14.59	48.11	15.55
1979	14.92	13.09	25.20	22.65	19.17	0.48	1.28	1.72	62.73	22.07	11.63	9.30	19.73	56.87	17.44
1980	17.94	13.27	24.83	20.63	15.97	0.24	1.21	3.21	63.52	23.26	14.01	9.31	16.94	58.22	19.12
1981	16.49	13.96	24.82	31.13	27.26	0.38	1.35	2.14	64.47	23.40	12.04	10.44	18.59	58.54	19.42
1982	17.82	16.44	26.93	37.33	33.11	0.47	1.64	2.11	70.24	26.28	12.58	11.57	19.81	62.20	20.77
1983	19.79	18.59	32.12	37.79	33.58	0.74	1.86	1.61	82.57	31.62	14.29	13.32	23.34	71.53	24.70
1984	23.88	26.91	37.32	46.25	40.22	0.84	2.25	2.94	103.12	41.24	17.16	19.16	25.56	89.60	32.62
1985	26.09	30.23	45.81	42.26	36.89	1.03	2.71	1.63	120.07	52.52	18.51	21.10	27.94	102.14	40.71
1986	38.35	35.25	47.80	37.90	30.41	2.86	2.72	1.91	128.27	52.06	24.15	23.48	28.58	108.90	39.01
1987	40.71	29.85	69.87	39.06	23.66	3.69	1.04	10.67	137.98	56.41	26.48	19.22	35.87	118.09	42.54
1988	49.56	41.74	81.18	48.54	30.36	3.21	1.71	13.26	163.30	67.64	31.77	25.99	37.90	142.24	53.40
1989	51.05	55.60	94.87	63.75	42.62	2.50	5.37	13.26	188.72	81.97	31.61	31.76	43.38	169.05	68.55
1990	60.27	57.60	100.37	80.81	54.08	3.15	6.76	16.82	210.07	100.36	38.82	32.37	38.52	186.61	84.77
1991	76.44	58.59	90.01	68.77	61.71	2.91	1.62	2.53	236.28	109.52	48.20	35.12	43.44	210.81	92.52
1992	98.87	70.62	123.05	82.94	72.94	3.27	1.32	5.41	289.26	117.51	60.54	48.76	62.45	259.42	100.10
1993	104.03	86.53	158.05	97.27	78.94	5.35	-0.26	13.24	366.36	161.93	56.14	68.36	79.93	326.85	139.50
1994	108.40	122.72	191.58	123.85	90.30	6.92	-0.10	26.73	440.81	212.74	64.63	93.79	69.65	390.17	176.55
1995	134.58	152.03	244.02	168.69	110.17	7.10	0.18	51.24	545.13	284.62	79.75	108.50	72.26	487.05	243.67

Year	v13b1ii	v13b1iii	v13b1iv	v13b2	v13b2i	v13b2ii	v13b2iii	v13b2iv	v13c	v13ci	v13cii	v13ciii	v13civ	v13c1
1952														
1953														
1954														
1955														
1956														
1957														
1958														
1959														
1960														
1961														
1962														
1963														
1964														
1965														
1966														
1967														
1968														
1969														
1970														
1971														
1972														
1973														
1974														
1975														
1976														
1977														
1978	9.87	8.54	14.15	3.34	2.52	0.33	0.05	0.44	18.34	10.20	2.59	2.11	3.44	2.72
1979	11.30	9.21	18.92	5.86	4.63	0.33	0.09	0.81	21.05	11.98	2.81	2.51	3.75	3.78
1980	13.66	9.23	16.21	5.30	4.14	0.35	0.08	0.73	24.61	13.49	3.69	2.75	4.68	6.26
1981	11.63	10.29	17.20	5.93	3.98	0.41	0.15	1.39	26.11	15.78	4.07	2.17	4.09	4.24
1982	12.05	11.28	18.10	8.04	5.51	0.53	0.29	1.71	31.65	18.64	4.77	3.23	5.01	6.22
1983	13.64	12.56	20.63	11.04	6.92	0.65	0.76	2.71	34.70	19.36	4.76	3.41	7.17	7.33
1984	16.15	17.92	22.91	13.52	8.62	1.01	1.24	2.65	48.05	27.85	5.88	5.50	8.82	13.30
1985	17.47	19.74	24.22	17.93	11.81	1.04	1.36	3.72	56.66	27.45	6.55	6.42	16.24	14.97
1986	22.38	22.07	25.44	19.37	13.05	1.77	1.41	3.14	68.94	31.24	11.34	9.05	17.31	17.73
1987	24.68	17.55	33.32	19.89	13.87	1.80	1.67	2.55	80.19	36.73	10.54	9.59	23.33	18.74
1988	29.69	23.93	35.22	21.06	14.24	2.08	2.06	2.68	104.85	46.21	14.58	14.04	30.02	22.19
1989	29.72	29.32	41.46	19.67	13.42	1.89	2.44	1.92	123.79	50.15	16.94	18.47	38.23	22.67
1990	36.07	28.83	36.94	23.46	15.59	2.75	3.54	1.58	138.39	56.59	18.30	18.47	45.03	24.99
1991	45.43	31.13	41.73	25.47	17.00	2.77	3.99	1.71	163.46	72.24	25.33	21.85	44.04	33.25
1992	57.09	45.58	56.65	29.84	17.41	3.45	3.18	5.80	197.92	87.13	35.06	20.54	55.19	43.82
1993	52.25	63.49	71.61	39.51	22.43	3.89	4.87	8.32	241.00	115.15	42.54	18.43	64.88	56.21
1994	59.98	87.19	66.45	50.64	36.19	4.65	6.60	3.20	289.11	128.03	36.85	29.03	95.20	70.54
1995	74.76	100.58	68.04	58.08	40.95	4.99	7.92	4.22	378.66	167.06	47.73	43.35	120.52	87.98

Year	v13c1i	v13c1ii	v13c1iii	v13c1iv	v13c2	v13c2i	v13c2ii	v13c2iii	v13c2iv	v13c3	v13c3i	v13c3ii	v13c3iii	v13c3iv
1952														
1953														
1954														
1955														
1956														
1957														
1958														
1959														
1960														
1961														
1962														
1963														
1964														
1965														
1966														
1967														
1968														
1969														
1970														
1971														
1972														
1973														
1974														
1975														
1976														
1977														
1978	0.78	0.45	0.59	0.90	4.81	2.04	0.43	1.49	0.85	1.71	0.09	0.01		1.61
1979	1.14	0.53	0.74	1.37	6.58	3.28	0.52	1.74	1.04	1.38	0.11	0.01		1.26
1980	1.93	0.89	1.35	2.09	5.11	2.35	0.63	1.36	0.77	1.97	0.26	0.01		1.70
1981	1.50	1.15	0.45	1.14	6.24	3.17	0.74	1.67	0.66	2.57	0.41	0.04		2.12
1982	2.34	1.50	1.12	1.26	6.49	3.90	0.99	2.03	-0.43	4.44	0.43	0.08		3.93
1983	3.24	1.17	1.34	1.58	8.30	4.10	1.03	1.97	1.20	4.63	0.46	0.09		4.08
1984	6.32	1.30	2.99	2.69	9.87	4.88	1.07	2.44	1.48	5.29	0.69	0.12	0.00	4.48
1985	5.10	1.16	2.89	5.82	13.08	5.82	1.00	2.80	3.46	7.53	0.53	0.15	0.52	6.33
1986	5.40	4.26	3.86	4.21	15.55	6.01	1.69	4.18	3.67	10.15	0.53	0.22	0.76	8.64
1987	5.82	4.69	3.14	5.09	17.29	8.25	1.34	4.54	3.16	16.18	0.81	0.24	1.17	13.96
1988	7.51	5.58	3.98	5.12	25.69	9.20	3.12	7.29	6.08	21.11	1.16	0.38	1.64	17.93
1989	8.03	6.72	3.50	4.42	26.79	8.19	3.54	10.56	4.50	30.95	1.37	0.54	2.45	26.59
1990	9.07	7.29	2.72	5.91	29.06	10.35	3.76	11.17	3.78	37.24	1.47	0.72	2.95	32.10
1991	9.98	10.05	3.38	9.84	34.71	19.24	6.93	13.63	-5.09	42.69	1.75	1.36	3.25	36.33
1992	12.58	15.44	4.09	11.71	44.31	26.01	8.73	9.65	-0.08	46.38	3.16	1.65	3.42	38.15
1993	20.84	21.47	6.03	7.87	52.46	35.80	9.31	5.26	2.09	58.47	4.27	1.38	4.70	48.12
1994	26.28	12.34	6.45	25.47	66.35	26.20	4.81	13.51	21.83	47.80	7.62	2.04	5.62	32.52
1995	36.71	17.46	13.92	19.89	84.96	35.99	7.87	15.94	25.16	80.39	8.76	1.74	6.98	62.91

Year	v13c4	v13c4i	v13c4ii	v13c4iii	v13c4iv	v13c5	v13c5i	v13c5ii	v13c5iii	v13c5iv	v13c6	v13c6i	v13c6ii	v13c6iii
1952														
1953														
1954														
1955														
1956														
1957														
1958														
1959														
1960														
1961														
1962														
1963														
1964														
1965														
1966														
1967														
1968														
1969														
1970														
1971														
1972														
1973														
1974														
1975														
1976														
1977														
1978	1.10	0.07	1.03			0.65	0.44	0.10	0.03	0.08	1.05	0.94	0.11	
1979	1.11	0.07	1.04			0.71	0.49	0.11	0.03	0.08	1.09	0.97	0.12	
1980	1.50	0.07	1.43			0.85	0.57	0.12	0.04	0.12	1.12	1.02	0.10	
1981	1.32	0.09	1.23			1.29	0.90	0.17	0.05	0.17	1.34	1.21	0.13	
1982	1.27	0.10	1.17			1.76	1.22	0.21	0.08	0.25	1.64	1.49	0.15	
1983	1.34	0.09	1.25			2.04	1.42	0.21	0.10	0.31	1.51	1.34	0.17	
1984	1.98	0.09	1.89			3.51	3.05	0.30	0.05	0.11	1.99	1.81	0.18	
1985	2.41	0.10	2.31			3.20	1.96	0.40	0.21	0.63	2.16	1.89	0.27	
1986	2.81	0.18	2.63			3.73	2.28	0.41	0.25	0.79	2.44	2.25	0.19	
1987	3.13	0.21	2.92			4.21	2.45	0.42	0.31	1.03	2.78	2.55	0.23	
1988	3.47	0.21	3.26			5.43	3.48	0.42	0.96	0.57	3.46	3.18	0.28	
1989	3.84	0.21	3.63			6.38	2.15	0.56	1.27	2.40	4.14	3.86	0.28	
1990	4.08	0.21	3.87			7.20	2.38	0.62	1.44	2.76	4.24	3.91	0.33	
1991	4.00	0.22	3.78			6.97	2.32	0.64	1.38	2.63	5.13	4.73	0.40	
1992	5.56	0.28	5.23		0.05	8.70	3.66	0.77	1.62	2.65	6.00	4.79	0.42	0.18
1993	6.05	0.45	5.52	0.14	-0.06	12.01	5.40	0.93	1.47	4.21	7.76	6.13	0.63	0.19
1994	7.20	0.40	6.13	0.19	0.48	14.62	3.98	0.72	1.72	8.20	8.60	6.22	0.81	
1995	8.17	0.50	6.90	0.54	0.23	19.55	10.48	1.75	2.14	5.18	10.29	6.85	0.90	0.88

Year	v13c6iv	v13c7	v13c7i	v13c7ii	v13c7iii	v13c7iv	v13c8	v13c8i	v13c8ii	v13c8iii	v13c8iv	v13c9	v13c9i	v13c9ii
1952														
1953														
1954														
1955														
1956														
1957														
1958														
1959														
1960														
1961														
1962														
1963														
1964														
1965														
1966														
1967														
1968														
1969														
1970														
1971														
1972														
1973														
1974														
1975														
1976														
1977														
1978		2.44	2.20	0.24			0.58	0.49	0.09			1.57	1.44	0.13
1979		2.44	2.20	0.24			0.55	0.45	0.10			1.66	1.52	0.14
1980		2.57	2.32	0.25			0.76	0.65	0.11			1.75	1.60	0.15
1981		3.33	3.03	0.30			0.91	0.80	0.11			2.53	2.33	0.20
1982		3.90	3.57	0.33			0.94	0.82	0.12			2.79	2.57	0.22
1983		3.82	3.45	0.37			0.99	0.87	0.12			2.92	2.57	0.35
1984		4.72	4.21	0.43	0.02	0.06	1.06	0.89	0.17			3.75	3.33	0.42
1985		4.93	4.49	0.44			0.94	0.83	0.11			4.42	3.71	0.71
1986		5.56	4.90	0.66			1.72	1.48	0.24			6.34	5.30	1.04
1987		5.97	5.56	0.31	0.03	0.07	2.31	1.81	0.08	0.40	0.02	7.01	6.70	0.31
1988		7.63	6.78	0.47	0.14	0.24	3.89	3.34	0.44	0.03	0.08	8.88	8.25	0.63
1989		8.92	7.86	0.66	0.11	0.29	5.14	4.07	0.46	0.58	0.03	11.30	10.75	0.55
1990		9.34	8.16	0.83	0.12	0.23	5.93	5.11	0.50	0.07	0.25	12.11	11.73	0.38
1991		11.27	9.84	1.00	0.15	0.28	5.40	4.65	0.64	0.06	0.05	15.60	15.07	0.53
1992	0.61	13.48	11.11	1.25	0.17	0.95	5.29	4.03	0.58	0.14	0.54	18.45	15.62	0.95
1993	0.81	16.22	14.02	1.55	0.13	0.52	5.49	3.74	0.58	0.15	1.02	19.82	18.05	1.11
1994	1.57	24.25	18.63	2.77	0.10	2.75	10.95	7.34	2.07	0.29	1.25	30.93	23.55	5.10
1995	1.66	29.53	22.09	3.37	1.04	3.03	13.45	9.49	2.06	0.44	1.46	35.69	27.61	5.61

Year	v13c9iii	v13c9iv	v13c10	v13c10i	v13c10ii	v13c10iii	v13c10iv
1952							
1953							
1954							
1955							
1956							
1957							
1958							
1959							
1960							
1961							
1962							
1963							
1964							
1965							
1966							
1967							
1968							
1969							
1970							
1971							
1972							
1973							
1974							
1975							
1976							
1977							
1978			1.71	1.71			
1979			1.75	1.75			
1980			2.72	2.72			
1981			2.34	2.34			
1982			2.20	2.20			
1983			1.82	1.82			
1984			2.58	2.58			
1985			3.02	3.02			
1986			2.91	2.91			
1987			2.57	2.57			
1988			3.10	3.10			
1989			3.66	3.66			
1990			4.20	4.20			
1991			4.44	4.44			
1992	1.27	0.61	5.93	5.89	0.04		
1993	0.36	0.30	6.51	6.45	0.06		
1994	1.15	1.13	7.87	7.81	0.06		
1995	1.47	1.00	8.65	8.58	0.07		

5

Inner Mongolia

Year	v1	v1a	v1b	v1b1	v1b2	v1c	v1c1	v1c2	v1c3	v2	v2a	v2b	v2b1	v2b2	v2c
1952	19.62	12.06	2.18	1.63	0.55	5.38	0.48	0.89	4.01						
1953	25.30	14.35	3.75	2.55	1.20	7.20	0.70	1.51	4.99	115.4	106.0	170.3	152.0	217.0	127.4
1954	31.42	16.77	6.05	3.77	2.28	8.60	0.97	1.79	5.84	117.5	109.7	162.9	147.8	189.8	117.6
1955	31.32	15.60	6.44	4.41	2.03	9.28	1.03	1.76	6.49	99.0	94.0	105.7	117.5	89.3	107.4
1956	42.00	19.52	9.83	6.05	3.78	12.65	1.47	2.29	8.89	130.8	124.2	153.0	135.1	185.7	131.4
1957	32.88	11.18	9.37	6.33	3.04	12.33	1.17	2.67	8.49	92.4	84.1	97.7	110.7	80.4	106.2
1958	47.38	15.60	17.03	12.03	5.00	14.75	2.39	3.19	9.17	139.8	132.2	176.5	183.1	164.5	127.1
1959	63.17	18.14	26.03	18.78	7.25	19.00	3.75	3.85	11.40	125.7	111.4	152.4	156.0	145.0	125.2
1960	71.75	16.57	36.05	28.57	7.48	19.13	3.49	4.08	11.56	103.0	88.9	136.2	151.2	103.2	86.5
1961	52.41	17.04	18.87	15.93	2.94	16.50	2.09	3.02	11.39	72.7	86.0	48.7	51.6	39.3	95.5
1962	47.51	17.05	15.93	14.26	1.67	14.53	2.30	2.81	9.42	87.5	94.1	78.3	83.5	56.7	86.5
1963	59.60	17.43	26.14	21.26	4.88	16.03	2.63	3.12	10.28	126.4	111.7	167.3	147.1	292.7	115.0
1964	67.22	20.82	28.70	23.05	5.65	17.70	2.95	3.62	11.13	115.2	120.8	111.3	109.8	115.7	111.3
1965	71.74	19.39	33.02	26.79	6.23	19.33	3.17	4.02	12.14	104.8	91.0	121.2	124.9	110.1	107.3
1966	77.14	20.93	36.71	29.56	7.15	19.50	3.53	4.62	11.35	109.0	107.9	116.7	117.3	114.9	99.7
1967	65.47	21.46	26.15	20.28	5.87	17.86	2.81	3.61	11.44	88.0	102.6	72.4	69.6	82.0	91.2
1968	67.24	22.08	27.18	21.19	5.99	17.98	2.79	3.88	11.31	99.1	95.0	105.1	106.1	102.1	98.3
1969	66.48	19.95	28.43	22.32	6.11	18.10	2.76	3.97	11.37	98.5	90.4	107.4	109.1	102.0	99.8
1970	80.41	24.04	36.04	27.80	8.24	20.33	3.62	5.37	11.34	124.1	120.5	140.3	142.1	134.8	105.6
1971	84.85	23.67	40.23	31.09	9.14	20.95	3.90	5.95	11.10	107.5	98.4	114.7	115.9	110.9	108.7
1972	84.02	21.17	40.80	31.57	9.23	22.05	3.82	6.00	12.23	98.1	87.5	100.1	101.6	94.7	110.4
1973	94.11	27.72	43.27	32.67	10.60	23.12	4.26	6.89	11.97	112.9	130.2	105.8	103.5	114.8	105.0
1974	93.40	29.57	40.04	29.78	10.26	23.79	4.01	6.65	13.13	97.9	102.1	92.4	91.2	96.8	101.8
1975	104.21	30.83	48.67	36.89	11.78	24.71	4.47	7.59	12.65	110.5	102.5	121.7	123.9	114.8	103.1
1976	106.80	31.29	49.77	37.61	12.16	25.74	4.47	7.80	13.47	102.5	101.3	103.0	103.0	103.2	103.2
1977	112.01	28.43	57.06	44.08	12.98	26.52	4.63	8.27	13.62	104.3	90.9	114.4	116.6	106.7	103.7
1978	123.94	28.35	67.35	52.96	14.39	28.24	4.98	9.08	14.18	107.8	100.2	114.9	115.9	110.9	101.6
1979	137.13	31.58	72.80	57.40	15.40	32.75	5.18	11.48	16.09	107.9	105.7	105.9	105.6	107.0	116.0
1980	145.57	30.68	74.64	59.39	15.25	40.25	7.77	13.81	18.67	102.4	86.7	101.5	102.1	99.0	122.9
1981	156.04	39.42	74.99	61.76	13.23	41.63	7.13	16.23	18.27	104.0	119.8	97.6	100.3	86.8	103.4
1982	189.08	47.16	91.49	73.73	17.76	50.43	9.84	18.77	21.82	118.5	115.8	118.4	115.1	134.2	121.1
1983	217.31	52.43	102.67	81.53	21.14	62.21	12.42	21.20	28.59	111.0	107.2	109.6	109.6	109.7	116.7
1984	260.52	61.28	115.94	90.02	25.92	83.30	15.62	27.31	40.37	116.4	112.1	111.6	108.1	125.6	128.1
1985	340.03	73.20	148.30	112.94	35.36	118.53	20.34	36.21	61.98	121.1	110.3	118.4	116.7	124.3	133.0
1986	370.56	77.25	162.52	126.46	36.06	130.79	23.81	42.34	64.64	109.4	94.7	106.1	109.6	94.9	122.5
1987	435.12	87.74	188.10	150.84	37.26	159.28	24.09	49.66	85.53	109.4	104.1	108.9	112.5	95.6	112.5
1988	551.92	122.38	239.76	193.86	45.90	189.78	27.92	63.18	98.68	108.9	114.2	112.1	113.9	103.8	103.3
1989	635.26	128.32	290.97	243.13	47.84	215.97	33.32	67.58	115.07	106.8	99.5	109.4	112.6	94.2	107.2
1990	679.77	156.92	312.40	263.33	49.07	210.45	37.14	64.07	109.24	105.8	118.7	102.9	104.1	95.8	103.4
1991	774.80	164.08	373.84	304.43	69.41	236.88	48.49	70.99	117.40	109.0	103.8	111.9	108.1	132.6	108.5
1992	942.96	180.27	468.11	363.72	104.39	294.58	60.81	90.78	142.99	113.3	105.8	116.0	111.3	136.9	114.4
1993	1259.22	220.80	670.69	520.01	150.68	367.73	83.14	98.00	186.59	112.4	107.2	115.8	112.8	126.6	110.7
1994	1565.51	309.32	802.43	640.04	162.39	453.76	102.99	124.71	226.06	111.2	103.3	112.6	115.6	102.9	114.1
1995	1898.23	387.20	957.45	781.72	175.73	553.58	131.82	149.90	271.86	110.7	104.1	112.0	113.3	107.1	112.5

Year	v2c1	v2c2	v3'	v3	v3a	v3b	v3b1	v3b2	v3c	v3c1	v3c2	v3c3	v3c4	v3c5	v3c6
1952			12.16	12.16	8.64	1.37	0.99	0.38	2.15	0.41	0.59				
1953	147.8	170.7	15.57	15.57	10.44	2.25	1.57	0.68	2.88	0.56	1.02				
1954	139.1	118.5	19.46	19.46	12.37	3.65	2.57	1.08	3.44	0.77	1.20				
1955	106.1	97.7	17.49	17.49	10.25	3.53	2.73	0.80	3.71	0.78	1.18				
1956	142.7	130.8	24.60	24.60	14.11	5.43	3.95	1.48	5.06	1.05	1.57				
1957	78.8	116.5	21.27	21.27	11.29	5.05	3.80	1.25	4.93	0.65	1.78				
1958	206.4	119.4	28.10	28.10	12.55	9.65	7.04	2.61	5.90	1.54	2.17				
1959	156.1	120.4	35.76	35.76	14.75	13.41	9.90	3.51	7.60	2.59	2.65				
1960	93.3	106.0	35.56	36.56	11.80	17.11	13.17	3.94	7.65	2.17	2.81				
1961	59.7	74.1	25.25	25.25	11.40	7.25	6.06	1.19	6.60	1.44	2.18				
1962	110.6	93.1	25.12	25.12	12.75	6.56	5.80	0.76	5.81	1.29	1.61				
1963	113.6	110.8	29.02	29.02	12.71	9.90	8.24	1.66	6.41	1.49	2.04				
1964	112.5	116.3	32.55	32.55	14.04	11.43	9.37	2.06	7.08	1.67	2.30				
1965	107.4	110.9	35.41	35.41	15.21	12.08	9.65	2.43	8.12	2.26	2.57				
1966	111.3	115.0	38.32	38.32	17.12	13.01	10.33	2.68	8.19	2.00	2.71				
1967	79.9	78.2	31.80	31.80	13.87	10.43	8.46	1.97	7.50	1.58	2.16				
1968	99.3	107.6	32.96	32.96	14.87	10.54	8.49	2.05	7.55	1.57	2.11				
1969	99.0	102.0	32.90	32.90	14.78	10.52	8.40	2.12	7.60	1.56	2.07				
1970	130.5	135.6	39.17	39.17	17.69	12.94	9.87	3.07	8.54	2.03	2.69				
1971	108.0	110.7	41.61	41.61	16.82	15.99	12.50	3.49	8.80	2.18	2.56				
1972	93.5	96.5	39.36	39.36	14.56	15.54	12.12	3.42	9.26	2.13	2.66				
1973	111.5	114.8	44.07	44.07	16.22	18.14	14.29	3.85	9.71	2.38	2.58				
1974	94.1	96.5	43.26	43.26	15.97	17.30	13.35	3.95	9.99	2.24	2.74				
1975	111.5	114.1	48.55	48.55	18.15	20.02	15.52	4.50	10.38	2.49	2.66				
1976	100.0	102.8	48.09	48.09	18.51	18.77	15.11	3.66	10.81	2.49	2.69				
1977	103.6	106.0	51.65	51.65	18.91	21.60	16.48	5.12	11.14	2.56	2.73				
1978	107.6	109.8	58.04	58.04	18.96	26.37	21.84	4.53	12.71	2.76	2.87	1.15	0.48	0.46	0.29
1979	104.0	126.4	64.14	64.14	21.03	28.37	23.52	4.85	14.74	2.85	3.25	1.75	0.59	0.68	0.31
1980	150.0	120.3	68.40	68.40	18.03	32.26	27.30	4.96	18.11	4.12	4.01	1.90	0.64	0.74	0.35
1981	91.8	117.5	77.91	77.91	27.14	32.04	27.92	4.12	18.73	3.71	4.00	2.10	0.69	0.80	0.52
1982	138.0	115.7	93.22	93.22	33.32	37.21	32.35	4.86	22.69	5.12	5.20	2.14	0.83	0.81	0.67
1983	115.4	107.9	105.88	105.88	35.90	41.98	35.90	6.08	28.00	6.58	6.32	3.21	1.10	1.02	0.83
1984	119.2	123.4	128.20	128.20	42.98	47.74	39.04	8.70	37.48	8.28	10.34	5.01	1.67	1.33	1.00
1985	128.5	122.1	163.83	163.83	53.54	56.95	45.90	11.05	53.34	10.85	19.65	5.95	1.86	1.66	1.29
1986	116.7	114.4	181.58	181.58	54.64	61.55	49.74	11.81	65.39	12.59	24.11	8.16	2.17	2.12	1.58
1987	95.9	107.9	211.38	212.27	62.21	70.42	58.26	12.16	79.64	12.77	32.91	8.25	2.61	2.54	2.52
1988	115.8	107.1	270.34	270.81	90.20	85.72	70.28	15.44	94.89	14.30	38.88	11.40	2.99	3.94	3.08
1989	111.4	104.0	292.62	292.69	89.08	98.96	83.66	15.30	104.65	18.63	35.58	19.46	3.35	3.08	3.13
1990	101.4	106.0	319.19	319.31	112.57	102.43	87.18	15.25	104.31	20.69	24.92	20.88	3.93	3.72	3.89
1991	121.7	108.6	359.50	359.66	117.19	124.03	102.74	21.29	118.44	26.84	27.76	21.30	4.04	4.57	4.31
1992	114.3	112.0	421.46	421.68	126.86	152.56	120.85	31.71	142.26	32.65	35.04	24.05	4.73	5.01	5.20
1993	115.1	109.1	532.53	532.70	149.96	208.05	162.53	45.52	174.69	46.14	38.71	28.12	6.25	7.38	6.38
1994	116.2	106.7	681.83	681.92	208.53	261.79	205.98	55.81	211.60	53.56	48.15	33.85	7.38	9.72	8.02
1995	116.0	112.4	832.77	832.88	260.18	314.90	254.88	60.02	257.80	67.12	57.28	40.77	8.85	12.15	9.88

Year	v3c7	v3c8	v3c9	v3c10	v3d	v4'	v4	v4a	v4b	v4b1	v4b2	v4c	v4c1	v4c2	v4c3
1952				1.15	173										
1953				1.30	211	116.3	116.3	107.5	159.9	153.7	176.3	127.4	140.6	174.3	
1954				1.47	249	119.4	119.4	111.3	160.4	162.3	156.1	117.6	137.8	117.1	
1955				1.75	213	90.7	90.7	83.7	97.5	107.0	74.8	107.4	101.6	98.0	
1956				2.44	283	138.7	138.7	136.6	152.3	143.2	183.3	131.4	133.3	133.8	
1957				2.50	232	110.9	110.9	117.5	98.3	101.7	89.1	106.2	61.9	113.1	
1958				2.19	292	125.3	125.3	105.3	184.0	178.6	200.5	127.1	238.5	121.9	
1959				2.36	349	122.9	122.9	112.6	139.2	140.7	135.0	125.2	166.9	122.0	
1960				2.67	325	95.8	95.8	77.9	126.6	132.1	111.2	86.5	84.1	106.0	
1961				2.98	215	65.3	65.3	80.7	39.3	42.6	28.0	95.5	66.1	77.6	
1962				2.91	215	94.7	94.7	105.2	84.3	89.1	59.9	86.5	90.4	73.7	
1963				2.88	243	119.7	119.7	108.9	148.6	140.0	214.3	115.0	114.4	126.7	
1964				3.11	262	113.2	113.2	111.8	117.1	115.5	125.5	111.3	112.6	112.9	
1965				3.29	275	109.8	109.8	105.9	113.6	110.8	126.8	112.6	135.1	111.8	
1966				3.48	289	110.0	110.0	112.4	114.4	113.7	117.4	99.7	88.4	105.6	
1967				3.76	233	83.3	83.3	81.1	81.2	83.0	74.5	91.2	79.4	79.8	
1968				3.87	235	99.9	99.9	98.9	102.6	102.0	105.4	98.3	99.2	97.8	
1969				3.97	227	100.8	100.8	99.5	103.4	102.5	107.4	99.8	99.2	97.7	
1970				3.82	263	123.3	123.3	119.7	140.2	134.0	164.8	105.6	129.6	130.0	
1971				4.06	271	102.1	102.1	95.0	106.5	109.1	98.2	108.7	108.0	95.3	
1972				4.47	247	107.8	107.8	117.0	97.2	97.0	97.9	110.4	93.1	99.4	
1973				4.75	269	111.7	111.7	110.8	116.8	117.9	112.8	105.0	111.7	96.9	
1974				5.01	256	96.2	96.2	94.3	95.4	93.5	102.6	101.8	94.0	106.1	
1975				5.23	280	111.3	111.3	111.7	115.7	116.2	113.9	103.1	111.1	97.3	
1976				5.63	272	99.4	99.4	101.8	94.7	98.4	82.1	103.2	100.0	100.9	
1977				5.85	287	107.0	107.0	102.2	114.5	108.5	139.2	103.7	103.2	101.5	
1978	1.38	0.19	1.00	2.13	317	108.0	108.0	98.8	117.2	127.3	84.6	108.9	107.7	105.2	
1979	1.59	0.39	1.20	2.14	343	109.8	109.8	107.7	108.6	108.4	110.0	116.0	103.3	113.1	151.9
1980	2.02	0.41	1.82	2.12	361	101.7	101.7	76.0	113.3	116.6	97.6	122.9	144.5	123.5	108.6
1981	2.32	0.39	2.08	2.13	407	110.6	110.6	141.8	96.3	98.2	85.7	103.4	90.1	99.9	110.8
1982	2.64	0.69	2.43	2.16	480	118.6	118.6	118.2	117.4	117.3	117.9	121.1	138.1	129.9	102.0
1983	2.80	0.82	3.13	2.19	535	109.8	109.8	105.0	109.9	108.5	118.8	116.7	117.4	116.1	143.3
1984	3.24	0.88	3.74	1.99	640	116.1	116.1	114.0	110.2	107.3	127.7	128.1	119.3	156.8	149.5
1985	4.15	1.13	4.99	1.82	809	117.2	117.2	114.1	108.2	105.5	121.7	133.0	129.3	175.1	109.3
1986	4.98	1.67	6.36	1.65	888	105.9	105.9	91.7	105.4	106.4	101.2	120.4	115.6	120.0	134.3
1987	6.46	2.30	7.63	1.66	1025	108.7	109.0	106.8	107.0	109.3	96.5	112.5	96.2	125.6	93.0
1988	7.83	2.68	7.98	1.82	1291	110.1	109.8	117.3	111.2	108.1	126.6	103.2	111.9	99.5	116.3
1989	8.02	2.16	9.23	2.02	1377	102.7	102.7	95.1	105.0	107.2	94.9	106.8	121.6	102.6	147.3
1990	8.91	3.81	10.95	2.61	1478	107.5	107.5	124.4	99.4	99.2	100.5	103.1	101.1	93.4	104.3
1991	10.00	4.98	11.66	2.98	1642	107.5	107.5	104.0	110.9	108.2	126.0	107.9	121.4	102.5	99.0
1992	11.86	5.58	13.56	3.58	1906	111.0	111.0	104.1	115.4	110.7	138.8	113.8	118.4	117.1	104.7
1993	13.82	6.85	16.64	4.40	2382	110.6	110.6	105.0	114.6	112.3	123.6	111.7	124.4	114.9	102.0
1994	18.83	8.56	18.58	4.95	3013	110.1	110.1	103.2	113.7	114.8	109.7	112.4	113.1	110.8	113.3
1995	22.26	10.38	22.91	6.20	3639	109.0	109.1	103.9	111.5	112.7	106.9	110.6	115.7	109.8	107.2

Year	v4c4	v4c5	v4c6	v4c7	v4c8	v4c9	v4c10	v5	v5a	v5a1	v5a1a	v5a1b	v5a2	v5b	v5b1
1952								12.16	7.53	6.91	5.42	1.49	0.63	1.66	0.91
1953								15.57	8.25	7.63	5.82	1.81	0.63	2.68	1.48
1954								19.46	9.13	8.30	6.02	2.28	0.84	4.01	2.44
1955								17.49	9.09	8.33	5.76	2.57	0.76	2.70	1.66
1956								24.60	11.22	10.26	6.89	3.37	0.96	5.14	3.34
1957								21.27	11.98	11.03	7.31	3.72	0.95	5.26	3.36
1958								28.10	13.02	12.03	7.58	4.45	0.99	14.46	12.24
1959								35.76	14.28	13.40	7.69	5.71	0.88	20.38	13.00
1960								36.56	14.76	14.20	7.32	6.88	0.56	19.16	16.76
1961								25.25	15.00	14.66	7.82	6.84	0.34	6.47	3.74
1962								25.12	14.56	14.18	8.46	5.71	0.39	3.99	2.83
1963								29.02	14.57	14.18	8.47	5.70	0.40	5.92	4.20
1964								32.55	15.38	14.61	9.11	5.50	0.77	8.28	5.88
1965								35.41	16.46	15.35	9.14	6.22	1.11	10.78	7.71
1966								38.32	18.50	17.34	10.02	7.32	1.17	10.30	7.31
1967								31.80	20.21	18.95	10.83	8.12	1.27	4.90	3.47
1968								32.96	19.73	18.54	10.28	8.26	1.19	5.70	4.17
1969								32.90	19.90	18.65	9.32	9.33	1.24	5.89	4.19
1970								39.17	21.90	20.70	10.54	10.15	1.20	9.66	7.26
1971								41.61	24.14	22.42	10.89	11.53	1.72	10.87	8.06
1972								39.36	26.93	24.81	11.05	13.76	2.12	10.30	7.32
1973								44.07	29.87	27.74	13.21	14.53	2.13	11.61	8.37
1974								43.26	31.21	28.70	13.95	14.74	2.51	13.04	9.83
1975								48.55	34.74	31.07	15.09	15.98	3.67	14.10	10.59
1976								48.09	37.48	33.60	16.18	17.42	3.88	15.50	11.70
1977								51.65	40.77	35.92	17.21	18.71	4.85	16.53	12.77
1978								58.04	42.91	37.75	17.72	20.03	5.15	21.20	16.56
1979	122.9	147.8	105.5	115.2	205.3	120.2	100.5	64.14	50.83	44.68	20.96	23.72	6.16	23.18	17.65
1980	108.5	108.4	113.2	127.0	105.1	151.5	99.1	68.40	62.07	55.83	28.22	27.61	6.24	18.88	15.78
1981	107.8	107.9	149.2	114.6	96.1	114.3	100.5	77.91	76.51	67.09	34.53	32.56	9.43	18.80	15.53
1982	120.3	102.0	129.0	114.1	176.1	116.8	101.4	93.22	88.01	79.07	43.66	35.41	8.94	26.10	20.94
1983	126.7	119.8	118.6	101.3	113.5	123.4	96.9	105.88	94.01	83.78	46.16	37.62	10.22	35.58	29.66
1984	145.5	125.5	115.7	110.9	102.6	114.4	87.1	128.20	106.57	89.38	48.79	40.58	17.19	45.81	40.85
1985	102.4	114.7	118.6	117.9	118.5	122.9	84.3	163.83	127.04	105.12	57.88	47.24	21.92	61.60	50.94
1986	114.6	125.3	120.1	117.5	143.9	124.8	88.7	181.58	144.84	118.22	59.54	58.68	26.62	60.22	47.57
1987	110.4	110.3	146.8	119.3	126.7	110.3	92.6	212.27	166.12	135.28	68.71	66.57	30.84	67.84	53.32
1988	96.6	130.4	102.7	102.1	98.1	88.2	92.3	270.81	184.46	149.57	77.59	71.98	34.89	110.15	72.05
1989	96.6	67.3	87.8	88.4	69.6	99.7	95.8	292.69	199.14	160.50	81.50	79.00	38.64	115.48	70.68
1990	113.9	117.5	120.6	107.9	171.4	115.3	125.5	319.31	216.70	169.79	86.44	83.35	46.91	124.68	70.77
1991	100.5	118.6	105.1	109.9	126.5	103.0	110.3	359.66	245.90	188.61	93.35	95.26	57.29	137.00	100.66
1992	115.4	124.3	116.1	111.8	107.3	110.9	116.3	421.68	271.06	208.08	101.90	106.18	62.98	195.10	149.24
1993	112.1	103.7	106.7	106.3	105.0	105.8	102.7	532.70	320.92	245.90	116.98	128.92	75.02	283.52	219.40
1994	110.0	111.4	109.9	110.1	112.3	110.6	110.2	670.99	406.88	313.88	144.06	169.82	93.00	331.11	250.23
1995	106.0	114.1	111.0	108.9	106.5	107.5	107.1	815.82	505.84	395.88	194.48	201.40	109.96	372.98	273.16

Year	v5b2	v5c	v5c1	v5c2	v6a1	v6a2	v6a3	v6a4	v6b2	v6b3	v6b4	v7	v7a	v7a1	v7a2
1952	0.75	2.96													
1953	1.20	4.64										109.6	110.4	107.4	121.6
1954	1.57	6.32										110.7	108.8	103.4	126.0
1955	1.04	5.70										99.6	100.4	95.8	112.7
1956	1.80	8.24										123.4	123.1	119.5	131.3
1957	1.90	4.03										106.8	107.5	106.1	110.5
1958	2.22	0.62										108.7	109.1	103.7	119.5
1959	7.38	1.10										109.7	111.4	101.4	128.4
1960	2.40	2.64										103.4	106.0	95.2	120.4
1961	2.73	3.78										101.6	103.3	106.9	99.4
1962	1.16	6.57										97.1	96.7	108.2	83.6
1963	1.72	8.53										100.1	100.0	100.1	99.8
1964	2.40	8.88										105.6	103.1	107.6	96.4
1965	3.07	8.17										107.0	105.1	100.2	113.0
1966	2.99	9.52										112.4	112.9	109.7	117.7
1967	1.43	6.69										109.2	109.3	108.1	111.0
1968	1.53	7.54										97.6	97.9	95.0	101.7
1969	1.70	7.11										100.9	100.6	90.7	113.0
1970	2.40	7.61										110.0	111.0	113.1	108.8
1971	2.81	6.61										110.3	108.3	103.3	113.6
1972	2.98	2.13										111.6	110.6	101.5	119.3
1973	3.24	2.59										110.9	111.8	119.6	105.6
1974	3.21	-0.99										104.5	103.5	105.6	101.5
1975	3.51	-0.29										111.3	108.2	108.1	108.4
1976	3.80	-4.90										107.9	108.2	107.2	109.0
1977	3.76	-5.65										108.8	106.9	106.4	107.4
1978	4.64	-6.07			5.66	10.38	1.42	0.27	18.27	1.37	0.40	105.2	105.1	103.0	107.1
1979	5.53	-9.88			6.69	12.27	1.68	0.32	21.63	1.62	0.47	118.5	118.3	118.3	118.4
1980	3.10	-12.55			9.01	16.52	2.26	0.43	25.18	1.89	0.55	122.1	125.0	134.7	116.4
1981	3.27	-17.40			11.02	20.22	2.76	0.52	29.69	2.22	0.64	119.9	116.8	117.8	115.7
1982	5.16	-20.89			13.94	25.57	3.49	0.66	32.29	2.42	0.70	114.5	117.3	126.7	107.5
1983	5.92	-23.71			14.74	27.09	3.69	0.64	34.34	2.53	0.75	107.1	106.1	107.3	104.5
1984	4.96	-24.18			15.58	28.38	3.90	0.93	37.01	2.77	0.81	107.6	101.3	100.0	102.8
1985	10.66	-24.81			18.80	33.48	3.71	1.89	42.71	3.75	0.78	108.8	106.4	106.0	106.9
1986	12.65	-23.48			20.25	33.61	4.08	1.60	52.84	4.72	1.12	110.7	109.0	101.8	117.7
1987	14.52	-21.69			21.27	40.91	4.69	1.84	60.20	5.22	1.15	106.6	106.5	108.4	104.6
1988	38.10	-23.80			23.41	45.97	6.22	1.99	64.48	6.23	1.27	94.6	95.3	98.0	92.4
1989	44.80	-21.93			25.29	47.31	6.72	2.18	70.04	7.40	1.56	94.4	93.8	90.4	97.9
1990	53.91	-22.07			35.71	41.14	7.01	2.58	73.49	7.99	1.87	103.6	101.0	98.1	103.9
1991	36.34	-23.24			36.71	45.87	7.93	2.84	83.05	9.85	2.36	110.0	108.5	109.0	108.0
1992	46.86	-45.50			37.69	50.27	8.77	5.17	93.71	9.32	3.15	104.5	104.1	105.0	103.2
1993	69.12	-76.74			45.39	55.07	10.40	6.12	113.58	11.37	3.97	104.0	103.7	101.2	106.4
1994	80.88	-67.00	267.00	334.00	53.17	68.99	13.12	8.78	145.12	17.89	6.81	104.0	103.2	100.0	106.4
1995	99.82	-63.00	322.00	385.00	73.38	91.94	17.71	11.45	172.15	21.15	8.10	105.5	106.8	112.5	101.4

Year	v7b	v8	v8a	v8b	v9	v9a	v9b	v10a1	v10a2	v10a3	v10a3a	v10a3b	v10a4	v10b1	v10b2
1952		99	88	171											
1953	100.0	103	93	165	105.0	105.1	96.4								
1954	133.3	106	93	173	102.8	100.1	105.0								
1955	90.8	101	85	179	95.3	91.5	103.5								
1956	126.1	118	98	205	116.3	114.9	114.5								
1957	98.9	120	99	209	102.1	101.5	102.0								
1958	104.7	125	99	228	104.0	99.9	109.2								
1959	88.9	131	99	232	104.5	99.9	101.4								
1960	63.8	126	93	205	96.5	93.8	88.6								
1961	60.8	125	96	191	98.6	103.0	92.9								
1962	112.9	121	98	187	97.5	102.9	97.9								
1963	102.9	119	96	183	97.7	97.7	98.0								
1964	194.4	118	96	190	99.2	99.7	103.9								
1965	144.3	119	95	190	101.2	99.2	100.3								
1966	105.0	131	102	212	109.7	107.6	111.1								
1967	108.5	139	108	225	106.3	105.8	106.2								
1968	93.9	132	100	221	94.9	92.3	98.2								
1969	104.6	129	88	236	97.5	88.6	107.2								
1970	96.5	139	99	241	108.0	111.7	101.9								
1971	143.1	146	98	273	105.0	99.1	113.1								
1972	123.7	156	97	303	106.8	99.3	111.2								
1973	100.5	169	113	305	108.5	116.9	100.5								
1974	117.5	170	115	310	100.3	101.2	101.6								
1975	146.5	179	122	321	105.6	106.3	103.6								
1976	105.7	190	128	343	106.1	105.2	107.0								
1977	124.9	200	135	355	105.1	105.5	103.5								
1978	106.2	207	138	370	103.4	101.8	104.2	13.75	0.58	2.24	0.58	1.66		2.51	2.13
1979	119.5	239	161	420	115.8	116.8	113.4	14.65	0.62	2.38	0.62	1.76		2.99	2.54
1980	101.3	295	213	484	123.2	132.5	115.3	13.10	0.55	2.13	0.56	1.57		1.68	1.42
1981	148.5	350	257	567	115.5	116.2	115.0	12.18	0.54	2.81	0.73	2.08		1.77	1.50
1982	94.3	407	318	619	115.7	124.1	107.9	17.43	1.72	1.79	0.37	1.42		2.79	2.37
1983	116.1	423	334	632	104.1	106.3	100.4	25.28	1.01	3.37	0.56	2.81		3.20	2.72
1984	158.6	446	349	671	100.1	99.0	101.1	30.33	1.40	9.12	0.86	8.26		2.68	2.28
1985	121.3	519	412	762	105.2	105.5	104.3	37.62	2.51	10.81	2.07	8.74		5.77	4.89
1986	118.5	578	418	942	107.9	100.5	117.2	37.00	2.52	8.05	2.05	6.00		6.84	5.81
1987	106.9	653	480	1039	105.2	107.9	101.6	39.06	3.07	11.19	2.33	8.86		7.86	6.66
1988	91.9	713	541	1086	94.1	97.7	89.4	49.23	4.44	18.38	3.47	14.91		20.61	17.49
1989	96.6	755	565	1157	92.6	89.9	95.0	52.92	3.98	13.78	2.94	10.84		24.24	20.56
1990	114.6	786	592	1189	99.3	97.0	101.3	56.77	3.06	10.94	2.81	8.13		29.17	24.74
1991	115.4	861	633	1330	107.0	107.9	105.7	81.63	4.72	14.31	3.28	11.03		19.66	16.68
1992	105.8	941	686	1461	103.1	104.2	101.6	123.61	6.52	19.11	5.84	13.27		25.35	21.51
1993	104.8	1100	779	1754	102.6	100.1	105.2	180.16	17.88	21.35	7.37	13.98		37.40	31.73
1994	107.0	1387	948	2283	101.8	98.8	104.7	187.39	24.00	27.82	7.49	20.33	11.02	41.74	8.70
1995	101.3	1729	1264	2682	70.0	111.1	100.4	207.71	12.46	44.06	7.56	36.50	8.93	53.72	9.13

Year	v10b4	v11a	v11a1	v11a2	v11b	v11b1	v11b2	v11c	v11c1	v11c2	v12	v12a	v12b	v13	v13i
1952															
1953											160.7	161.3	160.0		
1954											149.8	165.3	130.8		
1955											67.3	68.0	66.3		
1956											190.6	201.5	173.0		
1957											102.4	100.7	105.5		
1958											274.7	363.8	116.9		
1959											140.9	106.2	332.4		
1960											94.0	128.9	32.5		
1961											33.8	22.3	113.8		
1962											61.6	75.6	42.5		
1963											148.6	148.7	148.2		
1964											139.9	140.0	139.6		
1965											130.2	131.1	127.9		
1966											95.5	94.8	97.4		
1967											47.6	47.5	47.8		
1968											116.2	120.0	107.0		
1969											103.4	100.6	111.1		
1970											164.0	173.3	141.2		
1971											112.4	110.9	117.1		
1972											94.8	90.9	106.0		
1973											112.7	114.3	108.7		
1974											112.4	117.5	99.1		
1975											108.1	107.7	109.3		
1976											109.9	110.5	108.3		
1977											106.6	109.1	98.9		
1978		1.76	0.70	1.06	10.81	8.16	2.65	8.63	7.70	0.93	128.3	129.7	123.4	58.04	32.14
1979		1.92	0.77	1.15	11.82	8.93	2.89	9.44	7.95	1.49	109.4	106.6	119.2	64.14	35.59
1980		1.56	0.63	0.93	9.63	7.27	2.36	7.69	7.88	-0.19	81.5	89.4	56.1	68.40	35.49
1981		1.56	0.62	0.94	9.59	7.24	2.35	7.65	7.67	-0.02	99.6	98.4	105.5	77.91	41.87
1982		2.17	0.86	1.31	13.31	10.05	3.26	10.62	10.03	0.59	138.8	134.8	157.8	93.22	50.06
1983		2.95	1.18	1.77	18.15	13.70	4.45	14.48	14.78	-0.30	136.3	141.6	114.7	105.88	55.10
1984		3.81	1.52	2.29	23.36	17.64	5.72	18.64	21.69	-3.05	118.7	126.6	78.0	128.20	67.86
1985		5.11	2.04	3.07	31.42	23.72	7.70	25.07	25.18	-0.11	127.4	118.9	198.9	163.83	86.29
1986		5.00	1.99	3.01	30.71	23.19	7.52	24.51	22.39	2.12	92.9	88.0	115.0	181.58	95.45
1987		5.63	2.25	3.38	34.60	26.12	8.48	27.61	24.95	2.66	105.6	107.8	102.1	212.27	111.69
1988		9.14	3.65	5.49	56.18	42.41	13.77	44.83	25.99	18.84	65.6	126.2	223.8	270.81	144.94
1989		9.59	3.82	5.77	58.89	44.47	14.42	47.00	22.39	24.61	207.5	86.0	109.6	292.69	157.77
1990		10.35	4.13	6.22	63.59	48.01	15.58	50.74	18.63	32.11	104.2	104.3	110.2	319.31	180.02
1991		11.37	4.54	6.83	69.87	52.75	17.12	55.76	43.37	12.39	111.5	144.8	68.2	359.66	197.08
1992		16.28	6.49	9.79	100.02	75.52	24.50	79.80	67.23	12.57	126.5	127.6	123.3	421.68	231.86
1993		22.50	9.52	12.98	147.11	111.02	36.09	118.91	98.85	20.06	121.9	122.6	119.7	532.70	291.52
1994	30.44	40.28	15.49	24.34	178.75	134.64	44.11	112.08	99.65	12.43	102.6	102.5	102.9	681.92	385.04
1995	31.97	29.65	4.64	25.01	212.72	159.29	53.43	130.61	109.23	21.38	106.5	105.4	109.7	832.88	472.31

Year	v13ii	v13iii	v13iv	v13a	v13ai	v13aii	v13aiii	v13aiv	v13b	v13bi	v13bii	v13biii	v13biv	v13b1	v13b1i
1952															
1953															
1954															
1955															
1956															
1957															
1958															
1959															
1960															
1961															
1962															
1963															
1964															
1965															
1966															
1967															
1968															
1969															
1970															
1971															
1972															
1973															
1974															
1975															
1976															
1977															
1978	6.01	5.83	14.05	18.96	13.83	0.17	0.61	4.35	26.37	10.91	3.66	4.76	7.05	21.84	7.92
1979	6.62	6.35	15.58	21.03	15.50	0.17	0.67	4.69	28.37	11.73	3.95	5.11	7.58	23.52	8.50
1980	8.48	6.88	17.55	18.03	13.25	0.17	0.33	4.28	32.26	12.07	5.09	5.87	9.23	27.30	9.11
1981	9.45	7.21	19.38	27.14	19.22	0.89	0.68	6.35	32.04	11.95	5.31	5.84	8.94	27.92	9.10
1982	12.22	8.14	22.79	33.32	24.22	1.09	1.05	6.96	37.21	13.06	6.99	6.24	10.93	32.35	9.75
1983	14.90	9.49	26.38	35.90	25.56	1.50	1.08	7.76	41.98	14.38	8.18	7.32	12.10	35.90	11.09
1984	17.70	10.48	32.16	42.98	31.19	1.59	1.02	9.18	47.74	17.55	9.08	7.74	13.37	39.04	11.03
1985	20.58	14.30	42.65	53.54	36.52	1.94	1.10	13.98	56.95	22.69	9.14	10.31	14.81	45.90	14.90
1986	24.43	14.78	46.92	54.64	37.11	2.21	1.12	14.20	61.55	25.47	10.78	10.04	15.26	49.74	17.54
1987	28.63	17.48	54.47	62.21	42.10	2.56	1.03	16.52	70.42	28.42	12.54	11.82	17.64	58.26	19.89
1988	33.88	21.87	70.12	90.20	63.00	3.15	1.26	22.79	85.72	31.69	15.02	14.96	24.05	70.28	21.62
1989	39.90	28.24	66.78	89.08	68.80	3.30	1.41	15.57	98.96	36.52	18.77	20.55	23.12	83.66	26.20
1990	43.72	28.94	66.63	112.57	86.00	3.78	2.19	20.60	102.43	40.61	21.38	21.74	18.70	87.18	29.88
1991	50.61	36.26	75.71	117.19	87.80	4.48	2.06	22.85	124.03	48.20	24.58	28.79	22.46	102.74	33.54
1992	60.38	45.47	83.97	126.86	93.28	6.57	2.49	24.52	152.56	61.91	29.33	34.62	26.70	120.85	39.43
1993	67.32	62.29	111.58	149.96	103.08	7.45	3.78	35.65	208.05	92.85	28.57	48.39	38.24	162.53	63.22
1994	85.20	65.46	146.22	208.53	139.87	11.86	5.14	51.66	261.79	125.64	36.19	46.94	53.02	205.98	93.12
1995	101.16	83.59	175.82	260.18	177.16	13.00	6.73	63.29	314.90	150.05	43.81	57.97	63.07	254.88	114.56

Year	v13b1ii	v13b1iii	v13b1iv	v13b2	v13b2i	v13b2ii	v13b2iii	v13b2iv	v13c	v13ci	v13cii	v13ciii	v13civ	v13c1
1952														
1953														
1954														
1955														
1956														
1957														
1958														
1959														
1960														
1961														
1962														
1963														
1964														
1965														
1966														
1967														
1968														
1969														
1970														
1971														
1972														
1973														
1974														
1975														
1976														
1977														
1978	3.49	4.36	6.07	4.53	2.98	0.17	0.40	0.98	12.71	7.41	2.18	0.46	2.66	2.76
1979	3.77	4.70	6.55	4.85	3.23	0.18	0.41	1.03	14.74	8.35	2.50	0.57	3.31	2.85
1980	4.91	5.45	7.83	4.96	2.96	0.18	0.42	1.40	18.11	10.17	3.22	0.68	4.04	4.12
1981	5.10	5.67	8.05	4.12	2.85	0.21	0.17	0.89	18.73	10.70	3.25	0.69	4.09	3.71
1982	6.61	6.04	9.95	4.86	3.30	0.38	0.20	0.98	22.69	12.79	4.14	0.85	4.91	5.12
1983	7.58	6.88	10.35	6.08	3.29	0.60	0.44	1.75	28.00	15.16	5.22	1.09	6.52	6.58
1984	8.61	7.38	12.02	8.70	6.52	0.47	0.36	1.35	37.48	19.12	7.03	1.72	9.61	8.28
1985	8.01	9.92	13.07	11.05	7.78	1.13	0.39	1.75	53.34	27.09	9.50	2.89	13.86	10.85
1986	9.22	9.71	13.27	11.81	7.94	1.56	0.33	1.99	65.39	32.87	11.44	3.62	17.46	12.59
1987	10.97	11.33	16.07	12.16	8.53	1.57	0.49	1.57	79.64	41.17	13.53	4.63	20.32	12.77
1988	13.02	14.04	21.60	15.44	10.07	2.00	0.92	2.45	94.89	50.25	15.71	5.65	23.28	14.30
1989	16.45	19.51	21.50	15.30	10.32	2.32	1.04	1.62	104.65	52.45	17.83	6.28	28.08	18.63
1990	19.43	20.36	17.51	15.25	10.73	1.95	1.38	1.19	104.31	53.41	18.56	5.01	27.33	20.69
1991	22.39	26.81	20.00	21.29	14.66	2.19	1.98	2.46	118.44	61.08	21.55	5.41	30.40	26.84
1992	26.37	31.81	23.24	31.71	22.48	2.96	2.81	3.46	142.26	76.67	24.48	8.36	32.75	32.65
1993	26.40	43.59	29.32	45.52	29.63	2.17	4.80	8.92	174.69	95.59	31.30	10.12	37.69	46.14
1994	33.45	41.75	37.66	55.81	32.52	2.74	5.19	15.36	211.60	119.53	37.15	13.38	41.54	53.56
1995	40.76	52.51	47.05	60.02	35.49	3.05	5.46	16.02	257.80	145.10	44.35	18.89	49.46	67.12

Year	v13c1i	v13c1ii	v13c1iii	v13c1iv	v13c2	v13c2i	v13c2ii	v13c2iii	v13c2iv	v13c3	v13c3i	v13c3ii	v13c3iii	v13c3iv
1952														
1953														
1954														
1955														
1956														
1957														
1958														
1959														
1960														
1961														
1962														
1963														
1964														
1965														
1966														
1967														
1968														
1969														
1970														
1971														
1972														
1973														
1974														
1975														
1976														
1977														
1978	1.01	0.90	0.04	0.81	2.87	1.42	0.30	0.32	0.82	1.15	0.18	0.05	0.39	0.83
1979	1.04	0.93	0.04	0.84	3.25	1.61	0.34	0.36	0.93	1.75	0.27	0.08	0.14	1.26
1980	1.51	1.34	0.06	1.21	4.01	1.99	0.42	0.45	1.15	1.90	0.29	0.08	0.15	1.37
1981	1.36	1.21	0.05	1.09	4.00	1.98	0.42	0.45	1.15	2.10	0.32	0.09	0.17	1.52
1982	1.87	1.67	0.07	1.51	5.20	2.58	0.55	0.58	1.49	2.14	0.33	0.09	0.17	1.55
1983	2.40	2.14	0.09	1.94	6.32	3.13	0.67	0.71	1.81	3.21	0.49	0.14	0.25	2.33
1984	3.03	2.69	0.12	2.44	10.34	5.12	1.09	1.16	2.96	5.01	0.77	0.22	0.40	3.63
1985	3.97	3.53	0.15	3.20	19.65	9.73	2.07	2.21	5.63	5.95	0.91	0.26	0.47	4.31
1986	4.60	4.10	0.18	3.71	24.11	11.94	2.54	2.71	6.91	8.16	1.25	0.35	0.55	5.91
1987	4.67	4.16	0.18	3.76	32.91	16.30	3.47	3.70	9.44	8.25	1.27	0.36	0.55	5.97
1988	5.23	4.66	0.20	4.21	38.88	21.26	4.10	4.37	9.15	11.40	1.75	0.49	0.90	8.25
1989	6.81	6.06	0.26	5.49	35.58	19.94	4.11	4.37	7.16	19.46	2.99	0.84	1.54	14.09
1990	7.57	6.74	0.29	6.10	24.92	14.88	2.73	2.90	4.41	20.88	3.21	0.90	1.56	15.12
1991	9.75	8.77	0.38	7.94	27.76	16.75	2.93	3.12	4.96	21.30	3.27	0.92	1.59	15.42
1992	13.25	9.88	1.32	8.20	35.04	21.09	3.27	4.53	6.15	24.05	4.62	1.20	2.12	16.11
1993	18.72	13.96	1.87	11.59	38.71	25.77	3.62	5.00	4.32	28.12	5.40	1.40	2.48	18.84
1994	21.63	16.44	2.70	12.79	48.15	34.98	5.02	5.63	2.52	33.85	7.28	1.75	3.22	21.60
1995	27.54	20.50	3.39	15.69	57.28	40.48	5.63	8.81	2.36	40.77	9.50	1.99	3.38	25.30

Year	v13c4	v13c4i	v13c4ii	v13c4iii	v13c4iv	v13c5	v13c5i	v13c5ii	v13c5iii	v13c5iv	v13c6	v13c6i	v13c6ii	v13c6iii
1952														
1953														
1954														
1955														
1956														
1957														
1958														
1959														
1960														
1961														
1962														
1963														
1964														
1965														
1966														
1967														
1968														
1969														
1970														
1971														
1972														
1973														
1974														
1975														
1976														
1977														
1978	0.48	0.03	0.44		0.01	0.46	0.22	0.06	0.03	0.16	0.29	0.25	0.04	
1979	0.59	0.04	0.54		0.01	0.68	0.33	0.08	0.04	0.23	0.31	0.26	0.04	
1980	0.64	0.05	0.58		0.01	0.74	0.35	0.09	0.05	0.25	0.35	0.30	0.04	
1981	0.69	0.05	0.63		0.01	0.80	0.38	0.10	0.05	0.27	0.52	0.44	0.06	
1982	0.83	0.06	0.76		0.02	0.81	0.39	0.10	0.05	0.28	0.67	0.57	0.08	
1983	1.10	0.08	1.00	-0.01	0.02	1.02	0.49	0.12	0.06	0.34	0.83	0.71	0.10	
1984	1.67	0.12	1.53	-0.01	0.03	1.33	0.64	0.16	0.08	0.45	1.00	0.86	0.13	
1985	1.86	0.13	1.70	-0.01	0.04	1.66	0.79	0.20	0.10	0.56	1.29	1.10	0.16	
1986	2.17	0.16	1.99	-0.01	0.04	2.12	1.02	0.26	0.13	0.72	1.58	1.36	0.20	
1987	2.61	0.19	2.38	-0.01	0.05	2.54	1.22	0.31	0.16	0.86	2.52	2.16	0.32	-0.01
1988	2.99	0.21	2.73	-0.01	0.06	3.94	1.89	0.47	0.24	1.34	3.08	2.64	0.39	-0.01
1989	3.35	0.24	3.06	-0.02	0.07	3.08	1.47	0.37	0.19	1.04	3.13	2.69	0.39	-0.01
1990	3.93	0.28	3.58	-0.02	0.08	3.72	1.78	0.45	0.23	1.26	3.89	3.34	0.49	-0.01
1991	4.04	0.29	3.69	-0.02	0.08	4.57	2.19	0.55	0.28	1.55	4.31	3.70	0.54	-0.01
1992	4.73	0.40	4.24	0.00	0.09	6.01	2.85	0.67	0.41	2.08	5.20	4.47	0.63	-0.02
1993	6.25	0.53	5.19	0.28	0.25	7.39	3.51	0.82	0.50	2.55	6.37	5.48	0.77	-0.02
1994	7.38	0.71	6.00	0.35	0.32	9.72	4.31	1.19	1.06	3.16	8.02	6.80	0.74	0.13
1995	8.85	0.99	7.18	0.33	0.35	12.15	5.55	1.40	1.82	3.38	9.88	7.95	1.02	0.16

Year	v13c6iv	v13c7	v13c7i	v13c7ii	v13c7iii	v13c7iv	v13c8	v13c8i	v13c8ii	v13c8iii	v13c8iv	v13c9	v13c9i	v13c9ii
1952														
1953														
1954														
1955														
1956														
1957														
1958														
1959														
1960														
1961														
1962														
1963														
1964														
1965														
1966														
1967														
1968														
1969														
1970														
1971														
1972														
1973														
1974														
1975														
1976														
1977														
1978	0.01	1.38	1.18	0.22	-0.02		0.19	0.14	0.03		0.01	1.00	0.85	0.15
1979	0.01	1.59	1.36	0.25	-0.02		0.39	0.29	0.07	0.01	0.03	1.20	1.02	0.18
1980	0.01	2.02	1.72	0.32	-0.02		0.41	0.31	0.07	0.01	0.03	1.82	1.54	0.27
1981	0.01	2.32	1.98	0.37	-0.03		0.39	0.29	0.07	0.01	0.03	2.08	1.76	0.30
1982	0.01	2.64	2.25	0.42	-0.03		0.69	0.52	0.12	0.01	0.04	2.43	2.06	0.36
1983	0.02	2.80	2.39	0.44	-0.03		0.82	0.61	0.14	0.02	0.05	3.13	2.66	0.46
1984	0.02	3.24	2.76	0.52	-0.04		0.88	0.66	0.15	0.02	0.06	3.74	3.18	0.55
1985	0.02	4.15	3.54	0.66	-0.05		1.13	0.84	0.19	0.02	0.07	4.99	4.24	0.73
1986	0.03	4.98	4.25	0.79	-0.05		1.67	1.24	0.28	0.03	0.11	6.36	5.41	0.93
1987	0.05	6.46	5.51	1.03	-0.07	-0.01	2.30	1.71	0.39	0.05	0.15	7.63	6.48	1.12
1988	0.06	7.83	6.67	1.24	-0.09	-0.01	2.68	1.99	0.46	0.05	0.17	7.98	6.79	1.17
1989	0.06	8.02	6.84	1.28	-0.09	-0.01	2.16	1.61	0.37	0.04	0.14	9.23	7.84	1.35
1990	0.07	8.91	7.60	1.42	-0.10	-0.01	3.81	2.84	0.65	0.08	0.24	10.95	9.31	1.61
1991	0.08	10.00	8.53	1.59	-0.11	-0.01	4.98	3.71	0.85	0.10	0.32	11.66	9.91	1.71
1992	0.12	11.86	10.27	1.72	-0.12	-0.01	5.58	4.43	0.95	0.11	0.09	13.56	11.71	1.92
1993	0.15	13.82	11.97	2.00	-0.14	-0.01	6.84	5.44	1.17	0.14	0.10	16.64	14.37	2.36
1994	0.35	18.83	16.39	2.07	0.06	0.31	8.56	6.59	1.51	0.15	0.31	18.58	15.89	2.43
1995	0.75	22.26	19.37	2.13	0.08	0.68	10.38	7.72	1.72	0.19	0.75	22.91	19.30	2.78

Year	v13c9iii	v13c9iv	v13c10	v13c10i	v13c10ii	v13c10iii	v13c10iv
1952							
1953							
1954							
1955							
1956							
1957							
1958							
1959							
1960							
1961							
1962							
1963							
1964							
1965							
1966							
1967							
1968							
1969							
1970							
1971							
1972							
1973							
1974							
1975							
1976							
1977							
1978		0.01	2.13	2.13			0.03
1979		0.01	2.14	2.14			
1980		0.01	2.12	2.12			
1981		0.01	2.13	2.13			
1982		0.01	2.16	2.16			
1983	-0.01	0.02	2.19	2.19			
1984	-0.01	0.02	1.99	1.99			
1985	-0.01	0.03	1.82	1.82			
1986	-0.01	0.03	1.65	1.65			
1987	-0.01	0.04	1.66	1.66			
1988	-0.01	0.04	1.82	1.82			
1989	-0.02	0.05	2.02	2.02			
1990	-0.02	0.06	2.61	2.61			
1991	-0.02	0.06	2.98	2.98			
1992	0.01	-0.08	3.58	3.58			
1993	0.01	-0.10	4.40	4.40			
1994	0.08	0.18	4.95	4.95			
1995	0.13	0.20	6.20	6.20			

6

Liaoning

Year	v1	v1a	v1b	v1b1	v1b2	v1c	v1c1	v1c2	v1c3	v2	v2a	v2b	v2b1	v2b2	v2c
1952	77.51	16.60	50.10	44.20	5.90	10.81	3.50	6.00	1.31		114.2		144.3	312.5	
1953	100.99	16.90	67.40	57.80	9.60	16.69	5.00	9.80	1.89	129.6	100.6	133.6	129.6	170.0	158.8
1954	109.03	18.80	73.60	64.20	9.40	16.63	5.50	8.90	2.23	109.2	108.2	111.0	111.8	105.9	102.4
1955	110.76	19.40	75.50	67.80	7.70	15.86	6.10	7.30	2.46	102.6	101.6	106.6	109.5	85.6	85.8
1956	136.17	22.10	95.00	83.50	11.50	19.07	7.00	8.90	3.17	133.0	108.0	140.9	141.1	139.0	122.0
1957	145.46	21.20	104.80	94.40	10.40	19.46	6.70	9.30	3.46	107.3	94.1	112.3	115.6	81.3	89.9
1958	198.35	21.20	155.70	138.90	16.80	21.45	7.50	10.70	3.25	144.1	117.7	155.7	160.5	106.1	100.1
1959	262.13	24.60	212.80	198.60	14.20	24.73	10.50	10.80	3.43	124.3	109.4	128.4	129.7	107.7	103.5
1960	307.23	19.20	261.80	243.10	18.70	26.23	11.80	10.50	3.93	117.0	68.7	121.2	121.8	109.8	127.4
1961	156.16	19.60	114.70	107.90	6.80	21.86	8.70	8.90	4.26	50.8	87.5	44.7	43.2	77.2	93.5
1962	149.96	21.20	110.10	107.40	2.70	18.66	4.90	10.00	3.76	86.7	108.6	87.4	93.0	22.1	69.4
1963	164.05	21.80	122.50	117.90	4.60	19.75	5.20	10.70	3.85	112.3	116.4	112.1	111.7	133.3	110.0
1964	189.94	22.60	145.60	138.20	7.40	21.74	5.90	11.70	4.14	117.6	106.8	120.0	118.6	175.0	112.8
1965	227.39	26.50	177.20	170.50	6.70	23.69	7.20	12.10	4.39	122.3	112.2	124.6	125.1	110.2	115.4
1966	254.49	29.40	199.80	193.60	6.20	25.29	7.60	12.90	4.79	113.8	100.0	116.5	117.4	87.0	105.9
1967	195.64	29.30	142.70	137.90	4.80	23.64	5.90	12.70	5.04	78.4	100.9	73.9	73.9	76.6	97.3
1968	173.34	30.40	120.30	115.80	4.50	22.64	6.10	11.80	4.74	89.1	100.9	86.5	86.4	91.7	95.2
1969	249.45	30.00	193.00	186.10	6.90	26.45	9.60	11.90	4.95	150.2	95.8	164.8	165.3	145.5	116.4
1970	302.77	37.70	235.30	226.40	8.90	29.77	11.80	11.80	6.17	124.1	124.2	125.3	125.2	127.1	114.1
1971	334.48	35.50	266.70	252.50	14.20	32.28	13.30	12.60	6.38	111.2	92.6	113.2	112.3	154.1	108.8
1972	348.30	33.00	280.60	265.20	15.40	34.70	13.70	13.90	7.10	104.5	92.0	105.8	105.8	105.8	107.1
1973	385.18	40.30	305.80	289.30	16.50	39.08	14.50	15.40	9.18	111.1	121.4	109.7	110.0	104.1	113.0
1974	410.84	43.90	326.90	307.30	19.60	40.04	14.10	16.90	9.04	107.1	109.2	107.5	107.1	115.8	102.1
1975	440.31	48.30	349.10	325.50	23.60	42.91	14.90	18.60	9.41	107.4	108.4	107.3	106.8	117.0	107.2
1976	456.46	47.40	366.10	343.20	22.90	42.96	14.10	19.00	9.86	104.0	96.8	105.4	106.1	94.2	100.1
1977	446.90	46.60	356.30	337.00	19.30	44.00	14.60	19.70	9.70	98.7	99.8	98.1	99.0	82.0	102.4
1978	496.25	49.20	397.00	376.80	20.20	50.05	16.30	21.20	12.55	111.2	106.5	111.4	111.9	101.9	113.5
1979	545.53	59.80	429.80	396.00	33.80	55.93	18.30	21.40	16.23	108.2	103.4	108.5	106.2	163.0	111.2
1980	646.96	73.56	493.44	452.61	40.83	79.96	27.32	23.22	29.42	113.1	107.5	110.4	110.4	109.5	140.2
1981	683.11	78.60	507.06	461.06	46.00	97.45	25.02	34.83	37.60	103.2	102.1	100.9	100.2	112.5	118.1
1982	738.33	85.36	539.11	482.30	56.81	113.86	29.17	35.82	48.87	107.2	103.7	106.4	105.9	111.3	113.8
1983	826.45	106.53	584.61	527.71	56.90	135.31	34.40	42.36	58.55	110.6	121.0	108.2	109.0	100.2	115.2
1984	962.69	117.60	677.04	612.53	64.51	168.05	46.64	53.30	68.11	113.7	104.3	113.8	114.0	111.9	119.5
1985	1201.75	118.05	866.85	774.57	92.28	216.85	63.72	83.65	69.48	116.5	90.8	119.3	118.4	129.4	120.5
1986	1414.33	142.03	982.15	874.99	107.16	290.15	77.95	102.42	109.78	111.3	106.9	109.5	109.6	108.4	120.5
1987	1704.92	169.22	1174.33	1043.73	130.60	361.37	89.69	114.36	157.32	114.6	105.1	112.9	113.1	110.6	124.8
1988	2155.01	227.39	1464.94	1304.84	160.10	462.68	124.99	145.85	191.84	114.3	111.1	114.8	115.3	109.7	113.7
1989	2536.98	237.68	1704.76	1546.43	158.33	594.54	152.76	182.34	259.44	105.3	95.7	105.1	105.9	95.9	109.4
1990	2725.45	273.75	1785.04	1606.92	178.12	666.66	161.02	194.81	310.83	104.5	115.2	103.3	103.0	106.8	105.6
1991	3149.09	302.29	2058.04	1860.57	197.47	788.76	184.41	250.62	353.73	108.2	106.8	109.1	109.7	102.9	106.4
1992	3950.21	340.75	2606.83	2337.85	268.98	1002.63	221.38	327.57	453.68	117.2	109.1	119.1	119.3	117.8	115.5
1993	5794.19	442.70	3966.47	3503.90	462.57	1385.02	275.89	475.64	633.49	124.0	114.1	127.1	125.9	138.7	119.1
1994	7531.23	602.12	5145.63	4598.65	546.98	1783.48	348.26	578.21	857.01	122.4	103.4	126.8	128.6	111.2	116.0
1995	8754.91	761.80	5856.74	5280.22	576.52	2136.37	409.13	754.89	972.35	108.6	111.5	107.6	108.3	100.5	111.1

Year	v2c1	v2c2	v3'	v3	v3a	v3b	v3b1	v3b2	v3c	v3c1	v3c2	v3c3	v3c4	v3c5	v3c6
1952	134.6	155.9	41.38	41.38	12.00	20.00	18.13	1.87	9.38	2.64	5.60				
1953	145.7	169.8	52.85	52.85	12.30	26.14	22.77	3.37	14.41	3.39	9.39				
1954	115.7	91.1	56.90	56.90	14.00	29.33	25.94	3.39	13.57	3.73	8.02				
1955	86.4	81.7	59.37	59.37	14.60	32.18	29.40	2.78	12.59	4.32	6.32				
1956	117.6	123.9	72.04	72.04	16.60	39.47	35.00	4.47	15.97	5.32	8.08				
1957	83.3	91.6	78.69	78.69	16.00	46.62	42.39	4.23	16.07	4.88	8.33				
1958	104.5	102.3	105.64	105.64	16.20	70.82	64.38	6.44	18.62	5.97	9.83				
1959	108.6	102.2	136.69	136.69	18.40	95.21	89.41	5.80	23.08	9.53	10.35				
1960	132.9	119.8	158.14	158.14	14.70	119.39	112.04	7.35	24.05	10.28	10.17				
1961	96.0	81.7	75.86	75.86	14.80	41.60	38.97	2.63	19.46	7.35	8.32				
1962	51.5	87.6	74.06	74.06	15.80	41.02	39.90	1.12	17.24	4.12	9.65				
1963	106.0	114.1	76.08	76.08	16.80	42.05	40.17	1.88	17.23	4.31	9.56				
1964	113.2	113.5	87.21	87.21	18.00	50.50	47.44	3.06	18.71	4.78	10.37				
1965	125.0	110.9	103.15	103.15	20.20	62.60	59.75	2.85	20.35	5.96	10.62				
1966	104.0	106.3	112.61	112.61	22.60	69.47	66.90	2.57	20.54	5.96	10.69				
1967	88.5	98.3	93.35	93.35	22.60	51.65	49.66	1.99	19.10	4.61	10.42				
1968	102.9	91.5	86.89	86.89	23.50	45.05	43.13	1.92	18.34	4.72	9.78				
1969	149.3	100.0	113.78	113.78	22.10	70.07	67.25	2.82	21.61	7.68	9.89				
1970	121.7	100.9	136.82	136.82	28.50	85.31	81.66	3.65	23.01	8.91	9.33				
1971	112.4	107.4	148.60	148.60	26.30	97.57	91.81	5.76	24.73	10.03	9.81				
1972	103.0	109.4	153.96	153.96	24.50	103.55	97.25	6.30	25.91	10.25	10.36				
1973	105.8	111.5	171.98	171.98	31.40	113.60	106.89	6.71	26.98	10.42	10.22				
1974	97.2	109.0	185.14	185.14	33.10	123.79	115.74	8.05	28.25	10.12	11.75				
1975	105.7	110.1	198.51	198.51	36.00	132.69	123.08	9.61	29.82	10.36	12.92				
1976	94.6	102.2	203.99	203.99	34.70	140.28	130.99	9.29	29.01	9.69	12.66				
1977	103.5	103.7	203.77	203.77	34.33	138.74	130.92	7.82	30.70	10.58	13.35				
1978	111.6	107.1	229.22	229.20	32.40	162.90	155.20	7.70	33.90	12.80	12.60	2.70	0.64	0.71	1.16
1979	111.7	100.5	244.96	244.96	40.70	166.36	157.96	8.40	37.90	13.10	13.80	3.80	1.31	1.01	1.18
1980	146.3	103.7	281.00	281.00	46.05	192.33	182.68	9.65	42.62	14.80	14.06	4.06	1.83	1.47	1.36
1981	89.9	150.5	288.61	288.61	49.13	187.54	174.04	13.50	51.94	14.80	16.10	5.00	3.69	2.35	2.10
1982	114.2	100.2	315.07	315.07	54.67	199.71	185.58	14.13	60.69	15.20	17.59	8.00	4.63	3.36	2.76
1983	113.5	113.6	364.02	364.02	72.24	219.66	202.20	17.46	72.12	17.92	20.80	8.80	6.03	4.17	3.28
1984	128.7	121.7	438.17	438.17	80.40	268.20	243.30	24.90	89.57	24.30	26.17	10.40	5.90	5.58	3.90
1985	119.2	147.1	518.59	518.59	74.90	328.11	299.21	28.90	115.58	30.20	35.78	16.80	6.23	6.07	4.62
1986	105.6	111.0	605.39	605.33	92.85	357.83	326.04	31.79	154.65	40.61	49.29	27.28	7.07	6.93	5.00
1987	113.9	109.6	719.67	719.12	109.52	416.99	375.64	41.35	192.61	52.73	61.12	32.55	8.94	7.66	6.22
1988	128.5	115.1	881.74	881.02	141.92	492.49	444.37	48.12	246.61	64.12	71.61	46.13	11.42	12.21	7.92
1989	104.7	107.3	1004.64	1003.81	141.86	545.06	492.59	52.47	316.89	79.59	89.53	66.22	11.60	12.17	9.30
1990	129.4	102.3	1061.91	1062.74	168.57	540.84	482.90	57.94	353.33	83.89	95.44	72.69	15.15	18.08	11.66
1991	105.9	117.0	1200.02	1200.10	180.82	590.10	526.81	63.29	429.18	96.20	124.07	87.80	14.15	23.51	13.99
1992	123.9	106.5	1472.95	1472.95	194.58	741.90	661.19	80.71	536.47	111.52	167.92	103.98	19.89	32 14	17.46
1993	119.5	117.5	2010.82	2010.82	260.77	1039.29	920.55	118.74	710.76	127.43	237.37	131.79	36.40	46 16	23.63
1994	115.9	116.1	2461.78	2461.78	318.95	1259.05	1109.88	149.17	883.78	160.20	287.61	149.27	51.21	61 57	31.65
1995	108.7	114.4	2793.37	2793.37	392.17	1390.00	1233.37	156.63	1011.20	176.86	339.58	162.79	56.37	72 12	40.39

Year	v3c7	v3c8	v3c9	v3c10	v3d	v4'	v4	v4a	v4b	v4b1	v4b2	v4c	v4c1	v4c2	v4c3
1952				1.14	218										
1953				1.63	266	130.8	130.8	101.6	139.6	130.7	219.8	151.2	122.8	167.7	
1954				1.82	272	109.4	109.4	109.4	119.3	117.5	129.0	91.4	105.9	82.9	
1955				1.95	272	106.5	106.5	102.9	112.6	117.8	86.8	96.0	123.7	79.8	
1956				2.57	319	128.7	128.7	107.7	136.4	134.6	148.0	130.9	125.0	132.0	
1957				2.86	335	108.5	108.5	92.4	116.2	120.6	90.0	100.7	92.1	101.7	
1958				2.82	437	143.7	143.7	116.6	159.7	155.4	208.7	115.8	120.1	119.2	
1959				3.20	553	123.4	123.4	109.3	127.2	130.1	102.1	119.2	151.0	102.0	
1960				3.60	625	111.1	111.1	68.2	119.4	119.0	124.7	105.6	111.4	98.4	
1961				3.79	299	42.9	42.9	88.7	33.1	32.7	36.9	71.8	68.1	68.5	
1962				3.47	292	89.7	89.7	106.9	87.9	95.4	19.3	83.4	57.7	104.8	
1963				3.36	293	108.6	108.6	120.6	107.0	106.2	142.3	103.1	102.8	104.3	
1964				3.56	324	116.8	116.8	110.7	120.3	118.3	187.4	113.3	113.6	115.1	
1965				3.77	372	122.8	122.8	107.6	130.9	131.8	110.6	114.1	127.9	109.2	
1966				3.89	397	112.7	112.7	101.4	117.8	119.1	84.8	105.9	103.8	106.8	
1967				4.07	323	83.5	83.5	101.2	75.7	75.6	79.5	96.8	90.3	96.7	
1968				3.84	295	99.9	99.9	101.1	101.0	101.6	82.6	95.5	102.0	92.3	
1969				4.04	378	129.9	129.9	95.6	145.8	145.7	150.0	114.0	141.4	99.7	
1970				4.77	447	124.6	124.6	126.1	126.8	126.7	131.8	114.9	131.7	100.0	
1971				4.89	478	110.4	110.4	85.5	115.1	114.0	156.1	111.5	118.6	108.2	
1972				5.30	489	103.5	103.5	92.3	106.0	106.0	107.2	105.0	103.2	105.2	
1973				6.34	538	113.1	113.1	127.7	111.1	111.5	104.5	107.5	106.2	102.4	
1974				6.38	572	108.1	108.1	105.7	109.7	109.3	117.3	104.2	93.6	117.5	
1975				6.54	607	108.2	108.2	107.4	109.2	108.7	117.8	105.1	102.0	109.0	
1976				6.66	619	103.4	103.4	95.4	106.9	107.9	92.7	96.8	97.6	95.5	
1977				6.77	612	100.5	100.5	97.9	100.0	100.6	90.5	105.6	108.3	105.1	
1978	1.71	0.18	1.40		680	110.7	110.7	96.6	115.4	116.6	92.6	103.4	107.1	90.6	
1979	1.81	0.42	1.47		717	104.9	104.9	106.9	103.3	103.2	106.5	111.2	103.2	104.2	143.9
1980	2.90	0.54	1.60		811	109.2	109.2	103.8	110.0	110.0	109.4	109.9	104.7	104.2	112.1
1981	4.26	0.94	2.20		823	98.4	98.4	98.1	94.0	92.8	123.5	119.4	106.0	108.1	110.3
1982	5.34	1.11	2.70		884	105.3	105.3	106.6	102.5	101.8	113.5	113.8	105.4	102.0	135.7
1983	6.36	1.36	3.40		1012	113.3	113.3	128.3	108.8	109.1	104.4	115.2	114.2	118.3	124.3
1984	7.56	1.66	4.10		1203	116.8	116.8	105.0	119.5	120.1	109.3	119.5	116.9	116.7	135.6
1985	8.94	2.04	4.90		1413	113.3	113.3	84.0	118.7	118.2	127.8	120.5	122.8	120.9	139.0
1986	9.65	3.34	5.48		1633	108.3	108.3	111.7	103.5	103.1	109.6	120.5	114.5	124.0	135.2
1987	11.31	4.99	7.09		1917	114.1	114.0	106.0	111.4	111.5	110.4	124.8	123.7	127.0	136.4
1988	14.60	6.31	10.28	2.01	2285	111.7	111.7	106.9	111.7	111.5	114.9	113.7	109.1	119.5	109.1
1989	18.39	9.12	18.08	2.89	2574	103.1	103.1	95.7	101.6	102.0	95.4	109.3	106.3	103.2	112.5
1990	20.04	11.95	21.18	3.25	2698	100.9	101.1	114.5	97.0	96.6	104.0	104.8	102.9	102.9	103.1
1991	22.85	13.37	29.33	3.91	3027	106.1	106.1	104.2	104.3	103.6	110.9	110.2	113.3	115.5	107.0
1992	29.89	14.48	34.23	4.96	3693	112.1	112.1	104.2	113.5	114.5	104.4	113.6	113.2	116.1	111.1
1993	44.37	15.46	41.31	6.84	5015	114.9	114.9	110.7	116.4	116.0	120.4	114.3	113.3	114.1	115.6
1994	48.34	31.95	53.03	8.95	6103	111.2	111.2	102.1	113.8	114.3	109.3	111.1	111.9	110.8	105.0
1995	56.07	37.23	60.08	9.71	6880	107.1	107.1	104.9	107.1	107.8	100.1	107.8	106.8	112.7	105.3

Year	v4c4	v4c5	v4c6	v4c7	v4c8	v4c9	v4c10	v5	v5a	v5a1	v5a1a	v5a1b	v5a2	v5b	v5b1
1952								41.38	26.31	23.10	11.25	11.85	3.21	14.67	8.57
1953								52.85	32.89	28.45	12.75	15.70	4.44	19.36	10.76
1954								56.90	35.14	30.40	13.90	16.50	4.74	19.26	14.16
1955								59.37	34.84	30.10	14.70	15.40	4.74	10.43	11.13
1956								72.04	40.26	34.90	16.00	18.90	5.36	13.38	12.78
1957								78.69	43.91	38.10	16.20	21.90	5.81	18.18	12.68
1958								105.64	45.61	39.80	17.90	21.90	5.81	34.33	26.83
1959								136.69	53.10	45.60	19.30	26.30	7.50	48.19	34.09
1960								158.14	58.43	49.10	18.00	31.10	9.33	55.51	39.61
1961								75.86	51.64	44.45	15.55	28.90	7.19	8.52	7.62
1962								74.06	51.47	45.35	19.35	26.00	6.12	-3.11	5.79
1963								76.08	52.40	47.20	23.80	23.40	5.20	21.08	14.78
1964								87.21	54.43	47.70	25.00	22.70	6.73	25.78	19.08
1965								103.15	56.48	49.75	24.85	24.90	6.73	29.37	20.67
1966								112.61	53.66	47.85	27.95	19.90	5.81	24.55	16.35
1967								93.35	57.65	50.15	25.15	25.00	7.50	21.90	12.00
1968								86.89	57.59	50.55	26.75	23.80	7.04	21.40	12.30
1969								113.78	62.95	55.15	28.65	26.50	7.80	25.73	14.83
1970								136.82	67.56	59.60	33.70	25.90	7.96	32.96	17.36
1971								148.60	69.67	60.95	32.25	28.70	8.72	44.13	21.83
1972								153.96	72.88	63.70	32.60	31.10	9.18	36.18	24.68
1973								171.98	75.50	65.40	31.80	33.60	10.10	43.38	29.28
1974								185.14	81.66	68.65	32.95	35.70	13.01	50.18	31.98
1975								198.51	84.68	70.30	33.20	37.10	14.38	62.33	33.23
1976								203.99	94.53	77.85	37.95	39.90	16.68	62.86	30.46
1977								203.77	98.31	82.70	40.90	41.80	15.61	48.06	30.56
1978								229.20	109.37	90.22	40.20	50.02	19.15	62.33	33.63
1979	207.9	144.3	108.3	112.4	247.1	108.9		244.96	129.30	107.55	46.40	61.15	21.75	64.68	45.38
1980	132.1	135.6	106.8	155.2	121.4	107.5		281.00	157.43	124.79	53.01	71.78	32.64	56.82	42.94
1981	201.7	192.7	152.4	140.9	166.7	125.3		288.61	177.41	142.53	59.27	83.26	34.88	53.80	43.10
1982	122.8	114.7	126.6	123.0	109.9	118.4		315.07	185.21	148.54	60.89	87.65	36.67	67.87	63.03
1983	108.6	121.1	115.2	117.2	113.5	122.2		364.02	208.15	162.51	67.86	94.65	45.64	86.81	71.55
1984	113.3	132.2	113.2	116.0	111.1	118.5		438.17	236.89	188.42	80.66	107.76	48.47	127.59	92.63
1985	105.4	110.0	116.9	113.5	120.0	102.6		518.59	276.19	225.51	90.99	134.52	50.68	174.24	130.91
1986	119.3	112.0	122.8	106.2	119.6	116.7		605.33	314.75	257.88	100.04	157.84	56.87	215.95	158.58
1987	110.7	112.5	118.4	104.8	149.8	133.3		719.12	371.81	296.93	113.00	183.93	74.88	256.83	210.23
1988	111.0	105.4	104.1	109.6	153.2	117.3		881.02	459.39	379.61	131.15	248.46	79.78	335.39	260.30
1989	112.4	101.9	107.8	134.9	112.1	124.6	121.8	1003.81	543.60	434.09	148.43	285.66	109.51	356.47	241.89
1990	101.7	110.0	108.6	107.8	112.2	111.8	175.5	1062.74	574.24	450.76	140.60	310.16	123.48	392.74	262.39
1991	111.4	102.9	103.5	103.0	106.0	103.3	118.5	1200.10	640.51	502.22	156.02	346.20	138.29	452.62	323.66
1992	104.8	122.2	120.6	114.5	105.4	112.7	107.8	1472.95	769.94	614.28	200.54	413.74	155.66	561.81	405.18
1993	112.7	119.9	111.7	113.2	108.3	115.7	116.9	2010.82	962.51	770.19	240.22	529.97	192.32	901.26	731.60
1994	123.8	110.2	116.5	113.0	124.4	108.9	112.0	2461.78	1239.61	965.96	302.29	663.67	273.65	1024.66	887.99
1995	97.7	105.8	110.2	110.5	109.7	101.2	102.8	2793.37	1501.84	1177.59	350.38	827.21	324.25	1046.60	884.95

Year	v5b2	v5c	v5c1	v5c2	v6a1	v6a2	v6a3	v6a4	v6b2	v6b3	v6b4	v7	v7a	v7a1	v7a2
1952	6.10	0.40													
1953	9.10	0.10										120.7	117.6	102.9	131.6
1954	5.10	2.50										106.4	106.4	107.2	105.8
1955	-0.70	14.10										96.4	95.8	105.5	88.5
1956	0.60	18.40										115.2	115.6	110.8	119.9
1957	5.50	16.60										106.7	107.4	98.4	114.9
1958	8.00	25.20										104.2	103.6	106.5	101.4
1959	14.10	35.40										115.5	113.9	107.5	118.9
1960	15.90	44.20										102.3	99.3	89.2	106.4
1961	1.00	15.60										70.5	71.7	72.6	71.2
1962	-8.90	25.70										114.0	119.0	133.1	110.5
1963	6.30	2.60										108.5	108.8	112.3	106.3
1964	6.70	7.00										104.9	104.4	105.8	103.4
1965	9.20	16.80										105.1	105.1	104.8	105.3
1966	8.20	34.40										86.7	86.3	81.7	89.8
1967	9.90	13.80										101.7	100.0	98.1	101.3
1968	9.10	7.90										101.9	99.5	95.6	102.1
1969	10.90	25.10										108.5	108.6	116.7	103.4
1970	15.60	36.30										120.1	123.2	137.2	113.0
1971	22.30	34.80										103.3	102.4	95.8	108.3
1972	11.50	44.90										102.1	102.1	99.7	103.9
1973	14.10	53.10										103.8	102.9	97.1	107.3
1974	18.20	53.30										108.0	104.8	104.9	104.7
1975	29.10	51.50										103.5	102.4	103.0	102.0
1976	32.40	46.60										109.6	108.4	110.2	107.2
1977	17.50	57.40										103.9	106.1	107.9	104.9
1978	28.70	57.50			16.88	21.71	0.58	1.03	42.80	6.26	0.96	112.3	110.4	97.9	119.3
1979	19.30	50.98			19.49	24.76	0.96	1.19	53.52	6.43	1.20	115.7	116.4	108.7	120.9
1980	13.88	66.75			22.18	28.07	1.51	1.25	65.42	4.89	1.47	115.4	110.3	117.1	106.7
1981	10.70	57.40			21.68	34.15	1.80	1.64	73.86	7.77	1.63	110.2	111.5	108.6	113.7
1982	4.84	61.99			21.88	35.45	1.90	1.66	77.69	8.24	1.72	102.8	102.6	101.0	103.7
1983	15.26	69.06			25.04	37.98	2.42	2.42	84.16	8.78	1.71	110.5	107.4	109.3	106.2
1984	34.96	73.69			26.75	47.31	3.50	3.10	95.63	10.19	1.94	109.9	112.1	115.3	109.9
1985	43.33	68.16			28.66	54.17	3.90	4.26	120.61	11.71	2.20	104.2	107.0	102.9	110.0
1986	57.37	74.63			30.03	60.63	4.10	5.28	141.55	13.47	2.82	107.9	108.4	105.7	110.2
1987	46.60	90.48			30.39	71.04	5.45	6.12	164.98	15.73	3.22	110.1	107.3	106.6	107.7
1988	75.09	86.24	176.81	90.57	31.89	86.75	6.02	6.49	219.87	24.65	3.94	105.2	109.2	104.7	112.2
1989	114.58	103.74	201.27	97.53	35.45	97.35	8.50	7.13	251.30	29.31	5.05	101.2	100.7	98.2	102.3
1990	130.35	95.76	194.51	98.75	33.92	87.76	11.00	7.92	261.49	42.05	6.62	101.5	99.8	90.5	105.3
1991	128.96	106.97	211.90	104.93	40.94	91.74	14.61	8.73	292.67	43.52	10.01	106.2	106.0	105.1	106.5
1992	156.63	141.20	268.13	126.93	61.43	110.24	16.59	12.28	338.00	59.98	15.76	111.9	113.0	112.7	113.2
1993	169.66	147.05	330.96	183.91	70.50	135.80	19.54	14.38	429.35	77.42	23.20	109.9	109.3	108.2	109.8
1994	136.67	197.51	427.97	230.46	94.21	156.77	22.59	28.72	551.06	91.59	21.02	111.4	109.5	108.2	110.0
1995	161.65	244.93	472.93	228.00	113.49	179.30	25.98	31.61	670.97	111.57	44.67	108.1	106.9	102.0	109.1

Year	v7b	v8	v8a	v8b	v9	v9a	v9b	v10a1	v10a2	v10a3	v10a3a	v10a3b	v10a4	v10b1	v10b2
1952		120	76	262											
1953	143.1	143	87	299	113.3	103.9	113.4								
1954	106.5	145	96	253	101.5	108.9	85.2								
1955	100.0	137	100	214	91.3	103.5	80.2								
1956	112.7	155	106	255	112.7	107.9	116.3								
1957	102.6	163	106	268	103.5	97.9	104.2								
1958	108.3	165	118	242	100.0	107.5	91.4								
1959	125.8	186	131	268	112.3	110.5	109.8								
1960	120.3	194	128	276	96.2	93.7	92.6								
1961	64.4	176	110	260	72.2	72.0	72.3								
1962	86.9	179	126	259	118.1	122.4	122.2								
1963	106.0	173	135	242	101.3	98.1	110.5								
1964	108.6	177	146	232	105.9	108.8	102.1								
1965	105.3	179	140	249	101.9	100.9	103.2								
1966	90.0	169	153	197	84.1	79.5	89.1								
1967	114.0	173	137	235	97.8	97.8	96.1								
1968	117.1	172	142	225	98.5	93.1	102.7								
1969	108.3	183	141	270	105.3	107.4	111.6								
1970	103.9	195	160	274	122.1	133.3	117.1								
1971	109.2	196	149	304	100.6	93.1	108.5								
1972	102.1	202	150	318	100.6	99.1	100.3								
1973	110.2	205	146	333	101.7	97.2	104.0								
1974	129.7	212	148	349	103.4	102.9	103.3								
1975	109.9	215	148	362	101.6	101.9	101.7								
1976	115.6	236	167	388	107.0	108.2	106.8								
1977	93.3	248	177	408	105.5	106.7	105.3								
1978	123.3	267	173	476	108.5	97.6	116.3	24.21	5.72	3.70	0.45	3.25		18.94	9.38
1979	112.5	315	202	546	115.3	109.7	113.6	32.68	7.71	4.99	0.55	4.44		12.74	6.31
1980	141.2	355	235	573	107.2	119.1	95.2	30.82	7.46	4.66	0.54	4.12		9.16	4.48
1981	105.4	400	264	632	108.1	109.1	105.5	31.73	6.42	4.95	0.77	4.18		8.49	1.89
1982	103.5	410	270	641	101.1	100.8	100.2	42.14	8.75	12.14	0.50	11.64		0.40	4.41
1983	122.8	443	301	669	106.1	108.6	103.1	56.35	4.00	11.20	0.56	10.64		8.50	6.76
1984	102.1	510	362	735	111.8	115.9	107.1	63.53	15.52	13.58	0.29	13.29		13.23	21.73
1985	93.5	605	414	880	106.3	104.7	105.8	94.92	21.48	14.51	0.50	14.01		21.17	21.29
1986	105.9	686	454	1012	107.6	105.7	108.5	126.81	15.67	16.10	2.30	13.80		28.11	29.26
1987	123.0	780	508	1160	106.3	105.1	106.7	170.32	20.64	19.27	2.81	16.46		26.75	19.85
1988	89.3	985	589	1530	107.6	104.6	108.9	205.31	29.16	25.83	8.81	17.02		40.90	34.19
1989	103.3	1113	662	1722	122.3	157.4	99.9	194.34	21.43	26.12	8.59	17.53		78.70	35.88
1990	109.3	1144	622	1849	83.7	56.8	109.9	211.27	25.94	25.18	7.18	18.00		98.03	32.32
1991	107.0	1267	687	2045	105.3	104.5	105.5	251.91	39.27	32.48	10.79	21.69		88.91	40.05
1992	107.1	1540	884	2407	112.4	112.9	111.5	323.98	50.51	30.69	12.45	18.24		98.76	57.87
1993	112.3	1921	1065	3021	108.7	108.9	107.6	548.28	76.19	33.35	12.89	20.46	73.78	78.67	38.94
1994	118.6	2397	1348	3704	108.8	108.9	107.7	592.98	98.62	41.11	12.49	28.62	155.28	27.53	56.51
1995	112.1	2900	1566	4540	106.2	102.3	107.3	584.39	95.46	48.92	13.82	35.10	156.18	59.94	71.18

Year	v10b4	v11a	v11a1	v11a2	v11b	v11b1	v11b2	v11c	v11c1	v11c2	v12	v12a	v12b	v13	v13i
1952															
1953											135.4	125.2	149.8		
1954											99.8	135.7	57.8		
1955											59.5	86.5	100.0		
1956											133.2	119.2	100.0		
1957											128.8	94.1	863.4		
1958											212.4	234.6	161.1		
1959											141.7	130.1	180.9		
1960											112.2	113.2	109.7		
1961											13.5	16.8	5.1		
1962															
1963															
1964											128.2	135.3	111.7		
1965											133.1	124.4	157.8		
1966											80.5	77.5	87.3		
1967											85.5	70.3	115.7		
1968											95.5	100.1	89.8		
1969											126.4	126.7	125.9		
1970											132.8	121.5	148.3		
1971											127.9	120.2	136.4		
1972											60.9	67.1	50.9		
1973											119.0	117.8	121.7		
1974											114.3	107.9	127.6		
1975											105.0	87.9	135.1		
1976											108.1	98.3	119.4		
1977											80.3	105.4	56.8		
1978	0.38	2.68	0.67	2.01	37.58	17.49	20.09	22.07	15.47	6.60	127.3	109.7	161.1	229.20	75.80
1979	0.25	2.26	0.91	1.35	37.11	23.60	13.51	25.31	20.87	4.44	98.4	128.1	63.7	244.96	84.88
1980	0.24	1.83	0.86	0.97	32.05	22.33	9.72	22.94	19.75	3.19	88.0	94.8	72.1	281.00	97.81
1981	0.32	1.61	0.86	0.75	29.90	22.41	7.49	22.29	19.83	2.46	91.5	97.7	72.5	288.61	105.49
1982	0.03	1.60	1.26	0.34	36.16	32.78	3.38	30.11	28.99	1.12	117.5	135.3	43.0	315.07	122.94
1983		2.50	1.43	1.07	47.89	37.21	10.68	36.42	32.91	3.51	126.4	112.1	315.7	364.02	147.51
1984		4.30	1.85	2.45	72.64	48.17	24.47	50.65	42.61	8.04	145.0	127.6	226.3	438.17	172.08
1985	0.87	5.65	2.62	3.03	98.40	68.07	30.33	70.19	60.22	9.97	125.6	130.1	113.7	518.59	188.89
1986		7.19	3.17	4.02	122.62	82.46	40.16	86.14	72.95	13.19	116.7	111.6	117.3	605.33	218.53
1987		7.47	4.20	3.27	141.94	109.32	32.62	107.42	96.71	10.71	107.7	119.3	78.1	719.12	257.10
1988		10.46	5.20	5.26	187.92	135.36	52.56	137.01	119.74	17.27	115.9	110.3	137.8	881.02	332.93
1989		11.64	4.84	6.80	193.76	125.78	67.98	151.07	111.27	39.80	100.6	93.8	121.8	1003.81	374.39
1990		12.97	5.25	7.72	213.69	136.44	77.25	166.08	120.70	45.38	107.4	103.2	117.3	1062.74	437.42
1991		13.21	6.47	6.74	235.66	168.31	67.35	203.75	148.88	54.87	108.0	108.2	107.5	1200.10	489.36
1992		15.39	8.10	7.29	283.64	210.70	72.94	262.78	186.38	76.40	113.1	111.7	116.4	1472.95	621.92
1993	52.05	26.80	15.34	11.46	456.75	348.90	107.85	417.71	337.36	80.35	123.1	124.7	119.2	2010.82	894.89
1994	52.63	28.24	17.44	10.80	530.85	487.67	43.18	465.57	382.88	82.69	106.5	116.5	82.3	2461.78	1122.59
1995	30.53	75.26	15.94	59.32	521.94	459.59	62.35	449.40	409.42	39.98	98.0	97.0	103.5	2793.37	1323.27

Year	v13ii	v13iii	v13iv	v13a	v13ai	v13aii	v13aiii	v13aiv	v13b	v13bi	v13bii	v13biii	v13biv	v13b1	v13b1i
1952															
1953															
1954															
1955															
1956															
1957															
1958															
1959															
1960															
1961															
1962															
1963															
1964															
1965															
1966															
1967															
1968															
1969															
1970															
1971															
1972															
1973															
1974															
1975															
1976															
1977															
1978	28.72	41.90	82.78	32.40	27.82	1.27	0.68	2.63	162.90	35.95	22.87	36.09	67.99	155.20	31.30
1979	31.53	43.64	84.91	40.70	34.44	1.78	0.94	3.54	166.36	37.54	23.76	37.46	67.60	157.96	32.47
1980	34.11	48.70	100.38	46.05	39.56	1.79	0.97	3.73	192.33	42.90	25.74	42.60	81.09	182.68	37.08
1981	38.59	48.05	96.48	49.13	43.08	1.93	1.05	3.07	187.54	43.47	27.15	40.88	76.04	174.04	35.33
1982	39.35	49.36	103.42	54.67	46.96	2.13	1.15	4.43	199.71	54.07	26.36	41.88	77.40	185.58	45.55
1983	44.57	53.87	118.07	72.24	62.05	2.82	1.52	5.85	219.66	59.14	28.75	45.15	86.62	202.20	48.61
1984	53.04	64.95	148.10	80.40	69.07	3.12	1.69	6.52	268.20	71.46	35.04	54.73	106.97	243.30	56.45
1985	68.03	85.09	176.58	74.90	64.34	2.93	1.57	6.06	328.11	82.18	47.97	71.75	126.21	299.21	64.11
1986	73.68	94.95	218.17	92.85	79.74	3.56	1.99	7.56	357.83	85.38	49.33	77.61	145.51	326.04	66.19
1987	85.97	111.52	264.53	109.52	93.84	3.65	2.61	9.42	416.99	102.54	58.26	92.26	163.93	375.64	79.55
1988	103.70	130.04	314.35	141.92	118.10	4.16	3.68	15.98	492.49	131.68	67.68	107.75	185.38	444.37	104.47
1989	127.83	144.25	357.34	141.86	119.95	4.59	4.91	12.41	545.06	155.37	81.75	116.72	191.22	492.59	125.56
1990	147.37	160.43	317.52	168.57	135.86	5.65	6.75	20.31	540.84	181.48	93.25	126.57	139.54	482.90	148.07
1991	178.45	179.95	352.34	180.82	146.84	6.48	6.70	20.80	590.10	195.09	114.43	140.42	140.16	526.81	159.31
1992	210.58	228.27	412.18	194.58	157.56	8.36	7.55	21.11	741.90	276.89	134.37	173.51	157.13	661.19	225.84
1993	237.74	305.65	572.54	260.77	196.14	11.45	11.58	41.60	1039.29	427.08	159.51	223.84	228.86	920.55	348.86
1994	283.25	378.27	677.67	318.95	235.32	14.25	15.78	53.60	1259.05	521.64	165.04	273.41	298.96	1109.88	423.15
1995	339.87	397.42	732.81	392.17	297.88	15.93	17.42	60.94	1390.00	573.64	188.13	267.97	360.26	1233.37	470.23

Year	v13b1ii	v13b1iii	v13b1iv	v13b2	v13b2i	v13b2ii	v13b2iii	v13b2iv	v13c	v13ci	v13cii	v13ciii	v13civ	v13c1
1952														
1953														
1954														
1955														
1956														
1957														
1958														
1959														
1960														
1961														
1962														
1963														
1964														
1965														
1966														
1967														
1968														
1969														
1970														
1971														
1972														
1973														
1974														
1975														
1976														
1977														
1978	22.36	35.47	66.07	7.70	4.65	0.51	0.62	1.92	33.90	12.03	4.58	5.13	12.16	12.80
1979	23.19	36.79	65.51	8.40	5.07	0.57	0.67	2.09	37.90	12.90	5.99	5.24	13.77	13.10
1980	25.08	41.83	78.69	9.65	5.82	0.66	0.77	2.40	42.62	15.35	6.58	5.13	15.56	14.80
1981	26.23	39.80	72.68	13.50	8.14	0.92	1.08	3.36	51.94	18.94	9.51	6.12	17.37	14.80
1982	25.39	40.75	73.89	14.13	8.52	0.97	1.13	3.51	60.69	21.91	10.86	6.33	21.59	15.20
1983	27.57	43.75	82.27	17.46	10.53	1.18	1.40	4.35	72.12	26.32	13.00	7.20	25.60	17.92
1984	33.34	52.74	100.77	24.90	15.01	1.70	1.99	6.20	89.57	31.55	14.88	8.53	34.61	24.30
1985	46.01	69.52	119.57	28.90	18.07	1.96	2.23	6.64	115.58	42.37	17.13	11.77	44.31	30.20
1986	47.19	75.06	137.60	31.79	19.19	2.14	2.55	7.91	154.65	53.41	20.79	15.35	65.10	40.61
1987	54.72	89.08	152.29	41.35	22.99	3.54	3.18	11.64	192.61	60.72	24.06	16.65	91.18	52.73
1988	64.25	103.23	172.42	48.12	27.21	3.43	4.52	12.93	246.61	83.15	31.86	18.61	112.99	64.12
1989	76.75	111.49	178.79	52.47	29.81	5.00	5.23	12.43	316.89	99.07	41.49	22.62	153.71	79.59
1990	87.22	120.17	127.44	57.94	33.41	6.03	6.40	12.10	353.33	120.08	48.47	27.11	157.67	83.89
1991	107.43	133.93	126.14	63.29	35.78	7.00	6.49	14.02	429.18	147.43	57.54	32.83	191.38	96.20
1992	126.63	165.75	142.97	80.71	51.05	7.74	7.76	14.16	536.47	190.47	67.85	47.21	230.94	111.52
1993	151.76	210.65	209.28	118.74	78.22	7.75	13.19	19.58	710.76	276.67	66.78	70.23	297.08	127.43
1994	155.11	257.20	274.42	149.17	98.49	9.93	16.21	24.54	883.78	365.63	103.96	89.08	325.11	160.20
1995	177.70	250.95	334.49	156.63	103.41	10.43	17.02	25.77	1011.20	451.75	135.81	112.03	311.61	176.86

Year	v13c1i	v13c1ii	v13c1iii	v13c1iv	v13c2	v13c2i	v13c2ii	v13c2iii	v13c2iv	v13c3	v13c3i	v13c3ii	v13c3iii	v13c3iv
1952														
1953														
1954														
1955														
1956														
1957														
1958														
1959														
1960														
1961														
1962														
1963														
1964														
1965														
1966														
1967														
1968														
1969														
1970														
1971														
1972														
1973														
1974														
1975														
1976														
1977														
1978	3.24	2.64	1.66	5.26	12.60	5.22	0.59	3.18	3.61	2.70	0.14	0.16	0.26	2.14
1979	3.43	2.85	1.79	5.03	13.80	5.42	0.97	3.08	4.33	3.80	0.16	0.19	0.31	3.14
1980	4.11	2.95	1.89	5.85	14.06	5.79	0.97	2.78	4.52	4.06	0.17	0.20	0.34	3.35
1981	3.56	3.02	1.74	6.48	16.10	6.99	1.44	3.85	3.82	5.00	0.17	0.20	0.34	4.29
1982	4.66	3.10	1.79	5.65	17.59	6.86	1.42	3.78	5.53	8.00	0.26	0.21	0.53	7.00
1983	5.97	3.48	2.07	6.40	20.80	7.72	1.62	4.25	7.21	8.80	0.29	0.20	0.58	7.73
1984	7.74	4.89	2.81	8.86	26.17	8.51	1.77	4.68	11.21	10.40	0.33	0.19	0.61	9.27
1985	11.50	5.49	3.18	10.03	35.78	12.94	2.67	7.12	13.05	16.80	0.49	0.20	0.99	15.12
1986	15.97	7.27	4.17	13.20	49.29	16.48	3.00	8.95	20.86	27.28	0.82	0.23	1.70	24.53
1987	16.37	8.87	3.14	24.35	61.12	18.24	2.92	10.21	29.75	32.55	1.04	0.40	2.73	28.38
1988	18.03	11.53	3.51	31.05	71.61	23.10	3.70	10.01	34.80	46.13	2.99	0.85	3.42	38.87
1989	19.77	17.49	5.32	37.01	89.53	26.65	4.77	10.34	47.77	66.22	4.29	1.22	4.90	55.81
1990	23.12	20.11	6.12	34.54	95.44	29.59	5.73	12.41	47.71	72.69	5.29	1.51	6.36	59.83
1991	25.43	21.76	6.79	42.22	124.07	38.41	8.15	16.18	61.33	87.80	6.47	2.05	6.37	72.41
1992	32.71	26.06	7.16	45.59	167.92	50.40	10.49	26.26	80.77	103.98	9.34	2.86	8.48	83.30
1993	43.93	24.89	8.08	50.53	237.37	78.42	9.23	38.48	111.24	131.79	14.71	3.01	11.79	102.28
1994	53.10	41.70	13.88	51.52	287.61	117.35	13.47	44.14	112.65	149.27	19.38	4.93	14.66	110.30
1995	62.42	55.67	16.28	42.49	339.58	150.79	17.31	56.72	114.76	162.79	24.03	6.42	18.18	114.16

Year	v13c4	v13c4i	v13c4ii	v13c4iii	v13c4iv	v13c5	v13c5i	v13c5ii	v13c5iii	v13c5iv	v13c6	v13c6i	v13c6ii	v13c6iii
1952														
1953														
1954														
1955														
1956														
1957														
1958														
1959														
1960														
1961														
1962														
1963														
1964														
1965														
1966														
1967														
1968														
1969														
1970														
1971														
1972														
1973														
1974														
1975														
1976														
1977														
1978	0.64	0.11	0.52		0.01	0.71	0.43	0.21	0.02	0.05	1.16	0.64	0.10	
1979	1.31	0.11	1.17		0.03	1.01	0.62	0.21	0.04	0.14	1.18	0.70	0.10	
1980	1.83	0.23	1.45	0.02	0.13	1.47	0.71	0.33	0.06	0.37	1.36	0.87	0.10	
1981	3.69	0.37	3.13	0.04	0.15	2.85	1.38	0.70	0.11	0.66	2.10	1.35	0.15	
1982	4.63	0.47	3.92	0.05	0.19	3.36	1.60	0.88	0.13	0.75	2.76	1.76	0.22	
1983	6.03	0.59	5.01	0.06	0.37	4.17	1.97	1.12	0.17	0.91	3.28	2.10	0.25	
1984	5.90	0.59	5.01	0.06	0.24	5.58	2.66	1.17	0.29	1.46	3.90	2.50	0.29	
1985	6.23	0.62	5.30	0.06	0.25	6.07	2.89	1.26	0.32	1.60	4.62	2.95	0.36	
1986	7.07	0.68	6.10	0.05	0.24	6.93	3.21	1.75	0.38	1.59	5.00	3.19	0.39	
1987	8.94	0.62	7.45	0.03	0.84	7.66	3.50	1.58	0.41	2.17	6.22	4.17	0.52	
1988	11.42	1.94	7.54	0.46	1.48	12.21	5.62	2.32	0.37	3.90	7.92	6.81	1.03	
1989	11.60	1.97	7.66	0.46	1.51	12.17	5.52	2.69	0.43	3.53	9.30	7.99	1.21	
1990	15.15	2.04	7.92	0.48	4.71	18.08	8.32	3.44	0.54	5.78	11.66	10.03	1.52	
1991	14.15	2.42	9.39	0.59	1.75	23.51	10.73	4.54	0.61	7.63	13.99	12.00	1.80	
1992	19.89	3.89	11.09	1.45	3.46	32.14	14.20	3.87	1.35	12.72	17.46	14.78	2.12	
1993	36.40	9.70	12.02	4.56	10.12	46.16	21.91	2.96	3.40	17.89	23.63	20.91	2.19	
1994	51.21	11.51	20.84	6.18	12.68	61.57	31.14	6.02	5.05	19.36	31.65	26.83	2.93	0.17
1995	56.37	14.81	26.01	7.42	8.13	72.12	41.53	8.03	6.74	15.82	40.39	35.93	3.92	0.23

Year	v13c6iv	v13c7	v13c7i	v13c7ii	v13c7iii	v13c7iv	v13c8	v13c8i	v13c8ii	v13c8iii	v13c8iv	v13c9	v13c9i	v13c9ii
1952														
1953														
1954														
1955														
1956														
1957														
1958														
1959														
1960														
1961														
1962														
1963														
1964														
1965														
1966														
1967														
1968														
1969														
1970														
1971														
1972														
1973														
1974														
1975														
1976														
1977														
1978	0.42	1.71	1.06	0.24		0.41	0.18	0.15	0.02	0.00	0.01	1.40	1.04	0.10
1979	0.38	1.81	1.11	0.30		0.40	0.42	0.26	0.08	0.01	0.07	1.47	1.09	0.12
1980	0.39	2.90	1.99	0.34	0.02	0.55	0.54	0.28	0.11	0.01	0.14	1.60	1.20	0.13
1981	0.60	4.26	2.93	0.50	0.02	0.81	0.94	0.56	0.19	0.01	0.18	2.20	1.63	0.18
1982	0.78	5.34	3.66	0.65	0.02	1.01	1.11	0.65	0.23	0.02	0.21	2.70	1.99	0.23
1983	0.93	6.36	4.36	0.76	0.03	1.21	1.36	0.80	0.28	0.03	0.25	3.40	2.52	0.28
1984	1.11	7.56	5.19	0.91	0.03	1.43	1.66	0.99	0.32	0.03	0.32	4.10	3.04	0.33
1985	1.31	8.94	6.14	1.06	0.04	1.70	2.04	1.21	0.39	0.04	0.40	4.90	3.63	0.40
1986	1.42	9.65	6.62	1.16	0.04	1.83	3.34	2.38	0.44	0.04	0.48	5.48	4.06	0.45
1987	1.53	11.31	7.99	1.27	0.05	2.00	4.99	3.72	0.52	0.07	0.68	7.09	5.07	0.53
1988	0.08	14.60	11.53	2.34	0.15	0.58	6.31	3.72	1.14	0.38	1.07	10.28	8.34	1.23
1989	0.10	18.39	12.95	2.62	0.16	2.66	9.12	5.38	1.64	0.55	1.55	18.08	13.02	1.93
1990	0.11	20.04	15.76	3.26	0.20	0.82	11.95	7.05	2.15	0.72	2.03	21.18	17.16	2.54
1991	0.19	22.85	18.04	3.55	0.28	0.98	13.37	7.84	2.47	0.80	2.26	29.33	23.79	3.48
1992	0.56	29.89	24.36	4.01	0.35	1.17	14.48	10.12	2.90	1.11	0.35	34.23	28.08	3.97
1993	0.53	44.37	37.40	4.67	0.56	1.74	15.46	10.69	2.73	1.90	0.14	41.31	35.01	4.41
1994	1.72	48.34	38.99	5.43	0.96	2.96	31.95	18.06	3.73	2.80	7.36	53.03	44.09	4.16
1995	0.31	56.07	43.17	7.42	1.31	4.17	37.23	22.69	4.71	3.54	6.29	60.08	50.60	5.34

Year	v13c9iii	v13c9iv	v13c10	v13c10i	v13c10ii	v13c10iii	v13c10iv
1952							
1953							
1954							
1955							
1956							
1957							
1958							
1959							
1960							
1961							
1962							
1963							
1964							
1965							
1966							
1967							
1968							
1969							
1970							
1971							
1972							
1973							
1974							
1975							
1976							
1977							
1978	0.01	0.25					
1979	0.01	0.25					
1980	0.01	0.26					
1981	0.01	0.38					
1982	0.01	0.47					
1983	0.01	0.59					
1984	0.02	0.71					
1985	0.02	0.85					
1986	0.02	0.95					
1987	0.01	1.48					
1988	0.21	0.50	2.01	1.07	0.18	0.10	0.66
1989	0.32	2.81	2.89	1.53	0.26	0.14	0.96
1990	0.42	1.06	3.25	1.72	0.29	0.16	1.08
1991	0.52	1.54	3.91	2.30	0.35	0.19	1.07
1992	0.68	1.50	4.96	2.59	0.48	0.37	1.52
1993	0.88	1.01	6.84	3.99	0.67	0.58	1.60
1994	0.46	4.32	8.95	5.18	0.75	0.78	2.24
1995	0.59	3.55	9.71	5.78	0.98	1.02	1.93

7

Jilin

Year	v1	v1a	v1b	v1b1	v1b2	v1c	v1c1	v1c2	v1c3	v2	v2a	v2b	v2b1	v2b2	v2c
1952	30.10	12.42	11.80	10.48	1.32	5.88	1.30	1.70	2.88						
1953	36.96	12.54	15.61	13.28	2.33	8.81	1.63	2.99	4.19	116.9	93.3	131.4	126.0	176.5	143.7
1954	40.41	12.40	18.24	15.11	3.13	9.77	1.85	2.95	4.97	108.2	97.5	116.1	112.1	139.9	109.9
1955	40.62	13.34	16.53	13.89	2.64	10.75	1.94	2.94	5.87	102.3	105.4	96.7	98.4	88.7	109.6
1956	47.09	13.43	21.15	16.93	4.22	12.51	2.10	3.38	7.03	116.1	92.8	133.1	126.7	167.5	116.5
1957	50.64	12.84	23.91	20.80	3.11	13.89	2.04	3.82	8.03	107.2	95.0	111.5	120.8	73.8	111.5
1958	64.40	12.38	36.84	30.88	5.96	15.18	2.56	4.00	8.62	132.1	119.2	152.5	146.1	196.8	105.7
1959	80.36	13.92	49.91	41.84	8.07	16.53	2.84	4.43	9.26	125.6	109.7	135.6	135.5	136.1	113.6
1960	98.33	12.89	66.34	57.33	9.01	19.10	3.63	5.39	10.08	119.6	83.0	131.6	135.8	109.6	113.5
1961	69.62	14.89	35.88	32.71	3.17	18.85	2.91	4.74	11.20	63.3	106.3	51.2	54.3	31.4	80.1
1962	66.82	14.24	32.93	30.05	2.88	19.65	3.09	4.62	11.94	93.5	95.8	89.9	90.2	86.8	99.8
1963	76.22	16.07	39.64	35.47	4.17	20.51	3.49	3.90	13.12	116.9	110.8	120.9	118.6	147.0	113.4
1964	86.14	16.93	46.69	40.31	6.38	22.52	3.45	4.89	14.18	114.0	104.2	117.4	113.1	156.8	114.1
1965	93.85	17.75	53.12	47.49	5.63	22.98	3.65	4.50	14.83	110.8	105.3	117.6	122.2	87.5	99.4
1966	105.21	22.67	58.89	53.95	4.94	23.65	4.36	4.83	14.46	115.1	109.6	120.9	124.5	86.9	103.9
1967	91.01	24.14	43.96	40.01	3.95	22.91	3.69	3.91	15.31	84.3	106.5	74.5	74.2	79.4	97.0
1968	81.49	23.23	35.23	31.76	3.47	23.03	3.36	3.57	16.10	89.9	96.2	83.1	82.8	87.3	100.7
1969	100.88	19.82	56.91	52.42	4.49	24.15	3.55	4.50	16.10	127.3	85.3	156.0	158.3	128.5	105.3
1970	122.18	26.86	69.48	63.47	6.01	25.84	5.08	5.27	15.49	124.0	135.5	123.0	121.1	151.0	119.1
1971	136.37	27.48	81.76	74.25	7.51	27.13	5.80	5.58	15.75	113.8	101.0	118.5	117.7	128.2	109.3
1972	140.63	26.06	86.49	78.96	7.53	28.08	5.86	6.28	15.94	102.4	91.5	105.6	106.9	92.4	103.5
1973	154.33	31.55	93.33	84.91	8.42	29.45	6.25	6.59	16.61	110.0	120.5	108.7	108.1	116.0	104.9
1974	161.60	37.44	93.86	84.90	8.96	30.30	6.41	7.06	16.83	102.7	108.1	101.0	100.5	106.5	102.9
1975	175.75	35.27	109.03	99.31	9.72	31.45	6.84	7.69	16.92	111.6	102.8	117.0	117.9	108.4	103.8
1976	175.59	31.17	112.12	103.39	8.73	32.30	6.87	7.60	17.83	100.3	87.4	103.5	104.7	89.8	102.7
1977	177.05	31.25	111.92	104.34	7.58	33.88	7.13	7.51	19.24	100.5	99.5	99.6	100.6	87.0	104.4
1978	200.26	37.78	126.08	112.87	13.21	36.40	8.20	8.78	19.42	113.7	119.2	113.7	109.3	179.8	109.2
1979	227.30	42.02	143.36	125.74	17.62	41.92	10.38	7.74	23.80	108.8	96.7	111.1	108.3	136.0	111.9
1980	247.02	47.47	151.77	134.67	17.10	47.78	12.42	9.42	25.94	105.7	104.0	104.9	105.8	97.8	110.2
1981	260.58	56.89	152.89	136.64	16.25	50.80	10.28	12.30	28.22	101.1	107.0	99.3	101.2	84.1	102.6
1982	286.83	60.58	170.37	148.75	21.62	55.88	12.35	13.90	29.63	108.4	105.8	109.5	107.4	129.9	107.5
1983	340.48	78.11	194.03	172.04	21.99	68.34	15.11	21.03	32.20	117.5	129.2	112.8	114.3	101.7	119.8
1984	408.35	88.99	236.70	208.84	27.86	82.66	17.98	26.68	38.00	115.4	110.5	116.8	116.0	123.7	116.7
1985	495.98	85.89	297.02	256.75	40.27	113.07	23.09	37.35	52.63	113.5	92.0	117.4	116.0	128.7	125.1
1986	562.53	98.43	326.80	282.48	44.32	137.30	30.29	46.42	60.59	108.6	104.4	106.8	107.4	102.8	117.0
1987	715.35	120.81	413.33	359.46	53.87	181.21	37.03	52.98	91.20	118.4	114.4	117.6	118.1	113.8	123.4
1988	894.03	140.91	516.92	454.24	62.68	236.20	43.44	77.35	115.41	113.6	105.4	116.3	118.2	101.1	112.5
1989	1009.12	133.79	586.22	530.36	55.86	289.11	48.40	97.40	143.31	102.2	88.4	103.2	106.3	73.9	108.0
1990	1081.00	189.09	616.05	552.36	63.69	275.86	47.65	83.23	144.98	102.7	126.7	102.4	101.9	109.5	91.5
1991	1202.64	188.38	687.64	614.38	73.26	326.62	60.10	101.44	165.08	106.1	99.5	105.9	105.4	109.9	111.6
1992	1464.92	204.39	865.90	767.81	98.09	394.63	65.45	121.65	207.53	113.9	102.9	117.3	117.2	117.4	114.3
1993	1929.84	243.95	1201.13	1033.25	167.88	484.76	85.52	155.32	243.92	115.1	110.0	118.9	116.5	139.0	110.1
1994	2482.60	405.48	1442.30	1280.88	161.42	634.82	118.06	209.20	307.56	113.1	110.2	113.4	116.7	90.3	114.2
1995	2951.39	490.28	1649.26	1434.16	215.10	811.85	155.32	275.64	380.89	112.0	105.9	113.4	112.0	124.8	112.5

Year	v2c1	v2c2	v3'	v3	v3a	v3b	v3b1	v3b2	v3c	v3c1	v3c2	v3c3	v3c4	v3c5	v3c6
1952			16.55	16.55	9.19	4.54	4.19	0.35	2.82	0.78	1.03				
1953	117.7	169.4	18.97	18.97	8.94	6.00	5.19	0.81	4.03	0.92	1.84				
1954	115.7	97.2	20.43	20.43	9.10	6.96	5.89	1.07	4.37	1.05	1.58				
1955	104.5	99.3	21.13	21.13	9.87	6.48	5.54	0.94	4.78	1.06	1.69				
1956	109.2	114.8	24.58	24.58	10.56	8.20	6.62	1.58	5.82	1.28	2.08				
1957	96.5	113.8	25.22	25.22	8.81	10.08	8.91	1.17	6.33	1.29	2.23				
1958	125.5	100.5	31.18	31.18	9.30	15.00	13.08	1.92	6.88	1.57	2.38				
1959	110.9	116.4	37.15	37.15	9.91	19.67	17.78	1.89	7.57	1.79	2.63				
1960	127.8	119.2	41.83	41.83	8.26	24.64	22.17	2.47	8.93	2.17	3.05				
1961	74.1	69.6	31.89	31.89	10.34	13.22	11.87	1.35	8.33	1.83	2.69				
1962	104.1	91.6	31.35	31.35	9.92	12.89	11.47	1.42	8.54	1.92	2.50				
1963	111.4	96.8	35.94	35.94	11.68	15.67	14.06	1.61	8.59	2.05	2.02				
1964	100.6	128.0	38.45	38.45	11.72	17.95	16.12	1.83	8.78	1.96	1.86				
1965	101.3	90.0	42.93	42.93	13.19	20.68	19.11	1.57	9.06	2.06	1.88				
1966	117.3	107.1	46.67	46.67	16.26	20.96	19.63	1.33	9.45	2.46	2.01				
1967	86.9	82.0	44.25	44.25	17.66	17.48	16.42	1.06	9.11	1.99	1.58				
1968	91.7	91.6	42.49	42.49	17.16	16.16	15.31	0.85	9.17	1.82	1.45				
1969	106.1	126.6	45.18	45.18	14.30	21.12	19.99	1.13	9.76	1.97	1.88				
1970	161.3	129.5	56.07	56.07	18.73	26.57	25.29	1.28	10.77	2.67	2.32				
1971	117.3	105.8	60.90	60.90	19.56	29.86	28.41	1.45	11.48	2.92	2.63				
1972	101.0	112.5	56.02	56.02	15.53	29.26	27.66	1.60	11.23	2.95	1.96				
1973	106.7	104.9	63.33	63.33	21.28	30.27	28.45	1.82	11.78	3.20	2.15				
1974	102.6	107.1	65.11	65.11	22.11	30.88	28.94	1.94	12.12	3.16	2.01				
1975	106.7	108.9	72.31	72.31	21.24	38.49	36.37	2.12	12.58	3.62	1.94				
1976	100.4	98.8	67.32	67.32	16.81	37.47	35.34	2.13	13.04	3.53	2.03				
1977	103.8	98.2	72.91	72.91	19.76	39.20	36.98	2.22	13.95	3.88	2.10				
1978	115.0	113.1	81.98	81.98	23.98	42.96	40.34	2.62	15.04	4.46	2.69	1.41	1.52	1.10	0.66
1979	126.6	89.6	91.12	91.12	25.34	49.22	44.56	4.66	16.56	5.13	2.56	1.54	1.54	1.39	0.71
1980	119.7	115.3	98.59	98.59	27.24	52.24	47.42	4.82	19.11	5.62	2.78	1.85	1.64	1.93	0.87
1981	82.8	126.3	111.16	111.16	34.31	56.53	51.29	5.24	20.32	4.33	3.88	2.42	1.73	2.31	0.93
1982	120.1	109.8	121.67	121.67	38.40	60.36	54.21	6.15	22.91	5.19	3.34	3.86	1.80	2.39	1.08
1983	122.4	147.3	150.14	150.14	56.74	65.38	58.75	6.63	28.02	5.78	6.13	4.54	1.86	2.49	1.14
1984	116.4	121.9	174.39	174.39	60.04	80.46	72.10	8.36	33.89	6.75	7.54	5.74	2.73	2.72	1.21
1985	119.7	127.5	200.43	200.44	55.74	97.21	85.29	11.92	47.49	8.25	13.95	8.69	3.06	2.90	1.62
1986	130.9	118.0	227.13	227.15	64.35	104.30	91.28	13.02	58.50	10.89	18.28	10.02	3.59	3.61	1.85
1987	122.2	104.8	297.47	297.49	80.57	139.36	123.49	15.87	77.56	15.15	21.01	16.80	4.61	4.81	2.33
1988	117.3	121.2	368.64	368.67	92.59	173.57	155.12	18.45	102.51	18.56	29.98	22.30	5.21	5.85	3.26
1989	111.4	107.7	391.61	391.65	80.53	181.02	164.09	16.93	130.10	22.18	39.47	29.23	6.03	7.56	4.59
1990	92.0	82.3	425.21	425.28	124.99	182.15	163.82	18.33	118.14	21.11	25.47	28.56	6.15	7.97	4.87
1991	114.1	116.0	463.52	463.47	120.47	203.02	181.71	21.31	139.98	25.19	32.26	32.68	6.73	8.62	5.43
1992	106.4	112.5	558.25	558.06	130.82	257.01	227.17	29.84	170.23	30.17	41.63	38.55	8.64	10.78	6.39
1993	115.6	114.7	718.43	717.95	156.05	351.99	308.10	43.89	209.91	39.98	52.81	40.02	10.65	12.71	8.30
1994	121.1	117.3	937.34	936.78	259.40	398.83	354.70	44.13	278.55	54.47	72.61	50.02	14.72	13.97	10.59
1995	117.8	115.4	1129.98	1129.20	303.99	479.46	413.85	65.61	345.75	70.07	93.15	48.45	19.46	19.43	14.21

Year	v3c7	v3c8	v3c9	v3c10	v3d	v4'	v4	v4a	v4b	v4b1	v4b2	v4c	v4c1	v4c2	v4c3
1952				1.01	153										
1953				1.27	166	108.5	108.5	91.2	129.5	121.3	231.4	137.6	111.5	172.8	
1954				1.74	176	106.4	106.4	100.7	115.4	112.0	137.0	106.4	114.9	84.3	
1955				2.03	177	103.8	103.8	105.9	98.0	99.0	92.8	108.5	101.0	106.7	
1956				2.46	200	115.9	115.9	98.5	137.4	131.3	171.8	122.3	120.8	123.8	
1957				2.81	202	101.1	101.1	82.2	118.4	128.4	75.1	106.0	100.8	103.5	
1958				2.93	243	128.3	128.3	117.2	149.6	147.6	165.8	107.4	121.7	102.7	
1959				3.15	280	118.3	118.3	105.1	129.1	133.0	101.0	112.1	114.0	116.2	
1960				3.71	289	109.3	109.3	76.3	123.9	123.5	127.6	113.4	121.2	113.2	
1961				3.81	213	68.8	68.8	112.5	51.8	52.4	46.8	79.6	77.0	68.4	
1962				4.12	210	97.1	97.1	96.8	96.2	95.3	105.1	99.1	104.2	89.8	
1963				4.52	235	116.2	116.2	115.7	122.5	122.8	119.5	105.3	105.2	91.9	
1964				4.96	246	106.4	106.4	100.7	111.1	110.9	112.2	103.9	97.3	94.1	
1965				5.12	262	113.3	113.3	110.9	119.2	123.0	84.9	103.1	100.6	99.4	
1966				4.98	277	108.3	108.3	105.6	110.7	112.7	84.3	106.0	120.1	108.8	
1967				5.54	257	92.6	92.6	108.6	83.3	83.6	78.8	96.1	81.4	78.0	
1968				5.90	240	97.5	97.5	97.2	96.3	97.2	79.6	100.6	92.0	91.9	
1969				5.91	250	108.4	108.4	83.3	125.6	125.3	132.4	107.0	108.7	129.8	
1970				5.78	303	126.9	126.9	131.0	126.3	126.5	122.5	123.7	156.6	136.7	
1971				5.93	319	108.6	108.6	103.6	113.0	113.5	103.9	106.6	109.4	113.4	
1972				6.32	286	91.0	91.0	76.2	97.9	97.3	111.3	97.8	101.0	74.5	
1973				6.43	316	113.0	113.0	136.6	104.2	103.6	115.5	104.9	108.5	109.7	
1974				6.95	319	102.3	102.3	101.7	102.5	102.3	106.4	102.9	98.8	93.5	
1975				7.02	350	112.8	112.8	98.0	125.9	126.8	111.5	103.8	114.6	96.5	
1976				7.48	321	93.5	93.5	78.1	98.1	98.0	100.0	103.7	97.5	104.6	
1977				7.97	343	107.1	107.1	116.4	103.5	103.6	103.0	106.5	109.9	103.0	
1978	2.07	0.18	0.94	0.01	381	112.8	112.8	119.7	111.6	110.9	123.4	107.2	114.9	126.8	
1979	2.25	0.20	1.19	0.05	417	105.6	105.6	92.0	110.6	106.5	177.5	110.3	115.0	95.5	109.4
1980	2.86	0.24	1.21	0.11	445	106.5	106.5	98.8	108.1	108.5	103.7	111.0	109.6	102.8	113.8
1981	3.07	0.26	1.22	0.17	496	105.8	105.8	114.7	101.9	102.1	99.6	104.2	77.1	135.2	126.7
1982	3.48	0.27	1.26	0.24	538	107.7	107.7	111.8	104.5	103.6	114.5	110.1	119.9	83.7	155.3
1983	3.64	0.33	1.81	0.30	658	121.7	121.7	147.4	107.0	106.9	107.7	119.4	111.4	178.3	114.1
1984	4.21	0.37	2.27	0.35	760	112.5	112.5	104.3	117.6	117.0	123.2	116.7	115.2	118.0	121.2
1985	5.27	0.41	2.94	0.40	868	106.8	106.8	87.6	112.8	110.7	131.7	126.9	112.9	170.6	133.8
1986	5.50	0.46	3.88	0.42	977	107.3	107.3	104.3	103.9	104.4	100.0	118.3	131.7	124.3	114.1
1987	6.75	0.58	5.01	0.51	1269	118.8	118.8	115.3	118.8	119.7	111.6	122.7	138.2	106.1	147.6
1988	9.19	1.05	6.39	0.72	1559	115.9	115.9	103.4	121.1	123.9	96.3	119.4	114.9	133.4	116.0
1989	10.74	1.24	8.02	1.04	1636	97.5	97.5	82.8	96.0	97.8	76.0	113.4	107.9	119.2	114.9
1990	11.55	1.92	9.16	1.38	1746	103.4	103.4	136.7	97.9	97.5	103.0	90.7	106.7	56.4	99.0
1991	12.36	3.34	11.85	1.52	1878	106.0	106.0	100.0	105.8	105.5	108.6	113.0	111.6	120.6	109.0
1992	14.24	4.24	13.67	1.92	2246	112.2	112.2	101.8	118.2	117.4	125.1	114.0	116.7	121.1	109.2
1993	18.27	7.38	17.61	2.18	2868	112.8	112.8	107.7	117.3	117.0	119.7	110.6	117.2	112.7	94.2
1994	22.76	13.53	22.91	2.97	3703	114.3	114.3	110.0	115.6	118.3	94.5	115.9	119.5	121.0	109.2
1995	28.70	17.73	30.46	4.09	4414	109.8	109.7	105.0	111.6	111.7	110.6	111.1	115.3	112.3	96.5

Year	v4c4	v4c5	v4c6	v4c7	v4c8	v4c9	v4c10	v5	v5a	v5a1	v5a1a	v5a1b	v5a2	v5b	v5b1
1952								16.55	11.76	11.25	7.18	4.07	0.51	3.91	1.87
1953								18.97	14.54	13.98	8.25	5.73	0.56	5.12	3.22
1954								20.43	14.68	14.11	8.08	6.03	0.57	8.63	5.39
1955								21.13	15.05	14.47	8.24	6.23	0.58	7.10	5.57
1956								24.58	17.04	16.38	9.53	6.85	0.66	6.52	6.47
1957								25.22	16.22	15.44	7.84	7.60	0.78	6.40	4.28
1958								31.18	17.10	16.22	7.89	8.33	0.88	10.65	8.37
1959								37.15	19.72	18.77	8.23	10.54	0.95	13.68	10.74
1960								41.83	20.94	19.80	7.45	12.35	1.14	11.94	11.09
1961								31.89	22.45	21.64	8.58	13.06	0.81	7.82	5.11
1962								31.35	22.90	22.15	9.59	12.56	0.75	3.76	3.92
1963								35.94	26.16	25.21	10.79	14.42	0.95	7.39	5.24
1964								38.45	27.23	26.01	11.07	14.94	1.22	7.34	7.01
1965								42.93	28.88	27.86	12.77	15.09	1.02	9.82	7.50
1966								46.67	30.95	29.71	13.65	16.06	1.24	9.59	6.94
1967								44.25	32.44	30.93	14.96	15.97	1.51	8.40	5.36
1968								42.49	32.06	30.28	14.65	15.63	1.78	8.74	5.27
1969								45.18	35.42	33.31	16.07	17.24	2.11	10.42	6.46
1970								56.07	39.88	37.40	18.19	19.21	2.48	13.41	8.88
1971								60.90	40.45	37.84	17.97	19.87	2.61	16.48	11.64
1972								56.02	40.08	37.20	16.24	20.96	2.88	17.17	11.59
1973								63.33	41.76	38.94	16.83	22.11	2.82	19.34	13.39
1974								65.11	43.58	39.74	17.09	22.65	3.84	20.37	13.68
1975								72.31	47.37	43.02	19.51	23.51	4.35	24.86	15.44
1976								67.32	50.69	45.88	20.73	25.15	4.81	17.48	12.43
1977								72.91	54.51	49.53	22.76	26.77	4.98	19.03	11.74
1978								81.98	57.91	53.02	24.47	28.55	4.89	32.77	18.16
1979	101.3	126.9	107.7	108.8	117.7	125.5	500.0	91.12	69.54	61.86	29.85	32.01	7.68	26.68	19.54
1980	100.7	86.1	115.7	120.7	110.0	95.8	180.0	98.59	76.92	67.76	31.84	35.92	9.16	28.96	20.80
1981	102.4	115.9	103.4	104.2	104.2	103.3	154.5	111.16	85.12	75.13	36.41	38.72	9.99	28.02	20.98
1982	100.6	100.9	113.2	110.0	104.0	95.2	141.2	121.67	94.77	83.49	39.76	43.73	11.28	35.65	27.67
1983	100.6	100.9	101.9	101.8	119.2	139.2	120.8	150.14	112.22	96.66	49.28	47.38	15.56	38.59	29.33
1984	140.7	104.8	101.9	111.0	106.5	120.4	113.8	174.39	131.64	111.76	55.81	55.95	19.88	57.17	40.93
1985	103.3	98.3	114.0	112.6	103.0	113.4	106.1	200.44	145.02	120.53	56.42	64.11	24.49	81.15	62.38
1986	111.6	109.7	101.6	101.4	105.9	117.1	102.9	227.15	165.27	137.86	61.35	76.51	27.41	86.83	63.40
1987	112.9	126.2	128.2	108.0	111.1	112.7	102.8	297.49	196.18	161.49	69.36	92.13	34.69	111.93	76.70
1988	98.7	106.4	122.6	119.1	157.5	112.3	116.2	368.67	242.39	203.47	83.21	120.26	38.92	134.61	92.85
1989	101.3	113.2	123.1	106.0	119.1	112.7	130.2	391.65	266.94	223.29	91.47	131.82	43.65	148.26	81.73
1990	103.5	106.8	107.5	106.9	118.7	127.6	130.4	425.28	279.73	232.73	95.86	136.87	47.00	182.57	93.97
1991	104.2	103.0	106.2	101.9	293.8	117.8	107.2	463.47	308.40	255.85	101.03	154.82	52.55	193.05	117.43
1992	119.0	109.5	109.7	107.4	115.2	110.1	122.3	558.06	364.56	306.32	111.67	194.65	58.24	213.10	152.57
1993	111.7	113.4	117.1	116.5	163.6	109.1	96.1	717.95	436.06	364.91	125.93	238.98	71.15	287.05	252.94
1994	113.6	118.4	111.4	107.9	114.0	115.3	121.3	944.44	577.59	473.63	156.13	317.50	103.96	389.93	320.45
1995	114.8	121.7	117.4	110.4	113.6	114.6	118.5	1124.00	703.38	586.17	191.08	395.09	117.21	451.02	358.14

Year	v5b2	v5c	v5c1	v5c2	v6a1	v6a2	v6a3	v6a4	v6b2	v6b3	v6b4	v7	v7a	v7a1	v7a2
1952	2.04	0.88	4.11	3.23											
1953	1.90	-0.69	4.74	5.43								116.5	116.7	108.1	134.4
1954	3.24	-2.88	5.98	8.86								98.9	98.8	94.8	105.5
1955	1.53	-1.02	7.53	8.55								100.1	100.0	99.1	101.4
1956	0.05	1.02	9.24	8.22								110.5	110.5	110.0	111.3
1957	2.12	2.60	10.25	7.65								93.2	91.6	78.3	110.6
1958	2.29	3.42	11.63	8.21								109.3	109.1	108.7	109.6
1959	2.94	3.75	13.24	9.49								114.4	114.6	103.8	124.8
1960	0.85	8.95	15.47	6.52								98.5	97.5	83.2	108.8
1961	2.71	1.62	13.48	11.86								88.2	89.4	96.2	85.3
1962	-0.16	4.69	14.24	9.55								102.1	103.0	110.7	97.8
1963	2.15	2.39	16.67	14.28								113.5	113.3	113.5	113.2
1964	0.33	3.88	18.41	14.53								112.7	111.6	109.0	113.6
1965	2.32	4.23	21.35	17.12								103.6	104.7	111.6	99.7
1966	2.65	6.13	23.14	17.01								109.6	108.9	110.8	107.3
1967	3.04	3.41	23.45	20.04								102.5	101.7	105.9	98.1
1968	3.47	1.69	25.38	23.69								98.9	97.9	96.1	99.6
1969	3.96	-0.66	26.53	27.19								113.8	113.5	115.2	112.0
1970	4.53	2.78	27.66	24.88								113.8	113.7	105.0	121.6
1971	4.84	3.97	28.32	24.35								101.5	101.3	98.8	103.2
1972	5.58	-1.23	28.95	30.18								102.4	101.7	97.8	105.2
1973	5.95	2.23	29.87	27.64								103.5	103.9	102.5	105.2
1974	6.69	1.16	30.65	29.49								104.9	104.2	103.0	105.2
1975	9.42	0.08	31.22	31.14								105.8	104.4	103.1	105.5
1976	5.05	-0.85	34.33	35.18								100.5	100.3	99.1	101.2
1977	7.29	-0.63	39.72	40.35								107.6	107.8	109.9	106.3
1978	14.61	-8.70	40.02	48.72	13.54	9.56	0.55	0.82	26.74	1.08	0.73	106.7	107.9	110.0	106.2
1979	7.14	-5.10	51.38	56.48	16.78	11.54	0.66	0.87	29.76	1.20	1.05	111.3	109.3	110.7	108.1
1980	8.16	-7.29	61.31	68.60	14.38	15.74	0.79	0.93	33.58	1.34	1.00	109.3	109.3	106.1	112.0
1981	7.04	-1.98	76.21	78.19	14.25	20.29	0.86	1.01	36.42	1.31	0.99	107.8	107.4	107.6	107.2
1982	7.98	-8.75	80.80	89.55	16.17	21.48	0.97	1.14	41.16	1.47	1.10	110.6	109.7	110.0	109.4
1983	9.26	-0.67	91.95	92.62	18.89	27.74	0.92	1.73	43.87	2.35	1.16	112.3	110.1	119.6	101.3
1984	16.24	-14.42	95.87	110.29	21.32	31.39	1.02	2.08	51.86	2.40	1.69	114.6	113.0	112.9	113.2
1985	18.77	-25.73	115.54	141.27	18.63	33.66	1.57	2.56	59.46	2.93	1.72	104.6	102.8	96.7	109.5
1986	23.43	-24.95	117.34	142.29	18.83	37.61	2.10	2.81	69.46	4.72	2.33	107.3	105.8	100.8	110.6
1987	35.23	-10.62	99.47	110.09	20.37	42.74	2.58	3.67	83.10	6.45	2.58	109.8	109.2	108.8	109.5
1988	41.76	-8.33	118.94	127.27	22.10	54.12	3.09	3.90	109.09	8.11	3.06	106.3	104.7	101.2	107.8
1989	66.53	-23.55	130.27	153.82	23.42	59.14	3.98	4.93	119.44	9.31	3.07	94.3	93.8	91.3	96.0
1990	88.70	-37.12	140.69	177.81	25.35	59.72	5.06	5.73	123.67	9.99	3.21	101.3	100.8	98.4	102.8
1991	75.62	-37.98	147.74	185.72	24.97	63.70	5.85	6.51	140.10	11.17	3.55	104.3	104.1	99.4	107.4
1992	60.53	-19.60	175.37	194.97	26.71	70.24	7.21	7.51	169.85	19.17	5.63	106.4	106.8	103.0	109.3
1993	34.11	-5.16	228.80	233.96	26.35	81.59	9.60	8.39	207.78	24.07	7.13	107.2	106.5	103.1	108.6
1994	69.48	-23.08	275.25	298.33	29.67	91.05	18.48	16.93	259.33	38.80	19.37	115.0	112.9	107.4	115.9
1995	92.88	-30.40	290.52	320.92	39.36	103.38	26.51	21.83	323.64	48.48	22.97	107.9	109.1	107.6	109.9

Year	v7b	v8	v8a	v8b	v9	v9a	v9b	v10a1	v10a2	v10a3	v10a3a	v10a3b	v10a4	v10b1	v10b2
1952		104	86	165											
1953	109.8	123	100	180	110.4	110.0	103.6								
1954	101.8	121	96	186	96.9	92.7	104.1								
1955	101.8	121	97	181	97.6	97.1	95.5								
1956	110.3	133	108	195	107.5	107.1	108.8								
1957	132.8	123	90	201	89.9	79.3	102.7								
1958	112.8	127	90	207	106.7	108.4	103.0								
1959	110.2	142	93	237	110.2	103.3	113.0								
1960	117.5	136	81	233	89.3	79.6	91.0								
1961	69.3	145	91	246	86.4	93.2	82.2								
1962	82.3	149	100	237	103.7	110.1	101.7								
1963	118.5	165	109	269	110.7	109.2	112.4								
1964	140.3	167	108	280	108.9	104.8	114.0								
1965	81.5	171	120	266	100.0	108.1	93.4								
1966	127.3	176	120	296	105.9	103.2	112.7								
1967	120.5	180	128	288	99.3	104.1	95.8								
1968	117.0	172	123	275	95.8	94.1	97.0								
1969	117.1	184	129	303	110.3	110.5	112.1								
1970	115.1	202	143	334	111.3	101.9	120.4								
1971	105.2	199	136	338	98.8	95.3	101.0								
1972	111.6	190	120	345	99.0	95.6	101.8								
1973	97.6	194	122	354	101.0	100.0	102.3								
1974	115.2	194	134	329	102.5	101.6	103.7								
1975	123.7	208	142	355	103.5	102.3	103.9								
1976	103.0	219	143	389	98.6	97.0	100.8								
1977	104.8	233	155	409	106.8	108.5	105.0								
1978	94.0	246	165	427	106.3	108.5	104.0	15.60	1.85	0.71	0.44	0.27		8.72	1.61
1979	135.8	283	203	449	107.7	111.8	101.4	17.21	1.56	0.77	0.51	0.26		6.92	0.42
1980	109.4	305	214	491	107.5	105.3	109.0	17.58	1.94	1.28	0.59	0.69		4.10	1.26
1981	111.7	335	245	513	106.3	107.2	103.9	17.05	2.26	1.67	0.68	0.99		3.39	1.27
1982	118.9	369	267	564	108.9	110.1	106.5	22.21	2.41	3.05	0.80	2.25		4.11	1.46
1983	130.0	424	331	599	109.3	119.5	99.3	21.99	3.39	3.95	1.26	2.69		4.87	1.44
1984	125.2	487	376	691	112.3	113.1	110.7	25.50	2.16	13.27	1.48	11.79		13.64	2.60
1985	115.9	522	384	765	102.3	97.7	105.8	37.58	4.43	20.37	2.14	18.23		12.33	4.60
1986	115.5	593	420	884	104.9	101.5	107.0	42.12	4.33	16.95	2.76	14.19		16.18	3.41
1987	113.1	689	476	1038	108.3	109.1	106.7	53.66	6.37	16.67	3.43	13.24		21.10	6.10
1988	114.0	860	573	1316	103.7	101.6	104.8	67.58	7.30	17.97	4.66	13.31		27.86	11.27
1989	96.2	933	628	1405	92.8	91.0	93.6	59.20	4.84	17.69	4.44	13.25		45.33	15.50
1990	102.8	955	649	1427	99.0	96.9	100.4	67.38	2.84	23.75	4.07	19.68		79.30	10.97
1991	105.3	1037	678	1585	102.8	98.5	105.5	88.81	5.17	23.45	3.90	19.55		28.47	10.96
1992	104.3	1233	749	1958	106.0	103.0	107.4	122.87	12.46	17.24	3.08	14.16		29.83	18.71
1993	110.7	1458	850	2341	105.8	103.8	105.8	189.78	26.37	22.56	9.80	12.76	14.23	11.75	8.99
1994	125.5	1872	1062	2995	111.7	108.3	111.6	251.07	26.69	27.28	12.35	14.93	15.41	31.36	21.63
1995	102.2	2292	1291	3665	108.0	106.9	108.0	275.65	25.40	40.85	10.55	30.30	16.24	42.25	18.20

Year	v10b4	v11a	v11a1	v11a2	v11b	v11b1	v11b2	v11c	v11c1	v11c2	v12	v12a	v12b	v13	v13i
1952															
1953											123.6	173.2	80.1		
1954											170.7	165.3	180.9		
1955											86.8	108.3	49.5		
1956											102.7	128.7	3.9		
1957											83.5	56.9	3281.9		
1958											170.0	192.1	119.4		
1959											130.0	128.0	136.9		
1960											85.5	100.3	34.2		
1961											57.9	57.5	245.0		
1962											51.1	60.0			
1963											193.4	133.2			
1964											97.3	128.6	11.0		
1965											142.0	114.7	1024.8		
1966											96.8	91.6	115.5		
1967											86.7	76.5	115.4		
1968											103.6	97.4	115.4		
1969											119.0	121.1	115.4		
1970											128.4	136.3	115.5		
1971											124.4	132.7	108.1		
1972											104.3	99.7	115.5		
1973											112.8	115.7	106.8		
1974											105.5	102.3	112.6		
1975											122.3	113.2	140.9		
1976											70.6	80.8	53.8		
1977											108.7	94.4	144.3		
1978	4.28	0.64	0.36	0.28	26.19	14.51	11.68	5.94	3.29	2.65	172.1	154.5	200.2	81.98	45.70
1979	-0.20	0.75	0.55	0.20	19.69	14.42	5.27	6.24	4.57	1.67	80.7	106.7	48.4	91.12	48.40
1980	2.80	0.85	0.61	0.24	20.27	14.60	5.67	7.84	5.59	2.25	108.5	106.4	114.3	98.59	52.88
1981	2.38	0.66	0.49	0.17	18.54	13.88	4.66	8.82	6.61	2.21	92.0	94.3	86.3	111.16	61.84
1982	2.41	0.95	0.72	0.23	22.94	17.58	5.36	11.76	9.37	2.39	122.3	129.0	102.1	121.67	68.10
1983	2.95	0.46	0.35	0.11	27.21	20.68	6.53	10.92	8.30	2.62	106.0	104.7	110.9	150.14	91.09
1984		0.58	0.42	0.16	38.42	27.50	10.92	18.17	13.01	5.16	139.6	127.0	184.5	174.39	100.27
1985	1.84	0.73	0.56	0.17	54.53	41.92	12.61	25.89	19.90	5.99	132.8	142.1	109.9	200.44	105.82
1986	3.84	0.52	0.38	0.14	60.94	44.58	16.36	25.37	18.44	6.93	101.6	96.3	118.5	227.15	128.06
1987	8.03	1.00	0.69	0.31	86.68	59.27	27.41	24.25	16.74	7.51	125.0	117.8	143.4	297.49	159.98
1988	2.63	1.42	0.93	0.49	103.80	68.06	35.74	29.39	23.86	5.53	111.0	110.1	112.8	368.67	198.24
1989	5.70	1.50	0.84	0.66	109.84	61.27	48.57	36.92	19.62	17.30	97.0	74.8	142.8	391.65	202.61
1990	-1.57	1.68	0.88	0.80	138.11	72.47	65.64	42.88	20.62	22.26	122.1	113.1	131.7	425.28	253.92
1991	36.19	2.34	1.43	0.91	138.56	84.87	53.69	52.15	31.13	21.02	104.8	123.6	84.8	463.47	273.08
1992	11.99	2.83	2.05	0.78	156.64	113.05	43.59	53.63	37.47	16.16	100.4	115.2	77.4	558.06	286.20
1993	13.37	3.98	3.50	0.48	201.67	177.46	24.21	81.40	71.98	9.42	116.1	144.0	52.2	717.95	389.37
1994	16.49	16.63	7.25	9.38	214.54	169.26	45.28	158.76	143.94	14.82	110.9	104.3	156.6	936.78	572.09
1995	32.43	30.61	7.31	23.30	273.05	212.46	60.59	147.36	138.37	8.99	107.5	104.4	122.0	1129.20	676.53

Year	v13ii	v13iii	v13iv	v13a	v13ai	v13aii	v13aiii	v13aiv	v13b	v13bi	v13bii	v13biii	v13biv	v13b1	v13b1i
1952															
1953															
1954															
1955															
1956															
1957															
1958															
1959															
1960															
1961															
1962															
1963															
1964															
1965															
1966															
1967															
1968															
1969															
1970															
1971															
1972															
1973															
1974															
1975															
1976															
1977															
1978	9.68	11.87	14.73	23.98	18.70	0.61	1.56	3.11	42.96	17.93	5.55	8.45	11.03	40.34	14.90
1979	10.83	13.34	18.55	25.34	19.06	0.84	1.84	3.60	49.22	19.51	6.31	9.52	13.88	44.56	16.21
1980	11.43	14.24	20.04	27.24	21.02	0.79	1.98	3.45	52.24	20.55	6.49	10.17	15.03	47.42	17.15
1981	14.58	14.70	20.04	34.31	27.09	0.88	2.08	4.26	56.53	22.03	9.18	10.43	14.89	51.29	18.35
1982	16.18	18.20	19.19	38.40	31.12	1.00	4.20	2.08	60.36	22.81	10.28	11.77	15.50	54.21	18.56
1983	17.47	19.58	22.00	56.74	50.56	1.49	1.54	3.15	65.38	23.91	10.53	15.01	15.93	58.75	19.06
1984	20.71	24.60	28.81	60.04	53.06	1.58	2.09	3.31	80.46	27.88	12.20	19.58	20.80	72.10	21.83
1985	24.79	32.82	37.01	55.74	42.85	1.42	6.58	4.89	97.21	36.38	14.58	23.01	23.24	85.29	27.59
1986	28.09	31.32	39.68	64.35	56.70	1.60	3.16	2.89	104.30	39.13	15.62	24.01	25.54	91.28	29.57
1987	39.54	39.25	58.72	80.57	72.51	2.08	2.16	3.82	139.36	46.38	23.10	32.10	37.78	123.49	38.83
1988	45.82	52.63	71.98	92.59	81.66	3.07	2.71	5.15	173.57	64.33	26.13	45.13	37.98	155.12	51.49
1989	51.87	50.08	87.09	80.53	69.91	3.06	2.60	4.96	181.02	72.44	29.31	41.92	37.35	164.09	60.83
1990	57.50	56.05	57.81	124.99	106.74	3.40	4.12	10.73	182.15	81.22	32.95	48.78	19.20	163.82	67.80
1991	69.15	62.16	59.08	120.47	104.25	3.61	3.99	8.62	203.02	92.59	40.59	54.73	15.11	181.71	77.32
1992	80.72	56.94	134.20	130.82	110.20	5.60	2.85	12.17	257.01	84.18	46.37	47.56	78.90	227.17	66.08
1993	91.03	82.50	155.05	156.05	136.44	4.94	5.46	9.21	351.99	139.23	49.83	68.86	94.07	308.10	116.12
1994	119.47	97.09	148.13	259.40	220.71	8.36	6.77	23.56	388.83	203.24	60.93	77.39	57.27	354.70	174.89
1995	160.50	135.96	156.21	303.99	261.20	9.40	6.53	26.86	479.46	230.73	82.86	110.98	54.89	413.85	194.50

Year	v13b1ii	v13b1iii	v13b1iv	v13b2	v13b2i	v13b2ii	v13b2iii	v13b2iv	v13c	v13ci	v13cii	v13ciii	v13civ	v13c1
1952														
1953														
1954														
1955														
1956														
1957														
1958														
1959														
1960														
1961														
1962														
1963														
1964														
1965														
1966														
1967														
1968														
1969														
1970														
1971														
1972														
1973														
1974														
1975														
1976														
1977														
1978	5.22	8.32	11.90	2.62	3.03	0.33	0.13	-0.87	15.04	9.07	3.52	1.86	0.59	4.46
1979	5.77	9.30	13.28	4.66	3.30	0.54	0.22	0.60	16.56	9.83	3.68	1.98	1.07	5.13
1980	5.93	9.94	14.40	4.82	3.40	0.56	0.23	0.63	19.11	11.31	4.15	2.09	1.56	5.62
1981	8.55	10.19	14.20	5.24	3.68	0.63	0.24	0.69	20.32	12.72	4.52	2.19	0.89	4.33
1982	9.53	11.45	14.67	6.15	4.25	0.75	0.32	0.83	22.91	14.17	4.90	2.23	1.61	5.19
1983	9.75	14.68	15.26	6.63	4.85	0.78	0.33	0.67	28.02	16.62	5.45	3.03	2.92	5.78
1984	11.12	19.19	19.96	8.36	6.05	1.08	0.39	0.84	33.89	19.33	6.93	2.93	4.70	6.75
1985	13.23	21.81	22.66	11.92	8.79	1.35	1.20	0.58	47.49	26.59	8.79	3.23	8.88	8.25
1986	14.13	23.34	24.24	13.02	9.56	1.49	0.67	1.30	58.50	32.23	10.87	4.15	11.25	10.89
1987	21.02	31.21	32.43	15.87	7.55	2.08	0.89	5.35	77.56	41.09	14.36	4.99	17.12	15.15
1988	23.94	43.75	35.94	18.45	12.84	2.19	1.38	2.04	102.51	52.25	16.62	4.79	28.85	18.56
1989	27.02	40.55	35.69	16.93	11.61	2.29	1.37	1.66	130.10	60.26	19.50	5.56	44.78	22.18
1990	31.04	47.07	17.91	18.33	13.42	1.91	1.71	1.29	118.14	65.96	21.15	3.15	27.88	21.11
1991	38.44	52.59	13.36	21.31	15.27	2.15	2.14	1.75	139.98	76.24	24.95	3.44	35.35	25.19
1992	43.24	45.02	72.83	29.84	18.10	3.13	2.54	6.07	170.23	91.82	28.75	6.53	43.13	30.17
1993	46.56	63.35	82.07	43.89	23.11	3.27	5.51	12.00	209.91	113.70	36.26	8.18	51.77	39.98
1994	57.33	71.60	50.88	44.13	28.35	3.60	5.79	6.39	278.55	148.14	50.18	12.93	67.30	54.47
1995	77.46	102.47	39.42	65.61	36.23	5.40	8.51	15.47	345.75	184.60	68.24	18.45	74.46	70.07

Year	v13c1i	v13c1ii	v13c1iii	v13c1iv	v13c2	v13c2i	v13c2ii	v13c2iii	v13c2iv	v13c3	v13c3i	v13c3ii	v13c3iii	v13c3iv
1952														
1953														
1954														
1955														
1956														
1957														
1958														
1959														
1960														
1961														
1962														
1963														
1964														
1965														
1966														
1967														
1968														
1969														
1970														
1971														
1972														
1973														
1974														
1975														
1976														
1977														
1978	1.23	0.63	0.85	1.75	2.69	3.34	0.64	0.93	-2.22	1.41	0.23	0.08		1.10
1979	1.27	0.69	0.85	2.32	2.56	3.41	0.56	0.95	-2.36	1.54	0.30	0.10		1.14
1980	1.33	0.75	0.94	2.60	2.78	3.49	0.65	0.97	-2.33	1.85	0.46	0.11		1.28
1981	1.57	0.84	0.73	1.19	3.88	4.10	0.68	1.21	-2.11	2.42	0.52	0.12		1.78
1982	1.88	1.00	0.88	1.43	3.34	4.12	0.72	1.27	-2.77	3.86	0.86	0.14		2.86
1983	2.41	1.11	0.98	1.28	6.13	5.25	0.99	1.29	-1.40	4.54	0.88	0.15	0.52	2.99
1984	2.88	1.32	1.06	1.49	7.54	6.06	1.09	0.86	-0.47	5.74	1.18	0.16	0.75	3.65
1985	4.52	1.61	0.79	1.33	13.95	9.08	1.95	1.02	1.90	8.69	1.71	0.22	1.15	5.61
1986	5.80	2.28	0.76	2.05	18.28	10.99	2.38	1.85	3.06	10.02	2.50	0.24	1.20	6.08
1987	8.47	3.64	0.60	2.44	21.01	13.22	2.49	1.70	3.60	16.80	2.87	0.81	2.45	10.67
1988	10.31	4.76	0.35	3.14	29.98	18.13	2.72	0.86	8.27	22.30	2.97	0.91	2.83	15.59
1989	12.36	5.72	0.48	3.62	39.47	20.35	3.39	1.02	14.71	29.23	3.04	0.96	2.96	22.27
1990	13.34	6.02	-0.87	2.62	25.47	22.22	3.68	-0.45	0.02	28.56	3.16	1.16	3.04	21.20
1991	14.39	7.57	-0.16	3.39	32.26	25.99	4.21	-1.00	3.06	32.68	3.49	1.30	3.29	24.60
1992	16.99	8.50	0.14	4.54	41.63	31.48	4.88	0.69	4.58	38.55	4.76	1.66	3.98	28.15
1993	19.78	10.78	0.32	9.10	52.81	39.62	6.02	0.92	6.25	40.02	5.88	2.08	3.55	28.51
1994	23.09	16.24	1.00	14.14	72.61	51.95	8.91	1.27	10.48	50.02	6.79	2.63	5.83	34.77
1995	30.48	22.33	2.14	15.12	93.15	59.11	12.94	1.76	19.34	48.45	8.37	3.02	7.54	29.52

Year	v13c4	v13c4i	v13c4ii	v13c4iii	v13c4iv	v13c5	v13c5i	v13c5ii	v13c5iii	v13c5iv	v13c6	v13c6i	v13c6ii	v13c6iii
1952														
1953														
1954														
1955														
1956														
1957														
1958														
1959														
1960														
1961														
1962														
1963														
1964														
1965														
1966														
1967														
1968														
1969														
1970														
1971														
1972														
1973														
1974														
1975														
1976														
1977														
1978	1.52	0.11	1.41			1.10	0.73	0.33	0.08	-0.04	0.66	0.61	0.05	
1979	1.54	0.12	1.42			1.39	0.82	0.42	0.18	-0.03	0.71	0.65	0.06	
1980	1.64	0.15	1.49			1.93	1.22	0.52	0.18	0.01	0.87	0.80	0.07	
1981	1.73	0.16	1.57			2.31	1.40	0.63	0.25	0.03	0.93	0.85	0.08	
1982	1.80	0.20	1.60			2.39	1.55	0.67	0.08	0.09	1.08	0.99	0.09	
1983	1.86	0.23	1.63			2.49	1.52	0.68	0.24	0.05	1.14	1.05	0.09	
1984	2.73	0.26	2.47			2.72	1.68	0.75	0.26	0.03	1.21	1.11	0.10	
1985	3.06	0.29	2.77			2.90	1.82	0.77	0.27	0.04	1.62	1.49	0.13	
1986	3.59	0.31	3.28			3.61	2.22	0.99	0.34	0.06	1.85	1.70	0.15	
1987	4.61	0.42	4.29	0.02	-0.12	4.81	3.07	1.07	0.20	0.47	2.33	2.15	0.18	
1988	5.21	0.42	4.49	0.06	0.24	5.85	3.46	1.25	0.51	0.63	3.26	2.82	0.24	0.02
1989	6.03	0.57	4.85	0.20	0.41	7.56	3.86	0.78	0.53	2.39	4.59	3.95	0.37	0.05
1990	6.15	0.60	4.97	0.24	0.34	7.97	3.92	0.76	0.87	2.42	4.87	4.19	0.59	0.07
1991	6.73	0.87	5.22	0.27	0.37	8.62	4.55	1.00	0.67	2.40	5.43	4.78	0.67	0.02
1992	8.64	1.30	6.04	0.49	0.81	10.78	5.63	1.34	0.89	2.92	6.39	5.68	0.81	0.03
1993	10.65	1.23	7.45	1.10	0.87	12.71	6.05	1.61	1.17	3.88	8.30	6.95	1.05	0.04
1994	14.72	1.75	9.99	1.63	1.35	13.97	5.82	2.00	1.91	4.24	10.59	8.81	1.42	0.05
1995	19.46	2.37	12.93	2.44	1.72	19.43	8.58	3.12	2.42	5.31	14.21	11.28	2.20	0.20

Year	v13c6iv	v13c7	v13c7i	v13c7ii	v13c7iii	v13c7iv	v13c8	v13c8i	v13c8ii	v13c8iii	v13c8iv	v13c9	v13c9i	v13c9ii
1952														
1953														
1954														
1955														
1956														
1957														
1958														
1959														
1960														
1961														
1962														
1963														
1964														
1965														
1966														
1967														
1968														
1969														
1970														
1971														
1972														
1973														
1974														
1975														
1976														
1977														
1978		2.07	1.78	0.29			0.18	0.16	0.02			0.94	0.87	0.07
1979		2.25	1.93	0.32			0.20	0.18	0.02			1.19	1.11	0.08
1980		2.86	2.46	0.40			0.24	0.21	0.03			1.21	1.11	0.10
1981		3.07	2.63	0.44			0.26	0.23	0.03			1.22	1.14	0.08
1982		3.48	2.98	0.50			0.27	0.24	0.03			1.26	1.18	0.08
1983		3.64	3.12	0.52			0.33	0.29	0.04			1.81	1.64	0.17
1984		4.21	3.61	0.60			0.37	0.33	0.04			2.27	1.95	0.32
1985		5.27	4.52	0.75			0.41	0.36	0.05			2.94	2.49	0.45
1986		5.50	4.72	0.78			0.46	0.40	0.06			3.88	3.26	0.62
1987		6.75	5.73	0.94	0.02	0.06	0.58	0.52	0.06			5.01	4.25	0.76
1988	0.18	9.19	8.02	1.04	0.02	0.11	1.05	0.79	0.16	0.06	0.04	6.39	4.36	0.93
1989	0.22	10.74	8.58	1.77	0.12	0.27	1.24	0.94	0.16	0.10	0.04	8.02	6.09	1.35
1990	0.02	11.55	9.27	1.87	0.13	0.28	1.92	1.56	0.30	0.05	0.01	9.16	6.99	1.60
1991	-0.04	12.36	9.76	2.09	0.14	0.37	3.34	2.19	0.89	0.13	0.13	11.85	9.45	1.77
1992	-0.13	14.24	11.33	2.27	0.15	0.49	4.24	2.69	1.02	0.23	0.30	13.67	10.99	1.96
1993	0.26	18.27	14.50	2.91	0.19	0.67	7.38	4.54	1.50	0.85	0.49	17.61	14.05	2.53
1994	0.31	22.76	19.14	3.11	0.10	0.41	13.53	9.42	2.30	0.89	0.92	22.91	19.77	3.14
1995	0.53	28.70	23.69	3.98	0.30	0.73	17.73	11.98	2.99	1.31	1.45	30.46	26.14	4.02

Year	v13c9iii	v13c9iv	v13c10	v13c10i	v13c10ii	v13c10iii	v13c10iv
1952							
1953							
1954							
1955							
1956							
1957							
1958							
1959							
1960							
1961							
1962							
1963							
1964							
1965							
1966							
1967							
1968							
1969							
1970							
1971							
1972							
1973							
1974							
1975							
1976							
1977							
1978			0.01	0.01			
1979			0.05	0.04	0.01		
1980			0.11	0.08	0.03		
1981			0.17	0.12	0.05		
1982			0.24	0.17	0.07		
1983			0.30	0.23	0.07		
1984			0.35	0.27	0.08		
1985			0.40	0.31	0.09		
1986			0.42	0.33	0.09		
1987			0.51	0.39	0.12		
1988	0.06	0.54	0.72	0.47	0.12	0.02	0.11
1989	0.01	0.57	1.04	0.52	0.15	0.09	0.28
1990	-0.05	0.62	1.38	0.71	0.20	0.12	0.35
1991	-0.06	0.69	1.52	0.77	0.23	0.14	0.38
1992	-0.24	0.96	1.92	0.97	0.27	0.17	0.51
1993	-0.17	1.20	2.18	1.10	0.33	0.21	0.54
1994			2.97	1.60	0.44	0.25	
1995			4.09	2.30	0.71	0.34	0.74

8

Heilongjiang

Year	v1	v1a	v1b	v1b1	v1b2	v1c	v1c1	v1c2	v1c3	v2	v2a	v2b	v2b1	v2b2	v2c
1952	44.05	16.37	21.30	17.88	3.42	6.38	1.78	3.36	1.24	122.3	115.8	144.1	149.6	121.2	113.6
1953	57.15	18.28	29.10	25.10	4.00	9.77	2.94	4.85	1.98	110.3	93.1	135.0	132.3	148.5	139.3
1954	63.16	20.25	32.83	28.23	4.60	10.08	2.92	4.79	2.37	105.4	103.2	109.4	109.0	111.5	103.2
1955	64.70	22.42	31.51	26.87	4.64	10.77	3.23	5.10	2.44	104.7	108.3	99.7	99.3	101.8	104.9
1956	74.30	24.42	36.64	31.33	5.31	13.24	3.59	5.85	3.80	110.7	96.2	125.7	127.8	116.7	126.7
1957	77.54	23.89	39.47	35.03	4.44	14.18	3.87	6.31	4.00	102.3	95.0	108.3	113.0	86.2	108.0
1958	111.82	22.95	72.74	61.81	10.93	16.13	5.20	7.36	3.57	152.5	132.6	187.1	174.5	265.7	118.1
1959	144.76	22.84	100.12	89.68	10.44	21.80	7.10	9.19	5.51	119.2	96.0	132.1	141.6	93.1	133.0
1960	163.25	17.91	121.04	107.33	13.71	24.30	8.41	8.41	7.48	105.5	76.8	119.1	117.5	128.9	110.2
1961	108.46	18.59	67.77	62.18	5.59	22.10	7.32	7.92	6.86	56.9	83.9	44.6	46.7	32.8	70.0
1962	95.99	22.35	54.01	49.69	4.32	19.63	6.78	7.02	5.83	94.5	102.6	91.7	91.8	91.0	88.5
1963	104.99	24.01	62.75	55.47	7.28	18.23	5.52	5.59	7.12	118.5	117.5	118.0	111.6	170.8	121.6
1964	123.86	23.42	78.92	69.91	9.01	21.52	6.41	7.76	7.35	113.7	112.8	117.7	118.7	112.4	105.0
1965	147.48	24.93	98.07	88.54	9.53	24.48	7.85	8.86	7.77	116.0	105.7	123.4	126.5	107.1	114.0
1966	178.52	32.36	120.00	108.35	11.65	26.16	8.23	10.27	7.66	122.7	131.3	122.6	122.4	124.2	107.7
1967	168.78	36.30	107.87	97.39	10.48	24.61	7.55	9.65	7.41	96.9	112.2	89.2	89.8	85.2	90.9
1968	162.17	34.94	103.69	93.62	10.07	23.54	7.25	8.97	7.32	96.2	96.4	96.1	96.0	96.4	96.0
1969	183.51	33.71	121.47	108.70	12.77	28.33	9.19	9.93	9.21	115.6	96.9	127.7	126.9	133.5	123.8
1970	215.88	34.97	151.48	136.84	14.64	29.43	10.03	10.63	8.77	115.5	111.0	121.4	122.4	115.1	103.5
1971	227.39	50.38	145.86	130.56	15.30	31.15	10.91	10.58	9.66	102.4	100.6	103.0	103.1	102.1	104.2
1972	225.59	42.99	151.31	137.07	14.24	31.29	10.34	10.01	10.94	98.0	85.5	103.6	105.0	93.8	102.0
1973	241.34	47.10	161.77	147.70	14.07	32.47	10.21	10.09	12.17	107.4	109.5	107.0	107.8	100.4	105.1
1974	260.58	51.03	173.44	158.33	15.11	36.11	10.91	10.93	14.27	108.2	108.7	107.1	107.1	107.2	111.7
1975	286.30	56.35	193.97	176.06	17.91	35.98	10.60	10.18	15.20	109.9	110.3	112.1	111.2	119.3	100.5
1976	286.51	48.30	201.52	186.60	14.92	36.69	10.73	11.45	14.51	99.8	87.0	103.9	106.0	87.4	107.3
1977	304.76	49.33	217.14	202.09	15.05	38.29	10.83	12.21	15.25	104.9	101.2	107.5	108.5	97.8	99.6
1978	337.16	60.90	232.85	212.14	20.71	43.41	12.44	11.04	19.93	113.3	120.6	111.2	108.6	138.3	111.5
1979	369.18	69.93	254.53	230.74	23.79	44.72	13.09	12.02	19.61	105.0	100.3	107.5	106.6	115.1	101.5
1980	409.26	85.61	271.90	244.17	27.73	51.75	16.15	13.59	22.01	107.5	108.8	106.8	105.5	116.5	108.8
1981	437.09	87.01	289.97	254.19	35.78	60.11	19.46	17.18	23.47	105.4	98.2	106.9	103.7	129.5	111.0
1982	486.30	94.34	319.18	273.77	45.41	72.78	21.85	23.78	27.15	108.4	104.6	109.3	106.9	122.5	110.1
1983	542.78	106.88	354.07	305.90	48.17	81.83	23.32	26.12	32.39	108.8	116.2	106.7	107.8	101.2	107.8
1984	608.93	121.54	392.77	336.55	56.22	94.62	24.61	27.21	42.80	109.8	109.4	110.4	110.1	111.7	107.9
1985	705.89	114.31	464.07	391.95	72.12	127.51	31.79	34.98	60.74	105.6	92.4	108.3	110.9	95.1	114.0
1986	839.82	137.18	545.03	468.58	76.45	157.61	36.21	40.99	80.41	108.8	113.4	107.5	107.9	105.3	108.7
1987	984.73	137.00	650.13	563.97	86.16	197.60	42.91	55.72	98.97	108.5	97.4	110.3	111.0	106.2	115.5
1988	1233.63	151.72	793.57	686.04	107.53	288.34	58.36	92.27	137.71	112.5	104.5	113.5	114.5	107.3	117.5
1989	1451.81	162.18	923.28	804.77	118.51	366.35	68.21	117.62	180.52	103.5	96.1	104.8	106.1	96.3	105.3
1990	1650.97	245.38	980.70	863.51	117.19	424.89	76.93	139.17	208.79	105.1	125.1	101.9	101.8	102.5	99.5
1991	1855.77	247.71	1124.99	983.73	141.26	483.07	89.24	163.73	230.10	105.9	100.9	105.7	105.1	110.5	112.8
1992	2157.48	285.20	1291.02	1103.10	187.92	581.26	100.92	201.18	279.16	106.7	108.3	107.8	106.2	118.8	100.4
1993	2656.44	330.59	1621.60	1394.35	227.25	704.25	114.80	235.11	354.34	107.2	102.4	107.2	106.6	111.1	112.5
1994	3485.84	537.87	2099.12	1814.34	284.78	848.85	138.91	276.88	433.06	113.0	114.7	110.5	109.4	117.5	117.3
1995	4281.90	670.03	2577.72	2236.69	341.03	1034.15	187.74	308.47	537.94	111.4	109.2	111.6	111.5	112.4	112.0

Year	v2c1	v2c2	v3'	v3	v3a	v3b	v3b1	v3b2	v3c	v3c1	v3c2	v3c3	v3c4	v3c5	v3c6
1952	113.3	103.1	26.00	26.00	11.92	7.84	6.96	0.88	6.24	1.64	2.46				
1953	148.9	130.2	31.99	31.99	12.92	10.72	9.30	1.42	8.35	2.11	3.35				
1954	95.3	99.2	36.66	36.66	14.99	13.14	11.53	1.61	8.53	2.12	3.12				
1955	112.0	103.9	38.18	38.18	16.61	12.13	10.55	1.58	9.44	2.29	3.70				
1956	113.2	116.4	42.19	42.19	17.95	13.19	11.35	1.84	11.05	2.53	4.22				
1957	111.1	110.9	44.42	44.42	17.16	14.95	13.36	1.59	12.31	2.72	4.39				
1958	144.5	126.0	61.64	61.64	18.21	29.72	26.87	2.85	13.71	3.46	5.43				
1959	133.2	121.5	73.50	73.50	17.44	38.10	34.74	3.36	17.96	5.33	6.45				
1960	116.4	90.2	80.45	80.45	11.72	48.08	43.62	4.46	20.65	6.49	6.57				
1961	70.3	75.7	54.17	54.17	10.88	25.45	23.34	2.11	17.84	4.73	5.01				
1962	97.8	75.1	54.62	54.62	14.52	23.10	21.18	1.92	17.00	4.49	4.84				
1963	85.7	141.9	61.82	61.82	17.85	28.13	25.16	2.97	15.84	3.62	4.08				
1964	112.9	99.5	68.16	68.16	16.81	33.01	29.43	3.58	18.34	4.44	5.40				
1965	123.8	115.6	78.86	78.86	19.63	40.13	36.44	3.69	19.10	4.82	5.47				
1966	106.5	117.6	92.06	92.06	23.29	48.55	44.10	4.45	20.22	5.59	5.57				
1967	87.0	88.9	90.91	90.91	25.98	45.07	41.02	4.05	19.86	5.33	5.48				
1968	95.9	93.5	88.89	88.89	25.19	44.48	40.57	3.91	19.22	5.28	5.35				
1969	133.5	116.1	100.97	100.97	24.43	55.88	51.01	4.87	20.66	6.39	5.65				
1970	110.0	107.9	111.21	111.21	25.56	64.02	58.47	5.55	21.63	6.87	5.68				
1971	106.0	97.3	115.59	115.59	25.93	66.67	60.86	5.81	22.99	7.38	5.61				
1972	95.7	95.5	115.70	115.70	27.52	64.56	59.11	5.45	23.62	7.13	5.53				
1973	100.2	102.0	123.47	123.47	30.10	69.28	63.85	5.43	24.09	7.20	5.53				
1974	107.0	108.2	131.43	131.43	32.58	73.59	67.79	5.80	25.26	7.56	5.71				
1975	97.9	93.9	141.52	141.52	33.41	81.59	74.79	6.80	26.52	8.50	6.15				
1976	106.1	118.0	144.15	144.15	33.92	84.98	79.20	5.78	25.25	7.58	5.61				
1977	97.8	103.2	155.67	155.67	37.95	92.05	86.18	5.87	25.67	7.69	5.68				
1978	101.9	92.5	174.78	174.78	41.01	106.61	100.56	6.05	27.16	9.64	5.04	3.39	1.46	0.35	0.98
1979	107.0	106.8	187.16	187.16	44.27	113.93	107.33	6.60	28.96	10.95	5.71	2.76	1.57	1.02	0.99
1980	116.2	107.6	221.04	221.04	55.27	131.09	122.46	8.63	34.68	12.21	6.47	3.54	1.73	1.76	1.12
1981	116.9	115.4	228.30	228.30	57.78	132.40	122.57	9.83	38.12	11.87	8.51	3.41	1.96	2.20	1.44
1982	106.9	93.1	248.42	248.42	63.75	140.77	127.27	13.50	43.90	13.39	7.19	6.76	2.18	2.63	1.72
1983	103.9	111.3	276.94	276.94	78.93	150.67	135.37	15.30	47.34	14.86	7.20	6.42	2.39	3.08	1.93
1984	101.5	100.5	318.34	318.34	86.00	175.01	154.94	20.07	57.33	16.85	9.94	8.23	3.15	3.42	2.22
1985	119.4	117.5	355.04	355.04	77.06	205.07	180.92	24.15	72.91	20.08	15.32	11.80	3.98	3.77	2.76
1986	110.8	104.5	392.52	400.82	92.68	212.61	186.98	25.63	95.53	24.73	17.78	14.26	5.17	4.96	5.62
1987	106.9	144.7	449.34	454.60	90.72	261.61	231.94	29.67	102.27	26.37	20.68	14.69	5.48	5.24	5.81
1988	113.4	112.1	549.62	551.98	94.26	295.65	258.59	37.06	162.07	36.28	47.41	31.94	6.71	7.34	4.60
1989	104.5	99.4	627.56	630.61	93.86	345.51	307.00	38.51	191.24	40.53	50.42	43.60	8.48	8.34	5.92
1990	98.9	97.9	713.11	715.23	160.34	362.68	323.86	38.82	192.21	34.48	48.02	40.17	10.95	10.24	6.94
1991	113.7	115.6	823.38	824.23	150.18	413.34	369.52	43.82	260.71	45.98	79.86	49.73	12.76	11.07	8.99
1992	102.1	111.4	963.99	964.04	171.28	493.13	440.03	53.10	299.63	49.18	97.40	51.48	15.57	14.72	10.67
1993	120.1	115.3	1206.65	1203.22	203.31	649.73	580.40	69.33	350.18	56.90	113.58	65.89	17.19	16.17	12.75
1994	113.3	118.7	1622.36	1618.63	316.32	852.97	764.27	88.70	449.34	70.70	144.77	77.82	21.67	22.97	19.70
1995	108.4	111.4	2018.14	2014.53	388.15	1054.77	949.05	105.72	571.61	86.37	174.59	104.33	32.78	29.77	25.41

Year	v3c7	v3c8	v3c9	v3c10	v3d	v4'	v4	v4a	v4b	v4b1	v4b2	v4c	v4c1	v4c2	v4c3
1952				2.14	234										
1953				2.89	269	113.9	113.9	98.4	137.1	133.9	161.4	120.8	98.8	129.1	
1954				3.29	293	112.6	112.6	106.1	128.6	130.3	118.6	102.9	109.9	91.5	
1955				3.45	289	105.0	105.0	111.1	95.9	94.8	103.6	109.0	105.6	116.8	
1956				4.30	297	109.3	109.3	95.8	122.3	122.1	123.6	115.7	105.1	113.8	
1957				5.20	300	108.8	108.8	106.8	110.8	114.7	113.5	109.1	109.3	100.5	
1958				4.82	394	144.9	144.9	133.4	175.9	178.7	153.7	114.1	130.9	127.1	
1959				6.18	437	116.5	116.5	93.3	125.0	126.1	115.0	128.9	150.3	115.9	
1960				7.59	445	107.6	107.6	66.1	123.9	123.3	130.6	113.3	119.4	100.0	
1961				8.10	286	54.9	54.9	74.8	43.4	43.9	38.2	70.4	58.8	61.5	
1962				7.67	288	102.7	102.7	120.6	119.0	101.5	106.5	93.2	95.7	92.7	
1963				8.14	313	114.3	114.3	121.9	117.4	113.6	157.0	103.6	93.1	94.7	
1964				8.50	331	114.9	114.9	113.5	115.4	116.1	109.3	115.2	113.7	132.3	
1965				8.81	370	115.7	115.7	116.7	121.5	123.8	102.9	104.6	108.4	101.3	
1966				9.06	421	116.7	116.7	118.7	121.1	121.1	120.6	105.7	116.2	101.1	
1967				9.05	402	98.7	98.7	111.6	92.6	92.9	91.1	97.9	95.2	98.7	
1968				8.59	379	97.8	97.8	96.9	98.7	98.9	96.5	96.9	99.1	98.1	
1969				8.62	414	113.5	113.5	96.9	125.6	125.7	124.5	107.3	121.0	105.7	
1970				9.08	441	116.2	116.2	110.9	121.4	121.5	120.9	108.5	118.1	102.9	
1971				10.00	434	102.8	102.8	100.3	103.0	102.9	103.6	105.7	102.6	100.8	
1972				10.96	425	100.9	100.9	85.8	103.0	106.3	103.3	108.4	112.9	101.2	
1973				11.36	438	106.1	106.1	109.3	107.4	108.1	99.8	99.4	93.5	99.6	
1974				11.99	454	106.4	106.4	108.2	106.1	106.1	106.6	104.9	105.3	103.6	
1975				11.87	478	107.5	107.5	110.2	109.4	110.3	99.1	98.6	97.4	99.6	
1976				12.06	477	101.9	101.9	94.5	105.5	105.9	100.2	101.3	102.9	99.8	
1977				12.30	507	107.9	107.9	111.9	108.3	108.8	101.3	101.6	101.1	101.8	
1978	2.85	0.66	2.03	0.26	564	111.1	111.1	105.3	118.2	119.1	105.2	100.6	128.0	94.1	
1979	2.94	0.73	1.96	0.33	594	103.0	103.0	92.9	108.6	108.5	110.9	103.7	110.5	110.1	79.2
1980	3.69	0.93	2.43	0.80	691	110.0	110.0	112.1	108.1	107.2	122.8	113.3	105.5	107.3	121.2
1981	3.87	1.22	2.65	0.99	709	103.8	103.8	102.8	103.8	102.9	117.1	105.3	93.1	126.0	92.3
1982	4.36	1.56	2.92	1.19	762	106.6	106.6	107.8	104.8	102.4	135.3	111.0	108.8	81.5	191.0
1983	4.60	2.06	3.41	1.39	841	108.6	108.6	124.5	102.1	101.4	108.1	102.8	105.8	95.6	90.5
1984	5.36	2.56	4.00	1.60	959	111.1	111.1	102.0	116.2	114.5	131.2	113.7	106.4	129.5	120.3
1985	5.74	3.22	4.38	1.86	1062	106.0	106.0	87.4	112.3	111.9	115.3	120.0	112.4	145.4	135.3
1986	9.84	4.54	6.51	2.12	1189	103.5	103.5	117.9	91.9	91.6	94.1	120.5	113.3	106.7	111.1
1987	10.48	4.60	6.58	2.34	1335	108.6	108.6	95.5	114.3	115.2	107.6	112.6	112.2	139.4	114.2
1988	11.61	4.22	9.14	2.82	1602	108.6	108.6	97.6	101.6	100.2	112.3	138.5	120.2	175.9	180.2
1989	12.85	5.05	12.29	3.76	1808	106.3	106.3	89.6	111.2	112.6	101.4	110.8	104.9	99.9	128.2
1990	15.43	5.69	15.77	4.52	2028	105.8	105.8	141.8	97.4	97.7	94.7	97.7	82.7	92.6	89.6
1991	18.50	7.50	21.19	5.13	2316	106.9	106.9	93.1	110.7	111.6	103.7	113.1	111.2	138.7	103.2
1992	21.20	8.80	24.47	6.14	2684	106.8	106.8	107.1	106.4	106.4	107.3	107.0	99.6	113.5	96.4
1993	22.59	11.37	26.46	7.28	3320	107.6	107.6	104.9	108.7	108.3	111.7	107.6	110.6	108.8	109.8
1994	27.07	18.00	36.77	9.87	4427	108.7	108.7	108.9	108.8	109.0	107.7	108.6	104.9	104.6	106.0
1995	32.22	22.07	50.74	13.33	5465	109.6	109.6	109.0	110.2	110.0	111.9	109.0	108.8	105.5	113.0

Year	v4c4	v4c5	v4c6	v4c7	v4c8	v4c9	v4c10	v5	v5a	v5a1	v5a1a	v5a1b	v5a2	v5b	v5b1
1952								26.00	17.40	16.57	9.54	7.03	0.83	6.92	4.21
1953								31.99	22.09	20.80	11.36	9.44	1.29	11.04	5.98
1954								36.66	23.62	22.16	12.83	9.33	1.46	10.57	7.46
1955								38.18	23.75	22.23	13.13	9.10	1.52	9.62	7.59
1956								42.19	30.48	28.56	16.24	12.32	1.92	6.23	8.96
1957								44.42	33.23	31.20	15.58	15.62	2.03	11.94	8.08
1958								61.64	31.72	31.27	17.45	13.82	0.45	22.28	15.78
1959								73.50	37.50	36.98	19.34	17.64	0.52	25.87	19.23
1960								80.45	35.64	34.96	15.49	19.47	0.68	29.95	24.07
1961								54.17	43.25	42.65	19.23	23.42	0.60	8.96	7.96
1962								54.62	42.02	41.51	16.69	24.82	0.51	4.48	6.28
1963								61.82	43.66	41.51	18.92	24.22	0.52	13.62	9.97
1964								68.16	52.62	45.73	16.18	29.55	6.89	13.13	12.46
1965								78.86	56.37	47.62	18.50	29.12	8.75	12.25	12.08
1966								92.06	63.41	54.19	24.68	29.51	9.22	10.97	10.17
1967								90.91	72.53	62.24	31.53	30.71	10.29	8.75	8.12
1968								88.89	68.98	58.34	26.95	31.39	10.64	8.51	7.45
1969								100.97	64.08	54.73	22.06	32.67	9.35	16.10	10.38
1970								111.21	75.84	65.52	30.69	34.83	10.32	18.82	12.23
1971								115.59	83.85	72.33	34.31	38.02	11.52	16.97	12.08
1972								115.70	80.61	69.83	27.23	42.60	10.78	18.65	14.17
1973								123.47	91.79	78.94	33.43	45.51	12.85	22.02	16.42
1974								131.43	94.59	80.39	34.11	46.28	14.20	24.17	17.96
1975								141.52	97.25	81.58	35.14	46.44	15.67	29.36	20.08
1976								144.15	90.65	76.33	26.79	49.54	14.32	29.35	21.76
1977								155.67	103.16	87.98	33.77	54.21	15.18	27.05	23.48
1978								174.78	103.18	93.79	35.46	58.33	9.39	41.23	26.89
1979	104.5	117.0	98.3	100.4	107.6	94.0	123.4	187.16	112.18	101.35	39.54	61.81	10.83	45.21	28.64
1980	104.0	163.1	106.9	118.8	120.3	117.4	229.6	221.04	132.25	119.53	49.96	69.57	12.72	48.01	38.01
1981	108.7	119.9	123.1	100.5	126.0	104.5	118.8	228.30	140.72	131.71	56.89	74.82	9.01	57.21	46.64
1982	107.1	115.4	115.3	108.9	123.2	106.2	115.8	248.43	145.29	135.59	59.40	76.19	9.70	77.30	62.13
1983	104.8	111.6	106.8	100.6	125.9	111.4	110.9	276.94	157.94	145.73	65.62	80.11	12.21	93.46	70.83
1984	123.7	104.2	108.2	109.4	116.9	110.0	107.4	318.34	180.33	164.68	69.63	95.05	15.65	108.86	87.02
1985	119.2	103.8	117.4	101.1	118.5	103.3	110.6	355.04	209.19	190.42	74.72	115.70	18.77	136.20	109.88
1986	119.4	121.1	187.2	157.5	129.7	136.9	105.0	400.82	227.19	205.15	80.12	125.03	22.04	164.21	121.64
1987	111.5	111.2	108.7	103.6	106.5	106.3	115.8	454.60	261.62	229.81	91.31	138.50	31.81	181.83	138.60
1988	107.0	122.4	69.2	104.8	80.2	121.3	105.5	551.98	331.16	264.92	103.70	161.22	66.24	209.77	159.54
1989	118.6	106.7	120.8	103.9	112.3	126.3	125.2	630.61	389.97	308.08	106.23	201.85	81.89	235.36	157.02
1990	125.6	119.3	114.0	116.7	109.6	124.8	116.8	715.23	435.91	366.16	128.97	237.19	69.75	272.84	169.27
1991	97.2	90.1	108.1	100.0	109.8	112.0	94.7	824.23	538.79	447.20	151.21	295.99	91.59	280.10	196.18
1992	113.6	123.8	110.4	106.7	109.3	107.5	111.4	964.04	617.68	518.85	169.79	349.06	98.83	338.62	246.18
1993	104.0	101.7	110.6	98.7	119.6	100.1	109.6	1203.22	763.17	633.43	207.42	426.01	129.74	431.42	335.00
1994	106.8	118.0	112.7	116.8	114.5	115.3	116.3	1617.83	1019.21	853.15	264.95	588.20	166.06	566.21	435.73
1995	109.1	113.0	112.5	103.8	114.5	111.4	117.8	2006.48	1201.53	976.62	295.29	681.33	224.91	724.45	558.80

Year	v5b2	v5c	v5c1	v5c2	v6a1	v6a2	v6a3	v6a4	v6b2	v6b3	v6b4	v7	v7a	v7a1	v7a2
1952	2.71	1.68													
1953	5.06	-1.14										123.1	121.9	117.1	126.8
1954	3.11	2.47										104.4	103.9	111.2	97.2
1955	2.03	4.81										99.1	98.9	101.0	96.6
1956	-2.73	5.48										129.3	129.5	124.2	135.5
1957	3.86	-0.75										109.0	109.4	94.5	124.5
1958	6.50	7.64										95.4	99.9	112.7	90.0
1959	6.64	10.13										119.0	119.1	110.2	127.6
1960	5.88	14.86										96.3	95.8	79.5	109.3
1961	1.00	1.96										102.2	102.8	111.9	97.2
1962	-1.80	8.12										94.7	94.9	84.7	102.1
1963	3.65	4.54										106.0	106.0	119.7	98.0
1964	0.67	2.41										122.5	107.8	86.5	122.9
1965	0.17	10.24										107.9	104.8	116.9	98.8
1966	0.80	17.68										112.1	113.4	134.2	101.1
1967	0.63	9.63										113.5	114.0	126.6	104.1
1968	1.06	11.40										95.4	94.0	85.5	102.2
1969	5.72	20.79										93.2	94.2	81.9	104.1
1970	6.59	16.55										117.7	119.0	139.0	106.4
1971	4.89	14.77										110.9	110.7	112.4	109.3
1972	4.48	16.44										95.9	96.4	79.3	110.8
1973	5.60	9.66										113.3	112.4	122.3	106.5
1974	6.21	12.67										102.6	101.4	101.7	101.2
1975	9.28	14.91										102.7	101.3	102.9	100.2
1976	7.59	24.15										93.0	93.4	75.9	105.9
1977	3.57	25.46										113.0	114.4	125.7	108.6
1978	14.34	30.37			13.12	18.94	2.34	1.06	49.22	7.36	1.75	99.8	106.3	105.0	107.1
1979	16.57	29.77			16.43	19.51	2.41	1.19	52.17	7.79	1.85	106.6	105.9	110.2	103.4
1980	10.00	40.78			18.49	26.67	3.30	1.50	58.71	8.77	2.09	111.3	111.3	121.5	104.9
1981	10.57	30.37			21.05	30.38	3.75	1.71	63.14	9.44	2.24	104.3	108.0	111.7	105.3
1982	15.17	25.84			21.98	31.72	3.92	1.78	64.29	9.61	2.29	100.4	100.2	101.9	98.9
1983	22.63	25.54			24.28	35.04	4.33	1.97	67.61	10.10	2.40	106.5	105.3	108.7	102.6
1984	21.84	29.15			25.76	37.18	4.60	2.09	80.21	11.99	2.85	109.3	107.4	102.0	111.8
1985	26.32	9.65			27.65	39.90	4.93	2.24	97.64	14.59	3.47	114.3	114.3	101.9	123.7
1986	42.57	9.42			33.04	39.49	4.89	2.70	105.66	15.79	3.58	96.2	95.9	103.8	91.0
1987	43.23	11.15			32.90	48.98	6.05	3.40	117.51	17.56	3.43	104.7	101.6	102.2	101.2
1988	50.23	11.05	337.45	326.40	39.93	53.30	6.59	3.88	138.66	18.17	4.39	109.4	99.4	101.2	98.1
1989	78.34	5.28	388.93	383.65	43.73	52.20	6.45	3.85	171.33	25.60	4.92	101.6	100.2	87.9	109.4
1990	103.57	6.48	378.70	372.22	52.97	64.47	7.97	3.56	201.80	30.15	5.24	103.4	110.9	114.2	108.9
1991	83.92	5.34	400.72	395.38	55.75	81.24	10.04	4.18	252.47	37.73	5.79	115.3	113.8	111.3	115.3
1992	92.44	7.74	454.78	447.04	58.56	94.73	11.71	4.79	297.95	44.52	6.59	105.7	107.3	106.0	108.0
1993	96.42	8.63	521.86	513.23	65.73	121.03	14.89	5.77	362.31	53.49	10.21	110.4	109.2	115.6	105.5
1994	130.48	32.41	666.34	633.93	82.46	140.42	21.58	20.49	490.34	74.15	23.71	106.0	106.6	104.0	108.0
1995	165.66	80.49	796.14	715.65	71.98	161.39	35.48	26.44	549.83	96.38	35.12	108.0	105.7	103.3	107.0

Year	v7b	v8	v8a	v8b	v9	v9a	v9b	v10a1	v10a2	v10a3	v10a3a	v10a3b	v10a4	v10b1	v10b2
1952		152	120	236											
1953	146.1	181	142	270	115.7	116.3	107.2								
1954	112.5	182	159	227	97.9	110.1	83.7								
1955	102.1	173	156	204	93.9	97.3	89.3								
1956	125.9	208	182	258	121.5	116.7	125.4								
1957	102.9	215	170	293	103.5	92.2	109.5								
1958	22.8	206	173	268	95.2	102.5	94.7								
1959	114.0	228	193	285	111.4	110.5	105.1								
1960	129.2	200	168	236	89.1	86.8	80.5								
1961	72.6	230	188	282	97.0	100.9	97.3								
1962	82.0	219	147	327	92.6	76.1	110.5								
1963	112.0	223	159	325	104.0	114.6	100.9								
1964	1357.1	227	129	388	103.4	82.0	118.2								
1965	128.3	227	142	368	100.8	112.4	95.9								
1966	105.3	251	196	328	109.9	138.3	90.4								
1967	110.6	280	252	316	110.7	127.7	97.7								
1968	103.5	254	203	322	90.9	80.7	100.5								
1969	87.8	229	152	349	90.6	74.6	107.0								
1970	110.3	264	195	384	114.7	128.3	111.5								
1971	111.9	281	211	401	106.7	108.8	104.9								
1972	93.1	261	163	426	92.7	77.1	102.8								
1973	118.7	285	193	438	108.7	118.3	103.4								
1974	110.0	281	189	441	98.4	97.4	100.3								
1975	110.3	279	188	441	98.9	99.5	100.0								
1976	90.9	255	139	465	91.3	73.8	102.9								
1977	105.4	289	172	503	112.3	123.1	108.1								
1978	61.7	302	177	534	104.4	103.0	105.5	22.20	2.82	1.87	0.29	1.58		7.41	6.93
1979	113.3	322	196	546	104.4	109.5	100.1	23.65	1.98	3.01	0.37	2.64		10.11	6.46
1980	111.3	375	249	591	109.9	121.9	101.8	31.38	4.41	2.22	0.54	1.68		7.88	2.12
1981	69.4	409	283	618	106.8	111.7	102.8	38.51	5.53	2.60	0.63	1.97		6.31	4.26
1982	104.6	416	294	614	99.0	101.6	96.6	51.30	8.15	2.68	0.12	2.56		12.71	2.46
1983	123.2	444	326	633	104.6	109.0	101.0	58.48	10.49	1.86	0.82	1.04		9.08	13.55
1984	133.0	501	349	737	107.1	102.8	109.0	71.97	9.98	5.07	1.24	3.83		7.11	14.73
1985	114.7	577	377	877	113.8	102.7	119.5	90.43	11.26	8.19	2.36	5.83		18.69	7.63
1986	98.9	618	406	928	95.4	104.3	89.8	101.21	10.92	9.51	4.54	4.97		30.86	11.71
1987	133.8	687	463	1007	100.7	102.2	99.1	120.56	10.49	7.55	4.57	2.98		27.83	15.40
1988	180.2	783	525	1144	98.4	101.1	95.9	133.61	13.11	12.82	5.79	7.03		31.16	19.07
1989	107.2	900	536	1401	99.1	87.7	105.7	128.03	15.77	13.22	7.95	5.27		54.48	23.86
1990	76.3	1056	645	1616	109.4	113.2	107.2	127.76	25.67	15.84	5.32	10.52		72.11	31.46
1991	123.2	1278	753	1983	112.7	110.9	113.2	153.34	33.15	9.69	0.44	9.25		72.44	11.48
1992	97.9	1475	847	2305	106.7	106.3	106.4	205.32	29.65	11.21	3.83	7.38		72.55	19.89
1993	116.5	1792	1037	2780	108.8	115.7	104.7	295.67	30.22	9.11	4.72	4.39		61.55	34.87
1994	103.2	2334	1293	3660	105.6	104.2	105.6	356.92	20.53	29.26	5.11	24.15	29.02	2.68	17.50
1995	119.7	2650	1450	4132	104.9	103.9	104.3	404.06	16.17	41.76	10.31	31.45	96.81	39.07	7.09

Year	v10b4	v11a	v11a1	v11a2	v11b	v11b1	v11b2	v11c	v11c1	v11c2	v12	v12a	v12b	v13	v13i
1952															
1953											150.4	133.5	176.8		
1954											93.5	121.9	59.9		
1955											95.0	107.1	65.9		
1956											71.0	128.3	100.0		
1957											195.3	91.8	100.0		
1958											177.1	181.4	168.1		
1959											113.1	121.4	94.4		
1960											114.1	123.4	87.3		
1961											23.8	26.2	13.7		
1962											57.5	90.6			
1963											309.0	161.7			
1964											90.8	117.7	17.4		
1965											96.0	99.7	27.6		
1966											89.3	84.1	437.5		
1967											79.9	79.9	80.2		
1968											97.2	91.8	165.7		
1969											193.6	151.8	489.5		
1970											121.1	114.5	135.6		
1971											97.6	106.9	80.2		
1972											109.8	117.2	91.5		
1973											118.2	116.0	125.2		
1974											109.7	109.3	110.9		
1975											121.3	111.7	149.1		
1976											100.0	108.4	81.9		
1977											92.2	107.9	47.1		
1978		5.66	3.77	1.89	24.37	16.60	7.77	11.20	6.52	4.68	158.0	118.8	415.2	174.78	79.93
1979		6.11	4.07	2.04	26.05	17.25	8.80	13.05	7.32	5.73	108.2	105.0	114.3	187.16	82.31
1980		7.36	5.08	2.28	27.28	22.85	4.43	13.37	10.08	3.29	105.9	131.9	61.1	221.04	102.71
1981		7.78	5.31	2.47	31.89	27.86	4.03	17.54	13.47	4.07	117.0	120.9	102.3	228.30	113.40
1982		8.84	5.86	2.98	45.04	37.72	7.32	23.42	18.55	4.87	133.6	131.7	141.9	248.42	122.21
1983		13.73	7.26	6.47	51.51	40.37	11.14	28.22	23.20	5.02	117.4	91.8	222.1	276.94	135.90
1984		16.06	7.91	8.15	54.87	46.89	7.98	3.92	32.22	5.71	115.7	132.7	86.9	318.34	169.56
1985		10.07	7.08	2.99	73.64	54.94	18.70	52.49	47.86	4.63	119.9	119.0	122.2	355.04	183.53
1986		18.72	8.52	10.20	79.41	56.96	22.45	66.08	56.16	9.92	103.1	99.8	111.4	400.82	216.00
1987		18.41	8.34	9.07	93.30	70.09	26.21	68.12	60.17	7.95	100.9	104.7	92.1	454.60	250.89
1988		18.28	8.66	9.62	108.12	79.21	28.91	83.37	71.67	11.70	101.0	101.4	100.0	551.98	288.95
1989		20.31	8.63	11.68	133.71	92.57	41.14	81.34	55.82	25.52	100.4	84.8	140.7	630.61	330.04
1990		28.96	14.74	14.22	149.97	97.17	52.80	93.91	57.36	36.55	105.4	102.0	110.6	715.23	367.58
1991		9.83	13.80	-3.97	129.73	110.74	48.99	110.54	71.64	38.90	93.3	104.3	77.5	824.23	383.87
1992		14.13	15.74	-1.61	184.76	132.12	52.64	139.73	98.32	41.41	109.4	110.1	108.1	964.04	401.28
1993		31.21	18.66	12.55	227.66	174.08	53.58	172.55	142.26	30.29	106.4	110.3	98.7	1203.22	497.16
1994	110.30	70.92	19.31	51.61	256.63	244.64	11.99	238.66	171.78	66.88	108.2	110.0	103.8	1618.63	669.86
1995	119.50	170.14	61.56	108.58	285.24	239.11	46.13	269.08	258.13	10.95	112.1	111.3	114.2	2014.53	964.42

Year	v13ii	v13iii	v13iv	v13a	v13ai	v13aii	v13aiii	v13aiv	v13b	v13bi	v13bii	v13biii	v13biv	v13b1	v13b1i
1952															
1953															
1954															
1955															
1956															
1957															
1958															
1959															
1960															
1961															
1962															
1963															
1964															
1965															
1966															
1967															
1968															
1969															
1970															
1971															
1972															
1973															
1974															
1975															
1976															
1977															
1978	17.12	19.10	58.63	41.01	35.44	0.95	2.30	2.32	106.61	28.63	11.39	14.15	52.44	100.56	24.32
1979	19.57	20.12	65.16	44.27	34.62	0.93	2.37	6.35	113.93	30.84	13.37	14.74	54.98	107.33	26.04
1980	26.66	21.40	70.27	55.27	44.42	1.77	1.28	7.80	131.09	38.18	18.67	16.70	57.54	122.46	31.94
1981	30.81	23.88	60.21	57.78	53.51	1.28	2.52	0.47	132.40	37.65	22.15	17.85	54.75	122.57	30.32
1982	34.30	27.03	64.88	63.75	52.96	1.90	2.35	6.54	140.77	44.65	24.17	20.80	51.15	127.27	34.21
1983	39.50	32.03	69.51	78.93	66.15	1.99	2.63	8.16	150.67	43.21	28.15	24.52	54.79	135.37	34.34
1984	40.89	37.31	70.58	86.00	77.96	2.15	2.66	3.23	175.01	57.87	28.73	27.68	60.73	154.94	43.27
1985	51.61	46.47	73.43	77.06	69.40	3.58	2.87	1.21	205.07	72.61	35.11	36.13	61.22	180.92	55.57
1986	57.57	70.71	56.36	92.68	75.39	3.99	3.88	9.42	212.61	82.66	37.01	59.23	33.71	186.98	63.04
1987	62.31	65.32	76.08	90.72	70.40	4.03	4.94	11.35	261.61	116.70	36.69	53.71	51.51	231.94	93.98
1988	83.64	76.76	102.63	94.26	72.08	4.32	5.31	12.55	295.65	129.09	51.14	58.01	57.41	258.59	102.85
1989	97.26	96.63	106.68	93.86	72.40	3.82	5.39	12.25	345.51	158.58	62.34	73.98	50.61	307.00	130.95
1990	104.86	102.71	140.08	160.34	137.22	4.12	6.86	12.14	362.68	132.63	63.52	76.36	90.17	323.86	103.61
1991	112.31	141.28	186.77	150.18	136.42	4.76	6.10	2.90	413.34	142.13	67.30	121.00	82.91	369.52	111.73
1992	156.67	166.49	239.60	171.28	150.42	5.29	-1.57	17.14	493.13	124.27	107.70	148.26	112.90	440.03	98.26
1993	139.92	215.83	350.31	203.31	185.31	5.83	6.09	6.08	649.73	164.85	84.02	187.03	213.83	580.40	126.41
1994	198.65	281.36	498.76	316.32	266.44	7.84	4.22	37.82	852.97	202.65	130.98	245.65	273.69	764.27	156.30
1995	276.98	380.19	392.94	388.15	325.30	11.35	12.63	38.87	1054.77	359.11	168.13	322.02	205.51	949.05	302.62

Year	v13b1ii	v13b1iii	v13b1iv	v13b2	v13b2i	v13b2ii	v13b2iii	v13b2iv	v13c	v13ci	v13cii	v13ciii	v13civ	v13c1
1952														
1953														
1954														
1955														
1956														
1957														
1958														
1959														
1960														
1961														
1962														
1963														
1964														
1965														
1966														
1967														
1968														
1969														
1970														
1971														
1972														
1973														
1974														
1975														
1976														
1977														
1978	10.78	14.12	51.34	6.05	4.31	0.61	0.03	1.10	27.16	15.86	4.78	2.65	3.87	9.64
1979	12.80	14.71	53.78	6.60	4.80	0.57	0.03	1.20	28.96	16.85	5.27	3.01	3.83	10.95
1980	17.87	16.68	55.97	8.63	6.24	0.80	0.02	1.57	34.68	20.11	6.22	3.42	4.93	12.21
1981	21.47	17.81	52.97	9.83	7.33	0.68	0.04	1.78	38.12	22.24	7.38	3.51	4.99	11.87
1982	22.86	20.79	49.41	13.50	10.44	1.31	0.01	1.74	43.90	24.60	8.23	3.88	7.19	13.39
1983	26.54	23.36	51.13	15.30	8.87	1.61	1.16	3.66	47.34	26.54	9.36	4.88	6.56	14.86
1984	26.84	26.72	58.11	20.07	14.60	1.89	0.96	2.62	57.33	33.73	10.01	6.97	6.62	16.85
1985	32.31	34.93	58.11	24.15	17.04	2.80	1.20	3.11	72.91	41.52	12.92	7.47	11.00	20.08
1986	34.09	58.40	31.45	25.63	19.62	2.92	0.83	2.26	95.53	57.95	16.75	7.60	13.23	24.73
1987	36.50	52.05	49.41	29.67	22.72	3.19	1.66	2.10	102.27	63.79	18.59	6.67	13.22	26.37
1988	47.20	55.57	52.97	37.06	26.24	3.94	2.44	4.44	162.07	87.78	28.18	13.44	32.67	36.28
1989	58.72	70.51	46.82	38.51	27.63	3.62	3.47	3.79	191.24	99.06	31.10	17.26	43.82	40.53
1990	59.57	73.22	87.46	38.82	29.02	3.95	3.14	2.71	192.21	97.73	37.22	19.49	37.77	34.48
1991	63.56	116.62	77.61	43.82	30.40	3.74	4.38	5.30	260.71	105.32	40.25	14.18	100.96	45.98
1992	100.97	139.62	101.18	53.10	26.01	6.73	8.64	11.72	299.63	126.59	43.68	19.80	109.56	49.18
1993	79.67	176.24	198.08	69.33	38.44	4.35	10.79	15.75	350.18	147.00	50.07	22.71	130.40	56.90
1994	125.17	230.30	252.50	88.70	46.35	5.81	15.35	21.19	449.34	200.77	59.83	31.49	157.25	70.70
1995	162.00	303.09	181.34	105.72	56.49	6.13	18.93	24.17	571.61	280.01	97.50	45.54	148.56	86.37

Year	v13c1i	v13c1ii	v13c1iii	v13c1iv	v13c2	v13c2i	v13c2ii	v13c2iii	v13c2iv	v13c3	v13c3i	v13c3ii	v13c3iii	v13c3iv
1952														
1953														
1954														
1955														
1956														
1957														
1958														
1959														
1960														
1961														
1962														
1963														
1964														
1965														
1966														
1967														
1968														
1969														
1970														
1971														
1972														
1973														
1974														
1975														
1976														
1977														
1978	3.72	1.77	1.37	2.78	5.04	4.87	0.76	1.26	-1.85	3.39	0.46	0.04		2.89
1979	4.17	2.07	1.56	3.15	5.71	5.08	0.75	1.43	-1.55	2.76	0.52	0.04		2.20
1980	4.49	2.37	1.77	3.58	6.47	5.02	1.05	1.62	-1.22	3.54	0.99	0.04		2.51
1981	3.96	2.96	1.46	3.49	8.51	5.97	1.30	2.02	-0.78	3.41	1.23	0.04		2.14
1982	4.04	3.26	1.27	4.82	7.19	6.22	1.39	2.54	-2.96	6.76	1.49	0.06		5.21
1983	3.60	3.49	2.03	5.74	7.20	6.54	1.69	2.78	-3.81	6.42	1.89	0.08		4.45
1984	4.91	2.79	3.58	5.57	9.94	9.49	1.90	2.68	-4.13	8.23	2.46	0.29	0.61	4.87
1985	6.35	3.83	3.13	6.77	15.32	12.65	2.95	3.18	-3.46	11.80	3.31	0.29	0.84	7.36
1986	8.70	4.75	2.41	8.87	17.78	13.64	3.76	3.78	-3.40	14.26	5.55	0.29	1.04	7.38
1987	10.14	5.41	1.66	9.16	20.68	17.02	4.22	3.36	-3.92	14.69	5.64	0.33	1.21	7.51
1988	15.76	7.57	2.23	10.72	47.41	31.67	10.17	8.62	-3.05	31.91	5.70	0.47	2.04	23.73
1989	17.34	9.68	2.62	10.89	50.42	33.51	8.63	10.50	-2.22	43.60	5.76	0.51	3.53	33.80
1990	13.07	10.82	3.04	7.55	48.02	27.36	9.91	12.15	-1.40	40.17	5.82	0.73	3.63	29.99
1991	17.23	14.05	-0.72	15.42	79.86	26.11	4.93	9.50	39.32	49.73	5.88	1.52	3.93	38.40
1992	21.17	14.49	-1.43	14.95	97.40	31.54	5.72	14.45	45.69	51.48	7.49	1.62	4.08	38.29
1993	25.18	15.42	-2.03	18.33	113.58	38.08	8.32	15.21	51.97	65.89	8.26	2.69	7.23	47.71
1994	33.08	16.91	-1.99	22.70	144.77	48.65	9.03	21.08	66.01	77.82	11.45	3.42	8.82	54.13
1995	54.67	29.42	0.65	1.63	174.59	74.54	17.87	24.06	58.12	104.33	11.04	4.10	12.95	76.24

Year	v13c4	v13c4i	v13c4ii	v13c4iii	v13c4iv	v13c5	v13c5i	v13c5ii	v13c5iii	v13c5iv	v13c6	v13c6i	v13c6ii	v13c6iii
1952														
1953														
1954														
1955														
1956														
1957														
1958														
1959														
1960														
1961														
1962														
1963														
1964														
1965														
1966														
1967														
1968														
1969														
1970														
1971														
1972														
1973														
1974														
1975														
1976														
1977														
1978	1.46	0.12	1.34			0.85	0.71	0.07	0.02	0.05	0.98	0.90	0.08	
1979	1.57	0.14	1.43			1.02	0.88	0.09	0.02	0.03	0.99	0.90	0.09	
1980	1.73	0.16	1.57			1.76	1.51	0.16	0.03	0.06	1.12	1.06	0.06	
1981	1.96	0.22	1.74			2.20	1.82	0.21	0.03	0.14	1.44	1.33	0.11	
1982	2.18	0.24	1.94			2.63	2.16	0.28	0.07	0.12	1.72	1.60	0.12	
1983	2.39	0.26	2.13			3.08	2.51	0.32	0.07	0.18	1.93	1.70	0.23	
1984	3.15	0.29	2.86			3.42	2.69	0.32	0.10	0.31	2.22	1.83	0.39	
1985	3.98	0.37	3.42	0.19		3.77	2.92	0.39	0.13	0.33	2.76	2.28	0.48	
1986	5.17	0.64	4.29	0.24		4.96	3.50	0.95	0.13	0.38	5.62	5.06	0.56	
1987	5.48	0.73	4.45	0.30		5.24	3.57	1.06	0.14	0.47	5.81	5.10	0.71	
1988	6.71	0.97	5.38	0.36		7.34	5.01	1.48	0.19	0.66	4.60	4.16	0.44	
1989	8.48	1.24	6.84	0.40		8.34	5.79	1.62	0.21	0.72	5.92	5.39	0.53	
1990	10.95	1.33	9.20	0.42		10.24	7.16	1.92	0.25	0.91	6.94	6.33	0.61	
1991	12.76	1.38	9.79	0.25	1.34	11.07	5.76	1.27	0.54	3.50	8.99	7.69	0.94	-0.02
1992	15.57	2.16	10.61	0.52	2.28	14.72	7.21	1.51	1.00	5.00	10.67	9.21	1.11	-0.02
1993	17.19	2.38	10.79	0.59	3.43	16.17	7.76	1.81	1.06	5.54	12.75	10.55	1.38	0.03
1994	21.67	3.84	13.35	0.81	3.67	22.97	11.43	3.00	1.84	6.70	19.70	15.97	2.11	0.08
1995	32.78	5.25	22.48	1.55	3.50	29.77	17.02	4.08	2.82	5.85	25.41	20.60	2.72	0.12

Year	v13c6iv	v13c7	v13c7i	v13c7ii	v13c7iii	v13c7iv	v13c8	v13c8i	v13c8ii	v13c8iii	v13c8iv	v13c9	v13c9i	v13c9ii
1952														
1953														
1954														
1955														
1956														
1957														
1958														
1959														
1960														
1961														
1962														
1963														
1964														
1965														
1966														
1967														
1968														
1969														
1970														
1971														
1972														
1973														
1974														
1975														
1976														
1977														
1978		2.85	2.43	0.42			0.66	0.57	0.09			2.03	1.82	0.21
1979		2.94	2.48	0.46			0.73	0.63	0.10			1.96	1.72	0.24
1980		3.69	3.12	0.57			0.93	0.80	0.13			2.43	2.16	0.27
1981		3.87	3.31	0.56			1.22	1.07	0.15			2.65	2.34	0.31
1982		4.36	3.74	0.62			1.56	1.36	0.20			2.92	2.56	0.36
1983		4.60	3.89	0.71			2.06	1.76	0.30			3.41	3.00	0.41
1984		5.36	4.70	0.66			2.56	2.17	0.39			4.00	3.59	0.41
1985		5.74	5.03	0.71			3.22	2.79	0.43			4.38	3.96	0.42
1986		9.84	8.89	0.95			4.54	4.05	0.49			6.51	5.80	0.71
1987		10.48	9.32	1.16			4.60	4.12	0.48			6.58	5.81	0.77
1988		11.61	10.30	1.31			4.22	3.13	0.48		0.61	9.14	8.26	0.88
1989		12.85	11.25	1.60			5.05	3.81	0.61		0.63	12.29	11.21	1.08
1990		15.43	13.39	2.04			5.69	4.26	0.71	0.00	0.72	15.77	14.49	1.28
1991	0.38	18.50	14.34	2.68	0.28	1.20	7.50	5.40	1.26	0.16	0.68	21.19	17.62	3.13
1992	0.37	21.20	16.47	2.90	0.37	1.46	8.80	6.51	1.41	0.23	0.65	24.27	20.35	3.45
1993	0.79	22.59	17.04	3.21	0.41	1.93	11.37	8.85	1.61	0.21	0.70	26.46	22.66	3.80
1994	1.54	27.07	21.18	4.08	0.54	1.27	18.00	14.14	2.32	0.31	1.23	36.77	32.51	4.26
1995	1.97	32.22	25.21	4.86	0.64	1.51	22.07	18.66	2.12	0.95	0.34	50.74	43.60	7.14

Year	v13c9iii	v13c9iv	v13c10	v13c10i	v13c10ii	v13c10iii	v13c10iv
1952							
1953							
1954							
1955							
1956							
1957							
1958							
1959							
1960							
1961							
1962							
1963							
1964							
1965							
1966							
1967							
1968							
1969							
1970							
1971							
1972							
1973							
1974							
1975							
1976							
1977							
1978			0.26	0.26			
1979			0.33	0.33			
1980			0.80	0.80			
1981			0.99	0.99			
1982			1.19	1.19			
1983			1.39	1.39			
1984			1.60	1.60			
1985			1.86	1.86			
1986			2.12	2.12			
1987			2.34	2.34			
1988			2.82	2.82			
1989			3.76	3.76			
1990			4.52	4.52			
1991	0.34	0.10	5.13	3.91	0.68	-0.08	0.62
1992	0.39	0.28	6.14	4.48	0.86	0.21	0.59
1993			7.28	6.24	1.04		
1994			9.87	8.52	1.35		
1995			13.33	9.42	2.71	1.80	-0.60

9

Shanghai

Year	v1	v1a	v1b	v1b1	v1b2	v1c	v1c1	v1c2	v1c3	v2	v2a	v2b	v2b1	v2b2	v2c
1952	91.80	3.43	69.48	66.60	2.88	18.89	2.28	12.07	4.54						
1953	125.20	3.70	96.76	91.50	5.26	24.74	3.03	16.78	4.93	135.7	109.9	139.3	136.9	195.8	126.9
1954	130.69	3.36	100.41	96.37	4.04	26.92	3.62	18.11	5.19	103.4	94.7	103.9	105.2	83.0	102.8
1955	126.01	3.79	96.82	91.42	5.40	25.40	3.29	16.64	5.47	96.7	120.7	96.6	97.2	84.6	93.3
1956	151.58	3.78	116.71	113.92	2.79	31.09	3.53	20.93	6.63	129.6	92.8	132.5	134.3	89.9	123.9
1957	158.41	4.13	123.08	118.82	4.26	31.20	3.55	20.39	7.26	104.4	97.7	106.4	104.9	158.1	96.5
1958	223.55	5.71	182.25	176.44	5.81	35.59	5.09	22.39	8.11	137.2	117.9	149.2	150.0	127.7	92.6
1959	308.65	6.61	262.02	254.68	7.34	40.02	7.11	23.07	9.84	140.2	105.1	144.8	145.0	138.4	116.4
1960	356.12	6.69	306.76	298.97	7.79	42.67	8.23	22.12	12.32	117.5	100.6	119.8	120.3	104.5	101.9
1961	234.29	6.73	190.84	187.43	3.41	36.72	6.25	18.23	12.24	66.4	96.3	60.8	61.2	44.7	113.1
1962	193.79	7.61	154.32	151.98	2.34	31.86	5.57	14.64	11.65	81.0	107.2	78.8	79.1	64.8	88.2
1963	210.10	7.66	171.74	168.91	2.83	30.70	5.87	14.45	10.38	109.3	103.9	113.0	112.9	118.4	93.8
1964	243.21	9.61	201.08	196.95	4.13	32.52	6.70	15.52	10.30	118.9	120.9	120.4	120.0	146.7	110.9
1965	279.47	10.61	234.69	230.77	3.92	34.17	6.80	16.44	10.93	120.5	114.3	123.3	123.8	97.2	105.3
1966	309.26	10.77	263.24	259.59	3.65	35.25	7.05	17.13	11.07	113.6	101.7	115.9	116.2	94.0	101.0
1967	273.13	11.09	229.31	226.88	2.43	32.73	6.11	15.85	10.77	91.9	98.8	90.0	90.3	66.3	105.0
1968	301.68	12.34	254.00	251.87	2.13	35.34	6.55	16.39	12.40	113.9	113.1	114.7	115.0	89.2	108.0
1969	337.32	12.54	287.36	284.42	2.94	37.42	6.84	18.27	12.31	115.1	103.4	117.4	117.3	135.0	100.8
1970	366.92	12.29	316.51	312.18	4.33	38.12	7.45	18.00	12.67	113.7	96.7	115.2	114.9	149.8	104.3
1971	392.99	12.71	340.37	336.52	3.85	39.91	7.93	18.09	13.89	108.9	102.2	109.3	109.6	88.7	107.5
1972	414.72	14.24	359.72	355.39	4.33	40.76	8.59	18.94	13.23	106.3	108.0	107.0	106.9	112.5	99.5
1973	449.02	13.89	388.70	383.33	5.37	46.43	9.56	20.86	16.01	108.9	96.5	109.2	109.0	124.3	110.2
1974	470.35	14.96	405.87	398.40	7.47	49.52	10.47	22.36	16.69	106.8	102.4	106.8	106.4	141.2	107.5
1975	497.91	14.17	430.63	420.37	10.26	53.11	12.09	23.08	17.94	106.1	92.3	106.1	105.5	138.5	109.6
1976	506.68	15.95	432.93	423.45	9.48	57.80	13.06	24.22	20.52	102.6	104.9	101.9	102.1	92.2	108.2
1977	544.98	14.72	466.00	458.40	7.60	64.26	17.31	25.72	21.23	107.2	85.3	108.1	108.7	79.9	104.4
1978	617.70	18.26	527.47	514.01	13.46	71.97	20.94	28.31	22.72	113.3	132.6	113.1	112.1	177.2	111.5
1979	672.98	20.41	573.61	556.30	17.31	78.96	23.42	31.02	24.52	108.4	101.4	108.9	108.6	120.1	105.8
1980	730.10	18.90	618.87	598.75	20.12	92.33	25.72	38.59	28.02	107.2	90.8	106.6	106.5	108.4	116.3
1981	764.29	20.33	644.16	620.12	24.04	99.80	27.44	40.61	31.75	104.9	108.6	104.2	103.7	118.6	109.1
1982	794.23	23.97	660.71	634.65	26.06	109.55	29.80	38.76	40.99	106.4	117.4	104.8	104.7	108.2	114.7
1983	835.20	22.68	691.10	663.53	27.57	121.42	32.07	43.15	46.20	107.0	93.6	106.9	107.0	105.7	109.9
1984	934.49	26.59	763.06	728.12	34.94	144.84	38.51	51.50	54.83	110.6	113.3	110.2	109.9	119.3	112.1
1985	1128.29	31.38	910.25	862.73	47.52	186.66	48.67	71.33	66.66	113.2	90.8	113.4	113.5	110.6	115.7
1986	1261.71	33.76	1014.49	952.21	62.28	213.46	54.78	80.61	78.07	106.3	106.0	105.8	105.5	113.7	109.1
1987	1478.65	38.84	1175.31	1073.84	101.47	264.50	67.05	89.48	107.97	107.8	102.3	107.1	106.7	114.4	112.2
1988	1800.88	53.12	1425.44	1304.66	120.78	322.32	82.06	109.08	131.18	111.1	106.4	110.2	110.5	103.7	116.3
1989	2065.95	60.63	1645.27	1524.67	120.60	360.05	92.52	100.75	166.78	103.4	101.3	102.5	103.0	92.4	107.9
1990	2252.10	68.16	1770.26	1642.75	127.51	413.68	118.07	104.27	191.34	103.7	105.7	103.9	104.0	101.3	102.7
1991	2791.06	73.65	2077.98	1947.18	130.80	639.43	163.41	193.18	282.84	112.4	104.8	113.4	114.1	94.3	112.4
1992	3531.86	80.01	2595.64	2429.96	165.68	856.21	212.61	270.64	372.96	118.3	105.8	120.0	120.2	115.8	112.9
1993	4914.90	96.20	3621.54	3327.04	294.50	1197.16	256.76	390.78	549.62	119.7	95.6	121.0	119.7	143.9	116.8
1994	6536.08	140.24	4733.18	4255.19	477.99	1662.66	332.84	456.52	873.30	119.1	107.8	119.6	118.2	139.3	117.8
1995	7749.16	182.47	5378.05	4741.09	636.96	2188.64	408.20	561.31	1219.13	116.2	112.0	116.6	117.1	111.1	114.4

Year	v2c1	v2c2	v3'	v3	v3a	v3b	v3b1	v3b2	v3c	v3c1	v3c2	v3c3	v3c4	v3c5	v3c6
1952			36.66	36.66	2.17	19.22	18.22	1.00	15.27	1.79	10.49				
1953	131.6	134.0	51.71	51.71	2.51	28.75	26.91	1.84	20.45	2.56	14.66				
1954	124.7	98.3	54.70	54.70	2.26	29.67	28.38	1.29	22.77	3.11	16.30				
1955	88.8	91.1	53.64	53.64	2.71	29.39	28.02	1.37	21.54	2.88	15.06				
1956	106.0	128.5	63.61	63.61	2.38	35.25	34.41	0.84	25.98	2.93	18.67				
1957	102.8	91.1	69.60	69.60	2.70	40.83	39.57	1.26	26.07	2.97	18.34				
1958	157.2	74.9	95.61	95.61	3.57	64.66	62.93	1.73	27.38	3.69	18.24				
1959	159.9	97.0	128.49	128.49	4.29	94.82	92.98	1.84	29.38	4.52	18.15				
1960	119.3	75.7	158.39	158.39	4.23	123.36	121.47	1.89	30.80	4.71	17.22				
1961	66.6	174.1	101.78	101.78	4.43	71.06	70.10	0.96	26.29	3.68	13.88				
1962	79.5	89.5	84.72	84.72	4.51	58.80	58.05	0.75	21.41	3.02	10.22				
1963	109.9	92.6	90.69	90.69	4.54	65.72	64.77	0.95	20.43	3.08	10.28				
1964	121.0	112.9	100.70	100.70	6.24	72.17	70.97	1.20	22.29	3.63	11.73				
1965	106.0	103.3	113.55	113.55	6.50	82.92	81.83	1.09	24.13	4.08	12.59				
1966	92.3	101.5	124.81	124.81	6.80	92.27	91.27	1.00	25.74	4.47	13.60				
1967	109.5	106.7	110.04	110.04	7.20	79.51	78.97	0.54	23.33	3.50	12.46				
1968	110.4	100.0	123.24	123.24	8.31	89.20	88.73	0.47	25.73	3.85	12.91				
1969	109.3	96.7	142.30	142.30	7.91	106.08	105.37	0.71	28.31	4.13	15.21				
1970	112.3	99.8	156.67	156.67	7.42	120.82	119.86	0.96	28.43	4.50	14.74				
1971	113.7	102.1	164.86	164.86	7.57	128.23	127.10	1.13	29.06	4.83	14.25				
1972	110.2	98.1	170.98	170.98	8.54	132.82	131.70	1.12	29.62	5.34	15.18				
1973	115.3	98.9	185.35	185.35	8.97	142.39	141.02	1.37	33.99	5.95	16.82				
1974	107.9	109.4	193.45	193.45	9.45	147.86	145.95	1.91	36.14	6.30	18.13				
1975	113.2	109.9	204.12	204.12	8.22	157.54	155.35	2.19	38.36	7.34	18.58				
1976	108.3	102.2	208.12	208.12	8.79	158.89	156.96	1.93	40.44	7.82	18.47				
1977	111.4	103.9	230.36	230.36	7.98	176.98	175.09	1.89	45.40	10.84	19.97				
1978	123.2	107.8	272.81	272.81	11.00	211.05	207.47	3.58	50.76	12.04	23.15	7.02	0.27	2.90	0.72
1979	109.7	107.3	286.43	286.43	11.39	221.21	216.62	4.59	53.83	13.43	23.70	7.42	0.33	3.21	0.73
1980	108.2	121.6	311.89	311.89	10.10	236.10	230.87	5.23	65.69	15.45	31.62	7.82	0.36	3.58	0.89
1981	103.5	112.5	324.76	324.76	10.58	244.34	237.12	7.22	69.84	16.34	32.73	8.29	0.43	4.38	0.97
1982	110.6	103.0	337.07	337.07	13.31	249.32	240.75	8.57	74.44	17.28	29.18	13.36	0.48	4.72	1.27
1983	103.7	109.0	351.81	351.81	13.52	255.32	246.26	9.06	82.97	20.04	31.66	14.98	0.48	4.96	1.52
1984	108.3	115.8	390.85	390.85	17.26	275.37	263.19	12.18	98.22	22.93	38.22	17.21	0.52	6.31	1.81
1985	111.1	120.8	466.75	466.75	19.53	325.63	311.12	14.51	121.59	25.75	51.82	20.53	0.58	7.44	2.28
1986	107.0	105.7	490.83	490.83	19.69	336.02	318.89	17.13	135.12	31.51	51.56	25.59	0.53	8.63	2.33
1987	113.5	104.5	545.46	545.46	21.60	364.38	336.54	27.84	159.48	34.89	53.74	34.03	3.13	10.76	3.16
1988	106.8	119.1	648.30	648.30	27.36	433.05	399.53	33.52	187.89	42.08	64.19	41.88	3.37	10.53	4.07
1989	102.1	108.8	696.54	696.54	29.63	466.18	432.92	33.26	200.73	49.31	41.14	63.48	4.84	10.65	4.80
1990	104.3	99.3	756.45	756.45	32.60	482.68	446.88	35.80	241.17	62.44	51.84	71.07	3.75	14.80	6.01
1991	106.5	112.5	893.77	893.77	33.36	551.34	515.49	35.85	309.07	79.77	63.68	83.18	12.19	23.47	6.34
1992	109.6	114.0	1114.32	1114.32	34.16	677.39	636.68	40.71	402.77	95.92	96.31	98.93	20.48	30.84	8.24
1993	107.6	113.8	1511.61	1511.61	38.21	900.33	844.71	55.62	573.07	119.21	158.82	140.51	26.38	45.57	12.73
1994	111.6	99.4	1971.92	1971.92	48.59	1143.24	1069.31	73.93	780.09	148.44	206.44	214.75	39.09	61.74	17.74
1995	109.0	108.9	2462.57	2462.57	61.68	1409.85	1298.97	110.88	991.04	169.76	269.49	245.45	91.29	83.01	23.88

Year	v3c7	v3c8	v3c9	v3c10	v3d	v4'	v4	v4a	v4b	v4b1	v4b2	v4c	v4c1	v4c2	v4c3
1952				2.99	436										
1953				3.23	590	138.5	138.5	117.5	146.1	143.2	198.0	131.9	145.3	137.3	
1954				3.36	580	103.2	103.2	94.1	105.0	107.2	75.8	102.0	120.8	98.4	
1955				3.60	589	100.0	100.0	128.8	101.8	101.8	101.3	94.1	91.1	92.0	
1956				4.38	681	123.7	123.7	81.2	128.2	131.4	68.4	123.5	105.2	127.4	
1957				4.76	713	107.9	107.9	101.6	116.2	114.9	162.5	95.1	99.7	91.1	
1958				5.45	952	132.0	132.0	103.7	159.6	160.5	129.4	91.8	108.8	83.5	
1959				6.71	1268	136.4	136.4	102.9	150.0	151.2	104.9	103.3	123.2	91.4	
1960				8.87	1521	129.1	129.1	96.9	136.2	136.9	101.2	104.6	134.7	82.0	
1961				8.73	966	63.1	63.1	101.8	53.9	53.9	56.1	106.2	67.9	130.8	
1962				8.17	803	73.6	73.6	101.4	69.7	69.7	66.0	81.1	64.8	80.0	
1963				7.07	851	112.4	112.4	97.9	121.7	121.8	115.6	93.5	103.8	96.6	
1964				6.93	933	116.4	116.4	136.5	115.9	115.8	125.1	115.1	130.2	121.2	
1965				7.46	1042	122.6	122.6	104.0	128.0	128.3	99.8	109.5	128.2	104.7	
1966				7.67	1140	112.5	112.5	111.2	113.6	113.7	95.0	109.1	120.0	106.4	
1967				7.37	999	91.7	91.7	99.8	88.8	89.1	58.0	100.6	99.4	102.3	
1968				8.97	1113	114.0	114.0	122.1	114.2	114.4	81.7	112.2	119.9	101.9	
1969				8.97	1292	115.0	115.0	93.9	119.6	119.5	140.5	103.6	104.3	104.4	
1970				9.19	1446	112.1	112.1	92.5	115.3	115.2	147.6	103.2	114.6	97.7	
1971				9.98	1541	106.1	106.1	102.3	106.4	106.3	119.8	105.4	114.9	99.4	
1972				9.10	1605	102.5	102.5	104.7	103.4	103.4	99.1	98.2	108.5	99.7	
1973				11.22	1737	109.8	109.8	96.5	110.0	109.9	125.4	112.5	120.5	102.1	
1974				11.71	1905	110.9	110.9	102.3	112.2	111.9	142.0	107.2	106.2	108.9	
1975				12.44	1898	104.1	104.1	87.0	104.0	103.8	122.7	108.0	111.6	108.1	
1976				14.15	1929	101.4	101.4	106.9	100.3	100.4	87.6	105.4	105.6	98.7	
1977				14.59	2125	109.5	109.5	78.1	112.4	112.6	102.3	102.9	104.3	104.2	
1978	2.06	1.79	0.81		2498	115.8	115.8	127.0	116.6	115.8	189.7	110.6	110.0	114.3	106.9
1979	2.08	2.02	0.91		2568	107.4	107.4	99.3	108.6	108.8	97.9	103.0	110.8	103.1	88.0
1980	2.54	2.41	1.02		2738	108.4	108.4	99.4	106.0	106.1	101.4	122.2	120.2	126.8	121.9
1981	2.77	2.79	1.14		2813	105.6	105.6	100.3	104.9	104.1	139.2	108.9	104.6	110.2	107.3
1982	3.60	3.06	1.49		2877	107.2	107.2	126.2	104.6	104.2	118.7	113.4	113.7	98.3	165.0
1983	4.33	3.07	1.93		2963	107.8	107.8	100.0	107.6	107.5	108.9	109.8	114.5	106.5	109.0
1984	5.12	3.80	2.30		3259	111.6	111.6	125.2	110.0	109.7	119.3	114.7	109.3	116.4	115.8
1985	5.82	4.67	2.70		3855	113.4	113.4	77.8	114.8	115.0	111.1	114.7	108.6	121.4	112.6
1986	6.89	5.04	3.04		4008	104.4	104.4	99.8	104.0	103.7	111.7	106.0	104.0	100.7	115.2
1987	7.77	8.37	3.63		4396	107.5	107.5	97.3	107.4	106.8	122.2	108.9	103.5	101.0	120.6
1988	8.42	9.12	4.23		5161	110.1	110.1	104.6	109.4	109.3	112.1	112.6	105.7	115.9	121.3
1989	10.73	10.68	5.10		5489	103.0	103.0	100.3	101.6	101.9	95.6	107.1	103.8	101.0	126.3
1990	12.73	10.60	5.71	2.22	5910	103.5	103.5	104.3	102.8	102.7	105.1	105.3	112.6	100.3	106.3
1991	17.33	12.74	8.08	2.29	6955	107.1	107.1	100.4	106.8	108.8	81.3	108.5	107.8	117.1	102.5
1992	21.55	17.60	10.49	2.41	8652	114.9	114.9	100.4	117.2	117.8	107.7	112.0	109.2	117.7	109.1
1993	29.51	22.58	14.75	3.01	11700	114.9	114.9	97.3	116.7	116.9	113.8	113.2	107.3	112.9	118.1
1994	39.81	28.48	19.84	3.76	15204	114.3	114.3	102.9	114.2	114.2	114.1	115.8	101.6	110.5	129.7
1995	44.80	33.65	25.01	4.70	18943	114.1	114.1	106.4	114.8	114.3	125.0	113.1	108.0	114.7	105.4

Year	v4c4	v4c5	v4c6	v4c7	v4c8	v4c9	v4c10	v5	v5a	v5a1	v5a1a	v5a1b	v5a2	v5b	v5b1
1952								36.66	22.43	19.57	2.28	17.29	2.86	7.63	2.28
1953								51.71	26.94	23.12	2.42	20.70	3.82	5.58	3.91
1954								54.70	26.04	22.34	2.28	20.06	3.70	6.14	3.50
1955								53.60	24.83	21.50	2.20	19.30	3.33	6.64	3.75
1956								63.61	26.64	22.94	2.39	20.55	3.70	1.90	4.84
1957								69.60	28.86	25.05	2.75	22.30	3.81	15.87	5.58
1958								95.61	30.55	26.15	2.66	23.49	4.40	24.51	12.33
1959								128.49	33.24	28.16	3.23	24.93	5.08	40.08	16.66
1960								158.39	34.16	28.55	3.78	24.77	5.61	35.64	18.36
1961								101.78	33.89	29.62	4.15	25.47	4.27	12.35	7.86
1962								84.72	32.31	28.42	4.19	24.23	3.89	-2.07	4.35
1963								90.69	32.06	27.84	4.40	23.44	4.22	12.05	5.80
1964								100.70	34.43	29.15	5.13	24.02	5.28	15.69	7.94
1965								113.55	35.63	30.13	5.42	24.89	5.32	3.07	8.30
1966								124.81	37.93	32.59	5.94	26.65	5.34	24.78	7.90
1967								110.04	37.95	33.06	6.28	26.78	4.89	7.64	5.28
1968								123.24	37.04	32.39	7.24	25.15	4.65	23.41	5.18
1969								142.30	38.95	34.00	7.02	26.98	4.95	8.24	8.10
1970								156.67	37.69	32.95	6.97	25.98	4.74	18.24	11.53
1971								164.86	39.66	33.99	7.46	26.53	5.67	26.62	12.66
1972								170.98	41.05	35.61	8.44	27.17	5.44	36.67	14.62
1973								185.35	44.65	38.12	9.27	28.85	6.53	38.60	17.72
1974								193.45	47.40	40.69	10.23	30.46	6.71	42.66	23.89
1975								204.12	50.74	42.70	10.79	31.91	8.04	39.72	34.24
1976								208.12	53.33	44.05	11.25	32.80	9.28	29.76	25.71
1977								230.36	53.90	44.55	11.49	33.06	9.35	30.61	19.72
1978	122.7	112.3	101.4	101.5	101.1	106.6		272.81	59.06	48.25	12.82	35.43	10.81	47.96	31.69
1979	129.6	115.8	95.8	95.6	106.7	111.1		286.43	71.34	58.80	17.02	41.78	12.54	43.61	39.05
1980	114.3	113.7	116.2	116.2	113.7	105.6		311.89	81.24	66.31	19.43	46.88	14.93	66.52	45.57
1981	119.4	121.2	104.5	103.9	110.8	109.8		324.76	89.73	73.69	23.25	50.44	16.04	76.68	55.10
1982	118.6	114.1	133.3	132.2	111.6	130.4		337.07	92.90	75.02	26.41	48.61	17.88	90.27	70.49
1983	98.0	102.0	124.2	124.6	104.0	130.1		351.81	101.19	81.64	26.91	54.73	19.55	71.86	74.51
1984	106.0	125.1	111.7	110.8	116.1	117.0		390.85	117.25	94.56	31.10	63.46	22.69	101.63	90.70
1985	98.1	104.1	119.8	107.9	116.7	105.7		466.75	155.15	124.78	38.35	86.43	30.37	189.13	116.70
1986	92.3	116.3	102.4	118.7	107.9	112.8		490.83	181.74	145.73	42.49	103.24	36.01	228.12	144.41
1987	110.4	114.1	130.8	109.1	148.1	115.5		545.46	200.74	161.09	47.23	113.86	39.65	241.02	183.79
1988	101.9	102.3	114.9	95.8	111.0	107.5		648.30	255.42	211.04	55.97	155.07	44.38	335.56	236.92
1989	107.4	92.7	100.0	108.1	104.4	105.2		696.54	298.62	244.60	61.15	183.45	54.02	351.68	232.22
1990	79.3	117.0	107.3	110.8	94.6	107.2		756.45	316.80	257.16	58.83	198.33	59.64	321.89	248.34
1991	154.4	105.5	101.8	111.5	102.7	105.3	93.2	893.77	386.06	311.09	72.17	238.92	74.97	340.03	276.08
1992	120.9	121.3	113.4	104.8	109.7	111.6	100.2	1114.32	476.57	366.09	84.86	281.23	110.48	487.63	382.01
1993	112.0	119.4	123.6	109.5	107.9	117.0	103.9	1511.61	679.35	537.71	114.18	423.53	141.64	740.47	624.31
1994	124.5	114.3	113.3	112.4	108.5	110.3	106.0	1971.92	873.89	693.04	139.12	553.92	180.85	1151.61	996.48
1995	270.7	114.9	114.8	102.3	103.9	107.6	113.1	2462.57	1085.33	872.67	167.39	705.28	212.66	1551.20	1380.85

Year	v5b2	v5c	v5c1	v5c2	v6a1	v6a2	v6a3	v6a4	v6b2	v6b3	v6b4	v7	v7a	v7a1	v7a2
1952	5.35	6.60													
1953	1.67	19.19										118.5	115.2	104.4	116.7
1954	2.64	22.52										95.9	95.1	92.9	95.3
1955	2.89	22.13										95.0	95.7	94.6	95.8
1956	-2.94	35.07										106.3	105.9	108.6	105.6
1957	10.29	24.83										107.6	108.1	114.1	107.4
1958	12.18	40.55										106.2	104.8	97.3	105.7
1959	23.42	55.17										109.0	107.8	141.3	106.3
1960	17.28	88.59										102.9	101.3	100.0	99.3
1961	4.49	55.54										98.0	102.9	109.0	102.0
1962	-6.42	54.48										89.7	90.5	94.6	89.9
1963	6.25	46.58										99.6	98.8	111.2	96.7
1964	8.75	49.58										109.7	106.6	113.5	105.3
1965	-0.23	69.85										104.8	102.9	104.8	102.5
1966	16.88	62.10										109.3	110.8	113.0	110.3
1967	2.36	64.45										98.9	100.9	104.9	100.0
1968	18.23	62.79										95.2	95.2	116.5	90.2
1969	0.14	95.11										108.2	108.6	96.7	112.1
1970	6.71	100.74										99.4	99.2	101.4	98.6
1971	13.96	98.58										105.8	103.2	107.3	102.1
1972	22.05	93.26										100.5	101.6	109.8	99.3
1973	20.88	102.10										111.1	109.6	112.3	108.8
1974	18.77	103.39										105.9	107.0	110.5	105.8
1975	5.48	113.66										107.5	105.0	105.6	104.8
1976	4.05	125.03										106.1	103.8	105.0	103.4
1977	10.89	145.85										100.7	100.8	101.4	100.6
1978	16.27	165.79			4.58	7.59	0.13	0.52	30.05	3.19	2.19	110.2	108.8	114.3	106.9
1979	4.56	171.48			4.49	11.73	0.24	0.56	35.78	3.75	2.25	118.3	119.5	127.9	116.5
1980	20.95	164.13			3.92	14.57	0.35	0.59	39.80	4.73	2.35	109.0	107.3	108.9	106.6
1981	21.58	158.35			4.20	17.82	0.48	0.75	42.38	5.68	2.38	109.0	109.6	118.2	106.0
1982	19.78	153.90			4.51	20.60	0.52	0.78	39.98	6.16	2.47	103.4	101.7	101.5	101.8
1983	-2.65	178.76			4.78	20.54	0.58	1.01	44.57	7.26	2.90	111.0	108.5	114.4	105.8
1984	10.93	171.97			5.63	23.74	0.67	1.06	51.94	8.44	3.08	113.5	113.6	113.0	113.5
1985	72.43	122.47			5.18	30.91	0.80	1.46	73.17	10.21	3.05	115.8	114.3	105.3	119.0
1986	83.71	80.97			5.94	33.82	0.91	1.82	86.04	13.82	3.38	109.7	109.8	103.8	112.4
1987	57.23	103.70			6.28	38.04	1.04	1.87	93.52	16.62	3.72	103.1	102.4	103.2	102.1
1988	98.64	57.32			4.85	47.35	1.74	2.03	127.48	24.31	3.28	109.3	111.6	104.0	114.6
1989	119.46	46.24			4.56	51.89	2.41	2.29	150.39	29.10	3.96	102.6	101.5	99.8	101.8
1990	73.55	117.76			5.13	47.68	3.53	2.49	156.25	37.42	4.66	100.0	98.4	91.3	101.4
1991	63.95	167.68			5.54	59.16	4.85	2.62	182.57	48.59	7.76	110.0	108.9	113.3	107.6
1992	105.62	150.12			6.02	68.65	6.23	3.96	213.10	60.19	7.94	107.4	106.8	107.2	106.7
1993	116.16	91.79			6.73	89.07	13.26	5.12	320.85	92.13	10.55	118.1	121.4	112.3	124.2
1994	155.13	-53.58			7.98	107.63	17.12	6.39	421.42	118.12	14.38	109.2	109.2	103.5	110.8
1995	170.35	-173.96			16.49	117.31	21.97	11.62	545.28	136.40	23.60	108.1	109.7	104.2	111.2

Year	v7b	v8	v8a	v8b	v9	v9a	v9b	v10a1	v10a2	v10a3	v10a3a	v10a3b	v10a4	v10b1	v10b2
1952		232	100	281											
1953	140.6	264	106	320	110.8	104.0	111.0								
1954	100.7	240	99	287	89.9	92.3	88.5								
1955	91.1	228	94	272	94.4	93.7	94.2								
1956	108.7	246	98	298	106.9	103.3	108.5								
1957	105.0	257	107	311	103.4	107.5	103.2								
1958	114.5	260	110	308	101.7	104.0	99.7								
1959	114.7	278	117	338	106.9	105.8	110.0								
1960	110.8	274	115	347	98.5	99.1	102.5								
1961	76.3	281	124	354	101.6	106.4	101.2								
1962	85.0	269	122	340	90.5	92.2	90.6								
1963	104.3	261	123	331	97.9	106.5	97.0								
1964	128.2	270	140	337	105.2	110.5	104.8								
1965	113.9	276	144	349	102.0	102.4	102.3								
1966	102.8	298	155	374	110.4	110.9	110.9								
1967	94.7	300	162	375	100.4	104.2	99.7								
1968	95.1	293	187	350	94.6	116.1	89.3								
1969	106.4	309	177	383	109.2	94.8	114.6								
1970	100.5	304	172	384	100.7	98.8	102.5								
1971	119.8	318	179	406	104.5	104.3	105.8								
1972	95.3	334	200	423	102.0	108.3	101.0								
1973	118.7	357	216	453	109.5	110.4	109.6								
1974	101.1	380	236	477	106.6	109.9	105.7								
1975	120.0	397	247	499	104.5	105.0	104.7								
1976	115.6	408	255	514	103.5	103.4	103.6								
1977	100.4	411	255	521	100.3	99.6	101.2								
1978	115.6	442	286	551	108.0	114.6	105.5	26.97	3.20	0.88	0.10	0.78	0.64	12.67	3.60
1979	113.0	527	379	627	117.2	127.6	112.3	34.85	2.42	1.08	0.14	0.94	0.70	3.55	1.01
1980	117.1	582	438	675	104.9	110.3	102.2	39.40	3.58	1.58	0.16	1.42	1.01	16.31	3.66
1981	106.4	638	521	711	108.2	117.6	103.9	44.50	5.43	4.17	0.20	3.97	1.00	16.82	4.10
1982	110.9	640	590	671	100.2	101.1	99.7	59.50	5.11	4.59	0.29	4.30	1.27	18.84	0.36
1983	119.7	688	599	742	107.2	114.1	103.9	62.26	6.20	4.73	0.25	4.48	1.32	-4.84	1.54
1984	113.0	789	697	843	112.4	113.9	111.2	73.92	8.98	7.52	0.24	7.28	0.28	4.19	6.38
1985	122.5	1030	868	1124	113.3	106.2	116.5	92.23	10.44	12.20	0.20	12.00	1.83	57.75	14.12
1986	108.8	1190	977	1307	108.6	105.5	109.4	114.42	13.99	10.48	0.18	10.30	5.52	71.89	7.48
1987	105.9	1298	1104	1400	101.1	104.9	99.1	140.71	18.66	13.20	0.53	12.67	11.22	48.25	4.79
1988	100.3	1680	1317	1866	110.2	104.7	112.2	179.17	28.84	17.56	0.66	16.90	11.35	87.98	4.74
1989	107.5	1928	1449	2166	100.4	100.5	99.8	174.45	20.77	14.96	0.64	14.32	22.04	107.39	-4.12
1990	105.1	2009	1401	2306	97.6	91.8	99.9	183.92	21.37	16.57	0.60	15.97	26.48	56.36	5.27
1991	114.6	2421	1727	2756	108.4	113.7	106.7	210.29	27.70	14.87	0.70	14.17	23.32	23.93	21.28
1992	110.0	2842	2045	3221	106.6	108.0	105.9	225.46	63.99	17.55	0.55	17.00	75.01	30.22	66.39
1993	107.4	4162	2805	4786	121.0	114.5	122.5	444.53	119.97	19.13	2.13	17.00	40.68	68.44	18.64
1994	109.2	5343	3522	6141	108.8	106.7	108.7	637.39	174.12	11.61	1.21	10.40	173.36	97.30	25.22
1995	102.3	6713	4359	7700	109.4	107.2	109.4	898.65	224.85	13.83	0.72	13.11	243.52	20.41	57.40

Year	v10b4	v11a	v11a1	v11a2	v11b	v11b1	v11b2	v11c	v11c1	v11c2	v12	v12a	v12b	v13	v13i
1952															
1953											74.3	180.5	29.0		
1954											113.1	93.5	165.2		
1955											111.2	113.7	107.3		
1956											42.0	135.5			
1957											611.5	117.3			
1958											151.5	210.9	115.0		
1959											165.4	142.6	191.1		
1960											92.9	109.8	78.6		
1961											34.8	42.8	25.5		
1962												53.8			
1963												133.7			
1964											132.6	138.6	140.9		
1965											55.7	108.2			
1966											289.6	96.8			
1967											32.2	68.0	13.6		
1968											281.8	99.5	754.3		
1969											40.8	158.0			
1970											221.1	146.7			
1971											149.6	111.8	221.6		
1972											136.9	117.7	155.3		
1973											98.5	122.1	80.4		
1974											120.6	137.7	102.1		
1975											96.6	142.9	28.3		
1976											74.1	74.7	69.1		
1977											94.5	74.5	255.2		
1978		1.90	1.88	0.02	23.41	21.21	2.20	22.65	8.60	14.05	169.4	161.7	187.5	272.81	62.03
1979		2.00	2.36	-0.36	30.90	26.73	4.17	10.71	9.96	0.75	90.3	119.7	29.1	286.43	68.15
1980	0.98	2.69	2.75	-0.06	36.69	31.12	5.57	27.14	11.70	15.44	149.1	111.5	453.3	311.89	74.47
1981	0.66	3.95	2.73	1.22	43.31	35.97	7.34	29.42	16.40	13.02	116.2	123.4	102.1	324.76	78.99
1982	0.58	1.64	2.40	-0.76	52.09	49.45	2.64	36.54	18.64	17.90	113.1	127.9	77.7	337.07	85.00
1983	0.65	3.35	3.39	-0.04	50.25	49.56	0.69	18.26	21.56	-3.30	84.6	106.2		351.81	90.36
1984	0.36	1.51	1.79	-0.28	69.70	60.61	9.09	30.42	28.30	2.12	132.8	117.4		390.85	108.79
1985	0.56	3.73	3.02	0.71	123.86	74.34	49.52	61.54	39.34	22.20	173.6	117.3	602.8	466.75	125.99
1986	4.34	3.43	2.62	0.81	145.63	90.23	55.40	79.06	51.56	27.50	111.7	114.4	108.1	490.83	141.95
1987	4.19	1.59	2.07	-0.48	136.72	112.14	24.58	102.71	69.58	33.13	91.3	118.1	63.3	545.46	163.88
1988	5.92	3.23	2.38	0.85	203.63	146.13	57.50	128.70	88.41	40.29	117.6	114.0	128.1	648.30	197.69
1989	15.69	4.30	3.94	0.36	217.27	146.31	70.96	130.11	81.97	48.14	93.4	88.5	106.1	696.54	223.35
1990	11.42	3.86	3.36	0.50	226.89	156.13	70.76	91.14	88.85	2.29	87.4	102.6	58.7	756.45	244.03
1991	18.74	4.75	4.70	0.05	242.18	159.29	82.89	93.10	112.09	-18.99	98.8	104.0	81.3	893.77	302.94
1992	9.01	6.39	6.39	0.00	311.97	197.80	114.17	169.27	177.82	-8.55	130.3	125.4	151.2	1114.32	397.72
1993	29.08	6.33	5.88	0.45	393.37	287.87	105.50	340.77	330.56	10.21	120.6	127.2	96.8	1511.61	559.56
1994	32.61	16.58	15.97	0.61	454.52	352.58	101.94	680.51	627.93	52.58	135.9	139.3	120.3	1971.92	681.80
1995	92.54	9.14	8.37	0.77	605.67	438.49	167.18	936.39	933.99	2.40	124.2	128.3	101.8	2462.57	880.66

Year	v13ii	v13iii	v13iv	v13a	v13ai	v13aii	v13aiii	v13aiv	v13b	v13bi	v13bii	v13biii	v13biv	v13b1	v13b1i
1952															
1953															
1954															
1955															
1956															
1957															
1958															
1959															
1960															
1961															
1962															
1963															
1964															
1965															
1966															
1967															
1968															
1969															
1970															
1971															
1972															
1973															
1974															
1975															
1976															
1977															
1978	10.60	45.53	154.65	11.00	8.13	0.36	0.23	2.28	211.05	40.37	7.79	45.96	116.93	207.47	38.09
1979	11.13	45.61	161.54	11.39	8.31	0.35	0.24	2.49	221.21	44.71	7.84	47.87	120.79	216.52	41.77
1980	13.05	49.49	174.88	10.10	7.98	0.41	0.24	1.47	236.10	49.01	9.13	50.69	127.27	230.37	45.70
1981	14.70	54.52	176.55	10.58	8.80	0.41	0.26	1.11	244.34	51.46	10.31	54.11	128.46	237.12	46.56
1982	16.30	57.09	178.68	13.31	10.01	0.40	0.44	2.46	249.32	52.64	11.21	56.01	129.46	240.75	47.49
1983	17.92	57.51	186.02	13.52	10.31	0.45	0.44	2.32	255.32	54.47	13.41	56.57	130.87	246.26	49.13
1984	20.81	68.74	192.51	17.26	13.20	0.57	0.57	2.92	275.37	64.56	15.05	64.96	130.80	263.19	57.09
1985	26.16	87.36	227.24	19.53	15.03	0.57	0.60	3.33	325.63	75.21	18.27	80.94	151.21	311.12	66.68
1986	33.42	86.31	229.15	19.69	16.14	0.59	0.69	2.27	336.02	84.57	21.80	79.99	149.66	318.89	73.72
1987	40.73	98.61	242.24	21.60	18.20	0.64	0.87	1.89	364.38	97.84	26.47	94.26	145.81	336.54	79.61
1988	71.85	126.95	251.81	27.36	22.40	1.14	0.88	2.94	433.05	120.48	48.84	109.42	154.31	399.53	98.99
1989	79.79	136.01	257.39	29.63	23.33	1.38	1.33	3.59	466.18	135.92	55.63	121.73	152.90	432.92	112.25
1990	92.93	149.35	270.14	32.60	25.91	1.49	1.27	3.93	482.68	143.02	62.74	131.62	145.30	446.88	117.69
1991	126.62	170.42	293.79	33.36	25.95	1.53	1.29	4.59	551.34	173.36	83.80	145.59	148.59	515.49	147.34
1992	160.36	207.40	348.84	34.16	26.04	1.31	1.32	5.49	677.39	234.57	108.70	162.48	171.64	636.68	207.30
1993	158.49	256.72	536.84	38.21	32.55	1.93	1.48	2.25	900.33	337.69	98.28	206.16	258.20	844.71	299.23
1994	241.31	355.59	693.22	48.59	36.94	1.64	2.00	8.01	1143.24	393.76	162.97	266.14	320.37	1069.31	341.95
1995	332.29	428.07	821.55	61.68	45.20	2.04	2.45	11.99	1409.85	503.77	218.78	337.95	349.35	1298.97	441.48

Year	v13b1ii	v13b1iii	v13b1iv	v13b2	v13b2i	v13b2ii	v13b2iii	v13b2iv	v13c	v13ci	v13cii	v13ciii	v13civ	v13c1
1952														
1953														
1954														
1955														
1956														
1957														
1958														
1959														
1960														
1961														
1962														
1963														
1964														
1965														
1966														
1967														
1968														
1969														
1970														
1971														
1972														
1973														
1974														
1975														
1976														
1977														
1978	7.59	45.83	115.96	3.58	2.28	0.20	0.13	0.97	50.76	13.53	2.45	-0.66	35.44	12.04
1979	7.59	47.72	119.54	4.59	2.94	0.25	0.15	1.25	53.83	15.13	2.94	-2.50	38.26	13.43
1980	8.75	50.53	125.89	5.23	3.31	0.38	0.16	1.38	65.69	17.48	3.51	-1.44	46.14	15.45
1981	9.85	53.90	126.81	7.22	4.90	0.46	0.21	1.65	69.84	18.73	3.98	0.15	46.98	16.34
1982	10.64	55.67	126.95	8.57	5.15	0.57	0.34	2.51	74.44	22.35	4.69	0.64	46.76	17.28
1983	12.71	56.26	128.16	9.06	5.34	0.70	0.31	2.71	82.97	25.58	4.06	0.50	52.83	20.04
1984	14.16	64.34	127.60	12.18	7.47	0.89	0.62	3.20	98.22	31.03	5.19	3.21	58.79	22.93
1985	16.87	80.13	147.44	14.51	8.53	1.40	0.81	3.77	121.59	35.75	7.32	5.82	72.70	25.75
1986	20.35	78.98	145.84	17.13	10.85	1.45	1.01	3.82	135.12	41.24	11.03	5.63	77.22	31.51
1987	25.09	92.00	139.84	27.84	18.23	1.38	2.26	5.97	159.48	47.84	13.62	3.48	94.54	34.89
1988	45.90	106.33	148.42	33.52	21.60	2.94	3.09	5.89	187.89	54.81	21.87	16.65	94.56	42.08
1989	52.39	118.22	150.06	33.26	23.67	3.24	3.51	2.84	200.73	64.10	22.78	12.95	100.90	49.31
1990	58.80	127.77	142.62	35.80	25.33	3.94	3.85	2.68	241.17	75.10	28.70	16.46	120.91	62.44
1991	79.75	141.06	147.34	35.85	26.02	4.05	4.53	1.25	309.07	103.63	41.29	23.54	140.61	79.77
1992	104.23	157.64	167.51	40.71	27.27	4.47	4.84	4.13	402.77	137.11	50.35	43.60	171.71	95.92
1993	94.54	198.69	252.25	55.62	38.46	3.74	7.47	5.95	573.07	189.32	58.28	49.08	276.39	119.21
1994	157.66	255.66	314.04	73.93	51.81	5.31	10.48	6.33	780.09	251.10	76.70	87.45	364.84	148.44
1995	210.00	319.45	328.04	110.88	62.29	8.78	18.50	21.31	991.04	331.69	111.47	87.67	460.21	169.76

Year	v13c1i	v13c1ii	v13c1iii	v13c1iv	v13c2	v13c2i	v13c2ii	v13c2iii	v13c2iv	v13c3	v13c3i	v13c3ii	v13c3iii	v13c3iv
1952														
1953														
1954														
1955														
1956														
1957														
1958														
1959														
1960														
1961														
1962														
1963														
1964														
1965														
1966														
1967														
1968														
1969														
1970														
1971														
1972														
1973														
1974														
1975														
1976														
1977														
1978	3.23	1.40	0.78	6.63	23.15	4.50	0.51	-2.16	20.30	7.02	0.14	0.01	0.31	6.56
1979	3.68	1.62	0.86	7.27	23.70	5.29	0.55	-4.12	21.98	7.42	0.18	0.01	0.31	6.92
1980	4.17	1.80	0.93	8.55	31.62	6.03	0.72	-3.29	28.16	7.82	0.21	0.01	0.36	7.24
1981	4.27	2.31	1.13	8.63	32.73	6.51	0.43	-2.03	27.82	8.29	0.24	0.01	0.42	7.62
1982	4.56	2.72	1.36	8.64	29.18	8.01	0.45	-2.11	22.83	13.36	0.27	0.01	0.58	12.40
1983	5.08	2.42	1.64	10.90	31.66	9.44	0.51	-2.67	24.38	14.98	0.33	0.01	0.76	13.88
1984	6.68	2.51	2.00	11.74	38.22	11.05	0.46	-0.52	27.23	17.21	0.42	0.02	0.38	15.89
1985	7.36	3.53	2.03	12.83	51.82	12.39	0.84	1.66	36.93	20.53	0.61	0.03	1.38	18.51
1986	8.86	5.62	2.87	14.16	51.56	13.88	1.31	-0.39	36.76	25.59	0.86	0.05	1.75	22.93
1987	10.14	6.68	3.06	15.01	53.74	14.69	1.42	-3.84	41.47	34.03	1.16	0.08	2.31	30.48
1988	12.37	11.80	3.19	14.72	64.19	16.03	2.25	7.69	38.22	41.88	1.68	0.14	3.50	36.56
1989	14.73	12.17	2.83	19.58	41.14	18.36	2.33	2.52	17.93	63.48	2.05	0.26	4.63	56.54
1990	15.91	16.34	4.68	25.51	51.84	20.20	2.85	2.36	26.43	71.07	2.17	0.23	5.78	62.89
1991	20.53	21.09	6.48	31.67	63.68	32.17	4.11	8.00	19.40	83.18	2.32	0.48	5.97	74.41
1992	25.02	26.34	7.54	37.02	96.31	44.92	4.82	26.86	19.71	98.93	2.59	0.63	7.98	87.73
1993	35.96	30.58	10.73	41.94	158.82	62.86	5.00	16.67	74.29	140.51	3.62	0.87	20.71	115.31
1994	47.31	42.80	13.27	45.06	206.44	75.14	6.58	23.09	101.63	214.75	8.08	2.57	48.66	155.44
1995	31.61	52.31	17.72	37.79	269.49	101.19	9.66	22.71	135.93	245.45	9.76	6.58	40.20	188.91

Year	v13c4	v13c4i	v13c4ii	v13c4iii	v13c4iv	v13c5	v13c5i	v13c5ii	v13c5iii	v13c5iv	v13c6	v13c6i	v13c6ii	v13c6iii
1952														
1953														
1954														
1955														
1956														
1957														
1958														
1959														
1960														
1961														
1962														
1963														
1964														
1965														
1966														
1967														
1968														
1969														
1970														
1971														
1972														
1973														
1974														
1975														
1976														
1977														
1978	0.27	0.22	0.11	0.05	-0.11	2.90	1.42	0.29	0.25	0.94	0.72	0.70	0.02	
1979	0.33	0.23	0.15	0.06	-0.11	3.21	1.63	0.38	0.25	0.95	0.73	0.70	0.03	
1980	0.36	0.26	0.17	0.07	-0.14	3.58	1.94	0.45	0.29	0.90	0.89	0.85	0.04	
1981	0.43	0.29	0.25	0.08	-0.19	4.38	2.14	0.52	0.32	1.40	0.97	0.92	0.05	
1982	0.48	0.33	0.58	0.09	-0.52	4.72	2.32	0.50	0.34	1.56	1.27	1.23	0.04	
1983	0.48	0.36	0.81	0.10	-0.79	4.96	2.48	0.57	0.37	1.54	1.52	1.47	0.05	
1984	0.52	0.40	0.86	0.11	-0.85	6.31	3.03	0.67	0.39	2.22	1.81	1.70	0.06	
1985	0.58	0.45	1.19	0.02	-1.08	7.44	3.57	0.56	0.40	2.91	2.28	2.10	0.01	0.01
1986	0.53	0.48	1.64	0.03	-1.62	8.63	4.46	0.71	0.91	2.55	2.33	2.23	0.10	
1987	3.13	0.63	1.84	0.32	0.34	10.76	5.52	1.57	0.75	2.92	3.16	2.78	0.29	0.02
1988	3.37	0.67	2.90	0.32	-0.52	10.53	6.29	1.78	0.93	1.53	4.07	3.44	0.53	0.03
1989	4.84	0.82	3.06	0.32	0.64	10.65	6.86	1.83	1.21	0.75	4.80	3.85	0.59	0.04
1990	3.75	0.92	3.23	0.29	-0.69	14.80	9.34	2.11	1.67	1.68	6.01	4.46	0.88	0.05
1991	12.19	1.47	4.98	0.89	4.85	23.47	14.95	3.65	0.33	4.54	6.34	5.01	0.98	0.11
1992	20.48	3.59	5.47	1.56	9.86	30.84	20.49	4.85	-2.83	8.33	8.24	6.04	1.26	0.34
1993	26.38	4.84	6.05	2.17	13.32	45.57	27.12	6.35	-4.45	16.55	12.73	9.35	1.45	0.07
1994	39.09	7.18	7.37	7.84	16.70	61.74	36.46	7.32	-9.79	27.75	17.74	13.19	1.75	0.09
1995	91.29	11.49	22.80	8.83	47.87	83.01	51.22	8.46	-9.68	33.01	23.88	17.72	2.13	1.27

Year	v13c6iv	v13c7	v13c7i	v13c7ii	v13c7iii	v13c7iv	v13c8	v13c8i	v13c8ii	v13c8iii	v13c8iv	v13c9	v13c9i	v13c9ii
1952														
1953														
1954														
1955														
1956														
1957														
1958														
1959														
1960														
1961														
1962														
1963														
1964														
1965														
1966														
1967														
1968														
1969														
1970														
1971														
1972														
1973														
1974														
1975														
1976														
1977														
1978		2.06	1.97	0.06	0.03		1.79	0.55	0.04	0.08	1.12	0.81	0.80	0.01
1979		2.08	1.93	0.10	0.05		2.02	0.59	0.09	0.09	1.25	0.91	0.90	0.01
1980		2.54	2.30	0.16	0.07	0.01	2.41	0.73	0.14	0.12	1.42	1.02	0.99	0.02
1981		2.77	2.43	0.20	0.09	0.05	2.79	0.82	0.19	0.13	1.65	1.14	1.11	0.02
1982		3.60	3.06	0.18	0.11	0.25	3.06	1.12	0.18	0.16	1.60	1.49	1.45	0.03
1983		4.33	3.28	0.22	0.12	0.71	3.07	1.27	0.23	0.17	1.40	1.93	1.87	0.05
1984	0.05	5.12	4.03	0.28	0.13	0.68	3.80	1.48	0.28	0.21	1.83	2.30	2.24	0.05
1985	0.16	5.82	4.78	0.60	0.11	0.33	4.67	1.85	0.51	0.20	2.11	2.70	2.64	0.05
1986		6.89	5.45	0.91	0.12	0.41	5.04	2.14	0.55	0.32	2.03	3.04	2.88	0.14
1987	0.07	7.77	6.40	0.80	0.13	0.44	8.37	3.14	0.72	0.70	3.81	3.36	3.38	0.22
1988	0.07	8.42	6.85	1.29	0.15	0.13	9.12	3.52	0.95	0.80	3.85	4.23	3.96	0.23
1989	0.32	10.73	8.47	1.25	0.26	0.75	10.68	4.16	1.04	1.09	4.39	5.10	4.80	0.25
1990	0.62	12.73	9.71	1.56	0.42	1.04	10.60	4.86	1.16	1.15	3.43	5.71	5.31	0.34
1991	0.24	17.33	12.13	3.00	0.60	1.60	12.74	6.07	1.98	1.10	3.59	8.08	6.69	1.02
1992	0.60	21.55	15.36	3.33	0.66	2.20	17.60	7.88	2.44	1.41	5.87	10.49	8.81	1.21
1993	1.86	29.51	20.48	3.66	1.20	4.17	22.58	10.28	3.05	1.89	7.36	14.75	11.80	1.27
1994	2.71	39.81	29.15	4.06	1.89	4.71	28.48	14.67	3.40	2.30	8.11	19.84	16.16	0.85
1995	2.76	44.80	35.03	4.32	2.33	3.12	33.65	17.52	3.81	2.74	9.58	25.01	20.82	1.40

Year	v13c9iii	v13c9iv	v13c10	v13c10i	v13c10ii	v13c10iii	v13c10iv
1952							
1953							
1954							
1955							
1956							
1957							
1958							
1959							
1960							
1961							
1962							
1963							
1964							
1965							
1966							
1967							
1968							
1969							
1970							
1971							
1972							
1973							
1974							
1975							
1976							
1977							
1978							
1979							
1980	0.01						
1981	0.01						
1982	0.01						
1983	0.01						
1984	0.01						
1985	0.01						
1986	0.02						
1987	0.03						
1988	0.04						
1989	0.05						
1990	0.06		2.22	2.22			
1991	0.06	0.31	2.29	2.29			
1992	0.08	0.39	2.41	2.41			
1993	0.09	1.59	3.01	3.01			
1994	0.10	2.73	3.76	3.76			
1995	1.55	1.24	4.70	4.70			

10

Jiangsu

Year	v1	v1a	v1b	v1b1	v1b2	v1c	v1c1	v1c2	v1c3	v2	v2a	v2b	v2b1	v2b2	v2c
1952	81.54	31.87	27.19	25.53	1.66	22.48	1.31	11.12	10.05						
1953	92.06	32.31	32.51	29.81	2.70	27.24	1.81	12.43	13.00	109.5	100.9	121.9	117.6	158.2	117.5
1954	94.00	32.45	34.81	31.66	3.15	26.74	2.08	12.76	11.90	101.5	100.7	108.7	107.5	115.8	97.6
1955	100.53	36.22	35.77	32.82	2.95	28.54	2.15	12.94	13.45	108.1	111.3	101.4	102.6	94.6	107.8
1956	107.08	33.60	41.43	38.60	2.83	32.05	2.41	14.93	14.71	103.9	93.4	120.8	125.1	93.5	109.5
1957	114.15	36.81	44.63	41.01	3.62	32.71	2.76	15.08	14.87	101.9	103.4	104.4	102.3	122.3	97.6
1958	158.03	38.74	82.66	75.22	7.44	36.63	5.07	13.89	17.67	114.0	101.7	160.4	159.2	169.4	92.2
1959	182.82	37.35	104.12	96.00	8.12	41.35	6.68	15.16	19.51	112.1	93.3	134.9	139.3	105.7	109.3
1960	188.33	36.76	110.66	100.32	10.34	40.91	6.95	12.93	21.03	101.7	92.1	111.3	109.6	125.8	97.7
1961	140.88	35.73	67.20	62.50	4.70	37.95	4.60	15.06	18.29	80.3	96.9	60.8	62.3	48.8	99.6
1962	133.12	40.15	56.38	53.36	3.02	36.59	4.63	12.90	19.06	91.9	101.1	81.0	82.9	62.4	93.7
1963	141.37	46.77	58.36	54.66	3.70	36.24	4.82	12.77	18.65	110.4	119.5	105.1	103.3	127.6	102.9
1964	166.61	56.62	72.53	68.17	4.36	37.46	5.19	12.71	19.56	116.4	118.5	125.5	126.4	116.2	102.1
1965	192.52	57.27	97.49	88.08	9.41	37.76	6.16	14.60	17.00	116.1	105.7	140.7	134.1	216.9	101.3
1966	224.09	66.08	115.05	104.19	10.86	42.96	7.07	15.67	20.22	118.4	116.6	121.5	122.1	117.4	115.7
1967	196.39	61.19	93.06	84.80	8.26	42.14	5.89	14.66	21.59	89.7	92.4	82.0	82.6	77.8	100.5
1968	202.00	65.38	93.28	85.48	7.80	43.34	6.11	15.86	21.37	102.7	103.4	102.0	103.0	94.4	102.7
1969	228.23	65.60	114.59	102.80	11.79	48.04	6.90	16.86	24.28	111.8	99.3	127.2	124.6	149.5	109.7
1970	273.85	71.33	149.65	135.47	14.18	52.87	7.88	18.23	26.76	119.1	107.7	135.7	137.8	120.2	106.1
1971	320.40	79.90	184.61	167.15	17.46	55.89	8.33	19.56	28.00	116.5	111.0	123.6	123.8	121.9	108.4
1972	342.65	83.24	202.18	183.38	18.80	57.23	10.42	20.57	26.24	106.2	102.7	110.0	110.4	106.9	101.7
1973	377.87	89.71	227.95	208.10	19.85	60.21	10.43	20.87	28.91	109.8	106.7	113.2	114.1	105.1	104.7
1974	377.82	89.88	227.00	205.39	21.61	60.94	10.21	21.35	29.38	100.5	100.2	100.3	99.3	109.5	101.7
1975	412.28	91.66	260.23	235.28	24.95	60.39	11.50	21.03	27.86	108.3	100.9	115.4	115.5	114.6	98.4
1976	438.59	100.71	271.19	247.59	23.60	66.69	12.69	21.21	32.79	107.9	103.9	108.8	110.3	95.9	112.0
1977	487.98	89.16	326.37	297.12	29.25	72.45	13.99	22.33	36.13	110.2	90.0	120.3	120.1	122.8	107.6
1978	566.85	105.87	378.99	337.65	41.34	81.99	14.20	22.39	45.40	117.3	121.5	116.5	113.8	142.7	114.3
1979	661.26	145.25	427.36	386.05	41.31	88.65	15.69	29.12	43.84	110.1	110.9	111.7	113.9	94.3	102.0
1980	750.12	138.45	515.71	467.82	47.89	95.96	16.03	32.37	47.56	112.1	94.5	120.0	120.9	112.1	104.7
1981	816.27	153.62	557.41	504.94	52.47	105.24	17.29	34.47	53.48	109.1	107.9	108.8	108.3	113.6	112.2
1982	897.85	188.11	593.52	534.87	58.65	116.22	20.21	35.47	60.54	109.6	114.9	108.0	107.7	110.8	110.1
1983	1014.55	206.86	679.67	600.70	78.97	128.02	23.69	43.11	61.22	113.2	105.9	115.9	113.9	134.8	110.4
1984	1239.44	253.82	836.02	745.36	90.66	149.60	31.05	52.99	65.56	120.1	116.4	122.0	123.3	112.1	114.9
1985	1642.70	288.55	1157.52	1036.67	120.85	196.63	38.84	62.44	95.35	126.5	103.1	132.7	133.4	127.1	125.4
1986	1960.44	332.66	1380.16	1235.38	144.78	247.62	49.56	75.83	122.23	115.7	106.3	116.5	116.7	114.7	122.2
1987	2472.22	380.25	1771.85	1590.31	181.54	320.12	73.05	113.59	133.48	119.8	103.1	122.2	123.9	107.4	123.9
1988	3409.56	497.95	2370.81	2152.93	217.88	540.80	101.05	220.49	219.26	125.5	106.6	125.6	125.7	124.4	142.0
1989	3839.67	522.25	2713.50	2507.42	206.08	603.92	106.20	218.49	279.23	103.9	100.4	103.1	104.7	86.1	110.4
1990	4208.23	580.53	2978.51	2764.10	214.41	649.19	107.86	219.68	321.65	108.2	102.5	109.5	110.0	102.8	105.7
1991	4820.22	580.93	3416.59	3161.60	254.99	822.70	137.17	300.50	385.03	113.1	98.9	114.4	114.5	112.8	120.3
1992	6862.87	673.82	5089.59	4673.57	416.02	1099.46	174.76	415.46	509.24	141.0	113.0	149.0	149.2	145.9	125.7
1993	10245.27	875.37	7757.28	7096.46	660.82	1612.62	252.82	634.18	725.62	135.5	111.3	140.1	142.0	112.5	127.1
1994	14163.89	1335.23	10601.01	9826.50	774.51	2227.65	355.95	816.07	1055.63	128.3	112.1	132.0	133.7	101.4	116.1
1995	18328.00	1686.78	13681.15	12623.34	1057.81	2960.07	482.52	1104.21	1373.34	118.8	113.7	119.6	119.5	122.3	116.4

Year	v2c1	v2c2	v3'	v3	v3a	v3b	v3b1	v3b2	v3c	v3c1	v3c2	v3c3	v3c4	v3c5	v3c6
1952			48.41	48.41	25.49	8.53	7.63	0.90	14.39	0.89	7.14				
1953	134.4	108.4	53.42	53.42	25.86	10.26	9.21	1.05	17.30	1.18	8.48				
1954	114.2	102.1	53.77	53.77	25.81	10.98	9.84	1.14	16.98	1.35	8.10				
1955	103.2	102.4	58.96	58.96	29.69	11.29	10.06	1.23	17.98	1.40	8.61				
1956	110.3	112.5	61.90	61.90	27.76	13.79	12.44	1.35	20.35	1.56	9.73				
1957	109.7	96.6	65.11	65.11	29.94	14.40	12.51	1.89	20.77	1.79	9.72				
1958	151.3	75.9	75.30	75.30	29.05	23.17	21.29	1.88	23.08	3.19	9.54				
1959	131.6	105.7	79.62	79.62	25.79	27.57	25.30	2.27	26.26	4.21	10.61				
1960	99.4	84.2	86.80	86.80	25.68	35.96	33.12	2.84	25.16	4.38	9.61				
1961	71.1	125.0	72.20	72.20	25.78	22.89	21.20	1.69	23.53	2.90	10.14				
1962	98.0	83.3	69.20	69.20	29.10	17.34	15.69	1.65	22.76	2.92	9.65				
1963	108.1	102.9	75.52	75.52	35.27	18.14	16.35	1.79	22.11	2.94	9.28				
1964	106.3	98.3	89.55	89.55	42.50	24.01	22.18	1.83	23.04	3.16	9.58				
1965	119.2	115.4	95.10	95.10	41.20	30.26	26.87	3.39	23.64	3.76	9.29				
1966	116.7	109.2	109.89	109.89	47.53	35.51	32.25	3.26	26.85	4.28	10.58				
1967	85.3	95.8	99.20	99.20	44.13	29.53	26.64	2.89	25.54	3.56	10.52				
1968	103.6	108.1	102.84	102.84	47.04	29.45	26.95	2.50	26.35	3.70	10.82				
1969	111.7	105.2	111.75	111.75	47.22	35.42	31.89	3.53	29.11	4.17	11.86				
1970	114.1	108.0	129.23	129.23	51.03	46.16	42.33	3.83	32.04	4.76	12.88				
1971	104.6	106.1	148.04	148.04	57.24	56.43	51.73	4.70	34.37	5.12	13.76				
1972	124.2	104.5	157.31	157.31	60.20	61.74	56.83	4.91	35.37	5.40	14.00				
1973	99.7	101.0	170.93	170.93	64.74	69.28	64.02	5.26	36.91	5.58	14.70				
1974	98.4	102.8	171.94	171.94	65.50	69.45	63.57	5.88	36.99	5.34	14.95				
1975	111.8	97.8	184.16	184.16	67.59	79.61	72.70	6.91	36.96	6.12	14.15				
1976	111.9	102.3	187.97	187.97	62.38	85.04	78.48	6.56	40.55	6.75	15.48				
1977	109.5	105.3	202.40	202.40	53.22	105.35	97.15	8.20	43.83	8.05	16.00				
1978	102.2	100.3	249.24	249.24	68.71	131.09	117.10	13.99	49.44	6.85	13.63	10.43	5.50	2.89	1.44
1979	104.2	122.8	298.55	298.55	104.04	141.14	126.25	14.89	53.37	7.19	17.64	10.27	5.42	2.85	1.42
1980	101.5	110.4	319.80	319.80	94.24	167.41	151.22	16.19	58.15	8.10	18.04	11.52	6.08	3.20	1.60
1981	107.4	107.5	350.02	350.02	109.39	178.01	161.11	16.90	62.62	9.14	19.24	12.32	6.50	3.42	1.71
1982	116.5	102.0	390.17	390.17	135.15	185.52	168.09	17.43	69.50	10.48	20.84	13.74	7.25	3.81	1.91
1983	117.4	121.6	437.65	437.65	150.41	210.81	191.52	19.29	76.43	12.36	23.86	14.47	7.64	4.02	2.01
1984	128.9	120.1	518.85	518.85	179.00	250.39	228.58	21.81	89.46	16.67	29.66	15.52	8.19	4.30	2.15
1985	119.4	112.4	651.82	651.82	195.66	339.56	307.89	31.67	116.60	26.07	32.98	18.91	11.93	5.47	2.92
1986	123.8	116.2	744.94	744.94	224.26	376.32	337.77	38.55	144.36	33.76	40.09	25.56	13.50	6.73	3.69
1987	141.3	145.6	922.33	922.33	246.86	493.69	443.23	50.46	181.78	43.25	61.60	25.14	14.59	7.79	3.98
1988	126.4	177.3	1208.85	1208.85	319.18	586.82	526.92	59.90	302.85	59.62	103.63	47.44	21.25	16.91	8.42
1989	95.6	90.2	1321.85	1321.85	324.18	657.06	599.91	57.15	340.61	62.66	102.69	65.45	24.72	16.69	10.00
1990	102.6	99.4	1416.50	1416.50	355.17	692.59	634.13	58.46	368.74	63.64	103.25	72.53	27.02	19.88	11.66
1991	120.0	131.3	1601.38	1601.38	345.14	793.92	725.83	68.09	462.32	80.27	140.27	77.81	33.51	25.96	13.92
1992	113.2	131.7	2136.02	2136.02	393.82	1119.26	1017.94	101.32	622.94	100.55	201.91	109.27	43.89	35.79	17.74
1993	123.8	132.3	2998.16	2998.16	490.59	1598.05	1451.97	146.08	909.52	144.11	308.21	144.81	74.56	59.79	25.43
1994	123.3	105.9	4057.39	4057.39	671.94	2186.77	2002.22	184.55	1198.68	187.19	389.41	200.34	99.26	82.36	33.53
1995	115.0	118.4	5155.25	5155.25	848.35	2715.26	2467.63	247.63	1591.64	253.52	516.89	270.50	143.61	102.98	44.16

Year	v3c7	v3c8	v3c9	v3c10	v3d	v4'	v4	v4a	v4b	v4b1	v4b2	v4c	v4c1	v4c2	v4c3
1952				6.36	131										
1953				7.64	141	106.9	106.9	101.0	121.0	119.0	132.6	116.6	128.8	115.2	
1954				7.53	140	100.1	100.1	100.0	108.4	108.8	106.4	97.5	113.0	95.0	
1955				7.97	150	111.1	111.1	114.7	101.7	101.9	100.8	107.0	105.0	107.3	
1956				9.06	153	102.1	102.1	94.1	129.9	131.7	120.0	110.4	108.4	110.2	
1957				9.26	157	100.4	100.4	101.8	100.5	95.5	130.9	97.6	109.7	95.5	
1958				10.35	178	98.8	98.8	93.7	139.7	143.1	124.5	91.5	147.1	80.8	
1959				11.44	186	100.2	100.2	85.9	129.8	136.9	93.9	110.2	127.8	107.7	
1960				11.17	203	103.6	103.6	93.2	136.9	140.4	110.9	94.6	102.6	89.5	
1961				10.49	170	89.2	89.2	100.1	63.7	63.8	62.6	100.4	71.2	113.2	
1962				10.19	161	93.2	93.2	101.5	73.5	72.8	80.8	94.0	97.8	92.6	
1963				9.89	172	114.0	114.0	124.3	105.6	103.9	119.4	100.9	104.6	99.9	
1964				10.30	200	116.4	116.4	117.9	134.1	139.5	94.0	102.9	106.3	101.9	
1965				10.59	208	107.1	107.1	101.3	130.8	120.8	241.7	103.1	119.5	97.5	
1966				11.99	235	117.3	117.3	116.5	121.1	122.3	114.6	115.4	115.6	115.8	
1967				11.46	206	91.8	91.8	92.7	84.4	83.0	92.1	97.4	85.3	101.8	
1968				11.83	209	102.8	102.8	103.1	101.8	104.0	90.2	103.0	103.8	102.6	
1969				13.08	221	107.0	107.0	99.3	124.6	124.6	124.8	109.3	111.6	108.4	
1970				14.40	249	114.9	114.9	107.1	136.5	137.5	130.6	110.1	114.1	108.6	
1971				15.49	279	113.3	113.3	111.1	122.7	123.2	119.3	106.1	106.5	105.7	
1972				15.97	291	105.4	105.4	103.7	110.1	111.3	101.9	102.2	104.6	101.1	
1973				16.63	312	108.0	108.0	106.5	112.9	113.9	105.1	103.9	102.9	104.5	
1974				16.70	311	101.0	101.0	101.2	100.9	99.0	115.9	100.7	96.2	102.2	
1975				16.69	329	106.1	106.1	102.1	115.6	117.1	105.4	99.2	113.8	94.0	
1976				18.32	332	101.0	101.0	87.3	112.0	113.7	98.8	111.3	111.8	111.0	
1977				19.78	353	106.3	106.3	86.7	123.9	123.8	125.3	107.1	118.1	102.4	
1978	4.65	1.45	2.60		430	124.6	124.6	132.1	124.6	123.3	135.7	113.9	96.8	81.4	
1979	4.59	1.42	2.57		509	112.0	112.0	122.9	107.1	108.0	100.4	105.7	102.8	126.7	96.4
1980	5.13	1.60	2.88		541	104.8	104.8	89.5	118.2	119.7	105.2	101.6	105.1	95.3	104.5
1981	5.51	1.70	3.08		586	110.9	110.9	112.9	107.3	107.3	106.8	117.9	123.6	116.7	117.1
1982	6.14	1.90	3.43		645	109.8	109.8	116.0	105.8	106.1	102.8	110.4	114.1	107.8	111.0
1983	6.45	2.00	3.62		716	112.3	112.3	107.2	115.3	115.7	110.9	113.6	121.8	118.2	108.8
1984	6.94	2.15	3.88		843	115.7	115.7	112.9	117.9	114.6	151.8	114.6	122.0	112.5	114.6
1985	9.73	2.69	5.90		1053	117.3	117.3	99.2	128.1	131.5	101.5	118.1	153.3	109.0	101.1
1986	11.44	3.30	6.29		1193	110.4	110.4	105.4	109.6	108.8	118.1	119.3	124.8	117.2	130.3
1987	14.06	5.10	6.27		1462	113.5	113.5	100.5	118.1	117.3	125.3	116.7	118.7	142.4	91.1
1988	19.17	7.81	18.60		1816	119.6	119.6	104.3	117.8	118.2	114.2	140.1	115.9	141.4	158.6
1989	21.92	8.97	27.51		1951	102.5	102.5	97.2	100.5	102.1	85.8	111.2	103.9	97.8	136.4
1990	24.79	11.09	34.88		2016	105.0	105.0	101.0	105.4	105.9	99.7	106.9	100.1	99.4	109.5
1991	28.89	14.06	40.90	6.73	2347	108.3	108.3	96.1	108.9	108.8	110.4	119.0	117.0	126.7	104.8
1992	35.49	17.92	51.05	9.33	3097	125.6	125.6	110.7	131.9	130.9	143.5	126.2	117.3	138.3	133.1
1993	45.68	24.75	70.26	11.92	4308	119.9	119.8	102.6	123.3	123.2	125.0	125.1	129.3	133.0	113.3
1994	65.37	34.42	97.79	9.01	5785	116.5	116.5	105.2	122.3	122.9	116.7	111.4	118.5	105.5	111.9
1995	88.37	47.50	112.12	11.99	7299	115.4	115.4	113.6	116.1	115.4	125.1	114.9	115.3	115.2	118.1

Year	v4c4	v4c5	v4c6	v4c7	v4c8	v4c9	v4c10	v5	v5a	v5a1	v5a1a	v5a1b	v5a2	v5b	v5b1
1952								48.41	31.49	28.99	23.25	5.74	2.50	8.60	5.13
1953								53.42	33.24	30.34	23.77	6.57	2.90	9.73	7.90
1954								53.77	33.99	30.93	24.35	6.58	3.06	9.18	4.84
1955								58.96	35.93	32.58	25.79	6.79	3.35	11.90	5.93
1956								61.90	37.49	33.05	25.01	8.04	4.44	12.41	7.71
1957								65.11	39.87	34.98	26.88	8.10	4.89	12.62	8.77
1958								75.30	41.74	35.82	24.85	10.97	5.92	18.82	12.46
1959								79.62	43.22	36.42	26.14	10.28	6.80	23.21	15.56
1960								86.80	48.55	42.87	28.22	14.65	5.68	25.15	21.22
1961								72.20	46.31	41.41	27.76	13.65	4.90	12.05	11.24
1962								69.20	45.18	40.85	27.08	13.77	4.33	7.83	9.28
1963								75.52	47.88	43.81	30.47	13.34	4.07	13.27	10.19
1964								89.55	56.17	51.58	35.87	15.71	4.59	19.40	11.63
1965								95.10	54.83	50.03	34.05	15.98	4.80	20.91	11.86
1966								109.89	60.91	55.63	39.56	16.07	5.28	27.19	12.31
1967								99.20	61.43	56.55	40.00	16.55	4.88	17.27	10.20
1968								102.84	65.62	60.63	42.89	17.74	4.99	18.44	9.86
1969								111.75	65.86	60.01	42.39	17.62	5.85	20.97	11.47
1970								129.23	68.59	61.42	43.45	17.97	7.17	34.32	15.52
1971								148.04	77.56	69.52	49.99	19.53	8.04	41.39	19.22
1972								157.31	85.77	76.34	54.79	21.55	9.43	40.86	22.03
1973								170.93	93.57	83.26	59.76	23.50	10.31	47.26	24.02
1974								171.94	94.69	83.41	59.43	23.98	11.28	46.56	22.17
1975								184.16	99.43	87.81	62.59	25.22	11.62	52.25	25.85
1976								187.97	108.07	95.94	64.08	31.86	12.13	53.60	28.41
1977								202.40	111.54	98.14	62.52	35.62	13.40	56.92	29.68
1978								249.24	130.55	115.15	76.11	39.04	15.40	77.98	40.40
1979	96.5	96.2	96.2	96.7	96.2	96.8		298.55	161.08	142.89	96.16	46.73	18.19	85.56	46.28
1980	104.7	104.9	105.3	104.3	104.6	104.4		319.80	175.47	154.72	105.13	49.59	20.75	97.44	58.25
1981	117.1	117.2	116.9	117.5	116.3	117.0		350.02	198.64	174.30	121.83	52.47	24.34	97.03	56.83
1982	111.0	110.7	111.2	111.0	111.3	111.0		390.17	232.12	203.38	147.65	55.73	28.74	133.09	95.71
1983	108.7	108.9	108.7	108.5	108.7	108.8		437.65	251.98	215.96	158.02	57.94	36.02	142.21	105.49
1984	114.7	114.4	114.2	113.0	112.9	108.1		518.85	297.65	257.86	188.60	69.26	39.79	193.62	131.39
1985	120.9	105.6	113.2	118.4	105.5	133.9		651.82	353.72	300.86	219.98	80.88	52.86	271.42	193.25
1986	109.1	118.7	121.6	113.4	118.3	102.7		744.94	393.05	339.37	241.01	98.36	53.68	341.74	240.37
1987	100.2	107.1	100.0	113.8	143.5	92.4		922.33	478.89	406.84	282.48	124.36	72.05	411.70	303.45
1988	122.4	182.7	177.8	114.7	128.6	250.1		1208.85	594.76	501.62	352.23	149.39	93.14	523.45	390.46
1989	114.9	97.5	117.3	113.0	113.5	145.7		1321.85	662.01	557.60	386.40	171.20	104.41	523.44	336.24
1990	108.1	117.8	115.4	111.8	122.4	124.8		1416.50	717.36	608.29	403.29	205.00	109.07	583.44	374.12
1991	118.3	125.3	114.6	112.0	121.6	114.4		1601.38	835.07	656.99	423.60	233.39	178.08	694.80	461.98
1992	117.9	112.0	120.1	115.6	120.2	116.2	130.1	2136.02	960.21	735.62	459.99	275.63	224.59	1069.20	747.29
1993	149.8	114.1	119.9	111.6	115.5	114.6	120.2	2998.16	1251.08	984.44	569.94	414.50	266.64	1589.93	1201.41
1994	108.1	115.6	110.6	115.9	119.1	116.8	63.5	4000.90	1721.45	1350.89	782.19	568.70	370.56	2018.95	1434.95
1995	125.0	102.9	113.7	118.2	113.8	100.3	116.3	5091.46	2172.95	1728.72	1003.55	725.17	444.23	2529.30	1756.88

Year	v5b2	v5c	v5c1	v5c2	v6a1	v6a2	v6a3	v6a4	v6b2	v6b3	v6b4	v7	v7a	v7a1	v7a2
1952	3.47	8.32													
1953	1.83	10.45										103.5	102.6	100.8	110.0
1954	4.34	10.60										101.0	100.7	101.3	98.5
1955	5.97	11.13										103.9	103.6	103.9	102.5
1956	4.70	12.00										103.6	100.8	96.4	118.1
1957	3.85	12.62										105.0	104.5	106.5	98.2
1958	6.36	14.74										103.4	101.1	91.2	135.1
1959	7.65	13.19										103.6	101.7	105.1	93.8
1960	3.93	13.10										110.7	116.1	106.7	140.6
1961	0.81	13.84										89.8	90.9	92.2	88.2
1962	-1.45	16.19										94.4	95.6	94.8	97.2
1963	3.08	14.37										109.1	110.0	115.4	99.1
1964	7.77	13.98										117.6	118.2	118.1	118.5
1965	9.05	19.36										99.9	99.2	95.8	107.3
1966	14.88	21.79										111.8	112.0	117.4	100.5
1967	7.07	20.50										101.1	101.9	101.5	103.0
1968	8.58	18.78										106.9	107.2	107.2	107.2
1969	9.50	24.92										100.7	99.3	99.4	99.3
1970	18.80	26.32										104.1	102.3	102.5	102.0
1971	22.17	29.09										113.5	113.6	114.9	110.4
1972	18.83	30.68										110.4	109.5	110.0	108.5
1973	23.24	30.10										109.1	109.1	109.1	109.0
1974	24.39	30.69										101.3	100.3	99.6	102.2
1975	26.40	32.48										105.1	105.4	105.4	105.4
1976	25.19	26.30										106.9	107.5	99.7	126.7
1977	27.24	33.94										105.0	104.0	100.1	111.8
1978	37.58	40.71			28.31	37.48	4.43	5.89	33.18	5.11	0.75	116.9	117.2	121.6	109.5
1979	39.28	51.91			35.00	46.22	5.24	9.70	39.95	5.88	0.90	121.9	122.6	124.9	118.1
1980	39.19	46.89			35.06	54.39	5.68	10.00	42.20	6.43	0.96	104.5	103.9	104.8	102.0
1981	40.20	54.35			44.83	59.96	6.13	10.91	45.00	6.44	1.03	112.9	112.3	115.9	104.7
1982	37.38	24.96			54.04	74.67	7.94	11.00	48.26	6.39	1.08	115.7	115.5	119.9	105.3
1983	36.72	43.46			58.20	77.66	9.97	12.19	50.15	6.41	1.38	108.8	106.5	107.6	103.5
1984	67.23	22.58			70.81	95.15	11.75	10.89	58.99	8.69	1.58	115.6	116.9	117.6	114.8
1985	78.17	26.68			77.57	117.73	12.20	12.48	69.58	9.63	1.67	107.1	104.6	103.9	106.6
1986	101.37	10.15			84.65	123.71	19.28	13.37	83.75	11.65	2.96	106.9	107.8	105.5	114.3
1987	108.25	31.74			91.99	143.66	28.90	17.93	103.76	17.21	3.39	112.4	110.7	107.4	119.1
1988	137.99	85.64			118.16	180.18	31.07	22.82	125.55	19.71	4.13	101.4	99.7	99.9	99.3
1989	192.20	131.40			136.33	193.07	33.54	23.46	142.79	23.48	4.93	99.7	98.2	96.5	102.1
1990	214.32	110.70			144.96	197.79	38.62	21.92	163.47	36.09	5.44	106.3	107.3	104.5	113.5
1991	232.82	71.51			149.83	208.63	40.72	24.42	188.14	38.41	6.84	112.0	104.0	103.1	105.7
1992	321.91	106.61			159.07	228.28	43.56	29.08	225.50	40.42	9.71	112.6	110.4	106.6	117.9
1993	388.52	157.15			159.47	300.24	45.43	64.80	305.25	87.15	22.10	113.6	114.7	107.4	127.3
1994	584.00	260.50	1393.48	1132.98	265.06	344.82	76.75	95.56	403.39	130.72	34.59	112.2	112.2	112.8	111.3
1995	772.42	389.21	1874.87	1485.66	327.11	436.84	96.99	142.61	561.04	117.72	46.41	109.3	110.7	110.8	110.1

Year	v7b	v8	v8a	v8b	v9	v9a	v9b	v10a1	v10a2	v10a3	v10a3a	v10a3b	v10a4	v10b1	v10b2
1952		79	74	106											
1953	113.8	80	74	118	101.1	98.9	107.2								
1954	104.1	80	74	118	97.9	98.9	98.5								
1955	107.4	83	76	121	102.2	101.2	101.5								
1956	131.4	82	72	142	97.9	93.1	117.2								
1957	108.8	85	76	136	102.2	104.9	93.0								
1958	119.9	85	70	166	98.9	90.6	121.9								
1959	114.9	85	74	141	100.0	105.2	84.8								
1960	82.1	100	80	192	117.2	108.6	134.4								
1961	81.2	98	79	186	90.8	92.1	92.1								
1962	83.9	95	75	198	95.0	91.4	109.6								
1963	100.5	100	81	207	107.5	112.2	100.0								
1964	110.7	115	94	244	115.8	115.7	118.5								
1965	107.1	109	87	246	97.4	93.8	106.2								
1966	110.0	107	98	243	108.8	114.4	98.8								
1967	92.3	118	96	252	99.2	98.1	103.9								
1968	103.6	123	100	271	104.9	104.0	107.2								
1969	117.2	119	96	275	96.9	96.2	101.8								
1970	122.8	118	95	295	100.0	99.0	106.9								
1971	112.1	131	106	320	110.4	112.0	110.4								
1972	117.6	141	115	346	108.0	108.0	106.5								
1973	109.2	152	124	372	107.4	108.3	97.8								
1974	109.7	151	123	351	99.4	98.5	103.7								
1975	103.0	157	127	374	103.8	103.9	106.8								
1976	102.8	176	129	465	106.7	98.5	124.9								
1977	112.3	171	124	512	102.8	99.2	110.2								
1978	114.8	225	150	547	115.5	120.6	106.7	29.67	7.03	3.70	0.00	3.70		26.04	11.54
1979	116.7	244	189	602	121.5	124.7	108.5	34.80	7.42	4.06	0.06	4.00		27.21	12.07
1980	109.4	262	207	591	103.2	105.1	94.4	43.35	10.56	4.34	0.07	4.27		27.15	12.04
1981	117.0	292	238	607	111.1	115.0	101.7	38.90	13.00	4.93	0.08	4.85		23.32	16.88
1982	116.9	328	286	623	114.1	118.9	101.7	50.03	25.89	19.79	0.76	19.03		21.31	16.07
1983	125.6	353	305	626	105.4	107.1	100.0	46.79	21.41	37.29	0.83	36.46		20.57	16.15
1984	108.2	409	363	727	116.0	117.2	111.5	53.85	37.44	40.10	1.66	38.44		28.47	38.76
1985	123.3	486	423	817	103.9	103.9	102.6	81.75	59.06	52.44	1.55	50.89		40.49	37.68
1986	101.5	544	467	912	106.9	106.2	105.0	100.11	61.28	78.98	2.07	76.91		53.40	47.97
1987	122.3	645	548	1073	109.5	107.7	110.8	120.03	75.07	108.35	4.95	103.40		62.78	45.47
1988	109.9	785	682	1216	98.4	99.8	93.6	164.97	101.11	112.88	4.32	108.56	11.50	76.65	46.00
1989	107.1	860	749	1289	96.9	96.7	94.5	134.83	72.60	116.94	3.92	113.02	11.87	109.32	62.16
1990	102.2	903	760	1433	103.2	101.5	105.3	145.63	81.92	133.78	3.25	130.53	12.79	122.08	69.18
1991	156.7	963	789	1604	102.7	101.9	104.0	185.42	118.54	144.14	4.11	140.03	13.88	131.44	76.04
1992	120.5	1067	852	1838	109.2	105.9	114.4	306.47	293.28	125.26	4.98	120.28	22.28	175.01	110.17
1993	109.9	1415	1062	2604	113.6	107.9	119.9	426.63	521.17	138.43	9.41	129.02	115.18	140.24	186.65
1994	112.4	1926	1467	3382	111.3	113.5	105.4	477.86	603.97	175.06	12.26	162.80	178.06	193.34	287.09
1995	104.9	2448	1886	4163	109.8	111.0	106.3	622.10	500.25	255.42	14.42	241.00	379.11	217.77	370.61

Year	v10b4	v11a	v11a1	v11a2	v11b	v11b1	v11b2	v11c	v11c1	v11c2	v12	v12a	v12b	v13	v13i
1952															
1953											109.7	149.4	51.0		
1954											107.1	60.8	307.7		
1955											114.7	124.1	106.7		
1956											101.6	126.7	76.7		
1957											97.2	108.6	78.5		
1958											122.9	117.2	135.9		
1959											119.4	120.9	116.7		
1960											106.9	134.7	50.6		
1961											51.4	56.9	22.1		
1962											63.3	80.4	-173.6		
1963											175.8	113.9	-221.9		
1964											144.3	112.7	248.7		
1965											108.2	102.1	117.4		
1966											132.3	106.0	166.6		
1967											65.0	84.8	48.6		
1968											106.7	96.7	121.2		
1969											112.6	115.2	109.5		
1970											163.5	135.0	198.0		
1971											119.3	122.6	116.6		
1972											98.0	113.7	84.4		
1973											115.2	108.7	122.8		
1974											99.0	92.8	105.5		
1975											111.4	115.7	107.5		
1976											104.0	111.5	96.8		
1977											105.2	103.5	107.1		
1978		6.36	2.23	4.13	53.94	27.26	26.68	17.68	10.91	6.77	135.6	132.3	139.3	249.24	116.91
1979		7.55	3.23	4.32	58.02	30.13	27.89	19.99	12.92	7.07	109.6	120.2	98.6	298.55	152.45
1980		6.95	2.44	4.51	67.72	39.70	28.02	22.77	16.11	6.66	106.1	113.8	96.5	319.80	152.29
1981		7.84	3.22	4.62	64.95	36.21	28.74	24.24	17.40	6.84	104.9	103.9	106.4	350.02	171.50
1982		8.17	3.76	4.41	79.99	53.64	26.35	44.93	38.31	6.62	139.9	172.7	92.2	390.17	197.45
1983		8.29	3.85	4.44	80.46	54.46	26.00	53.46	47.18	6.28	109.1	113.1	98.3	437.65	222.33
1984		11.60	3.51	8.09	108.91	61.18	47.73	78.11	66.70	11.41	132.9	118.2	178.9	518.85	266.40
1985		12.86	4.50	8.36	145.25	89.82	55.43	113.31	98.93	14.38	125.2	132.1	110.9	651.82	321.08
1986		12.54	6.29	6.25	192.05	114.86	77.19	137.15	119.22	17.93	127.8	129.3	124.1	744.94	374.70
1987		16.30	8.50	7.80	215.64	141.10	74.54	179.76	153.85	25.91	111.2	114.4	103.0	922.33	429.08
1988	15.34	21.74	12.49	9.25	225.51	146.03	79.48	281.20	231.94	49.26	116.7	116.4	117.4	1208.85	583.96
1989	20.72	19.60	10.76	8.84	256.83	125.75	131.08	252.01	199.73	52.28	101.0	90.3	131.4	1321.85	625.53
1990	23.06	26.32	11.97	14.35	286.30	139.92	146.38	275.82	222.23	53.59	108.6	109.8	106.3	1416.50	693.86
1991	25.34	27.37	12.94	14.43	336.72	196.80	139.92	330.71	252.24	78.47	115.7	121.4	105.6	1601.38	731.05
1992	36.73	36.29	15.69	20.60	593.59	399.80	193.79	439.32	331.80	107.52	140.8	145.3	131.7	2136.02	1015.80
1993	61.63	45.58	21.87	23.71	923.38	669.43	253.95	620.97	510.11	110.86	120.4	123.2	114.1	2998.16	1383.03
1994	103.57	86.38	48.26	38.12	1073.66	736.45	337.21	858.91	650.24	208.67	110.1	104.3	124.0	4057.39	1964.18
1995	184.04	113.74	41.94	71.80	1274.85	829.54	445.31	1140.71	885.40	255.31	114.6	114.0	115.7	5155.25	2578.57

Year	v13ii	v13iii	v13iv	v13a	v13ai	v13aii	v13aiii	v13aiv	v13b	v13bi	v13bii	v13biii	v13biv	v13b1	v13b1i
1952															
1953															
1954															
1955															
1956															
1957															
1958															
1959															
1960															
1961															
1962															
1963															
1964															
1965															
1966															
1967															
1968															
1969															
1970															
1971															
1972															
1973															
1974															
1975															
1976															
1977															
1978	19.98	31.79	80.56	68.71	62.24	2.28	1.78	2.41	131.09	37.24	8.72	24.58	60.55	117.10	28.56
1979	22.82	38.21	85.07	104.04	94.25	3.47	2.70	3.62	141.14	39.29	10.15	28.98	62.72	126.25	30.06
1980	23.90	45.96	97.65	94.24	85.38	3.14	2.45	3.27	167.41	46.34	10.56	36.66	73.85	151.22	36.31
1981	27.33	49.22	101.97	109.39	99.11	3.62	2.84	3.82	178.01	50.08	12.73	39.12	76.08	161.11	39.61
1982	31.44	52.68	108.60	135.15	122.45	4.47	3.51	4.72	185.52	50.53	14.73	41.26	79.00	168.09	39.73
1983	35.69	56.98	122.65	150.41	136.27	4.98	3.91	5.25	210.81	59.66	17.13	44.21	89.81	191.52	47.71
1984	41.05	66.79	144.61	179.00	162.26	5.62	4.73	6.39	250.39	73.46	19.52	51.17	106.24	228.58	59.94
1985	48.80	89.26	192.68	195.66	177.37	6.12	5.17	7.00	339.56	102.25	21.64	69.51	146.16	307.89	82.75
1986	59.80	101.78	208.66	224.26	199.50	6.52	4.92	13.32	376.32	122.23	28.22	78.69	147.18	337.77	98.14
1987	104.98	96.76	291.51	246.86	214.61	8.57	6.78	16.90	493.69	153.75	60.58	69.73	209.63	443.23	122.37
1988	137.54	141.31	346.04	319.18	276.62	14.17	8.40	19.99	586.82	190.41	72.23	92.30	231.88	526.92	153.06
1989	164.39	169.13	362.80	324.18	278.97	16.08	8.23	20.90	657.06	209.51	90.57	113.44	243.54	599.91	174.73
1990	186.92	192.85	342.87	355.17	309.49	16.39	8.67	20.62	692.59	226.94	102.41	135.06	228.18	634.13	190.03
1991	217.55	183.48	469.40	345.14	303.75	11.60	8.41	21.38	793.92	251.80	124.72	164.63	252.77	725.83	208.34
1992	280.87	268.62	570.73	393.82	350.58	12.96	9.99	20.29	1119.26	394.46	157.56	242.56	324.68	1017.94	326.65
1993	331.02	426.14	857.97	490.59	427.02	18.49	13.49	31.59	1598.05	583.57	172.60	314.78	527.10	1451.97	486.41
1994	452.89	547.95	1092.37	671.94	595.71	24.94	16.30	34.99	2186.77	834.50	235.25	419.62	697.40	2002.22	712.43
1995	710.45	624.93	1241.30	848.35	758.93	31.40	19.39	38.63	2715.26	1120.25	401.97	461.39	731.65	2467.63	974.51

Year	v13b1ii	v13b1iii	v13b1iv	v13b2	v13b2i	v13b2ii	v13b2iii	v13b2iv	v13c	v13ci	v13cii	v13ciii	v13civ	v13c1
1952														
1953														
1954														
1955														
1956														
1957														
1958														
1959														
1960														
1961														
1962														
1963														
1964														
1965														
1966														
1967														
1968														
1969														
1970														
1971														
1972														
1973														
1974														
1975														
1976														
1977														
1978	8.30	23.74	56.50	13.99	8.68	0.42	0.84	4.05	49.44	17.43	8.98	5.43	17.60	6.85
1979	9.70	28.09	58.40	14.89	9.23	0.45	0.89	4.32	53.37	18.91	9.20	6.53	18.73	7.19
1980	10.06	35.69	69.16	16.19	10.03	0.50	0.97	4.69	58.15	20.57	10.20	6.85	20.53	8.10
1981	12.21	38.11	71.18	16.90	10.47	0.52	1.01	4.90	62.62	22.31	10.98	7.26	22.07	9.14
1982	14.19	40.22	73.95	17.43	10.80	0.54	1.04	5.05	69.50	24.47	12.24	7.91	24.88	10.48
1983	16.53	43.06	84.22	19.29	11.95	0.60	1.15	5.59	76.43	26.40	13.58	8.86	27.59	12.36
1984	18.86	49.86	99.92	21.81	13.52	0.66	1.31	6.32	89.46	30.68	15.91	10.89	31.98	16.67
1985	20.71	67.51	136.92	31.67	19.50	0.93	2.00	9.24	116.60	41.46	21.04	14.58	39.52	26.07
1986	26.86	75.15	137.62	38.55	24.00	1.36	3.54	9.56	144.36	52.97	25.06	18.17	48.16	33.76
1987	57.85	66.37	196.64	50.46	31.38	2.73	3.36	12.99	181.78	60.72	35.83	20.25	64.98	43.25
1988	68.31	88.51	217.04	59.90	37.35	3.92	3.79	14.84	302.85	116.93	51.14	40.61	94.17	59.62
1989	85.99	109.24	229.95	57.15	34.78	4.58	4.20	13.59	340.61	137.05	57.74	47.46	98.36	62.66
1990	98.31	130.52	215.27	58.46	36.91	4.10	4.54	12.91	368.74	157.43	68.12	49.12	94.07	63.64
1991	120.19	158.80	238.50	68.09	43.46	4.53	5.83	14.27	462.32	175.50	81.23	10.34	195.25	80.27
1992	151.35	232.93	307.01	101.32	67.81	6.21	9.63	17.67	622.94	270.71	110.35	16.07	225.76	100.55
1993	164.07	299.11	502.38	146.08	97.16	8.53	15.67	24.72	909.52	372.44	139.93	97.87	299.28	144.11
1994	224.84	399.55	665.40	184.55	122.07	10.41	20.07	359.98	1198.68	533.97	192.70	112.03	359.98	187.19
1995	388.25	436.29	668.58	247.63	145.74	13.72	25.10	63.07	1591.64	699.39	277.08	144.15	471.02	253.52

Year	v13c1i	v13c1ii	v13c1iii	v13c1iv	v13c2	v13c2i	v13c2ii	v13c2iii	v13c2iv	v13c3	v13c3i	v13c3ii	v13c3iii	v13c3iv
1952														
1953														
1954														
1955														
1956														
1957														
1958														
1959														
1960														
1961														
1962														
1963														
1964														
1965														
1966														
1967														
1968														
1969														
1970														
1971														
1972														
1973														
1974														
1975														
1976														
1977														
1978	2.53	0.81	0.71	2.80	13.63	5.03	0.97	3.68	3.95	10.43	0.36	0.07	0.68	9.32
1979	2.65	0.85	0.75	2.94	17.64	6.52	1.26	4.76	5.10	10.27	0.36	0.07	0.67	9.17
1980	2.98	0.96	0.84	3.32	18.04	6.67	1.28	4.87	5.22	11.52	0.40	0.08	0.75	10.29
1981	3.50	1.09	0.86	3.69	19.24	7.12	1.36	5.19	5.57	12.32	0.43	0.09	0.80	11.00
1982	3.76	1.25	0.95	4.52	20.84	7.70	1.48	5.62	6.04	13.74	0.48	0.10	0.89	12.27
1983	3.86	1.90	1.00	5.60	23.86	8.82	1.68	6.44	6.92	14.47	0.51	0.10	0.94	12.92
1984	5.07	3.10	1.36	7.14	29.66	10.90	2.07	8.00	8.69	15.52	0.54	0.11	1.01	13.86
1985	10.38	3.30	3.25	9.14	32.98	11.07	2.30	9.44	10.17	18.91	0.69	0.13	1.30	16.79
1986	14.45	5.03	3.50	10.78	40.09	14.56	2.70	10.97	11.86	25.56	0.92	0.20	2.83	21.61
1987	13.28	12.39	4.89	12.69	61.60	18.84	4.15	11.99	26.62	25.14	1.02	0.35	2.56	21.21
1988	23.62	12.77	5.12	18.11	103.63	43.72	8.37	30.09	21.45	47.44	1.38	0.48	3.68	41.90
1989	25.25	14.34	5.62	17.45	102.69	49.70	9.72	34.31	8.96	65.45	1.85	0.72	5.45	57.43
1990	27.06	14.15	5.24	17.19	103.25	58.37	15.54	34.18	-4.84	72.53	2.16	1.06	6.66	62.65
1991	25.27	17.61	3.66	33.73	140.27	49.05	14.08	-2.50	79.64	77.81	5.75	2.46	6.58	63.02
1992	45.59	21.54	10.76	22.66	201.91	96.73	26.73	-8.31	86.76	109.27	8.45	3.19	8.07	89.56
1993	71.50	28.43	14.18	30.00	308.21	118.77	24.33	49.77	115.34	144.81	12.76	3.71	23.05	105.29
1994	95.22	43.68	18.23	30.06	389.41	177.82	30.86	55.85	124.88	200.34	21.49	6.15	17.53	155.17
1995	134.35	59.77	22.22	37.18	516.89	238.76	49.38	76.02	152.73	270.50	25.13	8.59	22.52	214.26

Year	v13c4	v13c4i	v13c4ii	v13c4iii	v13c4iv	v13c5	v13c5i	v13c5ii	v13c5iii	v13c5iv	v13c6	v13c6i	v13c6ii	v13c6iii
1952														
1953														
1954														
1955														
1956														
1957														
1958														
1959														
1960														
1961														
1962														
1963														
1964														
1965														
1966														
1967														
1968														
1969														
1970														
1971														
1972														
1973														
1974														
1975														
1976														
1977														
1978	5.50	0.16	5.25	0.02	0.07	2.89	1.43	0.44	0.28	0.74	1.44	1.22	0.14	0.00
1979	5.42	0.16	5.17	0.02	0.07	2.85	1.41	0.43	0.28	0.73	1.42	1.20	0.14	0.00
1980	6.08	0.18	5.80	0.02	0.08	3.20	1.58	0.49	0.31	0.82	1.60	1.35	0.16	0.00
1981	6.50	0.19	6.20	0.02	0.09	3.42	1.70	0.52	0.33	0.87	1.71	1.45	0.17	0.00
1982	7.25	0.21	6.92	0.02	0.10	3.81	1.88	0.58	0.37	0.98	1.91	1.61	0.19	0.00
1983	7.64	0.22	7.29	0.02	0.11	4.02	1.99	0.61	0.39	1.03	2.01	1.70	0.20	0.00
1984	8.19	0.24	7.81	0.02	0.12	4.30	2.13	0.66	0.42	1.09	2.15	1.81	0.22	
1985	11.93	0.34	11.38	0.04	0.17	5.47	2.66	0.85	0.43	1.53	2.92	2.40	0.32	
1986	13.50	0.44	12.65	0.05	0.36	6.73	3.29	0.99	0.68	1.77	3.69	3.11	0.37	0.01
1987	14.59	0.71	13.62	0.09	0.17	7.79	3.64	1.18	0.56	2.41	3.98	3.34	0.43	0.01
1988	21.25	0.61	19.36	0.12	1.16	16.91	7.01	3.95	1.16	4.79	8.42	5.98	0.81	0.01
1989	24.72	0.76	22.51	0.26	1.19	16.69	7.98	2.97	1.24	4.50	10.00	7.11	0.95	0.01
1990	27.02	0.84	24.55	0.40	1.23	19.88	8.77	3.82	1.58	5.71	11.66	7.74	1.24	0.08
1991	33.51	1.59	29.33	0.62	1.97	25.96	11.36	3.47	1.58	9.55	13.92	11.93	1.50	-0.10
1992	43.89	2.45	37.19	1.07	3.18	35.79	18.35	4.47	2.53	10.44	17.74	12.28	2.30	0.23
1993	74.56	4.62	55.20	3.64	11.10	59.79	30.61	7.88	4.27	17.03	25.43	17.71	3.19	0.44
1994	99.26	7.35	72.75	6.69	12.47	82.36	45.70	10.55	9.00	17.11	33.53	25.98	4.34	0.46
1995	143.61	10.72	107.32	8.35	17.22	102.98	57.85	12.52	9.35	23.26	44.16	33.23	5.91	0.40

Year	v13c6iv	v13c7	v13c7i	v13c7ii	v13c7iii	v13c7iv	v13c8	v13c8i	v13c8ii	v13c8iii	v13c8iv	v13c9	v13c9i	v13c9ii
1952														
1953														
1954														
1955														
1956														
1957														
1958														
1959														
1960														
1961														
1962														
1963														
1964														
1965														
1966														
1967														
1968														
1969														
1970														
1971														
1972														
1973														
1974														
1975														
1976														
1977														
1978	0.08	4.65	3.74	0.63	0.02	0.26	1.45	0.96	0.38	0.01	0.10	2.60	2.00	0.29
1979	0.08	4.59	3.69	0.62	0.02	0.26	1.42	0.94	0.37	0.01	0.10	2.57	1.93	0.29
1980	0.09	5.13	4.13	0.69	0.02	0.29	1.60	1.06	0.42	0.01	0.11	2.88	2.22	0.32
1981	0.09	5.51	4.43	0.75	0.02	0.31	1.70	1.12	0.45	0.01	0.12	3.08	2.37	0.35
1982	0.11	6.14	4.94	0.83	0.02	0.35	1.90	1.25	0.50	0.01	0.14	3.43	2.64	0.39
1983	0.11	6.45	5.19	0.87	0.02	0.37	2.00	1.32	0.53	0.01	0.14	3.62	2.79	0.40
1984	0.12	6.94	5.58	0.94	0.03	0.39	2.15	1.42	0.57	0.01	0.15	3.88	2.99	0.43
1985	0.20	9.73	7.71	1.32	0.05	0.65	2.69	1.70	0.75	0.02	0.22	5.90	4.51	0.69
1986	0.20	11.44	9.20	1.54	0.05	0.65	3.30	2.15	0.88	0.02	0.25	6.29	4.85	0.70
1987	0.20	14.06	11.78	1.72	0.07	0.49	5.10	2.78	1.26	0.08	0.98	6.27	5.33	0.73
1988	1.62	19.17	14.41	2.33	0.12	2.31	7.81	4.41	1.75	0.15	1.50	18.60	15.79	1.32
1989	1.93	21.92	16.39	2.62	0.15	2.76	8.79	4.58	1.99	0.21	2.19	27.51	23.43	1.92
1990	2.60	24.79	17.89	3.02	0.20	3.68	11.09	5.34	2.25	0.44	3.06	34.88	29.26	2.49
1991	0.59	28.89	22.20	4.88	0.22	1.59	14.06	8.93	2.39	0.49	2.25	40.90	35.50	4.81
1992	2.93	35.49	26.82	5.10	0.30	3.27	17.92	11.82	2.65	0.62	2.83	51.05	42.92	6.26
1993	4.09	45.68	34.19	5.24	0.45	5.80	24.75	15.03	3.60	1.00	5.12	70.26	59.95	7.10
1994	2.75	65.37	51.94	7.53	0.83	5.07	34.42	21.48	6.01	1.78	5.15	97.79	80.89	9.79
1995	4.62	88.37	70.02	10.18	1.28	6.89	47.50	28.55	8.86	2.60	7.49	112.12	92.77	13.01

Year	v13c9iii	v13c9iv	v13c10	v13c10i	v13c10ii	v13c10iii	v13c10iv
1952							
1953							
1954							
1955							
1956							
1957							
1958							
1959							
1960							
1961							
1962							
1963							
1964							
1965							
1966							
1967							
1968							
1969							
1970							
1971							
1972							
1973							
1974							
1975							
1976							
1977							
1978	0.03	0.28					
1979	0.02	0.28					
1980	0.03	0.31					
1981	0.03	0.33					
1982	0.03	0.37					
1983	0.04	0.39					
1984	0.04	0.42					
1985	0.05	0.65					
1986	0.06	0.68					
1987	0.00	0.21					
1988	0.16	1.33					
1989	0.21	1.95					
1990	0.34	2.79					
1991	-0.36	0.95	6.73	3.92	0.70	0.15	1.96
1992	0.45	1.42	9.33	5.35	0.92	0.35	2.71
1993	0.74	2.47	11.92	7.30	1.25	0.33	3.04
1994	0.80	6.31	9.01	6.10	1.04	0.86	1.01
1995	0.87	5.47	11.99	8.01	1.54	0.54	1.90

11

Zhejiang

Year	v1	v1a	v1b	v1b1	v1b2	v1c	v1c1	v1c2	v1c3	v2	v2a	v2b	v2b1	v2b2	v2c
1952	38.07	21.77	9.30	8.24	1.06	7.00	1.28	3.24	2.48						
1953	43.50	22.01	13.16	11.71	1.45	8.33	1.48	4.17	2.68	114.0	102.7	129.5	129.0	134.0	121.1
1954	46.13	23.44	14.33	12.97	1.36	8.36	1.50	4.03	2.83	106.1	107.6	107.7	109.2	93.7	99.3
1955	48.52	25.05	14.07	12.57	1.50	9.40	1.53	4.74	3.13	107.0	107.6	103.1	102.5	110.5	112.8
1956	55.36	25.79	18.64	16.35	2.29	10.93	1.58	5.66	3.69	112.8	102.6	125.8	123.2	153.1	115.7
1957	62.51	26.48	23.98	20.88	3.10	12.05	1.92	6.08	4.05	111.7	110.0	115.6	113.6	132.0	108.2
1958	84.97	26.09	45.18	38.25	6.93	13.70	2.81	6.70	4.19	137.4	97.8	193.9	189.6	222.4	113.3
1959	100.41	25.68	58.32	50.33	7.99	16.41	3.75	7.24	5.42	115.9	96.4	125.9	128.0	114.1	119.0
1960	103.00	23.03	62.60	54.33	8.27	17.37	4.40	6.54	6.43	103.6	86.6	110.6	112.1	100.8	104.8
1961	81.39	24.14	41.28	37.56	3.72	15.97	3.39	5.65	6.93	71.1	90.9	61.1	64.0	40.6	83.2
1962	81.59	29.07	36.42	33.62	2.80	16.10	2.89	6.46	6.75	95.4	112.2	84.2	85.4	71.1	103.2
1963	85.78	32.53	37.81	33.97	3.84	15.44	3.05	6.30	6.09	107.2	114.4	104.8	102.3	138.4	101.8
1964	95.27	35.04	43.49	39.08	4.41	16.74	3.42	7.08	6.24	113.6	110.8	116.1	115.8	118.7	112.4
1965	103.95	37.46	48.60	44.01	4.59	17.89	3.47	7.39	7.03	112.3	108.0	116.5	117.5	106.5	109.6
1966	113.55	40.26	54.94	50.52	4.42	18.35	3.68	7.79	6.88	107.8	103.1	112.9	114.7	93.6	102.7
1967	108.92	39.78	51.07	47.27	3.80	18.07	3.38	7.29	7.40	95.8	99.0	93.1	93.7	85.0	98.3
1968	106.49	40.65	48.56	44.91	3.65	17.28	3.10	6.36	7.82	97.0	101.4	95.0	95.1	94.6	95.2
1969	124.74	42.76	62.85	57.85	5.00	19.13	3.65	6.89	8.59	117.6	103.8	129.5	128.8	139.0	110.7
1970	138.33	45.36	72.59	66.66	5.93	20.38	4.15	7.09	9.14	111.0	105.1	115.5	115.2	118.5	107.1
1971	145.61	45.21	78.68	70.59	8.09	21.72	3.93	7.41	10.38	109.4	99.0	117.3	115.0	141.3	107.8
1972	162.88	54.85	85.50	76.78	8.72	22.53	4.22	7.80	10.51	110.0	115.2	108.7	109.1	105.5	103.6
1973	172.39	53.85	94.78	85.56	9.22	23.76	4.34	8.20	11.22	105.9	98.2	110.9	111.5	105.4	105.5
1974	163.99	56.38	83.44	73.54	9.90	24.17	3.93	8.36	11.88	95.3	102.9	89.4	87.5	106.5	101.7
1975	166.25	52.73	88.53	77.59	10.94	24.99	3.95	8.68	12.36	100.9	91.9	106.0	105.5	109.5	103.3
1976	174.50	52.98	94.39	82.07	12.32	27.13	4.10	8.86	14.17	105.3	101.2	106.7	105.8	113.1	108.6
1977	204.99	54.00	121.88	107.62	14.26	29.11	4.56	10.01	14.54	117.8	101.9	129.3	131.2	116.3	107.2
1978	253.38	65.71	151.87	132.11	19.76	35.80	5.79	11.23	18.78	122.0	119.4	124.4	122.7	137.9	116.4
1979	313.00	91.84	179.98	158.22	21.76	41.18	7.46	12.90	20.82	114.7	112.3	116.6	118.2	105.8	110.4
1980	371.74	92.67	230.35	201.61	28.74	48.72	8.78	15.11	24.83	119.6	97.9	129.5	129.0	133.5	112.4
1981	422.67	95.56	263.69	232.98	30.71	63.42	12.88	21.62	28.92	111.8	100.8	113.6	115.0	103.2	124.9
1982	480.99	118.04	285.48	251.52	33.96	77.47	16.40	27.21	33.86	111.6	116.4	108.6	108.3	110.3	117.2
1983	539.50	118.68	328.50	293.55	34.95	92.32	20.14	31.67	40.51	111.1	96.8	115.5	117.4	100.6	115.2
1984	691.35	147.49	425.70	382.60	43.10	118.16	27.82	39.75	50.59	125.1	116.5	128.6	130.0	115.9	121.7
1985	959.54	174.05	622.86	550.62	72.24	162.63	36.53	57.39	68.71	130.7	103.9	141.0	139.5	156.2	119.7
1986	1160.83	192.04	761.56	674.86	86.70	207.23	44.93	70.07	92.23	116.7	105.4	119.0	119.8	111.3	117.3
1987	1450.59	228.12	966.56	853.10	113.46	255.91	53.00	86.70	116.21	118.7	103.7	122.9	123.1	121.2	111.9
1988	1909.33	282.62	1284.50	1141.03	143.47	342.21	65.18	123.81	153.22	118.9	102.4	122.9	124.4	107.3	111.2
1989	2186.29	307.84	1476.54	1333.87	142.67	401.91	78.04	142.97	180.90	104.0	101.7	105.4	106.9	88.4	97.0
1990	2357.50	336.04	1581.00	1434.15	146.85	440.46	80.95	156.49	203.02	106.7	104.0	107.6	108.6	94.1	103.2
1991	2957.70	368.64	1983.19	1801.39	181.80	605.87	108.00	250.01	247.86	122.8	108.6	122.7	123.4	115.6	133.9
1992	3913.65	404.79	2696.95	2447.62	249.33	811.91	144.89	343.14	323.88	125.1	103.2	128.9	129.6	121.4	125.9
1993	5803.27	499.70	4195.31	3812.39	382.92	1108.26	199.87	471.61	436.78	125.6	104.8	131.6	132.8	117.6	116.1
1994	8596.21	707.21	6345.37	5784.93	560.44	1543.63	264.98	675.06	603.59	124.6	105.6	128.8	129.1	125.0	117.3
1995	11965.49	891.71	8978.42	8199.06	779.36	2095.36	370.89	933.13	791.34	123.8	109.8	126.8	126.6	129.7	117.2

Year	v2c1	v2c2	v3'	v3	v3a	v3b	v3b1	v3b2	v3c	v3c1	v3c2	v3c3	v3c4	v3c5	v3c6
1952			24.53	24.53	16.28	2.78	2.29	0.49	5.47	0.98	2.55				
1953	113.3	134.3	27.24	27.24	16.55	3.86	3.27	0.59	6.83	1.16	3.47				
1954	100.7	95.6	28.65	28.65	17.76	4.13	3.62	0.51	6.76	1.18	3.29				
1955	104.1	117.5	30.53	30.53	18.78	3.88	3.30	0.58	7.87	1.21	4.04				
1956	101.3	119.2	33.54	33.54	18.91	5.60	4.43	1.17	9.03	1.26	4.72				
1957	121.4	105.5	37.27	37.27	19.29	7.93	6.49	1.44	10.05	1.51	5.16				
1958	147.3	109.5	43.75	43.75	18.27	14.37	11.80	2.57	11.11	2.25	5.46				
1959	132.5	107.5	47.35	47.35	17.80	16.89	14.17	2.72	12.66	2.74	5.74				
1960	113.8	90.4	47.25	47.25	15.94	18.12	15.43	2.69	13.19	3.44	4.87				
1961	70.0	72.8	40.56	40.56	16.95	12.27	11.02	1.25	11.34	2.38	4.04				
1962	79.2	126.1	43.35	43.35	20.24	11.76	10.61	1.15	11.35	1.99	4.60				
1963	107.9	111.4	46.60	46.60	23.37	12.26	10.79	1.47	10.97	2.14	4.50				
1964	115.4	117.8	51.75	51.75	24.92	14.68	12.98	1.70	12.15	2.39	5.23				
1965	104.6	107.7	55.67	55.67	25.97	16.93	15.09	1.84	12.77	2.46	5.42				
1966	102.0	112.5	58.28	58.28	28.01	17.01	15.28	1.73	13.26	2.58	5.39				
1967	91.8	88.6	56.35	56.35	27.55	15.69	14.23	1.46	13.11	2.34	5.40				
1968	90.7	87.2	54.94	54.94	28.57	13.78	12.41	1.37	12.59	2.11	4.78				
1969	117.8	109.2	62.70	62.70	30.27	18.84	17.01	1.83	13.59	2.45	5.03				
1970	114.1	103.6	69.17	69.17	32.28	22.42	20.30	2.12	14.47	2.75	5.23				
1971	98.6	105.6	70.43	70.43	31.98	23.49	20.71	2.78	14.96	2.39	5.42				
1972	104.4	105.6	84.39	84.39	39.78	29.22	26.34	2.88	15.39	2.47	5.74				
1973	102.6	105.1	86.99	86.99	39.22	31.89	28.98	2.91	15.88	2.42	5.96				
1974	89.7	101.9	86.57	86.57	42.10	28.34	25.34	3.00	16.13	2.09	6.11				
1975	85.2	103.8	84.23	84.23	39.20	28.63	25.48	3.15	16.40	2.03	6.26				
1976	104.5	102.2	87.27	87.27	39.57	30.72	27.00	3.72	16.98	2.05	6.06				
1977	120.0	112.9	100.00	100.00	39.18	41.52	37.07	4.45	19.30	2.51	7.15				
1978	137.4	112.2	123.72	123.72	47.09	53.52	46.97	6.55	23.11	3.22	7.98	1.89	3.75	0.84	0.73
1979	111.8	112.3	157.64	157.64	67.56	64.07	55.59	8.48	26.01	4.15	8.72	2.13	3.97	0.99	0.83
1980	122.2	108.6	179.68	179.68	64.61	84.07	73.71	10.36	31.00	4.88	10.55	2.88	4.19	1.23	1.04
1981	139.7	136.9	204.45	204.45	69.06	94.68	84.08	10.60	40.71	7.16	15.35	3.54	4.80	1.77	1.18
1982	121.4	121.4	233.41	233.41	84.88	98.44	87.21	11.23	50.09	9.12	19.43	5.31	5.21	1.96	1.35
1983	120.6	110.8	256.23	256.23	82.89	113.12	102.55	10.57	60.22	11.20	23.12	7.05	5.84	2.59	1.51
1984	133.1	118.4	322.07	322.07	104.40	141.48	127.91	13.57	76.19	15.47	28.42	9.14	6.63	3.96	1.75
1985	121.5	124.1	427.50	427.50	123.88	198.91	178.68	20.23	104.71	20.31	40.52	13.61	7.85	5.87	2.31
1986	114.7	113.4	500.06	500.06	136.29	230.89	206.63	24.26	132.88	24.98	48.77	19.67	9.83	7.98	2.92
1987	112.0	113.2	603.71	603.71	159.41	281.47	249.69	31.78	162.83	29.47	58.78	25.89	11.73	10.26	3.58
1988	112.8	114.8	765.76	765.76	195.68	354.39	315.36	39.03	215.69	36.24	81.96	33.22	14.24	13.37	4.75
1989	86.6	92.7	843.72	843.72	210.95	386.25	346.50	39.75	246.52	43.39	88.50	39.44	16.27	14.31	5.92
1990	99.5	97.2	897.99	897.99	225.04	408.18	363.74	44.44	264.77	45.01	91.86	44.48	17.21	16.95	6.88
1991	131.5	154.9	1081.75	1081.75	245.22	494.11	438.36	55.75	342.42	60.04	127.94	52.87	17.71	21.03	7.44
1992	128.5	128.5	1365.06	1365.06	262.67	653.43	581.73	71.70	448.96	80.03	174.33	62.80	22.76	29.03	9.63
1993	119.7	115.9	1909.49	1909.49	317.84	980.42	873.92	106.50	611.23	110.33	239.58	78.54	32.57	40.57	13.07
1994	125.1	117.8	2666.86	2666.86	443.87	1388.06	1236.74	151.32	834.93	147.17	335.60	100.99	40.65	57.05	20.37
1995	120.5	120.6	3524.79	3524.79	559.80	1834.47	1632.37	202.10	1130.52	204.59	473.35	139.69	56.05	86.48	30.75

Year	v3c7	v3c8	v3c9	v3c10	v3d	v4'	v4	v4a	v4b	v4b1	v4b2	v4c	v4c1	v4c2	v4c3
1952				1.94	112	115.0	115.0	116.6	114.3	111.8	133.0	111.3	134.0	99.2	
1953				2.20	122	109.8	109.8	101.8	123.0	124.0	118.4	127.0	116.3	142.0	
1954				2.29	125	103.6	103.6	105.6	105.0	108.8	86.2	98.0	100.9	93.9	
1955				2.62	130	108.6	108.6	105.3	109.5	108.4	116.0	116.7	104.3	122.6	
1956				3.05	139	107.5	107.5	101.0	124.9	111.9	200.0	114.2	102.5	116.5	
1957				3.38	151	109.6	109.6	104.2	130.5	134.1	119.0	109.3	119.5	107.4	
1958				3.40	173	117.7	117.7	96.5	174.0	173.3	177.3	110.2	150.0	105.2	
1959				4.18	183	107.3	107.3	95.6	117.4	120.1	104.8	113.1	121.0	104.6	
1960				4.88	181	97.6	97.6	85.4	105.6	107.4	96.2	103.2	121.9	84.9	
1961				4.92	154	78.0	78.0	93.0	66.1	70.1	42.1	77.8	62.8	69.9	
1962				4.76	163	102.3	102.3	113.8	89.0	89.3	86.8	102.5	77.9	125.5	
1963				4.33	169	110.3	110.3	118.6	105.9	103.6	129.3	102.6	109.5	111.8	
1964				4.53	182	114.0	114.0	109.5	120.6	120.8	119.3	114.7	115.0	121.8	
1965				4.89	191	110.3	110.3	105.1	120.2	121.2	110.6	107.8	106.0	106.9	
1966				5.29	195	102.1	102.1	102.3	100.3	101.2	91.7	104.0	100.9	106.2	
1967				5.37	184	96.6	96.6	98.6	92.4	93.3	83.3	98.7	90.6	94.8	
1968				5.70	175	96.3	96.3	102.9	87.7	87.3	92.5	95.6	89.1	88.5	
1969				6.11	195	114.4	114.4	104.6	136.9	137.1	135.1	108.0	116.3	106.0	
1970				6.49	211	110.4	110.4	105.6	119.1	119.4	116.0	107.0	112.5	104.6	
1971				7.15	210	104.5	104.5	99.8	112.3	109.5	135.8	104.6	90.5	104.8	
1972				7.18	247	117.6	117.6	119.4	124.4	127.5	101.4	102.7	100.4	106.2	
1973				7.50	250	102.6	102.6	97.5	109.2	110.1	100.7	103.2	97.6	103.8	
1974				7.93	245	99.2	99.2	105.4	90.3	89.1	102.4	101.6	85.7	102.5	
1975				8.11	235	96.5	96.5	91.5	101.0	100.5	104.0	101.6	82.3	102.4	
1976				8.87	240	104.0	104.0	101.6	107.3	105.9	118.5	103.7	101.7	96.8	
1977				9.64	271	114.9	114.9	98.9	135.3	126.5	120.2	113.5	132.0	117.9	
1978	1.86	0.57	1.10	1.17	331	121.9	121.9	118.7	128.6	126.5	146.4	113.5	139.0	111.7	
1979	2.11	0.67	1.27	1.17	417	113.5	113.5	110.8	117.9	117.1	124.3	108.1	111.8	106.8	110.5
1980	2.65	0.77	1.58	1.23	470	116.2	116.2	97.3	132.1	133.3	123.5	112.9	122.0	112.2	126.5
1981	3.05	0.85	1.79	1.22	530	111.5	111.5	104.7	111.3	113.1	98.8	126.1	139.8	139.2	118.8
1982	3.41	0.95	2.00	1.35	597	111.4	111.4	116.5	104.9	104.9	105.7	118.1	121.4	122.1	143.9
1983	3.85	1.14	2.47	1.45	648	108.0	108.0	93.9	115.5	118.5	92.1	116.0	120.5	113.2	128.9
1984	4.65	1.45	3.12	1.60	807	121.7	121.7	119.3	124.0	124.4	120.7	120.3	133.2	116.0	123.0
1985	6.18	1.99	4.08	1.99	1063	121.7	121.7	101.9	135.3	135.0	138.9	119.2	121.5	122.6	126.4
1986	7.84	2.52	5.98	2.39	1231	112.1	112.1	104.0	114.0	114.2	111.2	116.8	114.7	111.7	131.3
1987	9.28	3.09	8.31	2.44	1470	111.8	111.8	101.0	115.8	116.4	121.4	110.9	112.0	110.3	115.8
1988	12.50	4.10	12.51	2.80	1842	111.2	111.2	99.0	116.3	117.5	104.2	109.8	112.8	112.1	104.6
1989	14.79	4.68	15.28	3.94	2009	99.4	99.4	100.2	100.8	101.7	90.5	94.9	86.6	86.7	107.1
1990	15.36	5.03	17.21	4.78	2122	103.9	103.9	102.7	105.2	105.4	102.3	101.4	99.6	92.1	109.8
1991	17.26	6.44	24.63	7.06	2540	117.8	117.8	107.9	118.2	118.4	117.1	125.6	131.5	135.1	115.4
1992	21.54	8.56	31.28	9.00	3187	119.0	119.0	100.6	125.2	126.6	113.9	123.4	127.7	127.5	111.4
1993	29.94	11.57	43.06	12.00	4431	122.0	122.0	104.8	133.2	135.3	113.7	115.8	119.6	115.9	107.2
1994	43.96	14.74	60.48	13.92	6149	120.0	120.0	104.4	127.5	128.0	121.4	115.7	117.6	115.9	105.7
1995	49.09	16.17	59.35	15.00	8075	116.7	116.7	107.6	118.4	117.8	124.6	118.1	120.1	123.5	121.9

Year	v4c4	v4c5	v4c6	v4c7	v4c8	v4c9	v4c10	v5	v5a	v5a1	v5a1a	v5a1b	v5a2	v5b	v5b1
1952								24.53	19.23	18.75	14.23	4.52	0.48	3.58	2.96
1953								27.24	20.76	20.07	14.84	5.23	0.69	4.48	3.23
1954								28.65	21.68	20.98	15.80	5.18	0.71	4.56	3.49
1955								30.53	23.73	22.65	17.32	5.33	1.08	4.50	3.61
1956								33.54	24.94	23.76	17.65	6.11	1.18	5.32	4.78
1957								37.27	25.86	24.94	18.05	6.89	0.92	8.05	5.65
1958								43.75	25.55	24.28	16.61	7.67	1.27	15.18	11.22
1959								47.35	25.82	24.43	15.70	8.73	1.39	18.20	12.75
1960								47.25	27.20	25.39	15.98	9.41	1.81	15.48	13.79
1961								40.56	28.53	27.01	17.48	9.53	1.52	6.81	7.50
1962								43.35	31.99	30.52	21.18	9.34	1.47	6.18	6.73
1963								46.60	32.52	31.07	22.70	8.37	1.45	8.40	7.26
1964								51.75	33.74	32.53	23.80	8.73	1.21	9.94	8.60
1965								55.67	35.60	34.31	25.29	9.02	1.29	11.45	9.19
1966								58.28	36.99	35.47	26.19	9.28	1.52	12.77	9.89
1967								56.35	37.34	35.86	26.39	9.47	1.48	12.03	9.17
1968								54.94	37.09	35.77	26.08	9.69	1.32	11.50	8.76
1969								62.70	39.96	38.53	28.58	9.95	1.43	15.69	12.17
1970								69.17	42.62	40.92	30.84	10.08	1.70	18.09	14.21
1971								70.43	43.99	42.01	31.09	10.92	1.98	18.37	15.01
1972								84.39	52.14	49.30	37.17	12.13	2.84	22.94	19.01
1973								86.99	54.21	50.99	38.25	12.74	3.22	22.27	18.49
1974								86.57	56.63	53.17	40.02	13.15	3.46	22.30	18.63
1975								84.23	55.81	51.92	38.60	13.32	3.89	20.35	17.94
1976								87.27	59.44	55.43	41.22	14.21	4.01	21.05	20.11
1977								100.00	64.36	59.82	44.80	15.02	4.54	27.15	22.09
1978								123.72	77.76	72.14	54.34	17.80	5.62	32.65	23.23
1979	103.5	115.8	112.1	110.7	113.5	114.1	98.1	157.64	90.82	81.69	61.13	20.56	9.13	37.56	26.11
1980	98.6	115.9	116.2	117.6	108.5	115.9	98.1	179.68	102.04	90.52	66.79	23.73	11.52	49.29	33.25
1981	110.5	139.0	109.6	110.9	106.5	109.5	95.9	204.45	132.52	119.56	92.51	27.05	12.96	51.53	34.16
1982	104.3	106.4	109.6	107.5	107.3	106.9	105.1	233.41	147.92	134.33	105.25	29.08	13.59	61.79	41.72
1983	108.7	128.0	108.8	109.5	115.9	120.0	104.8	256.23	161.58	145.73	114.59	31.14	15.85	59.50	44.04
1984	107.8	145.1	109.6	114.7	121.6	119.8	105.4	322.07	189.67	167.63	130.51	37.12	22.04	100.62	64.87
1985	100.5	125.7	112.1	112.8	116.1	110.9	105.1	427.50	248.16	221.27	166.67	54.60	26.89	148.52	102.20
1986	113.7	123.5	115.0	115.2	115.3	133.6	109.0	500.06	299.09	268.59	197.31	71.28	30.50	185.39	121.76
1987	104.9	113.1	107.8	104.1	107.8	122.1	90.4	603.71	356.85	317.66	234.06	83.60	39.19	236.11	156.20
1988	99.0	106.2	108.2	109.9	107.8	122.7	93.7	765.76	463.13	412.73	299.95	112.78	50.40	297.40	188.95
1989	103.1	96.5	112.5	106.8	103.1	110.3	126.3	843.72	516.08	458.58	334.38	124.20	57.50	300.14	179.49
1990	103.0	115.4	113.1	101.1	105.0	109.7	118.5	897.99	548.85	474.67	343.73	130.94	74.18	252.44	186.96
1991	96.6	120.6	105.1	109.2	124.5	139.1	143.5	1081.75	613.19	522.66	374.25	148.41	90.53	336.05	239.75
1992	124.2	128.9	120.9	116.6	124.1	118.5	119.1	1365.06	697.40	589.03	407.85	181.18	108.37	533.76	361.18
1993	121.3	118.5	115.0	117.8	114.5	116.7	113.0	1909.49	849.96	712.24	464.80	247.44	137.72	902.23	683.83
1994	117.1	112.7	125.0	117.7	114.7	112.6	93.0	2666.86	1173.68	975.36	616.70	358.66	198.32	1185.74	1006.39
1995	128.3	124.8	129.5	95.8	99.5	84.2	92.4	3569.15	1495.24	1235.98	762.32	473.66	259.26	1786.79	1357.90

Year	v5b2	v5c	v5c1	v5c2	v6a1	v6a2	v6a3	v6a4	v6b2	v6b3	v6b4	v7	v7a	v7a1	v7a2
1952	0.72	1.62													
1953	1.25	2.00										95.5	95.4	95.9	93.6
1954	1.17	2.31										106.9	105.8	103.2	114.2
1955	0.89	2.30										114.0	112.6	116.5	101.2
1956	0.54	3.28										105.0	104.8	101.9	114.5
1957	2.40	3.36										101.5	102.7	100.1	110.5
1958	3.96	3.02										97.9	96.4	90.7	111.2
1959	5.45	3.33										100.2	99.7	93.5	113.1
1960	1.69	4.57										104.7	103.2	100.7	107.7
1961	-0.69	5.22										90.5	91.4	96.5	83.0
1962	-0.55	5.18										106.1	107.0	111.2	98.8
1963	1.14	5.68										108.4	109.0	117.4	90.7
1964	1.34	8.07										106.7	107.7	108.6	105.3
1965	2.26	8.62										109.9	109.9	112.0	104.0
1966	2.88	8.52										105.0	104.3	104.9	102.5
1967	2.86	6.98										101.3	101.4	101.5	100.8
1968	2.74	6.35										99.0	99.4	98.9	101.0
1969	3.52	7.05										108.0	108.0	110.1	101.6
1970	3.88	8.46										108.0	107.5	108.8	102.9
1971	3.36	8.07										102.2	101.6	100.9	103.9
1972	3.93	9.31										122.0	121.0	121.2	120.4
1973	3.78	10.51										104.2	103.7	103.1	105.3
1974	3.67	7.64										104.5	104.3	104.6	103.2
1975	2.91	7.57										98.5	97.6	96.5	101.2
1976	0.94	6.78										106.4	106.7	106.6	106.9
1977	5.06	8.49										108.2	107.9	108.7	105.5
1978	9.42	13.31	112.68	99.37	19.20	29.23	3.15	2.76	14.30	1.99	1.51	120.8	120.7	121.4	118.5
1979	11.55	29.16	120.15	90.99	21.37	33.23	3.60	2.93	16.67	2.24	1.65	116.0	112.5	112.5	112.6
1980	16.04	28.35	129.47	101.12	23.07	36.56	4.04	3.12	19.36	2.58	1.79	109.4	107.8	108.6	105.5
1981	17.37	20.40	136.17	115.77	31.74	52.04	5.17	3.56	22.16	2.84	2.05	128.0	130.2	136.6	112.1
1982	20.07	23.70	140.93	117.23	37.49	56.55	7.32	3.89	23.04	3.74	2.30	111.6	111.8	113.6	105.5
1983	15.46	35.15	152.05	116.90	38.55	65.22	6.41	4.41	24.51	4.03	2.60	107.6	106.9	107.6	104.2
1984	35.75	31.78	168.70	136.92	42.42	74.55	8.59	4.95	29.47	4.73	2.92	115.2	112.5	111.9	115.0
1985	46.32	30.82	184.42	153.60	47.83	101.94	10.98	5.92	44.80	6.30	3.50	115.4	115.1	111.7	127.8
1986	63.63	15.58	228.60	213.02	48.96	127.53	13.39	7.43	58.06	8.85	4.37	113.7	114.2	111.6	122.8
1987	79.91	10.75	336.94	326.19	51.73	157.14	16.31	8.88	67.63	10.78	5.19	111.7	110.0	111.5	105.8
1988	108.45	5.23	337.07	331.84	56.98	213.66	18.65	10.66	92.30	14.26	6.22	108.4	107.5	107.0	109.3
1989	120.65	27.50	293.08	265.58	62.97	235.36	23.83	12.22	99.74	17.27	7.19	94.1	93.5	93.2	94.3
1990	65.48	96.70	424.25	327.55	64.06	241.16	25.18	13.33	103.01	20.36	7.57	103.9	101.4	100.8	103.3
1991	96.30	132.51	486.73	354.22	69.50	264.04	26.34	14.37	115.75	24.46	8.18	109.1	107.3	107.3	107.3
1992	172.58	133.90	606.56	472.66	66.24	289.14	35.07	17.40	139.23	31.99	9.96	108.0	106.1	104.0	111.8
1993	218.40	157.30	711.67	554.37	70.02	329.00	44.33	21.45	188.62	44.77	14.05	107.4	106.0	101.8	112.5
1994	179.35	307.44	972.69	665.25	66.36	459.71	63.73	26.90	265.27	74.41	18.98	113.4	110.5	107.0	118.3
1995	428.89	287.12	1193.83	906.71	89.58	514.60	125.86	32.28	334.22	111.66	27.78	110.1	108.9	106.9	113.1

Year	v7b	v8	v8a	v8b	v9	v9a	v9b	v10a1	v10a2	v10a3	v10a3a	v10a3b	v10a4	v10b1	v10b2
1952		86	77	138											
1953	102.1	90	78	156	93.0	93.5	91.3								
1954	146.9	91	81	150	102.5	100.0	111.1								
1955	151.4	96	87	150	109.8	113.9	97.9								
1956	110.1	98	86	165	102.2	100.0	110.2								
1957	78.3	101	87	173	101.1	98.8	103.3								
1958	139.1	96	79	174	94.1	89.7	100.0								
1959	109.4	95	75	182	97.9	93.6	104.6								
1960	129.3	97	76	189	102.2	100.0	103.9								
1961	78.5	103	82	193	90.5	95.9	83.0								
1962	92.3	114	96	199	105.8	107.1	104.5								
1963	97.7	113	99	186	105.5	112.0	94.5								
1964	85.2	115	98	211	104.2	103.6	114.9								
1965	110.1	118	100	235	107.0	106.9	111.9								
1966	122.5	118	101	238	101.9	102.2	101.0								
1967	99.3	117	99	238	98.2	98.9	98.5								
1968	89.7	114	95	240	97.2	96.8	99.5								
1969	106.9	120	102	249	105.8	106.6	103.1								
1970	120.7	125	107	254	105.5	106.2	103.5								
1971	116.5	125	106	268	99.2	99.1	101.2								
1972	143.9	144	124	289	118.5	118.9	117.1								
1973	113.7	146	125	300	102.0	100.8	104.0								
1974	107.7	150	128	312	102.7	102.4	103.8								
1975	112.3	145	122	321	96.1	95.4	102.8								
1976	102.3	152	128	338	105.4	104.8	105.4								
1977	113.5	162	137	356	106.4	106.9	105.4								
1978	123.3	193	164	409	118.7	120.1	114.8	12.27	8.50	2.46		2.46		4.25	4.54
1979	161.3	216	184	451	111.2	112.0	107.5	13.06	7.45	5.60		5.60		5.57	4.99
1980	124.2	237	200	482	106.8	108.0	99.8	15.99	8.76	8.50	0.08	8.42		7.46	6.78
1981	110.7	310	276	534	128.7	136.0	106.5	15.13	7.74	11.29	0.18	11.11		8.22	6.84
1982	109.5	344	312	544	110.5	112.9	100.0	20.74	10.06	10.92	0.69	10.23		9.31	7.67
1983	115.0	368	337	562	105.6	106.8	100.4	19.97	9.88	12.89	0.82	12.07	1.30	6.95	5.74
1984	139.2	420	382	651	111.5	111.3	112.0	25.21	16.57	21.02	1.47	19.55	2.07	12.55	17.20
1985	117.1	550	489	892	114.1	112.1	119.0	37.52	31.29	31.40	2.79	28.61	1.99	17.18	25.66
1986	109.9	661	579	1089	113.2	111.7	114.8	48.25	34.47	36.46	2.34	34.12	2.58	22.63	39.60
1987	124.1	774	681	1247	108.8	110.5	103.2	56.67	43.20	53.56	2.80	50.76	2.77	31.15	45.37
1988	114.0	993	864	1646	106.3	105.9	107.0	66.63	47.16	72.06	5.67	66.39	3.10	44.07	57.49
1989	97.8	1092	955	1780	92.6	92.3	92.6	64.10	40.49	70.40	3.84	66.56	4.50	60.87	54.78
1990	118.5	1122	975	1857	100.5	100.0	102.2	75.89	39.74	67.35	2.60	64.75	3.98	15.75	44.82
1991	120.8	1227	1055	2086	106.6	106.7	106.4	92.79	67.56	74.32	3.34	70.98	5.08	26.31	65.80
1992	119.0	1375	1146	2496	105.5	103.7	109.5	151.57	123.09	82.76	4.14	78.62	3.76	59.60	91.56
1993	114.4	1653	1305	3308	105.4	103.2	109.2	306.90	242.86	113.10	7.75	105.35	20.97	90.63	62.06
1994	126.7	2249	1730	4640	109.8	107.0	114.5	337.79	389.77	158.73	14.62	144.11	120.20	39.33	35.29
1995	115.2	2832	2138	5928	108.2	106.8	109.4	440.14	488.35	226.89	21.63	205.26	202.52	46.93	193.16

Year	v10b4	v11a	v11a1	v11a2	v11b	v11b1	v11b2	v11c	v11c1	v11c2	v12	v12a	v12b	v13	v13i
1952															
1953											119.3	106.4	172.2		
1954											102.3	106.3	91.9		
1955											98.0	105.1	77.2		
1956											118.2	132.7	60.2		
1957											151.3	117.8	447.2		
1958											192.3	202.7	167.9		
1959											116.9	110.8	134.2		
1960											82.4	104.8	29.9		
1961											42.6	52.5			
1962											83.8	83.0			
1963											142.1	113.6			
1964											115.1	114.4	119.4		
1965											119.0	110.5	173.5		
1966											111.1	107.5	126.1		
1967											94.3	92.8	99.2		
1968											94.9	94.9	94.9		
1969											138.4	141.1	129.5		
1970											115.9	117.4	110.6		
1971											104.3	108.2	89.9		
1972											123.4	125.2	115.5		
1973											96.7	96.9	95.8		
1974											100.4	101.1	97.2		
1975											92.8	95.6	78.9		
1976											101.2	112.5	32.4		
1977											134.5	110.3	645.8		
1978	0.63	6.40	3.85	2.55	14.82	11.22	3.60	11.43	8.16	3.27	114.7	103.6	154.7	123.72	68.14
1979	0.99	7.25	3.89	3.36	14.72	10.37	4.35	15.69	11.85	3.84	104.6	103.4	107.4	157.64	93.31
1980	1.80	7.79	3.17	4.62	19.20	12.93	6.27	22.30	17.15	5.15	138.6	134.5	148.1	179.68	101.21
1981	2.31	6.93	1.90	5.03	20.49	13.47	7.02	24.11	18.79	5.32	103.0	100.3	108.6	204.45	112.75
1982	3.09	7.79	2.30	5.49	27.04	18.77	8.27	26.96	20.65	6.31	117.2	117.8	116.0	233.41	133.17
1983	2.77	7.37	2.25	5.12	25.46	18.35	7.11	26.67	23.44	3.23	95.4	104.6	77.6	256.23	136.00
1984	6.00	12.60	2.36	10.24	43.67	25.97	17.70	44.35	36.54	7.81	165.5	140.5	230.9	322.07	172.36
1985	3.48	12.37	2.18	10.19	70.94	45.19	25.75	65.21	54.83	10.38	142.5	153.5	124.9	427.50	221.21
1986	1.40	7.31	3.29	4.02	96.30	51.76	44.54	81.78	66.71	15.07	120.7	114.2	133.4	500.06	258.93
1987	3.39	7.39	3.50	3.89	113.69	65.74	47.95	115.03	86.96	28.07	118.8	116.5	122.7	603.71	311.54
1988	6.89	7.65	4.56	3.09	144.32	77.26	67.06	145.43	107.13	38.30	112.5	104.6	125.2	765.76	397.25
1989	5.00	9.38	5.42	3.96	149.08	67.27	81.81	141.68	106.80	34.88	97.4	90.7	106.4	843.72	440.79
1990	4.91	10.25	6.13	4.12	113.03	66.42	46.61	129.16	114.41	14.75	85.9	105.7	63.4	897.99	476.40
1991	4.19	14.21	10.13	4.08	163.65	94.61	69.04	158.19	135.01	23.18	127.6	119.7	150.1	1081.75	554.45
1992	21.42	12.37	8.26	4.11	299.77	175.30	124.47	221.62	177.62	44.00	139.5	133.3	153.7	1365.06	670.05
1993	65.71	12.80	7.71	5.09	463.51	314.68	148.83	425.92	361.44	64.48	137.6	142.7	127.5	1909.49	877.13
1994	104.23	53.58	52.68	0.90	531.36	441.44	89.92	600.80	512.27	88.53	116.2	130.0	85.6	2666.86	1258.78
1995	188.80	188.99	168.87	20.12	816.71	466.14	350.57	781.09	722.89	58.20	134.6	120.4	181.9	3524.79	1683.28

Year	v13ii	v13iii	v13iv	v13a	v13ai	v13aii	v13aiii	v13aiv	v13b	v13bi	v13bii	v13biii	v13biv	v13b1	v13b1i
1952															
1953															
1954															
1955															
1956															
1957															
1958															
1959															
1960															
1961															
1962															
1963															
1964															
1965															
1966															
1967															
1968															
1969															
1970															
1971															
1972															
1973															
1974															
1975															
1976															
1977															
1978	11.30	14.05	30.23	47.09	40.51	0.99	1.62	3.97	53.52	18.95	4.75	10.82	19.00	46.97	14.04
1979	12.82	15.87	35.64	67.56	59.56	1.27	2.03	4.70	64.07	23.81	5.50	12.09	22.67	55.59	17.46
1980	15.09	18.36	45.02	64.61	57.71	1.29	1.73	3.88	84.07	31.58	7.17	14.51	30.81	73.71	23.86
1981	17.88	21.67	52.15	69.06	62.30	1.36	1.77	3.63	94.68	35.33	8.56	16.57	34.22	84.08	27.45
1982	19.74	24.91	55.59	84.88	78.24	1.68	1.84	3.12	98.44	36.55	9.16	18.83	33.90	87.21	28.20
1983	22.89	29.27	68.07	82.89	76.26	1.91	2.07	2.65	113.12	38.55	10.81	22.07	41.69	102.55	30.69
1984	28.21	36.05	85.45	104.40	94.65	2.30	2.51	4.94	141.48	50.38	13.72	27.17	50.21	127.91	40.27
1985	35.07	52.18	119.04	123.88	111.00	2.73	3.16	6.99	198.91	73.45	17.16	40.06	68.24	178.68	58.43
1986	44.57	61.27	135.29	136.29	122.59	3.07	3.43	7.20	230.89	88.66	22.61	46.52	73.10	206.63	70.67
1987	54.50	73.66	164.01	159.41	142.97	3.77	3.82	8.85	281.47	109.74	28.44	55.72	87.57	249.69	85.86
1988	67.37	97.39	203.75	195.68	177.29	4.56	5.16	8.67	354.39	137.73	35.70	73.75	107.21	315.36	108.49
1989	76.75	112.16	214.02	210.95	190.87	5.53	6.03	8.52	386.25	154.81	39.34	84.31	107.79	346.50	125.51
1990	89.08	121.02	211.49	225.04	201.58	5.85	6.46	11.15	408.18	170.30	46.67	91.32	99.89	363.74	137.87
1991	106.59	141.51	279.20	245.22	211.97	7.49	4.98	20.78	494.11	203.41	56.15	108.12	126.43	438.36	161.92
1992	137.05	178.18	379.78	262.67	230.43	9.19	4.94	18.11	653.43	251.97	73.90	133.44	194.12	581.73	200.36
1993	170.63	273.86	587.87	317.84	237.24	10.63	3.06	66.91	980.42	383.65	90.39	216.10	290.28	873.92	306.99
1994	257.66	352.19	798.23	443.87	346.67	15.21	6.70	75.28	1388.06	550.70	148.78	269.60	418.98	1236.74	440.59
1995	299.86	404.55	1137.10	559.80	449.09	19.67	7.99	83.05	1834.47	729.93	165.13	292.53	646.88	1632.37	588.20

Year	v13b1ii	v13b1iii	v13b1iv	v13b2	v13b2i	v13b2ii	v13b2iii	v13b2iv	v13c	v13ci	v13cii	v13ciii	v13civ	v13c1
1952														
1953														
1954														
1955														
1956														
1957														
1958														
1959														
1960														
1961														
1962														
1963														
1964														
1965														
1966														
1967														
1968														
1969														
1970														
1971														
1972														
1973														
1974														
1975														
1976														
1977														
1978	4.54	10.47	17.92	6.55	4.91	0.21	0.35	1.08	23.11	8.68	5.56	1.61	7.26	3.22
1979	5.23	11.62	21.28	8.48	6.35	0.27	0.47	1.39	26.01	9.94	6.05	1.75	8.27	4.15
1980	6.83	13.95	29.07	10.36	7.72	0.34	0.56	1.74	31.00	11.92	6.63	2.12	10.33	4.88
1981	8.21	15.99	32.43	10.60	7.88	0.35	0.58	1.79	40.71	15.12	7.96	3.33	14.30	7.16
1982	8.78	18.22	32.01	11.23	8.35	0.38	0.61	1.89	50.09	18.38	8.90	4.24	18.57	9.12
1983	10.45	21.49	39.92	10.57	7.86	0.36	0.58	1.77	60.22	21.19	10.17	5.13	23.73	11.20
1984	13.25	26.43	47.96	13.57	10.11	0.47	0.74	2.25	76.19	27.33	12.19	6.37	30.30	15.47
1985	16.44	38.95	64.86	20.23	15.02	0.72	1.11	3.38	104.71	36.76	15.18	8.96	43.81	20.31
1986	21.77	45.19	69.00	24.26	17.99	0.84	1.33	4.10	132.88	47.68	18.89	11.32	54.99	24.98
1987	27.37	53.91	82.55	31.78	23.88	1.07	1.84	5.02	162.83	58.83	22.29	14.12	67.59	29.47
1988	34.18	70.96	101.73	39.03	29.24	1.52	2.79	5.48	215.69	82.23	27.11	18.48	87.87	36.24
1989	37.66	81.15	102.18	39.75	29.30	1.68	3.16	5.61	246.52	95.11	31.88	21.82	97.71	43.39
1990	44.39	87.91	93.57	44.44	32.43	2.28	3.41	6.32	264.77	104.52	36.56	23.24	100.45	45.01
1991	53.29	104.02	119.13	55.75	41.49	2.86	4.10	7.30	342.42	139.07	42.95	28.41	131.99	60.04
1992	69.79	127.79	183.79	71.70	51.61	4.11	5.65	10.33	448.96	187.65	53.96	39.80	167.55	80.03
1993	84.66	206.82	275.45	106.50	76.66	5.73	9.28	14.83	611.23	256.24	69.61	54.70	230.68	110.33
1994	141.85	252.26	402.04	151.32	110.11	6.93	17.34	16.94	834.93	361.40	93.67	75.89	303.97	147.17
1995	157.48	271.31	615.38	202.10	141.73	7.65	21.22	31.50	1130.52	504.26	115.06	104.03	407.17	204.59

Year	v13c1i	v13c1ii	v13c1iii	v13c1iv	v13c2	v13c2i	v13c2ii	v13c2iii	v13c2iv	v13c3	v13c3i	v13c3ii	v13c3iii	v13c3iv
1952														
1953														
1954														
1955														
1956														
1957														
1958														
1959														
1960														
1961														
1962														
1963														
1964														
1965														
1966														
1967														
1968														
1969														
1970														
1971														
1972														
1973														
1974														
1975														
1976														
1977														
1978	1.60	0.38	0.21	1.03	7.98	2.47	0.44	1.23	3.84	1.89	0.11	0.04	0.10	1.64
1979	2.01	0.49	0.26	1.39	8.72	2.76	0.48	1.31	4.17	2.13	0.13	0.04	0.11	1.85
1980	2.39	0.57	0.30	1.62	10.55	3.31	0.55	1.60	5.09	2.88	0.18	0.06	0.13	2.51
1981	3.32	0.81	0.44	2.59	15.35	4.74	0.85	2.61	7.15	3.54	0.21	0.08	0.17	3.08
1982	4.09	0.99	0.56	3.48	19.43	6.24	1.06	3.29	8.84	5.31	0.32	0.11	0.26	4.62
1983	4.92	1.19	0.70	4.39	23.12	6.94	1.19	3.95	11.04	7.05	0.44	0.13	0.30	6.18
1984	6.67	1.61	1.01	6.18	28.42	9.12	1.49	4.73	13.08	9.14	0.58	0.19	0.35	8.02
1985	8.57	2.06	1.37	8.31	40.52	12.72	1.93	6.52	19.35	13.61	0.86	0.25	0.67	11.83
1986	10.54	2.46	1.74	10.24	48.77	16.87	2.30	7.94	21.66	19.67	1.12	0.34	1.09	17.12
1987	12.52	2.83	2.13	11.99	58.78	20.75	2.86	9.75	25.42	25.89	1.40	0.49	1.49	22.51
1988	15.91	4.12	2.72	13.49	81.96	29.99	3.57	12.47	35.93	33.22	2.13	0.65	2.11	28.33
1989	18.96	4.95	3.38	16.10	88.50	33.72	4.23	13.50	37.05	39.44	2.09	1.08	3.46	32.81
1990	21.11	6.55	3.64	13.71	91.86	36.47	5.26	13.99	36.14	44.48	2.68	1.45	3.67	36.68
1991	28.28	8.18	5.02	18.56	127.94	52.83	6.92	16.56	51.63	52.87	3.37	1.75	4.07	43.68
1992	38.39	10.90	6.96	23.78	174.33	73.57	8.94	23.86	67.96	62.80	5.17	2.51	5.13	49.94
1993	52.02	15.38	9.40	33.53	239.58	101.58	11.18	32.80	94.02	78.54	6.47	3.12	6.47	62.48
1994	68.39	26.03	13.02	39.73	335.60	142.21	12.65	46.04	134.70	100.99	11.97	4.01	9.32	75.69
1995	99.50	36.81	15.80	52.48	473.35	231.25	13.50	58.62	169.98	139.69	12.45	5.65	11.93	109.66

Year	v13c4	v13c4i	v13c4ii	v13c4iii	v13c4iv	v13c5	v13c5i	v13c5ii	v13c5iii	v13c5iv	v13c6	v13c6i	v13c6ii	v13c6iii
1952														
1953														
1954														
1955														
1956														
1957														
1958														
1959														
1960														
1961														
1962														
1963														
1964														
1965														
1966														
1967														
1968														
1969														
1970														
1971														
1972														
1973														
1974														
1975														
1976														
1977														
1978	3.75	0.08	3.63	0.02	0.02	0.84	0.24	0.07	0.05	0.48	0.73	0.65	0.08	
1979	3.97	0.10	3.82	0.02	0.03	0.99	0.28	0.08	0.05	0.58	0.83	0.74	0.09	
1980	4.19	0.12	4.02	0.02	0.03	1.23	0.34	0.09	0.07	0.73	1.04	0.94	0.10	
1981	4.80	0.13	4.61	0.02	0.04	1.77	0.50	0.12	0.09	1.06	1.18	1.08	0.10	
1982	5.21	0.15	5.00	0.02	0.04	1.96	0.55	0.14	0.10	1.17	1.35	1.24	0.11	
1983	5.84	0.16	5.62	0.02	0.04	2.59	0.74	0.18	0.13	1.54	1.51	1.38	0.13	
1984	6.63	0.18	6.37	0.03	0.05	3.96	1.17	0.29	0.20	2.30	1.75	1.57	0.17	
1985	7.85	0.21	7.53	0.04	0.07	5.87	1.74	0.51	0.28	3.34	2.31	2.07	0.22	
1986	9.83	0.29	9.43	0.04	0.07	7.98	2.35	0.76	0.37	4.50	2.92	2.52	0.36	
1987	11.73	0.38	11.09	0.04	0.22	10.26	3.10	0.90	0.51	5.75	3.58	3.07	0.40	
1988	14.24	0.60	13.04	0.07	0.53	13.37	4.10	1.13	0.80	7.34	4.75	4.07	0.48	0.01
1989	16.27	0.88	14.52	0.15	0.72	14.31	4.16	1.41	0.95	7.79	5.92	5.10	0.60	0.01
1990	17.21	1.04	15.00	0.24	0.93	16.95	5.19	1.80	1.16	8.80	6.88	5.67	0.76	0.01
1991	17.71	1.12	15.08	0.41	1.10	21.03	6.52	2.24	1.77	10.50	7.44	5.82	0.87	0.02
1992	22.76	1.88	18.19	0.65	2.04	29.03	8.96	2.87	2.41	14.79	9.63	7.48	1.08	0.03
1993	32.57	2.70	22.49	0.87	6.51	40.57	12.63	3.24	3.72	20.98	13.07	9.42	1.90	0.04
1994	40.65	3.52	28.77	1.17	7.19	57.05	18.69	5.15	4.72	28.49	20.37	14.68	2.25	0.06
1995	56.05	4.21	33.28	7.85	10.71	86.48	37.75	6.49	8.27	33.97	30.75	17.44	2.11	0.19

Year	v13c6iv	v13c7	v13c7i	v13c7ii	v13c7iii	v13c7iv	v13c8	v13c8i	v13c8ii	v13c8iii	v13c8iv	v13c9	v13c9i	v13c9ii
1952														
1953														
1954														
1955														
1956														
1957														
1958														
1959														
1960														
1961														
1962														
1963														
1964														
1965														
1966														
1967														
1968														
1969														
1970														
1971														
1972														
1973														
1974														
1975														
1976														
1977														
1978		1.86	1.45	0.32		0.09	0.57	0.45	0.12			1.10	0.74	0.36
1979		2.11	1.64	0.36		0.11	0.67	0.53	0.14			1.27	0.85	0.42
1980		2.65	2.06	0.44		0.15	0.77	0.60	0.16		0.01	1.58	1.08	0.50
1981		3.05	2.36	0.50		0.19	0.85	0.66	0.17		0.02	1.79	1.22	0.57
1982		3.41	2.64	0.55	0.01	0.21	0.95	0.75	0.18		0.02	2.00	1.40	0.60
1983		3.85	2.97	0.60	0.03	0.25	1.14	0.89	0.22		0.03	2.47	1.73	0.74
1984	0.01	4.65	3.57	0.71	0.04	0.33	1.45	1.13	0.27	0.01	0.04	3.12	2.22	0.90
1985	0.02	6.18	4.77	0.91	0.06	0.44	1.99	1.54	0.36	0.02	0.07	4.08	2.91	1.17
1986	0.04	7.84	6.05	1.12	0.10	0.57	2.52	1.89	0.44	0.04	0.15	5.98	4.58	1.40
1987	0.11	9.28	7.21	1.27	0.11	0.69	3.09	2.34	0.51	0.05	0.19	8.31	6.52	1.65
1988	0.19	12.50	10.00	1.44	0.13	0.93	4.10	3.08	0.63	0.08	0.31	12.51	10.59	1.71
1989	0.21	14.79	11.72	1.83	0.15	1.09	4.68	3.45	0.70	0.11	0.42	15.28	12.92	2.09
1990	0.44	15.36	11.87	2.14	0.21	1.14	5.03	3.39	0.19	0.19	0.72	17.21	14.58	2.30
1991	0.73	17.26	13.08	2.65	0.25	1.28	6.44	4.15	0.99	0.27	1.03	24.63	20.58	3.42
1992	1.04	21.54	16.35	3.21	0.33	1.65	8.56	5.41	1.20	0.37	1.58	31.28	25.93	4.11
1993	1.71	29.94	22.31	3.86	0.41	3.36	11.57	7.40	1.60	0.45	2.12	43.06	35.70	5.64
1994	3.38	43.96	33.47	4.70	0.51	5.28	17.74	9.59	1.92	0.67	2.56	60.48	52.05	6.55
1995	11.01	49.09	37.32	5.52	0.68	5.57	16.17	9.57	2.25	0.66	3.69	59.35	47.07	7.36

Year	v13c9iii	v13c9iv	v13c10	v13c10i	v13c10ii	v13c10iii	v13c10iv
1952							
1953							
1954							
1955							
1956							
1957							
1958							
1959							
1960							
1961							
1962							
1963							
1964							
1965							
1966							
1967							
1968							
1969							
1970							
1971							
1972							
1973							
1974							
1975							
1976							
1977							
1978			1.17	0.89	0.12		0.16
1979			1.17	0.90	0.13		0.14
1980			1.23	0.90	0.14		0.19
1981			1.22	0.90	0.15		0.17
1982			1.35	1.00	0.16		0.19
1983			1.45	1.02	0.17		0.26
1984			1.60	1.12	0.19		0.29
1985			1.99	1.37	0.24		0.38
1986			2.39	1.47	0.28		0.64
1987	0.04	0.10	2.44	1.54	0.29		0.61
1988	0.09	0.12	2.80	1.76	0.34		0.70
1989	0.11	0.16	3.94	2.11	0.47		1.36
1990	0.13	0.20	4.78	2.52	0.57		1.69
1991	0.24	0.39	7.06	3.32	0.85	-0.20	3.09
1992	0.42	0.82	9.00	4.51	0.95	-0.41	3.95
1993	0.54	1.18	12.00	6.01	1.20		4.79
1994	0.38	1.50	13.92	6.83	1.64		5.45
1995	0.03	4.89	15.00	7.70	2.09		5.21

12

Anhui

Year	v1	v1a	v1b	v1b1	v1b2	v1c	v1c1	v1c2	v1c3	v2	v2a	v2b	v2b1	v2b2	v2c
1952	35.39	22.17	7.80	6.50	1.30	5.42	0.90	3.60	0.92						
1953	42.59	25.88	10.07	7.86	2.21	6.64	0.94	3.96	1.74	103.8	100.2	125.1	115.9	148.7	104.0
1954	44.50	26.09	10.79	8.76	2.03	7.62	1.06	4.32	2.24	104.1	102.5	103.7	109.5	91.9	113.8
1955	57.98	36.90	12.63	9.80	2.83	8.45	1.12	4.78	2.55	125.6	131.6	115.1	108.0	131.9	106.0
1956	57.82	32.36	15.56	12.40	3.16	9.90	1.33	5.15	3.42	89.9	82.0	117.2	124.3	103.4	107.9
1957	65.35	35.20	18.60	15.40	3.20	11.55	1.80	5.70	4.05	117.8	116.4	121.4	127.9	106.1	120.0
1958	89.85	36.95	39.13	31.80	7.33	13.77	2.92	6.78	4.07	116.5	92.4	209.2	211.9	201.5	108.7
1959	111.51	35.09	58.42	49.33	9.09	18.00	3.55	8.27	6.18	102.8	84.8	126.2	133.2	105.4	115.5
1960	122.05	34.57	68.78	56.62	12.16	18.70	4.01	7.92	6.77	102.2	89.0	117.4	115.0	126.9	99.1
1961	78.50	29.67	32.53	28.24	4.29	16.30	2.94	6.93	6.43	63.7	78.3	45.2	48.5	33.9	85.7
1962	66.37	28.60	22.11	20.01	2.10	15.66	2.50	6.90	6.26	98.7	116.3	68.7	70.9	58.0	107.9
1963	68.37	29.39	22.81	20.13	2.68	16.17	2.70	6.97	6.50	103.7	105.6	102.1	98.6	123.5	100.6
1964	76.11	31.02	28.15	24.45	3.70	16.94	3.03	7.04	6.87	116.9	117.2	124.3	119.8	146.1	107.9
1965	89.67	37.74	35.10	31.80	3.30	16.83	3.00	7.10	6.73	118.7	123.2	122.4	130.5	90.3	100.4
1966	102.73	43.44	41.71	38.25	3.46	17.58	3.30	7.19	7.09	107.4	106.5	114.6	117.5	98.1	99.1
1967	92.32	46.11	28.47	26.29	2.18	17.74	2.80	7.48	7.46	96.5	106.7	69.8	70.3	66.4	104.8
1968	91.36	47.12	27.75	25.56	2.19	16.49	1.71	7.06	7.72	100.1	101.6	100.3	100.2	101.4	94.0
1969	99.99	42.84	39.99	36.49	3.50	17.16	1.93	7.41	7.82	102.1	90.6	141.6	140.2	151.6	100.9
1970	123.43	53.22	51.30	45.45	5.85	18.91	3.40	7.60	7.91	123.6	123.4	132.9	128.3	163.5	107.5
1971	141.89	57.26	63.36	56.67	6.69	21.27	4.19	8.25	8.83	110.8	104.5	122.8	124.5	114.4	111.9
1972	153.64	62.51	67.21	61.70	5.51	23.92	4.59	9.27	10.06	105.8	105.4	104.2	108.5	80.1	111.0
1973	171.69	66.22	79.90	73.71	6.19	25.57	4.96	10.13	10.48	108.0	102.7	118.3	119.6	108.4	105.5
1974	169.66	67.71	75.41	69.87	5.54	26.54	4.58	10.68	11.28	99.6	102.2	93.9	94.3	90.9	104.3
1975	188.93	67.87	89.59	81.80	7.79	31.47	4.69	14.90	11.88	108.4	98.9	119.4	122.7	91.0	118.6
1976	207.86	74.69	99.61	90.51	9.10	33.56	4.92	16.10	12.54	109.4	107.7	111.8	105.8	182.5	109.3
1977	212.93	69.57	107.46	98.86	8.60	35.90	5.03	17.10	13.77	98.8	90.2	107.0	109.0	92.8	105.9
1978	227.64	71.07	118.31	107.11	11.20	38.26	5.96	18.30	14.00	103.1	97.3	109.1	108.5	113.7	103.5
1979	251.99	79.34	130.88	119.18	11.70	41.77	5.91	20.90	14.96	108.7	108.9	109.7	110.3	104.8	106.0
1980	281.54	84.63	148.45	129.65	18.80	48.46	8.50	22.30	17.66	105.7	94.5	114.3	108.5	160.4	111.6
1981	328.62	119.76	156.01	136.41	19.60	52.85	10.70	21.51	20.64	114.9	131.4	104.7	104.8	104.2	107.2
1982	373.55	128.99	179.38	153.17	26.21	65.18	13.57	24.45	27.16	113.7	108.6	115.3	111.9	133.7	122.7
1983	427.05	137.05	209.34	172.95	36.39	80.66	17.76	28.41	34.49	108.4	100.0	111.6	108.7	125.2	119.8
1984	520.01	162.11	258.36	211.97	46.39	99.54	20.94	31.98	46.62	119.2	114.2	122.1	121.7	124.0	122.1
1985	660.24	198.24	333.26	277.27	55.99	128.74	26.46	41.40	60.88	118.6	110.1	123.5	125.3	116.6	122.6
1986	780.62	221.92	395.58	324.34	71.24	163.12	37.72	48.29	77.11	113.4	109.3	114.4	114.2	115.5	117.9
1987	927.67	255.34	473.03	394.88	78.15	199.30	42.02	66.12	91.16	108.9	99.6	112.5	114.4	104.6	115.0
1988	1185.74	315.25	611.67	518.13	93.54	258.82	53.52	93.65	111.65	110.5	99.4	116.9	119.0	107.1	111.2
1989	1371.55	341.53	703.77	627.72	76.05	326.25	54.37	134.57	137.31	107.5	103.4	106.3	112.5	75.0	115.1
1990	1450.61	370.94	759.77	670.33	89.44	319.90	60.38	112.58	146.94	102.1	103.9	104.6	104.6	104.9	94.9
1991	1599.17	317.26	878.30	765.95	112.35	403.61	82.61	146.18	174.82	108.7	85.4	114.6	114.5	115.2	122.0
1992	2046.20	390.05	1164.63	995.81	168.82	491.52	93.40	181.92	216.20	120.4	118.8	124.8	125.4	120.1	112.1
1993	2821.90	473.43	1756.19	1545.49	210.70	592.28	101.20	225.81	265.27	123.9	110.2	134.5	137.1	114.7	109.5
1994	3983.69	590.74	2593.75	2347.45	246.30	799.20	134.86	297.94	366.40	126.3	103.2	135.7	137.2	121.7	118.8
1995	5367.48	980.26	3490.59	3155.91	334.68	896.63	164.79	374.75	357.09	118.9	114.2	122.5	122.2	124.7	110.7

Year	v2c1	v2c2	v3'	v3	v3a	v3b	v3b1	v3b2	v3c	v3c1	v3c2	v3c3	v3c4	v3c5	v3c6
1952			22.88	22.88	17.18	2.27	1.77	0.50	3.43	0.70	2.15				
1953	90.8	95.8	26.99	26.99	19.94	2.90	2.10	0.80	4.15	0.73	2.32				
1954	115.0	109.9	27.76	27.76	20.01	3.03	2.32	0.71	4.72	0.83	2.48				
1955	99.6	104.9	37.15	37.15	28.24	3.71	2.61	1.10	5.20	0.88	2.57				
1956	109.7	99.2	35.27	35.27	24.69	4.55	3.29	1.26	6.03	1.05	2.81				
1957	141.9	116.6	41.37	41.37	28.06	6.38	5.07	1.31	6.93	1.42	2.98				
1958	142.6	104.5	51.31	51.31	29.41	13.55	10.60	2.95	8.35	2.25	3.55				
1959	104.0	103.9	57.97	57.97	27.45	19.71	16.08	3.63	10.81	2.65	4.35				
1960	106.8	90.6	59.76	59.76	25.60	23.00	18.31	4.69	11.16	2.90	4.09				
1961	70.5	84.4	43.65	43.65	22.96	11.15	9.56	1.59	9.54	2.04	3.51				
1962	101.7	118.5	39.47	39.47	22.68	7.91	7.10	0.81	8.88	1.66	3.40				
1963	103.3	97.6	40.81	40.81	22.79	8.68	7.59	1.09	9.34	1.87	3.48				
1964	118.9	106.4	44.97	44.97	23.64	11.32	9.78	1.54	10.01	2.19	3.59				
1965	100.0	102.3	52.75	52.75	28.09	14.56	13.13	1.43	10.10	2.27	3.65				
1966	102.5	93.7	59.82	59.82	32.13	17.08	15.63	1.45	10.61	2.47	3.73				
1967	88.8	109.8	56.88	56.88	34.21	12.11	11.18	0.93	10.56	2.09	3.92				
1968	63.1	95.3	56.09	56.09	35.17	11.28	10.42	0.86	9.64	1.29	3.63				
1969	105.1	99.9	58.09	58.09	32.39	15.70	14.46	1.24	10.00	1.49	3.73				
1970	172.7	100.4	71.79	71.79	40.08	20.52	18.59	1.93	11.19	2.59	3.76				
1971	123.1	108.5	79.99	79.99	42.56	24.81	22.58	2.23	12.62	3.13	4.12				
1972	107.3	110.0	85.88	85.88	45.98	25.97	24.06	1.91	13.93	3.31	4.66				
1973	105.6	106.7	92.18	92.18	49.00	28.33	26.16	2.17	14.85	3.51	5.13				
1974	92.4	105.7	91.44	91.44	50.31	25.85	23.86	1.99	15.28	3.17	5.44				
1975	99.9	135.8	97.01	97.01	50.03	29.11	26.05	3.06	17.87	3.28	7.57				
1976	108.3	112.0	105.77	105.77	55.27	31.39	28.02	3.37	19.11	3.40	8.30				
1977	100.7	104.5	108.01	108.01	52.88	34.64	31.35	3.29	20.49	3.52	9.04				
1978	104.0	105.1	113.96	113.96	53.77	40.51	36.26	4.25	19.68	3.67	7.38	1.94	2.13	0.45	0.62
1979	99.0	107.2	127.31	127.31	61.16	44.76	40.31	4.45	21.39	3.44	8.77	1.77	2.15	0.56	0.68
1980	143.9	101.2	140.88	140.88	64.68	50.06	44.09	5.97	26.14	4.98	10.30	1.68	2.58	0.76	0.81
1981	125.9	94.9	170.51	170.51	88.44	52.48	46.32	6.16	29.59	5.71	11.20	1.96	2.97	0.96	1.04
1982	126.7	112.5	187.02	187.02	89.97	59.66	51.70	7.96	37.39	7.43	13.78	3.46	3.60	1.08	1.20
1983	129.1	114.6	215.68	215.68	96.55	73.20	61.99	11.21	45.93	10.01	15.59	4.93	4.11	1.48	1.33
1984	114.7	110.4	265.74	265.74	116.26	92.83	79.30	13.52	56.65	12.19	17.58	8.94	4.17	2.13	1.59
1985	122.5	120.2	331.24	331.24	140.97	117.84	101.37	16.47	72.43	15.56	21.27	9.66	6.14	4.60	2.14
1986	134.9	111.3	382.78	382.76	155.91	137.57	117.26	20.31	89.28	20.02	24.50	12.19	7.58	5.10	2.71
1987	110.8	125.6	442.43	442.35	176.35	157.74	135.59	22.15	108.26	23.99	32.48	14.75	8.66	5.67	3.12
1988	123.3	111.8	546.97	546.94	210.53	200.95	174.27	26.68	135.46	29.90	42.46	18.43	10.03	6.51	3.57
1989	101.7	130.1	616.26	616.25	225.39	227.85	205.52	22.33	163.01	30.44	54.58	25.19	13.22	6.47	4.47
1990	99.9	83.5	658.03	658.02	246.17	251.48	223.31	28.17	160.37	32.36	43.94	23.66	15.51	7.29	4.72
1991	132.4	128.6	663.67	663.60	190.48	280.28	245.34	34.94	192.84	44.03	50.51	27.94	17.15	8.29	6.23
1992	108.3	111.9	801.23	801.16	230.51	333.00	293.01	39.99	237.65	47.96	67.28	36.37	19.75	11.05	7.67
1993	110.1	109.4	1069.92	1069.84	284.06	494.85	441.90	52.95	290.93	54.65	90.32	43.17	22.44	16.83	8.59
1994	125.2	109.1	1488.56	1488.47	336.72	744.16	680.76	63.40	407.59	77.30	120.96	69.50	33.48	24.88	11.29
1995	122.1	111.9	2003.66	2003.58	581.24	938.72	852.10	86.62	483.62	86.79	143.62	100.72	38.78	27.80	12.11

Year	v3c7	v3c8	v3c9	v3c10	v3d	v4'	v4	v4a	v4b	v4b1	v4b2	v4c	v4c1	v4c2	v4c3
1952				0.58	78										
1953				1.10	89	101.2	101.2	99.6	123.0	113.7	140.0	102.7	91.0	94.0	
1954				1.41	89	103.1	103.1	102.0	100.6	108.6	88.9	112.5	115.5	107.7	
1955				1.75	117	127.5	127.5	131.3	122.1	108.6	146.4	105.1	100.0	103.2	
1956				2.17	109	86.4	86.4	81.7	116.3	123.8	106.1	106.5	110.2	95.9	
1957				2.53	126	122.6	122.6	121.6	139.4	158.8	108.9	117.7	142.0	111.8	
1958				2.55	152	105.6	105.6	92.2	209.6	214.5	198.2	110.0	139.2	104.7	
1959				3.81	170	94.9	94.9	83.4	122.8	130.2	104.5	115.0	100.7	104.4	
1960				4.17	185	94.3	94.3	84.2	116.1	114.0	122.6	98.6	103.4	89.0	
1961				3.99	145	71.4	71.4	81.8	46.1	50.8	32.5	84.3	67.8	82.8	
1962				3.82	109	107.0	107.0	119.2	71.7	74.3	60.4	104.0	97.2	115.3	
1963				3.99	128	103.8	103.8	103.3	108.7	104.8	130.2	102.5	107.9	98.9	
1964				4.23	140	116.4	116.4	115.1	131.2	127.0	149.6	110.3	124.0	108.7	
1965				4.18	163	118.1	118.1	120.4	126.2	134.8	94.0	101.8	104.8	103.2	
1966				4.41	179	106.1	106.1	105.8	113.0	116.3	94.8	99.8	101.3	94.5	
1967				4.55	164	100.5	100.5	107.1	72.5	73.2	67.7	103.5	88.6	110.8	
1968				4.72	157	100.0	100.0	102.2	95.7	96.0	93.2	92.4	63.7	93.5	
1969				4.78	157	98.3	98.3	91.8	136.4	136.3	136.7	100.4	107.6	97.8	
1970				4.84	186	123.0	123.0	122.9	134.8	132.4	152.3	108.8	170.4	98.7	
1971				5.37	200	107.4	107.4	103.1	120.5	121.3	115.6	112.3	120.8	109.5	
1972				5.96	208	104.7	104.7	104.3	103.2	106.2	83.3	109.3	103.4	110.7	
1973				6.21	216	104.7	104.7	103.3	108.9	108.8	109.6	105.4	103.7	107.5	
1974				6.67	210	100.3	100.3	102.6	91.0	90.7	93.2	103.6	90.4	106.3	
1975				7.02	218	103.5	103.5	98.1	112.8	114.4	99.5	116.9	100.8	135.4	
1976				7.41	234	108.6	108.6	108.1	109.4	102.8	172.0	109.7	107.0	113.7	
1977				7.93	235	98.3	98.3	92.7	109.3	111.7	95.9	106.3	101.9	107.1	
1978	1.57	0.12	1.10	0.70	244	100.4	100.4	96.9	115.5	115.9	112.8	91.8	91.5	80.2	
1979	1.81	0.15	1.29	0.77	268	109.9	109.9	110.9	109.6	110.2	105.1	106.7	93.6	111.5	91.3
1980	2.29	0.18	1.65	0.91	291	102.4	102.4	93.7	112.2	109.1	133.9	118.4	144.8	111.4	95.1
1981	2.59	0.21	1.95	1.00	346	117.8	117.8	127.0	104.4	104.6	103.2	112.3	114.7	107.0	116.5
1982	3.18	0.25	2.28	1.13	375	109.4	109.4	102.6	113.8	111.2	129.2	125.9	130.0	121.8	176.4
1983	3.89	0.30	2.81	1.48	428	108.8	108.8	101.0	117.3	115.4	127.0	118.6	132.9	111.5	137.3
1984	4.45	0.37	3.51	1.72	523	120.1	120.1	116.3	125.3	127.0	117.3	121.9	118.5	110.6	177.6
1985	5.70	0.48	4.47	2.41	646	115.5	115.5	109.1	121.7	122.5	117.7	121.0	123.7	113.4	101.5
1986	7.12	1.08	6.10	2.88	738	111.1	111.1	108.0	112.7	112.9	112.0	115.1	121.8	109.0	119.8
1987	7.95	0.69	7.36	3.59	842	104.8	104.8	97.9	107.9	108.7	104.0	113.8	119.1	121.6	110.5
1988	9.81	0.88	9.33	4.54	1026	105.4	105.4	96.1	115.2	116.6	107.8	107.6	120.6	103.2	104.5
1989	11.34	1.02	10.85	5.43	1136	105.2	105.2	102.2	104.8	109.5	77.2	110.1	101.9	116.4	117.8
1990	12.29	1.27	14.24	5.09	1182	102.9	102.9	104.4	107.0	106.4	112.5	94.9	95.6	80.2	92.4
1991	14.40	1.33	15.91	7.05	1161	99.1	99.1	77.2	109.8	109.9	108.8	115.8	131.6	114.0	111.2
1992	17.48	1.85	19.50	8.74	1382	116.8	116.8	116.9	118.7	118.0	124.2	113.8	104.4	119.8	129.2
1993	19.63	2.15	24.84	8.31	1824	121.0	121.0	111.9	133.2	134.9	119.8	111.7	115.8	118.3	107.2
1994	26.70	11.35	29.12	3.01	2521	120.6	120.6	103.0	132.0	134.3	112.2	118.3	124.6	112.4	123.6
1995	28.00	12.22	31.02	2.56	3357	114.3	114.3	117.6	114.3	113.8	119.0	111.5	111.5	112.3	119.8

Year	v4c4	v4c5	v4c6	v4c7	v4c8	v4c9	v4c10	v5	v5a	v5a1	v5a1a	v5a1b	v5a2	v5b	v5b1
1952								22.88	20.02	18.84	16.08	2.76	1.18	2.87	2.38
1953								26.99	22.88	21.27	18.33	2.94	1.61	4.10	3.36
1954								27.76	23.47	21.63	17.71	3.92	1.84	4.31	3.55
1955								37.15	30.26	27.74	23.32	4.42	2.52	6.90	5.69
1956								35.27	27.91	24.61	19.79	4.82	3.30	7.38	5.54
1957								41.37	33.89	30.66	24.34	6.32	3.23	7.50	5.77
1958								51.31	34.32	24.65	18.24	6.41	9.67	17.00	14.26
1959								57.97	38.07	25.91	17.22	8.69	12.16	19.92	16.16
1960								59.76	40.16	24.11	14.72	9.39	16.05	19.62	15.24
1961								43.65	36.06	27.93	18.56	9.37	8.13	7.61	4.77
1962								39.47	37.37	33.52	27.11	6.41	3.85	2.10	0.40
1963								40.81	36.78	31.76	25.57	6.19	5.02	4.03	2.41
1964								44.97	36.68	30.55	24.15	6.40	6.13	8.31	5.41
1965								52.75	42.58	36.68	29.01	7.67	5.90	10.20	7.04
1966								59.82	49.38	42.43	33.76	8.67	6.95	10.45	6.72
1967								56.88	50.85	44.49	34.85	9.64	6.36	6.62	4.41
1968								56.09	49.81	46.35	37.23	9.12	3.46	7.05	4.44
1969								58.09	49.42	45.05	36.40	8.65	4.37	8.68	5.93
1970								71.79	56.71	52.26	42.04	10.22	4.45	13.91	8.94
1971								79.99	63.21	58.04	46.74	11.30	5.17	16.86	11.69
1972								85.88	68.83	62.81	50.74	12.07	6.02	18.07	12.64
1973								92.18	73.25	66.54	53.84	12.70	6.71	19.89	13.86
1974								91.44	70.39	62.86	51.50	11.36	7.53	21.07	14.64
1975								97.01	75.58	67.20	54.91	12.29	8.38	21.50	14.84
1976								105.77	86.01	75.81	61.57	14.24	10.20	22.50	15.47
1977								108.01	86.48	77.03	62.16	14.87	9.45	22.83	15.54
1978								113.96	88.75	77.17	62.03	15.14	11.58	24.02	15.85
1979	100.9	123.6	110.4	115.3	123.8	117.5	104.9	127.31	103.14	89.81	73.11	16.70	13.33	25.03	16.13
1980	119.9	136.4	118.8	126.5	119.2	128.4	120.9	140.88	119.12	106.93	85.91	21.02	12.19	28.17	18.24
1981	115.1	126.0	128.1	113.3	112.9	118.3	110.3	170.51	140.02	128.11	105.27	22.84	11.91	26.00	15.62
1982	121.3	112.7	115.7	122.8	117.1	116.6	115.7	187.02	153.54	141.26	116.65	24.61	12.28	43.02	31.91
1983	103.0	126.8	108.3	117.8	122.0	118.8	124.1	215.68	170.73	153.78	126.45	27.33	16.95	55.02	44.26
1984	98.6	155.6	116.1	112.3	120.0	122.7	114.6	265.74	177.90	158.34	127.07	31.27	19.56	79.31	65.50
1985	142.5	194.8	127.8	122.1	125.0	121.3	131.5	331.24	217.99	187.32	147.90	39.42	30.67	113.28	86.31
1986	112.3	91.3	120.5	118.7	212.0	130.1	114.8	382.76	259.85	215.94	168.47	47.47	43.91	134.09	102.99
1987	108.9	102.8	107.3	103.6	59.1	112.2	115.2	442.35	298.31	253.35	190.32	63.03	44.96	149.38	114.64
1988	103.4	102.9	98.8	106.9	109.6	109.3	110.0	546.94	360.62	312.56	230.57	81.99	48.06	182.00	127.05
1989	131.7	86.8	110.6	99.5	102.9	103.2	105.6	616.25	409.67	354.24	258.37	95.87	55.43	183.39	123.32
1990	114.4	106.3	100.9	107.0	119.8	124.6	89.1	658.02	433.77	373.01	269.95	103.06	60.76	204.70	138.18
1991	109.0	108.2	126.5	112.9	100.0	111.5	97.1	663.60	466.38	389.38	270.79	118.59	77.00	208.39	150.85
1992	107.3	112.6	95.6	102.0	121.3	113.2	131.0	801.16	515.22	440.45	291.03	149.42	74.77	272.06	200.30
1993	110.9	142.2	120.3	109.3	118.8	72.1	112.1	1069.84	664.74	569.62	342.21	227.41	95.12	413.59	324.83
1994	116.1	120.6	108.3	109.4	124.0	124.9	103.8	1488.47	882.64	740.27	476.40	263.87	142.37	598.87	474.00
1995	110.5	107.5	106.2	104.3	109.7	106.7	87.0	2003.58	1174.65	996.10	642.33	353.77	178.55	824.61	619.07

Year	v5b2	v5c	v5c1	v5c2	v6a1	v6a2	v6a3	v6a4	v6b2	v6b3	v6b4	v7	v7a	v7a1	v7a2
1952	0.49	-0.01													
1953	0.74	0.01										98.3	97.1	98.1	91.8
1954	0.76	-0.02										103.3	102.4	96.7	134.0
1955	1.21	-0.01										122.2	121.5	125.2	106.8
1956	1.84	-0.02										85.6	82.4	78.3	101.6
1957	1.73	-0.02										127.2	130.4	128.6	136.6
1958	2.74	-0.01										90.0	72.0	66.6	90.2
1959	3.76	-0.02										96.5	92.4	82.2	117.9
1960	4.38	-0.02										97.4	85.3	77.0	99.9
1961	2.84	-0.02										84.4	107.2	117.8	93.1
1962	1.70	0.00										119.6	138.1	171.5	81.4
1963	1.62	0.00										99.2	96.0	95.7	97.1
1964	2.90	-0.02										107.4	104.1	101.8	111.9
1965	3.16	-0.03										116.7	120.4	120.3	120.7
1966	3.73	-0.01										108.8	108.7	109.5	106.1
1967	2.21	-0.59										105.8	107.3	105.5	113.2
1968	2.61	-0.77										98.6	104.7	107.8	95.2
1969	2.75	-0.01										96.2	94.5	95.0	92.7
1970	4.97	1.17										115.7	117.2	116.6	119.4
1971	5.17	-0.08										108.1	107.5	110.8	95.8
1972	5.43	-1.02										106.1	105.4	105.9	103.5
1973	6.03	-0.96										104.3	103.9	104.1	102.9
1974	6.43	-0.02										96.5	94.9	96.1	89.7
1975	6.66	-0.07										110.8	111.1	110.6	113.1
1976	7.03	-2.74										107.0	104.8	104.1	107.5
1977	7.29	-1.30										97.6	98.5	98.0	100.6
1978	8.17	1.19			31.29	24.26	1.05	5.43	13.78	1.18	0.18	98.1	95.3	94.9	97.2
1979	8.90	-0.86			36.82	28.19	1.70	6.40	15.27	1.22	0.21	114.9	115.9	117.1	111.1
1980	9.93	-6.41			36.96	39.69	2.57	6.69	19.34	1.42	0.26	107.9	111.0	110.3	114.3
1981	10.38	4.49			43.39	51.23	2.63	8.02	20.80	1.75	0.29	111.7	113.5	115.9	103.6
1982	11.11	-9.54			49.05	56.15	2.80	8.65	22.32	1.98	0.31	110.0	110.7	111.3	108.2
1983	10.76	-10.07			49.17	65.00	2.82	9.46	24.79	2.19	0.35	107.3	104.7	104.0	107.8
1984	14.31	8.03			47.16	66.50	3.16	10.25	28.41	2.45	0.41	102.3	101.0	98.5	112.5
1985	26.97	-0.03			55.88	76.86	4.16	11.00	36.08	2.82	0.52	112.5	107.9	106.7	112.9
1986	31.10	-11.18			61.51	89.64	5.55	11.77	42.22	4.53	0.72	115.6	112.0	111.0	115.7
1987	34.74	-5.34			63.42	108.23	6.04	12.63	56.55	5.52	0.96	106.2	108.9	105.1	122.6
1988	54.95	4.32			70.60	135.84	10.58	13.55	73.94	7.03	1.02	103.0	106.5	105.4	110.0
1989	60.57	22.69			77.28	152.40	14.20	14.49	83.83	8.75	3.29	105.1	105.2	103.0	111.7
1990	66.52	19.55			83.09	152.85	16.55	17.46	88.37	10.65	4.04	100.5	99.2	98.0	102.5
1991	57.54	-11.17			84.72	145.14	19.02	21.91	101.64	11.62	5.33	120.7	119.9	116.5	128.7
1992	71.76	13.88			90.04	154.45	22.65	23.89	125.71	16.44	7.27	112.8	117.1	111.9	129.4
1993	88.76	-8.49			96.16	186.50	33.19	26.36	171.17	40.25	15.69	126.2	128.0	117.3	150.0
1994	124.87	6.96			138.11	258.68	45.26	34.35	200.54	45.86	17.47	108.9	106.7	106.5	107.1
1995	205.54	4.32			186.79	354.07	59.72	41.75	283.71	49.70	20.36	110.3	108.3	110.0	105.9

Year	v7b	v8	v8a	v8b	v9	v9a	v9b	v10a1	v10a2	v10a3	v10a3a	v10a3b	v10a4	v10b1	v10b2
1952		64	59	138											
1953	118.9	71	65	153	94.4	94.8	95.7								
1954	115.1	70	62	159	99.5	95.5	104.7								
1955	130.1	87	80	159	118.6	123.6	94.8								
1956	120.7	76	67	169	81.2	77.1	99.0								
1957	103.1	93	82	192	127.8	128.0	118.4								
1958	263.2	73	62	152	70.5	66.9	70.6								
1959	107.1	76	60	159	91.1	84.6	90.8								
1960	125.0	74	55	170	90.2	81.8	98.7								
1961	48.9	93	73	200	114.7	124.1	109.7								
1962	56.3	110	102	155	136.1	164.9	92.3								
1963	125.9	100	91	160	92.2	90.9	103.5								
1964	128.6	95	86	165	103.5	101.0	111.9								
1965	97.7	113	102	196	119.2	119.2	119.1								
1966	109.3	127	115	216	105.0	105.8	103.7								
1967	96.2	128	114	235	103.8	101.6	110.6								
1968	55.0	129	118	220	101.3	103.9	94.4								
1969	120.2	122	111	212	91.2	91.5	94.3								
1970	99.7	136	122	250	112.8	111.7	118.8								
1971	116.0	145	131	263	103.2	106.5	91.6								
1972	114.0	152	137	272	102.1	102.7	100.0								
1973	108.9	156	142	279	100.9	101.0	100.3								
1974	112.4	144	132	246	92.9	93.8	88.4								
1975	108.3	151	138	262	108.6	108.4	111.5								
1976	126.2	168	152	299	103.2	102.3	105.7								
1977	91.2	168	151	309	96.9	96.5	99.5								
1978	120.3	165	149	306	93.8	93.5	94.8	15.21	0.46				0.11	4.09	3.27
1979	108.1	189	172	323	113.8	115.4	106.2	15.58	0.42				0.13	4.45	3.56
1980	86.7	221	200	387	109.1	108.5	108.8	17.60	0.52				0.12	4.97	3.97
1981	96.1	260	242	397	111.6	114.8	97.8	10.46	0.60	4.35	0.21	4.14	0.21	5.19	3.11
1982	102.1	283	266	409	109.3	110.5	103.4	17.78	4.88	8.46	0.43	8.03	0.79	5.56	3.33
1983	136.1	305	286	442	103.7	103.1	104.9	20.70	6.35	15.95	1.11	14.84	1.26	5.38	3.23
1984	113.1	312	286	487	100.2	98.1	108.5	30.79	8.40	22.66	1.09	21.57	3.66	7.16	4.29
1985	146.9	365	333	570	106.8	106.8	104.9	50.06	5.98	23.11	2.65	20.46	7.16	13.49	8.09
1986	135.5	416	379	641	110.8	110.8	107.9	58.70	11.14	24.90	1.36	23.54	8.24	15.55	9.33
1987	93.9	482	425	818	107.6	104.2	117.9	61.91	15.32	29.18	1.89	27.29	8.24	13.90	8.69
1988	84.4	586	508	1031	104.9	104.1	106.7	64.80	19.40	35.27	1.70	33.57	7.58	21.98	13.74
1989	104.4	653	561	1176	103.4	101.4	108.9	56.73	17.98	39.90	1.66	38.24	8.71	24.23	15.14
1990	109.2	670	570	1236	96.7	95.5	100.2	62.18	20.25	45.01	1.63	43.38	10.74	26.61	16.63
1991	125.8	683	559	1379	117.0	113.9	124.8	64.41	29.24	42.55	3.30	39.25	14.65	23.02	14.39
1992	87.3	762	597	1646	115.6	111.3	122.6	82.63	40.64	59.88	3.87	56.07	17.15	23.68	21.53
1993	112.1	973	700	2389	126.3	116.9	143.1	166.43	65.90	68.46	8.29	60.17	24.03	34.27	16.33
1994	120.8	1254	969	2668	105.9	106.3	103.1	242.88	96.17	91.35	13.27	78.08	43.60	48.27	26.63
1995	119.9	1669	1300	3441	107.2	109.4	101.8	311.45	113.97	124.76	21.15	103.61	68.89	58.18	46.55

Year	v10b4	v11a	v11a1	v11a2	v11b	v11b1	v11b2	v11c	v11c1	v11c2	v12	v12a	v12b	v13	v13i
1952															
1953											124.9	122.9	142.2		
1954											105.6	106.2	100.8		
1955											152.7	152.3	155.8		
1956											96.5	89.6	148.8		
1957											107.4	109.8	96.7		
1958											208.6	217.6	162.3		
1959											99.0	96.3	117.9		
1960											93.5	89.5	116.8		
1961											36.1	29.9	63.2		
1962											26.2	10.1	59.6		
1963											219.8	580.0	93.8		
1964											217.5	236.3	176.8		
1965											126.1	131.9	109.2		
1966											94.7	88.7	115.5		
1967											66.6	68.9	60.4		
1968											106.7	101.8	121.8		
1969											120.5	127.2	103.5		
1970											157.9	148.9	186.1		
1971											122.2	129.5	103.9		
1972											105.5	105.8	104.6		
1973											107.0	105.6	111.4		
1974											106.9	107.3	106.0		
1975											80.6	72.2	106.4		
1976											133.0	147.8	102.4		
1977											100.1	98.9	103.7		
1978	0.81	5.40	2.55	2.85	15.46	11.42	4.04	3.09	1.81	1.28	103.4	100.3	112.1	113.96	71.32
1979	0.89	5.74	2.48	3.26	16.10	11.81	4.29	3.20	1.84	1.36	99.1	95.5	108.2	127.31	78.95
1980	0.99	6.31	2.69	3.62	18.42	13.61	4.81	3.44	1.94	1.50	107.0	105.8	109.7	140.88	90.23
1981	2.08	6.07	2.45	3.62	16.48	11.35	5.13	3.45	1.82	1.63	92.7	86.5	106.1	170.51	115.06
1982	2.22	7.68	2.80	4.88	31.09	26.36	4.73	4.24	2.74	1.50	169.1	204.4	106.5	187.02	123.29
1983	2.15	7.22	2.49	4.73	43.93	39.35	4.58	3.86	2.41	1.45	118.2	125.1	94.7	215.68	136.63
1984	2.86	9.99	3.70	6.29	64.33	58.24	6.09	5.49	3.56	1.93	141.7	143.9	131.7	265.74	172.30
1985	5.39	16.27	4.81	11.46	86.81	75.71	11.10	10.20	5.79	4.41	136.3	127.3	180.1	331.24	210.24
1986	6.22	19.61	5.83	13.78	105.18	91.85	13.33	9.29	5.30	3.99	107.2	105.5	113.1	382.76	243.43
1987	12.16	27.76	13.73	14.03	107.90	92.94	14.96	13.73	7.98	5.75	105.4	105.5	105.0	442.35	275.45
1988	19.23	40.08	20.08	20.00	116.91	92.55	24.36	25.01	14.42	10.59	106.9	95.4	144.2	546.94	333.58
1989	21.20	43.33	17.63	25.70	116.65	92.78	23.87	23.91	12.91	11.00	97.7	96.5	100.1	616.25	373.04
1990	23.28	40.89	16.88	24.01	115.93	93.21	22.72	47.88	28.09	19.79	110.5	110.6	110.3	658.02	430.53
1991	20.14	40.08	24.13	15.95	105.72	81.29	24.43	62.59	45.43	17.16	78.7	68.7	99.5	663.60	379.28
1992	26.55	50.28	29.62	20.66	121.95	94.76	27.19	99.83	75.92	23.91	112.0	111.2	113.2	801.16	447.60
1993	38.16	71.30	58.47	12.83	154.24	105.48	48.76	188.05	160.88	27.17	124.4	136.3	107.5	1069.84	617.98
1994	49.97	110.20	89.94	20.26	238.92	167.63	71.29	249.75	216.43	33.32	137.3	137.4	137.2	1488.47	742.38
1995	100.81	158.16	124.85	33.31	337.22	224.84	112.38	329.23	269.38	59.85	120.3	119.7	122.5	2003.58	1016.73

Year	v13ii	v13iii	v13iv	v13a	v13ai	v13aii	v13aiii	v13aiv	v13b	v13bi	v13bii	v13biii	v13biv	v13b1	v13b1i
1952															
1953															
1954															
1955															
1956															
1957															
1958															
1959															
1960															
1961															
1962															
1963															
1964															
1965															
1966															
1967															
1968															
1969															
1970															
1971															
1972															
1973															
1974															
1975															
1976															
1977															
1978	11.38	12.12	19.13	53.77	48.66	3.12	1.31	0.68	40.51	11.71	5.51	10.28	13.01	36.26	8.73
1979	12.41	15.46	20.49	61.16	55.29	3.24	1.68	0.95	44.76	12.82	6.23	12.37	13.34	40.31	9.70
1980	13.28	16.19	21.18	64.68	58.86	3.32	1.48	1.02	50.06	16.23	6.49	12.29	15.05	44.09	11.93
1981	14.88	18.21	22.36	88.44	81.60	3.36	1.90	1.58	52.48	16.84	7.17	12.91	15.56	46.32	12.28
1982	17.16	20.52	26.05	89.97	83.07	3.41	1.88	1.61	59.66	19.31	8.30	14.42	17.63	51.70	3.26
1983	21.17	23.51	34.37	96.55	89.20	3.49	2.44	1.42	73.20	27.54	10.41	16.75	18.50	51.99	18.71
1984	23.50	28.74	41.20	116.26	107.59	3.94	3.45	1.28	92.83	41.44	10.83	19.23	21.32	79.30	29.69
1985	31.33	37.57	52.10	140.97	130.56	4.12	3.83	2.46	117.84	48.93	13.86	25.15	29.90	101.37	34.94
1986	39.37	43.20	56.77	155.91	144.32	4.63	4.09	2.87	137.57	60.09	16.67	27.94	32.87	117.26	43.08
1987	45.38	51.43	70.10	176.35	160.86	4.86	4.97	5.66	157.74	67.54	19.36	32.82	38.02	135.59	49.02
1988	58.62	64.02	90.72	210.53	191.14	5.44	6.15	7.80	200.95	85.07	25.02	42.87	47.99	174.27	62.69
1989	67.31	83.71	92.19	225.39	196.38	5.98	9.87	13.16	227.85	103.31	26.38	46.89	51.27	205.52	84.40
1990	74.40	91.33	61.76	246.17	220.04	5.84	9.23	11.06	251.48	115.51	31.72	48.95	55.30	223.31	91.53
1991	81.92	72.38	130.02	190.48	168.22	5.08	7.12	10.06	280.28	137.72	34.31	51.96	56.29	245.34	107.44
1992	100.15	102.22	151.19	230.51	203.88	5.96	9.79	10.88	333.00	153.71	47.81	71.95	59.53	293.01	124.16
1993	141.82	151.14	158.90	284.06	246.40	10.06	9.82	17.78	494.85	226.38	71.59	107.64	89.24	441.90	187.25
1994	181.58	217.09	347.42	336.72	289.48	14.34	9.29	23.61	744.16	262.82	82.30	160.44	238.78	680.76	215.80
1995	225.29	274.59	486.97	581.24	499.87	25.50	18.55	37.32	938.72	330.75	100.95	200.38	306.64	852.10	270.12

Year	v13b1ii	v13b1iii	v13b1iv	v13b2	v13b2i	v13b2ii	v13b2iii	v13b2iv	v13c	v13ci	v13cii	v13ciii	v13civ	v13c1
1952														
1953														
1954														
1955														
1956														
1957														
1958														
1959														
1960														
1961														
1962														
1963														
1964														
1965														
1966														
1967														
1968														
1969														
1970														
1971														
1972														
1973														
1974														
1975														
1976														
1977														
1978	5.47	10.11	1.95	4.25	2.98	0.04	0.17	1.06	19.68	10.95	2.75	0.53	5.44	3.67
1979	6.18	12.19	12.24	4.45	3.12	0.05	0.18	1.10	21.39	10.84	2.94	1.41	6.20	3.44
1980	6.43	12.05	13.68	5.97	4.30	0.06	0.24	1.37	26.14	15.14	3.47	2.42	5.11	4.98
1981	7.10	12.66	14.28	6.16	4.56	0.07	0.25	1.28	29.59	16.62	4.35	3.40	5.22	5.71
1982	8.22	17.09	16.13	7.96	6.05	0.08	0.33	1.50	37.39	20.91	5.45	4.22	6.81	7.43
1983	10.27	16.02	16.99	11.21	8.83	0.14	0.73	1.51	45.93	19.89	7.27	4.32	14.45	10.01
1984	10.66	18.67	20.28	13.52	11.76	0.17	0.55	1.04	56.65	23.27	8.73	6.07	18.58	12.19
1985	13.18	24.49	28.76	16.47	13.98	0.68	0.67	1.14	72.43	30.75	13.35	8.59	19.74	15.56
1986	15.31	27.17	31.70	20.31	17.01	1.36	0.77	1.17	89.28	39.02	18.07	11.17	21.02	20.02
1987	17.75	31.88	36.94	22.15	18.52	1.61	0.94	1.08	108.26	47.05	21.16	13.64	26.41	23.99
1988	23.35	41.29	46.94	26.68	22.38	1.67	1.58	1.05	135.46	57.37	28.16	15.00	34.93	29.90
1989	24.90	45.62	50.60	22.33	18.91	1.48	1.27	0.67	163.01	73.35	34.95	26.95	27.75	30.44
1990	30.02	47.18	54.58	28.17	23.98	1.70	1.77	0.72	160.37	94.98	36.84	33.15	-4.60	32.36
1991	32.55	49.31	56.04	34.94	30.28	1.76	2.65	0.25	192.84	73.34	42.53	13.30	63.67	44.03
1992	45.02	67.25	56.58	39.99	29.55	2.79	4.70	2.95	237.65	90.01	46.38	20.48	80.78	47.96
1993	67.90	101.42	85.33	52.95	39.13	3.69	6.22	3.91	290.93	145.20	60.17	33.68	51.88	54.65
1994	77.87	163.13	233.78	63.40	47.02	4.43	7.31	4.82	407.59	190.08	84.94	47.36	85.21	77.30
1995	97.14	191.72	293.12	86.62	60.63	3.81	8.66	13.52	483.62	186.11	98.84	55.66	143.01	86.79

Year	v13c1i	v13c1ii	v13c1iii	v13c1iv	v13c2	v13c2i	v13c2ii	v13c2iii	v13c2iv	v13c3	v13c3i	v13c3ii	v13c3iii	v13c3iv
1952														
1953														
1954														
1955														
1956														
1957														
1958														
1959														
1960														
1961														
1962														
1963														
1964														
1965														
1966														
1967														
1968														
1969														
1970														
1971														
1972														
1973														
1974														
1975														
1976														
1977														
1978	1.81	0.26	0.14	1.46	1.34	4.76	0.14	0.25	2.24	1.94	0.21	0.01	0.02	1.70
1979	1.98	0.32	0.32	0.81	8.77	3.81	0.16	0.93	3.87	1.77	0.28	0.01	0.02	1.46
1980	2.33	0.37	0.52	1.77	10.30	6.59	0.19	1.66	1.86	1.68	0.32	0.01	0.02	1.33
1981	2.36	0.62	0.67	2.07	11.20	6.67	0.23	2.47	1.82	1.96	0.60	0.02	0.03	1.26
1982	2.58	0.68	0.86	3.32	13.78	9.52	0.43	3.04	0.79	3.46	0.76	0.03	0.10	2.57
1983	2.38	1.37	1.04	5.22	15.59	6.43	0.67	2.43	6.06	4.93	1.35	0.08	0.54	2.96
1984	3.45	2.01	1.34	5.39	17.58	7.00	0.74	3.75	6.09	8.94	1.37	0.10	0.53	6.88
1985	4.38	2.98	1.59	6.61	21.27	8.28	1.88	4.94	6.17	9.68	1.71	0.14	1.14	6.69
1986	5.33	4.38	1.93	8.38	24.50	11.12	2.54	6.91	3.93	12.19	2.40	0.21	1.23	8.34
1987	6.92	5.17	1.58	10.31	32.48	13.70	3.10	9.13	6.54	14.75	3.58	0.30	1.83	9.04
1988	9.06	5.47	2.11	13.27	42.46	16.62	3.99	11.56	10.28	18.43	5.48	0.29	2.60	10.06
1989	10.98	6.17	2.54	10.75	54.58	23.39	4.33	23.45	3.41	25.19	9.80	0.41	4.49	10.49
1990	11.42	7.15	2.53	11.26	43.94	37.03	6.65	24.02	-23.76	23.66	11.19	0.53	4.87	7.07
1991	11.77	10.70	3.53	18.03	50.51	19.31	5.93	5.83	19.44	27.94	4.10	1.51	2.77	19.56
1992	13.72	9.93	4.16	20.15	67.28	23.19	6.36	10.98	26.75	36.37	5.60	1.77	3.22	25.78
1993	28.21	13.88	3.28	9.28	90.32	49.56	10.37	23.78	6.61	43.17	2.84	2.17	4.17	33.99
1994	30.29	17.39	7.87	21.75	120.96	64.10	18.63	28.94	9.29	69.50	12.66	2.34	7.35	47.15
1995	18.07	18.02	9.61	41.09	143.62	76.12	22.12	34.33	11.05	100.72	10.45	3.08	8.61	78.58

Year	v13c4	v13c4i	v13c4ii	v13c4iii	v13c4iv	v13c5	v13c5i	v13c5ii	v13c5iii	v13c5iv	v13c6	v13c6i	v13c6ii	v13c6iii
1952														
1953														
1954														
1955														
1956														
1957														
1958														
1959														
1960														
1961														
1962														
1963														
1964														
1965														
1966														
1967														
1968														
1969														
1970														
1971														
1972														
1973														
1974														
1975														
1976														
1977														
1978	2.13	0.03	2.10			0.45	0.30	0.05	0.05	0.05	0.62	0.59	0.02	0.01
1979	2.15	0.04	2.11			0.56	0.37	0.06	0.07	0.06	0.68	0.65	0.02	0.01
1980	2.58	0.05	2.53			0.76	0.51	0.08	0.09	0.08	0.81	0.77	0.03	0.01
1981	2.97	0.05	2.92			0.96	0.69	0.10	0.09	0.08	1.04	0.96	0.07	0.01
1982	3.60	0.05	3.54	0.01		1.08	0.82	0.13	0.10	0.03	1.20	1.11	0.08	0.01
1983	4.11	0.05	4.05	0.01		1.48	0.92	0.21	0.23	0.12	1.33	1.21	0.11	0.01
1984	4.17	0.06	4.10	0.01		2.13	1.36	0.37	0.31	0.09	1.59	1.40	0.17	0.02
1985	6.14	0.11	6.02	0.01		4.60	3.13	0.60	0.70	0.17	2.14	1.91	0.20	0.03
1986	7.58	0.15	7.41	0.02		5.10	3.24	0.91	0.80	0.15	2.71	2.31	0.36	0.03
1987	8.66	0.17	8.49			5.67	3.69	1.00	0.75	0.23	3.12	2.69	0.39	0.04
1988	10.03	0.15	9.88			6.51	4.54	1.07	0.66	0.24	3.57	3.05	0.47	0.05
1989	13.22	0.18	13.04			6.47	4.42	1.08	0.78	0.19	4.47	3.83	0.59	0.05
1990	15.51	0.20	15.00	0.08	0.23	7.29	4.83	1.15	1.10	0.21	4.72	3.99	0.67	0.06
1991	17.15	0.48	16.22	0.22	0.23	8.29	3.24	1.01	0.67	3.37	6.23	5.26	0.62	0.01
1992	19.75	0.70	18.44	0.36	0.25	11.05	4.34	1.28	0.95	4.48	7.67	6.40	0.98	0.02
1993	22.44	0.35	20.98	0.31	0.80	16.83	11.69	2.13	1.95	1.06	8.59	7.25	1.34	
1994	33.48	1.48	31.16	0.42	0.42	24.88	15.19	2.63	2.46	4.60	11.29	9.06	2.19	0.04
1995	38.78	0.73	37.54	0.01	0.50	27.80	16.99	2.95	2.67	5.19	12.11	8.74	0.32	0.05

Year	v13c6iv	v13c7	v13c7i	v13c7ii	v13c7iii	v13c7iv	v13c8	v13c8i	v13c8ii	v13c8iii	v13c8iv	v13c9	v13c9i	v13c9ii
1952														
1953														
1954														
1955														
1956														
1957														
1958														
1959														
1960														
1961														
1962														
1963														
1964														
1965														
1966														
1967														
1968														
1969														
1970														
1971														
1972														
1973														
1974														
1975														
1976														
1977														
1978		1.57	1.49	0.07	0.01		0.12	0.11	0.01			1.10	1.03	0.06
1979		1.81	1.71	0.09	0.01		0.15	0.12	0.02	0.01		1.29	1.20	0.08
1980		2.29	2.17	0.09	0.03		0.18	0.16	0.01	0.01		1.65	1.53	0.09
1981		2.59	2.39	0.17	0.03		0.21	0.19	0.02			1.95	1.82	0.11
1982		3.18	2.87	0.28	0.03		0.25	0.21	0.04			2.28	2.12	0.13
1983		3.89	3.34	0.45	0.01		0.30	0.25	0.05			2.81	2.57	0.21
1984		4.45	3.63	0.68	0.01	0.13	0.37	0.30	0.07			3.51	3.11	0.36
1985		5.70	4.83	0.71	0.08	0.08	0.48	0.37	0.11			4.47	3.91	0.50
1986		7.12	5.95	1.04	0.10	0.03	1.08	0.71	0.14	0.06	0.18	6.10	5.31	0.70
1987		7.95	6.50	1.27	0.12	0.06	0.69	0.55	0.14	0.01		7.36	6.47	0.79
1988		9.81	7.93	1.68	0.14	0.06	0.88	0.69	0.18	0.01		9.33	7.82	1.38
1989		11.34	8.87	2.23	0.16	0.08	1.02	0.79	0.22	0.01		10.85	9.19	1.52
1990		12.29	9.77	2.27	0.18	0.07	1.27	0.97	0.26	0.01	0.03	14.24	12.28	1.77
1991	0.34	14.40	11.55	2.27	0.12	0.46	1.33	0.84	0.29	0.06	0.14	15.91	12.87	2.38
1992	0.27	17.48	14.30	2.58	0.18	0.42	1.85	1.16	0.33	0.12	0.24	19.50	15.68	2.92
1993		19.63	15.63	3.96	0.04		2.15	1.70	0.45			24.84	21.87	2.97
1994		26.70	21.20	4.21	0.12	1.17	10.35	7.86	2.50	0.16	0.83	29.12	25.42	3.70
1995	3.00	28.00	21.31	5.06	0.22	1.41	12.22	8.41	2.74	0.16	0.91	31.02	22.88	6.86

Year	v13c9iii	v13c9iv	v13c10	v13c10i	v13c10ii	v13c10iii	v13c10iv
1952							
1953							
1954							
1955							
1956							
1957							
1958							
1959							
1960							
1961							
1962							
1963							
1964							
1965							
1966							
1967							
1968							
1969							
1970							
1971							
1972							
1973							
1974							
1975							
1976							
1977							
1978	0.01		0.70	0.63	0.03	0.03	
1979	0.01		0.77	0.68	0.06	0.03	
1980	0.02		0.91	0.71	0.06	0.06	0.09
1981	0.02		1.00	0.88	0.09	0.02	
1982	0.03		1.13	0.87	0.11	0.04	0.11
1983	0.03		1.48	1.39	0.08	0.01	
1984	0.04		1.72	1.58	0.13	0.01	
1985	0.06		2.41	2.13	0.22	0.02	0.04
1986	0.08	0.02	2.88	2.49	0.37	0.02	
1987	0.10		3.59	2.77	0.51	0.08	0.23
1988	0.12		4.54	3.37	0.63	0.11	0.42
1989	0.14		5.43	3.93	0.91	0.18	0.41
1990	0.19	5.09	5.09	3.30	1.39	0.29	
1991	0.52	0.14	7.05	3.92	1.60	-0.43	1.96
1992	0.66	0.24	8.74	4.92	1.79	-0.17	2.20
1993			8.31	6.10	1.92	0.15	0.14
1994			3.01	2.82	0.19		
1995		1.28	2.56	2.41	0.15		

13

Fujian

Year	v1	v1a	v1b	v1b1	v1b2	v1c	v1c1	v1c2	v1c3	v2	v2a	v2b	v2b1	v2b2	v2c
1952	18.43	11.07	4.70	4.20	0.50	2.66	0.47	1.78	0.41	124.5	118.3	130.2	131.3	122.0	139.3
1953	21.49	11.89	6.18	5.43	0.75	3.42	0.68	2.24	0.50	115.9	105.0	133.0	130.2	156.0	124.4
1954	23.58	11.97	7.16	6.12	1.04	4.45	0.97	3.09	0.39	111.6	101.6	117.0	113.5	141.0	131.1
1955	26.57	12.92	7.95	6.35	1.60	5.70	1.20	3.92	0.58	112.4	105.5	112.3	104.3	157.3	128.6
1956	33.71	14.94	11.63	7.32	4.31	7.14	1.24	4.98	0.92	125.6	112.6	142.6	116.0	242.2	125.1
1957	35.64	17.05	10.59	8.57	2.02	8.00	1.44	5.00	1.56	105.5	113.5	95.0	117.2	55.1	109.5
1958	41.44	15.47	16.20	12.94	3.26	9.77	2.39	5.32	2.06	115.3	90.1	153.2	151.5	160.4	110.1
1959	52.34	15.29	24.52	19.56	4.96	12.53	3.73	6.51	2.29	128.1	100.3	149.9	151.8	142.6	128.4
1960	57.35	12.61	31.22	25.01	6.21	13.52	3.15	6.17	4.20	109.7	78.5	127.2	128.3	122.5	107.6
1961	42.10	13.49	16.86	13.77	3.09	11.75	2.66	4.52	4.57	67.2	82.4	54.1	55.2	49.1	88.1
1962	42.16	14.81	13.84	11.23	2.61	13.51	2.25	5.85	5.41	98.4	111.4	82.7	81.8	87.4	112.7
1963	43.66	15.71	14.24	11.33	2.91	13.71	2.05	5.59	6.07	105.7	114.4	103.5	101.3	113.6	101.7
1964	48.15	16.35	18.00	13.94	4.06	13.80	2.40	4.74	6.66	116.2	116.0	126.3	123.4	138.4	104.7
1965	54.35	18.80	21.45	17.24	4.21	14.10	2.81	3.99	7.30	113.4	113.1	121.0	124.2	108.9	103.0
1966	60.37	20.67	25.61	21.57	4.04	14.09	2.95	4.08	7.06	111.1	106.9	120.1	125.5	97.1	100.5
1967	60.60	18.79	21.48	19.11	2.37	20.33	3.09	5.87	11.37	100.6	90.9	84.1	88.7	58.7	144.0
1968	46.20	18.01	14.87	13.37	1.50	13.32	3.23	3.35	6.74	75.7	95.9	71.0	71.9	63.3	67.0
1969	58.09	19.91	23.52	20.96	2.56	14.66	3.39	4.50	6.77	127.1	110.4	155.7	154.1	170.7	108.9
1970	67.81	21.12	29.79	24.41	5.38	16.90	3.55	5.37	7.98	118.0	106.4	126.7	116.9	210.2	114.9
1971	79.79	25.11	36.30	28.45	7.85	18.38	3.72	5.39	9.27	114.6	110.0	122.0	115.7	143.5	107.6
1972	87.80	27.12	42.04	33.64	8.40	18.64	3.87	5.35	9.42	110.2	108.0	116.2	119.1	105.8	101.2
1973	88.09	25.84	46.47	39.16	7.31	15.78	4.05	2.83	8.90	100.4	94.9	110.9	117.1	85.2	84.4
1974	91.73	26.71	47.67	39.88	7.79	17.35	4.24	3.55	9.56	104.3	103.6	102.7	102.4	104.2	110.2
1975	96.03	27.06	51.33	43.37	7.96	17.64	4.44	2.77	10.43	104.8	101.2	108.0	109.4	100.3	101.4
1976	98.40	26.54	50.69	43.55	7.14	21.17	5.05	5.53	10.59	103.1	97.5	99.2	101.0	88.3	122.9
1977	109.97	29.27	58.83	51.68	7.15	21.87	5.75	5.73	10.39	112.0	109.9	116.8	119.4	98.6	102.9
1978	138.83	36.33	73.71	63.14	10.57	28.79	6.54	10.97	11.28	121.7	111.6	122.5	119.7	145.5	132.6
1979	155.69	43.11	83.80	72.01	11.79	28.78	6.87	9.06	12.85	107.6	106.7	111.6	111.9	109.0	98.6
1980	169.83	45.49	95.85	81.45	14.40	28.49	7.56	8.59	12.34	108.8	105.2	113.8	113.0	119.5	98.6
1981	204.17	56.11	103.73	87.76	15.97	44.33	9.59	21.16	13.58	115.5	105.8	108.8	109.3	107.6	154.4
1982	229.65	63.73	116.27	95.77	20.50	49.65	10.90	22.07	16.68	110.1	107.6	111.0	107.3	132.3	111.1
1983	253.07	68.08	126.43	103.97	22.46	58.56	13.58	22.95	22.03	107.8	105.1	107.3	108.8	100.2	112.1
1984	306.08	80.66	159.41	131.11	28.30	66.01	16.94	28.34	20.73	117.9	113.9	123.8	125.3	116.4	108.4
1985	399.54	99.05	210.91	173.13	37.78	89.58	19.55	39.42	30.61	122.3	108.4	124.8	125.4	121.7	131.1
1986	466.22	107.07	249.31	205.10	44.21	109.84	25.45	44.89	39.50	109.5	102.2	113.5	115.4	102.8	106.3
1987	603.52	132.97	316.59	265.87	50.72	153.96	34.29	57.25	62.42	119.6	109.1	120.2	123.1	101.3	127.5
1988	838.36	182.00	451.80	388.85	62.95	204.56	50.90	83.50	70.16	119.0	107.7	129.2	133.2	97.8	101.8
1989	1040.95	209.92	554.54	488.96	65.58	276.49	69.57	102.59	104.33	113.0	106.5	113.0	115.2	90.5	117.9
1990	1177.37	228.70	600.94	531.49	69.45	347.73	79.39	108.26	160.08	112.0	104.3	111.3	112.8	90.8	119.7
1991	1431.59	256.74	747.33	658.86	88.47	427.52	91.90	145.28	190.34	117.6	108.7	121.6	122.4	115.1	117.0
1992	1915.60	300.72	1053.44	915.51	137.93	561.44	118.40	193.36	249.68	128.5	108.8	136.5	137.3	129.6	127.0
1993	3055.24	395.66	1756.70	1522.37	234.33	902.88	195.35	293.00	414.53	136.4	111.3	147.4	149.4	129.3	129.2
1994	4364.08	591.35	2460.92	2128.61	332.31	1311.81	254.55	374.26	683.00	131.6	114.6	138.0	136.3	155.4	125.7
1995	5752.23	765.38	3320.73	2881.47	439.26	1666.12	395.32	510.17	760.63	119.1	114.0	122.0	123.3	110.6	114.1

Year	v2c1	v2c2	v3'	v3	v3a	v3b	v3b1	v3b2	v3c	v3c1	v3c2	v3c3	v3c4	v3c5	v3c6
1952	136.0	141.6	12.70	12.73	8.39	2.42	2.17	0.25	1.92	0.27	1.00				
1953	144.7	120.8	14.34	14.38	8.89	3.16	2.83	0.33	2.33	0.36	1.20				
1954	144.1	138.6	14.82	14.86	8.82	3.17	2.66	0.51	2.87	0.49	1.56				
1955	125.5	126.8	16.43	16.45	9.62	3.49	2.71	0.78	3.34	0.55	1.80				
1956	106.5	127.0	20.75	20.81	11.29	5.68	3.41	2.27	3.84	0.53	2.10				
1957	101.5	100.4	21.87	22.03	12.31	5.20	4.23	0.97	4.52	0.64	2.21				
1958	165.3	91.4	24.39	24.39	11.22	7.23	5.86	1.37	5.94	1.14	2.54				
1959	153.4	122.3	29.19	29.22	11.07	10.14	8.15	1.99	8.01	1.88	3.27				
1960	84.4	95.0	29.52	29.58	9.14	12.01	9.59	2.42	8.43	1.54	3.03				
1961	86.7	73.1	23.21	23.25	9.83	6.41	5.05	1.36	7.01	1.25	2.12				
1962	82.8	129.6	22.03	22.12	10.26	5.12	4.00	1.12	6.74	0.88	2.29				
1963	92.8	95.4	23.56	23.60	11.42	5.38	4.13	1.25	6.80	0.80	2.17				
1964	116.6	89.0	25.89	25.95	11.88	6.92	5.21	1.71	7.15	0.98	1.93				
1965	117.2	84.1	28.75	28.81	13.48	8.31	6.55	1.76	7.02	1.10	1.57				
1966	105.7	102.5	32.09	32.13	15.16	9.62	7.98	1.64	7.35	1.21	1.68				
1967	106.8	143.8	29.22	29.25	13.82	8.04	7.09	0.95	7.39	1.00	1.91				
1968	105.4	57.1	26.05	26.06	13.30	5.86	5.22	0.64	6.90	1.17	1.22				
1969	104.2	134.4	31.11	31.12	14.64	8.71	7.68	1.03	7.77	1.31	1.73				
1970	104.6	119.5	34.68	34.70	15.34	10.64	8.56	2.08	8.72	1.47	2.23				
1971	102.8	99.8	41.01	41.03	18.43	12.85	9.61	3.24	9.75	1.65	2.40				
1972	103.8	99.1	44.47	44.50	20.23	14.74	11.17	3.57	9.53	1.56	2.16				
1973	104.2	53.1	43.61	43.64	18.56	16.12	12.97	3.15	8.96	1.82	1.28				
1974	104.8	125.5	45.16	45.16	19.34	16.66	13.23	3.43	9.16	1.77	1.49				
1975	104.6	78.0	46.50	46.48	19.43	17.81	14.29	3.52	9.24	1.85	1.15				
1976	114.8	206.2	46.97	46.92	18.87	17.37	14.35	3.02	10.68	2.01	2.21				
1977	113.3	103.5	52.42	52.41	21.31	19.80	16.86	2.94	11.30	2.35	2.34				
1978	114.2	191.3	66.40	66.37	23.93	28.19	23.85	4.34	14.25	3.35	3.47	3.01	0.69	0.51	0.32
1979	102.2	82.6	74.30	74.11	27.97	31.37	26.20	5.17	14.77	3.32	3.29	3.08	0.81	0.73	0.34
1980	109.7	94.8	87.52	87.06	31.95	35.68	29.55	6.13	19.43	4.40	5.08	4.03	0.92	0.32	0.43
1981	126.9	243.7	106.31	105.62	39.30	39.75	33.16	6.59	26.57	6.01	7.01	5.49	1.26	1.11	0.60
1982	113.7	103.0	118.29	117.81	44.24	42.92	35.25	7.67	30.65	6.85	8.12	6.34	1.46	1.30	0.69
1983	124.6	95.5	128.27	127.76	47.27	46.05	37.76	8.29	34.44	7.29	9.38	7.19	1.65	1.48	0.78
1984	115.7	121.5	158.16	157.06	55.72	56.39	44.47	11.92	44.95	9.69	11.82	9.48	2.18	1.95	1.03
1985	110.9	135.1	201.65	200.48	68.13	72.56	62.09	10.47	59.79	12.53	15.17	13.00	2.98	2.66	1.41
1986	113.0	98.4	224.01	222.54	72.24	82.19	67.06	15.13	68.11	14.54	16.53	14.98	3.43	3.08	1.64
1987	121.8	116.3	280.70	279.24	89.24	101.28	82.69	18.59	88.72	19.37	23.14	18.71	4.29	3.83	2.03
1988	120.1	107.8	385.78	383.21	118.16	141.82	120.45	21.37	123.23	32.50	40.58	17.40	4.40	5.08	1.87
1989	114.8	109.6	461.46	458.40	135.77	163.82	142.45	21.37	158.81	42.60	41.31	29.06	5.23	8.47	3.82
1990	105.0	102.9	529.66	523.30	148.03	174.47	150.55	23.92	200.80	48.56	49.53	34.40	8.31	12.07	5.16
1991	109.4	128.3	632.42	622.02	170.79	217.74	188.29	29.45	233.49	55.05	60.46	40.52	12.50	13.68	6.14
1992	125.1	128.4	798.21	787.71	197.90	291.60	241.78	49.82	298.21	70.51	79.64	48.34	18.89	19.06	7.35
1993	120.7	132.9	1150.09	1133.49	259.56	463.93	387.92	76.01	410.00	101.91	116.81	55.10	33.23	28.01	8.80
1994	144.3	112.1	1706.42	1685.34	372.58	739.52	629.88	109.64	573.24	139.04	146.83	99.46	50.30	38.24	12.41
1995	114.4	110.8	2191.27	2160.52	479.42	910.56	764.64	145.92	770.54	196.53	201.42	113.11	66.05	56.44	17.70

Year	v3c7	v3c8	v3c9	v3c10	v3d	v4'	v4	v4a	v4b	v4b1	v4b2	v4c	v4c1	v4c2	v4c3
1952				0.65	102	123.3	123.3	112.1	131.5	145.7	138.9	119.3	142.1	147.1	
1953				0.77	112	112.6	112.6	103.8	131.8	131.3	136.0	121.4	133.3	115.0	
1954				0.82	121	104.4	104.4	100.0	101.3	94.5	155.9	122.7	138.9	130.4	
1955				0.99	122	110.0	109.8	106.3	111.5	102.6	156.6	116.8	112.0	116.0	
1956				1.21	150	124.7	124.8	113.5	159.4	126.6	269.9	114.4	98.2	116.1	
1957				1.67	154	106.2	106.7	109.5	95.3	124.2	50.4	117.3	107.3	105.4	
1958				2.26	166	110.1	109.3	89.6	136.7	138.9	126.8	122.8	176.6	98.6	
1959				2.86	192	117.8	118.3	96.4	134.0	139.7	107.3	134.4	162.8	128.9	
1960				3.86	190	102.0	101.7	82.1	116.6	118.1	107.6	106.2	82.1	92.9	
1961				3.64	147	71.7	71.7	82.7	57.1	52.9	85.9	82.1	83.4	69.7	
1962				3.57	137	98.4	98.6	107.6	94.2	79.4	155.7	94.6	68.3	108.2	
1963				3.83	142	104.1	103.9	118.6	90.6	103.6	62.6	101.1	93.0	94.4	
1964				4.24	153	116.8	116.8	115.5	128.7	126.6	135.3	108.2	121.3	93.5	
1965				4.35	166	111.0	110.9	111.5	120.3	126.2	101.2	100.4	112.4	81.0	
1966				4.46	180	111.6	111.6	109.2	118.0	122.3	100.6	107.0	111.9	107.8	
1967				4.48	159	90.9	90.9	91.0	83.7	89.0	57.9	100.6	83.6	113.2	
1968				4.51	138	88.9	88.9	97.0	74.7	75.7	67.4	93.9	117.6	64.0	
1969				4.73	160	120.1	120.1	109.6	145.1	143.3	160.9	112.2	111.7	141.8	
1970				5.02	173	109.9	109.9	105.0	123.2	112.9	201.9	101.0	111.9	128.8	
1971				5.70	198	114.0	114.0	110.7	121.4	111.5	155.8	111.4	110.2	107.2	
1972				5.81	208	108.4	108.4	109.7	114.6	117.1	107.1	97.7	94.4	89.5	
1973				5.86	200	98.6	98.3	91.8	109.7	116.8	86.5	94.3	116.3	59.3	
1974				5.90	202	103.4	103.6	104.2	103.8	102.6	109.0	102.1	97.2	116.5	
1975				6.24	203	102.9	102.9	100.5	106.6	108.7	98.2	101.1	104.0	77.0	
1976				6.46	201	99.9	99.9	96.2	95.3	101.0	84.7	116.3	110.0	199.1	
1977				6.61	220	115.6	115.7	112.9	118.1	118.2	95.6	116.6	116.2	105.7	
1978	1.39	0.19	1.16	0.06	273	117.8	117.8	101.5	132.4	138.7	90.4	121.5	147.8	162.9	
1979	1.59	0.19	1.36	0.06	300	105.7	105.5	104.9	109.7	107.0	137.4	99.0	93.8	86.8	
1980	1.86	0.26	1.56	0.07	348	118.8	118.4	113.9	118.1	113.5	155.1	125.7	132.5	143.7	124.5
1981	2.52	0.34	2.13	0.10	416	115.6	115.5	108.5	110.3	113.8	91.0	136.3	136.4	136.4	136.2
1982	2.92	0.40	2.46	0.11	457	109.0	109.3	106.8	108.2	104.5	134.9	114.2	114.2	114.1	114.1
1983	3.30	0.46	2.78	0.13	487	106.1	106.2	104.7	107.3	107.4	106.7	106.5	106.4	106.4	106.5
1984	4.36	0.60	3.67	0.17	591	118.3	117.9	110.1	120.3	124.9	93.7	124.3	124.3	124.2	124.3
1985	5.98	0.81	5.03	0.22	737	117.5	117.6	105.3	123.3	124.2	115.8	123.5	123.5	123.5	123.4
1986	6.90	0.95	5.81	0.25	809	105.8	105.7	102.1	113.0	105.2	177.0	99.4	100.5	96.7	100.1
1987	8.60	1.18	7.25	0.32	999	113.4	113.6	110.5	110.0	117.1	75.4	121.9	120.4	125.2	121.0
1988	9.15	1.64	10.32	0.29	1349	114.4	114.3	102.6	125.1	132.7	67.6	109.7	135.7	129.5	76.1
1989	11.07	2.85	14.02	0.38	1589	107.7	107.8	109.7	104.9	108.5	51.2	110.7	110.2	90.8	140.2
1990	15.02	5.05	21.24	1.46	1767	108.4	107.7	102.4	108.1	109.3	63.6	111.4	98.2	110.4	103.1
1991	15.61	4.12	23.83	1.58	2049	115.0	114.4	109.7	122.0	123.7	111.2	111.5	107.2	116.7	113.8
1992	18.86	5.59	28.04	1.93	2567	120.0	120.3	110.8	128.5	126.8	140.6	120.0	120.1	127.1	113.5
1993	22.79	7.71	33.50	2.14	3649	125.6	125.2	109.9	140.8	144.6	116.1	120.1	119.7	122.6	102.0
1994	32.78	8.84	38.19	7.15	5386	121.8	121.7	109.9	134.5	135.6	126.2	114.0	118.1	107.6	133.0
1995	43.42	11.73	59.42	4.72	6833	115.8	115.2	110.0	117.9	116.6	128.5	114.8	118.1	119.9	107.5

Year	v4c4	v4c5	v4c6	v4c7	v4c8	v4c9	v4c10	v5	v5a	v5a1	v5a1a	v5a1b	v5a2	v5b	v5b1
1952								12.73	11.86	10.96	8.68	2.28	0.90	1.42	0.85
1953								14.38	12.88	11.83	9.06	2.77	1.05	1.84	0.99
1954								14.86	13.99	12.91	9.42	3.49	1.08	3.40	1.75
1955								16.45	15.07	13.85	10.02	3.83	1.22	3.90	2.52
1956								20.81	17.27	15.59	11.39	4.20	1.68	8.74	6.74
1957								22.03	18.19	16.42	11.89	4.53	1.77	5.67	3.11
1958								24.39	19.39	17.36	12.50	4.86	2.03	11.53	7.06
1959								29.22	20.31	17.51	11.62	5.89	2.80	15.62	8.85
1960								29.58	20.18	17.36	10.36	7.00	2.82	15.91	10.31
1961								23.25	21.10	18.63	10.90	7.73	2.47	2.36	3.07
1962								22.12	21.87	19.44	12.30	7.14	2.43	0.13	2.11
1963								23.60	21.94	19.57	12.90	6.67	2.37	-0.18	2.74
1964								25.95	22.85	20.75	13.99	6.76	2.10	5.10	4.63
1965								28.81	24.38	21.73	14.77	6.96	2.65	6.31	4.79
1966								32.13	27.01	24.18	16.58	7.60	2.83	8.13	4.82
1967								29.25	28.10	25.35	17.41	7.94	2.75	1.35	-0.11
1968								26.06	26.98	24.81	16.38	8.43	2.17	2.13	-1.06
1969								31.12	30.19	27.46	18.58	8.88	2.73	3.68	1.42
1970								34.70	32.47	29.07	20.48	8.59	3.40	9.68	7.24
1971								41.03	32.72	29.32	20.36	8.96	3.40	14.55	10.96
1972								44.50	36.72	32.40	22.84	9.56	4.32	12.97	10.80
1973								43.64	35.48	31.01	21.00	10.01	4.47	11.51	9.76
1974								45.16	39.23	33.51	22.71	10.80	5.72	9.38	8.66
1975								46.48	39.66	33.89	22.69	11.20	5.77	10.54	7.35
1976								46.92	41.03	34.36	22.69	11.67	6.67	6.41	5.31
1977								52.41	46.39	38.84	25.64	13.20	7.55	9.05	5.02
1978								66.37	53.02	44.52	29.36	15.16	8.50	22.59	13.25
1979	114.3	117.6	102.8	111.7		113.8		74.11	60.44	51.01	34.33	16.68	9.43	23.07	16.35
1980	108.0	106.3	121.6	111.6	128.6	108.8	116.7	87.06	67.91	57.89	38.46	19.43	10.02	27.08	19.70
1981	136.8	136.5	137.8	135.9	129.6	136.6	142.9	105.62	78.75	68.15	47.49	20.66	10.60	28.48	19.64
1982	114.6	114.7	112.9	114.2	117.1	114.1	110.0	117.81	90.75	78.73	55.16	23.57	12.02	33.21	23.36
1983	106.0	106.8	107.1	106.4	107.3	106.4	109.1	127.76	97.71	84.44	60.06	24.38	13.27	35.61	28.71
1984	124.7	123.9	124.0	124.3	122.7	124.3	125.0	157.06	115.57	100.49	72.32	28.17	15.08	43.76	33.51
1985	123.4	123.3	123.7	123.6	122.2	123.5	120.0	200.48	144.66	126.56	89.90	36.66	18.10	64.54	45.16
1986	100.0	100.5	100.9	100.2	101.5	100.2		222.54	163.91	139.48	98.04	41.44	24.43	81.72	61.19
1987	121.0	120.6	119.8	120.9	120.9	120.9	122.2	279.24	191.02	161.14	113.72	47.42	29.88	97.92	73.76
1988	84.0	108.4	124.5	86.9	113.6	116.5	72.7	382.43	259.47	211.40	151.77	59.63	48.07	124.64	84.36
1989	99.6	140.0	171.4	101.6	145.7	114.0	112.5	457.45	322.14	257.50	183.65	73.85	64.64	139.14	90.45
1990	138.2	124.1	117.2	118.2	154.5	132.0		523.30	376.65	284.85	208.59	76.26	91.80	151.46	108.02
1991	145.4	109.4	115.1	100.4	78.8	108.4	104.8	622.02	437.88	332.90	234.43	98.47	104.98	190.40	143.21
1992	139.2	127.1	109.3	110.8	123.1	107.3	111.8	787.71	535.34	412.11	285.77	126.34	123.23	261.23	198.45
1993	162.4	137.2	111.7	112.1	138.2	111.5	103.5	1111.80	673.39	524.15	364.11	160.04	149.24	446.44	349.64
1994	111.5	108.9	107.7	105.9	109.9	108.3	105.1	1685.34	936.20	725.81	499.67	226.14	210.39	756.34	553.97
1995	113.6	117.1	118.1	113.8	103.5	103.6	132.3	2160.52	1160.68	930.89	651.55	279.34	229.79	996.17	716.17

Year	v5b2	v5c	v5c1	v5c2	v6a1	v6a2	v6a3	v6a4	v6b2	v6b3	v6b4	v7	v7a	v7a1	v7a2
1952	0.57	-0.55													
1953	0.85	-0.34										106.7	105.7	103.3	114.5
1954	1.65	-2.53										107.5	107.5	102.5	124.9
1955	1.38	-2.52										105.3	104.4	102.6	109.5
1956	2.00	-5.20										114.6	112.4	113.5	109.5
1957	2.56	-1.83										104.8	104.7	104.3	105.9
1958	4.47	-6.53										105.4	104.3	103.1	107.5
1959	6.77	-6.71										103.3	99.2	92.9	115.2
1960	5.60	-6.51										89.6	88.1	81.6	101.4
1961	-0.71	-0.21										88.6	89.8	88.9	91.4
1962	-1.98	0.12										105.0	106.3	113.3	95.2
1963	-2.92	1.84										109.2	111.4	111.0	112.1
1964	0.47	-2.00										106.5	108.7	109.6	106.8
1965	1.52	-1.88										111.8	109.9	109.8	109.9
1966	3.31	-3.01										109.5	109.9	110.1	109.5
1967	1.46	-0.20										104.2	105.1	105.3	104.6
1968	3.19	-3.05										95.9	97.9	93.6	106.0
1969	2.26	-2.75										112.7	111.3	114.3	106.2
1970	2.44	-7.45										107.4	105.6	110.2	96.9
1971	3.59	-6.24										100.3	100.3	98.6	104.4
1972	2.17	-5.19										111.9	110.1	111.8	106.5
1973	1.85	-3.45										96.4	95.5	91.6	104.6
1974	1.22	-3.95										110.2	107.6	107.8	107.2
1975	3.19	-3.72										101.0	101.0	99.8	103.4
1976	1.10	-0.52										103.3	101.2	99.9	103.9
1977	4.03	-3.03										112.1	111.9	112.9	109.9
1978	9.34	-9.24			13.29	13.19	0.78	2.10	13.09	1.21	0.86	113.2	113.3	112.9	114.2
1979	6.72	-9.40			14.76	14.70	0.91	3.96	14.18	1.48	1.02	108.5	108.3	108.4	108.0
1980	7.38	-7.93			16.02	16.88	1.30	4.26	16.49	1.70	1.24	107.7	108.2	108.2	108.4
1981	8.84	-1.61			18.24	23.01	1.37	4.87	17.29	1.81	1.56	113.5	115.0	120.7	103.8
1982	9.85	-6.15			20.64	27.91	1.60	5.01	19.66	1.97	1.94	108.5	109.0	110.5	105.4
1983	6.90	-5.56			22.31	30.80	1.53	5.42	19.91	2.10	2.37	108.7	108.5	109.7	105.7
1984	10.25	-2.27			26.08	38.15	2.22	5.87	22.89	2.42	2.86	111.7	111.0	110.9	111.1
1985	19.38	-8.72			29.68	50.78	3.43	6.01	30.60	2.84	3.22	117.7	118.4	119.8	114.7
1986	20.53	-23.09			28.86	58.86	3.78	6.54	34.23	3.59	3.62	107.1	104.0	103.3	105.8
1987	24.16	-9.70			32.10	67.91	6.81	6.90	39.46	4.12	3.84	107.9	105.6	106.0	104.7
1988	40.28	-1.68			38.70	96.58	9.39	7.10	50.18	5.33	4.12	109.2	104.0	105.9	99.0
1989	48.69	-3.83			58.59	105.98	11.66	7.42	62.16	7.36	4.33	104.9	102.4	101.8	104.3
1990	43.44	-4.81			65.26	120.66	14.76	7.91	62.78	8.96	4.52	115.9	107.2	109.3	101.7
1991	47.19	-6.26			69.12	139.07	17.84	8.40	82.87	10.88	4.72	112.2	112.8	108.5	124.6
1992	62.78	-8.86			85.57	169.94	20.60	9.66	106.63	14.72	4.99	117.5	119.3	119.8	118.1
1993	96.80	-8.03	389.11	397.14	101.84	202.26	38.38	21.63	128.30	20.39	11.35	109.8	110.6	111.5	108.3
1994	202.37	-7.20	544.75	551.95	127.32	285.20	51.79	35.36	148.48	60.98	16.68	108.5	109.4	108.2	112.6
1995	280.00	3.67	729.97	726.30	122.82	414.96	68.66	45.11	178.45	78.24	22.65	109.8	111.7	114.0	106.1

Year	v7b	v8	v8a	v8b	v9	v9a	v9b	v10a1	v10a2	v10a3	v10a3a	v10a3b	v10a4	v10b1	v10b2
1952		86	79	159											
1953	118.9	92	80	185	102.8	100.8	109.1								
1954	107.5	98	82	208	104.3	100.5	111.6								
1955	114.8	102	86	204	101.9	101.5	98.1								
1956	136.4	113	100	172	109.9	116.1	84.0								
1957	105.0	115	98	214	101.6	97.8	122.1								
1958	115.8	118	105	173	101.0	105.1	81.0								
1959	137.6	115	97	187	96.3	92.1	102.7								
1960	98.9	111	86	201	85.9	81.1	91.8								
1961	82.1	118	86	244	88.3	84.7	100.7								
1962	97.4	120	92	252	104.1	107.7	106.3								
1963	95.1	118	94	238	108.7	107.5	113.3								
1964	90.6	123	99	244	106.6	106.9	108.0								
1965	129.2	125	102	246	107.3	107.1	107.9								
1966	106.9	135	111	261	106.5	106.6	106.5								
1967	97.3	138	113	268	102.2	102.2	102.6								
1968	79.1	131	104	275	95.2	91.2	102.5								
1969	127.5	141	112	303	108.1	109.4	111.2								
1970	124.2	145	119	304	102.2	105.5	100.4								
1971	100.0	141	114	304	97.2	95.6	100.3								
1972	127.1	152	124	322	107.0	108.2	105.5								
1973	103.0	142	112	329	93.7	89.9	102.1								
1974	128.1	150	118	348	105.0	105.1	105.2								
1975	100.9	148	115	357	98.8	97.5	102.2								
1976	115.5	147	113	364	99.0	97.7	101.6								
1977	113.3	163	124	407	109.5	110.4	108.6								
1978	112.4	183	140	455	111.2	110.9	111.2	10.11	0.39	2.75	0.58	2.17		5.60	3.74
1979	109.6	206	162	473	106.6	107.4	102.0	13.42	0.37	2.56	0.54	2.02		3.89	2.83
1980	105.2	231	180	533	106.8	107.1	104.9	16.36	0.49	2.85	0.60	2.25		4.35	3.03
1981	104.6	269	220	546	113.4	119.5	100.0	13.31	3.65	2.68	0.57	2.11		5.30	3.54
1982	105.8	305	252	607	107.1	108.9	102.5	14.90	3.89	4.57	0.45	4.12		5.91	3.94
1983	110.0	322	270	609	106.8	108.2	102.7	18.48	5.21	5.02	0.77	4.25		3.99	2.91
1984	116.4	378	323	672	109.4	110.1	106.0	20.51	6.35	6.65	1.66	4.99		6.05	4.20
1985	113.4	465	396	818	115.7	118.1	107.4	30.38	7.28	7.50	1.90	5.60		12.79	6.59
1986	127.4	507	430	880	102.8	102.9	100.7	40.57	6.51	14.11	2.34	11.77		13.36	7.17
1987	119.7	577	491	987	104.0	104.4	102.6	38.32	21.63	13.81	4.11	9.70		15.72	8.44
1988	133.3	744	645	1218	102.3	104.2	97.2	44.92	26.57	12.87	2.86	10.01		29.96	10.32
1989	113.8	893	771	1473	100.9	100.4	101.8	44.89	27.22	18.34	2.52	15.82		34.05	14.64
1990	144.1	962	852	1486	104.4	106.4	99.4	62.56	19.98	25.48	3.66	21.82		23.02	20.42
1991	110.4	1096	932	1885	110.0	105.7	122.4	83.37	30.43	29.41	5.14	24.27		26.46	20.73
1992	111.7	1343	1127	2366	118.1	118.9	115.5	114.98	48.80	34.67	6.10	28.57		33.77	29.01
1993	106.9	1688	1419	2964	109.3	110.2	107.1	205.14	46.14	75.57	27.57	48.00	22.79	37.39	25.66
1994	105.3	2320	1965	3857	108.6	109.2	103.8	362.08	52.47	108.94	37.46	71.48	30.48	83.95	48.73
1995	103.1	2944	2544	4648	110.5	113.1	103.5	482.94	65.03	131.42	44.70	86.72	36.78	116.16	67.41

Year	v10b4	v11a	v11a1	v11a2	v11b	v11b1	v11b2	v11c	v11c1	v11c2	v12	v12a	v12b	v13	v13i
1952															
1953											130.3	117.6	149.1		
1954											183.8	179.0	189.4		
1955											119.4	149.7	85.7		
1956											238.9	275.7	167.4		
1957											63.7	47.0	117.3		
1958											203.9	226.4	176.6		
1959											128.6	115.6	148.9		
1960											102.4	116.8	84.8		
1961											14.3	30.3	-12.3		
1962											6.0	64.2			
1963											-107.7	118.4			
1964												179.9			
1965											131.3	107.4	367.5		
1966											131.6	102.4	215.6		
1967											16.7	-2.3	42.6		
1968											161.6		223.0		
1969											173.8		71.8		
1970											261.8	509.6	106.9		
1971											149.3	149.9	147.5		
1972											88.2	97.2	60.8		
1973											89.5	90.2	85.8		
1974											84.9	88.8	65.4		
1975											106.1	83.7	260.2		
1976											60.9	72.0	36.3		
1977											141.9	92.9	356.9		
1978		1.83	1.11	0.72	10.60	4.96	5.64	10.16	7.18	2.98	246.9	262.8	228.7	66.37	42.16
1979		1.90	1.38	0.52	10.18	6.12	4.06	10.99	8.85	2.14	97.3	120.7	66.6	74.11	47.78
1980		2.23	1.66	0.57	11.84	7.38	4.46	13.01	10.66	2.35	115.5	116.9	112.2	87.06	55.96
1981		2.33	1.65	0.68	12.70	7.36	5.34	13.45	10.63	2.82	102.5	96.5	118.7	105.62	68.13
1982		2.72	1.96	0.76	14.70	8.75	5.95	15.79	12.65	3.14	114.1	116.3	109.5	117.81	76.46
1983		2.94	2.41	0.53	14.92	10.75	4.17	17.75	15.55	2.20	104.4	120.0	68.6	127.76	82.74
1984		3.61	2.82	0.79	18.74	12.55	6.19	21.41	18.14	3.27	119.5	111.7	150.9	157.06	101.47
1985		5.29	3.80	1.49	28.63	16.92	11.71	30.62	24.44	6.18	128.4	116.1	165.1	200.48	126.06
1986		5.30	3.72	1.58	36.85	24.45	12.40	39.57	33.02	6.55	114.1	120.2	101.3	222.54	139.73
1987		8.18	6.32	1.86	50.27	35.68	14.59	39.47	31.76	7.71	109.6	109.8	109.1	279.24	175.22
1988		8.53	5.43	3.10	67.62	43.29	24.33	48.49	35.64	12.85	100.2	91.8	121.1	383.21	241.25
1989		9.22	5.47	3.75	70.12	40.71	29.41	59.80	44.27	15.53	105.4	92.8	130.3	458.40	281.50
1990		11.57	8.23	3.34	70.69	44.45	26.24	69.20	55.34	13.86	95.9	98.3	92.6	523.30	322.96
1991		14.37	10.73	3.64	90.84	62.34	28.50	85.19	70.14	15.05	116.6	119.8	108.9	622.02	378.82
1992		17.18	12.34	4.84	121.44	83.52	37.92	122.61	102.59	20.02	119.5	115.1	131.5	787.71	475.59
1993	33.75	28.00	20.54	7.46	203.43	144.96	58.47	215.01	184.14	30.87	141.6	142.8	138.7	1133.49	634.38
1994	69.69	36.64	24.70	11.94	306.31	201.70	104.61	413.39	327.57	85.82	149.7	147.7	154.9	1685.34	853.13
1995	96.43	47.56	31.04	16.52	352.74	208.00	144.74	595.87	477.13	118.74	119.9	119.4	120.9	2160.52	1134.84

Year	v13ii	v13iii	v13iv	v13a	v13ai	v13aii	v13aiii	v13aiv	v13b	v13bi	v13bii	v13biii	v13biv	v13b1	v13b1i
1952															
1953															
1954															
1955															
1956															
1957															
1958															
1959															
1960															
1961															
1962															
1963															
1964															
1965															
1966															
1967															
1968															
1969															
1970															
1971															
1972															
1973															
1974															
1975															
1976															
1977															
1978	5.85	7.07	11.29	23.93	21.66	0.70	0.63	0.94	28.19	13.27	3.19	5.58	6.15	23.85	9.63
1979	6.48	7.75	12.10	27.97	25.32	0.82	0.73	1.10	31.37	14.92	3.53	6.16	6.76	26.20	10.58
1980	7.55	8.97	14.58	31.95	28.92	0.94	0.84	1.25	35.68	17.07	4.00	6.96	7.65	29.55	11.93
1981	9.22	10.45	17.82	39.30	35.58	1.16	1.03	1.53	39.75	18.92	4.47	7.79	8.57	33.16	13.39
1982	10.21	11.34	19.80	44.24	40.05	1.30	1.16	1.73	42.92	20.66	4.78	8.32	9.16	35.25	14.23
1983	11.12	12.24	21.66	47.27	42.79	1.39	1.24	1.85	46.05	22.19	5.13	8.92	9.81	37.76	15.24
1984	13.84	14.80	26.95	55.72	50.44	1.64	1.46	2.18	56.39	27.95	6.14	10.62	11.68	44.47	17.95
1985	18.38	19.89	36.15	68.13	61.68	2.01	1.79	2.65	72.56	33.85	8.28	14.54	15.89	52.09	25.07
1986	20.54	21.78	40.49	72.24	65.40	2.13	1.89	2.82	82.19	39.76	9.11	15.87	17.45	57.06	27.07
1987	25.84	27.25	50.93	89.24	80.79	2.63	2.34	3.48	101.28	48.97	11.24	19.55	21.52	32.69	33.38
1988	35.49	39.27	67.20	118.16	106.97	3.48	3.10	4.61	141.82	66.57	16.10	28.18	30.97	120.45	48.63
1989	43.13	46.73	87.04	135.77	122.91	4.00	3.56	5.30	163.82	75.43	18.86	33.12	36.41	142.45	57.51
1990	51.27	50.93	98.14	148.03	134.01	4.36	3.88	5.78	174.47	80.84	19.99	35.08	38.56	150.55	60.78
1991	63.37	62.31	117.52	170.79	154.62	5.03	4.48	6.66	217.74	100.72	24.98	43.84	48.20	138.29	76.02
1992	79.88	80.66	151.58	197.90	179.16	5.83	5.19	7.72	291.60	139.39	32.64	56.94	62.63	241.78	97.61
1993	115.61	127.39	256.11	259.56	225.38	6.46	8.76	18.96	463.93	210.50	53.66	90.39	109.38	337.92	159.05
1994	157.39	189.20	485.62	372.58	322.89	9.14	11.63	28.92	739.52	322.76	70.91	140.56	205.29	629.88	252.51
1995	233.83	217.17	574.68	479.42	417.46	10.86	14.50	36.60	910.56	415.67	111.36	155.88	227.65	754.64	319.89

Year	v13b1ii	v13b1iii	v13b1iv	v13b2	v13b2i	v13b2ii	v13b2iii	v13b2iv	v13c	v13ci	v13cii	v13ciii	v13civ	v13c1
1952														
1953														
1954														
1955														
1956														
1957														
1958														
1959														
1960														
1961														
1962														
1963														
1964														
1965														
1966														
1967														
1968														
1969														
1970														
1971														
1972														
1973														
1974														
1975														
1976														
1977														
1978	2.99	5.35	5.88	4.34	3.64	0.20	0.23	0.27	14.25	7.23	1.96	0.86	4.20	3.35
1979	3.29	5.88	6.45	5.17	4.34	0.24	0.28	0.31	14.77	7.54	2.13	0.86	4.24	3.32
1980	3.71	6.63	7.28	6.13	5.14	0.29	0.33	0.37	19.43	9.97	2.61	1.17	5.68	4.40
1981	4.16	7.44	8.17	6.59	5.53	0.31	0.35	0.40	26.57	13.63	3.59	1.63	7.72	6.01
1982	4.42	7.91	8.69	7.67	6.43	0.36	0.41	0.47	30.65	15.75	4.13	1.86	8.91	6.85
1983	4.74	8.48	9.30	8.29	6.95	0.39	0.44	0.51	34.44	17.76	4.60	2.08	10.00	7.29
1984	5.58	9.98	10.96	11.92	10.00	0.56	0.64	0.72	44.95	23.08	6.06	2.72	13.09	9.69
1985	7.79	13.94	15.29	10.47	8.78	0.49	0.60	0.60	59.79	30.53	8.09	3.56	17.61	12.53
1986	8.41	15.06	16.52	15.13	12.69	0.70	0.81	0.93	68.11	34.57	9.30	4.02	20.22	14.54
1987	10.37	18.56	20.38	18.59	15.59	0.87	0.99	1.14	88.72	45.46	11.97	5.36	25.93	19.37
1988	15.10	27.04	29.68	21.37	17.94	1.00	1.14	1.29	123.23	67.71	15.91	7.99	31.62	32.50
1989	17.86	31.98	35.10	21.37	17.92	1.00	1.14	1.31	158.81	83.16	20.27	10.05	45.33	42.60
1990	18.88	33.80	37.18	23.92	20.06	1.11	1.28	1.47	200.80	108.11	26.92	11.97	53.80	48.56
1991	23.61	42.27	46.39	29.45	24.70	1.37	1.57	1.81	233.49	123.48	33.36	13.99	62.66	55.05
1992	30.32	54.28	59.57	49.82	41.78	2.31	2.66	3.06	298.21	157.04	41.41	18.53	81.23	70.51
1993	48.49	83.26	97.12	76.01	51.45	5.17	7.13	12.26	410.00	198.50	55.49	28.24	127.77	101.91
1994	63.67	129.67	184.03	109.64	70.25	7.24	10.89	21.26	573.24	207.48	77.34	37.01	251.41	139.04
1995	101.33	140.57	202.65	145.92	95.78	10.03	15.31	24.80	770.54	301.71	111.61	46.79	310.43	196.53

Year	v13c1i	v13c1ii	v13c1iii	v13c1iv	v13c2	v13c2i	v13c2ii	v13c2iii	v13c2iv	v13c3	v13c3i	v13c3ii	v13c3iii	v13c3iv
1952														
1953														
1954														
1955														
1956														
1957														
1958														
1959														
1960														
1961														
1962														
1963														
1964														
1965														
1966														
1967														
1968														
1969														
1970														
1971														
1972														
1973														
1974														
1975														
1976														
1977														
1978	1.41	0.62	0.30	1.02	3.47	2.51	0.18	0.29	0.49	3.01	0.25	0.08	0.21	2.47
1979	1.39	0.61	0.30	1.02	3.29	2.38	0.17	0.27	0.47	3.08	0.26	0.08	0.22	2.52
1980	1.85	0.81	0.39	1.35	5.08	3.68	0.26	0.42	0.72	4.03	0.34	0.10	0.28	3.31
1981	2.53	1.11	0.54	1.83	7.01	5.07	0.36	0.59	0.99	5.49	0.46	0.14	0.39	4.50
1982	2.88	1.26	0.61	2.10	8.12	5.88	0.41	0.68	1.15	6.34	0.53	0.16	0.44	5.21
1983	3.06	1.35	0.65	2.23	9.38	6.79	0.48	0.78	1.33	7.19	0.60	0.18	0.50	5.91
1984	4.07	1.79	0.86	2.97	11.82	8.56	0.60	0.99	1.67	9.48	0.79	0.24	0.57	7.78
1985	5.26	2.31	1.12	3.84	15.17	10.98	0.77	1.27	2.15	13.00	1.09	0.33	0.91	10.67
1986	6.10	2.68	1.29	4.47	16.53	11.96	0.84	1.38	2.35	14.98	1.25	0.38	1.05	12.30
1987	8.13	3.58	1.73	5.93	23.14	16.75	1.18	1.93	3.28	18.71	1.57	0.47	1.31	15.36
1988	13.64	6.00	2.90	9.96	40.58	29.37	2.06	3.39	5.76	17.40	1.46	0.44	1.22	14.28
1989	17.88	7.86	3.80	13.06	41.31	29.90	2.10	3.45	5.86	29.06	2.43	0.73	2.04	23.86
1990	20.38	8.96	4.33	14.89	49.53	35.85	2.52	4.14	7.02	34.40	2.88	0.87	2.41	28.24
1991	23.11	10.16	4.91	16.87	60.46	43.76	3.07	5.05	8.58	40.52	3.39	1.02	2.34	33.27
1992	29.60	13.01	6.29	21.61	79.64	57.65	4.05	6.65	11.29	48.34	4.04	1.22	3.39	39.69
1993	42.79	18.28	9.44	31.40	116.81	70.51	5.41	9.16	31.73	55.10	4.02	1.54	3.48	46.06
1994	46.18	23.77	12.79	56.30	146.83	52.84	9.39	10.94	73.66	99.46	7.76	2.71	6.64	82.35
1995	69.60	33.17	16.08	77.68	201.42	85.42	12.65	9.86	93.49	113.11	11.39	4.31	9.04	88.37

Year	v13c4	v13c4i	v13c4ii	v13c4iii	v13c4iv	v13c5	v13c5i	v13c5ii	v13c5iii	v13c5iv	v13c6	v13c6i	v13c6ii	v13c6iii
1952														
1953														
1954														
1955														
1956														
1957														
1958														
1959														
1960														
1961														
1962														
1963														
1964														
1965														
1966														
1967														
1968														
1969														
1970														
1971														
1972														
1973														
1974														
1975														
1976														
1977														
1978	0.69	0.04	0.65			0.61	0.40	0.07	0.04	0.10	0.32	0.25	0.04	
1979	0.81	0.04	0.77			0.73	0.49	0.09	0.05	0.10	0.34	0.27	0.04	
1980	0.92	0.05	0.87			0.82	0.54	0.10	0.06	0.12	0.43	0.34	0.05	
1981	1.26	0.07	1.19			1.11	0.72	0.14	0.08	0.17	0.60	0.47	0.07	
1982	1.46	0.08	1.38			1.30	0.86	0.16	0.09	0.19	0.69	0.54	0.09	
1983	1.65	0.09	1.56			1.48	0.97	0.18	0.10	0.23	0.78	0.61	0.10	
1984	2.18	0.12	2.06			1.95	1.28	0.24	0.14	0.29	1.03	0.81	0.13	
1985	2.98	0.16	2.82			2.66	1.75	0.33	0.18	0.40	1.41	1.11	0.17	
1986	3.43	0.18	3.25			3.08	2.03	0.38	0.21	0.46	1.64	1.29	0.20	
1987	4.29	0.23	4.06			3.83	2.52	0.47	0.27	0.57	2.03	1.59	0.25	
1988	4.40	0.23	4.17			5.08	3.34	0.62	0.35	0.77	1.87	1.47	0.23	
1989	5.23	0.28	4.95			8.47	5.57	1.04	0.59	1.27	3.82	3.00	0.47	
1990	8.31	0.44	7.87			12.07	7.94	1.48	0.84	1.81	5.16	4.05	0.64	
1991	12.50	0.66	11.84			13.68	9.00	1.68	0.95	2.05	6.14	4.81	0.76	
1992	18.89	0.79	14.07	0.58	3.45	19.06	12.54	2.34	1.32	2.86	7.35	5.76	0.91	
1993	33.23	3.02	18.70	3.22	8.29	28.01	16.17	3.21	2.30	6.33	8.80	6.89	0.94	0.12
1994	50.30	2.62	28.29	2.46	16.93	38.24	16.62	3.44	3.22	14.96	12.41	9.23	1.11	0.17
1995	66.05	4.84	40.90	4.40	15.91	56.44	26.39	5.40	4.98	19.67	17.70	13.11	1.66	0.21

Year	v13c6iv	v13c7	v13c7i	v13c7ii	v13c7iii	v13c7iv	v13c8	v13c8i	v13c8ii	v13c8iii	v13c8iv	v13c9	v13c9i	v13c9ii
1952														
1953														
1954														
1955														
1956														
1957														
1958														
1959														
1960														
1961														
1962														
1963														
1964														
1965														
1966														
1967														
1968														
1969														
1970														
1971														
1972														
1973														
1974														
1975														
1976														
1977														
1978	0.03	1.39	1.12	0.18	0.02	0.07	0.19	0.15	0.02		0.02	1.16	1.04	0.12
1979	0.03	1.59	1.28	0.21	0.02	0.08	0.19	0.15	0.02		0.02	1.36	1.22	0.14
1980	0.04	1.86	1.50	0.24	0.02	0.10	0.26	0.20	0.02		0.04	1.56	1.40	0.16
1981	0.06	2.52	2.03	0.33	0.03	0.13	0.34	0.27	0.03		0.04	2.13	1.91	0.22
1982	0.06	2.92	2.35	0.38	0.03	0.16	0.40	0.31	0.04	0.01	0.04	2.46	2.21	0.25
1983	0.07	3.30	2.65	0.43	0.04	0.18	0.46	0.36	0.04	0.01	0.05	2.78	2.50	0.28
1984	0.09	4.36	3.51	0.57	0.05	0.23	0.60	0.47	0.06	0.01	0.06	3.67	3.30	0.37
1985	0.13	5.98	4.81	0.78	0.07	0.32	0.81	0.63	0.07	0.01	0.10	5.03	4.52	0.51
1986	0.15	6.90	5.55	0.89	0.08	0.38	0.95	0.74	0.09	0.01	0.11	5.81	5.22	0.59
1987	0.19	8.60	6.92	1.11	0.10	0.47	1.18	0.92	0.11	0.02	0.13	7.25	6.51	0.74
1988	0.17	9.15	7.36	1.19	0.11	0.49	1.64	1.28	0.15	0.02	0.19	10.32	9.27	1.05
1989	0.35	11.07	8.90	1.43	0.13	0.61	2.85	2.23	0.26	0.04	0.32	14.02	12.59	1.43
1990	0.47	15.02	12.08	1.95	0.18	0.81	5.05	3.95	0.47	0.07	0.56	21.24	19.08	2.16
1991	0.57	15.61	12.55	2.02	0.19	0.85	4.12	3.22	0.38	0.05	0.47	23.83	21.40	2.43
1992	0.68	18.86	15.17	2.44	0.23	1.02	5.59	4.37	0.52	0.07	0.63	28.04	25.[illegible]9	2.85
1993	0.85	22.79	17.10	2.98	0.34	2.37	7.71	5.83	0.96	0.18	0.74	33.50	30.03	3.47
1994	1.90	32.78	25.30	3.32	0.34	3.82	8.84	5.94	0.96	0.45	1.49	38.19	33.84	4.35
1995	2.72	43.42	32.64	4.86	0.66	5.26	11.73	7.83	1.54	0.75	1.77	59.42	48.61	6.25

Year	v13c9iii	v13c9iv	v13c10	v13c10i	v13c10ii	v13c10iii	v13c10iv
1952							
1953							
1954							
1955							
1956							
1957							
1958							
1959							
1960							
1961							
1962							
1963							
1964							
1965							
1966							
1967							
1968							
1969							
1970							
1971							
1972							
1973							
1974							
1975							
1976							
1977							
1978			0.06	0.06			
1979			0.06	0.06			
1980			0.07	0.07			
1981			0.10	0.10			
1982			0.11	0.11			
1983			0.13	0.13			
1984			0.17	0.17			
1985			0.22	0.22			
1986			0.25	0.25			
1987			0.32	0.32			
1988			0.29	0.29			
1989			0.38	0.38			
1990			1.46	1.46			
1991			1.58	1.58			
1992			1.93	1.93			
1993			2.14	2.14			
1994			7.15	7.15			
1995	0.63	3.93	4.72	1.88	0.87	0.34	1.63

14

Jiangxi

Year	v1	v1a	v1b	v1b1	v1b2	v1c	v1c1	v1c2	v1c3	v2	v2a	v2b	v2b1	v2b2	v2c
1952	29.66	15.35	7.49	6.97	0.52	6.82	0.69	3.55	2.58	122.3	125.4	132.0	129.0	174.2	103.9
1953	31.40	15.14	8.78	7.86	0.92	7.48	1.08	3.60	2.80	101.7	98.5	123.2	117.3	183.1	107.3
1954	33.51	15.15	9.68	8.36	1.32	8.68	1.38	4.23	3.07	104.0	99.5	116.1	111.3	147.0	118.8
1955	36.05	16.17	10.25	8.85	1.40	9.63	1.24	5.00	3.39	107.3	105.8	110.7	111.2	108.2	111.6
1956	39.77	17.24	12.75	10.62	2.13	9.78	1.50	4.45	3.83	106.0	105.5	124.0	128.3	102.6	96.7
1957	43.91	19.06	13.76	11.70	2.06	11.09	1.96	4.80	4.33	110.9	108.2	120.4	115.4	151.9	114.7
1958	59.55	18.98	24.72	18.96	5.76	15.85	3.33	6.50	6.02	118.3	98.3	180.1	159.6	278.2	147.5
1959	70.04	18.52	31.57	24.84	6.73	19.95	5.21	7.50	7.24	109.3	95.6	123.8	129.0	109.5	131.2
1960	75.87	17.80	36.85	28.79	8.06	21.22	6.20	7.00	8.02	102.9	95.8	114.6	113.8	117.2	105.4
1961	61.93	22.45	24.28	19.06	5.22	15.20	3.01	5.50	6.69	81.4	103.9	64.8	65.0	63.9	58.5
1962	56.80	23.70	20.02	16.95	3.07	13.08	2.35	4.46	6.27	93.6	100.9	79.3	85.0	60.9	87.1
1963	58.74	24.05	21.47	18.07	3.40	13.22	2.40	4.20	6.62	105.0	105.8	104.9	103.1	112.6	102.2
1964	67.41	27.64	24.75	21.11	3.64	15.02	2.47	4.80	7.75	108.8	106.3	116.4	118.9	106.1	109.6
1965	80.30	31.96	31.11	24.10	7.01	17.23	2.61	5.20	9.42	114.0	112.3	130.9	124.0	162.7	100.3
1966	91.24	37.53	34.73	27.17	7.56	18.98	2.60	5.48	10.90	108.8	105.6	120.8	116.5	135.8	103.9
1967	83.73	35.03	30.75	22.96	7.79	17.95	2.11	5.64	10.20	95.6	97.8	89.9	85.5	103.0	96.4
1968	89.22	36.51	33.85	26.11	7.74	18.86	2.43	5.36	11.07	107.8	105.4	109.6	113.6	99.4	115.4
1969	107.74	37.78	44.15	33.98	10.17	25.81	2.73	9.46	13.62	114.9	103.1	130.0	129.5	131.4	137.3
1970	124.68	44.04	54.45	41.62	12.83	26.19	2.90	7.26	16.03	114.8	106.5	130.4	131.8	126.2	116.1
1971	138.60	42.72	64.67	50.31	14.36	31.21	3.15	9.92	18.14	105.2	99.5	121.0	121.4	119.8	94.4
1972	142.07	45.73	64.47	50.74	13.73	31.87	3.34	9.61	18.92	100.5	101.6	99.5	101.2	94.4	99.8
1973	142.64	43.46	68.09	56.14	11.95	31.09	3.33	8.45	19.31	96.9	94.1	103.2	108.9	85.2	91.6
1974	136.90	45.16	59.41	47.45	11.96	32.33	3.14	10.35	18.84	99.1	103.7	87.2	84.5	97.8	113.7
1975	147.58	45.32	67.19	54.66	12.53	35.07	3.51	10.91	20.65	108.9	104.2	112.5	115.2	102.8	115.1
1976	141.39	44.14	61.19	48.12	13.07	36.06	3.10	12.87	20.09	98.9	97.2	91.5	88.6	102.8	116.1
1977	168.25	46.71	80.76	63.97	16.79	40.78	4.07	12.43	24.28	111.1	105.3	131.5	133.0	126.6	94.3
1978	189.16	49.29	95.89	73.57	22.32	43.98	5.63	10.62	27.73	107.8	102.8	118.6	115.2	130.8	98.2
1979	223.92	66.52	106.41	83.31	23.10	50.99	6.28	11.45	33.26	113.8	114.8	109.8	110.9	106.4	120.4
1980	243.73	68.15	119.19	94.01	25.18	56.39	7.08	12.51	36.80	104.7	96.9	110.5	111.0	108.8	110.3
1981	256.58	74.26	122.53	100.02	22.51	59.79	7.64	12.84	39.31	103.1	103.9	101.8	106.1	87.3	104.2
1982	277.33	83.15	129.98	106.91	23.07	64.20	8.39	12.71	43.10	108.0	110.2	105.5	106.2	102.6	109.0
1983	301.61	86.08	144.55	116.97	27.58	70.98	9.51	13.94	47.53	105.7	101.5	111.0	109.7	116.1	103.6
1984	346.42	98.35	166.80	136.52	30.28	81.27	10.98	14.97	55.32	112.0	110.8	113.7	115.0	107.7	110.9
1985	434.53	114.50	217.72	181.10	36.62	102.29	17.40	19.53	65.36	115.9	107.2	125.3	127.7	116.1	112.0
1986	504.53	124.79	255.12	213.75	41.37	124.50	20.89	26.49	77.12	109.5	102.6	114.0	115.0	109.6	111.1
1987	560.77	144.35	305.22	258.95	46.27	111.28	22.92	26.71	61.65	110.9	108.8	112.4	114.5	102.2	110.7
1988	733.15	174.18	413.77	345.33	68.44	145.20	29.46	39.28	76.46	114.2	102.7	118.5	120.1	109.6	122.7
1989	859.75	197.93	466.97	406.16	60.81	194.92	34.90	78.66	81.36	107.7	105.4	107.8	109.7	96.8	110.5
1990	953.55	255.24	485.25	425.75	59.50	213.14	40.47	72.52	100.15	103.4	106.5	105.2	106.4	97.2	94.7
1991	1077.11	271.55	562.72	497.94	64.78	242.84	45.06	56.63	141.15	111.3	106.1	114.3	114.9	110.0	111.2
1992	1348.04	298.35	737.82	646.19	91.63	311.87	63.50	91.82	156.55	120.7	106.6	124.8	124.9	123.9	130.0
1993	1905.61	360.11	1117.55	974.06	143.49	427.95	76.59	153.72	197.64	126.1	107.3	135.7	137.8	118.7	123.1
1994	2329.73	527.86	1217.89	987.66	230.23	583.98	108.10	199.84	276.04	123.6	110.2	130.0	129.3	136.3	119.1
1995	3038.85	631.71	1623.53	1333.30	290.23	783.61	160.25	248.00	375.36	116.7	105.2	122.0	122.4	119.4	115.8

Year	v2c1	v2c2	v3'	v3	v3a	v3b	v3b1	v3b2	v3c	v3c1	v3c2	v3c3	v3c4	v3c5	v3c6
1952	117.8	101.4	18.86	18.86	12.38	2.47			4.01						
1953	163.9	96.8	19.71	19.71	12.26	2.89			4.56						
1954	129.6	114.7	20.66	20.66	12.22	3.19			5.25						
1955	91.4	118.4	21.86	21.86	13.02	3.45			5.39						
1956	123.9	89.0	22.04	22.04	12.35	4.23			5.46						
1957	137.7	105.6	27.73	27.73	15.45	5.13			7.15						
1958	170.4	135.3	31.21	31.21	15.82	6.73			8.66						
1959	156.0	115.4	34.63	34.63	15.35	7.90			11.38						
1960	119.6	92.8	36.83	36.83	14.81	9.46			12.56						
1961	48.5	69.1	35.50	35.50	18.00	7.71			9.79						
1962	77.0	94.4	33.06	33.06	18.70	6.53			7.83						
1963	102.1	101.7	32.69	32.69	18.66	7.01			7.02						
1964	102.9	113.4	35.20	35.20	19.56	7.92			7.72						
1965	105.7	96.8	42.98	42.98	24.16	10.22			8.60						
1966	99.6	105.9	48.40	48.40	27.14	11.26			10.00						
1967	82.2	104.4	44.46	44.46	25.17	9.93			9.36						
1968	159.7	94.8	45.95	45.95	25.98	10.67			9.30						
1969	82.8	178.5	51.92	51.92	26.56	14.03			11.33						
1970	106.7	119.1	58.37	58.37	30.03	17.15			11.19						
1971	108.5	89.6	62.24	62.24	29.14	18.83			14.27						
1972	106.0	96.9	66.61	66.61	31.99	20.38			14.24						
1973	99.7	87.9	66.84	66.84	31.13	22.36			13.35						
1974	94.3	122.5	64.73	64.73	32.40	18.37			13.96						
1975	111.8	116.1	68.12	68.12	33.40	19.88			14.84						
1976	89.3	125.2	64.34	64.34	32.09	17.98			14.27						
1977	130.1	84.9	74.78	74.78	34.23	24.20			16.35						
1978	138.3	82.2	87.00	87.00	36.18	33.08	23.16	9.92	17.74	2.54	4.91	1.18	1.90	2.01	0.71
1979	111.5	125.9	104.15	104.15	48.70	36.41	26.43	9.98	19.04	3.27	4.92	1.04	1.92	2.07	0.80
1980	112.9	108.3	111.15	111.15	48.31	41.00	30.84	10.16	21.84	3.92	5.78	1.39	1.29	2.27	1.10
1981	107.1	102.1	121.26	121.26	56.09	41.10	31.93	9.17	24.07	4.19	6.50	1.48	1.58	2.49	1.22
1982	107.4	109.5	133.96	133.96	63.91	42.64	33.44	9.20	27.41	5.39	7.04	1.98	1.80	2.61	1.42
1983	109.5	99.4	144.13	144.13	63.98	49.20	38.12	11.08	30.95	6.28	8.21	2.29	1.99	2.66	1.74
1984	116.9	106.3	169.11	169.11	71.89	61.31	49.89	11.42	35.91	6.47	8.62	4.19	2.42	2.95	1.90
1985	106.0	116.0	207.26	207.26	84.06	76.05	63.13	12.92	47.15	8.75	10.90	5.85	4.79	4.16	2.05
1986	110.5	111.1	227.23	227.23	90.27	83.60	71.21	12.39	53.36	9.15	12.06	7.37	5.28	4.85	2.70
1987	108.3	111.8	261.83	261.83	104.63	92.44	79.33	13.11	64.76	10.24	12.85	12.03	5.90	5.80	2.93
1988	115.1	127.2	321.36	321.36	119.18	117.38	100.73	16.65	84.80	13.94	17.32	19.56	6.18	7.12	3.94
1989	106.4	112.5	363.47	366.87	133.19	131.23	111.91	19.32	102.45	14.94	16.38	26.82	7.24	10.89	4.66
1990	105.8	88.0	417.15	419.54	175.96	133.56	116.50	17.06	110.02	17.29	11.06	27.80	7.84	13.52	5.63
1991	107.1	113.5	461.27	465.10	183.27	154.77	135.82	18.95	127.06	18.20	15.49	30.97	9.37	14.94	6.28
1992	126.4	112.1	557.98	559.52	200.81	199.40	168.14	31.26	159.31	21.06	26.01	35.85	11.07	19.26	6.94
1993	119.6	118.0	723.04	701.91	225.58	282.46	233.76	48.70	193.87	39.43	44.68	48.44	12.77	9.31	6.90
1994	120.1	110.3	983.67	948.16	314.35	338.23	269.16	69.07	295.58	55.93	57.76	61.71	22.89	13.44	9.01
1995	126.8	107.1	1244.04	1205.11	374.64	451.12	366.87	84.25	379.35	73.32	77.39	71.84	29.78	17.49	11.78

Year	v3c7	v3c8	v3c9	v3c10	v3d	v4'	v4	v4a	v4b	v4b1	v4b2	v4c	v4c1	v4c2	v4c3
1952					114	123.6	123.6	124.4	131.6	129.2	177.6	112.9	117.6	112.0	
1953					118	101.3	101.3	98.8	122.0	117.3	187.5	115.6	162.5	105.6	
1954					121	101.8	101.8	99.2	114.9	111.7	146.7	118.3	130.8	110.5	
1955					125	106.1	106.1	105.5	109.0	110.9	95.4	103.4	88.1	110.4	
1956					124	98.1	98.1	94.3	127.2	124.6	147.6	111.0	117.3	112.7	
1957					152	126.2	126.2	123.2	134.1	136.5	117.8	115.9	129.6	111.2	
1958					166	109.7	109.7	102.7	124.3	105.5	269.4	129.7	176.3	110.7	
1959					178	106.0	106.0	93.5	118.7	120.3	113.8	123.6	136.3	119.3	
1960					185	104.1	104.1	100.1	118.9	111.0	144.7	113.0	120.1	106.4	
1961					176	87.3	87.3	95.6	81.6	93.3	52.4	58.0	51.4	63.2	
1962					163	91.3	91.3	99.2	80.4	82.4	72.2	92.0	75.8	89.0	
1963					158	102.1	102.1	105.2	105.3	103.1	116.4	83.2	101.6	84.9	
1964					166	107.5	107.5	104.9	114.3	115.3	109.1	109.2	103.1	114.9	
1965					197	115.2	115.2	108.7	153.5	137.4	194.7	103.2	109.0	99.6	
1966					215	106.5	106.5	103.9	102.6	107.9	103.5	132.5	95.2	144.8	
1967					192	95.1	95.1	97.1	88.5	85.0	100.4	91.3	82.7	103.9	
1968					193	104.0	104.0	104.7	107.7	112.0	95.5	192.6	113.0	89.9	
1969					211	113.4	113.4	101.9	130.7	125.3	149.4	68.1	106.2	155.5	
1970					229	107.8	107.8	104.7	125.2	123.9	129.4	180.8	108.7	77.9	
1971					238	108.4	108.4	100.4	112.3	119.3	92.9	132.2	113.3	157.8	
1972					248	104.6	104.6	104.3	108.7	106.4	117.0	199.5	105.3	97.0	
1973					242	99.4	99.4	103.1	106.0	108.5	98.1	45.2	97.3	88.2	
1974					227	96.2	96.2	104.0	82.6	85.2	73.2	208.9	94.3	113.8	
1975					233	109.9	109.9	107.4	107.3	107.0	108.3	65.1	112.1	126.9	
1976					214	92.8	92.8	93.4	90.6	86.3	108.2	81.3	94.1	92.0	
1977					243	112.6	112.6	106.2	136.9	137.1	136.4	88.3	129.1	74.1	
1978	2.06	1.07	0.97	0.39	276	113.3	113.3	99.8	126.1			128.6			
1979	2.28	1.26	1.09	0.39	325	115.8	115.8	115.4	115.9	120.9	104.2	116.6	141.6	108.2	83.3
1980	2.79	1.45	1.35	0.50	342	104.2	104.2	100.9	111.9	114.9	103.7	98.1	103.9	98.1	117.8
1981	3.03	1.65	1.49	0.44	369	105.6	105.6	110.2	98.5	102.4	86.6	109.3	103.3	113.5	109.3
1982	3.49	1.63	1.61	0.44	403	109.3	109.3	112.3	102.9	103.0	103.0	113.1	133.1	108.9	132.1
1983	3.58	1.85	1.87	0.48	428	106.8	106.8	100.1	114.5	113.0	119.7	109.5	109.6	113.7	109.5
1984	4.38	2.19	2.27	0.52	497	115.4	115.4	109.5	121.2	127.5	100.0	118.2	106.4	105.0	202.5
1985	5.04	2.32	2.64	0.65	595	114.8	114.8	107.1	119.6	122.6	107.0	121.8	128.5	116.7	121.9
1986	5.12	2.78	3.39	0.66	641	106.7	106.7	101.1	107.3	110.9	94.7	115.2	103.1	115.2	134.4
1987	6.85	3.14	4.29	0.73	726	108.3	108.3	109.1	106.9	108.2	98.7	109.1	102.7	94.9	148.0
1988	7.64	3.49	4.86	0.75	879	111.4	111.4	102.7	116.4	116.4	116.4	116.9	116.9	116.9	141.5
1989	11.10	3.80	5.76	0.86	987	105.1	106.1	103.9	104.7	103.5	112.2	111.1	104.2	88.9	125.6
1990	13.17	5.06	7.73	0.92	1110	104.9	104.5	106.4	102.5	104.9	88.8	105.2	112.3	65.7	101.1
1991	15.66	5.56	8.80	1.79	1212	107.9	108.2	103.5	111.8	110.8	103.4	112.1	92.8	130.2	107.2
1992	18.49	6.80	12.09	1.74	1472	115.4	114.8	105.8	123.0	117.7	160.8	119.2	110.2	154.9	113.5
1993	16.83	6.79	24.04	5.81	1838	117.4	113.7	101.6	128.9	127.1	141.6	112.0	109.0	100.8	119.0
1994	25.14	9.72	32.27	7.71	2376	118.0	117.0	105.7	128.7	129.3	124.5	115.0	115.8	108.7	111.6
1995	35.44	11.60	40.69	10.02	2984	114.2	114.5	105.0	123.4	125.1	114.4	113.7	121.5	115.6	105.8

Year	v4c4	v4c5	v4c6	v4c7	v4c8	v4c9	v4c10	v5	v5a	v5a1	v5a1a	v5a1b	v5a2	v5b	v5b1
1952															
1953															
1954															
1955															
1956															
1957															
1958															
1959															
1960															
1961															
1962															
1963															
1964															
1965															
1966															
1967															
1968															
1969															
1970															
1971															
1972															
1973															
1974															
1975															
1976															
1977															
1978															
1979	106.1	116.4	115.8	116.4	136.3	104.0	118.3								
1980	58.7	89.3	123.0	106.5	98.0	98.1	145.1	111.15	81.02	68.45	49.22	19.23	12.57	36.34	31.28
1981	127.8	109.4	109.4	109.2	109.2	109.3	72.8	121.26	89.05	75.74	52.18	23.56	13.31	33.93	28.63
1982	96.9	113.1	112.8	113.2	97.3	113.4	54.7	133.96	103.72	88.54	63.62	24.92	15.18	38.91	32.31
1983	91.4	87.5	131.3	100.9	109.5	109.4	224.4	144.13	111.17	95.00	69.28	25.72	16.17	42.96	38.67
1984	137.8	118.4	98.9	118.4	118.0	118.0	108.7	169.11	127.36	105.81	77.13	28.68	21.55	53.05	44.81
1985	173.9	136.9	97.1	111.6	101.5	122.0	67.0	207.89	151.31	126.30	90.76	35.54	25.01	68.33	52.05
1986	115.1	115.2	144.4	104.5	115.3	115.5	116.4	230.82	165.63	137.54	96.46	41.08	28.09	80.91	61.63
1987	98.4	109.1	87.2	120.2	109.1	108.7	106.4	262.90	184.12	150.66	103.47	47.19	33.46	95.58	65.75
1988	90.8	103.8	146.3	95.7	93.6	116.9	236.1	325.83	219.19	182.06	120.81	61.25	37.13	129.06	71.66
1989	111.1	152.7	111.0	123.5	83.2	111.2	55.6	376.46	268.42	212.44	140.28	72.16	55.98	134.76	79.14
1990	105.3	114.8	105.1	126.2	175.5	122.7	105.5	428.62	310.12	250.02	172.83	77.19	60.10	126.99	78.87
1991	114.7	106.0	104.5	110.1	96.2	129.8	100.0	479.37	341.79	270.89	185.27	85.62	70.90	147.50	86.56
1992	110.4	121.7	104.3	111.2	118.4	124.9	100.0	572.55	381.98	299.37	196.36	103.01	82.61	219.50	136.93
1993	119.2	112.3	102.6	117.8	88.0	120.8	114.2	723.04	460.22	349.29	222.92	126.37	110.93	298.34	222.47
1994	125.4	119.0	105.0	119.9	106.5	117.3	127.0	944.75	597.07	471.91	291.17	180.74	125.16	368.52	282.84
1995	111.3	116.1	111.8	120.6	111.0	111.0	119.8	1191.53	764.76	609.38	378.77	230.61	155.38	444.93	325.55

Year	v5b2	v5c	v5c1	v5c2	v6a1	v6a2	v6a3	v6a4	v6b2	v6b3	v6b4	v7	v7a	v7a1	v7a2
1952															
1953														100.5	101.7
1954													103.7	102.0	109.2
1955													106.7	101.7	122.1
1956													106.2	111.2	93.7
1957													110.0	111.0	106.5
1958													88.6	86.7	94.7
1959													113.4	105.5	136.1
1960													100.5	95.2	112.7
1961													110.9	115.8	101.6
1962													100.6	101.9	97.6
1963													102.0	104.4	96.7
1964													108.8	110.7	104.1
1965													108.1	106.8	111.4
1966													101.5	99.2	107.4
1967													107.2	108.0	105.3
1968													100.0	101.7	96.1
1969													104.3	104.3	104.4
1970													103.8	102.3	107.7
1971													113.8	104.0	137.2
1972													109.8	123.7	84.6
1973													102.7	102.0	104.7
1974													108.5	109.5	105.8
1975													100.6	100.7	100.4
1976													101.3	101.2	101.6
1977													104.6	110.3	89.5
1978					22.44	16.65	0.18	2.95	13.07	1.20	0.39		118.7	114.9	130.8
1979					22.32	21.82	0.35	3.20	15.56	1.26	0.50		112.4	111.1	116.2
1980	5.06	-6.21			21.66	23.63	0.51	3.42	17.31	1.31	0.61	100.2	99.8	97.9	105.3
1981	5.30	-1.72			20.81	26.95	0.83	3.59	21.44	1.39	0.73	106.4	107.1	102.6	118.6
1982	6.60	-8.67			28.19	30.56	1.10	3.77	22.63	1.47	0.82	115.4	113.8	118.7	103.0
1983	4.29	-10.00			29.20	34.58	1.60	3.90	23.27	1.52	0.93	105.9	106.2	107.8	102.2
1984	8.24	-11.30			32.19	38.75	2.12	4.07	26.01	1.60	1.07	112.8	109.3	109.3	109.4
1985	16.78	-12.25			37.93	45.89	2.54	4.40	32.73	1.66	1.15	108.5	108.9	107.3	113.0
1986	19.28	-15.72			37.21	51.64	2.98	4.63	37.03	2.61	1.44	105.8	102.9	101.3	107.2
1987	29.93	-16.90			35.97	58.47	3.75	5.28	42.43	3.23	1.52	104.8	105.1	103.3	110.1
1988	57.40	-22.42	144.51	166.93	41.58	67.60	5.77	5.86	56.90	2.65	1.70	106.3	106.5	103.3	114.4
1989	55.62	-26.72	141.62	168.35	51.08	74.73	7.34	7.13	67.32	2.69	2.15	109.7	102.3	103.6	94.0
1990	48.12	-8.49	140.35	148.84	80.44	74.57	8.72	9.10	69.88	4.61	2.70	106.7	106.8	107.2	105.9
1991	61.04	-10.02	151.85	161.87	85.51	78.28	12.13	9.35	77.19	5.54	2.89	107.0	105.9	105.4	107.0
1992	82.57	-28.93	170.21	199.14	73.40	96.47	14.35	12.13	89.67	9.01	4.33	109.6	108.1	106.4	112.0
1993	75.87	-35.52	217.15	252.67	72.98	113.54	22.18	14.22	103.19	15.14	8.03	109.5	107.3	106.2	109.8
1994	85.78	-20.94	328.84	349.78	114.72	125.79	35.23	15.43	155.07	15.00	10.67	108.9	109.5	108.3	112.2
1995	119.38	-18.16	432.39	450.55	152.30	156.15	50.24	20.08	195.55	22.80	12.26	112.2	113.3	113.3	113.2

Year	v7b	v8	v8a	v8b	v9	v9a	v9b	v10a1	v10a2	v10a3	v10a3a	v10a3b	v10a4	v10b1	v10b2
1952		77	70	117											
1953		79	70	131	99.2	96.7	108.3								
1954		82	72	137	101.1	100.2	101.8								
1955		85	74	150	103.9	102.9	109.8								
1956		89	78	156	104.3	105.0	103.4								
1957		99	86	163	109.5	108.6	102.9								
1958		85	75	137	83.6	84.9	81.9								
1959		94	79	165	109.2	104.0	118.9								
1960		94	76	170	99.1	95.2	102.0								
1961		113	95	189	111.9	116.4	103.5								
1962		116	96	217	98.1	96.6	109.3								
1963		115	97	215	107.7	109.8	108.1								
1964		120	103	213	110.8	112.8	105.2								
1965		126	105	203	108.4	105.3	98.4								
1966		123	102	203	98.6	99.0	101.0								
1967		127	105	210	103.2	102.0	103.5								
1968		124	104	208	97.6	99.0	98.9								
1969		125	103	223	102.0	100.1	108.5								
1970		125	102	228	100.2	99.2	102.4								
1971		140	105	238	112.1	103.0	104.5								
1972		150	127	249	107.6	121.6	105.1								
1973		149	126	255	99.6	99.3	102.5								
1974		157	134	261	106.7	106.4	102.3								
1975		154	131	260	96.9	97.8	99.6								
1976		152	129	253	98.7	98.5	97.3								
1977		156	139	256	102.1	107.6	101.0								
1978		181	161	281	115.7	115.7	109.7								
1979		203	179	323	110.7	109.7	113.4								
1980	100.3	211	183	340	99.7	98.0	101.0								
1981	104.3	230	194	394	104.1	101.3	110.8								
1982	123.9	266	235	403	112.4	117.7	99.5								
1983	103.6	282	253	410	104.5	106.1	100.3								
1984	134.4	311	279	448	107.6	107.6	106.6								
1985	107.1	366	326	532	108.7	107.9	109.7								
1986	121.3	389	341	576	101.6	101.0	101.6								
1987	102.9	425	364	333	103.7	101.7	107.0								
1988	105.0	499	415	836	104.7	101.7	111.7								
1989	143.4	565	468	945	100.0	101.6	96.5								
1990	106.4	652	565	993	104.5	104.8	103.6								
1991	111.7	685	587	1068	103.6	103.2	104.6								
1992	115.7	752	620	1271	106.7	105.1	110.0								
1993	118.0	861	691	1520	105.9	105.0	107.8	155.68	20.87	25.03	1.43	23.60	20.89	31.84	8.02
1994	106.7	1182	923	2165	108.0	107.5	108.5	173.88	42.65	42.20	9.65	32.55	24.11	37.35	17.06
1995	108.1	1509	1194	2663	111.9	112.8	109.1	199.27	24.52	74.18	12.46	61.72	27.58	33.98	49.70

Year	v10b4	v11a	v11a1	v11a2	v11b	v11b1	v11b2	v11c	v11c1	v11c2	v12	v12a	v12b	v13	v13i
1952															
1953											90.2	89.9	101.5		
1954											74.5	70.0	79.2		
1955											81.8	101.7	58.6		
1956											210.2	165.8	146.1		
1957											128.1	269.4	151.7		
1958											176.5	144.6	359.6		
1959											199.4	123.5	158.5		
1960											129.8	151.1	102.1		
1961											20.1	27.0	8.8		
1962											87.5	79.2	155.4		
1963											97.8	89.3	109.6		
1964											100.8	131.7	31.0		
1965											193.6	127.7	419.8		
1966											107.2	137.3	224.5		
1967											91.4	85.4	50.0		
1968											100.4	101.5	100.0		
1969											138.1	107.2	260.9		
1970											229.0	211.9	144.0		
1971											77.2	113.4	43.4		
1972											75.1	80.4	82.0		
1973											94.4	92.8	87.8		
1974											89.9	93.1	69.9		
1975											104.0	80.8	270.3		
1976											94.4	115.1	52.9		
1977											140.8	97.5	312.1		
1978		3.07			23.20			8.25			145.1	196.3	71.5	87.00	57.36
1979		3.50			26.43			9.40			107.1	109.3	180.7	104.15	68.87
1980		3.23			24.42			8.69			93.7	99.3	57.5	111.15	73.40
1981		3.02			22.80			8.11			87.8	80.0	105.2	121.26	79.84
1982		3.46			26.15			9.30			128.7	131.5	138.5	133.96	89.26
1983		3.82			28.87			10.27			110.7	121.7	53.3	144.13	95.08
1984		4.72			35.65			12.68			119.1	110.1	209.8	169.11	115.06
1985		6.13			46.25			16.45			133.2	114.9	193.4	207.89	134.11
1986		7.20			54.37			19.34			109.0	131.2	64.9	230.82	143.36
1987		8.52			64.29			22.87			102.2	85.7	158.4	262.90	159.16
1988		11.49			86.73			30.84			131.9	80.0	251.7	325.83	192.43
1989		11.99			90.56			32.21			136.3	145.1	110.9	376.46	218.11
1990		11.30			85.34			30.35			93.5	97.4	89.7	428.62	265.24
1991		13.14			99.19			35.27			111.5	103.1	125.5	479.37	277.58
1992		19.54			147.50			52.46			142.1	147.9	134.3	572.55	358.84
1993	36.00	26.54	20.89	5.65	200.54	135.83	64.71	71.26	65.75	5.51	119.8	144.6	82.7	723.04	458.97
1994	31.37	33.10	27.85	5.25	193.48	129.38	64.10	142.04	125.61	16.43	123.4	122.8	124.8	948.16	613.87
1995	35.70	57.87	24.31	33.56	173.60	118.05	55.55	213.46	183.19	30.27	112.7	110.0	121.3	1205.11	732.97

Year	v13ii	v13iii	v13iv	v13a	v13ai	v13aii	v13aiii	v13aiv	v13b	v13bi	v13bii	v13biii	v13biv	v13b1	v13b1i
1952															
1953															
1954															
1955															
1956															
1957															
1958															
1959															
1960															
1961															
1962															
1963															
1964															
1965															
1966															
1967															
1968															
1969															
1970															
1971															
1972															
1973															
1974															
1975															
1976															
1977															
1978	8.19	7.62	13.83	36.18	32.34	1.13	0.82	1.89	33.08	17.29	3.14	4.85	7.80	23.16	8.00
1979	8.74	8.55	17.99	48.70	42.48	1.20	0.97	4.05	36.41	18.08	3.38	5.43	9.52	26.43	8.75
1980	9.06	9.05	19.64	48.31	42.48	1.27	0.92	3.64	41.00	20.41	3.73	6.15	10.71	30.34	10.88
1981	9.88	10.11	21.43	56.09	48.59	1.34	1.07	5.09	41.10	19.92	4.02	6.94	10.22	31.93	11.38
1982	10.66	10.79	23.25	63.91	54.21	1.87	1.22	6.61	42.64	20.33	4.17	7.35	10.79	33.44	12.13
1983	11.10	12.37	25.58	63.98	54.63	1.30	1.39	6.66	49.20	23.62	4.89	8.39	12.30	38.12	13.63
1984	12.78	14.12	27.15	71.89	64.89	1.75	1.40	3.85	61.31	31.24	5.81	9.74	14.52	49.39	21.76
1985	17.82	19.79	36.17	84.06	78.09	1.95	1.68	2.34	76.05	34.54	7.67	13.31	20.53	63.13	24.60
1986	19.71	24.56	43.19	90.27	83.52	2.25	2.10	2.40	83.60	34.12	8.38	16.75	24.35	71.21	24.30
1987	22.11	40.64	40.99	104.63	95.58	2.53	3.01	3.51	92.44	35.10	9.89	28.39	19.06	79.33	24.58
1988	25.94	32.75	74.71	119.18	110.18	3.00	1.77	4.23	117.38	47.55	11.77	22.11	35.95	100.73	33.89
1989	29.44	44.21	84.70	133.19	124.19	3.47	3.33	2.20	131.23	46.61	12.61	28.26	43.75	111.91	34.70
1990	33.85	42.61	86.92	175.96	158.60	3.69	3.08	10.59	133.56	49.20	15.27	27.90	41.19	116.50	38.68
1991	44.06	45.52	112.21	183.27	165.19	3.71	3.39	10.98	154.77	55.74	15.76	33.37	49.90	135.82	44.17
1992	55.87	50.56	107.28	200.81	186.72	5.02	4.55	4.52	199.40	100.94	23.20	34.78	40.48	168.14	81.28
1993	60.81	80.71	122.55	225.58	198.35	6.84	5.09	15.30	282.46	138.24	23.13	58.01	63.08	233.76	106.61
1994	97.04	106.10	131.15	314.35	278.20	8.14	7.52	20.49	338.23	186.22	46.20	71.63	34.18	269.16	138.05
1995	127.74	108.78	235.62	374.64	331.54	8.23	11.02	23.85	451.12	209.24	56.58	72.19	113.11	366.87	162.86

Year	v13b1ii	v13b1iii	v13b1iv	v13b2	v13b2i	v13b2ii	v13b2iii	v13b2iv	v13c	v13ci	v13cii	v13ciii	v13civ	v13c1
1952														
1953														
1954														
1955														
1956														
1957														
1958														
1959														
1960														
1961														
1962														
1963														
1964														
1965														
1966														
1967														
1968														
1969														
1970														
1971														
1972														
1973														
1974														
1975														
1976														
1977														
1978	3.00	4.85	7.31	9.92	9.29	0.14	0.00	0.19	17.74	7.73	3.92	1.95	4.14	2.54
1979	3.23	5.43	9.02	9.98	9.33	0.15	0.00	0.50	19.04	8.31	4.16	2.15	4.42	3.27
1980	3.58	6.15	10.23	10.16	9.53	0.15	0.00	0.48	21.84	10.51	4.06	1.98	5.29	3.92
1981	3.86	6.94	9.75	9.17	8.54	0.16	0.00	0.17	24.07	11.33	4.52	2.10	6.12	4.19
1982	3.99	7.35	9.97	9.20	8.20	0.18	0.00	0.82	27.41	14.72	4.62	2.22	5.85	5.39
1983	4.70	8.39	11.40	11.08	9.99	0.19	0.00	0.90	30.95	16.83	4.91	2.59	6.62	6.28
1984	5.81	9.27	13.15	11.42	9.48	0.10	0.47	1.37	35.91	18.93	5.22	2.98	8.78	6.47
1985	7.28	12.92	18.33	12.92	9.94	0.38	0.38	2.20	47.78	21.48	8.20	4.80	13.30	12.27
1986	7.95	16.33	22.93	12.39	9.82	0.43	0.42	1.72	56.95	25.72	9.08	5.71	16.44	13.53
1987	9.68	27.83	17.24	13.11	10.52	0.21	0.56	1.82	65.83	28.48	9.69	9.24	18.42	14.54
1988	11.23	21.53	34.08	16.65	13.66	0.54	0.58	1.87	89.27	34.70	11.17	8.87	34.53	20.30
1989	11.39	27.30	38.52	19.32	11.91	1.22	0.93	5.23	112.04	47.31	13.36	12.62	38.75	21.03
1990	14.02	26.85	36.95	17.06	10.52	1.25	1.05	4.24	119.10	57.44	14.89	11.63	35.14	25.18
1991	17.37	32.06	45.22	18.95	11.57	1.39	1.31	4.68	141.33	56.65	24.59	8.76	51.33	26.73
1992	22.02	33.48	31.36	31.26	19.66	1.18	1.30	9.12	172.34	71.18	27.65	11.23	62.28	31.61
1993	21.17	55.73	50.25	48.70	31.63	1.96	2.28	12.83	215.00	122.38	30.84	17.61	44.17	39.43
1994	39.56	65.82	25.73	69.07	48.17	6.64	5.81	8.45	295.58	149.45	42.70	26.95	76.48	55.93
1995	51.32	66.80	85.89	84.25	46.38	5.26	5.39	27.22	379.35	192.19	62.93	25.57	98.66	73.32

Year	v13c1i	v13c1ii	v13c1iii	v13c1iv	v13c2	v13c2i	v13c2ii	v13c2iii	v13c2iv	v13c3	v13c3i	v13c3ii	v13c3iii	v13c3iv
1952														
1953														
1954														
1955														
1956														
1957														
1958														
1959														
1960														
1961														
1962														
1963														
1964														
1965														
1966														
1967														
1968														
1969														
1970														
1971														
1972														
1973														
1974														
1975														
1976														
1977														
1978	1.39	0.39	0.27	0.49	4.91	1.93	0.56	1.27	1.15	1.18	0.37	0.02		0.79
1979	1.68	0.50	0.39	0.70	4.92	1.84	0.64	1.30	1.14	1.04	0.37	0.02		0.65
1980	1.92	0.81	0.42	0.77	5.78	2.26	0.81	1.36	1.35	1.39	0.54	0.03		0.82
1981	2.05	0.84	0.46	0.84	6.50	2.86	0.85	1.40	1.39	1.48	0.55	0.03		0.90
1982	2.86	0.60	0.53	1.40	7.04	4.82	0.85	1.43	-0.06	1.98	0.65	0.05		1.28
1983	3.56	0.55	0.54	1.63	8.21	5.77	0.85	1.47	0.12	2.29	0.68	0.08		1.53
1984	3.91	0.32	0.56	1.68	8.62	6.09	0.85	1.78	-0.10	4.19	0.73	0.10	0.00	3.36
1985	4.66	0.87	1.11	5.63	11.57	7.72	0.93	2.38	0.54	5.60	0.73	0.13	0.60	4.14
1986	6.09	0.95	0.98	5.51	13.47	7.95	1.05	2.77	1.70	7.50	0.81	0.18	1.08	5.43
1987	7.36	0.94	0.87	5.37	13.84	8.38	1.22	3.50	0.74	11.71	0.81	0.21	3.77	6.92
1988	9.35	1.46	1.02	8.47	19.23	9.84	1.35	4.95	3.09	19.63	0.78	0.30	1.55	17.00
1989	10.25	1.60	4.39	4.79	28.30	17.83	2.16	5.55	2.76	25.86	0.86	0.34	2.05	22.61
1990	14.11	1.89	3.44	5.74	19.74	19.33	2.77	8.17	-10.53	27.33	1.12	0.41	2.42	23.78
1991	7.35	5.35	2.22	11.81	27.86	12.51	3.31	3.05	8.99	31.17	2.46	0.93	2.46	25.32
1992	9.74	6.36	2.68	12.83	35.80	15.28	3.21	3.68	13.63	38.83	3.74	1.38	3.35	30.36
1993	22.81	7.74	3.09	5.79	44.68	44.34	6.42	10.05	-16.13	48.44	3.64	0.54	3.23	41.03
1994	15.34	7.52	10.65	22.42	57.76	57.27	3.93	6.61	-10.05	61.71	7.00	2.25	5.51	46.95
1995	34.55	21.48	5.39	11.90	77.39	56.06	4.00	10.10	7.23	71.84	9.97	2.51	5.85	53.51

Year	v13c4	v13c4i	v13c4ii	v13c4iii	v13c4iv	v13c5	v13c5i	v13c5ii	v13c5iii	v13c5iv	v13c6	v13c6i	v13c6ii	v13c6iii
1952														
1953														
1954														
1955														
1956														
1957														
1958														
1959														
1960														
1961														
1962														
1963														
1964														
1965														
1966														
1967														
1968														
1969														
1970														
1971														
1972														
1973														
1974														
1975														
1976														
1977														
1978	1.90	0.05	1.84		0.01	2.01	1.08	0.37	0.15	0.41	0.71	0.35	0.11	
1979	1.92	0.07	1.84		0.01	2.07	1.09	0.39	0.15	0.44	0.80	0.40	0.12	
1980	1.29	0.14	1.13	0.01	0.01	2.27	1.21	0.42	0.19	0.45	1.10	0.54	0.13	
1981	1.58	0.17	1.38	0.01	0.02	2.49	1.01	0.50	0.23	0.75	1.22	0.59	0.14	
1982	1.80	0.18	1.59	0.01	0.02	2.61	1.06	0.53	0.25	0.77	1.42	0.67	0.15	
1983	1.99	0.19	1.77	0.01	0.02	2.66	1.08	0.59	0.30	0.69	1.74	0.82	0.16	
1984	2.42	0.23	2.14	0.02	0.03	2.95	1.28	0.63	0.31	0.73	1.90	0.87	0.18	
1985	4.48	0.18	4.26	0.02	0.02	2.48	1.16	0.41	0.38	0.53	1.40	0.63	0.13	
1986	5.20	0.26	4.89	0.02	0.03	3.11	1.55	0.46	0.45	0.65	2.21	0.97	0.16	
1987	5.61	0.27	5.29	0.02	0.03	3.48	1.85	0.36	0.53	0.74	2.00	0.86	0.15	
1988	6.04	0.30	5.65	0.05	0.04	4.40	2.47	0.36	0.70	0.87	2.79	1.15	0.17	
1989	6.81	0.28	6.43	0.05	0.05	6.45	3.94	0.41	0.85	1.25	3.16	1.26	0.18	
1990	7.63	0.23	7.02	0.09	0.29	8.29	5.60	0.38	0.75	1.56	3.94	1.64	0.22	
1991	9.18	0.51	8.43	0.12	0.12	5.83	2.57	0.52	0.52	2.22	4.44	3.88	0.52	0.01
1992	10.23	0.68	9.31	0.17	0.07	7.44	3.30	0.65	0.72	2.77	5.54	4.87	0.58	0.01
1993	12.77	0.54	11.38	0.13	0.72	14.00	10.63	0.74	1.01	1.62	6.90	6.83	0.60	
1994	22.89	0.93	20.43	0.80	0.73	13.44	6.91	2.40	2.07	2.06	9.01	7.91	0.95	0.02
1995	29.78	1.50	26.18	1.06	1.04	17.49	7.78	1.54	1.84	6.33	11.78	10.37	1.30	0.02

Year	v13c6iv	v13c7	v13c7i	v13c7ii	v13c7iii	v13c7iv	v13c8	v13c8i	v13c8ii	v13c8iii	v13c8iv	v13c9	v13c9i	v13c9ii
1952														
1953														
1954														
1955														
1956														
1957														
1958														
1959														
1960														
1961														
1962														
1963														
1964														
1965														
1966														
1967														
1968														
1969														
1970														
1971														
1972														
1973														
1974														
1975														
1976														
1977														
1978	0.25	2.06	1.15	0.34		0.57	1.07	0.43	0.08	0.26	0.30	0.97	0.58	0.17
1979	0.28	2.28	1.27	0.36		0.65	1.26	0.52	0.08	0.31	0.35	1.09	0.76	0.18
1980	0.43	2.79	1.65	0.39		0.75	1.45	0.92	0.11		0.42	1.35	0.94	0.19
1981	0.49	3.03	1.79	0.43		0.81	1.65	0.94	0.11		0.60	1.49	1.04	0.20
1982	0.60	3.49	2.10	0.46		0.93	1.63	0.92	0.12		0.59	1.61	1.13	0.22
1983	0.76	3.58	2.08	0.50	0.01	0.99	1.85	0.98	0.12	0.26	0.49	1.87	1.31	0.24
1984	0.85	4.38	2.68	0.54	0.02	1.14	2.19	1.16	0.14	0.29	0.60	2.27	1.59	0.26
1985	0.64	3.43	2.14	0.39	0.02	0.88	0.42	0.21	0.03	0.13	0.05	4.67	3.27	0.50
1986	1.08	3.54	2.22	0.41	0.02	0.89	0.52	0.26	0.03	0.07	0.16	6.31	4.52	0.54
1987	0.99	4.73	2.95	0.47	0.03	1.27	0.58	0.29	0.03	0.07	0.19	7.68	5.37	0.56
1988	1.47	5.44	3.51	0.49	0.04	1.40	0.68	0.33	0.03	0.10	0.22	8.98	6.12	0.66
1989	1.72	7.57	4.52	0.95	0.03	2.07	0.70	0.32	0.03	0.18	0.17	10.23	7.03	0.76
1990	2.08	9.30	5.63	0.72	0.01	2.94	0.95	0.30	0.03	0.01	0.61	14.20	7.58	0.90
1991	0.03	11.18	8.96	1.59	0.15	0.45	4.46	3.35	0.54	0.20	0.37	16.31	12.36	2.96
1992	0.08	13.52	11.07	1.79	0.17	0.49	5.45	4.12	0.51	0.24	0.48	19.27	15.50	3.26
1993	-0.53	16.83	13.64	0.68	0.00	2.51	2.10	2.22	0.20	0.04	-0.36	24.04	18.24	2.96
1994	0.13	25.14	16.98	0.93		7.23	9.72	7.15	0.66	0.68	1.23	32.27	25.42	3.29
1995	0.09	35.44	26.15	0.82	0.96	7.51	11.60	8.86	1.16	0.35	1.23	40.69	31.05	3.50

Year	v13c9iii	v13c9iv	v13c10	v13c10i	v13c10ii	v13c10iii	v13c10iv
1952							
1953							
1954							
1955							
1956							
1957							
1958							
1959							
1960							
1961							
1962							
1963							
1964							
1965							
1966							
1967							
1968							
1969							
1970							
1971							
1972							
1973							
1974							
1975							
1976							
1977							
1978		0.12	0.39	0.30	0.04		0.05
1979		0.15	0.39	0.31	0.03		0.05
1980		0.22	0.50	0.39	0.04		0.07
1981		0.25	0.44	0.33	0.04		0.07
1982		0.26	0.44	0.33	0.05		0.06
1983		0.32	0.48	0.36	0.05		0.07
1984		0.42	0.52	0.39	0.06		0.07
1985		0.90	1.46	0.78	0.55	0.16	-0.03
1986	0.02	1.13	1.56	0.99	0.41	0.30	-0.14
1987	0.05	1.70	1.66	0.33	0.46	0.40	0.47
1988	0.06	2.14	1.78	0.85	0.70	0.40	-0.17
1989	0.11	2.33	1.93	1.02	0.50	-0.59	1.00
1990		5.62	2.14	1.80	0.55	-3.26	3.05
1991	0.19	0.30	4.20	2.20	0.44	-0.16	1.72
1992	0.37	0.14	4.65	2.88	0.50	-0.16	1.43
1993		2.84	5.81	3.41	0.26		2.14
1994	0.61	2.95	7.71	4.54	0.34		2.83
1995		6.14	10.02	5.90	0.44		3.68

15

Shandong

Year	v1	v1a	v1b	v1b1	v1b2	v1c	v1c1	v1c2	v1c3	v2	v2a	v2b	v2b1	v2b2	v2c
1952	75.80	40.00	21.54	20.08	1.46	14.26	1.42	6.86	5.98						
1953	80.49	37.04	27.33	25.41	1.92	16.12	1.52	7.48	7.12	99.2	89.9	127.3	126.9	131.6	112.7
1954	91.07	41.92	31.30	29.35	1.95	17.85	1.67	8.24	7.94	111.6	111.0	114.9	116.2	100.0	109.9
1955	97.19	44.97	31.97	30.10	1.87	20.25	1.78	9.54	8.93	107.8	108.3	102.3	102.9	95.5	113.0
1956	108.27	44.05	44.18	39.64	4.54	20.04	1.91	8.60	9.53	111.7	102.9	149.2	142.7	240.3	99.2
1957	106.77	36.44	47.43	43.31	4.12	22.90	2.05	9.80	11.05	98.7	84.7	124.4	128.4	91.3	106.4
1958	148.70	41.66	79.17	69.57	9.60	27.87	4.36	9.37	14.14	125.7	114.4	143.6	133.1	266.4	122.7
1959	178.53	39.32	104.03	92.98	11.05	35.18	6.57	10.14	18.47	113.3	95.2	129.6	132.2	114.9	124.9
1960	171.99	26.32	110.42	97.91	12.51	35.25	7.18	8.92	19.15	88.5	61.8	106.7	105.3	115.6	100.5
1961	120.50	31.84	58.88	55.04	3.84	29.78	5.22	6.70	17.86	66.3	97.0	50.0	53.1	31.0	69.5
1962	117.68	38.32	48.78	45.70	3.08	30.58	5.20	7.28	18.10	95.3	106.4	78.6	78.7	76.9	107.4
1963	121.80	40.21	53.23	49.10	4.13	28.36	3.94	6.67	17.75	110.1	115.4	110.8	108.9	130.3	99.3
1964	132.75	40.18	63.52	58.61	4.91	29.05	4.79	5.87	18.39	111.3	105.9	121.6	121.9	119.4	106.4
1965	158.03	50.49	78.53	71.38	7.15	29.01	4.78	5.62	18.61	123.0	124.7	130.3	128.3	148.8	105.6
1966	182.40	55.93	96.05	88.64	7.41	30.42	5.27	6.23	18.92	115.8	113.9	121.8	124.1	104.3	106.7
1967	191.78	55.81	103.02	96.60	6.42	32.95	5.66	8.12	19.17	102.4	100.1	106.4	109.0	82.3	98.0
1968	195.75	51.83	110.22	103.85	6.37	33.70	5.52	8.54	19.64	99.5	90.9	107.0	107.6	99.1	102.2
1969	207.37	58.70	113.76	105.79	7.97	34.91	5.71	8.99	20.21	106.1	110.2	103.3	101.8	123.3	104.0
1970	255.31	66.78	150.66	141.22	9.44	37.87	6.50	9.77	21.60	120.5	108.6	132.9	133.4	126.7	115.6
1971	279.23	75.63	162.76	147.91	14.85	40.84	7.35	9.74	23.75	112.8	110.7	115.5	112.8	146.8	108.6
1972	295.79	81.42	169.25	153.92	15.33	45.12	8.28	10.15	26.69	107.6	103.4	110.1	108.9	120.6	109.0
1973	310.00	84.59	178.18	162.94	15.24	47.23	8.08	11.77	27.38	104.6	104.0	104.4	105.9	92.6	106.3
1974	256.36	78.47	132.61	119.99	12.62	45.28	7.00	10.00	28.28	84.8	93.4	76.1	75.3	83.0	95.9
1975	347.41	93.43	205.55	189.78	15.77	48.43	7.67	11.35	29.41	133.5	118.7	154.8	158.3	124.9	106.8
1976	391.19	100.36	238.08	220.00	18.08	52.75	9.51	12.79	30.45	111.9	106.3	116.1	116.2	114.5	109.1
1977	443.42	99.27	279.85	262.24	17.61	64.30	10.61	13.31	40.38	112.3	99.2	117.6	119.5	97.2	122.2
1978	485.25	102.22	319.96	296.82	23.14	63.07	10.91	11.92	40.24	110.2	103.0	114.6	113.3	131.6	106.2
1979	553.21	135.92	349.74	314.34	35.40	67.55	15.11	17.85	34.59	107.9	109.4	108.2	104.7	148.5	103.3
1980	627.80	160.91	384.02	340.32	43.70	82.87	13.96	28.83	40.08	111.4	109.4	109.8	108.2	122.9	122.7
1981	721.51	198.50	407.25	358.37	48.88	115.76	21.62	34.14	60.00	104.5	103.2	103.6	104.5	97.5	110.5
1982	820.65	218.51	455.86	393.21	62.65	146.28	24.56	46.65	75.07	111.6	109.3	110.6	108.5	126.6	119.4
1983	940.57	259.50	509.17	441.85	67.32	171.90	30.65	60.33	80.92	111.4	114.4	110.4	111.2	105.3	110.1
1984	1154.94	310.11	625.74	534.91	90.83	219.09	39.78	74.25	105.06	118.4	119.1	116.6	114.4	131.3	123.9
1985	1422.24	335.42	810.72	682.78	127.94	276.10	50.52	91.37	134.21	117.9	103.7	124.1	122.3	135.1	118.4
1986	1618.37	361.19	938.30	784.38	153.92	318.88	62.62	99.71	156.55	111.5	100.3	115.5	116.4	110.5	112.1
1987	2019.13	413.18	1204.39	1032.88	171.51	401.56	86.15	122.38	193.03	116.6	108.0	120.9	123.8	104.0	111.1
1988	2692.79	494.53	1670.04	1455.24	214.80	528.22	102.38	176.96	248.88	122.3	103.4	130.7	133.7	110.1	110.9
1989	3344.83	548.30	2148.97	1920.94	228.03	647.56	122.28	225.27	300.01	112.0	101.4	115.6	118.0	95.3	106.2
1990	3859.33	647.49	2414.37	2200.85	213.52	797.47	147.42	263.27	386.78	108.3	105.6	111.1	113.1	90.0	96.6
1991	4648.67	793.03	2868.59	2599.17	269.42	987.05	188.22	340.80	458.03	116.4	116.6	116.4	117.1	110.0	116.3
1992	5548.82	840.71	3492.83	3115.45	377.38	1215.28	224.66	465.21	525.41	119.1	102.0	124.2	124.2	123.6	117.5
1993	7763.73	994.25	5249.45	4713.48	535.97	1520.03	367.28	655.87	496.88	126.3	114.3	131.5	131.9	127.3	118.0
1994	11435.43	1387.03	7745.96	7023.23	722.73	2302.44	476.24	919.97	906.23	125.4	117.6	127.3	128.2	116.6	123.8
1995	14873.16	1857.48	9812.85	8906.60	906.25	3202.83	665.12	1185.04	1352.67	123.5	112.5	122.8	123.1	118.6	133.5

Year	v2c1	v2c2	v3'	v3	v3a	v3b	v3b1	v3b2	v3c	v3c1	v3c2	v3c3	v3c4	v3c5	v3c6
1952			43.81	43.81	29.55	7.27	6.82	0.45	6.99	1.01	2.72				
1953	105.2	109.0	45.79	45.79	28.23	9.30	8.74	0.56	8.26	1.20	3.22				
1954	105.0	110.2	52.98	52.98	32.48	10.98	10.38	0.60	9.52	1.31	3.92				
1955	103.7	115.8	57.78	57.78	35.52	11.42	10.81	0.61	10.84	1.40	4.62				
1956	108.6	90.3	63.13	63.13	35.67	16.34	14.98	1.36	11.12	1.44	4.53				
1957	106.5	104.6	61.39	61.39	31.95	17.59	16.62	0.97	11.85	1.61	4.38				
1958	214.9	95.4	72.97	72.97	33.94	23.73	21.29	2.44	15.30	3.28	4.88				
1959	148.2	106.8	75.96	75.96	28.73	27.86	25.16	2.70	19.37	4.55	5.56				
1960	110.3	87.3	71.37	71.37	20.61	31.07	28.11	2.96	19.69	5.38	4.68				
1961	71.8	51.6	63.40	63.40	26.44	20.19	19.04	1.15	16.77	4.02	3.64				
1962	97.9	123.3	64.38	64.38	30.42	16.91	15.90	1.01	17.05	3.89	3.93				
1963	78.9	102.5	67.61	67.61	33.47	19.09	17.65	1.44	15.05	2.84	3.16				
1964	118.4	94.1	71.66	71.66	33.05	23.43	21.74	1.69	15.18	3.25	2.64				
1965	110.6	96.3	86.25	86.25	42.24	28.96	25.99	2.97	15.05	3.67	2.00				
1966	110.6	114.5	97.58	97.58	46.99	34.44	31.34	3.10	16.15	3.98	2.67				
1967	91.5	125.8	99.44	99.44	46.71	35.43	32.78	2.65	17.30	3.92	3.66				
1968	97.5	105.3	99.34	99.34	44.46	37.43	34.72	2.71	17.45	3.77	3.77				
1969	104.0	105.6	108.17	108.17	50.16	39.56	36.22	3.34	18.45	3.99	4.15				
1970	124.9	113.3	126.31	126.31	52.23	53.71	50.16	3.55	20.37	4.84	4.69				
1971	113.6	99.9	139.69	139.69	56.33	61.50	57.65	3.85	21.86	5.45	4.49				
1972	108.7	104.4	146.52	146.52	59.11	63.22	58.57	4.65	24.19	6.07	4.51				
1973	101.5	116.4	154.33	154.33	61.92	65.99	60.67	5.32	26.42	6.15	6.31				
1974	86.8	84.8	130.81	130.81	59.19	47.44	42.70	4.74	24.18	5.15	4.60				
1975	109.6	113.4	166.19	166.19	65.54	75.31	69.76	5.55	25.34	5.63	4.77				
1976	123.8	112.6	179.58	179.58	68.88	84.70	78.23	6.47	26.00	6.27	4.40				
1977	111.6	104.1	207.07	207.07	79.01	95.34	88.05	7.29	32.72	7.81	3.92				
1978	102.6	89.3	225.45	225.45	75.06	119.35	108.53	10.82	31.04	8.27	3.29	5.17	4.50	1.24	1.37
1979	137.5	142.9	251.60	251.60	91.12	127.68	114.67	13.01	32.80	9.50	4.18	3.31	5.01	1.49	1.52
1980	92.4	156.5	292.13	292.13	106.43	146.11	130.55	15.56	39.59	10.07	6.39	4.93	5.36	1.73	1.93
1981	126.3	104.3	346.57	346.57	132.21	155.41	138.09	17.32	58.95	13.18	16.56	5.93	6.84	1.98	2.16
1982	106.0	107.9	395.38	395.38	154.07	166.05	147.10	18.95	75.26	14.10	22.39	10.84	9.41	2.49	2.71
1983	115.0	122.9	459.83	459.83	185.57	178.75	159.15	19.60	95.51	17.12	32.07	13.93	9.60	3.32	3.14
1984	115.0	125.2	581.56	581.56	222.13	239.27	214.20	25.07	120.16	22.25	37.97	18.07	12.71	4.03	4.25
1985	111.2	113.7	680.46	680.46	235.96	293.07	259.42	33.65	151.43	28.22	46.14	26.64	16.06	5.62	4.99
1986	112.9	110.9	742.05	742.05	252.73	313.21	274.80	38.41	176.11	34.03	49.85	32.46	18.55	6.35	5.49
1987	116.4	114.6	892.29	892.29	287.31	384.57	341.31	43.26	220.41	47.45	60.58	41.08	20.92	9.76	6.19
1988	115.3	118.2	1117.66	1117.66	331.94	497.10	435.51	61.59	288.62	55.50	86.71	59.02	22.67	12.51	7.48
1989	110.0	96.6	1293.94	1293.94	359.14	579.65	513.97	65.68	355.15	66.55	108.51	76.44	23.44	16.03	10.01
1990	90.7	96.8	1509.62	1511.19	425.29	635.98	568.25	67.73	449.92	81.87	132.83	84.39	28.61	20.73	14.00
1991	125.0	126.0	1808.68	1810.54	521.85	745.90	663.90	82.00	542.79	98.97	161.00	96.24	36.36	25.15	16.24
1992	137.0	130.0	2194.49	2196.53	534.62	999.11	889.59	109.52	662.80	120.18	200.93	112.10	47.60	33.32	19.50
1993	129.2	133.0	2776.23	2779.49	596.63	1358.94	1204.58	154.36	823.92	151.35	188.93	187.24	85.95	33.71	29.13
1994	120.7	117.1	3868.27	3872.18	775.03	1900.46	1700.31	200.15	1196.69	214.36	325.90	247.84	110.31	46.70	31.12
1995	119.1	118.9	4996.87	5002.34	1010.13	2372.67	2113.34	259.33	1619.54	297.71	439.79	285.93	160.55	72.69	49.50

Year	v3c7	v3c8	v3c9	v3c10	v3d	v4'	v4	v4a	v4b	v4b1	v4b2	v4c	v4c1	v4c2	v4c3
1952				3.26	91										
1953				3.84	94	102.1	102.1	92.7	127.8	128.5	117.7	113.7	114.2	113.8	
1954				4.29	106	114.0	114.0	112.9	116.2	116.7	105.6	115.2	105.4	122.6	
1955				4.82	113	109.5	109.5	110.4	104.6	104.7	101.8	112.2	101.4	116.7	
1956				5.15	121	111.8	111.8	100.4	152.3	149.2	221.1	103.2	107.9	98.0	
1957				5.86	116	96.5	96.5	87.5	110.8	112.9	81.0	101.9	111.9	91.8	
1958				7.14	135	118.7	118.7	106.0	133.4	126.5	252.6	129.0	203.7	111.3	
1959				9.26	141	103.9	103.9	83.9	117.4	118.4	109.4	125.1	137.4	112.5	
1960				9.63	135	88.0	88.0	70.4	96.2	94.7	109.0	100.8	117.2	83.5	
1961				9.11	121	78.1	78.1	102.6	68.2	70.4	47.7	67.8	73.4	52.1	
1962				9.23	120	97.4	97.4	106.8	79.8	80.7	72.6	108.2	98.3	121.9	
1963				9.05	123	111.0	111.0	117.6	114.2	112.6	136.6	98.1	75.8	95.1	
1964				9.29	128	111.4	111.4	103.3	127.0	127.9	117.4	106.7	115.9	89.7	
1965				9.38	152	122.0	122.0	126.6	130.0	125.7	182.8	102.5	120.7	74.3	
1966				9.50	169	116.3	116.3	114.2	123.4	125.7	104.7	107.9	109.0	135.8	
1967				9.72	168	102.3	102.3	99.4	107.8	110.7	80.9	97.4	83.0	134.0	
1968				9.91	165	99.0	99.0	92.3	104.9	104.9	103.6	100.8	96.1	103.0	
1969				10.31	175	107.8	107.8	111.2	105.7	104.5	122.7	106.0	106.0	110.6	
1970				10.84	199	115.7	115.7	103.5	126.1	127.1	111.7	117.4	133.4	117.8	
1971				11.92	215	115.6	115.6	104.9	133.4	135.6	109.6	102.2	113.1	95.9	
1972				13.61	221	108.4	108.4	103.0	112.0	111.6	121.1	111.0	111.8	100.8	
1973				13.96	229	105.5	105.5	104.6	104.9	104.2	114.7	109.3	101.5	139.9	
1974				14.43	191	84.2	84.2	95.7	72.4	71.2	89.3	91.7	84.0	73.0	
1975				14.94	240	129.2	129.2	110.6	159.8	163.6	117.0	104.7	109.2	103.7	
1976				15.33	256	105.2	105.2	104.8	106.3	105.5	116.5	102.5	111.3	92.1	
1977				20.99	293	111.3	111.3	114.6	107.0	106.5	112.6	118.3	124.6	89.2	
1978	2.74	0.23	1.96	2.27	316	110.1									
1979	3.00	0.29	2.20	2.30	350	106.6	106.6	108.2	106.3	105.1	118.6	104.1	113.2	125.1	63.1
1980	3.80	0.35	2.86	2.17	402	112.2	112.2	109.8	112.0	111.4	117.2	118.9	104.5	150.1	146.7
1981	4.40	1.82	3.37	2.71	472	105.8	105.8	106.5	103.2	104.3	94.3	111.7	98.1	194.2	90.2
1982	4.89	1.97	3.46	3.00	531	111.3	111.3	110.8	105.6	104.9	111.6	127.2	106.6	134.8	182.3
1983	5.95	2.35	4.41	3.62	611	113.9	113.9	116.0	107.6	108.4	101.3	123.7	118.4	139.6	125.3
1984	7.68	2.99	5.92	4.29	765	117.4	117.4	118.3	117.7	116.7	125.8	115.3	119.0	108.5	118.8
1985	9.29	3.34	6.60	4.53	887	111.4	111.4	102.2	118.5	117.1	128.9	114.9	115.7	110.8	134.4
1986	11.33	4.25	8.27	5.53	956	106.3	106.3	99.4	110.7	111.5	104.9	108.7	112.1	101.0	113.9
1987	12.23	4.86	10.93	6.41	1131	113.8	113.8	107.4	117.1	118.8	104.0	117.0	130.4	113.6	118.4
1988	15.70	5.98	15.93	7.12	1395	112.5	112.5	99.8	122.7	122.2	126.2	109.6	97.9	119.8	120.3
1989	17.74	7.53	20.85	8.05	1595	104.0	104.0	99.4	107.1	108.5	94.9	102.8	100.1	104.5	108.2
1990	26.41	9.90	41.51	9.67	1815	105.3	105.3	105.4	107.2	108.0	99.1	100.7	97.7	97.3	87.7
1991	25.05	11.86	61.43	10.49	2122	114.6	114.6	114.2	114.0	115.0	105.6	116.0	116.2	116.6	109.7
1992	30.61	15.11	71.19	12.26	2557	116.9	116.9	100.2	128.6	129.4	120.6	116.3	115.7	118.9	110.9
1993	59.91	11.09	53.02	23.59	3222	121.9	121.9	106.1	130.6	130.7	129.7	121.2	114.7	114.0	136.2
1994	64.26	23.97	110.02	22.21	4473	116.3	116.3	107.3	117.5	117.6	116.1	120.6	120.4	116.6	124.7
1995	99.98	26.65	149.88	36.86	5758	114.1	114.2	108.9	115.1	115.1	115.4	115.9	118.6	116.9	105.9

Year	v4c4	v4c5	v4c6	v4c7	v4c8	v4c9	v4c10	v5	v5a	v5a1	v5a1a	v5a1b	v5a2	v5b	v5b1
1952								43.81	34.41	33.04	25.07	7.97	1.37	8.02	5.74
1953								45.79	36.01	34.25	24.81	9.44	1.76	9.60	6.93
1954								52.98	38.84	36.79	27.98	8.81	2.05	13.87	8.29
1955								57.78	41.44	38.99	29.11	9.88	2.45	16.01	11.24
1956								63.13	45.65	42.92	31.42	11.50	2.73	17.13	13.97
1957								61.39	43.00	40.54	29.17	11.37	2.46	17.82	14.41
1958								72.97	48.90	45.55	32.13	13.42	3.35	23.12	15.43
1959								75.96	45.83	41.81	26.94	14.87	4.02	28.53	19.44
1960								71.37	44.58	40.27	24.16	16.11	4.31	26.36	22.43
1961								63.40	47.49	44.67	28.07	16.60	2.82	12.20	9.18
1962								64.38	49.44	47.55	31.95	15.60	1.89	8.98	8.60
1963								67.61	49.97	48.17	33.77	14.40	1.80	10.60	7.55
1964								71.66	50.38	48.46	34.22	14.24	1.92	12.48	9.02
1965								86.25	55.95	53.61	36.94	16.67	2.34	21.75	14.17
1966								97.58	60.71	58.02	40.61	17.41	2.69	26.85	17.48
1967								99.44	62.15	59.32	41.48	17.84	2.83	23.78	15.75
1968								99.34	63.12	59.90	41.81	18.09	3.22	22.44	14.41
1969								108.17	68.10	64.51	46.03	18.48	3.59	29.70	19.21
1970								126.31	73.15	69.51	49.98	19.53	3.64	33.47	22.50
1971								139.69	73.65	70.21	50.44	19.77	3.44	34.78	22.93
1972								146.52	80.68	75.96	52.19	23.77	4.72	36.06	23.29
1973								154.33	90.17	83.42	57.84	25.58	6.75	43.81	24.86
1974								130.81	90.77	83.53	58.37	25.16	7.24	30.14	23.87
1975								166.19	100.32	88.98	61.81	27.17	11.34	54.72	43.01
1976								179.58	109.59	94.53	64.83	29.70	15.06	59.01	46.11
1977								207.07	123.79	106.30	74.67	31.63	17.49	69.18	55.67
1978								225.45	143.67	120.59	88.35	32.24	23.08	77.08	62.32
1979	109.7	118.4	109.4	108.0	126.1	110.7		251.60	155.83	133.42	98.38	35.04	22.41	81.05	65.45
1980	105.4	114.2	124.5	124.9	117.2	128.0	93.0	292.13	188.26	161.67	118.98	42.69	26.59	95.27	71.31
1981	95.6	86.0	84.3	86.8	391.3	88.3	93.7	346.57	212.91	181.79	134.59	47.20	31.12	100.41	81.95
1982	137.1	125.0	124.8	110.8	107.8	102.4	110.5	395.38	257.12	221.77	173.28	48.49	35.35	126.52	102.30
1983	99.5	130.2	113.1	118.5	116.5	124.1	117.6	459.83	285.15	242.31	192.16	50.15	42.84	142.59	121.09
1984	121.3	111.3	123.8	118.4	116.4	123.2	108.3	581.56	318.40	264.67	208.57	56.10	53.73	192.49	153.86
1985	115.2	127.0	107.0	110.2	101.9	101.7	96.3	680.46	365.69	297.92	225.91	72.01	67.77	253.68	195.39
1986	108.0	105.5	103.0	114.1	119.0	117.0	114.3	742.05	410.40	330.87	251.54	79.33	79.53	279.80	230.54
1987	105.5	143.7	105.3	100.9	106.9	123.7	108.4	892.29	481.01	377.18	282.74	94.44	103.83	371.44	293.40
1988	90.7	107.5	101.2	107.5	102.9	121.9	92.9	1117.66	592.91	471.31	334.84	136.47	121.60	458.97	335.12
1989	86.3	106.9	111.9	94.4	105.1	109.3	94.5	1293.94	700.93	522.40	344.28	178.12	178.53	537.52	333.27
1990	97.0	102.8	111.0	118.3	104.6	158.2	95.4	1511.19	807.32	588.46	383.95	204.51	218.86	638.78	412.59
1991	122.2	116.6	111.6	91.2	115.2	142.3	104.3	1810.54	914.36	667.63	423.32	244.31	246.73	815.00	555.76
1992	124.7	126.2	114.3	116.4	121.4	110.4	111.3	2196.53	1078.95	780.50	457.62	322.88	298.45	1045.40	758.28
1993	149.4	114.9	118.9	132.3	110.3	113.7	108.0	2735.68	1263.34	907.58	514.38	393.20	355.76	1374.39	1024.84
1994	131.2	120.3	109.0	121.3	116.7	119.6	117.1	3810.03	1889.34	1321.60	703.25	618.35	567.74	1784.52	1229.55
1995	119.4	120.9	123.3	124.5	115.6	115.9	116.4	4895.26	2479.05	1688.25	879.61	808.64	790.80	2247.58	1481.10

Year	v5b2	v5c	v5c1	v5c2	v6a1	v6a2	v6a3	v6a4	v6b2	v6b3	v6b4	v7	v7a	v7a1	v7a2
1952	2.28	1.38													
1953	2.67	0.18										101.7	100.6	96.8	115.8
1954	5.58	0.27										107.0	106.6	111.1	91.9
1955	4.77	0.33										107.0	106.2	104.5	112.8
1956	3.16	0.35										111.8	111.8	109.9	118.6
1957	3.41	0.57										93.0	93.3	91.9	97.9
1958	7.69	0.95										109.0	108.8	107.2	114.0
1959	9.09	1.60										92.2	90.2	83.6	110.5
1960	3.93	0.43										89.7	89.1	82.1	105.3
1961	3.02	3.71										94.9	98.4	104.6	87.3
1962	0.38	5.96										99.3	101.2	104.4	94.3
1963	3.05	7.04										106.6	107.0	113.0	92.9
1964	3.46	8.80										105.3	104.9	105.5	103.1
1965	7.58	8.55										113.3	113.3	111.8	117.5
1966	9.37	10.02										112.3	112.1	113.6	107.9
1967	8.03	13.51										103.5	103.4	103.3	103.7
1968	8.03	13.78										100.3	99.8	99.6	100.2
1969	10.49	10.37										107.2	107.0	107.7	104.8
1970	10.97	19.69										106.9	107.3	107.6	106.5
1971	11.85	31.26										104.5	104.5	103.9	106.3
1972	12.77	29.78										113.3	111.9	107.4	125.4
1973	18.95	20.35										111.9	110.0	110.9	107.7
1974	6.27	9.90										101.6	99.7	98.7	102.4
1975	11.71	11.15										110.7	108.1	109.4	104.9
1976	12.90	10.98										106.7	103.9	102.9	106.5
1977	13.51	14.10										109.9	109.3	112.3	101.5
1978	14.76	4.70			50.90	32.21	1.43	3.81	28.65	3.18	0.41	117.2	114.5	119.3	101.1
1979	15.60	14.72			56.05	36.28	1.83	4.22	30.52	3.99	0.53	101.9	104.0	103.0	107.5
1980	23.96	8.60			69.82	42.31	2.20	4.65	37.66	4.41	0.62	109.9	109.2	106.4	118.1
1981	18.46	33.25			75.46	51.26	2.63	5.24	42.56	3.91	0.73	107.5	110.6	110.8	109.9
1982	24.22	11.74			88.47	75.75	2.85	6.21	43.15	4.48	0.86	111.6	113.3	117.2	101.8
1983	21.50	32.09			94.26	86.31	3.09	8.50	44.37	4.78	1.00	108.8	109.7	112.3	101.0
1984	38.63	70.67			97.78	96.52	3.60	10.67	48.82	6.00	1.28	108.3	107.9	107.4	110.1
1985	58.29	61.09			97.20	109.28	5.17	14.26	63.08	7.55	1.38	108.1	105.9	102.6	118.0
1986	49.26	51.85			101.00	127.92	6.23	16.39	68.29	9.53	1.51	108.9	107.4	108.2	104.9
1987	78.04	39.84			113.55	144.33	7.22	17.64	80.87	11.83	1.74	107.7	103.5	101.7	109.1
1988	123.85	65.78			87.97	213.52	13.93	19.42	118.99	14.59	2.89	106.6	106.0	101.2	120.6
1989	204.25	55.49			91.59	219.53	12.57	20.59	158.02	17.13	2.97	97.7	97.5	91.1	113.9
1990	226.19	65.09			114.38	220.31	25.75	23.51	182.33	18.51	3.67	107.9	106.3	104.8	109.2
1991	259.24	81.18			136.49	239.31	21.85	25.67	218.80	20.82	4.69	113.4	107.1	105.6	110.1
1992	287.12	72.18			134.28	265.46	23.31	34.57	290.93	26.57	5.38	110.5	110.2	102.3	125.0
1993	350.05	97.45			156.96	271.26	41.79	44.37	342.22	36.28	14.70	110.2	110.5	107.1	115.7
1994	555.07	136.07	1759.24	1623.17	188.44	382.22	70.89	61.70	526.15	62.72	29.48	114.1	112.2	107.1	118.9
1995	766.48	168.63	1925.60	1756.97	220.17	484.32	99.07	76.05	670.64	94.62	43.38	114.8	113.0	108.4	118.5

Year	v7b	v8	v8a	v8b	v9	v9a	v9b	v10a1	v10a2	v10a3	v10a3a	v10a3b	v10a4	v10b1	v10b2
1952		69	56	284											
1953	125.3	70	54	318	99.0	95.1	109.7								
1954	113.9	74	60	282	103.2	109.0	87.3								
1955	121.1	76	61	283	104.1	102.4	101.0								
1956	113.0	82	65	301	109.8	108.1	108.5								
1957	89.6	76	59	277	92.0	90.4	90.7								
1958	111.7	84	66	256	107.8	108.2	89.5								
1959	120.4	77	56	250	91.0	84.8	97.1								
1960	96.5	76	51	286	92.1	83.3	111.4								
1961	59.8	85	59	330	98.9	104.6	97.7								
1962	68.5	89	65	358	97.8	100.0	108.8								
1963	97.0	87	66	341	103.3	110.3	96.0								
1964	115.4	87	66	324	103.2	104.0	99.0								
1965	114.2	95	71	371	112.5	110.3	115.0								
1966	117.8	100	76	384	109.3	110.5	106.8								
1967	106.9	100	76	393	100.9	101.1	103.7								
1968	112.4	99	75	398	98.3	97.9	100.0								
1969	110.9	104	80	405	104.3	105.3	104.4								
1970	100.1	109	85	419	104.1	104.0	104.2								
1971	105.7	108	84	393	101.6	101.9	98.6								
1972	141.9	115	86	450	110.9	105.7	119.4								
1973	142.8	124	93	479	107.7	109.0	106.4								
1974	124.4	122	93	461	98.7	97.5	100.2								
1975	136.7	129	97	489	106.6	107.6	102.8								
1976	128.7	135	101	518	102.5	102.4	103.5								
1977	113.8	150	115	538	108.4	110.8	98.9								
1978	133.0	169	136	529	110.0	113.9	97.5	49.71	8.42	4.19	0.21	3.98		7.78	6.98
1979	91.2	185	150	544	106.1	106.7	101.7	35.72	18.97	10.76	0.30	10.46		15.30	0.60
1980	114.1	223	181	632	107.6	106.3	110.8	37.17	22.24	11.90	0.43	11.47		16.33	7.63
1981	90.2	247	203	662	109.7	109.7	105.7	31.98	32.08	17.89	0.61	17.28		12.54	5.82
1982	100.4	298	259	642	111.3	116.2	96.2	60.59	23.38	18.33	0.87	17.46		19.46	4.76
1983	101.0	322	285	633	108.7	111.8	96.3	73.75	19.19	28.15	1.67	26.48		2.63	18.87
1984	111.3	348	310	642	106.7	107.2	99.8	80.79	25.29	47.78	3.35	44.43		-12.09	50.72
1985	126.2	388	338	737	104.7	102.8	105.5	101.49	30.21	63.69	5.18	58.51		46.64	11.65
1986	119.0	426	373	795	106.3	107.2	102.7	129.41	43.09	58.04	5.72	52.32		38.15	11.11
1987	134.0	478	415	933	102.3	101.3	107.7	151.28	78.75	63.37	7.32	56.05		25.32	52.72
1988	109.6	588	494	1160	105.0	101.9	105.6	163.51	94.97	76.64	11.81	64.83		47.80	76.05
1989	98.6	644	514	1277	72.3	92.0	101.9	190.53	69.68	73.06	11.06	62.00		85.00	119.25
1990	115.4	698	563	1310	137.3	104.0	92.2	248.39	79.21	84.99	12.14	72.85		95.41	130.78
1991	140.3	780	617	1501	105.5	104.2	107.1	315.82	122.85	117.09	19.63	97.46		101.35	157.89
1992	111.7	909	667	1893	108.5	102.5	115.3	477.75	202.45	78.08	19.23	58.85		104.67	182.45
1993	109.3	1052	760	2150	110.1	108.2	106.3	552.23	277.57	107.21	22.76	84.45	87.83	103.24	97.98
1994	118.6	1527	1058	3079	115.3	113.2	112.5	641.13	335.70	118.45	26.15	92.30	134.27	156.93	146.48
1995	118.9	1943	1342	3788	112.6	109.9	111.5	773.50	407.07	140.53	27.40	113.13	160.00	237.75	211.70

Year	v10b4	v11a	v11a1	v11a2	v11b	v11b1	v11b2	v11c	v11c1	v11c2	v12	v12a	v12b	v13	v13i
1952															
1953											116.9	117.9	114.3		
1954											142.2	118.7	205.8		
1955											116.1	132.9	88.1		
1956											109.0	129.1	65.8		
1957											103.0	102.0	106.8		
1958											149.3	135.0	214.3		
1959											123.1	125.7	118.0		
1960											86.3	107.8	40.4		
1961											40.8	36.1	67.9		
1962											69.5	88.5	11.9		
1963											129.5	92.5	926.7		
1964											124.1	135.0	108.5		
1965											168.4	135.8	221.5		
1966											127.6	138.5	127.6		
1967											89.6	91.1	86.6		
1968											93.3	90.3	99.0		
1969											131.2	132.2	129.4		
1970											109.0	115.7	98.6		
1971											110.6	111.7	111.1		
1972											107.0	104.7	111.4		
1973											121.5	106.8	148.4		
1974											67.3	95.0	31.5		
1975											187.7	184.2	198.0		
1976											105.5	101.9	114.2		
1977											114.0	120.9	96.1		
1978		10.57	8.90	1.67	24.58	18.80	5.78	41.93	34.62	7.31	108.6	109.2	106.4	225.45	108.18
1979		17.96	16.82	1.14	27.52	20.68	6.84	35.57	27.95	7.62	102.0	101.8	102.5	251.60	128.14
1980		17.55	16.22	1.33	33.16	26.07	7.09	44.56	29.02	15.54	113.1	104.8	147.8	292.13	154.89
1981		17.04	15.36	1.68	35.92	25.25	10.67	47.45	41.34	6.11	96.8	105.5	70.9	346.57	189.80
1982		12.54	10.09	2.45	43.08	31.80	11.28	70.90	60.41	10.49	124.5	123.2	130.1	395.38	212.52
1983		10.77	7.51	3.26	44.62	35.16	9.46	87.20	78.42	8.78	106.6	110.5	87.6	459.83	260.63
1984		21.78	13.21	8.57	71.10	53.90	17.20	99.61	86.75	12.86	133.7	127.1	171.5	581.56	324.18
1985		15.39	10.21	5.18	130.24	84.32	45.92	108.05	100.86	7.19	125.3	120.8	143.4	680.46	394.23
1986		14.03	10.93	3.10	132.58	112.47	20.11	133.19	107.14	26.05	103.8	109.4	83.3	742.05	407.98
1987		25.75	22.04	3.71	198.15	165.84	32.31	147.54	105.52	42.02	126.6	120.0	153.9	892.29	486.81
1988		21.93	18.08	3.85	272.37	206.03	66.34	164.67	111.01	53.66	105.6	101.6	120.7	1117.66	590.69
1989		27.43	23.28	4.15	303.23	159.13	144.10	206.86	150.86	56.00	114.9	92.6	172.9	1293.94	665.99
1990		45.22	26.93	18.29	251.89	186.40	65.49	341.67	199.26	142.41	105.1	105.5	103.0	1511.19	792.51
1991		62.89	35.53	27.36	338.89	237.55	101.34	413.22	282.68	130.54	113.1	118.4	103.4	1810.54	942.43
1992		56.51	23.66	32.85	495.30	337.23	158.07	493.59	397.39	96.20	124.6	133.1	106.8	2196.53	1000.58
1993	148.83	86.22	25.86	60.36	722.46	561.22	161.24	566.21	437.76	128.45	130.8	133.8	123.0	2779.49	1278.93
1994	241.66	111.02	24.22	86.80	905.94	618.76	287.18	767.66	586.57	181.09	113.7	111.4	120.3	3872.18	1754.43
1995	317.03	260.71	129.44	131.27	1165.23	778.86	386.37	821.64	572.80	248.84	113.6	111.4	119.3	5002.34	2285.80

Year	v13ii	v13iii	v13iv	v13a	v13ai	v13aii	v13aiii	v13aiv	v13b	v13bi	v13bii	v13biii	v13biv	v13b1	v13b1i
1952															
1953															
1954															
1955															
1956															
1957															
1958															
1959															
1960															
1961															
1962															
1963															
1964															
1965															
1966															
1967															
1968															
1969															
1970															
1971															
1972															
1973															
1974															
1975															
1976															
1977															
1978	22.72	21.71	72.84	75.06	61.83	1.14	3.10	8.99	119.35	33.54	13.64	23.79	48.38	108.53	26.86
1979	26.43	21.23	75.80	91.12	75.53	1.21	3.01	11.37	127.68	36.69	16.43	24.85	49.71	114.67	28.58
1980	30.56	23.24	83.44	106.43	89.73	1.62	3.04	12.04	146.11	46.13	19.08	27.00	53.90	130.55	36.78
1981	35.16	31.33	90.28	132.21	115.44	2.36	3.27	11.14	155.41	49.67	20.10	31.50	54.14	138.09	39.47
1982	42.34	34.27	106.25	154.07	129.54	3.69	3.17	17.67	166.05	54.91	21.97	34.69	54.48	147.10	44.01
1983	46.77	39.94	112.49	185.57	169.81	4.21	3.07	8.48	178.75	56.41	24.64	36.70	61.00	159.15	45.70
1984	60.08	50.55	146.75	222.13	203.93	4.87	3.87	9.46	239.27	77.35	30.96	44.88	86.08	214.20	61.18
1985	71.22	70.35	144.66	235.96	215.98	5.86	4.10	10.02	293.07	128.19	35.74	60.85	68.29	259.42	105.41
1986	85.21	78.46	170.40	252.73	223.35	7.07	3.30	19.01	313.21	124.92	42.35	68.19	77.75	274.30	99.31
1987	105.34	82.60	217.54	287.31	251.81	10.50	3.54	21.46	384.57	164.16	52.16	67.96	100.29	341.31	135.55
1988	125.77	119.76	281.44	331.94	283.91	10.04	7.41	30.58	497.10	209.93	68.12	94.02	125.03	435.51	170.49
1989	149.96	150.24	327.75	359.14	295.79	12.19	9.14	42.02	579.65	256.94	82.63	116.99	123.09	513.97	215.76
1990	182.12	191.41	345.15	425.29	355.83	14.22	8.82	46.42	635.98	282.13	95.73	150.19	107.93	568.25	238.37
1991	220.78	219.11	428.22	521.85	434.21	16.77	10.84	60.03	745.90	323.68	116.24	166.62	139.36	663.90	269.76
1992	266.92	316.14	612.89	534.62	434.20	19.52	7.77	73.13	999.11	339.62	139.12	253.33	267.04	889.59	274.07
1993	385.99	458.46	656.11	596.63	483.27	25.69	9.80	77.87	1358.94	453.77	219.07	370.19	315.91	1204.58	376.34
1994	561.55	582.72	973.48	775.03	658.40	30.40	16.07	70.16	1900.46	614.74	308.99	453.70	523.03	1700.31	518.29
1995	655.73	563.20	1497.61	1010.13	868.34	35.45	20.26	86.08	2372.67	767.01	274.73	404.44	926.49	2113.34	637.03

Year	v13b1ii	v13b1iii	v13b1iv	v13b2	v13b2i	v13b2ii	v13b2iii	v13b2iv	v13c	v13ci	v13cii	v13ciii	v13civ	v13c1
1952														
1953														
1954														
1955														
1956														
1957														
1958														
1959														
1960														
1961														
1962														
1963														
1964														
1965														
1966														
1967														
1968														
1969														
1970														
1971														
1972														
1973														
1974														
1975														
1976														
1977														
1978	13.42	23.58	44.67	10.82	6.68	0.22	0.21	3.71	31.04	12.81	7.94	-5.18	15.47	8.27
1979	16.19	24.62	45.28	13.01	8.11	0.24	0.23	4.43	32.80	15.92	8.79	-6.63	14.72	9.50
1980	18.77	26.75	48.25	15.56	9.35	0.31	0.25	5.65	39.59	19.03	9.86	-6.80	17.50	10.07
1981	19.71	31.22	47.69	17.32	10.20	0.39	0.28	6.45	58.95	24.69	12.70	-3.44	25.00	13.18
1982	21.45	34.38	47.26	18.95	10.90	0.52	0.31	7.22	75.26	28.07	16.68	-3.59	34.10	14.10
1983	24.03	36.36	53.06	19.60	10.71	0.61	0.34	7.94	95.51	34.41	17.92	0.17	43.01	17.12
1984	29.63	44.73	78.66	25.07	16.17	1.33	0.15	7.42	120.16	42.90	24.25	1.80	51.21	22.25
1985	34.16	57.11	62.74	33.65	22.78	1.58	3.74	5.55	151.43	50.06	29.62	5.40	66.35	28.22
1986	40.47	64.12	70.90	38.41	25.61	1.88	4.07	6.85	176.11	59.71	35.79	6.97	73.64	34.03
1987	48.56	63.47	93.73	43.26	28.61	3.60	4.49	6.56	220.41	70.84	42.68	11.10	95.79	47.45
1988	61.38	88.89	114.75	61.59	39.44	6.74	5.13	10.28	288.62	96.85	47.61	18.33	125.83	55.50
1989	74.58	110.81	112.82	65.68	41.18	8.05	6.18	10.27	355.15	113.26	55.14	24.11	162.64	66.55
1990	87.05	143.80	99.03	67.73	43.76	8.68	6.39	8.90	449.92	154.55	72.17	32.40	190.80	81.87
1991	105.27	157.66	131.21	82.00	53.92	10.97	8.96	8.15	542.79	184.54	87.77	41.65	228.83	98.97
1992	128.13	243.12	244.27	109.52	65.55	10.99	10.21	22.77	662.80	226.76	108.28	55.04	272.72	120.18
1993	204.19	354.49	269.56	154.36	77.43	14.88	15.70	46.35	823.92	341.89	141.23	78.47	262.33	151.35
1994	295.20	434.50	452.32	200.15	96.45	13.79	19.20	70.71	1196.69	481.29	222.16	112.95	380.29	214.36
1995	257.46	378.18	840.67	259.33	129.98	17.27	26.26	85.82	1619.54	650.45	345.55	138.50	485.04	297.71

Year	v13c1i	v13c1ii	v13c1iii	v13c1iv	v13c2	v13c2i	v13c2ii	v13c2iii	v13c2iv	v13c3	v13c3i	v13c3ii	v13c3iii	v13c3iv
1952														
1953														
1954														
1955														
1956														
1957														
1958														
1959														
1960														
1961														
1962														
1963														
1964														
1965														
1966														
1967														
1968														
1969														
1970														
1971														
1972														
1973														
1974														
1975														
1976														
1977														
1978	2.38	0.81	0.84	4.24	3.29	2.51	0.82	-6.25	6.21	5.17	0.34	0.04		4.79
1979	3.19	0.97	0.81	4.53	4.18	3.89	0.90	-7.67	7.06	3.31	0.36	0.04		2.91
1980	3.40	1.33	1.28	4.06	6.39	4.85	1.08	-8.29	8.75	4.93	0.46	0.04		4.43
1981	3.88	1.97	1.34	5.99	16.56	6.73	1.43	-5.03	13.43	5.93	0.60	0.08		5.25
1982	4.24	2.09	1.45	6.32	22.39	8.25	2.09	-5.44	17.49	10.84	0.86	0.14		9.84
1983	4.89	2.32	1.55	8.36	32.07	10.02	2.38	-2.10	21.77	13.93	1.05	0.20	0.37	12.31
1984	6.49	4.07	1.83	9.86	37.97	11.79	2.60	-1.55	25.13	18.07	1.35	0.24	1.06	15.42
1985	7.70	5.39	2.52	12.61	46.14	13.06	2.63	0.11	30.34	26.64	2.31	0.31	2.23	21.79
1986	8.67	6.60	3.81	14.95	49.85	15.32	3.60	0.37	30.56	32.46	3.11	0.40	2.07	26.88
1987	10.88	8.36	5.65	22.56	60.58	18.34	4.80	1.48	35.96	41.08	3.70	0.54	2.58	34.26
1988	14.40	9.74	6.44	24.92	86.71	28.46	4.45	5.91	47.89	59.02	5.31	0.89	3.98	48.84
1989	16.43	12.56	6.71	30.85	108.51	32.92	6.59	8.59	60.41	76.44	6.19	1.29	6.29	62.67
1990	19.93	14.78	8.18	38.98	132.83	40.48	9.34	13.63	69.38	84.39	7.74	2.12	6.58	67.95
1991	24.90	16.76	9.39	47.92	161.00	49.65	10.10	19.18	82.07	96.24	9.23	3.23	7.39	76.39
1992	31.15	20.69	11.98	56.36	200.93	61.63	12.79	26.43	100.08	112.10	12.99	4.50	9.00	85.61
1993	94.45	25.13	9.30	22.47	188.93	94.48	32.51	38.52	23.42	187.24	9.17	5.73	15.49	156.85
1994	101.23	45.80	15.49	51.84	325.90	138.95	43.79	52.77	90.39	247.84	50.25	16.11	19.08	162.40
1995	115.55	82.08	19.23	80.85	439.79	163.55	62.63	64.20	146.41	285.93	63.48	22.30	25.14	170.01

Year	v13c4	v13c4i	v13c4ii	v13c4iii	v13c4iv	v13c5	v13c5i	v13c5ii	v13c5iii	v13c5iv	v13c6	v13c6i	v13c6ii	v13c6iii
1952														
1953														
1954														
1955														
1956														
1957														
1958														
1959														
1960														
1961														
1962														
1963														
1964														
1965														
1966														
1967														
1968														
1969														
1970														
1971														
1972														
1973														
1974														
1975														
1976														
1977														
1978	4.50	0.07	4.43			1.24	0.60	0.18	0.23	0.23	1.37	0.90	0.47	
1979	5.01	0.07	4.94			1.49	0.85	0.19	0.23	0.22	1.52	1.04	0.48	
1980	5.36	0.11	5.25			1.73	1.01	0.25	0.21	0.26	1.93	1.43	0.50	
1981	6.84	0.10	6.74			1.98	1.07	0.33	0.25	0.33	2.16	1.63	0.53	
1982	9.41	0.11	9.30			2.49	1.22	0.42	0.40	0.45	2.71	2.09	0.62	
1983	9.60	0.11	9.49			3.32	1.92	0.48	0.35	0.57	3.14	2.46	0.68	
1984	12.71	0.12	12.59			4.03	2.22	0.55	0.46	0.80	4.25	3.17	1.08	
1985	16.06	0.22	15.84			5.62	2.60	0.91	0.50	1.61	4.99	3.82	1.17	
1986	18.55	0.22	18.33			6.35	3.48	0.94	0.68	1.25	5.49	4.20	1.29	
1987	20.92	0.22	20.59		0.11	9.76	5.03	0.96	0.87	2.90	6.19	4.79	1.40	
1988	22.67	0.34	21.99		0.34	12.51	6.60	1.12	1.14	3.65	7.48	5.97	1.50	
1989	23.44	0.56	22.05	0.01	0.82	16.03	8.36	1.21	0.96	5.50	10.01	7.02	1.59	
1990	28.61	0.81	26.02	0.14	1.64	20.73	9.88	1.73	1.38	7.74	14.00	9.92	1.67	
1991	36.36	0.99	32.03	0.44	2.90	25.15	8.34	2.44	1.85	12.52	16.24	11.27	1.80	0.06
1992	47.60	1.66	39.65	0.85	5.44	33.32	11.11	3.33	2.61	16.27	19.50	13.81	2.19	0.08
1993	85.95	2.86	53.74	3.44	25.91	33.71	17.94	3.32	4.73	7.72	29.13	18.29	3.16	1.84
1994	110.31	4.80	64.63	5.52	35.36	46.70	24.76	4.88	6.37	10.69	31.12	19.61	3.59	2.28
1995	160.55	9.60	110.92	11.32	28.71	72.69	38.42	6.79	9.99	17.49	49.50	29.17	5.72	3.16

Year	v13c6iv	v13c7	v13c7i	v13c7ii	v13c7iii	v13c7iv	v13c8	v13c8i	v13c8ii	v13c8iii	v13c3iv	v13c9	v13c9i	v13c9ii
1952														
1953														
1954														
1955														
1956														
1957														
1958														
1959														
1960														
1961														
1962														
1963														
1964														
1965														
1966														
1967														
1968														
1969														
1970														
1971														
1972														
1973														
1974														
1975														
1976														
1977														
1978		2.74	2.18	0.56			0.23	0.09	0.14			1.96	1.47	0.49
1979		3.00	2.41	0.59			0.29	0.14	0.15			2.20	1.67	0.53
1980		3.80	3.15	0.65			0.35	0.17	0.18			2.86	2.23	0.58
1981		4.40	3.54	0.86			1.82	1.66	0.16			3.37	2.77	0.60
1982		4.89	3.79	1.10			1.97	1.73	0.24			3.46	2.73	0.68
1983		5.95	4.70	1.25			2.35	2.01	0.34			4.41	3.63	0.78
1984		7.68	6.27	1.41			2.99	2.46	0.53			5.92	4.74	1.18
1985		9.29	7.72	1.53	0.04		3.34	3.03	0.31			6.60	5.07	1.53
1986		11.33	9.70	1.59	0.04		4.25	3.57	0.68			8.27	5.91	2.36
1987		12.23	10.47	1.75	0.01		4.86	4.06	0.80			10.93	6.94	3.48
1988	0.01	15.70	13.75	1.91	0.04		5.98	5.04	0.94			15.93	9.86	5.07
1989	1.40	17.74	15.54	2.16	0.04		7.53	5.51	1.52	0.02	[illegible].48	20.85	12.68	6.17
1990	2.41	26.41	22.96	2.93	0.02	0.50	9.90	6.28	2.27	0.33	[illegible].02	41.51	27.88	10.63
1991	3.11	25.05	19.16	4.74	0.27	0.88	11.86	7.47	2.71	0.42	[illegible].26	61.43	44.45	13.11
1992	3.42	30.61	23.34	5.52	0.38	1.37	15.11	9.38	3.36	0.66	[illegible].71	71.19	51.95	15.23
1993	5.84	59.91	41.08	8.23	3.38	7.22	11.09	4.31	2.57	0.52	3.69	53.02	44.33	4.24
1994	5.64	64.26	40.14	11.46	3.02	9.64	23.97	13.06	4.31	1.07	5.53	110.02	75.18	25.15
1995	11.45	99.98	74.20	13.83	1.84	10.11	26.65	15.51	3.91	0.90	[illegible].33	149.88	107.14	32.54

Year	v13c9iii	v13c9iv	v13c10	v13c10i	v13c10ii	v13c10iii	v13c10iv
1952							
1953							
1954							
1955							
1956							
1957							
1958							
1959							
1960							
1961							
1962							
1963							
1964							
1965							
1966							
1967							
1968							
1969							
1970							
1971							
1972							
1973							
1974							
1975							
1976							
1977							
1978			2.27	2.27			
1979			2.30	2.30			
1980			2.17	2.17			
1981			2.71	2.71			
1982			3.00	3.00			
1983			3.62	3.62			
1984			4.29	4.29			
1985			4.53	4.53			
1986			5.53	5.53			
1987	0.51		6.41	6.41			
1988	0.82	0.18	7.12	7.12			
1989	1.49	0.51	8.05	8.05			
1990	2.14	0.86	9.67	8.67	0.68		0.32
1991	2.59	1.28	10.49	9.08	0.85	0.06	0.50
1992	2.95	1.06	12.26	9.74	1.02	0.10	1.40
1993	1.00	3.45	23.59	14.98	2.60	0.25	5.76
1994	6.22	3.47	22.21	13.31	2.44	1.13	5.33
1995	1.76	8.44	36.86	28.83	4.83	0.96	2.24

16

Henan

Year	v1	v1a	v1b	v1b1	v1b2	v1c	v1c1	v1c2	v1c3	v2	v2a	v2b	v2b1	v2b2	v2c
1952	50.15	27.74	14.22	9.98	4.24	8.19	1.17	1.84	5.18						
1953	59.78	31.54	18.37	11.90	6.47	9.87	1.40	2.39	6.08	113.2	105.6	127.5	120.3	151.2	118.0
1954	65.18	33.57	20.47	13.65	6.82	11.14	1.90	2.73	6.51	108.9	104.9	115.7	116.4	113.7	110.2
1955	69.57	36.02	21.37	14.49	6.88	12.18	2.30	2.87	7.01	107.5	107.4	106.7	107.9	103.4	109.0
1956	75.90	34.61	26.00	16.11	9.89	15.29	3.13	3.47	8.69	110.2	95.1	129.2	117.6	162.2	122.6
1957	83.45	31.57	34.98	16.63	18.35	16.90	3.53	3.28	10.09	112.0	107.7	115.9	105.8	136.7	114.6
1958	112.24	33.78	59.80	33.17	26.63	18.66	4.57	4.45	9.64	133.7	104.0	180.9	200.8	149.1	111.7
1959	132.17	32.46	81.85	50.16	31.69	17.86	3.64	4.03	10.19	117.1	91.4	141.4	150.5	121.9	94.1
1960	141.96	28.94	92.41	58.41	34.00	20.61	4.29	5.53	10.79	105.9	87.4	112.4	117.2	99.8	115.0
1961	91.49	24.81	46.44	31.20	15.24	20.24	3.57	4.94	11.73	56.3	67.9	43.7	50.9	21.2	88.9
1962	83.14	28.13	35.56	23.93	11.63	19.45	3.21	4.91	11.33	90.9	115.4	75.2	76.7	64.2	101.2
1963	83.19	25.33	37.94	26.65	11.29	19.92	3.55	4.88	11.49	105.6	91.0	120.7	107.9	234.8	104.2
1964	93.59	32.20	39.89	32.27	7.62	21.50	3.97	5.42	12.11	121.1	128.3	121.4	121.4	121.5	111.9
1965	117.13	42.17	51.54	42.24	9.30	23.42	4.84	5.95	12.63	126.0	128.2	135.2	136.9	128.3	106.1
1966	134.83	49.65	60.43	49.30	11.13	24.75	5.61	6.40	12.74	116.9	114.9	121.5	121.7	121.2	108.4
1967	137.44	58.02	55.06	46.15	8.91	24.36	4.56	6.78	13.02	99.3	114.2	92.0	94.7	80.0	95.4
1968	128.21	54.95	49.66	42.37	7.29	23.60	4.13	6.42	13.05	93.1	92.5	91.7	93.7	81.8	97.2
1969	149.88	57.73	66.56	54.25	12.31	25.59	5.28	7.52	12.79	120.5	102.6	137.8	132.6	168.8	109.4
1970	187.42	67.18	91.49	73.68	17.81	28.75	7.03	8.70	13.02	128.2	110.3	142.4	142.0	144.7	112.9
1971	209.35	71.21	107.79	91.54	16.25	30.35	7.50	9.72	13.13	108.9	104.8	111.4	116.1	89.8	107.1
1972	221.75	72.50	115.79	100.75	15.04	33.46	7.91	11.09	14.46	105.6	101.0	106.7	109.3	91.5	110.1
1973	243.17	83.31	124.47	106.07	18.40	35.39	8.33	12.13	14.93	107.8	113.1	106.5	104.6	119.8	105.8
1974	256.42	83.21	135.97	115.62	20.35	37.24	8.75	13.07	15.42	106.1	100.0	109.0	109.0	108.1	105.0
1975	278.72	85.98	153.91	130.46	23.45	38.83	9.58	13.41	15.84	109.5	103.1	112.8	112.8	113.1	106.9
1976	258.86	87.17	131.44	107.99	23.45	40.25	9.72	13.92	16.61	90.7	100.7	85.0	82.8	98.4	107.3
1977	317.17	82.70	189.20	161.69	27.51	45.27	12.57	15.33	17.37	124.7	94.3	142.2	147.3	115.5	106.2
1978	349.25	95.38	199.73	170.82	28.91	54.14	16.62	17.87	19.65	109.5	109.6	107.1	107.6	103.5	118.2
1979	397.36	113.48	225.93	193.49	32.44	57.95	16.50	19.50	21.95	108.2	101.2	109.7	109.7	109.6	116.1
1980	449.88	134.62	247.42	209.23	38.19	67.84	17.48	21.12	29.24	110.0	105.0	110.4	109.3	117.5	113.6
1981	497.44	151.24	264.65	223.50	41.15	81.55	18.69	23.25	39.61	108.3	113.0	105.4	105.0	108.0	116.3
1982	530.96	151.06	292.59	246.28	46.31	87.31	22.41	21.89	43.01	106.8	97.6	109.1	108.6	112.5	106.2
1983	613.40	187.02	318.00	268.14	49.86	108.38	28.06	25.45	54.87	113.5	122.0	108.8	109.1	107.1	119.4
1984	703.22	208.68	364.13	307.58	56.55	130.41	32.98	34.20	63.23	112.3	108.4	112.5	113.7	105.4	115.7
1985	911.57	241.54	487.03	401.32	85.71	183.00	43.57	53.20	86.23	123.4	104.3	123.9	122.7	132.1	136.5
1986	1038.75	259.49	577.92	478.09	99.83	201.34	46.72	58.63	95.99	110.7	95.7	113.9	114.4	110.9	109.8
1987	1289.19	323.62	709.86	594.64	115.22	255.71	54.03	70.88	130.80	116.8	118.4	117.2	118.0	112.2	116.9
1988	1631.60	370.67	929.30	779.90	149.40	331.63	73.15	107.35	151.13	115.7	98.5	120.0	120.3	118.3	107.8
1989	1933.73	449.88	1086.24	953.56	132.68	397.61	93.45	134.23	169.93	106.1	109.9	106.3	110.4	80.8	103.7
1990	2163.91	502.01	1193.52	1036.73	156.79	468.38	107.52	115.20	245.66	107.7	107.8	107.5	106.9	109.7	109.0
1991	2480.11	531.05	1412.91	1222.68	190.23	536.15	124.08	152.39	259.68	113.0	100.5	114.8	115.3	110.6	113.4
1992	3082.59	573.65	1869.78	1628.63	241.15	639.16	144.66	176.46	318.04	121.7	102.5	126.0	126.7	119.1	112.2
1993	4258.85	671.69	2775.36	2434.37	340.99	811.80	181.80	210.44	419.56	122.6	111.1	128.6	129.9	119.0	113.7
1994	5749.54	883.32	3853.10	3436.80	416.30	1013.12	204.23	291.41	517.48	119.9	103.3	125.8	127.6	110.6	113.8
1995	7947.73	1304.25	5217.64	4721.61	496.03	1425.84	307.64	399.56	713.60	118.9	117.6	120.6	121.9	109.0	113.7

Year	v2c1	v2c2	v3'	v3	v3a	v3b	v3b1	v3b2	v3c	v3c1	v3c2	v3c3	v3c4	v3c5	v3c6
1952			36.09	36.09	22.46	8.23	4.77	3.46	5.40	0.52	1.26				
1953	125.6	123.9	41.30	41.30	25.08	10.16	4.88	5.28	6.06	0.64	1.18				
1954	137.4	111.8	44.02	44.02	26.45	10.88	5.98	4.90	6.69	0.86	1.35				
1955	122.8	105.5	46.53	46.53	28.14	11.12	6.31	4.81	7.27	1.04	1.42				
1956	139.9	120.8	48.12	48.12	27.05	12.07	6.83	5.24	9.00	1.44	1.74				
1957	118.7	92.3	52.55	52.55	24.27	18.08	6.87	11.21	10.20	1.64	1.66				
1958	131.1	135.7	60.76	60.76	25.64	24.24	9.89	14.35	10.88	2.13	2.26				
1959	79.3	90.4	64.03	64.03	22.92	30.32	14.08	16.24	10.79	1.82	2.11				
1960	118.7	136.7	66.15	66.15	20.08	33.74	16.75	16.99	12.33	2.17	2.91				
1961	83.1	78.5	46.29	46.29	14.61	19.36	11.15	8.21	12.32	1.85	2.62				
1962	88.6	115.7	43.02	43.02	17.00	14.05	8.54	5.51	11.97	1.74	2.62				
1963	110.7	107.4	42.45	42.45	15.11	15.15	10.07	5.08	12.19	1.86	2.61				
1964	112.1	110.6	51.40	51.40	22.40	15.56	13.08	2.48	13.44	2.12	2.90				
1965	121.6	91.7	62.96	62.96	29.58	19.10	16.27	2.83	14.28	2.45	3.20				
1966	116.0	108.2	76.39	76.39	35.07	26.64	21.33	5.31	14.68	2.52	3.45				
1967	82.3	107.2	78.54	78.54	41.13	22.82	18.98	3.84	14.59	2.16	3.67				
1968	91.6	94.6	72.19	72.19	38.40	19.53	16.71	2.82	14.26	1.96	3.52				
1969	127.4	118.3	80.88	80.88	39.80	25.78	21.47	4.31	15.30	2.45	4.12				
1970	133.9	117.8	97.19	97.19	44.49	36.06	30.04	6.02	16.64	2.98	4.82				
1971	106.7	111.5	104.80	104.80	47.53	39.72	34.16	5.56	17.55	3.30	5.21				
1972	105.5	114.2	111.41	111.41	49.05	43.09	37.69	5.40	19.27	3.51	5.75				
1973	105.5	109.3	117.05	117.05	53.77	43.10	36.14	6.96	20.18	3.77	6.08				
1974	104.9	107.7	119.92	119.92	53.97	44.94	37.00	7.94	21.01	4.03	6.31				
1975	109.6	113.0	127.77	127.77	55.71	50.34	41.54	8.80	21.72	4.41	6.35				
1976	102.5	110.8	125.52	125.52	59.98	42.39	33.46	8.93	23.15	4.81	6.85				
1977	128.0	96.4	144.11	144.11	55.91	62.51	51.48	11.03	25.69	5.45	7.72				
1978	105.9	116.2	162.92	162.92	64.86	69.45	59.20	10.25	28.61	6.91	7.88	3.30	2.84	0.79	1.21
1979	100.8	127.4	190.09	190.09	77.30	80.52	68.64	11.88	32.27	7.79	8.88	3.72	3.21	0.89	1.36
1980	106.4	107.4	229.16	229.16	93.23	94.44	80.51	13.93	41.49	10.02	11.42	4.78	4.12	1.15	1.75
1981	106.7	106.7	249.69	249.69	106.04	95.79	82.61	13.18	47.86	11.96	12.00	5.97	4.92	1.96	1.75
1982	119.5	94.1	263.30	263.30	108.18	102.76	88.62	14.14	52.36	13.09	13.13	6.53	5.38	2.15	1.91
1983	110.9	117.4	327.95	327.95	143.49	116.36	100.35	16.01	68.10	17.02	17.08	8.49	7.00	2.79	2.49
1984	125.9	127.6	370.04	370.04	155.28	136.29	116.66	19.63	78.47	19.71	18.29	10.78	7.86	3.32	2.93
1985	129.3	148.3	451.74	451.74	173.43	170.07	144.39	25.68	108.24	24.82	27.34	15.15	12.38	4.44	3.89
1986	108.6	110.6	502.91	502.91	179.02	202.15	174.47	27.68	121.74	26.31	31.17	18.66	14.09	3.40	4.19
1987	114.8	111.2	609.60	609.60	220.22	230.25	195.75	34.50	159.13	30.08	42.11	27.85	19.74	5.82	4.81
1988	112.3	105.6	749.09	749.09	240.72	299.83	258.38	41.45	208.54	42.02	65.25	31.05	15.93	6.78	8.98
1989	107.6	100.7	850.71	850.71	289.95	317.13	281.71	35.42	243.63	51.18	71.14	41.03	19.36	8.17	9.34
1990	102.4	93.9	934.65	934.65	325.77	331.85	288.58	43.27	277.03	59.65	58.17	48.25	23.94	9.78	11.68
1991	116.5	117.2	1045.73	1045.73	334.61	388.09	336.26	51.83	323.03	72.68	73.82	52.74	28.10	11.55	12.84
1992	109.4	111.6	1279.75	1279.75	353.92	545.21	481.11	64.10	380.62	82.52	84.95	65.85	32.60	15.19	15.51
1993	113.6	114.0	1662.76	1662.76	410.45	768.89	681.65	87.24	483.42	103.82	101.64	87.47	49.83	19.36	17.85
1994	107.4	116.9	2232.17	2224.43	546.68	1071.74	958.00	113.74	606.01	113.06	136.13	100.33	63.72	32.32	24.54
1995	118.5	109.9	3013.86	3002.74	762.99	1420.25	1274.89	145.36	819.50	164.03	182.75	141.10	82.53	49.96	37.08

Year	v3c7	v3c8	v3c9	v3c10	v3d	v4'	v4	v4a	v4b	v4b1	v4b2	v4c	v4c1	v4c2	v4c3
1952				3.62	83	106.1	106.1	101.1	138.3	158.1	112.0	129.2	119.4	111.7	
1953				4.24	94	107.0	107.0	103.7	126.3	104.5	167.4	113.8	135.1	89.6	
1954				4.48	98	105.4	105.4	103.9	112.0	124.0	97.9	109.1	136.0	112.6	
1955				4.81	101	106.6	106.6	106.5	105.0	106.8	102.5	109.2	123.5	106.0	
1956				5.82	103	101.3	101.3	95.1	119.0	115.9	123.7	127.0	145.2	121.1	
1957				6.90	110	109.2	109.2	105.9	119.0	96.3	152.0	116.0	121.3	93.3	
1958				6.49	124	109.6	109.6	102.6	142.1	144.6	139.8	104.7	129.1	136.7	
1959				6.86	129	97.5	97.5	84.9	133.2	141.6	125.2	99.6	82.2	95.8	
1960				7.25	135	96.8	96.8	85.7	111.0	120.2	101.1	113.2	119.7	135.7	
1961				7.85	96	140.6	59.4	57.4	50.1	64.8	31.2	88.7	89.4	83.0	
1962				7.61	88	100.5	100.5	118.4	70.8	76.4	55.9	100.2	89.9	118.0	
1963				7.72	85	99.6	99.6	89.7	121.5	113.8	149.5	105.2	106.0	109.5	
1964				8.42	101	132.9	132.9	150.1	116.3	126.4	88.3	112.3	124.4	103.8	
1965				8.63	122	124.5	124.5	129.4	128.7	130.8	120.5	104.5	115.1	88.0	
1966				8.71	144	120.8	120.8	115.7	146.9	137.0	189.9	103.1	93.0	116.5	
1967				8.76	144	104.5	104.5	114.6	85.7	90.0	72.2	99.9	85.9	107.4	
1968				8.78	129	91.0	91.0	91.1	86.4	89.8	73.3	98.1	90.7	95.7	
1969				8.73	140	109.9	109.9	101.2	137.1	133.5	154.2	107.4	128.9	117.6	
1970				8.84	164	117.3	117.3	106.0	145.8	147.1	140.7	109.7	126.6	118.2	
1971				9.04	172	105.1	105.1	105.7	104.0	108.6	84.5	105.6	111.1	107.4	
1972				10.01	178	105.2	105.2	102.3	107.7	109.9	95.6	110.4	105.6	110.6	
1973				10.33	182	104.7	104.7	107.9	99.6	95.4	126.1	105.1	107.9	106.5	
1974				10.67	182	102.1	102.1	100.4	104.1	102.5	111.7	104.3	105.5	104.9	
1975				10.96	191	106.3	106.3	102.9	111.9	112.7	108.5	106.1	109.9	113.8	
1976				11.49	185	99.2	99.2	106.8	84.0	80.4	100.8	109.0	110.1	115.6	
1977				12.52	209	110.2	110.2	92.5	145.4	152.0	121.3	106.1	118.3	98.6	
1978	3.24	0.50	1.94		232	111.3	111.3	110.6	112.1	116.4	92.6	111.3	119.4	119.0	
1979	3.66	0.57	2.19		267	108.7	108.7	101.7	112.6	113.5	107.6	119.7	112.2	120.2	111.7
1980	4.70	0.73	2.82		317	115.4	115.4	109.2	117.2	116.6	121.3	126.9	121.6	123.8	123.7
1981	5.63	0.85	2.82		340	107.8	107.8	111.7	101.3	102.2	95.9	113.7	113.8	103.4	122.9
1982	6.16	0.93	3.08		353	104.3	104.3	100.5	106.1	105.7	108.6	109.0	109.6	107.8	109.5
1983	8.01	1.21	4.01		433	123.8	123.8	130.2	113.5	113.9	111.2	131.3	110.4	129.3	129.7
1984	9.17	1.88	4.53		482	110.1	110.1	105.5	115.0	115.0	115.1	110.7	112.4	101.5	121.0
1985	11.02	3.26	5.94		580	113.5	113.5	100.8	117.0	116.8	117.7	131.9	120.1	136.0	135.1
1986	13.16	3.41	7.35		635	104.6	104.6	92.1	114.0	115.7	103.2	108.6	106.6	108.3	117.8
1987	14.75	5.43	8.54		756	115.0	115.0	116.9	108.6	106.9	120.2	123.5	118.7	124.1	139.7
1988	18.71	4.94	14.88		910	109.8	109.8	97.4	120.1	121.8	109.6	109.4	116.1	108.6	94.3
1989	18.19	6.61	18.08	0.53	1012	104.4	104.4	109.2	97.6	105.5	90.1	110.3	97.2	121.1	139.4
1990	22.92	8.58	32.93	1.13	1091	104.5	104.5	105.4	102.3	100.1	119.4	106.8	107.6	73.4	113.4
1991	23.47	9.52	36.30	2.01	1201	106.9	106.9	97.4	113.3	113.8	109.3	110.4	117.5	123.0	97.0
1992	27.55	11.40	42.74	2.31	1452	113.7	113.7	101.5	125.4	126.5	117.1	111.1	107.2	109.2	116.8
1993	32.83	15.91	51.35	2.86	1867	115.8	115.8	110.4	122.1	123.1	113.5	111.6	110.2	109.7	118.0
1994	45.98	17.85	68.96	3.12	2475	113.8	113.8	101.3	121.6	122.5	113.7	112.9	105.9	112.6	112.5
1995	56.03	22.37	77.51	6.14	3313	114.8	114.8	111.9	117.2	117.7	112.2	113.1	117.6	109.2	113.0

Year	v4c4	v4c5	v4c6	v4c7	v4c8	v4c9	v4c10	v5	v5a	v5a1	v5a1a	v5a1b	v5a2	v5b	v5b1
1952								36.09	29.50	27.93	24.61	3.32	1.57	6.63	4.90
1953								41.30	32.46	30.50	26.86	3.64	1.96	7.98	3.55
1954								44.02	33.43	31.36	27.18	4.18	2.07	8.17	4.53
1955								46.53	35.20	33.15	28.80	4.35	2.05	10.73	8.14
1956								48.12	36.83	33.91	28.81	5.10	2.92	12.04	10.16
1957								52.55	36.87	33.94	27.82	6.12	2.93	16.49	11.17
1958								60.76	40.38	37.34	30.32	7.02	3.04	30.02	22.91
1959								64.03	37.26	33.72	25.14	8.58	3.54	38.59	29.27
1960								66.15	36.64	32.61	22.55	10.06	4.03	31.54	32.64
1961								46.29	38.79	34.67	23.62	11.05	4.12	5.11	11.07
1962								43.02	40.12	36.46	25.28	11.18	3.66	3.41	8.24
1963								42.45	41.03	37.08	25.82	11.26	3.95	10.34	8.76
1964								51.40	40.71	36.71	24.63	12.08	4.00	12.32	10.36
1965								62.96	42.36	38.13	25.93	12.20	4.23	14.91	12.21
1966								76.39	46.15	41.83	29.44	12.39	4.32	23.55	16.53
1967								78.54	50.11	46.05	33.58	12.47	4.06	18.38	11.89
1968								72.19	49.67	45.58	33.24	12.34	4.09	15.19	9.06
1969								80.88	52.34	48.00	34.55	13.45	4.34	22.84	15.57
1970								97.19	56.98	52.56	38.24	14.32	4.42	39.21	26.05
1971								104.80	61.29	55.97	41.71	14.26	5.32	35.09	25.60
1972								111.41	67.80	60.03	43.95	16.08	7.77	35.95	25.81
1973								117.05	71.54	63.04	46.12	16.92	8.50	40.69	29.36
1974								119.92	75.53	66.34	48.21	18.13	9.19	43.11	33.18
1975								127.77	80.08	68.60	49.67	18.93	11.48	46.34	35.85
1976								125.52	87.77	76.41	57.04	19.37	11.36	37.47	28.47
1977								144.11	90.57	79.57	59.63	19.94	11.00	53.25	38.57
1978								162.92	107.07	94.34	70.45	23.89	12.73	52.49	40.66
1979	113.0	112.7	111.4	111.9	112.9	111.8		190.09	127.10	113.01	86.10	26.91	14.09	60.46	46.37
1980	128.3	128.7	123.9	123.7	123.3	124.0		229.16	151.48	135.23	104.36	30.87	16.25	69.20	57.70
1981	119.4	167.4	98.4	117.9	114.6	98.4		249.69	164.83	147.09	112.62	34.47	17.74	76.12	55.20
1982	109.3	107.9	109.3	109.5	109.5	109.3		263.30	183.01	159.95	123.33	36.62	23.06	71.15	66.10
1983	129.6	130.8	129.8	129.6	130.1	129.5		327.95	194.43	165.43	125.63	39.80	29.00	115.21	88.14
1984	104.4	109.2	109.5	106.7	144.3	105.4		370.04	222.17	187.89	139.32	48.57	34.28	130.82	101.87
1985	139.1	124.1	123.8	111.7	161.6	122.4		451.74	275.95	231.11	166.16	64.95	44.84	173.43	138.19
1986	107.3	70.0	100.9	112.0	98.2	116.0		502.91	307.91	256.87	182.68	74.19	51.04	184.00	158.84
1987	135.7	160.8	107.2	104.7	147.9	108.2		609.60	344.68	285.09	201.05	84.04	59.59	223.78	174.20
1988	100.7	95.5	110.8	117.7	105.8	117.1		749.09	410.63	348.87	235.34	113.53	61.76	307.85	222.33
1989	121.0	138.7	116.1	109.9	126.9	129.6		850.71	466.33	395.47	264.82	130.65	70.86	345.19	209.62
1990	113.8	117.3	122.8	123.7	120.7	137.6		934.65	527.43	447.97	309.33	138.64	79.46	364.81	225.73
1991	114.8	111.8	105.2	97.9	109.4	102.0	138.9	1045.73	572.63	479.04	325.30	153.74	93.59	421.32	279.06
1992	105.7	108.4	121.4	113.0	125.3	114.7	105.7	1279.75	641.79	531.59	357.89	173.70	110.20	571.96	346.67
1993	116.2	106.9	111.0	109.1	104.7	110.9	115.1	1662.76	879.25	673.10	453.61	219.49	206.15	684.59	485.19
1994	119.4	127.2	113.2	115.9	137.2	112.0	122.0	2224.43	1198.86	929.14	597.12	332.02	269.72	883.44	670.35
1995	122.8	135.7	108.7	102.4	105.8	103.7	158.4	3000.26	1595.23	1253.06	819.64	433.42	342.17	1244.31	874.87

Year	v5b2	v5c	v5c1	v5c2	v6a1	v6a2	v6a3	v6a4	v6b2	v6b3	v6b4	v7	v7a	v7a1	v7a2
1952	1.73	-0.04													
1953	4.43	0.86										110.1	109.2	109.1	109.6
1954	3.64	2.42										103.0	102.8	101.2	114.8
1955	2.59	0.59										105.3	105.7	106.0	104.1
1956	1.88	-0.75										104.6	102.3	100.0	117.2
1957	5.32	-0.81										100.0	99.9	96.6	120.0
1958	7.11	-9.64										103.8	104.0	104.1	103.7
1959	9.32	-11.82										92.0	89.9	82.6	124.8
1960	-1.10	-2.03										97.8	96.0	89.7	116.3
1961	-5.96	2.39										104.9	105.4	104.4	107.7
1962	-4.83	-0.51										100.6	102.6	103.2	101.1
1963	1.58	-8.92										101.7	101.1	101.2	100.8
1964	1.96	-1.63										100.9	100.8	95.0	115.1
1965	2.70	5.69										105.7	105.7	105.9	105.1
1966	7.02	6.69										112.3	113.1	116.6	105.8
1967	6.49	10.05										108.9	110.4	114.2	102.0
1968	6.13	7.33										98.9	98.7	99.0	98.0
1969	7.27	5.70										105.5	105.4	104.0	109.0
1970	13.16	1.00										109.5	110.1	111.6	106.4
1971	9.49	8.42										108.7	107.5	110.8	99.7
1972	10.14	7.66										111.3	107.9	106.1	112.9
1973	11.33	4.82										105.8	105.3	105.3	105.2
1974	9.93	1.28										105.7	105.3	104.6	107.2
1975	10.49	1.35										105.9	103.3	102.9	104.3
1976	9.00	0.28										109.4	111.2	114.7	102.1
1977	14.68	0.29										103.0	104.0	104.4	102.6
1978	11.83	3.36			42.37	22.66	2.27	3.15	22.29	1.12	0.48	118.3	118.7	118.3	119.9
1979	14.09	2.53			49.16	30.89	2.30	3.75	24.90	1.45	0.56	118.6	119.6	122.1	112.6
1980	11.50	8.48			48.10	48.89	2.18	5.19	28.50	1.73	0.64	113.7	114.2	116.4	107.5
1981	20.92	8.74			51.59	51.77	2.77	6.49	30.59	3.21	0.67	107.5	107.5	107.1	108.8
1982	5.05	9.14			57.28	55.52	2.89	7.64	32.61	3.29	0.72	109.6	107.3	108.2	104.4
1983	27.07	18.31			56.28	58.46	2.92	7.97	35.31	3.69	0.80	104.7	102.0	101.0	105.6
1984	28.95	17.05			59.16	68.30	3.78	8.08	44.36	3.36	0.85	113.6	112.9	100.9	119.7
1985	35.24	2.36			73.00	75.73	5.13	12.30	55.68	8.11	1.16	118.8	117.8	115.2	125.7
1986	25.16	11.00			76.03	86.20	6.76	13.69	63.04	9.38	1.77	106.4	106.1	105.7	107.2
1987	49.58	41.14			78.76	91.25	11.57	19.47	72.60	9.72	1.72	105.6	104.8	104.8	104.9
1988	85.52	30.61			79.64	120.42	14.93	20.35	96.24	14.07	3.22	104.3	104.4	102.2	110.6
1989	135.57	39.19			84.97	134.62	21.28	23.95	110.07	16.83	3.75	102.1	102.1	102.0	102.3
1990	139.08	42.41			115.85	143.86	21.17	28.45	113.94	20.35	4.35	104.6	103.8	102.9	106.7
1991	142.26	51.78			121.63	146.62	24.57	32.48	125.63	22.27	5.84	106.0	104.9	104.6	105.6
1992	225.29	66.00			137.37	153.58	32.61	34.33	140.26	26.37	7.07	107.7	106.4	104.6	110.3
1993	199.40	98.92			193.68	169.52	42.53	47.88	180.46	28.39	10.64	122.7	119.6	118.8	121.3
1994	213.09	142.13			239.62	235.92	56.05	65.53	279.03	39.06	13.93	112.8	108.4	107.8	109.6
1995	369.44	160.72			301.73	380.85	66.68	70.38	350.78	56.45	26.19	111.2	111.0	111.5	109.9

Year	v7b	v8	v8a	v8b	v9	v9a	v9b	v10a1	v10a2	v10a3	v10a3a	v10a3b	v10a4	v10b1	v10b2
1952		64	60	132											
1953	124.8	69	65	135	108.2	108.4	102.5								
1954	105.6	70	65	129	100.6	100.2	95.6								
1955	99.0	72	68	121	103.1	104.1	93.7								
1956	142.4	72	66	149	100.4	97.7	123.0								
1957	100.3	71	62	186	97.9	94.2	125.1								
1958	103.8	76	68	176	101.8	103.4	85.0								
1959	116.9	68	56	179	88.7	82.8	104.0								
1960	113.7	67	52	194	97.2	91.7	107.8								
1961	101.2	72	54	234	107.3	105.3	118.5								
1962	84.6	75	56	287	101.3	99.9	122.1								
1963	107.4	74	56	298	98.7	98.3	104.0								
1964	101.5	72	53	302	99.2	93.8	108.8								
1965	106.3	74	55	291	103.6	104.0	100.1								
1966	105.5	79	60	290	110.0	113.3	104.0								
1967	94.4	85	67	291	107.7	111.2	101.5								
1968	100.5	82	65	289	96.2	96.3	98.5								
1969	105.9	83	65	316	102.1	100.5	109.2								
1970	102.7	88	70	326	106.8	108.2	103.2								
1971	121.8	92	74	294	104.6	108.4	90.2								
1972	146.6	96	76	316	105.2	103.6	107.3								
1973	109.8	98	78	333	102.6	102.4	105.6								
1974	108.1	101	79	351	102.9	102.1	105.5								
1975	124.8	102	80	362	101.5	101.0	103.1								
1976	98.8	112	91	365	109.6	113.0	100.6								
1977	96.8	115	94	369	102.5	103.0	100.5								
1978	115.7	135	109	428	116.9	116.7	116.3	19.82	12.10	8.74	0.82	7.92		8.38	2.95
1979	110.7	159	132	447	117.6	120.8	104.4	19.51	14.35	12.51	1.55	10.96		11.14	2.95
1980	109.4	187	159	471	112.5	115.5	98.6	21.37	14.71	21.62	5.73	15.89		8.82	2.68
1981	107.5	200	169	496	106.0	106.0	102.7	25.12	18.74	11.34	0.82	10.52		10.59	10.33
1982	128.1	214	183	502	105.6	106.9	99.4	30.09	22.44	13.57	0.98	12.59		-0.44	5.49
1983	123.6	218	185	523	100.4	99.7	101.4	39.94	6.09	24.14	1.12	23.02	17.97	9.43	17.64
1984	117.2	244	202	605	111.3	109.8	113.5	57.70	29.53	14.64	1.46	13.18		4.73	13.68
1985	124.1	297	240	750	116.2	114.5	116.4	75.06	15.65	37.26	3.56	33.70	10.22	25.14	9.99
1986	108.4	324	257	817	104.4	104.4	102.3	89.82	20.18	48.84	3.91	44.93		27.20	-2.04
1987	109.8	353	284	898	102.8	103.0	101.4	104.15	24.34	45.71	5.49	40.22		23.42	26.16
1988	103.7	424	325	1148	102.3	100.6	105.1	110.05	28.17	52.74	6.88	45.86	31.37	46.77	38.75
1989	102.0	471	360	1256	100.0	100.3	88.7	105.06	24.66	53.11	7.01	46.10	26.79	99.49	36.08
1990	108.0	523	413	1273	101.8	101.3	111.7	122.46	28.19	55.03	6.18	48.85	20.05	98.67	26.40
1991	112.4	550	429	1362	103.2	103.3	101.8	164.06	25.56	62.28	6.93	55.35	27.16	78.46	39.76
1992	115.1	603	469	1478	105.1	103.8	106.0	223.86	39.43	60.23	9.50	50.73	23.15	107.64	105.39
1993	138.6	756	592	1762	118.4	118.4	114.4	284.04	79.89	98.35	18.41	79.94	22.91	80.27	104.36
1994	132.2	1034	781	2476	107.3	108.0	101.8	421.42	102.21	90.34	22.63	67.71	56.38	-15.35	174.21
1995	112.0	1382	1075	3016	110.1	111.8	102.6	478.44	171.25	123.90	32.59	91.31	101.28	40.60	300.39

Year	v10b4	v11a	v11a1	v11a2	v11b	v11b1	v11b2	v11c	v11c1	v11c2	v12	v12a	v12b	v13	v13i
1952															
1953											110.5	66.9	250.7		
1954											69.0	136.9	80.0		
1955											195.7	165.1	71.5		
1956											120.2	133.9	73.8		
1957											133.8	110.5	277.5		
1958											183.1	201.9	137.0		
1959											128.4	124.9	140.8		
1960											83.9	112.6			
1961											17.3	28.9			
1962											67.1	83.0			
1963											276.3	118.1			
1964											127.3	120.6	192.3		
1965											125.2	124.4	130.0		
1966											157.4	138.5	266.5		
1967											76.9	71.2	93.8		
1968											81.5	75.4	95.5		
1969											155.8	174.7	121.7		
1970											173.7	168.6	186.8		
1971											88.5	96.8	69.1		
1972											101.3	99.7	106.6		
1973											111.7	111.8	111.3		
1974											104.2	109.5	87.7		
1975											108.3	107.8	110.3		
1976											91.9	92.9	88.2		
1977											120.8	112.8	152.4		
1978		6.99	5.68	1.31	33.25	28.79	4.46	12.25	6.19	6.06	103.9	111.6	81.4	162.92	91.39
1979		7.72	6.88	0.84	34.00	29.78	4.22	18.74	9.71	9.03	108.3	104.1	125.3	190.09	111.91
1980		7.54	6.91	0.63	39.95	39.74	0.21	21.71	11.05	10.66	113.9	123.5	81.9	229.16	134.18
1981		1.62	3.03	-1.41	40.64	37.04	3.60	33.86	15.13	18.73	109.1	95.3	178.6	249.69	151.29
1982		2.30	2.81	-0.51	50.39	42.27	8.12	18.46	21.02	-2.56	93.4	119.3	23.9	263.30	155.38
1983		8.03	4.31	3.72	73.83	62.25	11.58	33.35	21.58	11.77	159.6	131.1	539.7	327.95	196.92
1984	10.54	8.63	4.65	3.98	84.48	72.10	12.38	37.71	25.12	12.59	104.7	104.6	105.0	370.04	217.59
1985	0.11	1.01	1.26	-0.25	119.53	96.12	23.41	52.89	40.81	12.08	118.7	120.4	113.1	451.74	266.09
1986		9.40	5.94	3.46	118.24	107.48	10.76	56.36	45.42	10.94	101.8	111.1	69.8	502.91	307.14
1987		13.90	6.82	7.08	141.48	123.56	17.92	68.40	43.82	24.58	106.8	95.9	166.2	609.60	373.25
1988		18.83	7.07	11.76	201.20	164.64	36.56	87.82	50.62	37.20	136.2	136.2	163.9	749.09	444.21
1989		6.75	1.01	5.74	225.69	168.82	56.87	112.75	39.79	72.96	103.8	90.7	138.3	850.71	476.53
1990	14.01	8.30	0.86	7.44	234.48	170.12	64.36	122.03	54.75	67.28	101.2	100.2	103.0	934.65	554.91
1991	24.04	13.25	0.70	12.55	269.61	213.06	56.55	138.46	65.30	73.16	108.8	112.8	108.2	1045.73	606.59
1992	12.26	32.75	1.78	30.97	329.47	233.15	96.32	209.74	111.74	98.00	121.9	118.2	128.1	1279.75	706.32
1993	14.77	84.18	12.51	71.67	398.09	310.93	87.16	202.32	161.75	40.57	106.0	115.3	91.5	1662.76	909.42
1994	54.23	129.59	38.41	91.18	430.59	333.90	96.69	323.26	298.04	25.22	112.4	119.7	98.2	2224.43	1422.74
1995	28.45	302.54	62.52	240.02	515.12	433.04	82.08	426.65	379.31	47.34	122.2	118.6	130.8	3002.74	1964.75

Year	v13ii	v13iii	v13iv	v13a	v13ai	v13aii	v13aiii	v13aiv	v13b	v13bi	v13bii	v13biii	v13biv	v13b1	v13b1i
1952															
1953															
1954															
1955															
1956															
1957															
1958															
1959															
1960															
1961															
1962															
1963															
1964															
1965															
1966															
1967															
1968															
1969															
1970															
1971															
1972															
1973															
1974															
1975															
1976															
1977															
1978	16.23	24.03	31.27	64.86	56.96	1.02	1.53	5.35	69.45	23.60	8.66	19.03	18.16	59.20	17.36
1979	17.93	24.00	36.25	77.30	67.70	2.04	1.25	6.31	80.52	31.17	9.34	18.82	21.19	68.54	23.40
1980	22.77	28.57	43.64	93.23	82.55	1.46	1.53	7.69	94.44	35.97	11.77	22.01	24.69	80.51	27.49
1981	22.99	30.42	44.99	106.04	97.23	1.56	1.52	5.73	95.79	34.55	12.62	21.79	26.83	82.51	25.50
1982	27.49	32.40	48.03	108.18	97.59	3.32	1.52	5.75	102.76	36.80	14.23	23.18	28.55	88.52	27.08
1983	37.45	37.38	56.20	143.49	130.35	3.43	2.03	7.68	116.36	41.16	16.60	26.31	32.29	100.35	30.86
1984	41.88	46.64	63.93	155.28	141.06	3.71	2.20	8.31	136.29	44.27	19.44	33.10	39.48	116.56	31.63
1985	53.62	60.91	71.12	173.43	167.80	4.94	0.09	0.60	170.07	57.66	22.23	44.16	46.02	144.39	40.06
1986	57.72	67.99	70.06	179.02	166.61	5.60	6.69	0.12	202.15	83.31	24.71	47.62	46.51	174.47	61.35
1987	60.36	86.10	89.89	220.22	205.79	5.94	8.31	0.18	230.25	93.69	20.75	62.51	53.30	195.75	66.29
1988	71.15	107.56	126.17	240.72	229.81	7.36	2.75	0.80	299.83	121.16	28.47	74.22	75.98	258.38	89.52
1989	106.87	116.95	150.36	289.95	249.76	8.16	4.29	27.74	317.13	128.71	44.52	76.24	67.66	281.71	101.21
1990	119.13	107.04	153.57	325.77	276.72	9.19	4.51	35.35	331.85	147.15	48.32	71.70	64.68	288.58	113.40
1991	141.93	140.99	156.22	334.61	290.68	9.65	4.31	29.97	388.09	162.35	57.16	105.30	63.28	336.26	125.99
1992	184.36	186.24	202.83	353.92	311.43	10.71	4.17	27.61	545.21	222.22	89.70	142.11	91.18	481.11	178.01
1993	236.01	224.01	293.32	410.45	382.57	12.54	5.29	10.05	768.89	311.54	100.53	177.47	179.35	681.65	263.46
1994	301.73	256.16	243.80	546.68	502.46	12.92	9.67	21.63	1071.74	607.88	151.23	207.78	104.85	958.00	542.16
1995	343.01	356.58	338.40	762.99	695.58	15.32	12.12	39.97	1420.25	827.97	152.26	282.46	157.56	1274.89	740.18

Year	v13b1ii	v13b1iii	v13b1iv	v13b2	v13b2i	v13b2ii	v13b2iii	v13b2iv	v13c	v13ci	v13cii	v13ciii	v13civ	v13c1
1952														
1953														
1954														
1955														
1956														
1957														
1958														
1959														
1960														
1961														
1962														
1963														
1964														
1965														
1966														
1967														
1968														
1969														
1970														
1971														
1972														
1973														
1974														
1975														
1976														
1977														
1978	7.67	18.14	16.03	10.25	6.24	0.99	0.89	2.13	28.61	10.83	6.55	3.47	7.76	6.91
1979	8.99	17.70	18.55	11.88	7.77	0.35	1.12	2.64	32.27	13.04	6.55	3.93	8.75	7.79
1980	10.42	20.80	21.80	13.93	8.48	1.35	1.21	2.89	41.49	15.66	9.54	5.03	11.26	10.02
1981	12.08	20.87	24.16	13.18	9.05	0.54	0.92	2.67	47.86	19.51	8.81	7.11	12.43	11.96
1982	13.68	22.18	25.68	14.14	9.72	0.55	1.00	2.87	52.36	20.99	9.94	7.70	13.73	13.09
1983	14.98	25.26	29.25	16.01	10.30	1.62	1.05	3.04	68.10	25.41	17.42	9.04	16.23	17.02
1984	17.60	31.70	35.73	19.63	12.64	1.84	1.40	3.75	78.47	32.26	18.73	11.34	16.14	19.71
1985	20.50	42.47	41.36	25.68	17.60	1.73	1.69	4.66	108.24	40.63	26.45	16.66	24.50	24.82
1986	24.04	45.77	43.31	27.68	21.96	0.67	1.85	3.20	121.74	57.22	27.41	13.68	23.43	26.31
1987	20.05	60.17	49.24	34.50	27.40	0.70	2.34	4.06	159.13	73.77	33.67	15.28	36.41	30.08
1988	26.95	69.80	72.11	41.45	31.64	1.52	4.42	3.87	208.54	93.24	35.32	30.59	49.39	42.02
1989	42.57	73.36	64.57	35.42	27.50	1.95	2.88	3.09	243.63	98.06	54.19	36.42	54.96	51.18
1990	45.95	67.78	61.45	43.27	33.75	2.37	3.92	3.23	277.03	131.04	61.62	30.83	53.54	59.65
1991	53.66	98.62	57.99	51.83	36.36	3.50	6.68	5.29	323.03	153.56	75.12	31.38	62.97	72.68
1992	87.29	130.75	85.06	64.10	44.21	2.41	11.36	6.12	380.62	172.67	83.95	39.96	84.04	82.52
1993	94.97	166.18	157.04	87.24	48.08	5.56	11.29	22.31	483.42	215.31	122.94	41.25	103.92	103.82
1994	147.09	197.37	71.38	113.74	65.72	4.14	10.41	33.47	606.01	312.40	137.58	38.71	117.32	113.06
1995	143.76	270.52	120.43	145.36	87.79	8.50	11.94	37.13	819.50	441.20	175.43	62.00	140.87	164.03

Year	v13c1i	v13c1ii	v13c1iii	v13c1iv	v13c2	v13c2i	v13c2ii	v13c2iii	v13c2iv	v13c3	v13c3i	v13c3ii	v13c3iii	v13c3iv
1952														
1953														
1954														
1955														
1956														
1957														
1958														
1959														
1960														
1961														
1962														
1963														
1964														
1965														
1966														
1967														
1968														
1969														
1970														
1971														
1972														
1973														
1974														
1975														
1976														
1977														
1978	1.57	1.37	1.21	2.76	7.88	3.29	0.54	1.86	2.19	3.30	0.43	0.07	0.29	2.51
1979	1.85	1.26	1.43	3.25	8.88	3.62	0.81	2.04	2.41	3.72	0.57	0.07	0.34	2.74
1980	2.28	1.98	1.76	4.00	11.42	4.77	0.79	2.69	3.17	4.78	0.62	0.11	0.43	3.62
1981	2.46	1.64	2.79	5.07	12.00	5.54	0.90	3.58	1.98	5.97	0.83	0.09	0.40	4.65
1982	2.63	2.04	2.99	5.43	13.13	6.04	1.01	3.92	2.16	6.53	0.67	0.10	0.43	5.33
1983	2.64	5.92	3.00	5.46	17.08	7.75	1.54	5.02	2.77	8.49	0.83	0.14	0.56	6.96
1984	4.64	5.82	3.44	5.81	18.29	9.62	1.58	6.78	0.31	10.78	1.09	0.18	0.61	8.90
1985	6.31	7.68	6.09	4.74	27.34	10.47	2.37	9.10	5.40	15.15	1.16	0.20	0.92	12.87
1986	13.07	7.43	1.56	4.25	31.17	16.25	1.93	10.46	2.53	18.66	1.65	0.30	1.32	15.39
1987	17.91	4.75	1.65	5.77	42.11	23.19	3.53	10.69	4.70	27.85	2.51	0.43	2.05	22.86
1988	18.61	6.98	3.99	12.44	65.25	30.01	4.31	22.32	8.61	31.05	1.78	0.53	2.25	26.49
1989	21.21	12.28	4.61	13.08	71.14	28.88	13.09	25.40	3.77	41.03	1.93	0.69	3.58	34.83
1990	22.08	17.65	5.82	14.10	58.17	36.63	8.61	18.34	-5.41	48.25	3.86	0.92	3.81	39.66
1991	22.14	21.51	9.26	19.77	73.82	52.07	9.74	14.59	-2.58	52.74	6.55	2.00	4.39	39.80
1992	24.14	23.80	10.74	23.84	84.95	53.40	9.88	19.88	1.79	65.85	7.43	2.27	5.40	50.75
1993	28.33	42.26	11.71	21.52	101.64	71.41	11.37	17.06	1.80	87.47	7.99	2.39	7.90	69.19
1994	55.14	28.60	13.79	15.53	136.13	97.06	15.80	11.60	11.67	100.33	15.14	3.55	8.92	72.72
1995	96.19	43.09	15.15	9.60	182.75	130.31	20.77	28.43	3.24	141.10	16.73	5.48	14.14	104.75

Year	v13c4	v13c4i	v13c4ii	v13c4iii	v13c4iv	v13c5	v13c5i	v13c5ii	v13c5iii	v13c5iv	v13c6	v13c6i	v13c6ii	v13c6iii
1952														
1953														
1954														
1955														
1956														
1957														
1958														
1959														
1960														
1961														
1962														
1963														
1964														
1965														
1966														
1967														
1968														
1969														
1970														
1971														
1972														
1973														
1974														
1975														
1976														
1977														
1978	2.84	0.06	2.78			0.79	0.53	0.06	0.06	0.14	1.21	0.96	0.23	
1979	3.21	0.52	2.69			0.89	0.60	0.06	0.06	0.17	1.36	1.12	0.22	
1980	4.12	0.08	4.04			1.15	0.75	0.09	0.08	0.23	1.75	1.38	0.34	
1981	4.92	0.56	4.35		0.01	1.96	1.21	0.13	0.18	0.44	1.75	1.48	0.25	
1982	5.38	0.60	4.77		0.01	2.15	1.33	0.15	0.19	0.48	1.91	1.61	0.28	
1983	7.00	0.10	6.90			2.79	1.73	0.21	0.24	0.61	2.49	2.05	0.40	
1984	7.86	0.04	7.82			3.32	2.28	0.26	0.26	0.52	2.93	2.47	0.42	
1985	12.38	0.11	12.27			4.44	2.91	0.65	0.42	0.46	3.89	3.33	0.48	
1986	14.09	0.13	13.96			3.40	2.58	0.33	0.31	0.18	4.19	3.49	0.64	
1987	19.74	0.15	19.59			5.82	3.82	0.52	0.67	0.81	4.81	4.07	0.66	
1988	15.93	0.18	15.73		0.02	6.78	5.27	0.38	0.72	0.41	8.98	7.03	1.19	0.54
1989	19.36	0.17	19.17		0.02	8.17	4.82	0.90	1.36	1.09	9.34	7.18	1.35	0.56
1990	23.94	0.21	23.27	0.03	0.43	9.78	6.19	0.98	1.12	1.49	11.68	9.08	1.48	0.70
1991	28.10	0.42	26.85	0.15	0.68	11.55	6.44	1.97	1.23	1.91	12.84	9.98	1.64	0.77
1992	32.60	0.54	30.90	0.24	0.92	15.19	7.99	2.22	1.59	3.39	15.51	12.29	1.88	0.91
1993	49.83	0.58	47.77	0.38	1.10	19.86	11.05	2.46	1.64	4.71	17.85	14.50	1.98	0.83
1994	63.72	0.82	60.61	0.90	1.39	32.32	17.53	6.59	2.04	6.16	24.54	18.15	2.91	0.04
1995	82.53	2.36	78.68	1.41	0.08	49.96	34.52	9.75	1.57	4.12	37.08	31.54	1.12	0.08

Year	v13c6iv	v13c7	v13c7i	v13c7ii	v13c7iii	v13c7iv	v13c8	v13c8i	v13c8ii	v13c8iii	v13c8iv	v13c9	v13c9i	v13c9ii
1952														
1953														
1954														
1955														
1956														
1957														
1958														
1959														
1960														
1961														
1962														
1963														
1964														
1965														
1966														
1967														
1968														
1969														
1970														
1971														
1972														
1973														
1974														
1975														
1976														
1977														
1978	0.02	3.24	2.00	1.13	0.05	0.06	0.50	0.30	0.18		0.02	1.94	1.69	0.19
1979	0.02	3.66	2.43	1.09	0.06	0.08	0.57	0.39	0.17		0.01	2.19	1.94	0.18
1980	0.03	4.70	2.89	1.64	0.07	0.10	0.73	0.44	0.27		0.02	2.82	2.45	0.28
1981	0.02	5.63	4.23	1.05	0.16	0.19	0.85	0.61	0.22		0.02	2.82	2.59	0.18
1982	0.02	6.16	4.61	1.15	0.17	0.23	0.93	0.67	0.24		0.02	3.08	2.83	0.20
1983	0.04	8.01	5.83	1.67	0.22	0.29	1.21	0.83	0.35		0.03	4.01	3.65	0.29
1984	0.04	9.17	6.81	1.80	0.25	0.31	1.88	1.31	0.47		0.10	4.53	4.00	0.38
1985	0.08	11.02	8.42	1.88	0.13	0.59	3.26	2.64	0.49		0.13	5.94	5.28	0.43
1986	0.06	13.16	10.52	1.95	0.03	0.66	3.41	2.92	0.40		0.09	7.35	6.61	0.47
1987	0.08	14.75	11.37	2.03	0.22	1.13	5.43	3.92	0.61		0.90	8.54	6.83	1.55
1988	0.22	18.71	14.78	2.83	0.39	0.71	4.94	3.30	0.94	0.21	0.49	14.88	12.28	2.43
1989	0.25	18.19	13.79	2.85	0.29	1.26	6.61	4.53	1.16	0.29	0.63	18.08	15.15	2.60
1990	0.42	22.92	17.22	3.69	0.36	1.65	8.58	5.91	1.29	0.33	1.05	32.93	29.06	3.49
1991	0.45	23.47	17.06	4.37	0.37	1.67	9.52	7.08	1.25	0.42	0.77	36.30	30.51	5.37
1992	0.43	27.55	21.23	4.02	0.45	1.85	11.40	7.24	3.08	0.52	0.56	42.74	36.82	5.45
1993	0.54	32.83	24.91	5.65	0.53	1.74	15.91	9.33	2.96	0.64	2.98	51.35	45.24	5.55
1994	3.44	45.98	34.96	7.53	0.50	2.99	17.85	11.68	2.82	0.59	2.76	68.96	59.86	8.58
1995	4.34	56.03	42.91	5.17	0.22	7.73	22.37	14.92	4.93	0.81	1.71	77.51	70.24	5.82

Year	v13c9iii	v13c9iv	v13c10	v13c10i	v13c10ii	v13c10iii	v13c10iv
1952							
1953							
1954							
1955							
1956							
1957							
1958							
1959							
1960							
1961							
1962							
1963							
1964							
1965							
1966							
1967							
1968							
1969							
1970							
1971							
1972							
1973							
1974							
1975							
1976							
1977							
1978		0.06					
1979		0.07					
1980		0.09					
1981		0.05					
1982		0.05					
1983		0.07					
1984		0.15					
1985		0.23					
1986		0.27					
1987		0.16					
1988	0.17						
1989	0.33		0.53	0.40	0.10		0.03
1990	0.38		1.13	0.80	0.24	-0.06	0.15
1991	0.42		2.01	1.31	0.42	-0.22	0.50
1992	0.47		2.31	1.59	0.45	-0.24	0.51
1993	0.56		2.86	1.97	0.55		0.34
1994	0.52		3.12	2.06	0.59	-0.19	0.66
1995	0.19	1.26	6.14	1.48	0.62		4.04

17

Hubei

Year	v1	v1a	v1b	v1b1	v1b2	v1c	v1c1	v1c2	v1c3	v2	v2a	v2b	v2b1	v2b2	v2c
1952	44.61	16.59	11.49	9.99	1.50	16.53	1.08	7.02	8.43						
1953	55.83	19.64	15.90	13.60	2.30	20.29	1.61	8.33	10.35	109.7	107.7	124.3	132.5	88.2	103.4
1954	48.06	16.13	16.79	14.69	2.10	15.14	2.19	5.23	7.72	93.2	82.7	112.2	112.5	110.4	91.4
1955	59.16	21.57	19.30	16.26	3.04	18.29	2.88	6.08	9.33	121.8	129.6	113.6	111.8	126.0	121.1
1956	77.25	26.13	25.79	20.66	5.13	25.33	3.05	9.36	12.92	127.7	115.1	139.7	135.6	164.4	131.4
1957	85.31	28.60	30.55	24.31	6.24	26.16	3.37	9.45	13.34	105.9	106.7	113.9	112.9	119.0	98.3
1958	112.42	31.80	50.33	34.93	15.40	30.29	4.62	10.22	15.45	127.0	107.3	160.1	141.8	242.2	115.6
1959	123.96	29.29	61.83	49.57	12.26	32.84	5.97	10.12	16.75	108.4	87.2	122.3	139.3	77.9	110.2
1960	134.03	26.97	76.33	59.92	16.41	30.73	6.31	8.75	15.67	105.8	86.0	124.5	120.4	143.9	93.2
1961	90.87	29.28	38.59	33.55	5.04	23.00	4.21	7.06	11.73	62.4	95.8	47.2	53.0	24.7	69.0
1962	98.15	33.66	38.14	34.83	3.31	26.35	5.09	7.82	13.44	106.6	113.0	96.1	99.8	65.8	114.5
1963	107.11	39.19	43.74	39.19	4.55	24.18	3.99	7.86	12.33	102.0	116.2	115.0	113.1	139.2	73.5
1964	116.05	39.87	50.36	44.85	5.51	25.82	4.50	8.15	13.17	110.8	103.4	118.3	118.5	116.2	109.0
1965	137.71	47.48	59.50	52.90	6.60	30.73	6.38	8.68	15.67	119.3	115.7	124.9	123.0	144.8	113.9
1966	164.23	60.68	74.37	66.71	7.66	29.18	5.37	8.93	14.88	111.1	108.3	120.3	120.4	119.2	96.1
1967	154.25	57.08	68.35	60.95	7.40	28.82	4.93	9.19	14.70	93.4	93.1	91.9	91.4	96.3	98.0
1968	132.39	55.38	51.44	45.81	5.63	25.57	4.58	7.95	13.04	84.5	97.1	75.1	75.2	74.7	88.1
1969	149.63	51.78	66.89	59.46	7.43	30.96	5.31	9.86	15.79	114.0	89.8	130.3	129.8	134.4	121.6
1970	196.73	51.27	106.50	86.27	20.23	38.96	8.83	10.26	19.87	143.3	115.7	163.5	145.1	317.1	132.7
1971	217.03	60.56	118.16	95.31	22.85	38.31	7.24	11.53	19.54	109.6	105.3	117.1	120.6	104.1	97.8
1972	219.92	63.62	116.57	96.97	19.60	39.73	7.97	11.50	20.26	103.6	102.8	103.7	108.1	84.9	104.5
1973	243.27	72.13	128.92	110.92	18.00	42.22	8.24	12.45	21.53	109.3	110.1	110.1	114.4	86.6	105.7
1974	237.01	76.67	118.99	100.78	18.21	41.35	7.50	12.76	21.09	97.1	105.7	92.0	90.9	100.1	98.2
1975	280.72	74.68	156.20	127.99	28.21	49.84	9.65	14.77	25.42	118.3	97.4	130.9	128.6	145.7	120.3
1976	275.19	78.87	143.79	114.84	28.95	52.53	9.59	16.15	26.79	97.7	106.8	91.0	88.9	103.4	105.2
1977	301.35	78.68	168.81	139.15	29.66	53.86	12.51	13.88	27.47	109.5	98.3	118.5	121.2	105.1	102.2
1978	343.08	84.46	201.25	167.21	34.04	57.37	14.08	14.03	29.26	113.1	104.1	119.4	120.3	114.7	105.9
1979	410.91	109.85	234.57	200.82	33.75	66.49	14.82	17.76	33.91	113.0	109.6	114.6	117.7	96.5	112.0
1980	440.52	94.95	268.55	228.02	40.53	77.02	15.57	22.17	39.28	109.6	88.8	115.8	116.3	112.4	115.8
1981	488.12	111.68	287.34	249.72	37.62	89.10	15.86	28.69	44.55	108.7	111.2	106.1	109.7	85.2	114.6
1982	529.01	128.35	310.39	272.08	38.31	90.27	21.34	29.21	39.72	108.8	113.3	109.6	111.3	97.4	100.3
1983	600.35	134.09	361.65	319.21	42.44	104.61	25.51	33.07	46.03	112.0	100.1	115.4	115.2	117.7	116.9
1984	742.13	169.20	421.79	371.93	49.86	151.14	42.22	42.42	66.50	121.8	120.9	116.7	117.4	110.3	140.9
1985	902.19	192.32	535.37	467.22	68.15	174.50	53.08	51.62	69.80	115.0	106.2	120.0	119.3	126.2	109.5
1986	1033.21	219.10	612.33	538.29	74.04	201.78	58.47	58.56	84.75	108.7	103.5	109.7	110.9	100.1	110.5
1987	1238.56	249.68	746.11	659.19	86.92	242.77	69.08	69.30	104.39	111.7	102.7	114.8	115.5	108.5	110.4
1988	1516.43	297.51	935.63	834.84	100.79	283.29	72.59	91.72	118.98	111.4	97.2	117.6	119.0	103.3	103.2
1989	1740.88	335.04	1055.91	976.93	78.98	349.93	87.97	102.19	159.77	105.7	105.0	104.3	106.7	77.2	111.9
1990	1929.46	402.23	1100.91	1008.20	92.71	426.32	114.01	137.52	174.79	105.5	107.1	101.9	101.8	103.0	116.9
1991	2183.59	405.04	1245.20	1136.03	109.17	533.35	156.49	163.52	213.34	108.4	99.2	109.2	109.1	110.2	115.0
1992	2617.24	435.42	1523.00	1373.66	149.34	658.82	192.54	189.33	276.95	113.8	107.0	116.2	116.2	116.0	113.1
1993	3599.25	501.17	2230.27	1992.31	237.96	867.81	228.67	253.78	385.36	112.1	106.7	127.1	126.6	132.8	116.5
1994	5184.32	786.84	3317.12	3024.72	292.40	1080.36	287.80	306.44	486.12	125.3	109.8	133.4	134.9	116.9	112.7
1995	6847.21	988.53	4440.03	4045.19	394.84	1418.65	296.76	433.17	688.72	119.7	114.1	123.0	122.9	124.3	112.3

Year	v2c1	v2c2	v3'	v3	v3a	v3b	v3b1	v3b2	v3c	v3c1	v3c2	v3c3	v3c4	v3c5	v3c6
1952			24.51	24.51	13.90	3.83	3.17	0.66	6.78	0.49	5.09				
1953	143.5	114.6	30.23	30.23	16.41	5.33	4.31	1.02	8.49	0.83	6.23				
1954	136.2	61.6	25.51	25.51	12.97	5.97	5.26	0.71	6.57	1.16	3.86				
1955	130.0	115.2	34.05	34.05	18.14	7.45	6.25	1.20	8.46	1.62	4.59				
1956	105.8	151.8	44.60	44.60	22.29	10.24	8.42	1.82	12.07	1.68	7.41				
1957	110.0	88.6	48.86	48.86	24.33	11.59	9.03	2.56	12.94	1.85	7.61				
1958	137.6	105.9	61.50	61.50	26.80	19.69	12.73	6.96	15.01	2.60	8.35				
1959	130.6	97.6	64.22	64.22	24.77	22.59	18.96	3.63	16.86	3.08	8.29				
1960	104.6	82.0	63.61	63.61	23.60	23.62	17.59	6.03	16.39	3.25	7.19				
1961	66.7	73.2	48.91	48.91	25.86	10.20	8.52	1.68	12.85	2.12	5.51				
1962	120.9	108.6	52.13	52.13	29.30	10.63	9.10	1.53	12.20	2.02	5.37				
1963	39.2	102.1	56.30	56.30	32.25	12.28	10.31	1.97	11.77	1.86	5.47				
1964	112.9	106.2	61.43	61.43	32.22	16.94	14.59	2.35	12.27	2.05	5.49				
1965	141.7	86.3	72.43	72.43	37.74	21.16	17.36	3.80	13.53	2.82	5.51				
1966	78.5	132.0	83.95	83.95	45.77	24.58	21.44	3.14	13.60	2.38	5.79				
1967	90.5	102.6	78.92	78.92	43.65	20.88	18.00	2.88	14.39	2.35	6.36				
1968	93.1	86.5	73.12	73.12	42.86	16.59	14.41	2.18	13.67	2.11	5.42				
1969	116.1	124.0	76.09	76.09	39.52	21.45	18.41	3.04	15.12	2.28	5.88				
1970	172.1	103.8	88.15	88.15	44.41	26.90	21.79	5.11	16.84	3.63	5.98				
1971	80.6	112.8	100.12	100.12	45.41	36.89	28.67	8.22	17.82	3.29	6.53				
1972	107.6	100.1	102.84	102.84	47.45	38.37	31.03	7.34	17.02	3.24	6.29				
1973	104.3	107.9	113.29	113.29	52.55	43.06	35.47	7.59	17.68	3.45	6.62				
1974	93.4	102.4	107.34	107.34	56.80	32.05	24.14	7.91	18.49	3.30	7.12				
1975	127.5	115.8	120.10	120.10	53.71	45.48	32.68	12.80	20.91	4.10	8.20				
1976	99.2	109.3	114.64	114.64	57.87	34.48	21.33	13.15	22.29	4.01	9.45				
1977	129.2	85.8	131.11	131.11	57.52	49.35	39.08	10.27	24.24	4.80	9.71				
1978	112.2	100.4	151.00	151.00	61.11	63.71	52.17	11.54	26.18	4.30	9.69	4.54	1.42	1.42	0.65
1979	105.3	124.1	188.46	188.46	85.15	73.03	58.98	14.05	30.28	4.53	11.21	5.26	1.62	1.50	0.75
1980	105.1	120.0	199.38	199.38	71.22	91.67	75.63	16.04	36.49	4.85	14.09	5.51	2.83	2.14	0.83
1981	112.4	122.6	219.75	219.75	87.00	92.85	77.60	15.25	39.90	4.90	14.96	6.02	3.19	2.31	0.91
1982	134.5	97.9	241.55	241.55	101.73	94.97	80.28	14.69	44.85	5.66	16.82	6.50	3.10	2.40	1.34
1983	118.1	119.5	262.58	262.58	105.40	106.50	92.89	13.61	50.68	6.65	20.24	7.09	2.53	3.30	1.52
1984	152.0	129.6	328.22	328.22	126.36	136.50	119.69	16.81	65.36	9.24	24.90	9.04	3.89	3.61	3.40
1985	127.2	109.4	396.26	396.26	144.44	174.35	152.88	21.47	77.47	14.77	30.16	10.71	4.61	3.09	2.95
1986	106.6	108.1	442.04	442.04	163.61	187.96	164.93	23.03	90.47	16.98	33.20	13.68	5.97	3.61	3.44
1987	105.2	109.0	517.77	517.77	183.99	224.53	197.66	26.87	109.25	18.94	40.67	17.09	7.39	4.69	4.30
1988	93.9	112.0	628.06	626.52	214.66	271.25	244.17	27.08	140.61	23.03	47.95	20.82	8.88	6.23	5.02
1989	104.1	99.4	718.55	717.08	239.07	300.46	276.46	23.99	177.55	33.05	58.01	28.14	9.18	6.98	6.50
1990	126.7	126.3	825.83	824.38	289.45	313.39	284.15	29.24	221.54	37.25	69.35	33.77	11.38	10.26	9.41
1991	113.5	112.6	915.00	913.38	279.30	359.86	327.50	32.36	274.22	47.37	86.66	40.30	13.61	14.02	11.68
1992	115.1	109.3	1090.59	1088.39	303.00	444.61	402.59	42.02	340.78	56.53	112.25	48.07	17.22	18.95	14.52
1993	109.8	121.4	1427.47	1424.38	346.39	627.69	564.54	63.15	450.30	68.85	149.98	63.42	25.23	35.26	18.55
1994	111.9	113.1	1882.66	1878.65	501.44	812.56	733.25	79.31	564.65	87.46	175.32	86.68	36.69	39.33	23.44
1995	112.4	114.8	2396.77	2391.42	619.77	1029.85	925.75	104.10	741.80	114.92	239.16	107.01	40.15	55.49	30.67

Year	v3c7	v3c8	v3c9	v3c10	v3d	v4'	v4	v4a	v4b	v4b1	v4b2	v4c	v4c1	v4c2	v4c3
1952				1.20	90	113.8	113.8	109.6	127.4	136.2	103.2	118.5	114.1	139.2	
1953				1.43	109	114.0	114.0	107.4	129.4	126.3	144.4	122.7	157.0	118.2	
1954				1.55	90	83.9	83.9	79.5	112.2	122.4	69.2	75.8	145.8	60.7	
1955				2.25	118	127.1	127.1	135.5	104.9	99.8	143.1	127.1	137.9	117.8	
1956				2.98	152	129.8	129.8	116.7	159.5	156.4	175.7	141.8	103.7	159.3	
1957				3.48	162	107.4	107.4	106.4	115.3	109.2	143.1	102.6	109.8	90.3	
1958				4.06	198	123.2	123.2	106.3	174.6	144.9	279.1	114.1	140.1	107.5	
1959				5.49	203	96.0	96.0	87.5	97.0	126.0	44.2	111.1	119.4	97.9	
1960				5.95	201	100.0	100.0	92.1	117.2	104.1	186.0	92.1	104.6	82.2	
1961				5.22	154	70.0	70.0	94.0	47.9	53.7	30.8	65.8	65.2	69.5	
1962				4.81	161	100.9	100.9	112.3	84.0	86.0	73.9	94.0	95.7	95.4	
1963				4.44	170	110.0	110.0	109.8	116.1	113.9	129.2	104.6	45.9	103.5	
1964				4.73	182	111.8	111.8	101.4	142.4	146.2	122.6	107.9	109.7	102.8	
1965				5.20	209	118.1	118.1	111.5	132.5	126.1	171.8	114.9	138.3	81.7	
1966				5.43	236	103.3	103.3	104.8	102.2	108.7	72.6	101.2	78.7	134.5	
1967				5.68	216	94.2	94.2	95.4	85.0	83.9	91.8	106.1	97.4	109.2	
1968				6.14	195	92.2	92.2	98.3	79.0	79.5	75.4	95.1	89.4	85.1	
1969				6.96	197	103.7	103.7	89.1	130.2	128.7	139.9	110.4	108.4	108.5	
1970				7.23	222	126.9	126.9	112.2	161.2	152.1	216.5	111.3	165.0	101.5	
1971				8.00	245	113.8	113.8	104.0	134.8	129.4	158.1	106.2	89.0	109.5	
1972				7.49	246	101.9	101.9	102.5	103.9	108.2	89.2	96.1	96.6	96.6	
1973				7.61	266	110.0	110.0	110.7	112.1	114.1	103.3	103.6	107.1	104.9	
1974				8.07	248	92.8	92.8	104.7	73.1	66.9	102.4	104.4	98.5	107.5	
1975				8.61	274	111.4	111.4	94.5	139.0	132.6	158.5	116.0	122.8	115.1	
1976				8.83	258	94.8	94.8	107.8	74.4	64.1	100.7	103.9	97.8	115.2	
1977				9.73	292	115.8	115.8	99.1	150.2	192.3	81.9	108.6	118.2	102.5	
1978	2.00	0.63	1.44	0.09	332	113.5	113.5	103.4	128.4	128.5	128.4	107.4	107.5	107.4	
1979	2.31	0.70	2.31	0.09	409	115.6	115.6	118.9	113.1	115.7	83.4	114.4	104.2	114.3	114.5
1980	2.61	0.92	2.61	0.10	428	106.4	106.4	86.9	123.5	119.4	188.6	111.0	98.4	115.7	96.3
1981	2.85	1.01	3.65	0.10	466	106.5	106.5	113.3	101.5	100.5	111.7	104.9	96.9	101.9	104.8
1982	3.14	1.10	4.70	0.09	506	112.1	112.1	115.7	104.7	104.7	104.7	121.6	124.8	121.5	116.9
1983	3.34	1.30	4.55	0.11	549	105.8	105.8	99.6	109.9	109.8	111.2	111.5	116.1	119.1	107.5
1984	4.35	1.32	5.51	0.10	676	120.9	120.9	114.4	125.0	125.2	123.2	125.2	134.8	119.1	123.8
1985	5.16	1.56	4.34	0.12	808	116.2	116.2	108.3	124.7	125.9	113.3	112.4	151.6	114.9	112.4
1986	6.49	1.82	5.07	0.21	891	105.5	105.5	103.3	105.2	105.4	103.1	110.2	104.3	103.8	120.5
1987	8.07	2.12	5.62	0.36	1031	108.4	108.4	103.1	111.3	104.2	185.1	110.7	106.3	112.3	114.5
1988	10.52	3.49	14.19	0.48	1228	108.2	107.8	94.9	113.7	119.8	77.9	114.3	106.9	106.8	107.0
1989	11.83	5.10	17.27	1.49	1383	104.5	104.5	105.2	102.1	104.0	85.3	109.3	125.9	92.7	121.8
1990	16.58	7.38	25.16	1.00	1556	105.0	105.0	107.5	99.0	99.0	99.2	114.8	103.4	117.9	108.9
1991	19.17	9.34	29.93	2.14	1689	106.6	106.6	95.1	111.1	111.1	111.1	115.4	107.1	118.6	114.4
1992	22.65	11.80	36.24	2.54	1986	114.1	114.1	108.2	116.6	117.1	112.1	116.9	109.1	123.9	111.5
1993	24.66	14.50	46.81	3.04	2565	114.3	114.3	105.8	119.6	119.5	120.1	115.3	106.9	118.0	112.0
1994	34.50	16.59	61.59	3.05	3341	115.3	115.2	107.1	122.1	122.3	119.5	112.6	117.1	110.6	113.9
1995	48.23	23.10	79.02	4.05	4162	114.6	114.6	108.9	118.9	118.7	120.4	112.7	118.3	110.7	113.9

Year	v4c4	v4c5	v4c6	v4c7	v4c8	v4c9	v4c10	v5	v5a	v5a1	v5a1a	v5a1b	v5a2	v5b	v5b1
1952								24.51	21.32	19.78	15.52	4.26	1.54	3.89	1.66
1953								30.23	24.94	22.52	17.72	4.80	2.42	5.27	3.21
1954								25.51	22.78	20.29	15.54	4.75	2.47	5.45	3.69
1955								34.05	28.32	25.03	19.47	5.56	3.29	6.08	4.44
1956								44.60	34.95	30.92	23.81	7.11	4.03	9.43	7.23
1957								47.64	36.72	32.59	24.87	7.72	4.13	13.61	9.53
1958								62.32	37.49	32.13	23.40	8.73	5.36	21.41	14.94
1959								65.72	38.04	32.93	20.53	12.40	5.11	24.22	16.57
1960								63.34	36.12	30.90	17.74	13.16	5.22	20.55	20.13
1961								47.96	28.91	25.48	14.60	10.88	3.43	6.13	4.73
1962								51.99	36.60	34.14	23.17	10.97	2.46	5.83	4.35
1963								57.00	39.65	37.51	27.03	10.48	2.14	9.07	4.46
1964								61.09	42.94	40.67	29.51	11.16	2.27	6.32	4.67
1965								71.30	45.08	42.89	31.25	11.64	2.19	13.09	5.88
1966								84.21	47.55	44.84	32.74	12.10	2.71	15.95	10.21
1967								77.67	47.72	45.13	31.85	13.28	2.59	11.57	8.79
1968								74.67	50.18	47.45	33.32	14.13	2.73	9.75	5.39
1969								78.13	48.75	45.73	30.84	14.89	3.02	18.23	10.68
1970								90.61	52.00	48.41	33.95	14.46	3.59	34.42	28.82
1971								99.77	55.10	50.76	35.06	15.70	4.34	39.86	27.91
1972								100.69	56.86	52.52	35.75	16.77	4.34	27.77	23.24
1973								112.57	60.96	55.83	38.34	17.49	5.13	33.93	18.96
1974								109.73	64.41	58.70	40.17	18.53	5.71	31.84	21.22
1975								123.11	65.50	59.40	40.34	19.06	6.10	48.04	31.62
1976								111.14	70.06	63.91	43.82	20.09	6.15	49.52	34.78
1977								134.60	74.33	68.06	46.13	21.93	6.27	52.12	40.35
1978								151.19	81.70	74.70	50.89	23.81	7.00	43.11	31.40
1979	112.7	104.2	113.8	114.0	109.5	158.3	150.0	193.26	99.77	87.01	59.80	27.21	12.76	47.71	29.49
1980	160.6	131.8	102.7	103.9	121.7	103.9	111.1	200.19	107.79	93.51	61.47	32.04	14.28	40.10	33.19
1981	108.2	103.5	105.1	104.9	105.7	134.6	81.8	214.48	122.14	106.26	72.84	33.42	15.88	49.28	31.31
1982	105.2	112.4	159.8	119.4	117.4	139.0	100.0	243.52	144.99	126.75	90.67	36.08	18.24	65.47	45.60
1983	80.3	135.7	112.2	104.9	116.7	95.7	100.0	270.45	164.19	141.49	101.17	40.32	22.70	69.56	53.01
1984	149.6	106.3	217.0	126.3	98.4	117.5	88.9	328.30	202.86	172.19	120.41	51.78	30.67	97.35	74.00
1985	112.3	81.1	82.1	112.5	112.1	74.7	125.0	386.76	240.02	203.23	129.78	73.45	36.79	135.43	96.71
1986	122.2	110.2	110.3	118.7	110.1	110.1	720.0	454.28	291.48	247.13	158.31	88.82	44.35	146.73	104.74
1987	113.4	119.1	114.5	113.9	106.5	101.6	38.9	499.85	320.46	271.22	172.47	98.75	49.24	168.02	130.98
1988	105.6	116.6	102.4	114.5	144.8	222.0	117.9	612.63	399.38	328.82	204.21	124.61	70.56	223.31	149.87
1989	93.2	101.0	116.8	111.3	133.5	119.5	275.8	718.07	478.66	398.09	255.09	143.00	80.57	201.39	115.50
1990	109.7	129.9	127.8	119.3	126.0	124.3	70.3	818.89	535.49	434.62	273.27	161.35	100.87	261.95	147.13
1991	114.7	121.2	119.0	110.9	112.1	120.6	123.0	913.22	597.42	475.85	286.08	189.77	121.57	281.92	176.32
1992	117.8	128.4	116.2	110.3	115.8	113.1	152.0	1089.68	689.93	546.61	301.60	245.01	143.32	355.46	235.63
1993	119.4	127.1	107.1	108.7	113.7	118.2	122.5	1437.95	870.27	700.07	370.94	329.13	170.20	514.65	377.95
1994	125.3	117.9	106.5	109.0	111.6	108.2	96.1	1895.71	1058.13	858.77	445.95	412.82	199.36	746.91	571.68
1995	119.1	114.0	114.4	113.5	115.7	103.9	108.6	2435.04	1333.82	1122.60	564.83	557.77	211.22	937.03	778.25

Year	v5b2	v5c	v5c1	v5c2	v6a1	v6a2	v6a3	v6a4	v6b2	v6b3	v6b4	v7	v7a	v7a1	v7a2
1952	2.23	-0.70		0.70											
1953	2.06	0.02	1.92	1.90								115.2	112.2	113.1	108.7
1954	1.76	-2.72	0.06	2.78								88.8	87.6	85.0	97.4
1955	1.64	-0.35	0.61	0.96								122.9	122.0	123.5	117.1
1956	2.25	0.17	6.66	6.49								121.8	121.8	119.9	128.6
1957	4.08	-2.69	6.24	8.93								100.8	101.2	101.3	100.7
1958	6.47	3.42	8.29	4.87								99.6	96.0	90.6	113.6
1959	7.65	3.46	4.54	1.08								95.7	95.9	87.0	118.8
1960	0.42	6.67	6.67									89.0	87.8	83.9	95.1
1961	1.40	12.92	12.92									72.2	75.3	70.8	82.6
1962	1.48	9.56	10.49	0.93								125.8	133.1	152.7	105.1
1963	4.61	8.28	12.06	3.78								124.5	126.6	138.2	102.7
1964	1.65	11.83	16.21	4.38								105.5	105.3	103.5	110.2
1965	7.21	13.13	18.67	5.54								109.4	109.9	110.6	108.1
1966	5.75	20.70	26.62	5.92								106.5	105.5	105.7	104.8
1967	2.78	18.38	23.18	4.80								100.7	101.0	97.9	109.5
1968	4.37	14.73	18.69	3.96								105.3	105.2	104.8	106.3
1969	7.55	11.15	16.52	5.37								96.9	96.1	92.5	104.9
1970	5.60	4.19	10.03	5.84								106.8	106.0	110.0	97.6
1971	11.95	4.81	10.81	6.00								106.3	105.2	103.7	108.9
1972	4.53	16.06	25.30	9.24								103.8	104.1	102.7	107.2
1973	14.97	17.68	23.22	5.54								106.9	106.0	106.9	104.0
1974	10.62	13.48	26.43	12.95								105.6	105.1	104.7	106.0
1975	16.42	9.57	40.62	31.05								101.8	101.3	100.5	103.0
1976	14.74	-8.44	34.40	42.84								106.9	107.5	108.5	105.4
1977	11.77	8.15	52.38	44.23								105.9	106.3	105.1	109.1
1978	11.71	26.38	66.71	40.33	18.32	27.98	3.22	1.37	20.01	3.35	0.45	109.4	109.2	109.7	108.3
1979	18.22	45.78	94.61	48.83	21.51	33.68	2.94	1.67	22.86	3.83	0.52	120.7	115.1	116.7	111.8
1980	6.91	52.30	105.34	53.04	22.13	34.42	3.08	1.84	25.63	5.77	0.64	102.7	102.2	99.5	108.2
1981	17.97	43.06	138.72	95.66	24.76	40.06	5.91	2.11	28.41	4.34	0.67	113.8	114.5	120.9	102.2
1982	19.87	33.06	152.81	119.75	32.60	47.15	8.20	2.72	30.67	4.73	0.68	116.0	116.3	120.5	107.0
1983	16.95	36.30	172.82	136.52	38.40	58.67	1.17	2.93	35.88	3.67	0.77	111.8	110.2	110.3	109.9
1984	23.35	28.09	192.37	164.28	44.55	68.63	3.74	3.49	46.08	4.61	1.09	116.6	114.2	110.1	124.8
1985	38.72	11.31	249.30	237.99	53.21	72.16	0.49	3.92	66.84	5.00	1.61	110.1	111.1	103.3	128.6
1986	41.99	16.07	304.37	288.30	57.01	88.16	8.23	4.91	78.39	8.47	1.96	116.4	115.9	116.7	114.6
1987	37.04	11.37	350.65	339.28	62.27	96.05	7.84	6.31	90.43	6.23	2.09	104.7	103.9	103.0	105.6
1988	73.44	-10.36	450.68	460.74	65.09	113.17	19.94	6.01	108.65	13.20	2.76	105.1	102.2	100.8	104.7
1989	85.89	38.02	431.08	393.06	86.25	146.81	13.69	8.34	126.20	13.13	3.67	102.6	103.7	106.4	99.0
1990	114.82	21.45	456.94	435.49	95.43	152.26	16.84	8.74	140.09	17.91	3.35	103.7	104.2	102.8	106.9
1991	105.60	33.88	584.65	550.77	118.17	129.40	26.71	11.80	162.75	23.14	3.88	106.7	104.6	101.1	110.7
1992	119.83	44.29	679.36	635.07	117.20	137.97	33.81	12.62	181.07	54.14	9.80	108.9	106.5	99.0	118.1
1993	136.70	53.03	787.34	734.31	114.85	169.54	67.49	19.06	234.20	78.13	16.80	107.2	105.5	102.2	109.9
1994	175.23	90.67	902.11	811.44	119.23	225.59	75.08	26.05	306.36	79.55	26.91	111.9	113.3	109.7	117.7
1995	208.78	114.19	1080.05	965.86	180.85	268.12	88.81	27.05	400.89	112.20	44.68	110.1	111.8	107.8	116.3

Year	v7b	v8	v8a	v8b	v9	v9a	v9b	v10a1	v10a2	v10a3	v10a3a	v10a3b	v10a4	v10b1	v10b2
1952		73	64	139											
1953	154.5	90	73	147	109.6	112.5	102.2								
1954	100.4	72	62	137	86.3	83.3	91.5								
1955	130.5	87	77	148	111.8	121.7	108.5								
1956	121.8	105	94	184	119.5	119.2	124.8								
1957	98.2	108	96	192	99.0	98.9	96.9								
1958	127.8	104	87	200	93.5	88.4	104.7								
1959	94.3	104	77	253	94.1	86.9	106.0								
1960	96.6	97	68	242	87.4	86.3	85.4								
1961	55.1	81	55	207	75.9	69.8	85.7								
1962	70.9	106	85	231	130.2	147.7	116.0								
1963	94.7	113	95	225	123.2	132.3	105.0								
1964	110.1	120	101	235	103.0	101.2	107.9								
1965	100.0	124	106	240	107.7	109.2	105.9								
1966	125.5	126	107	244	102.7	102.1	102.8								
1967	95.1	124	102	261	98.3	95.9	106.7								
1968	105.6	127	103	274	102.7	101.1	104.6								
1969	110.1	118	92	291	93.1	89.4	105.6								
1970	119.1	122	98	280	102.8	107.1	97.0								
1971	121.4	125	100	279	102.5	102.0	99.6								
1972	100.7	126	100	285	101.6	101.0	102.5								
1973	117.5	131	104	303	103.9	104.0	105.9								
1974	111.2	136	107	319	103.8	103.0	105.6								
1975	107.1	136	106	323	100.0	99.1	101.2								
1976	100.5	144	114	328	105.8	107.5	101.5								
1977	101.9	151	119	345	104.8	104.3	105.2								
1978	111.1	164	131	362	107.9	109.2	104.6	31.03	0.37					7.92	3.14
1979	180.0	189	153	392	114.0	116.0	105.8	28.86	0.63					13.38	4.02
1980	106.3	201	156	437	101.1	98.7	102.6	31.96	1.23					4.08	2.09
1981	109.7	225	184	440	112.9	119.7	98.6	27.60	3.45	0.26	0.26			9.80	6.05
1982	114.0	265	227	463	115.0	119.1	104.2	32.18	7.89	5.53	0.46	5.07		10.37	7.03
1983	122.8	294	252	503	109.2	109.8	106.9	34.65	8.35	10.01	0.83	9.18		7.52	6.97
1984	131.1	355	302	596	113.3	111.0	115.2	44.96	10.92	18.12	7.13	10.99		9.93	11.08
1985	104.9	414	332	744	108.8	105.1	113.2	57.95	16.39	22.37	8.30	14.07		22.59	10.87
1986	119.3	498	406	834	114.6	117.1	106.2	62.43	14.93	27.38	9.98	17.40		25.87	9.10
1987	109.9	540	439	901	102.7	102.4	102.7	79.78	20.86	30.34	12.17	18.17		19.57	11.70
1988	119.6	644	515	1104	100.5	99.7	101.6	95.46	22.99	31.42	13.76	17.66		45.52	19.20
1989	97.6	769	636	1227	102.1	105.2	96.0	75.64	14.73	25.13	10.21	14.92		64.59	13.29
1990	101.0	820	665	1353	101.9	100.3	104.4	102.22	15.88	29.03	10.80	18.23		85.91	21.10
1991	115.6	879	682	1559	102.6	99.1	108.6	124.83	20.43	31.06	11.71	19.35		70.37	28.44
1992	118.1	998	713	1949	105.1	98.2	114.2	179.23	21.95	34.45	13.03	21.42		80.76	31.10
1993	113.1	1261	873	2520	104.2	101.5	105.8	271.62	29.16	40.38	9.88	30.50	36.79	83.23	21.71
1994	107.5	1527	1052	2984	111.8	109.8	111.0	415.71	32.92	56.62	15.08	41.54	66.43	105.85	30.54
1995	104.2	1954	1325	3759	109.4	107.3	108.5	545.37	33.65	99.90	41.23	58.67	99.33	115.81	40.92

Year	v10b4	v11a	v11a1	v11a2	v11b	v11b1	v11b2	v11c	v11c1	v11c2	v12	v12a	v12b	v13	v13i
1952															
1953											126.0	179.5	86.1		
1954											106.7	118.8	88.0		
1955											107.1	115.5	89.3		
1956											152.3	158.9	134.4		
1957											140.6	129.2	176.8		
1958											134.5	134.3	134.8		
1959											111.0	108.6	116.5		
1960											91.2	130.6	5.8		
1961											24.0	18.9	275.3		
1962											95.1	92.1	104.9		
1963											159.3	106.3	315.9		
1964											65.9	97.6	34.3		
1965											250.8	152.4	529.0		
1966											125.0	178.8	82.1		
1967											72.1	85.7	48.0		
1968											82.7	60.2	153.5		
1969											194.5	206.1	180.2		
1970											215.6	308.2	84.7		
1971											106.7	89.2	196.6		
1972											69.0	82.5	37.5		
1973											115.2	76.9	311.6		
1974											92.9	110.8	70.2		
1975											141.9	140.1	145.5		
1976											124.9	142.7	90.4		
1977											94.1	96.8	85.9		
1978	0.65	2.17	2.08	0.09	26.84	23.44	3.40	14.10	5.88	8.22	78.8	74.1	94.7	151.00	86.58
1979	0.82	2.44	2.34	0.10	26.37	19.56	6.81	18.90	7.59	11.31	107.8	91.4	151.6	188.46	113.45
1980	0.74	2.04	2.03	0.01	23.58	20.98	2.60	14.48	10.18	4.30	75.1	99.5	35.7	199.38	110.72
1981	2.12	1.36	1.27	0.09	26.97	20.37	6.60	20.95	9.67	11.28	117.5	91.2	236.3	219.75	125.84
1982	2.47	2.09	1.98	0.11	36.16	28.41	7.75	27.22	15.21	12.01	134.9	147.9	112.2	241.55	140.92
1983	2.46	2.18	2.09	0.09	40.14	33.55	6.59	27.64	17.37	10.27	106.9	116.3	85.3	262.58	151.93
1984	2.34	3.00	2.80	0.20	54.94	45.86	9.08	39.41	25.34	14.07	137.5	131.1	157.6	328.22	185.51
1985	5.26	4.10	3.40	0.70	73.46	58.41	15.05	57.87	34.90	22.97	126.9	120.8	142.8	396.26	223.45
1986	7.02	4.47	3.91	0.56	80.87	63.90	16.97	61.39	36.93	24.46	100.3	98.6	104.0	442.04	245.21
1987	5.77	5.09	4.68	0.41	100.84	84.17	16.67	62.09	42.13	19.96	106.4	117.7	83.1	517.77	288.19
1988	8.72	5.74	5.06	0.68	138.80	100.25	38.55	78.77	44.56	34.21	110.2	101.4	136.2	626.52	347.59
1989	8.01	4.90	4.01	0.89	124.15	74.44	49.71	72.34	37.05	35.29	95.1	87.1	112.8	717.08	420.50
1990	7.81	6.70	5.73	0.97	153.41	88.69	64.72	101.84	52.71	49.13	114.1	107.0	126.1	824.38	498.23
1991	6.79	6.63	5.63	1.00	179.53	105.96	73.57	95.76	64.73	31.03	103.6	114.3	89.8	913.38	543.76
1992	7.97	8.56	7.44	1.12	227.06	137.92	89.14	119.84	90.27	29.57	115.2	122.0	104.1	1088.39	551.05
1993	31.76	32.35	31.34	1.01	260.18	207.04	53.14	222.12	139.57	82.55	121.1	128.8	106.4	1424.38	708.66
1994	38.84	40.94	39.59	1.35	410.24	338.43	71.81	295.73	193.66	102.07	126.5	132.6	112.4	1878.65	948.39
1995	52.05	32.09	29.29	2.80	533.88	419.17	114.71	421.06	329.79	91.27	120.7	120.6	121.0	2391.42	1291.82

Year	v13ii	v13iii	v13iv	v13a	v13ai	v13aii	v13aiii	v13aiv	v13b	v13bi	v13bii	v13biii	v13biv	v13b1	v13b1i
1952															
1953															
1954															
1955															
1956															
1957															
1958															
1959															
1960															
1961															
1962															
1963															
1964															
1965															
1966															
1967															
1968															
1969															
1970															
1971															
1972															
1973															
1974															
1975															
1976															
1977															
1978	13.70	11.72	39.00	61.11	51.42	5.14	1.56	2.99	63.71	22.74	5.12	8.04	27.81	52.17	14.09
1979	17.00	13.72	44.29	85.15	71.74	7.18	2.09	4.14	73.03	26.90	5.97	9.35	30.81	58.98	16.51
1980	18.41	16.40	53.85	71.22	59.92	6.04	1.71	3.55	91.67	33.21	6.91	11.77	39.78	75.63	21.18
1981	20.66	17.73	55.52	87.00	73.19	7.26	2.22	4.33	92.85	33.35	7.27	12.37	39.86	78.73	22.90
1982	22.91	19.21	58.51	101.73	86.02	6.90	2.73	6.08	94.97	33.06	8.73	12.84	40.34	82.69	23.98
1983	24.02	21.80	64.83	105.40	89.06	7.91	2.99	5.44	106.50	38.40	9.15	14.42	44.53	92.19	27.67
1984	33.74	29.05	79.92	126.36	106.29	10.39	3.38	6.30	136.50	48.84	12.91	20.37	54.38	120.32	37.35
1985	29.26	26.51	117.04	144.44	130.86	3.19	4.11	6.28	174.35	57.90	15.06	16.37	85.02	152.88	41.51
1986	45.97	43.56	107.30	163.61	138.63	12.33	4.52	8.13	187.96	63.47	19.72	29.23	75.54	164.93	46.08
1987	53.85	52.61	123.12	183.99	157.04	13.49	5.22	8.24	224.53	77.53	23.55	34.91	88.54	197.66	58.44
1988	60.15	62.35	156.43	214.66	184.81	14.59	5.40	9.86	271.25	96.35	26.55	41.16	107.19	244.17	75.79
1989	76.68	73.17	146.73	239.07	202.47	13.92	7.69	14.99	300.46	118.96	34.51	44.37	102.62	276.46	101.08
1990	97.92	84.45	143.78	289.45	243.56	13.34	9.45	23.10	313.39	121.02	44.72	47.78	99.87	284.15	100.51
1991	122.35	101.14	146.13	279.30	246.76	9.06	9.33	14.15	359.86	133.42	59.01	61.57	105.86	327.50	113.82
1992	152.36	130.54	254.44	303.00	253.26	11.09	14.29	24.36	444.61	148.56	73.47	80.41	142.17	402.59	126.03
1993	137.74	169.60	408.38	346.39	288.63	8.72	8.48	40.56	627.69	213.53	70.19	119.83	224.14	564.54	180.06
1994	170.66	239.07	520.53	501.44	416.17	12.87	12.52	59.88	812.56	261.12	80.07	175.45	295.92	733.25	217.21
1995	283.65	325.76	490.19	619.77	514.38	15.91	17.47	72.01	1029.85	349.66	146.84	233.08	300.27	925.75	274.23

Year	v13b1ii	v13b1iii	v13b1iv	v13b2	v13b2i	v13b2ii	v13b2iii	v13b2iv	v13c	v13ci	v13cii	v13ciii	v13civ	v13c1
1952														
1953														
1954														
1955														
1956														
1957														
1958														
1959														
1960														
1961														
1962														
1963														
1964														
1965														
1966														
1967														
1968														
1969														
1970														
1971														
1972														
1973														
1974														
1975														
1976														
1977														
1978	4.54	7.83	25.71	11.54	8.65	0.58	0.21	2.10	26.18	12.42	3.44	2.12	8.20	4.30
1979	5.13	8.85	28.49	14.05	10.39	0.84	0.50	2.32	30.28	14.81	3.85	2.28	9.34	4.53
1980	6.05	11.34	37.06	16.04	12.03	0.86	0.43	2.72	36.49	17.59	5.46	2.92	10.52	4.85
1981	6.29	11.79	37.75	14.12	10.45	0.98	0.58	2.11	39.90	19.30	6.13	3.14	11.33	4.90
1982	8.09	12.40	38.22	12.28	9.08	0.64	0.44	2.12	44.85	21.84	7.28	3.64	12.09	5.66
1983	8.30	13.82	42.40	14.31	10.73	0.85	0.60	2.13	50.68	24.47	6.69	4.39	14.86	6.65
1984	11.81	19.57	51.59	16.18	11.49	1.10	0.80	2.79	65.36	30.38	10.44	5.30	19.24	9.24
1985	13.94	15.72	81.71	21.47	16.39	1.12	0.65	3.31	77.47	34.69	11.01	6.03	25.74	14.77
1986	17.91	27.84	73.10	23.03	17.39	1.81	1.39	2.44	90.47	43.11	13.92	9.81	23.63	16.98
1987	21.51	33.46	84.25	26.87	19.09	2.04	1.45	4.29	109.25	53.62	16.81	12.48	26.34	18.94
1988	23.97	39.71	104.70	27.08	20.56	2.58	1.45	2.49	140.61	66.43	19.01	15.79	39.38	23.03
1989	31.64	42.75	100.99	23.99	17.89	2.87	1.65	1.65	177.55	99.07	28.25	21.11	29.12	33.05
1990	41.54	45.48	96.62	29.24	20.51	3.18	2.30	3.25	221.54	133.65	39.86	27.22	20.81	37.25
1991	54.73	58.22	100.73	32.36	19.60	4.28	3.35	5.13	274.22	163.58	54.28	30.24	26.12	47.37
1992	68.09	76.02	132.45	42.02	22.53	5.38	4.39	9.72	340.78	149.23	67.80	35.84	87.91	56.53
1993	65.59	112.50	206.39	63.15	33.47	4.60	7.33	17.75	450.30	206.50	58.83	41.29	143.68	68.85
1994	73.59	165.71	276.74	79.31	43.91	6.48	9.74	19.18	564.65	271.10	77.72	51.10	164.73	87.46
1995	139.19	219.21	293.12	104.10	75.43	7.65	13.87	7.15	741.80	427.78	120.90	75.21	117.91	114.92

Year	v13c1i	v13c1ii	v13c1iii	v13c1iv	v13c2	v13c2i	v13c2ii	v13c2iii	v13c2iv	v13c3	v13c3i	v13c3ii	v13c3iii	v13c3iv
1952														
1953														
1954														
1955														
1956														
1957														
1958														
1959														
1960														
1961														
1962														
1963														
1964														
1965														
1966														
1967														
1968														
1969														
1970														
1971														
1972														
1973														
1974														
1975														
1976														
1977														
1978	2.09	0.71	0.47	1.03	9.69	4.71	0.76	1.08	3.14	4.54	0.54		0.40	3.60
1979	2.17	0.75	0.57	1.04	11.21	5.40	0.89	1.23	3.69	5.26	0.60		0.46	4.20
1980	2.35	0.80	0.54	1.16	14.09	6.97	1.12	1.69	4.31	5.51	0.63		0.48	4.40
1981	2.36	0.81	0.56	1.17	14.96	7.30	1.19	1.79	4.68	6.02	0.72		0.50	4.80
1982	2.75	0.93	0.68	1.30	16.82	8.33	1.34	2.12	5.03	6.50	0.85	0.01	0.57	5.07
1983	3.25	1.06	0.74	1.60	20.29	9.94	1.62	2.43	6.30	7.09	0.70	0.09	0.63	5.67
1984	4.45	1.52	0.96	2.31	24.90	11.55	1.87	3.21	8.27	9.04	0.90	0.10	0.81	7.23
1985	6.97	2.42	1.13	4.25	30.16	12.83	2.27	3.57	11.49	10.71	1.23	0.18	0.98	8.32
1986	7.81	2.80	1.78	4.59	33.20	16.55	2.70	6.50	7.45	13.68	2.81	0.26	1.20	9.41
1987	8.96	3.40	2.08	4.50	40.67	20.48	3.07	8.00	9.12	17.09	4.90	0.33	1.41	10.45
1988	11.58	4.01	2.20	5.24	47.95	19.49	3.02	9.97	15.47	20.82	5.75	0.38	1.78	12.91
1989	15.91	7.50	3.90	5.74	58.01	37.05	5.27	13.07	2.62	28.14	8.44	0.54	2.86	16.30
1990	19.34	9.04	4.50	4.37	69.35	44.72	7.20	17.43	0.00	33.77	15.84	1.11	5.15	11.67
1991	18.35	12.17	4.54	12.31	86.66	65.42	14.47	21.14	-14.37	40.30	18.20	1.58	5.45	15.07
1992	16.73	14.78	6.93	18.09	112.25	71.13	17.43	24.57	-0.88	48.07	4.68	1.88	5.77	35.74
1993	36.91	10.53	5.50	15.91	149.98	71.45	7.70	20.45	50.38	63.42	3.07	3.66	6.76	49.93
1994	36.07	20.78	7.85	22.76	175.32	83.52	9.00	23.91	58.89	86.68	6.60	5.15	9.56	65.37
1995	72.53	24.53	9.78	8.08	239.16	150.36	31.89	33.15	23.76	107.01	13.65	6.18	16.52	70.66

Year	v13c4	v13c4i	v13c4ii	v13c4iii	v13c4iv	v13c5	v13c5i	v13c5ii	v13c5iii	v13c5iv	v13c6	v13c6i	v13c6ii	v13c6iii
1952														
1953														
1954														
1955														
1956														
1957														
1958														
1959														
1960														
1961														
1962														
1963														
1964														
1965														
1966														
1967														
1968														
1969														
1970														
1971														
1972														
1973														
1974														
1975														
1976														
1977														
1978	1.42	0.15	1.27			1.42	0.75	0.15	0.17	0.35	0.65	0.34	0.31	
1979	1.62	0.17	1.45			1.50	0.98	0.16	0.02	0.34	0.75	0.70	0.05	
1980	2.83	0.29	2.54			2.14	1.15	0.23	0.21	0.55	0.83	0.79	0.04	
1981	3.19	0.32	2.87			2.31	1.20	0.25	0.29	0.57	0.91	0.83	0.08	
1982	3.10	0.40	2.70			2.40	1.25	0.28	0.27	0.60	1.34	1.16	0.18	
1983	2.53	0.28	2.25			3.30	1.40	0.36	0.55	0.99	1.52	1.30	0.22	
1984	3.89	0.26	3.63			3.61	1.80	0.40	0.31	1.10	3.40	2.85	0.55	
1985	4.61	0.74	3.86		0.01	3.09	1.24	0.39	0.33	1.13	2.95	2.60	0.35	
1986	5.97	0.19	5.65	0.06	0.07	3.61	1.89	0.42	0.26	1.04	3.44	3.08	0.36	
1987	7.39	0.23	7.01	0.07	0.08	4.69	2.61	0.54	0.33	1.21	4.30	3.84	0.46	
1988	8.88	1.18	7.23	0.07	0.40	6.23	3.49	0.67	0.41	1.66	5.02	4.21	0.50	
1989	9.18	0.32	8.69	0.06	0.11	6.98	4.29	0.66	0.46	1.57	6.50	6.09	0.41	
1990	11.38	0.35	10.64	0.12	0.27	10.26	6.19	1.09	0.85	2.13	9.41	8.30	1.11	
1991	13.61	0.48	12.70	0.14	0.29	14.02	8.99	1.24	0.90	2.89	11.68	10.65	1.03	
1992	17.22	0.53	16.08	0.18	0.43	18.95	8.62	1.72	1.24	7.37	14.52	7.72	1.48	
1993	25.23	5.57	16.39	0.57	2.70	35.26	18.49	2.47	10.37	3.93	18.55	11.55	1.54	
1994	36.69	6.55	23.68	2.52	3.94	39.33	25.91	2.21	7.26	3.95	23.44	17.42	2.30	
1995	40.15	7.01	27.49	1.41	4.24	55.49	37.98	5.92	12.17	-0.58	30.67	23.39	5.35	0.13

Year	v13c6iv	v13c7	v13c7i	v13c7ii	v13c7iii	v13c7iv	v13c8	v13c8i	v13c8ii	v13c8iii	v13c8iv	v13c9	v13c9i	v13c9ii
1952														
1953														
1954														
1955														
1956														
1957														
1958														
1959														
1960														
1961														
1962														
1963														
1964														
1965														
1966														
1967														
1968														
1969														
1970														
1971														
1972														
1973														
1974														
1975														
1976														
1977														
1978		2.00	1.96	0.04			0.63	0.55			0.08	1.44	1.24	0.20
1979		2.31	2.29	0.02			0.70	0.63			0.07	2.31	1.78	0.53
1980		2.61	2.60	0.01			0.92	0.82			0.10	2.61	1.89	0.72
1981		2.85	2.66	0.19			1.01	0.89	0.01		0.11	3.65	2.92	0.73
1982		3.14	2.96	0.18			1.10	0.91	0.10		0.09	4.70	3.14	1.56
1983		3.34	3.23	0.11			1.30	0.80	0.16	0.04	0.30	4.55	3.46	1.09
1984		4.35	3.90	0.45			1.32	0.80	0.18	0.01	0.33	5.51	3.77	1.74
1985		5.16	4.38	0.78			1.56	0.92	0.22	0.02	0.40	4.34	3.67	0.53
1986		6.49	5.78	0.71			1.82	0.39	0.39	0.00	1.04	5.07	4.44	0.63
1987		8.07	7.24	0.83			2.12	0.10	0.47	0.57	0.98	5.62	4.92	0.70
1988	0.31	10.52	9.05	1.10		0.37	3.49	2.40	0.50	0.11	0.48	14.19	11.72	1.92
1989		11.83	10.30	1.53			5.10	3.78	0.74	0.10	0.48	17.27	15.24	2.03
1990		16.58	14.30	2.28			7.38	3.59	1.82	0.15	1.82	25.16	22.02	3.14
1991		19.17	16.87	2.30			9.34	2.00	1.91	0.20	5.23	29.93	26.74	3.19
1992	5.32	22.65	15.51	2.72		4.42	11.80	7.13	2.36	0.26	2.05	36.24	24.09	3.87
1993	5.46	24.66	17.21	2.84		4.61	14.50	9.48	2.71	0.42	1.89	46.81	32.31	4.61
1994	3.72	34.50	26.23	5.74		2.53	16.59	12.38	2.53	0.00	1.68	61.59	53.65	6.05
1995	1.80	48.23	38.15	6.37	0.58	3.13	23.10	16.21	3.44	1.33	2.12	79.02	64.84	9.34

Year	v13c9iii	v13c9iv	v13c10	v13c10i	v13c10ii	v13c10iii	v13c10iv
1952							
1953							
1954							
1955							
1956							
1957							
1958							
1959							
1960							
1961							
1962							
1963							
1964							
1965							
1966							
1967							
1968							
1969							
1970							
1971							
1972							
1973							
1974							
1975							
1976							
1977							
1978			0.09	0.09			
1979			0.09	0.09			
1980			0.10	0.10			
1981			0.10	0.10			
1982			0.09	0.09			
1983			0.11	0.11			
1984			0.10	0.10			
1985		0.14	0.12	0.11	0.01		
1986			0.21	0.17		0.01	0.03
1987			0.36	0.34		0.02	
1988		0.55	0.48	-2.44	-0.32	1.25	1.99
1989			1.49	-2.35	0.88	0.66	2.30
1990			1.00	-1.00	2.43	-0.98	0.55
1991			2.14	-4.12	3.69	-2.13	4.70
1992		8.28	2.55	-6.91	5.48	-3.11	7.09
1993		9.89	3.04	0.46	6.38	-2.78	-1.02
1994		1.89	3.05	2.77	0.28		
1995	0.14	4.70	4.05	3.66	0.39		

18

Hunan

Year	v1	v1a	v1b	v1b1	v1b2	v1c	v1c1	v1c2	v1c3	v2	v2a	v2b	v2b1	v2b2	v2c
1952	39.34	23.79	9.09	8.19	0.90	6.46	1.32	2.79	2.35		121.3	151.9	132.3	236.8	
1953	42.63	23.71	11.39	10.10	1.29	7.53	1.92	3.90	1.71	108.2	100.1	130.6	129.1	143.3	112.1
1954	43.86	21.97	13.54	11.94	1.60	8.35	2.05	4.48	1.82	101.3	91.7	120.3	119.3	127.9	107.2
1955	49.24	25.83	14.47	12.11	2.36	8.94	2.39	4.50	2.05	115.1	118.5	111.8	105.8	154.5	110.2
1956	53.66	25.67	17.19	14.65	2.54	10.80	2.72	5.73	2.35	109.6	97.4	126.4	128.8	114.9	121.1
1957	66.03	32.88	19.74	16.99	2.75	13.41	3.08	5.46	4.87	117.6	120.1	111.8	112.6	107.5	121.4
1958	86.51	31.68	39.51	32.41	7.10	15.32	4.16	5.70	5.46	130.3	104.1	204.6	176.2	258.1	113.7
1959	103.48	29.79	52.35	42.63	9.72	21.34	7.01	7.60	6.73	117.0	91.9	130.0	132.4	119.3	137.5
1960	113.37	27.78	62.58	48.85	13.73	23.01	6.90	8.45	7.66	105.2	84.7	117.1	112.3	140.5	105.3
1961	76.77	26.29	31.72	28.56	3.16	18.76	4.20	6.59	7.97	59.9	84.8	47.1	53.5	22.5	66.0
1962	80.42	33.61	28.56	26.42	2.14	18.25	3.62	6.79	7.84	97.7	119.3	85.1	87.0	67.5	90.1
1963	80.55	31.92	31.43	28.21	3.22	17.20	4.30	4.70	8.20	103.2	94.2	111.2	109.2	135.6	106.0
1964	94.08	38.05	38.19	32.38	5.81	17.84	5.46	5.20	7.18	117.4	113.9	124.5	118.6	180.7	109.7
1965	107.35	42.70	45.55	38.90	6.65	19.10	5.93	5.35	7.82	115.5	104.4	126.1	127.9	114.5	112.2
1966	123.98	47.87	55.52	47.94	7.58	20.59	6.61	5.92	8.06	118.4	111.7	127.1	129.0	114.0	108.0
1967	120.70	50.35	49.33	42.98	6.35	21.02	6.16	6.24	8.62	97.2	105.1	91.0	91.9	83.8	101.9
1968	118.55	55.79	41.80	36.72	5.08	20.96	5.09	5.88	9.99	95.6	107.5	81.8	82.0	80.1	109.9
1969	134.39	55.30	55.51	47.83	7.68	23.58	6.24	7.07	10.27	116.8	97.9	139.4	138.1	151.0	106.1
1970	162.14	58.22	78.40	68.94	9.46	25.52	7.16	7.71	10.65	124.3	105.0	142.3	144.6	123.3	109.9
1971	177.75	60.29	90.37	77.35	13.02	27.09	8.01	8.28	10.80	110.9	99.9	116.2	115.5	137.6	109.6
1972	194.62	64.84	99.73	87.05	12.68	30.05	8.89	9.26	11.90	110.2	106.6	112.3	114.7	97.4	111.0
1973	216.29	70.82	113.61	100.63	12.98	31.86	9.60	10.22	12.04	109.3	108.3	110.8	112.0	102.4	106.0
1974	202.91	72.33	97.37	83.66	13.71	33.21	8.56	10.59	14.06	92.5	102.1	83.5	80.7	105.6	104.2
1975	234.10	76.06	120.60	105.34	15.26	37.44	9.25	11.23	16.96	117.4	104.6	128.4	131.2	111.3	112.9
1976	233.23	76.44	118.53	104.52	14.01	38.26	8.72	11.54	18.00	98.6	100.4	96.5	97.1	91.8	102.1
1977	256.72	77.59	138.02	124.44	13.58	41.11	10.12	12.76	18.23	111.2	101.5	118.4	121.2	96.9	107.4
1978	289.79	81.91	160.32	142.78	17.54	47.56	11.40	14.45	21.71	114.8	110.2	117.0	115.6	130.3	115.8
1979	347.74	109.18	186.04	164.12	21.92	52.52	12.12	16.05	24.35	110.4	106.3	112.9	112.1	120.0	108.7
1980	376.14	111.14	206.57	177.85	28.72	58.43	12.60	17.81	28.02	105.8	98.1	109.8	108.0	123.6	104.8
1981	408.13	126.36	214.61	187.02	27.59	67.16	12.68	19.77	34.71	105.6	106.1	103.2	104.0	98.4	112.9
1982	449.11	142.71	235.37	205.78	29.59	71.03	13.63	22.68	34.72	108.7	110.1	109.2	109.6	106.3	104.4
1983	498.03	158.16	261.66	221.15	40.51	78.21	15.14	22.84	40.23	108.9	105.0	111.4	107.8	137.6	108.2
1984	562.67	171.26	299.00	255.06	43.94	92.41	18.54	28.72	45.15	110.7	105.7	112.2	112.6	104.3	115.1
1985	698.36	198.44	372.89	314.68	58.21	127.03	26.00	40.52	60.51	114.5	104.9	116.1	116.4	114.3	125.9
1986	810.42	222.68	437.15	368.88	68.27	150.59	28.44	48.42	73.73	110.6	105.4	112.1	113.0	106.3	113.6
1987	980.08	253.39	540.92	456.74	84.18	185.77	32.68	58.96	94.13	113.3	103.3	116.2	116.9	111.4	117.8
1988	1239.59	303.01	690.19	581.85	108.34	246.39	43.09	80.03	123.27	111.0	100.5	114.6	115.3	110.0	112.6
1989	1390.89	337.48	768.85	680.09	88.76	284.56	51.37	85.79	147.40	104.3	105.1	103.1	106.7	76.6	107.2
1990	1571.34	397.42	809.86	712.67	97.19	364.06	56.35	136.70	171.01	103.9	101.9	104.7	105.0	100.9	103.8
1991	1777.40	425.58	928.67	803.71	124.96	423.15	70.50	157.16	195.49	109.5	103.9	111.9	111.2	117.3	110.5
1992	2247.41	471.22	1184.05	1006.79	177.26	592.14	90.01	232.92	269.21	114.5	103.8	120.0	119.9	121.5	113.6
1993	2938.67	563.47	1685.35	1438.92	246.43	689.85	142.87	289.82	257.16	116.4	105.3	121.0	123.2	105.8	116.5
1994	4110.56	792.90	2243.62	1925.35	318.27	1074.04	227.34	393.00	453.70	118.0	106.4	120.0	120.8	113.8	123.5
1995	5282.23	1046.97	2854.10	2451.47	402.63	1381.16	283.72	506.55	590.89	114.4	110.2	116.9	117.2	114.6	111.3

Year	v2c1	v2c2	v3'	v3	v3a	v3b	v3b1	v3b2	v3c	v3c1	v3c2	v3c3	v3c4	v3c5	v3c6
1952	129.3	107.7	27.81	27.81	18.72	3.43	2.94	0.49	5.66	1.10	2.50				
1953	150.4	130.1	30.29	30.29	18.48	4.28	3.53	0.75	7.53	1.64	3.54				
1954	107.3	114.0	30.51	30.51	17.03	5.13	4.22	0.91	8.35	1.77	3.98				
1955	118.8	99.5	35.83	35.83	21.13	5.76	4.25	1.51	8.94	2.07	3.83				
1956	112.7	127.2	37.93	37.93	20.56	6.57	5.19	1.38	10.80	2.38	4.83				
1957	113.2	91.4	45.20	45.20	26.41	7.45	5.94	1.51	11.34	2.71	4.51				
1958	134.0	104.0	55.85	55.85	26.65	16.63	12.40	4.23	12.57	3.51	4.58				
1959	173.6	133.2	61.95	61.95	23.60	21.57	16.57	5.00	16.78	5.45	6.04				
1960	96.6	109.8	64.07	64.07	20.58	25.47	19.22	6.25	18.02	5.42	6.60				
1961	57.6	55.6	46.64	46.64	20.78	11.69	10.25	1.44	14.17	3.20	4.95				
1962	84.4	92.4	51.19	51.19	27.17	10.59	9.46	1.13	13.43	2.73	4.93				
1963	125.8	81.1	48.08	48.08	25.11	11.37	10.31	1.06	11.60	3.25	2.82				
1964	123.0	132.3	57.36	57.36	30.41	15.60	13.50	2.10	11.35	2.57	3.45				
1965	109.6	105.0	65.32	65.32	34.00	19.17	16.86	2.31	12.15	2.98	3.68				
1966	110.8	111.0	72.73	72.73	37.30	22.16	19.67	2.49	13.27	3.14	4.41				
1967	92.1	105.4	73.51	73.51	40.07	19.89	17.46	2.43	13.55	3.03	4.54				
1968	81.3	94.1	75.67	75.67	44.85	17.31	15.03	2.28	13.51	2.92	4.22				
1969	124.2	120.3	81.26	81.26	44.08	21.98	19.39	2.59	15.20	3.37	5.20				
1970	116.6	109.1	93.05	93.05	44.62	31.98	28.83	3.15	16.45	3.96	5.67				
1971	112.4	107.3	99.10	99.10	46.31	35.33	30.35	4.98	17.46	4.34	5.63				
1972	111.7	112.1	107.01	107.01	47.73	39.91	34.31	5.60	19.37	4.89	6.68				
1973	107.5	110.3	115.80	115.80	51.91	43.35	37.92	5.43	20.54	5.01	7.23				
1974	87.4	103.6	108.17	108.17	53.17	34.87	29.21	5.66	20.13	4.34	6.98				
1975	109.6	106.3	118.40	118.40	54.97	41.96	35.58	6.38	21.47	4.92	7.29				
1976	92.9	102.7	118.53	118.53	55.07	41.47	34.95	6.52	21.99	4.83	7.17				
1977	116.9	110.5	129.17	129.17	55.95	49.59	43.14	6.45	23.63	5.33	8.06				
1978	113.2	113.2	146.99	146.99	59.83	59.82	51.94	7.88	27.34	5.91	9.71	2.55	2.03	0.62	1.05
1979	106.6	109.5	178.01	178.01	79.40	68.42	59.23	9.19	30.19	6.47	10.85	2.50	2.10	0.68	1.24
1980	102.6	104.8	191.72	191.72	81.14	76.99	65.31	11.68	33.59	6.77	11.73	2.70	2.32	0.83	1.54
1981	98.8	109.2	209.68	209.68	93.29	77.78	67.19	10.59	38.61	6.93	13.42	3.60	3.56	0.95	1.72
1982	108.3	112.8	232.52	232.52	107.99	82.51	71.31	11.20	42.02	7.61	12.81	5.02	3.96	1.06	1.96
1983	110.3	107.6	257.43	257.43	117.79	93.37	78.84	14.53	46.27	8.16	12.56	5.66	5.18	1.17	2.33
1984	122.3	121.9	287.29	287.29	128.28	104.34	90.79	13.55	54.67	9.30	15.40	6.53	5.76	1.58	2.58
1985	140.3	127.0	349.95	349.95	147.72	127.08	110.05	17.03	75.15	13.23	22.94	8.85	7.84	3.34	2.87
1986	111.6	114.1	397.68	397.68	165.28	143.31	124.30	19.01	89.09	15.00	27.60	12.55	7.93	3.39	3.26
1987	109.2	110.1	469.44	469.44	187.09	172.45	149.67	22.78	109.90	20.13	34.56	15.94	8.53	3.91	3.84
1988	118.7	107.8	584.07	584.07	217.03	221.28	190.40	30.88	145.76	24.12	46.61	20.91	9.96	6.55	5.08
1989	109.7	90.8	640.80	640.80	234.31	238.15	212.21	25.94	168.34	26.81	45.48	26.94	11.00	8.73	6.04
1990	109.4	91.2	744.44	744.44	279.09	249.98	220.69	29.29	215.37	32.27	62.94	31.01	16.25	10.84	7.98
1991	112.9	110.4	833.30	833.30	301.02	281.95	242.96	38.99	250.33	41.68	73.91	38.26	17.73	10.88	9.02
1992	121.5	132.4	997.70	997.70	323.91	347.89	295.38	52.51	325.90	51.29	104.96	49.01	20.57	16.52	11.35
1993	119.6	109.4	1278.28	1278.28	383.68	488.98	417.52	71.46	405.62	72.47	123.71	63.47	25.73	18.54	14.08
1994	110.8	109.0	1694.42	1694.42	532.89	618.07	525.77	92.30	543.46	99.63	167.75	73.60	32.30	24.84	20.72
1995	108.1	111.6	2195.70	2195.70	685.30	815.82	699.03	116.79	694.58	132.39	211.37	90.15	40.90	29.39	25.47

Year	v3c7	v3c8	v3c9	v3c10	v3d	v4'	v4	v4a	v4b	v4b1	v4b2	v4c	v4c1	v4c2	v4c3
1952				2.06	86										
1953				2.35	91	108.4	108.4	99.9	131.5	127.7	153.1	128.1	150.7	131.7	
1954				2.60	90	98.2	98.2	89.9	120.1	120.0	121.3	110.1	109.6	111.6	
1955				3.04	104	118.5	118.5	122.8	120.3	107.6	178.5	106.6	116.5	95.4	
1956				3.59	109	105.4	105.4	96.4	119.3	128.7	92.9	120.7	116.6	126.2	
1957				4.12	127	115.1	115.1	121.4	111.7	112.4	109.6	103.4	115.3	89.6	
1958				4.48	154	119.8	119.8	101.3	206.3	184.1	292.6	110.3	126.1	101.5	
1959				5.29	168	108.8	108.8	86.7	126.5	134.6	104.0	134.2	157.4	131.6	
1960				6.00	176	99.0	99.0	79.7	115.9	113.6	124.1	105.2	98.7	108.2	
1961				6.02	132	64.5	64.5	91.6	43.4	49.5	22.8	64.8	58.5	53.9	
1962				5.77	144	103.0	103.0	122.9	85.6	86.6	78.7	88.7	85.6	89.6	
1963				5.53	131	96.4	96.4	91.1	107.9	110.6	85.7	97.2	118.7	67.1	
1964				5.33	153	118.8	118.8	115.5	141.0	135.8	195.1	103.0	79.2	144.6	
1965				5.49	170	113.1	113.1	104.3	129.1	131.9	109.2	110.9	115.2	108.8	
1966				5.72	184	112.8	112.8	109.1	119.9	121.4	107.9	109.2	105.0	119.9	
1967				5.98	181	100.3	100.3	107.4	91.1	90.4	97.6	101.8	96.4	103.0	
1968				6.37	181	98.6	98.6	108.7	83.9	82.8	94.0	99.4	96.0	92.9	
1969				6.63	189	110.6	110.6	97.2	133.7	136.2	113.4	112.6	115.6	123.2	
1970				6.82	211	117.6	117.6	100.9	147.0	149.8	121.4	106.2	117.6	108.9	
1971				7.49	218	105.6	105.6	100.6	111.6	107.7	156.8	102.8	109.5	99.3	
1972				7.80	230	108.0	108.0	101.8	114.4	114.7	112.5	110.8	112.4	118.7	
1973				8.30	244	106.8	106.8	108.0	106.0	107.4	97.2	105.5	102.4	107.1	
1974				8.81	223	92.6	92.6	102.4	78.7	75.2	104.3	98.4	86.7	97.6	
1975				9.26	239	110.4	110.4	102.9	123.7	126.0	112.2	106.6	113.3	104.8	
1976				9.99	236	99.5	99.5	100.1	97.3	96.4	102.5	102.2	98.1	98.2	
1977				10.24	254	109.6	109.6	101.5	121.1	125.1	98.9	107.3	110.3	112.5	
1978	3.21	0.20	1.86	0.20	286	116.4	116.4	111.7	121.8	121.6	123.3	115.5	110.7	120.4	115.3
1979	3.72	0.28	2.10	0.25	343	109.1	109.1	106.8	111.4	111.3	112.1	109.0	109.3	110.1	96.5
1980	4.46	0.31	2.63	0.30	365	105.2	105.2	98.9	111.0	109.7	119.9	105.5	104.5	102.5	97.8
1981	4.83	0.36	2.89	0.35	394	105.5	105.5	107.0	100.2	101.4	92.7	113.3	102.6	112.6	131.0
1982	5.60	0.39	3.21	0.40	430	109.4	109.4	113.0	106.0	106.1	105.0	107.5	109.6	94.0	137.3
1983	6.40	0.49	3.87	0.45	470	109.2	109.2	103.7	116.7	114.8	130.2	108.2	107.2	95.8	110.1
1984	7.57	0.57	4.88	0.50	519	109.4	109.4	106.6	109.7	113.0	89.8	115.6	113.9	119.3	111.9
1985	9.13	0.68	5.67	0.60	626	112.0	112.0	103.7	113.6	114.3	108.7	127.2	140.6	134.8	122.1
1986	10.80	0.84	6.75	0.97	703	108.1	108.1	105.2	107.7	108.5	101.6	114.1	112.6	114.6	135.3
1987	12.61	0.99	8.14	1.25	818	109.3	109.3	102.9	112.8	113.3	108.6	114.0	127.1	113.8	114.9
1988	17.61	3.99	10.93		999	108.2	108.2	97.7	115.0	115.3	112.6	112.6	120.4	108.9	104.6
1989	21.61	6.07	13.86	1.80	1074	103.6	103.6	105.7	101.2	103.0	79.3	105.0	97.3	90.6	150.6
1990	17.43	7.36	26.51	2.78	1228	104.0	104.0	103.2	104.6	104.5	106.1	103.8	113.7	83.7	109.0
1991	19.14	7.45	29.08	3.18	1357	107.9	107.9	105.6	108.5	107.4	116.7	110.5	118.6	112.0	115.5
1992	23.02	9.41	34.72	5.05	1613	112.4	112.4	103.5	121.1	121.2	120.4	114.1	112.8	110.0	130.3
1993	27.55	10.93	43.96	5.18	2053	113.1	113.1	104.3	119.2	121.1	105.5	116.1	125.2	110.8	121.3
1994	42.37	15.78	59.70	6.77	2701	111.0	111.0	105.4	116.3	116.9	111.7	110.3	105.4	109.0	105.7
1995	55.99	19.86	79.98	9.08	3470	110.9	110.9	106.5	114.7	114.7	114.6	110.4	116.3	109.1	106.0

Year	v4c4	v4c5	v4c6	v4c7	v4c8	v4c9	v4c10	v5	v5a	v5a1	v5a1a	v5a1b	v5a2	v5b	v5b1
1952								27.81	24.87	24.12	20.98	3.14	0.75	1.63	1.24
1953								30.29	26.30	25.44	21.61	3.83	0.86	2.69	1.93
1954								30.51	26.61	25.46	21.43	4.03	1.15	3.10	2.41
1955								35.83	29.84	28.52	24.26	4.26	1.32	5.36	1.93
1956								37.93	32.23	30.56	25.28	5.28	1.67	5.09	3.28
1957								45.20	34.18	32.42	26.31	6.11	1.76	7.99	3.81
1958								55.85	36.98	35.16	27.57	7.59	1.82	18.84	14.06
1959								61.95	37.16	34.76	24.93	9.83	2.40	24.54	16.43
1960								64.07	37.96	35.47	24.92	10.55	2.49	21.39	17.98
1961								46.64	41.38	39.12	28.36	10.76	2.26	3.69	4.62
1962								51.19	45.28	43.51	33.32	10.19	1.77	0.89	2.73
1963								48.08	40.92	39.32	28.50	10.82	1.60	6.83	3.91
1964								57.36	43.61	41.32	30.59	10.73	2.29	11.39	8.46
1965								65.32	47.29	45.18	33.84	11.34	2.11	12.69	9.39
1966								72.73	51.61	49.26	37.93	11.33	2.35	16.31	11.20
1967								73.51	54.81	52.56	40.95	11.61	2.25	13.93	9.41
1968								75.67	55.30	53.27	41.60	11.67	2.03	12.69	7.52
1969								81.26	55.90	53.52	42.09	11.43	2.38	16.78	10.81
1970								93.05	58.04	55.60	43.54	12.06	2.44	27.05	18.54
1971								99.10	62.19	59.04	45.36	13.68	3.15	33.51	22.12
1972								107.01	67.40	63.76	47.81	15.95	3.64	28.60	18.23
1973								115.80	71.30	67.28	50.71	16.57	4.02	28.24	19.00
1974								108.17	74.50	69.54	51.98	17.56	4.96	24.50	19.32
1975								118.40	76.87	72.16	53.89	18.27	4.71	26.36	21.31
1976								118.53	78.41	73.13	53.94	19.19	5.28	24.80	19.33
1977								129.17	86.16	79.74	60.13	19.61	6.42	28.00	17.83
1978	104.0		113.4	115.8	115.1	116.9		146.99	100.83	93.93	70.87	23.06	6.90	42.41	27.68
1979	101.7	101.9	115.9	113.6	137.9	111.2	125.0	178.01	118.77	109.67	83.37	26.30	9.10	41.32	29.81
1980	110.4	104.8	113.5	110.0	103.7	115.3	112.0	191.72	136.94	125.42	93.15	32.27	11.52	40.02	32.76
1981	146.4	151.3	110.4	106.6	114.5	108.2	116.7	209.68	155.72	142.77	107.33	35.44	12.95	41.19	27.95
1982	110.3	110.2	112.1	114.3	105.8	109.1	111.4	232.52	174.68	159.45	121.93	37.52	15.23	50.33	34.07
1983	128.5	128.5	116.0	111.8	124.7	117.7	112.8	257.43	195.09	178.56	137.91	40.65	16.53	56.53	43.89
1984	110.0	108.8	107.9	114.9	114.0	122.7	106.8	287.29	218.09	199.24	152.95	46.29	18.85	59.06	42.15
1985	128.4	125.9	100.9	109.5	109.0	106.1	110.6	349.95	263.11	240.71	182.85	57.86	22.40	92.19	58.14
1986	100.9	97.4	109.4	113.0	118.6	113.7	157.7	397.68	290.14	265.54	196.12	69.42	24.60	115.02	75.57
1987	105.0	99.4	107.0	106.2	107.4	109.8	118.3	469.44	328.34	298.85	218.93	79.92	29.49	139.84	91.79
1988	109.5	149.8	107.1	112.6	131.1	108.5	112.4	584.07	399.15	364.37	256.19	108.18	34.78	184.75	114.73
1989	86.7	122.5	113.6	117.5	146.3	120.8	101.8	640.80	439.54	393.49	270.81	122.68	46.05	169.41	83.19
1990	109.0	104.3	110.2	107.3	108.9	110.4	115.3	744.44	564.70	454.90	314.05	140.85	109.80	184.12	122.82
1991	106.1	100.0	107.8	104.9	100.0	106.0	107.6	833.30	621.93	500.84	340.27	160.57	121.09	224.80	160.49
1992	110.6	116.7	104.4	106.3	108.7	116.8	107.8	997.70	725.60	582.91	379.23	203.68	142.69	301.76	228.29
1993	124.0	107.1	116.8	113.1	108.4	113.3	101.0	1278.28	885.05	706.55	442.35	264.20	178.50	414.73	330.54
1994	112.0	107.4	117.9	123.2	125.5	109.2	104.6	1694.42	1113.62	883.46	534.34	349.12	230.16	581.52	422.61
1995	114.7	102.4	106.5	104.4	104.4	116.0	116.2	2195.70	1396.88	1108.78	674.09	434.69	288.10	800.50	534.12

Year	v5b2	v5c	v5c1	v5c2	v6a1	v6a2	v6a3	v6a4	v6b2	v6b3	v6b4	v7	v7a	v7a1	v7a2
1952	0.39	1.31													
1953	0.76	1.30										97.3	97.0	94.8	111.2
1954	0.69	0.80										100.5	99.5	99.1	101.9
1955	3.43	0.63										111.0	110.9	112.2	103.7
1956	1.81	0.61										103.9	103.0	100.2	119.4
1957	4.18	3.03										101.2	101.1	98.6	113.8
1958	4.78	0.03										106.8	107.0	102.7	125.4
1959	8.11	0.25										100.5	98.8	91.2	129.2
1960	3.41	4.72										96.8	96.9	94.2	103.7
1961	-0.93	1.57										79.1	80.0	85.4	68.1
1962	-1.84	5.02										101.0	102.7	107.6	89.1
1963	2.92	0.33										101.8	101.6	96.3	119.9
1964	2.93	2.36										115.7	114.0	116.8	106.3
1965	3.30	5.34										118.9	119.9	120.6	117.7
1966	5.11	4.81										109.4	109.1	111.6	101.4
1967	4.52	4.77										104.3	104.8	105.7	101.5
1968	5.17	7.68										100.3	100.8	101.0	100.1
1969	5.97	8.58										101.6	100.9	101.7	98.0
1970	8.51	7.96										104.5	104.6	104.2	106.1
1971	11.39	3.40										107.1	106.0	103.8	114.0
1972	10.37	11.01										107.7	107.4	105.0	115.0
1973	9.24	16.26										105.4	105.1	105.4	104.2
1974	5.18	9.17										102.0	100.9	99.9	103.7
1975	5.05	15.17										103.5	104.1	104.1	104.2
1976	5.47	15.32										100.6	99.9	98.4	103.9
1977	10.17	15.01										110.4	109.6	111.9	103.1
1978	14.73	3.75			46.07	19.35	1.91	3.54	20.96	1.59	0.51	112.5	112.9	111.0	118.7
1979	12.01	17.42			47.76	28.51	1.85	5.25	23.90	1.82	0.58	112.3	10.8	110.3	112.2
1980	7.26	14.76			50.67	33.72	1.77	6.99	29.40	2.19	0.68	108.9	108.5	109.2	106.5
1981	13.24	12.77			53.77	42.82	2.48	8.26	32.36	2.34	0.74	111.2	111.3	113.0	106.5
1982	16.46	7.31			62.42	46.58	0.49	12.44	34.07	2.59	0.86	111.8	111.3	113.4	105.0
1983	12.74	5.71			62.06	56.82	3.03	16.00	37.16	2.56	0.93	107.5	107.7	108.8	104.2
1984	16.91	10.14			69.44	63.17	3.82	16.52	42.40	2.83	1.06	108.9	108.8	108.3	110.2
1985	34.05	-5.35			81.13	89.85	2.87	9.00	51.75	4.77	1.34	108.3	108.4	107.6	111.3
1986	39.45	-7.48			82.54	100.88	3.56	9.14	61.92	6.29	1.21	104.5	104.5	101.8	113.3
1987	48.05	1.26			85.01	117.40	6.38	10.14	70.46	7.64	1.82	102.3	102.1	101.2	104.5
1988	70.02	0.17			89.98	145.58	8.94	11.69	97.08	8.95	2.15	98.3	98.2	95.6	105.4
1989	86.22	31.85			90.88	154.75	11.81	13.37	109.30	9.82	3.56	97.7	96.8	97.0	96.2
1990	61.30	-4.38			136.03	152.46	12.44	13.12	125.82	11.06	3.97	105.9	105.0	101.7	113.8
1991	64.31	-13.43			145.00	166.39	14.44	14.44	142.58	13.50	4.49	105.4	105.3	104.1	108.0
1992	73.47	-29.66			153.78	173.94	35.72	15.79	169.99	27.59	6.10	103.9	103.5	101.4	108.3
1993	84.19	-21.50			173.97	203.25	46.55	18.58	221.65	35.39	7.16	105.3	104.5	100.7	112.2
1994	158.91	-0.72			218.72	239.01	54.05	22.56	282.11	54.49	12.52	105.8	105.9	100.6	115.5
1995	266.38	-1.68			256.35	311.44	70.56	34.74	362.77	56.61	15.31	108.6	108.7	109.2	107.8

Year	v7b	v8	v8a	v8b	v9	v9a	v9b	v10a1	v10a2	v10a3	v10a3a	v10a3b	v10a4	v10b1	v10b2
1952		75	71	113											
1953	108.8	77	72	130	94.6	92.9	104.5								
1954	127.0	75	70	123	97.2	97.6	91.9								
1955	113.8	83	78	130	108.9	110.0	103.5								
1956	123.4	88	80	156	101.9	99.3	115.8								
1957	103.8	91	82	167	99.2	97.4	105.2								
1958	104.5	97	86	172	103.6	102.5	104.1								
1959	131.9	94	79	183	97.6	91.7	106.1								
1960	95.3	98	80	199	98.3	95.6	104.9								
1961	65.4	111	92	230	82.1	86.2	77.5								
1962	70.9	122	106	248	102.3	105.2	101.2								
1963	105.3	107	87	272	98.7	92.9	123.9								
1964	158.0	110	92	263	111.2	114.0	103.8								
1965	101.3	118	99	274	117.0	117.5	115.8								
1966	115.6	125	107	268	106.0	108.3	99.5								
1967	95.1	129	113	269	101.9	102.7	99.3								
1968	89.2	127	111	271	98.1	97.9	100.3								
1969	118.5	125	108	277	98.2	98.2	102.2								
1970	103.2	126	109	289	101.8	101.2	105.0								
1971	129.2	130	111	305	103.2	101.6	105.9								
1972	115.1	137	114	339	104.9	102.8	109.6								
1973	110.4	141	119	343	102.7	103.1	101.6								
1974	120.5	143	119	354	98.8	97.9	100.8								
1975	95.2	146	121	360	102.2	102.3	101.9								
1976	110.4	146	120	371	98.3	97.0	102.1								
1977	122.1	157	132	374	108.3	110.6	101.7								
1978	107.7	183	154	427	111.7	110.0	115.4	20.21	4.65	2.82	0.05	2.77		9.41	4.52
1979	131.4	211	181	454	109.6	110.0	104.5	20.69	4.77	4.35	0.06	4.29		6.76	4.37
1980	112.8	239	201	523	107.3	108.8	100.1	20.67	4.39	7.70	0.13	7.57		3.32	2.53
1981	109.9	268	229	552	109.9	112.0	102.4	15.60	4.81	7.54	0.13	7.41		7.26	3.43
1982	116.5	295	257	567	109.5	111.8	101.7	21.50	5.04	7.53	0.31	7.22		8.76	5.35
1983	104.7	326	287	603	106.2	107.4	102.4	19.49	4.56	19.58	0.53	19.05	0.26	4.64	4.41
1984	110.6	360	317	650	107.7	108.0	104.3	19.47	4.76	16.95	0.98	15.97	0.97	6.43	7.07
1985	106.6	430	379	751	107.3	107.6	102.9	29.07	7.97	19.65	1.98	17.67	1.45	17.26	10.79
1986	104.3	469	404	866	103.3	101.1	108.9	36.73	10.13	27.05	3.02	24.03	1.66	21.18	11.56
1987	104.5	521	446	969	100.7	100.0	101.6	45.71	13.86	29.83	4.68	25.15	2.39	26.38	13.65
1988	99.4	623	514	1256	96.4	94.2	101.0	56.91	15.49	39.46	7.22	32.24	2.87	40.40	16.59
1989	107.9	660	534	1372	100.0	103.6	91.8	44.76	8.49	28.94	3.65	25.29	1.00	54.40	20.26
1990	114.0	750	611	1533	103.6	100.0	111.9	69.68	13.31	29.24	4.29	24.95	10.59	33.29	19.37
1991	106.0	816	654	1714	104.0	102.9	105.9	96.46	19.80	34.36	3.93	30.43	9.87	42.52	13.48
1992	105.4	942	726	2106	102.7	101.1	104.9	145.66	31.59	43.78	5.17	38.61	7.26	46.52	15.95
1993	108.9	1134	849	2598	103.9	100.8	106.6	210.81	46.06	56.61	6.87	49.74	17.06	32.41	10.75
1994	105.6	1408	1027	3260	105.1	100.7	109.7	250.96	56.55	87.38	11.08	76.30	27.72	76.38	52.29
1995	108.4	1752	1294	3884	107.8	109.0	103.2	316.90	39.83	128.34	13.94	114.40	49.05	87.52	53.31

Year	v10b4	v11a	v11a1	v11a2	v11b	v11b1	v11b2	v11c	v11c1	v11c2	v12	v12a	v12b	v13	v13i
1952															
1953											162.2	159.4	191.3		
1954											115.0	126.3	87.5		
1955											172.8	84.5	514.0		
1956											102.1	178.4	52.4		
1957											149.8	113.9	222.0		
1958											253.3	388.3	114.4		
1959											125.1	113.2	166.6		
1960											86.5	106.0	40.0		
1961											15.9	23.1			
1962											23.3	56.7			
1963											696.2	142.7			
1964											180.9	227.1	103.6		
1965											119.4	120.8	114.1		
1966											130.6	122.6	161.0		
1967											85.4	85.6	87.8		
1968											85.0	76.8	108.3		
1969											140.9	151.2	121.5		
1970											169.6	177.2	149.1		
1971											127.3	124.6	135.0		
1972											86.2	84.3	91.3		
1973											97.9	101.8	87.4		
1974											84.7	95.2	54.0		
1975											113.5	115.8	99.6		
1976											90.4	87.9	105.6		
1977											110.3	95.2	188.6		
1978	0.80	4.59	3.43	1.16	20.15	17.68	2.47	17.67	6.57	11.10	154.2	156.3	148.0	146.99	91.13
1979	0.88	4.74	3.73	1.01	18.85	17.83	1.02	18.23	8.25	9.98	98.0	106.2	75.9	178.01	113.89
1980	1.41	3.58	3.31	0.27	16.23	15.36	0.87	20.21	14.09	6.12	96.1	105.9	58.4	191.72	120.77
1981	2.55	1.49	1.40	0.09	16.25	14.53	1.72	23.45	12.02	11.43	95.8	84.2	176.5	209.68	134.16
1982	2.35	2.36	1.60	0.76	21.84	18.09	3.75	26.33	14.38	11.95	122.7	122.4	123.7	232.52	152.04
1983	3.69	1.40	1.67	-0.27	26.11	24.49	1.62	29.12	17.73	11.39	113.5	125.0	75.4	257.43	165.48
1984	3.41	4.37	1.56	2.81	38.97	23.94	15.03	15.72	16.65	-0.93	99.6	93.9	130.4	287.29	186.96
1985	6.00	2.71	1.45	1.26	38.93	32.73	6.20	50.55	23.96	26.59	138.0	125.6	185.8	349.95	225.99
1986	6.71	6.28	1.51	4.77	58.05	47.08	10.97	50.69	26.98	23.71	119.7	123.6	110.1	397.68	257.04
1987	8.02	6.37	2.48	3.89	69.19	59.48	9.71	64.28	29.83	34.45	113.7	113.7	113.3	469.44	296.68
1988	13.03	5.24	3.56	1.68	92.67	75.03	17.64	86.84	36.14	50.70	114.1	109.7	127.4	584.07	373.76
1989	11.56	13.70	2.41	11.29	101.59	56.24	45.35	54.12	24.54	29.58	81.2	68.6	113.3	640.80	415.54
1990	8.64	7.99	3.45	4.54	110.18	78.61	31.57	65.95	40.76	25.19	88.1	90.9	86.0	744.44	458.40
1991	8.21	12.01	3.91	8.10	116.64	99.02	17.62	96.15	57.56	38.59	115.4	121.4	103.4	833.30	505.93
1992	10.90	16.97	8.45	8.52	134.41	119.42	14.99	150.38	100.42	49.96	117.3	122.1	106.1	997.70	548.15
1993	41.03	37.00	15.73	21.27	199.25	127.78	71.47	178.48	187.03	-8.55	117.2	123.2	101.1	1278.28	722.76
1994	29.74	87.04	69.37	17.67	200.99	145.74	55.25	293.49	207.50	85.99	119.7	112.6	143.2	1694.42	1057.86
1995	125.55	160.92	95.46	65.46	232.28	158.33	73.95	407.30	280.33	126.97	123.0	114.5	145.1	2195.70	1479.29

Year	v13ii	v13iii	v13iv	v13a	v13ai	v13aii	v13aiii	v13aiv	v13b	v13bi	v13bii	v13biii	v13biv	v13b1	v13b1i
1952															
1953															
1954															
1955															
1956															
1957															
1958															
1959															
1960															
1961															
1962															
1963															
1964															
1965															
1966															
1967															
1968															
1969															
1970															
1971															
1972															
1973															
1974															
1975															
1976															
1977															
1978	12.78	19.26	23.82	59.83	55.70	1.50	1.73	0.90	59.82	22.07	6.66	15.16	15.93	51.94	14.98
1979	14.02	20.81	29.29	79.40	74.60	1.80	1.80	1.20	68.42	24.60	6.49	16.45	20.88	59.23	16.35
1980	16.27	22.52	32.16	81.14	75.92	2.15	1.57	1.50	76.99	27.83	7.90	18.13	23.13	65.31	17.27
1981	17.82	23.61	34.09	93.29	87.52	2.20	1.67	1.90	77.78	27.33	7.88	18.70	23.87	67.19	17.82
1982	18.47	24.35	37.66	107.99	101.27	2.50	1.72	2.50	82.51	29.84	7.76	19.45	25.46	71.31	20.19
1983	22.44	28.09	41.42	117.79	110.62	2.70	1.87	2.60	93.37	33.43	9.44	21.79	28.71	78.84	22.08
1984	24.22	32.91	43.20	128.28	120.46	2.92	2.10	2.80	104.34	37.55	10.23	25.74	30.82	90.79	26.42
1985	28.23	40.48	55.25	147.72	140.17	2.20	2.25	3.10	127.08	44.89	12.02	30.85	39.32	110.05	30.84
1986	31.36	45.86	63.42	165.28	156.57	2.48	2.73	3.50	143.31	53.12	13.30	34.85	42.04	124.30	36.67
1987	36.75	60.44	75.57	187.09	176.45	2.82	3.08	4.74	172.45	66.94	15.55	41.35	48.61	149.67	47.79
1988	44.58	87.95	77.78	217.03	202.12	4.01	5.56	5.34	221.28	94.42	18.83	61.79	46.24	190.40	68.81
1989	50.52	99.88	74.86	234.31	218.00	4.61	5.93	5.77	238.15	100.70	20.80	68.63	48.02	212.21	78.99
1990	58.88	90.91	136.25	279.09	260.14	4.74	8.26	5.95	249.98	112.51	22.36	69.36	45.75	220.69	90.23
1991	75.18	127.90	124.29	301.02	280.30	6.23	8.08	6.41	281.95	125.30	27.72	102.80	26.13	242.96	97.22
1992	100.15	131.28	218.12	323.91	298.08	7.73	9.32	8.78	347.89	119.44	39.58	100.14	88.73	295.38	84.26
1993	132.90	147.71	274.91	383.68	350.68	10.67	8.88	13.45	488.98	195.29	51.19	108.62	133.88	417.52	142.99
1994	177.69	249.26	209.61	532.89	472.10	11.12	11.70	37.97	618.07	313.66	91.23	187.88	25.30	525.77	243.75
1995	240.05	225.68	250.68	685.30	590.90	20.59	15.20	58.61	815.82	477.48	108.30	135.25	94.79	699.03	387.91

Year	v13b1ii	v13b1iii	v13b1iv	v13b2	v13b2i	v13b2ii	v13b2iii	v13b2iv	v13c	v13ci	v13cii	v13ciii	v13civ	v13c1
1952														
1953														
1954														
1955														
1956														
1957														
1958														
1959														
1960														
1961														
1962														
1963														
1964														
1965														
1966														
1967														
1968														
1969														
1970														
1971														
1972														
1973														
1974														
1975														
1976														
1977														
1978	6.21	15.05	15.70	7.88	7.09	0.45	0.11	0.23	27.34	13.36	4.62	2.37	6.99	5.91
1979	6.09	16.32	20.47	9.19	8.25	0.40	0.13	0.41	30.19	14.69	5.73	2.56	7.21	6.47
1980	7.48	17.98	22.58	11.68	10.56	0.42	0.15	0.55	33.59	17.02	6.22	2.82	7.53	6.77
1981	7.45	18.64	23.28	10.59	9.51	0.43	0.06	0.59	38.61	19.31	7.74	3.24	8.32	6.93
1982	7.35	19.29	24.48	11.20	9.65	0.41	0.16	0.98	42.02	20.93	8.21	3.18	9.70	7.61
1983	8.90	21.09	26.77	14.53	11.35	0.54	0.70	1.94	46.27	21.43	10.30	4.43	10.11	8.16
1984	9.80	24.84	29.73	13.55	11.13	0.43	0.90	1.09	54.67	28.95	11.07	5.07	9.58	9.30
1985	11.23	29.91	38.07	17.03	14.05	0.79	0.94	1.25	75.15	40.93	14.01	7.38	12.83	13.23
1986	12.49	33.92	41.22	19.01	16.45	0.81	0.93	0.82	89.09	47.35	15.58	8.28	17.88	15.00
1987	14.74	39.77	47.37	22.78	19.15	0.81	1.58	1.24	109.90	53.29	13.38	16.01	22.22	20.13
1988	17.77	59.34	44.48	30.88	25.61	1.06	2.45	1.76	145.76	77.22	21.74	20.60	26.20	24.12
1989	19.64	66.36	47.22	25.94	21.71	1.16	2.27	0.80	168.34	96.84	23.11	25.32	21.07	26.81
1990	20.95	64.81	44.70	29.29	22.28	1.41	4.55	1.05	215.37	85.75	31.78	13.29	84.55	32.27
1991	25.24	96.52	23.98	38.99	28.08	2.48	6.28	2.15	250.33	100.33	41.23	17.02	91.75	41.68
1992	37.00	94.36	79.76	52.51	35.18	2.58	5.78	8.97	325.90	130.63	52.84	21.82	120.61	51.29
1993	46.06	100.36	128.11	71.46	52.30	5.13	8.26	5.77	405.62	176.79	71.04	30.21	127.58	72.47
1994	83.42	176.40	22.20	92.30	69.91	7.81	11.48	3.10	543.46	272.10	75.34	49.68	146.34	99.63
1995	100.70	122.56	87.86	116.79	89.57	7.60	12.69	6.93	694.58	410.91	111.16	75.23	97.28	132.39

Year	v13c1i	v13c1ii	v13c1iii	v13c1iv	v13c2	v13c2i	v13c2ii	v13c2iii	v13c2iv	v13c3	v13c3i	v13c3ii	v13c3iii	v13c3iv
1952														
1953														
1954														
1955														
1956														
1957														
1958														
1959														
1960														
1961														
1962														
1963														
1964														
1965														
1966														
1967														
1968														
1969														
1970														
1971														
1972														
1973														
1974														
1975														
1976														
1977														
1978	2.26	1.09	0.28	2.28	9.71	4.71	0.57	2.08	2.35	2.55	0.20	0.06		2.29
1979	2.48	1.20	0.31	2.48	10.85	5.36	0.74	2.24	2.51	2.50	0.33	0.03		2.14
1980	2.74	1.02	0.43	2.58	11.73	5.78	1.00	2.36	2.59	2.70	0.34	0.07	0.01	2.28
1981	2.80	1.03	0.44	2.66	13.42	6.74	1.16	2.63	2.89	3.60	0.69	0.08	0.15	2.68
1982	3.08	1.08	0.49	2.96	12.81	6.48	1.09	2.45	2.79	5.02	0.86	0.08	0.22	3.86
1983	3.30	1.16	0.53	3.17	12.56	4.68	1.67	3.60	2.61	5.66	1.06	0.09	0.28	4.23
1984	4.45	1.17	0.53	3.15	15.40	7.94	1.57	3.56	2.33	6.53	1.61	0.14	0.93	3.85
1985	7.85	1.64	0.55	3.19	22.94	11.98	1.73	5.22	4.01	8.85	2.07	0.17	1.26	5.35
1986	9.01	2.05	0.87	3.07	27.60	12.60	2.75	5.04	7.21	12.55	3.16	0.26	1.97	7.16
1987	7.81	3.25	3.29	5.78	34.56	15.39	3.19	9.47	6.51	15.94	3.36	0.34	2.77	9.47
1988	10.27	3.62	4.01	6.22	46.61	22.36	3.57	11.49	9.19	20.91	6.33	0.35	4.42	9.81
1989	13.39	5.11	3.24	5.07	45.48	24.36	3.77	14.72	2.63	26.94	8.29	0.41	6.22	12.02
1990	8.47	6.13	2.31	15.36	62.94	21.81	5.25	6.86	29.02	31.01	2.36	0.50	3.26	24.89
1991	10.84	8.01	2.90	19.93	73.91	27.85	5.99	8.71	31.36	38.26	2.95	1.12	3.66	30.53
1992	14.00	10.57	3.68	23.04	104.96	37.89	7.92	11.40	47.75	49.01	6.74	2.16	4.06	36.05
1993	36.39	19.48	7.94	8.66	123.71	44.73	9.37	13.44	56.17	63.47	8.22	2.69	5.66	46.90
1994	65.67	12.56	14.52	6.88	167.75	60.66	12.70	18.22	76.17	73.60	13.32	3.84	7.45	48.99
1995	90.79	29.24	15.96	-3.60	211.37	127.66	19.76	37.34	26.61	90.15	16.73	4.55	10.63	58.24

Year	v13c4	v13c4i	v13c4ii	v13c4iii	v13c4iv	v13c5	v13c5i	v13c5ii	v13c5iii	v13c5iv	v13c6	v13c6i	v13c6ii	v13c6iii
1952														
1953														
1954														
1955														
1956														
1957														
1958														
1959														
1960														
1961														
1962														
1963														
1964														
1965														
1966														
1967														
1968														
1969														
1970														
1971														
1972														
1973														
1974														
1975														
1976														
1977														
1978	2.03	0.02	2.01			0.62	0.46	0.08	0.01	0.07	1.05	0.88	0.17	
1979	2.10	0.03	2.07			0.68	0.49	0.10	0.01	0.08	1.24	1.04	0.20	
1980	2.32	0.03	2.29			0.83	0.62	0.11	0.02	0.08	1.54	1.32	0.22	
1981	3.56	0.03	3.53			0.95	0.71	0.13	0.02	0.09	1.72	1.47	0.25	
1982	3.96	0.04	3.92			1.06	0.82	0.13	0.02	0.09	1.96	1.68	0.28	
1983	5.18	0.04	5.14			1.17	0.90	0.15	0.02	0.10	2.33	2.02	0.31	
1984	5.76	0.05	5.71			1.58	1.13	0.15	0.05	0.25	2.58	2.23	0.35	
1985	7.84	0.06	7.78			3.34	2.50	0.21	0.35	0.28	2.87	2.51	0.36	
1986	7.93	0.13	7.80			3.39	2.40	0.15	0.40	0.44	3.26	2.97	0.29	
1987	8.53	0.13	8.38	0.02		3.91	2.81	0.19	0.45	0.46	3.84	3.46	0.38	
1988	9.96	0.20	9.68	0.03	0.05	6.55	5.26	0.33	0.57	0.39	5.08	4.70	0.38	
1989	11.00	0.25	10.66	0.04	0.05	8.73	7.09	0.41	0.92	0.31	6.04	5.66	0.38	
1990	16.25	0.90	13.97	0.02	1.36	10.84	4.35	0.65	0.79	5.05	7.98	5.45	0.40	
1991	17.73	1.00	15.44	0.16	1.13	10.88	4.85	1.31	1.17	3.55	9.02	7.70	0.90	0.02
1992	20.57	1.29	18.32	0.24	0.72	16.52	6.05	1.63	1.46	7.38	11.35	9.28	1.08	0.05
1993	25.73	1.65	22.81	0.36	0.91	18.54	6.79	1.83	1.63	8.29	14.08	11.51	1.34	0.06
1994	32.30	2.75	26.97	1.37	1.21	24.84	9.10	2.45	7.39	5.90	20.72	16.64	2.01	0.07
1995	40.90	3.11	34.21	1.70	1.88	29.39	10.77	2.90	8.74	6.98	25.47	21.91	3.39	0.04

Year	v13c6iv	v13c7	v13c7i	v13c7ii	v13c7iii	v13c7iv	v13c8	v13c8i	v13c8ii	v13c8iii	v13c8iv	v13c9	v13c9i	v13c9ii
1952														
1953														
1954														
1955														
1956														
1957														
1958														
1959														
1960														
1961														
1962														
1963														
1964														
1965														
1966														
1967														
1968														
1969														
1970														
1971														
1972														
1973														
1974														
1975														
1976														
1977														
1978		3.21	3.14	0.07			0.20	0.14	0.06			1.86	1.36	0.50
1979		3.72	2.97	0.75			0.28	0.20	0.08			2.10	1.55	0.55
1980		4.46	3.66	0.80			0.31	0.21	0.10			2.63	2.03	0.60
1981		4.83	4.01	0.82			0.36	0.25	0.11			2.89	2.27	0.62
1982		5.60	4.76	0.84			0.39	0.27	0.12			3.21	2.56	0.65
1983		6.40	5.50	0.90			0.49	0.34	0.15			3.87	3.16	0.71
1984		7.57	6.58	0.99			0.57	0.41	0.16			4.88	4.08	0.80
1985		9.13	8.03	1.10			0.68	0.50	0.18			5.67	4.85	0.82
1986		10.80	9.55	1.25			0.84	0.66	0.18			6.75	5.93	0.82
1987		12.61	11.12	1.49			0.99	0.78	0.21			8.14	7.22	0.92
1988		17.61	15.52	2.09			3.99	2.86	0.51	0.08	0.54	10.93	9.72	1.21
1989		21.61	19.51	2.10			6.07	4.24	0.66	0.18	0.99	13.86	12.55	1.31
1990	2.13	17.43	13.50	2.15		1.78	7.36	5.06	1.08	0.05	1.17	26.51	22.43	1.34
1991	0.40	19.14	14.73	3.37	0.20	0.84	7.45	5.50	1.24	0.16	0.55	29.08	23.41	3.50
1992	0.94	23.02	18.08	4.12	0.28	0.54	9.41	6.77	1.90	0.46	0.28	34.72	28.78	4.66
1993	1.17	27.55	21.64	4.93	0.34	0.64	10.93	7.62	2.20	0.54	0.57	43.96	36.44	5.90
1994	2.00	42.37	36.14	5.18	0.35	0.70	15.78	12.26	2.50	0.31	0.71	59.70	53.21	6.49
1995	0.13	55.99	47.82	7.31	0.16	0.70	19.86	15.92	2.62	0.52	0.80	79.98	73.05	6.32

Year	v13c9iii	v13c9iv	v13c10	v13c10i	v13c10ii	v13c10iii	v13c10iv
1952							
1953							
1954							
1955							
1956							
1957							
1958							
1959							
1960							
1961							
1962							
1963							
1964							
1965							
1966							
1967							
1968							
1969							
1970							
1971							
1972							
1973							
1974							
1975							
1976							
1977							
1978			0.20	0.19	0.01		
1979			0.25	0.24	0.01		
1980			0.30	0.29	0.01		
1981			0.35	0.34	0.01		
1982			0.40	0.38	0.02		
1983			0.45	0.43	0.02		
1984			0.50	0.47	0.03		
1985			0.60	0.58	0.02		
1986			0.97	0.94	0.03		
1987			1.25	1.21	0.03		
1988							
1989			1.80	1.50	0.30		
1990		2.74	2.78	1.42	0.31		1.05
1991	0.04	2.13	3.18	1.50	0.35		1.33
1992	0.19	1.09	5.05	1.75	0.48		2.82
1993	0.24	1.38	5.18	1.80	0.49		2.89
1994			6.77	2.35	0.64		3.78
1995	0.14	0.47	9.08	3.15	0.86		5.07

19

Guangdong

Year	v1	v1a	v1b	v1b1	v1b2	v1c	v1c1	v1c2	v1c3	v2	v2a	v2b	v2b1	v2b2	v2c
1952		19.35	16.90	15.70	1.20		1.21	5.46			116.1	114.4	113.1	127.3	
1953		26.59	24.37	20.98	3.39		1.76	6.95			106.7	143.0	127.5	282.8	
1954		31.04	27.01	24.60	2.41		2.22	7.96			110.9	109.6	119.0	71.1	
1955		30.76	28.03	25.60	2.43		2.45	8.12			102.3	104.5	105.1	100.6	
1956		33.53	31.85	28.55	3.30		2.86	8.89			105.4	119.8	117.6	135.2	
1957		35.05	37.37	33.86	3.51		3.43	9.60			105.1	112.8	113.8	106.5	
1958		37.69	55.86	47.88	7.98		4.45	10.80			104.2	154.7	143.8	226.1	
1959		33.82	78.44	69.19	9.25		5.60	11.87			84.6	136.9	142.0	115.2	
1960		31.42	84.08	73.05	11.03		5.94	11.76			91.8	106.6	104.3	118.5	
1961		34.75	51.58	46.53	5.05		4.57	10.18			68.4	58.6	61.5	45.5	
1962		37.90	49.32	45.72	3.60		5.21	11.85			152.3	91.7	94.9	71.8	
1963		46.70	53.16	48.42	4.74		5.51	12.77			118.1	110.4	108.2	127.8	
1964		48.81	65.24	57.58	7.66		5.70	13.61			110.1	127.7	123.2	158.8	
1965		49.74	77.03	70.75	6.28		6.03	14.95			115.2	115.0	121.4	81.0	
1966		54.61	83.90	78.71	5.19		6.64	16.45			105.3	113.6	117.7	81.1	
1967		56.83	76.90	72.65	4.25		6.24	17.19			104.2	93.2	94.3	81.0	
1968		54.88	62.38	59.05	3.33		5.39	15.65			93.6	83.3	83.7	77.2	
1969		57.28	86.06	80.55	5.51		6.41	18.34			103.5	140.7	139.1	163.9	
1970		60.94	109.38	98.80	10.58		7.28	19.08			108.3	130.8	126.0	190.2	
1971		64.59	113.58	102.15	11.43		7.84	19.39			101.2	104.9	104.8	106.0	
1972		65.77	119.41	106.98	12.43		8.35	20.39			100.2	104.5	104.2	107.0	
1973		66.68	137.43	123.71	13.72		9.37	21.86			99.0	113.3	113.9	108.5	
1974		72.43	147.18	132.16	15.02		10.23	22.45			106.7	108.2	108.2	107.6	
1975		71.27	172.80	154.14	18.66		11.80	23.57			100.0	115.6	114.8	122.3	
1976		70.70	181.62	162.09	19.53		12.69	24.33			106.4	108.5	109.5	100.1	
1977		74.85	198.08	174.77	23.31		14.13	23.83			106.9	108.7	108.1	114.1	
1978		85.89	222.35	200.25	22.10		15.14	26.93			102.1	106.1	107.2	96.9	
1979		100.46	243.03	217.64	25.39		17.39	32.55			99.1	108.2	107.5	114.4	
1980		122.18	255.87	223.02	32.85		18.75	46.54			111.1	111.7	109.2	132.9	
1981		139.32	319.75	270.09	49.66		19.83	55.14			102.4	117.9	115.1	137.6	
1982		170.08	358.54	293.95	64.59		22.11	55.28			116.3	110.4	108.3	122.6	
1983		173.57	402.36	329.23	73.13		23.94	59.29			102.6	111.1	111.8	107.5	
1984		201.87	502.63	405.98	96.65		29.66	69.30			109.3	119.5	119.9	117.2	
1985		245.34	658.27	532.71	125.56		37.52	105.66			107.3	127.1	127.9	122.8	
1986		279.16	771.73	631.10	140.63		44.51	117.39			106.2	114.5	115.8	107.4	
1987		348.61	1038.67	878.29	160.38		60.14	148.60			109.6	129.5	133.1	107.5	
1988		473.78	1538.21	1318.92	219.29		69.29	206.23			107.7	132.2	135.0	110.5	
1989		548.60	1905.06	1647.24	257.82		79.27	224.24			107.8	114.8	116.3	100.5	
1990		600.71	2160.79	1902.25	258.54		108.75	223.65			107.4	115.8	117.1	102.3	
1991		654.82	2821.13	2524.12	297.01		134.51	279.63			106.1	126.8	128.6	113.5	
1992	6434.74	737.11	4081.00	3479.39	601.61	1616.63	169.27	353.05			106.1	138.1	136.0	150.0	
1993	9338.35	899.03	6244.94	5237.36	1007.58	2194.38	246.33	498.58		128.3	103.8	136.8	139.3	117.7	
1994	12542.76	1151.38	8424.65	7204.20	1220.45	2966.73	382.35	685.53		128.7	104.5	131.8	133.2	118.6	136.4
1995	16343.36	1445.48	11190.91	9720.55	1470.36	3706.97	502.94	885.91		123.7	108.3	124.3	124.9	118.5	126.6

Year	v2c1	v2c2	v3'	v3	v3a	v3b	v3b1	v3b2	v3c	v3c1	v3c2	v3c3	v3c4	v3c5	v3c6
1952	128.6	122.0	29.52	29.52	14.39	6.70			8.43						
1953	145.2	121.4	41.23	41.23	21.03	9.26			10.94						
1954	126.5	108.3	46.80	46.80	24.35	9.75			12.70						
1955	110.1	96.4	47.59	47.59	24.44	10.16			12.99						
1956	116.9	103.7	53.04	53.04	27.02	11.69			14.33						
1957	120.1	101.8	58.64	58.64	28.84	14.60			15.20						
1958	129.8	107.5	67.09	67.09	30.44	19.15			17.50						
1959	125.8	105.2	73.50	73.50	27.39	26.68			19.43						
1960	106.1	94.5	72.76	72.76	25.50	28.12			19.14						
1961	76.9	82.7	62.18	62.18	28.24	18.93			15.01						
1962	115.3	112.5	72.39	72.39	31.03	23.16			18.20						
1963	104.6	110.7	81.81	81.81	36.78	23.25			21.78						
1964	103.4	110.7	81.63	81.63	37.02	24.12			20.49						
1965	106.4	114.8	87.00	87.00	37.29	27.83			21.88						
1966	109.5	108.3	96.40	96.40	41.04	32.81			22.55						
1967	93.9	103.6	95.99	95.99	41.82	31.56			22.61						
1968	86.5	90.2	87.29	87.29	38.81	28.46			20.02						
1969	118.8	116.1	98.60	98.60	39.58	36.56			22.46						
1970	113.8	103.2	112.07	112.07	44.09	44.14			23.84						
1971	107.5	100.5	113.23	113.23	43.28	45.41			24.54						
1972	106.5	104.2	118.47	118.47	43.94	47.44			27.09						
1973	112.2	106.1	128.96	128.96	44.51	54.29			30.16						
1974	109.2	101.7	138.20	138.20	47.72	58.23			32.25						
1975	115.3	104.1	157.66	157.66	48.58	71.75			37.33						
1976	107.5	101.5	156.38	156.38	46.55	72.23			37.60						
1977	111.4	96.7	168.90	168.90	47.49	79.18			42.23						
1978	107.2	108.2	184.73	184.73	55.31	85.68	75.30	10.38	43.74	9.66	18.80	5.87	1.05	2.45	1.36
1979	113.6	124.3	207.07	207.07	66.62	90.68	81.49	9.19	49.77	10.71	22.06	6.11	1.19	2.79	1.59
1980	100.9	137.9	245.71	245.71	82.97	100.97	88.50	12.47	61.77	12.86	26.71	8.36	1.54	3.58	2.04
1981	101.7	105.8	284.24	284.24	94.30	118.59	102.09	16.50	71.35	15.49	29.26	9.20	2.00	4.42	2.57
1982	107.8	97.4	331.27	331.27	118.17	133.18	111.30	21.88	79.92	16.79	31.81	10.95	2.40	5.20	3.04
1983	108.3	106.3	357.43	357.43	121.24	149.58	123.60	25.98	86.61	17.59	33.18	12.46	2.86	6.07	3.46
1984	109.9	115.4	441.81	441.81	145.25	183.84	151.28	32.56	112.72	22.85	42.00	16.60	3.50	8.02	4.73
1985	112.3	133.9	553.05	553.05	171.87	225.44	182.27	43.17	155.74	31.86	61.52	18.89	4.23	10.32	6.20
1986	109.2	106.2	637.72	637.72	188.37	248.92	202.79	46.13	200.43	35.23	68.57	31.07	7.96	18.33	9.90
1987	129.0	112.6	807.70	807.70	232.14	318.43	263.89	54.54	257.13	45.74	77.92	51.11	10.99	28.15	10.78
1988	115.2	107.3	1098.61	1098.61	306.50	443.56	372.40	71.16	348.55	55.41	107.58	69.37	15.12	41.39	12.63
1989	106.9	89.9	1311.67	1311.67	351.73	528.16	442.31	85.85	431.78	65.81	95.17	109.92	26.79	49.31	14.98
1990	108.7	104.3	1471.84	1471.84	384.59	587.04	498.92	88.12	500.21	83.56	105.22	119.73	27.36	62.13	17.19
1991	118.2	123.2	1780.56	1780.56	416.00	749.65	647.05	102.60	614.91	113.51	127.72	135.75	34.33	84.11	19.57
1992	115.8	120.4	2293.54	2293.54	465.83	1053.63	861.12	192.51	774.08	140.88	160.55	176.67	51.27	101.39	23.08
1993	137.8	119.5	3225.30	3225.30	559.67	1625.29	1318.82	306.47	1040.34	188.95	223.31	234.05	78.27	129.86	31.75
1994	159.7	115.7	4240.56	4240.56	694.65	2139.89	1763.48	376.41	1406.02	272.27	305.24	314.49	104.36	167.28	41.82
1995	109.0	115.8	5381.72	5381.72	868.99	2786.05	2337.73	448.32	1726.68	353.17	396.94	312.63	139.26	228.98	50.79

Year	v3c7	v3c8	v3c9	v3c10	v3d	v4'	v4	v4a	v4b	v4b1	v4b2	v4c	v4c1	v4c2	v4c3
1952					101	116.3	116.3	113.3	117.1			123.0			
1953					139	114.9	114.9	106.0	141.0			123.0			
1954					153	109.7	109.7	110.0	107.9			110.1			
1955					152	101.8	101.8	103.6	104.9			97.0			
1956					166	107.9	107.9	105.2	123.2			105.1			
1957					179	109.5	109.5	112.2	112.1			102.3			
1958					200	110.1	110.1	99.3	146.5			109.0			
1959					215	102.4	102.4	84.8	135.9			107.0			
1960					210	97.3	97.3	92.0	106.5			95.0			
1961					178	78.0	78.0	91.7	63.5			76.0			
1962					204	110.3	110.3	120.1	94.3			109.6			
1963					225	114.1	114.1	113.8	115.0			113.7			
1964					219	114.1	114.1	108.4	128.7			111.6			
1965					227	111.5	111.5	111.5	116.0			106.3			
1966					245	103.6	103.6	100.3	107.3			106.1			
1967					238	100.2	100.2	102.0	97.6			99.8			
1968					211	90.2	90.2	90.0	92.4			88.0			
1969					232	115.1	115.1	106.6	132.0			111.4			
1970					258	110.1	110.1	102.0	125.7			102.9			
1971					254	102.4	102.4	98.9	105.0			104.6			
1972					260	104.1	104.1	101.5	103.8			109.6			
1973					277	106.0	106.0	97.4	112.1			110.5			
1974					291	106.6	106.6	105.3	108.0			106.2			
1975					326	110.9	110.9	103.5	117.8			109.5			
1976					319	104.6	104.6	102.8	106.0			104.5			
1977					340	107.5	107.5	103.0	110.5			107.8			
1978	1.75		1.49	1.31	367	100.4	100.4	105.3	96.4	115.2	56.2	102.0			
1979	2.04		1.69	1.59	405	107.8	107.8	106.7	104.9	108.3	90.0	114.8	112.3	119.8	103.2
1980	2.59		2.16	1.93	473	116.0	116.0	112.6	116.1	112.3	135.9	120.1	117.5	115.2	134.2
1981	3.42		2.64	2.35	537	108.4	108.4	104.6	112.4	110.3	121.4	106.2	105.6	102.3	105.1
1982	4.00		3.12	2.61	615	111.3	111.3	115.6	110.1	106.7	123.3	108.6	114.9	102.3	109.6
1983	4.76		3.46	2.77	653	106.7	106.7	100.1	110.8	110.4	112.4	107.5	104.6	103.4	112.8
1984	7.17		4.87	2.98	796	114.8	114.8	113.4	117.5	119.2	111.6	111.6	102.8	111.2	117.1
1985	12.41		6.99	3.32	979	120.1	120.1	104.1	120.1	120.3	119.4	139.0	137.2	135.0	136.5
1986	13.91	0.40	10.42	4.64	1116	111.3	111.3	105.6	107.5	108.2	104.9	122.8	111.2	116.5	130.9
1987	15.71	1.29	12.42	3.02	1381	117.7	117.7	107.5	124.3	128.3	109.2	115.9	112.9	106.2	137.6
1988	22.40	4.18	16.77	3.70	1864	115.6	115.6	104.9	123.2	126.3	109.7	111.2	119.2	104.7	112.4
1989	29.63	10.81	25.60	3.76	2191	107.0	107.0	107.2	107.5	109.8	95.6	106.0	116.5	75.6	131.5
1990	32.29	19.20	29.49	4.04	2395	111.3	111.3	107.0	112.2	113.9	102.2	112.7	104.1	110.4	115.7
1991	38.22	19.62	37.41	4.67	2823	117.3	117.3	105.4	124.4	123.7	129.1	117.9	127.9	119.8	105.7
1992	45.46	24.59	45.18	5.01	3575	122.0	122.0	105.6	133.5	131.0	148.7	118.7	120.8	119.3	123.1
1993	58.27	32.27	55.92	7.69	4938	122.3	122.3	102.6	136.0	139.6	116.3	115.1	124.2	118.6	112.3
1994	78.04	39.95	71.75	10.82	6380	119.0	119.0	103.2	126.0	127.3	117.4	116.1	127.4	116.7	109.9
1995	98.29	47.40	86.73	12.49	7973	114.9	114.9	105.5	120.1	120.8	115.6	110.1	118.5	115.0	87.8

Year	v4c4	v4c5	v4c6	v4c7	v4c8	v4c9	v4c10	v5	v5a	v5a1	v5a1a	v5a1b	v5a2	v5b	v5b1
1952															
1953															
1954															
1955															
1956															
1957															
1958															
1959															
1960															
1961															
1962															
1963															
1964															
1965															
1966															
1967															
1968															
1969															
1970															
1971															
1972															
1973															
1974															
1975															
1976															
1977															
1978								187.97	119.97	102.26	65.45	36.81	17.71	54.79	37.93
1979	114.7	112.9	115.1	114.9		111.5	118.8	207.86	137.40	119.95	80.09	39.86	17.45	53.89	40.75
1980	133.9	125.7	124.7	123.0		124.2	118.0	249.46	177.47	156.06	101.38	54.68	21.41	63.63	51.77
1981	127.7	112.0	113.6	118.9		110.2	109.5	293.26	194.66	170.17	106.22	63.95	24.49	90.03	70.29
1982	118.2	114.1	114.9	113.7		114.9	107.6	335.47	222.84	193.28	119.92	73.36	29.56	108.30	93.48
1983	117.5	111.7	113.6	118.8		110.7	106.3	352.56	240.18	208.60	126.57	82.03	31.58	110.25	96.70
1984	106.4	108.4	120.7	133.3		124.4	95.0	426.41	275.31	239.24	141.96	97.28	36.07	142.52	129.59
1985	148.1	137.4	138.7	173.6		143.9	126.5	541.61	344.67	297.04	179.86	117.18	47.63	214.97	160.28
1986	159.8	154.4	116.3	105.6		140.5	116.5	617.82	406.21	340.34	203.75	136.59	65.87	234.43	181.19
1987	127.8	138.9	112.8	101.7	290.8	107.3	58.7	773.74	500.20	422.75	240.33	182.42	77.45	287.70	205.07
1988	124.7	112.4	103.6	110.3	251.3	104.4	94.1	1070.51	663.77	560.66	322.20	238.46	103.11	406.20	288.79
1989	138.0	98.2	93.8	111.9	218.7	129.1	86.6	1271.84	773.76	635.45	356.40	279.05	138.31	477.01	320.01
1990	95.5	113.5	119.4	113.5	184.8	119.9	111.6	1450.34	831.30	675.43	375.06	300.37	155.87	511.35	393.26
1991	113.5	127.8	113.3	117.8	107.9	126.2	115.1	1736.27	975.59	787.93	410.05	377.88	187.66	601.05	457.32
1992	146.2	108.6	111.3	113.2	106.2	113.5	100.4	2283.27	1297.07	1013.42	500.48	512.94	283.65	948.19	759.16
1993	126.4	101.8	111.8	109.9	112.2	106.7	128.1	3216.48	1617.35	1289.06	614.62	674.44	328.29	1548.93	1275.44
1994	126.3	108.9	111.2	112.5	109.2	108.7	115.4	4239.65	2182.43	1793.72	826.92	966.80	388.71	1981.07	1639.83
1995	121.4	118.3	108.9	112.3	107.7	109.1	108.1	5367.83	2859.84	2318.88	1022.79	1296.09	540.96	2381.31	2059.43

Year	v5b2	v5c	v5c1	v5c2	v6a1	v6a2	v6a3	v6a4	v6b2	v6b3	v6b4	v7	v7a	v7a1	v7a2
1952															
1953															
1954															
1955															
1956															
1957															
1958															
1959															
1960															
1961															
1962															
1963															
1964															
1965															
1966															
1967															
1968															
1969															
1970															
1971															
1972															
1973															
1974															
1975															
1976															
1977															
1978	16.86	13.21			20.19	41.54	2.85	0.87	33.71	2.45	0.65				
1979	13.14	16.57			24.92	51.27	2.82	1.08	36.31	2.86	0.69	109.7	112.0	117.5	104.0
1980	11.86	8.36			31.55	64.92	3.54	1.37	50.04	3.70	0.94	123.5	123.1	124.0	121.7
1981	19.74	8.57			32.52	67.69	4.40	1.61	58.31	4.51	1.13	107.4	106.7	104.0	111.4
1982	14.82	4.33			35.25	76.47	6.06	2.14	66.71	5.10	1.55	110.7	109.6	109.0	110.4
1983	13.55	2.13			41.33	76.42	5.72	3.10	72.01	7.77	2.25	107.7	107.9	106.6	110.0
1984	12.93	8.58			45.45	84.92	7.11	4.48	85.13	9.57	2.58	113.1	113.3	112.0	115.2
1985	54.69	-18.03			54.36	111.50	9.40	4.60	100.86	12.61	3.71	114.3	112.0	111.3	113.0
1986	53.24	-22.82			59.95	124.79	12.77	6.24	118.39	13.45	4.75	112.5	109.1	104.2	116.2
1987	82.63	-14.16			63.40	149.03	20.38	7.52	157.73	18.44	6.25	108.1	108.0	103.4	113.8
1988	117.41	0.54			85.38	193.89	33.41	9.52	203.92	27.45	7.09	103.8	104.1	106.6	101.2
1989	156.78	21.07			74.65	222.15	45.55	14.05	218.69	51.03	9.33	105.5	104.3	106.5	101.6
1990	118.09	107.69			76.05	223.86	57.92	17.23	229.90	58.92	11.55	110.4	109.7	108.2	111.5
1991	143.73	159.63			85.85	242.18	64.13	17.89	291.40	73.27	13.21	116.5	115.7	109.6	123.4
1992	189.03	38.01			114.79	269.70	90.49	25.50	384.39	105.76	22.79	124.2	120.0	115.5	125.1
1993	273.49	50.20			148.27	359.99	63.09	43.27	553.24	85.92	35.28	107.3	108.7	106.7	110.8
1994	341.24	76.15			204.05	451.10	102.22	69.55	746.37	150.23	70.20	108.5	110.4	108.1	112.6
1995	321.88	126.68			220.26	564.81	148.65	89.07	959.56	234.18	102.35	117.3	117.0	109.0	124.6

Year	v7b	v8	v8a	v8b	v9	v9a	v9b	v10a1	v10a2	v10a3	v10a3a	v10a3b	v10a4	v10b1	v10b2
1952															
1953															
1954															
1955															
1956															
1957															
1958															
1959															
1960															
1961															
1962															
1963															
1964															
1965															
1966															
1967															
1968															
1969															
1970															
1971															
1972															
1973															
1974															
1975															
1976															
1977															
1978		203	157	426				27.92	1.17	8.84		8.84		11.44	4.40
1979	95.0	234	190	439	110.3	116.6	99.0	28.90	1.37	10.48		10.48		8.80	3.36
1980	126.7	300	239	575	121.2	122.9	116.2	34.78	2.27	14.72		14.72		9.53	1.75
1981	112.1	322	247	648	104.9	102.6	107.3	40.09	7.28	20.95	2.08	18.87	1.97	16.14	2.56
1982	118.4	359	275	722	107.7	107.5	107.2	58.10	8.77	23.44	2.03	21.41	3.17	10.76	2.92
1983	106.3	381	286	784	106.2	105.2	106.9	57.16	11.89	20.98	1.82	19.16	6.67	5.19	5.95
1984	112.1	431	320	878	111.7	111.6	108.7	79.61	16.24	26.27	2.32	23.95	7.47	-5.92	12.91
1985	129.9	528	406	972	110.4	111.7	103.9	104.53	21.86	25.52	5.25	20.27	8.37	37.73	10.90
1986	132.1	596	460	1066	107.6	104.1	109.3	117.85	25.78	28.18	5.83	22.35	9.38	31.28	13.37
1987	109.1	724	545	1277	105.6	103.9	102.1	130.05	33.20	28.77	5.95	22.82	13.05	47.69	19.22
1988	102.3	951	720	1680	103.2	105.1	101.9	180.44	51.93	42.12	19.93	22.19	14.30	65.91	27.15
1989	111.2	1061	786	1920	102.7	105.1	99.3	204.47	52.81	44.84	14.21	30.63	18.11	75.11	37.39
1990	113.5	1099	807	2002	106.8	105.6	108.0	259.95	62.39	54.03	11.04	42.99	16.89	45.99	29.13
1991	119.7	1249	863	2428	112.8	107.2	118.9	300.64	77.81	60.33	12.70	47.63	18.54	66.41	28.17
1992	141.8	1580	1047	3139	118.0	114.7	119.1	487.52	167.34	68.58	22.15	46.43	35.72	60.89	42.41
1993	102.3	1973	1291	3804	106.8	107.2	102.1	755.53	253.84	145.33	40.33	105.00	120.74	88.84	52.30
1994	101.5	2699	1741	5096	109.9	108.3	107.9	896.17	336.53	198.70	48.72	149.98	208.43	8.76	90.64
1995	118.1	3435	2158	6448	113.8	109.3	114.8	1074.80	380.15	253.56	58.06	195.50	350.92	-71.02	41.76

Year	v10b4	v11a	v11a1	v11a2	v11b	v11b1	v11b2	v11c	v11c1	v11c2	v12	v12a	v12b	v13	v13i
1952															
1953															
1954															
1955															
1956															
1957															
1958															
1959															
1960															
1961															
1962															
1963															
1964															
1965															
1966															
1967															
1968															
1969															
1970															
1971															
1972															
1973															
1974															
1975															
1976															
1977															
1978	1.02													184.73	107.35
1979	0.98										94.1	103.5	76.4	207.07	122.75
1980	0.58										110.4	120.9	83.6	245.71	147.61
1981	1.04										128.7	122.4	152.0	284.24	170.42
1982	1.14										117.7	132.3	74.0	331.27	202.03
1983	2.41										98.6		91.1	357.43	215.74
1984	5.94										117.4	121.3	94.8	441.81	265.36
1985	6.06										143.3	113.8	364.7	553.05	333.83
1986	8.59										105.4	110.7	93.1	637.72	377.20
1987	15.72										113.7	106.1	135.0	807.70	466.22
1988	24.35										116.7	119.5	110.5	1098.61	638.00
1989	44.28										106.7	105.8	108.9	1311.67	736.65
1990	42.97										104.8	115.7	79.9	1471.84	825.24
1991	49.15										116.8	115.5	121.0	1780.56	981.73
1992	85.73										136.7	140.5	124.3	2293.54	1228.06
1993	132.35	58.15	17.43	40.72	876.65	690.25	186.40	614.13	567.76	46.37	138.5	143.0	112.4	3225.30	1716.27
1994	241.84	79.89	23.28	56.61	723.05	480.94	242.11	1178.13	1135.61	42.52	119.6	123.1	104.9	4240.56	2051.28
1995	351.14	96.79	26.35	70.44	949.33	593.56	355.77	1335.19	1439.52	-104.33	112.0	114.4	100.3	5381.72	2723.38

Year	v13ii	v13iii	v13iv	v13a	v13ai	v13aii	v13aiii	v13aiv	v13b	v13bi	v13bii	v13biii	v13biv	v13b1	v13b1i
1952															
1953															
1954															
1955															
1956															
1957															
1958															
1959															
1960															
1961															
1962															
1963															
1964															
1965															
1966															
1967															
1968															
1969															
1970															
1971															
1972															
1973															
1974															
1975															
1976															
1977															
1978	22.36	28.30	26.72	55.31	45.91	2.77	1.11	5.52	85.68	38.19	13.84	23.63	10.02	75.30	32.38
1979	24.43	30.46	29.43	66.62	55.41	3.28	1.35	6.58	90.68	40.31	14.62	25.12	10.63	81.49	35.15
1980	28.06	33.91	36.13	82.97	69.16	4.03	1.71	8.07	100.97	45.30	15.97	27.28	12.42	88.50	38.28
1981	32.77	38.97	42.08	94.30	78.76	4.51	1.97	9.06	118.59	53.60	18.48	31.39	15.12	102.09	44.29
1982	37.03	43.02	49.19	118.17	98.91	5.57	2.50	11.19	133.18	60.80	20.36	34.27	17.75	111.30	48.43
1983	40.50	47.22	53.97	121.24	101.69	5.63	2.60	11.32	149.58	68.67	22.60	37.87	20.44	123.60	53.95
1984	50.41	57.92	68.12	145.25	122.09	6.65	3.16	13.35	183.84	84.73	27.51	46.01	25.59	151.28	66.23
1985	63.54	70.92	84.76	171.87	144.77	7.76	3.79	15.55	225.44	104.61	33.30	55.30	32.23	182.27	80.03
1986	74.98	80.49	105.05	188.37	159.00	8.38	4.21	16.78	248.92	115.64	36.53	60.77	35.98	202.79	89.31
1987	95.00	103.50	142.98	232.14	196.36	10.17	5.27	20.34	318.43	147.77	46.54	77.83	46.29	263.89	116.57
1988	124.37	140.94	195.30	306.50	259.80	13.24	7.05	26.41	443.56	205.80	64.46	108.27	65.03	372.40	164.99
1989	153.01	167.52	254.49	351.74	298.77	14.97	8.21	29.79	528.16	245.90	76.08	127.53	78.65	442.31	196.55
1990	172.81	187.48	286.31	384.59	327.37	16.13	9.10	31.99	587.04	273.14	84.06	141.71	88.13	498.92	222.37
1991	215.25	236.56	347.02	415.99	354.85	17.19	9.98	33.97	749.65	348.52	106.67	180.97	113.49	647.05	289.26
1992	294.70	337.39	433.39	465.84	396.89	16.77	11.65	40.53	1053.63	480.40	157.44	264.65	151.14	861.12	371.46
1993	397.84	459.79	651.40	559.68	480.20	24.63	12.87	41.98	1625.29	789.15	215.25	370.69	250.20	1318.32	606.11
1994	550.53	601.79	1036.96	694.64	589.76	30.37	16.82	57.69	2139.89	838.22	303.52	480.38	517.77	1763.48	623.86
1995	782.34	795.29	1080.71	868.99	752.55	37.12	17.84	61.48	2786.05	1204.74	452.71	603.48	525.12	2337.73	936.48

Year	v13b1ii	v13b1iii	v13b1iv	v13b2	v13b2i	v13b2ii	v13b2iii	v13b2iv	v13c	v13ci	v13cii	v13ciii	v13civ	v13c1
1952														
1953														
1954														
1955														
1956														
1957														
1958														
1959														
1960														
1961														
1962														
1963														
1964														
1965														
1966														
1967														
1968														
1969														
1970														
1971														
1972														
1973														
1974														
1975														
1976														
1977														
1978	12.80	22.59	7.53	10.38	5.81	1.04	1.04	2.49	43.74	23.25	5.75	3.56	11.18	9.66
1979	13.69	24.21	8.44	9.19	5.16	0.93	0.91	2.19	49.77	27.03	6.53	3.99	12.22	10.71
1980	14.69	26.05	9.48	12.47	7.02	1.28	1.23	2.94	61.77	33.15	8.06	4.92	15.64	12.86
1981	16.75	29.76	11.29	16.50	9.31	1.73	1.63	3.83	71.35	38.06	9.78	5.61	17.90	15.49
1982	18.04	32.13	12.70	21.88	12.37	2.32	2.14	5.05	79.92	42.32	11.10	6.25	20.25	16.79
1983	19.80	35.34	14.51	25.98	14.72	2.80	2.53	5.93	86.61	45.38	12.27	6.75	22.21	17.59
1984	23.95	42.85	18.25	32.56	18.50	3.56	3.16	7.34	112.72	58.54	16.25	8.75	29.18	22.85
1985	28.51	51.13	22.60	43.17	24.58	4.79	4.17	9.63	155.74	84.45	22.48	11.83	36.98	31.86
1986	31.34	56.34	25.80	46.13	26.33	5.19	4.43	10.18	200.43	102.56	30.07	15.51	52.29	35.23
1987	40.31	72.62	34.39	54.54	31.20	6.23	5.21	11.90	257.13	122.09	38.29	20.40	76.35	45.74
1988	56.21	101.50	49.70	71.16	40.81	8.25	6.77	15.33	348.55	172.40	46.67	25.62	103.86	55.41
1989	65.97	119.41	60.38	85.85	49.35	10.11	8.12	18.27	431.77	191.98	61.96	31.78	146.05	65.81
1990	73.53	133.41	69.61	88.12	50.77	10.53	8.30	18.52	500.21	224.73	72.62	36.67	166.19	83.56
1991	94.23	171.36	92.20	102.60	59.26	12.44	9.61	21.29	614.92	278.36	91.39	45.61	199.56	113.51
1992	132.28	245.52	111.86	192.51	108.94	25.16	19.13	39.28	774.07	350.77	120.49	61.09	241.72	140.88
1993	178.33	342.53	191.85	306.47	183.04	36.92	28.16	58.35	1040.33	446.92	157.96	76.23	359.22	188.95
1994	261.13	446.60	431.89	376.41	214.36	42.39	33.78	85.88	1406.03	623.30	216.64	104.59	461.50	272.27
1995	402.47	522.80	475.98	448.32	268.26	50.24	80.68	49.14	1726.68	766.09	292.51	173.97	494.11	353.17

Year	v13c1i	v13c1ii	v13c1iii	v13c1iv	v13c2	v13c2i	v13c2ii	v13c2iii	v13c2iv	v13c3	v13c3i	v13c3ii	v13c3iii	v13c3iv
1952														
1953														
1954														
1955														
1956														
1957														
1958														
1959														
1960														
1961														
1962														
1963														
1964														
1965														
1966														
1967														
1968														
1969														
1970														
1971														
1972														
1973														
1974														
1975														
1976														
1977														
1978	3.13	2.19	0.78	3.56	18.80	14.29	1.17	1.62	1.72	5.86	0.40	0.14	0.53	4.79
1979	3.49	2.42	0.87	3.93	22.06	16.80	1.38	1.86	2.02	6.12	0.43	0.15	0.56	4.98
1980	4.21	2.90	1.06	4.69	26.71	20.37	1.67	2.21	2.46	8.35	0.59	0.20	0.76	6.80
1981	5.11	3.48	1.29	5.61	29.26	22.36	1.85	2.37	2.68	9.20	0.66	0.24	0.83	7.47
1982	5.57	3.76	1.40	6.06	31.81	24.36	2.01	2.52	2.92	10.95	0.80	0.28	0.99	8.88
1983	5.87	3.93	1.48	6.31	33.18	25.46	2.11	2.57	3.04	12.46	0.92	0.33	1.13	10.08
1984	7.68	5.09	1.94	8.14	42.00	32.29	2.68	3.19	3.84	16.59	1.24	0.44	1.49	13.42
1985	10.77	7.07	2.73	11.29	61.52	47.39	3.95	4.58	5.60	18.89	1.43	0.52	1.69	15.25
1986	11.98	7.80	3.04	12.41	68.57	52.93	4.42	5.00	6.22	31.07	2.40	0.86	2.78	25.03
1987	15.65	10.09	3.99	16.01	77.92	60.27	5.05	5.56	7.04	51.10	4.00	1.45	4.56	41.09
1988	19.08	12.19	4.87	19.27	107.58	83.37	7.00	7.52	9.69	69.36	5.50	2.01	6.17	55.68
1989	22.80	14.44	5.83	22.74	95.17	73.90	6.22	6.51	8.54	109.91	3.85	3.25	9.75	88.06
1990	29.13	18.28	7.46	28.69	105.22	81.87	6.91	7.05	9.39	119.72	9.78	3.61	10.59	95.74
1991	39.81	24.76	10.22	38.72	127.72	99.57	8.43	8.38	11.34	135.75	11.25	4.18	11.98	108.34
1992	54.44	29.86	14.79	41.79	160.55	130.98	11.32	7.88	10.37	176.67	11.07	4.95	13.53	147.12
1993	60.67	39.66	17.08	71.54	223.31	175.37	13.38	14.75	19.81	234.05	13.05	7.86	21.69	186.45
1994	93.84	63.29	20.32	94.82	305.24	225.20	20.61	24.93	34.50	314.49	34.23	9.68	30.02	240.56
1995	128.46	94.34	30.08	100.29	396.94	246.18	28.45	66.31	56.00	312.63	42.83	15.37	34.62	219.81

Year	v13c4	v13c4i	v13c4ii	v13c4iii	v13c4iv	v13c5	v13c5i	v13c5ii	v13c5iii	v13c5iv	v13c6	v13c6i	v13c6ii	v13c6iii
1952														
1953														
1954														
1955														
1956														
1957														
1958														
1959														
1960														
1961														
1962														
1963														
1964														
1965														
1966														
1967														
1968														
1969														
1970														
1971														
1972														
1973														
1974														
1975														
1976														
1977														
1978	1.05	0.05	0.64	0.11	0.25	2.45	1.23	0.37	0.32	0.53	1.36	0.82	0.27	0.01
1979	1.19	0.07	0.72	0.12	0.28	2.79	1.39	0.42	0.36	0.62	1.59	0.96	0.32	0.01
1980	1.54	0.09	0.92	0.16	0.37	3.58	1.78	0.54	0.46	0.80	2.04	1.23	0.40	0.01
1981	2.00	0.12	1.19	0.21	0.48	4.42	2.19	0.67	0.56	1.00	2.57	1.56	0.50	0.01
1982	2.40	0.15	1.41	0.26	0.58	5.20	2.56	0.79	0.65	1.20	3.04	1.98	0.63	0.02
1983	2.86	0.19	1.67	0.31	0.69	6.07	2.98	0.93	0.75	1.41	3.46	2.28	0.71	0.02
1984	3.50	0.23	2.03	0.39	0.85	8.02	3.92	1.25	0.99	1.86	4.73	3.03	0.94	0.03
1985	4.23	0.30	2.44	0.48	1.01	10.32	5.03	1.59	1.25	2.45	6.20	4.06	1.24	0.03
1986	7.96	0.58	4.56	0.92	1.90	18.33	9.35	2.99	2.32	3.67	9.90	5.86	1.77	0.05
1987	10.99	0.83	6.25	1.28	2.63	28.15	13.62	4.39	3.36	6.78	10.78	7.01	2.09	0.06
1988	15.12	1.19	8.53	1.79	3.61	41.39	19.96	6.47	4.89	10.07	12.63	7.85	2.31	0.06
1989	26.79	2.20	14.99	3.22	6.38	49.31	23.69	7.75	5.77	12.10	14.98	9.34	2.71	0.08
1990	27.36	2.34	15.20	3.33	6.49	62.13	29.74	9.80	7.21	15.38	17.19	10.76	3.08	0.09
1991	34.33	3.05	18.93	4.25	8.10	84.11	40.12	13.32	9.66	21.01	19.57	12.29	3.48	0.10
1992	51.27	3.87	26.57	8.21	12.62	101.39	49.88	17.47	15.34	18.70	23.08	14.48	4.87	0.08
1993	78.27	7.69	43.29	8.57	18.72	129.86	57.26	20.42	12.41	39.77	31.75	19.46	5.34	0.19
1994	104.36	9.72	60.83	10.60	23.21	167.28	83.29	24.37	16.37	43.25	41.82	26.91	6.43	0.25
1995	139.26	11.47	78.76	15.04	33.99	228.98	119.19	30.13	22.49	57.17	50.79	34.19	7.21	0.55

Year	v13c6iv	v13c7	v13c7i	v13c7ii	v13c7iii	v13c7iv	v13c8	v13c8i	v13c8ii	v13c8iii	v13c8iv	v13c9	v13c9i	v13c9ii
1952														
1953														
1954														
1955														
1956														
1957														
1958														
1959														
1960														
1961														
1962														
1963														
1964														
1965														
1966														
1967														
1968														
1969														
1970														
1971														
1972														
1973														
1974														
1975														
1976														
1977														
1978	0.26	1.76	0.90	0.67	0.18	0.01						1.49	1.12	0.30
1979	0.30	2.03	1.04	0.78	0.20	0.01						1.69	1.26	0.34
1980	0.40	2.60	1.34	1.00	0.25	0.01						2.16	1.61	0.43
1981	0.50	3.42	1.75	1.33	0.33	0.01						2.64	1.96	0.52
1982	0.41	4.00	1.98	1.61	0.40	0.01						3.12	2.31	0.61
1983	0.45	4.76	2.35	1.92	0.47	0.02						3.46	2.56	0.67
1984	0.73	7.18	3.58	2.88	0.70	0.02						4.87	3.59	0.94
1985	0.87	12.41	7.02	4.32	1.04	0.03						6.99	5.13	1.35
1986	2.22	13.91	6.96	5.58	1.33	0.04	0.40	0.23	0.09	0.02	0.06	10.42	7.63	2.00
1987	1.62	15.72	7.88	6.31	1.49	0.04	1.29	0.74	0.29	0.04	0.22	12.42	9.07	2.37
1988	2.41	22.42	17.17	4.01	0.10	1.14	4.17	2.38	0.97	0.14	0.68	16.77	12.20	3.18
1989	2.85	29.64	22.74	5.26	0.13	1.51	10.80	6.13	2.52	0.38	1.77	25.60	18.57	4.82
1990	3.26	32.30	24.82	5.69	0.14	1.65	19.20	10.92	4.52	0.67	3.09	29.49	21.33	5.53
1991	3.70	38.23	29.44	6.67	0.17	1.95	19.62	11.18	4.65	0.69	3.10	37.41	26.98	6.97
1992	3.65	45.45	34.26	9.02	0.18	1.99	24.59	13.86	6.64	1.04	3.05	45.18	32.92	9.79
1993	6.76	58.26	44.23	10.29	0.29	3.45	32.27	18.22	7.26	0.92	5.87	55.92	38.28	10.46
1994	8.23	78.05	62.20	11.62	0.34	3.89	39.95	23.25	8.65	1.31	6.74	71.75	53.84	11.16
1995	8.84	98.29	80.89	12.87	1.11	3.42	47.40	27.19	10.42	1.62	8.17	86.73	64.55	13.61

Year	v13c9iii	v13c9iv	v13c10	v13c10i	v13c10ii	v13c10iii	v13c10iv
1952							
1953							
1954							
1955							
1956							
1957							
1958							
1959							
1960							
1961							
1962							
1963							
1964							
1965							
1966							
1967							
1968							
1969							
1970							
1971							
1972							
1973							
1974							
1975							
1976							
1977							
1978	0.01	0.06	1.31	1.31			
1979	0.01	0.08	1.59	1.59			
1980	0.01	0.11	1.93	1.93			
1981	0.01	0.15	2.35	2.35			
1982	0.01	0.19	2.61	2.61			
1983	0.02	0.21	2.77	2.77			
1984	0.02	0.32	2.98	2.98			
1985	0.03	0.48	3.32	3.32			
1986	0.05	0.74	4.64	4.64			
1987	0.06	0.92	3.02	3.02			
1988	0.08	1.31	3.70	3.70			
1989	0.11	2.10	3.76	3.76			
1990	0.13	2.50	4.04	4.04			
1991	0.16	3.30	4.67	4.67			
1992	0.04	2.43	5.01	5.01			
1993	0.33	6.85	7.69	7.69			
1994	0.45	6.30	10.82	10.82			
1995	2.15	6.42	12.49	11.14	1.35		

20

Guangxi

Year	v1	v1a	v1b	v1b1	v1b2	v1c	v1c1	v1c2	v1c3	v2	v2a	v2b	v2b1	v2b2	v2c
1952	19.10	11.49	4.71	4.05	0.66	2.90	0.33	1.38	1.19	116.2	113.8	116.5	131.5	71.8	127.8
1953	22.76	12.34	6.44	5.42	1.02	3.98	0.50	1.78	1.70	118.3	107.0	136.5	133.9	150.8	142.2
1954	25.99	13.45	7.75	6.62	1.13	4.79	0.63	2.14	2.02	114.8	107.4	124.2	125.9	116.0	126.6
1955	28.77	14.23	8.98	7.66	1.32	5.56	0.71	2.32	2.53	109.4	105.1	112.4	113.1	108.3	117.7
1956	32.95	15.33	10.26	8.59	1.67	7.36	0.91	2.59	3.86	114.0	108.2	111.9	113.9	101.3	131.7
1957	35.84	16.75	10.89	9.19	1.70	8.20	1.13	2.44	4.63	111.1	111.6	107.5	107.8	105.1	114.2
1958	43.03	18.60	15.26	12.15	3.11	9.17	1.71	2.58	4.88	124.0	112.0	161.4	158.1	175.5	107.1
1959	50.62	16.08	22.39	17.44	4.95	12.15	2.39	3.14	6.62	118.7	84.5	150.8	147.3	163.9	137.4
1960	54.36	14.65	25.55	19.49	6.06	14.16	2.83	3.53	7.80	108.3	87.2	117.7	111.5	139.0	118.6
1961	38.48	14.44	13.12	10.53	2.59	10.92	1.70	2.19	7.03	65.5	80.1	44.0	49.2	29.6	90.1
1962	38.16	17.08	11.23	9.53	1.70	9.85	1.38	2.06	6.41	92.5	114.3	80.7	84.6	62.8	84.4
1963	39.63	16.76	12.61	10.49	2.12	10.26	1.46	2.47	6.33	106.3	106.9	105.2	103.0	118.7	106.7
1964	46.15	20.13	15.01	11.94	3.07	11.01	1.91	2.28	6.82	111.8	121.3	125.5	120.6	152.0	89.8
1965	54.69	23.66	18.72	15.59	3.13	12.31	2.85	2.33	7.13	103.3	110.7	128.7	133.9	106.3	62.7
1966	59.78	23.02	23.12	19.36	3.76	13.64	3.18	3.12	7.34	119.4	98.4	126.1	126.2	125.7	160.7
1967	57.62	24.08	19.75	17.04	2.71	13.79	2.47	3.81	7.51	105.0	104.1	86.9	91.0	64.6	140.2
1968	49.67	23.89	13.66	12.15	1.51	12.12	1.72	2.98	7.42	84.5	99.6	67.4	69.3	52.7	85.3
1969	66.65	25.58	25.98	22.33	3.65	15.09	2.98	4.55	7.56	141.5	106.9	199.4	191.4	279.7	138.9
1970	76.24	26.85	32.72	27.41	5.31	16.67	3.69	4.83	8.15	117.3	104.8	133.0	129.0	160.4	110.8
1971	88.01	30.23	38.97	33.30	5.67	18.81	4.40	5.35	9.06	114.4	113.0	116.7	120.7	97.1	112.7
1972	102.04	35.80	43.56	37.48	6.08	22.68	4.93	5.86	11.89	111.9	107.8	111.1	112.6	101.5	120.9
1973	112.12	38.97	49.10	42.77	6.33	24.05	5.36	6.59	12.10	108.5	106.6	113.1	114.9	100.7	103.5
1974	117.19	40.72	49.98	42.73	7.25	26.49	5.33	8.67	12.49	108.7	103.6	109.6	110.1	105.4	115.7
1975	132.64	44.28	61.41	52.31	9.10	26.95	5.47	8.63	12.85	108.0	108.2	111.9	111.5	115.3	100.5
1976	137.11	43.39	65.98	56.71	9.27	27.74	5.29	8.99	13.46	103.8	97.2	108.0	109.7	94.0	105.8
1977	149.01	44.62	74.06	63.90	10.16	30.33	6.04	10.09	14.20	109.7	103.3	114.4	115.6	104.2	109.1
1978	166.10	46.17	83.24	69.97	13.27	36.69	6.74	10.46	19.49	113.8	102.5	110.5	109.6	120.3	137.1
1979	180.65	55.57	88.85	74.47	14.38	36.23	6.46	9.51	20.26	102.6	105.5	103.4	103.3	104.1	98.3
1980	197.00	63.31	94.04	78.64	15.40	39.65	6.68	10.31	22.66	103.6	104.0	106.0	107.4	92.7	98.6
1981	219.52	74.41	98.80	85.07	13.73	46.31	7.00	17.08	22.23	104.7	100.0	104.0	109.7	75.3	114.4
1982	252.34	88.23	109.85	92.73	17.12	54.26	8.83	19.37	26.06	113.3	117.0	110.9	108.9	126.1	112.5
1983	267.75	89.50	118.64	98.51	20.13	59.61	9.56	19.98	30.07	105.5	100.0	108.1	106.6	117.6	108.9
1984	298.77	95.02	131.22	109.48	21.74	72.53	11.81	22.26	38.46	108.2	99.7	108.2	109.6	100.2	120.7
1985	364.55	108.02	169.67	139.40	30.27	86.86	13.69	25.83	47.34	112.9	102.1	121.5	120.8	126.0	109.8
1986	414.73	118.69	201.31	164.79	36.52	94.73	16.29	25.85	52.59	106.7	103.4	111.4	111.9	108.6	100.6
1987	498.25	137.92	247.74	207.45	40.29	112.59	20.26	30.32	62.01	111.8	104.9	115.8	118.3	100.2	110.7
1988	661.56	168.94	325.24	272.00	53.24	167.38	30.00	53.23	84.15	107.7	98.0	115.7	115.8	114.9	99.1
1989	804.39	212.17	372.42	326.99	45.43	219.80	38.92	82.15	98.73	103.5	110.3	103.1	106.2	80.3	97.1
1990	925.06	252.22	398.57	353.44	45.13	274.27	49.20	107.50	117.57	104.7	108.0	107.2	108.2	97.6	93.3
1991	1082.89	278.15	478.90	421.47	57.43	325.84	73.97	116.02	135.85	113.4	108.1	116.5	115.4	125.1	113.7
1992	1418.78	329.58	671.32	582.81	88.51	417.88	95.06	146.17	176.65	125.2	114.9	134.8	135.3	130.7	120.1
1993	2018.55	390.11	1058.86	877.94	180.92	569.58	124.82	204.10	240.66	121.6	107.2	131.3	127.8	157.2	117.3
1994	2911.98	537.21	1621.32	1380.69	240.63	753.45	141.81	267.83	343.81	121.8	108.0	133.1	135.7	117.4	111.0
1995	3720.51	743.50	2009.81	1735.84	273.97	967.20	183.29	348.73	435.18	114.1	117.2	114.9	115.4	111.1	109.9

Year	v2c1	v2c2	v3'	v3	v3a	v3b	v3b1	v3b2	v3c	v3c1	v3c2	v3c3	v3c4	v3c5	v3c6
1952	140.9	129.2	12.81	12.81	8.34	2.95	2.53	0.42	1.52	0.15	0.70				
1953	174.0	130.8	14.24	14.24	8.71	3.48	2.99	0.49	2.05	0.21	0.87				
1954	139.1	125.7	16.21	16.21	9.60	4.13	3.54	0.59	2.48	0.25	1.09				
1955	113.7	110.1	17.43	17.43	9.96	4.47	4.05	0.42	3.00	0.27	1.29				
1956	131.2	110.6	19.51	19.51	10.63	4.97	4.40	0.57	3.91	0.36	1.37				
1957	125.7	96.2	21.57	21.57	11.45	5.54	4.91	0.63	4.58	0.46	1.50				
1958	140.8	101.9	24.52	24.52	12.71	6.79	5.79	1.00	5.02	0.81	1.45				
1959	153.7	124.6	26.75	26.75	11.68	8.88	7.58	1.30	6.19	0.87	1.56				
1960	113.2	116.1	26.15	26.15	10.63	8.39	7.38	1.01	7.13	1.06	1.65				
1961	65.4	73.5	23.79	23.79	10.46	7.51	5.55	1.96	5.82	0.69	1.14				
1962	78.7	87.2	23.82	23.82	12.44	6.08	5.34	0.74	5.30	0.60	1.07				
1963	104.2	123.6	24.49	24.49	12.13	6.87	6.01	0.86	5.49	0.60	1.30				
1964	131.8	74.5	27.18	27.18	14.40	7.09	5.99	1.10	5.69	0.81	1.02				
1965	150.8	41.6	31.45	31.45	17.13	8.46	7.26	1.20	5.86	1.17	0.65				
1966	130.9	224.8	31.68	31.68	16.50	8.73	7.71	1.02	6.45	1.42	0.87				
1967	70.7	203.4	31.18	31.18	17.51	6.96	6.31	0.65	6.71	1.05	1.40				
1968	68.4	75.9	28.46	28.46	17.37	5.11	4.77	0.34	5.98	0.65	1.12				
1969	177.0	173.4	35.22	35.22	18.52	9.14	8.04	1.10	7.56	3.39	1.87				
1970	127.7	105.9	39.36	39.36	19.27	11.47	9.85	1.62	8.62	1.88	2.12				
1971	118.3	110.8	45.75	45.75	21.60	14.56	13.14	1.42	9.59	2.16	2.30				
1972	112.0	109.8	53.47	53.47	25.57	16.01	14.78	1.23	11.89	2.54	2.60				
1973	99.2	111.8	58.53	58.53	27.72	18.32	16.67	1.65	12.49	2.78	2.85				
1974	102.8	138.3	62.27	62.27	28.55	19.78	17.96	1.82	13.94	2.76	4.09				
1975	96.8	99.5	67.02	67.02	30.36	22.72	20.25	2.47	13.94	2.76	3.90				
1976	114.1	103.5	67.32	67.32	29.74	23.56	21.55	2.01	14.02	2.65	3.73				
1977	109.9	113.2	68.75	68.75	30.18	24.41	22.17	2.24	14.16	3.05	4.29				
1978	95.8	123.6	75.85	75.85	30.88	25.81	23.29	2.52	19.16	3.67	4.43	1.81	1.45	0.48	0.59
1979	103.5	89.1	84.59	84.59	37.43	27.98	25.12	2.86	19.18	3.71	3.98	1.49	1.88	0.59	0.59
1980	104.7	95.5	97.33	97.33	43.91	30.79	27.78	3.01	22.63	4.79	5.00	1.95	2.45	0.72	0.59
1981	97.8	163.4	113.46	113.46	52.39	33.01	29.71	3.30	28.06	5.06	10.40	1.44	2.61	0.85	0.73
1982	104.7	111.7	129.15	129.15	62.93	34.72	30.98	3.74	31.50	5.36	11.36	2.66	2.76	1.03	0.84
1983	100.0	103.3	134.60	134.60	63.36	37.09	32.39	4.70	34.15	5.93	11.17	3.52	2.94	1.39	0.92
1984	123.5	110.5	150.27	150.27	66.01	43.26	36.97	6.29	41.00	6.88	12.31	5.69	3.12	1.61	1.27
1985	109.7	105.7	180.97	180.97	77.18	54.69	45.92	8.77	49.10	7.70	14.56	8.69	3.31	2.01	1.35
1986	112.8	92.2	205.46	205.46	85.27	69.03	58.41	10.62	51.16	9.04	12.30	7.74	3.55	2.78	1.70
1987	121.0	108.6	241.56	241.56	99.53	81.79	70.96	10.83	60.24	11.53	13.55	10.06	3.91	3.46	1.84
1988	107.6	115.1	313.28	313.28	117.72	100.69	86.38	14.31	94.87	15.72	28.23	18.21	4.31	4.84	2.70
1989	104.5	93.9	383.44	383.44	148.99	109.97	97.11	12.86	124.48	20.44	44.41	19.30	4.65	5.25	3.40
1990	101.7	97.3	449.06	449.06	175.61	118.45	104.79	13.66	155.00	25.79	57.53	19.73	5.18	7.07	4.24
1991	129.8	106.2	518.59	518.59	192.68	141.02	123.66	17.36	184.89	38.65	62.03	23.51	9.47	8.04	5.25
1992	120.2	117.4	646.60	646.60	229.13	187.48	161.44	26.04	229.99	49.14	74.92	27.83	12.11	11.71	6.62
1993	113.0	119.8	893.58	893.58	266.62	321.96	273.89	48.07	305.00	61.16	101.66	38.31	17.69	14.70	9.10
1994	114.5	104.3	1241.83	1241.83	357.74	485.57	420.35	65.22	398.52	69.52	130.96	51.15	22.23	24.33	13.41
1995	109.7	111.5	1606.15	1606.15	488.97	605.12	530.51	74.61	512.06	93.02	168.97	67.30	25.14	31.22	17.99

Year	v3c7	v3c8	v3c9	v3c10	v3d	v4'	v4	v4a	v4b	v4b1	v4b2	v4c	v4c1	v4c2	v4c3
1952				0.67	67										
1953				0.97	73	108.8	108.8	104.0	107.5	106.1	117.6	140.1	159.1	128.2	
1954				1.14	81	113.7	113.7	108.7	118.8	118.8	118.9	126.5	125.3	130.2	
1955				1.44	86	109.2	109.2	103.0	115.3	121.8	72.2	122.4	112.1	119.8	
1956				2.18	94	109.8	109.8	107.2	102.4	102.1	106.1	129.7	131.6	105.1	
1957				2.62	102	112.4	112.4	109.6	112.5	112.7	110.2	119.8	127.6	112.6	
1958				2.76	113	115.0	115.0	112.6	125.4	120.8	159.5	108.9	169.7	96.5	
1959				3.76	122	108.7	108.7	89.7	130.7	130.7	130.5	125.0	121.5	107.2	
1960				4.42	119	98.6	98.6	87.1	104.1	96.7	146.2	110.7	68.6	109.4	
1961				3.99	110	85.7	85.7	80.1	75.7	85.3	39.6	106.6	119.1	86.0	
1962				3.63	109	100.4	100.4	113.1	93.9	96.5	73.1	93.4	83.1	97.3	
1963				3.59	108	105.9	105.9	103.2	112.6	112.2	117.4	103.0	100.3	120.3	
1964				3.86	117	106.7	106.7	118.9	99.7	97.0	127.1	98.9	133.6	74.8	
1965				4.04	131	109.9	109.9	113.0	117.0	117.2	115.1	98.1	145.7	61.0	
1966				4.16	127	100.3	100.3	97.5	95.7	97.1	84.8	110.7	127.5	133.6	
1967				4.26	122	98.7	98.7	105.7	83.4	85.6	63.5	104.6	74.9	160.5	
1968				4.21	109	89.1	89.1	99.4	69.9	71.3	52.8	89.5	60.5	80.5	
1969				2.30	131	126.6	126.6	106.6	176.9	168.1	322.1	127.1	224.9	167.6	
1970				4.62	142	114.8	114.8	103.9	130.8	128.9	146.9	115.5	143.4	113.0	
1971				5.13	160	116.6	116.6	110.6	131.8	139.4	87.5	111.9	115.6	108.9	
1972				6.75	182	115.0	115.0	114.4	109.6	112.6	81.8	124.4	118.0	114.0	
1973				6.86	194	104.9	104.9	100.6	114.0	112.7	130.3	102.4	95.3	110.0	
1974				7.09	201	105.4	105.4	101.1	107.2	107.7	101.8	112.0	99.3	143.5	
1975				7.28	212	106.8	106.8	105.2	113.8	112.9	124.2	100.2	100.0	95.6	
1976				7.64	208	101.1	101.1	97.9	103.7	106.5	74.3	103.6	110.8	96.0	
1977				6.82	208	105.0	105.0	101.8	107.5	107.6	107.2	107.1	100.0	115.2	
1978	2.47	0.65	1.31	2.30	225	109.4	109.4	102.3	100.4	100.0	103.6	146.7	119.5	123.6	
1979	2.53	0.76	1.33	2.32	246	103.9	103.9	105.5	105.6	105.2	109.1	98.4	100.7	91.8	79.6
1980	2.56	0.82	1.38	2.37	278	110.4	110.4	112.6	106.7	108.5	92.1	111.0	129.3	114.9	123.5
1981	2.86	0.91	1.56	1.64	317	108.0	108.0	102.5	105.5	106.9	92.7	123.0	105.7	205.7	74.3
1982	3.10	0.98	1.75	1.66	354	112.5	112.5	118.5	105.1	104.1	114.7	110.6	106.1	107.2	179.7
1983	3.34	1.05	1.98	1.91	363	103.3	103.3	99.3	106.9	105.0	125.6	107.0	107.3	99.0	129.8
1984	4.08	1.35	2.50	2.19	399	106.9	106.9	97.9	113.6	112.6	122.0	115.5	115.6	109.1	150.1
1985	4.76	1.49	2.74	2.49	471	111.0	111.0	105.0	119.0	117.8	128.2	111.1	107.8	109.2	139.8
1986	5.97	1.78	3.55	2.75	525	106.4	106.4	105.7	118.1	119.4	109.2	93.7	107.5	79.2	78.1
1987	6.86	2.04	4.23	2.76	607	109.2	109.2	105.7	112.0	114.6	92.6	110.8	120.8	102.4	122.6
1988	8.36	2.50	7.14	2.86	770	104.5	104.5	93.8	108.8	108.1	115.0	114.2	115.4	139.6	116.0
1989	9.56	3.68	10.32	3.47	927	103.6	103.6	112.4	99.2	100.7	86.1	99.0	102.4	82.9	119.0
1990	11.31	4.40	15.39	4.36	1066	107.0	107.0	108.5	106.4	106.6	104.3	105.8	93.4	96.8	100.5
1991	12.97	4.89	18.79	1.29	1211	112.7	112.7	108.8	115.9	114.8	125.0	114.8	131.7	106.2	117.2
1992	15.59	6.23	23.86	1.98	1490	118.3	118.3	112.9	128.0	127.9	128.5	116.6	119.7	112.8	110.5
1993	18.87	8.16	28.67	6.68	2031	121.2	121.2	106.6	146.3	146.6	143.8	115.1	108.4	116.9	118.8
1994	28.89	11.54	37.52	8.97	2772	116.0	116.0	105.8	130.2	131.6	120.0	110.7	106.5	104.2	108.1
1995	38.21	12.18	46.84	11.19	3543	115.3	115.3	115.9	118.3	119.1	111.4	111.1	116.0	111.2	113.7

Year	v4c4	v4c5	v4c6	v4c7	v4c8	v4c9	v4c10	v5	v5a	v5a1	v5a1a	v5a1b	v5a2	v5b	v5b1
1952								12.81	10.45	9.72	7.76	1.96	0.73	2.20	1.99
1953								14.24	12.13	11.16	8.86	2.30	0.97	3.37	2.89
1954								16.21	13.64	12.51	10.17	2.34	1.13	4.84	3.76
1955								17.43	15.00	13.69	11.09	2.60	1.31	4.90	3.78
1956								19.51	16.63	15.04	12.32	2.72	1.59	5.70	4.66
1957								21.57	15.84	14.53	11.49	3.04	1.31	4.60	3.15
1958								24.52	19.95	18.16	14.67	3.49	1.79	7.37	5.96
1959								26.75	21.79	19.99	15.62	4.37	1.80	10.73	9.17
1960								26.15	21.57	19.25	14.07	5.18	2.32	8.94	7.78
1961								23.79	20.49	18.74	13.58	5.16	1.75	3.80	3.57
1962								23.82	20.52	18.77	13.70	5.07	1.75	4.00	2.90
1963								24.49	22.48	20.61	14.58	6.03	1.87	5.54	4.01
1964								27.18	23.59	21.51	15.22	6.29	2.08	5.71	4.67
1965								31.45	27.41	25.22	18.88	6.34	2.19	7.72	6.44
1966								31.68	29.48	26.91	20.00	6.91	2.57	10.25	8.94
1967								31.18	29.76	27.04	20.08	6.96	2.72	5.38	5.45
1968								28.46	27.67	25.00	18.64	6.36	2.67	8.07	6.66
1969								35.22	30.40	27.02	19.57	7.45	3.38	12.10	10.22
1970								39.36	31.70	27.65	20.21	7.44	4.05	13.16	10.74
1971								45.75	35.43	30.35	22.14	8.21	5.08	15.75	12.41
1972								53.47	40.77	35.02	26.24	8.78	5.75	16.21	12.68
1973								58.53	45.35	38.84	29.57	9.27	6.51	18.04	14.98
1974								62.27	46.06	40.00	30.20	9.80	6.06	18.92	14.06
1975								67.02	50.88	44.86	34.56	10.30	6.02	23.23	18.00
1976								67.32	52.44	45.60	34.39	11.21	6.84	23.02	18.00
1977								68.75	53.87	46.92	35.34	11.58	6.95	25.38	19.36
1978								75.85	59.22	50.14	38.55	11.59	9.08	26.80	20.89
1979	125.2	118.9	96.0	98.3	112.9	98.4	97.7	84.59	65.41	55.19	41.75	13.44	10.22	26.21	20.57
1980	121.4	114.4	93.4	94.5	101.0	95.7	94.2	97.33	77.79	65.62	49.28	16.34	12.17	29.08	26.76
1981	105.6	117.5	122.2	110.3	110.2	111.5	68.2	113.46	87.29	74.09	56.28	17.81	13.20	32.73	26.97
1982	103.8	118.8	113.1	106.5	105.7	109.7	99.0	129.15	105.45	89.60	71.17	18.43	15.85	30.56	19.11
1983	104.4	132.5	107.3	105.6	105.1	110.5	112.4	134.60	111.40	93.87	73.94	19.93	17.53	32.40	23.30
1984	99.3	108.1	129.2	114.3	120.1	118.8	107.9	150.27	126.73	102.82	80.34	22.48	23.91	36.51	34.42
1985	97.8	114.6	98.0	107.6	101.4	101.6	105.4	180.97	152.73	123.92	96.13	27.79	28.81	61.80	42.22
1986	94.3	121.3	110.7	110.3	104.9	115.0	98.0	205.46	169.14	137.65	102.06	35.59	31.49	72.04	55.21
1987	103.9	117.4	102.0	108.3	108.1	112.4	94.6	241.56	189.66	154.31	112.71	41.60	35.35	79.69	62.72
1988	78.1	91.5	119.1	98.9	84.7	126.1	77.4	313.28	251.93	196.36	134.04	62.32	55.57	104.29	75.63
1989	98.7	117.1	102.0	92.7	148.4	97.5	81.8	383.44	296.29	228.80	157.25	71.55	67.49	111.54	70.81
1990	106.8	131.6	130.9	124.1	118.3	130.5	110.0	449.06	346.68	265.41	180.03	85.38	81.27	107.40	72.60
1991	180.2	111.5	121.7	112.9	109.4	120.0	29.9	518.59	394.07	297.08	195.00	102.08	96.99	137.14	99.38
1992	122.5	136.8	118.2	113.0	120.1	119.0	142.4	646.60	445.12	328.31	212.95	115.36	116.81	227.39	150.11
1993	129.5	109.2	118.7	105.5	113.8	104.3	286.0	893.58	586.55	422.30	257.72	164.58	164.25	353.30	278.07
1994	112.4	135.1	120.5	125.4	123.0	107.2	108.5	1241.83	817.21	588.47	336.66	251.81	228.74	477.82	382.59
1995	98.3	111.4	116.0	114.7	117.0	108.2	107.5	1606.15	1041.93	754.12	430.25	323.87	287.81	632.47	423.37

Year	v5b2	v5c	v5c1	v5c2	v6a1	v6a2	v6a3	v6a4	v6b2	v6b3	v6b4	v7	v7a	v7a1	v7a2
1952	0.21	0.16	3.59	3.43								106.2	104.3	100.3	123.3
1953	0.48	-1.26	3.99	5.25								113.5	112.3	111.6	115.1
1954	1.08	-2.27	4.54	6.81								108.7	108.5	111.4	97.6
1955	1.12	-2.47	4.88	7.35								109.8	109.5	109.5	109.1
1956	1.04	-2.82	5.46	8.28								110.3	109.3	110.3	105.0
1957	1.45	1.13	6.04	4.91								91.2	92.3	88.8	108.5
1958	1.41	-2.80	6.86	9.66								125.5	124.5	127.1	115.0
1959	1.56	-5.77	7.49	13.26								108.1	108.8	104.7	125.8
1960	1.16	-4.36	7.32	11.68								93.2	90.9	86.2	107.2
1961	0.23	-0.50	6.66	7.16								91.5	92.7	94.7	87.0
1962	1.10	-0.70	6.67	7.37								99.0	98.8	97.9	101.3
1963	1.53	-3.53	6.86	10.39								112.8	111.9	111.7	118.1
1964	1.04	-2.12	7.61	9.73								102.6	102.2	100.6	106.5
1965	1.28	-3.68	8.81	12.49								111.3	112.6	117.1	101.0
1966	1.31	-8.05	8.87	16.92								105.5	104.4	103.7	106.5
1967	0.43	-4.46	8.73	13.19								104.8	104.3	104.2	104.6
1968	1.41	-7.28	7.97	15.25								88.3	87.8	88.7	85.3
1969	1.88	-7.28	9.86	17.14								110.5	108.6	105.8	117.0
1970	2.42	-5.50	11.02	16.52								107.2	105.0	105.8	102.6
1971	3.34	-5.43	12.81	18.24								115.1	112.9	112.8	113.2
1972	3.53	-3.51	14.97	18.48								115.2	115.4	118.5	107.0
1973	3.06	-4.86	16.39	21.25								107.5	107.1	108.9	101.6
1974	4.86	-2.71	17.44	20.15								100.1	101.4	100.6	104.0
1975	5.23	-7.09	18.77	25.86								113.6	115.4	118.2	106.8
1976	5.02	-8.14	18.85	26.99								105.2	103.6	101.6	110.5
1977	6.02	-10.50	19.25	29.75								105.6	105.7	105.5	106.4
1978	5.91	-10.17	22.05	32.22	17.46	17.48	2.64	0.97	10.38	0.90	0.31	110.0	106.7	108.3	101.7
1979	5.64	-7.03	28.90	35.93	18.98	18.63	3.12	1.02	11.96	1.14	0.34	101.6	100.3	97.3	110.4
1980	2.32	-9.54	31.80	41.34	22.45	22.23	3.43	1.17	14.72	1.20	0.42	117.3	117.1	117.7	115.3
1981	5.76	-6.56	41.63	48.19	25.69	25.89	3.23	1.47	15.87	1.48	0.46	111.5	112.2	114.1	106.4
1982	11.45	-6.86	47.99	54.85	32.23	32.32	5.03	1.59	16.36	1.53	0.54	117.6	118.0	123.9	98.8
1983	9.10	-9.20	47.97	57.17	28.10	38.48	5.59	1.77	17.95	1.49	0.49	104.3	103.5	102.9	105.9
1984	2.09	-12.97	50.85	63.82	34.77	36.74	6.35	2.48	20.32	1.56	0.60	110.3	105.3	103.5	112.1
1985	19.58	-33.56	46.74	80.30	39.75	46.64	6.33	3.41	24.81	2.10	0.88	110.8	111.3	110.4	114.6
1986	16.83	-35.72	51.44	87.16	38.85	52.87	6.82	3.52	31.24	3.20	1.15	103.4	103.1	102.1	106.8
1987	16.97	-27.79	95.15	122.94	39.92	60.82	8.02	3.95	36.22	3.90	1.48	104.6	104.5	102.9	110.2
1988	28.66	-42.94	94.36	137.30	40.35	79.52	9.84	4.33	55.92	4.54	1.86	106.7	104.5	100.2	117.9
1989	40.73	-24.39	133.66	158.05	45.67	94.55	12.30	4.73	63.28	5.88	2.39	95.6	98.8	100.7	93.6
1990	34.80	-5.02	169.73	174.75	65.72	96.87	12.11	5.33	75.52	6.89	2.97	108.0	107.1	104.3	115.1
1991	37.76	-12.62	207.63	220.25	72.58	100.40	16.09	5.93	87.07	11.05	3.96	113.0	111.3	108.6	116.8
1992	77.28	-25.91	371.14	397.05	88.26	95.46	19.37	9.86	96.57	13.19	5.60	110.5	105.8	104.6	108.1
1993	75.23	-46.27	564.56	610.83	107.22	117.39	22.79	10.32	137.33	17.54	9.71	110.8	109.2	102.0	122.8
1994	95.23	-53.20	805.56	858.76	124.07	160.96	34.89	16.74	206.12	27.92	17.77	112.7	113.6	106.8	124.3
1995	209.10	-68.25	1025.85	1094.10	157.87	207.93	45.39	19.06	266.98	33.35	23.54	112.1	113.7	115.9	110.7

Year	v7b	v8	v8a	v8b	v9	v9a	v9b	v10a1	v10a2	v10a3	v10a3a	v10a3b	v10a4	v10b1	v10b2
1952	140.2	51	46	84	104.1	97.9	127.3								
1953	129.8	57	51	106	109.8	108.7	125.0								
1954	111.1	63	57	109	105.4	108.0	98.1								
1955	114.3	67	61	119	108.5	107.4	106.8								
1956	121.5	73	66	125	106.3	108.6	105.5								
1957	80.4	69	61	134	91.2	87.3	104.3								
1958	136.5	84	77	140	120.3	124.6	104.5								
1959	100.9	91	82	156	108.4	105.3	112.1								
1960	119.0	88	74	179	91.1	86.3	103.8								
1961	82.2	87	72	183	93.9	95.7	89.6								
1962	101.4	86	71	200	97.4	95.5	112.3								
1963	107.6	91	72	249	109.3	107.9	123.8								
1964	106.7	92	73	253	98.8	97.1	103.9								
1965	99.4	105	88	248	109.9	113.6	97.6								
1966	116.9	108	90	259	101.1	100.0	102.4								
1967	109.8	106	88	250	101.1	101.3	100.0								
1968	92.3	95	80	231	85.7	86.8	86.7								
1969	126.5	100	80	283	105.1	101.5	121.9								
1970	123.6	100	80	280	102.4	103.0	101.3								
1971	129.8	106	86	293	109.0	110.0	107.5								
1972	114.0	119	100	293	112.8	115.9	100.0								
1973	109.5	129	109	301	104.1	106.9	98.7								
1974	91.9	129	108	316	98.4	97.2	103.4								
1975	101.8	142	121	325	113.5	116.0	104.6								
1976	116.4	141	118	341	101.4	99.2	106.2								
1977	105.2	142	119	342	103.4	104.1	103.5								
1978	132.2	149	128	329	104.7	106.3	97.7	9.60	10.18	1.11	0.08	1.03		4.51	1.40
1979	108.6	161	136	360	98.1	95.6	104.3	9.80	8.59	2.18	0.15	2.03		5.52	0.12
1980	118.1	187	158	417	114.9	115.5	109.7	12.18	10.63	3.95	0.28	3.67		1.62	0.70
1981	107.9	207	177	440	110.2	112.0	102.9	10.19	14.38	2.40	0.17	2.23		2.10	3.66
1982	115.7	246	220	443	115.5	121.5	96.3	13.93	1.80	3.38	0.24	3.14		4.29	7.16
1983	108.7	253	225	468	101.7	101.4	103.4	15.55	1.05	6.70	0.32	6.38		3.93	5.17
1984	137.8	273	241	513	103.7	102.3	109.1	22.68	1.37	10.37	0.83	9.54		-1.90	3.99
1985	108.8	323	284	607	109.2	108.5	109.4	24.18	2.47	15.57	1.88	13.69		13.72	5.86
1986	104.4	352	298	741	101.5	100.8	102.0	30.36	3.83	21.02	2.49	18.53		13.71	3.12
1987	104.9	388	324	832	102.5	101.2	105.8	39.04	6.17	17.51	2.33	15.18		12.17	4.80
1988	116.2	483	384	1074	102.5	100.0	101.6	51.11	8.22	16.30	3.77	12.53		22.59	6.07
1989	83.5	553	446	1177	96.9	99.6	89.3	45.47	7.29	18.05	3.71	14.34		30.62	10.11
1990	112.2	630	502	1364	105.3	102.8	111.8	45.20	5.47	21.93	3.11	18.82		26.31	8.49
1991	118.5	694	534	1615	109.4	106.8	115.7	63.96	6.40	29.02	4.69	24.33		27.67	10.09
1992	124.9	756	579	1740	104.5	103.7	103.0	88.05	14.76	32.82	6.47	26.35	14.48	43.15	13.98
1993	114.9	960	690	2475	110.1	104.1	122.4	169.36	37.86	36.22	13.44	22.78	34.63	42.04	8.11
1994	110.7	1314	896	3483	111.5	106.1	114.3	193.97	56.00	83.38	25.98	57.40	49.24	32.43	15.48
1995	108.1	1664	1141	4245	111.5	106.1	114.3	216.28	57.00	90.28	27.23	63.05	59.81	46.86	54.80

Year	v10b4	v11a	v11a1	v11a2	v11b	v11b1	v11b2	v11c	v11c1	v11c2	v12	v12a	v12b	v13	v13i
1952											69.6	72.5	50.6		
1953											217.8	207.2	316.7		
1954											138.2	129.3	192.3		
1955											117.1	118.0	113.1		
1956											96.9	95.6	102.4		
1957											79.4	71.7	110.0		
1958											172.5	195.6	122.3		
1959											146.6	141.9	162.6		
1960											119.6	91.8	203.6		
1961											27.3	41.8	7.5		
1962											111.5	80.9	343.3		
1963											139.0	132.5	150.7		
1964											93.1	112.1	63.3		
1965											124.3	128.0	114.0		
1966											136.7	142.6	118.4		
1967											50.5	57.7	23.5		
1968											151.2	123.0	412.3		
1969											156.9	163.8	137.8		
1970											111.8	109.6	119.0		
1971											127.1	122.2	149.1		
1972											98.8	96.5	107.2		
1973											104.1	104.8	101.7		
1974											105.4	92.5	148.9		
1975											112.2	116.2	103.7		
1976											95.7	94.7	97.9		
1977											114.6	111.1	122.7		
1978		4.84	3.36	1.48	15.88	13.50	2.38	6.08	4.03	2.05	109.2	109.2	109.4	75.85	46.39
1979		4.64	3.21	1.43	12.90	10.89	2.01	8.67	6.47	2.20	91.8	92.3	90.8	84.59	54.68
1980		4.24	3.61	0.63	13.84	13.02	0.82	11.00	10.13	0.87	95.7	121.5	41.8	97.33	64.16
1981		4.80	3.53	1.27	15.04	12.93	2.11	12.89	10.51	2.38	99.9	89.4	220.8	113.46	73.68
1982		4.94	2.28	2.66	13.23	9.15	4.08	12.39	7.68	4.71	95.2	67.3	225.6	129.15	88.75
1983		4.05	1.78	2.27	16.44	13.24	3.20	11.91	8.28	3.63	106.3	130.1	73.1	134.60	91.09
1984		2.85	2.26	0.59	20.15	19.42	0.73	13.51	12.74	0.77	102.9	135.1	23.0	150.27	100.49
1985		6.91	2.21	4.70	31.10	24.00	7.10	23.79	16.01	7.78	161.1	115.0	833.1	180.97	118.39
1986		6.64	2.43	4.21	36.28	29.96	6.32	29.12	22.82	6.30	109.8	122.3	84.7	205.46	134.36
1987		6.67	2.42	4.25	44.49	37.77	6.72	28.53	22.53	6.00	102.5	105.1	94.7	241.56	155.94
1988		10.27	3.06	7.21	61.42	48.35	13.07	32.60	24.22	8.38	90.4	78.1	129.7	313.28	189.84
1989		8.05	2.73	5.32	60.16	45.18	14.98	43.33	22.90	20.43	110.9	97.1	137.5	383.44	231.88
1990		9.80	2.82	6.98	55.98	42.56	13.42	41.62	27.22	14.40	102.5	89.0	120.9	449.06	273.22
1991		12.12	2.98	9.14	55.80	39.75	16.05	69.22	56.65	12.57	112.5	115.7	105.9	518.59	304.23
1992	20.15	16.83	4.71	12.12	89.68	60.04	29.64	120.88	85.36	35.52	153.6	135.8	194.2	646.60	386.76
1993	25.08	29.84	7.90	21.94	130.57	113.70	16.87	192.89	156.47	36.42	118.9	122.5	105.7	893.58	546.88
1994	47.32	35.19	12.05	23.14	193.59	151.76	41.83	249.04	218.78	30.26	118.9	122.5	105.7	1241.83	807.78
1995	107.44	92.81	12.69	80.12	254.15	156.17	97.98	285.51	254.51	31.00	121.9	107.0	185.6	1606.15	1207.21

Year	v13ii	v13iii	v13iv	v13a	v13ai	v13aii	v13aiii	v13aiv	v13b	v13bi	v13bii	v13biii	v13biv	v13b1	v13b1i
1952															
1953															
1954															
1955															
1956															
1957															
1958															
1959															
1960															
1961															
1962															
1963															
1964															
1965															
1966															
1967															
1968															
1969															
1970															
1971															
1972															
1973															
1974															
1975															
1976															
1977															
1978	7.26	8.86	13.34	30.88	27.62	0.92	0.92	1.42	25.81	8.95	3.12	6.56	7.18	23.29	7.01
1979	8.82	9.23	11.86	37.43	33.78	0.98	0.93	1.74	27.98	9.59	3.95	6.84	7.60	25.12	7.38
1980	10.03	10.75	12.39	43.91	39.87	1.07	0.93	2.04	30.79	10.67	4.09	7.80	8.23	27.78	8.35
1981	10.87	11.63	17.28	52.39	48.56	1.17	0.91	1.75	33.01	10.79	4.28	8.53	9.41	29.71	8.24
1982	12.11	12.35	15.94	62.93	59.18	1.28	0.98	1.49	34.72	11.35	5.05	8.74	9.58	30.98	8.46
1983	12.75	12.94	17.82	63.36	59.69	1.40	0.99	1.28	37.09	12.30	5.16	9.18	10.45	32.39	8.62
1984	14.93	14.32	20.53	66.01	62.40	1.52	1.01	1.08	43.26	14.58	6.65	10.04	11.99	36.97	9.55
1985	16.09	17.97	28.52	77.18	73.38	1.66	1.23	0.91	54.69	19.54	7.03	12.91	15.21	45.92	12.23
1986	19.02	22.85	29.23	85.27	81.09	1.82	1.59	0.77	69.03	24.47	8.85	16.41	19.30	58.41	15.57
1987	21.42	28.00	36.20	99.53	94.63	2.11	1.96	0.83	81.79	28.30	9.67	20.29	23.53	70.96	19.24
1988	27.59	35.05	60.80	117.72	112.38	2.36	2.00	0.98	100.69	38.47	11.41	24.09	26.72	86.38	27.27
1989	34.48	40.74	76.34	148.99	141.90	3.33	2.53	1.23	109.97	39.44	14.19	27.01	29.33	97.11	29.45
1990	41.51	44.25	90.08	175.61	167.16	3.85	3.06	1.54	118.45	40.56	17.59	28.78	31.52	104.79	29.97
1991	50.03	63.88	100.45	192.68	180.07	5.00	4.36	3.25	141.02	48.15	21.14	45.11	26.62	123.56	35.64
1992	60.53	87.88	111.43	229.13	213.89	5.57	4.53	5.14	187.48	75.28	26.56	62.96	22.68	161.44	56.15
1993	67.30	111.72	167.68	266.62	248.54	6.64	5.49	5.95	321.96	164.09	24.85	80.99	52.03	273.39	130.25
1994	86.86	152.07	195.12	357.74	335.03	7.47	7.48	7.76	485.57	204.96	36.56	107.25	136.80	420.35	157.93
1995	134.50	171.73	92.71	488.97	455.29	11.48	11.15	11.05	605.12	395.51	65.15	117.03	27.43	530.51	340.78

Year	v13b1ii	v13b1iii	v13b1iv	v13b2	v13b2i	v13b2ii	v13b2iii	v13b2iv	v13c	v13ci	v13cii	v13ciii	v13civ	v13c1
1952														
1953														
1954														
1955														
1956														
1957														
1958														
1959														
1960														
1961														
1962														
1963														
1964														
1965														
1966														
1967														
1968														
1969														
1970														
1971														
1972														
1973														
1974														
1975														
1976														
1977														
1978	2.94	6.46	6.88	2.52	1.94	0.18	0.10	0.30	19.16	9.82	3.22	1.38	4.74	3.67
1979	3.75	6.73	7.26	2.86	2.21	0.20	0.11	0.34	19.18	11.31	3.89	1.46	2.52	3.71
1980	3.88	7.68	7.87	3.01	2.32	0.21	0.12	0.36	22.63	13.62	4.87	2.02	2.12	4.79
1981	4.05	8.40	9.02	3.30	2.55	0.23	0.13	0.39	28.06	14.33	5.42	2.19	6.12	5.06
1982	4.81	8.59	9.12	3.74	2.89	0.24	0.15	0.46	31.50	18.22	5.78	2.63	4.87	5.36
1983	4.90	8.99	9.88	4.70	3.68	0.26	0.19	0.57	34.15	19.10	6.19	2.77	6.09	5.93
1984	6.37	9.78	11.27	6.29	5.03	0.28	0.26	0.72	41.00	23.51	6.76	3.27	7.46	6.88
1985	6.74	12.52	14.43	8.77	7.31	0.29	0.39	0.78	49.10	25.47	7.40	3.83	12.40	7.70
1986	8.54	15.94	18.36	10.62	8.90	0.31	0.47	0.94	51.16	28.80	8.35	4.85	9.16	9.04
1987	9.33	19.69	22.70	10.83	9.06	0.34	0.60	0.83	60.24	33.01	9.64	5.75	11.84	11.53
1988	10.96	23.27	24.88	14.31	11.20	0.45	0.82	1.84	94.87	38.99	13.82	8.96	33.10	15.72
1989	13.69	26.12	27.85	12.86	9.99	0.50	0.89	1.48	124.48	50.54	16.96	11.20	45.78	20.44
1990	16.86	27.82	30.14	13.66	10.59	0.73	0.96	1.38	155.00	65.50	20.07	12.41	57.02	25.79
1991	19.71	43.95	24.36	17.36	12.51	1.43	1.16	2.26	184.89	76.01	23.89	14.41	70.58	38.65
1992	24.01	60.97	20.31	26.04	19.13	2.55	1.99	2.37	229.99	97.59	28.40	20.39	83.61	49.14
1993	21.98	75.30	46.36	48.07	33.84	2.87	5.69	5.67	305.00	134.25	35.81	25.24	109.70	61.16
1994	33.13	102.25	136.80	65.22	47.03	3.43	4.71	10.05	398.52	267.79	42.83	37.34	50.56	69.52
1995	60.83	111.51	17.39	74.61	54.73	4.32	5.52	10.04	512.06	356.41	57.87	43.55	54.23	93.02

Year	v13c1i	v13c1ii	v13c1iii	v13c1iv	v13c2	v13c2i	v13c2ii	v13c2iii	v13c2iv	v13c3	v13c3i	v13c3ii	v13c3iii	v13c3iv
1952														
1953														
1954														
1955														
1956														
1957														
1958														
1959														
1960														
1961														
1962														
1963														
1964														
1965														
1966														
1967														
1968														
1969														
1970														
1971														
1972														
1973														
1974														
1975														
1976														
1977														
1978	1.12	0.82	0.51	1.22	4.43	1.85	0.39	0.81	1.38	1.81	0.09	0.02		1.70
1979	1.35	0.93	0.59	0.84	3.98	2.90	0.45	0.79	-0.16	1.49	0.10	0.02		1.37
1980	1.50	1.26	0.59	1.44	5.00	4.75	0.52	1.34	-1.61	1.95	0.16	0.02		1.77
1981	1.56	1.49	0.59	1.42	10.40	5.57	0.60	1.49	2.74	1.44	0.18	0.03		1.23
1982	1.81	1.55	0.62	1.38	11.36	8.56	0.69	1.87	0.24	2.66	0.21	0.05		2.40
1983	1.98	1.58	0.67	1.70	11.17	8.32	0.80	1.72	0.33	3.52	0.22	0.07	0.20	3.03
1984	2.70	1.73	0.75	1.70	12.31	9.87	0.92	2.05	-0.53	5.69	0.30	0.09	0.25	5.05
1985	3.10	1.95	0.78	1.87	14.56	9.95	1.06	2.42	1.13	8.69	0.34	0.11	0.35	7.89
1986	3.80	2.33	0.64	2.27	12.30	9.44	1.22	3.36	-1.72	7.74	0.36	0.11	0.49	6.78
1987	4.61	2.82	0.85	3.25	13.55	10.77	1.44	3.78	-2.44	10.06	0.48	0.12	0.67	8.79
1988	3.79	2.58	0.83	8.52	28.23	7.24	1.70	3.34	15.95	18.21	9.15	1.35	3.74	3.97
1989	4.96	3.40	1.08	11.00	44.41	11.35	2.76	5.27	25.03	19.30	10.24	1.30	3.60	4.16
1990	6.22	4.24	1.36	13.97	57.53	14.73	3.52	6.82	32.46	19.73	13.00	0.92	2.58	3.23
1991	9.24	6.26	2.05	21.10	62.03	15.88	3.79	7.35	35.01	23.51	14.58	1.17	3.28	4.48
1992	12.48	7.14	4.70	24.82	74.92	20.55	4.95	9.01	40.41	27.83	13.11	1.69	4.23	3.80
1993	15.50	8.82	5.86	30.98	101.66	27.89	6.72	12.22	54.83	38.31	26.57	1.99	3.94	5.81
1994	54.61	11.20	5.38	-1.67	130.96	67.28	7.23	21.37	35.08	51.15	46.90	3.15	5.42	-4.32
1995	69.35	17.06	5.62	0.99	168.97	88.09	9.65	26.29	44.94	67.30	58.88	3.71	6.98	-2.27

Year	v13c4	v13c4i	v13c4ii	v13c4iii	v13c4iv	v13c5	v13c5i	v13c5ii	v13c5iii	v13c5iv	v13c6	v13c6i	v13c6ii	v13c6iii
1952														
1953														
1954														
1955														
1956														
1957														
1958														
1959														
1960														
1961														
1962														
1963														
1964														
1965														
1966														
1967														
1968														
1969														
1970														
1971														
1972														
1973														
1974														
1975														
1976														
1977														
1978	1.45		1.45			0.48	0.27	0.05	0.03	0.13	0.59	0.50	0.05	
1979	1.88	0.01	1.87			0.59	0.35	0.06	0.04	0.14	0.59	0.50	0.05	
1980	2.45	0.01	2.44			0.72	0.44	0.06	0.05	0.17	0.59	0.50	0.05	
1981	2.61	0.01	2.60			0.85	0.51	0.07	0.07	0.20	0.73	0.63	0.06	
1982	2.76	0.02	2.74			1.03	0.60	0.09	0.10	0.24	0.84	0.72	0.06	
1983	2.94	0.04	2.90			1.39	0.84	0.12	0.13	0.30	0.92	0.79	0.07	
1984	3.12	0.03	3.09			1.61	0.91	0.15	0.17	0.38	1.27	1.13	0.07	
1985	3.31	0.03	3.28			2.01	1.13	0.18	0.22	0.48	1.35	1.20	0.07	
1986	3.55	0.04	3.51			2.78	1.67	0.24	0.30	0.57	1.70	1.46	0.12	
1987	3.91	0.04	3.87			3.46	2.16	0.27	0.37	0.66	1.84	1.56	0.13	
1988	4.31	0.01	4.12		0.18	4.84	1.91	0.84	0.53	1.56	2.70	2.29	0.29	
1989	4.65	0.01	4.43		0.21	5.25	2.06	0.91	0.58	1.70	3.40	2.89	0.36	
1990	5.18	0.04	4.82	0.03	0.29	7.07	2.78	1.23	0.77	2.29	4.24	3.60	0.45	
1991	9.47	0.20	5.30	0.13	3.84	8.04	3.16	1.40	0.88	2.60	5.25	4.46	0.56	
1992	12.11	0.49	5.88	0.34	5.40	11.71	4.40	1.80	1.21	4.30	6.62	5.63	0.71	
1993	17.69	1.51	7.32	0.74	8.12	14.70	5.53	2.26	1.52	5.39	9.10	7.74	0.97	
1994	22.23	1.93	9.06	0.95	10.29	24.33	14.13	2.69	3.03	4.48	13.41	10.93	1.02	0.06
1995	25.14	2.03	10.48	1.19	11.44	31.22	27.06	2.72	2.50	-1.06	17.99	16.78	1.12	0.09

Year	v13c6iv	v13c7	v13c7i	v13c7ii	v13c7iii	v13c7iv	v13c8	v13c8i	v13c8ii	v13c8iii	v13c8iv	v13c9	v13c9i	v13c9ii
1952														
1953														
1954														
1955														
1956														
1957														
1958														
1959														
1960														
1961														
1962														
1963														
1964														
1965														
1966														
1967														
1968														
1969														
1970														
1971														
1972														
1973														
1974														
1975														
1976														
1977														
1978	0.04	2.47	2.12	0.18	0.03	0.14	0.65	0.56	0.06		0.03	1.31	1.04	0.20
1979	0.04	2.53	2.14	0.18	0.04	0.17	0.76	0.68	0.06		0.02	1.33	1.04	0.22
1980	0.04	2.56	2.15	0.18	0.04	0.19	0.82	0.71	0.06		0.05	1.38	1.12	0.23
1981	0.04	2.86	2.33	0.21	0.04	0.28	0.91	0.78	0.07		0.06	1.56	1.24	0.23
1982	0.06	3.10	2.52	0.23	0.04	0.31	0.98	0.84	0.08		0.06	1.75	1.39	0.24
1983	0.06	3.34	2.67	0.26	0.05	0.36	1.05	0.90	0.08		0.07	1.98	1.59	0.25
1984	0.07	4.08	3.30	0.30	0.05	0.43	1.35	1.17	0.09		0.09	2.50	2.07	0.26
1985	0.08	4.76	3.86	0.33	0.06	0.51	1.49	1.30	0.10		0.09	2.74	2.21	0.26
1986	0.12	5.97	4.89	0.37	0.06	0.65	1.78	1.58	0.12		0.08	3.55	2.89	0.27
1987	0.15	6.86	5.42	0.47	0.08	0.89	2.04	1.82	0.13		0.09	4.23	3.49	0.32
1988	0.12	8.36	6.36	1.35	0.11	0.54	2.50	1.69	0.55	0.11	0.15	7.14	5.66	0.83
1989	0.15	9.56	7.27	1.55	0.12	0.62	3.68	2.50	0.80	0.16	0.22	10.32	8.13	1.19
1990	0.19	11.31	8.60	1.83	0.14	0.74	4.40	2.99	0.95	0.19	0.27	15.39	12.19	1.78
1991	0.23	12.97	9.87	2.10	0.16	0.84	4.89	3.33	1.03	0.21	0.32	18.79	14.89	2.18
1992	0.28	15.59	11.94	2.41	0.21	1.03	6.23	4.37	1.08	0.28	0.50	23.86	19.03	2.62
1993	0.39	18.87	14.45	2.91	0.26	1.25	8.16	5.73	1.46	0.38	0.59	28.67	22.86	3.15
1994	1.40	28.89	23.49	3.35	0.37	1.68	11.54	8.53	1.57	0.44	1.00	37.52	31.26	3.32
1995		38.21	31.46	6.52	0.22	0.01	12.18	9.75	1.71	0.54	0.18	46.84	42.10	4.62

Year	v13c9iii	v13c9iv	v13c10	v13c10i	v13c10ii	v13c10iii	v13c10iv
1952							
1953							
1954							
1955							
1956							
1957							
1958							
1959							
1960							
1961							
1962							
1963							
1964							
1965							
1966							
1967							
1968							
1969							
1970							
1971							
1972							
1973							
1974							
1975							
1976							
1977							
1978		0.07	2.30	2.27			0.03
1979		0.07	2.32	2.24	0.05		0.03
1980		0.03	2.37	2.28	0.05		0.04
1981		0.09	1.64	1.52	0.06		0.06
1982		0.12	1.66	1.55	0.05		0.06
1983		0.14	1.91	1.75	0.06		0.10
1984		0.17	2.19	2.03	0.06		0.10
1985		0.27	2.49	2.35	0.06		0.08
1986		0.39	2.75	2.67	0.06		0.02
1987		0.42	2.76	2.66	0.07		0.03
1988	0.10	0.55	2.86	0.89	0.21	0.20	1.56
1989	0.15	0.80	3.47	1.08	0.26	0.24	1.89
1990	0.22	1.20	4.36	1.35	0.33	0.30	2.38
1991	0.26	1.46	1.29	0.40	0.10	0.09	0.70
1992	0.26	1.95	1.98	0.59	0.12	0.15	1.12
1993	0.32	2.34	6.68	6.47	0.21		
1994	0.32	2.62	8.97	8.73	0.24		
1995	0.12		11.19	10.91	0.28		

21

Hainan

Year	v1	v1a	v1b	v1b1	v1b2	v1c	v1c1	v1c2	v1c3	v2	v2a	v2b	v2b1	v2b2	v2c
1952															
1953															
1954															
1955															
1956															
1957															
1958															
1959															
1960															
1961															
1962															
1963															
1964															
1965															
1966															
1967															
1968															
1969															
1970															
1971															
1972															
1973															
1974															
1975															
1976															
1977															
1978															
1979															
1980															
1981															
1982															
1983															
1984															
1985															
1986															
1987															
1988															
1989															
1990	215.29	68.72	69.23	44.32	24.91	77.34	10.03	32.42	34.89						
1991	261.93	75.79	88.26	56.49	31.77	97.88	12.56	39.69	45.63	120.1	111.4	123.6	122.4	125.1	122.8
1992	386.17	87.16	134.62	75.54	59.08	164.39	16.98	59.90	87.51	145.7	114.8	140.9	134.2	149.2	154.5
1993	622.24	120.25	248.52	128.27	120.25	253.47	28.32	99.64	125.51	131.2	111.3	153.6	138.5	172.9	123.6
1994	803.50	169.99	315.92	164.75	151.17	317.59	37.05	129.29	151.25	115.4	113.9	120.5	117.6	123.5	111.2
1995	889.59	202.52	333.02	197.84	135.18	354.05	42.76	145.71	165.58	107.8	112.5	106.4	114.8	97.2	106.8

Year	v2c1	v2c2	v3'	v3	v3a	v3b	v3b1	v3b2	v3c	v3c1	v3c2	v3c3	v3c4	v3c5	v3c6
1952															
1953															
1954															
1955															
1956															
1957															
1958															
1959															
1960															
1961															
1962															
1963															
1964															
1965															
1966															
1967															
1968															
1969															
1970															
1971															
1972															
1973															
1974															
1975															
1976															
1977															
1978															
1979															
1980															
1981															
1982															
1983															
1984															
1985			42.26	42.26	21.80	9.30	5.88	3.42	11.16	1.75	4.01	1.66	0.54	0.43	0.47
1986			46.73	46.73	24.05	9.92	6.67	3.25	12.76	2.07	4.29	1.93	0.65	0.68	0.54
1987			57.30	57.30	28.68	10.89	7.69	3.20	17.73	3.23	5.73	2.47	0.94	1.00	0.69
1988			77.13	77.13	38.59	14.15	9.94	4.21	24.39	4.01	8.64	3.74	1.08	1.54	0.83
1989			91.40	91.40	42.85	18.25	11.53	6.72	30.30	4.76	10.23	4.23	1.26	2.37	1.14
1990			102.49	102.49	46.02	20.12	12.91	7.21	36.35	6.02	11.35	5.31	1.40	3.24	1.52
1991	120.7	120.1	120.51	120.51	50.22	24.65	14.86	9.79	45.64	7.70	15.05	6.49	2.02	4.16	1.79
1992	134.1	190.3	181.71	181.71	54.13	38.34	20.36	17.98	89.24	10.85	29.32	11.68	16.05	8.25	2.00
1993	135.6	133.1	258.08	258.08	77.73	66.29	34.37	31.92	114.06	15.72	38.76	17.37	15.30	10.81	2.56
1994	109.7	106.1	330.95	330.95	107.55	83.66	42.84	40.82	139.74	22.60	47.84	23.06	12.36	13.17	2.97
1995	110.4	106.7	364.17	364.17	130.86	78.64	42.13	36.51	154.67	24.54	51.83	27.89	9.44	15.87	3.55

Year	v3c7	v3c8	v3c9	v3c10	v3d	v4'	v4	v4a	v4b	v4b1	v4b2	v4c	v4c1	v4c2	v4c3
1952															
1953															
1954															
1955															
1956															
1957															
1958															
1959															
1960															
1961															
1962															
1963															
1964															
1965															
1966															
1967															
1968															
1969															
1970															
1971															
1972															
1973															
1974															
1975															
1976															
1977															
1978															
1979															
1980															
1981															
1982															
1983															
1984															
1985	0.88	0.08	1.16	0.18	729										
1986	1.01	0.08	1.30	0.21	798	106.3	106.3	106.8	101.8	105.8	95.0	109.5	107.2	105.7	115.1
1987	1.55	0.13	1.69	0.30	939	112.5	112.5	109.2	108.6	115.4	98.4	121.7	134.8	120.3	120.2
1988	1.93	0.12	2.06	0.44	1241	110.3	110.3	103.8	119.6	123.2	110.9	115.2	106.1	118.0	124.7
1989	2.54	0.15	2.95	0.67	1444	105.7	105.7	103.1	113.9	105.2	134.4	105.0	110.0	96.6	104.3
1990	3.12	0.17	3.41	0.81	1598	110.6	110.6	109.2	100.5	110.0	111.5	112.6	104.6	110.3	118.0
1991	3.66	0.21	3.58	0.98	1836	114.9	114.9	108.7	120.1	120.0	120.2	119.9	118.3	128.6	117.7
1992	4.63	0.51	4.45	1.52	2727	140.2	140.2	110.0	138.3	131.8	148.2	174.6	137.6	179.2	166.8
1993	5.80	0.76	5.54	1.44	3815	120.9	120.9	110.5	150.6	136.1	167.0	114.4	121.0	106.7	124.2
1994	7.84	2.96	6.94		4820	116.0	116.0	105.8	130.2	131.6	120.0	110.7	106.5	104.2	108.1
1995	10.15	3.49	7.91		5225	104.3	104.3	111.5	94.4	94.1	94.6	104.6	108.0	103.8	108.1

Year	v4c4	v4c5	v4c6	v4c7	v4c8	v4c9	v4c10	v5	v5a	v5a1	v5a1a	v5a1b	v5a2	v5b	v5b1
1952															
1953															
1954															
1955															
1956															
1957															
1958															
1959															
1960															
1961															
1962															
1963															
1964															
1965															
1966															
1967															
1968															
1969															
1970															
1971															
1972															
1973															
1974															
1975															
1976															
1977															
1978															
1979															
1980															
1981															
1982															
1983															
1984															
1985															
1986	111.1	128.4	106.4	103.7	100.0	105.2	111.1								
1987	109.2	130.9	107.4	105.7	112.5	106.9	114.3								
1988	107.5	121.0	111.6	102.6	92.3	105.9	113.3								
1989	107.4	122.1	109.6	104.7	116.7	113.6	118.2								
1990	109.5	130.8	118.4	109.5	113.3	113.2	113.4	102.49	59.76	48.45	29.12	19.33	11.31	60.72	52.21
1991	137.9	118.5	113.2	112.8	117.7	101.7	114.8	120.67	72.87	56.86	34.54	22.32	15.93	67.01	56.80
1992	574.3	183.7	103.0	116.5	219.1	114.6	139.8	182.07	95.58	75.18	42.83	32.35	20.40	124.79	104.73
1993	123.0	116.5	110.0	107.8	127.5	107.0	81.6	258.55	127.92	98.04	56.14	41.90	29.88	171.65	144.82
1994	112.4	135.1	120.5	125.4	123.0	107.2	108.5	330.95	156.47	124.55	66.93	57.62	31.92	224.17	198.35
1995	83.1	108.6	105.4	111.7	107.5	108.4		364.17	188.50	153.09	82.87	70.22	35.41	219.21	192.64

Year	v5b2	v5c	v5c1	v5c2	v6a1	v6a2	v6a3	v6a4	v6b2	v6b3	v6b4	v7	v7a	v7a1	v7a2
1952															
1953															
1954															
1955															
1956															
1957															
1958															
1959															
1960															
1961															
1962															
1963															
1964															
1965															
1966															
1967															
1968															
1969															
1970															
1971															
1972															
1973															
1974															
1975															
1976															
1977															
1978															
1979															
1980															
1981															
1982															
1983															
1984															
1985															
1986															
1987															
1988															
1989															
1990	8.51	-17.99	91.41	109.40											
1991	10.21	-19.13	118.57	137.70								113.4	112.6	113.6	111.0
1992	20.06	-38.30	133.90	172.20								121.3	119.9	118.7	128.4
1993	26.83	-41.02	104.11	145.13								119.2	120.6	117.5	127.6
1994	25.82	-49.69	108.48	158.17	10.64	42.12	7.63	6.54	42.19	9.66	5.77	97.9	101.2	94.9	109.5
1995	26.57	-43.54	112.55	156.09	9.86	58.15	7.97	6.89	52.61	11.09	6.52	105.6	107.2	104.6	110.2

Year	v7b	v8	v8a	v8b	v9	v9a	v9b	v10a1	v10a2	v10a3	v10a3a	v10a3b	v10a4	v10b1	v10b2
1952															
1953															
1954															
1955															
1956															
1957															
1958															
1959															
1960															
1961															
1962															
1963															
1964															
1965															
1966															
1967															
1968															
1969															
1970															
1971															
1972															
1973															
1974															
1975															
1976															
1977															
1978															
1979															
1980															
1981															
1982															
1983															
1984															
1985															
1986															
1987															
1988															
1989															
1990		751	571	1436				31.42	1.01	3.35	0.52	2.83	16.43	4.39	0.25
1991	116.7	866	667	1609	110.7	111.9	107.7	34.08	1.33	3.25	0.41	2.84	18.14	5.82	0.45
1992	119.6	1128	819	2252	124.9	118.7	128.4	68.07	2.45	3.64	0.64	3.00	30.57	12.84	0.57
1993	118.7	1449	1064	2813	120.6	117.5	127.6	102.36	3.82	6.38	1.81	4.57	32.26	18.97	3.20
1994	87.3	1814	1259	3723	99.7	94.2	105.4	151.10	4.03	8.90	2.99	5.91	34.32	17.19	2.29
1995	99.7	2197	1548	4345	105.6	103.8	105.5	134.83	4.58	15.49	5.87	9.62	37.74	18.21	2.04

Year	v10b4	v11a	v11a1	v11a2	v11b	v11b1	v11b2	v11c	v11c1	v11c2	v12	v12a	v12b	v13	v13i
1952															
1953															
1954															
1955															
1956															
1957															
1958															
1959															
1960															
1961															
1962															
1963															
1964															
1965															
1966															
1967															
1968															
1969															
1970															
1971															
1972															
1973															
1974															
1975															
1976															
1977															
1978															
1979															
1980															
1981															
1982															
1983															
1984															
1985															
1986															
1987															
1988															
1989															
1990	3.87	3.75	3.23	0.52	13.15	11.43	1.72	43.82	37.55	6.27				102.49	69.81
1991	3.94	3.63	3.04	0.59	13.04	11.02	2.02	50.34	42.74	7.60	105.9	105.4	109.2	120.51	78.99
1992	6.65	5.10	3.19	1.91	33.69	28.96	4.73	86.00	72.58	13.42	143.8	139.0	167.4	181.71	93.44
1993	4.66	7.01	4.41	2.60	50.62	33.26	17.36	114.02	107.15	6.87	86.1	86.4	83.6	258.08	152.97
1994	6.34	6.86	4.53	2.33	45.43	39.24	6.19	171.88	154.58	17.30	129.0	138.1	80.2	330.95	195.23
1995	6.32	40.98	38.60	2.38	63.70	57.73	5.97	114.53	96.31	18.22	97.3	97.7	94.3	364.17	212.62

Year	v13ii	v13iii	v13iv	v13a	v13ai	v13aii	v13aiii	v13aiv	v13b	v13bi	v13bii	v13biii	v13biv	v13b1	v13b1i
1952															
1953															
1954															
1955															
1956															
1957															
1958															
1959															
1960															
1961															
1962															
1963															
1964															
1965															
1966															
1967															
1968															
1969															
1970															
1971															
1972															
1973															
1974															
1975															
1976															
1977															
1978															
1979															
1980															
1981															
1982															
1983															
1984															
1985															
1986															
1987															
1988															
1989															
1990	8.94	9.07	14.67	46.02	42.12	1.74	1.07	1.09	20.12	11.30	2.49	4.99	1.34	12.91	5.39
1991	10.80	10.73	19.99	50.22	44.41	2.16	1.46	2.19	24.65	14.47	2.77	5.39	2.02	14.86	6.42
1992	17.50	15.89	54.88	54.13	44.77	2.92	1.71	4.73	38.34	20.46	5.70	6.28	5.90	20.36	7.46
1993	29.16	24.31	51.64	77.73	62.91	5.09	2.17	7.56	66.29	35.78	10.96	9.60	9.95	34.37	13.43
1994	34.31	37.92	63.49	107.55	83.26	7.35	3.94	13.00	83.66	45.48	8.94	15.12	14.12	42.84	20.99
1995	45.86	44.25	61.44	130.86	97.92	10.80	4.54	17.60	78.64	38.92	12.87	16.34	10.51	42.13	16.98

Year	v13b1ii	v13b1iii	v13b1iv	v13b2	v13b2i	v13b2ii	v13b2iii	v13b2iv	v13c	v13ci	v13cii	v13ciii	v13civ	v13c1
1952														
1953														
1954														
1955														
1956														
1957														
1958														
1959														
1960														
1961														
1962														
1963														
1964														
1965														
1966														
1967														
1968														
1969														
1970														
1971														
1972														
1973														
1974														
1975														
1976														
1977														
1978														
1979														
1980														
1981														
1982														
1983														
1984														
1985														
1986														
1987														
1988														
1989														
1990	2.21	4.28	1.03	7.21	5.91	0.28	0.71	0.31	36.35	16.39	4.71	3.01	12.24	6.02
1991	2.37	4.47	1.60	9.79	8.05	0.40	0.92	0.42	45.64	20.11	5.87	3.88	15.78	7.70
1992	4.88	4.59	3.43	17.98	13.00	0.82	1.69	2.47	89.24	28.21	8.88	7.90	44.25	10.83
1993	7.24	5.94	7.76	31.92	22.35	3.72	3.66	2.19	114.06	54.28	13.11	12.54	34.13	17.84
1994	6.90	9.00	5.95	40.82	24.49	2.04	6.12	8.17	139.74	66.49	18.02	18.86	36.37	22.60
1995	10.70	10.83	3.62	36.51	21.94	2.17	5.51	6.89	154.67	75.78	22.19	23.37	33.33	24.54

Year	v13c1i	v13c1ii	v13c1iii	v13c1iv	v13c2	v13c2i	v13c2ii	v13c2iii	v13c2iv	v13c3	v13c3i	v13c3ii	v13c3iii	v13c3iv
1952														
1953														
1954														
1955														
1956														
1957														
1958														
1959														
1960														
1961														
1962														
1963														
1964														
1965														
1966														
1967														
1968														
1969														
1970														
1971														
1972														
1973														
1974														
1975														
1976														
1977														
1978														
1979														
1980														
1981														
1982														
1983														
1984														
1985														
1986														
1987														
1988														
1989														
1990	2.32	1.14	0.41	2.15	11.35	4.50	0.95	1.28	4.62	5.31	0.82	0.46	0.69	3.34
1991	2.98	1.45	0.52	2.75	15.05	5.96	1.26	1.70	6.13	6.49	1.00	0.57	0.84	4.08
1992	3.90	2.08	0.61	4.24	29.32	8.93	1.99	3.23	15.17	11.68	1.37	0.67	1.04	8.60
1993	9.29	2.68	1.84	4.03	38.76	23.25	2.62	4.27	8.62	18.10	3.08	1.13	2.87	11.02
1994	10.19	4.81	1.57	6.03	47.84	28.45	4.09	10.73	4.57	23.06	3.21	1.17	2.92	15.76
1995	11.40	5.34	2.31	5.49	51.83	30.42	4.88	10.89	5.64	27.89	4.11	1.36	3.10	18.66

Year	v13c4	v13c4i	v13c4ii	v13c4iii	v13c4iv	v13c5	v13c5i	v13c5ii	v13c5iii	v13c5iv	v13c6	v13c6i	v13c6ii	v13c6iii
1952														
1953														
1954														
1955														
1956														
1957														
1958														
1959														
1960														
1961														
1962														
1963														
1964														
1965														
1966														
1967														
1968														
1969														
1970														
1971														
1972														
1973														
1974														
1975														
1976														
1977														
1978														
1979														
1980														
1981														
1982														
1983														
1984														
1985														
1986														
1987														
1988														
1989														
1990	1.40	0.28	0.18	0.28	0.66	3.24	1.34	0.58	0.27	1.05	1.52	1.35	0.13	
1991	2.02	0.40	0.26	0.40	0.96	4.16	1.72	0.75	0.34	1.35	1.79	1.59	0.15	
1992	16.05	0.96	0.96	2.11	12.02	8.25	3.07	1.22	0.65	3.31	2.00	1.75	0.18	
1993	15.30	1.34	4.01	1.67	8.28	9.69	4.37	1.30	1.88	2.14	2.31	2.14	0.17	
1994	12.36	1.02	3.85	1.26	6.23	13.17	5.95	1.50	2.29	3.43	2.97	2.71	0.21	
1995	9.44	2.09	5.30	2.31	-0.26	15.87	6.92	1.65	4.62	2.68	3.55	3.11	0.37	0.01

Year	v13c6iv	v13c7	v13c7i	v13c7ii	v13c7iii	v13c7iv	v13c8	v13c8i	v13c8ii	v13c8iii	v13c8iv	v13c9	v13c9i	v13c9ii
1952														
1953														
1954														
1955														
1956														
1957														
1958														
1959														
1960														
1961														
1962														
1963														
1964														
1965														
1966														
1967														
1968														
1969														
1970														
1971														
1972														
1973														
1974														
1975														
1976														
1977														
1978														
1979														
1980														
1981														
1982														
1983														
1984														
1985														
1986														
1987														
1988														
1989														
1990	0.04	3.12	2.45	0.54		0.13	0.17	0.11	0.03	0.01	0.02	3.41	2.68	0.55
1991	0.05	3.66	2.87	0.64		0.15	0.21	0.13	0.04	0.01	0.03	3.58	2.81	0.57
1992	0.07	4.63	3.52	0.75	0.04	0.32	0.51	0.20	0.09	0.02	0.20	4.45	3.62	0.71
1993		5.80	5.04	0.76			0.76	0.71	0.05			4.54	4.21	0.33
1994	0.05	7.84	6.38	1.46			2.96	2.29	0.28	0.09	0.30	6.94	6.29	0.65
1995	0.06	10.15	8.14	2.01			3.49	2.62	0.34	0.13	0.40	7.91	6.97	0.94

Year	v13c9iii	v13c9iv	v13c10	v13c10i	v13c10ii	v13c10iii	v13c10iv
1952							
1953							
1954							
1955							
1956							
1957							
1958							
1959							
1960							
1961							
1962							
1963							
1964							
1965							
1966							
1967							
1968							
1969							
1970							
1971							
1972							
1973							
1974							
1975							
1976							
1977							
1978							
1979							
1980							
1981							
1982							
1983							
1984							
1985							
1986							
1987							
1988							
1989							
1990	0.06	0.12	0.81	0.54	0.15	0.01	0.11
1991	0.06	0.14	0.98	0.65	0.18	0.01	0.14
1992	0.14	-0.02	1.52	0.89	0.23	0.06	0.34
1993			0.96	0.85	0.06	0.01	0.04
1994							
1995							

22

Sichuan

Year	v1	v1a	v1b	v1b1	v1b2	v1c	v1c1	v1c2	v1c3	v2	v2a	v2b	v2b1	v2b2	v2c
1952	59.16	29.48	18.54	15.63	2.91	11.14	0.90	4.48	5.76		109.0				
1953	70.85	32.61	25.58	21.76	3.82	12.66	1.74	4.20	6.72	118.8	110.1	142.1	142.2	141.6	112.2
1954	83.31	36.45	31.65	27.36	4.29	15.21	2.05	5.96	7.20	116.3	109.5	128.1	129.1	122.6	119.2
1955	92.37	39.21	36.08	31.24	4.84	17.08	2.40	6.92	7.76	107.9	100.9	117.7	117.0	122.0	110.1
1956	111.14	47.15	42.61	36.08	6.53	21.38	2.85	9.14	9.39	116.6	109.3	124.0	119.3	150.0	121.8
1957	129.13	56.83	48.22	41.59	6.63	24.08	3.49	10.13	10.46	104.9	106.0	113.8	115.3	107.1	111.6
1958	154.79	56.93	71.44	59.08	12.36	26.42	5.09	11.43	9.90	120.4	107.1	146.3	140.1	124.8	102.0
1959	183.37	58.07	94.58	76.75	17.83	30.72	6.63	13.96	10.13	109.6	89.0	132.4	130.0	144.3	94.9
1960	203.56	58.03	113.60	94.66	18.94	31.93	8.55	14.08	9.30	107.6	89.0	120.2	123.3	106.2	100.8
1961	152.03	60.05	63.98	55.05	8.93	28.00	5.80	13.58	8.62	65.9	83.4	53.3	54.4	47.1	92.2
1962	132.00	62.05	46.34	41.72	4.62	23.61	4.37	11.47	7.77	85.3	108.5	71.4	74.2	55.2	78.6
1963	141.65	68.85	51.17	45.35	5.82	21.63	4.18	10.07	7.38	108.2	113.1	106.9	107.0	106.9	97.2
1964	160.85	72.24	65.52	56.54	8.98	23.09	5.75	9.86	7.48	117.7	107.8	130.0	126.3	160.0	113.2
1965	190.00	79.68	86.39	68.87	17.52	23.93	7.22	9.94	6.77	120.9	104.6	139.9	130.2	200.5	106.8
1966	227.62	90.49	110.27	82.92	27.35	26.86	7.66	11.80	7.40	121.6	110.1	132.0	127.1	151.6	110.3
1967	201.45	88.72	87.28	68.20	19.08	25.45	5.91	12.01	7.53	87.1	98.0	79.7	82.2	71.1	93.5
1968	153.34	80.94	52.20	42.96	9.24	20.20	3.91	9.15	7.14	73.6	91.1	60.1	62.9	49.1	79.3
1969	196.07	82.74	89.70	67.50	22.20	23.63	5.40	11.18	7.05	133.5	102.2	171.5	157.3	243.1	117.4
1970	253.06	89.29	134.97	103.15	31.82	28.80	7.13	13.45	8.22	133.9	109.4	122.4	152.9	142.3	129.5
1971	278.08	97.09	150.61	119.99	30.62	30.38	8.35	14.51	7.52	116.8	102.9	109.3	130.1	95.8	121.9
1972	276.97	96.39	148.33	121.18	27.15	32.25	8.97	14.93	8.35	99.5	99.3	98.0	101.0	88.6	103.6
1973	280.69	102.56	145.78	121.07	24.71	32.35	8.58	15.65	8.12	100.6	104.4	98.3	99.9	90.5	99.6
1974	271.95	104.92	134.99	113.62	21.37	32.04	7.68	15.56	8.80	95.9	100.3	92.4	93.9	85.0	98.7
1975	312.46	103.91	172.40	148.01	24.39	36.15	10.17	16.79	9.19	116.2	115.5	127.8	130.2	113.7	112.5
1976	286.48	98.54	156.98	133.72	23.26	30.96	7.74	15.82	7.40	93.4	93.4	94.0	92.4	95.5	86.0
1977	361.89	110.18	208.73	180.12	28.61	42.98	11.81	21.42	9.75	123.5	105.7	131.5	134.7	122.9	139.0
1978	453.98	127.10	261.94	225.57	36.37	64.94	13.69	26.25	25.00	124.9	118.8	123.3	122.9	126.5	150.8
1979	535.90	163.92	294.08	253.76	40.32	77.90	15.36	32.23	30.31	111.9	109.9	111.4	111.7	109.8	118.0
1980	591.83	181.27	317.07	273.65	43.42	93.49	15.36	32.23	45.90	107.3	106.6	105.9	106.4	102.2	114.7
1981	625.03	196.35	331.45	280.56	50.89	97.23	15.33	36.83	45.07	118.5	104.9	102.9	104.1	115.9	111.5
1982	710.22	233.10	367.25	313.24	54.01	109.87	16.80	38.12	54.95	108.1	111.0	108.9	110.1	101.7	99.1
1983	789.27	254.01	411.50	350.19	61.31	123.76	18.94	43.88	60.94	112.3	107.1	113.0	112.7	114.6	122.2
1984	926.11	281.65	488.61	420.15	68.46	155.85	21.00	52.02	82.83	112.8	107.8	115.8	116.6	110.6	112.6
1985	1146.61	313.06	637.10	531.51	105.59	196.45	26.32	69.69	100.44	117.3	103.2	122.7	119.4	144.2	125.5
1986	1266.24	338.98	710.53	598.61	111.92	216.73	31.03	79.34	106.36	108.8	105.6	108.9	109.9	103.4	113.2
1987	1506.31	388.94	859.58	725.06	134.52	257.79	38.74	99.21	119.84	112.5	103.2	115.4	115.6	114.4	116.7
1988	1916.99	475.98	1132.19	964.10	168.09	308.82	50.02	125.95	132.85	115.1	102.7	118.7	120.5	107.9	119.3
1989	2199.57	527.67	1317.44	1147.29	170.15	354.46	57.53	138.53	158.40	105.1	103.7	103.8	105.0	96.2	111.3
1990	2666.76	637.07	1418.68	1222.96	195.72	611.01	94.94	214.53	301.54	110.6	105.6	106.2	106.0	107.5	131.6
1991	3134.62	680.13	1664.76	1434.20	230.56	789.73	126.40	269.76	393.57	114.5	104.8	113.8	115.1	105.7	125.8
1992	3902.26	744.79	2186.12	1849.82	336.30	971.35	149.42	335.48	486.45	117.9	103.6	125.5	143.2	143.1	116.6
1993	5388.20	876.37	3365.51	2825.92	539.59	1146.32	164.39	423.70	558.23	124.5	101.8	136.8	136.5	139.1	116.2
1994	7543.52	1229.14	4726.05	4039.47	686.58	1588.33	205.55	541.49	841.29	116.2	104.0	120.5	121.4	115.0	113.2
1995	9334.20	1520.26	5742.91	4857.00	885.91	2071.03	276.22	698.88	1095.93	112.8	107.8	114.0	114.5	110.6	112.4

Year	v2c1	v2c2	v3'	v3	v3a	v3b	v3b1	v3b2	v3c	v3c1	v3c2	v3c3	v3c4	v3c5	v3c6
1952			42.10	42.10	27.50	6.69	4.87	1.82	7.91	0.80	4.45				
1953	171.1	92.6	48.31	48.31	30.42	8.90	7.04	1.86	8.99	1.46	4.17				
1954	129.9	140.8	55.77	55.77	33.63	11.34	9.33	2.01	10.80	1.66	5.87				
1955	125.5	113.0	60.81	60.81	35.49	13.19	11.07	2.12	12.13	1.91	6.82				
1956	131.5	128.9	72.05	72.05	41.60	15.27	12.25	3.02	15.18	2.14	8.96				
1957	113.0	107.8	81.84	81.84	47.88	16.86	13.78	3.08	17.10	2.76	10.29				
1958	164.8	111.7	90.10	90.10	44.39	26.95	18.29	8.66	18.76	4.01	11.90				
1959	128.7	121.5	93.77	93.77	40.38	31.58	24.62	6.96	21.81	5.16	14.10				
1960	121.6	99.7	83.98	83.98	28.18	33.13	26.87	6.26	22.67	6.23	14.24				
1961	68.4	62.3	69.70	69.70	31.56	18.26	14.76	3.50	19.88	3.68	13.65				
1962	69.5	67.7	77.44	77.44	45.40	15.28	13.25	2.03	16.76	2.78	11.05				
1963	96.5	118.2	89.02	89.02	55.50	18.16	15.80	2.36	15.36	2.59	9.42				
1964	120.3	122.0	95.95	95.95	57.25	22.30	18.92	3.38	16.40	3.80	8.96				
1965	141.2	102.9	110.51	110.51	63.14	30.38	23.06	7.32	16.99	4.86	8.11				
1966	107.5	107.9	125.44	125.44	72.50	33.87	22.76	11.11	19.07	4.87	10.25				
1967	78.3	105.2	113.15	113.15	71.35	23.73	15.84	7.89	18.07	3.34	10.44				
1968	66.2	76.2	91.44	91.44	64.49	12.61	8.57	4.04	14.34	1.88	7.71				
1969	135.5	122.7	107.81	107.81	65.54	25.49	16.24	9.25	16.78	3.05	9.60				
1970	134.5	120.6	132.01	132.01	71.47	40.09	25.93	14.16	20.45	4.38	9.16				
1971	117.1	107.3	138.03	138.03	72.85	43.61	30.40	13.21	21.57	5.09	12.86				
1972	107.4	103.9	139.45	139.45	70.95	45.60	33.74	11.86	22.90	5.47	12.56				
1973	95.7	105.8	148.28	148.28	78.15	47.16	35.86	11.30	22.97	4.97	13.33				
1974	89.5	99.5	142.30	142.30	79.42	40.13	30.73	9.40	22.75	4.22	12.97				
1975	132.4	107.9	163.05	163.05	76.58	60.80	49.78	11.02	25.67	6.42	13.64				
1976	76.1	94.0	138.87	138.87	72.88	44.01	33.80	10.21	21.98	4.01	11.69				
1977	152.6	143.9	186.57	186.57	90.61	65.44	53.38	12.06	30.52	6.88	12.77				
1978	115.9	118.8	244.83	244.83	104.97	93.75	81.06	12.69	46.11	9.13	16.33	3.16	3.34	2.40	1.64
1979	107.5	112.5	290.52	290.52	120.56	114.65	99.86	14.79	55.31	9.59	19.98	4.09	5.36	3.22	1.88
1980	104.3	103.6	322.11	322.03	134.11	121.55	106.32	15.23	66.37	10.50	24.22	5.06	6.94	3.96	2.03
1981	99.8	113.4	333.13	332.93	138.45	125.45	108.41	17.04	69.03	11.12	25.36	4.51	7.16	4.07	2.13
1982	109.6	101.1	379.69	379.13	163.71	137.41	118.85	18.56	78.01	12.73	28.23	5.74	7.33	5.19	2.56
1983	111.1	114.3	421.51	420.78	175.38	157.53	135.40	22.13	87.87	14.54	30.12	8.06	8.22	6.21	2.91
1984	109.5	117.2	498.70	497.58	200.44	186.49	160.88	25.61	110.65	16.33	36.45	10.05	12.08	8.17	3.60
1985	116.5	122.8	607.71	606.40	224.59	242.33	203.97	38.36	139.48	20.82	46.17	13.95	13.50	11.34	4.07
1986	113.7	110.6	656.23	654.62	234.23	266.51	225.77	40.74	153.88	22.33	51.96	15.31	13.93	12.72	4.86
1987	110.6	114.1	749.14	746.94	263.70	300.21	253.77	46.44	183.03	25.39	59.75	20.68	18.10	14.41	5.41
1988	107.7	110.4	924.97	922.62	312.20	391.16	326.86	64.30	219.26	30.36	73.37	24.55	19.81	15.90	7.51
1989	100.9	102.6	998.49	995.65	339.20	404.78	346.61	58.17	251.67	36.29	67.27	44.02	23.13	15.74	8.12
1990	103.8	104.5	1188.87	1186.22	417.71	428.56	356.18	72.38	339.95	50.50	96.15	61.05	24.07	31.15	12.16
1991	113.2	108.5	1386.21	1382.96	452.15	493.75	413.79	79.96	437.06	70.31	118.05	82.03	25.59	44.85	15.11
1992	117.5	111.2	1635.71	1624.51	480.27	608.99	504.87	104.12	535.25	79.40	146.81	107.19	35.35	49.69	17.79
1993	115.5	118.6	2109.31	2096.48	569.95	892.79	730.62	162.17	633.74	87.44	185.42	129.80	41.47	55.49	21.96
1994	122.2	120.1	2796.00	2777.88	788.39	1166.22	950.22	216.00	823.27	108.94	235.54	164.49	50.85	77.11	30.93
1995	110.5	114.6	3560.50	3534.00	976.96	1486.63	1215.00	271.63	1070.41	135.09	308.99	208.00	69.62	104.86	41.08

Year	v3c7	v3c8	v3c9	v3c10	v3d	v4'	v4	v4a	v4b	v4b1	v4b2	v4c	v4c1	v4c2	v4c3
1952				2.66	67	108.8	108.8	105.4	137.6	146.9	153.8	106.6	167.5	127.3	
1953				3.36	75	113.3	113.3	109.1	138.0	145.1	111.7	112.3	180.0	92.6	
1954				3.27	85	112.2	112.2	106.8	129.7	131.3	121.6	119.1	113.2	139.6	
1955				3.40	90	106.1	106.1	101.2	120.7	120.6	120.8	110.0	112.3	113.7	
1956				4.08	105	111.6	111.6	105.3	123.0	116.8	155.0	121.8	109.8	128.0	
1957				4.05	117	112.0	112.0	109.5	112.1	113.3	107.3	120.6	137.3	122.9	
1958				2.85	127	111.6	111.6	102.0	146.9	124.8	279.1	102.0	135.1	108.4	
1959				2.55	134	90.6	90.6	75.7	117.6	131.4	80.5	94.9	108.6	99.3	
1960				2.20	124	86.6	86.6	65.1	106.6	110.4	89.9	100.8	113.1	94.7	
1961				2.55	107	77.1	77.1	100.7	51.6	50.9	55.8	92.1	62.2	100.7	
1962				2.93	120	102.4	102.4	132.1	78.4	83.9	51.3	78.7	70.5	75.5	
1963				3.35	135	110.3	110.3	110.8	120.2	120.3	118.7	97.2	98.5	90.5	
1964				3.64	141	114.4	114.4	110.3	124.9	121.8	150.0	113.2	155.6	100.8	
1965				4.02	157	116.2	116.2	106.3	142.6	130.8	220.3	106.8	131.8	93.3	
1966				3.95	173	114.8	114.8	122.6	105.1	94.3	147.7	110.3	98.8	124.2	
1967				4.29	151	90.0	90.0	99.5	71.4	71.1	72.3	93.5	67.6	100.5	
1968				4.75	118	74.0	74.0	81.1	52.6	53.0	51.8	79.3	56.1	73.9	
1969				4.13	136	122.9	122.9	101.5	210.7	202.2	231.8	117.4	163.2	124.8	
1970				6.91	161	126.7	126.7	107.1	161.4	165.5	152.2	129.5	152.4	101.4	
1971				3.62	163	106.2	106.2	101.7	104.8	80.7	92.7	122.0	134.4	160.2	
1972				4.87	160	103.2	103.2	96.4	115.0	125.1	89.9	105.5	106.5	97.2	
1973				4.67	166	108.1	108.1	109.1	110.8	115.5	94.7	99.6	89.6	105.4	
1974				5.56	155	94.2	94.2	100.1	82.7	80.7	91.4	98.7	93.2	97.3	
1975				5.61	174	115.1	115.1	96.4	152.7	162.3	116.9	112.5	152.0	104.5	
1976				6.28	146	88.5	88.5	95.2	81.7	79.5	93.0	85.3	62.4	86.0	
1977				10.87	194	127.9	127.9	124.2	128.5	130.9	117.8	139.0	171.6	126.5	
1978	4.44	0.31	5.11	0.25	253	130.2	130.2	113.7	143.3	149.3	114.3	150.8	120.8	124.6	208.1
1979	4.78	0.46	5.64	0.31	298	115.6	115.6	110.3	120.2	121.1	114.6	118.0	103.4	120.4	127.3
1980	5.85	1.21	6.21	0.39	329	108.5	108.5	108.1	106.0	106.5	103.0	114.7	104.7	115.9	118.1
1981	6.06	1.27	6.91	0.44	337	98.0	96.8	88.6	100.4	99.2	108.8	111.6	113.6	112.4	95.7
1982	6.72	1.55	7.47	0.49	381	109.4	109.3	109.8	108.1	108.2	107.5	110.4	111.8	108.7	124.3
1983	7.41	1.70	8.19	0.51	419	110.5	110.5	105.3	115.9	115.2	120.5	111.8	113.4	106.1	139.4
1984	10.09	3.30	10.04	0.54	494	115.8	115.7	110.9	116.9	116.3	120.4	123.1	109.7	118.2	121.9
1985	12.99	4.30	11.75	0.59	599	115.3	115.3	104.1	125.3	123.3	137.1	118.0	119.1	119.0	129.9
1986	14.10	5.09	12.95	0.63	640	106.5	106.4	104.6	107.3	107.2	108.0	107.6	105.2	109.4	107.2
1987	15.60	6.90	16.14	0.65	721	109.9	109.8	102.6	114.3	114.9	111.2	112.8	107.5	109.0	127.9
1988	19.73	8.40	18.94	0.69	879	108.7	108.7	101.4	115.4	116.8	107.8	106.5	106.4	109.1	105.7
1989	23.75	9.58	23.05	0.72	937	102.8	102.7	101.8	102.3	103.4	95.9	104.7	109.0	82.1	163.5
1990	27.18	5.38	31.21	1.10	1105	104.3	104.3	104.2	103.4	102.8	107.2	106.3	102.2	105.8	107.0
1991	30.37	6.96	40.92	2.87	1278	108.8	108.7	106.4	109.6	107.0	126.2	110.9	114.4	102.3	110.7
1992	36.44	8.89	49.98	3.71	1498	113.2	112.6	102.6	120.0	118.6	127.4	116.3	109.4	124.8	124.0
1993	44.19	9.07	55.07	3.83	1922	113.9	113.9	100.6	125.7	125.0	129.0	113.6	112.9	113.8	116.1
1994	61.98	12.87	75.68	4.97	2516	111.4	111.1	102.8	116.0	117.4	109.1	112.6	115.0	112.3	108.7
1995	81.53	17.52	96.85	6.87	3177	110.4	110.0	105.5	112.4	113.0	109.7	110.6	111.8	112.8	106.7

Year	v4c4	v4c5	v4c6	v4c7	v4c8	v4c9	v4c10	v5	v5a	v5a1	v5a1a	v5a1b	v5a2	v5b	v5b1
1952								42.10	34.71	32.46	24.81	7.65	2.25	6.33	6.30
1953								48.31	38.51	35.41	26.92	8.49	3.10	9.38	4.28
1954								55.77	43.80	40.21	31.15	9.06	3.59	13.46	6.45
1955								60.81	46.77	43.34	33.27	10.07	3.43	11.49	7.13
1956								72.05	56.57	53.02	40.92	12.10	3.55	15.49	9.83
1957								81.84	62.82	59.63	45.50	14.13	3.19	18.16	13.83
1958								90.10	67.42	63.38	46.62	16.76	4.04	26.20	17.08
1959								93.77	63.01	57.93	33.20	24.73	5.08	43.94	33.77
1960								83.98	61.94	57.00	40.28	16.72	4.94	34.12	27.77
1961								69.70	69.20	66.46	45.44	21.02	2.74	0.84	0.31
1962								77.44	75.75	71.81	54.14	17.67	3.94	-4.88	2.08
1963								89.02	79.46	74.76	58.91	15.85	4.70	9.47	8.98
1964								95.95	81.74	76.64	59.71	16.93	5.10	16.99	14.08
1965								110.51	90.98	82.53	61.65	20.88	8.45	39.20	31.20
1966								125.44	100.92	90.90	67.73	23.17	10.02	59.61	47.33
1967								113.15	105.39	95.78	70.18	25.60	9.61	27.21	27.45
1968								91.44	94.71	86.87	64.48	22.39	7.84	11.98	10.70
1969								107.81	102.74	91.98	67.30	24.68	10.76	40.24	32.00
1970								132.01	104.74	97.45	70.55	26.90	7.29	68.19	49.28
1971								138.03	107.15	100.23	72.26	27.97	6.92	57.12	41.27
1972								139.45	115.63	101.90	71.90	30.00	13.73	54.85	42.45
1973								148.28	120.88	107.47	76.62	30.85	13.41	54.23	46.03
1974								142.30	125.12	110.85	77.28	33.57	14.27	47.97	45.67
1975								163.05	126.54	110.84	76.02	34.82	15.70	73.78	65.47
1976								138.87	124.78	109.53	73.99	35.54	15.25	45.14	44.85
1977								186.57	137.27	114.72	78.31	36.41	22.55	73.01	53.73
1978	208.3	208.9	205.1	207.7	214.3	208.1	209.8	244.83	162.06	141.41	95.71	45.70	20.65	90.98	72.06
1979	157.8	129.9	115.6	106.0	146.7	108.6	120.8	290.52	195.11	173.36	121.15	52.21	21.75	101.13	77.90
1980	124.0	119.4	100.5	117.0	152.3	105.2	120.7	322.03	213.52	192.29	134.53	57.76	21.23	106.06	80.38
1981	110.5	110.2	112.4	111.0	112.6	119.3	122.9	332.93	239.18	215.98	151.70	64.28	23.20	101.25	76.60
1982	100.1	124.5	117.7	108.4	119.2	105.7	109.3	379.13	262.33	236.87	168.25	68.62	25.46	118.90	89.46
1983	111.2	118.9	112.6	109.5	108.7	108.6	104.3	420.78	289.60	259.67	184.64	75.03	29.93	130.50	104.69
1984	143.8	128.4	121.3	133.1	190.1	120.0	102.0	497.58	335.90	302.40	219.48	82.92	33.50	157.89	123.60
1985	104.5	129.1	105.7	120.5	121.8	109.4	104.0	606.40	397.89	353.02	253.02	100.00	44.87	199.80	154.62
1986	100.7	110.3	116.6	105.9	115.5	107.3	107.7	654.62	438.27	388.24	270.49	117.75	50.03	209.80	162.55
1987	123.3	107.4	105.6	104.9	128.6	117.9	105.4	746.94	510.92	452.20	313.01	139.19	58.72	253.41	207.76
1988	97.3	98.2	123.3	112.5	108.1	103.9	106.8	922.62	655.38	564.78	396.24	168.54	90.60	323.03	228.98
1989	106.5	90.3	98.9	109.7	104.2	110.5	104.4	995.65	725.49	621.17	427.25	193.92	104.32	306.67	187.57
1990	102.8	116.7	119.4	104.9	100.5	101.6	138.6	1186.22	841.53	711.73	481.09	230.64	129.80	359.94	235.07
1991	102.4	111.5	102.3	100.9	106.0	105.2	189.6	1382.96	971.47	814.07	540.86	273.21	157.40	439.34	307.09
1992	104.8	109.4	111.8	102.0	118.0	118.0	138.1	1624.51	1086.52	908.84	588.31	320.53	177.68	538.13	400.91
1993	110.6	116.5	118.4	112.4	116.2	108.4	109.0	2096.48	1282.10	1045.49	656.33	389.16	236.61	797.30	609.38
1994	111.6	116.5	117.8	117.3	109.5	112.9	106.7	2777.88	1699.41	1392.52	877.19	515.33	306.89	1064.07	822.54
1995	107.8	112.9	111.8	110.8	110.4	109.9	112.0	3534.00	2193.23	1806.84	1122.12	584.72	386.39	1346.15	1042.79

Year	v5b2	v5c	v5c1	v5c2	v6a1	v6a2	v6a3	v6a4	v6b2	v6b3	v6b4	v7	v7a	v7a1	v7a2
1952	0.53	0.56													
1953	5.10	0.42										109.5	107.7	107.1	109.5
1954	7.01	-1.49										112.9	112.7	114.8	105.8
1955	4.36	2.55										104.6	105.6	104.7	108.9
1956	5.66	-0.01										117.8	119.1	119.8	117.1
1957	4.33	0.86										106.9	108.2	107.0	112.4
1958	9.12	-3.52										105.8	104.8	101.0	116.9
1959	10.17	-13.18										92.9	90.8	70.8	146.6
1960	6.33	-12.08										95.9	96.0	118.4	66.0
1961	0.53	-0.34										90.3	94.2	91.2	101.6
1962	-6.96	6.57										102.0	100.6	111.0	78.3
1963	0.49	0.09										111.2	110.4	115.4	95.1
1964	2.91	-2.78										109.1	108.7	107.5	113.2
1965	8.00	-19.67										114.7	111.0	106.4	127.1
1966	12.28	-35.09										109.0	108.2	107.9	109.0
1967	-0.24	-19.45										103.0	103.9	102.2	109.0
1968	1.28	-15.25										89.9	90.7	91.9	87.5
1969	8.24	-35.17										108.8	106.2	104.7	110.6
1970	18.91	-40.92										102.2	106.3	105.1	109.3
1971	15.85	-26.24										102.1	102.6	102.2	103.8
1972	12.40	-31.03										107.3	101.1	98.9	106.6
1973	8.20	-26.83										103.8	104.7	105.8	102.1
1974	2.30	-30.79										103.2	102.9	100.6	108.5
1975	8.31	-37.27										100.8	99.7	98.1	103.4
1976	0.29	-31.05										98.2	98.4	96.9	101.6
1977	19.28	-23.71										110.1	104.8	105.9	102.5
1978	18.92	-8.21			50.78	39.78	1.89	3.26	40.08	4.97	0.65	118.6	123.8	122.7	126.1
1979	23.23	-5.72			57.46	57.93	2.09	3.67	46.32	4.90	0.99	114.3	116.3	120.1	108.4
1980	25.68	2.45			58.51	67.68	3.92	4.42	49.96	6.28	1.52	101.2	102.6	102.7	102.4
1981	24.65	-7.50			70.08	73.58	3.81	4.23	56.62	6.01	1.65	110.0	110.3	110.7	109.3
1982	29.44	-2.10			81.66	77.39	4.33	4.87	58.83	8.15	1.64	107.2	107.2	108.4	104.4
1983	25.81	0.68			85.93	87.58	5.61	5.52	63.59	9.40	2.04	109.6	108.8	109.0	108.5
1984	34.29	3.79			100.31	106.07	6.44	6.66	70.55	10.34	2.03	113.4	113.9	116.2	108.0
1985	45.18	8.71			109.14	128.05	6.91	8.92	85.02	12.43	2.55	110.9	109.3	107.9	112.9
1986	47.25	6.55			115.26	137.13	7.57	10.53	100.77	14.08	2.90	106.0	105.9	102.9	113.3
1987	45.65	-17.39			133.55	158.84	9.34	11.28	117.07	18.71	3.41	108.4	108.3	107.6	110.0
1988	94.05	-55.79	245.25	301.04	6149.36	216.14	14.49	16.25	147.60	15.54	5.40	106.9	104.1	105.5	100.9
1989	119.10	-36.51	256.51	293.02	157.03	233.58	16.82	19.82	167.34	19.88	6.70	93.6	93.0	91.1	97.2
1990	124.87	-15.25	279.74	294.99	197.04	242.76	19.93	21.36	194.73	27.88	8.03	105.0	105.1	104.1	107.4
1991	132.25	-27.85	342.60	370.45	215.19	275.17	26.93	23.57	231.08	31.01	11.12	105.6	104.5	102.8	108.3
1992	137.22	-0.14	376.77	376.91	233.75	285.77	32.68	36.11	269.20	36.19	15.12	108.2	108.0	106.1	112.1
1993	187.92	17.08	452.39	435.31	272.11	309.40	35.30	39.52	325.35	45.41	18.40	104.7	104.2	101.7	109.2
1994	241.53	14.40	596.77	582.37	363.68	403.37	47.18	62.96	430.37	60.60	24.36	108.8	108.4	107.6	109.9
1995	303.36	-5.38	691.52	696.90	452.01	515.08	69.83	85.20	542.92	106.21	35.59	109.6	109.9	107.2	114.9

Year	v7b	v8	v8a	v8b	v9	v9a	v9b	v10a1	v10a2	v10a3	v10a3a	v10a3b	v10a4	v10b1	v10b2
1952		52	42	187											
1953	136.0	55	45	164	103.8	104.8	86.6								
1954	115.0	61	51	170	111.1	113.6	103.1								
1955	93.5	64	54	182	101.7	104.0	104.8								
1956	100.9	77	65	201	118.0	117.3	107.4								
1957	96.4	85	72	216	105.6	106.6	103.2								
1958	124.7	90	73	234	105.3	100.0	106.7								
1959	125.1	83	54	310	91.2	73.8	131.9								
1960	94.9	84	68	199	98.6	120.8	62.6								
1961	44.7	102	79	259	98.6	94.8	105.3								
1962	134.2	111	94	246	101.4	110.9	88.3								
1963	126.7	113	100	235	108.3	113.1	101.3								
1964	114.9	113	97	255	105.1	102.9	115.5								
1965	170.9	118	97	318	108.5	102.8	128.5								
1966	116.4	125	103	339	103.4	104.1	104.6								
1967	94.6	128	103	367	101.1	98.7	106.8								
1968	81.7	113	92	317	88.2	89.3	86.1								
1969	137.5	116	93	350	103.7	101.5	110.9								
1970	68.0	119	94	384	102.4	101.5	110.2								
1971	94.7	118	93	387	98.9	98.6	100.4								
1972	197.2	117	90	398	98.8	95.6	102.5								
1973	96.9	120	94	401	101.2	104.6	100.0								
1974	106.1	121	92	432	101.2	97.1	107.3								
1975	109.8	118	88	448	96.6	95.5	103.5								
1976	96.7	115	85	456	97.6	96.8	101.2								
1977	147.9	119	89	463	103.7	103.3	101.5								
1978	92.0	146	108	566	123.5	122.2	122.7	43.27	18.61	7.67	1.45	6.22	2.51	11.84	6.89
1979	100.0	178	136	616	115.2	119.5	103.5	46.78	20.12	8.28	1.57	6.71	2.72	14.54	8.46
1980	90.3	196	156	485	101.7	106.5	72.8	48.27	20.76	8.55	1.62	6.93	2.80	16.07	9.36
1981	107.3	218	175	516	109.8	110.2	104.6	46.00	19.79	8.14	1.54	6.60	2.67	15.43	8.98
1982	107.3	238	193	543	106.7	108.3	102.8	53.72	23.11	9.51	1.80	7.71	3.12	18.43	10.72
1983	116.7	258	211	577	107.6	107.7	105.5	62.87	27.04	11.13	2.11	9.02	3.65	16.16	9.40
1984	109.5	300	251	614	113.5	116.7	104.0	74.22	31.93	13.14	2.49	10.65	4.31	21.46	12.49
1985	125.4	348	290	697	108.5	108.2	106.4	92.85	39.94	16.43	3.11	13.32	5.40	28.28	16.46
1986	107.3	378	308	790	104.7	102.5	108.9	97.61	41.99	17.28	3.27	14.01	5.67	29.58	17.21
1987	109.2	435	352	926	107.0	106.1	109.1	124.76	53.66	22.09	4.18	17.91	7.25	28.57	16.63
1988	128.6	537	441	1094	102.8	104.6	98.5	137.51	59.15	24.33	4.61	19.72	7.99	58.87	34.26
1989	97.3	583	470	1236	91.8	90.1	95.5	112.64	48.45	19.94	3.78	16.16	6.54	74.55	43.39
1990	104.6	662	525	1454	109.9	108.0	114.0	141.17	60.71	24.99	4.74	20.25	8.20	78.16	45.49
1991	111.4	750	585	1700	110.8	109.1	114.3	184.41	79.32	32.64	6.19	26.45	10.72	82.78	48.18
1992	109.1	833	635	1941	104.5	102.1	107.2	240.76	103.56	42.60	8.07	34.53	13.99	85.89	49.98
1993	107.3	953	709	2274	100.4	98.0	103.0	365.95	157.40	64.77	12.27	52.50	21.26	117.63	68.46
1994	110.7	1261	947	2895	107.8	107.6	105.7	540.68	170.48	80.49	17.20	63.29	30.89	151.19	87.98
1995	108.0	1624	1211	3689	109.0	107.3	110.1	565.67	225.74	131.79	27.01	104.78	119.59	144.48	140.28

Year	v10b4	v11a	v11a1	v11a2	v11b	v11b1	v11b2	v11c	v11c1	v11c2	v12	v12a	v12b	v13	v13i
1952															
1953											135.6	67.1	949.1		
1954											142.4	149.4	136.6		
1955											83.5	108.2	60.8		
1956											131.4	134.4	126.6		
1957											112.8	135.4	73.5		
1958											142.3	121.7	208.0		
1959											166.6	196.5	110.8		
1960											75.8	80.3	60.9		
1961											2.0	0.9	6.8		
1962												613.6			
1963												456.3			
1964											190.3	166.4	623.5		
1965											237.8	228.4	283.0		
1966											149.4	149.0	150.8		
1967											45.0	67.2			
1968											44.0	39.0			
1969											336.7	299.7	646.2		
1970											169.9	154.5	230.0		
1971											83.6	83.6	83.6		
1972											95.5	102.3	77.8		
1973											98.2	107.7	65.6		
1974											88.2	98.9	28.0		
1975											153.3	142.9	360.6		
1976											60.9	68.2	3.5		
1977											161.8	119.9	6447.6		
1978	0.19	9.69	6.44	3.25	41.74	33.46	8.28	39.55	32.16	7.39	125.2	134.7	98.5	244.83	145.71
1979	0.23	10.96	6.97	3.99	46.33	36.17	10.16	43.84	34.76	9.08	105.5	102.6	116.5	290.52	169.13
1980	0.25	11.61	7.19	4.42	48.56	37.33	11.23	45.89	35.86	10.03	97.0	95.4	102.3	322.03	189.06
1981	0.24	11.08	6.85	4.23	46.35	35.57	10.78	43.82	34.18	9.64	93.8	93.6	94.3	332.93	195.88
1982	0.29	13.06	8.00	5.06	54.42	41.54	12.88	51.42	39.92	11.50	114.8	114.2	116.7	379.13	226.42
1983	0.25	13.81	9.37	4.44	59.90	48.61	11.29	56.79	46.71	10.08	109.0	116.2	87.0	420.78	246.77
1984	0.34	16.95	11.06	5.89	72.40	57.40	15.00	68.54	55.14	13.40	118.3	115.4	129.9	497.58	287.29
1985	0.44	20.79	13.03	7.76	91.57	71.80	19.77	87.44	69.79	17.65	118.5	117.1	123.4	606.40	343.50
1986	0.46	22.66	14.54	8.12	96.15	75.48	20.67	90.99	72.53	18.46	101.1	101.2	100.6	654.62	364.19
1987	0.45	26.42	18.58	7.84	116.45	96.48	19.97	110.54	92.70	17.84	112.4	118.9	89.9	746.94	403.71
1988	0.92	36.64	20.48	16.16	147.48	106.33	41.15	138.91	102.17	36.74	106.2	91.9	171.7	922.62	485.29
1989	1.16	37.24	16.78	20.46	139.20	87.10	52.10	130.23	83.69	46.54	80.3	69.2	107.1	995.65	532.74
1990	1.22	42.48	21.03	21.45	163.79	109.16	54.63	153.67	104.88	48.79	110.2	108.6	114.3	1186.22	666.15
1991	1.29	50.19	27.47	22.72	200.46	142.60	57.86	188.69	137.02	51.67	115.8	121.6	102.1	1382.96	757.59
1992	1.35	59.38	35.60	23.78	246.07	186.17	59.90	232.68	179.14	53.54	116.5	121.5	102.4	1624.51	930.70
1993	1.83	86.73	54.44	32.29	318.10	235.89	82.21	392.47	319.05	73.42	130.4	132.9	122.0	2096.48	1206.48
1994	2.36	99.68	73.56	26.12	508.44	381.96	126.48	455.95	367.02	88.93	115.9	115.7	116.7	2777.88	1632.07
1995	18.60	166.57	71.66	94.91	565.90	396.33	169.57	613.68	574.80	38.88	112.9	113.6	110.4	3534.00	2008.53

Year	v13ii	v13iii	v13iv	v13a	v13ai	v13aii	v13aiii	v13aiv	v13b	v13bi	v13bii	v13biii	v13biv	v13b1	v13b1i
1952															
1953															
1954															
1955															
1956															
1957															
1958															
1959															
1960															
1961															
1962															
1963															
1964															
1965															
1966															
1967															
1968															
1969															
1970															
1971															
1972															
1973															
1974															
1975															
1976															
1977															
1978	31.79	23.49	43.84	104.97	95.52	2.13	2.83	4.49	93.75	31.96	19.15	15.36	27.28	81.36	23.71
1979	35.69	29.20	56.50	120.56	108.50	2.41	3.25	6.40	114.65	39.22	20.20	19.62	35.61	99.36	29.35
1980	40.25	34.28	58.44	134.11	120.91	2.77	3.97	6.46	121.55	42.03	22.20	22.90	34.42	106.32	32.27
1981	41.75	34.40	60.90	138.45	124.61	2.98	4.60	6.26	125.45	43.80	22.74	22.01	36.90	108.41	32.69
1982	47.15	38.64	66.92	163.71	148.15	3.23	5.42	6.91	137.41	47.11	27.23	23.49	39.58	118.85	34.98
1983	50.15	46.04	77.82	175.38	157.84	3.46	6.23	7.85	157.53	55.14	27.94	28.23	46.22	135.40	40.51
1984	59.16	55.91	95.22	200.44	178.14	3.70	7.45	11.15	186.49	66.41	30.85	34.89	54.34	160.88	49.56
1985	67.38	73.37	122.15	224.59	200.30	4.58	7.58	12.13	242.33	91.38	35.13	45.46	70.36	203.97	65.40
1986	73.45	85.61	131.37	234.23	208.24	4.98	8.41	12.60	266.51	97.40	38.49	53.26	77.36	225.77	70.96
1987	87.49	101.20	154.54	263.70	224.94	5.98	13.71	19.07	300.21	110.23	45.59	61.07	83.32	253.77	79.75
1988	102.40	133.10	201.83	312.20	265.07	7.82	16.55	22.76	391.16	135.72	53.01	84.42	118.01	326.86	89.94
1989	115.44	145.08	202.39	339.20	288.69	8.73	14.47	27.31	404.78	146.78	58.61	96.00	103.39	346.61	104.86
1990	128.66	148.11	243.30	417.71	358.70	8.81	15.34	34.86	428.56	175.98	66.07	103.35	83.16	356.18	124.64
1991	161.39	172.91	291.07	452.15	381.99	10.45	15.85	43.86	493.75	189.48	81.31	124.96	98.00	413.79	134.57
1992	226.30	188.47	279.04	480.27	430.54	10.69	16.06	22.98	608.99	266.08	123.84	129.59	89.48	504.87	195.34
1993	261.74	236.89	391.37	569.95	506.65	14.57	13.44	35.29	892.79	403.42	138.32	168.36	182.69	730.62	292.91
1994	349.67	327.41	468.73	788.39	696.50	18.27	22.37	51.25	1166.22	529.84	179.24	219.61	237.53	950.22	380.95
1995	437.99	397.81	689.67	976.96	864.58	22.37	28.92	61.09	1486.63	654.69	228.89	279.26	323.79	1215.00	489.11

Year	v13b1ii	v13b1iii	v13b1iv	v13b2	v13b2i	v13b2ii	v13b2iii	v13b2iv	v13c	v13ci	v13cii	v13ciii	v13civ	v13c1
1952														
1953														
1954														
1955														
1956														
1957														
1958														
1959														
1960														
1961														
1962														
1963														
1964														
1965														
1966														
1967														
1968														
1969														
1970														
1971														
1972														
1973														
1974														
1975														
1976														
1977														
1978	17.11	15.12	25.12	12.69	8.25	2.04	0.24	2.16	46.11	18.23	10.51	5.30	12.07	9.13
1979	18.05	19.33	33.13	14.79	9.87	2.15	0.29	2.48	55.31	21.41	13.08	6.33	14.49	9.59
1980	19.74	22.51	31.80	15.23	9.76	2.46	0.39	2.62	66.37	26.12	15.28	7.41	17.56	10.50
1981	20.27	21.50	33.95	17.04	11.11	2.47	0.51	2.95	69.03	27.47	16.03	7.79	17.74	11.12
1982	24.69	22.84	36.34	18.56	12.13	2.54	0.65	3.24	78.01	31.16	16.69	9.73	20.43	12.73
1983	25.25	27.26	42.38	22.13	14.63	2.69	0.97	3.84	87.87	33.79	18.75	11.58	23.75	14.54
1984	27.92	33.40	50.00	25.61	16.85	2.93	1.49	4.34	110.65	42.74	24.61	13.57	29.73	16.33
1985	31.45	43.40	63.72	38.36	25.98	3.68	2.06	6.64	139.48	51.82	27.67	20.33	39.66	20.82
1986	34.00	51.00	69.81	40.74	26.44	4.49	2.26	7.55	153.88	58.55	29.98	23.94	41.41	22.33
1987	41.27	58.49	74.26	46.44	30.48	4.32	2.58	9.06	183.03	68.54	35.92	26.42	52.15	25.39
1988	48.53	81.28	107.11	64.30	45.78	4.48	3.14	10.90	219.26	84.50	41.57	31.13	61.06	30.36
1989	54.04	92.40	95.31	58.17	41.92	4.57	3.60	8.08	251.67	97.27	48.10	34.61	71.69	36.29
1990	60.13	96.15	75.26	72.38	51.34	5.94	7.20	7.90	339.95	131.47	53.78	29.42	125.28	50.50
1991	74.34	116.82	88.06	79.96	54.91	6.97	8.14	9.94	437.06	186.12	69.63	32.10	149.21	70.31
1992	110.86	117.36	81.31	104.12	70.74	12.98	12.23	8.17	535.25	234.08	91.77	42.82	166.58	79.40
1993	124.42	153.55	159.74	162.17	110.51	13.90	14.81	22.95	633.74	296.41	108.85	55.09	173.39	87.44
1994	161.82	199.70	207.75	216.00	148.89	17.42	19.91	29.78	823.27	405.73	152.16	85.43	179.95	108.94
1995	207.76	256.40	261.73	271.63	165.58	21.13	22.86	62.06	1070.41	489.26	136.73	89.63	304.79	135.09

Year	v13c1i	v13c1ii	v13c1iii	v13c1iv	v13c2	v13c2i	v13c2ii	v13c2iii	v13c2iv	v13c3	v13c3i	v13c3ii	v13c3iii	v13c3iv
1952														
1953														
1954														
1955														
1956														
1957														
1958														
1959														
1960														
1961														
1962														
1963														
1964														
1965														
1966														
1967														
1968														
1969														
1970														
1971														
1972														
1973														
1974														
1975														
1976														
1977														
1978	2.78	2.40	1.10	2.85	16.33	4.91	2.02	3.43	5.97	3.16	0.43	0.14	0.60	1.99
1979	2.94	2.44	1.24	2.97	19.98	6.15	2.25	4.04	7.54	4.09	0.55	0.14	0.82	2.58
1980	3.26	2.57	1.40	3.27	24.22	7.91	2.40	4.67	9.24	5.06	0.64	0.15	1.01	3.26
1981	3.59	2.66	1.48	3.39	25.36	8.27	2.43	5.01	9.65	4.51	0.65	0.15	0.94	2.77
1982	3.82	2.82	1.78	4.31	28.23	8.92	2.51	6.42	10.38	5.74	0.80	0.16	1.10	3.68
1983	4.18	3.01	2.17	5.18	30.12	9.23	2.77	7.08	11.04	8.06	1.02	0.20	1.75	5.09
1984	4.60	3.24	2.59	5.90	36.45	11.45	2.89	8.07	14.04	10.05	1.25	0.25	2.17	6.38
1985	5.42	3.38	3.21	8.81	46.17	12.70	3.14	13.34	16.99	13.95	1.42	0.31	2.78	9.44
1986	5.95	3.60	3.47	9.31	51.96	14.74	3.68	16.42	17.12	15.31	1.52	0.38	3.06	10.35
1987	6.95	3.86	4.32	10.26	59.75	16.21	4.22	17.17	22.15	20.68	2.13	0.43	3.83	14.29
1988	8.22	6.73	4.92	10.49	73.37	20.14	4.70	22.27	26.26	24.55	2.61	0.54	3.73	17.67
1989	9.09	7.48	4.93	14.79	67.27	22.95	5.82	22.71	15.79	44.02	4.58	1.40	5.45	32.59
1990	13.20	9.98	4.56	22.76	96.15	37.58	7.76	15.91	34.90	61.05	5.77	1.64	6.01	47.63
1991	15.55	13.56	4.96	36.24	118.05	51.88	14.46	16.02	35.69	82.03	13.75	2.14	6.42	54.72
1992	17.48	16.56	5.71	39.65	146.81	72.39	21.94	22.57	29.91	107.19	23.78	2.91	7.36	73.14
1993	21.11	19.82	8.35	38.16	185.42	94.03	25.36	29.24	36.79	129.80	32.81	4.37	9.15	83.47
1994	54.80	28.97	11.35	13.82	235.54	119.54	32.51	37.40	46.09	164.49	29.17	15.86	24.47	94.99
1995	69.53	39.19	14.94	11.43	308.99	129.84	30.78	30.63	117.74	208.00	35.62	18.00	28.86	125.52

Year	v13c4	v13c4i	v13c4ii	v13c4iii	v13c4iv	v13c5	v13c5i	v13c5ii	v13c5iii	v13c5iv	v13c6	v13c6i	v13c6ii	v13c6iii
1952														
1953														
1954														
1955														
1956														
1957														
1958														
1959														
1960														
1961														
1962														
1963														
1964														
1965														
1966														
1967														
1968														
1969														
1970														
1971														
1972														
1973														
1974														
1975														
1976														
1977														
1978	3.34	0.08	3.26			2.40	1.13	0.77	0.12	0.38	1.64	1.29	0.22	
1979	5.36	0.10	5.26			3.22	1.65	0.92	0.16	0.49	1.88	1.51	0.23	
1980	6.94	0.12	6.78		0.04	3.96	2.01	1.12	0.23	0.60	2.03	1.59	0.25	
1981	7.16	0.13	6.98		0.05	4.07	2.05	1.18	0.23	0.61	2.13	1.69	0.25	0.01
1982	7.33	0.15	7.08		0.10	5.19	3.05	1.35	0.26	0.53	2.56	2.09	0.26	0.01
1983	8.22	0.15	7.90	0.02	0.15	6.21	3.79	1.51	0.35	0.56	2.91	2.37	0.27	0.01
1984	12.08	0.15	11.67	0.04	0.22	8.17	4.68	1.80	0.41	1.28	3.60	3.01	0.28	0.02
1985	13.50	0.18	12.96	0.06	0.30	11.34	6.86	2.04	0.68	1.76	4.07	3.41	0.35	0.02
1986	13.93	0.23	13.31	0.07	0.32	12.72	7.81	2.47	0.66	1.78	4.86	4.09	0.40	0.00
1987	18.10	0.28	17.34	0.11	0.37	14.41	9.05	2.90	0.64	1.82	5.41	4.54	0.46	0.00
1988	19.81	0.33	18.97	0.11	0.40	15.90	10.07	3.01	0.72	2.10	7.51	6.50	0.50	0.01
1989	23.13	0.35	22.24	0.12	0.42	15.74	9.39	3.06	0.82	2.47	8.12	7.06	0.53	0.00
1990	24.07	0.62	21.60	0.12	1.73	25.91	12.93	3.48	1.88	7.62	12.16	8.82	0.89	0.00
1991	25.59	1.23	22.60	0.40	1.36	36.11	16.47	3.50	2.25	13.89	15.11	12.47	1.44	0.03
1992	35.35	1.87	29.84	0.78	2.83	40.26	20.60	4.19	3.67	11.80	17.79	14.80	1.72	0.13
1993	41.47	2.21	35.75	0.84	2.67	45.09	30.43	5.88	4.41	4.37	21.96	17.00	1.98	0.19
1994	50.85	4.13	42.48	1.60	2.64	61.90	40.84	8.45	6.33	6.28	30.93	20.15	2.45	0.21
1995	69.62	5.22	50.58	4.06	9.76	84.23	39.54	17.77	5.52	21.40	41.08	27.76	4.60	0.25

Year	v13c6iv	v13c7	v13c7i	v13c7ii	v13c7iii	v13c7iv	v13c8	v13c8i	v13c8ii	v13c8iii	v13c8iv	v13c9	v13c9i	v13c9ii
1952														
1953														
1954														
1955														
1956														
1957														
1958														
1959														
1960														
1961														
1962														
1963														
1964														
1965														
1966														
1967														
1968														
1969														
1970														
1971														
1972														
1973														
1974														
1975														
1976														
1977														
1978	0.13	4.44	3.21	0.70	0.01	0.52	0.31	0.21	0.08		0.02	3.16	2.13	0.78
1979	0.14	4.78	3.55	0.74	0.02	0.47	0.46	0.33	0.10		0.03	3.57	2.40	0.85
1980	0.19	5.85	4.62	0.75	0.02	0.46	1.21	0.77	0.22	0.01	0.21	4.15	2.91	0.88
1981	0.18	6.06	4.78	0.76	0.02	0.50	1.27	0.77	0.26	0.01	0.23	4.15	3.11	1.18
1982	0.20	6.72	5.38	0.76	0.02	0.56	1.55	0.98	0.31	0.01	0.25	5.12	3.32	1.24
1983	0.26	7.41	5.64	1.10	0.02	0.65	1.70	1.09	0.32	0.02	0.27	5.70	3.51	1.48
1984	0.29	10.09	7.49	1.90	0.02	0.68	3.30	2.65	0.34	0.03	0.28	7.08	4.19	2.04
1985	0.29	12.99	9.36	2.67	0.03	0.93	4.30	3.50	0.44	0.04	0.32	8.36	5.28	2.18
1986	0.37	14.10	10.28	2.86	0.02	0.94	5.09	4.07	0.62	0.04	0.36	9.37	5.94	2.45
1987	0.41	15.60	11.37	3.01	0.02	1.20	6.90	5.65	0.77	0.05	0.43	12.04	7.92	2.71
1988	0.50	19.73	15.11	3.19	0.03	1.40	8.40	6.83	0.86	0.06	0.65	14.87	10.24	2.84
1989	0.53	23.75	18.90	3.34	0.03	1.48	9.58	7.71	1.08	0.08	0.71	18.06	11.85	2.91
1990	2.45	27.18	19.90	3.62	0.20	3.46	10.62	7.69	1.18	0.35	1.40	31.21	24.38	3.47
1991	1.17	30.37	23.72	3.97	0.34	2.34	15.70	9.91	3.07	0.72	2.00	40.92	35.09	4.41
1992	1.14	36.44	28.49	4.65	0.44	2.86	18.32	11.99	3.23	0.94	2.16	49.98	41.25	5.98
1993	2.79	44.19	36.46	4.85	0.50	2.38	19.47	13.52	3.78	1.08	1.09	55.07	47.18	6.27
1994	8.12	61.98	52.51	5.48	0.71	3.28	27.99	18.15	5.89	1.45	2.50	75.68	64.29	9.04
1995	8.47	81.53	67.81	8.97	1.04	3.71	38.15	27.63	5.37	2.12	3.03	96.85	83.15	10.65

Year	v13c9iii	v13c9iv	v13c10	v13c10i	v13c10ii	v13c10iii	v13c10iv
1952							
1953							
1954							
1955							
1956							
1957							
1958							
1959							
1960							
1961							
1962							
1963							
1964							
1965							
1966							
1967							
1968							
1969							
1970							
1971							
1972							
1973							
1974							
1975							
1976							
1977							
1978	0.04	0.21	2.20	2.06	0.14		
1979	0.05	0.27	2.38	2.23	0.15		
1980	0.07	0.29	2.45	2.29	0.16		
1981	0.09	0.36	2.61	2.43	0.18		
1982	0.13	0.43	2.84	2.65	0.19		
1983	0.16	0.55	3.00	2.81	0.19		
1984	0.21	0.64	3.50	3.27	0.20	0.01	0.02
1985	0.16	0.74	3.98	3.69	0.20	0.01	0.08
1986	0.18	0.80	4.21	3.92	0.21	0.02	0.06
1987	0.26	1.15	4.75	4.44	0.22	0.02	0.07
1988	0.27	1.52	4.76	4.45	0.23	0.01	0.07
1989	0.45	2.85	5.71	5.39	0.24	0.02	0.06
1990	0.34	3.02	1.10	0.58	0.16	0.05	0.31
1991	0.85	0.57	2.87	1.05	0.48	0.11	1.23
1992	1.21	1.56	3.71	1.43	0.77	0.01	1.50
1993	1.27	0.35	3.83	1.66	0.79	0.06	1.32
1994	1.83	0.52	4.97	2.15	1.03	0.08	1.71
1995	2.12	0.93	6.87	3.16	0.82	0.09	2.80

23

Guizhou

Year	v1	v1a	v1b	v1b1	v1b2	v1c	v1c1	v1c2	v1c3	v2	v2a	v2b	v2b1	v2b2	v2c
1952	12.87	7.28	4.03	3.04	0.99	1.56	0.76	0.80	0.00						
1953	15.06	7.95	4.90	3.67	1.23	2.21	0.94	0.89	0.38	122.9	110.8	123.2	123.0	123.8	178.4
1954	16.90	9.07	5.33	4.13	1.20	2.50	1.08	1.02	0.40	108.6	106.8	109.5	113.3	97.9	112.2
1955	17.66	9.00	5.84	4.59	1.25	2.82	1.18	1.21	0.43	108.4	106.3	109.8	111.3	104.4	111.7
1956	22.15	10.83	7.73	5.38	2.35	3.59	1.33	1.47	0.79	121.4	111.1	133.5	119.1	187.8	127.8
1957	24.67	11.82	8.47	6.05	2.42	4.38	1.48	1.70	1.20	111.7	107.5	110.9	114.3	102.9	122.8
1958	33.27	13.09	14.28	9.42	4.86	5.90	2.27	2.12	1.51	133.6	105.5	175.1	164.9	200.5	129.0
1959	39.08	12.68	19.44	13.42	6.02	6.96	3.03	2.21	1.72	109.6	83.0	131.2	134.7	124.1	111.7
1960	39.90	11.04	20.91	13.95	6.96	7.95	3.31	2.35	2.29	101.3	85.2	106.9	103.0	115.5	110.5
1961	27.90	11.68	10.86	8.46	2.40	5.36	3.01	2.06	0.29	55.9	80.1	44.7	56.0	22.2	58.9
1962	26.91	14.79	8.19	7.12	1.07	3.93	1.74	1.84	0.35	90.8	113.7	76.4	80.4	56.4	84.1
1963	27.60	14.85	8.60	7.32	1.28	4.15	1.71	1.91	0.53	108.7	113.4	104.1	102.5	115.4	107.2
1964	33.64	17.52	11.44	8.84	2.60	4.68	2.11	1.92	0.65	122.2	118.0	131.8	121.0	200.1	113.2
1965	42.83	19.84	17.19	11.43	5.76	5.80	2.17	2.38	1.25	126.6	108.7	150.4	129.4	230.9	117.3
1966	45.50	19.42	19.47	12.98	6.49	6.61	2.48	2.83	1.30	104.0	91.7	113.4	113.7	112.7	105.5
1967	41.95	20.46	15.90	12.28	3.62	5.59	1.87	2.48	1.24	90.4	105.4	82.2	94.2	56.2	85.5
1968	38.92	19.31	14.47	11.20	3.27	5.14	1.47	2.20	1.47	93.8	94.4	91.8	91.7	92.0	98.7
1969	36.98	18.68	13.44	10.12	3.32	4.86	1.34	2.06	1.46	94.7	96.7	92.6	90.2	101.5	95.8
1970	54.50	20.52	27.42	20.75	6.67	6.56	2.07	2.60	1.89	152.4	110.6	200.9	202.2	196.5	121.2
1971	64.92	22.64	34.18	22.94	11.24	8.10	2.76	3.10	2.24	128.5	108.0	146.8	139.9	168.3	116.3
1972	57.38	19.42	30.39	22.04	8.35	7.57	2.69	3.20	1.68	87.4	83.0	90.0	96.0	74.4	87.0
1973	57.14	23.61	24.91	19.21	5.70	8.62	2.27	3.73	2.62	97.5	120.8	82.8	87.2	68.1	113.3
1974	53.28	22.20	22.57	17.86	4.71	8.51	2.05	3.72	2.74	95.8	93.0	91.0	93.0	82.7	122.5
1975	63.87	22.80	30.52	24.97	5.55	10.55	2.85	4.07	3.63	119.5	101.8	136.5	139.9	120.1	108.7
1976	60.47	23.98	28.07	23.08	4.99	8.42	2.46	4.38	1.58	93.7	103.8	91.8	92.4	88.3	79.5
1977	76.55	26.44	38.42	32.15	6.27	11.69	3.61	4.43	3.65	128.5	110.3	137.7	139.4	127.6	138.9
1978	94.22	27.46	50.94	41.26	9.68	15.82	4.88	5.64	5.30	123.8	102.9	132.7	129.5	153.5	131.1
1979	104.83	31.74	56.32	45.72	10.60	16.77	5.08	5.67	6.02	107.2	101.0	109.4	109.4	109.6	108.2
1980	111.64	36.44	55.67	45.19	10.48	19.53	5.59	5.69	8.25	100.0	104.3	96.5	97.4	91.6	108.4
1981	118.84	41.93	55.76	44.83	10.93	21.15	6.36	6.59	8.20	102.3	106.9	97.8	96.4	103.7	106.8
1982	140.50	51.49	65.11	53.62	11.49	23.90	6.53	7.21	10.16	116.4	119.8	115.2	119.6	97.8	113.2
1983	156.76	52.66	76.66	64.26	12.40	27.44	7.75	8.62	11.07	112.2	102.6	119.4	120.5	114.1	111.8
1984	192.58	63.09	98.14	81.41	16.73	31.35	11.17	9.91	10.27	118.3	111.4	124.4	123.3	130.0	113.4
1985	231.37	70.24	120.29	98.19	22.10	40.84	13.87	12.34	14.63	111.8	100.4	115.0	113.2	123.9	122.2
1986	269.16	79.34	131.95	108.09	23.86	57.87	16.36	15.51	26.00	108.7	108.4	103.3	104.4	98.4	124.7
1987	319.01	92.25	156.74	126.53	30.21	70.02	17.72	16.89	35.41	112.1	104.0	114.6	114.2	116.3	116.2
1988	407.25	123.39	197.76	166.81	30.95	86.10	22.50	21.90	41.70	110.8	102.3	112.1	116.5	91.5	117.4
1989	471.01	133.69	232.25	201.45	30.80	105.07	26.67	21.66	56.74	104.4	104.8	104.8	107.4	89.3	103.2
1990	512.56	145.53	253.14	218.16	34.98	113.89	24.18	23.59	66.12	105.7	102.4	107.0	106.9	107.7	106.0
1991	579.70	165.34	286.73	246.76	39.97	127.63	26.66	27.07	73.90	109.7	113.1	108.5	109.0	105.5	108.1
1992	684.82	176.72	350.89	301.49	49.40	157.21	34.12	33.17	89.92	111.0	100.8	114.1	116.3	99.8	117.5
1993	873.43	201.40	448.11	381.26	66.85	223.92	54.78	62.03	107.11	111.6	104.2	113.0	114.3	103.2	117.3
1994	1078.68	277.13	545.40	461.49	83.91	256.15	49.16	74.94	132.05	109.0	103.7	113.0	113.0	112.8	106.2
1995	1296.13	344.85	665.00	565.47	99.53	286.28	53.01	83.28	149.99	107.1	103.0	108.4	108.2	109.9	108.1

Year	v2c1	v2c2	v3'	v3	v3a	v3b	v3b1	v3b2	v3c	v3c1	v3c2	v3c3	v3c4	v3c5	v3c6
1952			8.55	8.55	5.85	1.59	1.17	0.42	1.11	0.54	0.57				
1953	124.7	110.8	10.01	10.01	6.47	1.97	1.48	0.49	1.57	0.63	0.65				
1954	113.8	114.8	11.14	11.14	7.19	2.19	1.70	0.49	1.76	0.69	0.73				
1955	109.7	118.5	11.61	11.61	7.28	2.35	1.86	0.49	1.98	0.75	0.86				
1956	113.1	122.0	14.65	14.65	8.87	3.25	2.21	1.04	2.53	0.82	1.04				
1957	110.9	115.7	16.30	16.30	9.73	3.49	2.55	0.94	3.08	0.89	1.21				
1958	153.3	124.7	20.36	20.36	10.50	6.02	3.68	2.34	3.84	1.61	1.51				
1959	133.6	103.9	23.51	23.51	10.05	9.01	5.99	3.02	4.45	2.10	1.56				
1960	109.3	106.7	22.94	22.94	8.60	9.49	5.85	3.64	4.85	2.23	1.64				
1961	72.7	74.5	18.05	18.05	9.19	5.17	3.93	1.24	3.69	1.90	0.91				
1962	61.6	75.5	16.52	16.52	11.01	2.93	2.55	0.38	2.58	0.65	0.68				
1963	87.3	110.8	16.80	16.80	11.13	2.97	2.61	0.36	2.70	0.78	0.62				
1964	126.4	98.0	19.75	19.75	13.07	3.74	3.01	0.73	2.94	0.97	0.58				
1965	100.8	120.3	24.41	24.41	15.25	5.63	3.96	1.67	3.53	1.02	0.95				
1966	114.3	115.2	24.78	24.78	14.90	6.04	4.21	1.83	3.84	1.07	1.31				
1967	77.0	87.0	23.99	23.99	15.91	4.66	3.67	0.99	3.42	0.74	1.08				
1968	70.4	90.5	21.38	21.38	14.16	4.20	3.25	0.95	3.02	0.41	0.91				
1969	90.7	94.1	21.12	21.12	13.82	4.33	3.29	1.04	2.97	0.30	0.93				
1970	174.6	124.5	28.36	28.36	15.15	9.56	7.60	1.96	3.65	0.66	1.24				
1971	133.1	120.2	32.29	32.29	15.93	12.06	8.83	3.23	4.30	1.15	1.50				
1972	97.6	103.4	29.62	29.62	13.55	11.90	8.06	3.84	4.17	1.12	1.39				
1973	84.1	115.9	28.39	28.39	15.62	8.20	6.34	1.86	4.57	0.78	1.71				
1974	90.6	99.6	24.48	24.48	14.52	5.79	4.79	1.00	4.17	0.63	1.62				
1975	144.0	111.7	31.10	31.10	16.16	9.46	7.91	1.55	5.48	1.23	1.79				
1976	87.6	108.8	89.30	29.30	16.94	8.00	6.58	1.42	4.36	0.83	1.48				
1977	145.6	98.9	37.72	37.72	18.07	13.50	11.37	2.13	6.15	1.57	1.84				
1978	133.5	127.3	46.62	46.62	19.42	18.73	15.24	3.49	8.47	1.68	3.59	1.04	0.14	0.46	0.21
1979	102.1	100.9	55.28	55.28	23.29	22.41	18.33	4.08	9.58	1.86	3.40	1.03	0.25	0.46	0.34
1980	109.8	97.9	60.26	60.26	24.86	24.00	19.37	4.63	11.40	2.01	3.17	1.17	0.55	0.49	0.51
1981	113.9	106.7	67.89	67.89	29.90	24.95	20.36	4.59	13.04	2.56	3.93	1.00	0.55	0.50	0.59
1982	103.6	114.1	79.39	79.39	37.37	27.44	22.58	4.86	14.58	2.74	4.02	1.51	0.75	0.51	0.67
1983	115.4	127.2	87.38	87.38	37.76	33.14	28.16	4.98	16.48	3.76	5.33	1.95	0.53	0.75	0.54
1984	145.0	109.6	108.27	108.27	45.73	43.51	36.85	6.66	19.03	4.66	6.39	2.20	0.56	0.37	0.57
1985	121.0	110.3	123.92	123.92	50.45	49.88	41.96	7.92	23.59	5.86	8.16	2.93	0.52	1.06	0.60
1986	114.2	119.3	139.57	139.57	56.46	50.96	43.57	7.39	32.15	7.34	8.54	4.62	0.85	1.48	1.22
1987	104.3	105.4	165.50	165.50	66.46	60.11	49.93	10.18	38.93	7.74	10.33	6.18	1.37	1.32	1.52
1988	119.6	122.8	211.37	211.79	85.20	78.63	68.32	10.31	47.96	9.78	12.60	7.87	1.85	2.29	2.07
1989	100.8	91.2	235.54	235.84	92.88	86.74	77.26	9.48	56.22	12.36	9.52	12.83	2.14	2.16	2.68
1990	88.3	104.9	259.78	260.14	100.10	92.83	82.15	10.68	67.21	11.69	18.20	11.33	3.95	2.41	2.23
1991	107.6	110.3	295.50	295.90	115.71	101.54	88.96	12.58	78.65	13.98	20.97	12.56	4.50	3.11	2.56
1992	123.7	108.1	339.89	339.91	121.18	122.08	106.41	15.67	96.65	19.00	25.53	14.51	5.12	4.09	3.12
1993	118.9	173.2	415.99	416.07	133.40	155.47	135.35	20.12	127.20	24.82	32.40	21.11	6.08	5.36	4.91
1994	121.8	101.1	520.74	521.17	183.52	195.76	172.89	22.87	141.89	17.13	39.16	23.81	5.64	6.06	5.05
1995	111.5	102.2	636.40	630.07	227.06	234.10	208.50	25.60	168.91	21.11	46.41	28.52	6.90	12.59	6.47

Year	v3c7	v3c8	v3c9	v3c10	v3d	v4'	v4	v4a	v4b	v4b1	v4b2	v4c	v4c1	v4c2	v4c3
1952					58										
1953				0.29	66	124.5	124.5	114.2	122.0	130.3	98.5	182.2	116.7	109.9	
1954				0.34	72	106.3	106.3	103.6	111.3	116.4	92.6	110.2	109.0	113.4	
1955				0.37	74	108.2	108.2	107.2	107.4	110.2	94.4	112.2	109.4	116.6	
1956				0.67	91	119.0	119.0	110.9	136.1	118.5	231.7	127.1	108.9	120.5	
1957				0.98	99	108.0	108.0	103.9	107.7	118.2	78.4	119.1	108.5	117.5	
1958				0.72	120	119.9	119.9	103.2	163.3	140.6	224.7	123.4	181.4	123.9	
1959				0.79	136	105.0	105.0	81.2	141.2	155.3	117.3	113.4	130.8	103.2	
1960				0.98	135	96.2	96.2	83.3	103.5	96.4	119.3	107.2	105.9	105.1	
1961				0.88	110	62.6	62.6	82.8	46.3	60.7	20.2	62.3	68.4	37.2	
1962				1.25	100	88.5	88.5	112.7	60.6	63.1	46.6	78.6	36.8	67.0	
1963				1.30	100	108.6	108.6	112.8	99.5	100.8	90.5	106.1	105.6	91.8	
1964				1.39	114	117.4	117.4	116.9	126.3	115.8	212.5	109.9	124.2	89.2	
1965				1.56	136	119.7	119.7	110.6	149.8	131.4	231.5	114.9	105.7	175.0	
1966				1.46	134	97.4	97.4	91.4	106.9	107.3	105.9	101.9	104.6	140.6	
1967				1.60	125	95.7	95.7	108.0	78.1	86.7	56.3	88.9	70.6	81.2	
1968				1.70	108	90.2	90.2	89.2	90.0	88.6	95.3	94.1	49.5	82.0	
1969				1.74	102	99.0	99.0	97.6	102.5	100.9	108.6	99.1	72.5	106.7	
1970				1.75	132	135.3	135.3	110.8	205.8	218.6	162.0	118.3	249.0	137.2	
1971				1.65	145	125.0	125.0	110.4	151.3	148.0	164.0	116.5	173.9	122.0	
1972				1.66	129	95.9	95.9	90.3	96.2	81.9	146.3	116.5	120.2	159.5	
1973				2.08	119	97.9	97.9	119.1	69.2	76.5	54.9	113.5	68.1	123.6	
1974				1.92	101	89.8	89.8	93.4	68.4	72.3	57.8	115.3	80.4	160.0	
1975				2.46	124	110.6	110.6	91.9	168.1	178.8	131.5	100.9	203.3	64.0	
1976				2.05	110	93.4	93.4	105.1	85.0	81.7	100.2	80.2	66.8	78.7	
1977				2.74	144	128.5	128.5	101.7	170.2	183.1	121.1	136.8	191.3	129.3	
1978	0.58	0.28	0.47	0.02	175	123.7	123.7	106.6	137.3	139.7	123.7	132.7	133.6	155.8	
1979	1.02	0.41	0.77	0.04	204	111.0	111.0	102.8	117.3	119.1	105.2	111.4	107.2	92.4	120.0
1980	1.55	0.53	1.35	0.07	219	104.4	104.4	100.4	104.3	106.9	85.6	111.7	106.5	88.4	115.7
1981	1.74	0.55	1.45	0.07	242	106.5	106.5	109.9	101.7	99.1	112.7	109.5	109.8	103.4	90.9
1982	1.99	0.62	1.59	0.08	278	115.8	115.8	123.0	109.3	111.4	101.3	112.6	103.6	111.9	147.0
1983	1.59	0.53	1.43	0.07	302	112.6	112.6	104.6	122.9	126.4	108.8	112.3	134.6	157.0	117.2
1984	1.70	0.54	1.47	0.07	371	119.8	119.8	118.2	123.8	123.8	123.5	114.9	137.6	103.1	119.4
1985	1.97	0.67	1.73	0.09	420	107.9	107.9	98.8	112.8	112.0	116.6	117.8	124.3	116.6	128.2
1986	3.51	1.63	2.76	0.20	467	105.6	105.6	106.1	98.0	99.7	90.5	120.9	108.7	109.1	127.1
1987	4.27	2.13	3.46	0.11	546	110.8	110.8	102.9	116.2	113.8	128.6	114.8	113.9	123.4	114.4
1988	5.64	2.36	3.36	0.14	683	108.2	108.6	99.0	113.2	115.5	103.1	115.0	108.3	117.1	121.8
1989	7.00	3.16	4.13	0.24	750	104.9	104.5	106.3	103.9	106.8	89.4	103.3	113.0	90.0	131.2
1990	5.23	2.16	9.38	0.63	810	103.9	104.3	101.7	106.1	105.6	108.8	104.6	84.9	104.9	91.5
1991	6.32	2.29	11.50	0.86	896	109.2	109.2	113.2	103.5	103.5	103.8	111.2	106.8	109.2	107.3
1992	7.63	2.86	13.58	1.21	1034	108.2	108.1	99.2	115.0	116.0	108.0	112.6	121.1	109.3	107.3
1993	9.89	4.21	17.42	0.80	1255	109.9	109.9	103.9	113.8	115.7	97.5	113.0	112.3	117.9	119.7
1994	13.93	4.83	24.27	2.01	1553	108.4	108.5	103.7	111.8	112.4	105.8	109.9	111.9	108.3	113.6
1995	15.29	5.24	24.21	2.07	1853	108.6	107.5	102.4	110.5	111.1	104.0	109.3	107.8	103.0	107.2

Year	v4c4	v4c5	v4c6	v4c7	v4c8	v4c9	v4c10	v5	v5a	v5a1	v5a1a	v5a1b	v5a2	v5b	v5b1
1952								8.55	7.94	7.31	5.94	1.37	0.63	1.00	0.31
1953								10.01	8.76	8.07	6.51	1.56	0.69	1.47	0.70
1954								11.14	9.60	8.44	6.81	1.67	1.12	2.78	1.43
1955								11.61	10.00	8.81	6.98	1.83	1.19	1.69	0.81
1956								14.65	12.07	10.32	7.91	2.41	1.75	3.05	2.07
1957								16.30	13.46	11.79	9.07	2.72	1.67	5.14	2.07
1958								20.36	15.37	13.24	10.17	3.07	2.13	12.64	8.37
1959								23.51	14.95	12.47	8.61	3.86	2.48	11.00	9.85
1960								22.94	15.75	13.00	8.35	4.65	2.75	8.16	9.94
1961								18.05	15.71	13.84	9.01	4.83	1.87	1.18	1.65
1962								16.52	15.62	14.59	10.11	4.48	1.03	0.45	0.63
1963								16.80	16.38	14.86	10.49	4.37	1.52	3.80	2.32
1964								19.75	18.39	16.72	11.63	5.09	1.67	6.00	5.83
1965								24.41	20.80	19.00	13.41	5.59	1.80	15.18	13.05
1966								24.78	21.48	19.45	13.59	5.86	2.03	15.48	15.29
1967								23.99	21.45	19.59	14.02	5.57	1.86	7.77	8.88
1968								21.38	20.48	18.86	13.67	5.19	1.62	8.52	7.23
1969								21.12	20.17	18.37	13.87	4.50	1.80	10.24	9.34
1970								28.36	23.43	21.41	15.30	6.11	2.01	24.21	18.00
1971								32.29	26.09	23.75	16.64	7.11	2.34	27.43	23.89
1972								29.62	26.82	24.12	16.13	7.99	2.70	17.92	16.91
1973								28.39	28.45	25.56	17.09	8.47	2.89	16.52	11.53
1974								24.48	28.35	25.35	15.64	9.71	3.00	10.80	8.78
1975								31.11	29.66	26.57	16.16	10.41	3.09	11.04	11.21
1976								29.30	31.17	27.72	17.18	10.54	3.45	10.11	9.40
1977								37.72	34.05	30.53	19.49	11.04	3.52	15.85	11.27
1978								46.62	38.39	34.23	21.95	12.28	4.16	23.15	17.98
1979	212.4	120.7	191.5	211.6	179.4	194.9	183.2	55.28	42.56	37.87	24.53	13.34	4.69	22.78	18.13
1980	222.8	106.7	155.3	157.1	133.4	180.9	179.6	60.26	48.71	43.45	28.38	15.07	5.26	20.95	17.53
1981	108.1	131.4	123.5	119.6	110.9	114.5	110.0	67.89	59.45	53.85	37.60	16.25	5.60	13.31	17.34
1982	130.8	98.2	110.6	111.4	108.9	106.3	105.2	79.39	67.59	58.59	41.26	17.33	9.00	22.48	19.62
1983	64.2	112.0	73.7	71.9	77.0	81.4	85.6	87.38	74.67	64.79	46.27	18.52	9.88	23.02	21.58
1984	113.0	122.4	109.9	113.5	109.7	109.3	114.6	108.27	88.59	77.07	56.62	20.45	11.52	32.82	30.05
1985	87.6	117.3	102.2	111.9	118.6	113.3	103.7	123.92	100.12	87.33	60.92	26.41	12.79	43.62	40.06
1986	131.8	112.2	163.0	143.6	195.6	128.6	182.4	139.57	115.92	97.38	67.94	29.44	18.54	49.30	45.24
1987	139.7	105.3	107.2	104.5	113.4	107.5	45.9	165.50	131.77	110.53	76.64	33.89	21.24	55.89	50.20
1988	127.3	120.7	129.4	125.2	104.2	92.1	140.0	211.79	151.12	127.43	84.45	42.98	23.69	72.98	56.96
1989	93.1	75.7	104.1	100.2	108.1	99.0	126.1	235.84	169.09	142.91	98.63	44.28	26.18	81.85	54.13
1990	109.7	133.2	122.1	125.0	128.1	135.1	129.6	260.14	189.91	148.55	100.96	47.59	41.36	80.42	64.34
1991	111.3	122.6	112.7	116.1	103.6	119.6	130.6	295.90	213.30	172.63	114.33	58.30	40.67	83.99	74.23
1992	111.0	119.9	112.9	113.8	115.3	111.0	130.3	339.91	250.04	196.59	128.88	67.71	53.45	107.60	92.25
1993	114.7	100.2	118.4	102.1	122.0	108.6	62.9	416.07	302.10	243.69	162.24	81.45	58.41	143.68	122.11
1994	79.8	111.3	94.3	123.8	111.1	118.3	101.6	517.96	388.91	316.27	197.88	118.39	72.64	154.55	150.84
1995	121.7	155.2	125.2	116.9	100.0	102.0	112.6	648.34	513.46	427.66	269.16	158.50	85.80	233.94	183.09

Year	v5b2	v5c	v5c1	v5c2	v6a1	v6a2	v6a3	v6a4	v6b2	v6b3	v6b4	v7	v7a	v7a1	v7a2
1952	0.69	-0.38	3.57	3.95											
1953	0.77	-0.22	3.94	4.16								111.9	111.6	108.9	123.4
1954	1.35	-1.24	4.24	5.48								109.1	104.8	104.8	104.7
1955	0.88	-0.08	4.41	4.49								104.4	104.3	102.5	111.3
1956	0.98	-0.47	5.26	5.73								116.4	111.5	105.2	134.0
1957	3.07	-2.30	5.92	8.22								109.3	112.4	113.1	110.2
1958	4.27	-7.65	6.72	14.37								110.8	108.2	106.3	114.7
1959	1.15	-2.43	6.43	8.86								90.4	85.8	73.0	125.3
1960	-1.78	-0.97	6.73	7.70								104.9	103.9	94.8	120.2
1961	-0.47	1.17	6.89	5.72								78.4	83.8	82.6	85.5
1962	-0.18	0.46	7.03	6.57								101.5	106.8	101.1	114.7
1963	1.48	-3.37	7.29	10.66								112.9	108.7	116.7	99.1
1964	0.17	-4.64	8.19	12.83								113.5	113.8	110.9	117.9
1965	2.13	-11.58	9.28	20.86								109.5	109.9	110.8	108.7
1966	0.19	-12.18	9.55	21.73								99.0	97.7	95.1	101.2
1967	-1.11	-5.23	9.58	14.81								98.8	99.8	103.3	95.3
1968	1.29	-7.62	9.18	16.80								95.4	96.4	97.6	94.7
1969	0.90	-9.29	9.01	18.30								97.3	95.5	101.3	87.3
1970	6.21	-19.27	10.46	29.73								121.1	122.5	115.2	134.7
1971	3.54	-21.23	11.62	32.85								110.3	109.7	106.8	116.9
1972	1.01	-15.12	11.87	26.99								132.0	133.6	142.7	112.6
1973	4.99	-16.58	12.58	29.16								104.6	104.4	104.1	105.4
1974	2.02	-14.67	12.49	27.16								97.4	96.9	90.8	114.5
1975	-0.17	-9.59	13.07	22.66								103.6	103.7	102.0	107.3
1976	0.71	-11.98	13.70	25.68								103.7	103.0	104.4	100.0
1977	4.58	-12.17	15.03	27.20								109.4	110.0	112.2	105.1
1978	5.17	-14.92	16.91	31.83	11.74	8.96	0.95	0.30	10.85	1.18	0.25	113.1	112.7	113.4	110.9
1979	4.65	-10.05	18.74	28.79	13.60	9.41	1.16	0.36	11.53	1.54	0.27	101.8	100.9	98.0	108.2
1980	3.42	-9.40	21.47	30.87	14.09	12.16	1.74	0.39	13.27	1.52	0.28	104.2	103.9	103.6	104.7
1981	0.97	-9.87	26.42	36.29	16.79	18.07	1.99	0.75	14.34	1.64	0.27	118.9	119.7	122.3	115.0
1982	2.86	-10.69	29.52	40.21	18.07	20.51	1.80	0.88	15.36	1.68	0.29	139.3	136.8	141.4	127.6
1983	1.44	-10.31	32.64	42.95	21.93	21.05	2.10	1.19	15.94	2.26	0.32	110.9	110.8	120.0	90.6
1984	2.77	-13.14	38.80	51.94	28.94	23.73	2.58	1.37	17.72	2.39	0.34	106.2	105.1	103.7	109.2
1985	3.56	-19.82	43.82	63.64	31.94	24.69	2.97	1.32	23.34	2.69	0.38	106.3	106.0	104.7	109.5
1986	4.06	-25.65	49.98	75.63	34.65	28.11	3.64	1.54	26.05	2.95	0.44	111.2	106.2	106.8	104.7
1987	6.69	-23.16	56.77	79.93	39.00	32.10	3.87	1.67	29.68	3.68	0.53	101.8	103.1	102.5	104.9
1988	16.02	-12.31	65.15	77.46	42.63	36.19	3.72	1.91	36.51	5.79	0.68	103.3	103.3	101.8	107.2
1989	27.72	-15.10	74.45	89.55	53.91	37.67	4.75	2.30	36.55	6.97	0.76	98.1	96.7	100.4	87.5
1990	16.08	-10.19	85.77	95.96	55.12	38.32	5.06	2.46	38.62	8.08	0.89	107.0	99.3	97.3	105.0
1991	14.76	-6.39	108.64	115.03	63.16	41.90	5.79	3.48	46.87	9.89	1.54	110.3	113.7	111.3	118.7
1992	15.35	-17.73	144.28	162.01	72.11	45.15	7.79	3.83	56.37	8.25	3.09	108.9	104.6	104.0	105.8
1993	21.56	-29.71	160.34	190.05	92.77	50.11	11.02	8.34	66.37	11.28	3.80	107.7	109.7	110.8	107.5
1994	3.71	-25.50	200.84	226.34	102.45	71.46	12.84	11.13	93.64	19.49	5.26	112.6	109.8	107.7	114.2
1995	50.85	-99.06	242.81	341.87	139.54	97.49	18.37	13.76	123.55	27.51	7.44	106.3	107.8	105.3	112.5

Year	v7b	v8	v8a	v8b	v9	v9a	v9b	v10a1	v10a2	v10a3	v10a3a	v10a3b	v10a4	v10b1	v10b2
1952		50	44	124											
1953	115.2	54	47	134	108.7	106.3	117.0								
1954	158.2	55	48	141	102.5	102.4	103.0								
1955	105.3	56	49	144	102.2	100.9	103.4								
1956	152.9	64	54	180	109.0	103.1	127.0								
1957	92.9	71	60	181	109.2	110.8	98.5								
1958	129.3	78	69	142	105.4	107.8	79.7								
1959	118.1	72	59	147	84.2	73.7	103.3								
1960	109.0	77	58	187	106.0	96.2	126.5								
1961	55.0	85	63	224	86.9	84.2	98.6								
1962	68.6	89	69	237	106.1	98.5	131.1								
1963	150.5	88	70	232	106.1	113.4	99.7								
1964	111.4	96	76	253	110.9	108.6	110.3								
1965	106.3	106	85	253	106.0	107.7	98.9								
1966	108.6	105	84	259	94.8	92.3	99.0								
1967	92.6	102	83	239	96.4	99.8	92.4								
1968	88.3	95	78	218	93.0	93.9	92.7								
1969	111.4	89	76	182	91.9	97.5	84.1								
1970	111.9	100	81	237	118.1	111.1	128.9								
1971	116.4	107	86	259	105.8	103.3	110.1								
1972	115.8	105	80	278	129.4	138.6	107.5								
1973	107.0	107	82	288	100.4	99.9	102.8								
1974	102.8	104	73	330	95.1	88.8	114.5								
1975	103.0	106	73	353	100.7	98.8	107.0								
1976	110.4	104	73	343	96.8	97.8	96.1								
1977	103.5	117	84	368	111.9	114.1	107.5								
1978	117.7	128	93	404	110.6	111.3	109.4	13.16	1.94	2.87		2.87		3.53	1.12
1979	110.4	140	102	429	99.2	96.4	105.7	12.51	2.29	3.34		3.34		3.18	0.98
1980	106.4	158	116	472	102.2	102.0	102.0	12.67	3.71	1.15		1.15		2.33	0.73
1981	112.4	192	152	500	117.7	120.2	112.9	11.90	3.36	2.08	0.14	1.94		0.60	0.28
1982	161.1	205	164	525	134.5	139.0	125.7	12.45	4.07	3.10	0.19	2.91		1.95	0.64
1983	111.1	224	181	553	109.4	118.4	89.2	12.93	4.34	4.31	0.29	4.02		1.02	0.29
1984	114.6	264	220	591	104.1	103.1	105.7	17.21	4.79	8.04	0.56	7.48		1.92	0.56
1985	108.4	296	235	742	104.8	103.8	106.4	23.01	6.07	10.98	0.82	10.16		2.44	0.67
1986	144.2	326	259	802	104.9	105.7	101.6	27.13	6.63	11.48	1.08	10.40		2.74	0.88
1987	95.1	365	288	906	101.7	101.1	103.0	28.54	8.76	12.91	0.95	11.96		3.10	3.22
1988	103.4	411	311	1122	101.0	99.6	104.7	36.70	9.56	10.69	1.34	9.35		12.43	2.11
1989	105.5	455	358	1140	95.4	99.0	86.3	34.56	9.87	9.70	0.63	9.07		20.43	4.85
1990	144.5	463	359	1205	97.3	95.3	103.3	43.64	10.74	9.96	0.27	9.69		10.25	3.37
1991	98.2	535	404	1455	112.3	109.7	116.3	45.74	17.18	11.31	0.35	10.96		9.62	1.55
1992	126.8	598	448	1645	103.3	103.0	103.6	63.38	14.21	14.66	0.25	14.41		9.44	5.73
1993	101.1	735	560	1952	108.8	110.1	106.1	84.46	17.51	18.63	0.87	17.81	1.47	11.97	5.79
1994	123.5	942	678	2707	108.5	106.9	109.0	96.85	19.89	28.40	0.40	28.00	5.70	-2.34	-4.11
1995	101.2	1258	915	3463	103.6	100.2	107.5	114.94	26.45	35.77	1.47	34.30	5.93	22.87	12.22

Year	v10b4	v11a	v11a1	v11a2	v11b	v11b1	v11b2	v11c	v11c1	v11c2	v12	v12a	v12b	v13	v13i
1952															
1953											145.0	212.9	114.5		
1954											182.8	198.5	169.6		
1955											63.0	58.0	67.9		
1956											178.4	267.1	104.4		
1957											168.1	99.0	315.8		
1958											241.4	402.4	132.8		
1959											82.4	110.8	24.3		
1960											64.0	70.9			
1961											17.4	17.4			
1962											37.6	37.6			
1963											660.8	422.5			
1964											161.8	246.9	11.0		
1965											263.5	237.9	1283.4		
1966											101.3	113.8	8.8		
1967											55.7	56.3			
1968											97.5	85.0			
1969											121.7	129.4	69.3		
1970											228.4	190.1	715.7		
1971											133.2	157.8	62.0		
1972											72.7	78.7	28.1		
1973											89.1	69.2	501.0		
1974											66.3	75.5	40.0		
1975											106.6	126.4			
1976											88.9	83.8			
1977											152.5	121.9	657.1		
1978	0.52	9.70	8.40	1.30	9.87	6.44	3.43	3.58	3.14	0.44	147.7	158.8	112.6	46.62	25.16
1979	0.49	10.57	9.34	1.23	8.81	5.72	3.09	3.40	3.07	0.33	96.5	99.0	85.5	55.28	32.05
1980	0.36	7.84	6.80	1.04	8.67	6.54	2.13	4.44	4.19	0.25	88.9	92.2	73.1	60.26	36.57
1981	0.09	4.45	4.12	0.33	9.49	8.94	0.55	4.37	4.28	0.09	87.5	99.5	26.1	67.89	43.92
1982	0.26	5.25	4.24	1.01	9.98	8.35	1.63	7.25	7.03	0.22	120.6	111.4	300.2	79.39	50.63
1983	0.13	5.81	5.36	0.45	9.69	8.82	0.87	7.53	7.41	0.12	107.7	120.8	12.4	87.38	51.65
1984	0.29	7.71	6.89	0.82	14.39	12.67	1.72	10.72	10.49	0.23	132.2	123.3	761.4	108.27	62.07
1985	0.45	6.73	5.77	0.96	20.65	18.37	2.28	16.24	15.92	0.32	128.3	128.9	122.1	123.92	70.85
1986	0.44	7.51	6.40	1.11	24.18	21.67	2.51	17.60	17.16	0.44	89.8	87.5	117.8	139.57	86.91
1987	0.37	8.60	6.78	1.82	32.31	28.07	4.24	15.98	15.35	0.63	107.6	104.7	133.8	165.50	102.14
1988	1.48	12.86	8.29	4.57	43.20	33.27	9.93	16.92	15.40	1.52	115.8	106.5	180.9	211.79	124.72
1989	2.44	16.41	9.01	7.40	48.10	30.12	17.98	17.34	15.00	2.34	102.4	83.1	182.0	235.84	139.04
1990	2.46	17.40	13.07	4.33	46.89	36.25	10.64	16.13	15.02	1.11	93.0	112.2	56.8	260.14	154.27
1991	3.59	14.41	10.43	3.98	52.63	42.85	9.78	21.95	20.96	1.00	103.5	106.4	92.0	295.90	169.35
1992	0.18	15.50	11.88	3.62	59.53	51.90	7.63	32.57	28.47	4.10	106.0	107.7	97.9	339.91	194.12
1993	3.80	14.91	11.09	3.82	69.47	60.82	8.65	59.30	50.21	9.09	107.4	105.0	119.4	416.07	249.93
1994	10.16	17.70	10.70	7.00	94.50	82.75	11.75	42.35	57.39	-15.04	103.8	119.2	20.5	521.17	328.55
1995	15.76	29.91	16.80	13.11	110.53	96.35	14.18	93.50	69.94	23.56	131.0	97.8	1177.9	630.07	409.04

Year	v13ii	v13iii	v13iv	v13a	v13ai	v13aii	v13aiii	v13aiv	v13b	v13bi	v13bii	v13biii	v13biv	v13b1	v13b1i
1952															
1953															
1954															
1955															
1956															
1957															
1958															
1959															
1960															
1961															
1962															
1963															
1964															
1965															
1966															
1967															
1968															
1969															
1970															
1971															
1972															
1973															
1974															
1975															
1976															
1977															
1978	3.94	6.33	11.18	19.42	15.13	0.58	1.00	2.71	18.73	6.97	2.27	4.37	5.12	15.24	4.85
1979	4.47	6.24	12.52	23.29	18.58	0.70	0.98	3.03	22.41	9.24	2.51	4.37	6.29	18.33	6.37
1980	5.06	6.65	11.98	24.86	21.33	0.73	0.86	1.94	24.00	9.85	2.67	4.85	6.63	19.37	6.76
1981	6.47	7.51	9.99	29.90	26.71	0.90	0.89	1.40	24.95	10.70	3.66	5.59	5.00	20.36	7.55
1982	6.59	8.56	13.61	37.37	32.75	1.12	1.15	2.35	27.44	10.05	3.38	6.18	7.83	22.58	6.95
1983	7.97	10.66	17.10	37.76	33.04	1.13	1.37	2.22	33.14	10.70	4.59	7.62	10.23	28.16	7.47
1984	10.00	13.60	22.61	45.73	38.62	1.37	1.89	3.85	43.51	14.78	5.62	10.29	12.83	36.85	10.09
1985	11.36	17.80	23.91	50.45	44.15	1.51	1.37	3.42	49.88	16.11	6.16	14.59	13.02	41.96	10.79
1986	10.67	18.33	23.64	56.46	49.89	0.97	1.52	4.08	50.96	19.80	5.95	14.04	11.15	43.57	13.97
1987	13.50	22.78	27.08	66.46	58.74	2.07	1.80	3.85	60.11	22.79	6.98	17.39	12.95	49.93	14.90
1988	19.73	32.60	34.74	85.20	73.57	2.81	2.61	6.21	78.63	25.15	10.65	24.82	18.01	68.32	17.51
1989	23.62	41.84	31.34	92.88	81.72	4.13	2.49	4.54	86.74	27.13	11.91	32.43	15.27	77.26	20.29
1990	29.60	47.88	28.39	100.10	86.40	4.21	3.01	6.48	92.83	31.06	13.66	35.40	12.72	82.15	22.54
1991	32.63	49.36	44.56	115.71	99.89	5.26	3.83	6.74	101.54	34.52	15.69	39.80	11.53	88.96	25.45
1992	39.72	26.21	79.85	121.18	105.91	5.18	2.88	7.21	122.08	41.97	19.19	14.97	45.95	106.41	29.61
1993	45.32	67.67	53.15	133.40	110.11	6.78	3.83	12.68	155.47	69.24	19.40	50.31	16.52	135.35	55.57
1994	54.11	85.01	53.50	183.52	147.60	9.48	6.75	19.69	195.76	89.56	24.79	58.75	22.66	172.89	71.72
1995	71.82	97.02	52.19	227.06	183.51	11.42	7.99	24.14	234.10	122.00	37.95	72.46	1.69	208.50	102.42

Year	v13c1i	v13c1ii	v13c1iii	v13c1iv	v13c2	v13c2i	v13c2ii	v13c2iii	v13c2iv	v13c3	v13c3i	v13c3ii	v13c3iii	v13c3iv
1952														
1953														
1954														
1955														
1956														
1957														
1958														
1959														
1960														
1961														
1962														
1963														
1964														
1965														
1966														
1967														
1968														
1969														
1970														
1971														
1972														
1973														
1974														
1975														
1976														
1977														
1978	0.30	0.56	0.18	0.64	3.59	1.08	0.24	0.58	1.69	1.04	0.11	0.01	0.12	0.80
1979	0.34	0.56	0.20	0.76	3.40	1.20	0.24	0.50	1.46	1.03	0.12	0.01	0.12	0.78
1980	0.42	0.56	0.22	0.81	3.17	0.89	0.24	0.52	1.52	1.17	0.16	0.02	0.13	0.86
1981	0.45	0.74	0.28	1.09	3.93	1.47	0.28	0.56	1.62	1.00	0.20	0.02	0.12	0.66
1982	0.48	0.76	0.30	1.20	4.02	2.11	0.19	0.67	1.05	1.51	0.28	0.03	0.18	1.02
1983	0.62	1.11	0.42	1.61	5.33	2.71	0.27	0.91	1.44	1.95	0.29	0.03	0.23	1.40
1984	0.84	1.33	0.51	1.98	6.39	2.98	0.75	0.56	2.10	2.20	0.37	0.03	0.27	1.53
1985	1.11	1.77	0.66	2.32	8.16	3.80	0.96	0.71	2.69	2.93	0.46	0.05	0.36	2.06
1986	3.38	1.36	0.66	1.94	8.54	3.98	0.71	1.45	2.40	4.62	0.51	0.09	0.50	3.52
1987	3.00	1.45	0.94	2.35	10.33	5.29	0.58	1.78	2.68	6.18	0.72	0.13	0.69	4.64
1988	4.25	2.36	1.10	2.07	12.60	7.08	0.73	2.73	2.06	7.87	1.09	0.16	1.03	5.59
1989	5.39	2.70	1.34	2.93	9.52	7.28	0.79	3.35	-1.90	12.83	1.34	0.19	1.76	9.54
1990	4.64	3.45	1.19	2.41	18.20	12.31	1.69	6.12	-1.92	11.33	1.46	0.23	1.78	7.86
1991	4.04	2.82	1.82	5.30	20.97	6.35	1.83	2.70	10.09	12.56	2.15	0.49	0.85	9.07
1992	7.10	5.78	2.69	3.43	25.53	7.63	2.13	4.13	11.64	14.51	3.12	0.59	1.05	9.75
1993	13.82	5.96	3.12	1.92	32.40	18.30	2.45	7.90	3.75	21.11	1.31	0.59	1.66	17.55
1994	15.71	7.03	2.23	-7.84	39.16	17.91	2.60	13.58	5.07	23.81	5.66	1.18	2.86	14.11
1995	18.49	8.83	2.31	-8.52	46.41	22.85	2.66	8.88	12.02	28.52	6.23	1.16	3.66	17.47

Year	v13b1ii	v13b1iii	v13b1iv	v13b2	v13b2i	v13b2ii	v13b2iii	v13b2iv	v13c	v13ci	v13cii	v13ciii	v13civ	v13c1
1952														
1953														
1954														
1955														
1956														
1957														
1958														
1959														
1960														
1961														
1962														
1963														
1964														
1965														
1966														
1967														
1968														
1969														
1970														
1971														
1972														
1973														
1974														
1975														
1976														
1977														
1978	2.06	4.16	4.17	3.49	2.12	0.21	0.21	0.95	8.47	3.06	1.09	0.96	3.35	1.68
1979	2.27	4.17	5.52	4.08	2.87	0.24	0.20	0.77	9.58	4.23	1.26	0.89	3.20	1.86
1980	2.39	4.60	5.62	4.63	3.09	0.28	0.25	1.01	11.40	5.39	1.66	0.94	3.41	2.01
1981	3.38	5.36	4.07	4.59	3.15	0.28	0.23	0.93	13.04	6.51	1.91	1.03	3.59	2.56
1982	3.09	5.88	6.66	4.86	3.10	0.29	0.30	1.17	14.58	7.83	2.09	1.23	3.43	2.74
1983	4.29	7.31	9.09	4.98	3.23	0.30	0.31	1.14	16.48	7.91	2.25	1.67	4.65	3.76
1984	5.22	9.96	11.58	6.66	4.69	0.40	0.33	1.24	19.03	8.67	3.01	1.42	5.93	4.66
1985	5.68	14.14	11.35	7.92	5.32	0.48	0.45	1.67	23.59	10.59	3.69	1.84	7.48	5.86
1986	5.51	13.72	10.37	7.39	5.83	0.44	0.32	0.80	32.15	17.22	3.75	2.77	8.44	7.34
1987	6.35	16.87	11.81	10.18	7.89	0.63	0.52	1.14	38.93	20.61	4.45	3.59	10.28	7.74
1988	9.87	24.15	16.79	10.31	7.64	0.78	0.67	1.22	47.96	26.00	6.27	5.17	10.52	9.78
1989	11.05	31.67	14.25	9.48	6.84	0.86	0.76	1.02	56.22	30.19	7.58	6.92	11.54	12.36
1990	12.89	34.62	12.09	10.68	8.51	0.77	0.77	0.62	67.21	36.82	11.73	9.47	9.19	11.69
1991	14.45	38.64	10.43	12.58	9.07	1.24	1.17	1.10	78.65	34.94	11.68	5.73	26.30	13.98
1992	17.47	13.81	45.52	15.67	12.36	1.72	1.16	0.43	96.65	46.24	15.35	8.36	26.70	19.00
1993	18.25	48.53	13.00	20.12	13.67	1.15	1.78	3.52	127.20	70.58	19.14	13.53	23.95	24.82
1994	23.24	56.65	21.28	22.87	17.84	1.55	2.10	1.38	141.89	91.39	19.84	19.51	11.15	17.13
1995	36.28	70.23	-0.43	25.60	19.58	1.67	2.23	2.12	168.91	103.53	22.45	16.57	26.36	21.11

Year	v13c4	v13c4i	v13c4ii	v13c4iii	v13c4iv	v13c5	v13c5i	v13c5ii	v13c5iii	v13c5iv	v13c6	v13c6i	v13c6ii	v13c6iii
1952														
1953														
1954														
1955														
1956														
1957														
1958														
1959														
1960														
1961														
1962														
1963														
1964														
1965														
1966														
1967														
1968														
1969														
1970														
1971														
1972														
1973														
1974														
1975														
1976														
1977														
1978	0.14	0.00	0.14			0.46	0.17	0.03	0.07	0.19	0.21	0.20	0.01	
1979	0.25	0.01	0.24			0.46	0.20	0.03	0.06	0.17	0.34	0.32	0.02	
1980	0.55	0.01	0.54			0.49	0.21	0.04	0.06	0.18	0.51	0.48	0.03	
1981	0.55	0.01	0.54			0.60	0.30	0.05	0.06	0.19	0.59	0.55	0.04	
1982	0.75	0.01	0.74			0.61	0.38	0.04	0.07	0.12	0.67	0.63	0.04	
1983	0.53	0.01	0.52			0.75	0.44	0.05	0.10	0.16	0.54	0.51	0.03	
1984	0.56	0.01	0.55			0.87	0.47	0.06	0.07	0.27	0.57	0.54	0.03	
1985	0.52	0.01	0.51			1.06	0.56	0.07	0.09	0.34	0.60	0.56	0.04	
1986	0.85	0.02	0.83			1.48	1.02	0.08	0.09	0.29	1.22	1.15	0.07	
1987	1.37	0.02	1.35			1.82	1.22	0.10	0.12	0.38	1.52	1.44	0.08	
1988	1.85	0.04	1.81			2.29	1.44	0.21	0.18	0.46	2.07	1.94	0.13	
1989	2.14	0.04	2.09		0.01	2.16	1.51	0.24	0.21	0.20	2.68	2.50	0.18	
1990	3.95	0.12	3.81		0.02	2.41	1.51	0.41	0.21	0.28	2.23	2.03	0.20	
1991	4.50	0.11	4.17	0.06	0.16	3.11	1.33	0.37	0.13	1.28	2.56	2.45	0.11	
1992	5.12	0.16	4.63	0.10	0.23	4.00	1.76	0.41	0.36	1.56	3.12	3.02	0.10	
1993	6.08	0.19	5.50	0.19	0.20	5.56	3.40	1.15	0.62	0.39	4.91	4.52	0.39	
1994	5.64	0.27	5.12	0.23	0.02	6.06	5.31	0.52	0.58	-0.35	5.05	4.69	0.36	
1995	6.90	0.39	6.05	0.37	0.09	12.69	6.40	0.71	1.02	4.56	6.47	5.81	0.55	0.01

Year	v13c6iv	v13c7	v13c7i	v13c7ii	v13c7iii	v13c7iv	v13c8	v13c8i	v13c8ii	v13c8iii	v13c8iv	v13c9	v13c9i	v13c9ii
1952														
1953														
1954														
1955														
1956														
1957														
1958														
1959														
1960														
1961														
1962														
1963														
1964														
1965														
1966														
1967														
1968														
1969														
1970														
1971														
1972														
1973														
1974														
1975														
1976														
1977														
1978		0.58	0.54	0.04			0.28	0.22	0.02	0.01	0.03	0.47	0.44	0.03
1979		1.02	0.95	0.07			0.41	0.34	0.03	0.01	0.03	0.77	0.72	0.05
1980		1.55	1.46	0.09			0.53	0.45	0.03	0.01	0.04	1.35	1.26	0.09
1981		1.74	1.64	0.10			0.55	0.48	0.03	0.01	0.03	1.45	1.36	0.09
1982		1.99	1.88	0.11			0.62	0.53	0.04	0.01	0.04	1.59	1.48	0.11
1983		1.59	1.50	0.09			0.53	0.45	0.03	0.01	0.04	1.43	1.33	0.10
1984		1.70	1.59	0.11			0.54	0.45	0.03	0.01	0.05	1.47	1.37	0.10
1985		1.97	1.86	0.11			0.67	0.55	0.04	0.02	0.06	1.73	1.62	0.11
1986		3.51	2.99	0.24	0.06	0.22	1.62	1.48	0.10	0.01	0.03	2.76	2.59	0.17
1987		4.27	3.75	0.29	0.04	0.19	2.13	1.77	0.30	0.02	0.04	3.46	3.30	0.16
1988		5.64	4.95	0.29	0.10	0.30	2.35	1.97	0.32	0.02	0.04	3.36	3.14	0.22
1989		7.00	5.66	0.39	0.23	0.72	3.16	2.49	0.61	0.03	0.04	4.13	3.82	0.31
1990		5.23	4.30	0.25	0.15	0.53	2.16	1.77	0.36	0.02	0.01	9.38	8.25	1.13
1991		6.32	4.98	0.96	0.11	0.27	2.29	1.92	0.17	0.06	0.14	11.50	11.00	0.50
1992		7.63	7.16	0.44		0.03	2.86	2.44	0.33	0.03	0.06	13.58	12.99	0.59
1993		9.89	8.90	0.99			4.21	3.65	0.37	0.04	0.15	17.42	15.93	1.49
1994		13.93	12.94	0.99			4.83	4.30	0.36	0.03	0.14	24.27	22.79	1.48
1995	0.10	15.29	14.18	0.79	0.12	0.20	5.24	4.30	0.30	0.20	0.44	24.24	23.11	1.10

Year	v13c9iii	v13c9iv	v13c10	v13c10i	v13c10ii	v13c10iii	v13c10iv
1952							
1953							
1954							
1955							
1956							
1957							
1958							
1959							
1960							
1961							
1962							
1963							
1964							
1965							
1966							
1967							
1968							
1969							
1970							
1971							
1972							
1973							
1974							
1975							
1976							
1977							
1978			0.02	0.01	0.01		
1979			0.04	0.03	0.01		
1980			0.07	0.05	0.02		
1981			0.07	0.05	0.02		
1982			0.08	0.05	0.03		
1983			0.07	0.05	0.02		
1984			0.07	0.05	0.02		
1985			0.09	0.06	0.03		
1986			0.20	0.10	0.10		
1987			0.11	0.10	0.01		
1988			0.14	0.10	0.04		
1989			0.24	0.16	0.08		
1990			0.63	0.43	0.20		
1991			0.86	0.60	0.26		
1992			1.21	0.86	0.35		
1993			0.08	0.55	0.25		
1994			2.01	1.81	0.20		
1995			2.07	1.77	0.30		

24

Yunnan

Year	v1	v1a	v1b	v1b1	v1b2	v1c	v1c1	v1c2	v1c3	v2	v2a	v2b	v2b1	v2b2	v2c
1952	17.79	9.60	4.35	3.81	0.54	3.84	0.62	2.26	0.96						
1953	23.83	11.71	7.42	6.03	1.39	4.70	0.80	2.54	1.36	123.5	120.9	168.5	156.1	250.4	121.3
1954	27.86	13.09	9.32	7.60	1.72	5.45	1.04	2.78	1.63	115.4	111.5	124.6	125.0	123.7	115.9
1955	30.12	13.80	10.49	8.66	1.83	5.83	1.18	2.90	1.75	107.5	105.0	112.0	112.7	106.4	106.9
1956	34.84	15.33	12.35	9.64	2.71	7.16	1.31	3.57	2.28	115.0	110.9	125.0	123.3	148.1	122.8
1957	37.98	16.56	14.07	11.19	2.88	7.35	1.50	3.57	2.28	99.9	101.5	109.0	113.7	106.3	102.1
1958	49.33	13.67	24.69	17.64	7.05	10.97	2.77	4.00	4.20	114.3	87.5	165.5	158.2	244.0	115.7
1959	60.58	13.25	33.66	24.45	9.21	13.67	3.62	4.16	5.89	115.1	98.0	133.3	146.3	130.6	115.0
1960	65.56	13.33	38.09	27.77	10.32	14.14	3.70	3.85	6.59	103.1	98.3	106.2	105.4	112.1	102.0
1961	42.37	15.21	19.34	15.70	3.64	7.82	2.48	3.08	2.26	80.2	107.3	146.5	54.5	35.3	67.9
1962	42.17	18.83	16.29	14.46	1.83	7.05	2.06	2.88	2.11	99.0	110.1	85.0	85.7	50.3	94.0
1963	44.66	20.03	17.19	14.74	2.45	7.44	2.03	2.83	2.58	104.8	102.7	94.7	102.4	133.9	105.5
1964	51.07	22.52	20.49	16.36	4.13	8.06	2.29	2.94	2.83	112.5	112.1	115.7	111.8	168.5	107.6
1965	62.89	22.83	30.70	20.31	10.39	9.36	2.74	3.00	3.62	116.0	106.5	137.5	126.4	251.5	111.0
1966	71.09	24.04	36.35	23.46	12.89	10.70	3.00	3.34	4.36	109.5	104.8	123.0	122.8	124.1	111.7
1967	65.81	24.25	31.67	21.59	10.08	9.89	1.94	3.56	4.39	93.6	100.3	85.0	86.9	78.3	94.0
1968	42.99	23.17	13.11	7.04	6.07	6.71	0.88	3.24	2.59	74.3	96.0	46.5	30.1	60.3	82.5
1969	68.90	24.64	33.61	24.01	9.60	10.65	2.41	3.52	4.72	130.1	106.3	220.6	370.0	158.1	130.0
1970	79.77	24.89	42.75	30.82	11.93	12.13	3.02	3.77	5.34	113.8	99.8	125.2	132.8	124.1	109.9
1971	86.20	28.81	44.58	32.75	11.83	12.81	3.12	4.12	5.57	107.0	106.4	104.0	107.9	99.3	105.0
1972	95.92	32.81	49.00	36.94	12.06	14.11	3.46	4.61	6.04	109.0	111.4	109.0	112.8	101.9	107.9
1973	104.88	35.55	53.98	41.33	12.65	15.35	3.85	5.03	6.47	108.0	108.1	108.7	112.0	104.8	108.0
1974	102.86	32.91	54.14	41.59	12.55	15.81	3.93	5.43	6.45	99.0	95.1	100.3	100.5	99.3	100.5
1975	107.81	35.40	55.94	42.33	13.61	16.47	4.16	5.56	6.75	103.5	96.9	103.0	101.7	108.4	102.5
1976	94.64	33.92	45.21	32.60	12.61	15.51	3.49	6.01	6.01	91.0	98.3	82.4	124.6	92.7	99.0
1977	111.04	33.47	58.96	46.22	12.74	18.61	4.62	6.93	7.06	115.1	98.0	127.7	145.7	101.0	115.0
1978	135.18	40.02	73.12	55.43	17.69	22.04	5.63	7.89	8.52	117.5	112.4	126.7	124.8	138.9	116.1
1979	149.92	44.71	80.74	62.38	18.36	24.47	5.75	9.43	9.29	107.7	94.4	106.1	108.1	103.8	111.0
1980	161.41	48.20	85.87	65.35	20.52	27.34	6.32	9.84	11.18	106.7	106.8	110.0	102.0	111.8	103.2
1981	174.02	55.20	90.74	72.54	18.20	28.08	6.17	12.08	9.83	105.5	109.5	102.5	108.0	88.7	103.7
1982	200.63	61.84	103.60	83.60	20.00	35.19	7.15	14.60	13.44	113.9	108.0	111.1	112.5	110.0	115.3
1983	220.87	65.68	115.07	95.11	19.96	40.12	8.16	16.82	15.14	109.4	105.6	109.7	111.9	99.8	111.3
1984	263.21	77.36	138.30	112.27	26.03	47.55	9.23	18.94	19.38	116.5	115.2	117.6	115.0	130.4	117.1
1985	316.19	88.88	169.75	136.26	33.49	57.56	10.43	20.20	26.93	111.2	106.4	116.8	114.6	127.3	113.5
1986	349.31	96.01	182.93	147.02	35.91	70.37	12.74	24.29	33.34	107.1	99.0	108.3	108.6	107.2	107.5
1987	438.20	111.25	221.13	181.85	39.28	105.82	17.42	34.25	54.15	113.3	107.8	114.3	116.7	109.4	115.4
1988	578.79	135.39	292.95	244.63	48.32	150.45	21.04	52.27	77.14	117.1	109.0	118.7	116.7	123.0	116.7
1989	693.47	152.68	353.78	304.91	48.87	187.01	27.15	61.86	98.00	106.8	104.0	104.5	107.9	101.2	110.3
1990	821.51	211.72	399.73	345.26	54.47	210.06	29.03	63.22	117.81	109.0	108.5	108.7	108.9	105.9	118.4
1991	973.72	222.93	461.29	393.63	67.66	289.50	37.20	86.64	165.66	110.1	102.1	111.1	109.8	111.6	111.4
1992	1165.41	250.35	577.64	477.07	100.57	337.42	47.33	124.73	165.36	111.4	104.4	120.3	116.5	126.2	110.1
1993	1627.12	281.21	852.47	688.61	163.86	493.44	67.25	178.00	248.19	113.7	103.0	117.8	115.6	131.6	116.4
1994	2082.97	356.78	1138.87	948.71	190.16	587.32	84.39	210.40	292.53	125.9	106.2	138.4	137.4	144.3	121.0
1995	2621.76	474.46	1460.99	1230.01	230.98	686.31	92.88	245.47	347.96	113.4	106.5	113.7	112.5	120.2	116.9

Year	v2c1	v2c2	v3'	v3	v3a	v3b	v3b1	v3b2	v3c	v3c1	v3c2	v3c3	v3c4	v3c5	v3c6
1952			11.78	11.78	7.27	1.82	1.59	0.23	2.69	0.48	1.58				
1953	129.0	112.4	14.86	14.86	8.87	2.88	2.34	0.54	3.11	0.53	1.68				
1954	130.0	109.4	17.03	17.03	9.92	3.57	2.91	0.66	3.54	0.66	1.81				
1955	113.5	104.3	18.34	18.34	10.44	4.13	3.41	0.72	3.77	0.76	1.88				
1956	111.0	123.1	21.33	21.33	11.60	5.11	3.99	1.12	4.62	0.85	2.30				
1957	114.5	100.1	22.53	22.53	12.47	5.43	4.32	1.11	4.63	0.94	2.25				
1958	101.8	112.0	23.21	23.21	9.57	7.99	5.71	2.28	5.65	1.43	2.06				
1959	130.0	104.0	25.35	25.35	9.00	10.01	7.27	2.74	6.34	1.68	1.93				
1960	102.2	92.6	25.43	25.43	8.83	10.50	7.66	2.84	6.10	1.60	1.66				
1961	70.0	80.0	22.90	22.90	11.16	7.28	5.91	1.37	4.46	1.41	1.76				
1962	115.0	93.5	24.50	24.50	13.64	6.55	5.81	0.74	4.31	1.26	1.76				
1963	99.0	99.0	25.63	25.63	14.01	7.11	6.10	1.01	4.51	1.24	1.72				
1964	112.7	103.1	29.25	29.25	16.18	8.19	6.54	1.65	4.88	1.39	1.78				
1965	119.6	102.0	33.62	33.62	17.31	11.01	7.28	3.73	5.30	1.55	1.70				
1966	109.5	111.3	36.39	36.39	18.37	12.18	7.86	4.32	5.84	1.64	1.82				
1967	74.9	106.6	34.18	34.18	18.49	10.17	6.93	3.24	5.52	1.08	1.99				
1968	45.6	91.1	26.51	26.51	17.36	4.74	2.55	2.19	4.41	0.58	1.01				
1969	273.8	108.6	34.34	34.34	18.63	10.01	7.15	2.86	5.70	1.29	1.67				
1970	125.3	107.1	38.52	38.52	18.87	13.38	9.65	3.73	6.27	1.56	1.95				
1971	103.3	109.3	43.47	43.47	21.99	14.57	10.71	3.86	6.91	1.68	2.22				
1972	110.9	111.9	49.50	49.50	24.84	16.89	12.73	4.16	7.77	1.91	2.54				
1973	111.3	109.1	54.57	54.57	27.23	18.85	14.43	4.42	8.49	2.13	2.78				
1974	102.1	107.5	51.78	51.78	24.29	18.98	14.58	4.40	8.51	2.12	2.92				
1975	105.9	102.4	54.29	54.29	26.34	19.12	14.47	4.65	8.83	2.23	2.53				
1976	94.7	108.1	49.27	49.27	25.70	14.96	10.79	4.17	8.61	1.94	3.34				
1977	132.0	115.0	55.84	55.84	24.36	21.45	16.82	4.63	10.03	2.49	3.73				
1978	121.8	113.9	69.05	69.05	29.46	27.58	20.91	6.67	12.01	2.34	4.49	1.54	0.33	0.13	0.38
1979	102.1	119.5	76.83	76.83	32.38	30.50	23.56	6.94	13.95	2.72	5.21	1.79	0.38	0.15	0.44
1980	109.9	104.3	84.27	84.27	35.89	33.98	25.86	8.12	14.40	2.80	5.16	1.85	0.39	0.16	0.45
1981	97.6	122.0	94.13	94.13	41.23	35.80	28.62	7.18	17.10	3.33	6.09	2.20	0.47	0.19	0.54
1982	115.8	120.8	110.12	110.12	47.04	42.39	34.21	8.18	20.69	4.01	7.41	2.65	0.57	0.23	0.65
1983	114.1	115.2	120.07	120.07	49.33	47.28	39.08	8.20	23.46	4.56	8.37	3.01	0.65	0.26	0.74
1984	113.1	112.6	139.58	139.58	57.33	54.38	44.14	10.24	27.87	5.42	9.94	3.57	0.77	0.31	0.88
1985	113.0	106.7	164.96	164.96	66.07	65.41	52.51	12.90	33.48	6.51	11.94	4.29	0.92	0.37	1.06
1986	110.1	108.3	182.28	182.28	71.32	70.83	61.09	9.74	40.13	7.84	14.20	5.16	1.11	0.74	1.28
1987	109.2	112.6	229.03	229.03	84.06	84.30	73.30	11.00	60.67	11.80	21.66	7.77	1.67	0.93	1.92
1988	103.0	130.1	301.09	301.09	103.47	112.40	99.19	13.21	85.22	14.57	33.01	9.98	3.11	1.16	2.71
1989	115.6	106.0	363.05	363.05	119.01	138.06	124.73	13.33	105.98	18.47	39.48	13.03	4.55	1.64	3.13
1990	106.0	103.7	451.67	451.67	168.13	157.80	142.77	15.03	125.74	19.82	40.44	18.45	6.28	2.00	4.01
1991	105.1	118.3	517.41	517.41	169.48	179.56	162.32	17.24	168.37	23.70	52.76	26.45	8.42	4.98	6.48
1992	112.1	115.8	618.69	618.69	186.80	219.03	193.90	25.13	212.86	25.19	78.89	34.52	10.64	6.60	7.20
1993	129.2	118.4	779.21	779.21	191.71	327.06	283.64	43.42	260.44	30.41	99.93	50.03	11.20	9.90	7.26
1994	113.6	122.4	973.97	973.97	237.51	429.66	381.88	47.78	306.80	38.72	110.58	58.32	12.82	12.86	8.96
1995	108.7	119.4	1206.68	1206.68	305.27	536.63	477.84	58.79	364.78	49.33	128.41	68.25	15.01	16.05	11.52

Year	v3c7	v3c8	v3c9	v3c10	v3d	v4'	v4	v4a	v4b	v4b1	v4b2	v4c	v4c1	v4c2	v4c3
1952				0.63	70										
1953				0.90	87	120.8	120.8	114.7	157.8	146.7	224.7	112.5	126.5	107.7	
1954				1.07	97	115.1	115.1	113.2	121.9	122.0	120.2	113.9	123.5	111.3	
1955				1.13	103	108.8	108.8	107.8	114.9	115.7	109.1	105.4	111.3	104.3	
1956				1.47	117	117.6	117.6	110.7	133.0	117.0	154.9	119.8	108.5	130.3	
1957				1.44	121	99.6	99.6	97.5	104.8	105.2	99.2	98.7	100.1	97.6	
1958				2.16	122	106.8	106.8	85.0	151.2	147.5	192.3	112.7	190.7	114.9	
1959				2.73	133	109.2	109.2	91.2	129.0	139.4	117.2	114.2	134.7	107.2	
1960				2.84	134	96.7	96.7	93.7	99.8	100.1	96.3	96.0	102.4	90.8	
1961				1.29	121	85.2	85.2	114.9	68.8	72.4	59.3	68.9	42.7	78.8	
1962				1.29	127	98.4	98.4	109.5	85.2	89.9	70.0	93.7	79.5	95.0	
1963				1.55	129	104.4	104.4	101.7	108.8	104.1	134.1	105.4	113.7	102.4	
1964				1.71	142	114.5	114.5	116.1	115.7	110.7	131.0	107.5	110.6	102.8	
1965				2.05	158	116.5	116.5	106.8	136.0	108.5	210.1	110.8	106.8	103.7	
1966				2.38	166	109.7	109.7	106.1	114.1	106.9	130.4	110.8	112.8	111.0	
1967				2.45	151	92.1	92.1	100.6	81.0	89.2	78.7	93.4	83.0	106.3	
1968				2.82	114	75.9	75.9	93.9	46.6	45.3	75.5	79.1	42.6	89.6	
1969				2.74	144	132.2	132.2	107.3	211.1	219.4	121.3	130.9	204.3	112.1	
1970				2.76	156	114.6	114.6	99.7	140.1	134.9	145.1	110.9	114.3	107.1	
1971				3.01	171	107.8	107.8	105.7	109.3	110.0	103.0	111.2	111.3	107.9	
1972				3.32	188	112.7	112.7	110.6	116.3	117.1	106.8	111.3	110.1	111.6	
1973				3.58	202	110.2	110.2	109.3	111.8	112.1	105.3	109.3	109.2	108.4	
1974				3.47	186	96.3	96.3	91.7	100.7	100.8	99.7	100.3	104.7	104.3	
1975				4.07	190	105.2	105.2	109.3	100.6	99.9	103.7	104.4	102.7	103.1	
1976				3.33	169	90.6	90.6	97.6	77.7	77.0	92.7	98.9	95.5	105.7	
1977				3.81	187	113.6	113.6	94.4	144.7	148.7	108.1	114.3	121.1	117.5	
1978	1.21	0.81	0.78		226	121.7	121.7	113.7	131.4	122.5	137.1	119.2	93.9	134.4	
1979	1.41	0.94	0.91		247	103.1	103.1	93.0	107.6	108.1	103.1	114.8	115.7	102.9	112.7
1980	1.45	0.97	1.17		267	108.5	108.5	109.8	110.1	108.7	114.0	102.5	103.1	119.2	95.2
1981	1.73	1.16	1.39		294	107.8	107.8	109.3	102.3	104.2	91.4	117.2	119.2	120.1	110.3
1982	2.09	1.40	1.68		339	115.5	115.5	112.8	116.1	117.1	111.9	120.5	120.6	114.4	104.3
1983	2.37	1.59	1.91		363	108.4	108.4	104.2	110.5	111.0	100.2	113.3	113.5	100.1	104.8
1984	2.82	1.89	2.27		417	114.5	114.5	113.7	113.1	110.7	118.1	118.9	119.3	118.8	103.6
1985	3.39	2.27	2.73		486	113.0	113.0	106.8	115.8	113.7	121.2	119.6	119.5	119.0	106.0
1986	4.08	2.43	3.29		529	104.3	104.3	97.7	108.7	110.6	106.7	107.6	108.5	109.4	103.9
1987	6.16	2.80	5.96		653	112.3	112.3	107.7	111.9	112.4	111.0	120.1	120.3	119.8	107.1
1988	9.32	3.02	8.34		845	116.0	116.0	107.8	120.9	118.8	120.7	119.0	105.5	130.3	94.4
1989	11.08	3.16	11.44		1003	105.8	105.8	103.2	104.5	107.9	100.4	111.3	113.2	106.5	110.6
1990	12.98	3.35	17.44	0.97	1224	108.7	108.7	108.5	109.8	109.9	107.9	107.1	107.0	102.7	103.7
1991	16.00	3.40	24.78	1.40	1377	106.6	106.6	101.1	108.9	109.3	103.3	111.4	111.9	112.2	123.6
1992	18.71	3.50	25.97	1.64	1622	110.9	110.9	103.0	116.8	115.2	123.3	113.5	102.2	136.5	111.9
1993	19.84	3.56	26.39	1.92	2020	110.6	110.6	102.6	114.2	113.0	125.4	115.2	114.9	120.0	131.6
1994	21.42	12.79	28.07	2.26	2490	111.6	111.6	103.0	117.2	117.5	114.7	113.0	118.1	113.0	106.7
1995	30.93	13.91	28.49	2.88	3044	111.2	111.2	105.1	113.6	114.0	109.6	113.4	116.4	108.5	120.3

Year	v4c4	v4c5	v4c6	v4c7	v4c8	v4c9	v4c10	v5	v5a	v5a1	v5a1a	v5a1b	v5a2	v5b	v5b1
1952								11.78	9.42	9.01	7.16	1.85	0.41	1.49	0.84
1953								14.86	10.97	10.46	8.43	2.03	0.51	2.85	1.61
1954								17.03	12.25	11.76	9.42	2.34	0.49	4.39	1.81
1955								18.34	13.58	13.09	10.29	2.80	0.49	3.68	1.92
1956								21.33	16.98	16.24	12.07	4.17	0.74	5.25	2.85
1957								22.53	16.70	15.70	11.53	4.17	1.00	5.17	2.92
1958								23.21	17.49	16.21	10.48	5.73	1.28	8.66	8.15
1959								25.35	15.92	14.23	9.39	4.84	1.69	13.05	10.30
1960								25.43	16.43	14.58	9.07	5.51	1.85	14.04	11.83
1961								22.90	18.13	16.42	10.59	5.83	1.71	4.38	4.07
1962								24.50	19.61	18.15	13.10	5.05	1.46	2.08	1.67
1963								25.63	20.57	19.10	13.99	5.11	1.47	3.91	2.66
1964								29.25	22.12	20.62	14.59	6.03	1.50	6.89	5.09
1965								33.62	24.17	22.66	15.92	6.74	1.51	11.19	8.97
1966								36.39	25.81	24.14	16.96	7.18	1.67	13.80	11.45
1967								34.18	27.74	25.97	18.68	7.29	1.77	8.89	6.94
1968								26.51	27.25	25.78	18.40	7.38	1.47	8.49	7.07
1969								34.34	29.40	27.77	19.94	7.83	1.63	13.74	10.21
1970								38.52	30.35	28.54	21.57	6.97	1.81	16.86	13.19
1971								43.47	31.94	29.94	22.57	7.37	2.00	16.81	12.65
1972								49.50	35.46	33.26	23.16	10.10	2.20	16.57	13.31
1973								54.57	37.96	35.53	25.33	10.20	2.43	19.77	14.44
1974								51.78	41.26	38.20	27.83	10.37	3.06	17.46	14.21
1975								54.29	42.61	39.38	28.75	10.63	3.23	20.10	15.45
1976								49.27	44.46	40.95	30.04	10.91	3.51	13.31	12.55
1977								55.84	46.49	42.52	31.33	11.19	3.97	19.45	16.52
1978								69.05	52.03	47.80	33.76	14.04	4.23	26.96	20.55
1979	111.7	111.9	112.3	113.0	112.5	113.1		76.83	58.86	54.35	37.18	17.17	4.51	30.63	27.64
1980	94.6	98.3	94.2	94.8	95.1	118.5		84.27	63.35	58.87	39.13	19.74	4.48	30.30	28.70
1981	111.8	110.1	111.3	110.6	110.9	110.2		94.13	67.85	63.04	42.61	20.43	4.81	28.35	26.09
1982	105.0	104.8	104.2	104.6	104.5	104.6		110.12	84.44	78.72	55.24	23.48	5.72	35.33	29.01
1983	105.2	104.3	105.0	104.6	104.8	104.9		120.07	89.85	83.45	62.12	21.33	6.40	34.57	29.63
1984	103.5	104.2	103.9	104.0	103.9	103.8		139.58	101.28	93.70	67.57	26.13	7.58	48.01	41.97
1985	105.3	105.2	106.2	106.0	105.9	106.0		164.96	119.86	110.69	76.46	34.23	9.17	56.76	50.07
1986	104.2	103.6	104.0	104.0	103.9	103.8		182.28	133.08	121.36	81.27	40.09	11.72	63.21	55.66
1987	106.9	109.1	106.9	107.2	107.1	107.4		229.03	155.63	141.23	93.35	47.88	14.40	68.70	59.75
1988	137.2	124.9	117.8	111.3	77.2	105.7		301.09	197.01	178.00	119.38	58.62	19.01	93.77	77.51
1989	69.3	119.8	129.3	100.6	139.1	99.5		363.05	241.71	218.26	151.39	66.87	23.45	114.22	79.90
1990	230.6	114.5	90.8	109.5	83.7	127.5		451.67	298.97	269.68	191.16	78.52	29.29	132.16	89.25
1991	125.9	108.1	135.7	116.5	112.9	112.8	105.5	517.41	361.73	325.36	231.62	93.74	36.37	185.88	150.37
1992	109.3	121.6	112.7	96.8	105.2	97.7	103.9	618.69	413.48	365.98	247.25	118.73	47.50	254.18	208.41
1993	168.2	109.3	98.3	115.6	119.3	117.2	117.2	779.21	471.26	415.18	263.39	151.79	56.08	371.24	287.57
1994	131.5	127.5	114.8	104.1	115.5	107.2	107.0	973.97	570.45	493.41	312.18	181.23	77.04	433.59	334.00
1995	110.2	107.6	120.1	140.8	115.9	102.2	111.8	1206.68	689.39	588.14	360.48	227.66	101.25	492.77	395.03

Year	v5b2	v5c	v5c1	v5c2	v6a1	v6a2	v6a3	v6a4	v6b2	v6b3	v6b4	v7	v7a	v7a1	v7a2
1952	0.65	0.87													
1953	1.25	1.03										111.8	111.4	113.0	105.3
1954	2.58	0.39										111.7	112.4	111.7	115.3
1955	1.76	1.08										112.0	112.4	110.3	120.9
1956	2.41	-0.91										126.3	125.3	118.5	150.4
1957	2.25	0.66										90.5	88.9	87.9	92.0
1958	0.51	-2.94										109.9	108.4	95.4	144.3
1959	2.75	-3.62										91.0	87.8	89.6	84.7
1960	2.21	-5.04										103.2	98.3	92.7	109.3
1961	0.31	0.39										103.7	103.6	109.6	99.5
1962	0.41	2.81										99.5	101.7	113.8	79.7
1963	1.25	1.15										103.8	104.2	105.7	100.2
1964	1.80	0.24										108.6	109.0	105.3	119.2
1965	2.22	-1.74										111.5	112.1	111.3	114.0
1966	2.35	-3.22										107.8	107.6	107.6	108.7
1967	1.95	-2.45										105.3	105.4	107.9	99.5
1968	1.42	-9.23										94.3	95.3	94.6	97.2
1969	3.53	-8.80										111.1	110.9	111.6	109.3
1970	3.67	-8.69										105.3	104.8	110.3	90.8
1971	4.16	-5.28										99.9	99.7	99.4	100.5
1972	3.26	-2.53										109.9	109.9	101.6	135.7
1973	5.33	-3.16										106.0	105.8	108.3	99.9
1974	3.25	-6.94										114.1	112.9	115.4	106.8
1975	4.65	-8.42										93.9	93.8	94.0	93.3
1976	0.76	-8.50										118.9	118.5	119.1	117.0
1977	2.93	-10.10										126.5	125.6	126.2	124.1
1978	6.41	-9.94			19.99	13.28	0.40	0.09	13.23	0.47	0.34	114.1	114.7	109.9	128.0
1979	2.99	-12.66			22.02	14.62	0.44	0.10	16.17	0.58	0.42	113.0	114.0	111.6	119.5
1980	1.60	-9.38			23.17	15.39	0.46	0.11	18.63	0.67	0.44	103.9	104.6	105.3	103.0
1981	2.26	-2.07			23.10	18.90	0.54	0.07	19.39	0.65	0.39	106.7	106.7	107.4	105.1
1982	6.82	-10.15			29.71	24.74	0.70	0.09	22.28	0.75	0.45	121.1	121.4	128.0	106.6
1983	4.94	-4.35			30.82	30.44	0.74	0.12	20.23	0.69	0.41	109.2	109.1	110.3	105.8
1984	6.04	-9.71			29.84	36.73	0.85	0.15	24.63	0.93	0.57	108.2	107.7	105.5	113.9
1985	6.69	-11.66			26.01	49.20	1.08	0.17	32.33	1.22	0.68	108.3	108.4	107.8	110.1
1986	7.55	-14.01			26.33	53.49	1.01	0.44	37.69	1.72	0.68	102.8	101.6	100.8	107.4
1987	8.95	4.70			29.58	61.67	1.77	0.33	44.54	2.28	1.06	107.8	107.3	105.9	110.1
1988	16.26	10.31			31.27	84.97	2.68	0.46	53.99	3.26	1.37	108.3	107.7	109.3	104.6
1989	34.32	7.12			46.08	100.93	3.71	0.67	62.08	3.31	1.48	122.6	126.9	126.9	114.1
1990	42.91	20.54			72.47	111.53	4.06	3.10	66.32	9.35	2.85	144.7	147.7	147.7	137.5
1991	35.51	-30.20			86.44	134.18	5.77	5.23	79.07	11.30	3.37	112.5	112.2	112.7	111.1
1992	45.77	-48.97			89.43	134.15	16.82	6.85	98.26	16.69	3.78	108.9	107.7	105.2	113.8
1993	83.67	-63.29	100.86	164.15	100.68	134.98	19.36	8.37	124.01	21.99	5.79	106.8	106.3	103.0	113.8
1994	99.59	-30.07	145.44	175.51	112.87	166.09	22.95	10.27	143.11	27.18	10.94	103.6	103.1	102.1	105.1
1995	97.74	24.52	208.26	183.74	128.10	188.43	32.03	11.92	178.54	38.08	11.04	105.8	102.6	102.4	103.1

Year	v7b	v8	v8a	v8b	v9	v9a	v9b	v10a1	v10a2	v10a3	v10a3a	v10a3b	v10a4	v10b1	v10b2
1952		54	47	123											
1953	119.4	61	54	127	112.0	115.9	104.0								
1954	96.0	67	60	141	110.7	109.8	111.5								
1955	101.0	73	64	162	109.7	107.1	114.7								
1956	152.5	89	74	219	122.1	116.7	135.3								
1957	124.3	84	69	208	89.2	90.0	96.1								
1958	134.4	118	63	247	140.5	90.5	118.5								
1959	132.0	74	57	176	62.5	89.5	71.2								
1960	105.1	77	55	207	104.6	98.0	117.8								
1961	86.9	87	64	246	113.2	116.0	118.6								
1962	121.5	94	76	237	102.6	117.2	96.6								
1963	99.7	96	78	244	102.5	102.9	103.0								
1964	103.1	100	79	275	103.7	101.4	112.3								
1965	102.7	107	84	281	119.0	112.7	111.0								
1966	111.7	110	88	273	103.0	105.0	97.2								
1967	103.9	115	94	271	104.9	106.0	99.2								
1968	79.7	111	92	270	96.3	97.8	99.6								
1969	114.2	116	94	286	104.8	102.3	105.8								
1970	113.3	116	98	257	100.9	105.6	90.3								
1971	104.9	118	100	263	101.8	102.1	102.2								
1972	108.9	127	99	343	108.0	99.0	130.4								
1973	109.4	131	106	332	102.5	107.4	96.8								
1974	132.2	137	113	329	104.8	105.9	99.0								
1975	96.0	138	114	330	100.8	100.9	100.3								
1976	75.5	140	116	333	101.3	101.8	101.0								
1977	120.8	142	118	334	101.3	101.8	100.3								
1978	110.4	156	124	406	105.7	105.3	115.0	13.01	1.41	1.94	0.03	1.91	4.19	4.20	0.68
1979	101.9	175	135	479	112.2	109.2	117.6	17.50	1.89	2.62	0.04	2.58	5.63	1.36	0.32
1980	95.1	187	141	530	107.2	103.8	130.2	22.00	0.78	2.21	0.05	2.16	3.71	1.24	0.22
1981	106.4	197	151	540	105.1	99.3	100.9	16.52	1.78	2.48	0.07	2.41	5.31	1.48	0.24
1982	116.7	242	193	608	103.7	126.9	102.2	18.37	1.98	2.76	0.08	2.68	5.90	4.46	0.73
1983	111.2	253	214	537	114.9	111.8	88.3	18.77	2.02	2.82	0.10	2.72	6.02	3.23	0.53
1984	115.9	280	230	640	110.3	108.9	119.3	24.57	5.47	4.87	0.11	4.76	7.06	3.95	0.65
1985	107.1	327	258	814	119.5	112.1	127.3	34.41	3.84	5.09	0.27	4.82	6.73	4.27	0.21
1986	119.9	354	268	918	105.1	103.0	110.4	38.03	3.99	6.01	0.38	5.63	7.63	5.27	0.54
1987	113.8	405	308	1066	107.8	104.2	122.0	40.19	4.82	6.56	0.56	6.00	8.18	5.98	1.19
1988	112.8	495	381	1254	118.9	121.7	114.7	52.73	5.85	10.40	1.34	9.06	8.53	12.70	1.48
1989	123.6	599	483	1366	118.2	122.1	108.9	49.92	2.92	11.52	2.04	9.48	15.54	24.67	2.90
1990	146.2	731	601	1548	122.0	124.9	111.4	66.85	7.10	8.12	0.58	7.54	7.18	32.99	2.59
1991	115.4	862	712	1790	113.0	113.4	110.8	113.30	9.54	9.61	1.21	8.40	17.92	29.16	4.04
1992	120.8	957	753	2202	118.3	117.9	105.3	155.68	13.75	14.45	1.96	12.49	24.53	34.33	3.57
1993	110.4	1069	792	2715	123.1	119.6	129.1	201.44	47.83	19.35	3.63	15.72	18.95	63.73	15.80
1994	107.9	1261	933	3195	102.3	101.6	103.5	236.38	53.34	29.09	4.15	24.94	15.19	78.02	16.80
1995	129.3	1484	1064	3958	101.2	101.1	101.7	262.83	78.22	39.52	3.57	35.95	14.46	66.46	17.00

Year	v10b4	v11a	v11a1	v11a2	v11b	v11b1	v11b2	v11c	v11c1	v11c2	v12	v12a	v12b	v13	v13i
1952															
1953											149.7	149.5	105.0		
1954											130.4	95.5	175.4		
1955											76.3	96.5	62.0		
1956											120.1	124.7	115.0		
1957											94.5	98.3	89.6		
1958											127.3	267.9	17.2		
1959											122.1	96.0	215.8		
1960											103.3	89.7	77.1		
1961											48.0	52.9	21.6		
1962											51.8	44.7	143.8		
1963											178.6	151.3	289.6		
1964											151.5	164.6	123.8		
1965											128.2	139.2	97.4		
1966											106.2	109.8	91.0		
1967											71.5	67.3	92.1		
1968											148.9	158.9	113.4		
1969											98.7	88.1	151.6		
1970											99.4	105.9	85.3		
1971											94.7	91.1	107.7		
1972											88.7	94.7	74.4		
1973											120.5	98.7	148.8		
1974											89.1	94.0	61.6		
1975											120.9	114.2	150.2		
1976											75.5	92.6	18.6		
1977											124.2	111.9	328.3		
1978	1.53	11.32	8.63	2.69	10.75	8.19	2.56	4.89	3.73	1.16	113.7	102.0	179.3	69.05	43.13
1979	0.71	12.91	11.65	1.26	12.16	10.97	1.19	5.56	5.02	0.54	109.1	129.1	44.8	76.83	47.69
1980	0.14	12.90	12.22	0.68	12.22	11.57	0.65	5.18	4.91	0.27	92.9	97.6	50.3	84.27	52.50
1981	0.54	12.42	11.43	0.99	10.78	9.92	0.86	5.15	4.74	0.41	99.5	85.5	127.9	94.13	58.92
1982	1.63	15.31	12.40	2.91	13.79	11.17	2.62	6.73	5.44	1.29	83.2	98.9	274.4	110.12	68.19
1983	1.18	14.20	12.17	2.03	13.61	11.70	1.91	6.76	5.76	1.00	87.8	92.9	65.9	120.07	72.88
1984	1.44	19.72	17.24	2.48	18.70	15.71	2.99	9.59	9.02	0.57	119.4	121.8	105.1	139.58	85.28
1985	2.21	22.73	20.05	2.68	22.51	19.81	2.70	11.52	10.21	1.31	104.0	105.0	97.4	164.96	100.13
1986	1.74	25.27	22.25	3.02	25.09	22.09	3.00	12.85	11.32	1.53	105.9	105.7	107.3	182.28	108.08
1987	1.78	27.23	23.68	3.55	33.95	29.53	4.42	7.52	6.54	0.98	109.0	107.7	118.8	229.03	128.34
1988	2.08	36.18	29.91	6.27	39.29	32.61	6.68	18.30	14.99	3.31	121.4	115.4	161.8	301.09	159.69
1989	6.75	43.12	30.16	12.96	50.02	35.01	15.01	21.08	14.73	6.35	113.7	96.2	196.9	363.05	183.05
1990	7.33	56.11	37.89	18.22	52.67	35.29	17.38	23.38	16.07	7.31	124.5	120.2	134.5	451.67	244.66
1991	2.31	72.77	58.87	13.90	77.11	62.46	14.65	36.00	29.04	6.96	127.3	152.5	74.9	517.41	266.79
1992	7.87	93.10	76.33	16.77	109.15	89.50	19.65	51.93	42.58	9.35	129.9	130.9	125.7	618.69	299.07
1993	4.14	10.31	8.06	2.25	141.05	106.83	34.22	219.88	172.68	47.20	117.3	110.9	146.7	779.21	357.82
1994	4.77	12.11	9.27	2.84	162.51	120.10	42.41	258.97	204.63	54.34	109.6	107.7	116.2	973.97	427.11
1995	14.28	20.35	16.69	3.66	217.65	175.20	42.45	254.77	203.14	51.63	104.6	106.3	99.1	1206.68	557.23

Year	v13ii	v13iii	v13iv	v13a	v13ai	v13aii	v13aiii	v13aiv	v13b	v13bi	v13bii	v13biii	v13biv	v13b1	v13b1i
1952															
1953															
1954															
1955															
1956															
1957															
1958															
1959															
1960															
1961															
1962															
1963															
1964															
1965															
1966															
1967															
1968															
1969															
1970															
1971															
1972															
1973															
1974															
1975															
1976															
1977															
1978	3.42	7.32	15.18	29.46	27.72	0.32	0.76	0.66	27.58	8.51	1.74	5.25	12.08	20.91	4.19
1979	3.87	8.19	17.08	32.38	30.47	0.35	0.83	0.73	30.50	9.20	1.94	5.83	13.53	23.56	4.71
1980	3.70	7.11	20.96	35.89	33.77	0.39	0.92	0.81	33.98	10.48	1.69	4.61	17.20	25.86	5.23
1981	4.64	9.27	21.30	41.23	38.80	0.45	1.06	0.92	35.80	10.35	2.34	6.34	16.77	28.62	5.72
1982	5.49	10.99	25.45	47.04	44.27	0.51	1.20	1.06	42.39	12.09	2.78	7.54	19.98	34.21	6.81
1983	6.22	12.26	28.71	49.33	46.43	0.53	1.26	1.11	47.28	13.07	3.16	8.44	22.61	39.08	7.78
1984	7.53	14.03	57.33	57.33	53.96	0.62	1.47	1.28	54.38	15.39	4.00	9.53	25.46	44.14	8.78
1985	9.03	16.71	66.07	66.07	62.19	0.71	1.69	1.48	65.41	18.77	4.77	11.37	30.50	52.52	10.45
1986	10.57	19.62	71.32	71.32	67.14	0.76	1.82	1.60	70.83	18.47	5.52	13.02	33.82	61.09	12.18
1987	16.40	25.37	84.06	84.06	78.13	1.90	2.14	1.89	84.30	20.79	7.06	15.48	40.97	73.30	13.97
1988	18.65	66.60	103.47	103.47	95.82	2.44	2.91	2.30	112.40	24.99	5.90	53.37	28.14	99.19	16.97
1989	26.25	43.29	119.01	119.01	109.90	3.11	3.35	2.65	138.06	28.17	7.12	28.47	74.30	124.73	19.92
1990	36.28	99.74	168.13	168.13	153.59	5.25	4.61	4.68	157.80	33.81	11.91	83.29	28.79	142.77	23.59
1991	50.57	114.38	169.48	169.48	153.58	6.16	7.11	2.63	179.56	37.72	17.23	94.17	30.44	162.32	27.25
1992	64.47	125.47	186.80	186.80	166.63	7.07	7.58	5.52	219.03	44.89	26.67	102.33	45.14	193.30	30.00
1993	87.21	174.67	191.71	191.71	172.86	9.74	7.29	1.82	327.06	79.19	42.44	149.41	56.02	283.54	61.98
1994	114.54	232.62	237.51	237.51	202.83	15.96	10.47	8.25	429.66	101.57	55.88	198.54	73.67	381.88	84.01
1995	131.95	262.00	305.27	305.27	255.64	18.83	18.72	12.08	536.63	148.48	48.40	216.81	122.94	477.84	104.8

Year	v13b1ii	v13b1iii	v13b1iv	v13b2	v13b2i	v13b2ii	v13b2iii	v13b2iv	v13c	v13ci	v13cii	v13ciii	v13civ	v13c1
1952														
1953														
1954														
1955														
1956														
1957														
1958														
1959														
1960														
1961														
1962														
1963														
1964														
1965														
1966														
1967														
1968														
1969														
1970														
1971														
1972														
1973														
1974														
1975														
1976														
1977														
1978	1.59	4.43	10.70	6.67	4.32	0.15	0.82	1.38	12.01	6.90	1.36	1.31	2.44	2.34
1979	1.79	4.98	12.08	6.94	4.49	0.15	0.85	1.45	13.95	8.02	1.58	1.53	2.82	2.72
1980	1.53	4.32	14.78	8.12	5.25	0.16	0.29	2.42	14.40	8.25	1.62	1.58	2.95	2.80
1981	2.19	6.08	14.63	7.18	4.63	0.15	0.26	2.14	17.10	9.77	1.85	1.87	3.61	3.33
1982	2.61	7.24	17.55	8.18	5.28	0.17	0.30	2.43	20.69	11.83	2.20	2.25	4.41	4.01
1983	3.00	8.14	20.16	8.20	5.29	0.16	0.30	2.45	23.46	13.38	2.53	2.56	4.99	4.56
1984	3.80	9.15	22.41	10.24	6.61	0.20	0.38	3.05	27.87	15.93	2.91	3.03	6.00	5.42
1985	4.52	10.89	26.66	12.90	8.33	0.25	0.48	3.84	33.48	19.17	3.55	3.65	7.11	6.51
1986	5.25	12.66	31.00	9.74	6.29	0.27	0.36	2.82	40.13	22.47	4.29	4.78	8.59	7.84
1987	6.37	15.12	37.84	11.00	6.82	0.69	0.36	3.13	60.67	29.42	7.44	7.75	16.06	11.80
1988	5.01	52.71	24.50	13.21	8.02	0.89	0.66	3.64	85.22	38.88	10.31	10.32	25.71	14.57
1989	6.51	27.32	70.98	13.33	8.25	0.61	1.15	3.32	105.98	44.98	16.02	11.47	33.51	18.47
1990	10.49	81.90	26.79	15.03	10.22	1.42	1.39	2.00	125.74	57.26	19.12	11.84	37.52	19.82
1991	15.51	92.00	27.56	17.24	10.47	1.72	2.17	2.88	168.37	75.49	27.18	13.10	52.60	23.70
1992	23.92	100.10	39.88	25.13	14.89	2.75	2.23	5.26	212.86	87.55	30.73	15.56	79.02	25.19
1993	33.53	139.58	48.55	43.42	17.21	8.91	9.83	7.47	260.44	105.77	35.03	17.97	101.67	30.41
1994	45.83	187.12	64.92	47.78	17.56	10.05	11.42	8.75	306.80	122.71	42.70	23.61	117.78	38.72
1995	44.95	209.22	118.87	58.79	43.68	3.45	7.59	4.07	364.78	153.11	54.72	26.47	120.48	49.33

Year	v13c1i	v13c1ii	v13c1iii	v13c1iv	v13c2	v13c2i	v13c2ii	v13c2iii	v13c2iv	v13c3	v13c3i	v13c3ii	v13c3iii	v13c3iv
1952														
1953														
1954														
1955														
1956														
1957														
1958														
1959														
1960														
1961														
1962														
1963														
1964														
1965														
1966														
1967														
1968														
1969														
1970														
1971														
1972														
1973														
1974														
1975														
1976														
1977														
1978	0.68	0.52	0.55	0.59	4.49	3.46	0.35	0.55	0.13	1.54	0.12	0.04	0.15	1.23
1979	0.79	0.59	0.64	0.70	5.21	4.01	0.42	0.64	0.14	1.79	0.14	0.05	0.18	1.42
1980	0.81	0.61	0.66	0.72	5.16	3.92	0.42	0.66	0.16	1.85	0.14	0.06	0.19	1.46
1981	0.96	0.60	0.79	0.98	6.08	4.60	0.53	0.78	0.17	2.21	0.17	0.07	0.22	1.75
1982	1.13	0.68	0.95	1.25	7.41	5.63	0.65	0.94	0.19	2.65	0.20	0.08	0.26	2.11
1983	1.29	0.77	1.08	1.42	8.37	6.35	0.75	1.07	0.20	3.01	0.23	0.09	0.29	2.40
1984	1.57	0.88	1.28	1.69	9.94	7.54	0.83	1.27	0.30	3.57	0.27	0.11	0.34	2.85
1985	1.88	1.18	1.54	1.91	11.94	9.09	0.93	1.53	0.39	4.29	0.33	0.13	0.41	3.42
1986	2.27	1.48	1.85	2.24	14.20	9.66	1.06	2.38	1.10	5.16	0.40	0.16	0.49	4.11
1987	3.97	2.60	1.87	3.36	21.66	10.05	1.53	5.06	5.02	7.77	0.56	0.28	0.74	6.19
1988	5.04	3.15	1.90	4.48	33.01	11.69	2.28	7.43	11.61	9.98	1.24	0.33	0.38	7.53
1989	5.55	5.65	2.00	5.27	39.48	12.63	3.64	7.66	15.55	13.03	1.77	0.36	1.51	9.39
1990	6.69	5.70	2.02	5.41	40.44	12.85	3.92	7.73	15.94	18.45	4.36	0.55	1.71	11.83
1991	6.90	8.74	2.22	5.84	52.76	14.46	5.44	8.20	24.66	26.45	8.27	0.86	1.34	15.48
1992	7.24	8.94	2.41	6.60	78.89	20.35	6.22	9.77	42.55	34.52	10.96	1.04	2.10	20.42
1993	8.89	9.38	2.45	9.69	93.55	23.87	6.70	10.38	52.60	50.03	17.36	1.78	3.43	27.46
1994	11.63	11.18	3.44	12.47	110.58	29.19	8.55	13.25	59.59	58.32	22.29	2.29	4.41	29.33
1995	25.43	17.28	4.62	2.00	128.41	39.37	19.83	11.11	58.10	68.25	17.40	2.80	6.01	42.04

Year	v13c4	v13c4i	v13c4ii	v13c4iii	v13c4iv	v13c5	v13c5i	v13c5ii	v13c5iii	v13c5iv	v13c6	v13c6i	v13c6ii	v13c6iii
1952														
1953														
1954														
1955														
1956														
1957														
1958														
1959														
1960														
1961														
1962														
1963														
1964														
1965														
1966														
1967														
1968														
1969														
1970														
1971														
1972														
1973														
1974														
1975														
1976														
1977														
1978	0.33	0.00	0.33			0.13	0.13				0.38	0.29	0.02	0.02
1979	0.38	0.00	0.38			0.15	0.15				0.44	0.34	0.02	0.02
1980	0.39	0.01	0.38			0.16	0.16				0.45	0.35	0.02	0.02
1981	0.47	0.01	0.46			0.19	0.19				0.54	0.42	0.03	0.02
1982	0.57	0.02	0.55			0.23	0.21		0.01	0.01	0.65	0.50	0.04	0.02
1983	0.65	0.02	0.63			0.26	0.21	0.01	0.02	0.02	0.74	0.57	0.05	0.02
1984	0.77	0.02	0.75			0.31	0.25	0.01	0.02	0.03	0.88	0.68	0.06	0.02
1985	0.92	0.03	0.88		0.01	0.37	0.28	0.02	0.03	0.04	1.06	0.82	0.07	0.02
1986	1.11	0.04	1.05		0.02	0.74	0.62	0.04	0.03	0.05	1.28	0.97	0.09	0.02
1987	1.67	0.06	1.58		0.03	0.93	0.77	0.07	0.04	0.05	1.92	1.55	0.10	0.02
1988	3.11	0.10	2.80		0.21	1.16	0.94	0.10	0.05	0.07	2.71	2.15	0.18	0.02
1989	4.55	0.12	3.37	0.02	1.04	1.64	1.35	0.16	0.05	0.08	3.13	2.45	0.24	0.02
1990	6.28	0.14	4.96	0.05	1.13	2.00	1.46	0.18	0.07	0.29	4.01	3.04	0.38	0.02
1991	8.42	1.52	5.64	0.16	1.10	4.98	1.96	1.11	0.35	1.56	6.48	5.10	0.66	0.02
1992	10.64	1.70	5.80	0.22	2.92	6.60	2.76	1.20	0.64	2.00	7.20	5.29	0.84	0.03
1993	11.20	1.73	6.02	0.26	3.19	9.90	4.29	1.50	0.83	3.28	7.26	5.31	0.86	0.03
1994	12.82	2.10	6.32	0.39	4.01	12.86	5.14	1.79	1.08	4.85	8.96	5.77	1.42	0.05
1995	15.01	2.23	7.70	2.28	2.80	16.05	7.21	1.80	1.09	5.95	11.52	7.21	1.78	0.09

Year	v13c6iv	v13c7	v13c7i	v13c7ii	v13c7iii	v13c7iv	v13c8	v13c8i	v13c8ii	v13c8iii	v13c8iv	v13c9	v13c9i	v13c9ii
1952														
1953														
1954														
1955														
1956														
1957														
1958														
1959														
1960														
1961														
1962														
1963														
1964														
1965														
1966														
1967														
1968														
1969														
1970														
1971														
1972														
1973														
1974														
1975														
1976														
1977														
1978	0.05	1.21	1.10	0.05		0.06	0.81	0.49	0.03	0.04	0.25	0.78	0.63	0.02
1979	0.06	1.41	1.28	0.06		0.07	0.94	0.57	0.04	0.05	0.28	0.91	0.74	0.02
1980	0.06	1.45	1.32	0.06		0.07	0.97	0.59	0.04	0.05	0.29	1.17	0.95	0.03
1981	0.07	1.73	1.58	0.07		0.08	1.16	0.71	0.05	0.06	0.34	1.39	1.13	0.04
1982	0.09	2.09	1.91	0.09		0.09	1.40	0.86	0.06	0.07	0.41	1.68	1.37	0.05
1983	0.10	2.37	2.17	0.10		0.10	1.59	0.98	0.07	0.08	0.46	1.91	1.56	0.06
1984	0.12	2.82	2.58	0.12		0.12	1.89	1.17	0.08	0.10	0.54	2.27	1.85	0.07
1985	0.15	3.39	3.11	0.15		0.13	2.27	1.40	0.10	0.12	0.65	2.73	2.23	0.09
1986	0.20	4.08	3.74	0.18		0.16	2.43	2.08	0.12	0.01	0.22	3.29	2.69	0.11
1987	0.25	6.16	5.32	0.60		0.24	2.80	2.17	0.33	0.02	0.28	5.96	4.97	0.35
1988	0.36	9.32	8.36	0.70		0.26	3.02	2.29	0.36	0.04	0.33	8.34	7.07	0.41
1989	0.42	11.08	9.57	1.06	0.09	0.36	3.16	2.37	0.37	0.06	0.36	11.44	9.17	1.17
1990	0.57	12.98	11.33	1.07	0.09	0.49	3.35	2.45	0.41	0.08	0.41	17.44	14.34	1.85
1991	0.70	16.00	12.98	1.70	0.14	1.18	3.40	2.46	0.42	0.10	0.42	24.78	20.98	2.45
1992	1.04	18.71	14.50	2.74	0.17	1.30	3.50	2.49	0.45	0.12	0.44	25.97	21.26	3.26
1993	1.06	19.84	14.59	3.64	0.20	1.41	9.94	7.23	1.54	0.28	0.89	26.39	21.48	3.33
1994	1.72	21.42	14.94	4.27	0.33	1.88	12.79	8.69	2.43	0.49	1.18	28.07	21.84	4.03
1995	2.44	30.93	21.56	6.16	0.48	2.73	13.91	9.24	2.68	0.61	1.38	28.49	22.04	4.16

Year	v13c9iii	v13c9iv	v13c10	v13c10i	v13c10ii	v13c10iii	v13c10iv
1952							
1953							
1954							
1955							
1956							
1957							
1958							
1959							
1960							
1961							
1962							
1963							
1964							
1965							
1966							
1967							
1968							
1969							
1970							
1971							
1972							
1973							
1974							
1975							
1976							
1977							
1978		0.13					
1979		0.15					
1980		0.19					
1981		0.22					
1982		0.26					
1983		0.29					
1984		0.35					
1985		0.41					
1986		0.49					
1987		0.64					
1988		0.86					
1989	0.06	1.04					
1990	0.07	1.18	0.97	0.60	0.10		0.27
1991	0.07	1.28	1.40	0.86	0.16		0.38
1992	0.10	1.35	1.64	1.00	0.24		0.40
1993	0.11	1.47	1.92	1.02	0.28		0.62
1994	0.17	2.03	2.26	1.12	0.42		0.72
1995	0.18	2.11	2.88	1.42	0.53		0.93

25

Tibet

Year	v1	v1a	v1b	v1b1	v1b2	v1c	v1c1	v1c2	v1c3	v2	v2a	v2b	v2b1	v2b2	v2c
1952															
1953															
1954															
1955															
1956															
1957															
1958															
1959															
1960															
1961															
1962															
1963															
1964															
1965															
1966															
1967															
1968															
1969															
1970															
1971															
1972															
1973															
1974															
1975															
1976															
1977															
1978															
1979															
1980															
1981															
1982															
1983															
1984															
1985															
1986															
1987															
1988															
1989															
1990															
1991															
1992															
1993															
1994	90.56	26.83	25.64	7.62	18.02	38.09	5.01	14.02	19.06	113.8	100.2	125.9	113.1	130.3	116.2
1995	118.36	35.89	39.71	9.08	30.63	42.76	5.14	15.18	22.44	122.6	104.5	155.8	107.9	170.0	112.4

Year	v2c1	v2c2	v3'	v3	v3a	v3b	v3b1	v3b2	v3c	v3c1	v3c2	v3c3	v3c4	v3c5	v3c6
1952															
1953															
1954															
1955															
1956															
1957															
1958															
1959															
1960															
1961															
1962															
1963															
1964															
1965															
1966															
1967															
1968															
1969															
1970															
1971															
1972															
1973															
1974															
1975															
1976															
1977															
1978															
1979															
1980															
1981															
1982															
1983															
1984			13.68	13.68	6.38	2.80			4.50						
1985			17.76	17.76	8.87	3.08			5.81	0.01	1.07	0.14	0.08	0.34	0.55
1986			16.95	16.95	7.95	2.18			6.82	0.35	1.43	0.14	0.07	0.40	0.59
1987			17.71	17.71	8.07	2.13			7.51	0.73	1.72	0.19	0.10	0.37	0.75
1988			20.25	20.25	9.65	2.40			8.19	0.99	2.11	0.39	0.12	0.23	0.78
1989			21.86	21.86	10.04	2.84			8.97	1.22	2.30	0.56	0.13	0.24	0.74
1990			24.45	24.45	10.85	3.57			10.03	1.62	2.38	0.80	0.14	0.24	0.86
1991			30.53	30.53	15.50	4.17			10.86	1.73	2.86	0.63	0.14	0.32	0.78
1992			33.29	33.29	16.59	4.46			12.24	1.84	3.80	0.64	0.15	0.34	0.82
1993			37.28	37.28	18.27	5.51			13.50	1.95	4.28	0.85	0.15	0.32	0.84
1994	101.2	113.4	45.84	45.84	21.10	7.92	3.43	4.49	16.82	1.82	5.12	0.01	0.25	0.53	1.18
1995	102.7	108.3	55.98	55.98	23.44	13.33	4.09	9.24	19.21	2.77	7.55	-0.29	0.16	0.58	1.00

Year	v3c7	v3c8	v3c9	v3c10	v3d	v4'	v4	v4a	v4b	4b1	v4b2	v4c	v4c1	v4c2	v4c3
1952															
1953															
1954															
1955															
1956															
1957															
1958															
1959															
1960															
1961															
1962															
1963															
1964															
1965															
1966															
1967															
1968															
1969															
1970															
1971															
1972															
1973															
1974															
1975															
1976															
1977															
1978															
1979															
1980															
1981															
1982															
1983															
1984					702										
1985	0.86	0.09	1.22	1.45	894	111.5	111.5	113.5	107.9			111.0			
1986	1.00	0.12	1.39	1.33	842	90.8	90.8	91.8	67.2			100.3			
1987	1.03	0.09	1.30	1.23	863	100.1	100.1	101.5	104.2			97.6			
1988	1.13	0.13	1.56	0.75	964	104.2	104.2	106.3	100.0			103.3			
1989	1.14	0.16	1.87	0.61	1021	108.4	108.4	104.1	117.9			110.0			
1990	1.22	0.16	2.03	0.58	1276	108.9	108.9	106.5	114.2			109.5			
1991	1.33	0.17	2.24	0.66	1387	100.4	100.4	96.3	108.6			103.6			
1992	1.34	0.19	2.37	0.75	1486	107.3	107.3	103.5	105.7			113.1			
1993	1.48	0.13	2.37	1.13	1642	108.2	108.2	106.5	116.4			107.4			
1994	2.35	1.60	3.69	0.27	1984	115.6	115.6	104.0	128.9	108.6	148.4	125.5	95.2	119.6	
1995	2.22	1.46	3.59	0.17	2392	117.9	117.9	104.0	167.6	109.1	208.8	113.2	152.1	147.5	

Year	v4c4	v4c5	v4c6	v4c7	v4c8	v4c9	v4c10	v5	v5a	v5a1	v5a1a	v5a1b	v5a2	v5b	v5b1
1952															
1953															
1954															
1955															
1956															
1957															
1958															
1959															
1960															
1961															
1962															
1963															
1964															
1965															
1966															
1967															
1968															
1969															
1970															
1971															
1972															
1973															
1974															
1975															
1976															
1977															
1978															
1979															
1980															
1981															
1982															
1983															
1984															
1985															
1986															
1987															
1988															
1989															
1990															
1991															
1992								40.43	25.14	20.23	11.46	8.77	4.91	15.29	13.33
1993								43.24	27.09	21.13	11.57	9.56	5.96	16.15	12.94
1994	166.7	165.6	140.5	158.8	276.9	155.7	158.8	46.76	32.74	25.65	13.81	11.84	7.09	23.07	17.87
1995	64.0	109.4	84.8	94.5	75.0	97.3	63.0	69.65	37.14	28.13	15.39	12.74	9.01	32.56	29.72

Year	v5b2	v5c	v5c1	v5c2	v6a1	v6a2	v6a3	v6a4	v6b2	v6b3	v6b4	v7	v7a	v7a1	v7a2
1952															
1953															
1954															
1955															
1956															
1957															
1958															
1959															
1960															
1961															
1962															
1963															
1964															
1965															
1966															
1967															
1968															
1969															
1970															
1971															
1972															
1973															
1974															
1975															
1976															
1977															
1978															
1979															
1980															
1981															
1982															
1983															
1984															
1985															
1986															
1987															
1988															
1989															
1990															
1991															
1992	1.96				4.25	7.08	0.09	0.04	7.76	0.87	0.14				
1993	3.21				4.95	6.46	0.10	0.06	8.56	0.76	0.24	101.6	98.2	94.7	103.0
1994	5.20	-9.05	1.74	10.79	6.42	7.10	0.20	0.09	10.44	1.02	0.38	117.9	118.9	114.6	124.3
1995	2.84	-0.05	2.92	2.97	7.58	7.56	0.16	0.09	11.19	1.06	0.49	111.6	107.2	109.0	105.1

Year	v7b	v8	v8a	v8b	v9	v9a	v9b	v10a1	v10a2	v10a3	v10a3a	v10a3b	v10a4	v10b1	v10b2
1952															
1953															
1954															
1955															
1956															
1957															
1958															
1959															
1960															
1961															
1962															
1963															
1964															
1965															
1966															
1967															
1968															
1969															
1970															
1971															
1972															
1973															
1974															
1975															
1976															
1977															
1978															
1979															
1980															
1981															
1982															
1983															
1984															
1985															
1986															
1987															
1988															
1989															
1990															
1991															
1992		903	594	2825											
1993	115.9	931	591	3083	96.7	92.8	102.9	10.16	1.60	0.58	0.33	0.25	0.60	3.[illegible]6	0.05
1994	114.1	1110	694	3700	117.1	112.9	120.5	14.59	1.96	0.76	0.41	0.35	0.56	5.[illegible]8	0.02
1995	128.0	1202	762	3981	106.6	107.4	105.2	27.82	1.38	0.18	0.18		0.34	2.[illegible]1	0.73

Year	v10b4	v11a	v11a1	v11a2	v11b	v11b1	v11b2	v11c	v11c1	v11c2	v12	v12a	v12b	v13	v13i
1952															
1953															
1954															
1955															
1956															
1957															
1958															
1959															
1960															
1961															
1962															
1963															
1964															
1965															
1966															
1967															
1968															
1969															
1970															
1971															
1972															
1973															
1974															
1975															
1976															
1977															
1978															
1979															
1980															
1981															
1982															
1983															
1984														14.38	
1985														17.76	17.34
1986														16.93	15.90
1987														17.71	16.09
1988														20.25	18.45
1989														21.86	19.59
1990														24.45	21.25
1991														30.53	27.15
1992														33.29	28.75
1993											105.6	97.1	163.8	37.28	31.00
1994		2.33	2.31	0.02	6.01	5.32	0.69	14.73	10.24	4.49	142.8	138.1	162.0	45.84	37.13
1995		2.79	2.06	0.73	9.18	8.48	0.70	20.59	19.18	1.41	141.1	168.6	46.3	55.98	42.60

Year	v13ii	v13iii	v13iv	v13a	v13ai	v13aii	v13aiii	v13aiv	v13b	v13bi	v13bii	v13biii	v13biv	v13b1	v13b1i
1952															
1953															
1954															
1955															
1956															
1957															
1958															
1959															
1960															
1961															
1962															
1963															
1964															
1965															
1966															
1967															
1968															
1969															
1970															
1971															
1972															
1973															
1974															
1975															
1976															
1977															
1978															
1979															
1980															
1981															
1982															
1983															
1984															
1985	1.04	0.83	-1.45	8.87	8.81	0.08		-0.02	3.08	2.59	0.21	0.17	0.11		
1986	1.40	0.78	-1.15	7.95	7.73	0.27		-0.05	2.18	1.66	0.20	0.21	0.11		
1987	1.74	0.79	-0.91	8.07	7.79	0.28			2.13	1.78	0.25	0.19	-0.09		
1988	1.56	1.21	-1.01	9.65	9.38	0.27			2.40	1.97	0.30	0.31	-0.18		
1989	1.59	1.56	-0.88	10.04	9.73	0.31			2.84	2.47	0.25	0.30	-0.18		
1990	2.12	1.45	-0.37	10.85	10.47	0.34		0.04	3.57	2.46	0.66	0.31	0.14		
1991	2.30	1.40	-0.32	15.50	14.89	0.53	0.01	0.07	4.17	2.84	0.69	0.36	0.28		
1992	2.24	1.57	0.73	16.59	15.91	0.60	0.00	0.08	4.46	3.18	0.34	0.41	0.53		
1993	2.92	1.56	1.80	18.27	17.25	0.90	-0.02	0.14	5.51	3.54	0.40	0.43	1.14		
1994	3.85	0.86	4.00	21.10	18.44	1.26	0.01	1.39	7.92	4.55	0.41	0.56	2.40	3.13	1.52
1995	6.08	1.06	6.24	23.44	20.40	1.18	-0.01	1.87	13.33	7.55	2.07	0.86	2.85	4.09	1.56

Year	v13b1ii	v13b1iii	v13b1iv	v13b2	v13b2i	v13b2ii	v13b2iii	v13b2iv	v13c	v13ci	v13cii	v13ciii	v13civ	v13c1
1952														
1953														
1954														
1955														
1956														
1957														
1958														
1959														
1960														
1961														
1962														
1963														
1964														
1965														
1966														
1967														
1968														
1969														
1970														
1971														
1972														
1973														
1974														
1975														
1976														
1977														
1978														
1979														
1980														
1981														
1982														
1983														
1984														
1985									5.81	5.86	0.75	0.66	-1.46	
1986									6.82	6.49	0.93	0.57	-1.17	
1987									7.51	6.52	1.21	0.60	-0.82	
1988									8.19	7.13	0.99	0.90	-0.83	
1989									8.97	7.39	1.03	1.25	-0.70	
1990									10.03	8.32	1.12	1.14	-0.55	
1991									10.86	9.42	1.08	1.03	-0.67	
1992									12.24	9.66	1.30	1.16	0.12	
1993									13.50	10.21	1.62	1.15	0.52	
1994	0.34	0.25	1.32	4.49	3.03	0.07	0.31	1.08	16.82	14.14	2.18	0.29	0.21	1.82
1995	0.52	0.49	1.52	9.24	5.99	1.55	0.37	1.33	19.21	14.65	2.83	0.21	1.52	2.77

Year	v13c1i	v13c1ii	v13c1iii	v13c1iv	v13c2	v13c2i	v13c2ii	v13c2iii	v13c2iv	v13c3	v13c3i	v13c3ii	v13c3iii	v13c3iv
1952														
1953														
1954														
1955														
1956														
1957														
1958														
1959														
1960														
1961														
1962														
1963														
1964														
1965														
1966														
1967														
1968														
1969														
1970														
1971														
1972														
1973														
1974														
1975														
1976														
1977														
1978														
1979														
1980														
1981														
1982														
1983														
1984														
1985														
1986														
1987														
1988														
1989														
1990														
1991														
1992														
1993														
1994	2.05	0.55	0.17	-0.95	5.12	2.86	0.57	1.19	0.50	0.01	0.41	0.23	-1.[illegible]0	0.47
1995	2.19	0.76	0.17	-0.35	7.55	3.88	0.75	1.83	1.09	-0.29	0.48	0.49	-1[illegible]3	0.57

Year	v13c4	v13c4i	v13c4ii	v13c4iii	v13c4iv	v13c5	v13c5i	v13c5ii	v13c5iii	v13c5iv	v13c6	v13c6i	v13c6ii	v13c6iii
1952														
1953														
1954														
1955														
1956														
1957														
1958														
1959														
1960														
1961														
1962														
1963														
1964														
1965														
1966														
1967														
1968														
1969														
1970														
1971														
1972														
1973														
1974														
1975														
1976														
1977														
1978														
1979														
1980														
1981														
1982														
1983														
1984														
1985														
1986														
1987														
1988														
1989														
1990														
1991														
1992														
1993														
1994	0.25	0.10	0.15			0.53	0.30	0.06		0.17	1.18	1.15	0.03	
1995	0.16	0.01	0.15			0.58	0.32	0.07		0.19	1.00	0.95	0.05	

Year	v13c6iv	v13c7	v13c7i	v13c7ii	v13c7iii	v13c7iv	v13c8	v13c8i	v13c8ii	v13c8iii	v13c8iv	v13c9	v13c9i	v13c9ii
1952														
1953														
1954														
1955														
1956														
1957														
1958														
1959														
1960														
1961														
1962														
1963														
1964														
1965														
1966														
1967														
1968														
1969														
1970														
1971														
1972														
1973														
1974														
1975														
1976														
1977														
1978														
1979														
1980														
1981														
1982														
1983														
1984														
1985														
1986														
1987														
1988														
1989														
1990														
1991														
1992														
1993														
1994		2.35	1.98	0.37			1.60	1.51	0.07		0.02	3.69	3.[illegible]	0.14
1995		2.22	1.85	0.37			1.46	1.36	0.07	0.01	0.02	3.59	3.[illegible]	0.11

Year	v13c9iii	v13c9iv	v13c10	v13c10i	v13c10ii	v13c10iii	v13c10iv
1952							
1953							
1954							
1955							
1956							
1957							
1958							
1959							
1960							
1961							
1962							
1963							
1964							
1965							
1966							
1967							
1968							
1969							
1970							
1971							
1972							
1973							
1974							
1975							
1976							
1977							
1978							
1979							
1980							
1981							
1982							
1983							
1984							
1985							
1986							
1987							
1988							
1989							
1990							
1991							
1992							
1993							
1994			0.27	0.23	0.01	0.03	
1995			0.17	0.13	0.01	0.03	

26

Shaanxi

Year	v1	v1a	v1b	v1b1	v1b2	v1c	v1c1	v1c2	v1c3	v2	v2a	v2b	v2b1	v2b2	v2c
1952	21.12	10.75	5.61	4.95	0.66	4.76	0.28	1.63	2.85		97.2	129.1	129.6	126.5	
1953	28.74	14.23	7.96	6.63	1.33	6.55	0.49	2.18	3.88	125.7	117.2	141.6	133.7	200.5	144.1
1954	33.89	15.89	10.02	8.51	1.51	7.98	0.72	2.69	4.57	117.3	110.4	125.8	128.3	113.7	135.2
1955	35.22	14.51	12.07	9.37	2.70	8.64	0.87	3.02	4.75	103.8	93.5	120.4	109.6	179.0	112.7
1956	46.30	18.78	16.51	11.23	5.28	11.01	1.14	3.62	6.25	129.2	118.2	142.8	126.9	195.6	137.6
1957	44.17	17.72	15.27	11.34	3.93	11.18	1.50	3.72	5.96	96.5	98.6	92.2	100.2	74.4	100.5
1958	57.90	18.72	25.47	19.90	5.57	13.71	1.83	4.07	7.81	136.0	112.9	166.6	175.1	141.7	138.4
1959	72.12	18.29	36.66	29.49	7.17	17.17	2.85	4.59	9.73	124.3	96.0	142.9	147.0	128.7	145.8
1960	82.70	18.02	45.68	36.84	8.84	19.00	3.21	4.63	11.16	114.0	88.9	127.1	128.1	123.2	120.9
1961	62.30	22.22	24.29	21.19	3.10	15.79	2.44	4.94	8.41	62.5	86.1	49.7	53.1	35.2	70.1
1962	53.13	19.36	20.83	18.14	2.69	12.94	1.73	4.04	7.17	87.3	98.2	83.9	83.8	84.6	77.2
1963	53.22	18.31	22.43	19.69	2.74	12.48	1.98	3.32	7.18	106.2	108.9	108.7	109.8	102.0	94.8
1964	59.30	18.35	27.77	23.88	3.89	13.18	1.66	3.52	8.00	116.4	107.9	126.6	124.4	141.8	109.5
1965	74.10	23.66	35.10	29.65	5.45	15.34	1.82	3.52	10.00	133.8	136.0	139.4	139.3	140.1	111.7
1966	88.05	22.76	47.60	40.94	6.66	17.69	1.80	4.01	11.88	118.5	92.0	133.6	135.4	122.2	135.3
1967	76.87	22.98	37.94	33.08	4.86	15.95	1.60	3.98	10.37	86.8	100.9	80.5	81.6	73.0	83.8
1968	56.75	20.50	24.16	20.30	3.86	12.09	1.09	3.34	7.66	72.1	88.5	63.5	61.4	79.4	65.6
1969	92.28	23.10	50.44	42.69	7.75	18.74	1.72	4.57	12.45	169.4	112.7	209.5	212.5	200.6	200.0
1970	112.27	26.16	63.70	51.61	12.09	22.41	2.06	5.20	15.15	137.0	109.4	148.9	147.8	156.0	141.2
1971	136.93	30.78	79.40	62.46	16.94	26.75	2.31	5.96	18.48	119.4	105.1	123.6	120.6	140.1	122.5
1972	136.23	29.58	79.56	61.89	17.67	27.09	2.63	6.08	18.38	99.7	95.7	100.4	99.6	104.3	101.7
1973	141.34	30.96	81.90	66.05	15.85	28.48	3.10	6.31	19.07	105.5	104.1	106.8	110.3	89.7	102.1
1974	142.93	31.94	82.24	68.10	14.14	28.75	3.06	6.40	19.29	101.1	102.7	101.2	103.3	89.2	98.9
1975	154.53	33.95	89.85	75.36	14.49	30.73	3.41	6.47	20.85	108.5	106.1	109.6	110.6	102.5	106.7
1976	148.93	33.84	84.55	71.47	13.08	30.54	3.39	7.14	20.01	96.8	99.6	93.8	95.7	80.2	106.2
1977	163.79	33.67	96.74	82.08	14.66	33.38	3.68	7.60	22.10	110.2	99.2	114.6	114.9	112.1	105.6
1978	186.62	36.27	113.01	96.48	16.53	37.34	4.06	8.10	25.18	112.8	102.7	118.2	118.8	112.8	100.9
1979	211.12	45.86	122.22	105.79	16.43	43.04	4.88	9.67	28.49	108.5	112.9	105.3	105.8	100.6	119.1
1980	213.16	41.88	127.12	109.96	17.16	44.16	6.11	9.29	28.76	99.8	85.9	103.0	102.9	104.5	99.8
1981	218.37	46.47	125.73	108.64	17.09	46.17	6.06	10.64	29.47	100.9	105.6	98.8	98.7	99.6	106.1
1982	247.53	56.90	138.37	117.70	20.67	52.26	8.01	10.85	33.40	114.6	123.5	109.4	108.2	120.9	127.8
1983	272.49	60.95	154.47	131.77	22.70	57.07	8.12	12.18	36.77	107.4	100.4	113.2	113.6	109.8	93.2
1984	319.84	73.69	179.36	150.70	28.66	66.79	9.53	14.10	43.16	115.7	113.5	115.4	114.9	119.8	119.2
1985	396.56	79.58	231.66	192.08	39.58	85.32	12.63	19.18	53.51	118.5	102.8	122.0	121.8	123.5	117.2
1986	475.43	87.20	260.95	219.26	41.69	127.28	18.57	36.90	71.81	109.6	104.8	110.7	112.8	96.4	108.6
1987	557.78	103.39	306.29	258.44	47.85	148.10	22.06	41.10	84.94	111.4	102.7	113.2	114.1	103.9	110.0
1988	717.31	130.52	391.39	331.74	59.65	195.40	34.17	53.89	107.34	116.4	106.9	116.8	116.1	104.6	120.8
1989	840.19	147.81	468.59	406.71	61.88	223.79	40.70	54.25	128.84	107.3	105.9	108.4	109.7	92.8	103.3
1990	937.32	169.96	513.76	442.58	71.18	253.60	53.86	52.76	146.98	106.2	106.1	106.9	106.9	106.0	103.4
1991	1066.03	185.37	591.84	509.11	82.73	288.82	56.82	64.45	167.55	110.4	104.4	113.8	112.4	108.2	107.2
1992	1236.71	205.34	686.66	592.29	94.37	344.71	67.71	74.28	202.72	110.6	106.0	112.0	113.5	101.1	110.4
1993	1557.76	239.78	903.69	760.44	143.25	414.29	85.54	92.34	236.41	114.2	109.2	115.7	115.7	115.2	113.8
1994	2074.50	302.38	1142.16	963.89	178.27	629.96	123.05	177.20	329.71	111.3	99.6	112.4	112.5	111.1	116.2
1995	2539.33	381.65	1389.63	1182.72	206.91	768.05	152.10	210.72	405.23	111.8	104.0	114.3	115.0	108.3	110.2

Year	v2c1	v2c2	v3'	v3	v3a	v3b	v3b1	v3b2	v3c	v3c1	v3c2	v3c3	v3c4	v3c5	v3c6
1952	151.5	261.7	12.85	12.85	8.40	1.92	1.70	0.22	2.53	0.18	1.54				
1953	175.2	133.3	17.44	17.44	11.03	2.84	2.25	0.59	3.57	0.32	1.99				
1954	145.2	123.3	20.04	20.04	12.34	3.73	3.08	0.65	3.97	0.44	2.11				
1955	121.1	112.5	20.58	20.58	11.43	4.85	3.59	1.26	4.30	0.54	2.19				
1956	131.0	119.8	27.14	27.14	14.92	6.52	4.27	2.25	5.70	0.75	2.92				
1957	131.4	102.8	25.58	25.58	13.17	6.06	4.44	1.62	6.35	0.96	3.00				
1958	121.7	109.4	31.02	31.02	13.48	10.83	8.55	2.28	6.71	1.09	3.32				
1959	155.4	112.9	35.58	35.58	12.73	14.93	11.75	3.18	7.92	1.74	3.48				
1960	112.9	100.8	38.30	38.30	12.59	17.17	13.88	3.29	8.54	1.95	3.58				
1961	75.9	107.7	31.64	31.64	15.61	8.38	7.49	0.89	7.65	1.20	3.59				
1962	71.1	81.7	26.85	26.85	13.35	7.30	6.27	1.03	6.20	0.70	2.79				
1963	85.8	82.3	27.36	27.36	13.09	8.12	6.94	1.18	6.15	1.02	2.24				
1964	83.9	105.9	29.34	29.34	13.33	9.44	8.13	1.31	6.57	0.95	2.48				
1965	109.7	100.0	35.93	35.93	17.51	11.78	10.01	1.77	6.64	1.07	2.19				
1966	98.7	113.9	40.47	40.47	16.59	15.97	13.83	2.14	7.91	1.10	2.41				
1967	88.9	99.5	36.84	36.84	16.85	12.23	10.91	1.32	7.76	0.81	2.50				
1968	68.1	93.8	28.11	28.11	14.84	7.03	6.14	0.89	6.24	0.46	1.83				
1969	157.9	136.9	40.73	40.73	17.00	16.01	13.66	2.35	7.72	0.76	2.93				
1970	120.0	113.7	46.84	46.84	18.89	20.42	16.62	3.80	7.53	1.11	3.15				
1971	112.2	114.6	57.66	57.66	22.72	25.86	20.95	4.91	9.08	1.14	4.02				
1972	113.8	102.1	57.76	57.76	20.78	27.18	21.22	5.96	9.80	1.31	4.06				
1973	117.7	103.7	59.63	59.63	22.17	26.73	22.58	4.15	10.73	1.68	4.05				
1974	98.7	101.5	62.03	62.03	23.24	27.74	22.55	5.19	11.05	1.70	4.17				
1975	111.5	101.1	64.92	64.92	23.76	29.87	25.18	4.69	11.29	1.94	4.00				
1976	96.7	110.4	62.94	62.94	23.78	27.75	24.28	3.47	11.41	1.85	3.88				
1977	111.7	106.4	69.99	69.99	24.09	33.88	28.87	5.01	12.02	0.72	4.02				
1978	110.4	106.6	81.33	81.07	24.70	42.13	36.52	5.61	14.24	3.15	4.47	1.22	0.99	0.3[illegible]	0.54
1979	120.2	119.4	94.80	94.52	32.52	44.67	39.38	5.29	17.33	3.83	5.44	1.48	1.21	0.4[illegible]	0.66
1980	125.2	96.1	95.21	94.91	28.47	47.74	42.22	5.52	18.70	3.91	4.24	2.31	1.22	0.4[illegible]	1.44
1981	99.0	114.6	102.41	102.09	35.40	46.25	40.08	6.17	20.44	3.65	4.84	2.67	1.37	0.6[illegible]	1.57
1982	132.3	101.9	112.30	111.95	37.02	50.36	43.31	7.05	24.57	4.69	4.69	4.13	1.47	0.5[illegible]	1.19
1983	101.4	112.3	123.80	123.39	40.00	55.15	47.48	7.67	28.24	5.48	4.79	4.45	1.62	1.1[illegible]	1.42
1984	123.2	106.0	149.79	149.35	51.05	63.12	53.82	9.30	35.18	7.79	6.13	4.87	1.72	1.4[illegible]	2.21
1985	133.5	140.7	181.36	180.87	53.39	80.89	67.81	13.08	46.59	7.95	8.68	7.88	2.13	2.8[illegible]	2.14
1986	107.5	114.8	208.83	208.31	58.00	91.13	76.61	14.52	59.18	10.09	11.49	11.45	2.82	2.8[illegible]	2.38
1987	117.0	105.7	245.54	244.96	67.84	104.58	87.08	17.50	72.54	13.10	12.78	15.14	3.60	3.3[illegible]	2.71
1988	132.3	106.7	314.99	314.48	82.69	133.32	112.85	20.47	98.47	19.43	19.11	19.77	5.25	4.6[illegible]	3.27
1989	100.8	61.4	359.06	358.37	91.28	149.64	128.11	21.53	117.45	22.52	18.36	28.70	4.61	5.63	3.82
1990	106.5	93.0	405.10	404.30	105.56	157.14	134.10	23.04	141.60	30.54	22.15	32.29	5.40	7.5[illegible]	4.95
1991	99.8	113.2	467.72	466.84	116.88	185.81	157.31	28.50	164.15	31.48	30.17	38.14	5.16	7.94	6.50
1992	106.9	107.5	539.39	538.43	127.02	218.86	186.57	32.29	192.55	37.95	33.77	43.39	6.36	10.24	7.75
1993	122.8	116.3	662.77	661.42	148.67	279.41	231.93	47.48	233.34	48.33	37.18	49.84	7.07	12.[illegible]	7.66
1994	130.5	126.4	816.58	816.58	181.78	336.46	278.34	58.12	298.34	60.08	43.15	64.63	9.06	14.[illegible]	10.06
1995	113.2	107.2	1000.03	1000.03	227.25	405.53	338.95	66.58	367.25	74.10	61.90	71.75	9.93	20.34	12.50

Year	v3c7	v3c8	v3c9	v3c10	v3d	v4'	v4	v4a	v4b	v4b1	v4b2	v4c	v4c1	v4c2	v4c3
1952				0.81	85	109.9	109.9	98.4	134.0	136.6	117.7	185.9	150.0	265.7	
1953				1.26	111	123.6	123.6	117.0	147.8	132.3	167.4	135.7	171.8	124.0	
1954				1.42	123	113.3	113.3	110.5	131.4	137.1	109.9	109.3	134.8	104.2	
1955				1.57	122	102.7	102.7	94.9	129.2	115.6	193.1	108.6	123.2	104.1	
1956				2.03	156	126.7	126.7	119.0	141.7	125.4	188.0	136.3	142.8	137.2	
1957				2.39	144	95.9	95.9	92.3	92.2	103.2	71.3	111.1	127.1	102.4	
1958				2.30	171	128.6	128.6	114.4	187.1	201.4	148.6	106.4	114.1	111.6	
1959				2.70	192	107.2	107.2	88.6	130.4	130.0	131.0	117.4	159.4	104.1	
1960				3.01	200	104.0	104.0	89.2	118.1	121.3	106.5	106.9	110.8	102.1	
1961				2.86	162	66.6	66.6	87.8	45.5	50.3	25.1	75.7	52.0	84.6	
1962				2.71	135	89.8	89.8	95.8	85.0	81.6	113.0	84.3	60.7	80.9	
1963				2.89	135	109.3	109.3	112.5	112.0	111.5	115.2	98.6	144.8	79.7	
1964				3.14	141	112.0	112.0	109.6	119.3	120.1	114.4	107.3	93.9	111.4	
1965				3.38	169	132.0	132.0	137.1	138.0	136.2	148.9	108.3	120.3	94.8	
1966				4.40	187	110.3	110.3	91.7	134.3	136.8	119.9	122.2	105.3	112.8	
1967				4.45	166	91.5	91.5	100.5	76.6	78.8	61.7	103.2	77.3	109.1	
1968				3.95	124	75.8	75.8	88.1	57.5	56.3	67.6	77.2	54.9	70.2	
1969				4.03	175	145.2	145.2	114.5	229.9	224.7	266.2	123.0	162.9	159.6	
1970				3.27	196	124.5	124.5	107.7	153.3	146.2	193.9	99.6	149.5	109.6	
1971				3.92	234	118.4	118.4	108.1	126.7	126.1	129.5	116.6	100.1	123.8	
1972				4.43	229	102.7	102.7	94.9	106.4	102.6	122.7	108.5	115.3	101.3	
1973				5.00	231	102.6	102.6	102.7	100.8	109.1	71.3	109.3	128.0	99.5	
1974				5.18	236	103.6	103.6	103.9	103.8	99.9	125.3	101.9	100.1	102.0	
1975				5.35	243	105.0	105.0	102.2	107.7	111.6	90.4	101.4	113.1	95.1	
1976				5.68	233	97.6	97.6	100.1	94.1	97.6	74.9	106.1	99.9	101.9	
1977				7.28	256	112.3	112.3	101.4	122.1	118.9	144.7	100.9	37.1	99.2	
1978	1.72	0.73	1.05		291	111.0	111.0	98.4	114.7	114.7	114.7	122.2	122.2	122.2	
1979	2.09	0.88	1.28		336	107.5	107.5	109.1	102.7	102.7	102.7	123.7	121.6	121.7	121.3
1980	1.87	1.72	1.24	0.27	334	107.3	107.3	109.0	106.4	106.4	106.4	107.9	102.1	77.9	156.1
1981	2.05	1.53	1.37	0.75	356	104.5	104.5	113.7	96.3	96.2	96.3	108.1	92.3	113.0	114.3
1982	2.34	1.25	1.41	2.83	385	109.1	109.1	106.5	108.5	108.5	108.4	115.3	123.3	92.9	148.5
1983	2.90	1.57	1.47	3.42	420	107.3	107.3	101.5	109.5	109.5	109.6	112.7	114.6	100.2	105.6
1984	4.47	2.57	2.78	1.24	504	117.8	117.8	112.5	120.0	120.0	119.9	121.9	139.0	125.1	107.0
1985	6.90	3.04	3.61	1.42	604	116.5	116.5	99.3	121.9	121.9	122.0	131.0	101.0	140.1	160.0
1986	7.62	2.71	4.94	2.88	688	108.7	108.7	104.6	105.9	105.9	105.0	118.2	138.1	119.3	132.2
1987	8.84	2.75	6.13	4.10	794	110.0	110.0	101.8	110.8	110.8	110.2	116.6	128.8	103.6	127.0
1988	9.87	3.40	8.43	5.33	1004	120.8	121.0	105.3	125.0	125.0	121.0	127.9	132.3	138.1	128.5
1989	11.89	4.12	10.59	7.21	1124	103.3	103.3	106.5	102.8	104.0	95.4	101.6	102.9	68.2	122.4
1990	13.51	5.31	12.90	7.05	1241	103.4	103.4	105.3	101.8	102.2	96.1	104.5	112.2	116.9	109.1
1991	13.55	8.33	15.40	7.48	1410	107.0	107.0	106.8	112.6	112.5	113.4	100.8	99.5	128.1	94.6
1992	15.69	9.95	18.33	9.12	1591	109.8	109.8	103.1	109.0	111.2	101.7	116.1	106.7	106.1	122.0
1993	18.53	13.87	21.90	16.96	1926	112.0	112.0	109.6	114.5	114.5	114.6	110.9	120.5	101.3	103.3
1994	27.41	18.53	30.03	20.76	2344	107.9	108.1	97.5	115.2	116.5	107.2	106.9	118.0	96.6	101.2
1995	32.12	21.97	35.94	26.70	2843	109.0	109.0	104.5	114.0	114.8	108.6	105.2	111.3	106.1	94.9

Year	v4c4	v4c5	v4c6	v4c7	v4c8	v4c9	v4c10	v5	v5a	v5a1	v5a1a	v5a1b	v5a2	v5b	v5b1
1952								12.85	12.81	12.50	9.94	2.56	0.31	2.0[illegible]	0.74
1953								17.44	15.20	14.73	11.00	3.73	0.47	4.2[illegible]	2.04
1954								20.04	17.24	16.65	12.48	4.17	0.59	6.2[illegible]	2.60
1955								20.58	18.23	17.61	13.30	4.31	0.62	6.5[illegible]	3.14
1956								27.14	20.04	19.27	15.14	4.13	0.77	7.25	6.93
1957								25.58	21.24	20.48	15.00	5.48	0.76	5.8[illegible]	5.19
1958								31.02	22.12	21.13	15.47	5.66	0.99	9.2[illegible]	8.01
1959								35.58	23.09	21.89	15.06	6.83	1.20	17.3[illegible]	12.85
1960								38.30	23.81	22.33	14.76	7.57	1.48	17.54	13.71
1961								31.64	25.30	23.88	15.94	7.94	1.42	6.03	2.91
1962								26.85	26.71	25.37	17.76	7.61	1.34	1.8[illegible]	1.20
1963								27.36	26.45	24.78	17.42	7.36	1.67	3.05	2.30
1964								29.34	25.24	23.76	16.23	7.53	1.48	6.73	5.47
1965								35.93	29.57	27.90	19.95	7.95	1.67	9.37	7.12
1966								40.47	29.53	27.72	19.30	8.42	1.81	15.3[illegible]	11.36
1967								36.84	29.86	27.99	19.36	8.63	1.87	8.24	6.19
1968								28.11	27.25	25.29	16.53	8.76	1.96	7.82	4.87
1969								40.73	32.08	29.97	19.70	10.27	2.11	16.12	10.76
1970								46.84	34.12	32.04	21.29	10.75	2.08	23.33	18.42
1971								57.66	38.39	36.16	24.00	12.16	2.23	31.[illegible]	24.30
1972								57.76	39.49	37.10	24.08	13.02	2.39	29.36	23.04
1973								59.63	41.48	38.75	25.22	13.53	2.73	23.[illegible]1	20.75
1974								62.03	44.45	41.18	27.54	13.64	3.27	21.[illegible]8	18.73
1975								64.92	44.49	40.93	26.95	13.98	3.56	23.[illegible]6	19.60
1976								62.94	46.78	42.80	27.91	14.89	3.98	19.[illegible]2	16.38
1977								69.99	48.18	44.09	28.45	15.64	4.09	24.[illegible]1	19.09
1978								81.07	52.74	48.24	30.97	17.27	4.50	30.[illegible]5	23.18
1979	122.2	124.3	122.2	121.5	120.6	121.9		94.52	64.78	58.98	40.12	18.86	5.80	35.[illegible]8	26.00
1980	100.8	104.4	218.2	89.5	195.5	96.9		94.91	72.32	65.21	42.53	22.68	7.11	27.[illegible]8	26.35
1981	111.5	131.3	107.6	108.6	87.8	109.7	274.1	102.09	80.87	72.23	47.25	24.98	8.64	32.[illegible]2	27.38
1982	102.2	85.7	72.9	109.4	78.8	98.5	362.2	111.95	88.71	78.45	52.35	26.10	10.26	40.[illegible]5	33.49
1983	108.6	192.6	116.8	121.6	122.7	102.2	118.7	123.39	95.71	84.11	56.17	27.94	11.60	40.[illegible]5	39.90
1984	104.0	122.1	152.3	150.7	160.3	184.7	35.9	149.35	112.81	98.57	66.56	32.01	14.24	54.[illegible]5	46.17
1985	122.3	201.6	96.0	152.6	117.1	128.5	111.4	180.87	134.05	115.82	73.72	42.10	18.23	88.38	63.86
1986	131.3	84.4	97.9	97.3	78.1	122.8	177.9	208.31	151.34	127.72	77.43	50.29	23.62	98.12	72.01
1987	118.3	112.5	105.3	107.6	94.4	115.0	133.6	244.96	176.90	145.09	87.05	58.04	31.81	116.14	89.63
1988	173.5	127.2	107.5	101.4	119.8	118.1	120.2	314.48	233.37	192.97	110.74	82.23	40.40	142.59	102.74
1989	88.6	100.9	106.1	104.3	111.2	110.2	123.4	358.37	269.26	202.54	114.95	87.59	66.72	182.18	106.64
1990	53.3	113.5	94.7	101.2	101.5	111.1	79.0	404.30	300.64	220.39	125.55	94.84	80.25	169.37	120.84
1991	99.4	107.3	94.1	94.7	95.3	94.2	99.7	466.84	331.60	239.56	132.40	107.16	92.04	193.15	140.56
1992	97.8	134.5	114.2	102.4	111.2	128.5	111.2	538.43	372.42	270.51	142.52	127.99	101.91	196.30	165.22
1993	122.3	98.0	110.5	110.4	118.3	106.9	164.3	661.42	442.73	324.71	172.15	152.56	118.02	326.29	247.41
1994	112.5	102.2	105.3	118.3	110.5	105.1	101.4	816.58	570.34	420.88	220.81	200.07	149.46	398.55	300.27
1995	103.0	120.6	104.4	101.6	101.7	102.3	115.0	1000.03	673.42	503.25	264.35	238.90	170.17	480.48	358.75

Year	v5b2	v5c	v5c1	v5c2	v6a1	v6a2	v6a3	v6a4	v6b2	v6b3	v6b4	v7	v7a	v7a1	v7a2
1952	1.27	-1.97													
1953	2.17	-1.97										111.7	110.7	102.4	142.8
1954	3.64	-3.44										112.6	112.3	113.5	108.8
1955	3.38	-4.17										104.9	105.1	106.2	101.7
1956	0.32	-0.15										109.0	108.4	104.0	121.9
1957	0.64	-1.49										103.8	104.1	104.5	103.2
1958	1.23	-0.34										103.8	102.8	102.7	103.1
1959	4.52	-4.88										104.7	103.9	97.5	120.4
1960	3.83	-3.05										101.5	100.4	95.9	110.1
1961	3.12	0.31										94.0	94.4	92.5	97.8
1962	0.69	-1.75										106.1	106.8	114.4	93.7
1963	0.75	-2.14										99.5	98.1	98.8	96.9
1964	1.31	-2.68										97.4	97.9	95.0	104.1
1965	2.25	-3.01										116.6	116.7	121.4	107.3
1966	3.95	-4.37										98.8	98.2	94.8	106.0
1967	2.05	-1.26										102.1	101.9	101.0	103.8
1968	2.95	-6.96										91.6	90.6	85.1	101.5
1969	5.36	-7.47										119.7	120.7	122.1	118.4
1970	5.21	-10.91										107.0	107.6	109.0	105.3
1971	6.89	-11.92										112.1	112.4	112.0	113.2
1972	6.62	-11.39										104.0	103.6	101.2	107.8
1973	2.76	-5.36										104.3	103.7	104.0	103.4
1974	2.75	-3.90										106.6	105.5	108.0	101.4
1975	3.56	-2.73										100.5	99.8	98.2	102.6
1976	3.24	-3.46										105.7	105.1	104.4	106.4
1977	4.92	-2.20										103.4	103.5	102.6	105.1
1978	7.27	-2.12			12.34	14.61	4.02		13.96	3.31		108.3	108.2	106.8	110.4
1979	9.78	-6.04			18.24	16.47	5.41		14.96	2.97	0.93	114.8	113.6	117.6	107.4
1980	1.33	-5.09			18.58	17.70	4.96	1.29	18.25	3.36	1.07	108.4	107.4	103.1	114.8
1981	4.74	-10.90			20.07	20.27	6.91		19.94	3.89	1.15	109.6	108.6	109.2	107.7
1982	7.16	-17.41			22.89	21.78	6.13	1.55	20.63	3.72	1.75	107.4	107.1	109.3	103.6
1983	1.05	-13.27			24.88	23.02	6.59	1.68	22.21	3.91	1.82	107.1	105.4	105.5	105.3
1984	8.28	-17.91			31.67	25.29	7.82	1.78	25.20	4.59	2.22	113.7	112.8	113.4	111.7
1985	25.02	-42.06			31.68	31.33	8.59	2.12	33.75	6.17	2.18	114.5	112.9	106.6	123.2
1986	26.41	-41.45			32.24	33.27	9.37	2.55	39.72	7.91	2.66	106.9	104.5	99.9	112.6
1987	26.81	-48.38			33.40	39.82	10.51	3.32	45.38	9.64	3.02	108.4	105.5	104.8	106.7
1988	39.85	-61.48			36.78	55.59	14.52	3.85	62.93	10.88	8.42	113.1	114.4	109.2	122.5
1989	75.84	-93.37			41.80	64.15	4.50	4.50	71.48	8.24	7.87	98.6	90.5	89.6	91.7
1990	48.53	-65.70			45.98	68.06	6.15	5.36	76.54	9.62	8.68	109.2	106.4	107.0	105.5
1991	52.89	-58.21			43.93	75.33	7.68	5.46	87.79	9.89	9.48	104.2	102.7	103.0	105.3
1992	31.58	-30.79			44.56	82.88	8.57	6.51	105.45	9.49	13.05	103.8	105.2	100.7	108.0
1993	78.88	-107.60			62.66	91.46	10.93	7.10	124.14	12.64	15.78	103.6	103.2	101.5	105.3
1994	98.28	-152.31			93.87	105.91	12.85	8.18	161.69	18.91	19.47	101.1	101.3	97.9	105.4
1995	121.73	-153.87			108.64	128.96	16.92	9.83	192.15	24.06	22.69	101.8	101.7	99.7	104.0

Year	v7b	v8	v8a	v8b	v9	v9a	v9b	v10a1	v10a2	v10a3	v10a3a	v10a3b	v10a4	v10b1	v10b2
1952		81	72	159											
1953	154.4	91	79	161	105.5	101.9	100.6								
1954	123.0	100	88	173	109.6	110.3	105.0								
1955	101.9	103	90	182	101.6	102.5	102.7								
1956	125.7	109	93	203	105.5	101.7	111.9								
1957	96.9	113	97	208	101.5	101.6	100.9								
1958	130.7	116	98	221	102.2	101.6	106.4								
1959	121.3	118	95	249	102.1	96.1	112.5								
1960	121.9	116	91	254	96.5	93.4	101.1								
1961	88.3	121	96	258	92.8	91.2	94.3								
1962	94.1	127	104	264	104.7	110.6	100.4								
1963	123.4	121	98	271	96.3	95.7	102.8								
1964	90.2	114	90	269	96.1	92.7	101.2								
1965	114.8	131	108	273	113.7	119.6	103.1								
1966	108.3	127	103	281	96.5	92.6	103.0								
1967	104.2	126	101	276	99.3	99.1	99.6								
1968	104.8	111	85	270	88.9	83.0	102.5								
1969	108.4	128	99	305	118.3	119.4	113.8								
1970	98.9	133	103	302	104.2	106.3	99.4								
1971	107.2	145	114	320	108.8	108.5	106.3								
1972	109.2	145	112	323	101.2	99.2	101.8								
1973	112.5	148	115	330	101.2	101.6	101.7								
1974	121.0	155	123	333	103.6	106.2	101.4								
1975	108.7	152	118	342	98.2	96.4	102.5								
1976	112.3	157	120	363	103.6	103.0	106.3								
1977	102.1	160	121	381	102.9	101.5	104.6								
1978	109.9	173	131	409	106.7	105.8	107.6	21.00	2.18					7.1[illegible]	0.16
1979	126.5	210	169	431	112.6	117.1	103.4	19.67	3.52	2.81		2.81		9.5[illegible]	0.25
1980	116.7	230	178	498	106.5	102.9	110.6	23.88	3.46	2.17		2.17		-1.87	0.07
1981	117.8	252	197	528	106.9	108.5	102.4	19.58	1.93	3.15	0.10	3.05	2.72	2.8[illegible]	0.68
1982	109.7	270	216	535	104.5	108.4	96.9	24.86	-2.50	3.31	0.09	3.22	7.82	5.0[illegible]	-0.97
1983	119.5	286	230	562	105.9	104.8	106.7	26.51	1.12	4.74	0.21	4.53	7.53	-3.33	-0.09
1984	119.8	333	271	625	112.5	114.7	107.6	28.43	4.17	5.35	0.31	5.04	8.22	4.87	-0.57
1985	124.5	386	300	784	108.2	103.2	116.5	41.02	5.09	9.54	0.56	8.98	8.21	18.73	1.99
1986	122.2	422	312	921	103.3	99.2	110.7	49.49	4.85	8.20	0.75	7.45	9.47	20.44	0.84
1987	124.0	470	346	1018	103.5	103.1	102.2	62.28	8.12	9.50	1.04	8.46	9.73	12.27	4.83
1988	106.9	616	435	1396	112.7	108.4	118.5	71.38	9.38	13.97	1.31	12.66	8.01	18.47	5.26
1989	138.9	635	445	1450	88.9	88.1	89.4	71.14	8.66	15.60	1.56	14.04	11.24	53.13	4.92
1990	118.4	677	476	1525	104.0	104.8	102.5	82.37	9.57	17.24	1.39	15.85	11.66	38.61	4.55
1991	108.4	723	495	1685	100.9	101.5	103.0	91.66	12.39	23.71	1.29	22.42	12.80	36.45	7.57
1992	100.2	798	526	1899	103.1	99.4	101.8	121.92	10.88	17.90	2.11	15.79	14.52	16.0[illegible]	9.14
1993	104.6	945	627	2221	105.3	106.7	103.5	179.39	24.81	32.24	3.81	28.43	10.97	33.8[illegible]	9.62
1994	100.6	1208	793	2870	99.9	96.5	103.9	209.58	31.09	44.94	4.62	40.32	14.66	20.34	10.76
1995	101.9	1431	939	3398	100.7	98.8	103.1	242.27	37.49	58.34	4.22	54.12	20.65	41.1[illegible]	26.12

Year	v10b4	v11a	v11a1	v11a2	v11b	v11b1	v11b2	v11c	v11c1	v11c2	v12	v12a	v12b	v13	v13i
1952															
1953											209.6	283.8	170.1		
1954											139.8	108.3	167.8		
1955											110.5	142.1	92.4		
1956											112.7	229.5	10.0		
1957											81.0	75.1	199.6		
1958											156.3	151.5	192.7		
1959											179.1	148.4	363.3		
1960											105.4	113.0	86.9		
1961											29.9	15.7	75.1		
1962											25.6	31.5	21.6		
1963											181.3	254.7	110.3		
1964											238.7	265.4	179.2		
1965											174.4	168.9	192.4		
1966											155.8	150.2	172.2		
1967											57.1	59.0	52.2		
1968											80.1	57.6	144.4		
1969											241.7	292.9	183.2		
1970											181.2	215.1	119.2		
1971											130.3	129.8	132.0		
1972											95.5	95.1	96.7		
1973											81.5	93.6	43.0		
1974											89.8	88.4	99.8		
1975											106.5	102.6	130.1		
1976											85.9	84.7	91.9		
1977											119.9	112.7	152.1		
1978		4.75	2.91	1.84	16.53	14.32	2.21	9.17	5.95	3.22	125.0	118.0	148.2	81.07	45.90
1979		4.47	3.33	1.14	18.10	15.74	2.36	13.21	6.93	6.28	113.7	112.2	127.5	94.52	54.07
1980	-0.03	2.46	3.07	-0.61	18.06	16.98	1.08	7.16	9.46	-2.30	97.0	103.0	47.0	94.91	54.88
1981	1.24	5.36	4.28	1.08	17.32	17.92	-0.60	9.44	5.18	4.26	109.9	102.8	241.4	102.09	62.06
1982	3.12	9.15	7.82	1.33	20.43	17.15	3.28	11.07	8.52	2.55	111.9	103.2	180.7	111.95	67.19
1983	4.47	11.69	8.15	3.54	21.59	20.17	1.42	7.67	11.58	-3.91	79.4	96.6	2.1	123.39	74.11
1984	3.98	10.61	8.21	2.40	27.33	22.35	4.98	16.51	15.61	0.90	186.8	152.3	7425.0	149.35	90.52
1985	4.30	13.18	8.68	4.50	45.12	37.98	7.14	30.58	17.20	13.38	166.2	144.8	258.4	180.87	106.85
1986	5.13	17.18	12.00	5.18	65.79	47.17	18.62	15.45	12.84	2.61	125.3	133.7	105.1	208.31	121.26
1987	9.71	19.99	10.11	9.88	66.18	55.89	10.29	30.27	23.63	6.64	92.1	91.4	93.9	244.96	142.60
1988	16.12	22.24	8.98	13.26	88.88	68.63	20.25	31.47	25.13	6.34	119.1	106.9	155.8	314.48	179.41
1989	17.74	29.79	12.58	17.21	106.91	64.48	42.43	45.78	29.58	16.20	112.3	91.3	155.5	358.37	210.77
1990	5.37	15.73	13.39	2.34	111.38	77.65	33.73	42.26	29.80	12.46	81.5	95.9	64.2	404.30	244.89
1991	8.87	20.38	14.53	5.85	114.40	86.09	28.31	58.67	39.94	18.73	103.7	104.4	101.9	466.84	284.08
1992	6.44	20.59	13.72	6.87	87.99	74.05	13.94	88.22	77.45	10.77	97.4	111.3	63.7	538.43	314.64
1993	35.46	31.34	18.75	12.59	148.25	110.34	37.91	146.70	118.32	28.38	121.3	107.2	181.2	661.42	386.17
1994	66.98	47.28	23.59	23.69	180.85	142.53	38.32	170.42	134.15	36.27	104.6	106.3	100.4	816.58	513.65
1995	54.51	43.33	27.98	15.35	181.93	143.00	38.93	255.22	187.77	67.45	109.0	111.4	102.5	1000.03	616.80

Year	v13ii	v13iii	v13iv	v13a	v13ai	v13aii	v13aiii	v13aiv	v13b	v13bi	v13bii	v13biii	v13biv	v13b1	v13b1i
1952															
1953															
1954															
1955															
1956															
1957															
1958															
1959															
1960															
1961															
1962															
1963															
1964															
1965															
1966															
1967															
1968															
1969															
1970															
1971															
1972															
1973															
1974															
1975															
1976															
1977															
1978	8.02	10.58	16.57	24.70	21.09	1.52	0.70	1.39	42.13	17.92	3.48	7.68	13.05	36.52	13.51
1979	9.67	12.11	18.67	32.52	27.47	2.28	0.98	1.79	44.67	18.46	3.75	8.27	14.19	39.34	14.39
1980	9.29	11.26	19.48	28.47	24.47	1.58	0.81	1.61	47.74	20.11	4.24	8.42	14.97	42.22	15.92
1981	10.15	11.10	18.78	35.40	30.58	1.79	1.01	2.02	46.25	19.68	4.47	7.92	14.18	40.03	14.98
1982	11.92	12.18	20.66	37.02	32.14	1.70	1.06	2.12	50.36	21.27	5.15	8.48	15.46	43.30	16.05
1983	12.03	13.29	23.96	40.00	34.43	2.16	1.14	2.27	55.15	23.24	5.50	9.36	17.05	47.43	17.70
1984	14.63	15.70	28.50	51.05	45.58	1.39	1.63	2.45	63.12	26.75	7.12	10.26	18.99	53.82	19.92
1985	16.85	20.61	36.56	53.39	48.27	1.87	1.73	1.52	80.89	33.29	8.67	14.32	24.61	57.84	23.74
1986	19.67	24.03	43.35	58.00	52.44	2.03	1.88	1.65	91.13	37.42	9.78	16.18	27.75	76.64	26.82
1987	23.27	27.70	51.39	67.84	61.33	2.38	2.20	1.93	104.58	43.27	11.19	18.39	31.73	87.08	30.49
1988	30.68	36.91	67.48	82.69	74.76	2.90	2.68	2.35	133.32	54.46	14.33	23.83	40.70	112.85	39.51
1989	43.17	46.92	57.51	91.28	82.53	3.20	2.96	2.59	149.64	67.62	25.60	32.68	23.74	128.11	51.90
1990	48.97	49.37	61.07	105.56	95.44	3.70	3.42	3.00	157.14	71.15	26.84	34.22	24.93	134.10	54.33
1991	55.01	60.01	67.74	116.88	105.67	4.09	3.79	3.33	185.81	85.77	31.15	41.98	26.91	157.31	63.73
1992	70.22	69.36	84.21	127.02	109.25	5.80	3.82	8.15	218.86	100.57	36.83	49.69	31.77	186.57	75.58
1993	90.22	88.90	96.13	148.67	126.34	6.22	5.08	11.03	279.41	125.12	47.90	62.64	43.75	231.53	93.96
1994	106.74	63.77	132.42	181.78	145.19	9.32	9.25	18.02	336.46	178.34	42.77	44.38	70.97	278.34	146.66
1995	137.31	99.12	146.80	227.25	180.68	13.03	9.63	23.91	405.53	189.48	63.61	76.65	75.79	338.35	158.26

Year	v13b1ii	v13b1iii	v13b1iv	v13b2	v13b2i	v13b2ii	v13b2iii	v13b2iv	v13c	v13ci	v13cii	v13ciii	v13civ	v13c1
1952														
1953														
1954														
1955														
1956														
1957														
1958														
1959														
1960														
1961														
1962														
1963														
1964														
1965														
1966														
1967														
1968														
1969														
1970														
1971														
1972														
1973														
1974														
1975														
1976														
1977														
1978	3.25	7.68	12.08	5.61	4.41	0.23		0.97	14.24	6.89	3.02	2.20	2.13	3.15
1979	3.54	8.27	13.18	5.29	4.07	0.21		1.01	17.33	8.14	3.64	2.86	2.69	3.83
1980	3.97	8.42	13.91	5.52	4.19	0.27		1.06	18.70	10.30	3.47	2.03	2.90	3.91
1981	4.10	7.92	13.08	6.17	4.70	0.37		1.10	20.44	11.80	3.89	2.17	2.58	3.65
1982	4.74	8.48	14.03	7.06	5.22	0.41		1.43	24.57	13.78	5.07	2.64	3.08	4.69
1983	4.94	9.36	15.48	7.67	5.54	0.56		1.57	28.24	16.44	4.37	2.79	4.64	5.48
1984	6.51	10.23	17.16	9.30	6.83	0.61	0.03	1.83	35.18	18.19	6.12	3.81	7.06	7.79
1985	7.69	14.30	22.08	13.08	9.55	0.98	0.02	2.53	46.59	25.29	6.31	4.56	10.43	7.95
1986	8.69	16.16	24.94	14.52	10.60	1.09	0.02	2.81	59.18	31.40	7.86	5.97	13.95	10.09
1987	9.88	18.36	28.35	17.50	12.78	1.31	0.03	3.38	72.54	38.00	9.70	7.11	17.73	13.10
1988	12.80	23.80	36.74	20.47	14.95	1.53	0.03	3.96	98.47	50.19	13.45	10.40	24.43	19.43
1989	23.99	32.65	19.57	21.53	15.72	1.61	0.03	4.17	117.45	60.62	14.37	11.28	31.18	22.52
1990	25.11	34.18	20.48	23.04	16.82	1.73	0.04	4.45	141.60	78.30	18.43	11.73	33.14	30.54
1991	29.46	40.10	24.02	28.50	22.04	1.69	1.88	2.89	164.15	92.64	19.77	14.24	37.50	31.48
1992	34.94	47.56	28.49	32.29	24.99	1.89	2.13	3.28	192.55	104.82	27.59	15.85	44.29	37.95
1993	43.44	59.12	35.41	47.48	31.16	4.46	3.52	8.34	233.34	134.71	36.10	21.18	41.35	48.33
1994	38.91	40.75	52.02	58.12	31.68	3.86	3.63	18.95	298.34	190.12	54.65	10.14	43.43	60.08
1995	58.46	70.18	52.05	66.58	31.22	5.15	6.47	23.74	367.25	246.64	60.67	12.84	47.10	74.10

Year	v13c1i	v13c1ii	v13c1iii	v13c1iv	v13c2	v13c2i	v13c2ii	v13c2iii	v13c2iv	v13c3	v13c3i	v13c3ii	v13c3iii	v13c3iv
1952														
1953														
1954														
1955														
1956														
1957														
1958														
1959														
1960														
1961														
1962														
1963														
1964														
1965														
1966														
1967														
1968														
1969														
1970														
1971														
1972														
1973														
1974														
1975														
1976														
1977														
1978	0.93	0.70	0.59	0.93	4.47	1.86	0.58	1.51	0.52	1.22	0.44	0.02	0.08	0.68
1979	1.09	0.82	0.77	1.15	5.44	2.10	0.74	1.95	0.65	1.48	0.51	0.04	0.11	0.82
1980	1.15	0.82	0.78	1.16	4.24	2.19	0.62	1.06	0.37	2.31	0.83	0.02	0.15	1.31
1981	1.09	0.78	0.69	1.09	4.84	2.62	0.67	1.32	0.23	2.67	1.41	0.04	0.11	1.11
1982	1.43	0.91	0.91	1.44	4.69	2.83	1.32	1.41	-0.87	4.13	1.41	0.05	0.27	2.40
1983	1.73	0.93	1.09	1.73	4.79	2.51	0.36	1.42	0.50	4.45	2.24	0.06	0.20	1.95
1984	2.26	1.80	1.46	2.27	6.13	2.89	0.92	1.84	0.48	4.87	0.49	0.13	0.45	3.80
1985	2.69	1.29	1.29	2.68	8.68	3.84	0.56	2.62	1.66	7.88	2.61	0.14	0.48	4.65
1986	3.41	1.64	1.64	3.40	11.49	5.08	0.74	3.47	2.20	11.45	3.79	0.20	0.70	6.76
1987	4.43	2.13	2.13	4.41	12.78	5.65	0.82	3.86	2.45	15.14	5.01	0.27	0.22	8.94
1988	6.57	3.15	3.15	6.56	19.11	8.45	1.23	5.77	3.66	19.77	6.55	0.35	1.20	11.67
1989	7.62	3.65	3.65	7.60	18.36	8.12	1.18	5.54	3.52	28.70	9.51	0.51	1.25	16.93
1990	10.33	4.96	4.95	10.30	22.15	15.58	2.33	4.37	-0.13	32.29	10.70	0.57	1.57	19.05
1991	10.65	5.11	5.10	10.62	30.17	21.22	3.18	5.95	-0.18	38.14	12.63	0.68	2.22	22.51
1992	17.86	7.76	2.30	10.03	33.77	25.92	3.78	7.54	-3.47	43.39	3.62	1.92	[illegible]	34.10
1993	20.07	8.38	6.66	13.22	37.18	32.41	10.46	6.99	-12.68	49.84	3.51	2.10	[illegible]	39.10
1994	32.47	19.35	4.88	3.38	43.15	39.68	14.29	-4.09	-6.73	64.63	7.80	3.28	[illegible]	48.00
1995	37.98	24.91	6.73	4.48	61.90	58.17	10.83	-3.62	-3.48	71.75	8.73	4.49	[illegible]	51.74

Year	v13c4	v13c4i	v13c4ii	v13c4iii	v13c4iv	v13c5	v13c5i	v13c5ii	v13c5iii	v13c5iv	v13c6	v13c6i	v13c6ii	v13c6iii
1952														
1953														
1954														
1955														
1956														
1957														
1958														
1959														
1960														
1961														
1962														
1963														
1964														
1965														
1966														
1967														
1968														
1969														
1970														
1971														
1972														
1973														
1974														
1975														
1976														
1977														
1978	0.99	0.02	0.97			0.37	0.32	0.05	0.02	-0.02	0.54	0.45	0.09	
1979	1.21	0.02	1.19			0.46	0.34	0.06	0.03	0.03	0.66	0.54	0.12	
1980	1.22	0.02	1.20			0.48	0.46	0.04	0.04	-0.06	1.44	1.19	0.19	
1981	1.37	0.02	1.35			0.64	0.51	0.07	0.05	0.01	1.57	1.29	0.23	
1982	1.47	0.02	1.45			0.57	0.55	0.08	0.05	-0.11	1.19	0.98	0.19	
1983	1.62	0.03	1.59			1.12	0.80	0.09	0.08	0.15	1.42	1.20	0.18	
1984	1.72	0.03	1.69			1.40	1.01	0.11	0.06	0.22	2.21	1.98	0.17	
1985	2.13	0.12	2.00		0.01	2.84	1.58	0.16	0.17	0.93	2.14	1.91	0.15	
1986	2.82	0.16	2.65		0.01	2.80	1.56	0.16	0.16	0.92	2.38	2.12	0.17	
1987	3.60	0.20	3.38		0.02	3.39	1.88	0.19	0.20	1.12	2.71	2.42	0.19	
1988	5.25	0.30	4.93		0.02	4.61	2.57	0.26	0.28	1.50	3.27	2.92	0.23	
1989	4.61	0.26	4.33		0.02	5.63	3.13	0.32	0.34	1.84	3.82	3.41	0.27	
1990	5.40	0.30	5.07		0.03	7.50	4.18	0.42	0.44	2.46	4.95	4.42	0.35	
1991	5.16	0.29	4.85		0.02	7.94	4.42	0.45	0.47	2.60	6.50	5.80	0.45	
1992	6.36	0.31	6.02		0.03	10.24	6.11	1.15	1.71	1.27	7.75	6.88	0.61	
1993	7.07	0.44	6.01	0.40	0.22	12.00	7.17	1.34	2.00	1.49	7.66	7.22	0.44	
1994	9.06	0.65	7.23	0.72	0.46	14.63	13.23	1.61	2.47	-2.68	10.06	9.34	0.55	0.03
1995	9.93	1.44	8.42	0.57	-0.50	20.34	23.21	1.86	1.63	-6.36	12.50	11.87	0.63	

Year	v13c6iv	v13c7	v13c7i	v13c7ii	v13c7iii	v13c7iv	v13c8	v13c8i	v13c8ii	v13c8iii	v13c8iv	v13c9	v13c9i	v13c9iii
1952														
1953														
1954														
1955														
1956														
1957														
1958														
1959														
1960														
1961														
1962														
1963														
1964														
1965														
1966														
1967														
1968														
1969														
1970														
1971														
1972														
1973														
1974														
1975														
1976														
1977														
1978		1.72	1.43	0.28		0.01	0.73	0.54	0.18		0.01	1.05	0.90	0.15
1979		2.09	1.64	0.44		0.01	0.88	0.80	0.07		0.01	1.28	1.10	0.16
1980	0.06	1.87	1.63	0.24			1.72	1.53	0.13		0.05	1.24	1.07	0.17
1981	0.05	2.05	1.75	0.30			1.53	1.33	0.16		0.04	1.37	1.18	0.19
1982	0.02	2.34	1.97	0.37			1.25	1.10	0.14		0.01	1.41	1.22	0.19
1983	0.04	2.90	2.52	0.37		0.01	1.57	1.39	0.15		0.03	1.47	1.27	0.20
1984	0.06	4.47	4.01	0.42		0.04	2.57	1.99	0.52		0.06	2.78	2.53	0.20
1985	0.08	6.90	5.83	0.90		0.17	3.04	2.30	0.67		0.07	3.61	3.26	0.27
1986	0.09	7.62	6.44	0.99		0.19	2.71	2.05	0.60		0.06	4.94	4.46	0.37
1987	0.10	8.84	7.47	1.15		0.22	2.75	2.08	0.61		0.06	6.13	5.54	0.46
1988	0.12	9.87	8.34	1.29		0.24	3.40	2.57	0.75		0.08	8.43	7.61	0.63
1989	0.14	11.89	10.05	1.55		0.29	4.12	3.12	0.91		0.09	10.59	[illegible]	0.79
1990	0.18	13.51	11.41	1.76		0.34	5.31	4.02	1.17		0.12	12.90	11.65	0.96
1991	0.25	13.55	11.45	1.77		0.33	8.33	5.60	1.88	0.40	0.45	15.40	[illegible]	1.16
1992	0.26	15.69	12.92	2.45	0.03	0.29	9.95	6.81	2.15	0.52	0.47	18.33	16.24	1.45
1993		18.53	15.99	2.54			13.87	11.91	1.96			21.90	19.94	1.96
1994	0.14	27.41	23.36	3.61	0.10	0.34	18.53	14.89	2.66	0.47	0.51	30.03	28.42	1.59
1995		32.12	26.84	4.11	0.15	1.02	21.97	8.65	2.25	0.58	0.20	35.94	[illegible]	1.81

Year	v13c9iii	v13c9iv	v13c10	v13c10i	v13c10ii	v13c10iii	v13c10iv
1952							
1953							
1954							
1955							
1956							
1957							
1958							
1959							
1960							
1961							
1962							
1963							
1964							
1965							
1966							
1967							
1968							
1969							
1970							
1971							
1972							
1973							
1974							
1975							
1976							
1977							
1978							
1979		0.02					
1980			0.27	0.23	0.04		
1981			0.75	0.60	0.10		0.05
1982			2.83	2.27	0.37		0.19
1983			3.42	2.75	0.44		0.23
1984		0.05	1.24	1.00	0.16		0.08
1985		0.08	1.42	1.15	0.17		0.10
1986		0.11	2.88	2.33	0.34		0.21
1987		0.13	4.10	3.32	0.50		0.28
1988		0.19	5.33	4.31	0.63		0.39
1989		0.24	7.21	5.84	0.86		0.51
1990		0.29	7.05	5.71	0.84		0.50
1991		0.34	7.48	6.68	0.24		0.56
1992		0.64	9.12	8.15	0.30		0.67
1993			16.96	16.05	0.91		
1994	0.01	0.01	20.76	20.28	0.48		
1995	0.01		26.70	26.11	0.59		

27

Gansu

Year	v1	v1a	v1b	v1b1	v1b2	v1c	v1c1	v1c2	v1c3	v2	v2a	v2b	v2b1	v2b2	v2c
1952	18.19	8.93	4.57	2.48	2.09	4.69	1.10	2.18	1.41	111.7	110.8	121.8	120.9	123.3	105.8
1953	19.33	9.59	5.03	2.89	2.14	4.71	1.30	2.23	1.18	105.7	102.9	111.3	117.8	104.2	107.3
1954	21.99	10.53	6.41	3.51	2.90	5.05	1.41	2.43	1.21	118.8	117.2	130.6	124.5	139.2	107.2
1955	24.40	10.46	8.18	3.87	4.31	5.76	1.72	2.58	1.46	113.0	105.2	132.4	118.6	146.7	111.2
1956	29.70	10.90	12.81	4.83	7.98	5.99	1.82	3.19	0.98	125.8	110.7	145.9	120.0	194.0	113.6
1957	30.42	10.13	14.08	6.22	7.86	6.21	2.51	3.09	0.61	97.5	88.3	108.3	117.6	97.5	92.8
1958	37.93	11.58	18.90	9.49	9.41	7.45	3.26	3.34	0.85	122.0	110.1	140.6	160.4	122.2	120.4
1959	45.11	10.29	25.85	16.36	9.49	8.97	3.84	4.15	0.98	112.8	88.8	134.9	169.2	102.1	120.0
1960	45.40	7.17	28.92	19.45	9.47	9.31	3.76	4.42	1.13	93.5	69.2	107.3	116.7	92.5	102.6
1961	24.26	7.18	10.53	8.64	1.89	6.55	2.18	3.01	1.36	50.0	90.3	30.2	43.9	17.3	52.7
1962	28.87	8.24	13.65	11.87	1.78	6.98	2.06	3.21	1.71	111.8	104.6	116.7	128.3	93.9	107.9
1963	34.30	10.24	16.78	13.85	2.93	7.28	2.19	3.26	1.83	126.6	136.3	125.6	116.3	172.8	107.1
1964	42.47	10.60	22.94	18.75	4.19	8.93	2.41	3.29	3.23	122.1	111.7	138.7	135.5	145.4	108.9
1965	52.82	11.91	31.66	24.06	7.60	9.25	3.08	3.30	2.87	129.0	115.2	141.8	133.1	186.8	110.4
1966	56.10	10.20	36.13	27.81	8.32	9.77	2.68	3.26	3.83	103.7	85.7	116.9	119.1	112.5	101.3
1967	52.54	12.30	30.60	23.69	6.91	9.64	2.65	3.23	3.76	96.4	120.3	84.8	85.4	83.5	98.6
1968	50.61	11.47	30.15	24.57	5.58	8.99	2.36	3.17	3.46	95.2	92.9	109.8	104.2	78.9	96.7
1969	62.82	12.12	40.45	33.34	7.11	10.25	2.32	3.18	4.75	120.9	105.5	134.2	137.1	126.3	101.5
1970	80.80	13.73	56.76	47.58	9.18	10.31	2.62	3.30	4.39	130.0	113.1	139.7	144.4	131.7	107.8
1971	88.52	13.69	63.27	54.23	9.04	11.56	2.75	3.25	5.56	109.7	100.5	112.7	118.0	95.8	101.2
1972	90.81	16.25	61.27	52.59	8.68	13.29	3.06	4.08	6.15	104.0	106.9	101.2	101.3	99.6	116.2
1973	95.97	17.97	64.03	55.72	8.31	13.97	3.40	5.12	5.45	103.9	99.9	102.8	106.0	94.2	114.3
1974	104.56	21.93	67.34	58.91	8.43	15.29	3.40	5.12	6.77	110.6	122.0	104.8	107.5	98.6	111.2
1975	119.29	23.29	78.65	69.71	8.94	17.35	3.58	7.18	6.59	114.0	105.3	114.0	120.2	100.3	109.4
1976	119.25	22.22	78.34	70.16	8.18	18.69	3.58	7.18	7.93	99.1	95.4	97.6	101.1	89.1	107.8
1977	123.74	21.33	83.07	74.32	8.75	19.34	4.04	8.19	7.11	104.8	97.2	104.9	106.2	113.3	105.2
1978	134.06	22.45	90.53	79.38	11.15	21.08	4.25	7.97	8.86	108.0	104.1	109.4	107.6	125.4	105.4
1979	137.02	23.28	91.50	80.64	10.86	22.24	4.26	7.97	10.01	99.5	93.5	101.0	102.3	97.8	100.5
1980	147.19	27.39	90.55	78.60	11.95	29.25	5.34	10.75	13.16	104.8	111.1	105.2	97.3	118.1	110.3
1981	143.58	28.02	86.82	74.86	11.96	28.74	5.63	9.89	13.22	92.4	90.7	91.1	93.4	86.2	96.7
1982	155.68	30.33	95.04	81.32	13.72	30.31	6.12	10.25	13.94	109.3	112.6	109.0	108.4	109.9	104.3
1983	177.74	39.79	102.33	88.18	14.15	35.62	6.43	12.45	16.74	110.5	113.1	110.2	109.2	111.2	110.2
1984	202.26	40.32	118.45	101.36	17.09	43.49	7.96	14.81	20.72	112.9	113.0	112.9	111.0	120.0	114.3
1985	265.13	48.74	151.47	126.41	25.06	64.92	13.25	19.22	32.45	120.8	108.9	120.6	118.4	139.3	120.6
1986	307.69	56.40	171.72	144.00	27.72	79.57	16.06	22.93	40.58	112.0	107.3	110.4	108.6	112.0	118.3
1987	356.56	65.52	190.81	159.88	30.93	100.23	18.60	29.51	52.12	110.3	102.4	109.2	108.6	110.3	120.2
1988	456.55	84.72	243.30	203.94	39.36	128.53	21.78	39.24	67.51	117.0	107.8	117.6	115.8	123.2	128.4
1989	527.78	89.12	293.28	249.22	44.06	145.38	25.30	48.03	72.05	109.2	106.8	108.9	108.1	110.9	113.0
1990	583.18	103.05	323.97	278.70	45.27	156.16	25.69	52.39	78.08	108.0	107.3	108.6	108.5	109.1	108.8
1991	669.41	108.36	359.91	313.17	46.74	201.14	27.16	57.32	116.66	109.3	103.0	108.1	108.1	107.5	109.6
1992	792.99	122.70	423.26	369.27	53.99	247.03	30.20	77.13	139.70	111.5	107.5	114.0	114.4	107.6	117.3
1993	985.79	140.42	568.71	505.25	63.46	276.66	34.53	89.04	153.09	112.1	108.6	114.3	114.8	111.0	110.1
1994	1300.92	225.41	731.18	656.58	74.60	344.33	45.45	112.95	185.93	112.4	105.3	114.8	115.4	110.6	111.8
1995	1616.23	289.37	911.79	824.73	87.06	415.07	62.26	145.27	207.54	111.4	101.1	113.4	114.0	108.9	112.6

Year	v2c1	v2c2	v3'	v3	v3a	v3b	v3b1	v3b2	v3c	v3c1	v3c2	v3c3	v3c4	v3c5	v3c6
1952	111.6	99.6	13.53	13.32	8.66	1.73	0.86	0.87	2.93	0.70	1.23				
1953	117.0	102.5	14.08	13.86	8.87	1.80	0.92	0.88	3.19	0.82	1.26				
1954	107.8	107.1	16.52	16.30	10.43	2.44	1.20	1.24	3.43	0.89	1.32				
1955	121.3	106.1	18.05	18.12	10.51	3.75	1.69	2.06	3.86	1.10	1.36				
1956	105.2	119.5	21.41	21.17	11.22	5.08	2.20	2.88	4.87	1.08	1.62				
1957	137.5	99.6	20.35	20.11	9.65	5.63	2.74	2.89	4.83	1.06	1.68				
1958	131.2	111.3	23.05	22.81	9.26	8.07	4.61	3.46	5.48	1.71	1.73				
1959	118.3	121.7	23.98	23.73	7.59	10.21	6.54	3.67	5.93	2.15	1.97				
1960	96.2	104.9	18.08	17.82	4.57	8.91	6.26	2.65	4.34	2.04	1.13				
1961	49.8	53.6	12.02	11.75	4.70	3.76	2.97	0.79	3.29	0.98	1.62				
1962	98.6	111.0	12.84	12.57	5.15	3.90	3.21	0.69	3.52	0.91	1.82				
1963	106.9	108.0	16.53	16.25	6.66	5.85	4.65	1.20	3.74	0.93	1.85				
1964	114.9	102.1	19.95	19.66	6.88	8.65	7.14	1.51	4.13	1.05	1.87				
1965	129.1	98.3	25.27	24.98	7.74	12.74	9.86	2.88	4.50	1.42	1.74				
1966	86.9	102.8	24.53	24.59	6.78	13.08	9.98	3.10	4.73	1.37	1.78				
1967	100.5	97.5	23.40	21.08	6.77	9.92	7.33	2.59	4.39	1.26	1.68				
1968	90.2	99.0	23.71	23.39	7.95	11.70	9.83	1.87	3.74	1.11	1.49				
1969	97.8	102.2	27.63	27.28	7.91	15.00	12.63	2.37	4.37	1.17	1.58				
1970	112.1	102.1	34.86	34.50	8.28	21.05	18.04	3.01	5.17	1.33	1.72				
1971	102.3	101.0	38.24	37.87	8.33	24.62	21.64	2.98	4.92	1.50	1.73				
1972	112.6	125.7	41.54	41.17	9.88	24.70	21.67	3.03	6.59	1.74	2.29				
1973	106.7	120.8	44.23	43.85	10.96	25.43	22.46	2.97	7.46	1.87	2.84				
1974	102.5	117.4	49.99	49.59	13.39	28.27	25.16	3.11	7.93	1.89	3.22				
1975	103.6	114.4	57.78	57.37	14.34	33.85	31.03	2.82	9.18	1.99	3.89				
1976	105.0	108.4	56.88	56.45	13.55	34.43	31.65	2.78	8.47	1.82	3.90				
1977	108.7	104.6	59.15	58.72	13.51	35.28	32.48	2.80	9.93	2.67	3.99				
1978	105.5	105.9	65.17	64.73	13.21	39.04	34.66	4.38	12.48	3.23	4.55	1.18		0.18	0.53
1979	98.1	100.7	67.97	67.51	12.89	40.98	36.90	4.08	13.64	3.26	4.83	1.32		0.59	0.58
1980	132.1	129.2	74.38	73.90	16.46	39.85	35.25	4.60	17.59	3.27	6.86	1.95	0.09	0.59	0.60
1981	102.1	94.8	71.38	70.89	17.63	35.30	31.33	3.97	17.96	3.50	7.07	1.96	0.10	0.50	0.50
1982	106.4	104.2	77.39	76.88	19.68	38.54	33.63	4.91	18.66	3.74	7.18	2.17	0.10	0.55	0.52
1983	110.9	112.3	92.03	91.50	27.65	42.92	37.52	5.40	20.93	4.07	8.63	2.26	0.11	0.75	0.40
1984	115.5	117.7	103.73	103.17	27.83	49.99	43.66	6.33	25.35	5.14	10.16	2.52	0.12	0.38	0.44
1985	182.6	112.7	123.97	123.39	33.08	58.81	50.53	8.28	31.50	7.36	11.40	3.76	0.13	0.93	0.66
1986	112.5	144.9	141.41	140.74	38.02	65.27	56.01	9.26	37.45	9.33	12.71	5.54	0.13	1.30	0.80
1987	118.7	125.3	160.16	159.52	45.27	68.40	58.26	10.14	45.85	10.67	15.67	8.37	0.17	1.47	0.88
1988	116.4	133.2	192.46	191.84	52.77	81.33	67.28	14.05	57.74	10.94	22.55	10.50	0.45	1.90	1.28
1989	113.8	113.2	217.44	216.84	59.01	91.79	77.62	14.17	66.04	11.82	29.08	10.90	0.50	2.01	1.31
1990	108.9	106.4	243.26	242.81	64.06	98.34	83.93	14.41	80.41	12.01	30.64	12.02	2.56	3.27	2.42
1991	107.9	111.4	271.72	271.39	66.55	111.91	97.19	14.72	92.93	12.45	31.17	15.20	4.17	4.28	3.11
1992	116.1	121.9	318.02	317.79	74.21	128.66	110.22	18.44	114.92	14.18	39.15	18.89	5.72	5.44	3.92
1993	108.5	113.2	372.44	372.24	87.43	159.96	136.74	23.22	124.85	15.03	43.11	19.97	6.43	6.41	4.02
1994	112.1	115.2	451.85	451.66	103.81	199.32	174.62	24.70	148.53	20.22	50.26	24.02	7.83	7.60	5.17
1995	111.7	114.5	553.53	553.35	110.53	258.51	226.45	32.06	184.31	25.64	67.23	30.74	9.76	7.62	5.92

Year	v3c7	v3c8	v3c9	v3c10	v3d	v4'	v4	v4a	v4b	v4b1	v4b2	v4c	v4c1	v4c2	v4c3
1952				1.00	125										
1953				1.11	126	104.9	105.0	102.5	110.9	120.4	102.9	107.5	113.8	101.0	
1954				1.22	146	115.6	116.0	117.6	131.6	126.1	138.1	102.9	106.1	102.1	
1955				1.40	154	109.9	107.8	103.7	132.3	122.6	142.8	99.4	118.7	103.0	
1956				2.17	174	119.0	104.1	113.5	140.5	117.6	162.7	117.1	105.7	118.1	
1957				2.09	160	97.8	96.1	87.8	112.1	123.4	101.8	99.1	126.8	96.3	
1958				2.04	178	116.3	117.2	103.2	142.7	169.5	115.1	112.2	123.8	107.9	
1959				1.81	183	102.4	102.2	81.4	120.9	138.0	105.4	108.9	110.9	106.3	
1960				1.17	143	75.9	75.7	60.4	88.8	115.7	79.2	73.0	74.8	102.4	
1961				0.69	97	62.6	62.6	90.4	42.9	49.4	40.4	73.5	68.7	77.5	
1962				0.79	101	105.8	105.4	103.0	104.0	113.8	96.1	110.1	92.9	116.8	
1963				0.96	130	127.0	127.3	128.6	147.2	139.4	164.3	103.7	102.2	105.9	
1964				1.21	152	123.7	123.6	119.2	134.9	135.2	132.2	112.4	121.9	101.1	
1965				1.34	186	124.3	124.7	115.2	140.9	138.7	152.0	108.9	129.7	92.2	
1966				1.58	174	98.5	98.5	83.2	108.4	108.5	107.6	99.3	96.5	102.3	
1967				1.45	160	84.9	84.7	99.8	72.4	71.9	79.2	96.8	95.8	97.0	
1968				1.14	157	112.0	112.2	112.2	120.9	126.7	77.8	94.8	92.8	95.6	
1969				1.62	178	117.6	118.2	101.3	134.8	136.4	128.5	104.2	102.1	106.9	
1970				2.12	218	122.7	122.4	106.7	134.6	147.9	133.1	108.1	121.1	107.0	
1971				1.69	231	108.0	108.2	99.8	113.2	122.9	96.3	102.4	102.0	104.4	
1972				2.56	243	105.5	105.8	101.6	104.1	109.0	104.7	120.8	116.1	131.3	
1973				2.75	252	106.6	106.3	116.4	101.2	109.4	96.1	111.5	108.7	120.4	
1974				2.82	279	113.7	113.7	114.2	112.3	112.3	104.1	117.9	103.9	113.3	
1975				3.30	318	116.2	116.4	115.2	119.0	124.9	98.3	109.1	105.3	114.4	
1976				2.75	309	100.3	100.3	94.6	102.0	102.2	97.9	102.8	108.6	100.3	
1977				3.27	318	101.1	101.2	99.1	102.7	102.7	105.1	98.8	110.3	96.6	
1978	0.93	1.06	0.82		348	113.1	113.2	96.0	115.1	108.4	133.9	130.4	106.2	131.5	
1979	1.04	1.03	0.99		359	101.5	101.4	87.4	104.9	106.5	97.2	108.9	100.0	105.0	120.2
1980	1.86	1.19	1.18		388	109.2	109.1	123.9	98.0	95.9	112.1	127.9	104.4	136.7	128.4
1981	1.88	1.15	1.20		367	91.8	91.6	93.8	85.9	84.1	86.3	102.8	105.2	106.0	98.3
1982	1.87	1.27	1.16		393	108.9	108.9	116.1	108.3	107.2	113.3	103.4	103.0	101.8	109.4
1983	2.07	1.23	1.41		462	114.9	114.9	122.6	113.1	112.1	119.4	110.1	113.7	112.2	104.3
1984	2.95	1.26	1.88		515	113.7	110.7	111.2	112.9	112.0	110.9	118.7	121.0	117.9	108.9
1985	3.50	1.44	2.32		608	113.2	116.4	108.1	109.4	110.3	129.8	118.2	129.5	112.0	120.3
1986	3.55	1.33	2.76		684	110.7	111.0	106.9	110.1	106.1	113.2	124.9	109.7	150.0	136.2
1987	3.94	1.54	3.14		764	109.1	108.9	106.5	102.4	101.9	103.4	122.1	110.2	135.2	139.7
1988	4.45	2.38	3.29		905	113.6	113.7	107.6	113.9	111.2	118.8	117.8	111.1	124.3	123.2
1989	4.50	2.57	3.35		1007	108.8	108.8	106.0	109.8	108.8	108.2	109.3	112.2	114.2	109.0
1990	5.31	3.11	6.53	2.54	1099	105.6	105.6	105.0	105.4	106.1	102.4	106.5	97.3	105.6	109.3
1991	7.07	4.47	8.45	2.56	1204	106.5	106.6	101.6	109.0	108.9	108.9	107.7	105.4	109.2	109.4
1992	8.31	5.58	10.46	3.27	1384	109.8	109.9	105.8	110.2	109.1	109.9	112.8	108.0	120.1	106.4
1993	9.52	6.06	10.87	3.43	1600	111.6	111.6	108.8	113.6	114.1	110.2	111.1	109.6	116.7	109.4
1994	10.42	7.55	11.30	4.16	1925	110.4	110.4	106.0	111.4	111.3	112.1	112.3	114.1	115.4	111.1
1995	11.32	8.79	12.53	4.76	2288	109.9	109.9	103.1	110.4	110.1	112.0	114.1	116.1	116.4	115.8

Year	v4c4	v4c5	v4c6	v4c7	v4c8	v4c9	v4c10	v5	v5a	v5a1	v5a1a	v5a1b	v5a2	v5b	v5b1
1952								13.32	9.13	7.22	4.77	2.45	1.91	5.41	4.82
1953								13.86	10.57	8.18	5.55	2.63	2.39	6.94	5.98
1954								16.30	12.39	9.76	6.64	3.12	2.63	8.66	6.02
1955								17.82	13.37	10.58	6.93	3.65	2.79	11.07	6.37
1956								21.17	14.97	12.75	8.26	4.49	2.22	13.08	8.05
1957								20.11	17.23	14.25	9.43	4.82	2.98	12.37	9.54
1958								22.81	16.74	12.31	6.88	5.43	4.43	10.12	10.28
1959								23.73	15.88	12.62	5.69	6.93	3.26	15.07	13.53
1960								17.82	10.84	6.56	2.78	3.78	4.28	15.37	14.74
1961								11.75	4.73	3.55	1.96	1.59	1.18	11.32	11.35
1962								12.57	6.47	5.40	2.74	2.66	1.07	11.24	10.53
1963								16.25	12.29	11.23	5.86	5.37	1.06	10.83	9.38
1964								19.66	14.86	13.62	7.78	5.84	1.24	13.30	11.73
1965								24.98	18.96	15.06	9.04	6.02	3.90	13.59	12.04
1966								24.23	18.87	13.96	8.33	5.63	4.91	13.93	12.31
1967								23.08	18.89	14.63	9.65	4.98	4.26	12.68	11.09
1968								23.37	19.27	14.85	9.88	4.97	4.42	13.51	11.85
1969								27.28	20.68	16.08	10.75	5.33	4.60	15.20	13.03
1970								34.50	23.89	18.75	12.89	5.86	5.14	18.08	15.05
1971								37.87	26.15	19.96	13.54	6.42	6.19	20.40	16.67
1972								41.17	27.23	21.12	13.77	7.35	6.11	20.77	17.31
1973								43.85	28.61	22.02	14.10	7.92	6.59	23.56	19.25
1974								49.59	30.54	23.75	14.92	8.83	6.79	27.14	21.93
1975								57.37	32.84	25.67	15.79	9.88	7.17	31.06	23.96
1976								56.45	32.25	24.99	14.24	10.75	7.26	28.18	23.01
1977								58.72	38.26	28.30	16.31	11.99	9.96	27.59	22.76
1978								64.73	43.12	31.90	17.98	13.92	11.22	30.73	28.16
1979	111.3	109.2	110.5	113.2	110.8	110.2		67.51	46.57	34.98	19.74	15.24	11.59	30.04	27.42
1980	120.3	117.9	137.3	131.3	136.4	111.3		73.90	53.77	39.81	21.82	17.99	13.96	24.38	22.18
1981	97.9	101.8	97.6	99.9	101.2	102.6		70.89	57.24	42.74	24.50	18.24	14.50	22.32	19.79
1982	108.2	108.8	99.2	99.8	100.0	95.9		76.88	61.32	47.05	26.52	20.53	14.27	25.34	21.87
1983	105.3	104.7	104.7	102.2	105.7	122.9		91.50	68.10	51.54	29.44	22.10	16.56	31.28	26.54
1984	107.7	106.4	129.0	131.7	127.2	131.8		103.17	73.43	55.99	31.73	24.26	17.44	35.46	29.65
1985	118.8	112.3	119.0	112.8	115.4	113.7		123.39	86.23	66.10	37.98	28.12	20.13	47.16	39.17
1986	119.3	117.6	109.3	108.2	110.3	122.2		140.74	104.24	77.82	42.84	34.98	26.42	60.02	45.83
1987	118.8	128.1	111.7	108.9	111.0	113.0		159.52	119.56	90.63	49.94	40.69	28.93	62.02	52.19
1988	120.2	118.2	102.1	102.9	103.0	110.3		191.84	139.60	107.43	58.73	48.70	32.17	77.57	53.64
1989	107.2	108.0	104.3	103.9	104.0	111.5		216.84	158.00	120.26	67.34	52.92	37.74	90.06	59.78
1990	108.8	107.9	104.9	105.0	104.3	103.8		242.81	170.20	130.36	72.14	58.22	39.84	104.91	67.19
1991	109.0	107.6	104.9	105.3	103.8	103.9	101.8	271.39	195.73	147.60	82.55	65.05	48.13	113.17	76.47
1992	105.4	106.8	103.5	104.2	104.8	105.4	102.3	317.79	227.96	170.10	96.85	73.25	57.86	130.90	85.73
1993	111.4	106.5	106.0	105.6	106.3	108.5	100.1	372.24	263.00	194.69	105.48	89.21	68.31	152.27	98.42
1994	114.6	107.4	107.9	107.9	107.0	108.7	103.6	451.66	319.11	236.22	127.98	108.24	82.89	177.53	114.81
1995	117.4	110.5	109.8	108.9	108.9	107.2	106.0	553.35	376.81	283.40	151.39	132.01	93.41	222.57	141.98

Year	v5b2	v5c	v5c1	v5c2	v6a1	v6a2	v6a3	v6a4	v6b2	v6b3	v6b4	v7	v7a	v7a1	v7a2
1952	0.59	-1.22	1.88	3.10								113.3	113.5	104.9	156.8
1953	0.96	-3.65	1.59	5.24								103.7	103.7	101.7	108.5
1954	2.64	-4.75	1.33	6.08								123.7	125.7	120.5	141.1
1955	4.70	-6.62	1.72	8.34								114.7	114.4	111.4	121.8
1956	5.03	-6.88	3.07	9.95								124.0	121.9	115.4	139.1
1957	2.83	-9.49	1.76	11.25								105.1	105.4	106.7	102.3
1958	-0.16	-4.05	4.19	8.24								81.1	80.1	66.8	110.2
1959	1.54	-7.22	2.36	9.58								95.9	93.6	73.5	121.4
1960	0.63	-8.39	2.20	10.59								92.5	93.3	87.0	98.4
1961	-0.03	-4.30	5.34	9.64								91.0	89.7	100.1	82.5
1962	0.71	-5.14	6.44	11.58								102.1	106.0	124.7	88.7
1963	1.45	-6.87	6.88	13.75								111.8	109.5	116.8	100.5
1964	1.57	-8.50	6.94	15.44								109.1	109.9	110.4	109.1
1965	1.55	-7.57	9.71	17.28								110.3	111.8	117.5	103.0
1966	1.62	-8.57	10.79	19.36								101.0	100.0	103.8	93.1
1967	1.59	-8.49	12.09	20.58								101.9	100.7	105.6	91.0
1968	1.66	-9.41	13.87	23.28								98.3	97.2	97.3	97.0
1969	2.17	-8.60	16.75	25.35								109.2	108.9	109.5	107.3
1970	3.03	-7.47	20.97	28.44								118.6	118.4	122.8	108.4
1971	3.73	-8.68	24.10	32.78								106.0	106.0	99.4	119.6
1972	3.46	-6.83	29.52	36.35								104.7	104.9	103.2	108.2
1973	4.31	-8.32	33.22	41.54								103.3	103.3	101.7	106.4
1974	5.21	-8.09	37.09	45.18								108.1	108.2	104.8	114.7
1975	7.10	-6.53	41.79	48.32								110.2	110.2	108.9	112.6
1976	5.17	-3.98	47.35	51.33								97.9	97.2	90.3	108.7
1977	4.83	-7.13	47.22	54.35								107.5	107.2	108.7	106.4
1978	2.57	-9.12	49.12	58.24	9.17	7.86	0.28	0.67	12.34	1.32	0.26	110.6	109.0	109.7	108.4
1979	2.62	-9.10	54.47	63.57	10.07	8.63	0.31	0.73	13.52	1.43	0.29	111.8	110.9	112.0	108.7
1980	2.20	-4.25	63.18	67.43	11.13	9.54	0.34	0.81	15.87	1.80	0.32	107.2	106.4	103.6	111.1
1981	2.53	-8.67	62.95	71.62	12.54	10.71	0.38	0.87	15.98	1.90	0.36	107.0	106.8	109.6	101.4
1982	3.47	-9.78	65.56	75.34	13.57	11.59	0.41	0.95	18.03	2.11	0.39	106.6	106.7	105.7	110.2
1983	4.74	-7.88	70.68	78.56	15.06	12.87	0.46	1.05	19.29	2.38	0.43	112.8	111.8	111.0	112.9
1984	5.81	-5.72	77.01	82.73	14.42	15.76	0.45	1.10	21.07	2.73	0.46	107.6	107.8	106.9	110.1
1985	7.99	-10.00	78.40	88.40	15.74	20.30	0.67	1.27	24.60	3.02	0.50	112.7	110.2	113.7	106.9
1986	14.19	-23.52	68.99	92.51	16.01	24.53	0.88	1.42	30.56	3.79	0.63	113.0	111.4	106.8	118.7
1987	9.83	-22.06	75.28	97.34	18.21	28.55	1.64	1.54	35.45	4.48	0.76	108.7	109.7	110.0	110.2
1988	23.93	-25.33	78.12	103.45	22.55	32.21	2.23	1.74	42.80	5.03	0.87	102.0	102.3	103.8	100.4
1989	30.28	-31.22	77.70	108.92	27.84	35.12	2.47	1.91	46.65	5.28	0.99	101.2	100.9	101.4	100.1
1990	37.72	-32.30	83.01	115.31	31.33	35.86	2.85	2.10	51.67	5.51	1.04	99.4	99.0	99.0	99.6
1991	36.70	-37.51	85.50	123.01	36.56	39.29	3.93	2.77	57.11	6.63	1.31	109.4	109.1	107.9	110.6
1992	45.17	-41.07	87.95	129.02	43.94	45.06	4.36	3.49	63.71	7.98	1.56	108.4	107.9	106.3	110.0
1993	53.85	-43.03	90.98	134.01	44.52	51.40	5.29	4.27	78.09	9.26	1.88	111.6	110.3	109.0	111.9
1994	62.82	-45.08	94.85	139.93	54.03	62.36	6.42	5.17	94.73	11.24	2.27	110.1	109.6	109.5	109.8
1995	80.59	-46.03	99.00	145.03	63.91	73.87	7.52	6.09	115.49	13.75	2.77	109.0	108.9	108.4	109.6

Year	v7b	v8	v8a	v8b	v9	v9a	v9b	v10a1	v10a2	v10a3	v10a3a	v10a3b	v10a4	v10b1	v10b2
1952	102.5	80	61	229											
1953	123.4	82	62	240	103.1	101.1	106.9								
1954	117.3	93	69	281	113.9	110.2	114.6								
1955	116.6	99	73	302	105.6	106.2	108.0								
1956	137.4	108	79	341	110.5	110.1	113.5								
1957	101.9	115	87	330	105.7	109.2	96.4								
1958	84.1	108	62	341	93.7	69.9	103.7								
1959	122.3	107	52	385	99.4	82.8	113.0								
1960	88.1	106	50	374	98.1	63.7	97.4								
1961	99.2	101	51	351	95.0	102.2	93.8								
1962	75.1	108	62	382	109.4	128.3	108.7								
1963	130.7	110	66	413	101.9	103.4	108.2								
1964	99.6	117	72	412	104.7	109.8	99.5								
1965	93.4	123	82	399	103.6	113.4	96.1								
1966	110.2	117	79	360	94.8	94.7	90.3								
1967	109.6	110	77	321	92.7	97.2	89.2								
1968	105.0	107	75	313	98.0	95.7	97.8								
1969	105.5	115	81	337	101.0	107.5	106.8								
1970	121.6	130	96	366	115.4	118.1	109.2								
1971	104.7	133	95	398	101.0	101.2	108.9								
1972	106.0	136	97	401	100.8	102.4	100.5								
1973	104.9	140	99	417	103.2	101.2	104.1								
1974	108.1	145	101	438	106.8	103.9	112.4								
1975	110.4	156	107	470	106.8	102.2	107.3								
1976	103.6	150	98	496	99.3	95.6	104.8								
1977	109.8	159	105	513	100.7	102.3	102.7								
1978	122.0	168	112	535	112.8	103.3	102.2	19.71	4.51	2.52	0.23	2.29	1.42	1.34	0.85
1979	118.9	185	122	564	103.1	116.1	106.4	19.19	4.38	2.47	0.21	2.26	1.38	1.36	0.98
1980	109.3	208	133	647	111.6	103.7	114.7	15.53	3.54	1.99	0.18	1.81	1.12	1.14	0.82
1981	110.5	220	147	651	109.8	112.5	101.3	13.85	3.19	1.59	0.14	1.45	1.16	1.21	0.95
1982	104.8	238	157	707	105.5	104.8	106.4	15.31	3.53	1.80	0.23	1.57	1.23	1.56	1.30
1983	120.0	258	173	740	109.9	111.4	107.4	18.58	4.28	2.24	0.20	2.04	1.44	2.27	1.98
1984	106.3	277	185	788	111.2	111.6	103.7	20.76	4.78	2.53	0.22	2.31	1.58	2.78	2.08
1985	113.2	323	220	881	105.4	109.2	102.6	27.42	6.32	3.34	0.37	2.97	2.09	3.83	2.99
1986	120.0	376	247	1050	102.9	105.0	100.4	31.96	7.40	4.03	0.65	3.38	2.44	6.80	5.82
1987	107.3	431	284	1176	108.4	109.2	106.5	36.39	8.43	4.59	0.89	3.70	2.78	5.22	3.85
1988	101.6	503	330	1368	101.2	102.6	100.4	34.03	9.16	5.83	1.09	4.74	4.62	11.46	8.97
1989	103.3	555	373	1482	100.7	101.0	100.9	41.85	9.56	3.22	0.53	2.69	5.15	27.52	2.02
1990	101.9	590	392	1608	99.4	99.3	98.5	47.03	10.75	3.62	0.37	3.25	5.79	31.96	4.25
1991	110.6	655	440	1730	104.8	108.2	106.5	53.53	12.23	4.12	0.38	3.74	6.59	30.19	5.13
1992	110.2	741	508	1888	107.2	104.2	109.5	60.03	12.61	6.02	1.83	4.19	7.09	37.16	6.31
1993	111.4	837	547	2241	106.0	103.0	107.8	68.28	13.02	9.75	4.09	5.66	7.37	39.83	8.68
1994	111.5	1007	660	2666	108.7	108.8	107.6	79.65	15.19	11.37	4.77	6.60	8.60	46.46	10.13
1995	109.3	1172	764	3028	105.7	106.0	102.0	97.23	19.52	13.72	5.80	7.92	11.51	61.17	12.36

Year	v10b4	v11a	v11a1	v11a2	v11b	v11b1	v11b2	v11c	v11c1	v11c2	v12	v12a	v12b	v13	v13i
1952											117.3	116.5	120.7		
1953											156.3	154.2	156.8		
1954											151.2	107.2	287.6		
1955											164.0	114.1	220.8		
1956											138.2	210.3	90.6		
1957											72.7	87.0	52.5		
1958											112.5	161.8			
1959											125.5	111.1			
1960											94.0	101.3	38.7		
1961											16.5	17.7			
1962											90.2	59.7			
1963											185.3	170.1	214.9		
1964											169.7	201.2	107.4		
1965											168.5	187.5	97.3		
1966											92.7	94.1	106.7		
1967											91.6	88.4	103.6		
1968											96.0	93.9	101.9		
1969											117.3	115.2	126.9		
1970											127.3	123.4	136.9		
1971											110.2	106.5	122.7		
1972											90.7	89.3	91.6		
1973											109.5	105.0	120.8		
1974											110.8	106.3	122.0		
1975											118.0	109.4	135.4		
1976											87.9	97.0	72.9		
1977											95.9	97.5	93.2		
1978	0.38	2.39	2.18	0.21	16.29	14.66	1.63	12.05	11.32	0.73	124.3	153.8	53.6	64.73	35.49
1979	0.28	2.34	2.14	0.20	15.93	14.54	1.39	11.77	10.74	1.03	96.9	94.8	103.8	67.51	37.56
1980	0.24	2.04	1.84	0.20	13.18	11.86	1.32	9.16	8.48	0.68	71.9	68.9	79.6	73.90	41.97
1981	0.37	1.98	1.79	0.19	13.09	11.78	1.31	7.25	6.22	1.03	83.5	79.7	108.8	70.89	38.14
1982	0.51	2.27	1.34	0.93	14.87	13.38	1.49	8.20	7.15	1.05	114.8	109.6	138.2	76.88	41.79
1983	0.49	3.04	2.73	0.31	15.94	14.30	1.64	12.30	9.51	2.79	121.6	118.3	130.4	91.50	53.77
1984	0.95	3.45	3.07	0.38	18.07	16.08	1.99	13.94	10.50	3.44	131.8	131.9	124.2	103.17	57.29
1985	1.17	4.59	4.06	0.53	24.03	21.15	2.88	18.54	13.96	4.58	143.2	140.7	129.3	123.39	68.42
1986	1.57	5.84	5.17	0.67	30.58	25.21	5.37	23.60	15.45	8.15	128.5	117.0	173.4	140.74	75.95
1987	0.76	6.03	5.27	0.76	31.63	27.83	3.80	24.36	19.09	5.27	95.7	108.9	65.9	159.52	86.55
1988	3.50	7.54	5.58	1.96	39.56	30.81	8.75	30.47	17.25	13.22	125.4	94.7	242.0	191.84	103.36
1989	0.74	9.50	6.53	2.97	48.87	34.51	14.36	39.43	18.74	20.69	126.5	103.5	162.1	216.84	112.22
1990	1.51	9.69	7.01	2.68	53.62	40.17	13.45	41.60	20.01	21.59	104.5	101.6	105.8	242.81	128.77
1991	1.38	10.15	7.65	2.50	60.23	42.33	17.90	42.79	26.49	16.30	104.6	108.4	89.5	271.39	144.44
1992	1.70	11.68	8.01	3.67	71.52	46.50	25.02	47.70	31.22	16.48	110.4	110.4	110.1	317.79	164.75
1993	5.34	11.84	9.20	2.64	80.27	52.19	28.08	60.16	37.03	23.13	112.1	112.3	111.7	372.24	191.80
1994	6.23	15.81	10.73	5.08	93.64	60.88	32.76	68.18	43.20	24.98	111.5	110.2	114.4	451.66	230.72
1995	7.06	19.20	13.64	5.56	116.99	75.38	41.61	86.38	52.96	33.42	110.3	110.1	110.8	553.35	276.80

Year	v13ii	v13iii	v13iv	v13a	v13ai	v13aii	v13aiii	v13aiv	v13b	v13bi	v13bii	v13biii	v13biv	v13b1	v13b1i
1952															
1953															
1954															
1955															
1956															
1957															
1958															
1959															
1960															
1961															
1962															
1963															
1964															
1965															
1966															
1967															
1968															
1969															
1970															
1971															
1972															
1973															
1974															
1975															
1976															
1977															
1978	5.54	13.54	10.16	13.21	11.86	0.17	0.77	0.41	39.04	17.32	4.11	11.03	6.58	34.66	14.51
1979	5.86	14.35	9.74	12.89	11.70	0.17	0.75	0.27	40.98	18.96	4.29	11.76	5.97	36.90	16.27
1980	6.17	14.81	10.95	16.46	14.72	0.20	1.10	0.44	39.85	18.36	4.29	11.39	5.81	35.25	15.39
1981	7.10	12.76	12.89	17.63	15.68	0.32	1.15	0.48	35.30	13.52	4.96	9.19	7.63	31.33	10.98
1982	7.53	13.98	13.58	19.68	16.59	0.82	1.18	1.09	38.54	15.81	4.89	10.32	7.52	33.63	12.79
1983	9.44	15.37	12.92	27.65	22.96	1.95	1.20	1.54	42.92	20.40	5.49	11.26	5.77	37.52	16.99
1984	10.90	17.19	17.79	27.83	23.08	2.50	0.81	1.44	49.99	21.32	5.80	12.92	9.95	43.65	20.72
1985	14.32	19.62	21.03	33.08	27.21	3.68	0.96	1.23	58.81	25.66	7.29	14.82	11.04	50.54	20.72
1986	16.15	22.65	25.99	38.02	30.28	4.20	1.08	2.46	65.27	27.59	7.83	16.92	12.93	56.01	21.84
1987	17.67	25.21	30.09	45.27	36.32	4.60	1.11	3.24	68.40	29.91	8.32	17.91	12.26	58.26	23.89
1988	18.99	29.50	39.99	52.77	42.94	4.80	1.48	3.55	81.33	35.50	8.06	19.53	18.24	67.28	26.78
1989	21.31	34.86	48.45	59.01	44.78	5.63	2.48	6.12	91.79	39.09	9.25	22.89	20.56	77.52	30.19
1990	23.67	38.98	51.39	64.06	47.15	5.88	4.72	6.31	98.34	41.80	9.72	24.27	22.55	83.93	32.73
1991	27.13	42.60	57.22	66.55	49.17	6.13	4.91	6.34	111.91	47.94	10.22	26.53	27.22	97.19	38.10
1992	38.06	46.54	68.44	74.21	54.56	7.16	6.10	6.39	128.66	51.37	16.88	28.01	32.40	110.22	40.38
1993	46.65	55.12	78.67	87.43	64.33	8.42	7.20	7.48	159.96	64.92	20.89	34.40	39.75	136.74	51.07
1994	58.20	68.98	93.76	103.81	75.04	11.00	8.55	9.22	199.32	84.67	26.37	43.42	44.86	174.62	69.85
1995	70.82	89.72	116.01	110.53	79.76	11.71	9.42	9.64	258.51	109.81	35.30	57.36	56.04	226.45	90.58

Year	v13b1ii	v13b1iii	v13b1iv	v13b2	v13b2i	v13b2ii	v13b2iii	v13b2iv	v13c	v13ci	v13cii	v13ciii	v13civ	v13c1
1952														
1953														
1954														
1955														
1956														
1957														
1958														
1959														
1960														
1961														
1962														
1963														
1964														
1965														
1966														
1967														
1968														
1969														
1970														
1971														
1972														
1973														
1974														
1975														
1976														
1977														
1978	3.41	10.71	6.03	4.38	2.81	0.70	0.32	0.55	12.48	6.31	1.26	1.74	3.17	3.23
1979	3.64	11.39	5.60	4.08	2.69	0.65	0.37	0.37	13.64	6.90	1.40	1.84	3.50	3.26
1980	3.55	10.97	5.34	4.60	2.97	0.74	0.42	0.17	17.59	8.89	1.68	2.32	4.70	3.27
1981	4.23	8.85	7.27	3.97	2.54	0.73	0.34	0.36	17.96	8.94	1.82	2.42	4.78	3.50
1982	4.69	9.87	6.28	4.91	3.02	0.20	0.45	1.24	18.66	9.39	1.82	2.48	4.97	3.74
1983	5.27	10.87	4.39	5.40	3.41	0.22	0.39	1.38	20.93	10.41	2.00	2.91	5.61	4.07
1984	6.67	14.34	8.81	6.33	3.86	0.31	0.44	1.72	25.35	12.89	2.60	3.46	6.40	5.14
1985	6.67	14.34	8.81	8.28	4.95	0.62	0.48	2.23	31.50	15.55	3.35	3.84	8.76	7.36
1986	7.24	16.51	10.42	9.26	5.75	0.59	0.41	2.51	37.45	18.08	4.12	4.65	10.60	9.33
1987	7.69	17.32	9.36	10.14	6.02	0.63	0.59	2.90	45.85	20.32	4.75	6.19	14.59	10.67
1988	7.72	18.83	14.25	14.05	8.72	0.64	0.70	3.99	57.74	24.92	6.13	8.49	18.20	10.94
1989	8.55	21.47	17.41	14.17	8.90	0.70	1.42	3.15	66.04	28.35	6.43	9.49	21.77	11.82
1990	9.01	22.74	19.45	14.41	9.07	0.71	1.53	3.10	80.41	39.82	8.07	9.99	22.53	12.01
1991	9.46	24.92	24.71	14.72	9.84	0.76	1.61	2.51	92.93	47.33	10.78	11.16	23.66	12.45
1992	15.65	26.23	27.96	18.44	10.99	1.23	1.78	0.44	114.92	58.82	14.02	12.43	29.65	14.18
1993	19.42	32.08	34.17	23.22	13.85	1.47	2.32	5.58	124.85	62.55	17.34	13.52	31.44	15.03
1994	24.80	40.96	39.01	24.70	14.82	1.57	2.46	5.85	148.53	71.01	20.83	17.01	39.68	20.22
1995	32.16	53.12	50.59	32.06	19.23	3.14	4.24	5.45	184.31	87.23	23.81	22.94	50.33	25.64

Year	v13c1i	v13c1ii	v13c1iii	v13c1iv	v13c2	v13c2i	v13c2ii	v13c2iii	v13c2iv	v13c3	v13c3i	v13c3ii	v13c3iii	v13c3iv
1952														
1953														
1954														
1955														
1956														
1957														
1958														
1959														
1960														
1961														
1962														
1963														
1964														
1965														
1966														
1967														
1968														
1969														
1970														
1971														
1972														
1973														
1974														
1975														
1976														
1977														
1978	1.47	0.49	0.51	0.76	4.55	1.59	0.21	1.10	1.65	1.18	0.35	0.02	0.11	0.70
1979	1.49	0.48	0.53	0.76	4.83	1.64	0.22	1.16	1.81	1.32	0.42	0.03	0.12	0.75
1980	1.52	0.49	0.54	0.72	6.86	2.40	0.31	1.58	2.57	1.95	0.51	0.05	0.15	1.24
1981	1.63	0.48	0.56	0.83	7.07	2.46	0.36	1.62	2.63	1.96	0.58	0.07	0.17	1.14
1982	1.85	0.42	0.58	0.89	7.18	2.51	0.39	1.63	2.65	2.17	0.62	0.08	0.19	1.28
1983	2.18	0.41	0.63	0.85	8.63	2.99	0.41	1.98	3.25	2.26	0.66	0.05	0.21	1.34
1984	2.90	0.61	0.80	0.83	10.16	3.55	0.42	2.32	3.87	2.52	0.70	0.07	0.23	1.52
1985	3.97	1.04	0.84	1.51	11.40	3.94	0.48	2.58	4.40	3.76	0.74	0.08	0.29	2.65
1986	5.47	1.30	0.86	1.70	12.71	4.45	0.60	3.21	4.45	5.54	0.79	0.11	0.43	4.21
1987	5.65	1.62	1.60	1.80	15.67	5.45	0.67	3.82	5.73	8.37	0.84	0.16	0.60	6.77
1988	5.88	1.81	1.73	1.52	22.55	7.89	1.09	5.47	8.10	10.50	0.96	0.27	1.11	8.16
1989	6.26	1.84	1.18	2.54	29.08	10.18	1.29	6.88	10.73	10.90	1.21	0.34	1.24	8.11
1990	6.30	1.87	1.20	2.64	30.64	11.56	1.51	7.11	10.46	12.02	1.43	0.43	1.47	8.69
1991	6.45	2.43	1.43	2.14	31.17	12.98	1.83	7.79	8.57	15.20	1.69	0.51	1.61	11.39
1992	7.63	2.58	1.55	2.42	39.15	16.44	2.55	8.74	11.42	18.89	3.07	0.62	1.75	13.45
1993	7.48	2.94	1.77	2.84	43.11	18.11	3.76	9.33	11.91	19.97	3.69	0.78	1.95	13.55
1994	9.09	3.86	2.78	4.49	50.26	19.55	4.43	11.32	14.96	24.02	4.16	1.00	2.30	16.56
1995	11.53	4.18	3.57	6.36	67.23	27.38	5.13	15.68	19.04	30.74	5.34	1.28	2.95	21.17

Year	v13c4	v13c4i	v13c4ii	v13c4iii	v13c4iv	v13c5	v13c5i	v13c5ii	v13c5iii	v13c5iv	v13c6	v13c6i	v13c6ii	v13c6iii
1952														
1953														
1954														
1955														
1956														
1957														
1958														
1959														
1960														
1961														
1962														
1963														
1964														
1965														
1966														
1967														
1968														
1969														
1970														
1971														
1972														
1973														
1974														
1975														
1976														
1977														
1978						0.18	0.06	0.04	0.02	0.06	0.53	0.38	0.15	
1979						0.59	0.29	0.09	0.03	0.18	0.58	0.42	0.16	
1980	0.09	0.04	0.05			0.59	0.20	0.17	0.05	0.17	0.60	0.44	0.16	
1981	0.10	0.06	0.04			0.60	0.17	0.18	0.07	0.18	0.50	0.33	0.17	
1982	0.10	0.04	0.06			0.65	0.23	0.19	0.08	0.15	0.52	0.34	0.18	
1983	0.11	0.04	0.07			0.75	0.14	0.35	0.09	0.17	0.40	0.21	0.19	
1984	0.12	0.04	0.08			0.88	0.17	0.42	0.11	0.18	0.44	0.24	0.20	
1985	0.13	0.05	0.08			0.93	0.13	0.47	0.13	0.20	0.66	0.44	0.22	
1986	0.13	0.04	0.09			1.30	0.23	0.68	0.15	0.24	0.80	0.57	0.23	
1987	0.17	0.06	0.11			1.47	0.27	0.74	0.17	0.29	0.88	0.64	0.24	
1988	0.45	0.16	0.29			1.90	0.42	0.88	0.18	0.42	1.28	1.04	0.24	
1989	0.50	0.38	0.12			2.01	0.49	0.94	0.19	0.39	1.31	1.05	0.26	
1990	2.56	1.89	0.67	0.00	0.00	3.27	1.31	1.01	0.21	0.74	2.42	2.14	0.28	
1991	4.17	1.92	1.67	0.10	0.48	4.28	1.86	1.11	0.23	1.08	3.11	2.82	0.29	
1992	5.72	2.01	3.04	0.14	0.53	5.44	2.20	1.16	0.25	1.83	3.92	3.61	0.31	
1993	6.43	2.30	3.41	0.17	0.55	6.41	2.35	1.17	0.30	2.59	4.02	3.69	0.33	
1994	7.83	2.81	4.16	0.26	0.60	7.60	2.79	1.39	0.35	3.07	5.17	4.75	0.42	
1995	9.76	3.50	5.18	0.34	0.74	7.62	2.80	1.40	0.40	3.02	5.92	5.43	0.49	

Year	v13c6iv	v13c7	v13c7i	v13c7ii	v13c7iii	v13c7iv	v13c8	v13c8i	v13c8ii	v13c8iii	v13c8iv	v13c9	v13c9i	v13c9ii
1952														
1953														
1954														
1955														
1956														
1957														
1958														
1959														
1960														
1961														
1962														
1963														
1964														
1965														
1966														
1967														
1968														
1969														
1970														
1971														
1972														
1973														
1974														
1975														
1976														
1977														
1978		0.93	0.73	0.20			1.06	0.99	0.07			0.82	0.74	0.08
1979		1.04	0.81	0.23			1.03	0.94	0.09			0.99	0.89	0.10
1980		1.86	1.62	0.24			1.19	1.09	0.10			1.18	1.07	0.11
1981		1.88	1.61	0.27			1.15	1.03	0.12			1.20	1.07	0.13
1982		1.87	1.61	0.26			1.27	1.14	0.13			1.16	1.05	0.11
1983		2.07	1.83	0.24			1.23	1.10	0.13			1.41	1.26	0.15
1984		2.95	2.48	0.47			1.26	1.11	0.15			1.88	1.70	0.18
1985		3.50	2.90	0.60			1.44	1.26	0.18			2.32	2.12	0.20
1986		3.55	2.87	0.68			1.33	1.14	0.19			2.76	2.52	0.24
1987		3.94	3.22	0.72			1.54	1.34	0.20			3.14	2.35	0.29
1988		4.45	3.46	0.99			2.38	2.16	0.22			3.29	2.95	0.34
1989		4.50	3.50	1.00			2.57	2.32	0.25			3.35	2.96	0.39
1990		5.31	4.30	1.01			3.11	2.84	0.27			6.53	6.00	0.53
1991		7.07	5.56	1.51			4.47	4.17	0.30			8.45	7.34	0.61
1992		8.31	6.28	2.03			5.58	5.17	0.41			10.46	9.67	0.79
1993		9.52	6.64	2.88			6.06	5.51	0.55			10.87	9.86	1.01
1994		10.42	7.27	3.15			7.55	6.80	0.75			11.30	10.25	1.05
1995		11.32	7.89	3.43			8.79	7.93	0.86			12.53	11.37	1.16

Year	v13c9iii	v13c9iv	v13c10	v13c10i	v13c10ii	v13c10iii	v13c10iv
1952							
1953							
1954							
1955							
1956							
1957							
1958							
1959							
1960							
1961							
1962							
1963							
1964							
1965							
1966							
1967							
1968							
1969							
1970							
1971							
1972							
1973							
1974							
1975							
1976							
1977							
1978							
1979							
1980							
1981							
1982							
1983							
1984							
1985							
1986							
1987							
1988							
1989							
1990			2.54	2.05	0.49		
1991			2.56	2.04	0.52		
1992			3.27	2.74	0.53		
1993			3.43	2.92	0.51		
1994			4.16	3.54	0.62		
1995			4.76	4.06	0.70		

28

Qinghai

Year	v1	v1a	v1b	v1b1	v1b2	v1c	v1c1	v1c2	v1c3	v2	v2a	v2b	v2b1	v2b2	v2c
1952	2.39	1.61	0.32	0.26	0.06	0.46	0.05	0.28	0.13						
1953	2.85	1.68	0.55	0.35	0.20	0.62	0.10	0.29	0.23	113.9	97.6	155.3	129.8	218.4	148.7
1954	3.56	2.21	0.67	0.47	0.20	0.68	0.12	0.28	0.28	124.1	129.1	119.2	133.1	98.9	112.7
1955	4.62	2.43	1.23	0.71	0.52	0.96	0.23	0.36	0.37	132.2	110.4	182.4	141.4	263.2	150.0
1956	7.20	2.50	3.28	1.16	2.12	1.42	0.37	0.50	0.55	165.6	105.6	275.2	152.1	405.7	166.7
1957	6.96	2.80	2.50	1.27	1.23	1.66	0.46	0.54	0.66	91.3	100.3	71.0	104.0	57.8	122.6
1958	9.68	2.35	4.88	1.77	3.11	2.45	0.48	0.96	1.01	140.9	79.3	208.1	151.6	248.5	133.7
1959	15.14	2.41	9.57	4.96	4.61	3.16	0.64	1.20	1.32	156.2	101.0	183.6	277.8	142.5	143.3
1960	16.40	2.34	9.88	6.57	3.31	4.18	0.94	1.25	1.99	107.6	92.2	101.4	133.3	74.3	131.9
1961	9.68	2.64	3.75	3.17	0.58	3.29	0.74	1.10	1.45	54.7	96.7	38.0	45.9	25.9	72.1
1962	7.36	2.71	2.12	1.91	0.21	2.53	0.50	0.99	1.04	72.2	114.8	57.6	58.0	56.5	67.0
1963	7.66	3.29	2.25	1.88	0.37	2.12	0.34	0.88	0.90	108.9	126.3	118.9	98.7	175.1	82.4
1964	8.65	3.85	2.61	1.97	0.64	2.19	0.40	0.79	1.00	119.0	110.5	133.5	107.1	175.0	112.0
1965	9.93	4.16	3.41	2.42	0.99	2.36	0.56	0.74	1.06	109.5	111.0	103.8	129.2	137.6	115.9
1966	11.30	4.09	4.55	3.01	1.54	2.66	0.65	0.87	1.14	135.4	98.0	184.1	129.7	155.2	114.9
1967	11.75	4.56	4.42	3.11	1.31	2.77	0.67	0.94	1.16	99.1	109.3	92.5	104.6	83.4	102.8
1968	11.38	3.94	4.52	3.08	1.45	2.92	0.67	1.07	1.18	99.3	86.3	104.9	99.1	109.8	103.4
1969	13.03	4.37	5.54	3.48	2.06	3.12	0.77	1.05	1.30	121.4	113.5	131.9	119.6	142.3	106.9
1970	14.96	4.37	7.28	4.74	2.54	3.31	0.85	1.09	1.37	118.6	100.0	131.3	142.3	123.4	105.6
1971	18.20	4.66	9.69	7.23	2.46	3.85	0.95	1.30	1.60	112.2	102.2	114.3	131.9	99.7	115.5
1972	19.51	5.27	10.06	7.16	2.90	4.18	0.94	1.41	1.83	110.5	114.4	110.7	111.7	109.6	106.3
1973	19.74	5.30	11.02	8.51	2.51	3.42	0.97	1.42	1.03	105.0	107.8	104.5	119.4	87.9	104.3
1974	21.58	5.68	11.25	8.83	2.42	4.65	0.96	1.43	2.26	102.0	102.9	101.8	104.5	97.6	102.0
1975	23.96	5.63	13.35	10.16	3.19	4.98	0.95	1.55	2.48	114.4	99.1	121.9	115.7	132.1	104.7
1976	24.19	5.71	13.29	9.96	3.33	5.19	0.89	1.56	2.74	101.8	106.7	100.8	98.3	104.2	101.3
1977	26.70	5.71	15.35	11.34	4.01	5.64	0.96	1.69	2.99	112.7	99.9	117.4	114.9	120.7	107.8
1978	32.06	5.99	19.54	13.56	5.98	6.53	1.19	1.89	3.45	123.3	99.4	125.8	116.3	147.0	117.8
1979	34.72	6.52	21.31	13.73	7.58	6.89	1.33	1.98	3.58	109.4	96.0	113.2	99.8	126.6	102.2
1980	37.18	7.77	21.51	14.33	7.18	7.90	1.30	2.12	4.48	99.8	111.0	96.0	97.5	94.7	111.4
1981	34.75	7.30	18.85	12.25	6.60	8.60	1.12	2.37	5.11	91.8	93.1	89.1	85.5	92.0	102.6
1982	37.84	8.36	22.71	14.73	7.98	6.77	1.34	2.64	2.79	117.5	107.8	120.1	119.0	120.8	113.9
1983	43.34	8.67	24.14	15.37	8.77	10.53	1.80	3.00	5.73	108.3	102.5	106.3	101.4	109.9	119.6
1984	50.22	10.48	27.55	17.92	9.63	12.19	2.53	3.47	6.19	112.6	108.9	111.6	114.2	109.8	117.8
1985	62.18	12.25	35.27	22.65	12.62	14.66	3.10	4.34	7.22	106.9	111.1	106.8	119.7	97.5	105.3
1986	71.17	14.11	39.49	26.79	12.70	17.57	2.96	5.20	9.41	102.7	104.7	101.6	111.3	93.0	105.5
1987	81.13	15.94	45.11	31.30	13.81	20.08	3.32	5.97	10.79	106.8	103.9	106.5	113.0	99.7	109.3
1988	101.76	19.49	59.08	42.51	16.57	23.19	3.68	7.46	12.05	109.2	100.3	112.3	120.6	102.4	103.4
1989	123.31	21.60	68.76	54.18	14.58	32.95	4.59	7.93	20.43	95.7	102.4	96.3	108.1	79.8	93.7
1990	144.62	24.53	71.29	55.25	16.04	48.80	9.12	14.00	25.68	116.5	104.9	102.1	103.2	100.0	173.2
1991	155.73	25.24	78.08	60.51	17.57	52.41	10.32	16.96	25.13	108.0	102.3	100.0	105.7	88.7	126.2
1992	183.24	27.26	95.07	68.22	26.85	60.91	12.61	18.83	29.47	113.6	104.1	113.7	105.3	133.5	115.7
1993	235.22	31.00	127.03	94.09	32.94	77.19	14.55	21.51	41.13	106.7	100.2	109.9	113.5	102.6	107.0
1994	295.98	44.87	157.71	127.06	30.65	93.40	15.78	26.11	51.51	108.0	103.6	107.8	112.7	88.8	110.1
1995	356.18	55.10	184.58	149.46	35.12	116.50	19.21	31.11	66.18	108.1	99.8	109.3	109.0	110.4	109.8

Year	v2c1	v2c2	v3'	v3	v3a	v3b	v3b1	v3b2	v3c	v3c1	v3c2	v3c3	v3c4	v3c5	v3c6
1952			1.63	1.63	1.20	0.12	0.10	0.02	0.31	0.02	0.21				
1953	194.9	106.5	1.74	1.74	1.24	0.20	0.13	0.07	0.30	0.04	0.23				
1954	125.7	96.9	2.35	2.35	1.67	0.24	0.18	0.06	0.44	0.05	0.22				
1955	190.3	120.1	2.93	2.93	1.84	0.51	0.34	0.17	0.58	0.09	0.27				
1956	193.5	141.3	3.81	3.81	1.90	1.00	0.38	0.62	0.91	0.14	0.37				
1957	123.3	120.3	3.95	3.95	2.13	0.78	0.40	0.38	1.04	0.17	0.42				
1958	104.5	185.2	4.87	4.87	1.90	1.59	0.69	0.90	1.38	0.16	0.67				
1959	132.5	135.5	6.94	6.94	1.93	3.03	1.80	1.23	1.98	0.20	0.80				
1960	128.0	109.2	7.68	7.68	1.89	3.22	2.29	0.93	2.57	0.26	0.84				
1961	75.5	87.0	5.40	5.40	2.12	1.24	1.12	0.12	2.04	0.21	0.78				
1962	69.3	61.8	4.59	4.59	2.17	0.82	0.73	0.09	1.60	0.15	0.69				
1963	71.3	91.5	4.86	4.86	2.66	0.85	0.72	0.13	1.35	0.11	0.63				
1964	115.6	104.5	5.57	5.57	3.12	1.04	0.82	0.22	1.41	0.14	0.58				
1965	141.2	102.7	6.14	6.14	3.36	1.28	0.96	0.32	1.50	0.21	0.57				
1966	116.4	122.8	6.42	6.42	3.12	1.64	1.18	0.46	1.66	0.24	0.66				
1967	103.6	108.6	6.95	6.95	3.65	1.57	1.19	0.38	1.73	0.23	0.70				
1968	99.4	113.6	6.35	6.35	2.98	1.56	1.13	0.43	1.81	0.23	0.76				
1969	116.0	97.5	7.03	7.03	3.35	1.79	1.15	0.64	1.89	0.26	0.77				
1970	110.6	103.7	8.15	8.15	3.36	2.79	2.02	0.77	2.00	0.28	0.80				
1971	110.9	119.7	9.32	9.32	3.63	3.40	2.68	0.72	2.29	0.30	0.97				
1972	98.7	109.2	10.34	10.34	4.11	3.71	2.81	0.90	2.52	0.32	1.06				
1973	103.8	99.9	11.08	11.08	4.35	4.11	3.23	0.78	2.62	0.33	1.04				
1974	98.2	100.2	11.76	11.76	4.66	4.31	3.35	0.76	2.79	0.35	1.07				
1975	99.4	108.3	12.42	12.42	4.64	4.76	3.78	0.98	3.02	0.36	1.16				
1976	93.2	101.3	12.24	12.24	4.57	4.56	3.53	1.03	3.11	0.31	1.14				
1977	108.8	112.8	13.13	13.13	3.84	5.88	4.65	1.23	3.41	0.39	1.25				
1978	124.4	117.3	15.54	15.54	3.67	7.71	5.57	2.14	4.16	0.67	1.29	0.42	0.23	0.06	0.64
1979	111.5	97.8	15.19	15.19	3.97	7.44	5.40	2.04	3.78	0.49	1.32	0.28	0.22	0.06	0.33
1980	97.5	106.4	17.79	17.79	5.00	7.83	5.67	2.16	4.96	0.67	1.51	0.45	0.25	0.15	0.23
1981	86.3	107.9	17.49	17.49	4.63	7.23	5.21	2.02	5.63	0.54	1.90	0.52	0.25	0.15	0.28
1982	119.7	109.6	19.95	19.95	5.56	8.03	5.62	2.41	6.36	0.67	1.99	0.62	0.25	0.20	0.32
1983	134.7	111.3	22.45	22.45	5.90	8.98	6.38	2.60	7.57	0.93	2.33	0.73	0.25	0.22	0.39
1984	140.2	113.0	26.42	26.42	7.35	10.15	7.19	2.96	8.92	1.50	2.53	1.09	0.20	0.28	0.43
1985	97.1	112.5	33.01	33.01	8.64	13.39	8.90	4.49	10.98	1.79	2.93	1.68	0.21	0.76	0.45
1986	93.3	110.8	38.44	38.44	10.47	15.40	11.06	4.34	12.57	1.60	3.74	1.73	0.37	0.96	0.50
1987	104.8	109.5	43.38	43.38	11.74	16.61	12.09	4.52	15.03	1.47	4.24	2.67	0.38	1.22	0.57
1988	105.3	104.8	54.96	54.96	14.36	23.30	17.33	5.97	17.30	1.76	4.90	2.70	0.40	1.32	0.75
1989	118.2	92.6	60.37	60.37	15.73	25.29	20.07	5.22	19.35	1.93	4.53	4.24	0.50	0.88	0.91
1990	103.9	147.4	69.94	69.94	17.67	26.89	21.23	5.66	25.38	4.10	7.06	4.35	0.43	0.91	0.85
1991	98.3	121.1	75.10	75.10	17.96	29.84	23.49	6.35	27.30	4.48	7.27	5.26	0.41	0.91	0.85
1992	104.2	111.0	87.52	87.52	19.44	36.31	26.69	9.62	31.77	5.72	8.44	5.83	0.49	1.01	0.99
1993	115.3	114.3	109.62	109.62	21.61	48.39	36.77	11.62	39.62	6.47	10.32	8.22	0.72	1.09	1.18
1994	104.8	98.0	138.24	138.24	31.71	58.35	46.38	11.97	48.18	7.02	12.55	10.69	0.98	1.31	1.49
1995	106.9	101.7	165.31	165.31	38.79	65.54	52.05	13.49	60.98	8.97	14.74	14.37	1.32	1.68	1.94

Year	v3c7	v3c8	v3c9	v3c10	v3d	v4'	v4	v4a	v4b	v4b1	v4b2	v4c	v4c1	v4c2	v4c3
1952				0.08	101										
1953				0.03	106	101.8	101.8	96.8	166.7	130.0	350.0	96.8	200.0	109.5	
1954				0.17	138	133.9	133.9	133.1	120.0	138.5	85.7	146.7	125.0	95.6	
1955				0.22	164	124.0	124.0	110.6	200.0	172.2	283.3	131.8	180.0	122.7	
1956				0.40	199	131.7	131.7	105.6	197.9	106.5	364.7	156.9	155.6	137.0	
1957				0.45	193	97.3	97.3	100.5	74.7	100.0	61.3	114.3	121.4	113.5	
1958				0.55	225	121.3	121.3	84.5	212.0	186.5	236.8	133.0	94.1	166.7	
1959				0.98	284	142.3	142.3	99.4	127.7	260.9	136.7	144.0	125.0	118.6	
1960				1.47	30	109.6	109.6	93.5	159.6	128.3	75.6	129.1	130.0	104.8	
1961				1.05	233	63.6	63.6	95.9	36.7	46.3	12.9	75.6	80.8	80.5	
1962				0.76	218	87.1	87.1	114.5	63.9	75.0	75.0	78.3	71.4	90.0	
1963				0.61	232	109.1	109.1	127.5	105.3	100.0	144.4	88.4	73.3	101.6	
1964				0.69	257	112.2	112.2	110.8	125.0	116.4	169.2	107.3	127.3	98.4	
1965				0.72	271	112.5	112.5	110.5	127.0	121.8	145.5	106.1	150.0	98.4	
1966				0.76	270	107.1	107.1	92.9	133.1	129.5	143.8	112.8	114.3	119.4	
1967				0.80	281	106.8	106.8	114.6	96.4	101.6	82.6	104.5	95.8	106.8	
1968				0.82	246	92.9	92.9	81.8	99.4	95.2	113.2	106.0	100.0	111.4	
1969				0.86	262	112.4	112.4	114.4	118.5	108.4	148.8	104.6	113.0	102.3	
1970				0.92	303	119.6	119.6	100.3	162.5	183.6	120.3	106.9	107.7	106.7	
1971				1.02	320	105.8	105.8	102.8	106.5	106.8	93.5	105.5	107.1	101.0	
1972				1.14	341	115.5	115.5	114.5	119.5	117.8	125.0	110.8	106.7	109.3	
1973				1.25	352	109.2	109.2	113.3	108.8	115.8	86.7	103.5	103.1	99.1	
1974				1.37	361	103.8	103.8	103.0	102.9	104.3	97.4	106.4	106.1	102.9	
1975				1.50	371	107.8	107.8	99.8	116.2	113.4	129.0	108.1	102.9	108.3	
1976				1.66	356	100.3	100.3	81.0	95.9	93.6	105.1	102.9	86.1	97.4	
1977				1.77	371	107.7	107.7	107.2	130.0	133.0	119.4	109.5	125.8	108.8	
1978		0.50	0.35		428	114.9	114.9	96.9	128.1	116.3	174.0	122.6	171.8	100.8	
1979	0.49	0.30	0.29		410	90.9	90.9	106.1	81.6	76.4	95.3	80.7	71.6	98.5	65.1
1980	0.46	0.81	0.43	0.00	473	117.8	117.8	97.7	123.2	131.4	105.9	129.9	135.4	113.2	153.6
1981	0.55	0.94	0.50		459	98.6	98.6	94.8	92.5	92.4	93.5	122.2	80.6	117.4	113.3
1982	0.65	1.09	0.57		513	111.8	111.8	113.3	110.3	105.8	119.3	112.5	124.1	104.2	119.6
1983	0.77	1.29	0.66		569	110.4	110.4	106.8	109.1	110.8	107.9	115.9	134.3	114.2	114.8
1984	1.14	0.88	0.85	0.02	662	113.6	113.6	114.0	111.6	110.6	113.9	115.6	157.8	106.2	147.1
1985	1.18	1.04	0.94		808	110.8	110.8	108.1	115.2	118.8	107.1	107.9	104.2	101.7	135.0
1986	1.34	1.19	1.14		916	108.1	108.1	109.3	107.5	109.8	101.6	107.9	84.5	120.2	97.1
1987	1.47	1.58	1.39	0.04	1018	105.7	105.7	103.1	103.0	108.3	88.5	111.1	85.6	105.5	143.7
1988	1.93	1.76	1.72	0.06	1260	107.7	107.7	99.4	123.1	126.2	112.6	96.6	100.0	97.1	85.1
1989	2.17	2.11	1.99	0.09	1365	101.2	101.2	102.6	99.7	105.8	78.5	102.3	100.9	84.6	143.0
1990	2.46	1.45	3.21	0.56	1558	103.7	103.7	104.2	102.2	100.5	109.1	105.5	107.4	106.0	103.8
1991	2.53	1.52	3.37	0.70	1647	104.7	104.7	101.0	104.3	105.6	98.7	108.0	105.8	102.6	126.9
1992	2.93	1.69	4.02	0.66	1890	107.4	107.4	104.0	107.6	105.6	117.0	109.6	123.3	109.7	104.6
1993	3.49	2.24	5.26	0.63	2337	109.6	109.6	99.3	113.8	115.4	112.0	112.0	105.8	108.7	125.7
1994	4.20	2.66	6.53	0.75	2910	108.2	108.2	103.6	108.2	110.6	98.3	110.9	103.6	98.1	122.6
1995	5.63	3.46	7.92	0.95	3430	108.0	108.0	99.5	109.4	109.5	108.5	111.4	108.1	101.5	116.8

Year	v4c4	v4c5	v4c6	v4c7	v4c8	v4c9	v4c10	v5	v5a	v5a1	v5a1a	v5a1b	v5a2	v5b	v5b1
1952								1.63	1.13	1.03	0.75	0.28	0.10	0.70	0.33
1953								1.74	1.41	1.22	0.80	0.42	0.19	0.84	0.43
1954								2.35	1.77	1.54	1.00	0.54	0.23	1.46	0.74
1955								2.93	2.11	1.80	1.08	0.72	0.31	2.09	1.20
1956								3.81	3.15	2.67	1.23	1.44	0.48	4.75	3.70
1957								3.95	3.68	3.12	1.36	1.76	0.56	3.07	2.12
1958								4.87	4.05	3.31	1.16	2.15	0.74	1.86	1.72
1959								6.94	5.97	4.16	1.40	2.76	1.81	6.18	6.11
1960								7.68	6.79	4.64	1.11	3.53	2.15	6.70	5.37
1961								5.40	4.56	3.81	1.21	2.60	0.75	0.89	1.19
1962								4.59	4.49	3.79	1.50	2.29	0.70	0.14	0.60
1963								4.83	4.44	3.77	1.79	1.98	0.67	0.62	0.65
1964								5.57	4.69	3.95	1.97	1.98	0.74	1.17	0.96
1965								6.55	4.93	4.19	1.99	2.20	0.74	1.90	1.49
1966								6.42	5.16	4.34	1.98	2.36	0.82	3.40	2.60
1967								6.95	5.58	4.93	2.28	2.65	0.65	1.96	1.72
1968								6.35	4.43	3.91	1.21	2.70	0.52	2.35	1.67
1969								7.03	6.71	6.12	3.18	2.94	0.59	3.30	2.70
1970								8.45	5.70	5.05	1.97	3.08	0.65	3.42	3.32
1971								9.32	6.60	5.74	2.43	3.31	0.86	4.31	3.07
1972								10.34	7.05	6.08	2.44	3.64	0.97	9.44	6.37
1973								11.08	7.49	6.27	2.44	3.83	1.22	5.44	2.92
1974								11.76	8.65	7.25	2.58	4.67	1.40	3.53	3.72
1975								12.32	8.93	7.72	3.00	4.72	1.21	4.77	3.58
1976								12.43	9.38	8.08	3.14	4.94	1.30	4.43	3.95
1977								13.13	9.81	8.49	3.12	5.37	1.32	6.58	5.91
1978								15.54	11.37	9.33	3.80	5.53	2.04	9.38	8.90
1979	95.7		160.0		58.8	77.8		15.19	12.20	9.55	3.67	5.88	2.65	11.92	11.15
1980	109.1	233.3	71.9	97.8	260.0	146.4		17.79	13.63	11.58	4.48	7.10	2.05	8.89	7.65
1981	138.9		121.7	104.6	114.8	116.3		17.49	14.41	12.13	4.56	7.57	2.28	7.35	6.58
1982		133.3	114.3	116.4	116.1	112.0		19.95	15.75	13.29	5.36	7.93	2.46	10.70	10.20
1983		105.0	118.8	114.1	115.7	112.5		22.45	17.80	14.64	6.18	8.46	3.16	10.08	9.97
1984	80.0	123.8	107.9	148.0	66.4	127.0		26.42	20.83	16.59	6.67	9.92	4.24	12.39	10.37
1985		234.6	90.2	89.8	103.6			33.01	24.89	20.03	8.75	11.28	4.86	21.40	15.59
1986	140.0	123.0	105.4	111.3	107.0	112.5		38.44	29.20	23.08	9.36	13.72	6.12	19.58	15.30
1987	100.0	118.7	105.1		123.9	113.5		43.38	32.25	26.15	10.30	15.85	6.10	27.25	18.76
1988	85.7	89.9	112.2	109.3	93.9	104.0	200.0	54.96	36.90	29.66	12.83	16.83	7.24	30.12	21.34
1989	116.7	62.5	108.7	102.5	110.3	104.8	125.0	60.37	42.43	34.74	16.27	18.47	7.69	25.08	16.23
1990	71.4	107.3	102.0		84.8	109.1	60.0	69.94	53.79	36.44	17.68	18.76	17.35	28.60	20.44
1991	107.5	98.9	106.4	107.4	102.1	105.1	106.8	75.10	60.76	40.37	19.29	21.08	20.39	33.36	23.91
1992	111.6	107.3	109.6	109.4	105.5	113.0	70.8	87.52	65.18	46.94	22.07	24.87	18.24	38.03	29.04
1993	127.1	103.4	105.5	106.7	118.2	111.8	106.3	109.62	72.80	54.30	25.03	29.27	18.50	51.49	41.03
1994	126.2	112.2	117.7	113.6	117.1	119.9	112.0	138.25	92.17	68.66	29.80	38.86	23.51	60.10	47.76
1995	120.8	113.9	113.3	117.8	114.6	115.4	110.7	165.81	112.24	81.41	33.72	47.69	30.83	77.67	57.48

Year	v5b2	v5c	v5c1	v5c2	v6a1	v6a2	v6a3	v6a4	v6b2	v6b3	v6b4	v7	v7a	v7a1	v7a2
1952	0.37	-0.20		0.20											
1953	0.41	-0.51		0.51								86.4	79.9	105.6	54.1
1954	0.72	-0.88		0.88								110.5	126.1	125.3	127.5
1955	0.89	-1.27		1.27								135.4	117.2	108.5	133.3
1956	1.05	-4.09		4.09								149.8	148.8	113.7	201.5
1957	0.95	-2.80		2.80								116.4	116.6	110.3	121.9
1958	0.14	-1.04		1.04								111.5	107.1	85.9	123.4
1959	0.07	-5.21	1.33	6.54								147.3	125.6	120.9	128.2
1960	1.33	-5.81	2.12	7.93								113.9	111.6	79.0	128.0
1961	-0.30	-0.05	0.84	0.89								52.4	60.5	109.5	45.3
1962	-0.46	-0.04	0.55	0.59								117.6	118.9	123.5	124.8
1963	-0.03	-0.23	3.60	0.83								106.0	108.1	119.7	99.5
1964	0.21	-0.29	0.76	1.05								105.7	104.7	110.0	100.5
1965	0.41	-0.28	0.71	0.99								104.9	105.8	100.5	111.1
1966	0.80	-2.14	0.89	3.03								104.7	103.5	99.5	107.1
1967	0.24	-0.59	0.87	1.46								108.1	113.8	115.5	112.4
1968	0.68	-0.43	1.18	1.61								79.7	79.6	53.2	102.0
1969	0.60	-2.98	0.95	3.93								149.8	154.6	257.4	108.9
1970	0.10	-0.67	0.75	1.42								85.7	83.4	63.2	104.6
1971	1.24	-1.59	0.88	2.47								118.0	116.0	125.7	109.8
1972	3.07	-6.15	0.99	7.14								106.9	105.9	100.4	110.0
1973	2.52	-1.85	1.26	3.11								94.7	95.6	100.0	92.7
1974	-0.09	-0.52	1.33	1.85								123.0	124.7	105.5	138.5
1975	1.19	-1.38	1.75	3.13								103.2	106.4	116.5	100.9
1976	0.48	-1.38	1.63	3.01								105.0	104.7	104.5	104.8
1977	0.77	-3.36	1.99	5.35								104.7	105.2	99.7	108.7
1978	0.98	-5.71	2.32	8.03	1.25	2.20	0.15	0.20	4.97	0.43	0.13	115.8	109.8	121.5	103.1
1979	0.77	-8.93	2.10	11.03	1.20	2.13	0.15	0.19	5.28	0.47	0.13	107.8	102.4	96.7	106.3
1980	1.24	-4.73	2.39	7.12	1.47	2.60	0.18	0.23	6.38	0.56	0.16	111.1	121.2	122.0	120.7
1981	0.77	-4.27	2.15	6.42	1.50	2.64	0.18	0.24	6.79	0.60	0.18	104.5	103.1	99.8	105.2
1982	0.50	-6.50	2.48	8.98	1.76	3.11	0.21	0.28	7.13	0.62	0.18	107.9	107.9	116.7	102.7
1983	0.11	-5.43	1.26	6.69	2.03	3.58	0.25	0.32	7.60	0.67	0.19	112.4	109.1	113.7	106.0
1984	2.02	-6.80	1.37	8.18	2.19	3.87	0.26	0.35	8.92	0.78	0.22	114.3	110.2	105.4	113.7
1985	5.81	-13.28	3.12	16.40	2.87	5.07	0.35	0.46	10.13	0.89	0.26	118.6	121.6	136.4	111.6
1986	4.28	-10.34	3.20	13.54	3.07	5.43	0.37	0.49	12.32	1.08	0.32	120.8	118.7	107.5	127.8
1987	8.49	-16.12	4.31	20.43	3.38	5.97	0.41	0.54	14.23	1.25	0.37	110.0	112.6	110.5	114.0
1988	8.78	-12.06	4.89	7.17	4.21	7.44	0.51	0.67	14.82	1.57	0.44	103.8	103.1	112.8	96.6
1989	8.85	-7.14	3.85	10.99	4.62	10.41	0.54	0.70	16.35	1.66	0.46	114.7	117.0	125.0	110.9
1990	8.16	-12.45	16.26	28.71	5.66	10.43	0.68	0.91	16.57	1.70	0.49	116.5	104.6	119.1	101.9
1991	9.45	-19.02	19.51	38.53	5.83	11.08	0.82	0.96	18.83	1.70	0.55	106.8	106.0	104.8	107.2
1992	8.99	-15.69	18.09	33.78	6.86	13.12	0.88	1.21	22.54	1.75	0.58	100.1	107.7	111.4	107.7
1993	10.46	-14.67	18.57	33.24	9.09	13.75	0.91	1.28	25.98	2.68	0.61	102.3	105.5	104.5	106.6
1994	12.34	-14.02	20.54	34.56	10.30	16.67	1.00	1.83	32.72	5.10	1.04	106.4	103.3	98.4	107.8
1995	20.19	-24.10	30.04	54.14	11.32	18.35	1.39	2.66	39.48	6.57	1.64	101.8	100.5	98.0	102.5

Year	v7b	v8	v8a	v8b	v9	v9a	v9b	v10a1	v10a2	v10a3	v10a3a	v10a3b	v10a4	v10b1	v10b2
1952		94	52	426											
1953	200.0	74	55	221	78.2	104.5	52.1								
1954	121.1	90	67	260	121.8	121.9	116.5								
1955	134.8	101	70	306	112.1	104.9	118.0								
1956	155.2	139	77	468	138.5	109.4	153.7								
1957	115.6	153	82	450	109.5	107.5	96.0								
1958	136.5	153	71	404	100.9	86.7	90.7								
1959	243.7	170	82	376	111.4	115.6	93.0								
1960	119.1	181	64	433	106.4	77.4	115.2								
1961	35.0	164	74	385	66.8	116.3	54.7								
1962	93.1	180	92	480	137.1	125.0	176.6								
1963	95.5	180	107	477	108.6	115.9	114.3								
1964	110.9	182	114	449	101.2	107.0	94.1								
1965	100.0	185	111	459	101.0	96.9	102.3								
1966	111.3	183	106	463	98.9	95.9	100.6								
1967	78.5	199	118	496	108.7	111.0	107.4								
1968	80.7	152	60	482	76.5	51.2	97.2								
1969	114.0	228	149	497	148.3	248.2	103.0								
1970	108.8	181	90	506	80.1	60.5	101.7								
1971	133.9	197	108	507	111.2	121.6	102.4								
1972	113.3	201	105	509	101.7	97.8	100.3								
1973	125.3	199	102	505	92.2	97.2	87.3								
1974	114.4	223	105	590	120.6	102.2	132.7								
1975	86.7	230	118	581	103.3	113.0	98.4								
1976	106.8	235	121	592	102.0	101.8	102.0								
1977	101.6	240	117	621	102.4	97.3	104.8								
1978	155.1	257	139	622	107.0	118.5	100.3								
1979	132.5	258	132	639	100.3	95.2	102.7								
1980	76.6	308	160	737	119.2	121.3	115.2								
1981	112.5	318	162	765	101.8	99.0	102.4								
1982	107.6	342	185	794	105.7	113.8	101.8								
1983	129.8	371	211	838	107.6	112.1	104.8								
1984	131.9	416	227	940	109.0	105.4	108.9								
1985	107.7	493	299	911	119.3	136.8	103.5								
1986	129.4	550	314	1131	114.9	105.4	119.9								
1987	100.4	613	342	1264	110.8	109.5	110.3								
1988	106.9	685	420	1322	97.5	111.0	95.2								
1989	105.0	791	524	1437	120.2	122.9	109.9								
1990	117.5	812	558	1421	120.7	126.5	115.9								
1991	111.4	885	595	1597	103.0	102.5	104.4								
1992	86.5	1014	699	1870	105.4	104.4	106.9								
1993	94.4	1158	749	2168	104.1	103.2	105.0								
1994	115.0	1445	879	2857	102.0	96.9	107.0	41.02	2.47	3.49	0.43	3.06	0.78	2.19	1.53
1995	105.2	1689	983	3431	98.9	96.8	100.3	44.66	5.41	6.67	2.93	3.74	0.74	14.43	1.70

Year	v10b4	v11a	v11a1	v11a2	v11b	v11b1	v11b2	v11c	v11c1	v11c2	v12	v12a	v12b	v13	v13i
1952															
1953											120.0	130.3	111.6		
1954											173.8	172.1	175.5		
1955											143.5	162.2	123.7		
1956											227.3	308.3	117.8		
1957											64.4	57.3	89.7		
1958											60.1	81.1	12.8		
1959											335.3	355.2	12.9		
1960											106.0	87.9	24.9		
1961											13.6	22.2			
1962											28.1	50.4			
1963											247.8	108.3			
1964											185.5	147.7	633.3		
1965											160.9	155.2	199.5		
1966											178.9	174.5	175.1		
1967											58.3	66.2	28.6		
1968											117.6	97.1	349.3		
1969											142.3	161.7	85.8		
1970											105.6	123.0	16.6		
1971											126.1	92.5	1503.8		
1972											218.8	207.5	253.3		
1973											57.5	45.8	81.6		
1974											48.6	67.1			
1975											181.0	131.1			
1976											92.9	110.3	39.8		
1977											150.9	149.6	161.8		
1978		1.30	1.22	0.08	5.52	4.98	0.54	3.06	2.70	0.36	148.0	150.6	127.6	15.54	9.53
1979		1.51	1.44	0.07	6.73	6.13	0.60	3.68	3.58	0.10	120.7	125.3	78.4	15.19	9.57
1980		1.09	0.99	0.10	5.18	4.21	0.97	2.62	2.45	0.17	74.6	68.6	161.8	17.79	11.31
1981		0.92	0.86	0.06	4.22	3.62	0.60	2.21	2.10	0.11	80.7	83.8	61.8	17.49	10.98
1982		1.37	1.33	0.04	5.99	5.61	0.38	3.34	3.26	0.08	145.3	154.9	64.5	19.95	12.75
1983		1.31	1.30	0.01	5.52	5.48	0.04	3.25	3.19	0.06	94.2	79.7	20.4	22.45	14.20
1984		1.51	1.35	0.16	7.27	5.70	1.57	3.61	3.32	0.29	123.2	104.0	199.3	26.42	15.95
1985		2.48	2.03	0.45	11.10	8.57	2.53	7.82	4.99	2.83	170.5	147.3	198.9	33.01	20.19
1986		2.32	1.99	0.33	10.65	8.42	2.23	6.61	4.89	1.72	89.1	95.0	73.6	38.44	23.88
1987		3.08	2.43	0.65	14.93	10.31	4.62	9.24	6.02	3.22	139.3	121.6	198.0	43.38	27.01
1988		3.45	2.78	0.67	16.84	11.74	5.10	9.83	6.82	3.01	105.0	105.9	103.0	54.96	33.03
1989		2.79	2.11	0.68	15.83	8.93	6.90	6.46	5.19	1.27	88.0	81.4	100.9	60.37	36.08
1990		3.28	2.65	0.63	15.88	11.24	4.64	9.44	6.55	2.89	124.7	125.9	101.4	69.94	39.50
1991		3.71	3.11	0.60	19.34	13.15	6.19	10.31	7.65	2.66	107.0	98.3	116.3	75.10	43.75
1992		4.36	3.78	0.58	22.91	15.97	6.94	10.76	9.29	1.47	102.8	108.3	91.2	87.52	49.86
1993		4.80	5.30	-0.50	33.21	22.74	10.47	13.48	12.99	0.49	106.9	108.9	102.0	109.62	63.21
1994	8.62	13.85	4.72	9.13	22.48	25.15	-2.67	23.77	17.89	5.88	106.5	103.4	115.0	138.24	77.97
1995	4.06	8.22	3.85	4.37	42.64	34.71	7.93	26.81	18.92	7.89	112.8	114.2	109.2	165.31	94.79

Year	v13ii	v13iii	v13iv	v13a	v13ai	v13aii	v13aiii	v13aiv	v13b	v13bi	v13bii	v13biii	v13biv	v13b1	v13b1i
1952															
1953															
1954															
1955															
1956															
1957															
1958															
1959															
1960															
1961															
1962															
1963															
1964															
1965															
1966															
1967															
1968															
1969															
1970															
1971															
1972															
1973															
1974															
1975															
1976															
1977															
1978	1.52	1.76	2.73	3.67	3.23	0.17	0.17	0.10	7.71	4.15	0.70	1.40	1.46	5.57	2.19
1979	1.57	1.50	2.55	3.97	3.55	0.13	0.15	0.14	7.44	3.88	0.93	1.09	1.54	5.40	2.18
1980	1.90	1.87	2.71	5.00	4.51	0.19	0.15	0.15	7.83	4.13	0.95	1.23	1.52	5.67	2.61
1981	2.09	1.82	2.60	4.63	4.18	0.18	0.13	0.14	7.23	3.70	1.05	1.11	1.37	5.21	2.31
1982	2.33	1.85	3.02	5.56	5.01	0.21	0.16	0.18	8.03	4.18	1.16	1.19	1.50	5.62	2.49
1983	2.60	2.07	3.58	5.90	5.30	0.24	0.17	0.19	8.98	4.65	1.30	1.35	1.68	6.38	2.83
1984	3.01	2.32	5.14	7.35	6.30	0.30	0.16	0.59	10.15	4.95	1.28	1.43	2.49	7.19	3.22
1985	3.21	2.90	6.71	8.64	7.17	0.31	0.30	0.86	13.39	6.52	1.55	1.73	3.59	8.90	3.97
1986	4.17	4.10	6.29	10.47	8.96	0.52	0.26	0.73	15.40	7.42	2.01	2.58	3.39	11.06	4.19
1987	4.39	4.21	7.77	11.74	10.09	0.52	0.29	0.84	16.61	8.55	2.29	2.39	3.40	12.09	4.93
1988	5.53	5.94	10.45	14.36	12.80	0.50	0.14	0.92	23.20	10.70	3.02	4.02	5.56	17.33	6.17
1989	6.25	7.78	10.26	15.73	14.71	0.44	0.37	0.21	25.29	10.13	3.51	5.17	6.48	20.07	6.30
1990	9.86	8.48	12.10	17.67	16.47	0.49	0.48	0.23	26.89	11.63	4.42	6.03	4.81	21.23	7.39
1991	7.38	12.50	11.47	17.96	16.38	0.49	0.58	0.51	29.84	15.15	4.79	6.86	3.04	23.49	10.37
1992	14.32	10.87	12.47	19.44	17.82	0.53	0.51	0.58	36.31	17.06	7.63	7.88	3.74	26.59	10.30
1993	14.57	12.11	19.73	21.61	16.64	0.85	0.54	3.58	48.39	26.28	7.05	8.23	6.83	36.77	17.54
1994	19.37	14.19	26.71	31.71	23.27	1.22	0.66	6.56	58.35	30.45	10.75	10.22	6.93	46.38	21.42
1995	26.48	16.70	27.34	38.79	28.41	1.61	1.25	7.52	65.54	34.54	15.76	11.44	3.80	52.05	24.04

Year	v13b1ii	v13b1iii	v13b1iv	v13b2	v13b2i	v13b2ii	v13b2iii	v13b2iv	v13c	v13ci	v13cii	v13ciii	v13civ	v13c1
1952														
1953														
1954														
1955														
1956														
1957														
1958														
1959														
1960														
1961														
1962														
1963														
1964														
1965														
1966														
1967														
1968														
1969														
1970														
1971														
1972														
1973														
1974														
1975														
1976														
1977														
1978	0.56	1.40	1.42	2.14	1.96	0.14		0.04	4.16	2.15	0.65	0.19	1.17	0.67
1979	0.70	1.08	1.44	2.04	1.70	0.23	0.01	0.10	3.78	2.14	0.51	0.26	0.87	0.49
1980	0.73	1.22	1.11	2.16	1.52	0.22	0.01	0.41	4.96	2.67	0.76	0.49	1.04	0.67
1981	0.81	1.10	0.99	2.02	1.39	0.24	0.01	0.38	5.63	3.10	0.86	0.58	1.09	0.54
1982	0.90	1.18	1.05	2.41	1.69	0.26	0.01	0.45	6.36	3.56	0.96	0.50	1.34	0.67
1983	1.01	1.34	1.20	2.60	1.82	0.29	0.01	0.48	7.57	4.25	1.06	0.55	1.71	0.93
1984	1.02	1.42	1.53	2.96	1.73	0.26	0.01	0.96	8.92	4.70	1.43	0.73	2.06	1.50
1985	1.13	1.66	2.14	4.49	2.55	0.42	0.07	1.45	10.98	6.50	1.35	0.87	2.26	1.79
1986	1.47	2.46	2.94	4.34	3.23	0.54	0.12	0.45	12.57	7.50	1.64	1.26	2.17	1.60
1987	1.43	2.21	3.52	4.52	3.62	0.86	0.16	-0.12	15.03	8.37	1.58	1.55	3.53	1.47
1988	2.37	3.74	5.05	5.97	4.53	0.65	0.28	0.51	17.30	9.53	2.02	1.78	3.97	1.76
1989	2.85	4.82	6.14	5.22	3.83	0.70	0.35	0.34	19.35	11.24	2.30	2.24	3.57	1.93
1990	3.67	5.62	4.55	5.66	4.24	0.75	0.41	0.26	25.38	11.40	4.95	1.97	7.06	4.10
1991	4.15	6.36	2.61	6.35	4.78	0.64	0.50	0.43	27.30	12.22	5.06	2.10	7.92	4.48
1992	6.15	7.09	3.15	9.62	6.76	1.48	0.79	0.59	31.77	14.98	6.16	2.48	8.15	5.72
1993	5.45	7.23	6.55	11.62	8.74	1.60	1.00	0.28	39.62	20.29	6.67	3.34	9.32	6.47
1994	9.22	9.39	6.35	11.97	9.03	1.53	0.83	0.58	48.18	24.25	7.40	3.31	13.22	7.02
1995	14.18	10.54	3.29	13.49	10.50	1.58	0.90	0.51	60.98	31.84	9.11	14.01	16.02	8.97

Year	v13c1i	v13c1ii	v13c1iii	v13c1iv	v13c2	v13c2i	v13c2ii	v13c2iii	v13c2iv	v13c3	v13c3i	v13c3ii	v13c3iii	v13c3iv
1952														
1953														
1954														
1955														
1956														
1957														
1958														
1959														
1960														
1961														
1962														
1963														
1964														
1965														
1966														
1967														
1968														
1969														
1970														
1971														
1972														
1973														
1974														
1975														
1976														
1977														
1978	0.46	0.11	0.04	0.06	1.29	0.33	0.08	0.15	0.73	0.42	0.03	0.01		0.38
1979	0.27	0.13	0.08	0.01	1.32	0.42	0.10	0.18	0.62	0.28	0.03	0.01		0.24
1980	0.36	0.17	0.09	0.05	1.51	0.43	0.10	0.38	0.60	0.45	0.10	0.01		0.34
1981	0.26	0.19	0.02	0.07	1.90	0.67	0.12	0.54	0.57	0.52	0.11	0.01		0.40
1982	0.27	0.23	0.08	0.09	1.99	0.74	0.14	0.40	0.71	0.62	0.13	0.02		0.47
1983	0.42	0.27	0.12	0.12	2.33	0.82	0.14	0.40	0.97	0.73	0.15	0.02		0.56
1984	0.82	0.43	0.18	0.07	2.53	0.57	0.19	0.50	1.27	1.09	0.34	0.03	0.03	0.69
1985	0.81	0.47	0.26	0.25	2.93	1.34	0.22	0.50	0.87	1.68	0.53	0.04	0.07	1.04
1986	1.04	0.50	0.20	-0.14	3.74	1.39	0.24	0.92	1.19	1.73	0.56	0.06	0.08	1.03
1987	1.21	0.40	0.13	-0.27	4.24	0.74	0.27	1.09	2.14	2.67	0.77	0.06	0.26	1.58
1988	1.76	0.61	0.15	-0.76	4.90	0.89	0.30	1.38	2.33	2.70	0.93	0.08	0.19	1.50
1989	1.49	0.55	0.24	-0.35	4.53	0.95	0.32	1.56	1.70	4.24	1.81	0.11	0.34	1.98
1990	1.52	1.90	0.32	0.36	7.06	2.24	0.64	0.76	3.42	4.35	0.77	0.23	0.40	2.95
1991	1.69	1.93	0.35	0.51	7.27	2.58	0.68	0.80	3.21	5.26	0.80	0.24	0.42	3.80
1992	2.26	2.65	0.46	0.35	8.44	3.15	0.80	1.07	3.42	5.83	1.05	0.30	0.49	3.99
1993	3.44	2.87	0.41	-0.25	10.32	4.34	0.81	1.71	3.46	8.22	1.10	0.31	0.71	6.10
1994	3.72	2.85	0.49	-0.04	12.55	4.68	0.99	1.23	5.65	10.69	1.93	0.42	0.90	7.44
1995	5.76	3.70	0.58	-1.07	14.74	5.49	1.15	1.45	6.65	14.37	2.41	0.48	1.14	10.34

Year	v13c4	v13c4i	v13c4ii	v13c4iii	v13c4iv	v13c5	v13c5i	v13c5ii	v13c5iii	v13c5iv	v13c6	v13c6i	v13c6ii	v13c6iii
1952														
1953														
1954														
1955														
1956														
1957														
1958														
1959														
1960														
1961														
1962														
1963														
1964														
1965														
1966														
1967														
1968														
1969														
1970														
1971														
1972														
1973														
1974														
1975														
1976														
1977														
1978	0.23		0.23			0.06	0.05	0.01			0.64	0.55	0.09	
1979	0.22		0.22			0.06	0.05	0.01			0.33	0.32	0.01	
1980	0.25		0.24		0.01	0.15	0.08	0.01	0.02	0.04	0.23	0.21	0.02	
1981	0.25		0.24		0.01	0.15	0.07	0.02	0.02	0.04	0.28	0.26	0.02	
1982	0.25		0.24		0.01	0.20	0.10	0.02	0.02	0.06	0.32	0.30	0.02	
1983	0.25		0.24		0.01	0.22	0.10	0.03	0.03	0.06	0.39	0.36	0.03	
1984	0.20		0.20			0.28	0.17	0.06	0.02	0.03	0.43	0.40	0.03	
1985	0.21		0.20		0.01	0.76	0.59	0.04	0.04	0.09	0.45	0.42	0.03	
1986	0.37		0.35	0.01	0.01	0.96	0.79	0.05	0.05	0.07	0.50	0.44	0.05	
1987	0.38	0.01	0.36	0.01		1.22	1.05	0.05	0.05	0.07	0.57	0.52	0.04	
1988	0.40	0.01	0.38		0.01	1.32	0.29	0.10	0.06	0.87	0.75	0.68	0.05	
1989	0.50	0.01	0.43	0.05	0.01	0.88	0.52	0.13	0.05	0.18	0.91	0.78	0.07	
1990	0.43	0.02	0.39	0.01	0.01	0.91	0.43	0.22	0.09	0.17	0.85	0.70	0.15	
1991	0.41	0.03	0.35	0.01	0.01	0.91	0.45	0.22	0.09	0.15	0.85	0.71	0.15	-0.01
1992	0.49	0.07	0.39	0.02	0.01	1.01	0.57	0.24	0.10	0.10	0.99	0.84	0.15	
1993	0.72	0.09	0.60	0.02	0.01	1.09	0.90	0.28	0.13	-0.22	1.18	1.07	0.11	
1994	0.98	0.13	0.83	0.01	0.01	1.31	1.00	0.29	0.13	-0.11	1.49	1.34	0.15	
1995	1.32	0.16	1.04	0.06	0.06	1.68	1.30	0.32	0.15	-0.09	1.94	1.76	0.18	

Year	v13c6iv	v13c7	v13c7i	v13c7ii	v13c7iii	v13c7iv	v13c8	v13c8i	v13c8ii	v13c8iii	v13c8iv	v13c9	v13c9i	v13c9ii
1952														
1953														
1954														
1955														
1956														
1957														
1958														
1959														
1960														
1961														
1962														
1963														
1964														
1965														
1966														
1967														
1968														
1969														
1970														
1971														
1972														
1973														
1974														
1975														
1976														
1977														
1978							0.50	0.43	0.07			0.35	0.30	0.05
1979		0.49	0.48	0.01			0.30	0.29	0.01			0.30	0.29	0.01
1980		0.46	0.37	0.09			0.81	0.74	0.07			0.43	0.38	0.05
1981		0.55	0.44	0.11			0.94	0.85	0.09			0.50	0.44	0.06
1982		0.65	0.52	0.13			1.09	0.99	0.10			0.57	0.51	0.06
1983		0.77	0.61	0.16			1.29	1.19	0.10			0.66	0.60	0.06
1984		1.14	0.88	0.20			0.88	0.70	0.18			0.85	0.80	0.05
1985		1.18	1.00	0.18			1.04	0.93	0.11			0.94	0.88	0.06
1986	0.01	1.34	1.13	0.21			1.19	1.07	0.12			1.14	1.08	0.06
1987	0.01	1.47	1.26	0.21			1.58	1.45	0.13			1.39	1.32	0.07
1988	0.02	1.93	1.67	0.26			1.76	1.63	0.13			1.72	1.61	0.11
1989	0.05	2.17	1.81	0.36			2.11	1.95	0.16			1.99	1.83	0.16
1990		2.46	1.77	0.70	-0.01		1.45	1.10	0.27	0.03	0.05	3.21	2.79	0.42
1991		2.53	1.80	0.74	-0.02	0.01	1.52	1.16	0.28	0.03	0.05	3.37	2.94	0.43
1992		2.93	2.16	0.78	-0.01		1.69	1.29	0.32	0.03	0.05	4.02	3.50	0.49
1993		3.49	2.70	0.79	0.00	0.00	2.24	1.83	0.33	0.03	0.05	5.27	4.72	0.50
1994		4.20	3.31	0.89			2.66	2.09	0.36	0.05	0.16	6.53	5.95	0.58
1995		5.63	4.66	0.97			3.46	2.99	0.47	0.00	0.00	7.92	7.16	0.76

Year	v13c9iii	v13c9iv	v13c10	v13c10i	v13c10ii	v13c10iii	v13c10iv
1952							
1953							
1954							
1955							
1956							
1957							
1958							
1959							
1960							
1961							
1962							
1963							
1964							
1965							
1966							
1967							
1968							
1969							
1970							
1971							
1972							
1973							
1974							
1975							
1976							
1977							
1978							
1979							
1980							
1981							
1982							
1983							
1984			0.02	0.02			
1985							
1986							
1987			0.04	0.04			
1988			0.06	0.06			
1989			0.09	0.08	0.01		
1990	-0.01	0.01	0.56	0.06	0.03	0.38	0.09
1991	-0.02	0.02	0.70	0.07	0.03	0.42	0.18
1992	-0.03	0.06	0.66	0.08	0.03	0.36	0.19
1993	-0.02	0.07	0.63	0.10	0.07	0.35	0.11
1994			0.75	0.10	0.04	0.50	0.11
1995			0.95	0.15	0.04	0.63	0.13

29

Ningxia

Year	v1	v1a	v1b	v1b1	v1b2	v1c	v1c1	v1c2	v1c3	v2	v2a	v2b	v2b1	v2b2	v2c
1952	2.22	1.61	0.24	0.20	0.04	0.37	0.06	0.08	0.23	119.4	118.5	127.2	120.8	177.0	118.7
1953	2.29	1.53	0.31	0.26	0.05	0.45	0.06	0.11	0.28	103.1	96.0	124.3	125.8	116.6	120.2
1954	2.62	1.74	0.36	0.32	0.04	0.52	0.06	0.11	0.35	125.9	128.2	130.9	136.6	97.8	114.8
1955	3.06	2.02	0.42	0.37	0.05	0.62	0.09	0.14	0.39	106.6	104.0	105.6	103.3	123.3	117.4
1956	3.51	2.25	0.42	0.36	0.06	0.84	0.11	0.19	0.54	122.8	124.5	99.0	97.2	111.5	133.6
1957	3.57	2.09	0.52	0.46	0.06	0.96	0.14	0.25	0.57	95.6	86.2	121.1	123.8	105.6	112.8
1958	5.00	2.16	1.55	0.92	0.63	1.29	0.27	0.42	0.60	141.5	109.9	307.0	205.3	1006.4	128.4
1959	6.89	2.12	2.88	1.79	1.09	1.89	0.37	0.72	0.80	133.6	96.7	184.3	192.5	172.8	144.7
1960	7.87	1.79	3.76	2.38	1.38	2.32	0.43	0.80	1.09	110.7	84.1	128.3	128.2	127.3	119.8
1961	7.53	2.73	2.73	2.05	0.68	2.07	0.23	0.80	1.04	75.9	95.1	64.7	75.0	49.1	76.4
1962	6.07	2.60	1.97	1.53	0.44	1.50	0.15	0.50	0.85	84.3	98.5	78.9	84.8	64.8	74.8
1963	6.21	2.58	1.99	1.49	0.50	1.64	0.17	0.53	0.94	114.3	122.1	102.1	98.8	112.5	121.4
1964	6.50	2.59	2.13	1.59	0.54	1.78	0.19	0.55	1.04	110.4	111.2	107.6	107.0	109.3	112.9
1965	7.57	3.05	2.67	2.03	0.64	1.85	0.22	0.62	1.01	117.4	114.8	129.9	134.6	117.1	105.6
1966	9.04	3.03	3.94	3.08	0.86	2.07	0.30	0.74	1.03	124.6	100.9	157.4	164.3	135.9	114.0
1967	8.83	3.23	3.74	2.92	0.82	1.86	0.28	0.64	0.94	90.8	106.1	81.1	77.4	95.4	88.3
1968	8.13	2.72	3.64	2.87	0.77	1.77	0.27	0.56	0.94	94.4	84.4	103.5	106.8	93.7	94.9
1969	9.84	2.89	4.84	3.76	1.08	2.11	0.35	0.69	1.07	126.5	105.4	146.4	148.1	140.3	117.8
1970	11.86	2.80	6.49	5.01	1.48	2.57	0.47	0.85	1.25	124.7	97.3	140.7	141.8	136.8	122.0
1971	15.40	3.78	8.46	6.53	1.93	3.16	0.59	1.06	1.51	122.6	112.2	126.1	125.0	130.2	123.9
1972	16.95	3.77	9.70	7.50	2.20	3.48	0.67	1.08	1.73	111.8	99.8	116.3	116.9	114.0	110.2
1973	17.45	3.32	10.40	7.99	2.41	3.73	0.72	1.08	1.93	106.9	86.9	112.6	113.4	109.3	107.1
1974	21.48	4.80	12.60	9.68	2.92	4.08	0.85	1.18	2.05	115.3	141.0	111.3	108.7	121.4	109.5
1975	23.37	4.61	14.37	11.17	3.20	4.39	0.97	1.22	2.20	109.8	96.7	114.2	115.5	109.4	107.4
1976	21.51	3.73	13.45	10.45	3.00	4.33	0.92	1.06	2.35	95.2	80.8	97.8	98.9	93.9	98.6
1977	24.44	4.36	15.35	11.92	3.43	4.73	1.06	1.12	2.55	110.3	116.2	110.9	110.0	114.3	103.6
1978	28.07	4.81	17.76	13.85	3.91	5.50	1.19	1.22	3.09	116.6	112.6	117.5	118.4	114.2	116.2
1979	30.46	5.60	18.59	14.55	4.04	6.27	1.12	1.40	3.75	104.8	95.3	105.3	105.8	103.2	110.8
1980	31.48	6.41	17.72	13.92	3.80	7.35	1.30	1.65	4.40	100.9	114.1	95.7	96.1	94.1	112.0
1981	31.84	7.53	16.53	12.79	3.74	7.78	1.36	1.81	4.61	93.8	106.8	88.3	85.7	98.4	103.0
1982	36.76	7.78	19.37	14.75	4.62	9.61	1.73	2.07	5.81	113.8	100.6	115.1	114.6	116.5	120.0
1983	42.19	9.14	21.88	16.54	5.34	11.17	1.99	2.46	6.72	113.4	117.4	112.4	112.4	112.3	113.5
1984	51.10	10.99	25.72	19.11	6.61	14.39	2.28	3.69	8.42	119.3	117.4	114.4	113.8	116.4	133.9
1985	62.43	12.02	33.75	24.30	9.45	16.66	2.86	4.03	9.77	120.9	102.5	124.7	121.3	136.2	122.6
1986	74.50	14.16	39.74	28.24	11.50	20.60	3.28	4.87	12.45	108.2	107.8	113.2	112.2	116.0	96.7
1987	83.47	14.76	46.08	33.38	12.70	22.63	3.92	6.18	12.53	107.4	92.0	111.9	113.6	107.0	103.0
1988	106.62	19.67	56.51	44.00	12.51	30.44	5.01	9.74	15.69	110.8	114.2	109.0	117.0	84.4	114.5
1989	126.84	21.43	70.56	58.53	12.03	34.85	6.55	10.83	17.47	107.7	106.0	111.2	116.7	87.9	98.3
1990	140.67	24.69	78.24	64.74	13.50	37.74	7.11	11.78	18.85	106.4	104.3	106.8	106.6	107.7	106.1
1991	164.45	26.95	90.67	73.10	17.57	46.83	8.16	13.85	24.82	108.3	104.8	106.6	105.7	111.5	115.3
1992	197.46	28.37	113.05	89.36	23.69	56.04	9.54	16.43	30.07	113.1	97.0	116.8	114.4	129.6	109.0
1993	259.36	31.89	157.08	122.13	34.95	70.39	11.68	22.33	36.38	112.9	106.7	114.5	114.3	115.5	110.0
1994	326.67	45.80	191.63	150.63	41.00	89.24	14.48	27.77	46.99	107.1	102.1	107.7	101.5	108.9	108.5
1995	410.84	56.55	246.52	198.39	48.13	107.77	20.88	30.23	56.66	112.7	105.7	114.5	113.6	114.7	112.4

Year	v2c1	v2c2	v3'	v3	v3a	v3b	v3b1	v3b2	v3c	v3c1	v3c2	v3c3	v3c4	v3c5	v3c6
1952	125.9	105.4	1.73	1.73	1.43	0.08	0.07	0.01	0.22	0.04	0.07				
1953	115.0	115.1	1.68	1.68	1.31	0.11	0.10	0.01	0.26	0.05	0.08				
1954	99.1	103.4	2.14	2.14	1.68	0.15	0.14	0.01	0.31	0.05	0.10				
1955	137.9	120.3	2.24	2.24	1.71	0.17	0.15	0.02	0.36	0.06	0.11				
1956	125.1	132.8	2.57	2.57	1.91	0.18	0.16	0.02	0.48	0.07	0.15				
1957	127.8	118.6	2.58	2.58	1.80	0.22	0.20	0.02	0.56	0.09	0.18				
1958	194.8	179.5	3.29	3.29	1.84	0.65	0.44	0.21	0.80	0.18	0.33				
1959	135.9	167.2	4.36	4.36	1.82	1.34	0.94	0.40	1.20	0.25	0.56				
1960	114.9	108.0	4.80	4.80	1.52	1.99	1.28	0.71	1.29	0.26	0.48				
1961	53.2	85.5	4.15	4.15	2.12	0.86	0.82	0.04	1.17	0.14	0.52				
1962	64.8	64.8	4.02	4.02	2.32	0.75	0.65	0.10	0.95	0.11	0.37				
1963	114.6	119.4	3.96	3.96	2.06	0.85	0.70	0.15	1.05	0.13	0.41				
1964	111.3	108.1	4.09	4.09	1.98	0.97	0.79	0.18	1.14	0.14	0.43				
1965	119.0	114.5	4.66	4.66	2.24	1.24	0.98	0.26	1.18	0.16	0.47				
1966	133.4	122.3	5.41	5.41	2.42	1.64	1.33	0.31	1.35	0.20	0.58				
1967	93.6	84.1	5.47	5.47	2.62	1.63	1.33	0.30	1.22	0.18	0.51				
1968	95.2	87.1	5.06	5.06	2.23	1.68	1.38	0.30	1.15	0.16	0.47				
1969	130.5	121.0	5.86	5.86	2.31	2.14	1.75	0.39	1.41	0.25	0.58				
1970	134.9	122.9	6.52	6.52	2.07	2.71	2.20	0.51	1.74	0.36	0.69				
1971	126.4	126.1	8.12	8.12	2.70	3.35	2.71	0.64	2.07	0.44	0.80				
1972	113.4	101.8	8.83	8.83	2.69	3.84	3.18	0.66	2.30	0.50	0.85				
1973	107.3	100.0	8.96	8.96	2.40	4.15	3.41	0.74	2.41	0.48	0.86				
1974	118.5	108.8	11.40	11.40	3.47	5.32	4.36	0.96	2.61	0.52	0.96				
1975	113.3	103.3	12.06	12.06	3.35	5.90	5.03	0.87	2.81	0.61	0.99				
1976	95.3	86.5	11.10	11.10	2.72	5.60	4.78	0.82	2.78	0.56	0.92				
1977	114.5	98.5	12.13	12.13	2.93	6.25	5.35	0.90	2.95	0.61	0.93				
1978	112.8	108.0	13.00	13.00	3.06	6.60	5.59	1.01	3.34	0.66	0.96	0.43	0.08	0.16	0.11
1979	93.9	108.3	14.36	14.36	3.41	7.36	6.37	0.99	3.59	0.65	0.97	0.53	0.09	0.18	0.12
1980	116.5	110.5	15.96	15.96	4.26	7.27	6.17	1.10	4.43	0.82	1.12	0.73	0.10	0.20	0.15
1981	103.4	101.9	17.42	17.42	5.47	6.97	5.64	1.33	4.98	0.85	1.13	0.93	0.11	0.22	0.18
1982	126.2	106.2	18.22	18.22	5.66	7.02	5.69	1.33	5.54	1.05	1.19	1.05	0.12	0.24	0.21
1983	113.7	110.4	20.79	20.79	6.62	7.87	6.35	1.52	6.30	1.20	1.33	1.15	0.13	0.27	0.23
1984	113.2	121.4	24.78	24.78	7.82	9.46	7.46	2.00	7.50	1.38	1.61	1.52	0.15	0.32	0.26
1985	124.6	116.5	30.27	30.27	8.90	12.12	9.32	2.80	9.25	1.75	1.87	1.98	0.22	0.44	0.31
1986	113.4	110.6	34.54	34.54	10.36	12.97	9.99	2.98	11.21	1.96	2.22	2.55	0.27	0.52	0.40
1987	118.3	116.2	39.63	39.63	10.44	15.77	12.44	3.33	13.42	2.46	2.83	3.14	0.30	0.59	0.43
1988	120.0	129.4	50.29	50.29	13.39	19.74	16.14	3.60	17.16	2.65	4.41	4.02	0.36	0.71	0.53
1989	109.6	91.9	59.21	59.21	14.80	24.39	20.91	3.48	20.02	3.33	4.90	4.80	0.43	0.84	0.57
1990	104.0	116.0	64.84	64.84	16.84	25.34	21.29	4.05	22.66	3.49	5.32	5.57	0.50	1.03	0.72
1991	106.8	107.1	71.78	71.78	17.90	27.77	23.12	4.65	26.11	4.20	6.45	6.04	0.54	1.14	0.89
1992	102.6	108.7	83.14	83.14	18.31	34.05	27.24	6.81	30.78	4.76	7.60	7.08	0.79	1.41	1.07
1993	111.7	115.0	103.82	103.82	20.84	45.52	37.15	8.37	37.46	5.19	9.45	9.90	0.95	1.76	1.20
1994	109.0	103.6	133.97	133.97	29.93	55.78	45.89	9.89	48.26	6.14	11.72	13.38	1.23	2.03	1.61
1995	129.9	102.4	169.75	169.75	35.39	74.14	62.45	11.69	60.22	8.39	14.28	17.06	1.79	2.57	1.86

Year	v3c7	v3c8	v3c9	v3c10	v3d	v4'	v4	v4a	v4b	v4b1	v4b2	v4c	v4c1	v4c2	v4c3
1952				0.11	126	121.4	121.4	121.8	118.6	115.3	194.6	118.7	130.5	109.8	
1953				0.13	115	102.8	102.8	96.8	135.3	140.2	106.5	118.5	109.0	111.1	
1954				0.16	138	127.3	127.3	127.6	140.0	143.4	113.1	120.2	106.1	118.8	
1955				0.19	138	105.1	105.1	103.4	101.3	100.3	110.7	114.5	122.6	108.5	
1956				0.26	152	120.6	120.6	119.3	105.6	105.5	106.7	133.4	121.2	129.6	
1957				0.29	147	95.6	95.6	86.4	124.1	125.1	115.1	116.1	127.5	119.7	
1958				0.29	176	140.9	140.9	114.3	289.5	214.9	1011.8	143.0	191.1	180.6	
1959				0.39	217	136.6	136.6	97.8	207.0	216.7	187.2	151.0	141.1	166.8	
1960				0.55	227	105.5	105.5	83.5	128.0	116.9	154.4	106.8	105.1	102.2	
1961				0.51	199	73.4	73.4	97.3	42.8	63.8	5.0	91.0	37.4	74.7	
1962				0.47	200	89.7	89.7	98.0	91.0	82.8	278.7	80.9	75.2	74.8	
1963				0.51	195	119.3	119.3	121.2	128.0	120.1	181.8	111.2	116.1	122.8	
1964				0.57	194	109.9	109.9	109.6	116.0	115.0	120.3	105.5	112.1	110.3	
1965				0.55	211	116.8	116.8	117.0	132.0	129.1	144.7	103.3	115.4	111.2	
1966				0.57	234	116.2	116.2	100.9	139.0	141.7	128.5	114.2	138.8	128.3	
1967				0.53	228	95.0	95.0	106.7	87.0	87.6	84.6	90.0	92.2	86.0	
1968				0.52	202	96.2	96.2	85.8	110.0	111.1	105.2	94.8	88.6	90.5	
1969				0.58	225	123.3	123.3	105.2	141.0	139.9	146.2	122.5	150.3	120.9	
1970				0.69	241	118.9	118.9	96.3	132.0	131.2	135.6	124.0	146.5	119.2	
1971				0.83	288	115.5	115.5	108.0	120.0	119.7	121.3	118.5	121.9	117.5	
1972				0.95	302	109.2	109.2	100.1	115.0	117.7	103.5	111.0	114.0	105.6	
1973				1.07	296	103.3	103.3	86.5	114.0	113.2	118.0	104.2	92.3	101.3	
1974				1.13	365	120.5	120.5	142.1	116.0	115.6	118.0	108.4	107.1	111.7	
1975				1.21	374	105.6	105.6	97.0	110.0	114.4	90.1	107.5	117.4	102.3	
1976				1.30	333	95.7	95.7	85.0	100.0	100.2	99.9	98.9	92.0	95.8	
1977				1.41	354	107.1	107.1	106.0	108.0	108.4	105.5	106.1	108.9	94.1	
1978	0.29	0.11	0.33	0.21	370	108.9	108.9	166.0	110.0	108.8	118.2	109.0	109.3	103.1	
1979	0.34	0.12	0.36	0.23	399	106.4	106.4	91.3	112.8	115.3	99.9	107.0	104.5	102.2	123.2
1980	0.44	0.16	0.45	0.26	433	107.9	107.9	117.7	102.4	100.5	114.6	112.6	117.1	105.8	126.3
1981	0.49	0.19	0.56	0.32	460	102.0	102.0	122.8	88.9	84.8	112.1	106.3	103.4	101.8	120.2
1982	0.59	0.20	0.57	0.32	469	108.9	108.9	100.5	107.5	107.6	106.9	120.5	125.6	103.2	122.3
1983	0.63	0.25	0.72	0.39	525	115.4	115.4	119.8	111.4	110.9	113.7	117.0	113.9	109.7	112.8
1984	0.74	0.28	0.81	0.43	615	113.6	113.6	115.2	113.4	110.8	124.2	112.5	114.7	114.5	124.6
1985	0.92	0.30	1.05	0.41	737	117.8	117.8	108.0	122.6	119.6	133.8	120.8	126.8	111.4	112.4
1986	1.19	0.41	1.28	0.41	823	108.3	108.3	106.2	106.4	106.5	105.9	112.6	112.3	114.2	120.1
1987	1.28	0.51	1.46	0.42	922	107.9	107.9	92.4	108.9	111.6	100.0	119.4	125.2	121.6	122.5
1988	1.63	0.63	1.73	0.49	1143	112.1	112.1	109.1	113.2	117.3	97.9	112.8	107.8	133.2	112.9
1989	1.89	0.75	1.96	0.55	1317	107.7	107.7	106.1	111.7	117.2	87.3	104.2	98.8	111.1	106.7
1990	2.11	0.91	2.37	0.64	1393	103.7	103.7	103.4	102.5	100.4	115.0	105.3	97.6	108.6	108.0
1991	2.38	1.13	2.63	0.71	1511	104.8	104.8	102.7	103.2	102.3	108.0	108.4	113.2	121.3	102.0
1992	2.79	1.37	3.12	0.79	1718	108.6	108.6	95.7	112.5	110.1	124.6	113.8	109.5	117.9	106.4
1993	3.06	1.58	3.49	0.88	2123	110.1	110.1	106.5	113.1	113.3	112.2	109.1	111.7	112.6	108.6
1994	4.10	2.06	4.82	1.17	2685	108.2	108.2	102.1	108.5	109.5	102.6	111.8	103.1	104.2	118.8
1995	4.94	2.55	5.22	1.56	3328	109.0	109.0	101.1	113.0	113.8	107.9	108.9	115.5	105.8	110.6

Year	v4c4	v4c5	v4c6	v4c7	v4c8	v4c9	v4c10	v5	v5a	v5a1	v5a1a	v5a1b	v5a2	v5b	v5b1
1952								1.72	1.37	1.31	1.05	0.26	0.06	0.47	0.37
1953								1.65	1.45	1.38	1.13	0.25	0.07	0.50	0.39
1954								2.06	1.86	1.78	1.37	0.41	0.08	0.64	0.50
1955								2.19	1.99	1.91	1.47	0.44	0.08	0.67	0.51
1956								2.58	2.04	1.96	1.43	0.53	0.08	1.10	0.87
1957								2.52	2.04	1.95	1.31	0.64	0.09	1.05	0.83
1958								3.30	2.41	2.25	1.48	0.77	0.16	2.60	1.75
1959								4.31	2.88	2.62	1.46	1.16	0.26	3.63	2.32
1960								4.84	2.90	2.52	1.07	1.45	0.38	4.26	2.50
1961								4.09	3.21	2.80	1.60	1.20	0.41	1.58	1.24
1962								4.00	3.43	3.10	2.00	1.10	0.33	0.97	0.77
1963								3.98	3.28	2.94	1.88	1.06	0.34	1.14	0.92
1964								4.06	3.40	3.02	1.94	1.08	0.38	2.10	1.72
1965								4.57	3.63	3.18	2.04	1.14	0.45	2.74	2.25
1966								5.54	4.06	3.56	2.47	1.09	0.50	3.66	3.00
1967								5.57	4.10	3.59	2.56	1.03	0.51	3.48	3.07
1968								4.91	4.22	3.69	2.69	1.00	0.53	2.40	2.01
1969								5.51	4.92	4.30	2.93	1.37	0.62	3.37	2.86
1970								6.74	5.26	4.57	3.07	1.50	0.69	5.17	4.41
1971								8.32	5.51	4.76	3.12	1.64	0.75	6.26	5.38
1972								9.04	5.98	5.14	3.43	1.71	0.84	6.05	5.24
1973								9.44	6.43	5.77	3.62	2.15	0.66	6.31	5.51
1974								10.97	6.98	5.90	3.58	2.32	1.08	6.01	5.51
1975								12.83	7.09	6.04	3.50	2.54	1.05	8.45	7.48
1976								11.63	7.87	6.64	3.88	2.76	1.23	7.26	6.50
1977								12.64	8.29	6.61	3.82	2.79	1.68	8.78	7.98
1978								13.41	9.87	7.61	4.86	2.75	2.26	9.04	7.95
1979	115.6	113.7	111.0	116.0	109.8	109.1	109.9	15.34	10.90	8.11	4.63	3.48	2.79	9.37	8.78
1980	99.0	100.6	113.0	116.8	115.5	113.2	108.1	16.37	12.81	9.78	5.44	4.34	3.03	8.07	7.48
1981	104.1	105.1	113.5	106.2	113.7	119.0	114.4	17.19	14.38	10.72	6.19	4.53	3.66	6.81	5.50
1982	114.4	114.4	125.6	129.2	117.6	109.5	110.3	17.80	16.75	11.98	7.10	4.88	4.77	8.28	7.77
1983	114.3	115.9	116.0	110.9	125.3	128.9	124.9	19.48	18.78	13.25	8.11	5.14	5.53	9.74	8.98
1984	113.3	113.1	107.3	109.8	105.9	107.8	102.2	23.93	22.11	15.07	9.25	5.82	7.04	12.84	10.65
1985	120.3	119.4	103.0	108.6	92.2	110.9	84.7	31.66	25.72	17.67	10.60	7.07	8.05	19.12	17.05
1986	115.0	110.7	118.5	119.7	127.0	114.2	88.6	37.74	29.85	20.42	12.25	8.17	9.43	22.34	19.35
1987	113.1	113.2	108.6	107.2	124.8	113.0	105.3	43.31	33.34	23.74	13.46	10.28	9.60	25.27	21.98
1988	105.9	104.9	108.6	112.6	108.6	104.4	104.8	53.82	38.82	27.79	15.77	12.02	11.03	31.20	22.88
1989	105.7	106.5	96.0	103.5	106.3	101.6	98.2	61.43	44.44	31.73	17.38	14.35	12.71	33.59	22.96
1990	107.3	114.0	117.3	104.0	112.6	112.5	109.0	66.06	47.87	33.88	17.91	15.97	13.99	37.22	25.47
1991	102.2	104.3	115.8	105.9	117.5	104.4	106.0	73.13	53.85	38.07	19.72	18.35	15.78	40.55	31.74
1992	132.3	112.1	108.4	106.2	109.9	107.6	102.0	80.61	59.54	42.45	21.54	20.91	17.09	46.70	38.38
1993	115.7	109.9	106.1	106.8	104.4	105.7	104.3	104.22	72.16	50.51	24.42	26.09	21.65	61.64	52.67
1994	112.0	105.9	114.0	114.0	115.8	116.5	113.3	134.23	95.17	67.63	32.02	35.61	27.54	69.12	61.98
1995	123.8	111.1	99.1	105.0		102.4	114.1	169.75	113.31	83.81	41.01	42.80	29.50	82.45	70.12

Year	v5b2	v5c	v5c1	v5c2	v6a1	v6a2	v6a3	v6a4	v6b2	v6b3	v6b4	v7	v7a	v7a1	v7a2
1952	0.10	-0.12	1.13	1.25											
1953	0.11	-0.30	1.19	1.49								104.8	104.7	107.0	95.6
1954	0.14	-0.44	1.25	1.69								126.7	127.9	120.1	162.9
1955	0.16	-0.47	1.31	1.78								106.0	106.0	105.9	106.1
1956	0.23	-0.56	1.38	1.94								101.6	101.7	96.9	117.5
1957	0.22	-0.57	1.44	2.01								94.9	94.5	86.9	115.4
1958	0.85	-1.71	1.59	3.30								116.6	114.2	111.2	120.3
1959	1.31	-2.20	1.75	3.95								118.1	114.8	97.6	147.5
1960	1.76	-2.32	1.92	4.24								97.6	93.1	70.6	121.3
1961	0.34	-0.70	2.12	2.82								94.1	94.5	128.1	69.9
1962	0.20	-0.40	2.64	3.04								111.0	115.0	129.2	95.9
1963	0.22	-0.44	2.90	3.34								106.8	106.0	105.2	107.5
1964	0.38	-1.44	3.04	4.48								108.4	107.1	107.6	106.3
1965	0.49	-1.80	3.35	5.15								109.5	108.0	108.0	108.0
1966	0.66	-2.18	3.68	5.86								114.0	114.2	123.2	97.9
1967	0.41	-2.01	4.05	6.06								99.0	98.9	101.7	92.7
1968	0.39	-1.71	4.25	5.96								102.1	102.0	104.3	96.4
1969	0.51	-2.78	5.11	7.89								115.1	114.6	107.3	134.2
1970	0.76	-3.69	6.13	9.82								106.4	105.9	104.3	107.9
1971	0.88	-3.45	7.35	10.80								105.7	105.2	102.9	111.5
1972	0.81	-2.99	8.46	11.43								108.4	107.9	109.8	104.2
1973	0.80	-3.30	9.73	13.03								107.3	111.9	105.0	125.8
1974	0.50	-2.02	11.77	13.79								108.4	102.2	99.0	107.5
1975	0.97	-2.71	12.73	15.44								101.2	102.1	97.5	109.3
1976	0.76	-3.50	13.77	17.27								110.5	109.3	110.2	108.1
1977	0.80	-4.43	14.90	19.33								98.0	92.7	91.8	94.0
1978	1.09	-5.50	16.11	21.61	2.19	2.54	0.06	0.07	2.34	0.37	0.04	119.1	115.0	127.1	98.5
1979	0.59	-4.93	17.43	22.36	2.08	2.41	0.06	0.08	2.99	0.45	0.04	110.4	106.6	95.3	126.5
1980	0.59	-4.51	18.86	23.37	2.36	2.85	0.07	0.16	3.92	0.37	0.05	109.7	112.6	109.7	116.5
1981	1.31	-4.00	20.40	24.40	2.58	3.32	0.10	0.19	4.09	0.39	0.05	110.1	107.5	111.5	102.4
1982	0.51	-7.23	22.06	29.29	2.82	3.90	0.15	0.23	4.36	0.42	0.10	113.6	109.0	111.5	105.1
1983	0.76	-9.04	23.87	32.91	3.08	4.59	0.19	0.25	4.61	0.46	0.07	110.9	109.4	113.4	104.3
1984	2.19	-11.02	25.82	36.84	3.36	5.30	0.22	0.37	5.18	0.56	0.09	114.0	110.2	110.5	109.7
1985	2.07	-13.18	27.93	41.11	3.69	6.25	0.24	0.41	6.06	0.83	0.18	108.0	108.8	106.4	112.6
1986	2.99	-14.45	30.21	44.66	4.12	7.40	0.28	0.45	7.08	0.87	0.22	110.6	110.2	110.1	110.2
1987	3.29	-15.30	32.68	47.98	4.17	8.39	0.37	0.53	8.91	1.13	0.24	103.4	107.6	101.7	116.5
1988	8.32	-16.20	35.36	51.56	4.38	10.10	0.63	0.65	10.42	1.34	0.26	99.1	99.6	99.7	99.5
1989	10.63	-16.60	38.24	54.84	5.16	10.73	0.71	0.78	12.10	1.94	0.31	97.2	97.0	93.6	101.3
1990	11.75	-19.03	38.34	57.37	5.34	10.86	0.81	0.90	13.52	2.14	0.31	103.4	102.5	98.9	106.8
1991	8.81	-21.27	43.20	64.47	7.09	10.79	0.89	0.95	15.18	2.79	0.38	106.4	106.3	104.2	108.7
1992	8.32	-25.63	48.44	74.07	8.20	10.83	1.44	1.07	17.28	3.19	0.44	103.0	103.8	101.7	106.1
1993	8.97	-29.58	56.65	86.23	8.54	12.67	1.72	1.49	20.95	4.60	0.54	107.4	105.5	100.5	110.6
1994	7.14	-30.06	59.51	89.57	12.80	15.53	2.15	1.54	29.10	5.79	0.72	107.9	108.8	108.0	109.5
1995	12.33	-26.01	49.16	75.17	15.11	20.64	3.10	2.16	34.89	7.15	0.76	105.1	106.4	110.2	102.7

Year	v7b	v8	v8a	v8b	v9	v9a	v9b	v10a1	v10a2	v10a3	v10a3a	v10a3b	v10a4	v10b1	v10b2
1952		92	80	231	116.9	114.0	135.0								
1953	104.9	91	82	186	98.9	102.5	80.3								
1954	106.1	113	95	296	124.4	116.0	159.8								
1955	106.0	116	97	327	102.7	102.1	110.2								
1956	101.5	114	91	363	98.3	93.8	110.8								
1957	102.2	109	81	362	86.7	80.0	91.1								
1958	167.3	117	87	329	107.1	108.3	89.9								
1959	167.8	126	85	323	105.7	107.7	174.8								
1960	143.8	118	62	356	91.0	63.1	59.2								
1961	91.5	134	96	332	96.0	130.2	78.9								
1962	83.3	156	118	382	120.6	129.0	119.5								
1963	114.0	142	107	337	101.7	102.2	98.6								
1964	118.7	140	106	338	103.4	102.2	104.9								
1965	121.8	140	106	330	102.4	104.3	100.0								
1966	112.5	151	125	291	110.3	96.6	89.9								
1967	99.7	147	125	255	95.7	120.6	86.5								
1968	102.4	145	126	240	97.7	100.0	92.6								
1969	118.3	162	132	311	110.0	102.7	128.0								
1970	109.7	165	132	334	101.4	100.0	106.9								
1971	108.9	166	131	343	101.4	100.0	103.8								
1972	111.9	173	139	342	104.8	106.0	99.3								
1973	79.3	187	141	415	107.1	100.8	121.2								
1974	162.6	186	136	436	99.4	96.8	104.9								
1975	96.4	184	128	462	98.2	93.3	105.5								
1976	117.0	196	138	482	106.2	108.0	104.0								
1977	127.0	191	133	477	90.6	89.3	92.2								
1978	135.0	214	165	450	112.3	124.1	94.3	7.16	0.32	0.47	0.14	0.33		0.93	0.14
1979	123.4	223	155	539	102.9	92.5	118.3	7.90	0.35	0.53	0.16	0.37		0.50	0.07
1980	101.3	262	178	640	111.2	108.9	112.2	7.03	0.08	0.37	0.11	0.26		0.47	0.09
1981	118.5	280	198	638	104.5	108.9	97.7	5.13	0.29	0.08	0.03	0.05		1.05	0.20
1982	127.2	305	222	669	106.3	109.5	102.3	6.92	0.33	0.52	0.04	0.48		0.35	0.11
1983	114.6	332	251	679	108.1	112.4	100.6	8.14	0.36	0.48	0.03	0.45		0.52	0.17
1984	123.1	370	281	745	107.9	108.3	106.3	8.67	0.54	1.44	0.05	1.39		1.50	0.48
1985	106.3	426	320	849	107.0	108.7	105.8	14.12	1.19	1.68	0.15	1.53	0.06	1.42	0.45
1986	111.6	481	368	897	107.6	109.4	100.5	15.95	1.16	2.18	0.06	2.12	0.06	2.04	0.65
1987	94.2	546	398	1056	105.1	100.9	109.0	17.64	1.29	2.99	0.07	2.92	0.07	2.25	0.71
1988	97.9	625	461	1173	97.4	99.6	94.5	16.99	2.28	3.49	0.39	3.10	0.12	5.35	1.21
1989	97.8	698	500	1335	94.7	92.3	96.7	17.46	1.32	4.03	0.27	3.76	0.15	6.35	3.06
1990	105.6	728	506	1434	100.0	97.2	103.1	20.13	1.36	3.83	0.13	3.70	0.15	7.27	1.92
1991	106.7	803	548	1611	104.5	102.4	106.3	26.19	1.75	3.60	0.12	3.48	0.20	6.59	1.38
1992	100.9	880	589	1794	102.0	101.4	103.6	30.88	2.71	4.49	0.47	4.02	0.31	5.41	2.03
1993	112.3	1029	658	2182	103.6	98.2	107.8	41.28	4.81	6.05	0.41	5.64	0.53	3.80	2.72
1994	106.0	1355	865	2760	106.6	107.4	102.7	49.87	3.69	5.45	0.78	4.67	2.97	-0.33	2.47
1995	102.0	1643	1102	3101	104.1	109.6	96.0	51.40	4.18	10.69	0.69	10.00	3.85	7.22	0.91

Year	v10b4	v11a	v11a1	v11a2	v11b	v11b1	v11b2	v11c	v11c1	v11c2	v12	v12a	v12b	v13	v13i
1952															
1953											105.9	105.9	106.0		
1954											128.3	128.3	128.3		
1955											104.6	100.6	119.7		
1956											160.2	166.6	140.0		
1957											88.8	89.7	85.7		
1958											246.5	207.9	397.7		
1959											137.2	130.4	151.0		
1960											113.9	104.8	130.2		
1961											31.4	42.2	16.1		
1962											63.7	64.3	61.5		
1963											132.3	133.5	127.4		
1964											192.0	195.4	177.9		
1965											133.5	133.4	133.4		
1966											136.4	136.8	134.7		
1967											93.30	100.1	62.2		
1968											68.5	65.3	92.1		
1969											138.2	139.7	130.5		
1970											152.7	153.6	148.1		
1971											122.2	123.1	116.6		
1972											96.5	97.2	92.0		
1973											104.2	105.0	99.1		
1974											95.0	99.8	62.4		
1975											140.1	135.4	191.8		
1976											85.6	86.6	78.1		
1977											112.5	114.1	98.7		
1978	0.02	0.48	0.32	0.16	5.83	5.17	0.66	2.73	2.46	0.27	102.9	99.7	135.5	13.00	6.82
1979	0.02	0.46	0.35	0.11	6.03	5.71	0.32	2.88	2.72	0.16	102.3	109.0	53.7	14.36	7.34
1980	0.03	0.45	0.37	0.08	4.85	4.49	0.36	2.77	2.62	0.15	81.4	80.5	94.6	15.96	8.43
1981	0.06	0.46	0.27	0.19	3.98	3.19	0.79	2.37	2.04	0.33	82.7	72.1	216.3	17.42	10.14
1982	0.05	0.46	0.39	0.07	4.66	4.35	0.31	3.16	3.03	0.13	118.6	137.8	38.2	18.22	10.58
1983	0.07	0.56	0.45	0.11	5.40	4.94	0.46	3.78	3.59	0.19	116.3	114.3	146.8	20.79	12.39
1984	0.21	0.86	0.53	0.33	7.17	5.86	1.31	4.81	4.26	0.55	127.8	114.9	279.1	24.78	14.54
1985	0.20	1.17	0.86	0.31	10.44	9.20	1.24	7.51	6.99	0.52	138.2	148.5	87.9	30.27	16.85
1986	0.30	1.41	0.97	0.44	11.86	10.06	1.80	9.07	8.32	0.75	111.4	108.2	137.6	34.54	19.45
1987	0.33	1.72	1.10	0.62	12.97	10.99	1.98	10.58	9.89	0.69	104.7	105.2	101.9	39.63	21.32
1988	1.76	2.63	1.38	1.25	15.97	10.98	4.99	12.60	10.52	2.08	105.1	88.6	215.0	50.29	25.97
1989	1.22	4.30	1.38	2.92	14.55	10.56	3.99	14.74	11.02	3.72	91.4	85.2	108.5	59.21	29.20
1990	2.56	4.43	1.53	2.90	19.02	11.21	7.81	13.77	12.73	1.04	106.3	106.5	106.1	64.84	32.42
1991	0.84	2.79	1.90	0.89	18.77	13.33	5.44	18.99	16.51	2.48	103.1	117.9	70.9	71.78	35.39
1992	0.88	3.45	2.30	1.15	20.64	15.35	5.29	22.61	20.73	1.88	107.3	112.6	88.0	83.14	40.54
1993	2.45	4.49	3.06	1.43	23.30	17.28	6.02	33.85	32.33	1.52	117.7	122.6	95.6	103.82	51.88
1994	5.00	2.24	2.37	-0.13	27.29	23.42	3.87	39.59	36.19	3.40	96.7	102.1	69.5	133.97	72.84
1995	4.20	6.47	3.58	2.89	32.60	26.92	5.68	43.38	39.62	3.76	107.1	103.2	136.2	169.75	98.61

Year	v13ii	v13iii	v13iv	v13a	v13ai	v13aii	v13aiii	v13aiv	v13b	v13bi	v13bii	v13biii	v13biv	v13b1	v13b1i
1952															
1953															
1954															
1955															
1956															
1957															
1958															
1959															
1960															
1961															
1962															
1963															
1964															
1965															
1966															
1967															
1968															
1969															
1970															
1971															
1972															
1973															
1974															
1975															
1976															
1977															
1978	1.84	1.20	3.14	3.06	2.73	0.21	0.05	0.07	6.60	2.63	1.04	0.96	1.97	5.59	1.85
1979	2.13	1.51	3.38	3.41	3.03	0.23	0.06	0.09	7.36	2.73	1.26	1.27	2.10	6.37	1.98
1980	2.35	1.49	3.69	4.26	3.84	0.26	0.06	0.10	7.27	2.73	1.31	1.20	2.03	6.17	1.91
1981	2.60	1.34	3.34	5.47	4.97	0.29	0.08	0.13	6.97	3.08	1.48	1.00	1.41	5.64	2.07
1982	2.86	1.42	3.36	5.66	5.13	0.32	0.09	0.12	7.02	3.14	1.58	1.03	1.27	5.69	2.14
1983	3.26	1.56	3.58	6.62	6.00	0.36	0.10	0.16	7.87	3.63	1.82	1.11	1.31	6.35	2.46
1984	3.84	1.89	4.51	7.82	7.10	0.40	0.12	0.20	9.46	4.24	2.20	1.36	1.66	7.46	2.77
1985	4.36	2.20	6.86	8.90	8.08	0.42	0.14	0.26	12.12	4.93	2.52	1.59	3.08	9.32	3.01
1986	4.82	2.51	7.76	10.36	9.42	0.44	0.16	0.34	12.97	5.37	2.75	1.78	3.07	9.99	3.24
1987	5.61	3.37	9.33	10.44	9.61	0.46	0.19	0.18	15.77	6.42	3.26	2.28	3.81	12.44	4.05
1988	6.95	5.83	11.54	13.39	12.53	0.51	0.13	0.22	19.74	7.29	3.92	4.10	4.43	16.14	4.82
1989	8.39	7.75	13.87	14.80	13.67	0.57	0.23	0.33	24.39	8.45	4.86	5.40	5.68	20.91	6.14
1990	9.52	7.65	15.25	16.84	15.17	0.73	0.26	0.68	25.34	9.24	5.28	5.58	5.24	21.29	6.89
1991	10.68	6.42	19.29	17.90	15.93	0.58	0.27	1.12	27.77	10.79	6.16	3.66	7.16	23.12	7.91
1992	12.84	12.77	16.99	18.31	16.12	0.59	0.59	1.01	34.05	13.45	7.82	9.14	3.64	27.74	9.37
1993	15.28	14.33	22.33	20.84	18.78	0.67	0.48	0.91	45.52	19.28	9.61	10.25	6.38	37.15	14.51
1994	18.80	8.62	33.71	29.93	27.71	0.77	0.55	0.90	55.78	24.97	10.71	4.30	15.80	45.89	19.19
1995	25.79	20.71	24.64	35.39	32.81	0.88	0.69	1.01	74.14	38.02	15.97	17.52	2.63	62.45	29.53

Year	v13b1ii	v13b1iii	v13b1iv	v13b2	v13b2i	v13b2ii	v13b2iii	v13b2iv	v13c	v13ci	v13cii	v13ciii	v13civ	v13c1
1952														
1953														
1954														
1955														
1956														
1957														
1958														
1959														
1960														
1961														
1962														
1963														
1964														
1965														
1966														
1967														
1968														
1969														
1970														
1971														
1972														
1973														
1974														
1975														
1976														
1977														
1978	0.93	0.90	1.91	1.01	0.78	0.11	0.06	0.06	3.34	1.46	0.59	0.19	1.10	0.66
1979	1.14	1.20	2.05	0.99	0.75	0.12	0.07	0.05	3.59	1.58	0.64	0.18	1.19	0.65
1980	1.17	1.13	1.96	1.10	0.82	0.14	0.07	0.07	4.43	1.86	0.78	0.23	1.56	0.82
1981	1.33	0.93	1.31	1.33	1.01	0.15	0.07	0.10	4.98	2.09	0.83	0.26	1.80	0.85
1982	1.42	0.96	1.17	1.33	1.00	0.16	0.07	0.10	5.54	2.31	0.96	0.30	1.97	1.05
1983	1.65	1.03	1.21	1.52	1.17	0.17	0.08	0.10	6.30	2.76	1.08	0.35	2.11	1.20
1984	1.93	1.24	1.52	2.00	1.47	0.27	0.12	0.14	7.50	3.20	1.24	0.41	2.65	1.38
1985	2.16	1.42	2.73	2.80	1.92	0.36	0.17	0.35	9.25	3.84	1.42	0.47	3.52	1.75
1986	2.36	1.59	2.80	2.98	2.13	0.39	0.19	0.27	11.21	4.66	1.63	0.57	4.35	1.96
1987	2.85	2.06	3.48	3.33	2.37	0.41	0.22	0.33	13.42	5.29	1.89	0.90	5.34	2.46
1988	3.46	3.84	4.02	3.60	2.47	0.46	0.26	0.41	17.16	6.15	2.52	1.60	6.89	2.65
1989	4.39	5.05	5.33	3.48	2.31	0.47	0.35	0.35	20.02	7.08	2.96	2.12	7.86	3.33
1990	4.78	5.19	4.43	4.05	2.35	0.50	0.39	0.81	22.66	8.01	3.51	1.81	9.33	3.49
1991	5.56	3.23	6.42	4.65	2.88	0.60	0.43	0.74	26.11	8.67	3.94	2.49	11.01	4.20
1992	6.98	8.47	2.92	6.31	4.08	0.84	0.67	0.72	30.78	10.97	4.43	3.03	12.34	4.76
1993	8.96	8.94	4.74	8.37	4.77	0.65	1.31	1.64	37.46	13.82	5.00	3.60	15.04	5.19
1994	10.08	3.34	13.28	9.89	5.78	0.63	0.93	2.52	48.26	20.16	7.32	3.77	17.01	6.14
1995	14.70	16.02	2.20	11.69	8.49	1.27	1.50	0.43	60.22	27.78	8.94	2.50	21.00	8.39

Year	v13c1i	v13c1ii	v13c1iii	v13c1iv	v13c2	v13c2i	v13c2ii	v13c2iii	v13c2iv	v13c3	v13c3i	v13c3ii	v13c3iii	v13c3iv
1952														
1953														
1954														
1955														
1956														
1957														
1958														
1959														
1960														
1961														
1962														
1963														
1964														
1965														
1966														
1967														
1968														
1969														
1970														
1971														
1972														
1973														
1974														
1975														
1976														
1977														
1978	0.21	0.25	0.10	0.10	0.96	0.32	0.05	0.04	0.55	0.43	0.04	0.03	0.02	0.34
1979	0.20	0.26	0.09	0.10	0.97	0.34	0.06	0.04	0.53	0.53	0.05	0.03	0.02	0.43
1980	0.26	0.34	0.11	0.11	1.12	0.35	0.06	0.04	0.67	0.73	0.06	0.04	0.03	0.60
1981	0.26	0.33	0.13	0.13	1.13	0.37	0.07	0.05	0.64	0.93	0.07	0.04	0.04	0.78
1982	0.32	0.42	0.14	0.17	1.19	0.39	0.07	0.05	0.68	1.05	0.08	0.04	0.05	0.88
1983	0.36	0.46	0.16	0.22	1.33	0.49	0.10	0.06	0.68	1.15	0.10	0.05	0.07	0.93
1984	0.40	0.51	0.17	0.30	1.61	0.61	0.13	0.07	0.08	1.52	0.12	0.05	0.09	1.26
1985	0.44	0.57	0.19	0.54	1.87	0.76	0.15	0.07	0.89	1.98	0.15	0.06	0.11	1.66
1986	0.49	0.63	0.22	0.62	2.22	0.96	0.20	0.10	0.96	2.55	0.18	0.07	0.15	2.15
1987	0.61	0.70	0.24	0.91	2.83	0.99	0.27	0.35	1.22	3.14	0.22	0.08	0.19	2.65
1988	0.89	0.93	0.52	0.31	4.41	1.37	0.42	0.75	1.87	4.02	0.18	0.10	0.33	3.41
1989	1.10	1.02	0.78	0.43	4.90	1.48	0.55	0.83	2.04	4.80	0.30	0.12	0.40	3.98
1990	1.33	1.19	0.22	0.75	5.32	1.54	0.61	0.90	2.27	5.57	0.37	0.17	0.42	4.61
1991	1.24	1.26	0.78	0.92	6.45	1.81	0.64	1.09	2.91	6.04	0.41	0.27	0.45	4.91
1992	1.37	1.35	0.81	1.23	7.60	2.17	0.75	1.29	3.39	7.08	0.71	0.41	0.62	5.34
1993	2.81	1.40	0.42	0.56	9.45	2.84	0.89	1.77	3.95	9.90	0.71	0.50	0.85	7.84
1994	3.82	1.70	0.38	0.24	11.72	3.93	1.75	1.99	4.05	13.38	1.17	0.66	0.76	10.79
1995	4.72	2.83	0.79	0.05	14.28	5.67	1.30	-0.62	7.93	17.06	2.66	0.86	1.78	11.76

Year	v13c4	v13c4i	v13c4ii	v13c4iii	v13c4iv	v13c5	v13c5i	v13c5ii	v13c5iii	v13c5iv	v13c6	v13c6i	v13c6ii	v13c6iii
1952														
1953														
1954														
1955														
1956														
1957														
1958														
1959														
1960														
1961														
1962														
1963														
1964														
1965														
1966														
1967														
1968														
1969														
1970														
1971														
1972														
1973														
1974														
1975														
1976														
1977														
1978	0.08	0.01	0.07			0.16	0.03	0.06	0.03	0.04	0.11	0.08	0.02	
1979	0.09	0.01	0.08			0.18	0.04	0.06	0.03	0.05	0.12	0.09	0.02	
1980	0.10	0.01	0.09			0.20	0.04	0.06	0.04	0.06	0.15	0.10	0.03	
1981	0.11	0.01	0.10			0.22	0.05	0.07	0.04	0.06	0.18	0.12	0.03	
1982	0.12	0.01	0.11			0.24	0.05	0.07	0.06	0.06	0.21	0.14	0.04	
1983	0.13	0.01	0.12			0.27	0.07	0.08	0.07	0.05	0.23	0.17	0.04	
1984	0.15	0.01	0.14			0.32	0.08	0.09	0.08	0.07	0.26	0.20	0.04	
1985	0.22	0.01	0.21			0.44	0.10	0.09	0.09	0.16	0.31	0.23	0.06	
1986	0.27	0.01	0.26			0.52	0.13	0.10	0.11	0.18	0.40	0.27	0.07	
1987	0.30	0.02	0.28			0.59	0.16	0.11	0.13	0.19	0.43	0.32	0.08	
1988	0.36	0.02	0.33		0.01	0.71	0.30	0.10	0.07	0.24	0.53	0.35	0.10	
1989	0.43	0.02	0.40		0.01	0.84	0.35	0.12	0.08	0.29	0.57	0.41	0.13	
1990	0.50	0.04	0.43		0.03	1.03	0.42	0.14	0.23	0.24	0.72	0.53	0.15	
1991	0.54	0.03	0.47	0.01	0.03	1.14	0.44	0.16	0.13	0.41	0.89	0.55	0.17	
1992	0.79	0.05	0.52	0.05	0.17	1.41	0.66	0.17	0.21	0.37	1.07	0.70	0.19	
1993	0.95	0.04	0.55	0.14	0.22	1.76	0.81	0.19	0.35	0.41	1.20	0.79	0.21	
1994	1.23	0.06	0.92	0.09	0.11	2.03	0.94	0.24	0.45	0.40	1.61	1.26	0.28	0.45
1995	1.79	0.12	1.36	0.24	0.07	2.57	1.56	0.30	0.25	0.46	1.86	1.55	0.30	0.01

Year	v13c6iv	v13c7	v13c7i	v13c7ii	v13c7iii	v13c7iv	v13c8	v13c8i	v13c8ii	v13c8iii	v13c8iv	v13c9	v13c9i	v13c9ii
1952														
1953														
1954														
1955														
1956														
1957														
1958														
1959														
1960														
1961														
1962														
1963														
1964														
1965														
1966														
1967														
1968														
1969														
1970														
1971														
1972														
1973														
1974														
1975														
1976														
1977														
1978	0.01	0.29	0.27	0.01		0.01	0.11	0.09			0.02	0.33	0.2[illegible]	0.07
1979	0.01	0.34	0.30	0.02		0.02	0.12	0.10	0.01		0.01	0.36	0.2[illegible]	0.01
1980	0.02	0.44	0.37	0.03		0.04	0.16	0.13	0.01		0.02	0.45	0.3[illegible]	0.20
1981	0.03	0.49	0.41	0.05		0.03	0.19	0.15	0.01		0.03	0.56	0.4[illegible]	0.10
1982	0.03	0.59	0.46	0.06		0.07	0.20	0.17			0.03	0.57	0.4[illegible]	0.11
1983	0.02	0.63	0.51	0.07		0.05	0.25	0.21	0.01		0.03	0.72	0.5[illegible]	0.11
1984	0.02	0.74	0.59	0.09		0.06	0.28	0.24	0.01		0.03	0.81	0.6[illegible]	0.12
1985	0.02	0.92	0.72	0.11		0.09	0.30	0.25	0.01		0.04	1.05	0.8[illegible]	0.13
1986	0.06	1.19	0.90	0.14		0.15	0.41	0.35	0.01		0.05	1.28	1.0[illegible]	0.13
1987	0.03	1.28	0.99	0.17		0.12	0.51	0.46	0.01		0.04	1.46	1.1[illegible]	0.14
1988	0.08	1.63	0.90	0.35	0.12	0.26	0.63	0.49	0.02	0.02	0.10	1.73	1.2[illegible]	0.14
1989	0.03	1.89	1.13	0.41	0.02	0.33	0.75	0.53	0.02	0.01	0.19	1.96	1.3[illegible]	0.10
1990	0.04	2.11	1.28	0.50	0.02	0.31	0.91	0.56	0.09	0.01	0.25	2.37	1.5[illegible]	0.19
1991	0.17	2.38	1.40	0.56	0.02	0.40	1.13	0.68	0.14	0.01	0.30	2.63	1.6[illegible]	0.21
1992	0.18	2.79	1.66	0.63	0.03	0.47	1.37	1.17	0.11	0.01	0.08	3.12	1.9[illegible]	0.26
1993	0.20	3.06	1.83	0.66	0.06	0.51	1.58	1.30	0.16	0.01	0.11	3.49	2.1[illegible]	0.35
1994	0.40	4.10	3.15	0.88	0.06	0.01	2.06	1.48	0.38	0.04	0.16	4.82	3.4[illegible]	0.41
1995		4.94	3.98	0.94	0.02		2.55	2.07	0.45	0.03		5.22	4.0[illegible]	0.49

Year	v13c9iii	v13c9iv	v13c10	v13c10i	v13c10ii	v13c10iii	v13c10iv
1952							
1953							
1954							
1955							
1956							
1957							
1958							
1959							
1960							
1961							
1962							
1963							
1964							
1965							
1966							
1967							
1968							
1969							
1970							
1971							
1972							
1973							
1974							
1975							
1976							
1977							
1978			0.21	0.15	0.02		0.03
1979		0.01	0.23	0.19	0.02		0.02
1980		0.02	0.26	0.22	0.02		0.02
1981		0.06	0.32	0.26	0.03		0.03
1982		0.04	0.32	0.26	0.03		0.03
1983		0.08	0.39	0.32	0.04		0.04
1984		0.08	0.43	0.35	0.04		0.04
1985		0.10	0.41	0.34	0.04		0.03
1986		0.11	0.41	0.33	0.04		0.04
1987		0.13	0.42	0.34	0.04		0.04
1988		0.31	0.49	0.36	0.04		0.09
1989		0.42	0.55	0.39	0.04		0.12
1990		0.66	0.64	0.40	0.05		0.19
1991		0.75	0.71	0.45	0.05		0.21
1992		0.88	0.79	0.50	0.06		0.23
1993		0.99	0.88	0.54	0.09		0.25
1994		0.93	1.17	0.87	0.10		0.20
1995		0.73	1.56	1.45	0.11		

30

Xinjiang

Year	v1	v1a	v1b	v1b1	v1b2	v1c	v1c1	v1c2	v1c3	v2	v2a	v2b	v2b1	v2b2	v2c
1952	14.24	7.16	4.60	2.20	2.40	2.48	0.62	1.14	0.72						
1953	15.90	8.43	4.14	2.96	1.18	3.33	0.76	1.63	0.94	108.6	106.4	94.5	136.6	54.3	138.4
1954	18.54	9.35	5.19	3.43	1.76	4.00	1.07	1.78	1.15	114.1	107.6	126.2	118.4	144.8	117.9
1955	21.06	9.66	6.38	4.06	2.32	5.02	1.45	2.13	1.44	114.3	104.7	122.9	120.9	127.0	127.4
1956	25.27	10.59	8.29	4.03	4.26	6.39	2.01	2.53	1.85	122.1	110.9	129.9	97.4	190.6	135.5
1957	26.26	11.51	9.76	4.75	5.01	4.99	1.24	2.31	1.44	101.4	96.4	129.9	133.5	126.4	79.1
1958	32.28	12.51	14.22	7.10	7.12	5.55	1.35	2.59	1.61	127.9	121.8	143.6	150.1	137.0	112.7
1959	45.06	13.11	24.53	15.99	8.54	7.42	2.33	2.95	2.14	134.3	105.6	162.1	191.5	129.5	133.1
1960	51.64	14.11	29.93	20.17	9.76	7.60	2.36	3.05	2.19	117.2	101.7	122.0	127.2	113.5	130.3
1961	38.58	11.68	20.19	15.59	4.60	6.71	1.68	2.75	2.28	69.4	93.1	62.7	72.4	45.0	55.2
1962	31.80	11.60	14.24	12.19	2.05	5.96	1.59	2.35	2.02	82.9	100.1	67.0	74.4	45.0	90.4
1963	35.55	14.97	14.44	11.72	2.72	6.14	1.70	2.35	2.09	116.5	129.8	105.0	98.1	138.3	108.7
1964	38.23	16.93	14.97	11.18	3.79	6.33	1.79	2.39	2.15	115.0	113.6	120.7	116.9	133.7	107.3
1965	43.81	18.61	18.16	13.77	4.39	7.04	2.15	2.50	2.39	115.5	110.9	121.9	123.7	116.3	115.0
1966	49.70	20.51	20.97	17.27	3.70	8.22	2.33	2.77	3.12	113.7	110.0	115.6	125.1	85.0	119.9
1967	44.02	19.15	17.57	15.52	2.05	7.30	1.70	2.83	2.77	88.7	92.2	84.0	89.7	57.0	90.5
1968	39.83	16.70	16.18	13.89	2.29	6.95	1.46	2.84	2.65	91.8	88.8	94.0	91.3	114.3	95.3
1969	40.21	16.96	16.55	13.48	3.07	6.70	1.35	2.81	2.54	102.6	103.8	103.6	98.3	134.9	97.3
1970	49.03	18.42	21.90	18.10	3.80	8.71	2.48	2.93	3.30	122.3	109.4	134.2	136.5	124.4	130.4
1971	54.21	19.50	23.94	19.89	4.05	10.77	3.34	2.92	4.51	108.8	104.7	106.5	108.6	96.6	123.7
1972	50.52	18.40	21.48	17.47	4.01	10.64	3.25	2.93	4.46	93.1	95.1	88.6	87.5	94.1	98.7
1973	51.18	18.97	21.48	17.17	4.31	10.73	3.25	2.98	4.50	102.7	104.2	102.1	98.6	119.6	100.9
1974	50.13	17.47	22.49	17.38	5.11	10.17	3.01	2.91	4.25	98.2	92.0	106.6	102.3	124.5	94.8
1975	58.19	18.35	29.02	21.41	7.61	10.82	3.38	2.91	4.53	114.4	106.4	125.5	124.7	128.1	106.4
1976	63.04	19.12	30.71	24.08	6.63	13.21	4.10	2.91	6.20	108.7	103.6	107.0	109.2	99.9	122.5
1977	71.83	17.98	37.65	29.22	8.43	16.20	5.68	2.93	7.59	112.5	94.6	121.1	119.6	126.5	122.8
1978	81.90	20.97	43.14	33.90	9.24	17.79	6.16	3.28	8.35	111.1	113.0	111.3	113.6	103.5	108.3
1979	90.69	24.58	46.76	36.71	10.05	19.35	6.09	4.18	9.08	106.8	106.5	107.8	105.8	115.2	105.1
1980	105.82	30.89	51.27	40.71	10.56	23.66	6.52	6.05	11.09	107.9	108.8	105.6	111.2	86.2	112.0
1981	119.24	35.08	54.47	43.59	10.88	29.69	7.03	7.25	15.41	110.7	109.9	105.0	105.5	102.9	123.6
1982	133.14	38.76	60.95	49.63	11.32	33.43	7.59	8.49	17.35	110.8	109.4	110.3	112.4	100.9	113.1
1983	151.94	43.39	71.65	58.67	12.98	36.90	8.30	9.45	19.15	111.7	109.7	114.5	115.1	111.6	108.7
1984	174.86	49.89	82.37	67.22	15.15	42.60	9.60	10.89	22.11	112.0	111.2	112.5	112.8	111.2	112.0
1985	214.53	56.57	107.57	86.78	20.79	50.39	9.98	13.70	26.71	115.3	110.9	121.8	121.8	122.1	108.2
1986	250.92	65.52	120.90	97.71	23.19	64.50	12.38	17.35	34.77	109.4	112.4	108.8	109.8	104.0	107.4
1987	294.97	81.63	139.87	115.64	24.23	73.47	14.77	19.76	38.94	110.9	111.7	108.8	111.9	91.7	114.5
1988	385.84	108.46	182.22	149.09	33.13	95.16	18.01	26.72	50.43	113.3	106.6	117.3	116.5	122.2	113.1
1989	459.77	121.50	223.83	187.41	36.42	114.44	21.18	36.97	56.29	108.7	104.7	108.5	110.4	96.2	113.5
1990	576.42	144.66	262.94	219.92	43.02	168.82	37.22	61.11	70.49	113.9	115.1	109.4	109.1	111.4	121.6
1991	750.38	162.01	345.42	280.59	64.83	242.95	45.05	86.26	111.64	115.1	107.5	117.4	115.5	131.8	118.1
1992	891.23	172.42	437.23	317.22	120.01	281.58	56.57	110.32	114.69	113.9	105.5	115.3	108.6	157.5	118.7
1993	1165.38	198.20	636.68	448.40	188.28	330.50	66.40	129.48	134.62	111.7	102.5	113.5	110.8	122.5	116.6
1994	1559.46	306.47	804.98	590.52	214.46	448.01	83.73	172.30	191.98	109.6	110.9	109.7	110.9	106.4	108.5
1995	2038.45	405.73	1047.31	804.27	243.04	585.41	124.30	218.04	243.07	111.8	107.1	113.1	114.6	108.6	112.9

Year	v2c1	v2c2	v3'	v3	v3a	v3b	v3b1	v3b2	v3c	v3c1	v3c2	v3c3	v3c4	v3c5	v3c6
1952			7.91	7.91	5.12	1.74	1.09	0.65	1.05	0.22	0.43				
1953	108.8	160.6	8.74	8.74	5.51	2.10	1.50	0.60	1.13	0.25	0.45				
1954	285.6	124.2	10.54	10.54	6.26	2.70	1.82	0.88	1.58	0.38	0.63				
1955	123.1	118.3	12.31	12.31	6.69	3.22	2.10	1.12	2.40	0.47	0.84				
1956	134.2	114.9	14.09	14.09	7.51	3.71	1.65	2.06	2.87	0.61	0.92				
1957	57.4	113.5	14.67	14.67	7.88	3.82	1.75	2.07	2.97	0.73	1.01				
1958	141.6	107.2	16.90	16.90	8.80	4.72	2.28	2.44	3.38	0.77	1.07				
1959	156.6	114.7	21.37	21.37	8.73	8.48	5.99	2.49	4.16	1.03	1.16				
1960	115.1	103.5	25.20	25.20	9.27	11.06	8.12	2.94	4.87	1.20	1.23				
1961	63.0	84.1	21.46	21.46	8.21	9.11	6.97	2.14	4.14	0.72	1.15				
1962	95.0	86.1	17.72	17.72	8.26	6.11	5.01	1.10	3.35	0.75	0.88				
1963	107.5	98.5	19.01	19.01	9.79	5.66	4.28	1.38	3.56	0.88	0.91				
1964	105.2	104.1	21.55	21.55	11.29	6.29	4.33	1.96	3.97	0.89	1.10				
1965	122.2	103.8	24.20	24.20	12.48	7.32	5.03	2.29	4.40	0.97	1.16				
1966	109.7	107.5	26.78	26.78	13.80	8.17	6.25	1.92	4.81	1.06	1.30				
1967	75.0	106.6	22.45	22.45	10.91	7.51	5.71	1.80	4.03	0.83	1.38				
1968	82.0	101.0	19.78	19.78	9.20	6.77	4.79	1.98	3.81	0.73	1.43				
1969	94.0	103.4	19.84	19.84	9.26	6.89	4.80	2.09	3.69	0.68	1.45				
1970	184.9	101.5	23.08	23.08	10.35	8.67	6.19	2.48	4.06	0.89	1.34				
1971	141.4	100.2	26.14	26.14	11.42	9.96	7.47	2.49	4.76	1.00	1.43				
1972	96.6	100.4	24.38	24.38	10.79	8.96	6.78	2.18	4.63	0.91	1.44				
1973	94.1	100.4	24.67	24.67	10.73	9.27	6.59	2.68	4.67	0.90	1.49				
1974	92.5	95.3	25.05	25.05	10.25	10.15	7.13	3.02	4.65	0.89	1.52				
1975	116.4	104.9	28.12	28.12	11.21	12.20	8.86	3.34	4.71	0.98	1.53				
1976	123.6	100.4	31.78	31.78	12.35	14.01	10.43	3.58	5.42	1.11	1.66				
1977	131.0	100.4	35.67	35.67	13.10	16.52	12.79	3.73	6.05	1.24	1.75				
1978	107.6	114.3	39.07	39.07	13.97	18.35	14.48	3.87	6.75	1.18	2.07	1.21	0.04	0.24	0.28
1979	99.0	118.7	45.63	45.63	16.32	21.43	17.16	4.27	7.88	1.52	2.34	1.43	0.04	0.28	0.32
1980	116.1	140.2	53.24	53.24	21.52	21.44	17.48	3.96	10.28	1.91	2.91	1.79	0.06	0.36	0.42
1981	109.0	118.9	59.41	59.41	25.18	22.39	17.93	4.46	11.84	2.25	3.41	2.10	0.07	0.41	0.49
1982	109.1	121.0	65.24	65.24	28.11	23.35	18.66	4.69	13.78	2.53	3.84	2.47	0.08	0.48	0.57
1983	107.6	110.5	78.55	78.55	32.84	29.10	23.33	5.77	16.61	3.01	4.75	2.82	0.10	0.58	0.68
1984	113.2	111.8	89.75	89.75	36.67	31.66	25.46	6.20	21.42	4.01	6.29	3.80	0.11	0.69	0.81
1985	104.0	116.3	112.24	112.24	42.89	40.50	32.14	8.36	28.85	4.59	8.97	4.30	0.16	1.16	1.06
1986	108.9	110.7	129.04	129.04	46.00	45.63	36.79	8.84	37.41	5.98	10.49	7.02	0.73	1.93	1.29
1987	125.4	113.8	148.51	148.51	56.18	50.30	41.16	9.14	42.03	7.73	12.45	6.59	0.62	1.65	1.51
1988	116.2	113.4	192.72	192.72	72.27	66.02	53.53	12.49	54.43	11.60	16.11	7.91	0.88	1.90	1.67
1989	122.7	109.2	217.42	217.42	78.01	73.83	60.22	13.61	65.58	12.90	17.59	13.03	0.98	2.62	2.12
1990	95.6	98.0	274.00	274.00	94.61	83.50	68.09	15.41	95.89	19.73	27.70	14.13	1.01	4.12	3.30
1991	118.0	125.1	335.92	335.92	111.86	107.99	84.07	23.92	116.07	22.64	36.88	15.63	1.12	5.21	3.93
1992	127.9	112.6	402.31	402.31	114.50	147.65	106.30	41.35	140.16	28.33	39.85	22.30	1.59	7.30	4.75
1993	122.3	108.5	505.63	505.63	126.85	217.49	156.11	61.38	161.29	31.78	43.84	25.86	2.24	9.75	5.11
1994	103.8	105.9	673.68	673.68	187.69	265.38	190.47	74.91	220.61	42.24	58.69	39.57	4.28	14.70	6.71
1995	130.4	108.4	825.11	825.11	240.71	302.56	219.01	83.55	281.84	55.34	75.74	54.75	5.64	16.12	8.12

Year	v3c7	v3c8	v3c9	v3c10	v3d	v4'	v4	v4a	v4b	v4b1	v4b2	v4c	v4c1	v4c2	v4c3
1952				0.40	166										
1953				0.43	179	106.0	106.0	104.2	103.5	128.4	71.9	118.6	110.5	86.4	
1954				0.57	211	115.6	115.6	108.0	125.4	119.4	139.0	135.0	144.0	145.2	
1955				1.09	241	109.8	109.8	103.1	124.0	124.0	124.0	114.8	117.5	117.9	
1956				1.34	268	115.5	115.5	111.7	109.2	72.6	180.5	136.3	127.1	113.8	
1957				1.23	267	99.5	99.5	98.8	106.0	110.4	102.5	94.3	69.6	103.2	
1958				1.54	294	130.0	130.0	128.0	130.3	132.9	128.1	134.9	192.9	119.8	
1959				1.97	344	115.9	115.9	93.3	167.6	241.9	102.6	110.6	139.5	108.3	
1960				2.44	374	116.8	116.8	101.4	139.0	148.7	118.8	109.1	102.9	104.8	
1961				2.27	305	90.5	90.5	102.5	85.2	90.5	71.5	79.0	71.0	92.7	
1962				1.72	249	78.0	78.0	92.5	65.3	69.2	52.3	72.7	105.2	75.9	
1963				1.77	267	116.0	116.0	128.1	98.8	91.9	128.7	86.9	113.5	104.2	
1964				1.98	29	113.5	113.5	113.4	110.3	100.4	140.9	120.3	103.8	124.2	
1965				2.27	312	113.9	113.9	112.9	116.7	119.5	110.6	112.4	104.9	107.0	
1966				2.45	325	112.0	112.0	111.2	112.1	121.6	89.6	114.2	108.5	115.2	
1967				1.82	259	84.4	84.4	76.0	88.9	88.6	89.9	104.5	78.4	102.3	
1968				1.65	219	90.5	90.5	88.0	92.2	86.4	110.9	94.0	89.2	102.3	
1969				1.56	211	101.8	101.8	103.0	101.0	98.3	107.5	100.3	94.7	101.6	
1970				1.83	236	117.2	117.2	111.2	129.7	134.8	118.0	112.3	134.2	92.2	
1971				2.33	258	108.0	108.0	106.0	109.7	114.5	97.1	109.8	109.7	104.1	
1972				2.28	232	94.9	94.9	94.3	91.0	92.0	87.8	103.2	88.7	101.9	
1973				2.28	226	103.0	103.0	103.0	102.7	98.7	115.6	103.4	97.4	102.4	
1974				2.24	222	92.9	92.9	89.0	105.2	102.3	113.2	82.0	97.6	101.9	
1975				2.20	240	115.7	115.7	109.2	131.1	133.8	124.5	101.3	111.2	102.0	
1976				2.65	266	106.7	106.7	104.0	105.0	110.1	91.7	115.9	120.5	103.3	
1977				3.06	293	116.8	116.8	106.9	127.8	130.1	120.5	112.6	132.0	103.8	
1978	0.78	0.41	0.54		313	109.5	109.5	110.1	109.8	112.8	101.9	107.3	101.8	109.4	
1979	0.83	0.50	0.62		359	112.3	112.3	109.9	111.6	111.3	112.6	120.7	121.9	117.2	126.5
1980	1.19	0.66	0.98		410	107.2	107.2	106.0	104.3	108.5	93.1	116.6	115.8	125.5	103.9
1981	1.35	0.74	1.02		450	108.5	108.5	115.3	99.4	99.1	100.2	113.4	119.4	117.9	103.7
1982	1.62	0.88	1.31		488	109.8	109.8	111.3	104.2	104.7	102.8	117.1	119.1	119.8	111.6
1983	2.03	1.06	1.58		583	113.4	113.4	112.2	111.8	112.4	110.0	118.7	113.0	108.8	129.9
1984	2.56	1.26	1.89		661	114.0	114.0	113.6	114.6	115.1	112.8	114.1	100.2	109.2	137.4
1985	3.52	2.47	2.62		820	116.9	116.9	112.9	116.7	116.1	119.0	125.0	100.2	126.6	126.0
1986	4.32	2.53	3.12		924	111.5	111.5	108.3	109.1	111.0	102.6	120.7	124.9	110.0	127.2
1987	4.67	3.24	3.57		1053	109.7	109.7	110.7	104.8	108.6	91.3	114.7	119.1	111.1	111.1
1988	5.88	4.26	4.22		1347	109.6	109.6	103.3	114.9	113.6	120.3	112.9	118.8	114.7	107.4
1989	6.59	4.61	5.14		1493	105.9	105.9	101.8	104.5	106.9	94.5	113.5	112.7	107.6	142.1
1990	8.72	6.88	8.30	2.00	1799	111.7	111.7	116.0	106.8	106.4	108.5	112.0	106.7	104.4	106.9
1991	9.83	7.02	10.33	3.48	2101	114.4	114.4	111.2	117.0	113.1	134.9	115.7	129.0	104.7	114.8
1992	11.59	8.06	12.63	3.76	2477	113.1	113.1	105.5	119.4	112.6	145.4	115.7	125.7	112.6	105.1
1993	13.76	11.39	13.39	4.17	3019	110.3	110.3	101.1	114.0	111.3	122.1	116.7	115.4	122.4	124.3
1994	18.74	12.63	17.61	5.44	3953	110.9	110.9	111.2	110.2	111.1	107.9	111.2	103.0	106.5	121.7
1995	23.09	14.40	21.34	7.30	4764	109.0	109.0	104.9	111.7	113.6	106.6	110.0	116.6	109.9	118.2

Year	v4c4	v4c5	v4c6	v4c7	v4c8	v4c9	v4c10	v5	v5a	v5a1	v5a1a	v5a1b	v5a2	v5b	v5b1
1952								7.91	6.25	5.84	3.42	2.42	0.41	2.19	1.95
1953								8.74	7.08	6.36	3.81	2.55	0.72	1.99	1.65
1954								10.54	7.99	7.24	4.24	3.00	0.75	2.50	2.08
1955								12.31	8.85	8.03	4.57	3.46	0.82	3.67	3.28
1956								14.09	9.87	8.82	4.76	4.06	1.05	4.00	3.60
1957								14.67	11.54	10.53	5.47	5.06	1.01	4.10	3.72
1958								16.90	12.56	11.37	5.92	5.45	1.19	6.45	4.91
1959								21.37	15.62	13.98	6.82	7.16	1.64	8.56	6.56
1960								25.20	16.42	14.59	7.01	7.58	1.83	11.61	8.92
1961								21.46	15.64	14.13	7.08	7.05	1.51	5.75	3.95
1962								17.72	15.85	14.64	7.44	7.20	1.21	4.01	2.34
1963								19.01	16.05	14.75	7.53	7.22	1.30	5.00	3.46
1964								21.55	16.57	14.98	7.92	7.06	1.59	6.67	4.86
1965								26.78	18.23	16.55	6.96	9.59	1.68	6.90	5.41
1966								26.78	18.23	16.55	6.96	9.59	1.68	6.90	5.41
1967								22.45	18.86	17.41	6.89	10.52	1.45	5.36	4.01
1968								19.78	18.36	17.18	6.84	10.34	1.18	4.68	2.91
1969								19.84	19.43	18.17	6.85	11.32	1.26	5.61	3.56
1970								23.08	20.18	18.63	7.09	11.54	1.55	8.10	5.07
1971								26.14	21.54	19.36	7.33	12.03	2.18	8.96	5.82
1972								24.38	22.89	20.69	7.66	13.03	2.20	9.02	5.47
1973								24.67	24.46	21.43	7.24	14.19	3.03	9.65	6.22
1974								25.05	24.35	21.44	6.61	14.83	2.91	11.42	7.08
1975								28.12	26.07	22.68	7.34	15.34	3.39	12.65	7.53
1976								31.78	27.85	23.95	7.52	16.43	3.90	12.05	7.11
1977								35.67	29.76	25.41	8.60	16.81	4.35	13.86	9.48
1978								39.07	32.13	27.10	8.99	18.11	5.03	18.42	13.24
1979	124.5	124.9	124.9	113.9	133.1	121.8		45.63	37.91	31.57	11.32	20.25	6.34	20.27	14.52
1980	113.4	107.9	101.6	110.0	106.7	124.3		53.24	44.57	37.53	13.02	24.51	7.04	23.15	18.14
1981	105.3	104.6	109.4	105.9	104.4	103.3		59.41	50.96	42.89	15.00	27.89	8.07	25.56	19.35
1982	105.7	107.6	109.4	116.0	109.1	115.0		65.24	54.68	45.46	16.62	28.84	9.22	30.45	25.51
1983	137.2	137.2	137.2	142.3	137.2	137.2		78.55	60.43	49.36	18.96	30.40	11.07	33.94	30.30
1984	116.2	121.5	120.9	129.0	120.5	122.3		89.75	70.48	56.09	21.71	34.38	14.39	42.99	36.54
1985	163.9	171.0	152.5	127.4	164.0	130.0		112.24	87.81	68.28	25.68	42.60	19.53	58.42	46.78
1986	197.3	134.3	109.9	135.8	125.4	121.1		129.04	103.72	77.48	28.24	49.24	26.24	60.26	51.94
1987	150.0	106.4	113.4	109.9	128.9	123.1		148.51	117.31	89.59	33.02	56.57	27.72	69.94	55.78
1988	131.7	103.0	105.0	110.8	117.5	105.7		192.72	142.85	110.37	41.30	69.07	32.48	98.30	75.69
1989	108.5	120.1	110.1	103.7	108.6	105.9		217.42	156.67	126.42	48.55	77.87	30.25	117.84	86.73
1990	108.0	127.0	115.4	115.9	116.6	114.4		274.00	188.16	142.51	52.93	89.58	45.65	141.17	91.50
1991	120.1	111.2	106.8	106.2	126.9	130.0	133.1	335.91	221.11	170.09	62.38	107.71	51.02	169.13	124.76
1992	106.3	118.8	121.9	116.3	112.5	120.9	120.9	402.31	248.43	186.06	68.28	117.78	62.37	249.26	181.18
1993	122.6	129.8	113.2	109.9	103.1	107.1	107.8	505.63	300.75	228.61	81.96	146.65	72.14	356.16	264.90
1994	162.7	120.3	105.5	108.3	110.0	105.0	104.8	673.68	375.20	281.05	109.62	171.43	94.15	487.55	376.95
1995	110.5	91.7	103.2	105.1	93.9	103.8	114.9	825.11	497.56	373.63	149.50	224.13	123.93	560.88	422.53

Year	v5b2	v5c	v5c1	v5c2	v6a1	v6a2	v6a3	v6a4	v6b2	v6b3	v6b4	v7	v7a	v7a1	v7a2
1952	0.24	-0.53													
1953	0.34	-0.33										116.2	111.8	113.8	109.0
1954	0.42	0.05										111.3	112.3	112.0	112.7
1955	0.39	-0.21										112.3	112.6	109.0	117.6
1956	0.40	0.22										118.2	116.3	108.0	127.1
1957	0.38	-0.97										117.4	119.7	116.8	123.1
1958	1.54	-2.11										110.5	109.6	110.2	109.0
1959	2.00	-2.81										124.3	123.0	115.6	130.8
1960	2.69	-2.83										103.3	102.4	101.4	103.4
1961	1.80	0.07										78.0	79.5	80.9	78.1
1962	1.67	-2.14										103.0	105.2	106.7	103.8
1963	1.54	-2.04										107.6	107.2	109.8	104.6
1964	1.81	-1.69										107.3	105.7	109.4	101.7
1965	1.49	1.65										110.4	110.5	110.5	110.4
1966	1.49	1.65										106.1	106.5	87.6	127.6
1967	1.35	-1.77										105.3	107.0	99.8	112.5
1968	1.77	-3.26										97.8	99.1	97.8	100.0
1969	2.05	-5.20										106.6	106.5	101.2	110.1
1970	3.03	-5.20										104.1	102.8	103.6	102.3
1971	3.14	-4.36										106.6	103.9	103.4	104.3
1972	3.55	-7.53										106.2	106.8	104.6	108.1
1973	3.43	-9.44										106.7	103.6	94.4	109.0
1974	4.34	-10.72										99.2	99.7	91.4	103.9
1975	5.12	-10.60										107.0	105.8	111.2	103.3
1976	4.94	-8.12										107.1	105.8	102.7	107.4
1977	4.38	-7.95										75.6	106.2	114.3	102.4
1978	5.18	-11.48			5.12	3.40	0.43	0.04	15.61	2.24	0.26	151.0	105.5	103.9	106.3
1979	5.75	-12.55			5.85	4.95	0.48	0.04	17.51	2.47	0.27	114.5	113.2	120.6	109.5
1980	5.01	-14.48			6.08	6.32	0.57	0.05	21.40	2.81	0.30	112.9	114.1	111.6	115.5
1981	6.21	-17.11			6.30	8.06	0.59	0.05	24.61	2.97	0.31	112.2	112.0	113.9	111.1
1982	4.94	-19.89			7.42	8.51	0.64	0.05	25.37	3.03	0.44	107.0	105.8	110.2	103.3
1983	3.64	-15.82			8.06	10.13	0.69	0.08	26.71	3.22	0.47	108.7	106.8	113.0	103.1
1984	6.45	-23.72			8.91	11.95	0.74	0.11	30.33	3.54	0.51	113.2	110.5	110.4	110.5
1985	11.64	-33.99			9.69	14.24	1.61	0.14	37.23	4.73	0.64	114.8	112.1	110.6	113.1
1986	8.32	-34.94			10.60	15.83	1.63	0.18	42.80	5.57	0.87	110.5	106.3	103.2	108.2
1987	14.16	-38.74			12.95	17.88	1.72	0.47	49.18	6.47	0.92	105.5	107.8	110.9	105.9
1988	22.61	-48.43			16.99	21.91	1.90	0.50	60.29	7.79	0.99	104.8	105.4	105.1	105.5
1989	31.11	-57.09			22.58	22.57	2.52	0.88	67.44	9.32	1.11	92.7	96.7	95.6	97.3
1990	49.67	-55.33			25.53	23.39	3.07	0.94	74.77	13.10	1.71	115.4	108.3	105.3	110.1
1991	44.37	-54.33			30.06	27.74	3.36	1.22	90.59	15.00	2.12	108.4	109.9	109.8	110.1
1992	68.08	-95.38			31.35	30.84	4.39	1.70	96.64	18.50	2.64	105.0	102.6	105.8	100.7
1993	91.26	-151.28			34.48	38.08	7.66	1.74	116.42	26.90	3.33	107.4	108.9	107.8	109.7
1994	110.60	-189.07			51.12	44.72	10.64	3.14	124.02	43.33	4.08	96.1	93.9	98.3	91.3
1995	138.35	-233.33			73.22	56.26	11.60	8.42	157.92	60.93	5.28	109.8	110.2	107.7	111.9

Year	v7b	v8	v8a	v8b	v9	v9a	v9b	v10a1	v10a2	v10a3	v10a3a	v10a3b	v10a4	v10b1	v10b2
1952		122	87	281											
1953	181.3	130	96	277	109.1	111.7	101.8								
1954	102.2	145	105	316	110.3	110.4	109.2								
1955	110.1	157	111	353	110.1	107.0	114.0								
1956	137.2	168	113	390	112.7	105.1	119.7								
1957	97.6	191	127	429	114.5	114.2	108.5								
1958	119.5	198	135	398	104.8	108.9	93.9								
1959	136.7	225	156	391	113.8	115.3	97.9								
1960	110.7	217	163	313	94.7	103.1	78.3								
1961	66.0	201	162	264	75.8	79.9	70.8								
1962	82.0	206	164	280	104.1	102.2	107.7								
1963	113.4	207	165	281	107.1	109.5	104.7								
1964	126.7	203	174	251	102.1	109.7	93.0								
1965	109.3	206	182	241	104.9	108.2	99.8								
1966	102.5	201	147	278	100.2	85.9	113.6								
1967	88.0	201	140	281	101.7	96.1	104.8								
1968	81.4	190	133	264	94.9	93.9	95.6								
1969	108.2	193	128	277	102.6	97.5	105.7								
1970	123.5	191	128	273	99.0	99.6	98.9								
1971	140.3	191	128	274	100.3	100.0	100.2								
1972	101.1	197	130	283	102.8	101.9	103.0								
1973	137.5	196	120	291	99.8	91.9	102.9								
1974	95.9	190	107	293	96.6	89.2	100.2								
1975	116.6	194	115	291	102.0	107.6	99.2								
1976	115.5	201	114	307	103.5	99.6	104.5								
1977	111.5	209	127	310	104.3	111.7	105.4								
1978	114.2	217	131	323	102.8	102.2	104.7	9.50	3.65	0.09	0.01	0.08		4.66	0.52
1979	121.6	248	162	352	111.2	118.7	101.9	9.70	4.72	0.10	0.01	0.09		5.27	0.48
1980	106.6	289	186	410	111.7	111.1	111.1	13.67	4.34	0.13	0.01	0.12		4.43	0.58
1981	112.8	325	212	455	110.3	112.8	108.3	14.94	4.16	0.25	0.02	0.23		5.65	0.56
1982	114.1	340	232	465	104.4	108.9	102.1	21.33	3.69	0.49	0.09	0.40		4.26	0.68
1983	118.4	366	262	489	106.0	111.8	102.8	25.78	3.65	0.87	0.16	0.71		2.97	0.67
1984	126.0	413	296	549	109.6	109.3	109.8	28.98	6.33	1.23	0.22	1.01		3.22	3.23
1985	125.5	499	347	678	111.3	109.4	112.8	38.73	6.23	1.82	0.49	1.33		7.18	4.46
1986	126.0	555	376	761	104.0	101.7	105.0	41.84	7.32	2.78	0.86	1.92		7.37	0.95
1987	98.5	635	435	869	106.8	109.7	105.3	45.82	7.84	2.12	0.66	1.46		9.88	4.28
1988	103.1	771	537	1043	103.8	103.8	103.8	56.36	16.12	3.21	0.93	2.28		15.70	6.91
1989	79.2	868	623	1150	95.1	94.3	95.2	63.02	19.64	4.07	0.90	3.17		19.81	11.30
1990	145.0	936	662	1239	103.5	102.6	103.1	69.37	18.63	3.50	0.89	2.61		23.88	20.81
1991	103.5	1064	762	1381	104.7	107.3	101.9	96.69	23.77	4.30	0.70	3.60		23.84	15.53
1992	113.1	1146	824	1482	101.0	104.5	98.8	147.99	20.54	6.35	1.18	5.17	6.30	43.65	18.29
1993	102.7	1365	976	1756	105.7	106.5	104.4	214.28	17.72	13.65	2.92	10.73	19.25	62.97	19.21
1994	103.0	1649	1290	2007	92.4	97.1	89.3	288.46	34.32	26.57	3.42	23.15	27.60	73.60	20.43
1995	108.4	2157	1736	2573	108.4	106.4	109.7	316.21	55.99	25.82	5.23	20.59	24.51	35.03	89.60

Year	v10b4	v11a	v11a1	v11a2	v11b	v11b1	v11b2	v11c	v11c1	v11c2	v12	v12a	v12b	v13	v13i
1952															
1953											100.3	93.0	152.3		
1954											122.4	123.4	117.9		
1955											141.6	151.8	94.9		
1956											113.1	113.8	108.0		
1957											109.6	111.1	97.5		
1958											155.9	127.1	406.3		
1959											140.5	144.4	129.9		
1960											134.6	135.0	133.3		
1961											45.1	42.3	53.8		
1962											69.9	59.8	94.3		
1963											131.4	153.7	97.2		
1964											131.6	135.2	122.6		
1965											116.9	124.5	96.7		
1966											90.4	90.5	89.8		
1967											79.8	76.2	92.5		
1968											89.2	74.3	131.9		
1969											120.7	123.2	116.6		
1970											145.0	142.9	148.4		
1971											103.9	104.2	103.6		
1972											98.3	89.4	113.0		
1973											113.3	126.1	96.7		
1974											122.2	119.8	126.4		
1975											101.7	91.5	118.3		
1976											103.1	108.2	96.7		
1977											114.4	132.8	88.9		
1978		4.42	2.04	2.38	8.44	7.00	1.44	5.56	4.20	1.36	127.0	132.0	116.5	39.07	22.25
1979		5.14	2.50	2.64	8.71	7.11	1.60	6.42	4.91	1.51	113.4	116.1	107.2	45.63	26.09
1980		5.67	3.34	2.33	10.29	8.94	1.35	7.19	5.86	1.33	97.3	102.6	83.7	53.24	31.90
1981		3.03	1.54	1.49	10.56	10.97	-0.41	11.97	6.84	5.13	110.2	106.5	121.9	59.41	36.26
1982		3.13	2.63	0.50	14.35	13.25	1.10	12.97	9.63	3.34	114.9	127.9	79.5	65.24	40.20
1983		2.95	2.33	0.62	17.82	17.25	0.57	13.17	10.72	2.45	107.7	115.7	72.6	78.55	48.44
1984		5.31	3.91	1.40	21.80	18.93	2.87	15.88	13.70	2.18	121.9	114.8	171.8	89.75	55.99
1985		4.49	3.63	0.86	26.97	22.99	3.98	26.96	20.16	6.80	123.3	114.0	166.9	112.24	68.84
1986		5.18	3.90	1.28	30.93	25.33	5.60	24.15	22.71	1.44	94.9	103.6	67.0	129.04	76.93
1987		6.15	4.98	1.17	37.28	32.17	5.11	26.51	18.63	7.88	105.1	94.2	159.0	148.51	89.31
1988		11.74	5.15	6.59	50.31	41.38	8.93	36.25	29.16	7.09	125.9	121.3	139.2	192.72	117.59
1989		11.17	5.99	5.18	60.41	46.55	13.86	46.26	34.19	12.09	105.2	100.3	117.9	217.42	135.51
1990		12.40	7.31	5.09	71.41	58.00	13.41	57.36	26.19	31.17	134.8	127.6	150.4	274.00	154.17
1991		14.74	9.04	5.70	100.15	82.68	17.47	54.24	33.04	21.20	106.9	119.3	88.1	335.92	187.61
1992	6.14	21.08	14.61	6.47	141.37	114.58	26.79	86.81	51.99	34.82	136.1	133.9	141.9	402.31	229.13
1993	9.08	31.56	21.36	10.20	164.79	111.52	53.27	159.81	132.02	27.79	114.5	115.6	111.8	505.63	276.14
1994	11.56	59.65	33.12	26.53	215.55	182.06	33.49	212.34	161.77	50.57	110.9	116.9	96.4	673.68	355.50
1995	12.72	74.05	39.93	34.12	206.52	179.77	26.75	280.31	202.83	77.48	105.4	104.8	107.4	834.57	461.36

Year	v13ii	v13iii	v13iv	v13a	v13ai	v13aii	v13aiii	v13aiv	v13b	v13bi	v13bii	v13biii	v13biv	v13b1	v13b1i
1952															
1953															
1954															
1955															
1956															
1957															
1958															
1959															
1960															
1961															
1962															
1963															
1964															
1965															
1966															
1967															
1968															
1969															
1970															
1971															
1972															
1973															
1974															
1975															
1976															
1977															
1978	3.08	4.55	9.19	13.97	12.15	0.42	0.28	1.12	18.35	6.95	1.99	3.58	5.83	14.48	4.24
1979	3.71	5.36	10.47	16.32	14.20	0.49	0.33	1.30	21.43	8.22	2.43	4.23	6.55	17.16	5.23
1980	4.12	5.77	11.45	21.52	18.72	0.65	0.43	1.72	21.44	8.28	2.45	4.29	6.42	17.48	5.31
1981	4.52	6.13	12.50	25.18	21.91	0.75	0.51	2.01	22.39	8.74	2.58	4.41	6.66	17.93	5.62
1982	4.93	6.55	13.56	28.11	24.45	0.84	0.57	2.25	23.35	9.14	2.72	4.59	6.90	18.66	5.86
1983	6.18	8.10	15.83	32.84	28.57	0.98	0.66	2.63	29.10	11.73	3.55	5.74	8.08	23.33	7.69
1984	6.66	9.38	17.72	36.67	32.23	0.92	0.71	2.81	31.66	12.72	3.84	6.63	8.47	25.46	8.32
1985	8.03	12.18	23.19	42.89	38.31	0.98	1.21	2.39	40.50	15.35	4.96	7.88	12.31	32.14	9.37
1986	11.56	14.07	26.48	46.00	41.09	1.00	1.30	2.61	45.63	17.17	5.85	8.99	13.62	36.79	10.62
1987	12.25	14.33	32.62	56.18	50.19	1.06	1.52	3.41	50.30	18.66	6.58	9.03	16.03	41.16	12.13
1988	18.08	19.84	37.21	72.27	64.43	1.58	1.57	4.69	66.02	24.51	10.10	12.07	19.34	53.53	15.33
1989	16.05	23.26	42.60	78.01	69.74	1.50	1.70	5.07	73.83	29.90	8.23	14.66	21.04	60.22	19.92
1990	26.85	23.57	69.41	94.61	75.71	2.97	2.77	13.16	83.50	35.91	9.36	15.70	22.53	68.09	23.98
1991	32.75	26.93	88.63	111.86	87.88	3.56	2.90	17.52	107.99	47.97	12.15	17.79	30.08	84.07	31.13
1992	46.51	30.85	95.82	114.50	90.49	4.09	2.56	17.36	147.65	75.71	21.37	19.23	31.34	106.30	44.83
1993	64.83	44.54	120.12	126.85	97.75	5.30	4.87	18.93	217.49	105.89	34.86	29.21	47.53	156.11	63.93
1994	80.46	68.36	169.36	187.69	133.75	7.51	4.82	41.61	265.38	121.40	44.89	47.13	51.96	190.47	71.16
1995	121.06	81.96	170.19	250.17	175.88	10.55	4.96	58.78	302.56	138.62	69.16	50.60	44.18	219.01	77.64

Year	v13b1ii	v13b1iii	v13b1iv	v13b2	v13b2i	v13b2ii	v13b2iii	v13b2iv	v13c	v13ci	v13cii	v13ciii	v13civ	v13c1
1952														
1953														
1954														
1955														
1956														
1957														
1958														
1959														
1960														
1961														
1962														
1963														
1964														
1965														
1966														
1967														
1968														
1969														
1970														
1971														
1972														
1973														
1974														
1975														
1976														
1977														
1978	1.80	3.40	5.04	3.87	2.71	0.19	0.18	0.79	6.75	3.15	0.67	0.69	2.24	1.18
1979	2.22	4.04	5.67	4.27	2.99	0.21	0.19	0.88	7.88	3.67	0.79	0.80	2.62	1.52
1980	2.25	4.11	5.81	3.96	2.97	0.20	0.18	0.61	10.28	4.90	1.02	1.05	3.31	1.91
1981	2.36	4.21	5.74	4.46	3.12	0.22	0.20	0.92	11.84	5.61	1.19	1.21	3.83	2.25
1982	2.48	4.38	5.94	4.69	3.28	0.24	0.21	0.96	13.78	6.61	1.37	1.39	4.41	2.53
1983	3.26	5.48	6.90	5.77	4.04	0.29	0.26	1.18	16.61	8.14	1.65	1.70	5.12	3.01
1984	3.56	6.31	7.27	6.20	4.40	0.28	0.32	1.20	21.42	11.04	1.90	2.04	6.44	4.01
1985	4.45	7.55	10.77	8.36	5.98	0.51	0.33	1.54	28.85	15.18	2.09	3.09	8.49	4.59
1986	5.50	8.63	12.04	8.84	6.55	0.35	0.36	1.58	37.41	18.67	4.71	3.78	10.25	5.98
1987	6.18	8.55	14.30	9.14	6.53	0.40	0.48	1.73	42.03	20.46	4.61	3.78	13.18	7.73
1988	9.40	11.17	17.63	12.49	9.18	0.70	0.90	1.71	54.43	28.65	6.40	6.20	13.18	11.60
1989	7.44	13.62	19.24	13.61	9.98	0.79	1.04	1.80	65.58	35.87	6.32	6.90	16.49	12.90
1990	8.74	14.11	21.26	15.41	11.93	0.62	1.59	1.27	95.89	42.55	14.52	5.10	33.72	19.73
1991	10.24	16.03	26.67	23.92	16.84	1.91	1.76	3.41	116.07	51.76	17.04	6.24	41.03	22.64
1992	18.54	16.74	26.19	41.35	30.88	2.83	2.49	5.15	140.16	62.93	21.05	9.06	47.12	28.33
1993	30.94	23.88	37.36	61.38	41.96	3.92	5.33	10.17	161.29	72.50	24.67	10.46	53.66	31.78
1994	40.77	41.88	36.66	74.91	50.24	4.12	5.25	15.30	220.61	100.35	28.06	14.41	75.79	42.24
1995	64.91	44.95	31.51	83.55	60.98	4.25	5.65	12.67	281.84	146.86	41.35	26.40	67.23	55.34

Year	v13c1i	v13c1ii	v13c1iii	v13c1iv	v13c2	v13c2i	v13c2ii	v13c2iii	v13c2iv	v13c3	v13c3i	v13c3ii	v13c3iii	v13c3iv
1952														
1953														
1954														
1955														
1956														
1957														
1958														
1959														
1960														
1961														
1962														
1963														
1964														
1965														
1966														
1967														
1968														
1969														
1970														
1971														
1972														
1973														
1974														
1975														
1976														
1977														
1978	0.36	0.28	0.21	0.33	2.07	0.59	0.20	0.37	0.91	1.21	0.16	0.03	0.09	0.93
1979	0.56	0.33	0.24	0.39	2.34	0.61	0.23	0.43	1.07	1.43	0.21	0.04	0.11	1.07
1980	0.66	0.42	0.32	0.51	2.91	0.66	0.30	0.56	1.39	1.79	0.30	0.05	0.14	1.30
1981	0.82	0.49	0.36	0.58	3.41	0.82	0.34	0.65	1.60	2.10	0.36	0.06	0.16	1.52
1982	0.88	0.57	0.40	0.68	3.84	0.88	0.40	0.76	1.80	2.47	0.43	0.07	0.19	1.78
1983	1.09	0.69	0.51	0.72	4.75	1.11	0.48	0.91	2.25	2.82	0.54	0.08	0.23	1.97
1984	1.64	0.83	0.59	0.95	6.29	1.99	0.55	1.09	2.66	3.80	0.77	0.09	0.27	2.67
1985	1.97	0.86	0.64	1.12	8.97	2.49	0.56	1.99	3.93	4.30	0.85	0.11	0.35	2.99
1986	2.43	1.99	0.74	0.82	10.49	3.39	0.95	2.34	3.81	7.02	1.15	0.20	0.57	5.10
1987	2.60	2.02	0.61	2.50	12.45	3.80	0.86	2.46	5.33	6.59	1.00	0.18	0.59	4.82
1988	4.04	2.93	1.40	3.23	16.11	6.56	1.32	3.78	4.45	7.91	1.56	0.22	0.86	5.27
1989	4.88	2.63	1.74	3.65	17.59	10.55	1.12	3.27	2.65	13.03	1.63	0.24	1.73	9.43
1990	6.65	5.79	0.51	6.78	27.70	8.68	2.54	2.93	13.55	14.13	1.58	0.62	1.16	10.77
1991	7.60	6.65	0.58	7.81	36.88	11.55	3.38	3.92	18.03	15.63	1.75	0.69	1.28	11.91
1992	9.23	8.29	0.88	9.93	39.85	13.71	4.20	5.67	16.27	22.30	2.65	0.92	1.77	16.96
1993	10.35	9.29	0.99	11.15	43.84	15.08	4.63	6.24	17.89	25.86	3.07	1.07	2.05	19.67
1994	21.96	11.03	3.07	6.18	58.69	13.05	3.15	7.67	34.82	39.57	6.55	1.89	3.59	27.54
1995	29.25	16.11	4.44	5.54	75.74	31.49	7.75	16.03	20.47	54.75	7.39	2.09	4.06	41.18

Year	v13c4	v13c4i	v13c4ii	v13c4iii	v13c4iv	v13c5	v13c5i	v13c5ii	v13c5iii	v13c5iv	v13c6	v13c6i	v13c6ii	v13c6iii
1952														
1953														
1954														
1955														
1956														
1957														
1958														
1959														
1960														
1961														
1962														
1963														
1964														
1965														
1966														
1967														
1968														
1969														
1970														
1971														
1972														
1973														
1974														
1975														
1976														
1977														
1978	0.04	0.01	0.03			0.24	0.14	0.01	0.02	0.07	0.28	0.26	0.02	
1979	0.04	0.01	0.03			0.28	0.16	0.01	0.02	0.09	0.32	0.30	0.02	
1980	0.06	0.01	0.05			0.36	0.21	0.01	0.03	0.11	0.42	0.39	0.03	
1981	0.07	0.01	0.06			0.41	0.23	0.01	0.04	0.13	0.49	0.45	0.04	
1982	0.08	0.02	0.06			0.48	0.28	0.01	0.04	0.15	0.57	0.52	0.05	
1983	0.10	0.02	0.08			0.58	0.33	0.02	0.05	0.18	0.68	0.63	0.05	
1984	0.11	0.02	0.09			0.69	0.43	0.01	0.09	0.16	0.81	0.77	0.04	
1985	0.16	0.03	0.13			1.16	0.56	0.04	0.11	0.45	1.06	1.05	0.01	
1986	0.73	0.03	0.70			1.93	1.09	0.19	0.13	0.52	1.29	1.19	0.10	
1987	0.62	0.03	0.59			1.65	0.85	0.15	0.12	0.53	1.51	1.40	0.11	
1988	0.88	0.05	0.83			1.90	1.28	0.23	0.16	0.23	1.67	1.56	0.11	
1989	0.98	0.05	0.93			2.62	1.60	0.23	0.16	0.63	2.12	1.83	0.16	
1990	1.01	0.09	0.97	0.04	-0.09	4.12	1.71	0.54	0.37	1.50	3.30	2.85	0.34	
1991	1.12	0.10	1.07	0.04	-0.09	5.21	2.16	0.68	0.47	1.90	3.93	3.39	0.41	-0.02
1992	1.59	0.13	1.44	0.07	-0.05	7.30	2.99	1.01	0.67	2.63	4.75	4.10	0.47	-0.03
1993	2.24	0.19	2.02	0.09	-0.06	9.75	4.00	1.36	0.88	3.51	5.11	4.40	0.51	
1994	4.28	0.64	2.72	0.64	0.28	14.70	5.79	1.93	1.36	5.62	6.71	5.75	0.62	
1995	5.64	0.44	4.79	0.13	0.28	16.12	12.55	2.30	1.49	-0.22	8.12	7.41	0.70	0.01

Year	v13c6iv	v13c7	v13c7i	v13c7ii	v13c7iii	v13c7iv	v13c8	v13c8i	v13c8ii	v13c8iii	v13c8iv	v13c9	v13c9i	v13c9ii
1952														
1953														
1954														
1955														
1956														
1957														
1958														
1959														
1960														
1961														
1962														
1963														
1964														
1965														
1966														
1967														
1968														
1969														
1970														
1971														
1972														
1973														
1974														
1975														
1976														
1977														
1978		0.78	0.72	0.06			0.41	0.38	0.03			0.54	0.53	0.01
1979		0.83	0.75	0.08			0.50	0.47	0.03			0.62	0.60	0.02
1980		1.19	1.09	0.10			0.66	0.62	0.04			0.98	0.96	0.02
1981		1.35	1.23	0.12			0.74	0.69	0.05			1.02	1.00	0.02
1982		1.62	1.49	0.13			0.88	0.83	0.05			1.31	1.28	0.03
1983		2.03	1.87	0.16			1.06	1.00	0.06			1.58	1.55	0.03
1984		2.56	2.37	0.19			1.26	1.18	0.08			1.89	1.87	0.02
1985		3.52	3.28	0.24			2.47	2.38	0.09			2.62	2.57	0.05
1986		4.32	4.01	0.31			2.53	2.41	0.12			3.12	2.97	0.15
1987		4.67	4.38	0.29			3.24	3.01	0.23			3.57	3.39	0.18
1988		5.88	5.56	0.32			4.26	4.02	0.24			4.22	4.02	0.20
1989	0.13	6.59	6.15	0.44			4.61	4.34	0.27			5.14	4.84	0.30
1990	0.11	8.72	7.46	1.11		0.15	6.88	4.33	1.51	0.09	0.95	8.30	7.20	1.10
1991	0.15	9.83	8.64	1.25	-0.23	0.17	7.02	4.42	1.54	0.09	0.97	10.33	8.67	1.37
1992	0.21	11.59	10.33	1.37	-0.22	0.11	8.06	5.33	1.76	0.14	0.83	12.63	10.70	1.59
1993	0.20	13.76	12.00	1.63		0.13	11.39	7.53	2.48	0.21	1.17	13.39	11.71	1.68
1994	0.34	18.74	16.55	1.78		0.41	12.63	9.20	2.75	0.08	0.60	17.61	15.42	2.19
1995		23.09	21.02	2.04	0.03		14.40	11.34	2.90	0.18	0.02	21.34	18.67	2.67

Year	v13c9iii	v13c9iv	v13c10	v13c10i	v13c10ii	v13c10iii	v13c10iv
1952							
1953							
1954							
1955							
1956							
1957							
1958							
1959							
1960							
1961							
1962							
1963							
1964							
1965							
1966							
1967							
1968							
1969							
1970							
1971							
1972							
1973							
1974							
1975							
1976							
1977							
1978							
1979							
1980							
1981							
1982							
1983							
1984							
1985							
1986							
1987							
1988							
1989							
1990			2.00	2.00			
1991	0.11	0.18	3.48	3.48			
1992	0.11	0.23	3.76	3.76			
1993			4.17	4.17			
1994			5.44	5.44			
1995			7.30	7.30			

APPENDIX: Organizational Structure of the State Statistical Bureau (SSB)

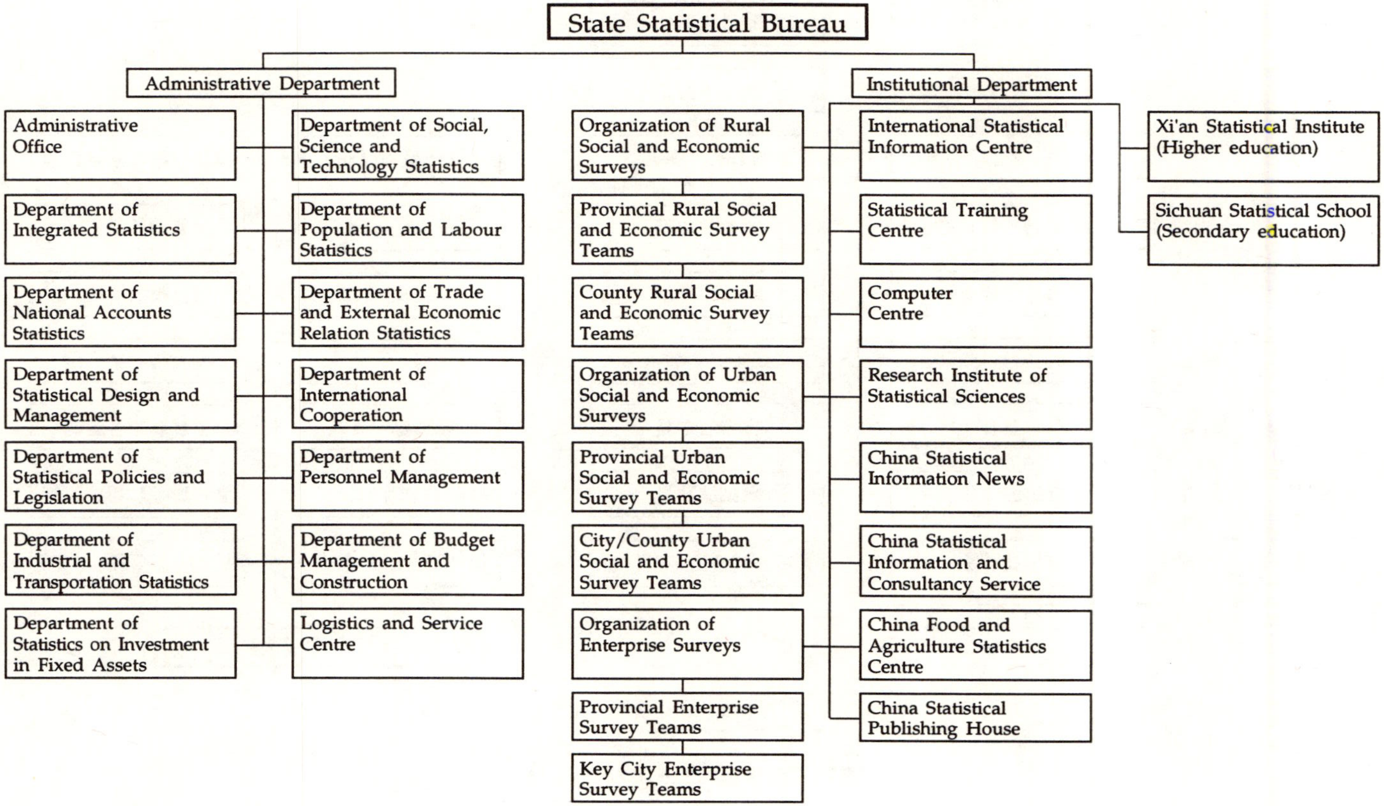

附件：國家統計局機構圖

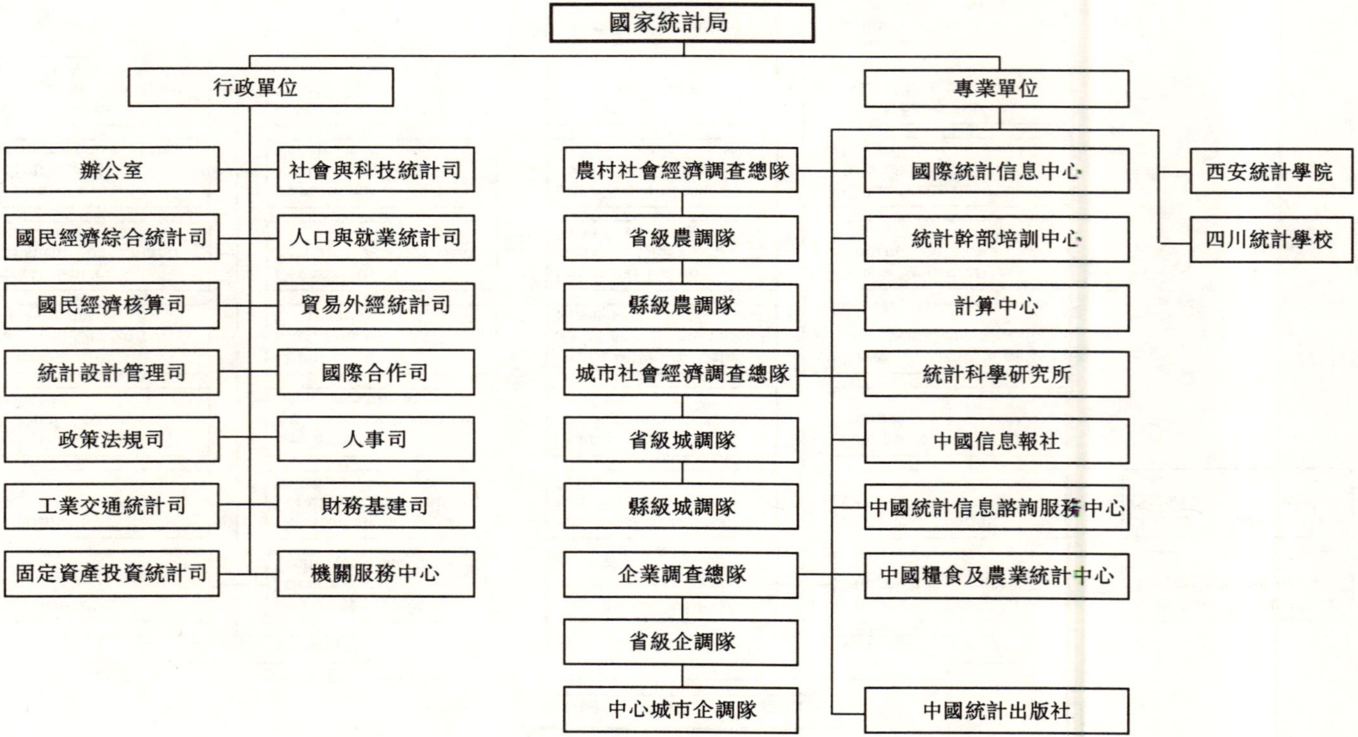
國家統計局
行政單位
專業單位
辦公室
社會與科技統計司
國民經濟綜合統計司
人口與就業統計司
國民經濟核算司
貿易外經統計司
統計設計管理司
國際合作司
政策法規司
人事司
工業交通統計司
財務基建司
固定資產投資統計司
機關服務中心
農村社會經濟調查總隊
省級農調隊
縣級農調隊
城市社會經濟調查總隊
省級城調隊
縣級城調隊
企業調查總隊
省級企調隊
中心城市企調隊
國際統計信息中心
統計幹部培訓中心
計算中心
統計科學研究所
中國信息報社
中國統計信息諮詢服務中心
中國糧食及農業統計中心
中國統計出版社
西安統計學院
四川統計學校

About the Book and Editors

The most complete set of the Chinese national income and its components based on SNA is contained in the volume, in which the non-material sector omitted in the MPS has been filled up so that the Chinese data are directly comparable with those of other countries all over the world. This book consists of two parts. Part I presents the information on the theoretical aspect of China's national income estimation in which five chapters are included: the establishment and evolution of China's national income; China's national income accounting in MPS; China's national economic accounting system — SNA; the interchange between SNA gross domestic product and its constituent elements and MPS national income and its constituent elements; and some explanations of the estimation of gross domestic product and its components and future improvements. Part II comprises the data of China's national income at both national and provincial levels. The materials recorded in the volume are the first hand and have never made their appearance anywhere, which are indispensable and absolutely necessary to the students of the field of China study around the world.

Hsueh Tien-tung is Professor in Economics Department and Director of China's Reform and Development Programme, Hong Kong Institute of Asia-Pacific Studies at the Chinese University of Hong Kong. Li Qiang is Director of the Department of National Accounts Statistics at the State Statistical Bureau, PRC.

Contributors

Hsueh Tien-tung
Department of Economics and China's Reform and Development Programme at Hong Kong Institute of Asia-Pacific Studies, The Chinese University of Hong Kong

Li Huaju
Department of National Accounts Statistics, State Statistical Bureau (SSB), The People's Republic of China (PRC)

Li Qiang
Department of National Accounts Statistics, SSB, PRC

Li Xiaochao
Department of National Accounts Statistics, SSB, PRC

Liu Liping
Department of National Accounts Statistics, SSB, PRC

Xu Xianchun
Department of National Accounts Statistics, SSB, PRC

Zhang Xiyun
Department of National Accounts Statistics, SSB, PRC